D1432473

PATHWAYS TO THE INFORMATION SOCIETY

Proceedings of the Sixth International Conference
on Computer Communication
London, 7-10 September, 1982

editor
M. B. WILLIAMS

Sponsored by

The International Council for Computer Communication (ICCC)

Hosted by

British Telecommunications

1982

NORTH-HOLLAND PUBLISHING COMPANY – AMSTERDAM • NEW YORK • OXFORD

Publishers:
NORTH-HOLLAND PUBLISHING COMPANY
AMSTERDAM • NEW YORK • OXFORD

Sole distributors for the U.S.A. and Canada:

ELSEVIER SCIENCE PUBLISHING COMPANY, INC.
52 Vanderbilt Avenue,
New York, N.Y. 10017

The views and the opinions presented in these Proceedings
are not necessarily endorsed by the
International Council for Computer Communications

PRINTED IN THE U.K.

Contents

ii

D10 NETWORK INTERCONNECTION

D11 NETWORK PERFORMANCE

Session Chairmen

A1 ISDN - planning & implementation

Prof R Meisel
FTZ, FRG

A2 ISDN - systems definition

R Parodi
SIP, Italy

A3 Public data networks - services

D J Horton
GTE Telenet, USA

A4 Public data networks - systems

A Texier
French PTT

A5 Local Networks - Architecture & standards

Prof A A S Danthine
University of Liege
Belgium

A6 The Bell System packet transport network

W E Strich
AT&T, USA

**A7 Local networks –
implementation &
experience**

Dr K Kuemmerle
IBM Research Lab
Switzerland

A10 Videotex

R Hooper
British Telecom

**A8 Intelligent network
services – I**

F R Zitzmann
AT&T, USA

**A11 Local networks
– access protocols**

D J Farber
University of
Delaware, USA

**A9 Intelligent network
services – II**

J R Harris
Bell Labs, USA

**A12 Public data
networks – operational
aspects**

Ph Picard
TRANSPAC, France

B1 Office systems strategy

Dr I G Dewis
BL Systems, UK

B4 Teletex services

K Katzeff
Swedish PTT

B2 Office systems – standards & systems

M B Naughton
Langton Information
Systems, UK

B5 Office systems – the PABX approach

D G Hunt
British Telecom

B3 Satellite systems definition & facilities

D N Gregory
British Aerospace
Dynamics Group

B6 The Universe project

Dr J H H Merriman
Consultant, UK

B7 Teletex - usage & users

D Tombs
Philips Business
Systems, UK

B8 Satellite systems - integrated networks

N Abramson
University of Hawaii,
USA

B9 Local radio networks

L Fratta
Milan Polytechnic,
Italy

B10 Applications in banking & EFT

I A Edmonds
Barclays Bank, UK

B11 Optical systems - I

L C Seifert
Western Electric, USA

B12 Optical systems - II

Prof W A Gambling
University of
Southampton, UK

C1 Human factors – man–machine interfaces

Prof B Shackel
Loughborough
University of
Technology, UK

C2 Regulation & public policy

Sir Henry Chilver
Cranfield Institute of
Technology, UK

C3 Human factors – the friendly system

Dr J G Axford
IBM UK Labs

C4 Applications in education

Dr M C Andrews,
IBM, USA

C5 Information network architecture

Dr P K Verma
AT&T, USA

C6 Human factors – office systems

D R Fairbairn
NCC, UK

C7 Transborder dataflow – legal & economic considerations

T J Myers
Peabody Lambert &
Myers, USA

C10 Transmission technology

Prof V G Lazarev
USSR Academy of
Sciences

C8 Pricing & allocation in communications networks

D S Sibley
Bell Labs, USA

C11 Network Management

S B Erskine
Bell Canada

C9 Applications in medical services

Dr M E Silverstein
George Washington
University, USA

D1 Distributed Systems – architecture & organisation

Prof M Paul
Technical University
of Munich, FRG

D 2 Open systems interconnection – I

L Pouzin
CNET, France

D5 Open systems interconnection – II

B M Wood
The CAP Group, UK

D3 Switch architecture

Dr M Kato
NTT, Japan

D6 Protocols – low level

R Blanc
National Bureau
of Standards, USA

D4 Distributed systems – implementation

D L A Barber
Logica, UK

D7 Protocols – low level

Dr E Raubold
GMD, FRG

D8 Protocol proving & validation

Dr T Kalin
COST II bis,
Yugoslavia

D10 Network interconnection

Prof P T Kirstein
University College
London, UK

D9 Routing & flow control

Dr W L Price
National Physical
Laboratory, UK

D11 Network performance

A W Coulter
University of
Queensland, Australia

Opening Ceremony

PATRON OF ICCC'82

HRH The Duke of Kent

CONFERENCE CHAIRMAN

J S Whyte
British Telecom

PRESIDENT, ICCC

D F Parkhill
Department of Communications,
Canada

CONFERENCE GOVERNOR

S Winkler
IBM, USA

Keynote & Theme Addresses

Rt Hon Kenneth Baker MP
Minister of State for
Information Technology, UK

F J M Laver CBE
Pro-Chancellor,
Exeter University, UK

T A Larsson
Deputy Director-General,
Swedish Telecomms
Administration, Sweden

I M Ross
President, Bell Labs,
USA

D M Leakey
Technical Director,
GEC Telecomms, UK

S Winkler
Director, Technical
Personnel Development,
IBM, USA

Computers + Communications + People = ?

F J M Laver
Exeter University, UK

Some light can be thrown on the purposes we hope to serve when enquiring into the 'social consequences' of using electronic computers and communications by asking Kipling's six questions: Why? Where? When? What? Who? and How?, plus a seventh: Whether?

WHETHER?

Any attempt to assess the economic, social and personal consequences of using information technology faces an inconvenient prior question: whether it is possible to predict what those consequences will be? Social inertia and the time required for capital projects to mature allow us to predict which applications and equipment are likely to come into service over the next five to ten years, but thereafter our extrapolations are seriously perturbed by the emergence of novelty. We can never know what will emerge, but that something will do so is quite certain. Moreover, in neither the short nor the long term does a knowledge of probable hardware and software, or of their likely applications, help when we are attempting to predict extra-technical effects.

We labour under four handicaps. First, economics and sociology are fearsomely difficult subjects, and our understanding of them is rudimentary; next, the technology itself will change substantially within the forecast period; thirdly, its very use will alter the circumstances to which the prediction must respond. Finally, the consequences we seek to predict are side-effects – unexpected and uncontrolled, unintended and unwanted – for no one has yet admitted planning to use information technology deliberately as a tool of social engineering.

Our difficulties are aggravated by ever-deepening specialization which engenders intellectual parochialism: it is alarmingly easy to be shown to be naive in someone else's subject. So, hardware and software designers deny their competence, and neglect their duty, to seek out the social and economic side-effects of the systems they contrive, and act as if they assumed that this could be performed by a separate set of specialists – those in the social sciences. Hence, when evaluating social consequences neither precision nor certainty is to be expected, and any policies we formulate must necessarily be tentative, subject to continual monitoring, and open to review.

WHY?

Why do we feel the need to examine the external consequences of using information technology? Our current concern is a new phenomenon; a century ago an entrepreneur would have been astonished to be censured for polluting the environment or disturbing the lives of his workers; he expected to be praised for providing work and adding to the nation's wealth. Our disquiet may derive from the more conspicuously nasty consequences of the industrial revolution, for these exposed the radiating public implications of private decisions. The applications of nuclear fission and fusion have also led men and women to fear other uses of the higher technology. Each age sees its problems by the light of a favourite paradigm, and that of our age is 'system'. Perhaps, therefore, it is our analyses of systems behaviour which have given us a keener insight into the inter-connection of seemingly separate activities, and revealed surprising richochets from actions taken in all innocence, and with quite different intent.

Robust sceptics, however, assert that the investigation of social implications is no more than a public relations ploy, also that those who preach the doctrine of social responsibility are (perhaps subconsciously) seeking to distance themselves from future reproach. They, themselves, see their attention to the wider implications of their work as a sign of professional maturity – but professionalism has occasionally been used as a stalking horse in the hunt for improved status and reward.

Whatever the reasons, it is now obligatory for our literature and conferences to allocate space and time to the examination of motives, achievements and future plans. I am in no way opposed to this critical introspection, so long as we do not allow it to degenerate into a sterile and enfeebling obsession.

WHERE? WHEN?

The questions Where? and When? invite those who speak or write about our subject to declare their context more clearly and precisely than has been usual.

Most contributors seem to have based their analyses on their own societies, predominantly those of the industrialized West, but information technology will impact differently on nations that differ in social tradition, economic development or political regime. Thus, in an underdeveloped country its use could perhaps enable the rate of economic advance to be accelerated, and bring material benefits to the entire population. In an industrialized nation, however, it can displace and devalue traditional skills, and create obstinate social problems. Again, information technology offers to play a larger and more fundamental part in a regime based on comprehensive planning and control by a central government than in one which, more or less, leaves economic activity to the interplay of independent initiatives.

Asking When? reminds us that it is as easy to be parochial in time as in space, for example, by believing that we find ourselves at the crucial point when computing, communications and micro-electronics are combining synergistically. Thinking that our present situation is unique could induce us to take hasty, fire-brigade, action to deal with what we had misread as a once-for-all crisis: it is far more likely that the future holds much more change, and much faster change, than any we have yet experienced.

WHAT?

In research and development, and in lesser investigations also, it is useful to assume success and ask what we would then do? The answer can be surprising, sometimes disconcerting, and may cause us to modify, or even abandon, our enquiries. Suppose we have managed to predict the economic, social and personal consequences of applying information technology in some specific context, what - apart from intellectual satisfaction and another learned paper - do we hope to have achieved? I cannot accept that the only purpose is the identification of obstacles to ever-rising sales of hardware, software and services: but I do accept that it would be sensible to attempt to foresee and forestall troubles that could otherwise afflict those who will use, or be used by, future information systems. We might, therefore, seek to formulate some principles of design which would ensure that the machine adapts to men and women, rather than vice versa - as so often happens. This adaptation must be conscious and deliberate, and we cannot avoid our responsibility as professionals by claiming to make our systems transparent. Every system imposes characteristics on its users, and information technology could dupe us into paying undue respect to those data that can be coded efficiently and manipulated formally. A moment's thought tells us that such data are neither logically nor empirically superior to qualitative information, and that programmable operations are not intrinsically better than others we use all the time but cannot encapsulate in algorithms.

WHO?

Who are we seeking to influence by our discussion of social consequences? If we fail to identify that target we may well influence no one but ourselves. The style, content, vocabulary and medium all need to be tailored to our intended audience or readership, and it contains at least seven groups with different requirements, interests and capacities.

(i)   Our fellow professionals, who have to be convinced that this is not just a coterie topic for those who like an easy option.

(ii) System users and suppliers, who have to finance whatever extra hardware, software or processing time may be required to make their systems more acceptable.

(iii) The officials and members of trade unions concerned about the effects of information technology on our working lives.

(iv) Ordinary men and women outside their roles as workers, who need sober and realistic information about the possible effects on such personal matters as privacy, surveillance, education and medicine.

(v)   Pressure groups of various kinds, who need solid information so that they can base their arguments on secure foundations - should they choose to do so.

(vi) The media of public information need authoritative data and clear analyses to weigh against the partial accounts that issue from interested parties and obscure experts.

(vii) The elected members of the legislature and their civil servants, who may have to frame laws or policies for information technology.

Even this preliminary list is enough to show that our target is far from being a monolith.

HOW?

How can any remedial action we recommend be made effective? Professional standards of practice and behaviour are efficaceous in medicine, but that profession operates a closed shop from which backsliders are expelled and excluded from practice. Information technology however, is far from being confined to members of its two main professions. In the last resort legislation may be unavoidable, but even good laws cannot create good systems, and detailed prescriptions could rapidly become irrelevant to so protean an art as information technology. The most appropriate kind of law may, therefore, be one which requires that for certain sensitive, and specified, applications information systems must be designed, and their operation controlled, by members of explicitly approved professional bodies.

The certain threat of expulsion would then be available to reinforce the uncertain promptings of conscience; and the professions should be able to exercise a control that stayed in step with the advance of the art.

CODA

Two final points.

First, we practice an ancillary art: no one computes or communicates for its own sake, but only to improve the performance of some more important task. Information technology, therefore, is not itself a primary cause of social change, although it undoubtedly brings forward and develops changes which were already latent, and may well do so before we are willing or able to adapt to them.

Second, I am opposed to discussing the social and other extra-technical consequences of using information technology without being clear about why we are doing so. If it is just an exercise in amateur sociology, then let us recognise and evaluate it as such. If, however, we want to shape the future use of information technology - and I can think of few more important objectives - then we must take Kipling's questions very seriously.

F J M LAVER, CBE, BSc, C Eng, FCEE, FBCS

MURRAY LAVER'S professional career began in radio engineering, but switched to organisation and methods and then to computing with the rapid introduction of large-scale computing in the British Post Office. He retired in 1976 as Member for Data Processing of the Post Office Board and as a member of the Board of the National Research Development Corporation.

Subsequently Visiting Professor at the Computing Laboratory of the University of Newcastle-upon-Tyne he is now Pro-Chancellor of the University of Exeter. Well known as a writer and speaker with a keen interest in probing the social and human consequences of technology, his book 'Computers and Social Change' was published last year.

Service & Business Aspects of Computer Communications

T A Larsson
Swedish Telecomms Administration

GENERAL EVOLUTION OF TELECOMMUNICATIONS AND DATA COMMUNICATIONS

The present status of telecommunications services is a result of a long evolution through more than a hundred years.

If you study the basic transmission technique used for different services, it is interesting to note that the old telegraph system utilized digital transmission. When many years later, telephony was introduced, analogue transmission was used. Telex, however, worked with digital technique and video transmission uses in principle analogue transmission. Data communication is digital and a successive transition is now taking place where all services - voice, text, data and picture - will be integrated in a basic digital network. The digital network will be an ideal carrier of data communications and will promote the growth of such communications.

Behind the technical evolution there is an economic background. Costs for electronics, memory and logic decrease at the same time as its capacity increases.

The willingness to allocate economic resources to telecommunications and data communications is expected to increase in most countries. In this connection I recollect the findings of an investigation made 10 years ago about economic resources for telecommunications up to the year 2000. The economic progress of the world today may not be exactly what was projected in the early 70's. Unlike the situation at that time, there is today an economic regression in many countries. Nevertheless I think that most of the findings in that investigation are still valid. They showed that, in Sweden, the GNP and the telecommunications part of the GNP are increasing. Telecommunications will require 2.7 % of the GNP in year 2000 as compared with 1.8 % in 1965 and 1979. At the same time the GNP expands considerably. (See fig 1.) Today we are also entering the post-industrial society - a service-oriented society which favours services such as telecommunications.

In many developed countries a certain saturation of the telephone density will occur. In turn this will mean that resources will be allocated to other telecommunications activities such as data communications.

The development of data communications' depends to a great extent upon the development of data processing. So far all signs indicate a trend towards distributed data processing which means great usage of data communications services.

Indeed a "marriage" of telecommunications and data processing will be the result. This "marriage" will hopefully result in a number of useful products some of which will be more influenced by telecommunications and others more by data processing. They will doubtlessly expand quickly and soon represent great economic interests which might create a struggle between the parties interested and difficulties to control in what direction the products will develop.

In addition to the basic data communication network services a range of specialized services are foreseen - in particular in the text communication field.

SOME EXAMPLES FROM SWEDEN

I should like to illustrate the development with some examples taken from my native country, Sweden. A similar development to that in Sweden can be found in most industrialized countries - at least in Europe.

- Data communication services were introduced early in Sweden - in 1962. Potential customers showed great interest in the new services, but very few subscriptions were made until about 1970 when the computer industry was ready to market on-line processing. Then quickly a number of fixed leased networks (20-30) were established. Geographically these networks seemed to have the same structure. A computer center - in most cases located in Stockholm - connected with terminals spread over the whole country. If you study the networks more closely you find, however, that they are different. Different standard protocols and network philosophies are used depending upon what computer manufacturer has delivered the centrally located equipment. Interworking between the different network was - and is still - impossible.

- From this it was easy to conclude that a better way to provide both compatibility and cost efficiency was to provide a Public Data Network - as recommended by e.g. the CEPT (European Conference of Postal and Telecommunications Administrations). A Public Data Network - as a result of a joint Nordic development was taken into operation about a year ago. This network is circuit switched and works in accordance with CCITT standards. It is believed that circuit switched technique will be used by most data terminals. Great emphasis is put on security and integrity of the network.

- A smaller packet switched network is also in operation. It will successively be replaced by a larger packet switched network compatible with the circuit switched network.

- A satellite network, offering point-to-point high speed data communication is planned to be taken into operation in the late 1980's.

- Great effort is made on the modernization and digitalization of the public switched telephone network. Because of the size of the network it will take some time before it can be digitized throughout the country and thus before nationwide access to a 64 kbit/s data communication service can be offered. Densely populated areas will, how ever be covered rather soon.

- A service integrated digital network (ISDN) is under study

- Digital PABX's offering data communication services will be compatible with the telex and teletex PABX services

- Local Area Networks (LAN) of the bus type may have a great impact

- A number of new text services are introduced or will be introduced shortly:

    A great interest is concentrated to the Teletex service, which is now being introduced

    The telefacsimile (Telefax, Group 2) service is well etablished. Group 3 terminals will be introduced within short

    Group 4 telefax terminals offering interworking with Teletex is under study

    The videotex service has been tested for some years and is now offered to business subscribers

    Message handling services including Mailbox functions are planned to be introduced

- Electronic fund transfer systems are under development

The use of the digital Public Switched Telephone Network (PSTN) will most likely be dominating in the future also for data communications services but a number of different networks and different services will exist side by side for a long time.

PUBLIC NETWORKS AND PUBLIC SERVICES

It is evident that a rapid development of networks and services will take place for some years to come. It is therefore essential to define as early as possible what is really meant by Public Networks and Public Services, so that a Telecommunications Administration or an Operating Company can clearly realize its responsibilities and duties. A Public telecommunications service should meet the following conditions:

- Communication between all terminals connected to the service possible without discrimination

- Reliable up-to-date directory information available to the public

- Uniform availability and technical quality throughout the country in accordance with public rules and regulations laid down for the service

- International interworking to the extent permitted by international agreements

- Interworking between different generations of equipment and interchangeability between generations

- Uniform charges throughout the country

- Uniform quality of service throughout the country

Typical examples of public services are telephony, telex and teletex.

In addition to public services the Administrations provide public networks which contain transmission and switching of a certain quality and at a certain price. The Administration/ Operating Company sets the technical conditions for connecting terminals to the network, but takes no responsibility, neither for their interworking with each other, nor for their operation.

EVENTUALLY AN INTEGRATED NETWORK

Technically it will be possible to integrate various types of telecommunication networks to form an Integrated Services Digital Network (ISDN). A number of public services and networks can be realized using the technical facilities of this network. Integration which up to now has mainly been limited to the transmission network will be extended to include switching technology in the 1980's. In addition, switching and transmission technology will be integrated in such a way that it will be difficult to define the boundary between them.

It is expected that CCITT will be able to
establish certain standards for digital subscriber lines in 1984. It would then be
possible to offer digital subscriber services
around 1990.

INTERWORKING PROBLEMS BETWEEN NETWORKS AND
SERVICES

Despite the development towards an ISDN, a
number of specialized networks will live side
by side for many years to come.

Looked upon from a customers' point of view,
it is therefore essential that networks and
services are compatible. It should be possible
to use one and the same terminal for different
services and to send traffic over different
networks. The question is, however, how this
can be realized. It is easy to see the need
for a number of conversion units converting
between the procedures of different networks
and terminals.

Could an intelligent network be designed to
handle the problems? We will hear more about
this in some of the sessions of this conference.

Even if a true intelligent network most likely
is a utopia, it might be possible to offer
very important conversion facilities to the
benefit of the customers. (See fig 2.)

A good help in designing these conversion
facilities is the Open System Interconnection
model (OSI) that seems universally accepted.

An internationally agreed standard for the
higher levels of the OSI model is found in the
CCITT recommendations for the Teletex service.

The standards adopted for the higher levels of
the Teletex procedures could be used as a
basis for procedures allowing interworking
between services such as Teletex, Telex,
Videotex and Telefax.

The Teletex service will successively be
supplied with suitable protocols for working
with data bases. This will imply an important
change as compared with the present situation
in which computer communication protocols are
decided by a few computer suppliers. In the
further development of the Teletex service,
CCITT will have a greater influence on the
standardization of protocols and the signalling relationship in the interworking between
data terminals and computers and also between
computers over the telecommunications network. This will certainly be an advantage to
the end users as well as to the telecommunications and computer industries as a whole. The
large international computer manufacturers
will of course be the first to realize the
advantages of such a standardization and will
probably quickly adhere to CCITT's recommendations.

It is my firm belief that continuous and
efficient international standardization
activities capable of developing necessary
standards in time, are indispensable in the
very dynamic world of data communication.

Changes of the components of GNP

Reference: Heet PTT—Bedrijf nr 2 Dec 1970

Figures are updated according
to development 1965—79

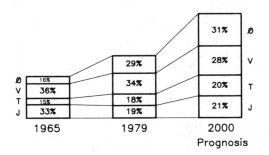

J=Domestic gross investments
T=Private consumption—services
V=Private consumption—durables and non durables
Ø=Public consumption

Telecommunications requirement of GNP	1965	1979	Prognosis 2000
Investments	0,4%	0,4%	0,7%
Operations	1,4%	1,4%	2,0%
Total	1,8%	1,8%	2,7%

Figure 1

CONCEPT OF A POSSIBLE "INTELLIGENT" NETWORK

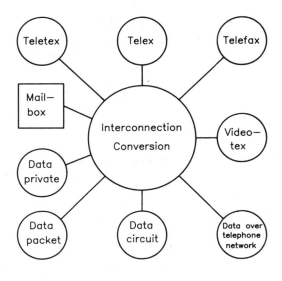

Figure 2

Possible Trends in Computer Communications

D M Leakey
GEC Telecommunications, UK

Computer communications are evolving in a manner characterised by considerable increases in complexity at the user requirement, system and technology levels. It is questionable to what extent our existing specification and design procedures will be able to cope adequately with this situation and it is suggested that modifications will be necessary to make systems less susceptible to errors introduced throughout the complete realisation process. In particular it is suggested that a radical change in multiplexing techniques might be beneficial to match more adequately the evolving communication requirements.

1. INTRODUCTION

As with any product or service, innovation in computer communications can result from the two primary forces of technology push and market pull. Both categories can be subdivided. Technology push can result from improvements in the basic technology or from the introduction of new system concepts. Market pull can result from responding to user identified needs or as a result of a thrust by a supplier to increase market share by introducing systems with potentially special customer appeal.

All of these forces can encourage innovation, although not necessarily in the same direction. However, at the present time there does appear to be one common theme which could lead to fundamental changes in communication system design. The common theme concerns complexity. Not only are systems now being asked to do more, but our basic technologies are increasingly capable of performing more. Unfortunately this match is being frustrated by our limited capability to design and operate such increasingly complex systems. A primary cause would appear to be that our existing specification and design approaches are generally unsuitable beyond some given level of complexity. This suggests that radically new approaches might be necessary if rapid progress is to be maintained.

To attempt to analyse the nature of possible future trends, the following topics will be considered :

(a) What will be the major technological innovations encouraging change.

(b) What will be the major user requirements encouraging change.

(c) How will these factors merge to form the broad system parameters of future communication systems.

The commercial pressures will be taken as self-evident. Many companies, and possibly countries, will wish to dominate the market. If major changes appear to be necessary to achieve a dominant position, then no doubt at least one company, or country, will ultimately achieve resolution of the many problems associated with such major changes.

2. SOME RELEVANT TECHNICAL TRENDS

In a very short space of time, we have already witnessed the move from the discrete device era to the integrated circuit era where many thousands of active devices can be accommodated on a single semiconductor chip. The advantages of high levels of integration in terms of space occupancy, power consumption and overall cost, are so significant that in many cases it has become necessary to reconfigure systems to reduce to a minimum the need for small scale integrated circuits and discrete components. An associated problem has also arisen in that, if all systems incorporate only LSI and VLSI devices, then for there to be any significant difference between systems considerably more than a limited range of standard devices has to be employed.

To give system designers the necessary freedom, a rapid increase is now occurring in the use of custom LSI, where the system designer is responsible for at least part of the device design, rather than leaving the design entirely to the semiconductor manufacturer. It is often considered that this customisation approach is a new phenomenon, but it is probably more realistic to regard it as a natural progression from the customisation which traditionally took place at the printed circuit board level and which is now being extended to include the component level.

To meet the potentially vast disparity in volume requirements for particular semiconductor device types, several custom approaches are employed ranging from ROM programmed microprocessors to fully handcrafted approaches. The various design techniques provide different compromises between the cost of design and the cost of making relatively inefficient use of silicon area in the final devices.

The uncommitted gate array approach has become a popular technique for custom LSI design where the quantity requirements for each design are relatively modest. Present commercially available devices contain up to some 2,000 gates. The generation about to enter the market will contain some 5,000 gates per device. At this complexity close attention has to be given to the testing aspects which must exert a considerable influence on the basic design. The 5,000 gate array represents no special technological limit and arrays incorporating 20,000 gates or more should become available to reasonable timescales if a demand exists. However, as the number of gates per device increases certain problems will become even more acute :

(a) The implied system complexity incorporated on a single chip suggests that we could be unable to specify performance requirements precisely.

(b) Even given a correct specification, it is possible that the achievement of a 100% correct design could be unrealistic.

(c) Even given a correct design, it is probable that at the manufacturing stage it will be desirable to accept devices which do not meet the specification precisely in order to achieve a reasonable yield.

(d) Even if the device did function correctly, it is likely that this could not be verified in a reasonable time.

Summarising, it would appear that at some future stage the concepts of precise specification, design, manufacturing and testing will have to be relaxed. To an extent this is already happening, but it will become essential to mould together the existing somewhat piecemeal approaches so as to provide an adequate overall solution to deal readily with the complexities which will be feasible when semiconductor device feature sizes decrease to the sub-micron level. This could lead to design approaches which are based on a reasonable probability of correct operation rather than a requirement for precise accuracy. Obviously such approaches must not be just theoretical niceties, but must be capable of meeting the needs of practising designers.

3. EVOLVING USER REQUIREMENTS

Three significant trends in user requirements can be identified which could be of considerable significance in the overall design of information systems.

The first trend concerns the interfaces between systems and users. Most existing systems require a user to stare at a cathode-ray tube displaying some 24 lines of 80 characters. Alternatively it is permissible to scan reams of printout containing masses of information with little or no indication of the possible significance. The occasional graph is provided, but pictures particularly in colour remain a rarity. These restricted forms of presentation give rise to several problems :

(a) They inhibit the human ability to scan several documents rapidly and to abstract relevant information by pattern matching.

(b) The human being has to be taught from a tender age to read conventional text whereas pictorial methods of presentation represent a more natural match.

(c) In normal communication the human being performs more naturally if allowed to make use of more than one sense. This is normally impossible with a typical computer terminal.

(d) Users have to undergo training, the magnitude of which is probably unacceptable for the rapidly growing class of occasional, non-technical users.

Similar problems occur with information retrieval, although several methods are now available to supplement the ubiquitous Qwerty keyboard. For example, hand-written character recognition is becoming more in evidence and direct speech input is emerging from the realms of research.

These improvements, although still in the early stages of introduction, illustrate a trend. There is a requirement for displays to contain a mixture of text, graphics and pictures as required. It should be possible to scan documents as is possible with normal paperwork. There is a requirement for speech input and output to be used in close association with the visual methods of communication.

An interesting communication problem could arise as a result of these requirements. This can be illustrated by considering a general purpose terminal capable of displaying high definition still colour pictures, each picture requiring some 2 – 10 MBits of information in an uncompressed form. Such a terminal might normally perform adequately with communication channel rates not exceeding some 9.6 KBits/sec, but when a picture display is required, this could increase to some 10 MBits/ sec for a single second in order to achieve a reasonably rapid picture refresh rate. Thus there is a potential requirement for base rate communication channels which infrequently can call up vast increases in bandwidth for relatively short periods.

The second likely trend concerns information coding. The problem can be illustrated by means of a rather trivial example. If it is required to transfer a large sum of money from one bank's computer file to another, it is possible that the required information can be coded in a form not exceeding some tens or hundreds of bits. In contrast a single frame of a colour television display requires some 2 MBits for satisfactory transmission. However, the loss of a single picture frame is unlikely to cause more than a flicker to the picture whereas the loss of information representing the money transfer could be serious.

This example exposes the rather inappropriate coding systems which we employ to transmit information. It is evident that the methods make little or no allowance for the possible significance of the data or of the significance of introducing errors. If average data rates are to increase considerably as a result of the extensive use of picture presentations, then it is likely that the coding of very significant information should be carried out in a manner more in accordance with this significance.

The third trend concerns systems specification. At present a potential user has to specify his understanding of his requirements in a precise manner even though the means of conveying this precision are conspicuous by their absence. The assumption also has to be made that the potential user is fully aware of his precise requirements before the equipment is introduced. As a result specification errors inevitably occur which often permeate through the complete realisation process to be discovered only when the equipment is installed and operational.

Two approaches to ease this problem are being given increased attention. The first approach assumes conventional design and realisation techniques and aims to provide specification languages in which the behavioural requirements can be stated unambiguously with the minimum reference to subsequent realisation approaches. Complete exclusion of subsequent realisation procedures is usually unrealistic in that complete decoupling is generally impractical where cost targets have to be met. A second approach assumes that the realisation will contain a degree of so-called artificial intelligence and will be able to adapt to the required specification in some automatic error correcting manner. In these cases the initial specification is more of a list of prohibited actions since the precise responses required are often unspecified. It is interesting to note that civilised society is organised on the basis of such negative specifications, which are commonly referred to collectively as the law.

4. COMMUNICATION SYSTEMS IMPLICATIONS

The influence of the technology trends and evolving user needs on computer communication systems might be summarised as follows :

(a) A need to incorporate devices with very high levels of integration and to adjust system structures accordingly.

(b) A need for large increases in channel capacity to cater particularly for picture transmission. This could be coupled with a need to alter channel capacity dynamically during a connection to cater for the transmission of occasional, single, high definition pictures.

(c) A need for systems to adapt rapidly to changes in information mix particularly between text, speech and picture.

(d) A need to adapt to a limited number of errors in system specification and realisation without system re-design.

How are existing communication systems to be adapted to meet these trends. An indication might be obtained by extrapolation from the discussion which is already raging concerning the relative merits of so-called circuit switching and packet switching for computer communications. This discussion is likely to continue for some time, and might expose the possibility of other systems which meet more adequately the evolving needs.

What is the likely nature of this possible alternative. Technological trends suggest that whilst sheer complexity need not be a problem it is important that the resultant systems should not be required to function in a precise manner. In simple terms this can be achieved by incorporating error detection and correction, but

there could be a limit to which such techniques can be used in the present rather simplistic manner.

The conventional combination of time division multiplex and circuit switching has poor inherent resilience to equipment malfunction, and extra equipment with suitable changeover arrangements has to be incorporated in any practical system. Time division multiplex also makes poor use of available channel capacity except in the fully loaded condition and is difficult to evolve to cater for large changes in the user's instantaneous bandwidth requirements. The capacity of an individual channel cannot be increased automatically to achieve faster transmission rates when the bearer as a whole is underloaded. The predetermined channel allocation also severely limits the flexibility to meet rapidly varying demands in individual message requirements.

Packet switching provides more flexibility. Rigidly defined multiplex structures are avoided and the system can more readily accommodate large changes in the nature of the messages offered. However, at the present time packet switching tends to be uneconomic for messages requiring high average bit rates such as speech and video due largely to the associated storage and storage access requirements. Nevertheless, with the increase in potential complexity of integrated circuits, it appears that packet switching could form a sounder basis for the very flexible systems required in the future.

A useful compromise could result from a combination of circuit and packet switching. A system can be visualised where a narrow bandwidth circuit path is established which can call upon commonly available wider bandwidth channels for limited periods when the wider bandwidth is required. Such a combined approach could be based on extensions of existing techniques or might be achieved by a more radical departure based on code division multiplex (CDM). In this approach pseudo-random sequences act as the message carriers and pattern recognition is used as the primary message separation mechanism rather than channel timing or header recognition. With such a system the necessity for sending messages in strict sequence is avoided and it is possible to offer all messages in a random manner to a common bearer with storage being required only to avoid gross overload.

The advantages of such a system could include :

(a) Channels would not have to be defined precisely thus giving a high degree of flexibility.

(b) A degree of inbuilt self optimisation could be incorporated, where the system could adapt to prevailing conditions caused either by traffic levels or by system imperfections.

(c) Each message would pervade the whole of the bearer capacity with messages overlapping both in the time and frequency domain and hence would be less susceptible to the more common types of interference.

The concept of such a system is of course not new, but the lack of suitable technologies has restricted its use mainly to special military systems. With the advance in technology these restrictions could reduce considerably with the result that CDM might represent a better match with the user requirements than can be offered by simpler evolutions of existing techniques.

The above comments have been made primarily in relation to communications between spaciously separated processing utilities. However, there are other parts of a complete information system which should be included under the general title of communications. The list includes :

(a) Links between spaciously separated processing utilities (communications in space).

(b) Links between past and present processing (communications in time – commonly called storage).

(c) Links with system users (the input and output interfaces).

(d) Links with system operators (for system configuration, operation and maintenance).

Although these categories might appear to have little in common, they are all influenced by advances in technology and evolving customer requirements and to that extent should develop along paths which show considerable similarity. This necessity for similarity appears to be overlooked somewhat in existing systems. For example, very little appears to be said about the necessity for common formats in space communication and storage and there is often a need for complex format converters which ideally should be unnecessary. The application of ad hoc data compression methods can also lead to unfortunate dissimilarities. Hopefully, the widescale use of optical fibres, bubble memories and similar high capacity techniques will combat the desire to reduce every message to a minimum bandwidth form with the resultant susceptibility to errors.

These trends could also influence our attitude towards conventional digital systems. If systems are to be designed which inherently deal with errors, then there seems little point in retaining very low error rate approaches if this puts a severe limitation on effective channel capacity. It is likely that multi-level systems will show considerable advantage and there could even be a return to analogue operation. However this does not infer that sinewaves should be resurrected.

5. CONCLUSIONS

The basic concept which appears to be emerging is that computer communication system design should move away from the idea of precise transmission of information to one where errors are catered for in an integrated manner with the necessary redundancy forming part of the actual message structure. Such an approach could be closely related to the techniques used in speech and picture recognition, and could be used throughout a complete information system. Information with considerable significance could be coded with additional redundancy, whilst information of lower significance could be coded in a less redundant manner.

All of these changes could dig deep into our basic understanding of information processing and communication, but have such potential advantage that their possible impact cannot be ignored. It is worth recalling that human communication has progressed almost precisely along the lines suggested, probably because very high levels of integration have been available, but with only limited assurance of accuracy. The degree of self programming or learning possible in human systems is very impressive and it is likely that this will be copied increasingly under titles such as Expert Systems. Similarly the self healing features contained in human systems suggests that our conventional ideas on maintenance and repair might be modified with considerable economic advantage.

The problems are formidable, but the rewards for achieving even the first step in the right direction could be very significant. The fifth generation of computers might be publicised as being based on novel programming languages, VLSI, distributed computing and picture manipulation, but the underlying impact could be very much greater than implied by these topics alone. It is difficult to see how computer communications can stand aside from these potentially radical changes which are promised elsewhere in information systems.

DAVID LEAKEY graduated from Imperial College in 1953 and joined the General Electric Company as a Graduate Trainee. In 1955 he returned to Imperial College to carry out research into human hearing under the guidance of Professor E C Cherry. He was awarded a Ph.D. in 1958.

From 1956 to 1963 Dr Leakey worked at the Hirst Research Centre, Wembley. He then returned to GEC Telecommunications Limited, where he has remained except for one year's sojourn into academic life. He is now the Technical Director of the Company.

Dr Leakey is an active member of the institution of Electrical Engineers, serving on various committees and being Past Chairman of the Electronics Division and the immediate Past Chairman of the Management and Design Division. He has close contacts with several Universities and Polytechnics, has been associated with the Sciences and Engineering Research Council and serves on several Advisory Committees.

In 1979 he was elected to the Fellowship of Engineering.

The Long-term Future of Circuit and Non-circuit Switching in Multiservice Networks

C J Hughes
British Telecom Research
Laboratories, UK

The distinction is made between circuit-switched systems which offer constant bit-rate channels and non-circuit switched systems, in which the bit-rate may be varied dynamically. The two approaches are compared in terms of the network characteristics in relation to the subscriber services. Real time considerations are particularly important and a synchronous slot allocation approach is preferred to one employing store-and-forward technology. A strategy for evolution from a circuit switched network to one providing variable bit-rate channels is outlined.

1   INTEGRATED SERVICES

In the past, switched networks have developed after most of the basic service requirements have been defined. The characteristics of the telephone network have been based on the use of the carbon microphone and the electron-magnetic earphone to give a voice service that is satisfactory for most commercial and social purposes. The telex network, which has developed separately in most countries, has been based on the 50-baud teleprinter.

It is now accepted that there are considerable economic advantages in moving towards a network that is capable of carrying a wide range of telecommunications services. This is possible mainly because techniques now exist for the economic conversion of all types of telecommunications signals to digital form. The concept has been embodied in the term 'Integrated Services Digital Network' or ISDN.

A nationwide (or worldwide) telecommunications network normally takes several decades to develop. Any 'new' network should therefore be designed to cater for not only the existing services but should incorporate sufficient flexibility to carry those services that might be developed in the future. So far, most development of ISDN has been based on circuit-switched 64 kbit/s channels and it is pertinent to ask whether such a network is likely to be adequate to meet the needs of the next century. In attempting to answer this question, it is necessary first to examine some basic aspects of switched network design.

2   FUNDAMENTAL CHARACTERISTICS OF A SWITCHED NETWORK

In theory, a switched network can be designed by mapping the network parameters on to the requirements for the customer services. Both economic design and physical limitations require that some impairments be tolerated by the user. The problems of carrying out the mapping operation for future unknown services might appear to be formidable. However the task should not be regarded as impossible since the range of even future human communications is limited by physiology and, in the case of machine communications, the design of future terminal equipment can to a certain extent be adapted to fit the network.

It is important to distinguish between the characteristics of the specific telecommunication services, as seen by the customer and those of the network services. In an ISDN, the network services should be defined from the outset, since changes are likely to be very costly, and should be sufficiently flexible to carry a wide range of user services, even those which may be defined at some time in the future.

2.1   Customer Service Characteristics

The main customer service characteristics to be defined are:

i)   call duration characteristics (holding times)

ii)   acceptable delays in setting up calls

iii)   acceptable losses in calls ("grade of service")

iv)   number and configuration of terminals involved; a simple call will involve only two terminals but more complex services may involve any number of terminals in a 1:n (selective broadcast) or a n:n-1 conference (mode)

v)   symmetry of information flow

vi)   bit-rate characteristics (ie the variations in bit-rate during the call)

vii)   storage required (eg if a terminal is not able to receive the information immediately)

viii)   acceptable delays in transmission through the network

ix)   acceptable loss of information during call

x)   acceptable errors during call

2.2   Network Characteristics

The process of mapping the service requirements on to the network then involves defining the general network characteristics including:

i)   call set-up capability (busy hour call attempts)

ii)   traffic handling capability (Erlangs)

iii)   call overload characteristics (loss of calls; delays)

iv)   switched connection configurations possible

v)   ability to handle asymmetric information flow

vi)   bit-rate characteristics of channels

vii)   transparency

viii)   delay characteristics (transmission delay plus delays at switching nodes)

ix)   probability of loss of information during call

x)   error characteristics (error probability and grouping)

In addition to the general characteristics, the network may have characteristics which are specific to particular services. These include:

i)   storage capability

ii)   signal processing

2.3   Signalling

In addition to the terminal-to-terminal communication, there is need for control signalling between the terminal and the network and between switching nodes within the network. This has presented considerable problems in the past but message-type digital signalling[1] now offers the prospect of a signalling system that can be expected to meet all the needs of future multiservice networks.

3   TAXONOMY OF SWITCHED NETWORKS

Most present day networks are based on metallic contact switches. They are circuit switched in that a two-way circuit of fixed bandwidth is established at the beginning of a call and this is retained for the duration of the call, irrespective of how much use is made of it. This has provided a satisfactory basis for voice communication and the high signal-to-noise available on most connections has enabled speeds of up to 9600 bit/s to be achieved for data transmission over most of the network.

The range of technologies now available has led to a wider range of network options, some of which have been implemented. An attempt has been made in Fig 1 to classify the types of network service in relation to the technologies employed.

For digital operation, only four basic network technologies need be considered. Circuit

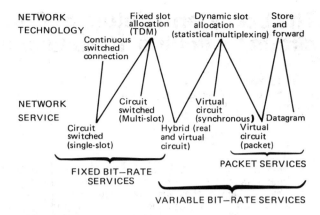

Fig 1 TAXONOMY OF SWITCHED NETWORKS (DIGITAL)

switching has already been dealt with. Both the conventional TDM and the dynamic slot allocation approaches are based on a fixed duration frame and are therefore synchronous. The distinction is shown in Fig 2. For cyclic TDM, a delay of up to one frame may be introduced at each (time-) switching stage but this is normally fixed at the beginning of each call and remains constant throughout the call. With dynamic slot allocation, the delay at each switching stage is variable but still restricted to one frame. Store and forward technology leads to virtually unrestricted and variable delays in transmission.

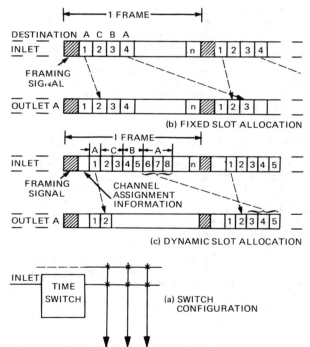

Fig 2 TIME SWITCHING

The types of network service resulting from the use of these technologies, either singly or in combination, are shown in Fig 1. A distinction is made between circuit-switched or 'fixed bit-rate' systems and the range of 'variable bit-rate' (VBR) systems.

Data & Text Services	Voice Services	Still Picture Services	Real - time Picture Services
Telegraph	Telephone	Facsimile	Slow Scan TV
Telex	Voicegram	—line drawing	High Definition
Teletex	Voicedata	—halftone	TV
Telemetry	Radiophone	—colour	Picturephone
Telecommand	Hi-Fi (music)	Picture	Confravision
Inter computer data	Stereophonic	Viewdata	Colour TV
Electronic Fund	Conference	Home	Stereo TV
Transfer	Etc	Newspaper	Moving
Home Newspaper		Still Hologram	Hologram
Radio Paging		Etc	Etc
Alarms			
Viewdata			
Etc			

Fig 3 CUSTOMER TELECOMMUNICATION SERVICES

4   NETWORK DESIGN

4.1   Telecommunication Services

A list of some of the customer telecommunication services that might be carried on an
integrated network is given in Fig 3. The services may be divided into groups, depending on
the human and machine characteristics of the
terminal.

4.1.1   Data and text services

These include the complete range of man-
machine and machine-communications. Bit-rates
of 256 kbit/s are normally adequate for text,
even when only a few words are read on each
page. For communication between machines, bit-
rates have tended to be low but development may
have been restricted by the limitations of current networks. Error rates are very important
for some data service and additional error
detection/correction may be necessary.

4.1.2   Voice services

Digital speech is now carried on 64 kbit/s (or
56 kbit/s) PCM channels and these channels form
the basis of current ISDN proposals. The
choice of 64 kbit/s is based on earlier technology together with the expectation that
several successive coding/decoding operations
would be required on some connections. It is
now possible, with improved coding techniques
and an all digital network, to transmit continuous commercial-quality speech at 24 kbit/s or
less.

On the other hand, 64 kbit/s may not be considered adequate for high-quality audio circuits.
However, any move to different standards must
be constrained by the widespread penetration
of equipment based on existing standards.

4.1.3   Still picture services

This type of service is relatively easy to deal
with since the full information is normally
available before the start of transmission.
Almost any combination of coding techniques and
transmission speeds may be used.

4.1.4   Real-time picture services

Real-time pictures require a wide variety of
transmission characteristics. Fig 4 shows the
range of bit-rates that might be required for
tranmission over a circuit-switched network.
However, real-time pictures contain a high
degree of redundancy that depends on the detail

that is required to be observed and the speed of
movement. The degree of redundancy varies
throughout the call and, although there is a
trade-off between movement and resolution, the
required bit-rate will also vary over a wide
range.

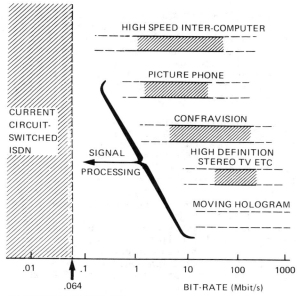

Fig 4 WIDEBAND SERVICES

4.2   Bit-Rate Profiles

The bit-rate characteristics form one of the
most important factors in designing the network
to carry a range of services. Since many of the
services are real-time, it is necessary to consider the variations in bit-rate with time and
to define both the mean and the peak bit-rate
for each service. The ratio of mean to peak
bit-rate may be defined as the "activity factor"
or "communication intensity"(2).

4.3   Delay Characteristics

For human response, the maximum tolerable round-
trip delay is about 500 milliseconds. Terrestrial cable systems can give delays up to 200
msec and, if both-way satellite transmission is
used, most of the tolerable delay is taken up by
the transmission system. The delay at the
switching nodes must then normally be limited
to a few milliseconds to give a satisfactory
service. Variations in delay are also undesirable although little quantitative information
is available on this aspect.

4.4   Tolerable Errors/Loss of Information

The error rates that may be regarded as
acceptable vary with the service. For computer
communications, with little redundancy, the
error rate should be extremely low. Human communication services normally involve considerable redundancy so that some errors can be
tolerated. However, if signal processing
removes some of the redundancy, the effects of
errors become more significant.

It is fortunate that errors and delays are
complementary for virtually all telecommunica-

tion services. If a very low error rate is required it is normally acceptable to introduce an additional delay while the errors are corrected by retransmission.

4.5   Congestion

All economic telecommunication networks suffer from the effects of traffic congestion. In a circuit switched network, the system is normally designed so that an arbitrary proportion of the calls are lost due to congestion during the busy hour, although it is possible to design the system so as to optimise the profit or the cost-benefit.(3)

For non-circuit-switched networks, the effects of traffic congestion are more complex. It is possible to design the system so that the initial effects of congestion are to cause a degradation in the performance of existing calls rather than a loss of new calls. Eventually, as congestion builds up, new calls have to be refused but the important advantage of the graceful degradation effect is that transmission capacity does not need to be engaged until the called subscriber answers. For real-time human communication services, this method of operation would result in savings in transmission capacity of about 25%.

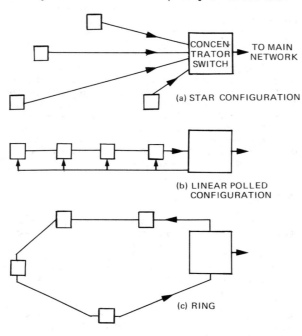

(a) STAR CONFIGURATION

(b) LINEAR POLLED CONFIGURATION

(c) RING

Fig 5 LOCAL DISTRIBUTION & CONCENTRATION

5   DESIGN OF SWITCHING NODES

5.1   Concentrator Stage

In any switched network, some form of local distribution system and concentrator switch are necessary to gather the traffic from the terminals and multiplex it into a form suitable for the main network. The distribution system may take several different forms as shown in the examples in Fig 5. In some cases the traffic concentration is inherent in the distribution. The basic operation, although

important, is common to both circuits and non-circuit switched networks and need not be considered further.

5.2   Circuit Switched Node

The main functions of a circuit switched node are shown in Fig 6. The basic design is similar irrespective of whether it is located adjacent to the concentrator switch or at an intermediate node in the network.

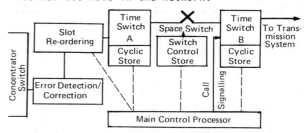

Fig 6 CONVENTIONAL CIRCUIT SWITCH

The signalling information sent at the beginning of the call enables the space- and time-switches to be set up to route the call to the required outgoing multiplexed transmission link. For a multiservice network, it is necessary to engage enough slots in the multiplex to carry the maximum bit-rate of the service required. Initially, the slots at the sending end will be in the correct order, although they may be interspersed with other channels in the multiplex. If time switching is involved, the sequence of the channels is liable to change (Fig 2) and it will be necessary to re-order the channels at the receiving end.

5.3   Variable Bit-Rate Node

Both dynamic slot allocations and store-and-forward technology may be considered as the basis for the design of a VBR node. An important consideration is the delay characteristic and, although store-and-forward (packet) systems have been used for voice service(4,5), it is very difficult to achieve satisfactory real-time performance in a large network. The framing inherent in synchronous dynamic slot-allocation imposes an upper limit to the delay and, for this reason, is regarded as the more fundamental technology for a multiservice network.

The provision of a packet switched network service is still desirable, particularly to provide the capability for error correction by retransmission. This can be achieved in a fundamentally dynamic slot-allocation system by adding the storage required to provide the necessary retransmission facility.

It is important to regard the synchronous dynamic slot-allocation technology as the fundamental basis of design and to add on the store and forward technology for those network services that require it rather than the other way round. Storage can be added; delay cannot be subtracted.

The outline design of a switching node is illustrated in Fig 7. The information offered by the concentrator or by an incoming multiplex link is first stored in the 'A' time-switch. It is then passed through a space switch as determined by the control, to the time-switch B, which is associated with a particular outgoing route.

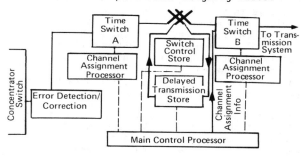

Fig 7 VARIABLE BIT−RATE SWITCH

If the total multiplexed information for the outgoing route exceeds the capacity of the frame, the control then has to decide whether to abandon the less significant information or to store it for transmission in a subsequent, less heavily loaded, frame. Information that may be required to be retransmitted in the event of errors is also stored.

An important design parameter is the length of the frame. The advantage of a long frame is that better statistical smoothing from the channel inputs is achieved. An upper limit to the frame length is set by the delay that can be tolerated at the switching node, since a delay of up to one frame may be introduced at each of the time switches A and B. Synchronization recovery and the cost of storage both tend to favour a short frame.

5.4 Hybrid Circuit and Variable Bit-Rate Switch

Hybrid circuit and variable bit-rate switched systems have been proposed. In some cases, the system effectively offers separate circuit switched and packet facilities(6,7); in others, a single slot circuit switched connection is established for each call and additional slots are seized as necessary to handle the instantaneous increases in bit-rate.(8)

6 COMPARISON BETWEEN CIRCUIT-SWITCHED AND VARIABLE BIT-RATE SYSTEMS

6.1 Switching and Signalling

Although the switching nodes shown in Figs 6 and 7 have much in common, there are considerable differences in their realization. For the circuit-switched node, once the time switches are set up by the main control, simple cyclic stores are sufficient to ensure that the time switches operate correctly throughout the call.

The switch control for a VBR system is more complex. It must first make the basic transmit/abandon/store decision for each slot in the multiplex and, in the case of the B switch transmit the channel assignment information as part of the frame. The decision algorithm is relatively complex for a multiservice system and, although some processing may be carried out as the frame is assembled, the final decisions must be made in a fraction of the frame interval.

There is no basic technical difficulty in achieving such rapid processing but the processor must be carefully designed and will add to the cost of the switching node.

6.2 Transmission

In a VBR system, the transmission capacity is used only to the extent that a particular channel has information to transmit. Apart from the small amount of channel assignment information, the transmission capacity so freed may be used to accommodate an increased number of channels.

For data, the gain is determined by the activity factor, which varies over a very wide range. A gain of about 2:1 in the number of channels carried has been shown to be feasible for a voice service.(9) For real-time picture services, much depends on the nature of the pictures to be transmitted. If there is normally little movement, a very considerable gain in channel may be expected since only the differences between successive frames need be sent. For example, an assessment(10) based on a picturephone service shows that gains of about 5:1 can be expected.

6.3 Economic Aspects

The basic economic trade-off is that of the cost of increased storage and processing in the switching node against the savings on the transmission links. Exact comparisons are difficult because relatively little equipment has been constructed for VBR systems. However preliminary studies have shown that the difference in the quantity of equipment required for a VBR switching node and that needed for a multiservice circuit switched node is not excessive. To some extent, the additional control and storage cost of statistical multiplexing in a VBR system is compensated by the slot reordering requirement in the circuit switched case for services requiring multislot operation.

Furthermore, the trend in technology is for the cost of digital processing equipment to fall at a much higher rate than the cost of transmission systems, and this will tend to make the VBR approach increasingly attractive.

More effective use of radio spectrum and satellite orbit space is a further point in favour of VBR systems but difficult to quantify in economic terms.

7 NETWORK EVOLUTION

Although there are considerable advantages in a VBR network, there remains the problem of progressing from an existing network, based predominantly on FDM transmission and space division switching but which contains an increasing amount of digital transmission and switching based on 64 kbit/s channels.

Fig 8 shows the main stages of evolution towards a multiservice VBR network. In the first stage, the 64 kbit/s channels are retained in the

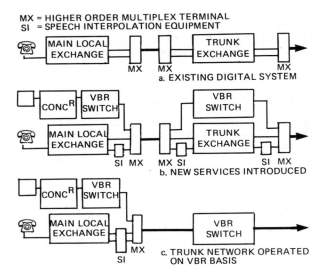

MX = HIGHER ORDER MULTIPLEX TERMINAL
SI = SPEECH INTERPOLATION EQUIPMENT

a. EXISTING DIGITAL SYSTEM

b. NEW SERVICES INTRODUCED

c. TRUNK NETWORK OPERATED ON VBR BASIS

Fig 8 EVOLUTION FROM CIRCUIT SWITCHED TO VBR NETWORK

switching nodes but more effective use is made of the transmission capacity by signal processing and time assignment for the transmission links only.

As wideband and new data services are introduced, separate switch units are used to provide the VBR switching capability. Common signalling is used for both systems and common higher-order multiplexes are used. Where interworking between the two systems is necessary (eg for some types of data service) gateway units are provided.

Finally, as the intermediate trunk switches are replaced, VBR operation may be extended to the whole of the main network. Existing circuit switched exchanges are retained mainly to switch locally and to concentrate voice traffic on to the main trunk network.

8 CONCLUSIONS

A study of the long-term requirements of an integrated services digital network has considered both circuit-switching and a range of non-circuit-switching techniques. The initial implementation of an ISDN will be based on 64 kbit/s (or 56 kbit/s) circuit-switched channels. This type of ISDN will serve as the basis for the introduction of a substantial range of voice and non-voice services. However, at some stage in the future, the demand for an even wider range of services may be expected to exert pressure to move away from the 64 kbit/s standard for the main trunk network.

A non-circuit-switched network would remove many of the constraints inherent in circuit switching. It could be designed to carry economically every conceivable telecommunication service and would facilitate the early exploitation of new technology.

In considering the options for a non-circuit-switched network, the limitation that might be imposed by any delay impairments is seen as a very important factor. For this reason, dynamic slot-allocation is preferred as the fundamental basis of design rather than a store-and-forward technology.

Although a non-circuit-switched network might appear to represent a radical departure from a circuit-switched digital network, it appears feasible to make the change in a controlled evolutionary manner. Existing message-type signalling can be extended without much difficulty and local exchanges would continue to be used, mainly for voice traffic. The non-circuit-switched trunk network would be introduced gradually by the addition of subsystems rather than by widespread plant replacement.

The implementation of a public telecommunications network normally takes a decade or more. The system definition and planning operations and the establishment of national and international standards therefore need to be started well in advance of the main service demand. The rate of advance of technology is such that demand may be with us sooner than hitherto expected.

9 ACKNOWLEDGEMENTS

Acknowledgement is made to the Director, System Evolution and Standards Department, British Telecom for permission to publish this paper. Discussions with many colleagues on non-circuit-switched systems are also gratefully acknowledged.

10 REFERENCES

1 "CCITT Signalling System No 7" CCITT Yellow Book, Vol 6 (1980).

2 RATZ H C and FIELD J A "Economic comparison of data communication services" Computer Networks, Vol 4, p.143 (Sept 80).

3 LITTLECHILD S C "Elements of telecommunications economics" p.151 (Pub Peter Peregrinus Ltd).

4 MINOLI D "Issues in packet voice communication" Proc IEE, Vol 126, No 8 (Aug 79).

5 FRANK H and GITMAN I "Study shows packet switching best for voice traffic too" Data Communications, Vol 8, Pt 3 (Mar 79).

6 GERLA M and MUELLER D "PACUIT the integrated packet and circuit alternative to packet switching" COMPCON 78 (San Francisco).

7 ROSS M J "Alternatives for integrating voice and data" International Switching Symposium, Montreal (1981).

8 HUGHES C J "Signal processing versus transmission in telecommunication networks" IERE Conference on Digital Processing of Signals in Communications (Loughborough 1981).

9 FRASER J M, BULLOCK D B and LONG N G "Overall characteristics of a TASI system" BSTJ, Vol 41, p.1439 (July 62).

10 HUGHES C J et al "Service characterization and modelling for variable bit-rate switching systems" International Switching Symposium, Montreal (1981).

Charles Hughes has Bachelor's and Master's degrees from London University and is a Fellow of the Institution of Electrical Engineers.

He has had a career in research and development laboratories with Cable and Wireless Limited and with British Telecom. In recent years he has been concerned with many aspects of telecommunications switching systems and is now a Deputy Director and Head of the Advanced Systems Unit at British Telecom Research Laboratories, Martlesham, near Ipswich.

Future Facilities in Digital Network

T Arita, K Imai, S Yoshida
Nippon Telegraph and Telephone
Public Corporation, Japan

This paper proposes, considering the actual result of DDX service commercial test in Japan and recent technical tendency of voice encoding, desirable facilities in the future digital network, and presents several realization techniques.
(1) Voice and non-voice services oriented communication facilities such as independent forward/backward path control (multi-address delivery without network storage, simultaneous send/receive communication with different terminals)
(2) Packet/circuit switched network interconnection and processing nodes in digital network
(3) Multi-purpose terminal/network interface (frame structure of Ax interface)
(4) A future digital network configuration example toward ISDN

1. Introduction

Circuit switching and Packet switching services have already been offered in Japan, and expansion of these networks to the whole country with enhanced service facilities is being planned now.

Existing telephone network is gradually changing from analog system to fully digital system.

It is expected that these networks will be organically combined and develope into a fruitful digital network in the future. Considering these circumstances, the authors propose desirable facilities in the future digital network.

2. Digital network merits

Digital network merits are considered as follows.

(1) 0 dB loss communication by digital 1 link connection
(2) Economical communication possibilities
(3) Widely selective communication services by multi-purpose terminal/network interface

Item (1) is essential in the digital network. Items (2) and (3) are discussed hereafter.

3. Digital communication economy

3.1 Voice/non-voice communication categories

Non-voice communication is classified into the following three categories.

(a) Bulk transfer (File transfer,Facsimile communication etc.)
(b) Conversational (Telemetering,Videotex etc.)
(c) Mixed (Data-base access etc.)

Data flow in non-voice communication is mostly one-directional at a time, and it is rare to use backword and forward circuits simultaneously.(Table 1)

Terminal to terminal bulk data transfer, which is common in Teletext communication, will become more and more popular, and one-directional data flow will retain the main position in non-voice communication.

Furthermore, many users, if there were a slightest bit cost diffrence in service classes, will utilize the service class whose tariff per bit is minimum.

When a circuit switching service is restricted to the bidirectional transmission, just like telephone communication, many users will select a packet switching for more efficient data transmission.

In the case of DDX system in Japan, circuit switching service tariff per bit is lower than that for Packet switching service, if the circuit switched both-way transmission lines are fully used.

However, in practical cases, the Circuit switched service transmission density cannot be so high.

Therefore, it is desirable to control backward and forward circuits independently, and also to shorten the call setup time.

3.2 Independent forward/backward circuit control

Independent control of each forward or backward path is easily realized in memory switch (T-switch).[1],[2]

The problem is to determine how the backward circuit can be prepared after the forward information is transmitted.

Three backward transmission categories are shown in Fig. 1.

(a) Lower bit-rate channel
A lower bit-rate channel is prepared for backward transfer. This category is appropriate for a call whose backward message amount is small, but is required frequently.

Facsimile communication and Videotex service are examples of this category.
(b) Packet mode channel
HDLC frame structured backward message are

Table I Communication Form

Category	Example	Communication Form
Bulk Transfer	File transfer Facsimile	
Conver-sational	Tele-metering Videotex	
Mixed	Data-base access	
Telephone		

transfered through a packet switched or common signaling network. This is suitable for a small amount and not frequent backward message calls.

(c) One-directional connection

This category fits to the call for rather long message transfered from each side alternatively.

Application fields for these three categories are shown in Fig. 2.

In case of category (a), there are two ways to lower bit-rate channel setup on subscriber line.(Fig. 3)

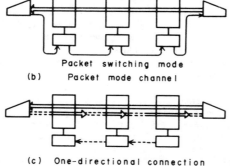

(a) Lower-bit-rate channel

V₁ : Low speed
V₂ : High speed

Circuit switching mode

Packet switching mode

(b) Packet mode channel

(c) One-directional connection

Fig.1 Backward transmission methods

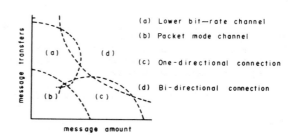

(a) Lower bit-rate channel
(b) Packet mode channel
(c) One-directional connection
(d) Bi-directional connection

Fig.2 Backward transmission methods application fields

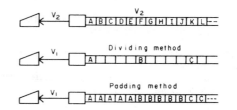

Dividing method

Padding method

Fig.3 Lower-bit rate channel setup on subscriber line

One is to use one V_1 channels divided from basic subscriber bit-rate V_2 $(V_1={1 \over N}V_2)$. Another is padding V_1 on V_2.

The selection of them is performed through the signaling channel in terminal/network interface, which will be discussed in Section 4.

Various signaling rate selection for the backward path can be extended to the communication service for a selective speed terminal. Selective speeds communication examples in a circuit switched service are shown in Fig. 4.

The packet mode backward message transfer (b) will be realized by multi-purpose interface discussed in Section 4.

Packet mode backward message transfer may realize the following efficient communication methods.

3.2.1 Multi-address call without storage

To realize a multi-address call in a circuit switching system, usually the same message is sent from the storage equipment in originating terminal or in the network to every destination terminal, one by one.

A digital network, however, contains the following characteristics.

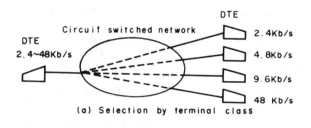

(a) Selection by terminal class

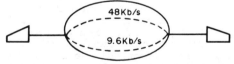

(b) Selection by communication content

Fig.4 Selective speeds communication examples

(a) Transmission quality will not be lowered by one-directional multi-connection (1 to N connection) because of 0 dB loss characteristics.
(b) The backward message can be transfered by packet multiplexed mode from every destination terminal to the originating terminal.

From the above conditions, the realtime multi-address call (Fig. 5) can be realized. The transfer time will be shortened (1/N) and the transmission line will be efficiently used.

3.2.2 Simultaneous different terminals connection

Although there are usually signal sender and receiver in a non-voice communication terminal, it is rare for both sender and receiver to be used at the same time.

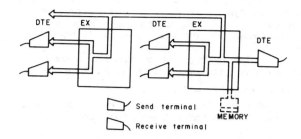

Fig.5 Multi-address calling (1 to N connection)

If the one-directional connection and packet mode backward message transfer techniques are applied to such a terminal, it will be possible to connect more than three terminals in a row at the same time.

This means the efficient use of terminal equipment and subscriber line.(Fig. 6)

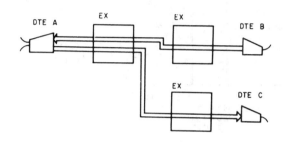

Fig.6 Sender/Receiver independent communication

3.3 Fast circuit switching

Figure 7 shows holding time examples of DDX Circuit switching service. Although samples are few, it shows that many calls are made in a short holding time.

These calls correspond to the path setting method shown in Fig. 1(c), which requires path connection and disconnection for every message transfer. Program controlled intelligent terminals may use such a call category more frequently.

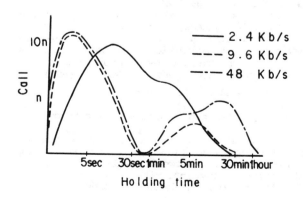

Fig.7 DDX circuit switching service holding time examples

In such a case, path setting procedure for every message transfer has the effect of an overhead to both subscriber and network, and simplified procedure and fast call setup are necessary.

The authors have already proposed a virtual call concept for a circuit switching service.(Fast Circuit Switching)[3]

Figure 8(a) shows the call setup time analysis for DDX Circuit switching service.

Fast Circuit Switching reduces the message setup time to one tenth of normal call setup time, as shown in Fig. 8(b), for a 2.4 Kbit/sec synchronous terminal.

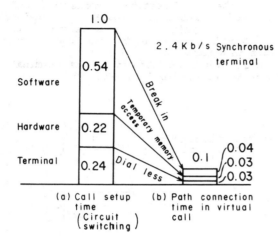

Fig.8 Fast path connection effect

This is one of the challenging ways to obtain information volume charge in a circuit switched service. Its application field versus a packet switched service should be surveyed, taking into account processing cost increase.

3.4 CS/PS common access, Store and forward service

Non-storage circuit switching (CS) and packet switching (PS) interconnection can be made by two methods. One is CS and PS selection by subscriber accommodation equipment (Line concentrator for CS, or Packet multiplexer for PS).(Fig. 9(a))

The other is CS and PS network interconnection through a gateway equipment.(Fig. 9(b))

To achieve more useful message handling services, a communication processing node is required. For this purpose, a Store-and-forward Processing Service Center (SSC) is being developed in NTT, Japan.[4]

4. Multi-purpose terminal/network interface

In addition to the economical communication techniques mentioned in Section 3, the future digital network will provide a multi-purpose terminal/network interface to offer the following wide user demands.

(1) Holding time proportional charging or transmitted information volume charging selection in every call

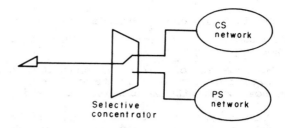

(a) CS and PS selection

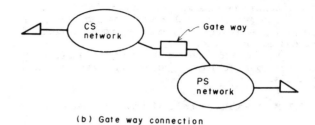

(b) Gate way connection

Fig.9 CS and PS interconnection

(2) Communication speed selection in every call
(3) Communication quality (e.g. voice encoding bit-rate) selection
(4) Other communication factors selection

Customer access arrangement discussed in CCITT (Ax) will support these facilities.[5]

Various multi-purpose interface utilizations are so much alike that various electric apparatuses can be used by connecting them to an outlet.

Ax interface image will be as follows.

(1) Interconnection with existing interface (e.g. X21) is possible by logical interface conversion.(Fig. 10)
(2) Four circuits physical connection by multiplexing data channels and a control channel.(Fig. 11) In this case, terminal equipment should extract clock signal and control channel. To connect with existing X21 interface, an additional interface adapter may be used to convert the four Ax circuits to eleven X21 circuits.

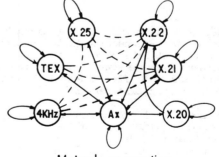

Mutual connection is possible

Connected through communication processing node

Fig.10 Ax interface and existing interface

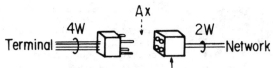

Arrester, Ping-pong transmission control
Wave form transformation, Test loop, etc

Fig.11 Multi-purpose outlet

(3) Time multiplexed frame structure example is shown in Fig. 12.

In the future, when optical fiber is commonly used, long frame structure will be useful. They will be exchanged by a wide-band electronic digital switch.

(4) As a protocol for control signal transmission, High level Data Link Control (HDLC) is preferable, owing to its data format flexibility and hardware cost reduction by dedicated LSI. The control channel, which transmits control signal for data channels, can also handle X25 user data by its HDLC function.

(5) Data channels can be used for circuit switched and/or packet switched channels, as appointed in the control channel.(Fig. 13) End to end signals to negotiate divided channels usage can also be carried on the control channel, just like terminal to network signals.

NB + D

(N ≥ 2)

```
F B B B --- B D
```

F : Framing bit
B : Information channel
D : Signal channel

Fig.12 Ax interface frame structure example

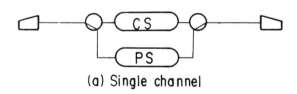

(a) Single channel

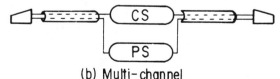

(b) Multi-channel
CS: Circuit Switching PS: Packet Switching

Fig.13 Circuit/Packet switched channel selection

5. Future digital network image

Network structure, composed by facilities described in Sections 3 and 4, are shown in Fig. 14.

Main features of this network structure are as follows.

(1) The whole network consists of real-time network by circuit switching, and store-and-forward network by packet switching.
(2) Existing X series interface terminals are accommodated in circuit switched and/or packet switched network.
(3) Multi-purpose interface (Ax) terminals can access either a circuit switched or a packet switched network through a new concentrating equipment.
(4) Circuit switched network offers various bit-rates transmission for non-voice communication.

It also has independent forward/backward channel control and virtual call setup functions. It uses packet switched network or common signaling network for backward signal transmission.
(5) Packet switched network also transfers end to end signals for Ax interface terminals.

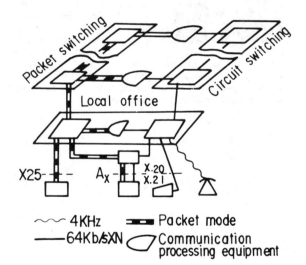

~~~ 4KHz   ▬▬ Packet mode
—— 64Kb/sXN ⬭ Communication
                processing equipment

Fig.14 Future network structure

6. Conclusion

Because of the recent progress in micro-computers, signal processing LSIs and semi-conductor memories, future intelligent terminals may have various functions which are provided in the network in these days, and may require the network to offer many communication modes to choose the mostly cost-effective one.
This paper proposes several basic functions to match the above mentioned user demands. One of the digital network main features is effective communication processing ability.

Future digital network must provide such useful features to meet customer requirements.

References

(1) S.Tomita, et al., "Some Aspects of Time-Division Data Switch Design" Proc. IEEE, Vol.65, No.9 (1977)

(2) K.Mawatari, et al., "A Distributed Control Digital Data Switching System", ISS'79

(3) M.Kato, et al., "Fast Circuit Switching", ICCC'80 (Oct. 1980)

(4) S.Matsushita, et al., "Message Handling Facilities for Public Use in DDX", ICCC'80 (Oct. 1980)

(5) CCITT SGXVIII, "Report on the Meeting of group of experts on ISDN Matters of Study Group XVIII (Munich, 17-25 Feb. 1982)", CCITT SGXVIII Temp. Doc. 27

Shinichro Yoshida is a staff engineer of Integrated Communication Division, Yokosuka Electrical Laboratory of NTT. He received the B.S. and M.S. degrees from Waseda Univercity in 1969 and 1971, respectively. Since joining ECL in 1971, he has been engaged in the development of a DDX circuit switching system and EPABXs. He is presently engaged in fundamental developmental studies on integrated switching systems and on new service features in digital EPABX He is a member of the Institute of Electronics and Communication Engineer of Japan.

Takemi Arita is a staff engineer of Switching Systems Development Division, Musashino Electrical Laboratory of NTT. He received the B.S. and M.S. degrees both from Tokyo Institute of Technology. Since joining the NTT in 1969, he was engaged in computer software development, and in DDX circuit and packet switching equipments. He is now engaged in developing satellite switching system. He is a member of the Institute of Electronics and Communication Engineer of Japan.

Kazuo Imai is an engineer of Switching Systems Development Division, Musashino Electrical communication Laboratory of NTT. He received the B.S. and M.S. degrees both from Kyoto Univercity in 1974 and 1976. Since joining the laboratory in 1976, he has been engaged in developmental research on digital data switching systems. He is a member of the Institute of Electronics and Communication Engineer of Japan.

Packet-switched Data Communication Services in the ISDN

V Frantzen
Siemens, Federal Republic of Germany

End-to-end digitalization of public telephone networks leads to the concept of an Integrated Services Digital Network (ISDN) that uses standard 64 kbit/s digital channels both for the transmission of PCM-coded speech and for a wide range of new and established non-voice services. Even though emphasis will be on a new service independent ISDN-type interface (S) that will enable new terminals to exploit the full range of ISDN features, ISDN will also provide for the connection of existing terminals in accordance with CCITT Recommendations X.21 and X.25. This paper deals with possible solutions for incorporating PS facilities into ISDN. Different degrees of integration of PS facilities within ISDN are discussed. In particular, various approaches for the access of X.25-DTEs to a PS facility within the ISDN are described.

1. INTRODUCTION

Advances in semiconductor technology and economic advantages have been leading towards an increasing use of digital techniques in public telephone networks. By applying digital techniques not only to interexchange transmission and switching but also to subscriber loops, due to the feasibility of incorporating the necessary analog/digital converters into the telephone terminal, public telephone networks will evolve into end-to-end digital telecommunications networks. In fact, pulse code modulation (PCM) techniques are being employed to convert analog telephone channels into digital channels with a bit rate of 64 kbit/s. However, the main attraction of complete digitalization is the possibility to use the standard 64 kbit/s channels employed throughout digital telephone networks not only for PCM encoded speech but also for a wide range of new and established non voice services. This leads to the concept of an Integrated Services Digital Network (ISDN) /1,2,3,4/.

Even though it is likely that existing dedicated data networks will continue to exist for a considerable time after the introduction of ISDN a demand for offering X.21 and X.25 data communication services to ISDN subscribers can be expected /5,6/. This paper deals with possible solutions for incorporating packet switched (PS) facilities into ISDN. Section 2 gives a survey of the functional structure and the related interfaces of the basic ISDN customer access. In section 3 different degrees of integration of PS facilities into ISDN are discussed such as interworking with dedicated PS networks, a PS overlay network within the ISDN. Furthermore, various approaches to the access of X.25 terminals to PS facilities in the ISDN are examined in section 4, the basic alternatives being the user information channel (B-channel) and the common signalling channel (D-channel).

2. SURVEY OF BASIC ISDN CUSTOMER ARRANGEMENTS AND ACCESS INTERFACES

The concept emerging for the basic customer access to the ISDN will be highlighted in this section, as seen from the present state of discussion at CCITT /7,8,9,/. Figure 1 shows the functional structure and the related interfaces at the customer's premises and at the corresponding termination of the digital local exchange. Due to the larger bandwidth resulting from the use of digital technology, a time division multiplexed channel structure of two B-channels and one D-channel will be available at the ISDN user/network interface via existing two-wire subscriber access lines.

2.1 The user information channel (B-channel)

B designates one of two independent circuit switched 64 kbit/s user information channels which may be used simultaneously towards different destinations. The standard bit rate of 64 kbit/s stems from the fact that digital transmission and switching systems are based on 64 kbit/s PCM channels as described in CCITT Recommendation G.703. As a consequence of the circuit-switched digital nature of the ISDN, B-channels are characterized by end-to-end transparency and correspond to the physical layer of the OSI model. Therefore, besides its original task of carrying PCM encoded digital voice (i.e. information type v) the B-channel can also be used for the transport of data information (i.e. information type d) or other types of non-voice information (e.g. text, facsimile, interactive videotex, etc.).

2.2 The common signalling channel (D-channel)

D designates a separate i.e. out-slot signalling channel which is shared by the set of terminals which may be attached to the particular ISDN network termination NT12 in various multiterminal installations. Besides the star access configuration depicted in Figure 1 bus and ring in house distribution schemes will also be foreseen. In contrast to the B-channel the D-channel is message interleaved and is primarily designed to carry the signalling information (i.e. information type s) that controls the handling of B-channels through

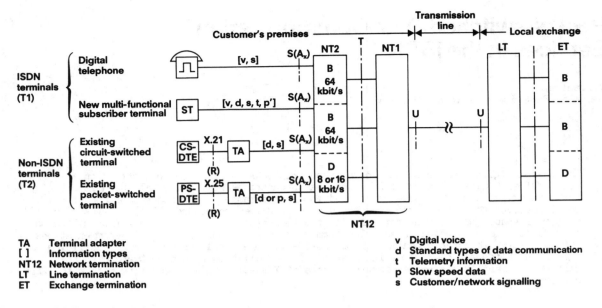

TA   Terminal adapter
[ ]   Information types
NT12 Network termination
LT   Line termination
ET   Exchange termination

v   Digital voice
d   Standard types of data communication
t   Telemetry information
p   Slow speed data
s   Customer/network signalling

Fig. 1   ISDN multiservice customer arrangements and access interfaces

the ISDN. The out-slot D-channel offers enhanced signalling capabilities to new ISDN services since the exchange of s-information does not interfere with the transport of user data (i.e. information type d) on the B-channels. In other words, signalling information may be conveyed during an established B-channel connection. In addition to carrying s-information the D-channel might optionally be used for the transport of low bit rate message-oriented data (i.e. information type p) and for telemetry information (i.e. information type t). This latter group includes new services such as remote meter reading, telecontrol, remote alarm monitoring, etc. As regards the use of the D-channel for p-information certain limitations concerning data throughput and the related quality of service (call set-up time, transit delay) have to be accepted, if significant performance and/or cost penalties for the prime task of the D-channel, i.e. carriage of s-information, are to be avoided. The bit rate of the D-channel will be 16 kbit/s.

2.3 Interfaces for the attachment of
    subscriber terminals

In the ISDN multiterminal and multiservice customer arrangement - as shown in Figure 1 - two different categories of subscriber terminals and related interfaces can be identified:

- New ISDN terminals will use a new universal interface S that is tuned to the ISDN channel structure of B + B + D and employs out-slot signalling. The S interface can be regarded as a service independent "ISDN type" interface to which voice terminals, i.e. digital telephone sets, as well as future non voice terminals can be directly connected. In this context a call control procedure is envisaged which would be common to all circuit switched ISDN services i.e. digital telephony and circuit switched data communications. New ISDN terminals comprise a future generation of multifunctional or even multiservice ISDN terminals exploiting

the full range of features offered by ISDN.

- Bearing in mind that circuit and packet switched services are already offered by dedicated data networks in many countries in accordance with adopted X.-series CCITT Recommendations, provisions have to be made for the connection of existing text and data terminal equipment, i.e. Non-ISDN terminals, to the ISDN. R implies existing X.-series interfaces such as X.21 and X.25 corresponding to circuit and packet switched user classes of service respectively, at bit rates lower than 64 kbit/s consistent with Rec. X.1. Terminals with interfaces X.21 or X.25 will be connected to the ISDN network termination NT12 by means of suitable terminal adapter (TA) functions.

2.4 The network termination (NT12)

Before looking more closely at the possible solutions for providing X.21 and X.25 data communications services, let us review in brief the essential functions allocated to the ISDN network termination NT12.

- NT1 performs "simple" functions associated with the proper physical and electrical termination of the network. NT1 functions that may be regarded as belonging to the physical layer (layer 1) of the OSI reference model include line transmission termination, maintenance (test loops), timing and power feeding, etc.

- NT2, in principle, also comprises functions belonging to the link and network layers (i.e. layers 2 and 3) of the OSI model. This applies to the "intelligent" NT2 which handles levels 2 and 3 of the D-channel protocol thus providing for the control and coordination of the customer's multiple terminal installation. In this case the local exchange need not be aware of the terminal configuration at the customer's premises and will only be required to support a point-to-point communication with the NT2. Another case currently under consideration regards the "transparent" NT2 which would be confined to layer 1 functions, e.g. contention resolution concerning D-channel access by several terminals for outgoing calls. In the case of a transparent NT2 the local exchange would have to support a point-to-multipoint (multidrop) configuration by operating multiple (parallel) logical links (LAPs) on the same D-channel. The different LAP end points would be located in the various subscriber terminals on one hand and in the local exchange on the other.

2.5 Adaption of X.21 to ISDN

The circuit switched B-channel connections with a bitrate of 64 kbit/s may be used to offer X.21 data communications services to ISDN customers without any impact on the network as such. The provisions necessary for the connection of X.21 terminals with user rates according to X.1 user classes 3 - 7 can be restricted to a suitable terminal adapter TA. Essentially, adaption functions for X.21 include

- Adaption of X.1 user rates to the 64 kbit/s bearer rate of the B-channel

- Mapping of the X.21 in-slot call control procedure to the out-slot signalling protocol on the D-channel

- In-slot synchronization procedure to be executed between the TA's involved, in order to enable synchronized entry in and leaving of the state "ready for data" for the communicating X.21 terminals, as provided by existing dedicated networks. Due to the message interleaved, i.e. not time transparent nature of the ISDN D-channel, a precise synchronization of through connection at both X.21 interfaces cannot be achieved by means of D-channel messages.

While X.21 can be completely integrated into ISDN as shown above, the provision of packet switched services with interface X.25 can be expected to have a greater impact on a circuit switched network like ISDN. This will be dealt with in the following sections.

3. DIFFERENT DEGREES OF INTEGRATION OF X.25 SERVICES AND FACILITIES INTO ISDN

Service integration being the key characteristic of ISDN, a need for offering X.25 data communication services to ISDN customers can be anticipated. In principle, this demand can be expected to continue after extensive introduction of circuit switched ISDN data communication services due to specific advantages of packet switching for interactive applications (bursty traffic i.e. low volume users with long connect times) and to the multichannel access facility of Recommendation X.25.

For the introduction of packet switched services into ISDN various integration models and related customer access arrangements can be conceived. In this context, it should be taken into account that ISDN will be based upon the digitized telephony network. In consequence,

when considering network functions and the provision of user facilities offered by an ISDN two categories can be identified:

- Basic functions related to circuit switched 64 kbit/s digital connections. These have to be provided by all ISDN exchanges for the purpose of digital telephony and can also be utilized for circuit switched data and text communication (X.21) as shown in the previous section.

- Additional functions which go beyond the network resources of the basic circuit switched version of ISDN. Included in this category are special features requiring store and forward capabilities.

Based on the above discussion a very pragmatic approach to the introduction of ISDN would be to restrict the functionality of the normal ISDN exchanges to basic circuit switched functions. Thus, additional ISDN functions such as packet switching would either continue to be provided by existing packet switched data networks (PSDNs) or could be performed by special equipment located at particular ISDN switching centers depending on the conditions in the various countries.

- In the case of the internetworking solution (see Figure 2a) the ISDN acts as a transparent access media to a PSDN. Access to the PSDN will be accomplished through an ISDN interworking unit of the PSDN. In other words, the DCE function is treated in the PSDN for the link (2) and packet (3) levels of X.25. Although packet switching functions are still separately handled by dedicated networks in this case, it provides for service integration in terms of an integrated access to packet switched facilities.

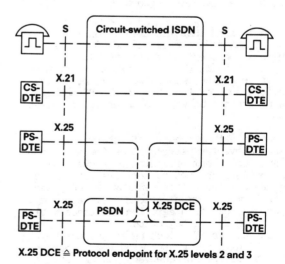

X.25 DCE ≙ Protocol endpoint for X.25 levels 2 and 3

CS-DTE Circuit-switched DTE
PS-DTE Packet-switched DTE

Fig. 2a   Internetworking solution

- Another solution is to include packet switching functions in the circuit switched

ISDN. In order to unburden the normal ISDN switches from X.25 handling this can be achieved by installing specialized equipment, hereafter called packet switching modules, in just a few suitable ISDN switching centers. Packet switching modules (PSM) of different ISDN switching centers could be interconnected by means of semipermanent 64 kbit/s ISDN channels i.e. by 64 kbit/s connections which are semipermanently switched through the switching networks of the involved ISDN switches. Thus, a set of PSM's interconnected by standard PS trunk protocols (i.e. CCITT Recommendation X.75) would form a packet switched overlay network within ISDN as shown in Figure 2b.

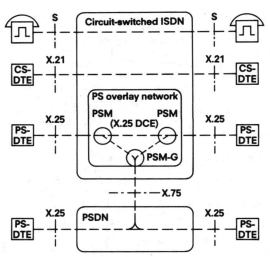

PSM   Packet switching module
PSM-G   Packet switching module (gateway)

Fig. 2b   PS overlay network within ISDN

Bearing in mind that the transition from present dedicated data networks to ISDN will require a long period of time, it is obvious that the capability for interworking between ISDN and existing data networks is essential. Therefore some of the PSMs of the PS subnetwork behave as gateways to an existing packet network.

To summarize the concepts of interworking and of the PS overlay network allow for an economic and short term provision of packet switched services to ISDN subscribers without causing a significant cost penalty to the predominant form of communications i.e. telephony. Deeper degrees of integration are conceivable such as complete integration of PS facilities by means of hybrid switching techniques, e.g. CS and PS data being supported within common switching equipment. However, taking into account that ISDN will be based on the digital telephone network, it does not appear economical, to integrate PS facilities into the local exchanges. For a considerable time PS services in the ISDN will rather remain centralized, i.e. they will be offered as a kind of "value added service" by dedicated equipment that can be accessed from the ISDN subscriber access via ISDN channels. Therefore the remainder of

this paper will be devoted to the internetworking and overlay network solutions with particular emphasis on the latter.

4. ACCESS OF X.25 TERMINALS TO PACKET-SWITCHED FACILITIES IN THE ISDN

Let us now consider the possible solutions for the access of packet terminals with X.25 interface to packet switched ISDN facilities e.g. to a packet switching module PSM. Recalling the customer access arrangements for the basic access from section 2 the choice lies between the B-channel (Figure 3a) and the D-channel (Figure 3b).

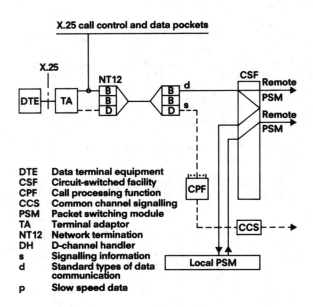

DTE	Data terminal equipment
CSF	Circuit-switched facility
CPF	Call processing function
CCS	Common channel signalling
PSM	Packet switching module
TA	Terminal adaptor
NT12	Network termination
DH	D-channel handler
s	Signalling information
d	Standard types of data communication
p	Slow speed data

Fig. 3a   PSM access through B-channel

The X.25 DTE may use one B-channel of the envisaged B + B + D access structure as a physical access path to a PSM that would be connected to the ISDN switch via a standard 64 kbit/s channel. Thus, X.25 call control and data transfer packets could be conveyed in-slot as d-type information between the X.25 terminal adaptor and the PSM. The B-channel connection employed for accessing the PSM could either be switched or non-switched. In the first case the same out-slot signalling procedure that is used for voice and circuit switched data communications could also be applied to establish the B-channel connection to the PSM. It should be noted that the PSM need not necessarily be located at the site of the ISDN local exchange to which the X.25 customer is connected. Instead X.25 packets could be routed further towards a remote PSM by means of B-channels on trunk lines.

The D-channel is designed primarily to carry the customer/network signalling information (information type s) that controls the handling of B-channels in the ISDN. Additionally, the D-channel may be used to transport slow speed user data (information type p) in a message interleaved manner with s information. In this way X.25 call control and data transfer packets would be conveyed out-slot as p-type

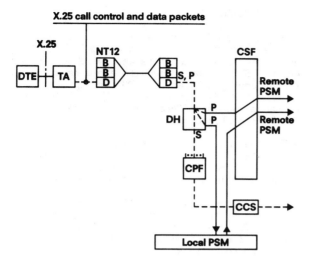

X.25 call control and data packets

Fig. 3b   PSM access through B-channel

information between the X.25 terminal adaptor
(TA) and the exchange terminal (ET) of the
ISDN local exchange. Bearing in mind that the
common channel signalling (CCS) network does
not seem appropriate for further routing of
X.25 packets onto a remote PSM a separation of
the respective information flows associated
with s and p is performed in a D-channel handler (DH) at the local exchange. Hence, in
accordance with the B-channel approach X.25
packets would be routed further using B-channels on trunk lines.

4.1 Access through the B-channel

Let us first examine the access of X.25 terminals or X.25 DTE's (data terminal equipment)
to a packet switching module PSM by means of
switched B-channels. In the case of switched
access the PSM could be connected to the ISDN
like a trunk exchange, i.e. digital trunks at

standard CCITT digital multiplex rates (e.g.
2 048 Mbit/s) and common channel signalling by
means of CCITT Signalling System No. 7 would
be used. With regard to minimizing the impact
of PS services on ISDN a two-phase call set-up
procedure is proposed (Figure 4). In a first
step a circuit switched 64 kbit/s channel is
established between the X.25 terminal adapter
TA and the PSM by means of regular out-slot
call control procedures (D-channel and CCS).
Once connected to an access port of the PSM
via a physical access path (in-slot), the X.25
DTE can exchange standard X.25 level 2 and
level 3 protocol elements with the PSM in
order to set-up virtual circuits to the called
X.25 terminal(s) as a second step. In Figure 4
the special case of interworking between X.25
DTE at the PS overlay network and a X.25 DTE
connected to a dedicated PS network (PSDN) is
illustrated. For calls originating from the
PSDN an escape code (digit) within the numbering plan for data networks, i.e. Rec. X.121,
may be employed to indicate that the called
X.25 DTE is located in the ISDN. In principle,
the double call request method shown in Figure
4 can also be applied to the previously mentioned internetworking solution.

When considering the B-channel access two conflicting requirements have to be dealt with

- efficient use of the 64 kbit/s channel

- real time properties i.e. minimal overall
  call set-up delay (CS and PS) for interactive applications.

Regarding the first requirement switched 64
kbit/s channels would be an optimum solution.
When taking into account that the ISDN topology will be similar to that of telephone networks and will deviate considerably from the
topology of dedicated networks it is obvious
that the second requirement will not be catered for. On the other hand, semipermanent 64
kbit/s access channels being dedicated to one
particular X.25 DTE, cannot be considered as
an efficient solution in terms of the first

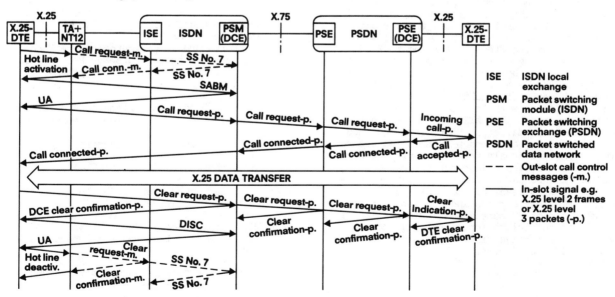

Fig. 4   Outgoing PS call/interworking ISDN→PSDN

ISE	ISDN local exchange
PSM	Packet switching module (ISDN)
PSE	Packet switching exchange (PSDN)
PSDN	Packet switched data network
- - -	Out-slot call control messages (-m.)
——	In-slot signal e.g. X.25 level 2 frames or X.25 level 3 packets (-p.)

requirement. Therefore, besides providing switched access for isolated X.25 terminals and semipermanent access for the connection of computer centers with high traffic volumes the following compromise solution is proposed for the access to PSM's:

In case of this mixed access switched 64 kbit/s connections will be used only up to the local ISDN exchange thus providing for a level 1 concentration of X.25 traffic. Between the local exchange and the PSM semipermanent connections will be used to carry the X.25 traffic.

In order to avoid significant changes to existing terminal equipment the X.25 DTE is only required to initiate the establishment of the 64 kbit/s access channel by means of a hot line type of signalling (e.g. direct call) in case of switched or mixed access.

4.2 Access through the D-channel

At first glance the possibility of devising common level 3 procedures for s, t and p information flows appears to be attractive. Furthermore, one might even think of using X.25 call control procedures as the common solution corresponding to the case of true integration of PS services into ISDN. However, the following considerations seem to preclude these solutions

- X.25 call control procedures are specifically designed to convey signalling information in an en-bloc fashion whereas digit-by-digit sending of selection information is required for telephone applications

- Mapping of X.25 level 3 procedures to any common solution other than X.25 would be required.

Therefore, a new call control procedure should be designed that would be common only to all circuit switched ISDN services i.e. digital telephony (v) and circuit switched data communications (d). The signalling messages of this out-slot call control procedure for circuit switching (s) would share the D-channel with packet information flows conforming to X.25 (p). Multiplexing of the s and p information flows can either be performed at layer 3 or at layer 2 of the D-channel. Multiplexing at layer 3 by means of a multiplexing sub layer would be in line with the OSI model but would require an intelligent NT2. Therefore, in the second case two different HDLC links are used for the transfer of s and p information according to the previously mentioned multiple LAP concept: LAP D (for s information, based on X.25 LAP B) and LAP B (for p information, conforming to X.25 level 2) could have different characteristics. For instance an information field length of 32 octets and a window size of 1 would be sufficient for signalling. Moreover, the respective link end points at the network side could possibly be located in different equipment, i.e. in the call processing function CPF for s and in the PSM for p (Figure 3b).

5. CONCLUSION

The concepts of internetworking and of the PS overlay network allow for an economic and short term provision of packet switched services to ISDN subscribers while avoiding significant cost penalties on ISDN. As regards the access to PS facilities by the X.25 DTE's the B-channel access offers some advantages over the D-channel access.

- The B-channel solution minimizes the impact of X.25 services and protocols on the circuit switched ISDN which is only aware of PS functions in terms of service requests.

- The B-channel solution will be needed anyhow, since the D-channel access does not allow for the connection of high speed X.25 DTE's, i.e. conforming to X.1 user class 11 corresponding to 48 kbit/s.

- The D-channel solution has a considerable influence on the protocols (additional complexity) and resources required for the D-channel.

- The quality of PS service obtainable via the D-channel will be lower as compared to the B-channel solution.

REFERENCES

/1/ F. Arnold: Die integrierende Rolle der Deutschen Bundespost. Funk-Technik 36(1981),pp.59-61.

/2/ P. Bocker, P.Gerke: Towards a Digital Communication Network. Siemens Rev.1981,pp.10-14.

/3/ J. Kanzow: Entwicklungspolitische Maßnahmen der Deutschen Bundespost im Bereich digitaler Dienste für die zweite Hälfte der achtziger Jahre. Informatik-Fachberichte 40(1981)

/4/ F. Arnold: Das Leistungsangebot der DBP unter Berücksichtigung des Einsatzes digitaler Technik. 22. Post- und Fernmeldetechnische Fachtagung des Verbandes Deutscher Postingenieure e.V.,2.und 3.4.1981. Tagungsband 1.1 bis 1.9

/5/ Deutsche Bundespost: Planning Aid for Data Communication, 2nd edition, January 1980

/6/ W. Tietz: Die Datenpaketvermittlung und Datex-P. Bürotechnik 11(1980),pp.1116-1127.

/7/ CCITT Recommendation G.705: Integrated Services Digital Network (ISDN).

/8/ CCITT Draft Recommendation I.XXX: ISDN User/Network Interfaces - Reference Configurations.

/9/ CCITT Draft Recommendation I.XXY: ISDN User/Network Interfaces - Channel Structure and Access Interfaces.

Voice/Data Integration Opportunities

A M Rybczynski, A C Chow
TransCanada Telephone System, Canada

Corporations are increasingly turning to the integration of their voice and data networks as a means of more cost effectively meeting their communication requirements. This paper examines the synergies between voice and data applications from end user and network manager perspectives, and identifies resulting technology integration opportunities. Examples are given of current developments which bring together voice and data. It is concluded that there is a merging of technologies for voice and data communications, that the majority of voice end user features apply, selectively, to some data applications, and that there may be significant operational and administrative economic benefits from integrating voice and data networks. With the merging of voice and data networks, truly integrated voice/data application will begin to be developed.

I. INTRODUCTION

Corporations typically operate segregated voice and data networks as a means of meeting their communications requirements. These networks consist of a broad range of shared and dedicated facilities for voice and data services. These networks are operated and managed as completely separate entities.

While voice services are based on a single application (i.e., the switching and transmission of a 4 kHz signal with a set of well understood characteristics), data services must accommodate a broad range of applications. In contrast to voice signals, data signals require considerably better error performance, are generally bursty in nature, and have application dependent delay and throughput requirements. While voice networks are being used for voiceband applications, economics and functional requirements dictate a need to establish segregated data networks. In fact, a typical corporation requires a number of data networks to meet its data communication requirements.

Over the last few decades, significant developments have taken place in the provisioning of voice services. Thus today, stored program control, digital switching and transmission and enhanced signalling systems are being deployed worldwide. At the same time, technology associated with data communications has moved even more rapidly (in step with the data processing industry) with the development of packet switching, intelligent multiplexers, terminals and modems.

This paper(1) addresses the opportunities associated with integrating voice and data networks. It does this first by comparing voice and data services and operational requirements from both the user and network manager perspectives. This is followed by a discussion on technology integration trends and opportunities. Current developments including digital data services on the telephone network, voice/data PBXs and satellite business serv-

ices are then described to illustrate the degree of integration that is currently possible. This paper concludes that there are opportunities in integrating transmission, switching, access, signalling control, operational and administrative systems to support multiple services, and that such integrated systems can not only provide network benefits but also serve as the vehicle for new and innovative services, such as integrated voice/ data messaging.

II. VOICE AND DATA COMMUNICATIONS REQUIREMENTS

Two trends are developing as corporations attempt to increase the utility, limit and perhaps decrease the costs of their networks.

The first is that a typical large corporation is integrating its several separate application-specific data networks, as a means of containing network costs, increasing network utilization, permitting increased functionality of terminals, and enhancing its capability of administering and operating its networks.

The second trend is that large and small corporations are looking at the total integration of their voice and data networks. Two major motivations are to permit data services to benefit from the economies of scale inherent in the voice network, and as a central strategy, to develop a vehicle aimed at increasing office productivity.

A. End User's Perspective

Voice and data services can essentially be mapped into the following five basic service elements: call based, transaction, store-and-forward, broadcast and conferencing.

The most important common element is that both data and voice services are call based. It is this single element that provides the basis of a significant level of service, operational and administrative integration.

With time, voice services in a business environment have become feature rich. The following classes of features have been identified: i) attendant, ii) station, iii) system, iv) networking, and v) value added. Attendant features are applicable only to voice calls, as data calls do not normally require operator intervention. Station features are those that provide enhanced functionality to the station set or data terminal. System features are provided on a broader scale and are often designed for an industry segment or application. Networking features allow a geographical distribution of a corporate network. Finally, value-added services are those which are not normally associated with real-time communication services. They often include storage and some level of processing.

Table 1 consists of a representative list of the last four feature sets for voice and data applications. It should not be interpreted to imply that features applicable to data apply to all classes of data terminals. Simple data terminals such as keyboards and printers are amenable to station features, while intelligent terminals, terminal controllers with limited data processing capabilities, minicomputers and large mainframes have little need for most station features. As can be seen from the comparison, many of the basic features are common to both data and voice. Even in the interface support area where data and voice are significantly different, the digital technology and international voice and data interface standards(2) being developed by CCITT will ensure a high degree of commonality.

In addition to the commonality of features for segregated voice and data applications, today's voice and data conversion techniques have made possible the integration of voice and data into a single application whereby

voice inputs are digitized, manipulated, stored and retrieved. Examples of such are voice mail and dictation(3). In the future when speech recognition and synthesis techniques become practical and economical, we expect to see a whole new set of applications involving voice and data interaction.

The basic premise of voice and data integration is that these common sets of requirements are being and will be realized by essentially the same set of networking hardware and software products made possible by the emerging technology integration. It is through this service synergy that the economics of voice and data integration will be realized.

B. Network Management Perspective

The purpose of this section is to show that although there are differences in operating voice and data networks, the basic network management philosophies are the same. Network management is the set of activities necessary to plan, organize, control, maintain and evolve a network at optimum cost and performance(4).

This discussion is divided into two parts, the first dealing with real-time management requirements, the second dealing with non-real-time considerations. No attempt is made to distinguish between segments of the network operated by the carrier(4) and corporate network manager. This latter role is currently often split between the telecommunication department for voice and the computer centre for data.

2. Real-time Network Management Requirements

For both voice and data networks, the network management system must provide continuous

Table 1
Service Feature Comparisons

	SYSTEM	STATION	NETWORK	VALUE ADDED
Common Features	. Account Code . Calling Restrictions . Closed User Group . Hunting . Broadcasting . Encryption	. Call Forwarding . Call Transfer . Call Waiting . Last Number Dial . Auto Dial . Busy Out . Speed Calling . Display of Signalling	. Direct Inward Dialing . Direct Outward Dialing . Least Cost Routing . Authorization Codes . Uniform Numbering Plan . Offnet Overflow	. Messaging . Directory . Text-voice Conversion . Electronic Filing
Voice only Features	. Conference Calls	. On Hook Dialing . Conference Phone		. Dictation Recording . Recorded Answering Device
Data Only Features	. Protocol, speed and code conversion	. Terminal dependent Interface Support . Keyboard Dialing	. Interworking of different networks	. Telemetry . Personal work space

network surveillance and configuration information, by monitoring network changes and reporting them to the control centre. System logs of status information, alarms and operator actions should be maintained. Furthermore, there is a need to convey prerecorded voice messages or system status text messages to the end users.

In a voice environment, emphasis has been traditionally placed on node alarms and trunk status, utilization and performance. In a data circuit switching environment, the same general requirements apply. However, performance expectations are higher, requiring more detailed monitoring capabilities (e.g., percentage error free seconds). In a packet switching environment, considerably more detail is required. For example, trunk utilization measurements may include packet length histograms, queue length distributions, number of packets sent and received, and call throughput distributions. Likewise, transmission facility performance can be monitored by measuring number of frames retransmitted and frames received in error.

Certain data applications require additional status information, such as terminal status, delay, and throughput performance and traffic monitoring of key terminals and their access lines.

The operations staff must have the ability to exert remote network control by activating or deactivating selected network components, transmission facilities and customer connections. The system must have the capability of diagnostic probing into the network to remotely check the status of equipment, and to trigger running of diagnostic analysis programs, to isolate the fault and initiate a restoration plan. For data applications, more sophisticated capabilities are required to permit sectionalization of the problems between the terminal intelligent devices and network. To accomplish this task, specialized skills are required to operate sophisticated testing equipment, such as protocol testers and monitors.

Network control is needed to change network routing and configurations to cope with peak traffic loads and network failures, and in a voice environment, to control (real-time) attendant/console work load. There may be a need to reconfigure the network bandwidth to make efficient use of resources: for example inquiry/response during business hours, batch during off hours. Control can be administered on a centralized or distributed basis. In addition, diversity and disaster recovery are major issues, this being due to the importance of key elements in data or voice networks (e.g., access to a corporation's DP resources, high priority voice communication).

2. Non-real-time Network Management Requirements

The network must collect usage data on a user or user group basis. These accounting records must be sent to an accounting centre for off-line bill and statistics processing. The

amount of data required for data applications is generally greater than that for voice, and may include: packets sent/received, packet size, etc. In addition, data tariffs are generally more varied and complex.

Statistics gathering and processing is another important network management area. The network is continuously generating performance data about its own behaviour. The control system automatically collects these figures on a periodic basis and makes them available for to the operating staff. The control centre also processes these data to produce historical reports for maintenance, administrative and planning purposes. For voice, trunk usage and availability statistics, and attendant statistics are most important. For data, the former are also important, but a new dimension is required on communications processing capacity utilization (e.g., packetizing, depacketizing). Network modelling tools are much more complex for data applications because of the increased number of variables, as well as the varied performance requirements of data applications. All networks have a requirement for a system of feature management, to ensure controlled network growth and reconfigurations and port feature changes. In voice networks, the types of changes that must be accommodated are typified by directory changes, station feature changes and attendant capabilities. Conceptually, data applications are similar and the opportunity exists for a common approach to feature management. Attention must also be given to routing and access restrictions that are required in both voice and data environments. For example, certain critical DP resources should not be accessible from some terminals. Likewise, routing of data calls may be impacted by protocol and performance requirements.

3. Network Management Opportunities

This brief review of voice and data network management requirements has indicated that the basic philosophies and techniques used in operating voice and data networks are fundamentally the same. The degree of commonality will become even higher with the emerging technology integration, which permits data and voice applications to be provided by the same station set, transmission medium and serving vehicle. Differences between various networks and applications (i.e., voice and data) could be masked out by a well-designed automated control system. This will no doubt present an opportunity and challenge to combine the two separate network management capabilities into a single more cost effective unit.

III. TECHNOLOGY INTEGRATION OPPORTUNITIES AND TRENDS

This discussion of technology integration opportunities is restricted to digital systems. The authors recognize the importance and widespread use of modems to provide typically up to 2.4 kbps on a 4 kHz path provided by the public switched telephone network. This mode of operation will continue to be exploited

33

particularly as a means of accessing digital networks.

A. Technology Integration Opportunities

1. Transmission Technologies

The public telephone network is based on the time division multiplexing (TDM) of 64 kbps PCM channels. In the future, more efficient coding schemes (e.g., at 32 kbps) may be used. Data transmission can be accomplished by rate adaption to the 64 kbps channels, which are becoming increasingly available in the public telephone network. Alternatively, sub-64 kbps data channels can be time division multiplexed into the 64 kbps channels. Character-interleaved and packet-interleaved Asynchronous TDM have been developed. These are extensively used in statistical multiplexers and in X.25 packet networks. Inter-office digital transmission systems are used to carry voice and data. The implementation of data services on the digital voice network is constrained by transparency and performance requirements. This is typically done(5) by selecting high performance trunks, using segregated trunk groups or introducing techniques such as majority voting and error correcting codes to improve performance.

Loop transmission systems used for accessing long-haul networks can likewise be designed to carry voice and data on an alternate use basis (e.g., for a 64 kbps digital stream), or on a concurrent use basis. Two basic schemes have been widely discussed to accomplish the latter: a hybrid scheme(6) which provides analog voice with above-band data, and a digital scheme(2) as discussed in subsection 3 below.

2. Network Switching Technologies

Switching of voice is normally achieved via circuit switching. Packet switching may prove increasingly cost effective for certain applications (e.g., transcontinental links). However, meeting voice delay requirements in a large network is a serious problem. Switching of data, on the otherhand, can be achieved by circuit, packet and message switching. Which of these switching techniques is most suitable for a particular application is primarily dependent on the traffic characteristics and delay requirements associated with that application. Circuit switching with 64 kbps paths, is not as cost effective as packet switching for bursty and low speed (e.g., 2.4 kbps) data traffic. Circuit switching with sub-64 kbps paths would increase the efficiency of handling sub-64 kpbs voice and data traffic. In order to serve a wide range of applications, it is expected that for some time to come, both packet and circuit switching technologies will be used to respond to the challenge of voice and data integration.

3. Network Interface and Signalling

Data users, equipment manufacturers, network managers and planners are faced with a large number of different data protocols and interfaces, resulting in high costs of development, maintenance and inventory. In packet switching, this is being achieved by the use of the widely accepted X.25 data link and network level protocols. However, at the physical level, a large number of voice and data interface standards exist, including X.21, V.24 and V.35 for data. The present voice and data standards are not suited to meet the emerging need for an integrated voice/data user/network interface. Therefore, the CCITT, as part of its work on the ISDN, is defining a family of interfaces, not to be confused with access loop transmission technologies discussed previously which are not addressed by the CCITT work. The "basic" digital ISDN interface operates at a fixed rate of 144 kbps and includes a 16 kbps D channel (for signalling, telemetry and low bit rate data supporting for example X.25), and a 128 kbps channel which is initially partitioned into two 64 kbps B channels. Both the D and B channels can be used for accessing a local or remote packet switch. The availability of these B channels depends on the subscriber's service and the capabilities of the loop transmission system, and in any event is signalled in the D channel. CCITT is also studying a multichannel ISDN interface for use by PABX's and communications controllers.

The conventional in-band telephony signalling scheme, with information and control signals sharing the same transmission bandwidth, poses significant limitations to accommodate new services and advanced features. To overcome these limitations, CCITT has developed the Common Channel Signalling #7 system(7) whereby the control signals, known as user parts, will be transmitted over high speed signalling links physically separated from the information channels. It has a wide variety of control signals to accommodate existing and future services. Common Channel Signalling is an important element in carrier plans to efficiently handle voice and data circuit switched services on the integrated digital network.

B. Current Developments

1. Circuit Switched Digital Data Service

A TransCanada Telephone System (TCTS) service called Datalink™ is based on a data capability developed for the Northern Telecom DMS 100™(5) using the digital network overlay of the voice network to transmit synchronous data at 2.4, 4.8, 9.6 and shortly 56 kbps. The access system for Datalink could evolve to support the ISDN interface as discussed in the previous section. AT&T(11) is planning a similar service over their digital voice network. The significant advantage of this incremental development approach is the economic and operational benefit of voice and data integration.

2. Satellite Business Networks

Satellite is another vehicle to integrate voice and data service. The advantages of satellite systems lie in their inherent distance insensitivity, multiple access capability, large geographical coverage including remote locations, and high data rates. Coupled with TDMA and small size earth stations, satellite networks can achieve a high degree of resource sharing and allow on demand configurability under customer control. Satellite Business System (SBS)(12) and the French Telecom 1(13) are examples of business satellite services.

In 1981, TCTS announced the development of an Integrated Service Business Network (ISBN) to be available in 1983. Together with terrestrial networks, ISBN will provide video, voice and data integrated services to large corporate customers. A key element of ISBN is the provision of integrated network management.

3. Business Communications Systems

PBXs have undergone a similar digital evolution. Customer located, computer controlled, PBXs are natural vehicles to facilitate voice and data integration. Today, virtually all PBX manufacturers consider data capability including X.25 interface support as a basic requirement for their existing and future product lines. For example, Northern Telecom's SL-1^{TM} PBX(14) provides simultaneous voice and data rates up to 9.6 kbps. Future PBXs will no doubt incorporate a much wider range of data capabilities. Baseband and broadband coaxial cable systems are emerging as alternative technologies.

The user's station set will also be the target for integration in the 1980's. Already the Displayphone^{TM} recently announced by Bell Canada is a combination of a telephone set, a terminal and an intelligent processor. In the future, the digitization of the local interface, the provision of enhanced signalling and improvements in voice and text conversion techniques would improve the range of possible services to include truly integrated voice and data applications.

IV. CONCLUSIONS

This paper has examined the opportunities of voice/data integration from the perspectives of technology, end user and the network manager. Significant technology integration opportunities result from the digitization of the voice network, being brought about by the need to contain costs and develop new services. Today, these opportunities are exploited in both the common carrier and private networking environments to provide an incremental data circuit switching capability. Common channel signalling is an important element in this integrated solution.

Segregation of circuit and packet switching elements will continue to be the norm, this being a result of the very significant differences between the application and performance characteristics of circuit and packet switching. While integrated switching technologies are beginning to emerge in the PBX environment, circuit switching in a public network environment will continue to be handled separately. However, circuit switching will

be used as one of the means of physically accessing a packet network and perhaps become the basis for peak load control for packet network trunking.

A review of basic end user services reveals that the call-based nature of voice and data applications provides the basis of a significant level of network integration. There are also definite advantages of offering a common set of station and system features to both voice and (non-intelligent) data terminals. The benefits to the end-user of integrating voice and data are economic and increased ease of use, which in turn results from an integrated numbering plan, uniform service feature definition and selection. By embedding intelligence and storage capabilities into these network products, value added services are being developed which enable end users to increase office productivity while, at the same time, contain operating costs. Integrated voice/data applications will also emerge in the future.

Furthermore, integrated voice/data terminals including capabilities for messaging, personal directories, auto-dialing, and display and control of network signalling should offer very visible benefits to the end user. These terminals are greatly enhanced with the support of a sophisticated network interface signalling system, such as the ISDN interface. In fact, feature commonality can also be viewed as having a significant positive effect on the administration of the network.

The network management advantages associated with integrated voice/data systems are most evident in the area of network surveillance and management systems, customer usage accounting and feature configuration, the latter as discussed above. Opportunities also exist, in network control and statistics gathering and processing systems. However, significant differences still remain in the area of resolving and sectionalizing network faults at the user interface, this due to application-dependency of data protocols.

Many large corporations have separate departments to plan, operate and administer their voice and data networks. Operating expenses can be as high as 30 to 40 percent of the annual equivalent network cost. With voice and data integration, the amalgamation of the two operating units into a single more efficient organization could result in significant reduction in operating costs.

The future direction is clear. Economic realities and market demands make the merging of voice and data inevitable. In the carrier environment, planning is being done under the ISDN banner. Similar concepts can apply in the private network environment. The integration of services, organizations and technologies is an evolving process in which each step depends on the prevailing requirements, technological capabilities, economic opportunities and acceptance by users and equipment vendors.

REFERENCES

(1) Rybczynski, A.M., and Chow, A.C., "Voice/
Data Integration Opportunities", Proc. of
the International Conference on Computer
Communications (ICCC), September 1982,
London, England.
(2) M. Kemp, L. Retallack, "Integrated Access
to the Evolving Digital Telephone Net-
work", Proc. of ICCC, September 1982,
London.
(3) I. Richer and M. Steiner, "Office
Communication and the Digital PBX",
Computer Networks Vol. 5, No. 6, pp
411-422, December 1981.
(4) F.M. Gilkinson, J.A. Kennedy, J.W. Snow,
"Network Management: A Common Carrier's
Persepctive", Proc. of ICCC, September
1982, London.
(5) A. Delorenzi, R. Vilis, R. DeHoog,
"Opportunities for Digital Data on
Digital Voice Network", Proc. of
International Switching Symposium (ISS),
September 1981, Montreal.
(6) E.A. Claire, "Field Trial Results of the
Vidon System: A New Multiple Service
System For The Telephone Local Loop",
Proc. of the National Telecommunications
Conference, Paper 23.3.1, November 1980,
Houston.
(7) R.K. Williams, M. Caskey, "CCITT No.7
Opportunities and Applications to Business Services", Proc. of ISS, September
1981, Montreal.
(8) F.A. Tobagi, "Multiaccess Protocols in
Packet Communication Systems", IEEE
Trans. Commun., Vol. COM-28, No. 4, pp
468-488, April 1980.
(9) R. Begbie, I. Cunningham, H. Williamson,
"iNet: The Intelligent Network", Proc.
of ICCC, September 1982, London.
(10) D.J. Horton, P.G. Bowie, "An Overview of
Dataroute, System and Performance",
International Conference on Communication, June 1974, Minneapolis.
(11) S.W. Johnston, B. Litofsky, "End-to-End
56 kb/s Switched Digital Connections in
the Stored Program Controlled Network",
Proc. of ISS, Paper 23.C.4, September
1981, Montreal.
(12) H. Schnipper, "The SBS System and Services", IEEE Communications Magazine,
Vol. 18, No. 5, September 1980.
(13) A Guenin, B. Ghillebaert, P. Montaudoin,
"Satellite Systems: A Means Towards
ISDN", Proc. of ISS, September 1981,
Montreal.
(14) R. Dayem, R. Faletti, "Electronic
Switched Network", Proc. of ISS, September 1981, Montreal.

Antony Rybczynski is Staff
Engineer - Network Planning
in the Computer Communications Group of the Trans-
Canada Telephone System.
He is responsible for the
development of long range
plans for CCG value-added
and transport networks, for
conducting engineering research and economic studies
in integrated voice/data
communications systems and for developing system architectures and protocol standards. He
has had a long association with the development of CCITT Recommendations X.25 and X.75
and with their implementations on the Datapac
network. Mr. Rybczynski is a member of APEO
and IEEE, and has been a sessional lecturer
at the University of Ottawa, Canada.

Anthony Chow received his
B.Sc (Special) degree in
physics from the University
of Hong Kong in 1969 and
Masters Mathematics degree
in Computer Science from
the University of Waterloo
in 1970. He also did graduate work in the University
of Calgary 1971-1972. Until
1974, he was a Systems Analyst with a geophysical data
processing consultant in Calgary. Since 1975,
he has been with the Computer Communications
Group of the TransCanada Telephone System and
has since been involved in the design and
development of CCG's data networks and services including Datapac and DATAlink. He is
currently Section Manager - Data Network Planning, responsible for the evolution planning
of CCG's data networks.

ISDN Capabilities in a Digital Local Exchange

M Romagnoli
SIP, Italy

S Giorcelli
CSELT, Italy

L Musumeci
ITALTEL, Italy

A number of technical characteristics need to be defined for the establishment of an ISDN; among them, the most important ones concern the subscriber's access features and the local ISDN exchange functions.

After some general considerations, this paper describes the main guidelines to be considered for the digital subscriber's line protocols in order to provide the basic communication types and the various services to be accomplished in the ISDN; a particular consideration is given to the provision of multi-terminal customer's installations. Moreover the additional functions to be provided in the local ISDN exchange are discussed with reference to an experimental realization being carried out in Italy on the basis of a UT 10/3 ITALTEL digital local exchange.

1. INTRODUCTION

A generally accepted concept is the evolution towards the ISDN starting from the telephone IDN and progressively incorporating additional functions and network features relating to both voice and non-voice services. No doubt that such an evolution will have to take into account different conditions that exist in various countries, and therefore its practical realization will involve a number of different solutions. However an unifying factor in this area will be represented by the digital local ISDN exchange: in fact, it will constitute the ISDN access point for the various customer categories (including small business installations, large PABX's, local area networks, etc.) and it will offer for this purpose standardized interfaces both in terms of services provided and of protocols to support them.

It is universally recognized that two basic communication capabilities have to be offered to ISDN customers, namely:

a) a 64 kbit/s user-to-user digital connectivity, based on circuit switching technique: this communication type, based on service-independent call control procedures, will provide to the customers the capability of transparently exchanging any kind of information (digitized voice, standardized and non standardized non-voice services, combined services,etc.);

b) a user-to-user transfer of message-oriented information: this will include presently standardized non-voice services such as packet switching, teletex, videotex, etc. as well as new services of future standardization.

It can be noted that for type a) communication it will be necessary and sufficient to provide all-digital interexchange paths through the network between the two involved local exchanges, with an enhanced signalling capability provided by CCITT No. 7 common channel signalling system. On the contrary, transfer of message-oriented information in the network will, in principle, be possible by means of a number of different facilities, i.e.

i)   specialized links between exchanges;

ii) existing packet switching facilities;

iii) CCITT No. 7 signalling network.

A choice between these solutions will be subject to different considerations of both technical and economical nature and it will be made time to time according to the characteristics of each type of message-oriented information.

In addition, the ISDN will need to include information processing and storage facilities to support advanced voice services and the various standardized telematic services (teletex, facsimile, etc.). The physical location of the corresponding functions should be allowed to migrate according to various factors (network structure, traffic patterns, etc.); this will, in turn, require the appropriate flexibility to be provided in signalling and protocols used (1,2,3).

From what precedes, it may be concluded that two points are of paramount importance in the evolution towards the ISDN:

1) the definition of the subscriber's accesses to the local ISDN exchange, including signalling and protocols for the two basic communication types and for the various services to be supported;

2) an appropriate identification and evaluation of the various functions to be implemented in the local ISDN exchange to accomplish the customer's services by using the available network facilities in the most suitable way.

In the following, a number of technical considerations will be presented concerning these two items, with particular reference to studies and implementations being carried out in Italy.

2. CHARACTERISTICS OF THE BASIC ISDN ACCESS

2.1 General

In addition to analog lines, two fundamental access types will exist in a local ISDN exchange (see Fig.1):

i) the <u>basic access</u>, consisting of one (or possibly two) 64 kbit/s channel (B-channel) and a message-oriented channel (D-channel) whose rate will probably be 16 kbit/s;

ii) the <u>extended access</u>, based on the existing primary PCM MUX, consisting of a number of B-channels and of one 64 kbit/s channel for signalling and other message-oriented information.

Although other access types may be envisaged (such as the so-called <u>hybrid access</u>, consisting of an analog line combined with a D-like channel carried over voice), the definition of the ISDN capabilities will be mainly determined by the two above indicated ones. In particular, even though the extended access will represent a very important item (considering the connection of service integrated PABX's, local area networks, communications controllers, etc.), the basic access represents the solution that may accomodate a large part of the residential and small business installations, provided that a sufficient flexibility is obtained in the related technical developments. For this reason, in the following we will concentrate on such an access type.

The B- and D - channels provided in the basic access can be used to carry various information types as follows:

- the B-channel can carry voice (<u>f</u>) and non-voice (<u>d</u>) information, where the latter may include a very broad range of different services; a combined <u>f+d</u> use is also possible;

- the D-channel can carry signalling for B-channel control (<u>s</u>), telemetry information for alarms or metering (<u>t</u>) and low activity data services compatible with the rate and characteristics of the D-channel (<u>d</u>').

It is to be noted that while some information types may only be carried on the B-channel (e.g. when their rate is greater than 16 kbit/s or when the activity factor is high), there are a rather large number of message-oriented applications that may in principle be supported by both B-and D-channels. The most suitable approach is therefore to develop technical solutions (in particular, signalling and protocols) that allow the most appropriate allocation to be determined time to time and to be changed when required. In fact, as depicted in Fig. 1, the local ISDN exchange will not only include 64 kbit/s circuit switching facilities (to be used for handling the B-channel), but also message handling facilities to deal with the message-oriented services carried in the D-channel; it may be expected that, according to technological evolutions, the processing capacity that may be made economically available for this purpose in the local exchange will increase, so to encourage a more and more extended use of the D-channel. This is, on the other side, also particularly attractive for the customer, since the D-channel will allow multiple calls relating to various services to be performed at the same time, together with a single circuit-switched call performed on the B-channel. The final effect of the flexibility allowed by the adopted technical solutions will therefore be that the customer will be able to choose the B- or the D-channel for a given service in accordance with the related implementation costs in the network as they will appear to him through the tariff aspect.

2.2 Signalling and protocols

The most evident implication of these considerations is the need to define a universal protocol to be used on the D-channel (D-protocol) which will meet the requirements of both <u>s</u> information type and of the various message-oriented applications, such as <u>t</u> information type, packet switched data, teletex, videotex, facsimile, etc. In addition to that, also service-dependent in-slot protocols on the B-channel will be used: a typical example is the case of a X.25 DTE acceding, through a circuit switched connection, the packet facilities of the ISDN. The definition of the D-protocol has to take into account various factors, such as:

- the capability to allow multiple communications from different terminals relating to the same or to different services, and

- the ability to support a wide range of customer's installation configurations, in terms of number and type of terminals, of in-house distribution schemes (bus, star, ring), etc.

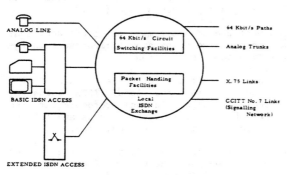

FIG. 1 - REFERENCE MODEL FOR LOCAL ISDN EXCHANGE

A key problem is represented by the definition of the level 2 of the D-protocol (LAP-D) in such a way as to meet all these requirements. A particularly suitable solution, which also represents the current trend of the international studies, is the following:

a) the HDLC frame format is used;

b) the LAP B error control method is adopted, possibly with some minor modifications (e.g. by using a window = 1 for simple terminals);

c) the level 2 Address field of the frames is used to differentiate various logical links, by assigning a different configuration to each terminal and for each basic information type (s,t,d'); this allows a straightforward separation between information flows belonging to various terminals and information types even when they are carried by the same level 1 facilities (such as when, for example, many terminals are connected to a single in-house distribution bus).

The concept of logical links allows a number of interesting features. As shown in Fig. 2a, in case of relatively simple customer's installations (i.e. with a limited number of terminals) it is possible to directly place in the local exchange the endpoints of the logical links of the various terminals: in this way, the complexity of the network termination (NT) at customer's premises is reduced to a minimum (only level 1 adaptation and some maintenance features are required). On the contrary, as shown in Fig. 2b, in larger installations where a complex network termination is required to perform level 3 functions (e.g. to provide internal calls, DDI, etc.), the NT itself acts as logical link endpoint towards the terminals; nevertheless also in this case more than one logical links between the NT and the exchange are used in order to separate the basic information types (e.g. s, t, d').

Some important advantages of this approach are:

- the same D-protocol is implemented in the exchange irrespectively of the NT type, the only difference being that in Fig. 2a the point-to-multipoint operation is used, while in Fig. 2b the point-to-point one;

- conveyance of the different basic information types by different logical links allows them to be easily separated and handled in different places in the local exchange (as it will be shown later).

Moreover, by an appropriate use of a "global" logical link identifier (i.e. addressed to all the terminals) and of unnumbered frames containing level 3 information it is possible to practically realize solutions where the exchange (or the NT in case 2b) is not aware of the terminal's population, but it learns it whenever required (e.g. on incoming calls). The technical and economical implications of such a feature are obvious.

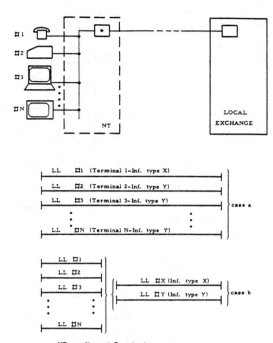

NT = Network Termination

• = {LEV. 1 functions (case a)
{LEV. 1, 2, 3 functions (case b)

LL = Logical Link (=configuration of the LEV. 2 Address).

FIGURE 2 - NT FUNCTIONS AND LOGICAL LINKS

Finally, the balanced operation of the LAP-D requires to solve the contention for access to the D-channel when a number of terminals in a customer's installation need to send frames at the same time. This can rather easily be provided as a level 1 indication, based for example on enhanced CSMA techniques (with a listen – before – talking method and collision detection).

3. IMPLEMENTATION ASPECTS

3.1 Structure of the UT 10/3 experiment

In accordance with the above indicated principles, an experimental realization is being developed by ITALTEL and CSELT in cooperation with SIP. This experiment, whose field trials are scheduled for 1983, will allow to verify the impacts of the introduction of ISDN features in a digital local exchange and it will provide first experimental feedbacks on the present solutions, emerging in the international and national studies. The experience that will be gained will also be essential in the light of further industrial developments and service provision policy.

The experiment is based upon the UT 10/3 local/transit exchange, developed by ITALTEL, modified with the addition of appropriate functional blocks for ISDN operation, as depicted in Fig.3. The general architecture of the exchange provides autonomous switching modules interconnected by high speed digital

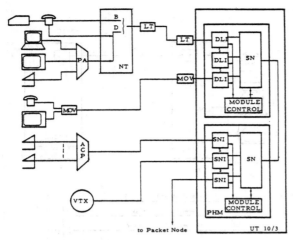

PA = Protocol Adaptor
DLI = Digital Line Interface
SN = 64 kbit/s Switching Network
MOV = Modem Over Voice
ACP = Packet Adaptor Concentrator
SNI = X.75 Synchronous Network Interface
LT = Line Termination
VTX = Videotex Center

FIG. 3 - STRUCTURE OF THE UT 10/3 EXPERIMENT

links carrying PCM voice and internal communication messages. The two basic functional blocks that will be added are:

- the Digital Line Interface (DLI), which supports the digital subscriber lines, and

- the Packet Handling Module (PHM), which is devoted to the handling of the message-oriented information.

In the following a short description of the subscriber's installation and of the implementation aspects in the exchange is given (4).

3.2 Subscriber's installation

Each experimental subscriber's installation will be connected to a (B+D) subscriber's line and will contain terminals accessing both the B-and the D-channels. The following terminals and services will be provided, as a typical configuration, in the experiment.

Channel	Terminal/service (+information type)
B	- digital telephone (A-law) (f) - combined slow video (48 kbit/s) and digital voice (16 kbit/s) (f+d) - X.25 computer (d)
D	- videotex (d') - interactive data terminal (d') - signalling for B-channel control (s)

As it appears in Figure 3, a Protocol Adapter (PA) is provided to connect the existing terminals using the D-channel, in order to perform protocol and rate adaptation. Similarly, a rate conversion for the X.25 computer accessing the B-channel is performed within the digital telephone set. It may be noted from the NT structure that the

D-channels coming from the PA and from the digital telephone set access a bus, where level 1 contention resolution is accomplished by a method including: 1) CSMA based on a steady bus state (all 1's); 2) collision detection with automatic backing-off by one contender, in such a way that the frame sent by the gaining contender is not corrupted. This method, although implemented in the experiment for only two D-channel contenders, is well suited to be extended to a whole in-house installation with multiple access points at a minimum cost.

It may also be noted that, in this approach, the NT functions are minimized and the situation is similar to the one depicted in Fig. 2a. In the experimental installation two level 2 logical links are established on the D-channel, respectively between the telephone set or the PA and the exchange, acting as common endpoint; in this way the two logical links also separate the s from the d' information types.

Concerning the call control procedures (level 3 of the D-protocol), basically level 3 of X.25 is used for d' and the communications to/from the various terminals connected to the PA are assigned different logical channel numbers; as for s information, ad-hoc procedures are used. In both the cases a Service Indication is carried in the first frame sent for a given call, so that the appropriate terminal is alerted.

Finally, the line transmission system (performed by the LT blocks) employs a burst technique with a line rate of 256 kbit/s; this technique has proven to be effective for some 93% of the Italian distribution network (5).

As a complement to the ISDN access, the experiment also includes a test on the hybrid access; in this case, the D-like channel will only carry d' information and it will be obtained on the analog subscriber's line by means of an over-voice modem.

3.3 Implementation aspects in the exchange

Connection of the digital subscriber's lines to the UT 10/3 exchange is made by the already mentioned Digital Line Interface (DLI), which is capable to serve a number of lines (presently 7). The main functions of the DLI are:

- to interface the B-channel to the 64 kbit/s switching network of the UT 10/3 module;

- to separate within the D-channel the s information from the d' information at level 2 and to deliver the former to the module control, to provide setup and cleardown of the 64 kbit/s connections;

- to concentrate the d' information from all the connected subscriber's lines on a unique 64 kbit/s SD-channel (SD = Sum of D-channels) towards the Packet Handling Module (PHM); the concentration is a statistical one (message-by-message) and the path towards the PHM is a semi-permanent 64 kbit/s connection in the switching network.

It may be noted that the already mentioned use of different logical links at level 2 for s and d' information types allows to minimize the analysis to be performed by the DLI for their discrimination. Moreover an appropriate pre-processing of the s information is performed at level 3 by the DLI, so reducing the extra complexities in the module control. It is also important to note that, even though not yet in the experiment, information to be sent via the No. 7 signalling network (e.g. telemetry) will also be passed by the DLI to the module control, which will access the signalling network either directly or via another module control.

The main functions of the PHM are:

- to handle the SD channels coming from DLI's and carrying d' information;

- to interface the 64 kbit/s switching network, to allow connection of non-voice terminals carried on the B-channel (the X.25 computer in the experimental installation);

- to provide X.75 ports for connection to the packet switching network. These ports can also be used to connect ACP equipment (ACP = Packet Adaptor and Concentrator) for connection of start-stop character terminals acceding, for example, a conventional telephone exchange; in the experiment, these ports will also be used for connection to the videotex centre.

The PHM is realized in such a way as to be introduced in the UT 10/3 instead of a normal module; therefore its interconnections and interactions with other modules are the standard ones. Moreover the PHM is characterized by a modular structure, so that its capacity can be optimized according to the needs with on overall throughput of some hundreds packet/s.

The main PHM blocks appear in Fig. 4 and are: the switching network, the module control and the X.75 Synchronous Network Interfaces (SNI).

The switching network is the same used in the other exchange modules and is fully duplicated; it connects the various Processing Units (PU) constituting the module control between themselves and with the 64 kbit/s channels to/from the other modules.

The module control can be configured up to 7 PU's, depending on the desired lines & traffic capacity. Each PU can handle up to 32 links at 64 kbit/s each being either a SD-channel or an inter-PU link. It basically consists of a duplicated MIC-20 computer, running in parallel mode; MIC-20 is a 16-bit microprocessor system with microprogrammed CPU, 200 ns cycle time, 15 DMA channels and a 1024 kbytes memory. A special interface (named HDLC multicontroller), which is also duplicated, provides for all the 32 links

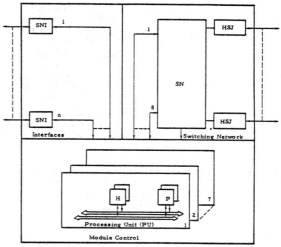

HSJ = High Speed Junctor
P = MIC-20 processor
H = HDLC multi-controller

FIG. 4 - STRUCTURE OF THE PACKET HANDLING MODULE

operations such as flag generation, bit stuffing, CRC handling, etc. One of the functions of the module control is, as usual, to control the switching network; this is performed, in addition to packet handling, by the first PU, while the other PU's are only used for packet handling.

3.4 Software aspects of the PHM

An appropriate operating system has been developed for the virtualization of the hardware structure towards the user. Moreover the applicative software is virtualized according to CCITT SDL rules; the reference model is based on the finite state machine concept (where each process represents an automate, activated as an instance after a message has been received from another process instance). In this model, the O.S. has to integrate the processing resource distribution aspects in the various system links; hence, the O.S. presents to the applicative programs a virtual machine where all the distribution resource problems have been solved.

The virtual machine Kernel has to manage the parallel evolution of the single process instances in concurrent processing of different links, and handle the synchronization and the message interchange among processes.

The I/O drivers send (through the system primitive GETIN) the message received from the enviroment to the process instances.
Solved in such a way the problems on duplication of processing units, this primitive loads the message in the system work queue.

According to the priority, the message is scheduled in the corresponding queue waiting for the execution. When the event happens, the message is conveyed to the process activator

41

that verifies the presence of the process in that unit. If this is the case, it activates the instance and sends the message, otherwise the process activator will communicate the same message to the destinator unit. The process instances activated can also send messages to other instances (SEND primitive), and toward the I/O peripheral and can change its state waiting for another message (RECEIVE primitive). Besides these support functions, when hardware breakdown or software fault happen the operating system handles the system diagnosis and reconfiguration.

Finally, in regard to applicative programs, the main PHM functions performed are: X25 and X75 protocol handling, routing, charging and a number of data user facilities.

4. CONCLUSIONS

This paper has presented an approach to the definition of ISDN access protocols and related handling functions in the digital local ISDN exchange, with particular reference to implementations being carried out in Italy. It appears that, at least from what can be foreseen at this stage, it is possible to define solutions capable of ensuring adequate cost-effectiveness as well as sufficient flexibility to meet various requirements in terms of customer services and operational features. This technical feasibility will be accompanied in the next years by extensive international standardization activities, so that the objective of ISDN can be expected to be reached in a limited period of time, at least as for its first development phase.

REFERENCES

1. M. Décina, R. Parodi, "Circuit and packet-switched data communication in integrated services digital networks", ICCC'80, Atlanta, October 1980.

2. C. Mossotto, D. Di Pino, "The role of signalling and protocols in the emerging ISDN", ICC'81, Denver, June 1981.

3. R. Parodi, D. Di Pino, L. Musumeci, "Evolutionary steps towards an Integrated Services Digital Network", ISS'81, Montreal, September 1981.

4. S. Dal Monte, J. Israel, "Proteo System: UT 10/3, a combined local and Toll exchange", ISS'81, Montreal, September 1981.

5. U. de Julio, A. Fausone, G. Pellegrini, "Experiments of digital transmission in subscriber loops", ICC'81, Denver, June 1981.

Marco Romagnoli received the Dr. Ing. degree in electrical engineering in the Politecnico of Milan in 1971. In the period 1972-1973 he worked in the field of electronic instrumentation and automatic controls. In 1974 the joined the New Techniques Division of SIP Headquarters, where at present he is head of the Signalling Section; his main interests are towards common channel signalling and the various signalling aspects relating to new supplementary telephone services and to the emerging ISDN. He is also active in various Groups of CCITT and CEPT working in such areas.

Silvano GIORGELLI was born in Crescentino (Vercelli) in 1944. He received the degree in Information Sciences from the University of Torino in 1970. From 1970 to 1971 he served as researcher in INFN at the University of Torino. Afterwards he joined the CSELT where he is currently head of the computer systems department.
Since 1971 he has been working in the field of SPC exchanges.
His main interests include: computer architecture, fault-tolerant systems, software application and maintenance.

Luigi Musumeci received the Dr. Ing. degree in electrical engineering in 1961 from the Politecnico of Milan, Italy. He joined ITALTEL in 1968. Since 1973 he has been working in the area of the new public data networks. At present he is involved in the realization of the Public Packet Switched Network in Italy.
Since 1972 he is a professor of Information Theory at the University of Pavia, in Italy.

Access to the British Telecom ISDN

J H M Hardy, C E Hoppitt
British Telecom Research
Laboratories, UK

In 1983 British Telecom plans to bring into service the initial installation of an Integrated Services Digital Network (ISDN). This network will provide customers with a variety of new services, via user-to-user digital connections based on 64kbit/s and 8kbit/s channels. Integrated Digital Access (IDA) will provide the customer with several forms of access connection via a single high capacity link to suit customers' varied communications needs. Services provided include voice, DATEL, and digital data at rates up to 64kbit/s via CCITT X21 and X21-bis interfaces, and operation in circuit and packet-switched modes. This paper outlines the facilities and features of the British Telecom ISDN and describes the call control signalling protocols being implemented for 1983.

1. INTRODUCTION

In the latter quarter of 1983 British Telecom plans to bring into service the initial installation of its Integrated Services Digital Network (ISDN) {1}{2}. This network will provide customers with a variety of new services and facilities {3}, many of which are made possible by the increased bandwidth provided by a wholly digital connection (Table 1). IDA (Integrated Digital Access) is the customer's digital link with the ISDN, via his local digital System X exchange. This paper describes the services and facilities provided to the user via IDA, and explains some of the ways in which they are implemented.

2. INTEGRATED DIGITAL ACCESS (IDA)

Each ISDN customer is provided with either an 80kbit/s or a 2048kbit/s digital link between his premises and the ISDN local exchange.

The 80kbit/s link {4} provides him with the following full duplex channels:-

- a 64kbit/s main channel
- an 8kbit/s secondary channel
and - an 8kbit/s signalling channel

The main channel is capable of supporting all CCITT X1 synchronous user data rates, as well as synchronous data at 8kbit/s and 64kbit/s (Table 2). This channel is also used for voice communication using network compatible A-law PCM encoding.

The secondary channel is used for carrying data at X1 synchronous rates of 2400 and 4800bit/s, asynchronous data sampled at 8kHz, and 8kbit/s synchronous data (Table 3). The secondary channel of 8kbit/s is reiterated at the exchange to form a 64kbit/s data stream which can be switched in the normal manner through the network. The converse process is performed in the reverse direction of transmission.

TABLE 1
ADVANTAGES OF ISDN DIGITAL CONNECTIONS

* CIRCUIT SWITCHED DATA
  AT RATES UP TO 64kbit/s

* TWO DUPLEX USER CHANNELS PER LOCAL LINE

* MULTIPLEXED (30 x 64kbit/s) INTERFACE
  WITH DIGITAL PABXs

* USE OF A SERVICE INDICATOR CODE TO CHECK
  TERMINAL COMPATIBILITY BEFORE CONNECTION

* MESSAGE BASED SIGNALLING SYSTEM

TABLE 2
SERVICES SUPPORTED ON THE 64KBIT/S CHANNEL

* **VOICE FREQUENCY SIGNALS**
(encoded using A-Law PCM)

Speech via integral digital telephone
Voice frequency modem signals via analogue port
X21bis to PCM-encoded modem signals via a MODEC

* **CCITT X1 SYNCHRONOUS DATA AT RATES OF:**

48kbit/s   9600bit/s   4800bit/s   2400bit/s

Status information is conveyed through the network.

* **SYNCHRONOUS DATA AT ADDITIONAL RATES OF:**

64kbit/s   8kbit/s

Status information is not conveyed.

* **DATA SAMPLED AT 8kHz**

Start-stop data at up to 1200 Baud

Acknowledgement is made to the Director, System Evolution and Standards Department, British Telecom for permission to publish this paper.

Data interfaces to CCITT Recommendations X21 (switched and leased circuit operation) and X21bis are supported. Where the user data rate is less than the digit rate of the channel then status information is also conveyed.

TABLE 3
SERVICES SUPPORTED ON THE 8KBIT/S CHANNEL

* **CCITT X1 SYNCHRONOUS DATA AT RATES OF:**

4800bit/s   2400bit/s

Status information is conveyed through the network.

* **SYNCHRONOUS DATA AT 8kbit/s**

Status information is not conveyed.

* **DATA SAMPLED AT 8kHz**

Start-stop data at up to 1200 Baud

3. NETWORK TERMINATING EQUIPMENT

In order for the customer to gain access to these channels he is provided with a Network Terminating Equipment {5}. The NTE performs the function of interfacing with the customer's terminal equipment, provides means for call control and contains the line transmission termination.

Fig. 1 shows a schematic diagram of the functional blocks within an NTE. The rate adapter (RA) converts between the lower data rates and that of the access channel (64 or 8kbit/s).

For the initial phase of ISDN service customers will be able to choose from a range of three Network Terminating Equipments. The range extends from an NTE with simple data port to one offering up to six full facility data ports. At present the NTEs are referred to as NTE1, NTE2, and NTE3.

NTE1
This NTE includes a digital telephone, keypad, display and a data port capable of operating at up to 64kbit/s using an X21bis interface.

NTE2
This NTE has all the facilities of NTE1 but the data ports are add-on units and include X21 as well as X21bis. The NTE can be configured with up to two data ports.

NTE3
This NTE is unlike the other NTEs in that it does not offer a built-in digital telephone. It is possible for it to be wall mounted remote from the terminals which it serves. It is in the form of a double height Eurocard crate into which are fitted certain common control equipment and up to six adapters selected from a range. The range at present includes:-

    X21 & X21bis
    2-wire analogue
    Modec (combined modem and codec)

3.1 NTE features

Considerable effort has gone into the design of the human interface aspects of the keypad, display (2 rows of 32 characters) and illuminated buttons for NTE1 and NTE2 so that as far as possible the operating procedures reflect established protocols. Guidance is also given by prompts on the display. This is essential because, for example in NTE2, the user has to control the following:-

    2 exchange connections
    1 telephone + loudspeaker
    2 data ports
    90 internal stores
    configuration of the port parameters (e.g.
    data speed, service indicator codes,
    fixed destination call numbers).

Although ISDN is aimed primarily at bringing data facilities to telephony exchanges, the importance of good telephony features and supplementary services has not been ignored. The user can program up to 90 stores in the NTE with sequences of up to 26 characters (0 to 9, * or #) for commonly used numbers or supplementary services. The programming sequence is:

    Enter characters to the display
    Hold down Memory Store (MS) button
    Enter two digit memory location
    Release MS button

The stored sequence can then be recalled by pressing Memory Recall (MR) followed by the two digit memory location. For more frequently used numbers several "user facility" buttons are provided; their contents can be recalled with a single press of the appropriate button. Additional digits can be appended to a displayed number either by keying the required digits or using further MR operations. This is of use, for example, in appending numbers to a Closed User Group code or in adding a particular in-dialling PABX code to the national (or international) prefix code. All of these short code dialling features can be used for data calls as well as telephony calls.

A built-in monitor loudspeaker is provided to facilitate on-hook dialling. On hearing the called party answer the caller can then lift the handset to converse. He may also revert to loudspeaker listening-only mode later in the call.

The specification of the digital telephone was compiled based on acoustic-to-digital measurements. Although derived from existing analogue telephony and codec requirements, greater freedom is given to the NTE designer if these two requirements are combined into a single specification. The sending and receiving sensitivities were chosen to enable optimum interworking with the Public Switched Telephone Network (PSTN) as well as to provide good communication with the other ISDN customers.

Calls between ISDN customers are completely 4-wire, low noise, low loss connections; sidetone between the earphone and its associated microphone is introduced in a controlled manner so that the telephone sounds "live".

The X21bis interface offers V24 100-series interchange circuits, including loopback, ring indication, direct call and auto-answer. Since there is no provision for passing other information over the interface, all call set-up is initiated from the keypad by means of a direct call. Synchronous data rates from 2.4 to 64kbit/s are available selected under the control of the keypad for NTE1 and NTE2, and by means of preset switches for NTE3. By sampling data at 8kHz it is possible to offer service to start-stop V24 terminals (e.g. RS232) at rates up to 1200 Baud.

The X21 interface is also specified for data rates from 2.4 to 64kbit/s. Selection and call progress information can be passed across the interface. Alternatively, keypad call set-up can be used in order to connect either full X21 terminals or X21 terminals limited to leased circuit operation.

The 2-wire analogue interface enables telephony apparatus, including answering machines, modems and existing Prestel sets, to interwork between ISDN and PSTN.

The modec interface is specifically to allow low speed, start-stop RS232 terminals to interwork with similar terminals connected to the PSTN via modems.

4. OTHER FUNCTIONAL BLOCKS OF THE ISDN

Fig. 2 shows the functional blocks of the ISDN.

The NTE is connected to the ISDN local exchange either directly via an existing local cable pair or via a local cable pair connected to a multiplexer. Such a multiplexer {6} would be situated remote from the exchange either in the customer's premises or in a nearby BT building and connected to the ISDN exchange via a 2048kbit/s digital link.

Customers with a suitable digital PABX (Integrated Services PABX or ISPBX) can be connected to the ISDN exchange directly via a 2048kbit/s digital link. In this event the customer is provided with 30 x 64kbit/s channels, and any knowledge of 8kbit/s secondary channels is internal to the PABX. The ISPBX extensions may be NTEs or equivalent, or the ISPBX may act as a "super-NTE" performing the functions normally carried out by an NTE.

5. CALL TYPES

In the initial phase of the British Telecom ISDN service there are two types of ISDN call. These are (i) an ISDN TELEPHONY call, which does not require an all digital routing and is appropriate for calls involving analogue terminals such as telephones and voice frequency data modems, and (ii) an ISDN DIGITAL call, which is given a transparent digital connection to the called ISDN terminal.

The ISDN DIGITAL call type is sub-divided into two further call types. These are VOICE/DATA and DATA.

The VOICE/DATA call is only provided using the 64kbit/s channel. It is initiated as a voice call but with an end-to-end digital connection. During such a call it is possible to switch from voice communication to data communication and back in much the same way as may be done on a Datel call.

The DATA call is set up for a specific data terminal and the network performs compatibility checks to ensure that the called NTE has a terminal capable of operating at the desired data rate. The check may also include verification of service parameters such as Teletex, Facsimile, Prestel, Slow Scan TV, etc.

Access to the Packet Switched Service (PSS) may be gained by means of a leased ISDN circuit to a PSE, or by using the Direct Call facility of the NTE.

6. CALL PROGRESS INFORMATION

The message based signalling system used in ISDN {7} permits the exchange to send call progress information to the customer for presentation in a form other than in-band tones or announcements. This is particularly necessary on Digital calls since no in-band announcements or tones are permitted on this type of call in order to avoid interference with data communication.

The call progress information (dependent upon the call type) may be conveyed to the customer by means of an alphanumeric display on the NTE, in-band tones, a tone-caller, or via the X21 interface to his data terminal.

Typical information on an outgoing call would be as follows:-

SUCCESSFUL CALL

Terminating Line Identity	0473643210
Answer	speech path
	Ready for Data
Clearing cause	CLEARED

UNSUCCESSFUL CALL

Reason for failure	INCOMPATIBLE TERMINAL
	NUMBER BUSY
	ACCESS BARRED
	TERMINAL UNAVAILABLE

Typical information, for example, on an incoming voice/data call would be as follows:-

Call type	VOICE/DATA
Closed user group indicator	*01*5# (CUG 5)
Originating line identity	0473643210

7. SIGNALLING INTERCHANGES

Customer-network control messages are transferred between the NTE and exchange on IDA links using the digital access signalling system (DASS). The transfers are in variable length blocks over the full duplex signalling channel.

For a single customer access channel DASS consists of a single link access procedure (LAP). Where control of multiple customer access channels is required (e.g. between a multiplexer or ISPBX and the exchange), a number of LAPs may be supported within DASS. Each LAP within DASS is based upon the technique of "compelled" signalling. This means that a confirmatory response is required to each transmitted signal, which is sent repeatedly until the response is recognised, before the next signal may be transmitted.

Wherever possible, the general provisions defined by the ISO in respect of High-level Data Link Control (HDLC) are followed.

The structure of the DASS is in three levels:-

Network	Level 3	Call handling, customer-network control messages
Link	Level 2	Link access protocol
Physical	Level 1	Transmission facility

Figs. 3-5 give a pictorial description of the Level 3 message interchanges between an NTE and the local ISDN exchange on a successful call. The signalling interchanges for an ISPBX are similar, but in addition the ISPBX may provide the identity of the calling extension (originating line identity OLI) and the network provides the necessary inward dialled digits.

Originating line identity (OLI) is provided on all DIGITAL calls when available. It is not provided when the customer is classmarked 'ex-directory'.

The Service Indicator Code (SIC) contained in the Initial Service Request and provided in the Incoming Call Indication message supplies the following information:-

Type of call	Telephony, Voice/data, or Data
Rate adaption method	6+2, 5-octet, etc.
DTE data rate	8kHz sampled, 2.4, 4.8, 8, 9.6, 48, 64 kbit/s
Service	Teletex, Videotex, Fax, Video, etc.

8. CONCLUSION

By exploiting existing digital switching and transmission equipment developments, the British Telecom ISDN will provide a timely introduction of end-to-end digital communication. It will provide evolutionary customer-network signalling for interconnection of digital services at rates up to 64kbit/s. The initial installation in late 1983 is likely to be extended rapidly during the following years and will provide advanced circuit and packet switched communications capable of supporting the needs of customers into the 21st century.

GLOSSARY OF TERMS

CUG	Closed User Group: supplementary service available on ISDN Digital calls to provide a degree of private network operation
Digital call	ISDN call between two ISDN users which is provided with a wholly digital end-to-end connection.
Telephony call	Call which may or may not involve one or more ISDN users: a digital end-to-end connection is not essential.
Voice/Data	ISDN Digital call type initiated in voice call mode with option of invoking digital data transmission during the call.
Data call	ISDN Digital call type initiated for a specific data transmission rate.
IDA	Integrated Digital Access: customer access to British Telecom's ISDN services and facilities over a single digital link.
ISDN	Integrated Services Digital Network
ISPBX	ISDN Private Automatic Branch Exchange: a PABX which is compatible with the ISDN service features.
NTE	Network Terminating Equipment.
PSTN	Public Switched Telephone Network.
OLI	Originating Line Identity, i.e. full national number of the calling line.
TLI	Terminating Line Identity, i.e. full national number of the called line.

REFERENCES

{1} G P Oliver and A G Orbell, System Evolution - Integrated Services Networks, ISS, Montreal, Sept 1981.
{2} G P Oliver, System X Evolution for ISDN, IEE Colloquium - Recent Developments In System X, London, April 1982.
{3} H R Brown, Services and terminals for the ISDN, ibid.
{4} M T Shortland, An 80kbit/s transmission system for the subscriber line, ibid.
{5} W B Deller, Network Terminating Equipment, ibid.
{6} D J Clothier and I G Sunman, The Remote Multiplexer, ibid.
{7} J H M Hardy, Call Handling for ISDN, ibid.

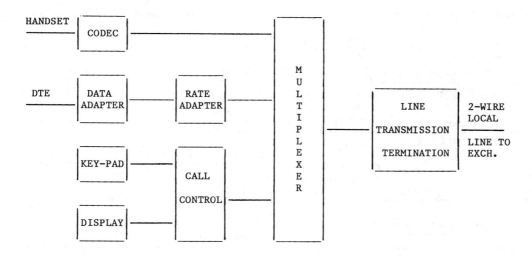

Fig. 1: FUNCTIONAL BLOCKS OF A NETWORK TERMINATING EQUIPMENT

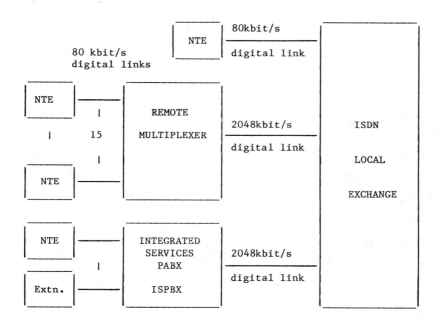

Fig. 2: FUNCTIONAL BLOCKS OF THE ISDN

Fig. 3: MESSAGE FLOWS AT THE ORIGINATING END

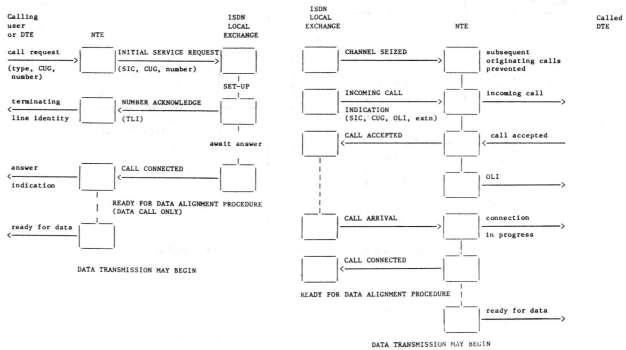

Fig. 5: MESSAGE FLOWS AT THE TERMINATING END : call to an X21 DTE

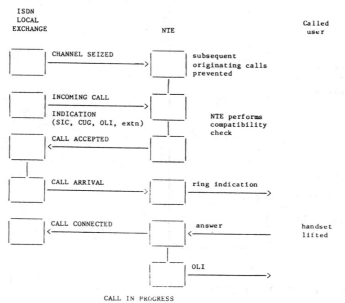

Fig. 4: MESSAGE FLOWS AT THE TERMINATING END : call to a voice terminal

48

Integrated Access to the Evolving Digital Telephony Network

M F Kemp, L J Retallack
Bell-Northern Research, Canada

The use of the existing telecommunications network for data communications is well established. Acceptance of international standards has lead to compatible communication equipment and protocols. As the telephone switching network evolves with digital technology, opportunities to provide carriage of digital information directly onto the customer premises arise with significant potential for additional services. This will introduce a new era of integration between telephony and data communication technologies. If full advantage is to be taken of this integration, a new range of standards and protocols must be defined.

This paper examines the digital network access mechanism and use of the digital network for data communications.

1. INTRODUCTION

The development of the telecommunications network has been driven by voice requirements through both its analog and digital phases of evolution. Convenient local accessibility and global switching capability have made the voice network a logical choice as a basis for data communications. Network interface devices (e.g. modem's) designed to international standards permit communication across the network in a variety of data and formats. The network interface functions can be incorporated in a proprietary terminal or be in a separate unit that connects to a terminal via a standard interface (e.g. V24). Through this standard interface, a data terminal can establish a physical data path through the network upon which higher levels of protocols can be superimposed.

As the need for more efficient data communication grows, the constraints of the limited bandwidth available with the existing network become apparent. As speed requirements increase, the number of unconditioned lines suitable for use diminishes and the cost of network interface devices rapidly increases.

Many of the growing needs of data communications are being met by alternative public and private data networks. The use of digital technology within the telecommunications network, however, is driving a re-evaluation of its role in data communications.

Telephony is evolving towards an integrated digital network. Major switching offices are using digital switches with control of the network being achieved using digital communications protocols; interconnection links increasingly are being achieved with digital transmission technologies. Digital technologies provide cost savings through time sharing of equipment, and increased flexibility in operational control and maintenance of the system. A logical step is to provide digital transmission onto the customer premises, allowing a whole new range of data services to be offered in addition to the basic voice service.

Transmission requirements for digitized speech are not the same as those for data because of the real time constraints for quality voice communication, and the relative immunity of digitized voice to line errors due to the redundancy of information and human perception. Data communications are more susceptible to errors, less intolerant to delays, and generally are of a bursty nature.

Since voice communications probably will be the major service offered by the telecommunication company (and required by the customer) for the forseeable future, the CCITT digital 64 K bit/sec PCM voice standard [1] is to be the basis of the digital customer access.

It is recognized that voice communications can be added to networks designed specifically for data but the economics of this probably will not compete for lower speed data and voice services offered by the telecommunications company.

2. ISDN

The evolution to an Integrated Services Digital Network (ISDN) is envisaged to be completed in two phases. First, an Integrated Digital Network (IDN) will appear as a dedicated service based upon transport of 64 K bit/sec through circuit switched channels. Voice and end to end data applications will use this transport facility. Secondly, the IDN will evolve to the ISDN and support many other services not all necessarily based upon 64 K bit/sec [2].

The ISDN is expected to contain a full range of packet and circuit switched data transport services plus a range of application services. User access to the ISDN will be via a limited set of standard multipurpose interface arrangements; the internal organization, however, will be transparent to the user.

A model partioning ISDN access into functional
entities and interfaces is under development
by CCITT SG XVIII [3] and is shown in Figure
1. The functions may vary in complexity
depending upon the final topology of the
access network. An objective of the ISDN is
that new terminals will support interface S or
T; existing terminals will be supported by the
R interface which includes current Data terminal network interface standards (e.g. V24,
X21). The basic access structure to the ISDN
is given by b channels (64 K bit/sec) for
voice and data, and a D channel which contains
signalling information that controls access to
the b channels and possibly can carry telemetry and low speed data. In addition b'
channels may be included for carriage of less
than 64 K bit/sec data.

The final configuration of the access network
and user interface have yet to be defined.
Bell-Northern Research is actively participating within CCITT study group XVIII whose
mandate is to define standards regarding
access to the ISDN by 1984.

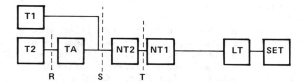

T1: Future Terminal (With S I/F) T2: Existing Terminal (With R I/F)

TA: Terminal Adapter NT1

                                    &

NT2: Network Termination

LT: Line Termination SET: Subscriber Exchange Termination

Fig. 1 Digital Access Functional Reference
Model

3. BNR EXPLORATORY EFFORT

3.1 Implementation

In preparation for implementation of the ISDN,
BNR has developed an integrated test vehicle
(2,6) to investigate key technical and system
issues relating to both private and public
digital networks. In North America, the T
interface is expected to be the demarcation
point between customer and network equipment.
Terminals that use the digital network facilities, therefore, must meet the T interface
specification.

In the test vehicle, the S interface is not
specified as this resides internal to the
customer terminal. The T interface, however,
is based upon an 'N+1' access structure, where
'N' is the number of b channels
(64 K bit/sec) and '+1' includes D
(signalling) and b' (< 64 K bit/sec) channels.
For convenience 'N' is made equal to 3 and the
total bit rate of the '+1' channel made
64 K bit/sec. These values can be changed as
standards are finalized.

A bus structure has been chosen as this provides flexibility in terminal positioning and
allows multiple terminals to share the same

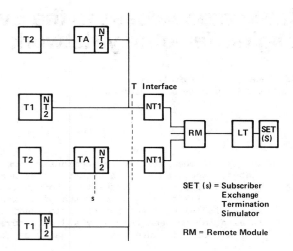

SET (s) = Subscriber
Exchange
Termination
Simulator

RM = Remote Module

NB S Interface Internal to Terminal

Fig. 2 Experimental Test Vehicle – Functional
Model

physical access loop thus permitting a saving
in copper over a star configuration. If
residential applications are included in the
ISDN a bus access will allow maximum use of
existing copper, since most residences (in
North America) are wired in a bus configuration. The functional access model for the
experimental test vehicle using a bus is shown
in Figure 2. RM is a Remote intelligent
concentrator Module supporting two and four
wire digital Multi-Channel (N+1) line cards.
It contains the network termination function,
NT1, which meets the T interface specification; terminals therefore must contain the
functions to support his interface.

Two distribution transmission formats have
been implemented based upon four and two
wires. The four wire distribution (Figure 3)
provides separate transmit and receive paths
at 320 K bit/sec. This includes the 'N+1'
data structure in frames of 125 usec, and
transmission overhead bits for synchronization
and guard time. The guard time is to allow
for the differential transmission delays of
terminals sitting at different distances from
a common point on the bus.

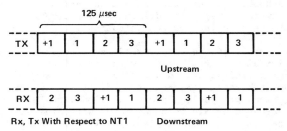

Rx, Tx With Respect to NT1 Downstream

1 – 3: 64 k bit/sec channels
+1: D (Signalling) and b' Channels

Fig. 3 4 Wire 'N+1' Digital Distribution

The two wire distribution (Figure 4) uses a technique called Time Compression Multiplex (TCM) to provide full duplex operation over one physical path. The loop controller sends a burst downstream (towards terminal) and all terminals synchronize to the burst. The data link then turns around and terminals can transmit upstream. Since there is a transmission delay, a line rate of 2.5 times 320 K bit/sec is used (e.g. 800 K bit/sec) to allow for a loop length of 2.5 km. The guard bits are used in a similar manner to the four wire case to allow for terminal differential distances.

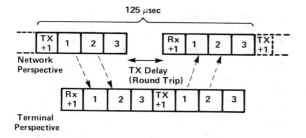

Fig. 4   2 Wire 'N+1' Digital Distribution

Both two and four wire distribution have advantages: four wire permits a lower line rate, and eases power considerations whereas two wire saves on copper and can use existing two wire links. Whatever distribution technique is used, the same ISDN access structure (i.e. b, b' and D channels) are available to the application. Higher levels using the service will be unaware of the distribution technique.

The basic access to the 'N+1' loop T interface is via the digital network access circuitry. This supplies a standard transmission interface independent of 2/4 wire distribution. A data terminal, terminal adapter, or basic digital telephone set adds application circuitry to utilize the information transported in the b, b' and D channels, e.g. Figure 5 shows the basic digital telephone set.

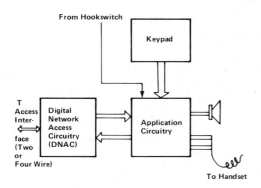

Fig. 5   Basic Digital Telephone Set

3.2 Services

The test vehicle provides 3 x b channels (64 K bit/sec) and a b' and D channel at every

bus outlet. This constitutes the T interface defined in Figure 2. Experimental data terminals with the necessary functions to support the T interface, Terminal Adapters (TA) which convert the T interface to an existing terminal standard interface (e.g. RS 232C), and digital telephone sets have been implemented and connected to the loop (Figure 6). Since the access loop provides only transport of data in the b or low bit rate data channels there is no restriction on terminal or service using the channel as long as the T interface specifications are met.

The flexible nature of the test vehicle has enabled a variety of voice or data services, access configurations, and access protocols to be investigated.

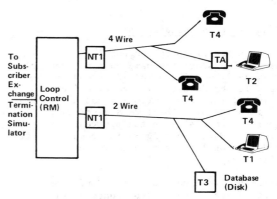

RM = Remote Module

TA = Terminal Adapter

T1 = Integrated Voice/Data Terminal

T2 = Existing Terminal

T3 = Database

T4 = Digital Telephone

Fig. 6   Experimental Test Vehicle

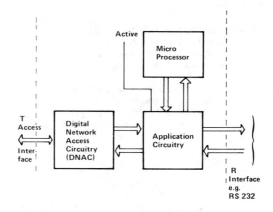

Fig. 7   Terminal Adapter

4. ACCESS PROTOCOL

4.1 Introduction

The access protocol definition is a key issue; it must not only meet telephony requirements, but those of data as well. Three protocols, each one optimized towards either data or telephone requirements are detailed and their effect on implementation complexity are examined.

In the test vehicle, the basic loop access protocol control functions reside in the Remote Module (RM); higher level access control functions reside in the Subscriber Exchange Termination (SET) simulator (Figure 2). The Remote Module performs protocol conversion between the loop access protocol and the internal network protocol.

In a practical implementation, the basic loop access protocol may propagate to the SET or even further into the network; the functional element that controls the loop access protocol is therefore referred to as the loop controller.

4.2 Multi Access Requirements

The bus structure proposed permits many terminals to time share the same common D channel for signalling and controlled access to the loop. In the downstream direction (towards terminal), the loop controller has a 1 to N configuration with absolute access to the 'D' signalling channel. In the upstream direction there is a N to 1 configuration requiring the access protocol to have multiple access facilities.

Polling has been chosen as this provides the network access loop control function with absolute control over the loop. It permits selective flow control, independent reassignment of terminal priorities, and controlled optimization of overload conditions. In addition, polling has potential for reducing the complexity of the terminal access mechanism, hence terminal complexity and cost.

4.3 Simple Access Protocol

4.3.1 Characteristics

The structure of the relevant higher levels of access protocol, i.e. link and network levels [6] depends upon the initial emphasis towards telephony or data requirements.

A simple access protocol has been developed based upon the requirement of providing cost effective basic telephony. This protocol must support all the functions required for basic telephony, i.e.:

- line supervision
- alerting
- call set up (network addressing)

It must provide real time operation at least equivalent to that provided by the existing analog service. It must also meet existing requirements for misdirected and abandoned calls. The error performance for the ISDN has been specified by the CCITT [7], although, where possible, a more rigorous specification may be met in order to meet national market requirements. The access protocol however,

must be able to work in this environment while still meeting the call integrity specification.

The characteristics of a simple protocol include:

- Bus arbitration mechanism of polling.

- Integral number of bytes per message. This fits in well with distribtuion schemes where the D channel is accessed in entities of one byte. Byte alignment is automatically provided by the synchronization mechanism.

- Fixed message length. This permits many simplifications to the link level procedures, i.e. frame synchronization can be achieved by a bit within the message. Frame delimitation is maintained by simply counting the integral number of bytes within a message. Fixed message length permits information field transparency without any additional functions. In addition, it permits efficient use of bandwidth for a full duplex channel since synchronized overlap of upstream and downstream messages can occur.

- Simple error correction procedures within the terminal. The access loop controller takes the major share of responsibility for loop error control.

- Sufficient flexibility to meet both basic and enhanced signalling requirements. Enhanced signalling includes feature set signalling, and possibly simple telemetry messages (e.g. alarms).

- No complex data messages to be transported. Although a simple protocol can support data messages, the overheads are extremely high. To meet data requirements therefore, the D channel is partitioned into two channels; i.e. signalling and data channels. This approach permits network signalling to be given a consistent priority (i.e. no data messages to contend with). It also makes removal of the data at the remote module a physical layer function allowing data message decoding to be carried out at another more convenient place in the network.

4.3.2 Two Byte Protocol

Based upon the above characteristics, two simple protocols have been investigated. The first of these is based upon two bytes, as shown in Figure 8. The frame structure consists of an address field to indicate to whom the mesage belongs or is from, a synchronization bit (F) used for frame synchronization, a parity bit (P) for error detection, an eight bit information field, and an indicator bit (I) which is used to indicate whether the information is basic or enhanced signalling.

The simple link level procedures consist of the loop controller transmitting a command frame downstream (towards terminal) and all terminals reading the frame. If parity is correct the address field is checked; the terminal to whom the command frame belongs reads the message and is compelled to transmit a response frame upstream (to the loop controller). The loop controller sets a timer when transmitting a command frame. If a response is not received within timeout it informs higher levels for error recovery.

Network level entitites using the data link for exchange of signalling require a greater degree of error protection than that afforded by a simple parity check. Retransmission of network messages for basic call set up procedures are therefore implemented to increase reliability.

Enhanced signalling is achieved by the network entity setting the I bit high. The information field then contains information that is defined by the relevant application requirements.

Basic telephony terminals will not have to handle enhanced signalling functions since this is transparent to the basic signalling; this permits a less complex basic digital telephone. Data terminals and featured voice terminals can use the enhanced signalling channel as defined by the appropriate higher level protocol.

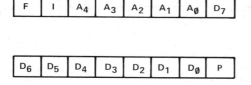

F: Frame Synchronization   P: Parity

I: Mode. Enhanced/Basic Signalling $D_7 - D_0$: Information Field

$A_4 - A_0$: Address Field

Fig. 8   Two Byte Protocol Format

4.3.3 Three Byte Protocol

The other simple protocol approach has been with three bytes (Figure 9). This protocol is similar to the two byte protocol but its philosophy is radically different. The link level provides a secure data link for transmission of higher level messages. This approach aligns itself more clearly with the principles laid down by the OSI reference model. As such it is better adapted to evolve to a new ISDN access standard.

The frame structure contains address information, and an enhanced signalling (I bit) field similar to that of the two byte protocol. In addition, it has an eight bit Cyclic Redundancy Code (CRC) appended to the frame for comprehensive error detection, and an 'N' bit which is used as the frame acknowledgement and retransmission mechanism.

The link level procedures are based on the loop controller transmitting a three byte command frame; all terminals read the command frame and if the cyclic redundancy check poly-

nominal is correct the terminal who owns the message is compelled to transmit a response frame. If the loop controller does not receive a response frame within timeout it retransmits the last command frame with the N bit set. A terminal receiving a command frame with the N bit set retransmits the last response frame sent. The N bit is not used in the upstream direction (terminal to loop controller) since an erroneous downstream message will be rejected by all terminals. The link layer within the loop controller uses the CRC error check on upstream response frames, and timeout on downstream command frames (i.e. no response) to provide the network layer with information about the performance of the data link.

Since the link level provides a reliable data link, Network level entities using the link for transport of signalling information need no further error protection capability. The network level uses the information derived from the link level to determine if the quality of the link is suitable.

The basic network signalling messages can now be defined without retransmission. Any enhanced signalling using the I bit is also protected by the data link in a similar manner. Use of the enhanced signalling capability is similar to that defined for the two byte approach.

Both simple protocols meet telephony call set up requirements over loops operating within error performance specifications with minimum bandwidth (e.g. 4 K bit/sec) requirements. The implementation complexity of both approaches is very similar (+20%); the two byte access protocol requiring network level retransmission comparison and the three byte requiring CRC checking/generation and frame retransmission capability.

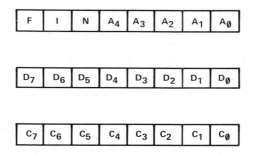

F: Frame Sychronization

I: Mode. Enhanced/Basic Signalling

N: Message Acknowledgement

$A_4 - A_0$:   Address Field

$D_7 - D_0$:   Information Field

$C_7 - C_0$:   Cyclic Redundancy Check (CRC) Field

Fig. 9   Three Byte Protocol Formal

4.4 Sophisticated Access Protocol

The philosophy behind ISDN is to support a growing number and wide range of applications.

With the simple protocol a two tier approach has been taken with enhanced signalling using the simple link level frame as a transparent transport mechanism. For transport of low bit rate data, it is assumed that a separate < 64 K bit/sec channel (b') will be available in the access loop.

The above approach is taken from a telephony viewpoint. To optimize the access protocol for basic telephony requirements, however, may restrict the operational flexibility of more demanding applications, e.g. intelligent terminals. These intelligent terminals may handle and require:

- Interleaving of signalling and low bit rate data

- Variable length messages

- Message sequencing facility

- Extensive error detection/correction facilities

- Sophisticated network level procedures.

High Level Data Link (HDLC) control procedures (8) have gained considerable support within Study Group XVIII as the link level protocol for access to the ISDN. This is a well established and understood standard protocol which meets the needs of the intelligent terminal.

Work has been undertaken investigating the effect of using a subset HDLC as the D channel link level access protocol on the basic digital telephony terminal complexity.

No alterations to the elements of the HDLC frame structure can be made since this must appear as standard for all terminals. Where savings can be made is in how applications use the link level, e.g. choice of classes of procedure, and elements of procedure. HDLC is very flexible with several options of operational classes, e.g. (asynchronous response mode, normal response mode), and procedures. By limiting the options for the basic telephony terminal to the minimum compatible with telephony signalling requirements, the most cost effective terminal is produced. Additional software will be required by the loop controller to handle the limited flexibility of the basic terminal, although the frame handling hardware will be identical. The loop controller will also have the task of separating signalling messages from data messages. The operation of HDLC for the basic terminal includes the following:

- The frame structure is to be implemented according to the HDLC specification [8].

- The terminal will operate in the Normal Response Mode (NRM). This will allow the loop controller to poll the terminals in the multiple drop configuration.

- The terminal will always return the "final" bit in the first response frame following a poll, i.e. it can only transmit one message per poll.

- If the terminal receives an erroneous frame (i.e. CRC not valid), it does nothing. It is the responsibility of the loop controller to recover from errors.

- The terminal will recognize a limited set of supervisory and unnumbered command frames to ensure the loop controller can exercise adequate control over the operation of the data link.

- The terminal can only send/receive one unacknowledged message removing the need to implement the send or receive message sequencing procedures.

- The terminal may only send or receive a fixed length information field (e.g. one byte). This information is optimized to basic telephony call set up requirements.

- The terminal will only interpret information frames (I) with an information field less than or equal to the permitted maximum.

The use of a subset of HDLC procedures to reduce complexity has indicated that the overheads in the basic terminal need not be excessive compared to the simple protocol approach. Flags detection and generation, zero insertion and removal, and control field decoding are the extra functions required by the basic digital terminal to support the use of HDLC. Information field processing remains the same as in the three byte case. The use of HDLC, however, for telephone call set up signalling impose bandwidth overheads that may prevent it meeting the real time operational telephony requirements. Further study is being undertaken in this area.

5. CONCLUSION

The digital telecommunications network is maturing with potential for its evolution to an Integrated Digital Services Network. Already digital data is being carried through the network [9] but before widespread access is ensured standards must be firmly defined.

Exploratory work within BNR has examined issues relating to customer access to the ISDN. One of these issues detailed in this paper relates to the access protocol required for establishment of a physical layer connection through the network.

The examples given of access protocols show the different approach a definition can take depending on initial requirements, i.e. flexibility for data signalling or low cost for basic terminals. The simple protocol will work but has overhead for data terminals. The reverse is true for HDLC but if a limited set of procedures are used with the basic terminal, optimization can occur.

There are many criteria to judge the suitability of the access protocol. If a subset of HDLC procedures is used for the basic cost sensitive terminal then complexity issues will not be the major issue; instead issues relating to bandwidth and facilities will predominate.

Network Architecture for Medium Term Digital Access of Multiservice Subscribers

S De Micheli, D Di Pino
CSELT - Centro Studi e Laboratori
Telecomunicazioni, Italy

The paper describes a network architecture with related functional partitioning studied and under experimental evaluation in CSELT for multiservice subscribers; the network architecture and the subscriber services are chosen for enhancement of capabilities in the short and medium term, with total compatibility in respect to ISDN trends. The proposed system allows the analogue telephone service to be offered simultaneously with the new services, and makes reference to Service Centers allocated in the network to carry out the main part of the applications. In particular, the use of a two-way digital channel with out-of-band modems on the subscriber loop, and an access network to the high hierarchy network are depicted. To obtain valid elements for the system performance evaluation, the CSELT laboratory experiment takes into account the following applications: - high quality digital access to specialized data network; - remote alarms and controls, with extension to remote metering; - information retrieval; - electronic text preparation and interchange.

1. INTRODUCTION - A LOOK TO NETWORK EVOLUTION

Telephone distribution networks, and especially subscriber lines, have up to now undergone only marginal changes in the general technological evolution, whilst other parts and subsystems of the telecommunications network have profited by a deep renewal. Subscriber line areas are indeed a high investment field, with the drawback of low activity periods over such links as well as of a scant utilization of the available bandwidth resource. Thus, substantial improvements in distribution areas (activity degree, bandwidth exploitation), not so important for telephony only, become more and more an evolution keypoint in view of the subscriber requirements driven by new services, such as data transmission (between user and host) and telematic services (Videotex, Teletex, facsimile, electronic mail).

In principle, these new services can be offered to the users within the framework of different solutions, each of which characterized by a technological time frame of the telecommunication networks; voiceband modems over analogue telephone network, specialized data networks, and now the emerging Integrated Services Digital Networks (ISDN) are the usual backgrounds against which services provision is depicted. The various development phases of the telecommunication network (Fig. 1) can thus start

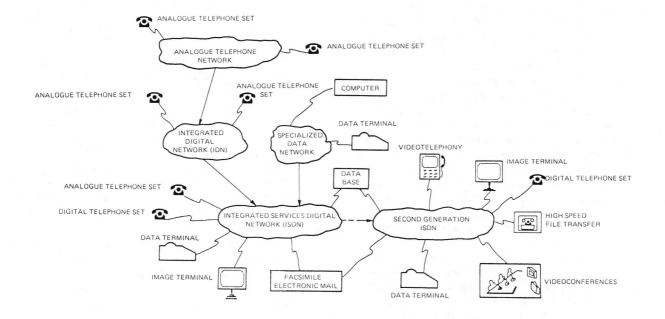

Fig. 1 - Network evolution

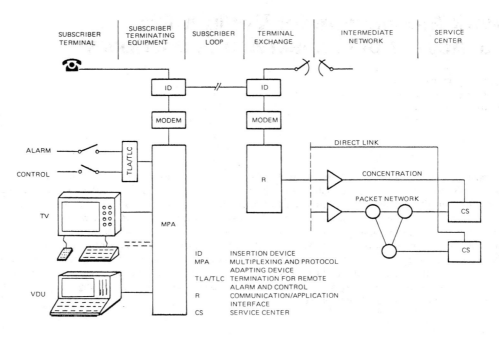

| SUBSCRIBER TERMINAL | SUBSCRIBER TERMINATING EQUIPMENT | SUBSCRIBER LOOP | TERMINAL EXCHANGE | INTERMEDIATE NETWORK | SERVICE CENTER |

ID   INSERTION DEVICE
MPA   MULTIPLEXING AND PROTOCOL ADAPTING DEVICE
TLA/TLC TERMINATION FOR REMOTE ALARM AND CONTROL
R   COMMUNICATION/APPLICATION INTERFACE
CS   SERVICE CENTER

Fig. 2 - General System Architecture

(phase 0) from analogue telephony, then pass to phase 1, characterized by the digitalization of transmission and switching telephone subsystems, with the exclusion of subscriber lines, and by the appearing of specialized data architectures. The next phase (phase 2) will follow, contemplating the digitalization also of the subscriber access in the framework of ISDN, so giving rise to the possibility of a wide range of services (data and telematics) over an all digital structure (first generation ISDN).

Broadband services, not yet offered at this stage, will be provided within the scenario of phase 3, second generation ISDN, when the use of media such as satellites and fiber optics can be envisaged for the implementation of a video-matic environment integrated with the existing services. Taking this as a rough trend for the network evolution, it appears that the ISDN remains at present the reference background for long term situations. Undoubtedly, ISDN, into which digital telephony and specialized data networks can merge, is the most interesting scenario from the technical point of view, but involves in turn high investment and a considerable amount of time for its diffusion; as a consequence, evolutionary approaches to the final objective can be pursued, based on the present structures and achieving intermediate short term results without impairing the compatibility with the ISDN. In this respect, the transition from phase 0 to phase 1, going on in these years, does not involve major changes in the provision of new services over the telephone structures: subscriber lines remain analogue and information data are in alternative with the voice; only a digitalization technique of some kind for the subscriber and the contemporaneous presence of voice and data on the line can pave the way leading to phase 2, anticipating not only some of phase 2 techniques, but above all the introduction of network centralized resources (Service Centers for information, messages, alarms and telemetry).

This paper refers to an experimental system system applying to this environment, exploiting the unused bandwidth over the subscriber line by means of a data over voice partial digitalization, yet providing a considerable bit rate if compared with the requirements of data and telematic services proposed. The data over voice technique developed in CSELT ("Infowire") (*) is associated in the system to a network architecture allowing the users to take benefit from new applications. As it will be pointed out later on, key features of this evolutionary approach are the simultaneous use of telephone sets and data/information terminals, the easy introduction of special equipment into digital as well as electromechanical exchange environment without any modifications to the existing network structure, the low-cost implementation of some sophisticated applications.

2. BASIC ELEMENTS FOR THE ARCHITECTURE OF THE PROPOSED SYSTEM

From the functional standpoint, the system, proposed in Fig. 2 in its most complete configuration, is composed of i) user terminals; ii) communication terminations on user and exchange side; iii) a transport network which can be regarded as comprising an intermediate access network and a data network; iv) Service Centers, interconnected and mutually cooperating, which are entrusted with the main part of the application-oriented support to the subscriber requirements.

Among the various applications which can be experimented over a laboratory structure of the system, the following ones have been tentatively identified:

a) high quality digital access to specialized data networks, for connection between users and between users and host

(*) *Patent pending*

b) remote alarm and remote control functions, with further extensions to meter reading
c) Videotex
d) electronic text preparation, editing, addressing and exchange between subscribers.

The basic architecture is studied in order to obtain a high flexibility degree for the introduction of further services, other than those above mentioned, or for the modification inherent to their subsequent development: in particular, the characteristics of the building blocks are centered upon this fundamental objective.

2.1 User termination and subscriber loop

As regards the subscriber loop, a high-speed (16 kbit/s full duplex) data channel is inserted, through "Infowire" data over voice technique, on the link, by means of low-cost FSK modems (see photo of Fig. 3), using frequency bands of 30 - 50 kHz and 90 - 110 kHz respectively in the two directions of information from the user and to the user. Mixing/demixing of voice and data is provided, at the subscriber end and at the exchange, by insertion devices ID.

Fig. 3 - Infowire modem (subscriber side)

Considering that the contemporaneous use of analogue telephone set is anyhow assured by this transmission technique, it is essential to define an overall structure of the subscriber termination able to support the different requirements of users equipped with simple or complex terminal configurations. First, the need for an ever-awake alarm/metering function imposes to adopt, for the other services to be supplied, some multiplexing principle on the line, so that alarms can have a permanent connection to the exchange regardless of the activity of other user terminals; second, the necessary compatibility with the emerging ISDN standards suggests to provide the user with a statistical multiplexing equipment, using on the data over voice channel the same link protocol (level 2) proposed for the D-channel of ISDN digital subscriber line and currently introduced in Italy in early ISDN experiments. As well known, D-channel link protocol is

based upon HDLC framing principles, and X.25 levels 2 and 3 can be considered a reference standard, also in view of an easier interconnection with the packet public data network, for the multiplexed structure.

In the system of Fig. 2, if low-cost character terminals are used for data and alarms, the main functions of the multiplexing/protocol adapting device MPA are the grouping of the characters flowing out of the terminals, their framing, their assignment to level 3 virtual channels (which, for sake of simplicity, can retain a fixed identity over the subscriber line) and the handling of all error detection and failed frame retransmission according to X.25 LAPB procedures. In the opposite direction, the equipment provides for the disaggregation of received frames into characters and for their distribution to the terminals.

This configuration is a point-to-point connection, particularly suitable to low-requirement subscribers. As an example, it is felt that a great part of domestic subscribers might be enabled to profit from some of the new services (in particular message and information services), just providing them with a TV set adapted for Videotex plus an additional low cost keyboard. Obviously, for this user class, only one service at a time can be activated simultaneously with analogue telephone and alarms. However, the general access configuration allowed by the system meets the basic needs also of the business subscribers, for which the simultaneous use of several terminals is necessary. From this point of view, higher requirement users can own either more character terminals, or be equipped also with some packet terminals. In the former case, the same basic statistical multiplexer with more inputs will be adopted, while in the latter a point to multipoint operation takes place between the user and the exchange, as the line has to mix informations originated by framing devices with the statistically framed flow of the character terminals. In this case, parallel link protocols are needed. This powerful extension capability is again quite in line with proposed Multilap ISDN standards, which introduce some special addressing modifications at level 2 with respect to LAPB, catering for a simpler and more direct connection between terminals and network. It can be stated at this point that the only difference between the ISDN D-channel and the data channel in the system under description is the absence from the latter of the ordinary telephone signalling, carried over the analogue channel.

2.2 Exchange equipment

Excluding the normal voiceband channel, extracted in the office and switched in analogue form or through digital conversion, the data interface between the subscriber and the high hierarchy network levels is represented by a device, R, placed in the terminal exchange, to which several functions are entrusted. The keypoint in the architectural role and in the design of such a device is its behaviour inherent both to communication control and to application-dependent local processing. From the communication point of view, the device provides for level 2 handling of the subscriber line data protocol, for the statistical multiplexing of several data channels and for the interconnection, through a standard X.25 interface, with the Service Centers. Service Centers, as depicted below, retain the most part of the service oriented functions, but it is conceivable to relieve them, and the terminal exchange/Service Centre links, which may be also long distance links, of the burden of local interest or general functions present for some kind of services. This concept leads to the inclusion into device R of more or less extended functions, depending on the specific service concerned, for the application handling. Typical examples of locally processable elements are the general menu of choices and the validation procedures for call set-up (e.g. for Videotex service) and the editing support functions (for message service).

Also in this case, however, the presence of these decentralizable portions of application handling in the exchange equipment must not influence the expandibility of the system, the evolution of service provision in terms of geographic location of Service Centres and in terms of availability of further services, and the subsequent adjustments in the procedures. Such a flexibility can be obtained by a modular software structure for the device R, in which residing application-oriented programs are based upon an almost invariant hardware backbone; the updating of the application routines, their modifications and their extension are brought about through a remote loading facility upon requests originated in the Service Centers every time a renewal is necessary. In a word, equipment R acts as a variable transparency communication equipment, which in dependence of the nature of the service and of its development is able to manage autonomously a part of the information. The maximum transparency degree may take place, for example, for the subscriber's access to the data network, as the R device in this case behaves as a pure communication controller.

2.3 Intermediate Network

In the system proposed the network which connects the R devices to the Service Centers must be able to fit the topological distribution and the growth of the subscribers and the allocation and capacity of Service Centers.

For different cases this network can consist, according to Fig. 2, of direct connections, connections through statistical concentrators, general purpose data network connections.

In the first two cases, great attention must be posed to the reliability and maintenance of the network, while the routing facilities of the data network connections assure a high degree of quality and reliability and the possibility of specialization of different Service Centers for various applications.

2.4 Service Centers

The Service Centers, which perform functions requiring a large storage amount and great computing resources to assure the proper application required by the subscriber, are located in the higher network level according to the general system architecture above mentioned.

The primary function performed by the Service Center is to interface the data base related to the subscriber selected application and the subscriber terminal (through R device) with its presentation characteristics, supporting at the same time all the statistical informations necessary to the carriers and to the application providers or useful for the subscriber.

3. EXPERIMENTAL ACTIVITIES

The general purpose structure of the communication architecture of the proposed system allows many applications to be supported. If the user terminal is defined as a multi-service one, a menu is initially presented by the R device in order to select the desired service. Then the user is connected to the appropriate application program of the Service Center. If instead the user terminal is a specialized one, this selection phase may be skipped. Some of the possible service and their relationship with the system architecture are the following:

- data retrieval. At present many Videotex coding and control techniques are used or studied in the world: the proposed system has not been designed specifically for a particular standard. Nevertheless some of its features are useful in general.
  For example many of the functions required for Videotex service may be carried out in the R device; the consequences are a reduction of the transmission cost on intermediate network, as some of the user commands do not require an access to the Service Center, and a reduction of the Service Center load, due to the fact that some of its functions (e.g. keeping track of the transactions of each user, temporary accounting, syntax checking of user requests) are decentralized.
  Moreover, the high bit-rate (compared to an access by voice-band modems) offered to the user allows very good performances due to the low transmission time necessary for each page.

- text communication. At present the message handling facility is a matter of study in CCITT and ISO, either as an independent service or as a feature offered by another service (Videotex, Teletex, facsimile). In particular the text structure elements and the message preparation and transfer facilities are to be defined. Some complex text handling functions have been identified; in the experimental system, these functions may be carried out by a simple terminal thanks to the presence of memory and computing resources connected to the user terminal by the over-voice channel on the subscriber loop. In fact the terminal can borrow the required resources from the R device, using the data channel obtained on the subscriber loop with the Infowire technique. The speed of this channel gives satisfactory response times (e.g. for updating the screen during an editing session); moreover the higher volume of data exchanged between the user terminal and the R device does not represent a large cost since it is limited to the subscriber loop.

- remote alarm. Present remote alarm systems make use either of the telephone network, or of a radio link, or of dedicated lines; most of the advantages of these systems are put together in the Infowire-based experiment. In fact the high security and reliability of a dedicated line are obtained at a lower cost since the remote alarm transmission is fully independent of the telephone service.
  A polling procedure can be used: at fixed time intervals the R device polls the alarm detector at the user premises; the polling message may be coded using cryptographic

techniques to detect the simulation of the responses by ill-intentioned people. When a status change of the alarm detector occurs or if the response to a polling is not received by the R device within a fixed time, or if it is wrong, an appropriate message is sent to the Service Center.

In the experimental system set up in CSELT laboratories, such applications are running for the performance evaluation, for the validation of protocols and functional partitioning, together with high quality digital access to data networks.

Commercial TV sets with standard alpha-mosaic coding and a full alphanumeric keyboard have been employed as subscriber terminals for information retrieval and electronic text preparation and interchange; data terminals (VDU or Teletype) (*) have been employed for digital access to data network and on-off switches interfaced by TLA/TLC subscriber terminating equipment are used for remote alarms and controls.

The network configuration is based on a PDP11/60 as Service Center using high speed serial interfaces for communication with two R devices on dedicated lines; the R devices are located in the CSELT private exchange and the link with subscriber terminals is obtained using the subscriber line and 16 kbit/s full duplex over voice modems. The service desired by the subscriber is obtained through a tree search as shown in the flow diagram of Fig. 4, for information retrieval, text preparation and interchange and digital access to data network, while remote alarm and control are always activated.

Some of the application functions required for information retrieval service are carried out by the R device, in order to minimize transmission cost on the intermediate network and to unburden the Service Center from keeping track of the transactions of each user, as required by the

_____

(*) *In addition also a low cost access is under evaluation contemplating the use of a TV set with keyboard.*

present systems using only a central computer. These functions are
- user identification
- syntax checking of user's requests
- translation of user's requests into Service Center format
- speed and protocol adapting.

In the same way some of the functions required for text preparation and interchange service are carried out by the R device; using the simple cursor commands (up, down, left, right, home, return) of a standard Videotex terminal, a screen oriented editing program resident in R has been developed. Some editing functions (character and line insert and delete), although involving a considerable amount of traffic between user terminal and R device for screen updating, minimize the cost/performances ratio of the service since the data flow is limited to the subscriber loop.

Once the message has been prepared, it is sent to the Service Center, giving the address number according to the mailbox philosophy, or is stored in it in the subscriber's own file for subsequent retrieval. The service also provides directory assistance, time stamping, sender number and message arrival notification.

Also for remote alarms and control some functions are performed by the R device; in particular it polls, at fixed intervals, the state of user's alarm detectors; in this case too the low resulting increase in traffic does not affect the overall cost-performance ratio being limited to the subscriber loop. When a change occurs or the response to a polling is wrong or is not received by the R device after a fixed time, an appropriate alarm message is sent to the Service Center. The Service Center, according to the priority or class given to the alarm message, sends to the appropriate organization a complete notification for a subsequent intervention.

No service applications are performed by the R device for high quality digital access to the data network.

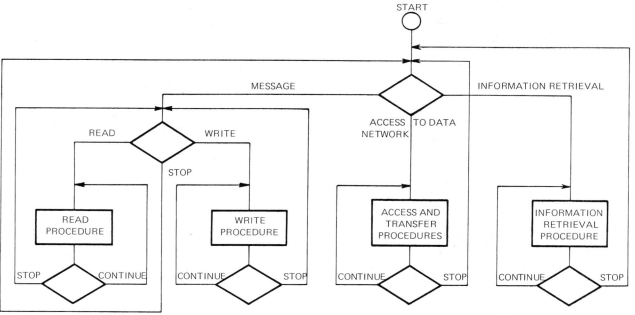

Fig. 4 - Flow diagram of application facilities

4. CONCLUSIONS

It is felt that the above proposed communication architecture may allow the introduction of telematic services even within an electromechanical or IDN environment. The system experimented by CSELT represents a cost-effective solution until ISDN has reached a sufficient diffusion degree, and is particularly attractive when several services are offered to the subscriber, realizing a true basic multiservice arrangement in line with ISDN emerging perspectives. The easy coexistence of telematic services and telephone service, due to the use of the Infowire, and the possibility of a near-term development and installation of telematic support Service Centers, make the proposal presented in this paper an interesting approach to bridge the gap between the analog and the fully digital. Laboratory trials and techno-economical evaluations carried out by CSELT are proving the feasibility and the effectiveness of the system described.

REFERENCES

[1] Artom, A.; De Micheli, S.; Dogliotti, R.: The possible use of customer loop for new services during the transition from analogue to digital, European Telecommunication Congress, Liège, September 1980.

[2] Artom, A.; Di Pino, D.; Dogliotti, R.: Medium term prospects for new services to the telephone customers, ICC '81, Denver, Colorado, June 1981.

[3] Bella, L.; Palmeri, M.: A medium-term network architecture for new services: problems and experimental results, International Symposium on Graphics and Text Communication, Paris, November 1981.

[4] Ghillebaert, B.; Guenin, J.P.; Invernici, I.C.; Loyez, P.: Presentation of the Nostradamus Systems, ISSLS '80, Munich, September 1980.

[5] Luetchford, I.C.; Han, B.: Loop evolution. The driving forces affecting system integration, Telecommunication Networks Planning, Paris, September 1980.

[6] Williamson, C.R.: Opening the Digital Pipe Bell System Overview, ICC '81, Denver, Colorado, June 1981.

[7] Mossotto, C.; Di Pino, D.: The role of signalling and protocols in the emerging ISDN, ICC '81, Denver, Colorado, June 1981.

Spiridione De Micheli, born in L'Aquila in 1941, obtained the doctorate in Electronic Engineering at the Politecnico of Turin in 1964. Since 1964 to 1972 he was research engineer with IEN (Istituto Elettrotecnico Nazionale G. Ferraris) working in the field of Electromagnetic Compatibility and Time and Frequency Standards. In 1972 he joined CSELT where his primary activity was in the field of large electronic systems to improve capabilities, performances and maintenance of electromechanical switching exchanges. Since 1978 his primary activities were in the field of data network and nonvoice new services. At present he is Section Head of the "Data and Terminals" Section in the "Networks and Systems" Division at CSELT.

Duccio Di Pino, born in Florence in 1946, received his Electronic Engineering doctorate at the Politecnico of Turin in 1971. In the same year he joined CSELT, working at the design of electronic experimental exchanges and control equipment until 1976. Since 1976 he was engaged in system definition of telecommunication equipment, with particular reference to signalling and protocols, and since 1979 he is active in the field of service integrated networks. At present, he is Deputy Section Head in the "Networks" Section of the "Networks and Systems" Division at CSELT.

Terminal Support in the DATEX-P Network

W Tietz
Deutsche Bundespost, Federal
Republic of Germany

The situation for operators of public packet-switched networks is about the
same in all countries - custormers need non-packet-mode terminals to access
the service. Start/stop terminals are considered for implementation with PAD
facilities described in CCITT Recommendations X.3, X.28 and X.29.
PAD-to-HOST connections duplicate circuit-switched network features. Other
non-packet-mode terminal families are candidates for further "additional
services". Most of these are either display- or batch-oriented devices,
operating with different protocols and dissimilar basic mode procedures.
The additional service P20 (X.28, X.29) was introduced into the Federal
Republic of Germany along with the basic service P10 (X.25) in August 1980.
The service group to follow is called P32 (IBM 3270-compatible), P33
(Siemens 8160-compatible) and P42 (IBM 2780/3780-compatible). Service
elements, charges, standards and forecasts are items dealt with in more
detail in this paper.

1. RANGE OF DATEX-P SERVICES OFFERED

DATEX-P is offered on the same terms in
the whole service area of the Deutsche
Bundespost.

The Deutsche Bundespost provides the
following:
- main stations, including Deutsche
  Bundespost-owned data communication
  equipment, operating at different
  signalling rates;
- access points for the connection of
  the public circuit-switched Datex
  network (DATEX-L) and the public
  switched telephone network;
- additional facilities for the various
  types of main stations;
- data transport facilities (error-
  controlled data transmission
  procedures, switching features).

Since in a data packet switching
network, calls between data stations are
not set up directly, they are termed
switched virtual calls. If the terminals
involved are communicating over
dedicated logical channels - that is,
without employing a dialling procedure -
then we speak of permanent virtual
circuits.

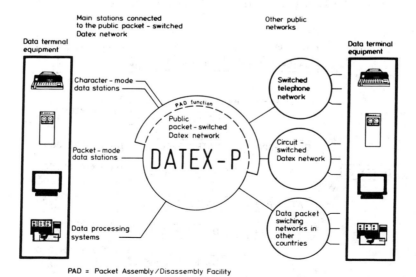

PAD = Packet Assembly/Disassembly Facility

Fig. 1 Interconnection between the public
packet-switched DATEX network and
other public networks

Normally, the above-described transmission principle requires the usage of equipment between the network nodes only if data packets are transmitted. In consequence, the transmission charge is determined by the data volume to be transmitted rather than the duration of the call.

Access to the DATEX-P network is made possible by PAD (packet assembly/disassembly) facilities which adapt and, in particular, assemble and disassemble the packets.

The DATEX-P network can switch and transmit only standardized data packets. Depending on the form in which the data can be sent and received by the data stations, a distinction is made between:

    the basic service P10 and

    the additional services P20, P32, P33, P42.

As a rule, packet switched Datex main stations of type P10H are equipped with interfaces conforming to CCITT Recommendation X.25. Transmission between these packet-mode stations can be regarded as the basic service. However, packet-switched DATEX main stations can likewise operate with non-packet-mode DTE if they are adapted through a PAD.

Also, circuit-switched networks (i.e., the public switched telephone network and circuit-switched DATEX network) can gain access to the packet-switched DATEX network via a PAD facility (see Fig. 1).

If PAD facilities are involved, we speak of "additional services".

The basic service DATEX-P10 and the additional service DATEX-P20 were introduced by the Deutsche Bundespost on 26 August 1980. In the year that followed, subscribers were given the opportunity of using the network free of charge in a trial operation. The objective of the latter was to familiarize customers with the new service and to enable manufactures to develop and market the equipment required. A DATEX-P user group was established with the aim to provide information on the technology used by the new service offered and to exchange first experience.

Meanwhile, the Deutsche Bundespost has issued a lot of publications and documentation on the new services rendered. Supply of information to prospective customers started already at a very early stage. To ensure reliable, long-term planning and to prepare manufactures and users for the new services, the tariff structure and rates charged were also made known well in advance.

Before going into some detail, we would now like to give you a survey of the information being essential in obtaining a picture of the DATEX-P service.

Table 1 lists a number of DATEX-P terms that are used to describe the individual service components.

Table 1 Designations of the DATEX-P services

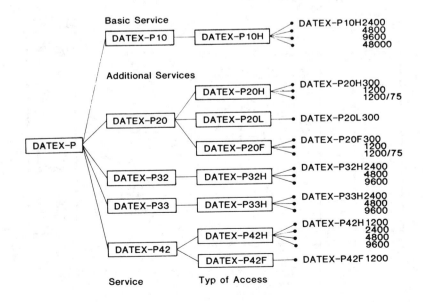

The Planning Aid for Data Communication contains the time frame within which the individual service elements are intended to be realized /1/. A reproduction of those tables has been dispensed with here.

Table 2 shows important characteristic features of DATEX-P. Special attention should be directed to the references indicated in the annexed bibliography, inclusive of the DATEX-P User Handbook /2/. In the following chapters we can give only a brief outline of the new service and an enumeration of its various facilities. In doing so, text passages selected from the aforementioned references are used for explanatory purposes. As even a cursory glance at the bulk of information available will show, any attempt at comprehensiveness would go beyond the scope of this paper.

DATEX-P10

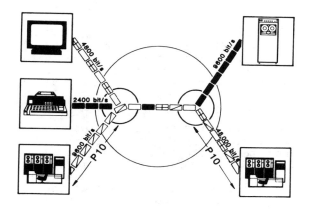

Fig. 2   Basic configuration of DATEX-P10

1.1 The basic service DATEX-P10

The basic service DATEX-P10 is destined for the connection of packet-mode data terminal equipment using a protocol conforming to CCITT Recommendation X.25. The data are sent and received in the form of standardized packets. This service is conceived for main stations of type DATEX-P10H, operating in the synchronous mode at 2400, 4800, 9600 and 48000 bit/s (see Fig. 2).

At the time of introduction of the new service on 26 August 1980, the basic service P10 was already available. Performance of tests had been possible even prior to that date.

1.2 Additional DATEX-P service in general

Additional service are destined for adaptation and connection of non-packet-mode DTE. The latter transmits and receives its data, which are passed through a PAD, character- or block-oriented (see also Tables 1 and 2).
Although new system and equipment families with interfaces and protocols conforming to CCITT Recommendation X.25 will no doubt be developed, it is safe to say that current terminals and their associated interfaces will still be offered and installed for a very long time.

For a modern packet-switched network to become more effective and largely independent of the development of new data terminal equipment, it is essential to find ways of making the old compatible with the new. This very principle has been implemented in the PAD facilities located at the periphery of data packet switching networks.

Table 2:   DATEX-P services offered characteristic features

service	data terminal equipment (DTE)	packet-mode	non-packet-mode	PAD facility required	communication protocol	main station	access from other switched networks	permanent virtual circuit	virtual call	other facilities	connection possibilities to and from main stations DATEX
DATEX-P10	intelligent synchronous	x	–	–	P10 P20B P32B P33B P42B	x	–	x	x	x	P10H P20H P32H P33H P42H
DATEX-P20	TTY-compatibel asynchronous	–	x	x	P20A	x	x 1200 bit/s	(x)	x	x	P10H P20H
DATEX-P32	IBM-3270-compatibel synchronous	–	x	x	P32A	x	–	x	–	(x)	P10H
DATEX-P33	Siemens-Transdata 8160-compatibel synchronous	–	x	x	P33A	x	–	x	–	(x)	P10H
DATEX-P42	IBM 2780/3780-compatibel synchronous	–	x	x	P42A	x	x 1200 bit/s	x	x	(x)	P10H P42H

So far, international standards have been set up only for the adaptation of character-mode, asynchronously operating DTE. CCITT Recommendations X.3, X.28 and X.29 form the basis for the additional service DATEX-P20. However, there are no such standards for certain producer-specific equipment families that operate synchronously and on a per block basis and employ basic modes such as BSC, MSV and the like. This is to be attributed, among other things, to the fact that different manufacturers frequently use dissimilar types of system architecture. The resultant product families nowadays represent a substantial part of the data terminal equipment in use. The largest portion is constituted by what is termed "teletype-compatible" equipment (printers and display units), which operates at signalling rates up to 1200 bit/s and employs start-stop procedures. In practice it is used primarily for communication with HOST computers.

Equipment belonging to, or compatible with, the IBM 3270 family makes up the second largest market segment. Further, though considerably smaller, portions are formed by the equipment families

Siemens 8160
IBM 2780/3780
manufacturer X
manufacturer Y.

Such producer-specific DTE can be adapted either with the aid of additional network services or by means of black boxes at the P10H main stations.

All additional services can also be run with stations in data networks of other Administrations, provided these services are similar and make use of compatible features.
The market potential for these additional services will become the smaller the more new and low-cost X.25-compatible product families are commercially available.

1.2.1 The DATEX-P20 service

For the connection of non-packet-mode DTE operating on a per character basis and using no X.25 interface, CCITT Recommendations X.28 and X.29 were drawn up. They enable certain character-mode DTE to interwork with packet-mode DTE. This additional service is called DATEX-P20. In the direction of the remote DTE its communication protocol is designated P20A (in conformity with X.28), in the direction of the central data processing system/HOST, P20B (in accordance with X.29).
The PAD equipment is designed in conformity with CCITT Recommendation X.3 (see Fig.3).

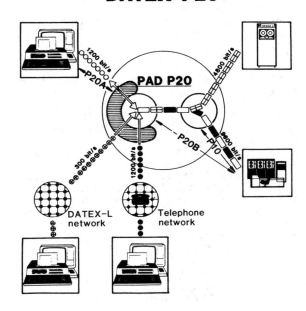

DATEX-P20

Fig. 3 Basic configuration of DATEX-P 20

Like the basic service P10, DATEX-P20 has been offered since 26 August 1980. Tests were conducted even before that date. In Canada the same service is operated under the name "DATAPAC 3101".

1.2.2 DATEX-P32

The family IBM 3270 along with compatible equipment has been supported in the DATEX-P network by the DATEX-P32 service since mid of 1982. As an international standard did not exist, use has been made of the solution implemented by the Canadian switching system manufacturer. In Canada the service is called "DATAPAC 3303" [3,4]. The concept of its associated protocol is similar to the structure in CCITT Recommendation X.29.

P32H main stations are offered for operation at 2400, 4800 and 9600 bit/s.

The communication protocols used on the remote DTE and HOST sides are called P32A and P32B, respectively. The HOST must be equipped with a P10H connection that fulfills additionally the requirements of the P32B protocol (see Fig.5).

The latter, which handles the transpost between the PAD facility and the HOST, must be available as a programme packet in or in front of the HOST. Like the P20B protocol, it is not provided by the Deutsche Bundespost.
In North America efforts are under way to further develop the protocol for the aforementioned terminals /5/.

DATEX-P32

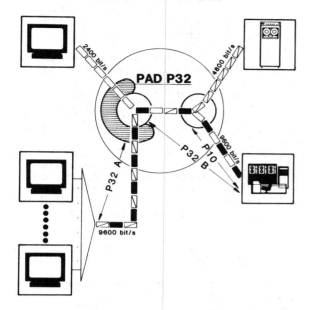

Fig. 4   Basic configuration of
         DATEX-P32

1.2.3 DATEX-P33

The families Siemens 8160 an 9750 along
with compatible equipment can be
supported in the DATEX-P network as
soon as an appropriate specification
has been completed and demand has increased to such an extent that an
economical implementation of this
additional service is ensured. Its
introduction could begin some 12 to 18
months later.

The P33 communication protocol is
structured in the same way as that of
P32.

1.2.4 DATEX-P42

The IBM 2780/3780 family and compatible
equipment has been supported in the
DATEX-P network by the DATEX-P42
service since mid of 1982. Because an
international standard was not available, use has been made of the
solution implemented by the switching
system manufacturer in Canada, where
the service is called "DATAPAC 3305"
/3,4/.

P42H main stations are offered for
operation at 2400, 4800 and 9600 bit/s.
Additionally, dialling access from the
public telephone network is provided at
1200 bit/s. The communication protocols
on the remote DTE and HOST sides are
called P42A and P42B, respectively. In
the case of version 1, the HOST must
be equipped with a P10H connection
that fulfills additionally the
requirements of the P42B protocol
(see Fig. 5).

DATEX-P42
Version 1

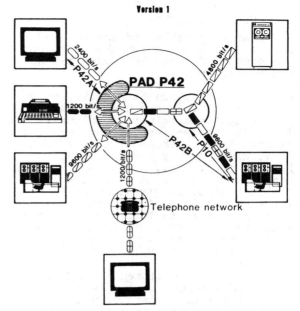

Fig. 5   Basic configuration of
         DATEX-P42, version 1

Version 2 uses the symmetrical
communication protocol P42A at either
end (see Fig. 6). For more detailed
information, please see the revised
DATEX-P User Handbook.

DATEX-P42
Version 2

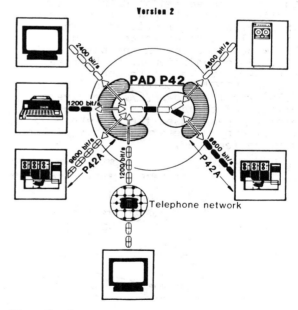

Fig. 6   Basic configuration of
         DATEX-P42, version 2

2. DATEX-P FACILITIES

The term "facility" is often used to
generally describe a system feature.
It is applied, for example, to the
types of connection "switched virtual
call" and "permanent virtual circuit".

65

The facilities will be upgraded
step by step to the version 1980
of recommendation X.25.

3. CHARGE STRUCTURE

All charges payable for the DATEX-P
service are included in the ordinance
"Verordnung für den Fernschreib- und
den Datexdienst".

DATEX-P charges are attractive, above
all, because they are distance-
independent and primarily volume-based.
The basic charges are of the same order
of magnitude as those of the DATEX-L
service and partly even identical.
Further fees, e.g., access and
adaptation charges, are to be paid for
the additional services. No doubt,
these charges are of interest to the
subscriber for the following reasons:

- the usage of current character- and
  block-mode data terminal equipment
  is possible without modifying the
  terminal;
- data terminal equipment required for
  DATEX-P10 main stations (with X.25
  interface) is either not yet
  available or too expensive at present;
  moreover, separate adaptation
  facilities (black boxes) are too
  complex and costly;
- the number of X.25-compatible
  products rises steadily;
- flexibility of application increases.

4. INTERNATIONAL CONNECTIONS VIA DATEX-P

The interconnection of DATEX-P with
public packet-switched data networks
in foreign countries is advancing
gradually. Such networks abroad are
likewise conceived on the basis of
CCITT Recommendation X.25. For the
purpose of their interconnection
another CCITT Recommendation (i.e.,
X.75) was laid down [6]. The diverse
origins of the switching techniques
employed has caused the emergence of
variations in the availability of the
service features.

However, the basic service should be
the same everywhere. Also, the range of
facilities offered to the user is
generally similar in all these networks.
Prior to the setting up of a traffic
relation, the Administrations concerned
conduct appropriate tests so as to
establish whether interworking of the
networks in question is feasible and
which peculiarities have to be considered in the setting up of calls and
transfer of data. The findings are
published in detail in the DATEX-P User
Handbook issued by the Deutsche Bundespost [2].
Fig. 7 gives a survey of the traffic
relations already in existence and of
those under preparation. Depending on
the availability of appropriate
services in other countries, DATEX-P
will help to increase international
coverage.

5. CURRENT RANGE OF DATEX-P APPLICATIONS

At the end of the trial period on
26 August 1981 the exceptional
regulation which provided exemption
from charges was lifted. Since the
beginning of commercial operation
subscriber have to pay for all DATEX-P
applications.

At the end of the trial period were
437 stations in operation. About 500
additional applications were in the
process of installation.

The technical equipment ordered in the
middle of 1979 and finished in mid-
1980 has now been used for some time
by the Deutsche Bundespost. As early
as at the beginning of 1981, expansion
measures had to be taken. Since then
the network has been extended gradually
to satisfy the steadily increasing
demand.
To date, the expectations of the
Deutsche Bundespost have in general
been met. In a period of somewhat

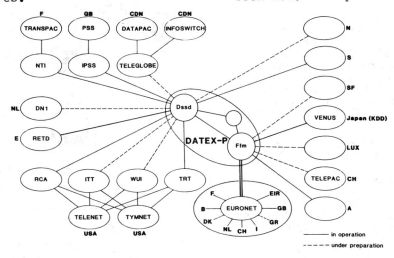

Fig. 7   International traffic relations of DATEX-P

more than one year a rather good result has been achieved: 350 customers from every important sector of the economy, science and administration (e.g., insurance companies, banks, saving banks, trading concerns, industrial firms, services enterprises, travel agencies, machine factories, pharmaceutical firms and building contractors). Many of these users have expressed the intention to employ data processing on an even greater scale in the future, so that DATEX-P will no doubt experience an large growth in the years ahead.

6. POSSIBLE FURTHER DEVELOPMENTS

The data packet switching network, whose range of data communication services has now been enlarged, will have to be developed further like the other networks.

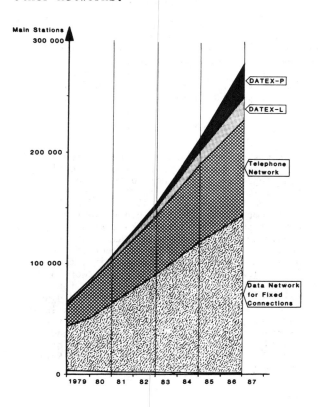

Fig. 8   Forecast of data stations in the public telecommunication networks

Figure 8 shows some tentative forecast figures. The 1980 CCITT Plenary Assembly has amended various existing recommendations and adopted new standards. Recommendation X.25, for example, was extended substantially. All this new specifications will have to be considered in the forthcoming technological development. Of course, equipment manufacturers will need some time to adapt their products to the new situation. The Deutsche Bundespost, on the other hand, will do its best to integrate novel applications properly into its services. Part of the technical evolution will take place relatively unnoticed by the user, in the background of the network technology, for instance, the
- increase in expansion capability and throughput of the network;
- increase in the number of nodes and trunks;
- development of the central network modules such as data network control centres, data collection centres and enlargement of the maintenance and testing functions;
- further development of the extension and transmission techniques.

Other technological advances will be reflected in improved and extended possibilities of applications available to the user, for example with additional facilities:
  investigation of new facilities such as
- multiple circuits of the same DTE
- multiple terminals with the same data number
- datagrams
- fast select
- end-to-emd control
- delayed delivery, mail box
- other adaptation services

A completion of the above-cited facilities by the following service features is conceivable:
- traffic relations with other countries,
- interconnection between the PSTN, telex network, circuit-switched Datex network and packet-switched Datex network to a greater extent.
Modern SPC switching systems with a high adaptability to new requirements offer ideal pre-conditions for the attainment of these objectives. The result of such an interconnection could be defined as a "virtual network" that will gradually produce a "distributed integration of services" in spite of the different technological concepts underlying the individual networks.

In addition to the further development of the networks, great efforts have to be undertaken so as to arrive at an optimum utilization of the new public services by a world-wide standardization of protocols exceeding the scope of pure transport functions.
    The complexity of the problems to be solved as well as the conflicting interests of manufacturers and the time-consuming procedure of co-ordination are serious obstacles to a fast completion of the standardization process.

The TRANSPAC Network Services in 1985

M Monnet
TRANSPAC, France

TRANSPAC, the french public packet switched network opened in 1978 with a set of services close to the ones defined through CCITT recommendations X.25, X.28, X.29. In 1980, these standards were enhanced according to the experience gained all around the world in operating a number of access lines, and the will of network responsibles to harmonize susbcribers services in different countries. However, the last published CCITT recommendations left for further study the definition of complementary services and facilities which, though remaining in the strict area of transport of information, excluding so called "value added services", would allow for a better handling of users requirements. Besides CCITT views on possible improvments of basic packet switching services, considerations based on a real experience of managing 5 000 subscribers lines at the end of 1981 lead TRANSPAC responsibles to study the introduction in next years of a set of extended services taking into consideration current and future users needs, plans regarding Telematic applications and the use of new technics for subscribers connection. Without precluding the decision to incorporate them among existing services, and the tariffs which would be then applied, we present the most significant basic service extensions which are currently being under study, and the expected benefits as well from users point of view as from network managers point of view.

"TRANSPAC...

TRANSPAC[1], the french Packet Switched Public Data Network has now reached a state of maturity with the following figures (april 1982) :

- 19 operationnal nodes

- 12366 ports capacity
- 9979 installed ports, including :
- 7450 X.25 ports,
- 2797 X.28 ports, including :
- 1947 X.28 dedicated ports,
- 663 X.28 telephone dial-in ports,
- 78 Telex ports,

- 6118 operationnal subscribers, including :
- 4734 X.25 subscribers,
- 1384 X.28 subscribers (through dedicated ports)

- 2,80 millions of bits per day (average figure per dedicated port)
- 13,2 virtual calls of 39 minutes per day (average figure per dedicated port).

...NETWORK...

Though packet switched technique is now recognized to be a comfortable basis in a variety of applications operable by PTT's or carriers (message switching, FAC-SIMILE services,...), this paper voluntarily restricts the discussions and issues to the kernel roughly described in the phrase "real time transport of transparent information". More precisely, this definition includes the activities required to operate this basic function in good conditions (registration procedures, maintenance operation, tax collection and advice,...), and ex-

cludes such activities as store and forward facilities, protocol conversion and terminal handling. One should feel contradictory that PAD[2] functions be considered here : if we consider that the basic activity of a PAD is to assemble characters within packets and to extract characters from packets with minimum knowledge of the meaning of characters (limited to the satisfactory functionnement of the packet/character interworking unit), then we feel allowed to quote PAD among network activities, though we recognize that its functionnalities logically belong to so called higher layers (higher than ISO defined network layer): Our meaning of "Network" refers to PTT's and Carriers responsability in this area, and knowingly is not restricted to the set of functions dedicated to the OSI defined Network layer[3].

... SERVICES...

It is not obvious to define the word "service" and a comparaison may be drawn on this topic between packet switched networks and time shared computers : basically, the key-word "service" refers to the specifications of a contract between a supplier and a customer, and defines the conditions under which a benefit is expected by the customer at a given cost in the respective areas of data transmission and data processing. In the two cases, the benefits expected by the users are almost impossible to be described as such in contractual terms : the contract will refer to "resources " that the supplier dedicates to the user and that participate in the process of satisfying users needs : Memory capacity, CPU time, available subprogramms,.. for data processing ; virtual circuit, available facilities, class of service,... for packet switching. These "resources" (in their respective areas) are assumed to have the widest meaning so that to avoid, in most cases, controversies between users and suppliers.

As for Public Data Networks, based upon packet switching technique, CCITT publishes Recommendations which contain a basis upon which PTT's and carriers on one side, customers on the other side, may establish contracts with a fairly common understanding of expectable results. These Recommendations define and describe classes of users (Recommendation X.1), user facilities (Recommendations X.2, X.3) procedures and interfaces between DTE and DCE (Recommendations X.29, X.25, X.28), tarification and charging principles (Recommendations D.10, D.11, D.12), maintenance (Recommendation X.150 and others to be published), administrative arrangements (X.180 and others to be published). It may be noted that consequent work has been undertaken to define elements of quality of service and expected figures.

In France, the services offered by TRANSPAC network are willingly in line with CCITT Recommendations. However, a number of characteristics which are not present (or have not to be present) in international Recommendations are detailed in a document (STUR [4]) which is the Bible for TRANSPAC connectable DTE's manufacturers and is the reference for provided services in the contract that customers subscribe to.

... IN 1985"

As mentionned in upper lines, TRANSPAC opened with a set of services very close to the CCITT defined services. However TRANSPAC also exhibits some complementary facilities which,though not referring to CCITT Recommendations, allow for an interesting use of packet switching technology. Among them, one may quote :

- The possibility to operate in a PAD to PAD mode, with a special configuration of one of the extremities : for those applications where asynchronous terminals would formerly access a computer through the switched telephone network, this facility allows, with minor modifications, to replace a long distance telephone call by a combination of a local telephone call and a virtual circuit, with fruitful benefit in termes of costs and transmission quality.

- The interface with the national Telex network, permitting the access of Telex terminals to X.25 or directly connected X.28 equipments, and the outgoing access towards Telex terminals from such equipments ; this function is operated by Telex-PAD which handles Telex procedures and performs code conversion between International Alphabets n°5 (ASCII) and n°2 (BAUDOT).

- The possibility to operate a multiline procedure as an alternative to LAP or LAP-B procedures, for X.25 equipments which require either a higher transmission speed than allowed with a single line, or a high degree of transmission security, the link level being not reset and the virtual calls not cleared since at least one line remains operationnal.

Since the opening of the network, some characteristics have moved from a former state which was closely tied either to the proper state of the international standardization at this time, or to a limited knowledge of the real needs of users :

As an example, the X.25 REJECT option (allowing a DTE to ask the network to retransmit packets) was left after a year of operation, when it was stated that practically no implementation would advocate the use of such a facility.

However, it appeared that the capabilities of extending network services were limited because of the packet switches hardware, or the need to modify too deeply current software implementations. At the same time, the decision was taken to prepare a second generation of TRANSPAC switches, to take advantage from the evolution of the technology (development of 16 bits microprocessors, high density memories,...), and to have at disposal a modular machine permitting, in small configurations to improve the distribution of network access points, and in medium or large configurations, to be installed instead of first generation switches.

Taking into consideration that a complete study was necessary for this second generation, it was then decided to include the development of a range of functions permitting to supply customers with an enhanced set of services, as soon as a sufficient distribution of second generation access points shall be ensured ; considering that the first switches in complete software configuration are to be installed at the beginning of 1984, it is estimated that a delay of at least twelve monthes is necessary to allow the opening of new public services with a satisfactory covering of customers geographical distribution.

WHY NEW SERVICES ?

Let us first consider the evolutions of international standardization :

On one hand, network implementations go along with more accurate definition of standardized interfaces and procedures, so that it is a real difficulty to find out the best compromises between the stability of supplied services and the compliance with recognized standards. In worst cases, this consideration leads to maintain a double mode of operation with a risk of proliferation of users parameters, and an unexpected complexity of the service definition and of the subscribing forms. As for TRANSPAC network, STUR supply manufacturers with indications relative to possible standardization issues, so that in most cases, this risk is avoided, at least for those manufacturers who take into consideration the provided warnings.

However, cases may remain where a duplication of interfaces is necessary, and as an example, it is envisaged that TRANSPAC second generation switches provide users with a double range of diagnostic codes selectable at subscription time.

On the other hand, enhancements of international standardization issuing a real improvement in the use of network services are generally considered in a very short delay, as in the examples above :

- LAP-B mode of operation, permetting a DTE implementation compatible with ISO balanced class among HDLC procedures was offered to TRANSPAC users at the end of 1979. This alternative mode of operation was supplied in a way that no contract modification was necessary, the DTE selecting LAP or LAP-B mode by proper command (SARM or SABM) each time the link level is initialized.

- Modifications are in course to ensure the availability of a set of facilities, such as the possibility to select a throughput class for each virtual call, independently from the negociation of packet maximum length and packet window size, when these facilities were tied at the opening of the network.

- The introduction of the so called D-bit, allowing a packet emitting-DTE to get a network insurance that the D-bit marked data packets have been delivered to the packet receiving DTE, in a way that no extra control packet (and no extra network charge) is required, is on the verge to be supplied among TRANSPAC services.

One should note that a number of X.2 facilities are simply quoted with a quite laconic definition which generally does not describe precisely neither the supplied service nor the procedures to be operated.

Moreover, this table is not complete, in the way that a number of improvments which are estimated of interest for customers, do not appear in the list. Following sections of this paper describe a range of services which may refer or not to X.2 Recommendation, and are planned within the second generation TRANSPAC switches.

However, the "new services" presented here refer to the technical possibilities (available functions) for supplying these services. Opening a new service assumes that a number of processes are achieved : tarification study, user definition of the services and interfaces, commercial and operational procedures definition (including billing), etc. Moreover the decision of opening a new service is closely tied to preliminary studies of profitability, compatibility with public service definition and industrialization capacities in the case where new specific equipments (e. g. modems) are needed.

For all these reasons, and because the current degree of definition is not similar for all these services, the reader should not take

these lines as a TRANSPAC advertisement, but as an examination of the capabilities of a public packet switched data network.

WHAT NEW SERVICES ?

... SHORT TRANSACTIONS

This service is dedicated to the applications which require a limited number of exchanges between DTE's (typically a question and a response), and so, which do not require neither the same level of network resource allocation as for virtual call service, nor the same tarification principles (minimum charge per call). The procedure for accessing this service is the same as for Virtual Call, but extended by the use of Fast Select and/or Fast Transmission[5]. Fast Transmission facility does not require a modification of packet formats, but allows to send data packets prior to the reception of the Call Confirmation and so does not limit the amount of user data that may be exchanged at call set up time. A combination of the two facilities is felt as the most sophisticated possibility for this service. The use of Datagram facility has been left, for this procedure appeared too far from Virtual Call procedure.

... PACKET MODE THROUGH TELEPHONE NETWORK

This definition covers 3 kinds of services :

- A so called "pseudo-direct" access, in which DTE's may advocate the use of almost the whole range of facilities as those available through an access via a leased line (but with limitation due to the current technology of modems), for those customers whose needs (in time of connection to the network) do not justify the installation of a dedicated line per DTE.

- A service of back-up access permitting to recover from access line failures for those applications who require a high degree of network services disponibility and cannot cope with the MTTR of access links. The back-up may be one-to-one (the same port is accessed either via the leased line or via the telephone network), or shared between several DTE's ; this last facility permits also to depart from long duration failures of the switches if the back-up access port is installed on a separate switch.

- A service of public packet mode telephone dial ports, which may be considered as an extension of asynchronous X.28 public dial ports, for those terminals which require a higher transmission speed and/or a better reliability permitted by the use of X.25 procedure. This service will not allow the advocation of all X.25 facilities (access link parameters predetermined, limited number of logical channels,...) ; but, as for existing Telex ports, incoming and outgoing dialling shall be available. French TELETEX terminals shall be among the first users of this service.

These services may require the implementation of a set of functions (half-duplex procedure, frame level identification procedure, telephone dialling capabilities,...) by DTE side. In order to ensure the acceptability of those services, and to prepare future implementations, TRANSPAC has developped external adapters which operate these functions and allow standard X.25 DTE's to use telephone accesses with no modification. Experiments are in course with some customers since july 1981 [6] .

...FACILITIES FOR PRIVATE NETWORKS MANAGEMENT

A number of facilities allow private networks having their own requirements about management of host-computers, terminals, private concentrators, ... interconnected by means of public packet networks, to handle these equipments in good conditions. Among these facilities, one may quote :

- Teleloading of terminals : the principle of this facility consists in the availability of a simple procedure (i. e. requiring a limited amount of ROM or PROM memories in terminals) which permits to load operational programs (including a complete network access software). The use of HDLC standardized commands such as RIM, SIM and the transfer or informations through UI frames is seen as the more suitable way to proceed when X.25 procedure cannot be directly handled by the terminal. A specific teleloading protocol is operated on top of Virtual Circuit service between the DTE owning the software to be teleloaded, and the packet switch which is accessed by the terminal to be teleloaded, the switch acting in this case as a relay in this host-to-terminal activity.

- Systematic failure report : In the case where a call cannot succeed because of subscriber line failure, power not supplied at the called DTE or distant modem side, link level not established,... the network issues a diagnostic (after timer has run out in order to prevent from temporary malfunctionnement) which is recorded in the access point context. Every new call directed to this user shall be cleared with a report to the calling DTE of the diagnostic issued by the network, until the malfunctionnement remains.

- Access to a subset of TRANSPAC operators language (this possibility refers to the "on line registration" facility defined in Recommendation X.2) : the main idea is to simplify contractual aspects with customers in the case where real time parameters modification is required at the network access point (e. g. modification of redirection address) or to permit customers to be informed with moving figures (e. g. taxation counters), or,

in certain cases, to operate maintenance procedures such as quality of service measurement, test of the access link, etc. It should be noted that these facilities are authorized to customers but with great care such as belonging to "administrative Closed Users Groups" and passwords associated with the class of the function to be operated. As for network operators, these functions can be handled using a Man-to-Machine language applying on top of Virtual Circuit service, i. e. operable from a standard X.28 access.

- Call Redirection : it is possible to associate with the access point, an address to which is redirected any call which cannot succeed because the user link is out of order and/or there are no more free outgoing logical channels, or systematically redirected at the subscriber request. The accurate definition of the associated procedures is in course within the CCITT ad-hoc study group. This facility is also used internally within the network to allow subscribers transfer without address modification and to supply users with a back-up service between direct access links.

... FACILITIES FOR PUBLIC SERVICE SUPPLIERS

Considering an expected growth of the number of the public information suppliers, especially thanks to the development of VIDEOTEX terminals, a number of facilities are planned to be of some help for these specific network subscribers :

- Complementary tax indication : This facility permits some carefully selected public service suppliers to notify the network with the specific tax issued (at the termination of each incoming call) by the access to its services, so that the network may charge the calling DTE, in addition with the proper network utilization taxes. The sum of complementary taxes notified to the network is substracted from the bill relative to the service supplier. This facility avoids the need for public service suppliers to know the population of users which access to its services.

- Tax indication at call termination : In Clear or Clear Confirmation packets, the DTE which is charged for the call is notified with figures (number of taxation segments, duration of the call, possible complementary taxes,...) which permit to estimate the cost ot the call. A specific PAD conversion is necessary for X.28 terminals.

- Calling party confidentiality : A study is undertaken about the need or the opportunity to protect users anonymity (i. e. calling DTE address) against possible misuses of this information by public service suppliers. The question is to know whether this facility is to be required by calling party or is a mandatory feature of some public service suppliers.

- Generic adressing for DTE'S : Though the first applications of this function are for network management facilities (access to directory, to packet generators,...) it is felt that it could be of some help for those service suppliers who provide the same facilities on a range of DTE's and so would take advantage of having a single network address. The function performed by the network is to route any call referring to such an address to the nearest involved DTE.

- Called DTE reselection :
This facility allows a DTE (at call clear time) to insert an address with which the calling DTE should attempt to reestablish a call. In the case of an X.28 calling DTE, the X.29 "invitation to clear" message is completed with the rerouting indication which is then handled by the PAD, with an indication to the X.28 DTE that rerouting has taken place : this facility permits, for example to DTE's providing a directory service, to reroute the initial call once the appropriate supplier has been selected by the customer.

... PAD EVOLUTION

Though some experts would predicated soon vanishing of asynchronous terminals, with the argument that technology would permit synchronous transmission at equivalent cost, it appears that the percentage of such connections remains almost constant among TRANSPAC users (1/4 of direct connections, plus telephone dialled accesses). Moreover the development of first generation VIDEOTEX terminals seems to cause a stimulus by terminals manufacturers side, and the fall out of the contracts negociated in France for Electronic Directory System [7] is strongly felt by the TRANSPAC marketting staff.

Beyond the opening of 1200 bits/s full duplex dialled access ports at the end of 1981, the following enhancements are planned :

- direct call extended to direct accesses :
This facility allows the PAD to establish a Virtual Call with a predefined address, as soon as the link level is set up.
Note : the extension of this facility to X.25 single channel DTE's is under study.

- Support of VIDEOTEX terminals, i. e. support of the V.23 75/1200 bits/s rate, and necessary modifications in recommendations X.3 and X.28 to handle specific characteristics of such terminals (S.100 code instead of ASCII code, functions generated by the keyboard).

- Terminal identification by means of NUI procedure permitting calls not to be restricted with reverse charging, and the introduction within Closed User Groups.

CONCLUSION

A common feature of the services described in upper lines is that they are expected to increase either the number of connectable terminals, or the traffic generated by installed terminals, or attract new customers with enhanced facilities. This network manager point of view goes along with national users requirements which shall have the possibility to interconnect a higher variety of terminals, to take advantage in the possibility of calling a higher number of correspondants, and to benefit from an improved basic Virtual Circuit service.

Moreover, a large subset of these new facilities may be supplied on an international basis provided a concensus is reached first on their usefulness, then on their accurate definition. May this paper be of some help to packet switchers in that first step.

GREETINGS

The author thanks Bernard JAMET, co-manager of the TRANSPAC Technical Division, Sylvie RITZENTHALER and Pierre MAIRESSE, for their precious help in the redaction of these lines.

BIBLIOGRAPHY

1 : "TRANSPAC 1981-1985 : évolution du réseau et des services ; impact sur les projets des utilisateurs" by J.F. GUILBERT, PARIS, 21-25 september 1981, published by Convention Informatique, 6 place de Valois 75001 PARIS FRANCE.

2 : "Terminal handling protocols in a public packet switched network" by B. JAMET and M. MONNET, EUROCOMP 78, published by ONLINE Conferences Ltd.

3 : "New telecommunication services and network architecture : a tentative survey", by A. TEXIER, IFIP 1980, published by North Holand Publishing Company.

4 : Specifications Techniques d'Utilisation du Réseau (STUR) available at : TRANSPAC, BP 145, 75755 PARIS CEDEX 15 FRANCE.

5 : CCITT-COM VII n°1-E : Questions entrusted to study group VII "Data communication Networks" for the period 1981-1984 (annex 1 to question 23/VII).

6 : "X.25 access through the Telephone Network", by B. JAMET and M. MONNET published in ICCC 80 proceedings (ATLANTA, 27-30 october 1980).

7 : "French Telematique Programme", Intelmatique, 98 rue de Sèvres, 75007 PARIS FRANCE.

Michel MONNET is graduated from l'Ecole Nationale Supérieure des Télécommunications. After three years in the Network System team of the french company CII-HB, he joinded the TRANSPAC technical division in 1976 where he is now responsible of the studies department. He is currently involved in the development of second generation TRANSPAC switches, the definition and experiment of new services, and in the standardization of users interfaces.

The Nordic Public Data Network – a Possible Multiservice Network

P Eikeset
Norwegian Telecommunications
Administration

O Sjøstrøm
Swedish Telecommunications
Administration

Abstract

The Nordic Public Data Network (NPDN), operating in Denmark, Finland, Norway and Sweden, is basically a synchronous, circuit switched network offering a transparent, real time circuit switched service to the users. Supervisory functions for fault location and efficient tools for operation and maintenance form part of the network functions.

The network meets key requirements of public data communication services such as

. good error performance
. high degree of availability
. integrity of data transferred
. short connection and disconnection times of circuits
. flexibility in offering different services
. flexibility in accepting new terminals

Dedicated circuits are also provided.

The paper discusses the application of the network to different types of services.

Special emphasis is put on the implementation of the packet-switched service using the circuit-switched part of the network as physical bearer channels.

The NPDN will fill the gap between the use of PSTN and leased circuits and a future integrated service digital network (ISDN). It is also likely to be a part of the ISDN for at least a period of time.

1. THE NORDIC PUBLIC DATA NETWORK - NPDN - SHORT INTRODUCTION

The NPDN is basically a star network with network components connected to each other in accordance with figure 1-1.

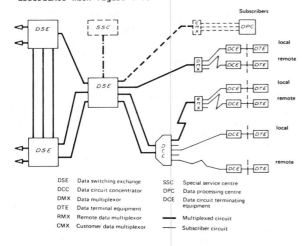

DSE	Data switching exchange	SSC	Special service centre
DCC	Data circuit concentrator	DPC	Data processing centre
DMX	Data multiplexor	DCE	Data circuit terminating equipment
DTE	Data terminal equipment		
RMX	Remote data multiplexor	——	Multiplexed circuit
CMX	Customer data multiplexor	——	Subscriber circuit

Figure 1-1   Main components in the NPDN

The circuit switched service now in operation is named DATEX and conforms to CCITT Rec. X.1 user classes of service 1-7 and Rec. X.2. The interfaces are in accordance with CCITT Rec. X.20 bis, X.21 and X.21 bis.

The network parameters are as follows:
- symmetrical duplex connections
- bit sequence independence
- bit timing and 8-bit-byte timing from the network with 8-bit-byte synchronization terminal to terminal (DTE to DTE) in data transfer phase
- automatic answering
- standardized call progress signals
- call charging of the calling subscriber
- automatic supervision and maintenance of customer connections
- short call set-up time (in the order of 100-200 ms)
- short call clear-down time (less than 100 ms)

2   INTERWORKING AND LOCAL ACCESS CAPABILITIES

The need for interworking capabilities as well as different local access possibilities is generally envisaged. How NPDN will comply with these demands on the basis of the work going on in CCITT is discussed in the following.

2.1 Interworking aspects

Needs and demands

Today, we are faced with a situation where different types of data networks, e.g. circuit switched public data networks (CSDN)

and packet switched public data networks (PSDN), are put into operation.

The Telecommunications Administrations will be responsible for offering international services through different types of networks, thus creating the need for interworking between different networks when terminals assigned to the same service, but connected to different networks, shall communicate. The situation is shown in figure 2-1.

Consequently, a firm need for interworking between the CSDN and the PSDN for the Teletex service has been identified.

In addition, the need for <u>interworking</u> <u>between different services</u> is foreseen, either

- between services using the same network, e.g. the Datex and Teletex services, see chapter 3.3

- between services using different networks, e.g. the Teletex and Telex services, see also chapter 3.3.

The general solution for interworking will be to conduct interworking on interexchange signalling levels. The interworking unit may be separated as a dedicated autonomous functional unit, generally applicable in other interworking situations than shown in figure 2-1, or as an integrated function in one of the networks.

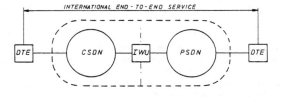

IWU : Interworking Unit
CSDN : Circuit Switched Data Network
PSDN : Packet Switched Data Network

Figure 2-1 Interworking between CSDN and PSDN

Functional_description

The interworking situation referred to in figure 2-1 is dealt with in the following. The functions of the Interworking Unit (IWU) consist of two main elements:

- conversion between different interexchange signalling schemes, e.g. CCITT Rec. X.60/X.71 and X.75

and/or

- adaptation and conversion between different network levels defined in the ISO model for Open System Interconnection.

In an interworking situation the networks are fully independent: The users (terminals) are subscribers only in the network to which they are connected, utilizing only user facilities in that network. This implies that the

subscriber (normally) has its user data resident in his own network, as shown in figure 2-2.

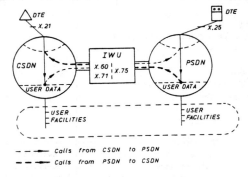

- - - ➤ Calls from CSDN to PSDN
- - ➤ Calls from PSDN to CSDN

Figure 2-2 Functional description of inter-working between CSDN and PSDN

It is normally assumed that in an interworking situation the user facilities (and network utilities) utilized in the two networks are compatible and symmetrical. The principles and procedures for international user facilities and network utilities are defined in CCITT Rec. X.87. Here the need is stressed for compatibility and desire for uniformity of the principles for the realization of international user facilities and network utilities in public data networks. As regards the closed user group facility e.g., interworking between different networks implies establishment of a common interlock code scheme in the two networks. In case of incompatibility, X.87 also gives rules and criteria for rejection and barring of calls forming part of the interworking functions.

As part of offering the Teletex service as an international service, interworking between the CSDN and the PSDN has been made feasible. The interworking implementation in the NPDN is in accordance with the principles defined above, based on CCITT Rec. S.70 and the rules for interworking specified in this recommendation, see chapter 3 below.

It is essential that interfaces and procedures for new terminals and services which will be introduced in coming years are equal. If these comply with CCITT recommendation S.70, we will have a unique situation in which the subscriber can disregard to what kind of network (or service) other terminals, with which we wishes to communicate, are connected.

2.2 Local access

Needs and demands

It would be most attractive to give packet-switched based terminals the possibility to use the CSDN as a pure access network, utilizing only the basic call establishment elements, to gain access to the PSDN, its user data and user facilities.

It should also be noted that the terminal market is evolving towards more intelligent multipurpose terminal installations. We foresee the need for such terminals to access either the CSDN or the PSDN on a per call basis, utilizing the user facilities in the CSDN or the PSDN. This enables the calling subscriber to choose the most suitable network, depending on actual traffic pattern and/or to which network the called subscriber is connected.

Functional aspects

The architectural approach defined above gives a packet-switched based subscriber equipment connected to the CSDN two possible modes of operation:

(i) The subscriber equipment is a pure CSDN subscriber utilizing only the user facilities in the CSDN. The terminal may use e.g. CCITT Rec. X.25 levels 2 and 3 procedures symmetrical end-to-end, the CSDN being transparent to these levels.

(ii) The subscriber equipment is to be considered as a PSDN subscriber utilizing the user facilities in this network. The main part of the user data is resident in the PSDN, and the CSDN is only a local access network where only the basic call establishment elements defined in CCITT Rec. X.21 are used.

The situation described above is depicted in figure 2-3.

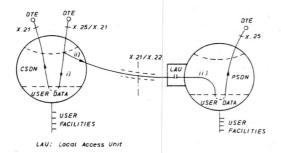

LAU: Local Access Unit

Figure 2-3   CSDN used as access to PSDN

Contrary to the interworking situation, the subscriber connected to the CSDN may be both a CSDN and a PSDN subscriber terminal. The service used is selectable from the terminal (X.25/X.21 DTE) at each call.

The local access situation (i.e. case ii) above) implies a two-step call establishment procedure:

1. Physical connection (level 1) is established to the PSDN using the X.21 call establishment procedure and conveying calling line identification (CLI) to the PSDN for identification and charging purposes. The PSDN is considered as a group of (equal) subscribers in the CSDN, i.e. a group number, shared by a larger number of X.25/X.21 DTEs.

2. Link and logical channels set-up is performed in the PSDN, the CSDN being transparent and the DTE considered as a subscriber in the PSDN.

To ease the connection to the PSDN and minimize the need for new functions in the PSDN already in operation, a separate Local Access Unit (LAU) as shown in figure 2-3, could functionally be introduced between the CSDN and the PSDN, preferable as a physical part of the PSDN. The LAU will then terminate the establishment of the physical connection (level 1) through the CSDN, transferring only signalling on level 2 (link level), including the conveyance of calling line identification (CLI), and level 3 towards the PSDN itself.

The approach described gives a solution to the questions raised in CCITT Rec. X.25 chapter 1.2, which defines the need for standardized interface characteristics and procedures for a DTE connected to a packet switched data transmission service through a circuit switched data transmission service, using the X.21 procedures for circuit switched access to the PSDN.

3.   TELETEX SERVICE IN THE NPDN

3.1 Short description

The Teletex service is a text communication service with a transmission bit rate of 2400 bit/s. The Teletex service could be implemented both in circuit switched and packet switched networks, as well as in the public switched telephone network. CCITT Rec. S.70 outlines the interworking procedures when the Teletex service is implemented in different networks.

The Teletex service is implemented in the Nordic countries using the NPDN as a carrier for the service. Interworking with telex is essential from the beginning. Future interworking with the Datex service and with the Teletex service in packet switched networks is foreseen.

3.2 Implementation

The teletex subscribers are connected to the NPDN as synchronous users with 2400 bit/s. There are two possibilities to handle the Teletex service as a service separate from the Datex service, either to use different user categories in the network and/or to use separate parts of the numbering plan.

3.3 Interworking

Actual interworking situations are shown in figure 3-1.

Interworking Teletex - telex

As already mentioned, interworking with the telex service is essential for the Teletex service. Already at the introduction of the Teletex service, this interworking enables the teletex users to communicate with the more than one million telex users all over the world, and vice versa.

As the Teletex service is a memory-to-memory service working at 2400 bit/s and the telex service is basically a keyboard-to-printer-service working at 50 bit/s, speed, code and protocol conversion is necessary.

The conversion is made with store-and-forward technique in a piece of equipment called Conversion Facility (CF). The teletex terminal is not kept busy during the entire message transfer between the Conversion Facility (CF) and the teletex terminal. The interworking is based on CCITT recommendations F.200, S.62 and S.70. The CF and the teletex terminal are connected only at the beginning and at the end of the telex transmission time. This applies to communication in both directions. The dialogue mode possible in telex is thus not possible in the interworking Teletex - telex.

Interworking Teletex - Datex

In providing the Teletex service, the Administration guarantees to a certain degree that communication between teletex users is possible. Assurance should be made, that the terminals used are able to operate in accordance with the recommendations. This is basically assured as the teletex terminals are provided by the Administration. The terminals provided are tested to act in accordance with the CCITT recommendations adopted for the Teletex service.

For other terminals (terminals provided by others than the Administration) this could be guaranteed either by a terminal approval system or by checking that the actual communication follows the teletex procedures at each individual call. In the latter case checking will take place in a separate piece of equipment, called IF (Interworking Facility), which the communication has to pass when a non-administration provided terminal belonging to the Datex service is involved in the communication.

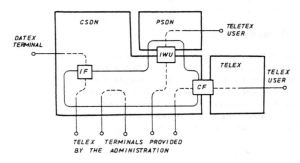

Figure 3-1 Teletex Interworking

Interworking between circuit switched and packet switched Teletex

It is foreseen that future Teletex terminals may be connected both to the circuit switched and the packet switched part of the NPDN. Teletex terminals in other countries may be connected either to a circuit switched or a packet switched network. These circumstances imply that there is a need for interworking

between the circuit switched and packet switched networks for the Teletex service. This will be done in a piece of equipment between the two networks, called the IWU (Inter-Working Unit). This unit works in accordance with CCITT Rec. S.70.

4 PACKET SWITCHED SERVICE IN NPDN

The NPDN will be extended to include a packet switched service, to complement the circuit switched service now in operation.

In figure 4-1 the functional structure, including main types of connections and interfaces, is shown. It should be emphasized that all types of connections and interfaces may not necessarily be present inter alia depending on point of time and/or implementation strategy.

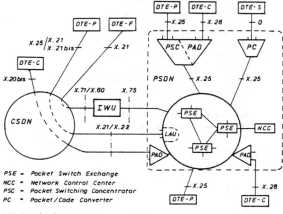

PSE = Packet Switch Exchange
NCC = Network Control Center
PSC = Packet Switching Concentrator
PC = Packet/Code Converter

DTE-P = Synchronous Packet mode DTEs
DTE-F = "Frame mode" DTEs
DTE-C = Asynchronous, Character mode DTEs
DTE-S = Synchronous, Dedicated BSC DTEs

Figure 4-1 PSDN functional network structure

4.1 Functional description

The Packet Switching Concentrator (PSC), including the Packet Assembly/Disassembly facility (PAD), could functionally be regarded as an extension of the PSE, and may be supervised and controlled by the PSE to which the PSC is connected. Main functions are:

- PAD functions
- call handling
- local switching
- concentration of traffic to the PSE.

If provided, the Packet/Code Converter (PC) converts other protocols and codes, e.g. IBM 3270, to X.25 level 2 and 3 protocols.

Both the PSC and the PC may be integral parts of the PSE itself.

4.2 Subscriber Connections and Interfaces

DTE-Ps may be connected to the PSDN in two alternative or complementary ways:

i) To the PSDN, either directly or via the PSC utilizing the concentration function

ii) To the PSDN via the CSDN utilizing a dedicated circuit or a switched circuit through the X.21 or X.21 bis interface, using the local access functions as described in chapter 2.2.

DTE-Cs may also be connected to the PSDN in two principle ways:

i) To the PSDN, either directly where the PAD function is part of the PSE or via the PSC/PAD. The connection may be a dedicated circuit or a dial-up connection in the PSTN.

ii) To the PSDN via the CSDN, where the DTE-C is connected to a PAD function in the PSDN through a circuit switched circuit through the X.20 bis interface, using the local access function in the same way as the DTE-P described above.

DTE-Fs may specifically be Teletex terminals conforming to S.70, or more general purpose terminals preferably using S.70, connected to the PSDN through the CSDN utilizing the interworking functional unit as described in chapter 2.1, based upon S.70 for demands on the general interworking protocol.

5   ISDN

5.1 The ISDN concept

ISDN - Integrated Services Digital Network - is discussed as the future network offering access to many different services such as telephony, telefax, videotex etc. Data communications services are among the services which will play an important role in such a network. Other papers presented at this conference describe the concept and the benefits of the ISDN. Today, standardization work is performed on the user access interface and the user access line. This work has resulted in a possible concept which can probably imply that at least the major parts of the network will have widely adopted standards. The discussions about the other parts of the network such as switches and the trunk network have not resulted in a generally adopted concept. There are also several different possibilities for realization of these parts in the network. It may prove important to use investment in development and equipment already done. This implies that there are benefits to use existing possibilities in public data networks when introducing ISDN with data services.

In the user interface there are different kinds of channels available:

- B-channel. A 64-kbit/s channel, basically circuit switched in at least the first switching point when accessing other networks.

- B'-channel. A digital channel with a bit rate less then 64 kbit/s.

- D-channel. A channel with a bit rate of 16 or 8 kbit/s primarily used for signalling purposes between the user and the network in establishing and clearing connections on the B- and B'-channels.

  Services available on the D-channel could be used simultaneously with the use of the B- and/or B'-channels.

5.2 Data communication and ISDN

There are many kinds of data communication services. In this paper we have restricted ourselves to describe primarily the data communication services defined in CCITT rec. X.1, possible extensions thereof and related recommendations. Both circuit and packet switched services, at present up to 48 kbit/s are included. 64 kbit/s will probably also be a standardized speed specially intended for use in the ISDN.

It is essential that services available today via public data networks also could be available to users connected to the ISDN. New services offered to users in the ISDN could also be envisaged. Interworking between these new services and services with users not able to be connected to the ISDN should be carefully studied, and interworking (both economic and technical) offered if possible.

5.3 NPDN as a component in ISDN

The interface towards the user in the ISDN is one of the essential subjects in present standardization studies. A common interface for all services offered is foreseen. Let us assume that this interface should be logically similar to CCITT Rec. X.21 for circuit switched services and CCITT Rec. X.25 for packet switched services.

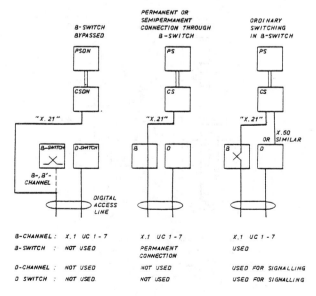

Figure 5-1 Usage of B-, B'-channel for circuit switched service according to CCITT Rec. X.1

User classes 1-7 in CCITT Rec. X.1 could be provided over the B- or B'-channels. If the channel is only used for one service and this is a data communication service also provided in the public data network (NPDN), the channel could either be "diverted" to the NPDN before the first switching point of the ISDN, or used as a permanent or semi-permanent connection through one or more switching points in the ISDN and then access the NPDN.

The B-channel could also be used for packet switching with the same arrangements.

If the B-channel is switched, the signalling system between the ISDN and the NPDN should be CCITT Rec. X.60 or X.71.

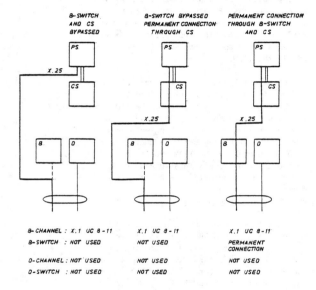

B-CHANNEL : X.1 UC 8-11   X.1 UC 8-11   X.1 UC 8-11

B-SWITCH : NOT USED   NOT USED   PERMANENT CONNECTION

D-CHANNEL: NOT USED   NOT USED   NOT USED

D-SWITCH : NOT USED   NOT USED   NOT USED

Figure 5-2   Usage of B-, B^1-channel for packet switched service according to CCITT Rec. X.1

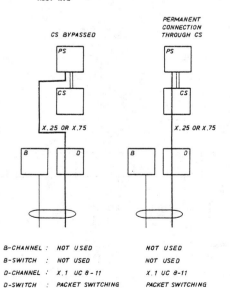

B-CHANNEL : NOT USED   NOT USED

B-SWITCH : NOT USED   NOT USED

D-CHANNEL: X.1 UC 8-11   X.1 UC 8-11

D-SWITCH : PACKET SWITCHING   PACKET SWITCHING

Figure 5-3   Usage of D-channel for packet switched service according to CCITT Rec. X.1.

The D-channel could be used for packet switching in addition to the signalling purpose which it is primarily intended for. The ISDN should then have the possibilities to differentiate between frames (HDLC-frames) in the packet switched service and forward them to the NPDN, and other frames (e.g. for signalling purposes) which should be treated in other ways. The protocol between the "ISDN – HDLC – frame switch" could be CCITT Rec. X.75 or perhaps even X.25.

Services such as Teletex and Datafax which also could use HDLC-frame format can be handled in the same way accessing the NPDN through the D-channel.

For the different alternatives see figures 5-1, 5-2 and 5-3.

6   CONCLUDING REMARKS

In this paper we have illustrated how the NPDN will be well suited as a bearer of different types of services

Special emphasis has been put on the interworking and local access functions. These functions should be looked upon as complementary functions giving the NPDN, including the packet-switching capabilities, a more complete and adequate service repetoir.

By complementing the circuit switched service in the NPDN with a packet switched service as described, it is our conviction that the NPDN will constitute an up-to-date network concept with a well-balanced service offering. The harmonized cooperation of circuit and packet switched services will give our subscribers advanced international data communication possibilities.

We have also described the suitability of the NPDN to be used as a component of the future service integrated digital network (ISDN).

PER EIKESET received his M.Sc (1964) and Ph.D. degrees (1970) from the Technical University of Trondheim in the field of digital transmission systems and digital signal processing.

He joined the Norwegian Telecommunications Administration Research Establishment in 1969 where he became leader of the research unit for Data Communication. In the last five years he has mainly been engaged in activities concerning the Nordic Public Data Network as project leader within the Norwegian Telecommunications Administration for establishing the network in Norway.

OLOV SJÖSTRÖM received his M.Sc (1967) from the Institute of Technology in Stockholm in electronic engineering.

He joined the Swedish Telecommunications Administration in 1967 and has since 1969 worked with public data networks including the Nordic Public Data Network. He is now head of the Data network office in the Technical department.

The Australian Digital Data Service

J A Lockwood, T J Poussard
Telecom, Australia

In December 1982 Telecom Australia will introduce a Digital Data Service providing synchronous private line facilities at speeds from 2400 bit/s to 48 kbit/s. The service will offer CCITT X21 and X22 interfaces. It aims to be more cost effective, of high performance, and greater network flexibility for users than the equivalent modem based facilities.

INTRODUCTION

During the period 1978/79 Telecom Australia undertook a comprehensive review of its involvement in the provision of data communications facilities within Australia. By the middle of 1978 the number of modems in Australia had increased from virtually zero at the beginning of the seventies to 19,000. Growth was continuing at the rate of about 30%/annum.

Although Telecom Australia by world standards offered a comprehensive range of modem based services as Telecom's Datel service, it was clear that there was disatisfaction in the market place with several aspects of this service. The main areas of complaint were related to quality of service, particularly speed of provision and fault restoration. In addition the cost of long distance inter-capital circuits was high by world standards. In a country whose development has been described as a continuous battle against the tyranny of distance this was a serious shortcoming. Finally there was a demand for new data services, for example packet switching, and a demand for more flexible regulations with respect to privately owned and integral modems.

Recognition that these perceived shortcomings had to be overcome rapidly if Telecom Australia was to continue to play a major part in the provision of data communications led to the development of a three pronged plan to be implemented in the period 1980-1982. Firstly it was decided to introduce a purpose designed data switch utilising packet switching techniques. By 1978/79 packet switching was established as a viable technique overseas offering clear benefits to users not least in Australia being the potential of distance independant tariffs. Secondly it was decided to allow privately owned modems including terminals with integral modems to be attached to Telecom Australia circuits. This was to be done in stages between mid 1980 and the end of 1982. The third element involved the introduction of the Digital Data Service which would provide for synchronous leased line users a better quality of service at lower cost than the equivalent Datel service. The development of the Digital Data Service as a technical entity and as a market package is the subject of this paper.

THE DIGITAL DATA NETWORK (DDN)

In 1978 tenders were sought for the supply of a synchronous Digital Data Network (DDN) which would support synchronous services from 1.2k bit/s - 48kbit/s and possibly asynchronous services as well. This network was to be X50 based, to employ both X21 and X21 bis user interfaces. DDN was to complement modem based services within the Datel service and aimed at:

. improving quality of service within the framework of the Datel service especially on inter-capital routes.

. reducing provisioning times since most of the long haul routes would be pre-provisioned.

. improving service restoration times through the use of centralised testing and fault diagnostic capabilities.

However when the project was reviewed in 1979 it was considered that these objectives were too limited both in the context of maximum exploitation of the technical capabilities of DDN and in terms of the market requirement. From the marketing standpoint the DDN strategy offered inter-capital circuit users the prospect of a gradual increase in quality of service in the most sensitive long haul areas and potential for lower tariffs over a five to seven year period. Quite clearly this was inadequate given the level of disatisfaction in the marketplace. Technically the project was constrained by being cast as an upgrade of Datel.

THE DIGITAL DATA SERVICE (DDS)

At the end of 1979 the decision was taken to follow a course of action which would ensure a more rapid introduction of the DDN network. This decision included a fundamental change of direction. DDN was to be established as a network supporting a new set of services, the Digital Data Service (DDS). This was to be differentiated from Datel in terms of quality of service and in terms of the available facilities. The market objective was by 1985 to make DDS the first choice of users implementing leased line networks at speeds from 2.4 kbit/s to 48 kbit/s. In addition the emerging CCITT Recommendation X.22 was to be a key feature of the service. This package is described below.

The DDS will offer synchronous, full duplex, leased line services that operate at data signalling rates of 2.4 kbit/s, 4.8 kbit/s, 9.6 kbit/s and 48 kbit/s. The basic range of point-to-point and multipoint services will be functionally similar to Datel Services.

New services that combine transmission and multiplexing facilities will offer advantages to users prepared to restructure their operations. The major new services will be NETPLEX and NETSTREAM.

DDS service and interface options are summarised in Table 1.

Data Rate (kbit/s)	Interface	Point-to-Point	Multipoint	NETPLEX	NETSTREAM
2.4	X21	X	X	X	X
	X21 bis (V24)	X	X	X	X
4.8	X21	X	X	X	X
	X21 bis (V24)	X	X	X	X
9.6	X21	X	X	X	X
	X21 bis (V24)	X	X	X	X
48	X21	X			X
	X21 bis (V35)	X			X
	X22	X		X	X

Table 1
DDS SERVICE OPTIONS

The access line from the Digital Data Network (DDN) to a user's office will terminate at a Network Terminating Unit (NTU) which will be provided by Telecom. The user's data terminal equipment (DTE), will interface the DDN at the NTU.

The interface between a DTE and NTU in public data networks is defined by CCITT Recommendation X21, but recognising that most users currently have terminals with data modem-compatible interfaces, Telecom will also support CCITT Recommendation X21 bis (V24 and V35). This means that some DDS Services will be plugcompatible with Datel Services and in these cases it will not be necessary for users to change their existing operations to take advantage of superior DDS facilities.

TERMINAL STATIONS

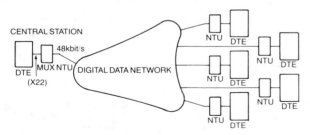

Fig 1
DDS NETPLEX SERVICE

A DDS NETPLEX service will multiplex data from a number of different terminal stations into a single multiplex stream that can be accepted directly by a central station. An exclusive, dedicated communications path is provided between each terminal station and the central station.

Telecom will supply a special multiplexing NTU that will provide timing to allow demultiplexing by a users front end equipment. Data will cross the DTE/NTU interface at the central station in a 48kbit/s multiplex stream. A multiplex time slot will be provided for each terminal station with the format of the multiplex stream defined by CCITT Recommendation X22. Fig. 1)

Initially, the X22 interface will be able to accommodate the following combinations of data circuits up to a maximum aggregate data rate of 48kbit/s:

. 20 x 2400 bit/s or
. 10 x 4800 bit/s or
. 5 x 9600 bit/s

NETPLEX will combine transmission and multiplexing functions to provide cost and control advantages to customers prepared to adopt the service. Networks based on NETPLEX can be readily re-configured by manual re-arrangements under network operator or user control. This will make the service particularly valuable to any user whose business viability might be threatened by any prolonged failure of his computer or communications facilities.

As well as the NTU, Telecom will supply special Test Access Equipment (TAE/X22) which can be inserted between the DTE and the NTU to provide a range of test facilities for the NETPLEX Service. The TAE allows the user to monitor the status of an individual channel within the NETPLEX stream or to divert a selected channel through the TAE to a local terminal or local test equipment. A facility is also provided on the TAE which permits remote activation of loops on the NTU's on terminal stations of the NETPLEX network. This allows data testing of NETPLEX point-to-point links. DDS NETPLEX Services will be provided from June 1983.

NETSTREAM is a pricing option that will assist customers to configure their networks to achieve maximum efficiency and cost savings.

A DDS NETSTREAM service will nominally aggregate separate data services operating between the same two centres into a higher speed data stream of 4.8, 9.6, 19.2 and 48 kbit/s for charging purposes. Charging benefits of up to 30% are available through this pricing option.

SERVICE OBJECTIVES

A comprehensive network management system, well protected digital links and high equipment reliability will be features of the DDN. The network has been designed to achieve fast provision and restoration of services and to meet the following performance objectives.

. A DDS long term target availability of 99.9%, with a low probability of an outage exceeding 4 hours in duration.

. A long term error performance of 99.5%
  error free seconds.

. A propagation delay through the network
  less than 20 ms for a typical service.
  However, the propagation delay will depend
  on the data rate of the service. The
  higher the data rate, the lower the delay.

Firm performance objectives will be set
following the engineering trials and national
introduction of the Digital Data Network.

DDS EXPANSION

The DDS will be expanded in stages. Since
September 1981 Sydney, Melbourne and Canberra
have been linked and the network is undergoing
engineering trials with live traffic. A full
intercapital service will be available when
the DDS is launched in December 1982. The
basic configuration of the DDN which will
support only intercapital services in its
first stage, is shown below (Fig. 2):

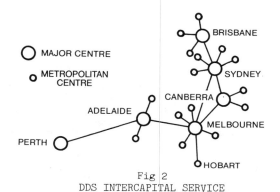

Fig 2
DDS INTERCAPITAL SERVICE

In December 1982, DDS service will be offered
between seven capital cities. However, the
network will be expanded rapidly to other
cities and country towns. By June 1985,
DDS service will be available in over 70
cities and towns throughout Australia.

DDS CHARGES

The DDS will provide end-to-end service from
user interface to user interface.

Prices are based on the following general
principles:

. The charging structure is simple, so that
  it can be easily understook by customers.

. Charges are designed to be attractive to
  operators of large teleprocessing leased
  networks. Most customers will find that
  DDS charges for long haul services will
  be substantially lower than Datel charges.

. The pricing structure is designed to
  enable customers to design their networks
  more flexibility.

. Charges increase with the data rate and
  are less distance dependent than Datel
  charges.

Although customers' total charges will depend
on their overall network configurations, the
pricing elements making up the totals are
designed to facilitate calculation of charges.
The three basic pricing elements that will
be used to construct DDS charges are:

. An installation charge for each NTU required
  to support a service.

. An annual access charge for each NTU
  required to support a service.

. An annual transmission charge for the aggregate data transmission capacity used by
  a customer on each chargeable route.

Australia has been divided into 9 zones for
charging purposes. Transmission charges within
a zone are dependant on speed but not distance.
Transmission charges between zones depends
on speed and on whether the distance is up
to 1145km or above. The one significant result
is that long distance charges between the
major Australian cities are as much as 50%
lower than the equivalent Datel charges.
Another cost saving feature is the Netplex
facility which reduces the access costs to
the DDS network by approximately 60%.

THE DIGITAL DATA NETWORK STRUCTURE

The Digital Data Network (DDN) is a digital
transmission and multiplex network to provide
point-to-point and multipoint links at the
synchronous rates of 2.4, 4.8, 9.6 and 48 k
bit/s with the CCITT user interfaces of X21
bis, X21 and X22 as listed in Table 1.

The basis network structure as shown in Fig 3
employs the CCITT multiplex streams of 64
kbit/s (X50 frame) and 2048 kbit/s (G732 Frame).
The current trial network linking Melbourne,
Sydney and Canberra is 64 kbit/s based. Full
2048 kbit/s operation will apply to the inter-
capital network at December 1982.

The DDN will be developed within a three level
hierarchy of network nodes as indicated below:

. main centres are fully intermeshed with at
  least 64 kbit/s links. They support both
  through connection and user collection
  functions. They also contain network
  synchronisation and network management
  systems.

. branch centres are parented off main centres
  and are not fully meshed. In other respects
  they are equivalent to main centres.

. terminal centres are parented off main
  or branch centres and carry out the user
  collection function only.

This architecture is arranged to limit cross
connections (user rate and 64 kbit/s) to
control delay and optimise operational
procedures. Direct routes between centres
will be established to meet high traffic
demands.

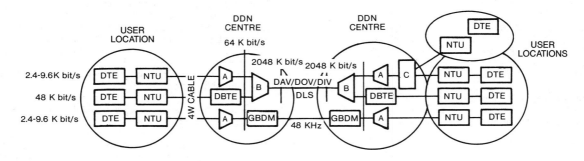

DTE   DATA TERMINAL EQUIPMENT
NTU   NETWORK TERMINATING UNIT
A - ZDME   ZERO ORDER DIGITAL MULTIPLEX EQUIPMENT
B - IDME   FIRST ORDER DIGITAL MULTIPLEX EQUIPMENT
    GBDM   GROUP BAND DATA MODEM
    DBTE   DIGITAL BASEBAND TRANSMISSION EQUIPMENT
C - MJE   MULTIPOINT JUNCTION EQUIPMENT
    DAV   DATE ABOVE VOICE
    DIV   DATA INVOICE
    DOV   DATA OVERVOICE
    DLS   DIGITAL LINE SYSTEM

Fig 3
DDN BASIC NETWORK STRUCTURE

Currently a 64 kbit/s trial network linking Melbourne, Sydney and Canberra is in operation supporting limited customer traffic and network evaluation testing. Fig 2 shows the network configuration for December 1982 when the DDS is launched offering inter-capital links on a national basis. DDN centres will then be interconnected by short haul 2048 kbit/s digital transmission links and long haul 2048 kbit/s and 64 kbit/s analogue based transmission. Long haul 2048 kbit/s digital transmission links are planned to support DDN development. During 1983 the number of terminal centres in the major cities will be increased and key regional centres connected to provide an intercapital service by December 1983.

LOCAL DISTRIBUTION SYSTEM

This consists of the user NTU operating over two unloaded cable pairs into the Zero Order Digital Multiplex Equipment (ZDME), (which generates a 64 kbit/s multiplex stream with an X50 frame structure) and the Multipoint Junction Equipment (MJE) which allows several NTU to operate to a single ZDME port.

The NTU performs several functions.

. extracts timing from the incoming network line signal to provide timing to the DTE

. provides CCITT synchronous interfaces of X21 bis, X21 or X22 to the DTE

. converts the DTE signals into a digital diphase signal for transmission over unloaded cable pairs to the ZDME in the terminal centre for 2.4 kbit/s - 9.6 kbit/s services.

. converts the DTE signals into a diphase signal for transmission over unloaded cable pairs to Digital Baseband Transmission Equipment (DBTE) and then to a first order multiplexer (1DME) for 48 kbit/s services.

. employs a 6+2 enveloping structure to provide network control signalling and framing. Thus the network rate is higher than the user interface rate.

. incorporates facilities that allow user initiated and network management initiated testing of the total data communications link.

Two NTU types are used, one for user rates 2.4 kbit/s to 9.6 kbit/s and another for 48 kbit/s.

The ZDME also interfaces directly to line thus carrying out both the user rate transmission interface and 64 kbit/s multiplex interface functions. The following user rate combinations can be supported.

```
20 x 2.4 k bit/s    (3.2 k bit/s)
10 x 4.8 k bit/s    (6.4 k bit/s)
 5 x 9.6 k bit/s    (13.2 k bit/s)
```

2048 kbit/s DIGITAL MULTIPLEXING

The First Order Digital Multiplex Equipment (1DME) generates a 2048 kbit/s multiplex stream from 31 x 64kbit/s input streams. The 2048 kbit/s interface is compatible with transmission links used for PCM telephony systems.

NETPLEX

A key element of DDS is the NETPLEX service
which provides a single 48 k bit/s multiplex
stream terminating data links consisting
of up to:

	20 x 2400 bit/s
or	10 x 4800 bit/s
or	5 x 9600 bit/s

This is achieved in the DDN by extending
to the user premises the X50 frame 64 kbit/s
interface from a DDN centre which has combined
these individual user links. Fig. 4 indicates
a typical network configuration. A 48 k bit/s
NTU with frame timing extracted in accordance
with CCITT interface X22 is employed. Fig. 5
shows the interface circuits and the use
of the Test Access Equipment/X22 (TAE/X22).
Single channels can be accessed via manual
timeslot selection at the TAE/X22, and remote
NTU looping established to enable testing
without disturbance of the other channels.
The framing signal across the interface is
achieved through detection of the X50 20
envelope frame (F) bit pattern. Allocation
of services is as follows:

2.4 kbit/s	1 envelope/frame
4.8 kbit/s	2 envelopes/frame
9.6 kbit/s	4 envelopes/frame

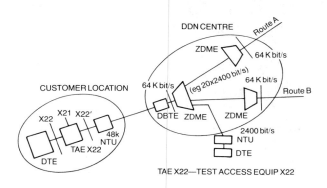

Fig 4
TYPICAL X22 PROVISION

DIGITAL TRANSMISSION

DDN centres are to be connected by digital
transmission links. The following transmission
links are to be provided initially.

. 2048 kbit/s digital line systems (used
  for PCM telephony) to connect terminal
  centres to branch or main centres in urban
  areas (short haul)

. 2048 kbit/s Data Above Voice (DAV) on
  radio bearers to interconnect main or
  branch centres (long haul). Short haul
  2048 kbit/s digital line systems extend
  DAV links from radio terminals to DDN
  centres.

. 64 kbit/s via data modems over group band
  telephony links to interconnect main or
  branch centres (long haul).

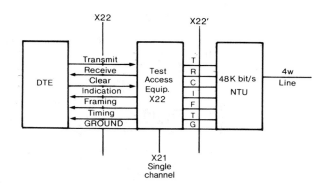

Fig 5
X22 INTERFACE CIRCUITS

The following additional transmission
facilities which will support DDN expansion
are planned for introduction by June 1985.

. 140 Mbit/s digital radio plus optical
  fibre system tails on all intercapital
  links

. 8 M bit/s on standard television link
  radio bearers (interim intercapital
  links)

. 2048 k bit/s Data In Voice (DIV) on
  two or three telephony supergroup allocations.

. 704 K bit/s DIV (within 2048 k bit/s
  stream) on a single telephony supergroup.

Automatic patch protection is provided
on a 1+1 basis and manual patching on an
N+1 basis for 64 kbit/s and 2048 kbit/s
links to avoid loss of intercentre links
due to transmission system failures. Diverse
routing and distribution of links across
multiple bearers is also employed.

NETWORK MANAGEMENT

The network management philosophy of DDN
is based upon each main and branch centre
being capable of local link supervision
and having network testing capability to
the users premises in each direction. These
functions also exist at Special Services
Restoration Centres (SSRC) which control
the user level service restoration activities.

Fig 6 shows the network management systems
as they relate to the transmission paths.

Every 64kbit/s link terminating at a main
or branch centre is monitored for failure
in each direction of transmission by the
Supervisory Alarm System (SAS) to enable
rapid network maintenance action.

User level testing is achieved through
access to an individual user channel by
time slot selection within a 64kbit/s
or 2048 kbit/s stream. Pattern generation
and analysis is implemented within the
processor based Subscriber Test System (STS)
and employed after the establishment by VDU
codeword control of test loops at the NTU, ZDME.

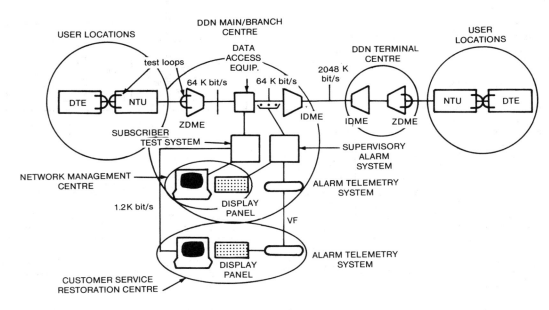

Fig 6
NETWORK MANAGEMENT SYSTEMS

In the monitor mode, only data stream status information can be extracted so that user data confidentiality is preserved.

64 kbit/s level testing is also implemented in the STS. In the monitor mode an indication of error performance can be gained from analysis of the X50 framing pattern.

NETWORK SYNCHRONISATION

The network is synchronised through a master slave hierarchy centred on a master clock in the Melbourne main centre. Slave clocks reside in every other main and branch centre. Both the master clock and the slave clocks are triplicated for security. Clock distribution is achieved within data streams and priority selection of timing sources carried out for maximum continuity of the clocking system. Failure of the master clock results in main service areas being driven by their slave clocks and operating pleisiochronously with each other. Slave clock failure results in the equipment clocks taking over.

CONCLUSION

The introduction of the Digital Data Service is expected to have a substantial impact on the cost, availability and error performance of leased line synchronous data services in Australia. In doing so it will also be enabling the establishment of responsive access paths for the AUSTPAC packet switching service scheduled for public service in December 1982. In addition, by laying down a national centrally managed 64 kbit/s transmission grid, the early development of an Integrated Services Digital Network (ISDN) could be greatly facilitated.

BIOGRAPHY

Mr T.J. POUSSARD has been engineering manager of the Digital Data Service network in Telecom Australia since early 1980. Initially involved in telephony transmission design and implementation, he moved to the data communications area in 1971 and was involved in the introduction of 2400 bit/s and 4800 bit/s modem based synchronous services. From 1977-1979 he carried out planning studies on packet switching services for Telecom Australia. He graduated from the Royal Melbourne Institute of Technology in 1964 and also holds a Bachelor of Commerce degree from Melbourne University and an M.Sc (Telecommunications Systems) degree from the University of Essex.

Mr A.J. LOCKWOOD is the Data Products Marketing Manager in Telecom Australia. He started his career in British Telecom in the Data Communications Marketing Division where he was involved, amongst other projects, in the Experimental Packet Switched Service Project. In 1980 he has had product marketing responsibilities for Datel, the Digital Data Service and Austpac. He graduated from Bristol University in 1970 and also holds a MSc (Eng) from University College London.

Interconnection of National Packet Switched Data Networks in Europe and their Impact on New Services

P T F Kelly

British Telecommunications, UK

Within Europe a packet switched data network to enable users within the European Economic Community to gain access to scientific, technical and socio-economic databases was established in late 1979 and is known as EURONET. In addition, some 17 countries are planning national packet switched data networks to be operational by the end of 1984 and four are already fully operational.

Within the Conference of European Postal and Telecommunications Administrations an Action Plan has been agreed which will ensure not only the interconnection of these networks but also their connection to EURONET and to overseas networks on a bi-lateral basis or on a transit basis as appropriate.

The paper outlines the plans and indicates the role of international gateways in easing the problems of the interconnection of the various networks. Some indication is also given of the impact of such interconnection on the provision of telex, teletex and videotex services.

1. THE EURONET NETWORK

In March 1980 the EURONET telecommunications network (1) was brought into full commercial operation. It is a packet based network initially provided to enable low cost access to be obtained to scientific, technical and socio-economic databases within the European Economic Community (EEC). Originally the name "EURONET" was assigned not only to the telecommunications network but also to the information aspects covering data terminals and the databases. However, the name "DIANE", Direct Information Access Network - Europe, was subsequently assigned to the information aspects of the network.

Since the network was opened it has been expanded and enhanced. In 1980 the network itself was extended to Switzerland and during 1982 Greece will gain access following the admission of the latter country to the EEC in 1981. The French national network, TRANSPAC, (2), was connected to EURONET in late 1979 via a gateway node known as a Node Transit Internationale (NTI).

The capacity of the network itself has been increased and now, in terms of the number of ports, is some 3 times larger than at opening date having about 600 access ports of which over 200 are for X25 connections. Of these X25 ports some 90 are currently operational and some 1700 Network User Identifiers (NUIs) have been issued to users who access EURONET via their respective national public switched telephone networks. The standards adopted for the telecommunications network were those defined by the International Telegraph and Telephone Consultative Committee (CCITT), at the date the development contract was placed, namely, June 1977. At that date only the 1976 version of CCITT Recommendation X25 existed, and there were not any Recommendations relating to the connection of character mode terminals to a packet switched data network. Specifications for such connections had thus to be defined by the Data Communications Group (CD) of the Conference of European Postal and Telecommunications Administrations (CEPT). These specifications became, with certain modifications, the CCITT Provisional Recommendations X3, X28 and X29 in 1978, (3). Also because at that time no CCITT Recommendation existed for a numbering plan or for an inter-node protocol, EURONET had to adopt the concepts used on TRANSPAC.

During 1981 and the early part of 1982, EURONET was modified to comply fully with the international numbering plan for public data networks, X121, and to include modifications to bring it closer into line with the CCITT 1980, (4), Recommendations X3, X25, X28 and X29. In addition, at each of the 5 switching nodes, ports were made available for the connection of national networks to EURONET by means of the international internetwork protocol X75, (4).

2. PLANS FOR EURONET AND USER IMPLICATIONS

Some indications of the future plans for EURONET have been given in a previous article (1). However, in June 1981, some significant decisions in regard to the future of EURONET were taken by the Consortium of PTT Administrations, which operates EURONET, and the Commission of the EEC. In effect it was decided that because of the rapid growth in national packet switched data networks in Europe, that EURONET should be frozen at its present size and configuration and that plans should be made to enable the DIANE traffic to be transferred over a 3 year period ending in 1984 to not only the respective national networks, but also to the network established to interconnect them. Such integration of the EURONET/DIANE traffic into the emerging interconnected national networks was, of course, always envisaged when the contract between the Commission of the EEC and the Community based PTTs was signed in 1975.

The key to this integration, and thus the effective disappearance of EURONET, but not of course DIANE, was the adoption of the full CCITT international numbering plan to X121 and the introduction of X75 access to each EURONET switching node; CCITT Recommendation X75 relating to the international internetwork signalling system. During 1981 the necessary software development was undertaken and tested on a "test" network before being introduced onto the live network. Because of uncertainies in regard to the actual availability of the various national networks it was decided at this stage to modify the implementation to enable EURONET itself to carry transit traffic thus permitting, if necessary, two national networks to be connected via EURONET even though this contravened the spirit of Recommendation X92 (4) in regard to the number of transit exchanges involved in an international connection. This latter decision caused some delay to the introduction of X75 onto EURONET but was considered by all concerned to be advantageous in the longer term.

Modifications to operational networks are often difficult to implement without causing some disruption to the service as seen by the users. On EURONET the changes were quite significant but by trying out the concepts on the "test" network and introducing the software changes over a weekend disruption of the network was avoided. However, as far as the users were concerned all addresses on the network were changed. Prior to the introduction of X121 the calling address was 0 DCC 3 followed by a 3 digit address, plus, where needed, an additional 2 digit sub-address. Since EURONET is in effect an "international" network, with users directly connected to it, the prefix "0" is superfluous and was thus dropped at the time of changeover and all addresses on EURONET are now as shown in table. 1.

When any country connects its national network to EURONET however, then users in that country may need to use an international prefix digit, which is absorbed by the national network, to gain access to EURONET. However, if the distant user is also connected to a national network the fourth digit of the DNIC will change from a 3 to whatever digit is allocated by that Administration for its respective national network.

Naturally the continual changes in calling and called addresses can be confusing to users but given adequate warning and publication of the revised international codes, changeover to the new codes and addresses was achieved without any difficulty.

At the same time as the numbering changes were made, changes were made to the procedures adopted by users who access EURONET through their national switched telephone network. These changes brought EURONET closer, but not fully, into line with X28 and were also achieved without any difficulty or disruption to traffic, mainly due to careful planning and adequate user awareness of the proposals and the reason for their introduction.

Prior to the modification users input firstly the called Network User Address (NUA) followed by his own Network User Identifier (NUI). After the modification the sequence was reversed, the NUI being input first followed by the called address, namely, the NUA. This change was implemented simultaneously with the dropping of the prefix "0" on called addresses as indicated in table. 2.

In accordance with CCITT Recommendation X28 the NUI is not echoed back to the calling terminal.

As mentioned previously these changes affected some 1700 users simultaneously as and from the changeover date in December 1981.

The introduction of X75 however, although extremely complicated, did not affect EURONET users, at least not initially. However, once a national packet network was connected to EURONET via the X75 connection there were significant changes. Firstly, users who accessed EURONET via their national telephone network could now achieve access via their nearest national packet network node. In some countries this involved a local telephone call charge rather than a long distance one with consequent financial benefits, but of course, the access code was changed. Users with X25 connections could also be re-terminated on their national packet network. This could involve a change in access charges since national rather than EURONET charges applied. However, it also enabled national calls to a particular DIANE database to be charged at national rather than EURONET rates. Overall the impact on the user was to lower his costs for rentals and call charges. With the transfer of the X25 connections to a given national network, users however, now had to conform to X25 as implemented on that network rather than that implemented on EURONET. This could involve adoption of X25 Lap 'B' in many cases and full compliance to CCITT X25 (1980) Recommendations.

In practice it was found that once a national network opened, a given DIANE host tended to initiate an X25 connection to the new network

Table. 1.
EURONET address structure

DCC	3	XXX
Data Country Code	EURONET Network Code	Terminal Address
3 digits	One digit	3 digits

←------------- DNIC ----------------→

Data Network Identification Code

Table. 2.
EURONET - User identifier structure

			NUA				DN		NUI				CR

OLD   NUA |02343001| DN   NUI |2340000ABCDE| CR

NEW   N |2340000ABCDE| NUI   -   NUA |2343001| CR

yet retaining the existing connection to EURONET. Once the new link was fully operational and carrying national originated traffic, notification of the new address, DCC N YYYYYYYYY rather than DCC 3 ZZZ was all that was necessary to ensure the new access was used. After a few weeks of parallel operation the user's direct link to EURONET was discontinued.

Currently the national networks in the United Kingdom, France and the Federal Republic of Germany are connected to EURONET via appropriate international gateway exchanges. Countries such as Sweden, Spain, Portugal and Finland now gain access to and from EURONET via one of these gateways. Greece, although an EEC country, differs from all other EEC countries in that they also gain access to and from EURONET via the NTI in Paris so as to ease the eventual disappearance of EURONET itself. In consequence all calls to and from Greece do not have the EURONET network code "3" but utilise the Data Network Identification Code (DNIC) specified by Greece, namely, 2022.

By the end of 1982 the EURONET network is expected to be as shown in fig. 1.

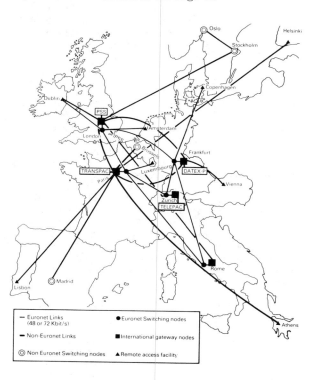

Fig.1. EURONET layout at end 1982

3. GROWTH OF NATIONAL PACKET SWITCHED DATA NETWORKS IN EUROPE

Within Western Europe some 17 countries currently plan to introduce national packet switched data networks (5). Of these some 4 had national networks in full operation at the end of 1981, and some 5 others had single nodes in operation prior to the implementation of a full network. During 1982 some 8 more countries expect to open national networks as can be seen from table. 3. These various networks have been obtained from some 7 different contractors.

In 1981 some 4 networks/nodes were interconnected using either extended X25 procedures or early X75 procedures. Interconnection to full X75 procedures began in earnest at the end of 1981 and during the early part of 1982. Among the early connections established was a link between Norway and Sweden, links from Spain to France and the UK, links from the FRG to both France and the UK and a link between the UK, France and Sweden. Early in 1982 the national network in the FRG was joined to EURONET as was the national network in the UK both via international gateway exchanges using the X75 international internetwork protocol.

As can be realised with so many contractors involved the facilities available on the various networks varies considerably. The development timescales were such in many cases that development had to be frozen before the 1980 CCITT Recommendations were published. Many of the newer networks for instance will only offer X25 Lap 'B' whereas others will offer both Lap and Lap 'B'. However, as part of the CEPT's plans for harmonisation of networks and services it is currently expected that all national networks will fully conform to CCITT Recommendation X25 (1980) by mid 1983. This will be of considerable advantage to terminal manufacturers who will then be able to manufacture equipment knowing that it can be readily connected to networks in any of the CEPT countries without modification, other than to meet national safety standards. Connection procedure approval should thus be expedited.

One major problem when networks are interconnected using X75 is that the facilities implemented in each country may vary or be introduced at different times. Within the CEPT countries discussions are in hand to see to what extent certain 'A' facilities in the CCITT Recommendation X2 can be designated as an 'E' facility, and thus implemented in all CEPT countries perhaps by mid 1983. However, if implemented nationally they may still not be available internationally for policy reasons and this can cause implementation problems.

Plans of European Administrations for National Packet Switched Data Networks

Country	Date for National Network	Network Name	Contractor for National Network	Date for single node
Austria	1982	DATEX-P	B	–
Belgium	1982	DCS	F	–
Denmark	1983	–	*	–
Finland	1983	–	*	1982
France	1978	TRANSPAC	A	–
F R Germany	1980	DATEX-P	B	1979+
Greece	1983	–	*	1982
Ireland	1983	IRPAK	*	1981
Italy	1982	–	F	1979+
Luxembourg	1982	–	A	–
Netherlands	1982	–	G	–
Norway	1982	NORPAK	D	1980
Portugal	1982	TELEPAC	*	1981
Spain	1971 (Non-X25)	RETD I	E	–
	1982 (X25)	RETD II	E	
Sweden	1983	TELEPAK	*	1979
Switzerland	1982	TELEPAC	B	1980+
United Kingdom	1977 (Non-X25)	EPSS	C	–
	–	IPSS	D	1978
	1980 (X25)	PSS	D	1979+

*   Contract for national network not yet placed.

+   Single node as part of EURONET.

For instance, "reverse charging" may be offered in country A and in country B, but not on calls between those countries. If a user requests the reverse charging facility from where should the "reverse charge refused" notice be returned? From the outgoing gateway or the incoming gateway exchange? If the former then it must know the status of international reverse charging to all other countries. If at the distant gateway then the international X75 link could carry excess call set-up packets. It seems now however, if agreement is reached within the CEPT countries, that some facility requests such as "reverse charging" will be checked at the outgoing gateway and others, such as calls to international based closed user groups at the incoming gateway in order to avoid excessive and non-revenue earning international traffic.

A major problem with the introduction of X75 as the protocol between national networks and between national networks and EURONET is the number of different contractors involved as can be seen from table. 3. Recommendation X75 was first issued in 1978 by the CCITT and was updated in 1980. Nevertheless it is still, as was X25, liable to be implemented with some variants by the many contractors involved. However, since X75 has to be implemented between networks made by different contractors, variants are simply not permissible. Implementation needs to be made in such a way that the basic implementation is common, but that the software implementation at the various gateways is flexible enough to take up the varying requirements applicable to individual routes. In the case of the UK, for instance, with X75 routes planned to most Western European countries the basic CCITT X75 specification of some 66 pages had to be augmented by some additional 30 pages to clarify certain

aspects including parameter settings for the various routes. Even then a "facilities" specification had to be agreed with each and every distant Administration to reflect the variants in regard to incoming and outgoing facilities which of course may need to be changed with time as enhancements are made to the various networks. The mere fact that interconnection of several networks has been achieved is due, no doubt, to the extreme care taken by the various project engineers in defining the gateway parameters.

4. CEPT EUROPEAN ACTION PLAN

Within the CEPT several Action Plans have been agreed in relation to data transmission services. These action plans relate not only to packet switched data services but also to circuit switched and leased line services – in fact to all services appropriate to Public Data Networks as defined by the CCITT.

The Action Plan includes inter-alia several significant proposals relevant to the packet switched data services. Firstly it proposed the maximum harmonisation of services and facilities provided by the various Administrations. Secondly, it proposed the early interconnection of national networks either on a bilateral basis or via transit working via a third country and thirdly, it recommended harmonisation in relation to tariffs within Europe.

As has been mentioned the first two proposals are now in the course of implementation and should be completed by the mid 1980's. As far as tariffs were concerned this represented a problem. Tariffs for EURONET had been decided by the members of the EURONET Consortium – some 10 of the 17 countries known to be planning and implementing national networks. Whilst technically feasible to absorb the EURONET/DIANE traffic into the emerging European packet switched data service, users would not agree to transfer if there was to be an increase in tariffs. Thus it was accepted that the tariffs between the EURONET countries would not change when the traffic was transferred. In addition, it was necessary to ensure that no user within the Community countries was discriminated against due to location and this meant in effect common tariffs for calls between Community countries. Each Administration has to add national access charges where appropriate and this does mean that tariffs between any two countries vary slightly but the international (common) element, allowing for currency fluctuations, is broadly the same. In the case of the UK this results in tariffs for UK originated traffic of £1.32/hour and £1.20/k segments.

5. SERVICES USING THE NETWORKS

The first type of service to use EURONET was, of course, database access traffic and this led to a high proportion of character mode (X28) terminal connections to the network compared to packet mode (X25) terminal connections. However, there is a limited market for database access traffic and for networks to be viable it is necessary for them to carry other types of traffic. Whilst X25 to X25 type traffic is feasible on EURONET it has not grown significantly during the early years of EURONET. It is difficult to analyse the reason for this but some companies seem reluctant to use EURONET until is has a greater geographical coverage. This will, of course, be a practical realisation once national networks are connected to EURONET and to each other.

Analysis of the growth patterns of the various national packet networks shows a completely different story. In all countries demand for the national service is much greater than originally forecast. This is particularly so in relation to the demand for connection at X25 and for interworking between X25 terminals. In some countries the demand for connection at X25 exceeds the demand at X28.

This could be due in some way to the fact that X25 is now respectable and supported by the data processing industry. Adoption of X25 could mean therefore, an increase in not only "data" traffic but also in regard to "text" traffic perhaps at the expense of telex traffic.

The introduction in Europe of a Teletex service is expected to increase the amount of traffic on the various packet switched data networks since not only do many Administrations intend to offer a Teletex service on their national networks, since Teletex is an X25 based service, but they intend to use their international packet links for communication to other countries. In this context it is significant that the X75 protocol is recommended by the CCITT (6) for international working. However, some Administrations in Europe envisage their national Teletex service being provided on their circuit switched data service.

Currently the technical problem of interworking between a Teletex service on a packet switched network and one on a circuit switched network has not yet been fully resolved although some Administrations are now considering implementing a CS/PS conversion facility. However, interconnection needs to be implemented in such a way as to not degrade the principles inherent in X25 based networks and the principle of Open Systems Interconnection, (7). The location of the conversion facility in the PS country or in the CS country is a problem, but one which may resolve itself when the international tariffs for both circuit and packet transmission are known. It is, however, the author's firm view that packet based networks are ideally suited both technically and cost wise for carrying a Teletex service and probably eventually, a "packeted" telex service.

Although Administrations intend to offer a Teletex service on either their circuit or packet switched data service some intend, in addition, to offer it on their Public Switched Telephone Networks, PSTN. The current position of the various Administrations is shown in table. 4.

Table. 4.
Plans of European Administrations for a
Teletex service

Country	PSTN	PDN	
		Circuit	Packet
Austria	–	1982	–
Belgium	–	–	1983
Denmark	–	1983/84	–
Finland	–	1983	–
France	1983	–	1983
F R Germany	–	1981	–
Italy	1983	1983+	1983+
Netherlands	1983+	–	1983+
Norway	–	1983	–
Portugal	–	–	1983
Spain	–	–	1983
Sweden	–	1982	–
Switzerland	1982/83*	–	1982/83
United Kingdom	1982	–	1982

NOTES: + – Choice of network to be used
not yet decided

* – Initial trial period

Since a basic requirement of a Teletex service is that communication should be feasible to and from telex terminals, this opens up some interesting internetworking problems. In the UK, for example, a Teletex service is being provided on both the PSTN and on the national Packet Switched Data Network (PSDN). Interworking between these networks and the telex network is needed and will be available in 1983. In the case of interworking to the telex network a Store and Forward facility needs to be implemented but between the PSTN and the PSDN because Teletex uses X25 procedures the interworking can be achieved in real time. With similar interworking facilities provided in overseas countries international interworking presents some interesting routing, numbering and tariff problems which are still under consideration. The concepts of Teletex networking is shown in fig. 2.

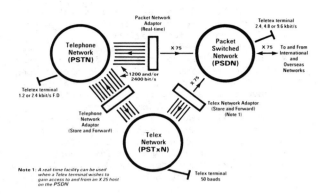

Fig. 2.   Teletex networking in the UK

Many Administrations are also planning, or
have implemented, Videotex services. In the
UK and in the FRG access to a Videotex centre
is generally via the PSTN. Calls to databases
not available at the centre are switched via
the national packet switched networks to third
party databases. It seems reasonable to presume therefore, that international Videotex
service will be implemented via the international packet service. A major problem however, is that the tariffs for a packet service
being volume based are not ideally suited to
the tree search concepts adopted on Videotex.
However, where keyboard versions exist then,
of course, access can be direct to the necessary "pages" if known. Availability of keyboard Videotex terminals, of course, also enables them to access packet networks direct
without the need to route their calls via a
Videotex centre. Such direct access has already been demonstrated on EURONET but necessitates some changes to the HOST software to
accommodate the Videotex repertoire.

6. CONCLUSIONS

By the mid 1980's a European-wide packet based
data transmission service should be available
to full CCITT Recommendations which will provide an ideal transmission medium for the
transmission of both data and text. The extension of these European plans to other parts
of the world could see the establishment of a
world-wide packet switched data network to
complement the existing switched telephone
and telex networks.

7. ACKNOWLEDGEMENTS

Acknowledgement is due to the many members of
the various European Administrations who have
worked together so earnestly not only to bring
EURONET into full operation, but who have also
formulated the plans for its gradual integration into a European-wide packet based data
transmission service. Acknowledgement is also
due to the many people throughout the world
who have contributed to the establishment of
CCITT Recommendations.

8. REFERENCES

(1) Kelly, P.T.F., EURONET/DIANE - A European
    Harmonisation Project Proc ICCC-80
    pp 658-663.

(2) Picard, Ph., et al, The Industrial Comple-
    tion of TRANSPAC Revue Sotelec - Special
    Number, Geneva 1979, pp 73-86.

(3) Provisional CCITT Recs X3, X25, X28 and
    X29. Grey Book. International Telecom-
    munications Union - Geneva 1978.

(4) CCITT "Recommendations for Data Communica-
    tion Networks" - Yellow Book Vol VIII.2
    and 3. International Telecommunications
    Union - Geneva 1981.

(5) Public Data Networks - Plans of the Euro-
    pean Telecommunications Administrations -
    4th Edition 1981 - Eurodata Foundation,
    London, England.

(6) CCITT "Recommendations for Telegraph and
    Telematic Services Terminal Equipment" -
    Yellow Book Vol VII.2. International
    Telecommunications Union - Geneva 1981.

(7) Wood, B,M., Open System Interconnection -
    basic concepts and current status.
    Proc ICCC-82.

BIOGRAPHY

Philip Kelly is a Deputy
Director in the Network
Executive of the Head-
quarters of British Tele-
communications which was
formerly part of the
British Post Office. His
responsibilities cover the
planning, development,
maintenance and operations
of national non-voice net-
work services, including telex as well as
packet, circuit and leased line data services.
He has represented British Telecommunications
at SG VII of the CCITT and at the CEPT Special
Committee on Data Transmission (CSTD). He is
also a Vice-Chairman of the CEPT Data Transmission Group and Chairman of the multinational committee established to oversee the
planning and implementation of the telecommunications network for EURONET. He has an
honours degree in electrical engineering, and
is a member of the Institution of Electrical
Engineers and of the British Computer Society.
In March 1981 he was elected a Governor of the
International Council for Computer
Communications.

The Public Packet Switched Service in Italy

R Parodi
SIP, Italy
A Micciarelli
PT Administration, Italy
L Musumeci
Italtel, Italy

The Italian Administration and SIP (Operating Company) have defined a joint plan for the introduction of a public network providing both circuit and packet switched data services.
The network organization and the basic technical choices have been defined on the basis of the principles of the emerging ISDN. This will favour the subsequent incorporation of the future equipment and network evolutions in the ISDN.
A basic principle adopted in the definition of the network structure is the specification of a precise interface between the (subscriber) access function and the (network) transit function. Two types of equipment have been defined to perform such functions, respectively Packet Adaptor Concentrator (ACP) and Packet Switching Node (NCP).
Operation and maintenance will be provided by means of Maintenance Centers (CM), whose functions will be gradually integrated in the correspondent centers for the telephone service, and of a Network Management Center (CGM) for the general supervision of the network.
After a description of the network, the paper focuses on the implementation aspects of the concerned equipment.

1. INTRODUCTION

The rapid development of data services in Italy creates a need to establish a public telecommunication network providing a wide range of data communication facilities.

It is foreseen that, aligned with the general trend in most countries, the network structure will be based on the principles of the Integrated Services Digital Network (ISDN). According to this evolutionary principle a joint plan between the Administration and SIP have been defined for the introduction of a public network providing both circuit and packet switched data services. The paper refers in particular to the development for the packet switched service which will be introduced by 1983 with an initial installation capacity of 5000 subscribers and planned expansion for 12000 subscribers. The paper focuses on the implementation aspects of the equipment which have been realized with the objective of a future incorporation in the ISDN.

Finally reference is made to the realizations under development which will be introduced in a second stage to cope with the progressive expansion of the provided services.

2. NETWORK ARCHITECTURE FOR PACKET SWITCHED SERVICE

2.1 ISDN perspective

It is generally recognised that both circuit and packet switching techniques should be incorporated in the ISDN (Integrated Services Digital Network) to provide sufficient flexibility in handling the various voice and non-voice services. (1)(2)
Present trends in the development of distributed control structures for telephony

exchanges confirm the technical possibility to introduce data capability into digital telephony exchanges.
The international activity on the ISDN is now concentrating in the definition of suitable standards for the customer access to the digital local exchange with the aim to allow full integration of the various services, at least in the access part of the ISDN.
Concerning packet switched service it is felt that, at least for now, the integration process will invest the access network while at the transit network level dedicated resources will continue to be used (e.g. packet nodes of dedicated networks).

Fig. 1 shows the general ISDN architecture as we see in Italy (3). The backbone of the network is formed by the telephony IDN (Integrated Digital Network) with full use of common channel signalling system CCITT n° 7 between exchanges.
Concerning packet switching, a Packet Handling Module (PHM) is introduced at local exchange level; it may also be centralised at transit level depending on subscriber density and distribution.

The multiservice subscriber access, via a digital subscriber line, consists of a transparent 64 kbit/s in-slot channel (B) and a message oriented out-slot channel (D) at 16 kbit/s.
Subscriber access to data services may be performed: i) by using the B-channel, in which case the user rate may be up to 64 kbit/s and the service may be provided in alternative to telephony or concurrently (e.g. 16 kbit/s for digital voice and 48 kbit/s for data service), ii) by exploiting the message transport capability of the D channel which may provide performances similar to those offered through an X.25 connection.

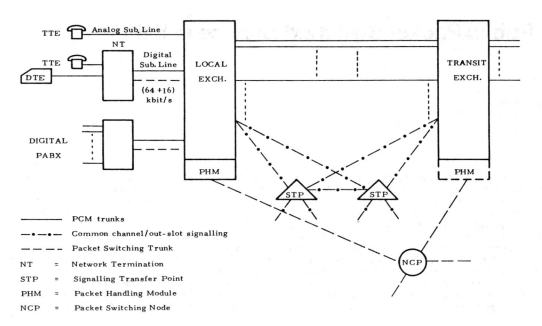

TTE 📞 Analog Sub. Line
NT
TTE 📞 Digital Sub. Line
DTE
(64 +16) kbit/s
LOCAL EXCH.
TRANSIT EXCH.
DIGITAL PABX
PHM
PHM
STP
STP
NCP

```
———————    PCM trunks
—•—•—     Common channel/out-slot signalling
— — — —    Packet Switching Trunk
NT    =    Network Termination
STP   =    Signalling Transfer Point
PHM   =    Packet Handling Module
NCP   =    Packet Switching Node
```

FIGURE 1 - ISDN NETWORK ARCHITECTURE

In the ii) case, the D channel conveys, in statistical multiplexing, signalling information for the B-channel and packetized data or other message oriented information (e.g. telemetry) (4).
Of course the B channel may be used to carry packet calls; in this case it offers a circuit switched access at 64 kbit/s to the PHM.

A companion paper presented to this conference (5) more deeply presents our considerations on the introduction of data services into the ISDN. It is outlined the ISDN field-trial, planned by 1983, which will include a PHM function fully integrated in the ITALTEL UT 10/3 digital telephony exchange.

2.2 Short term developments

The joint plan between the Administration and SIP (Operating Company) foresees a network structure which is based on the principles described above. Already from the first stages the network organization and the basic technical choices are defined in coherence with those principles (6).
A basic principle adopted in the definition of the network structure is the specification of a precise interface between the (subscriber) access function and the (network) transit functions. In this way, it is expected that future equipment and network evolutions (including the achievement of the final ISDN objective) can be easily incorporated.

The resulting network architecture for packet switched service is shown in fig. 2. Four types of equipment are identified, namely; i) Packet Adaptor and Concentrator (ACP), ii) Packet Switching Node (NCP), iii) Maintenance Center (CM), iv) Network Management Center (CGM).

The ACP is a relatively small size equipment (about 100 user terminations), which provides

adaptation of non-packet mode DTEs and packet concentration also for packet DTEs. Initially it supports start-stop DTEs, according to CCITT Rec. X.28, and X.25 DTEs with access through both direct connections and circuit switched connections.
Further developments already in progress relate to an ACP characterized by enhanced capabilities in terms of higher capacity (256 user terminations) local switching, support of other non-packet mode DTEs (e.g. BSC DTEs).
A ratio of 4 between start-stop and packet DTEs has been adopted for the specification of the network equipment. However, taking into account the increasing diffusion of X.25 DTEs, it is already foreseen that the above said ratio will consequently decrease in the further development (in the new ACP type the ratio of 1 will also be supported).

The network nodes (NCPs) handle virtual circuits (both switched and permanent) generally established through the ACPs. It is also foreseen that high throughput X.25 DTEs may be directly connected to the NCP.

At the opening time the network has an initial capacity of about 5000 subscribers and planned expansion to 12000 subscribers and will consist of 3 nodes, placed respectively in Rome, Milan and Naples, and some one hundred of ACPs distributed on the territory. It is already planned to introduce two other NCPs and an adequate number of ACPs for the further expansion of the network.
The NCPs are interconnected among themselves and with the ACPs generally by means of 64 kbit/s PCM links; for connections towards ACPs also 9.6 kbit/s links are used for analogue transmission facilities. The corresponding signalling procedures adopted throughout all the network are consistent with X.75 with some adaptation in particular concerning the introduction of signalling procedures for PVC.

Network Control and Maintanance is provided by means of the Network Management Center

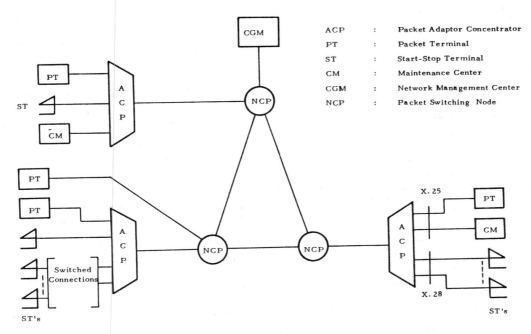

ACP	:	Packet Adaptor Concentrator
PT	:	Packet Terminal
ST	:	Start-Stop Terminal
CM	:	Maintenance Center
CGM	:	Network Management Center
NCP	:	Packet Switching Node

FIGURE 2 - NETWORK ARCHITECTURE FOR PACKET SWITCHED SERVICE

(CGM) and of the Maintenance Centers (CMs).
CGM and CMs are linked to the network equipment via permanent virtual circuits. They perform control and supervision; in particular CMs are foreseen for the control and management of the peripheral part of the network including the subscriber lines.
A general approach is foreseen in which real-time functions requiring a 100% availability target (e.g. alarms collection and displaying, reconfiguration command sending) are decentralized in the network while functions requiring high computing resources and large storage support (e.g. statistic collection and processing, report preparation) are centralized.

3. SERVICE CHARACTERISTICS

The basic services provided by the network are virtual call and permanent virtual circuits for user classes up to 1.2 kbit/s in the start-stop mode and 9.6 kbit/s in the packet mode. Moreover, the synchronous class at 64 kbit/s is being considered as an alternative to 48 kbit/s.

3.1 Optional user facilities

The optional user facilities are a subset of those specified by Rec. X.2. A list of them is given in table 1.

3.2 Performances

The system performance is determined essentially by parameters related to traffic handling capacity, introduced transit delay and reliability. Detailed values assumed as design objectives are shown in table 2.

Optional user facilities	User class
Closed user group	All
Incoming/outgoing calls barred	All
Throughput class selection	Packet
Window size selection	Packet
Calling line identification	All
One way logical channel	Packet
Reverse charging	All
Reverse charging acceptance	All
Pad Parameters	Start-stop

Table 1: Optional User facilities

Performance parameters		Values
Throughput:	NCP	>400 packet/s
	ACP	40 packet/s
Packet transit delay		250 ms (50%)
Service Availability		98%
Call set up time		500 ms (50%)
Clear down time		250 ms (50%)

Table 2: Performance parameters

3.3 Interfaces and protocols

Basically X.28 and X.25 interfaces, aligned to the status of CCITT Rec.s in 1980, have been adopted. For the packet interface the following main parameters have been chosen:
i) link access protocol (level 2) = LAPB,
ii) 128 octets for maximum packet length,
iii) default window size = 2

4. NETWORK EQUIPMENT

The network equipment are supplied by ITALTEL and FACE-SUD Selettronica. In the following a short description of the characteristics of each network equipment is given.

4.1 Packet Switching Node (NCP)

The global capacity of the NCP is of about 500 line/junctions. In the first stage the NCP has a net throughput of about 400 packet/s (64 bytes per packet) in addition to the one required for network control and supervision.

Fig. 3 shows the basic hardware of the node. Every Terminator Group may be equipped with a maximum of 31 line/junction terminators. The line/junction terminators are equipped with the line interfaces which implement the interfaces to the connected line. In particular the line/junction terminator uses a microprocessor whose main job is the implementation of level 2 procedures of X.25/X.75 Recommendations.

The Central Processor provides the real time functions for the set-up and clear down of the virtual connections and for the forwarding of the packets through the line/junction terminator.
Two types of processors may be supplied: both these types are powerful 16 bit processing units with a Main Memory capacity of 256 kbytes or 1 Mbyte respectively.
In both cases the use of a Cache Memory increases considerably the throughput rate of the Central Processor.
Communication between the Line Terminators and the Central Processor is via the Communication Controller which has direct access to the Main Memory.

The Communication Controller scans the Line Terminators and transfers line status reports, control information and data to Central Processor. It also forwards control commands and data, received by the central processor, to the Line Terminators.

In order to ensure continuity of service, the node is provided in duplicate mode. The duplication method operates on the hot stand-by principle.
When the switchover procedure is activated the following actions take place:
i) existing virtual connections are either resetted or cleared down;
ii) virtual connections which are in the set-up phase are cleared down;
iii) permanent virtual connections are resetted.

As it is shown in figure 3, the duplication starts at the level of the Terminator Groups. The Bus Link permits mutual supervision and updating of the duplicated system modules.

4.2 Packet Adaptior-Concentratore (ACP)

The ACP (fig. 4) consists of a central processor and of dedicated line terminators which are grouped into four subsystems (7).
The ACP may be equipped with different ratios of asynchronous and synchronous ports, replacing one synchronous port with four asynchronous ports.
The typical configuration provides 32 asynchronous ports plus 8 synchronous ports.
To obtain the desired configuration, no changes or modification are required; it is only necessary to equipe the ACP with the appropriate line terminators.

In any case the ACP may be connected to the node with up to four trunks which employ the X.75 protocol. The basic central processing hardware structure is composed of a CPU module, two 64 kbyte RAM modules, a diagnostic bootstrap and bus terminator module and a floppy disk driver controller.

The communication interface units are grouped into up to four subsystems. A subsystem is an autonomous structure which includes its bus interface, watch dog timer and typically up to 12 asynchronous interfaces and 2 synchronous interfaces (DMA).
Two subsystems are contained in a single card cage. Each subsystem can be separately isolated from the ACP bus both by manual switch and by software control.
This provides service continuity for the remaining lines whenever a fault occurs or maintenance is needed.

4.3 Network control centers (CM and CGM)

A network control center consists of a central processor with a main memory and an adequate number of peripheral devices, namely console typewriters, video display units, disk storage and magnetic tape units.
The main tasks of the control centers are remote loading and bootstrapping, remote dumping, recording of accounting and statistical data, network monitoring and management.
The man-machine interactions for the provision of the various functions are performed in accordance with the CCITT Rec.s for MML (Z. series).

4.4 The Software System

The software of the packet switching system is characterized by an accurate and efficient partitioning in program modules. This approach makes the software more flexible in order to allow enhancements or modifications.
The functions implemented by the various program modules may be classified as follows: network management and network monitoring functions, which are performed in the control centers, and switching functions, which are

performed in the nodes and in the concentrators.

In line with the distribution of the functions it is appropriate the use of a standard executive in the control center and of a dedicated executive, particularly optimized for packet switching applications, in the nodes and in the concentrators.

The software structure makes reference to the layers organization.
In the packet switching network up to five levels are considered: the nodes and the concentrators utilize all the levels, while the control center uses only the Level 5, as the other levels are handled by its Front-End.
The level 1,2,3 programs . include all the switching-oriented functions for handling the procedures according to adopted CCITT Recommendations (X.28, X.25, X.75).
The level 4 programs provide the trasport mechanism for the exchange of messages between the control center, the nodes and the concentrators. In the nodes and in the concentrators the level 5 programs provide for

the transmission of accounting information and of statistical data and alarms. It also includes the functions to execute operator commands received from the control center and to send the appropriate responses to the commands. In the control center the level 5 programs provide for the processing of accounting information and of statistical data received from the nodes and concentrators, of the network monitoring and of the command/response functions of the network.
Therefore connections between users in the network will be handled by the relevant software modules up to level 3, while connections between the nodes (or the concentrators) and the control center are governed by the protocols up to level 5.

To complete the list of the software modules, it is worthwhile to mention the I/O system and the safeguard system.
The I/O system contains the software drivers for connecting peripheral devices.
In the nodes and in the concentrators the safeguard system is principally responsible for handling the recovery functions (start up,

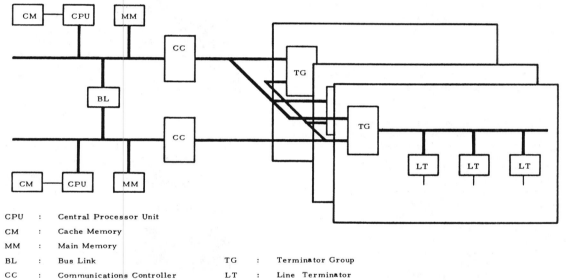

CPU	:	Central Processor Unit			
CM	:	Cache Memory			
MM	:	Main Memory			
BL	:	Bus Link	TG	:	Terminator Group
CC	:	Communications Controller	LT	:	Line Terminator

FIGURE 3 – NODE STRUCTURE

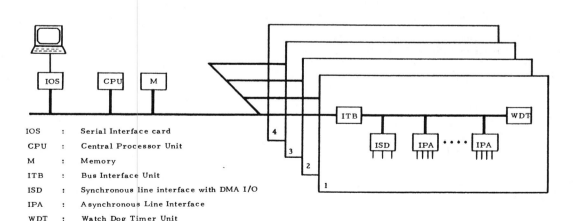

IOS	:	Serial Interface card
CPU	:	Central Processor Unit
M	:	Memory
ITB	:	Bus Interface Unit
ISD	:	Synchronous line interface with DMA I/O
IPA	:	Asynchronous Line Interface
WDT	:	Watch Dog Timer Unit

FIGURE 4 – ACP STRUCTURE

restart and switchover procedures) and for monitoring the operating condition of the apparatus.
In the control center the safeguard system comprises all the software modules required for system recovery (start up, restart, switchover procedures) and for functional checks.

6. CONCLUSION

An outline has been given of the characteristics of the public packet switched service which will be introduced in Italy by 1983.

Since the initial stage the realizations, which have been described in the paper, are in full accordance with the relevant CCITT Recommendation, in particular concerning user interfaces and network signalling.

The network organization and the basic technical choices have been done in accordance with the basic principles emerging for the ISDN, so that gradual incorporation of the dedicated resources for packet switched service in the ISDN will be simplified.

REFERENCE

(1) M. Dècina, R. Parodi: "Circuit and packet switched data communication in integrated services digital networks" ICCC '80 Atlanta, October 1980
(2) COMM.X.VIII - No R8 "Report of the meeting of the group of experts on ISDN matters of Study Group XVIII" - Munich 17.25 February 1982.
(3) D. Di Pino, L. Musumeci, R. Parodi: "Evolutionary steps towards and Integrated Services Digital Network (ISDN)" ISS '81 Montreal, September 1981.
(4) C. Mossotto, D. Di Pino: "The role of signalling and protocols in the emerging ISDN" ICC '81, Denver Colorado, June 1981.
(5) Giorcelli, L. Musumeci, M. Romagnoli: "ISDN capabilities in a digital local exchange" to be presented at ICCC '82.
(6) A. Cardarelli, M.L. D'Atri, A. Micciarelli, R. Parodi: "Servizi di telematica in Italia nel quadro della rete multiservizio" IIC '80, Genova, October 1980.
(7) N. Corsi, L. Musumeci, R. Parodi: "Design and performance of subscriber access equipment for packet switched networks" ISS '81, Montreal, September 1981.

Roberto PARODI received the Dr. Ing. degree in electrical engineering in 1972. Since 1973 he is working in the New Techniques Division of the SIP Headquarters where at present he is head of the Data Section. Among various aspects his interest is now focused on the introduction of data services in the emerging ISDN. He has been for a long time an active member of CEPT W.G. Data Communication and of CCITT S.G. VII where at present he is Rapporteur for ISDN matters.

Antonio MICCIARELLI Technical manager in the PTT Administration – Services Automatization Central Direction. He is the head of the department for the project and installation of Telex and data switching exchanges. He is presently deeply involved in the assessment for the establishment of the public packet switched service in Italy. He is national coordinator for the international activity in the area of data communication.

Luigi MUSUMECI received the Dr. Ing. degree in electrical engineering in 1961 from the Politecnico of Milan, Italy. He joined ITALTEL in 1968. Since 1973 he has been working in the area of the new public data networks. At present he is involved in the realization of the Public Packet Switched Network in Italy. Since 1972 he is a professor of Information Theory at the University of Pavia, in Italy.

Telex-packet Switching Interworking in the United Kingdom

R S Brown
British Telecommunications, UK

This paper describes the new British Telecom interworking facility which enables users of the UK telex network to communicate with users of the Packet switched public data network. The equipment is based on the Plessey Controls Limited 4660/20 telex switch and is known within British Telecom as the "Telex Network Adaptor" (TNA). The facility is due to become operational in early 1983. The paper begins with a discussion of the design constraints and then describes the Telex and Packet interfaces. The paper goes on to describe the methods of calling customer and called customer identification and the charging principles employed. The methods of accessing the TNA are described and the selection numbering schemes for both Packet and Telex originated traffic. The Call Set Up, Data Transfer, and Clear-Down phases of interworking calls are discussed. The paper closes with a description of the hardware and the traffic handling capability of the unit.

INTRODUCTION

It is recognised by British Telecom (BT) that as the various networks, Public Switched Telephone Network (PSTN), Integrated Services Digital Network (ISDN), Public Switched Data Network (PSDN) and the Public Switched Telex Network (PSTxN) develop there is a need to interwork between them mainly to meet non-voice requirements.

An interworking capability from the PSTN to the PSDN has existed for some time but not as yet in the reverse direction although work is in hand. Following the PSDN becoming fully operational British Telecom identified a user need for access to and from the PSDN for telex terminals. Although as with the introduction of any new service it was difficult to accurately forecast the demand, it seemed clear that what was needed was the capability to provide interworking to enable users who have a telex terminal to access hosts connected to the PSDN, in particular those offering electronic mail and databases.

Thus this interworking combination enables users of the UK telex network and users of the PSDN to communicate with each other. The equipment is known within British Telecom as the Telex Network Adaptor (TNA) and is the result of speculative development by Plessey Controls Ltd (PCL) and based on the 4660/20 telex switch with a moderate amount of additional software development. This paper describes the TNA and the way in which the network interworking problems were overcome.

In addition to the network interworking situations outlined above, service interworking requirements are also receiving attention. For instance, the newly recommended Teletex service has been defined to have a basic requirement of interworking with the Telex service. Telex-Teletex interworking requires processing of data above the network protocol layers which a network inetworking device such as the TNA is not designed to provide. As a result the telex-teletex service interworking facility is the subject of a separate development within the UK.

DESIGN CONSTRAINTS

A primary aim was that by the use of the discreet "black box" approach the function would be performed with minimal or no change to either network. Additional facilities were restricted in order to minimise the software development timescale and introduce the service as early as possible. The need to provide service at an early stage necessitated making minimum changes and compromising the engineering implementation. The TNA was introduced as a stop-gap before the function is provided as an integral feature of modernised (SPC) Inland Telex Exchanges.

It is possible for a telex customer to initiate a call to a packet terminal, or to a character terminal via a Packet Assembler/Disassembler (PAD). It is similarly possible for a customer of the packet network to initiate a call to a telex terminal. The TNA will act as a Packet Assembler Disassembler (PAD), and perform code and speed conversion. Telex to telex working by this method was not an objective and not technically feasible. No call charging facilities were required within the TNA equipment since this was accomplished by external means.

With 90,000 UK telex terminals and a rapidly growing PSDN a significant traffic level between both networks was anticipated. However, until a service is offered the traffic could not be easily estimated and hence a relatively small provision was initially planned. The TNA is provided with two X75 links and 64 telex ports which can be easily expanded to 128 telex ports without major change. It would also be possible to provide a second TNA to meet user demand, although as indicated earlier it was anticipated that modernised SPC Inland Exchanges would take over this function before this became necessary.

PHYSICAL NETWORK INTERFACES

Telex Interface

It was necessary to choose an access code which would route calls from anywhere in the telex network to a common point in order to access the TNA. The selection chosen was the International Telex Assistance level "200" and access to the TNA equipment is provided off level "8". It was decided to site the TNA in a London exchange because this had a number of advantages which include: a. Direct telex routes from London exchanges to and from all other inland exchanges, b. Direct access to and from international telex gateway exchanges may be required, and c. The expected large proportion of London Based interworking traffic.

The exchange chosen was Fleet in the City of London. There are 32 telex trunks into the TNA and 32 telex trunks from it and the general signalling protocol is to CCITT Recommendation U1 Type B using dial selection as currently used in the inland telex network.

Packet Interface

The TNA is connected to the PSDN by two tandem X75 links operating at 48 kbit/s to one Packet Switch Exchange (PSE). Only one of the links is used at any time and the second is provided for redundancy. The PSE chosen was Baynard House. The TNA appears to the PSDN to act as a remote PAD, in accordance with CCITT Recommendations X3, X28 and X29. Recommendations X3, X28 and X29 respectively define: the PAD facility, the interface for a start stop mode asynchronous terminal accessing a PAD, and the procedures for the exchange of control information and user data between a PAD and a packet mode terminal or another PAD. Full implementation of Rec X3, X28 and X29 was not necessary. The TNA provides a fixed PAD profile with the exception of a single parameter thus avoiding the full complexity of Rec X28. The value of acting as a PAD is that it warns other DTEs of the type of service the TNA provides, the low data signalling rate, enables them to interrogate the PAD parameters, and make use of PAD command facilities. It also provides a fixed framework within which to handle the PSDN/PSTxN interface.

CALL SET UP PROCEDURES

The overall call set up procedures described in the following paragraphs are summarised for reference in Figure 2.

ACCESSING THE TNA

Telex to PSDN

The telex customer uses a two stage selection procedure. Access to the TNA is gained using the chargeable code 2008. Following this the first selection input to the TNA by the telex caller is a single dial digit which allows access to the PSDN. Following 2008 the use of a single dial digit other than the PSDN access code allows access to TNA special services.

Packet to Telex

Calls from terminals on PSDN or an overseas packet network to telex terminals in the UK are routed to the TNA by the use of the digit 8 defined in X121 for use with interworking with telex networks. The 8 becomes the first digit of the four digit field normally filled by a DNIC within the called DTE address field.

SELECTION NUMBERING SCHEMES

Telex to Packet

Following the TNA access procedure the remainder of the selection is the "keyboard" second stage selection delimited by an end of selection (EOS) character. The selection is in the form: "DNIC + Network Terminal Number". This mode of selection applies to all telex originated calls and thus even calls to a UK DTE use the full international address including the UK DNIC (2342) where 234 is the data country code and 2 is the digit allocated to the UK PSDN.

Several problems were identified for the overseas telex to UK PSS category of traffic. These were associated with inter-network accounting, transfer of telex answerbacks, and transit calls.

Initially it is not planned to offer access to the TNA to incoming international telex customers but this category of traffic may be introduced later when the above questions have been resolved.

Packet to Telex

For UK PSS originated calls in accordance with X121 the TNA access procedure is followed by the F69 code and the national telex number of the called terminal. Thus to call a UK telex terminal the selection would be 51< UK national telex number >.

Initially the use of the UK telex DNIC code 2348 followed by the telex number was proposed which is also in accordance with X121 but this was abandoned in favour of the F69 code. The reason for this approach was operational. The aim was to identify the called party using the normal international number used to identify that customer on the normal destination network. Most international numbers are found either from directories dedicated to a particular service or from letterheads. Thus it is unreasonable (and is in many cases complex) to expect a PSS customer calling a telex customer to carry out a manual translation and replace the destination F69 found from a directory or letterhead by a DNIC, particularly as the fourth digit of a DNIC is not internationally standardised with a single value set aside for Telex.

However for calls originated from terminals on an overseas packet network to telex terminals in the UK the selection does consist of the UK telex DNIC code followed by the UK national telex number of the called terminal.

CUSTOMER IDENTIFICATION

Customer identification is used during call establishment to inform the calling terminal of the identity of the called terminal and to identify the calling terminal for charging purposes.

Calling Customer Identification

In the telex to packet direction the telex callers identity is provided by the terminal's answerback captured during call establishment. The national identification code letters from the answerback are converted to the international telex country code (F69 code) appropriate to the calling telex terminal which may be 2 or 3 digits in length. For example the UK national telex identification code is a G and this is converted to the UK F69 code, ie 51. The complete Network User Address (NUA) consists of the prefix digit 8 in accordance with X121, followed by the F69 code, followed by the national telex number of the calling terminal, also obtained from the answerback. The format of the NUA is defined as commencing with a 4 digit Data Network Identification Code (DNIC), followed by the telex number unique to each user. To satisfy this requirement the DNIC is represented by the digits 8510 and this is followed by the national telex number which may be 5, 6 or 7 digits in length.

Consideration was given to the question of the use of a customer input Network User Identity (NUI) instead of using the telex answerback. This NUI would have been converted to a NUA from tables of valid NUIs by the TNA. Use of a NUI offers advantages from the point of view of being able to give telex customers security against fraudulent use, and makes charging an easier problem to overcome. It also makes it possible for the telex customer to make use of a number of telex terminals and be charged on a single NUI account. The use of NUIs ensures that only known users, issued with a NUI could use the facility and would allow the Packet Switched Service (PSS) billing system to directly issue billing advices based on the registered customer's name and address. The use of the NUI would also have the advantage of compatibility with current PSS practice for terminals accessing via the PSTN.

However the NUI concept was eventually abandoned as it had a significant impact on timescales due to the requirement for more complex protocols and the additional complexity due to the necessary tables and commands. Implementation of the NUI facility would have limited the TNA in capacity due to the need to search for the input NUI for validation and to obtain the NUA. A maximum of only 5,000 customers could have been accommodated. Use of the NUI facility also has the disadvantages of the overhead of maintaining the NUI list, and a longer call set up.

Use of the answerback involves validation of format and speed, and extraction of the numeric part for use as the calling address but far less processing is involved and no limit is put on the number of customers, but extention to certain overseas telex customers who do not have numeric answerbacks is difficult. The protocol is however telex-compatible.

In the packet to telex direction the identification of the calling DTE is given by the NUA provided in the calling DTE address field of the call request packet. It is stored for the duration of the call to generate a pseudo answerback if requested by the calling telex terminal.

Called Customer Identification

In the telex to packet direction when the "call connect" packet is received by the TNA, the called DTE address is used to form the called terminal's identity. This identity is returned to the calling telex terminal as a pseudo answerback. The format of this pseudo answerback is:

FS CR LF FS FS $\langle$ 14 character NUA $\rangle$ LS

Where FS = Figure Shift   LF = Line Feed

              CR = Carriage Return   LS = Letter Shift

where the NUA is extracted from the called DTE address field of the "call connect" packet. NUAs which are less than 14 characters in length are padded out using LS characters. The NUA is stored by the TNA for the duration of the call to allow the generation of the pseudo answerback during the data transfer phase of the call if requested by the calling telex terminal.

In the packet to telex direction the called terminal identity is not derived from the called terminal's answerback but instead from the called DTE address field of the Call Request packet. However a terminal on the PSDN can verify connection to the correct telex terminal customer by use of the "ENQ" character. This will be converted by the TNA to the ITA-2 character WRU which triggers the telex terminal's answerback which is then transmitted to the PSDN terminal in a separate data packet.

DATA TRANSFER PHASE

The data transfer stage is entered following the successful completion of the call set up procedures. During this phase the TNA performs packet assembly, disassembly and code conversion in accordance with X3, X28, X29 and X30.

Telex to Packet

Telex characters are converted from ITA-2 to IA5 with even parity and stored sequentially in data packets. ITA-2 shift characters are used to regulate the conversion. A fixed PAD profile is used by the TNA to describe telex terminals and only one PAD parameter, number 8, may be altered by remote PAD or Packet Mode terminals on the PSDN.

Packets are forwarded, subject to flow control, when they reach their permitted size (128 data characters) or on expiry of a delay (7.5 seconds) without receipt of a telex character. Packets are also forwarded following the receipt of reserved telex characters or special combinations of characters and on receipt of the 5 W's break sequence.

When flow control prevents the forwarding of further data packets the TNA stores up to a limited number of packets from the calling telex terminal. When this limit is exceeded the TNA transmits a sequence of P characters to the telex terminal until receipt of telex data ceases and then transmits the service message "MOM" to the telex terminal.

Packet to Telex

The contents of the user data field of data packets received by the TNA will be transmitted to the telex user. The characters are converted from IA5 to ITA-2 ignoring parity, according to CCITT Recommendation S18, and transmitted at 50 baud. The TNA inserts CR LF sequence when a sequence of 69 characters is received without a CR.

The TNA detects data packets with the Q bit set to 1, which are interpreted as PAD messages and acted upon by the TNA. Flow control is used to regulate the receipt of packets. The TNA acknowledges the receipt of each data packet with a 'Receive Ready' packet when all the contents of the data packet have been transmitted successfully to the called telex terminal.

RESET

When a 'Reset Request' packet is received from the packet terminal all current user data held in the TNA is discarded. The TNA transmits a reset service signal to the telex terminal and a 'Reset Confirmation' packet to the originator of the 'Reset Request' packet.

The TNA will transmit a 'Reset Request' packet itself when packet level protocol errors occur as required by CCITT Recommendation X75, and the reset service signal will be sent to the telex terminal. The TNA will also transmit a 'Reset Request' when the break sequence is received from the telex terminal. The TNA then awaits receipt of a 'Reset Confirmation' packet.

CLEAR DOWN PHASE

Clearing initiated by the packet terminal or network.

The TNA will clear the call on receipt of a 'Clear Request' packet, or an invitation to clear PAD message, or on receipt of an error PAD message. On receipt of a 'Clear Request' packet the TNA returns a 'Clear Confirmation' packet. On receipt of an invitation to clear PAD message the TNA continues transmission to the telex terminal until all packet data has been output before initiating clearing. On receipt of a PAD error message the TNA clears the call in both directions.

Clearing initiated by the telex terminal.

The TNA will clear the call, and transmit a 'Clear Request' packet with the clearing cause set to "DTE Clearing".

Clearing initiated by the TNA

The TNA will clear the call and generate a 'Clear Request' packet in a number of circumstances which include call set up failures, system failures due to internal congestion and restart. The TNA inserts a diagnostic code field relevant to the packet network in the 'Clear Request' packet which identifies the clearing cause. On receipt of a restart request the TNA returns confirmation and clears all calls. The TNA may decide to initiate a restart itself under some conditions of equipment failure.

CHARGING

No charging functions are performed by the TNA since this is handled by equipment in the telex and packet networks. Briefly the principles of charging are as follows.

For telex originated calls the customer is charged separately for the PSTxN, and PSTN portions of the call. For the telex portion of the call the customer is metered on a distance dependent basis from the time the TNA is accessed. This follows the same principle as applied to calls accessing the PSDN from the PSTN where a customer has his telephony call metered from the moment that access to a PAD is provided. For the PSDN portion of the call, the telex answerback is used to identify the calling telex terminal. This approach required the output of the PSS billing program to be processed manually by Telex Billing Centres so that the appropriate telex customer can be identified. The PSS billing program charges the telex customer a fixed PSDN access charge, and in addition he is charged for the data transmitted on the basis of both volume and duration in accordance with normal PSDN practice.

For PSDN originated calls the PSS customer pays normal PSDN volume and duration charges. In addition the PSDN customer has to pay for the telex element of the call on a distance dependent basis. Billing for the entire call is undertaken as part of the PSS billing program suite.

EQUIPMENT DESCRIPTION

The equipment is based on the Plessey Controls Ltd 4660/20 Telex Switch which had already been installed in the UK telex network as Inland Telex Line Concentrators. This is the smallest version of Plessey's 4660 systems; a larger version, the 4660/70 has been in operation for some years providing international gateway facilities. Minimal hardware development was required.

The basic 4660/20 system comprises a fully redundant, stored program control, non-blocking time division multiplexed switch. The equipment is controlled by a General Automation 16/240 microprocessor through which all signalling and data traffic passes. Dual redundancy extends down to the terminator module controllers. The module controllers are under the control of a duplicate pair of terminator cabinet controllers. The terminator module controllers themselves control four terminator group controllers (TGC). Each TGC serves 4 terminator cards, each of which comprises four trunk terminations. The TGC performs certain low level tasks associated with character transmission and signalling, thus relieving the load on the centre microprocessor. Typical of these tasks are the serial to parallel and parallel to serial conversion of characters, decoding of dial selection information, character distortion measurement, and detection of calling and clearing conditions.

The equipment was supplied with 128K words of Main (RAM) Memory. The system is backed up by 128K words of bubble memory for use in the event of a cold restart being required. There is no secondary storage eg magnetic drum or disc or disc and no magnetic tape storage units.

The TNA equipment is configured on the on-line/warm standby principle. Any item of equipment affecting more than 16 ports is duplicated. The HDLC (X75 link) ports are duplicated. The on-line system handles all functions of the TNA. Any on-line component failure likely to cause degradation or loss of service is detected by hardware or software and causes a switchover. The warm standby then takes over. All calls in progress are lost but the warm standby has a record of the calls which have been cleared and sends service signals to the customers affected.

A block diagram of the TNA configuration is shown in Figure 1.

TRAFFIC HANDLING

It has been assumed that during the data transfer phase that data will normally flow in one direction only since telex terminals are half-duplex. It has also been assumed that half the traffic will be in each direction. Call set up times are estimated to average 20 seconds and the data transfer phase estimated to average 60 seconds. The average busy hour telex trunk occupancy is 0.85 erlangs. Based on these assumptions the TNA is expected to handle 2 call attempts/second.

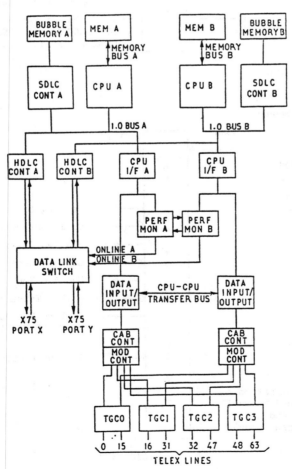

FIG.I. BLOCK DIAGRAM OF *TN*A CONFIGURATION

FIGURE 2 CALL SET UP PROCEDURES

Telex to Packet - Call Set Up Sequence

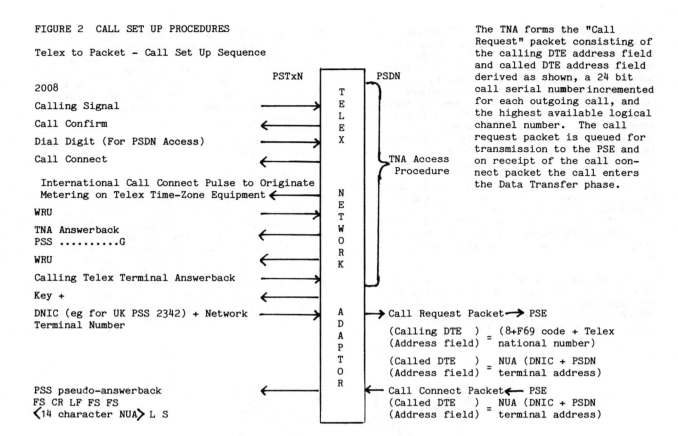

The TNA forms the "Call Request" packet consisting of the calling DTE address field and called DTE address field derived as shown, a 24 bit call serial number incremented for each outgoing call, and the highest available logical channel number. The call request packet is queued for transmission to the PSE and on receipt of the call connect packet the call enters the Data Transfer phase.

Packet to Telex - Call Set Up Sequence

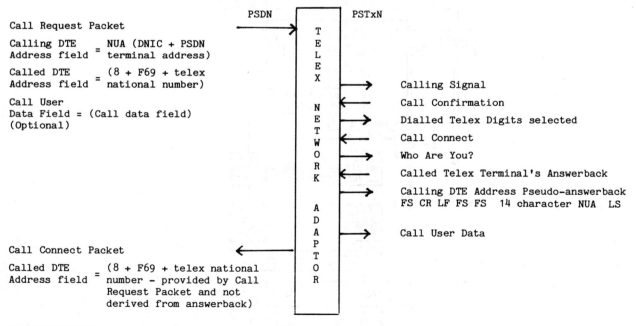

ACKNOWLEDGEMENT

The author wishes to acknowledge the contribution made by PCL of Poole, Dorset, to the production of this paper by the provision of technical information on the 4660 Modem 20.

BIOGRAPHY

Bob Brown obtained an Honours Degree in General Engineering at the University of Leicester, and a Masters Degree in Electronics at the University of Southamptom. He has worked in Computer Systems Engineering for BT since 1972.

A Leased Line Digital Data Network for the 80's

W H F Green
Marconi Communication Systems, UK

J F S Forster, L A Redburn
British Telecom, UK

This paper describes the plans of British Telecommunications (BT) for the introduction in early 1983 of a new dedicated all-digital synchronous network which will extend the advantages of digital transmission to customers, and bring improved leased-line facilities to all the country's main business areas. The network will support a range of new services. Foremost of these is the Kilostream service which will cater initially for customers requiring leased lines over a wide range of data signalling rates. The demand for such a service is discussed together with the availability of suitable transmission plant. The new items of equipment that have been developed for this network are described and the comprehensive alarm and supervisory arrangements explained. Finally, the scope for future enhancements and developments is explored.

1 INTRODUCTION

Data transmission is at a point of change. Since the early 1960's Datel services provided by means of modems attached to analogue telephony circuits have become an accepted and flexible method of providing customers data communications needs over the ubiquitous telephone network. During this period modem designs have evolved to become today's complex and sophisticated devices, providing up to 16 kbit/s transmission over analogue voiceband circuits and up to 168 kbit/s over groupband circuits. Such services however, provided on a network originally designed primarily for voice traffic, exhibit many well known technical and economic disadvantages. It would be overstating the case to suggest that this approach will change overnight, but there is a growing realisation that digital transmission capability can be made available down to the customer offering improved performance and much higher bit rate transmission at lower inherent cost.

2 PENETRATION OF DIGITAL TRANSMISSION SYSTEMS FOR TELEPHONY

The last 20 years has seen the steady penetration of digital telephony transmission systems into the junction and trunk telephone networks in the UK. Initially this was done to increase circuit capacity between telephone exchanges utilising existing cables and ducts, but more recently the trend towards digital working has occurred as a means of creating a more flexible and economical telephone network. Currently BT are installing in the telephone system over 1000 short-haul digital transmission systems each year using Pulse Code Modulation (PCM) techniques for encoding the analogue voice signals. The position in 1982 with some 11,000 systems now in service is shown in Figure 1. Additionally, by March 1983 digital trunk systems operating at 8 Mbit/s, 120 Mbit/s and 140 Mbit/s will have been provided in rapidly increasing numbers and will have linked together the main business centres of the UK by using pair or coaxial cables, fibre optic cables or microwave radio systems. It will then be possible to extend the benefits of full digital data transmission to important sections of the business community by installing suitable digital multiplexing equipment in local telephone exchanges and by providing an appropriate digital transmission system to the customers premises.

FIG 1. PCM SYSTEMS IN SERVICE 1982

The integration of digital transmission with time-division System X-type switching systems is already under way, and will lead to a reduction in overall costs and an improvement in operational flexibility and capability, and to the realisation of an Integrated Digital Network (IDN).

The evolution of this is to provide a single network to cover all likely future customer needs, whether voice, data or video, i.e. the concept of an Integrated Services Digital Network (ISDN) is the ultimate goal, but will take some years to establish and provide full geographical coverage.

Meanwhile, it is the intention of BT to exploit the availability of digital plant on routes provided for telephony to establish a dedicated digital data transmission network which will carry a range of new services. Foremost of these is the Kilostream service which will be introduced early in 1983.

3 KILOSTREAM SERVICE

This service will cater initially for customers requiring private circuits (leased lines) for synchronous duplex transmission at CCITT Rec X1 data signalling rates of 2400, 4800, 9600 and 48,000 bit/s. Presentation to the customer will be by the CCITT recommended digital interface X21. But in order to cater for existing Datel customers with V interface terminals, it is intended to offer an interworking X21 bis (V compatible) interface for a limited period. A number of enhanced services are under consideration for later introduction and are discussed elsewhere in the paper.

4 THE NETWORK

Long-distance transmission in the network will be provided by means of standard 2048 kbit/s digital paths derived from the national digital transmission network. Local telephone exchanges in areas of high data demand will be designated "Multiplexing Sites" where equipment will assemble 31 data tributaries into a 2048 kbit/s digital stream employing the standard frame format used in 30 channel PCM telephony. Users will be connected to the Multiplexing Site by means of a baseband digital local transmission system over 4-wire physical circuits for which existing pairs in the telephony local network will be employed.

The CCITT 6 + 2 envelope format is used and each user is allocated an exclusive 64 kbit/s time slot irrespective of his data rate. For every 6 bits of user data, 2 network bits - alignment (F) and status (S) are added by the terminating unit at the users premises to form the 6 + 2 envelopes. In consequence the line bit rate becomes higher than the user rate in the ratio 4:3.

The status bit will be controlled by the customer and will identify changes from data to signalling and the framing bit will identify the start of each 6 + 2 envelope. Strategically-placed Multiplexing Sites, called Cross Connect Sites (CCS), will be used as flexibil-ity points for the interconnexion of channel timeslots. The muldex equipments at these sites being connected to a Digital Distribution Frame (DDF). Separate "local access" equipment will be provided at each CCS to serve local users.

Historically, private circuits have always been provided individually on an ad hoc basis, utilising spare path capability derived from equipment in the telephone network. The approach being adopted for the provision of Kilostream private circuits is that a dedicated digital network incorporating advanced technology and sophisticated maintenance and management facilities will be provided in advance of demand to enable rapid provision of service to be given to customers.

The service is to open in early 1983 serving some 60 provincial exchanges and 40 London exchange areas in the first year, and rapidly expanding to cover some 100 provincial locations and a similar number of London exchanges by the end of 1985. In addition to meeting data users private circuit needs, the network may also be used beneficially to provide digital sections for other services eg Packet Switched, Prestel, Telex, out-of-area ISDN customers and terrestrial sections of satellite systems.

5 SYNCHRONISATION

The network will be synchronised using the master-slave principle. A central clock at each Cross Connect Site will be slaved to the national digital synchronisation hierarchy which is part of the System X switched network. A Multiplexing Site will derive timing via the 2 Mbit/s line from its serving Cross Connect Site.

6 BENEFITS

The new digital network will bring advantages and benefits to customers, the principle ones being:

- Reduced operating costs compared with equivalent-speed Datel services.

- Provision of service more quickly and at less cost than Datel.

- Significantly improved performance.

- Improved maintenance with quicker fault clearance.

There will be complementary advantages also to BT including:

- Easier and quicker circuit provision as the individual equalization of circuits is not required.

- Easier maintenance by reason of the built-in monitor and alarm facilities.

- Flexibility to enhance the system and provide new and improved digital services as customers needs arise and technology permits.

7 EQUIPMENT REALISATION

Reference to Figure 2 shows the functional
interconnection of the system and enables
three specific equipment areas to be
identified

7.1 Customer Located Equipment

At the customer's premises the Network Terminating Unit (NTU) provides the interface
between the Data Terminal Equipment (DTE) and
the line to the local telephone exchange, at
the rates described earlier. The CCITT
recommendations for these interfaces define
completely the multiwire interconnection
system between DTE and NTU, and the control
protocol used.

In addition to reiteration and enveloping the
NTU performs the circuit functions of data
scrambling, differential encoding and WAL2
modulation and their inverse, for transmission
to and reception from line. The use of
WAL2 modulation results in a line signal which
is simple to generate and is resistant to
interference. The signal has zero d.c.
content but contains excellent clock
information for all data patterns. The
circuit functions are implemented in the
form of two custom designed microcircuits,
giving the benefits of low power consumption
and increased reliability. Simple U-links
on the NTU enable the unit to be set up to
the appropriate user rate; no further
adjustments are necessary since within its
working range the transmission system is
independent of line length.

The standard physical realisation of any of
the three types of NTU is as a desk-top unit.
This consists of a moulded plastics case with
integral power circuit and a slide-in
Terminating Unit which performs all the NTU
functions described above. The unit is a.c.
mains powered and the mains lead and appropriate DTE connector are at the rear of the
unit. A front panel gives access to the
various controls and indicators which are
mounted on the Terminating Unit, together
with built-in test facilities.

The Terminating Unit may alternatively be
housed in a rack-mounted shelf in which up to
ten similar units may be fitted. These are
powered from a within-shelf power supply which
may be energised either from a.c. mains or
-50V d.c. A jack field on the shelf gives
test access to each bothway circuit.

7.2 Multiplexing Site

The next link in the network is the Multiplexing Site which is normally located at a
local exchange. The equipment which is
installed here and at the Cross Connect Site
to be discussed later, is housed in TEP 1E
equipment practice. It is not intended to
describe TEP 1E in this paper as this has
already been done elsewhere (Ref. 1).
Generally it has been found convenient to fit
the various equipment blocks into double
shelf units.

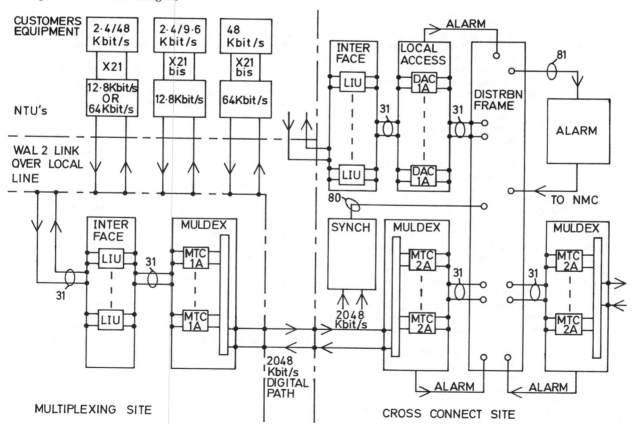

FIG. 2   TYPICAL SYSTEM REALISATION

The Digital Line Interface Equipment consists of up to thirty one identical Line Interface Units (LIU) together with a single Power Unit. The incoming WAL2 line signals are converted to binary and the signal is processed in a manner similar to that employed at the NTU. Absence of line signal is detected at the input to the unit and an alarm is raised. Wetting current for the local line pairs is injected and detected on this unit. This facility provides the means for detecting both a line fault and a power circuit failure at the NTU. Each LIU interfaces with a Muldex Tributary Card (MTC) and the equipment is arranged so that a Digital Line Interface Equipment is always adjacent to an Equipment Muldex on the same rack. This arrangement results in a simple interface between the two equipments.

The Equipment Muldex consists of a double shelf structure in which are accommodated up to thirty one MTCs, and a number of common equipment cards. These latter provide the necessary timing waveforms, multiplex/demultiplex functions and alarm processing facilities. They are implemented in the form of a Timing Card, Muldex Card and Alarm Card. A 64 kbit/s channel is assigned to each tributary and the multiplexed 2048 kbit/s signal produced is structured as CCITT recommendation G732 except that Timeslot 16 is used as a data channel. Timeslot 0 (TSO) is used for framing and the transmission of supervisory information in the normal way.

The MTC in this application provides the interface between the LIU signals at base rates and the Muldex aggregate signal at 2048 kbit/s. A single design of MTC is used with on-card linking to differentiate between structured and unstructured signals. Structured signals at base rate are reiterated to 64 kbit/s where appropriate. Envelope alignment is established with the Muldex timing and fault conditions in both directions of transmission are detected. These circuit functions are sufficiently complex to require the use of a third custom-designed device. Alarm signals from the associated LIU together with on-card detected alarms are buffered and fed onto an 8-bit alarm bus.

The bus is accessed by the Alarm Card where the alarm status of the various MTC/LIU pairs is scanned and the information, together with supervisory information in TSO is processed in a single-chip microcomputer. Fault status information is transmitted between Multiplex and Cross Connect Sites via TSO of the 2048 kbit/s signal. Local indications of fault status are provided by LED displays at the front of the Alarm Unit. In addition to the on-card displays, alarm indications appear at the end of shelf and rack top displays.

The individual tributary input and output signals are multiplexed and demultiplexed in the Muldex Card, together with TSO data. Alarms associated with the 2048 kbit/s transmission system are displayed on the front of the card. Timing waveforms for the Equipment Muldex are derived from the Timing Card whose basic clock is extracted from the incoming 2048 kbit/s signal.

The cards on the Equipment Muldex are powered from a DC/DC converter constructed as a single plug-in unit. A common design of converter has been adopted for the various equipment packages in the system. A comprehensive system of monitoring is employed which results in any potentially damaging fault condition causing the converter to shut down. Continual attempts to restart are made automatically, so that immediately the fault condition is removed, for example an external overload, the converter restores to normal operation.

7.3   Cross Connect Site

The third area to be considered is the Cross Connect Site (CCS). As has already been described, the purpose of this type of site is to provide a flexibility point for 64 kbit/s channels. The remote signal connections to this site are via standard 2048 kbit/s digital paths and the interface to these signals is the Equipment Muldex already described. However at the individual channel level of 64 kbit/s a simple interface is required which will tolerate cabling across a distribution frame, and the internationally recommended co-directional interface has been chosen for this purpose. This interface provides 64 kbit/s data, bit timing and octet timing on one pair of wires and is implemented by the MTC2A which also provides the standard alarm interfaces of the other MTCs.

Provision is made for local traffic generated at a CCS and the interface to line is made via the Digital Line Interface Equipment in the normal way. In order to interface the base rates obtained to the 64 kbit/s cross connection facility, an Equipment Local Access is employed. This consists of 2 shelves and is of similar layout to the Equipment Muldex, utilising identical common equipment cards. The difference lies in the provision of Digital Access Cards (DACs) rather than MTCs and the omission of the Muldex Card. The circuit functions of the DAC1A correspond exactly with those of the MTC1A except that co-directional interfaces are employed.

The Distribution Frame for the 64 kbit/s co-directional signals consists of a number of connection blocks mounted on a TEP 1E rack such that the terminations for up to 24 Muldex Equipments can be accommodated. Further racks may be added when it is required to expand the system. The connectors are of the insulation-displacement type and provide access points for test and maintenance purposes. The Frame is also used as a distribution point for synchronising signals and a collection point for alarm signals. These are cabled to the Equipment Synchronisation and the Equipment Alarm respectively.

The Equipment Synchronisation provides main and standby timing sources which are each synchronised to separate nominated incoming 2048 kbit/s paths. If a CCS is co-located with a System X exchange however, the main input is a feed from that source. It is essential that the equipment is secure and for this reason it is implemented as 2 identical shelves which function as main and standby in an operational equipment. Either shelf may be completely removed for maintenance purposes without affecting service. The status of the equipment in each shelf is monitored by an Alarm Unit which carries LED displays. This unit interfaces to the rack alarm system and to the Equipment Alarm via a 64 kbit/s co-directional channel.

In addition to this input the Equipment Alarm accepts up to 80 co-directional inputs from the Alarm Cards fitted in Muldex and Local Access Equipments. The information received via each interface is extracted and loaded onto a 14-bit alarm data bus, each input being scanned sequentially. A single-chip microcomputer is used to process the information received and control the front panel display. Under fault-free conditions the display is blank. On the occurrence of an alarm the identity of the faulty equipment and the nature of the fault is displayed and refreshed on each scan. If a second fault occurs a multiple fault indication is given either on an equipment or tributary basis. It is possible to step sequentially, using front panel controls, through each equipment identity and each faulty tributary within that equipment. In addition to the local display facility, all fault data is assembled into a form suitable for outputting via a 64 kbit/s co-directional interface. This is routed to the Distribution Frame where it may be linked via an appropriate Equipment Muldex to the Network Management Centre.

8   MAINTENANCE PHILOSOPHY

Considering the increased complexity and importance of customer located equipment a 'positive' maintenance policy has been adopted where all parts of the network, including customers lines, are permanently monitored so that most faults are brought to immediate notice - rather than a 'negative' policy of generally waiting until a fault is reported.

In keeping with the foregoing a 3-point philosophy has been adopted:

- Rapid indication of major equipment faults and of complete failure of individual users circuits.

- Rapid restoration of service following the occurrence of a fault.

- Rapid attention to users reports of difficulty.

It will be seen from **section 7 that a move** towards the 'positive' maintenance policy will be achieved by in-built monitors which provide local and centralized displays of a multiplicity of fault conditions. The speed at which faults will be located and service restored will be further enhanced by the following maintenance aids which are already available or in course of provision:

- In-built monitors on digital line sections to give early indication of major and/or incipient faults.

- Manual or automatic changeover to standby line plant in the event of failure.

- A comprehensive range of spare units to effect rapid replacements of faulty items which will subsequently be repaired at a central depot.

- Portable test equipment to monitor performance at 2 Mbit/s, 64 kbit/s and X21 interfaces. These testers can be operated in an in-service mode and are invaluable in locating intermittent faults eg those resulting in error bursts. A typical application would be to measure and record the errors in the frame-alignment signal at each distribution frame traversed by the circuit. It should be noted that the utility of these portable tests is dependent upon the use of structured signals that comply with current CCITT recommendations for the 6 + 2 format at 64 kbit/s and the 2 Mbit/s framing structure in G732 et seq. Customers who may wish to use other formats will be denied the rapid fault diagnostic facilities provided and could suffer delay in the restoration of service. Moreover, circuits may have to be taken out of service in order to connect equipment that generates recognisable test patterns, and this additional effort required to locate faults may present a significant penalty.

9   FUTURE ENHANCEMENTS

9.1   Services

It is envisaged that a wide range of additional services will be conveyed over the network eg.

- Submultiplexing. 64 kbit/s bearers will be submultiplexed into lower-rate data channels and/or encoded speech channels.

- NX64 kbit/s. This service will provide a high bit rate at NX64 kbit/s, the maximum value of N being 31. Regardless of the value of N it is proposed that an additional 64 kbit/s be added for in-service monitoring and end to end signalling.

- Multipoint services at various customer rates.

9.2   Maintenance

- The ability to access 64 kbit/s circuits from a remote test centre is under consideration; this will reduce the number of occasions where maintenance engineers are called upon to connect portable test equipment.

- Fault information displayed at each cross-
connect site will be conveyed to a National
centre together with data on the status of
the long-haul high capacity digital network.

9.3 Circuit provision

It is intended that the speed at which
circuits are provided and/or re-routed will be
increased by utilizing remotely controlled
through-connection equipment at Cross-Connect
Sites. Such equipment will, in effect, be a
digital switch having semi-permanent connections under BT control rather than under
customer control as in the case of a public
switched network. This switch would also
provide remote test access facilities and a
temporary reconfiguration of circuit routings
under fault conditions.

10   SUMMARY

The leased line network described will provide
a multiplicity of services more rapidly than
at present and will incorporate high speed
fault diagnostics. Further enhancements in
these areas are planned for the future. The
network will comprise building blocks that
can be readily adapted, by the use of interchangeable plug-in units, to provide new
services as and when demand arises. The
operational area of the network will cover
the major catchment areas in the UK by 1985
and the network will subsequently be
extended to the more remote centres.

Ref 1   A New Equipment Practice for Trans-
mission and Other Applications;
TEPIE.POEEJ Vol 72 page 160 Oct 1979
N G Crump.

Acknowledgements are made to the Deputy
Director for Non-Voice Services of British
Telecommunications and Technical Director
of Marconi Communications Systems Ltd for
permission to publish this paper.

Biographies

W H F Green B.Sc C.Eng
MIEE

Mr Green joined the
Baddow Research
Laboratories of the
Marconi Company in 1958
and worked on a wide
variety of communica-
tions projects. In
1967 he joined the
development team working
on 24 Channel PCM and
subsequently was engaged as a Section Leader
on a digital switching project. He was
responsible for the development of a number of
digital transmission systems including 30
Channel PCM and the Supergroup Codec equipment.
In his present position of Group Leader he has
a wider responsibility, in particular, the
Kilostream project and its future expansion.

Mr J F S Forster
C. Eng MIERE

Mr Forster joined BT in
1940 working on Telephone
exchange maintenance. In
1954 he joined a develop-
ment team on FDM terminal
equipments and entered
the TDM transmission field
in 1968. He is currently
managing several projects
covering PCM and digital
multiplexers, high speed digital line systems
and service protection switching equipment.

Mr L A Redburn

Mr Redburn has been with
BT since 1939. His whole
career spent in Telecomms
in the transmission field
covering such diverse
activities as development
of audio and FDM equipment
to planning and laying
deep water submarine
systems world wide. Since
early 1970's he has been
associated with the
engineering problems of data services over
analogue circuits and more recently with the
concept and introduction of dedicated digital
networks for specialised services. Project
Manager (Operations) for Kilostream Data
Services.

Report on ECMA LAN Standardisation

J B Brenner
ICL, UK

The paper reports the progress of Local Area Network standardization in ECMA, and gives a brief overview of the set of LAN standards ratified by ECMA in June 1982, with comment on their significance as a step towards Open System Interconnection.

1 INTRODUCTION

This paper is a personal report by the author, and presents a view of the rapidly evolving situation in mid June 1982.

ECMA, the European Computer Manufacturers' Association, has taken a leading role in the acceleration of world-wide agreement of LAN standards.

The ECMA Member Companies are: AEG-Telefunken, Burroughs, Cii Honeywell Bull, Digital Equipment Corporation, Ericsson Information Systems, Ferranti Computer Systems, IBM, ICL, Olivetti, NCR, Nixdorf, Philips, SEMS, Siemens, Sperry Univac and Xerox. They have world-wide interests, and participate actively in the work of standards bodies in Europe and the USA, and in ISO and the CCITT.

In June 1982, ECMA ratified a complete initial set of LAN standards, mainly as a result of intensive liaison with IEEE Project 802. Ratification of ECMA standards does not oblige anyone to implement them. However, the early availability of products from multiple suppliers, using these standards for interworking, can be predicted with some confidence.

Further ECMA standards are being developed for different types of LAN (again mostly through intensive liaison with IEEE Project 802), and for the interconnection of multiple wide area and local area networks in series (principally through a very productive liaison with the US National Bureau of Standards).

2 THE STANDARDS

The ECMA LAN standardization is within the framework of the ISO Reference Model for Open System Interconnection (1). It is concerned with the layers below the transport service. Higher layer interworking standards are generally considered to be independent of network characteristics, and therefore common to local and wide area networks.

The following set of inter-related specifications has been ratified:

- Standard ECMA 72 revised:

  Transport Protocol (2).

- Standard ECMA 80:

  Local Area Networks, Coaxial Cable System (CSMA/CD Baseband) (3).

- Standard ECMA 81:

  Local Area Networks, Physical Layer (CSMA/CD Baseband) (4).

- Standard ECMA 82:

  Local Area Networks, Link Layer (CSMA/CD Baseband) (5).

- Technical Report ECMA TR13:

  Network Layer Principles (6).

- Technical Report ECMA TR14:

  Local Area Networks, Layer 1-4 Architecture and Protocols (7).

The decision to make CSMA/CD standards first (Carrier Sense Multiple Access with Collision Detection) is because mature and well agreed specifications are available now. Standards for token access techniques will follow when proposals are sufficiently mature; likewise for broadband signalling techniques. A variety of such techniques is necessary to cover the full spectrum of LAN performance and cost requirements, and the technology is continually being enriched.

3 THE ARCHITECTURE

The distinctive features of the architecture defined in ECMA TR14 (with supporting information in ECMA TR13) are:

- Simple connectionless-data-transfer mode of LAN operation (layers 1 and 2);

- Simple inter-network datagram (ie connectionless) communication across multiple concatenated networks (layer 3c);

- Robust transport service provided by a network independent transport protocol (layer 4), with comprehensive self-contained error-detection and recovery. This is the class 4 protocol of ECMA 72 (which is identical to that in the ISO Draft Proposal).

The choice of connectionless lower layer operation and transport class 4 may be unexpected: current ISO and CCITT work generally assumes connection-like operation of the lower layers, and a less robust class of transport protocol. The main reasons for the choices in ECMA TR14 are:

- Class 4 transport protocol is particularly well suited for operation across multiple concatenated subnetworks, when it is impracticable generally to depend on error-free behaviour of multiple inter-network gateways.

- The combination of datagram and class 4 transport allow satisfactory avoidance of hazardous and complex problems of network deadlocks, network reconfiguration procedures and network error-indication reliability.

- The absence of layer 1 and 2 flow control is tolerable in a wide range of cases where there is adequate transport layer flow control. The absence of link layer delivery confirmation and recovery is likewise tolerable, particularly with low error-rate LANs.

The additional complexity of using the more sophisticated transport protocol is more than compensated by the corresponding lower layer and system simplifications, as is borne out by extensive implementation experience.

This is only one of the possible ways of layer 1-4 operation. Other different needs must also be recognised. Extension to include the alternatives of connection like working in the link and network layers is intended. Also, there is an initial restriction that operation is only across a single LAN, pending development of the inter-net protocol.

4 CSMA/CD

The ECMA CSMA/CD standards are based on the well known Xerox ethernet design, and its progression by IEEE Project 802. The logical, electrical and physical design has been thoroughly tested in the field. The specification is comprehensive and precise.

The differences from ethernet are minor. The only remaining significant difference between the ECMA specification and that of IEEE Project 802 concerns the "start of frame delimiter". Close liaison between ECMA and IEEE has ensured convergence on all other technical issues during the development of the standards.

Agreement on this last issue is also to be hoped for.

The role of ECMA has been to provide special expertise and to help form a broadly based consensus on which IEEE Project 802 could agree. ECMA has also been highly effective in rapid development and evaluation of the drafts. Equivalent IEEE CSMA/CD standards are expected later this year, and it is hoped that this will also be the basis for ISO standards.

REFERENCES

1) Draft International Standard, ISO/DIS 7498.

   Data Processing – Open Systems Interconnection-Basic Reference Model.

2) Standard ECMA 72: Transport Protocol (revised June 1972).

3) Standard ECMA 80: Local Area Networks, Coaxial Cable System (CSMA/CD Baseband).

4) Standard ECMA 81: Local Area Networks, Physical Layer (CSMA/CD Baseband).

5) Standard ECMA 82: Local Area Networks, Link Layer (CSMA/CD Baseband).

6) Technical Report ECMA TR13: Network Layer Principles.

7) Technical Report ECMA TR14: Local Area Networks, Layer 1-4 Architecture and Protocols.

Copies of ECMA documents may be obtained free from ECMA, 114 Rue du Rhone, CH 1204 Geneva, Switzerland.

J B Brenner graduated from Cambridge University 1961, MA, and joined his present Company, now International Computers Ltd (ICL) in a series of roles in sales technical support, project management, consultancy, special assignments, development and research. He has been an active contributor to Open System Interconnection standardization in BSI, ISO and ECMA. He is currently manager responsible for ICL network architecture and OSI standardization.

Standardisation Issues and Protocol Architecture for LANs in view of OSI Reference Model

T Kalin, G Le Moli
COST 11 bis, JRC, Ispra and
CREI-Politecnico, Italy

The paper first deals with the standardisation issue in the Local Area Network, where the present work may not lead to a solution which is favourable to the user. A shift of the emphasis to the definition of the services provided by the Communication Sub-System and standardisation of the service primitives is proposed. In the second part, a discussion of the protocol architecture of Local Area Networks leads to the conclusion that the Open System Interconnection Reference Model seems to be a sensible approach.

I. INTRODUCTION

The Local Area Network (LAN) can be defined as a digital communication facility carrying data at high speed among a potentially large number of host computers located in a single building or adjacent buildings. One is speaking of distances of the order of a few kilometers, speeds of 1 to 100 Mbits/s and the number of computers attached to a LAN could easily reach 1000. Terminals can only be connected via a host computer and they can only be attached directly if they are intelligent enough to qualify as "computers". At the present time, most of the traffic on the existing LANs consists of computer originated digital data. But for future use one can predict more diverse use of the LAN local area networks: we will digitise the voice, transmit it, compress it, store and forward it as messages, etc. The same will be true for high speed digital facsimiles and up to a point for video, even if today an immediate packet video application is not envisaged.

II. CONNECTION OF THE HOST

In the long haul networks, the connection of the hosts to the Communication Sub-System can be represented by the well known picture (1):

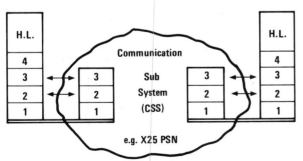

Fig.1.Protocol Architecture for Interconnection via Packet Switching Network.

*on leave from "J.Stefan"Institute,Ljubljana, Jugoslavia.

In the case of the LAN, the communication of the hosts connected to the same LAN is direct, as a consequence of the inherent full connectivity of the majority of present LANs. The equivalent becomes:

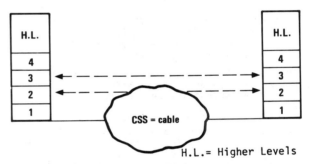

H.L.= Higher Levels

Fig.2. Protocol Architecture in a LAN.

Where CSS is reduced to a coaxial cable or twisted pair of wires. Peer-to-Peer communication in this case is end-to-end on the second level also or at least on the upper part of it. This is why many LAN designers assume that the end-to-end responsability at the higher levels is not required and that it is sufficient to rely on the end-to-end support from level two.

The main issues seem to be the methods and standardised approaches of the connection of hosts to LAN. The loose definition of the problem is the consequence of uncertainty about the point where the border between the CSS and the outside world should be drawn. This decision has big repercussions on the architecture of the LAN, on the compatibility of hosts made by different manufacturers and on the dependence of the user to one supplier. More precisely, while the OSI architecture is clearly defined, it is not yet clear how this architecture will be reflected on real devices which will be available on the market.

Two possibilities exist: either hosts contain all that is required for their direct connection to the CSS (e.g.the Cable), or some Network Access Unit (NAU) is required.

For this second case the following two problems will be considered here:

i) how to distribute layers between the host and the NAU and how to interconnect them;

ii) wether NAUs should be standardised or not.

Let us examine three possible approaches (1,2a and 2b):

1. Without NAUs (Fig.3)

To have different hosts talking to each other, one must standardise the signalisation on the media, protocols between peer entities on level 1 and level 2, or on sublayers which take the place of layer 2 in some recent (2) standardisation efforts of the communicating hosts.

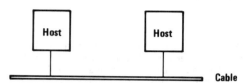

Fig.3. Direct Attachment of Hosts.

In practical terms, it means that the manufacturer of the hosts or workstations will have the appropriate hardware and software integrated in his equipment,which should

enable it to be attached to the cable, optical fibre, twisted pair or infrared transciever, which-ever method is used in the particular network.
But the above list, combined with the proposed access methods (CSMA/CD, token paasing etc. and some proprietary versions) makes for a very large number of combinations which would all be in accordance with the standard or de-facto standard, but incompatible.
There is one big advantage in this approach, that is, one can purchase the whole LAN, that is CSS + hosts, from the same manufacturer and have the highest assurance of compatibility. On the other hand, this approach leads to very strong dependence and it is mostly to the advantage of a large vendor of the whole line of automated office equipment, which will constitute the majority of the LANs of the near future.

2.With the Use of Network Adapter Units(Fig.4)

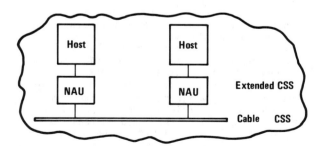

Fig.4. Use of Network Access Units.

Since CSS and NAUs constitute a sort of extended CSS (ECSS), this approach in its turn splits into two: 2a) ECSS is provided as a whole by a single manufacturer; 2b) CSS and NAUs may be provided separately by different manufacturers.

Before discussing separately points 2a) and 2b) let us state some more general considerations. NAU contains some of the levels, typically levels 1,2 and 3. According to the discussion in Paragraph III only the first three layers should be in a NAU. So, this second approach became as in Fig.5.

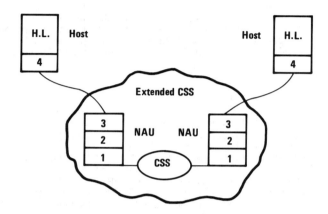

Fig.5.Simplified View of the Second Approach.

In the real implementation one cannot just simply connect two layers, as shown on Fig.5, but one has to introduce some simple discernable tiers of logic between the two otherwise adjacent protocol layers, as a consequence of the physical division of those, with one running in the NAU and another in the host. A practical arrangement is shown in Fig.6, where three tiers have been indicated.

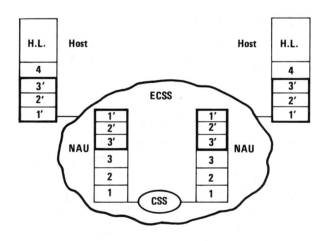

Fig.6.Shows the Auxiliary Layers between Layers 3 and 4.

Now let us examine the two following approaches:

2a) where the ECSS is provided as a whole by one manufacturer.

There are a number of consequences:
- one can connect the same host to any Extended Communication Sub System, regardless of the physical media and the techniques used for physical data transmission, of the CSS access method, etc.
- the cost of the NAUs will become comparable with the cost of laying the cabling for the LAN in the building. The choice of the vendor of the ECSS will be irrelevant as will be the consequences of a dependence on one particular manufacturer of NAUs;
- the third is a result of the first two; one could obtain hosts and ECSS from different sources, which is certainly not to the advantage of the large manufacturer.

To make this approach practical, the services offered by level 3,(running in the NAU) to level 4 running in the host must be defined and service primitives standardised.
Because hosts and NAU are usually very near, the connection between them is usually very short and highly reliable; therefore the levels 1', 2' and 3' are usually very simple and their task is simply to carry service primitives from level 4 in the host to level 3 in the NAU and viceversa. Furthermore level 3' may even be empty. Unfortunately, with some exceptions (3,4,5) little has been done in this respect up to now. One author (6) proposes the attachment of existing mainframes to LAN by a X25 (L3,L2,X21 bis) interface. Such solution is, for price reasons,at present less attractive for the connection of low priced microcomputer hosts, but it could become practical with the next generation of X25 chips.

In this approach there is no need to standardise the internal protocols of CSS analogously to the PSN s where several different internal protocols exist, which are of no concern to the user.

2b) CSS and NAU are provided separately by different manufacturers.
This approach is in fact a combination of the approaches 1 and 2a).
One should be able to connect NAUs of different origins into a common ECSS. On the other hand, any host complying with the rules could connect to the ECSS and use its services. The requirement for this is the existance of standards of the internal protocols in the ECSS (as in approach 1) and service primitives and 3'2'1' protocols (as in approach 2a).
We do not want to be particularly biased toward any of the three possibilities, but it is obvious that in order to remain flexible and to benefit the user, one should accept approaches 2a) or 2b).
At present much effort is being invested in the standardisation proposals for the first approach 2 , but unfortunately much less is being invested in the definition and standardisation of the services expected from the Extended Communication Sub System. One would hope that there is still a real possibility to take another road in the LAN standardisation field.

III.LAN AND THE OSI REFERENCE MODEL

In the previous paragraph nothing has been said about the higher level protocol architecture of the LAN. Implicitly it has been assumed that layering corresponds to OSI RM, but we would now like to discuss the question of compliance to OSI RM in some detail.

The designer of a LAN has to make a decision whether:
1. the LAN is a collection of open systems
2. the LAN as a whole acts as an open system relying on the functionality of the gateway.

The criteria to assess these two possibilities could be listed as:

- those internal to the LAN:
  a. cost of the software in the hosts connected to the LAN ;
  b. openness of LAN to connectability of heterogenous hosts;
- those relevant to the interconnection of LAN with other networks:
  c. complexity of the gateway design;
  d. addressing problems;
  e. end-to-end responsibility.

A further discussion of these criteria may clarify the picture:
As far as criterion a. is concerned it is a consensus that nearly all functions present in the OSI RM are needed to perform the communication. The main difference is whether these functions are grouped together in an orderly way, as in OSI RM, or spread in a random fashion through various software modules in the adhoc implementations.
Up to now there seems to be no proof that the second way leads to a cheaper software implementation or higher performance in terms of throughput and delays.
If we consider criterion b. as well, then it should become clear that there is no reason from the LAN internal point of view to reject the OSI architecture for protocols in a Local Area Network (7): in fact, one should be able to use the same higher level protocols and also the same implementations regardless of wether the host is connected to a long haul or local network.

The criteria regarding interconnection of LANs point in the same direction. It is obvious, concerning criterion c., that a gateway which must convert from some exotic internal protocols will be much more complex and expensive to design and implement, and sometimes possibly even unworkable.
The last two points (d. and e.) are connected since when the LAN as a whole is an Open System, ,the addresses inside the LAN are invisible to the outside world.One can only address the services on the transport level or above, which is not undesirable, but which involves a disadvantage: the transport (end-to-end) connection ends at the gateway and not at the transport entity in the host connected to the LAN. That fact alone is an argument strong enough to disqualify this approach, because the gateway has to accept the whole responsability to deliver data and to act on behalf of the end user. This is the reason for selecting only the first three layers for NAU as in Fig.5.

From this discussion one can conclude that
there are good reasons for the LAN design to
keep internal protocols in compliance with
the ISO OSI RM. There can be no doubt that
some enhancements to the RM are needed in
order to make it more suitable for use in LAN.
The most likely candidates would be connection.
less services, broadcasting and multicasting,
but the appropriate actions are already
underway.

IV. CONCLUSIONS

Without looking very far one can find a good
analogy in the satellite data transmission
field. There is a number of different fre-
quences, TDMA schemes, and codings in different private satellite transmission services
or experiments. It should not be long before
the PTTs in Europe or specialised carriers
elsewhere provide a uniform standardised
interface on the networks level to the user.
From this point, he would no longer be concerned with the peculiarities of satellite
transmission, with the exception of long
delays. Regardless of the quality of the
protocols imposed this will be a step forward.
We have no such authority in the LAN field,
but the keen commercial interest of many
companies.
What can be done?
We can do our best, so that at least the
scientific community understands the real
issues.

LITERATURE

1) Data Processing - Open System Interconnection - Basic Reference Model, ISO/TC97/SC16.
2) IEEE 802 Local Network Standard, DRAFT B,
   October 1981.
3) Local Area Network Architecture - Functional
   Layering, AFNOR, ISO/TC97/SC16-N 728.
4) C.A.Vissers, Service Types for Connectionless services, EWICS, SIG. S51/81.
5) E.Chen: Classes of Applications on the IEEE
   Standard Local Area Network. (Position
   Paper for IEEE 802 LAN Committee).
6) T.Stack: LAN Protocol Residency Alternatives
   for IBM Mainframe Open System Interconnection, Proc. On-line Conf. Local Networks
   & Distributed Office Systems, London 1981.
7) S.Schindler: Open Systems, Today and Tomorrow, Computer Networks 5 (1981)
   167-176.

Tomaz Kalin is a member of
of the research staff at
the "J.Stefan" Institute,
Ljubljana, Jugoslavia.
He has received Engineers
Degree as well as MSc.
and Doctors Degree from the
Physics Department of the
University of Ljubljana.

During his work in computational physics he
became involved in the computer science field.
His interest include computer performance
evaluation and modelling and computer networks. In the years 1977/78 he worked for the
Executive Body of the European Informatics
Network Project, Teddington, UK.

For the period 1981/83 he has been appointed
Project Leader of the COST 11 bis, European
Action in Teleinformatics. T.Kalin is
teaching a graduate course on Computer Networks at the University of Ljubljana.

Gesualdo Le Moli was born
in November 1940. He took
his degree in electronic
engineering in July 1963,
at the Politecnico di
Milano, where he entered
in the same year as assistant professor. In 1976 he
became full professor at
the University of Catania
where he was director of
the Istituto Elettrot-
ecnico up to November
1978, when he reentered in Politecnico di
Milano, where he presently is. Since 1974, he
is also director of the Centro Rete Europea di
Informatica (CREI) which has been responsible
for the whole Italian part of the EIN network.
Now CREI is involved in several national and
international research projects.

A Proposal for Broadcast Architecture Network (BANET)

H Yamazaki, I Yoshida, K Hasegawa
OKI Electric Industry Company, Japan

We propose Broadcast Architecture Network (BANET) which is suitable for the distributed office system. A major design goal for BANET is to realize the broadcast which can be thought as a generalization of the communication among multiple endpoints just like the conversation through a round table. For this purpose, BANET provides the commands to form and dissolve a group called "Communication Group". One remarkable feature of BANET is that the commitment control scheme is provided within a network layered structure.

1. INTRODUCTION

In recent years, people have shown great interest in the office automation systems. Particularly the number of installed office computers, workstations and associated devices has grown dramatically in these years.

Since the number of individual devices is growing, the communication technology which integrates these terminals and host computers into total system is going to be more and more important. Thus the way to apply computer network technology (especially the local network) to the office system becomes an important technical consideration now.

So far, various network architectures such as ISO reference model, etc. have been proposed [1] [2]. However, these architectures are not always suitable for varying applications in the office system.

It has been pointed out by the researchers in the distributed database and some of computer network architects [3] [7] that the broadcasting-within-a-group function is required as a communication facility (rather than application) when the distributed data is handled. However few existing computer network architectures include this function within their internal layered structures. The most of architectures include the mechanisms called a "session" or a "connection" to ensure the end to end data transmission. These mechanisms could be thought as a generalization of the communication between two endpoints via single physical link. On the other hand, the broadcasting-within-a-group function could be a generalization of the communication among multiple endpoints just like the conversation through a round table. This function is particularly important for the systems which handle distributed files or databases [3] [4] [5].

Based on this broadcasting-within-a-group function, we are going to implement the pilot local network system called BANET (Broadcast Architecture Network) which is suitable for distributed office system.

In this paper, the outline of BANET's architecture is described. It should be noted that some architecture such as the Ethernet [6] includes broadcasting-within-a-group function (multicast function) in a data link level. On the other hand, the most outstanding feature of BANET's architecture is that this function is further included in higher level structure in order to create or dissolve this group more dynamically.

2. OFFICE SYSTEM AND BROADCAST FUNCTION

The distributed office systems are expected to include the broad range of services; for example, distributed database, tele-conference, electric mail, document retrieval/maintenance etc. In such services, the broadcasting-within-a-group function is essential. The following examples describe the necessity of this function. Suppose a transaction which updates data A, B and C is received at the station S1 in the distributed database system. Then the update request must be transmitted to stations S2, S3 and S4 where data A, B and C reside respectively. In the conventional virtual circuit type network, S1 must have three connections to S2, S3, S4, and the update request is transmitted through these individual connections. Besides it should be ensured that the data are updated consistently, that is, the system must guarantee that the transaction will either reach everyone of S2, S3, S4 or none of them. The mechanism to insure this is easily and efficiently implemented in the network which provides both the group formation and the broadcasting-within-a-group functions.

Another example is the tele-conference system. Suppose the conference by four men at stations S1, S2, S3, S4, connections are required for every pair of stations, that is totally six connections in the conventional network. Messages (or speech data) are must be transmitted quickly and should be received simultaneously. However, to realize this service is fairly difficult as long as the conventional network is used, since the same messages (or speech data) must be separately transmitted through the individual connections. Obviously, the broadcasting-within-a-group function can be a solution for this difficulty and can reduce the volume of transmissions.

Since the most of the services in the office system must treat the distributed data in such a way, the group formation and the broadcasting-within-a-group functions are expected to be the key to construct an effective office system. Some proposed local network architectures include the higher level protocols as well as the data link level. They provide the conventional virtual circuit in the session level. However the virtual circuit is not compatible with broadcast but a generalization of the physical link between two ends. Some architectures provide virtual circuit function in higher level even though their data link level is implemented as the Ethernet-type broadcast architecture. This is our motivation to implement BANET.

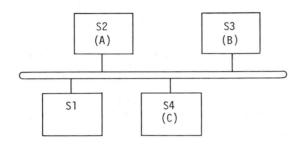

Fig. 1 A Sample Network

3. BROADCAST ARCHITECTURE NETWORK (BANET)

3.1 Overview

This section outlines the basic structure and functions of BANET.

3.1.1 Physical Structure

The physical structure of BANET is shown in Fig. 2. The coaxial cable and transceivers are compatible with the Ethernet [6]. The Network Interface Adaptor (NIA) can be connected to more than one host or terminal. The standard physical interfaces (e.g. RS232C) are adopted between a NIA and a host or terminal, so that various types of devices could be connected to BANET.

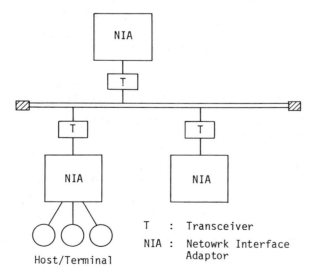

T   : Transceiver

NIA : Netowrk Interface Adaptor

Fig. 2 Physical Structure of BANET

3.1.2 Layered Structure

BANET consists of three levels-physical level, data link level and broadcast level (hereinafter we denote simply as BL) as shown in Fig. 3. BL provides functions to form and dissolve a group and to broadcast data in the group.

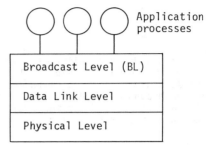

Fig. 3 Layered Structure of BANET

In our project, not the global network but the local network system is considered as the pilot system because of the feasibility and system cost. For the physical level of BANET's local network, we selected the bus type architecture with CSMA/CD. The reasons are as follows;

(1) Broadcasting-within-a-group function can be easily implemented in higher level, since the physical (and the data link) level basically provides the broadcast facility.
(2) In this type of network, the broadcast of data does not require any extra communication cost.
(3) The transmission delays within a network are uniform, so the atomicness of read/write operation of data is guaranteed. Therefore the implementation of the commitment control mechanism can be simplified.

3.1.3 Addressing Scheme

The following types of addresses are employed in BANET.

(1) Station address: a unique address in BANET which is given to NIA. Data link level treats only this address.
(2) Terminal address: an address given to each host or terminal connected to NIA. It is unique within a given NIA.
(3) Function address: an address given to each program or function (e.g. RJE, DB, E-mail etc.) in BANET.
(4) Process address: an identifier given to a process generated to perform a function in a specified host.

Thus, an address of a certain process within a certain host is specified by a quarter (S T f p) with station address S, terminal address T, function address f and process address p.

3.1.4 Commitment Control

For the system which the distributed data are shared by multiple users (e.g. database, file), the preservation of data consistency is a serious technical consideration. So far, many control mechanisms in distributed databases have been proposed in order to solve this problem [3] [4] [5].

However it should be noted that in these control mechanisms, two types of control each of which goal is essentially different are mixed within a single control algorithm. First type of control is called commitment control, and is required to complete a single job which might be decomposed and distributed over the network. For example, this type of control is required for the seat reservation in a travel schedule system, or updating the redundant copies of data in a distributed database system. On the other hand, the second control is called concurrency control, and is required for the system where the multiple processes share common resources, since this control determines which process should be executed first and which should be waited or aborted when the conflict occurs. These two types of control scheme should be implemented separatelly, since the commitment control is necessary even for the system with a single user, but concurrency control is required only for the system where the multiple processes could be executed simultaneously.

Since the commitment control ensures a reliable broadcasting, this control mechanism is implemented within a BANET's network layered structure. On the other hand, the concurrency control is excluded from BANET's layered structure, since this mechanism mostly depends on the applications and their priority handlings.

3.1.5 Three Types of Communication

Most network architectures support three types of virtual circuits, that is, simplex, half duplex and full duplex circuit. And the selection of the type is executed through command parameters in the connection initiation phase. Similarly, BANET supports three types of broadcast communication within a group; First type is called "fixed source" where only a fixed member process can be a source of broadcasting. Whereas the second is called "variable source" where any one of the members can be a broadcasting source. The third is called "multiple source" where multiple members can be sources simultaneously. Obviously there are the generalized concepts of simplex, half duplex and full duplex circuits. The selection of the type is done through command parameter in connection initiation phase analogous to the type selection of virtual circuit in the conventional network architecture.

3.1.6 Packet Format

The packet format of BANET is shown in Fig. 4. Data link level treats the DLH (Data Link Header) and frame check sequence field. DLH contains the DSA (Destination Station Address) and SSA (Source Station Address). The format of DLH is compatible with the Ethernet specification. BLH (Broadcast Level Header) contains command type, function, STA (Source Terminal Address), SPA (Source Process Address), CGID, DAL (Destination Address List) etc. DAL is the list of destination terminal and process addresses.

In the group formation phase, the request is broadcasted with DAL. Once the group is formed, CGID is used to broadcast packets in the group instead of DAL.

DLH (Data Link Header)   •DSA (Destination Station Address)   •SSA (Source Station Address)
BLH (Broadcast Level Header)   •Command Type   •Function   •STA (Source Terminal Address)   •SPA (Source Process Address)   •CGID(Communication Group Identifier)   •DAL (Destination Address List)
Data
Frame Check Sequence

Fig. 4 Packet Format of BANET

3.2 BL Operation and Functions

Hereinafter an initiating process which has station address I, terminal address Ti, function address f, process address p_1 is called an initiator and denoted by AP (I Ti f p_1). On the other hand, responding process is called a responder and assumed to have a station address R, terminal address Tr. Further, a BL and a data link level in a station I are expressed as BL(I) and DL(I), respectively.

3.2.1 Communication Group Formation

An application process AP (I Ti f p_1) in station I requests Communication Group formation to the BL(I) by issueing CGFORM command. This command must be accompanied with a candidate member list and transmission control parameters. One of these parameters specifies the one out of three transmission types (that is; fixed source, variable source, multiple source). In the fixed source transmission, only a process which requested the Communication Group formation can be allowed to broadcast data. In the variable source transmission, as described previously, any member in the group can broadcast data, but only one member can be a source at any given time. Therefore, BANET resolves the conflict by priorities. These priorities are specified by the candidate member list in the CGFORM command.

On receiving this CGFORM command, the BL(I) assigns a CGID = I#X and creates an entry of the Communication Group Table (CGT). The CGT includes the CGID, function, terminal and process addresses in this station, and the list of addresses for all members in other stations. BL(I) requests the DL(I) to transmit the following packet;

```
Command type   : CGFORM
Function       : f
SSA, STA, SPA  : I Ti p₁
DSA            : BR (Broadcast)
CGID           : I#X
DAL            : Candidate terminal list
```

117

On receiving the CGFORM packet, the BL(R) in
station R checks if the received candidate
terminal list includes a terminal in station R.
If so (suppose that the list includes the terminal Tr), the BL(R) issues the CGFORM command
to the management process p_0 of the function f
in terminal Tr in order to notify the process
that the group formation is requested. Then,
the notified management process AP (R Tr f p_0)
checks whether the group formation is possible
or not. If possible, the management process
AP (R Tr f p_0) creates process AP (R Tr f p_2) and
issues the CGACK command to the BL(R). Otherwise, AP (R Tr f p_0) issues the CGNACK command to
the BL(R) indicating the reason.

When the BL(R) receives the CGACK command, it
creates the entry of the CGT and transmits the
CGACK packet.

```
Command type  :  CGACK
Function      :  f
SSA, STA, SPA :  R Tr p₀
DSA           :  I
DAL           :  I Ti p₁
```

If the CGNACK command is received, the BL(R)
transmits the CGNACK packet.

```
Command type  :  CGNACK
Function      :  f
SSA, STA, SPA :  R Tr p₀
DSA           :  I
DAL           :  I Ti p₁
Data          :  reason
```

On the other hand, the BL(I) which receives
either CGACK or CGNACK marks the candidate
member list in the CGT in order to keep track
of individual responses. When all candidate
members return responses, the BL(I) creates
the list of processes which return CGACK.
Then, the BL(I) broadcasts this member list
(CGMEMBER packet) to all members.

```
Command type  :  CGMEMBER
Function      :  f
SSA, STA, SPA :  I Ti p₁
DSA           :  BR
CGID          :  I#X
DAL           :  member list
```

However, if the fixed source transmission is
used, this broadcast transmission of the member list is not necessary, and BL(I) terminates the group formation phase by responding
CGID and the member list to the AP (I Ti f p_1).
If BL(R) receives this CGMEMBER packet, the
BL(R) creates CGT and transmits the following
response to BL(I).

```
Command type  :  CGMEMBER-ACK
Function      :  f
SSA           :  R
DSA           :  I
DAL           :  I Ti p₁
```

When the BL(I) receives this response from all
members in the member list, it notifies the
successful completion code, CGID, member list
and other necessary information to the AP
(I Ti f p_1). Fig. 5 shows the summary of the
sequence described above.

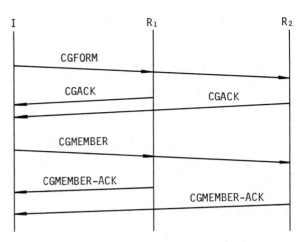

Fig. 5   Sequence of Group Formation

3.2.2 Data Transmission

In data transmission phase, three modes are
provided   commitment, monitoring and transaction mode. Application processes can select
any one of these modes depending on their purposes.

An application process can request the commitment mode data transmission to all members of
the Communication Group. In this mode, the
data is transmitted by "two-phase commit"
scheme [8]. Data transmission of this mode is
used to ensure that the data is received either
by all members or none of them. The updating
of redundant copies of data in distributed
database is typical example of this mode.

The monitoring mode provides only the delivery
confirmation facility, and the list of not-
confirmed (time-outed) members is returned to
the application process. In the transaction
mode, no delivery confirmation facility is provided.

The data transmission by commitment mode is a
little complicated, and the sequence of this
mode is outlined below;

(1) An application process AP (I Ti f p_1) can
    transmit the data to all the members of the
    Communication Group I#X by issueing the
    SEND command of the commitment mode. Then
    the BL(I) broadcasts the following packet;

```
    Command type  :  SECURE
    Function      :  f
    SSA, STA, SPA :  I Ti p₁
    DSA           :  BR
    CGID          :  I#X
```

(2) Receiving the SECURE packet, the BL(R)
    searches the CGT with key I#X, and finds
    the process address (R Tr f p_2) in this sta-
    tion. Then, the BL(R) transfers the re-
    ceived data to the AP (R Tr f p_2) by the
    Secure command. If the AP (R Tr f p_2) deter-
    mines that the received data can be pro-
    cessed, it saves the received data in tem-
    porary memory and issues the SECURED com-
    mand to the BL(R). Otherwise, it issues

the NOT-SECURED command. The BL(R) transmits the SECURE-ACK or SECURE-NACK packet depending on the command issued by AP (R Tr f p_2).

Command type	:	SECURE-ACK/SECURE-NACK
Function	:	f
SSA, STA, SPA	:	R Tr p_2
DSA	:	I
DAL	:	I Ti p_1
Data	:	reason (in case of SECURE-NACK)

(3) Receiving the above packet, the BL(I) marks the member list in the CGT in order to keep track of individual responses. When all members return the SECURE-ACK packet, the BL(I) broadcasts the following packet to all members.

Command type	:	COMMIT
Function	:	f
SSA, STA, SPA	:	I Ti p_1
DSA	:	BR
CGID	:	I#X

(4) If some stations return the SECURE-NACK packet or if timeout is detected, the BL(I) returns the status = Transmit - Fail to the AP (I Ti f p_1) and transmits the following packet to all members.

Command type	:	RECOVER
Function	:	f
SSA, STA, SPA	:	I Ti p_1
DSA	:	BR
CGID	:	I#X

(5) On receiving the COMMIT or RECOVER packet, the BL(R) notifies the AP (R Tr f p_2) of that. In the case of the COMMIT command, the AP (R Tr f p_2) completes the processing of data in temporary memory. On the other hand, the content of temporary memory is discarded in the case of RECOVER command.

The sequence of commitment mode data transmission described above is shown in Fig. 6.

4. CONCLUSIONS

In this paper, it has been shown that the broadcast type network architecture is required for the distributed office system rather than the conventional virtual circuit based network architecture. Thus, BANET is designed to satisfy such requirements. We have completed the basic design for BANET and are developing the software modules. We are also developing basic mechanisms for distributed database system. In the near future, we intend to construct the integrated office automation system which consists of many kinds of services such as distributed database, electronic mail and document retrieval. Furthermore, we are evaluating the performance of BANET in order to have quantitative estimation about how effective BANET works compared to the conventional virtual circuit based network where the commitment control is executed in application level.

REFERENCES

[1] ISO DP7498 "Data Processing - Open Systems Interconnection - Basic Reference Model"

[2] T. Kawaoka et. al. "A Logical Structure for Heterogeneous Computer Communication Network Architecture" ICCC-78, September, 1978.

[3] P.A. Bernstein et. al. "The Concurrency Control Mechanism of SDD-1: A System for Distributed Databases (The Fully Redundant Case" IEEE Trans on Software Engineering May, 1978.

[4] M. Stonebraker, "Concurrency Control and Consistency of Multiple Copies of Data in Distributed INGRES" IEEE Trans. on Software Engineering May, 1979.

[5] H. Yamazaki et. al. "A Hierarchical Structure for Concurrency Control in a Distributed Database System" 6th Data Communications Symposium 1979.

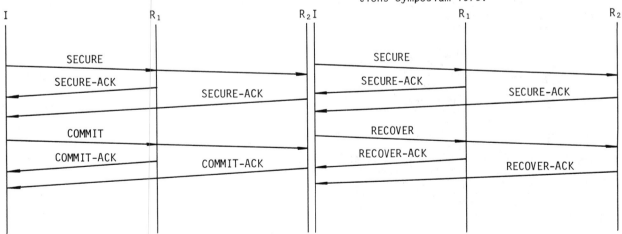

(a) Normal Case

(b) Recover Case

Fig. 6 Sequence of Commitment Mode

[6] The Ethernet, A Local Area Network: Data Link Layer and Physical Layer Specifications, Version 1.0, September 30, 1980.

[7] J.B. Brenner, "Preliminary View on Administration and Use of Logically Related Sessions", Contribution to ISO/TC97/SC16/WG2 N60.

[8] J.N. Gray, "Notes on Database Operating Systems", Operating Systems and Advanced Course. Berlin, Heidelberg: Springer-verlag, 1978.

Haruaki Yamazaki received the B.S. degree in mathematics in 1970 from Nagoya University, Japan. He subsequently joined OKI Electric Industry Co., Ltd. and has been engaged in research and development in the distributed processing systems. He received the M.S. degree in computer science in 1977 from the University of Illinois at Urbana-Champaign. His current interests are in distributed database system, Artificial intelligence and Software engineering. He is a member of the Information Processing Society of Japan, the Operations Research Society in Japan. He is presently a staff engineer of the research laboratory, OKI Electric Industry Co., Ltd.

Isamu Yoshida received the B.S. and M.S. degrees in Applied Mathematics from the University of Electro-Communications, Japan in 1973 and 1975, respectively. He joined OKI Electric Industry Co., Ltd. in 1975 and has been engaged in research and development of distributed systems. He is a member of the Institution of Electronics and Communication Engineers of Japan and the Information Processing Society of Japan.

Kiyoshi Hasegawa received the B.S. degree in Electrical Engineering in 1959 from Yokohama National University. He joined OKI Electric Industry Co., Ltd. in 1959 and has been engaged in research and development of time-division electronic exchange, memory systems and database systems. His current interest is in office automation systems. He is a member of IEEE.

Planning Packet Transport Capabilities in the Bell System

G J Handler, R L Snowden
American Telephone and Telegraph
Co., USA

As part of the plans for the evolution to an Integrated Services Digital Network (ISDN),
the Bell System has been planning the possible deployment of packet switching capabilities
in the Network. An internal packet switching network already exists to carry messages used
in the call set-up and disconnect procedures in the voice network. New plans include the
deployment of packet switches for commercially available long haul basic data transport, as
well as smart statistical multiplexers for support of local access. This talk will
describe the plans for deploying this capability, the protocols supported, and the possible
applications.

INTRODUCTION

In recent years the need for data
communications has skyrocketed. At first
only large businesses could afford computers
and usually only a few at their
headquarters. As the use of computing
became more important to their operation and
several computers were needed, the
requirement to transport data among them
shepherded in the era of data
communications. As the cost of computing
declined and computers of all sizes
proliferated further, the numbers of users
grew to the point where it became impossible
to co-locate users and the computer. This
necessitated the evolution of sophisticated
data communications much beyond the simple
transmission lines that were needed in the
beginning.

Today we are standing at the edge of an era,
where the need to send and receive data may
become universal. In addition, with the
advent of digital voice, data communications
may merge with voice communications to
create the requirement for a single
ubiquitous communications network.

If one analyzes the components of this
growing communication market, the following
picture arises: Applications such as bulk
data transfer, facsimile, and video data
transmission are characterized by high
information density, long holding time
messages. Requirement for another type of
data communications arises from applications
such as interactive computing, home
information, energy management, credit
verification etc. Such applications require
communication technology which responds to
traffic that is characterized by relatively
short holding times, low message density,
and bursty traffic patterns.
To serve data traffic with long holding
time, high message density characteristics,

it is economically advantageous to have a
physical transmission path available for the
entire time of the message. This means that
circuit switching is likely to be the best
technology for such traffic. However,
for short holding time bursty messages, the
technology that is most likely to be
economical is packet switching.

In this paper we discuss the planning in the
Bell System aimed at defining the
architecture for a network which
incorporates packet switching, and serves
the needs of this fast growing
communications market.

CUSTOMER NEEDS

To be able to define a network architecture,
the customer's needs must first be
understood. By examining customer
applications such as home information,
interactive computing, inquiry and response,
and energy management, a set of requirements
can be derived which guides the definition
of the architecture of the network. A
partial list of these requirements is given
below.

1. Ubiquity

    The number of potential
    participants gives rise to the need
    for universal access, and a network
    which allows these participants to
    freely communicate with each
    other.

2. Standard Interfaces.

    The complexity of the interfaces
    for data communications, along with
    the number of different vendors who
    manufacture terminal equipment and
    communications software, require

that the network interfaces be standard and well publicized.

3. Economic Data Transport.

It is expected that terminals and computers of varied complexity will require access to this network. Due to the various applications that may be involved, the traffic characteristics are expected to be highly variable. A wide range of speeds, holding times, and message densities will have to be economically carried by the network.

4. Multiple Simultaneous Services.

It is expected that customers of this data communications network will want to reach several services simultaneously. For example, customers may require voice communications simultaneously with several data services, or may require that data services such as energy management and home information operate simultaneously. The network therefore, must allow for simultaneous voice, and multiple logical data channels via a single access facility.

REGULATORY ENVIRONMENT

Another important consideration in defining the network architecture is the current regulatory environment in the United States. While at the writing of this paper the regulatory environment has not finalized, and legislation is still pending in the U.S. Congress, one can analyze recent decisions of the Federal Communication Commission and use that information in planning network capabilities. The FCC's Computer Inquiry II decision has two major aspects which impact the design of a data communications network. First, customer premises equipment must be offered by a separate subsidiary which is independent from the Bell regulated carrier's offerings of transport capabilities. This means that the regulated carrier cannot offer an end-to-end service which includes the customer premises equipment, but must offer a network service between two demarcation points, referred to as Network Channel Terminating Equipment (NCTE). Access to the network is then defined via interface specifications at the NCTE.

The second important aspect of the Computer Inquiry II decision is a differentiation between enhanced and basic services. Enhanced services include data communication services which involve storage and processing of customer information. Such services must also be offered by a separate subsidiary. Protocol conversion involving customer to customer information is

considered to be processing, and therefore an enhanced service. Since the regulated carrier can only offer basic services, protocol conversion involving customer to customer information cannot be offered. At the time of this writing, however, the exact definition of protocol conversion has not been specified by further action of the FCC.

Also, at the time of this writing, a consent decree was signed by AT&T and the US Government, in which it was agreed that AT&T would divest its local exchange access and intraexchange telecommunications business. The impact of this consent decree will be substantial on the planning and implementation of new network capabilities.

NETWORK TECHNOLOGY

In this section we will discuss the building blocks needed to create a network which best responds to the communications needs of the customers. These building blocks will be selected in light of the customer requirements, the regulatory environment, as well as the enormous capital investment already in place in the form of the existing voice and data telecommunications network. The primary components of interest of the existing network are access lines and switches. Ubiquity of a new data communications network can best be achieved by taking advantage of the ubiquity of the existing communications architecture. If the universally available access lines and the widely deployed electronic switching equipment can be employed in the creation of a new data communications network, then ubiquitous availability of this network can be achieved at a relatively fast pace. The customer applications described above can be best served by packet switching technology. Since the existing technology is circuit switched, new technology for packet switching must be integrated into the existing network. Our discussion of technology will be divided into four parts: access alternatives, interfaces, concentration, and switching.

1. Access Alternatives

The characteristics of the access line are dictated by the speed of transmission, the holding time, and the message frequency. Low speed access with multiple data channels can be achieved by putting special equipment at the ends of a normal telephone loop. Such channel equipment allows for the simultaneous transmission of voice and up to 8 kilobits per second (kbs) of data. The 8 kbs data stream can then be subdivided into several simultaneous logical data channels.

Low speed dial-up access can also become achieved via the normal analog voice network in conjunction with modems at the terminals. Such modems may allow full duplex low speed access to a packet data network.

High speed dial-up access in the Bell System may become available via 56 kbs Digital Data System facilities, and new capabilities,currently being planned, which allow the transmission of 56 kbs full duplex data on a standard voice loop. Local access to this new capability can be achieved via a new technology called time compression multiplexing. (1)

In addition to characterizing the access by its speed, the holding time and message frequency characterization leads us to require differentiation between dedicated and dial-up modes of access. That is, situations will exist in which customers require full time dedicated access to the data network. Applications, such as energy management and security services (e.g., burglar and fire alarms) may require the full time availability of the data channel. Other applications, such as home information, may only require occasional access, and therefore can be accomplished via a dial-up scenario. (2)

2. Interfaces

In light of the regulatory restriction regarding protocol conversion, a network service must only use a single protocol at all its interfaces. The international standard for packet transport communications is X.25. Therefore, all the network interfaces will use the X.25 protocol. In packet switched networks for example, for lower cost terminals with relatively low speeds, level two X.25 (LAPB) may be used. For more sophisticated access, which allows for simultaneously handling many calls, the full three level X.25 packet network protocol may be used. Interfacing of terminals using other protocols, such as asynchronous start/stop terminals, must be accomplished through an intermediate enhanced services vendor. This enhanced services vendor can offer protocol conversion, and then interface the network at the full three level X.25 protocol.

3. Concentration.

In order to economically handle many calls simultaneously, the network should offer some form of concentration. For the type of applications that we are considering, the concentration technology planned is the statistical multiplexer. Access to these multiplexers must be available via both dial-up and dedicated arrangements. In one direction, to low speed terminals, the multiplexers will offer the level 2, X.25 interface. In the other direction, a 56 kbs interface at the full three level X.25 protocol would be available to carry many simultaneous data channels.

4. Switching.

At this time, the switching technology for the applications described above is packet switching. Therefore, packet switches will be integrated with the access arrangements and concentrators to form a communications network. Access to these packet switches may be obtained by direct connections via the full X.25 interface at various access speeds. In addition, dial-up connections, directly into the packet switch, could also be made available. Indirect access, through concentration, is provided via the statistical multiplexers described above. The multiplexer itself can of course also be reached either by a direct dedicated connection, or a dial-up arrangement.

THE PACKET DATA NETWORK

In Figure 1 we depict an architecture for the proposed Packet Data Network. As can be seen, low speed access is available via a statistical multiplexer. This access is achieved either through a dedicated loop, or a dial-up arrangement. The dial-up arrangement passes through the existing voice network. High speed access to the packet switch may be achieved directly. Dedicated 56 kbs access is obtained by dedicated lines directly into the packet switch. Dial-up access may be desirable into the packet switch, and could be planned via a new 56 kbs circuit switching capability. This dialed 56 kbs circuit switching capability will be available via the existing Electronic Switching Systems in the Bell System and new channel equipment on the loops, which allow for full duplex 56 kbs data transmission.

The interface to this network is all X.25. The concentrators provide access to the customer via LAPB based interface. The HDLC frames within LAPB, arriving at the concentrators, are appropriately addressed in the multiplexers, and the multiplexers then interface to the packet switch via full X.25. The high speed direct access lines to the packet switch that do not go through the concentrators provide the full three level X.25 protocol. Therefore, no protocol conversion is offered in this network. Terminals which are not capable of using LAPB, or the full three levels of X.25, must interface to this network via an enhanced services vendor who offers protocol conversion capabilities. That enhanced services vendor then would interface to the network via either LAPB, or the full three levels of the X.25 protocol.

This architecture allows for universal access to packet switching capabilities after the placement of just a few packet switches. Because circuit switching, either at low speed or at 56 kbs, can be available universally through the existing circuit switched voice network, dial-up access to packet switching can be achieved after just a few high capacity packet switches are placed around the country. Then, depending on the growth of the applications, concentrators can be placed more ubiquitously to allow for an orderly growth of dedicated access. As the demand grows, the number of packet switches placed around the country can be increased giving rise to a larger backbone network. The customers already being served need not be affected by this transition strategy.

ISSUES

The evolution of a new data communication network is bound to bring with it new technical, operational, and economic concerns. For example, integration of the new technology, that is the new statistical multiplexers and packet switches, with the existing circuit switched network requires considerable technology development, as well as considerations of operational issues such as billing, maintenance, and administrations. While considerable experience exists in the Bell System for such activities within the circuit switched network, the introduction of new technology requires not only the development of new billing, maintenance and administration schemes, but also the integration of these with the existing operations in the circuit switched environment. It is only through such integration that the most economic approach can be achieved.

The performance characteristics of this entire network is another area of concern. In order to build data transport capabilities which will cover the entire United States, it is likely that complicated routing arrangements may have to be developed. Experience must also be obtained with respect to performance levels, e.g., delays and error characteristics. Because of potentially excessive delay, it is likely that the multilevel hierarchy of the circuit switched network cannot be duplicated for a packet switch arrangement. In addition, it is important to consider potential applications and the end-to-end performance they require, and then allocate transmission impairments among the access lines, trunks, multiplexers, and the packet switches delay and availability performance can then be built into the network design. The ability to gradually deploy this packet switching capability would allow for a careful consideration of all the factors stated above. With the experience gained from the first few switches, a high quality packet transport capability may be integrated into the Bell System Communications Network.
Then, the evolution of this network can be planned with the objective of developing the Integrated Services Digital Network.

REFERENCES

(1) Bell System Technical Reference - "Circuit Switched Digital Capability - Network Access Interface Specifications" - PUB 61310

(2) G. J. Handler - "Planning Switched Data Transport Capabilities in the Bell System." National Telecommunications Conference (NTC). November 1981

R. L. Snowden is a Director - Network Services Planning at AT&T, Basking Ridge, NJ. Mr. Snowden's current responsibilities include conception, planning, and project management of new network services and establishment of network performance objectives. In his previous position as Director of Systems Engineering at Long Lines, Mr. Snowden was responsible for the design and implementation of large Data Processing application used to support various internal Bell System Engineering and Operations Practices. Mr. Snowden received the B.S. degree in Electrical Engineering from Iowa State University in 1961.

G. J. Handler is a Division
Manager - Network Services
Project Management
at AT&T, Basking Ridge, NJ.
Mr. Handler currently has
network project management
responsibilities for major
new services being planned
for the Bell System network,
including packet and circuit
switched data networks.   He
started his Bell System
career in 1965 with Bell Telephone
Laboratories where he has worked in the
Operations Research department and later on
the implementation of private networks.   He
assumed his current position in 1980.
Mr. Handler has a BS and MS degree in EE
from Columbia University and MIT
respectively, and a PhD in Operations
Research from New York University.

PROPOSED DATA NETWORK ARCHITECTURE

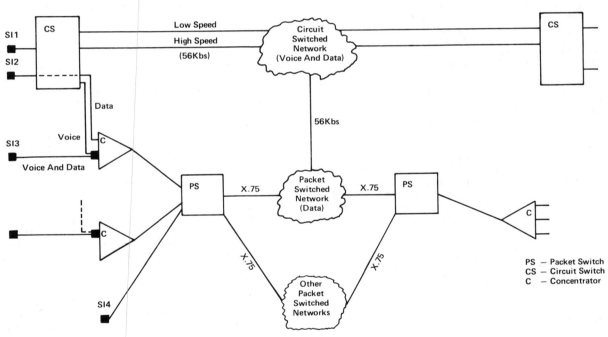

FIGURE 1

Systems Engineering Considerations in Bell System Packet Switching Networks

J J Mansell
Bell Telephone Laboratories, USA
R D Stubbs II
American Telephone & Telegraph Co.,
USA

The Bell System packet switching network is planned to consist of one or more packet switches, interconnecting trunks, and access lines to user's Data Terminal Equipment. The transmission paths will be provided by data communications facilities operating at speeds up to, and including, 56 kilo-bits per second. The internal network protocol used between the packet switches will be designed to provide for high data integrity and high data throughput. The interface between the network and the user will conform to the CCITT Recommendation X.25 protocol as approved by the VIIth Plenary Assembly in November of 1980. The use of high capacity packet switches will permit minimizing trunking costs, and allow for the most cost-effective tradeoffs between packet switch, trunking and access line costs.

1. INTRODUCTION

In planning for the Bell System packet switching network, the fundamental systems engineering task is to translate statements of customer needs into a technical plan for meeting those needs. As in any such endeavor however, there are many aspects to consider. First, from an external customer perspective, there exist many dimensions of customer needs including features supported, performance objectives, and traffic demands. Second, it is clear that these needs will change over time, both with respect to growth in total traffic demands and with respect to specific features needed. Third, in addition to the external customer perception, there exists an internal perspective of the network which incorporates both the routing/congestion control aspects and the operations aspects of the system. This third element is generally not visible to the customer directly, but has a strong influence on network design.

This paper addresses many of the systems engineering issues raised in planning the Bell System packet switching network and provides the technical rationale for the approach taken.

2. NETWORK ELEMENTS

The network consists of packet switches, interconnecting trunks, access lines to user's Data Terminal Equipment (DTE), and an optional Network Control Center System (NCCS).

Packet Switch

At the heart of the network is a Bell System packet switch. The packet switch is based on Electronic Switching System (ESS) processor technology and, as such, can be expected to provide highly reliable service.

Interconnecting Trunks

Data communications facilities which interconnect packet switches operate at 56 kilo-bits per second (kbps) and are referred to as trunks. The internal network protocol used between packet switches was designed to enable the network to meet stringent performance objectives for throughput and data integrity.

Access Lines

Data communications facilities which connect user's DTE to the network may operate at speeds of 9.6 or 56 kbps. These facilities are known as access lines. While CCITT Recommendation X.1 provides for data signalling rates of 2.4, 4.8, 9.6 and 48 kbps for packet mode operation, the network currently supports 56 kbps (instead of 48 kbps) because it is the standard speed in the U.S.A.

Network Control Center System (NCCS)

Finally, the NCCS is an optional network element which is desirable in larger networks (i.e., those having more than a few packet switches). The NCCS provides global network management functions which enhance the maintainability of networks with large numbers of packet switches.

Operations and maintenance functions may, however, be performed locally at each packet switch. This is made possible by the provision of tapes, disks, and maintenance and operations consoles at each packet switch. While centralized network management functions are desirable, and will be provided in larger networks, Bell System packet switches do not require the services of separate network control center systems. This design approach enables the network to meet stringent availability and mean-time-to-repair objectives economically over a range of network sizes.

3. NETWORK INTERFACE

The interface between user's DTEs and the network must be standard and widely supported. The obvious choice, therefore, is the 1980 CCITT Recommendation X.25. All mandatory facilities of this recommendation for both Virtual Call and Permanent Virtual Circuit Service are supported by the network. Beyond these essential facilities, X.25 specifies certain other facilities (termed additional) which may be provided by networks to offer additional choices to DTEs. The decisions as to which of these additional facilities and other features to support depended strongly on customer needs inputs. Based on analysis of potential customer applications it was decided to initially support the interface as follows:

Physical Level

The physical interface to the network is the DDS Customer Service Unit (CSU) (Reference Bell system Publication 41021). At 56 kbps the user may provide equipment which conforms to CCITT V.35, and at 9.6 kbps (and below) provide equipment which conforms to RS-232C.

Link Level

At the Link Level the network supports the CCITT Recommendation X.25 LAPB procedures, with a link level window size of seven frames in each direction of transmission.

Packet Level

At the Packet Level the network supports the packet level procedures and formats for Virtual Call and Permanent Virtual Circuit, as defined in the CCITT Recommendation X.25 protocol.

Virtual Circuits – User data flows are multiplexed across the DTE/DCE interface through the use of Virtual Circuits. A Virtual Circuit is identified throughout the network by Logical Channel Numbers which may be different on each access line and trunk in the path of a given Virtual Circuit. The network supports X.25 logical channels at the DTE/DCE interface in the following manner: Up to 511 simultaneous virtual circuits on access lines operating at 56 kbps, and up to 127 simultaneous virtual circuits on access lines operating at 9.6 kbps. Logical channel zero is reserved for control packets which affect the entire X.25 interface.

Address Validation – When a Virtual Call is placed the user must specify the calling address, and should in general specify the called address. The network performs address validation in accordance with CCITT Recommendation X.87 for both call requests and call acceptances.

User Data Fields – The network currently only supports user data fields which contain an integral number of octets.

Delivery Confirmation – The network supports the 1980 CCITT X.25 delivery confirmation procedures. In essence, the customer accepts responsibility for the delivery of data packets transmitted by the DTE with the D-bit set to one, and the network accepts responsibility for the delivery of data packets transmitted by the DTE with the D-bit set to zero. The network is designed to support the D-bit procedures while meeting a number of stringent performance objectives.

This method of operation provides faster response times to user data flows, allowing DTE buffer space to be released sooner. The high reliability of the network allows DTEs to eliminate time-consuming packet-level recovery procedures when using the delivery confirmation procedures. It is expected that D-bit equal to zero will be the usual mode of DTE operation.

Local Confirmation – The network has stringent objectives for response time requirements. In order to aid in meeting these objectives the network sends a confirmation to clear, reset and restart packets as soon as the network action is complete. The network will not wait for acknowledgement from the distant DTE prior to issuing confirmation to the requesting DTE.

Diagnostic Packet – The network supports the diagnostic packet, thus allowing the DTE more opportunity for error analysis and recovery. The diagnostic packet is used to indicate error conditions in the network that are not normally covered by other X.25 procedures.

X.25 User Facilities – In addition to the foregoing, there are a number of X.25 user facilities supported by the network. These facilities build upon the basic X.25 attributes and increase the utility of the network to its users.

Throughput Class Negotiation – The network will support throughput class negotiation for all classes up to and including 9.6 kbps. More importantly, the network is designed to ensure a high probability of an individual virtual circuit sustaining a 9.6 kbps throughput rate. The negotiated throughput class may be different in each direction of transmission.

Flow Control Parameter Negotiation – The flow control parameters are the packet size and packet level window size. DTEs negotiate these parameters on a per call basis, for each direction of transmission. The network currently supports packet sizes of 128 and 256 octets, and packet level window sizes of 2 and 3 outstanding packets.

It should be noted that there is a correlation between the selected window and packet sizes, and virtual circuit throughout. It is the responsibility of the user DTEs to select the appropriate flow control parameters to achieve the desired virtual circuit throughput. The network is designed to achieve high virtual circuit throughput with small packet and window sizes.

In order to better serve the permanent virtual circuit, the network supports non-standard default packet sizes and non-standard default window sizes. These facilities are established at service provisioning time and apply to each direction of transmission.

Fast Select/Fast Select Acceptance - Fast Select is a per-call facility which allows the DTE to send up to 128 octets of user data with the call request packet. One example of the usefulness of Fast Select is for DTEs wishing to sub-address beyond the access line. This allows the destination DTE the opportunity to determine the availability of the sub-addressed process prior to issuing a call accepted packet. Call Acceptance to a Fast Select is in the form of a Fast Select Acceptance. Fast Select Acceptance also allows up to 128 octets of user data to be sent to the originating DTE.

Other X.25 user facilities provided by the network are:

- Closed User Group
- One-way Logical Channel Outgoing
- Incoming Calls Barred
- Outgoing Calls Barred

The above facilities apply to Virtual Calls and are established by service provisioning.

4. NETWORK SERVICES

In addition to the X.25 access line procedures, the network provides several services to increase its utility for packet-mode DTE.

Access Line Addressing

There are two options available for assigning logical network addresses to access lines:

(1) One address per access line

(2) Multiple addresses per access line

It is anticipated that the majority of users will be host computers which run multiple processes and/or have a number of associated data terminals. In order to allow an originator to more easily address the host processes and/or terminals, the network supports an assignment of up to 1000 logical addresses to an individual access line. These addresses are assigned in blocks of 100, and must begin on addresses where the least significant digits are "00".

Multiple Line Hunt Group

The network supports up to twenty 56 kbps access lines in a hunt group. Incoming Virtual Calls are distributed among the lines of the hunt group so that the total of Virtual Calls and Permanent Virtual Circuits on each line are approximately equal. Consistent with ESS operations philosophy it is possible to add and delete lines from hunt groups without affecting other lines in the hunt group.

Access Line Take-Down

In order to aid the user in maintenance procedures, the network has both immediate and graceful access line take-down procedures.

Operations personnel located at the packet switch may enter commands on the local operations console to cause access lines to be taken out of service. This may take one of two forms:

(1) unconditional, where all Virtual Calls are cleared and Permanent Virtual Circuits are reset, and

(2) conditional, where no new Virtual Calls may be placed. Once the line activity has decayed to where only Permanent Virtual Circuits are on the access line, the unconditional command may be used to complete the out-of-service process.

This feature may be used on lines in hunt groups without affecting other lines in the hunt group. It is anticipated that users will request access line takedowns by placing a voice telephone call to a designated network contact.

Closed User Group

The network supports the CCITT Recommendation X.87 Closed User Group facility. This facility allows DTEs to establish logical subnetworks for the purpose of restricting communications with other DTEs outside the subnetwork. DTEs may be members of up to ten Closed User Groups.

Test Calls

For diagnostic purposes a DTE may place a call to its own logical network address. The network will perform normal routing functions, including access line selection in the case of a multiple line hunt group. The DTE may then pass data to itself, through the network, for test purposes.

5. NETWORK ARCHITECTURE CONSIDERATIONS

After the interface protocol selection is determined, and performance objectives have been established, decisions must be made which shape the architecture of the network. These are quite often aspects of the network which are transparent to the user. We discuss below the considerations which determined the resulting Network Architecture.

Internal Protocol

The Internal Protocol defines the rules for communication between the switches within the network, and the choice of X.25 as an access protocol does not, in itself, structure the nature of the Internal Protocol. In fact, there exist packet switched networks using various forms of virtual call oriented internal protocols, as well as packet switched networks which use different Datagram-oriented approaches. In the systems engineering work defining the Internal Protocol for the Bell System Packet Switching Network, both approaches were studied.

The major constraints placed on the decision process were:

- X.25 interface functions must be handled
- Performance objectives must be met
- System must be cost effective
- System must be reliable and extensible

Based on the studies performed, the fundamental conclusion reached was to use a virtual call oriented internal protocol.

This approach appears to have several attractive attributes. First, it clearly provides a more efficient mechanism for guaranteeing proper packet sequencing at the network interfaces. Second, it provides a convenient mechanism for maintaining the required call signaling and call supervision across the network. Third, it supplies a mechanism for analyzing traffic flows and tracing virtual calls. This last attribute appears to be very valuable for network congestion control and diagnosis of certain potential network faults.

Number Plan/Routing

In defining the number plan and the translations necessary to do routing, there were several major considerations. As in the case of the access protocol, a strong desire to be consistent with relevant international standards led to the plan of conforming with CCITT recommendation X.121. This recommendation allows addresses up to 14 digits in length, the first four of which are fixed as the Data Network Identification Code (DNIC). The decision was to use all 10 of the remaining digits and to format these digits in the same manner and with the same general meaning as telephone numbers are formatted and used in the Bell System domestic telephone network. This provides a degree of commonality with existing Bell System number plans which appears to be useful in possible future integration of digital services.

Another major influence on the number plan and consequent routing plan was a strong desire to provide a uniform number plan in which the actual topology of the network was not visible to the customer. This means that a customer does not need to address a fixed destination differently based on where the call originates, and that additions of network resources (packet switches or trunks) do not cause the customer to be affected by having to encounter a number change.

Based on these considerations, the Bell System Packet Network will have a uniform, X.121 compatible, 14 digit number plan. The 10 digits beyond the DNIC will be formatted in a manner similar to that of the Bell System domestic telephone network. Each switch is required to translate the digits to an internal representation, choose a route to the appropriate destination, and forward both the originating and termination addresses. Moreover, each switch is required to represent itself to the rest of the network as multiple different switch numbers. This

permits most aspects of network provisioning activity to be performed in a way that is not visible to the customer.

Traffic/Performance

A major input to systems engineering of any communications network is the expected traffic demand and the required system performance under that demand. Intuitively one expects that most traffic on a packet switched network will be bursty with relatively long idle times between bursts since packet switching is ideally suited for such traffic. If one expects, however, that the customer DTEs interfacing with the Bell System Packet Switching Network are either host computers or are some form of protocol conversion devices, the access lines to the packet switch are likely to be carrying a large number of simultaneous virtual calls. While each call may indeed be interactive, the combined packet data traffic as seen by the network interface is not light. This suggests that the per line (as opposed to per call) traffic may be rather heavy. Moreover, it suggests that a customer DTE will demand a high level of availability, reliability, and impairment performance, since a single line is carrying many calls.

When taken together these inputs suggest the following:

- Traffic per call is likely to be interactive and bursty in nature. The network must therefore supply rapid virtual call set up and provide only a small cross network delay in data transfers typically associated with the needs of interactive traffic.

- Many calls will be multiplexed onto a single high speed access line and that line will carry heavy traffic. Therefore, the network must be highly available and network generated restarts must be rare compared to customer equipment failures since the effect of a restart is significant.

- Many different customer lines will connect to a single packet switch. Hence, the switch must have a relatively large capacity, failures on one line should not affect other lines, and failures or disruption of an entire switch should be very rare.

Broadly, these requirements imply a switch structure with independent high capacity per line units, together with a highly reliable central processor capable of supporting many high-speed lines each generating heavy traffic.

Flow/Congestion Control

In determining the approach to be followed for flow and congestion control strategies, there were many factors to consider. First, it was recognized that traffic forecasts were highly dependent on how customers behaved in detail, and moreover, the customer behavior would change over time. Second, it was clear that there was a balance to be struck between providing more network resource and less sophisticated control versus less resources and more controls. Third, it seemed evident that the goal should be to provide high quality service and, if a DTE behaved poorly, attempt to guarantee that this did not affect other DTEs. Fourth, an appropriate balance was needed between automatic actions by the switch or switches and manual actions by a network management center.

These considerations led to a plan for flow and congestion control with the following major characteristics:

- Flow control on virtual circuits is a network end point to network end point function.

- Internal acknowledgement of receipt of packets is independent of internal window rotation.

- Internal windows can be (and usually are) larger than external windows.

- Real time controls on congestion handle the vast majority of cases but also provide time for manual actions where necessary.

- Manual actions are intended to be rare and are guided by traffic congestion and failure data automatically supplied to the network management center in near real time.

Simulation and analytic studies of networks using these approaches seem to confirm that this plan will provide a system that is robust to varying customer behavior and provides high quality performance.

Operations Approach

While much of the operations environment is not directly visible to the end user, it is very often true that this aspect of the system heavily influences customer perception of the service. In planning the operations approach to the Bell System Packet Switching Network, three major considerations drove the results. First, the goal was obviously to provide high performance service not only in terms of availability delay and similar objectives, but also in terms of responsiveness to customer requests or customer perceived troubles. Second, the ultimate goal was to integrate the operations for packet switching with similar operations for other Bell System services. Third, the approach chosen must recognize that the network would begin with only a few switches and evolve over time to a much larger network.

These considerations led to an approach which is a balance of centralized and local (i.e., at each switch) functions. Moreover, the approach is designed so that as the network grows in size, the number and types of functions done centrally can be altered to maintain a proper balance.

Functions performed centrally through the use of a mechanized support system include network management, network maintenance, and customer trouble localization. Network management's role is to observe network congestion and failure status and take necessary actions based on global network information. Typical actions include code blocking on originating traffic and forced routing around failures. The network maintenance function is provided for escalation of difficult troubles which cannot be resolved locally. An example is the inability to complete calls to certain destinations. By centralizing these functions, a broader view of switch to switch interaction is permitted. Moreover, people who perform this work must be highly trained and centralization reduces the number of people who must be trained. In addition, the provision of a single point of contact for customer trouble reporting and trouble localization provides a responsive customer interface.

Local functions include switch maintenance, line and trunk maintenance, traffic administration, and service provisioning activity. Maintenance capabilities exist locally for diagnosing hardware and software faults. The majority of these capabilities can be executed without impairing customer service. Since traffic data reports are often a source of maintenance information, that function is also implemented locally. Similarly, it is often true that troubles are introduced by activity associated with adding new services or changing existing services and hence this function is performed locally.

6. SUMMARY

The major systems engineering issues addressed in planning the Bell System Packet Switching Network have been described. The fundamental resolution of the issues is that the network has the following characteristics:

- X.25 interface with all essentials of virtual call and permanent virtual circuit service. A moderate number of additional features are supported.

- Virtual call oriented internal protocol and virtual call routing.

- High capacity switches with high quality performance.

- End to end flow control with internal acknowledgement decoupled from window rotation.

- A balanced operations approach with centralization of functions needing a global network view.

7. BIOGRAPHIES

J. J. Mansell is Head of the Packet Transport Systems Engineering Department at Bell Laboratories. His department is responsible for technical requirements for packet network services including interface requirements, performance objectives, network and operations requirements. Since joining Bell Laboratories in 1962, Mr. Mansell has participated in planning data communications services including economic technical studies of potential switched and private network services. Mr. Mansell received the BSEE degree from St. Louis University in 1962 and the MSE degree from the University of Pennsylvania in 1963.

R. D. Stubbs is District Manager-Network Switching & Operator Systems Design, Network Planning and Design Department, AT&T Basking Ridge, NJ. Mr. Stubbs is currently responsible for managing the design and initial implementation of packet switching networks for use in the Bell System. Prior to this current assignment, he was with Southern Bell Telephone Co., with the major responsibility for planning, designing and implementing a company-wide corporate packet switching network. He previously held positions as a digital systems design engineer. Mr. Stubbs received the BSEE Degree from the University of Florida in 1969, has done graduate studies in electrical engineering, and is currently enrolled in a graduate advanced management program.

Architectural Considerations in Bell System Packet Switching Network

E J Rodriguez
Bell Laboratories, USA

The Bell System Packet Switching Network supports the 1980 CCITT Recommendation X.25 Protocol. Access lines to customer interfaces and interconnecting trunks between packet switches make use of digital transmission facilities, such as Dataphone® Digital Service facilities. Operations and maintenance objectives are predicated on a seven day week, twenty-four hour day operating environment.

Software and hardware architectural issues considered in the design of this high speed, highly reliable packet switching network are described.

1. INTRODUCTION

The fundamental design of the Bell System Packet Switching Network is based on a highly reliable switch supporting 56 Kilobits per second (Kbps) digital transmission facilities, such as Dataphone® Digital Service facilities, as its primary source of input/output traffic.

The 1980 CCITT Recommendation X.25 network interface is supported at the physical, link and packet levels. Physical level data signaling rates of 56 Kbps and 9.6 Kbps are supported. The link level protocol is the bit oriented LAPB data link control procedures. The X.25 Virtual Call (VC) and Permanent Virtual Circuit (PVC) services are supported at the packet level. Initially, packet sizes of 128 and 256 octets are allowed with a maximum of 511 logical channels per 56 Kbps line (127 logical channels per 9.6 Kbps line). Additional features supported are described in the Bell System X.25 Interface Preliminary Technical Reference.[1]

Performance objectives such as response time, data transfer rates, serviceability, system availability and accuracy are similar to those imposed on other Bell System Electronic Switching Systems (ESS). Operations and maintenance objectives are predicated on a seven day week, twenty-four hour day operating environment.

The remainder of the paper describes critical design objectives and discusses architectural hardware and software considerations in the overall system design. Operations and maintenance features are also described.

2. DESIGN OBJECTIVES

The Bell System Packet Switching Network will adhere to applicable standards on service features and to Bell System standards on operations and maintenance capabilities.

The initial design objectives for a packet switch development include the following capabilities:

- Support the 1980 X.25 CCITT recommendation for VCs and PVCs for packet sizes of 128 and 256 octets and 511 logical channels per line.

- Support a network of packet switches with an internal network protocol capable of meeting stringent performance objectives on accuracy, response time and data transfer rate.

- Focus the design on a high capacity packet switch (hundreds to thousands of data packets per second) to be able to efficiently support the X.25 and the internal network protocols.

- Focus the design on access lines and trunks operating on 56 Kbps transmission facilities.

- Develop maintenance, administrative and other operational support locally (stand-alone operation) for each packet switch, as well as remote capabilities from a centralized location and be able to provide seven days a week, twenty-four hours a day service.

These capabilities played an important role in the selection of a hardware and software architecture for the Bell System Packet Switch. A number of other service, maintenance and operations capabilities are also provided.

3. ARCHITECTURAL CONSIDERATIONS

The above objectives clearly show the need for an architecture that has high capacity, high speed and high reliability. However, these objectives do not specify the performance characteristics of the 1980 X.25 and internal network protocols in terms of Central Processing Unit (CPU) real time and memory usage. These also play an important role in the software architecture.

3.1 CPU Usage

The X.25 interface consists of three independent layers of protocol (fig. 1):

    Level 1 - the physical level
    Level 2 - the link level
    Level 3 - the packet level

Level 1 specifies the physical/electrical interface of a full duplex point-to-point synchronous circuit. It does not play a role in CPU or memory usage. Level 2 specifies a data link control procedure compatible with the High-Level Data Link Control (HDLC) procedures. Hardware chips are available to provide interfaces, flags, etc. but CPU cycles and memory are required to handle the Level 2 procedures.

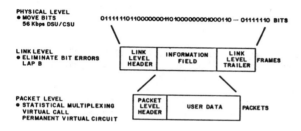

3 LEVEL X.25 PROTOCOL
FIGURE 1

Level 3, the Packet Level, provides for the concurrent operation of multiple calls over a single access line and manages the logical channel assignment and multiplexing functions. It also handles call setups, call clears and data flow. The level 3 also supports the Data Assurance ('D' bit), More Data ('M' bit) and the Qualifier ('Q' bit) facilities.

Analysis of Level 3 experimental software executed in various processors provided an insight into the X.25 protocol complexity. The protocol uses significant CPU resources to handle data packets and acknowledgments, as well as call setups, clears, etc. Therefore, considerable CPU resources are required to support Levels 2 and 3 of X.25. This is particularly evident when trying to serve the packet rate of 56 Kbps full duplex transmission facilities.

The X.25 protocol defines the interface between the customer and the network. In addition, an internal network protocol is required to manage the traffic flow within the network (via 56 Kbps trunks). In the Bell System Packet Switching network, the internal network protocol is based on X.25 at Levels 1 and 2 and has similar internal virtual circuits at Level 3. It connects logical channels in the access lines in support of VCs and PVCs and communicates all X.25 signaling during call setup, call clear, and data transfer. The internal network protocol also handles flow control for rate matching and

congestion control and provides end Packet Switch to end Packet Switch delivery assurance to minimize the loss of packets within the network.

The internal network protocol complexity is similar to the X.25 protocol. Therefore, considerable CPU resources are also required to handle it.

In summary, the 1980 X.25 Levels 2 and 3 protocol and the internal network protocol operating with access lines and trunks at 56 Kbps require a CPU intensive architecture.

3.2 Memory Usage

Another design objective is to be able to support at least 511 active X.25 Level 3 logical channels per 56 Kbps access line. Each channel requires a control block to keep state and window information, buffer pointers, etc.

In addition, buffers are required to handle the packet flow (up to 256 customer data octets per packet) through the system, to hold packets in the originating switch until packet delivery is confirmed and to hold packets for rate matching when necessary.

Thus, the large number of logical channels per access line and the buffers needed to support data flow require a memory intensive architecture.

3.3 Architecture Alternatives

Two general architecture approaches were considered.

A centralized architecture (fig. 2) where most or all the processing is done by a main CPU is technically feasible to meet the functional design objectives. Access lines and trunks interface to the main CPU through network interface (NI) units. NIs support the Level 1 of X.25 and possibly some or all X.25 Level 2 functions. However, since most or all of the processing takes place in a single CPU, a capacity limit will be reached depending on the CPU processing power. Flexible growth is hard to achieve in this architecture.

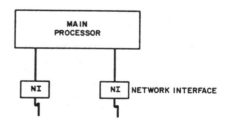

CENTRALIZED PACKET SWITCHING ARCHITECTURE
FIGURE 2

A decentralized architecture (fig. 3) where
protocol functions and memory space can be
moved to outboard processors is more flexible
and reduces the CPU bottleneck. In this
architecture the outboard processors connect
to a central control processor via an interconnect mechanism. Outboard processors can
be added to the interconnect mechanism until
its bandwidth or other physical constraints
are exceeded. This architecture introduces
the management and control of a multiple
number of processors with more complex reliability and recovery strategies.

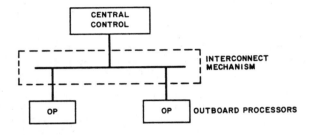

**DECENTRALIZED PACKET SWITCHING ARCHITECTURE
FIGURE 3**

4. HARDWARE ARCHITECTURE

The hardware selected for the Bell System
Packet Switching Network consists of a
decentralized arrangement where a central
control processor is the key to the reliability and maintainability of the switch and
where outboard processors are available to
handle the X.25 and internal network protocol
functions. An interconnect mechanism provides
the coupling between the central control and
the outboard processors. Phases of decentral-
ization from partial to full have been defined
in an evolutionary architecture design and
development.

4.1 Central Control

The central control unit is a Western Electric
3B-20 processor with duplicated control
units.[2] Each control unit consists of the
central processing unit, its memory (up to 16
megabytes), a direct memory access controller,
input/output channels, and local input/output
devices.

For normal operation, one control unit is
active and the other is in standby mode. A
main store update unit maintains consistency
between the main memory of the standby control
unit and the main memory of the on-line control unit. To recover from a failure of the
active control unit, a switch to the standby
unit will take place. The new on-line control
unit can then be used to diagnose the new

(failed) standby control unit. Service is
not disrupted during a processor switch.

Disk units as well as tape units are available
in each packet switch to store programs and
other data. A local maintenance terminal
attached to the 3B-20 processor is available
to control the operation of the switch.

4.2 Outboard Processors

The outboard processors perform most of the
protocol functions. The NI function is
incorporated in them. The outboard processors
are microprocessor based with provisions for
over 500 Kilobytes of memory. These processors are simplex units and can handle a
mix of 56 Kbps and lower speed transmission
facilities depending on the traffic mix and
other engineering factors.

Outboard processors communicate to the 3B-20
central control or to other outboard processors via an interconnect mechanism.
Hundreds of access lines and trunks can
physically be supported by adding outboard
processors as needed. An outboard processor
failure brings a few access lines or trunks
down but not the entire system. The central
control provides the diagnostics and other
recovery software to find the reasons for the
failure.

5. SOFTWARE ARCHITECTURE

In the decentralized architecture, software
functions are partitioned between the central
control and the outboard processors. Most
of the service affecting real time software
resides in the outboard processors. This
includes the X.25 Levels 1, 2 and 3 protocol
and the internal network protocol. The software in these processors has been optimized
to the characteristics of the various protocols. The control blocks to manage the logical channels and the buffers necessary to
support data flow reside in the outboard
processors.

The DMERT (Duplex Multi-Environment Real
Time) [3] operating system (OS) is provided
with the 3B-20 central control. Besides OS
services, DMERT provides diagnostic and recovery software to make the 3B-20 a highly
reliable processor. Under the DMERT operating
system, a large amount of operations and maintenance software is available to provide
system control and integrity. In addition,
routing tables and any other tables that
control the flow of packets throughout the
network reside in the 3B-20. Thus, the 3B-20
central control is used by the outboard processors to determine the path packets will
follow in the network.

The 3B-20 central control also manages an
interprocessor communications mechanism needed
to exchange maintenance and other administrative messages between the central control and
the outboard processors. All program down-
loads are also initialized from the 3B-20
central control. Fig. 4 shows the overall
hardware/software architecture.

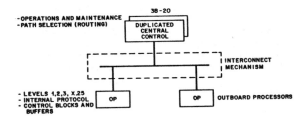

**BELL SYSTEM PACKET SWITCH HARDWARE/SOFTWARE ARCHITECTURE
FIGURE 4**

6. GENERAL OPERATIONS AND MAINTENANCE SUPPORT

In addition to redundancy in the 3B-20 central control, a large amount of nonprotocol software is provided to help meet the reliability goals. This requires careful initial systems planning in basic redundancy configurations, in the human interface to the switch, and in hardware-software tradeoffs. Approximately two-thirds of the total switch software is dedicated to maintenance and administrative programs that are used to manage system redundancy, control diagnostic routines, make performance measurements, and provide communications with the craftsperson responsible for the switch operation. It is the need to keep the packet switch operational during periods of growth and change of customer services, the need to maintain calls in progress during switches to standby equipment, the need to react to possible congestion conditions, and the requirement for providing simultaneous on-line communications with a number of craftspersons that adds extensively to the program structure and makes maintenance more than simply a matter of running diagnostics.

6.1 Operator Interface to Packet Switch

The major communications vehicle between the packet switch and the craftsperson is by a maintenance terminal. In addition, audible alarms and visual displays are used to alert the craftsperson to trouble conditions which are subsequently more fully reported on a printer. Manual controls are also available for taking restart action when the system has lost its "sanity" to the point where it can no longer interpret input commands.

6.2 Documentation

The human interface to the packet switch is built on a set of documents with which the craftsperson must be familiar.

The Input Message (IM) and Output Message (OM) Manuals define all possible messages which are programmed into the machine and list all acceptable input requests and the expected response to them.

7. MAINTENANCE SOFTWARE

Every hardware device has features to facilitate operation of the switch from the maintenance terminal.

The actual process of maintaining the switch (from a software point of view) consists of four areas: trouble detection, alarms, system recovery and diagnostics. Trouble detection is the process of recognizing the existence of a hardware error. Alarms provide an indication of a trouble condition. Recovery is the process of bypassing a hardware or software error by initiating some corrective action. Diagnostics is the process of isolating a fault to a particular device or circuit board. These four areas of maintenance are discussed in the next subsections.

7.1 Trouble Detection

Four techniques are used to detect errors: self-checking hardware, periodic testing, audits, and protocols. The self-checking hardware usually consists of encoding and decoding instructions and data words into an m-out-of-n code or a parity code. Periodic testing is the process of executing software tests on hardware that is not self-checking. Audit programs protect the switch software from the effects of data mutilation by detecting and correcting errors in the various control blocks and packet buffers.

Protocols are used to transmit and receive data from a remote station. Failures in the protocol indicate possible hardware errors. Protocol checks include block check character codes such as the Cyclic Redundancy Check (CRC), message length errors, format errors, or time-out errors.

In addition, detection of excessive transient error counts in a hardware device may indicate a trouble condition. A transient error is defined as an incorrect operation of a hardware device which does not reoccur on a subsequent retry of the same operation.

7.2 Alarms

Maintenance terminal output messages which report trouble conditions are assigned one of three alarm levels: critical, major, or minor. Also, audible alarms are activated according to the output message alarm level. Craft personnel are alerted by these alarms and appropriate steps are immediately taken according to the severity of the trouble.

7.3 System Recovery

Generally, hardware or software malfunctions can occur which result in improper processing actions. The purpose of recovery software is to respond to a report from a protocol processing program, from a maintenance program or from a hardware fault. In the case of a suspected hardware fault, the software will either confirm that the fault exists or it will consider it a transient error. If recovery software recognizes a device as being faulty, it will report the

135

trouble via a maintenance terminal message so that craft personnel can take appropriate repair actions. Alarms are also activated. Communication line(s) associated with the faulty hardware are removed from service, automatic diagnostics are started, and protocol processing software is alerted of the present hardware configuration.

In case of software faults, problems arise which are serious enough that severe recovery action, known as initialization, is necessary. The severity of an initialization determines the degree to which service is disrupted. Several levels of severity or phases are provided so that increasingly drastic initialization actions can be performed until proper operation is resumed. The goal, however, is to minimize service disruptions.

7.4 Diagnostics

The objective of diagnostics programs is to produce a maintenance terminal printout which isolates a fault to as few circuit packs, cables, power units, and wiring areas or installation options as possible.

The diagnostic programs are also used for restoring equipment to service after repair and for testing new equipment additions. A new piece of equipment is not allowed into service until diagnostics pass all tests.

8. ADMINISTRATIVE SOFTWARE

Administrative functions for the packet switch may be loosely categorized as either those dealing with system or customer changes and growth or those necessary for ongoing operations and system evaluation. Service order changes clearly belong in the first group, while maintenance and traffic measurements fit into the second.

Basically, the software administrative functions are:

(i) Service Order Changes. Service order change programs are required to provide a craftsperson or service order clerk with the means to update system memory to reflect changes which are subscriber-originated (e.g., initiate, cancel, or modify a service) as well as changes to system parameters resulting from relatively minor office equipment and network rearrangements (e.g., addition of new access lines in the form of outboard processors). The service order change procedures are designed for quick response and for daily use.

(ii) Maintenance and Traffic Measurements. Maintenance and traffic measurements are made by the packet switch as a result of trouble conditions and protocol processing. The data is used to engineer the system and to evaluate its performance.

(iii) Billing. Usage measurements provide the data necessary for determining usage charges.

(iv) Network Management. Network management provides a means of human intervention in real-time traffic management to handle exceptional conditions of an infrequent or unpredictable nature. Initially, local controls can be provided at each packet switch. As the network expands, network management and the other administrative and maintenance functions will also be allowed from a remote centralized location.

9. SUMMARY

The basic design objectives for the Bell System Packet Switching Network have been described. The design is centered around a decentralized architecture with a 3B-20 Duplex processor used as the central control and a large number of outboard processors providing most of the X.25 and internal network protocol processing. A large amount of administrative and maintenance software is available to insure operational integrity. The highlights of the architecture are flexible growth of CPU power and memory, high capacity and high reliability.

ACKNOWLEDGMENTS

H. C. Bauer, L. R. Beaumont, B. H. Heider, W. E. Omohundro, and R. W. Stubblefield have contributed in many ways to the fundamental design and architecture of the Bell System Packet Switching Network.

REFERENCES

[1] PUB54010 - AT&T Preliminary Technical Reference, X.25 Interface Specifications, August, 1981.

[2] Arnold, T. F., Toy, W. N., "Inside the 3B-20 Processor," Volume 59, Number 3, March, 1981, Bell Laboratories Record.

[3] Martellotto, N. A., "An Operating System for Reliable Real-Time Telecommunications Control," July 20-24, 1981, Fourth International Conference on Software Engineering, University of Warwick, England.

Ernie Rodriguez, B. S. Math., 1967, Michigan Technologial University; M.S.O.R., 1970, New York University; Bell Laboratories, 1967 - Mr. Rodriguez initially worked on various aspects of computer-access planning for PICTUREPHONE® service. He supervised a group responsible for developing software aids to help telephone companies in planning for the Digital Data System. He was also involved in the software development and design of the Transaction Network. Mr. Rodriguez has led a department responsible for design and development of a packet switching network.

Implementation of a Gateway between a Cambridge Ring Local Area Network and a Packet Switching Wide Area Network

I N Dallas
University of Kent at Canterbury, UK

With the increasing numbers of local area networks, a need has arisen to interconnect these networks with existing and planned wide area networks. This interconnection is by means of gateways, and this paper will show how one such gateway has been designed, and is currently being implemented. The gateway in question uses a standard manufacturer's operating system and X25 package and the paper as well as being a case study of the project, highlights some of the problems encountered with this approach.

1 INTRODUCTION

The University of Kent at Canterbury has had a Cambridge Ring as part of its Computer Service, since January 1980, and it forms the main communications medium on the campus. The hosts on the ring as at May 1982, number 3, being an ICL 2960 computer running the EMAS {1} operating system, a DEC VAX 11/780 and a DEC VAX 11/750 both running the UNIX operating system. (UNIX is the registered trade mark of Bell Telephone Laboratories, and VAX is the registered trade mark of the Digital Equipment Corporation.).

As the facilities of Kent Ring expand, with more hosts and servers, being added, it is logical to also allow access from it to a wide area network (WAN), in the case of Kent, the British Telecom, (BT), Packet Switching Service or PSS. Access to any such network is by means of a computer which acts as a node on each network, performing protocol conversion. Such a computer has become known as a gateway.

The remainder of the paper will be a case study of how this gateway between the Kent Ring and PSS has been implemented.

2 GENERAL DESIGN GOALS

The objective was to produce a true Transport Level gateway, which, by not requiring users to log on to it, was as far as possible invisible to them. Additionally, the gateway would ensure that at the operating site, only authorised use would be made of the WAN, whilst the system manager and users would be provided with the appropriate facts and figures.

It was decided that a minicomputer should form the basis of the gateway, and it should use one of the manufacturer's operating systems, and if available, X25 package. Since 1972, the Computing Laboratory at Kent has had a great deal of experience with DEC PDP-11 computers. So, not surprisingly, a PDP-11/34 was selected for use as the gateway.

The machine has 128K words of store, and 2 RL01 5 megabyte disc drives. These discs are used by the operating system, and also hold the gateway database. DEC's standard program interrupt interface, the DUP-11, allows access to the X25 network, whilst access to the Ring is by a general purpose interface board, which uses program interrupts, and was developed by Cambridge University. This board is the MDB1710, and has been used very successfully at Kent on other PDP-11s attached to the ring. The only other piece of equipment on the PDP-11/34, is the operator's Decwriter.

The gateway does not have a lineprinter. Any listings of accounts etc. will be produced using the lineprinter server on the Ring. If the gateway is used on a Ring which does not have such a facility, then optionally, the listings can be produced on the Decwriter.

Since the gateway had to operate in a real time environment, RSX-11M was chosen as the operating system. The only disadvantage of RSX-11M was that the Computing Laboratory at Kent had no experience of it, and so a period of acclimatisation and education on the new operating system was required.

An added bonus with RSX-11M was that we learned that DEC were hoping to produce an X25 package for it. (Note, although as at May 1982, this package is in field test, DEC have "no committment to produce, offer for sale, or support" such a package.)

Although the gateway database is held on the filestore on the gateway, if the ring on which the gateway operated had a file server, then this would become an alternative and perhaps more logical location for the database.

As far as we were concerned, the Transport Level, (Level 4 in the 7 layer reference model), was the only logical place to achieve the gateway, it being the first level where true network independence can be achieved. The protocol conversion, is then between X25 and the relevant ring protocols, with higher level protocols passing through the gateway unconverted.

In the UK, a definition of the Transport Service had been produced in 1979, and this was updated in 1980. It is known simply as the Yellow Book, (from the colour of its covers), though its full title can be found in reference 2. It was only natural, therefore, to use it as the basis of the gateway.

Whenever a local area network, which usually has no charging, is to be connected to a WAN where charging is in operation, it is necessary to control the access to the WAN, to prevent unauthorised usage. Similarly, accounting information from the use of the WAN needs to be compiled and used as part of the access control procedure, as well as being distributed to the users. Modules capable of doing this were included in the gateway. Both the access control module and the accounting module perform a very important role. The decisions taken in designing and implementing these modules will be covered in detail in a later section.

From the outset, the Kent Ring had what could be described as a "leased line gateway". This allowed crude communications between hosts on the Ring, and hosts attached via leased lines to this gateway. The protocols used on the leased lines were proprietary, (e.g. CDC UT-200, and ICL XBM), whilst the local Ring hosts used RCONET RJE protocol {3}, above the ring protocols. Communication through this gateway was achieved by placing the appropriate emulators back-to-back.

Because the hardware running the leased line gateway was 10 years old, and coming to the end of its useful life, the new gateway was designed with two functions in mind. In addition to being a gateway to X25 networks, it will be capable of being a gateway to any host connected by a leased line, providing the lower level protocol used on the lines is Yellow Book Transport Service above "PSS compatible X25". This approach will be very useful, since most host sites are moving in this direction, as well as using higher level protocols such as the Network Independent File Transfer Protocol {4}, and the Job Transfer and Manipulation Protocol (JTMP) {5}. One of the features of the DEC X25 package means that the gateway can only act as the DTE-end of the leased line connection.

The fact that higher level protocols pass through a Transport Level gateway without conversion, poses a small problem for interactive traffic. The interactive protocol in use around the Kent Ring, at least as far as the gateway is concerned, is TS29 {6}. This should pass through the gateway unconverted, but some hosts attached to PSS will support only X29.

To overcome this the gateway was designed with a module to carry out conversion between TS29 and X29 and vice versa, where necessary.

3 THE PROTOCOLS

The lower level protocols used on PSS are of course, X25. To achieve a realisation of the Transport Service over X25 for the gateway simply meant implementing the appropriate annex of the Yellow Book.

From its inception at Kent, the lower

level protocols used on the Ring were those which had been defined and used by Cambridge University, viz. Basic Block Protocol, (BBP), Byte Stream Protocol, (BSP), {7}, and Single Shot Protocol, (SSP), {8}. We found them to be most satisfactory for our needs, and we did not see the need for defining a new set of protocols for use with the gateway.

All that was needed was to define a realisation of the Yellow Book Transport Service for the ring, using the protocols, in much the same way as the annex in the Yellow Book had done for X25. The resulting protocol became known as Transport Service Byte Stream Protocol, or TSBSP {9}, {10}.

The realisation was a comparitively simple task, and was made so because BSP and its commands mirrored the Transport Service primitives very closely, so that many of the "hooks" required by the realisation already existed in the protocol.

Cambridge University have produced a driver for BSP for use with RSX-11M, so this will be used as the basis for TSBSP. Some work will have to be done to it, since some of the features of BSP exploited by TSBSP do not exist in the implementation, but the additions are minimal.

The structure of the gateway is shown in Fig. 1.

Access Control, Policing and Accounting Modules			
TS29—X29 Convertor	Transport Service	Transport Service	
X25 Level 3		TSBSP	
X25 Level 2			
X25 Level 1		BBP	

Fig. 1. Gateway Structure

4 ACCOUNTING & ACCESS CONTROL MODULES

4.1 Accounting

Since the gateway is connected to a WAN on which charging takes place, the compilation of the charges actually accrued is vital. This is because the user will often need to know the cost of a particular connection. Also, the total costs to date for any one user form an important part of the access control module, as will be seen in a later section.

PSS has a feature whereby call statistics may be returned to the user at the end of a call. The initial plan was to make use of these statistics for the accounting package. It was then found that the DEC X25 package did not make the statistics available to the user, in the case of the gateway, the Transport Service. As a result, the Transport Service has to compile its own usage statistics. The information compiled is identical to that provided by the network, and so it appears that there is unnecessary duplication, but it can be shown that independent statistics have several advantages. They serve as a checking mechanism for the subsequent billing information provided by the PTT each month or quarter. Secondly, the gateway can be used on X25 networks which do not provide call statistics. Only the charging algorithm need be changed.

There is a disadvantage to independent statistics. The data volume part of any accounting information has to be in terms of the data presented to and received from the X25 package. Normally, the PTT statistics and the independent statistics should agree, but if a coding or logical error, for example, in the X25 code results in spurious retransmissions of data packets, then the data volume charges could disagree, perhaps by a considerable margin.

The accounting information compiled has three main uses. Firstly, it will be returned to the user on a per connection basis, so that the user has an immediate indication of the costs etc. of the network usage. Secondly, it will be used to update the gateway database, which is used as part of the access control procedures. Finally, the compounded accounting information held in the database can be used to check bills for network usage received from the PTT, and to produce internal bills, sent to individual users.

4.2 Problems with the Production of Accounting Information

Ideally, the gateway would pass on accounting information to the user on the termination of a connection, using the text field in the Transport Service DISCONNECT message. However, there are complications in trying to provide the user with the appropriate statistics.

Firstly, there are two types of connection being made through the gateway, interactive connections, typified by a user on a terminal accessing a host, and host to host connections, originated on a user's behalf.

For interactive connections, any which are of the form of a remote user using a local host, can be ignored for the purposes of this discussion, since the remote end will be responsible for compiling the accounting information. Similarly for host to host connections initiated remotely.

Any connection where the DISCONNECT originates from the remote end is the previously defined "ideal situation", and the usage statistics can be placed in the text field of the DISCONNECT message as it passes through the gateway.

Most interactive connections should result in DISCONNECTs of this form, since typically the user will log out from the remote interactive service, which in turn should generate the DISCONNECT. With host to host connections which generate this form of

DISCONNECT, there is a problem that there may not by any "intelligence" in the local host to interpret the accounting information received.

If the DISCONNECT originates locally, then there is a more serious problem, since the DISCONNECT message returned to the local user has no text field in which to place the usage statistics. DISCONNECTs of this form will occur on interactive connections where logging out from an interactive service does not generate a DISCONNECT. With host to host connections, it is just as likely to occur as the other type of DISCONNECT.

To overcome the lack of a text field, the gateway could generate a DATA message which would contain the accounting information, before returning the DISCONNECT. This approach is not recommended, since the gateway would have to distinguish between interactive and host to host connections. For the latter, the extra DATA message could cause havoc in some high level protocol implementation, even to perhaps causing extra information to be added to some job or disc file.

Alternatively, the gateway could do nothing, other than update the accounting information in the database on the gateway. This is not acceptable, other than as a very short term solution.

An interim solution could be for the gateway to print out a daily list of all accounts, or just the over budget accounts. The system manager would then have a central record which could be consulted in case of a query by a user.

Much the best solution is to avoid using either the text field of DISCONNECTs or an extra DATA message. Instead the gateway sends mail to the user, to inform him/her of the network resources used during the connection. This approach does assume that a mail system exists on the local network, but as such systems become more widespread, particularly with the introduction of a UK mail "standard" {11}, this becomes a trivial restriction.

In all cases, the accounting information held in the gateway database, will always be updated.

5 ACCESS CONTROL

5.1 Features

Fig. 2 lists the possible functions which should be performed by the access control module. The list is governed by the fact that the gateway must stop at all costs, usage violations of the network.

Although at first sight the access control functions are all very desirable, closer examination will show that some are very difficult to implement and may in fact be unnecessary.

Unauthorised access to the WAN is clearly imperative, and relatively simple to implement. The mechanisms for checking access will be covered in a later section. The checking of users, however, only takes place where the connection is via the wide area network. No check is made on connections which are to be made via any leased lines which radiate from the gateway. This is because other than the rental charges, there are no charges for the use of the leased lines, so no stringent access control is required, There may be cases where a host is accessible via the WAN, and via a leased line. Users with no funding available to use the network could be barred from using the host via the network, but still be able to use a program package on the host, by means of the leased line, a very convenient facility.

1) Prevention of unauthorised users from accessing the network.
2) Checking the user has access permission for the type of connection requested.
3) Checking the user is not over budget, (i.e. funds are available for the connection).
4) Breaking any connection which has been inactive for M minutes.
5) As for 4), but the connection is an incoming reverse charge connection.
6) Breaking any locally initiated connection if the user goes N% over budget.

Fig. 2. Access Control Functions

The information about whether a user may access the network is part of the gateway database. The lack of an entry for a user implies that that user is not allowed access.

Once a user has been approved, a check has to be made that he/she has permission for the type of connection being requested. The sort of things which can be checked are whether the user can make reverse charge calls into the network, whether the user can make international calls, or whether the user can make a call to a specific Transport Service Address.

All the information for this checking is also held in the gateway database. The checking performed, can be on a global, group, or user basis. For example, restrictions could be set up, such that no users are allowed to make international calls, or all users within a particular group are not allowed to make reverse charge calls, or only a specific Calling Address is able to make a connection to a specific Called Address.

The check that the user is not over budget is straight forward, and uses the accounting information held in the gateway database. If the user has indicated that this connection is to be a reverse charge connection, then no such check is made. Conversely, if the gateway will accept reverse charge calls, then the budget checking is applied to any incoming reverse charge connection.

The remaining checks are those which are either difficult to implement, or can be shown

to be unnecessary. The breaking of idle connections will be considered first. The concept is very desirable, since it prevents unnecessary call duration charges. The first snag is how to distinguish an idle connection from one where the user is in a compute bound loop, since to the gateway, these appear the same. An argument could be made that if a connection is broken after 15 to 20 minutes, then a user accessing a remote host interactively, who is in a compute bound loop for that period of time is not using either the network or the remote host efficiently, and the gateway is quite justified in breaking such a connection. The user should be using the host via something like JTMP.

Further examination of the problem, however, shows that the feature is not required anyway. Most, if not all, interactive systems have a mechanism for aborting idle terminals, whether they be connected directly, or via a network. Hence, the gateway can leave this task for the remote (or local) host to perform. The breaking mechanism can, if required, be implemented in the gateway, and used for some other purpose, e.g. detecting connections which go down, due to hosts crashing etc.

Function 6 raises the problem of the choice of the algorithm for breaking the connection. There seems to be no ideal solution, the options being shown in Fig. 3.

(i) Prevent access to the wide area network, if the user´s budget is 99% used.
(ii) Warn the user that his/her budget is 95%, 96% ..... 99% used, and then break the connection as soon as the budget is exceeded.
(iii) Break the connection with no warning to the user, as soon as the budget is exceeded.
(iv) Allow the user to go over budget on the current connection, but then prevent all future access.

Fig. 3. Connection Breaking Options

Option (i) seems to be a fair solution, but it does not help if the user´s budget is only 98% used, and then the current connection gets out of control, and runs up a large bill.

Option (ii) is a neat solution in theory, but in practice, there is once again the problem of how the warning messages should be sent to the user. Extra DATA messages could be used, but they suffer the drawbacks of this approach which were discussed earlier.

Option (iii) is really (ii) with no warnings, something which could lead to irate users, and hence to be avoided.

Option (iv) is probably the best compromise. It is still subject to the problem cited in (i), where an out of control connection could run up quite high costs. This can be avoided to some extent, if a decision is made to break the connection if some, typically high, cost level is exceeded. This option, (which is the one to be implemented), has the added advantage that the first implementation can be quite simple, with features like the high cost cut off being added to subsequent releases.

5.2 Access Control Operation

Each potential user of the wide area network will be registered on the gateway, and will have an entry in the gateway database. The entry will initially consist of four items, viz.

A Username
A Password
Budget Details
Access Permissions

Once use of the network takes place, the accounting information will be added to the user's entry.

All entries in the database will be set up and modified by the system manager. Since it is not possible to log on to the gateway, the user is not able to change any of the entries, not even the password, which avoids "password cracking" by other users.

If, for any reason, as the access control checks take place, the gateway decides not to forward the connection to the WAN, a DISCONNECT is returned to the user, with the text field giving the reasons.

Any attempted connection by a user who does not have an entry in the gateway database is refused immediately. If an entry in the database exists, then the first check to be carried out is a confidence test on the user, i.e. to verify that the user is who he/she claims to be. This check is by means of the username and password. Although the user does not log on to the gateway, he/she must supply these, so that the verification can take place. They arrive in the Called Address field of the Transport Service CONNECT message, and are recognised by the gateway by being enclosed within special delimiters. (They are not forwarded into the WAN.) The mechanism for the transmission of the username and password in this manner is identical to that used on SERCNET {12}. This mechanism can also be used to transmit information to the gateway about the type of call or quality of service, (e.g. reverse charging or X25 window size etc.).

Having received the username and password, the gateway compares them with those held in the database. If they agree, further checks are made, otherwise, the connection is refused. Since there are both interactive and host to host connections through the gateway, the user verification is carried out in one of two ways. For the former, the verification is on username and password. For host to host connections, the gateway assumes that the local host has already performed the verification, and the check is merely to see if the user has access to the WAN.

Determining that the connection originates from a host, rather than from an interactive user, can be done in one of two ways, the latter being adopted for the gateway at Kent. Firstly, the host can supply a special password. This keeps the mechanism identical to the interactive case, but is then open to abuse if users "crack" the password. Alternatively, the gateway can keep a list of the Calling Addresses of all the hosts on its local network. These are then checked each time a CONNECT is received.

The next check is on the type of access requested. The mechanism is described in terms of reverse charging, but may, and will be applied to other types of access. The gateway database is interrogated to see if this is a legal request. Such a check will ascertain whether reverse charging is allowed from the site, and if so, if the user is allowed to make such a call, either because he has individual permission, or because he is a member of a select group who can make such a call. In this context, "the user" is widened to include the Calling Address, since reverse charge calls may be banned from certain locations.

If the type of access requested is legal, then a check is made to see if the user is over budget, and if so, the connection is rejected. Doing the check this way round, (i.e. access requested followed by over budget), means that a legal reverse charge call by a user who is over budget, will be allowed through the gateway.

6 INTERFACING TO THE X25 MODULE

Although the X25 package from DEC has had several delays, other commitments on the author have meant that the coding of the Transport Service module to interface to the package has also been delayed. Some documentation, albeit changing (though not drastically), on the X25 package was available at quite an early date, so the design of the user interface to the Transport Service {13} was completed at an early stage of the project.

The design makes use of many of the ideas and principles used by the X25 package one level below. This was done because many of the Transport Service functions have parallels at the lower level, and so to adopt the "tried and trusted" approach adopted by DEC, seemed better than trying to "reinvent the wheel".

Since the design of the Transport Service module was done at the RSX-11M educational stage, the advice of other RSX-11M users was sought. Their advice was that the module should be written as an Ancillary Control Processor, or ACP, which is a highly privileged task, and offers the protection required by something like the Transport Service, although it does not avoid the context switching overhead imposed by RSX-11M.

Two big disadvantages of the ACP approach seemed to be that ACPs were very difficult to write and test, and there was a lack of information and documentation about them, nevertheless, this approach was taken, and a definitive document on ACPs {14}, was located.

The fact that the Transport Service was being written as an ACP, meant that the user interface to the Transport Service could make use of the RSX-11M QIO directive as its means of communication.

As at May 1982, the field test version of the X25 package has been in operation at Kent for a few months. Due to initial delays, it has been decided to make the Transport Service a set of procedures. This means that the X25 package can be tested sooner than with the ACP approach, and it also means that if and when ACP development is resumed, the Transport Service encoding will be tried and tested, so that any new problems will be known to be associated with the ACP.

The data structures and user interface defined for the ACP approach have been retained wherever practical. To date only the communication via QIOs has been dropped, but the subsequent procedure call has been made to look almost identical.

The problems encountered with the DEC X25 package so far have been minimal, and have been mainly to do with unclear documentation, and missing software features.

7 CONCLUSION

This is an on-going project. So far, much of the design has been completed, and coding is under way. No problems have yet arisen which have proved to be unsolvable, and it is hoped that this will continue for the rest of the project. As the work progresses, it will be possible to say more about the performance of the manufacturer's X25 software, and to give further updates on the problems encountered with interfacing to it. Further, time will show whether some of the design decisions taken about the gateway, were the correct ones, or whether in the light of experience, they will require modification.

The gateway has given an insight into internetwork addressing problems. The Yellow Book overcomes these through its source routing approach to addressing, and it allows addresses to be transmitted across networks, so as to arrive at the destination as a valid Transport Service address. This requires intermediate nodes, typically gateways, to modify the address according to certain rules. This approach has not been fully understood by many people, and the rules can produce addresses which are valid, but impractical to use. Implementors are now enhancing the rules to avoid this.

8 REFERENCES

{1} Whitfield, H. and Wright, A.S., The Edinburgh Multi-Access System, Computer Journal. Volume 18. Number 2 (1975).

{2} A Network Independent Transport Service, prepared by Study Group Three of the Post Office, (now British Telecom), PSS User Forum, SG3/CP(80)2, 1980-2-16.

{3} Barry, P.T., RCONET Protocol Specifications, Edinburgh Regional Computer Centre (June 1977).

{4} A Network Independent File Transfer Protocol, revised by the File Transfer Protocol Implementors Group (February 1981).

{5} A Network Independent Job Transfer and Manipulation Protocol, prepared by the JTP Working Party of the Data Communication Protocols Unit (September 1981).

{6} Character Terminal Protocols on PSS, prepared by Study Group 3 of the British Telecom PSS User Forum, SG3/CP(81)/6 (February 1981).

{7} Johnson, M.A., Ring Byte Stream Protocol Specification, System Research Group Paper, Cambridge University Computing Laboratory (April 1980).

{8} Ody, N.J., A Protocol for "Single Shot" Ring Transactions, Systems Research Group Paper, Cambridge University Computing Laboratory (April 1979).

{9} Dallas, I.N., A Cambridge Ring Local Area Network Realisation of a Transport Service, in West, A. and Janson, P. (eds.), Local Networks For Computer Communications, the Proceedings of the IFIP Working Group 6.4 International Workshop on Local Area Networks, Zurich, August 27-29 1980, (North Holland Publishing Company, 1981).

{10} Dallas, I.N., Transport Service Byte Stream Protocol (TSBSP), Revision 3, University of Kent Computing Laboratory Report Number 1 (August 1981).

{11} Bennett, C.J., JNT Mail Protocol, Dept. of Computer Science, University College London (January 1982).

{12} Dunn, A.S., A User Authorisation Scheme for SRCNET (now SERCNET) - Proposal, Computing Division Rutherford Laboratory, TSIG 9.0 (January 1981).

{13} Dallas, I.N., RSX-11M Transport Service Module (For X25) Specification, University of Kent Computing Laboratory Report Number 8 (June 1981).

{14} Stamerjohn, R.W., Up Your ACP, Monsanto (April 1980).

Ian Dallas graduated in Computational Science at St. Andrews University in 1971, and then took up his current position as systems programmer at the University of Kent. Most of his time at Kent has been spent on communications work, and in 1975, he acquired the title of Communications Officer. He has worked on the Cambridge Ring at Kent since 1978, and he is a member of the Ring Advisory Group to the Joint Network Team.

Local Area Networks: Management and Quasi-Political Issues

E B Spratt
University of Kent at Canterbury, UK

The Cambridge Ring based Local Area Network at the University of Kent which has been fully operational since Christmas 1979 is described from technical and user viewpoints. Topics in management and control are discussed and the paper concludes with a short account of related work in the U.K. Higher Educational Sector.

1. INTRODUCTION

The Computing Laboratory at the University of Kent at Canterbury is responsible for the provision of a central computing service as well as for teaching and research in computer science and related fields such as software engineering and data processing. In May 1979 following a successful evaluation of a small Cambridge Data Ring system [6], which had been built following designs supplied by Cambridge University Computer Laboratory. It was decided to base all communications in the Laboratory on such a system by the end of 1979. This also entailed a change to the mainframe operating system on an ICL2960 from the ICL VME/K system to the EMAS system [11] (which had been developed at the University of Edinburgh). In the event this objective was met since then almost all the computing facilities in the Laboratory have been interconnected with Cambridge Ring Local Area Networks. In what follows the totality of these networks will be referred to as UKCNET.

This paper aims to consider some issues that are related both directly and indirectly to UKCNET. These relate to management (including user issues) and quasi-political matters. However certain items which fall into this category will not be treated here since they have been discussed in earlier papers, e.g. [2] and [3].

(1) The reasons for wishing to have a Local Area Network at Kent.

(2) The reasons for choosing a Cambridge Ring.

(3) A description of a Cambridge Ring.

(4) The techniques employed in moving services to a Local Area Network.

(5) Research work based on UKCNET.

The reader should note that although the discussion in this paper is in terms of a Cambridge Data Ring, that nevertheless much of what follows is applicable to other types of Local Area Network. It is the view of the present author that there are several viable technologies in this area and that it is better to address some of the higher level issues than have too much discussion on the relative merits of the actual technologies themselves.

2. THE CURRENT POSITION ON UKCNET

By the third quarter of 1982 UKCNET will consist of four interlinked Cambridge Rings, as shown in Fig. 1, whilst Table 1 gives the main devices which are attached to each of these Rings. The interconnection is achieved by joining pairs of rings by means of a Bridge, which is the name normally given to a device (in this case a microcomputer system) which connects two Local Area Networks of the same type. Similarly a Gateway is a device which connects two disparate networks.

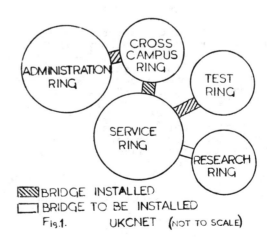

```
▨ BRIDGE INSTALLED
▢ BRIDGE TO BE INSTALLED
```
Fig.1.   UKCNET (NOT TO SCALE)

UKCNET DEVICES

SERVICE RING

UTILITIES
        BOOKING SERVER
        NAME SERVER
        ERROR LOGGER
        TERMINAL CONCENTRATORS (4)
        BRIDGES
        *Campus Ring
        *Test Ring
        *Registry Ring
        LEASED LINE GATEWAY
        *CDC7600 (LONDON)
        *ICL2980 (OXFORD)

USER DEVICES
        TIME SHARING HOSTS
        *ICL2960 (EMAS)   35
        *DEC 11/780 (UNIX)   45
        *DEC 11/750 (UNIX)   35
        PSS GATEWAY   8
        *BRITISH TELECOMM NETWORK

RESEARCH/DEVELOPMENT
        DEC PDP11/34
        *BACKUP FRONT END FOR 2960
        *REMOTE TERMINAL EMULATION
        *SOFTWARE DEVELOPMENT
        DEC PDP11/40
        *INGRES DATA BASE SYSTEM
        MICROPROGRAMMABLE SERVER
        (HEX 29)
        COMPILER SERVER
        (PASCAL MICROENGINE)
        DATA BASE MICRO SYSTEM
        ICL PERQ WORKSTATION

CAMPUS RING

        TERMINAL CONCENTRATORS (2)

TABLE 1.

3. THE USER VIEW OF UKCNET

Users on UKCNET can access various
services and these are shown in Table
2. It will be noted that they fall
into two main categories, Local and
Remote. In general the latter provide
a means of "topping up" the local
facilities, or provide various services
which cannot be economically offered
at a local level, e.g. heavy numerical
calculations (or "Number Crunching")
and specialist packages which cause
problems if they are run in-house
either in terms of software support or
machine resources. The local machines
provide an increasingly wide range of
facilities some of which are provided
on all the main systems, e.g. a
common editor, but there are always
definite limits with what can be
achieved with limited resources.
Although it is pleasing to see
increasing numbers on undergraduate
courses, it will probably be appreciated that the available resources are
not always in balance with the

USER VIEW OF UKCNET

USERS CAN

*LOGON TO THREE TIME SHARING HOSTS

*LOGON TO PSS GATEWAY, hence
        IPSS, ARPA and U.K. Universities

*FILE TRANSFER:UKCNET HOSTS TO
        University of London (CDC7600)
        University of Oxford (ICL2980)

*SUBMIT WORK FOR REMOTE PROCESSING

LOCAL FILESTORE	REMOTE SYSTEM
ICL2960 (EMAS)	LONDON CDC 7600
VAX 11/780 (UNIX)	OXFORD ICL 2980
CARDS PRINTER	

*ARCHIVE FILES ONTO MAGNETIC TAPE
 (EMAS)

*ACCESS UTILITIES
        Booking Server
        Plotter Server
        Paper Tape Server
        Printer Server

*USE COMMON EDITORS (EM-UNIX and
 CHEF)

*USE BOOKING SERVER
        Controls Access to Time Sharing
        ports at peak times.

TABLE 2.

4. RELIABILITY AND MAINTENANCE ISSUES

The user view of any computer system
also embraces other issues besides the
facilities offered. Specifically
reliability, maintenance procedures
(for hardware and software) and
facilities management are vital considerations. We will now discuss
various items under these headings in
relation to UKCNET.

The reliability of UKCNET has been good
and better than any of the attached
devices. Table 3 summarises this over
a 16 month period. The number of breaks
for system testing (which of course
includes the attachment of new devices)
is only considered acceptable in the
context of a system which is being
heavily used for development work. We
anticipate that these figures will
improve for two main reasons. Firstly
the connection of the Test Ring to the
main ring enables new devices to be
checked out with a minimum amount of
disturbance to the main and campus
extension rings and secondly the

availability of standard ring components such as repeaters, stations and interfaces from suppliers, rather than building them in-house. The maintenance philosophy which we have adopted can be summarised as "fast fix on fail", using tested spares with the work being carried out by our own staff. As a general point it would appear that whatever maintenance arrangements are made at a given site, it will presumably not be practicable in many cases to tolerate much delay if problems occur, and this seems to rule out the "on call" type of maintenance contract which is frequently used for mini and mainframe computer systems. Even though all the common Local Area Network technologies: Baseband (Rings, Ethers etc.) and Broadband are very reliable there are bound to be occasions when trouble occurs.

Another issue which must be faced is that of "mixed maintenance", or problems which occur when machines are supplied by different manufacturers and thus maintained by different organisations are connected together. These matters are simplest to deal with if one has in-house staff who are competent to discuss the issues with the relevant organisations in a balanced way. Even so there may be some things that cannot be resolved. For example we are currently unable to load test programs into minicomputers supplied by a well known manufacturer because we wish to hold them in one system on UKCNET and load them over this network. On the other hand the degree of electrical isolation afforded by the ring resolved another problem raised by an organisation maintaining a mainframe who had reservations about a certain minicomputer. It seems clear to the present writer that organisations of any size who wish to run local area networks will have to employ some specialist staff to look after them, perhaps with back-up from an outside contractor in the case of major problems. There may well be a role here (at least in the U.K.) for the so-called independent maintenance organisations, particularly if equipment from several suppliers is involved. It is interesting to note that similar views are expressed in the Preface of a publication which contains the Proceedings of an International Symposium on Local Area Networks [4].

RELIABILITY AND MAINTENANCE

PERIOD 2/12/1981 TO 22/11/1981

HARD ERRORS	16 BREAKS 1 of 3.5 hours Rest < 10 mins TOTAL DOWNTIME 5 hrs
SOFT ERRORS	User transparent and corrected by protocols. About 100 1 bit in 10 exp 11
SYSTEM WORK	33 Controlled Breaks Total Downtime 26 hrs testing 09-10 hrs, daily. Ring usually available.

*Pinpointing Errors can be problem error logger information can be imprecise.

*Maintenance Philosophy is fast fix on fail - using tested components and own staff.

TABLE 3.

5. MANAGEMENT AND TECHNICAL FACILITIES

We now turn to some of the UKCNET management facilities, as will be seen from what follows these are inevitably bound up with technical issues.

Partitioning UKCNET into subnetworks

This has been done for several reasons. The principal one being to ensure as far as possible that faults may be easily isolated and rectified. There are really two levels of partitioning involved in the sense that there are several interconnected rings at one level (Fig. 1), this allows for a service ring to which most of the servers are attached. A test ring for commissioning new equipment and providing a set of tested components, and a research ring. The campus ring provides a backbone network and is used to provide facilities for connecting "user devices", these will initially be terminal concentrators situated in various parts of the university but there is already one example of a departmental ring, which is being installed for the University Administration. As previously mentioned, the campus and service rings are linked by means of a bridge, and two more of these devices are being built and commissioned to link the service ring to the test ring and the administration ring. It is also planned to link in the research ring to the service ring in the same manner. It should be noted that our current bridges are not high throughput devices and are, in fact, based on some Zilog Z80 hardware that was originally developed for a terminal concentrator at Kent. The campus ring is, of course, considerably longer than the other rings and this is itself partitioned into petals or loops which can be cut out or lopped off in case of serious faults or a ring break on a petal.

It is considered that these arrangements will enable a reasonable amount of departmental autonomy, provided of course that there are appropriate rules about attaching devices and adequate tests are set out for the installation of new devices, since it is anticipated that some of these may well belong to individual departments. A set of such rules has been prepared and this is currently under discussion within the University. Essentially these are a simplified version of the BT/PSS connection permission rules.

The Booking Server

This is currently used to control access to the time sharing host ports at peak times. It is an essential facility in our environment to control undergraduates carrying out practical work and on timetabled classes, in order to make sure for example that the class can all log on together. An alternative way of doing this would have been to put a system on each host, the method we have adopted however, takes administrative overheads off the hosts and is conceptually simpler. As the name implies, the Booking Server also enables users in general to reserve console sessions. This scheme only comes into effect when there is contention for the host ports. The Booking Server is more fully described in [10].

The facilities on the Booking Server are currently being enhanced in order to provide facilities for the Operations staff in the context of records. A further development is likely to involve mechanisms for the authorisation of users when they logon to the network, this will replace the present arrangements whereby it is necessary to logon to the hosts separately. As with several other aspects of UKCNET, this is likely to draw on the work done by Cambridge on their Distributed Model Computer System [9].

The Error Logger

This device, which is a Zilog Z80 microcomputer system, outputs error messages from the ring hardware onto a hard copy device. This output is used by those responsible for maintaining the ring for fault diagnosis.

In particular it gives information on cable breaks, although it must be stated that this has not (yet) happened at Kent.

The Printing Server

This actually has two line printers (or more accurately a printer and a printer/plotter). Simple mechanisms are used to ensure that the server is used fairly, these are as follows. Firstly, it is not possible for a single user (i.e. from the same ring station address) to use both printers at the same time. Secondly, if a user has just used a line printer, it will not be possible for him/her to use the same printer until a timeout has occurred, currently this is set to 10 seconds. Thirdly, if a user is in conversation with the printer server and fails to send any new data for a predetermined period (currently 20 secs) then the server assumes that this user has either crashed or gone to sleep, and the printer is freed for other users. Note that in this case the user does not receive any indication from the server about the action taken.

The Name Server

The Name Server is a ring device which essentially converts names in the form of character strings to ring addresses. This is useful for at least two reasons. Firstly, it is not good programming practice to bury constants in programs and secondly, it is possible to change the address of a particular service in a way that is transparent to users, i.e. the system can be easily reconfigured.

Fault Logging

There is one aspect of Local Area management which is concerned with keeping manual records on problems or a Fault Log. We have instituted procedures by which our computer operators log all communications faults and pass them onto technical staff for their resolution. A Fault Investigation Report is produced for each one occurrence. Although it is possible that this will become partly automated (e.g. by having a status server) it will not remove the need for such actions by operations staff.

Thrust Meter

This is a simple device which gives a crude measure of ring traffic. As is customary in the Local Area Network Area this is normally about 2%/3% of the total capacity. However, there is a definite requirement for more refined information for diagnostic and monitoring purposes and provided the resources can be found, we plan to tackle some of these issues at an early date. There is, of course, much current interest in this field (e.g. [4].

PSS Gateway

This system consists of a DEC PDP11/34 Minicomputer system acting as an interface between UKCNET and the U.K. PTT Public Packet Switched Service (or PSS). At the present time we have an interim facility originating from Edinburgh Regional Computer Centre (ERCC). We ourselves are developing an alternative system under a contract from the Joint Network Team (JNT). (Note: The reader who maybe baffled by these acronyms will find more information about these bodies in a later section.) A description of the UKCNET/PSS Gateway is given in ([1], Proceedings ICCC82). Here we will merely remark that a vital management function, that of controlling PSS usage, will be carried out by this system.

6. RELATED WORK AT OTHER INSTITUTIONS

The developments at Kent have not, of course, been carried out in isolation. Most of the Universities, Polytechnics and Research Councils in the U.K. are heavily engaged in both local and wide area networking. This work is supported at the research level by the Science Engineering Research Council through the auspices of their Distributed Computer Systems programme, and at the development level by the Joint Network Team of the Computer Board and the Science Engineering Research Council. The names of these bodies are usually abbreviated in the U.K. to SERC, JNT and CBU respectively. The non-U.K. reader may care to note that these three entities are funded directly from central government via the department of Education and Science, and that the Computer Board is responsible for funding the provision of central computing facilities in Universities. The totality of involved staff in the Universities, Polytechnics and Research Councils is called the Network Community, or simply the "Community". Other papers in this conference (e.g. [6], [1] and [7]) should be referred to for more details. Here we will merely remark that a large scale effort is going on to standardise protocols and equipment in which members of the community are playing a vital role, either on standardisation committees, working and study groups or carrying out implementations of the various protocols which are involved. All this involves collaboration between the various bodies and a willingness to avoid unnecessary duplication.

At Kent we have been fortunate enough to have funding from both these sources. In particular the JNT have supported the Cambridge Ring work over the last four years. This has enabled us to establish the feasibility of running a Cambridge Ring, in a service/teaching research environment and to carry out work of benefit to the rest of the community. The PSS Gateway project which has already been referred to is one example, another is a Zilog Z80 based terminal concentrator which is now available commercially from SEEL of Livingston, Scotland. The interfaces to the EMAS and UNIX operating systems form another type of example. As regards work we have drawn upon from other members of the community, it will be appreciated that we owe an immense debt to Cambridge who gave us all the information we required and dealt patiently with our queries. At a later stage we drew upon work from University College, London (Printed Circuit Boards) the University of Edinburgh (Printed Circuit Boards and of course the EMAS operating system). In addition to this we have had discussions with some 12 other Universities. Apart from anything else, this has in the view of the present writer ensured that the cost falling to the public funding bodies has been minimized.

7. CONCLUSIONS

This paper has outlined some developments at the University of Kent in the Local Area Network field, these have led to a fully operational system with real users which has been working since January 1980. We have outlined the system from a user viewpoint, discussed some of the management/control issues and the importance to this work of developments elsewhere in the community. It seems to us at Kent that we have really adopted a systems approach in that we have freely drawn on what has been available, put it all together, done development work only as necessary and made it all work. In short we have eschewed a "not invented here" approach. There are two reasons for this, firstly it seemed the only sensible thing to do and secondly, some of us who have been involved with UKCNET are responsible with colleagues in the Electronics Labs at Kent for an undergraduate course on Computer Systems Engineering - thus we have attempted, in part at least, to practice what we preach!

The reader will appreciate that the UKCNET developments at Kent have been very much a team effort and that this paper has been written to record their efforts. It is a pleasure to thank them for all the work they have done.

Mr. S. E. Binns
Mr. D. J. Caul

147

Mr. I. N. Dallas
Mr. A. L. Ibbetson
Dr. R. P. A. Collinson
Mr. M. N. Lee
Mr. G. W. Tripp
Mr. T. Schutt·(1/4/80 - 15/3/81)
Dr. P. W. Riley

Brian Spratt is currently Director of the Computing Laboratory at the University of Kent. He graduated from the University of Nottingham (B.Sc.Hons Mathematics, 1952) and the University of Durham (Ph.D., 1956). After holding posts at the Ministry of Supply at the Royal Military College of Science (Shrivenham) he joined the University of Kent in 1965.

REFERENCES

[1] Dallas,I.N., Implementation of A Gateway between a Cambridge Ring Local Area Network, and a Packet Switched Local Area Network, Proc ICCC82.

[2] Spratt,E.B., Operational Experiences with a Cambridge Ring Local Area Network in a University Environment, in West,A. and Janson, P. (eds), Local Area Networks for Computer Communications, the Proceedings of the IFIP Working Group 6.4 on Local Area Networks, Zurich, August 27-29 1980, (North Holland Publishing Company, 1981).

[3] Binns,S.E., Dallas,I.N. and Spratt, E.B., Further Developments on the Cambridge Ring at the University of Kent, in [4] below.

[4] Ravasio,P., Hopkins,G and Naffah,N. (eds), Local Computer Networks, the Proceedings of the IFIP TC 6 International Symposium on Local Computer Networks, Florence, April 19-21, 1982.

[5] Dallas,I.N., Line Printer Server, University of Kent Computing Laboratory Note, January 1980.

[6] Wilkes,M.V. and Wheeler,D.J., The Cambridge Digital Communication Ring, in Proceedings of Local Area Communication Networks Symposium, Mitre Corpn and National Bureau of Standards, Boston, May 1979.

[7] Rosner,R., Towards OSI among UK universities, Proc. IEEE82.

[8] Heard,K.S., Local Area networks and practical aspects of interworking, Proc. IEEE82.

[9] Wilkes,M.V. and Needham,R.M., The Cambridge Model Distributed System, ACM Operating Systems Review, Vol. 14, No. 1, Jan. 1980.

[10] Binns,S.E., A Virtual Terminal Controller, UKC/INRIA School on Local Area Networks, Canterbury, March 30-April 3, 1982.

[11] Whitfield,H. and Wight,A.S., The Edinburgh Multi-Access System, Computer Journal, Vol 18, No. 2, 1975.

An Implementation of a Token Ring

P Willis
University of Bath, UK

A local communication network may be designed to meet various expectations and needs. Presented here is a ring structured network utilising a single type of node of a particularly simple, inexpensive design. To complement this a high-efficiency protocol is used, offsetting the modest bandwidth of the node. No central controller or specialised master node is needed, the network functioning correctly even with only a single node and being impervious to node switch-on or switch-off and resilient to noise induced in the cabling.

A prototype version exists and is currently the basis for experimentation. As the motivation for designing the ring was to meet a demand for inter-computer data interchange, it is intended to expand the prototype into a fully operational utility.

1. INTRODUCTION

The network to be described arose for that most pressing of reasons, necessity. The department possesses a number of disimilar small computers, each having its own storage medium and peculiar input-output capability. File transfers between machines became necessary and were achieved in the simplest manner possible: the back-to-back connection via RS-232 links, the only common, easy interface available. Although this achieved the immediate objective of information transfer, it was by no means satisfactory. For one thing, a loom of wires rapidly developed, a new wire for each machine pair, with much plugging and unplugging. Secondly, a variety of transfer programs were developed, usually in haste, with no overall co-ordination.

Very early on in this evolutionary process it became clear that a communication network was a desirable utility and, although the mesh of wires continued to grow, it did so with our expectation that it would be entirely replaced by a uniform expandable network. The options available at this early stage were deemed to be four. The first of these was to purchase Cambridge Ring {1-2} hardware and develop our own software to drive it. Eventually this was rejected, partly because of the then uncoordinated nature of those companies supplying such kit, but also because the cost of a node exceeded the cost of some of the small microcomputers we wished to connect. The second option was to wait for Ethernet {3-4} to become properly available and, more importantly, fully defined. We judged the time factor alone was sufficient reason to reject this option. Additionally, the software effort and node costs are also relatively large.

The remaining two options both centred around in-house development. Option number three was to use an existing PDP 11/34, an old machine no longer needed for its original teaching role, as the centre of a star network

{5}. This was quite attractive. By using RS-232 links all the machines would be able to communicate via the PDP-11 and the only additional hardware required was a multiple serial interface card. Eventually this too was rejected. The central PDP-11 would clearly be the life or death of the network: a failure here would put all communication at risk. More fundamentally, maintenance costs on the machine were sufficiently high to pay for a fully distributed network in its place. This left option four, to design and build a network of our own.

As with the other solutions, it would still be necessary to develop communication software for each type of host machine. Unlike the other solutions, factors such as node cost, bandwidth, topology and protocols are entirely under our control. This option was therefore selected with the intention that node hardware should be inexpensive; that a minimal amount of host software and interfacing capability should be assumed; that the communication network should be uniform and reliable; and that bandwidth was not a goal to be pursued unless and until the other factors had been met.

2. SPECIFYING THE DESIGN

Having made the decision to design a network, it was necessary to choose the topology. Stars were eliminated for the reason given earlier, as well as for being non-uniform and therefore requiring development of more than one type of node. Contention networks (Ethernet) and ring networks (Cambridge) both seemed to offer the kinds of characteristics sought, with drawbacks. The latter require on-the-fly comparison, insertion and deletion. While not arguing that this is grossly difficult, it does require extra components and design effort. The second drawback centres on uniformity. Ethernet cannot expand over larger distances without special repeaters, while the Cambridge ring structure requires a master node to delete uncollected packets.

On balance, it was felt that a ring better
served our purpose, provided that the nodes
could be simple and identical. Rather than
an empty slot with its additional hardware, it
was decided that a token ring should be
implemented. Further, to facilitate token
recognition, the token would circulate in its
own ring, independently of the data ring.
With this arrangement node hardware is greatly
simplified. In particular, a node which is
not participating in a data transfer has no
need to monitor the transfer to synchronise on
the next token and can, in effect, allow all
data to bypass itself at electronic speed.
Having taken this decision, it is a small step
to put all control information through the
token ring, permitting a richness of control
with a simplicity of implementation.

The final step in the basic design process was
the selection of the node hardware. The
specification had by this time eliminated the
need for specialised hardware, and so a
direct implementation based on serial ports
controlled by a Z80A microprocessor was chosen.
Protocol was, as far as possible, entrusted to
firmware. A node therefore consists of
(Fig. 1) - a microprocessor; firmware; input
and output ports on a data ring; input and
output ports on a token ring; and, at a
minimum, RS-232 connections to the host
computer. In addition, it must function as a
repeater, even in the absence of its host or
local power, to ensure ring integrity.

No mention has been made of ring bandwidth or
point-to-point performance. This is a
conscious design choice. As will be seen,
aids to getting the best performance from the
design have not been neglected, but performance was not a driving factor in the design.
In practice, the node firmware places an upper
limit on the usable bandwidth and so enhancement to meet this limit, but not beyond, is
considered justified.

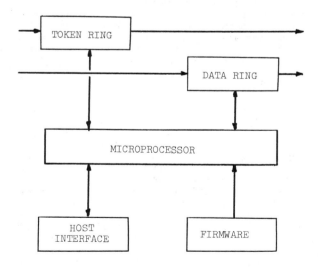

Fig. 1 Node Structure

3. SPECIFYING THE PROTOCOL

Having made decisions about the overall ring
design which underplay the performance, it was
felt appropriate to redress the balance by
implementing a protocol which used a high
proportion of the delivered bandwidth for useful data transfer. This immediately rules out
packets containing very short data items
wrapped in source address, destination address,
check-bits and so forth. Such protocols are
only appropriate where a high bandwidth is
available to carry the overhead. Instead, the
chosen protocol transfers blocks of data,
typically containing up to 256 useful data
bytes in a message 264 bytes long. Similarly,
acknowledgement of transfers is performed at
the message, rather than byte, level to avoid
delays between byte transmission and acknowledgement. If message transmission failed
significantly often performance would degrade
to an unacceptable degree, the cost of failure
being higher as the message size increases, so
it is important that ring implementation
ensures a reliable data channel. Being
intended as a local network, the system is
readily amenable to being engineered to the
necessary quality.

With these comments in mind, we may sketch the
protocol as follows: A computer host, wishing
to transfer information to another host, first
loads its attached node with a message of
information, including all necessary address
information. The node then monitors the token
ring until the token arrives. It then removes
the token from circulation, guaranteeing that
only that node has the right to transmit. The
node then transmits the message around the data
ring, whence the receiving node, recognising
the destination address as its own, removes and
acknowledges. The transmitting node then
releases the token so that other nodes may gain
access to the ring if they wish to do so. It
also reports success or failure back to its
host, which may subsequently wish to continue
transmitting to the same destination or start
a new transfer to another node.

This is the protocol adopted, but with finer
details hidden. Treating it as a high level
specification, it is, however, sufficient to
constrain the design of the nodes to the point
where implementation is possible. Interesting-
ly, an understanding of the node design then
feeds back into the protocol design at the more
detailed level and so it is to the node
implementation that we must now turn.

4. IMPLEMENTING THE NODES

For reasons already discussed, the node is constructed around conventional microprocessor
components with no reliance on dedicated logic:
every node action is directly firmware controlled. This results in a simple, inexpensive
implementation, of limited bandwidth.

The bandwidth limitation is brought about by
two factors. Firstly, serial interface chips
have a finite performance. In practice, this
performance is adequate and steadily improving.

Secondly, information passing into and out of a node under firmware control does so at a rate limited by the microprocessor cycle time multiplied by the number of firmware instruction cycles needed to perform this transfer. Although this need not be long, it is clearly much longer than the very slight delay introduced by a simple repeater. If there are many nodes in the path, a transfer will be unduly delayed, slowing down the overall transmit/acknowledge cycle.

Hence each node is designed to permit direct data bypass when it functions only as a repeater, as well as permitting in-line operation when all transfers are under firmware control. This affects the protocol, for nodes which are not participating in information transfer must be allowed to switch to bypass, and then later alerted to listen once more in case they are participating in the next transfer. Further, nodes which have just been switched on must power-up in bypass mode to prevent ring corruption. Finally, as the bypass is a repeater, it may be optically isolated from the remainder of the node and powered directly from the ring.

In practice, bypasses are provided for both the token and data rings. The token bypass is only used at switch on, so that no node may escape the control information provided by the token ring. The data bypass is used dynamically in the way just described, the gains here being substantially greater than are obtainable by dynamic token ring bypass. The latter would also require an increase in firmware out of all proportion to its only benefit, the small improvement in token acquisition latency.

One other node characteristic should be mentioned. Balanced drivers and receivers are used to connect to twisted pair rings, giving high immunity to corruption and the ability to drive long lines, eliminating the need for between-node repeaters. A modest bandwidth requirement actually improves this ability, other things being equal, allowing long runs of cable and avoiding the introduction of unwanted nodes purely to act as repeaters.

5. IMPLEMENTING THE PROTOCOL

Having developed an overall protocol specification and determined how the nodes interface to the rings with a bypass mechanism, we may now determine the protocol at a sufficiently fine level to permit implementation. Essentially we require that all nodes monitor the ring in the idle state. A node wishing to transmit seizes the token and must then compel all nodes except the presumed listener to switch to bypass. Having transmitted the message the converse problem must be resolved: that of compelling the bypassed nodes to listen once more, prior to token release.

The first of these two problems is easily resolved by presuming that the message contains a target address, obviously necessary, which all nodes sample. Every node which fails to match the target address with its own switches to bypass immediately. If a node of the target address is present it modifies a reserved bit in the address, guaranteeing no further matches and telling the transmitting node that its target is present. The target continues listening while the packet is transferred.

To overcome the second problem, that of bringing passive nodes out of bypass, we recall that control information passes through a second ring, the token ring, which is not normally bypassed. By releasing the token the transmitting node is, in effect, alerting all other nodes to the fact that the transmission has ended. To ensure that all nodes are alerted, this first circulation of the token is always allowed to complete, without a node removing the token. To compel node response, token arrival generates a high priority interrupt to the node hardware, a mechanism which also permits token circulation to be unimpeded by other node tasks. Indeed, so effective is this at circulating the token when the ring is idle that it may diminish the node's ability to perform other tasks when the ring has few nodes. Whether or not this is a genuine problem will be determined only when firmware implementation nears completion, so that the overall processing load at each node is known. However a solution which deliberately delays token passing is not infeasible. Performed statically, this means that latency in obtaining the token will never drop below that occurring in a ring of some number n of nodes, even if less than n are in use. Performed dynamically, tokens will only be delayed if the processing load threatens to saturate a node, an attractive graceful degradation in performance. Another view of the same problem is that token arrival is always a high priority event, but token passing need not be.

Message transfers thus proceed by a series of state changes within the network such that during any data transfer only the transmitter and receiver are active and all other nodes are temporarily ignoring the data ring. At the end of each transmission, the receiver acknowledges receipt, positively or negatively, and the transmitter reinstates the token. Token circulation ensures that no node may dominate the ring.

Within a transmitted message, information fields are provided to indicate the source address, destination address, sequence number (for extended transmission) and check digits (Fig. 2). Each message requires a single acknowledgement so the protocol overhead occupies only a small percentage of the available bandwidth.

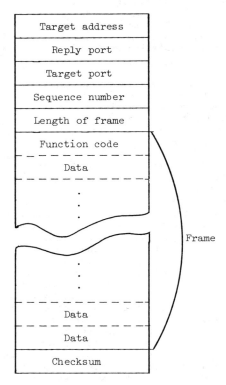

| Target address |
| Reply port |
| Target port |
| Sequence number |
| Length of frame |
| Function code |
| Data |
| . |
| . |
| . |
| . |
| . |
| . |
| Data |
| Data |
| Checksum |

Fig. 2 Logical packet
format

6. A FULLY DISTRIBUTED PROTOCOL

No mention has been made of a master node and
this is deliberate. The network does not
include a master controller and control is
fully distributed among the identical nodes.
This requires careful attention to exception
handling, notably at start-up and shut-down of
nodes, as well as that brought about by
possible token corruption.

Node start-up can occur in one of two forms:
either the node is switched on when the ring is
running smoothly, or it is switched on as the
ring itself is started. The difference is
that in the former case token circulation is
already occurring, while in the latter it is
not. It is quite simple to so arrange the
hardware that it powers up in bypass mode, so
ensuring that this has no damaging effect on
the ring. In this state the node monitors
the ring for signs of activity by listening
for a token. There is a guaranteed time by
which the token must arrive, so the node
incorporates a time-out for tokens. If a
valid token arrives the node recognises that it
is safe to join the network and does so. However, it continues to time-out token arrival.
Any token time-out then causes the node to try
to re-inject a new token in order to restore
normal network operation, but this cannot be
done indiscriminately in case several nodes
inject tokens simultaneously. Instead, a

special start-up sequence is used in which each
node first injects its own (unique) address.
If the node receives its own address back
after a complete circuit of the ring, it replaces it with the token. This is safe
because any node receiving an address, having
already transmitted its own, will remove it
if it is less than its own address, and will
pass it on and drop to standy-by if it is
greater than its own. In this manner a single
token will be injected. This is an
implementation of ideas presented in {6-7}.

Token corruption is handled by requiring each
node to filter out any unrecognisable tokens.
If this happens to remove the only item in the
token ring, the mechanism just described will
install a fresh token in due course.

7. CONSTRUCTION OF THE PROTOTYPE

A prototype two node ring was constructed as a
test vehicle for firmware development and for
detailed hardware evaluation. The ring
interfaces were constructed on a separate card
to the remaining, control section, of the node
to permit easy experimentation.

The control section is essentially a microcomputer incorporating small amounts of random
access memory for stack and variable items
needed by the firmware (held in erasable PROM)
with interfaces to the host computer.
Although not essential, there are light-
emitting diodes to indicate the status of the
node as an aid to fault location and monitoring.
The ring interfaces are serial devices,
initially running at 128 k bits/sec, connected
to interrupt lines on the processor. The
rings are twisted pairs connected to balanced
line drivers and receivers giving the
capability for long cable runs between nodes.
Power is also delivered through the ring cable
at 40 volts DC, local switching mode power
units being used to convert this to the 5
volts required by the logic.

The interfaces may be optically isolated from
the control section, allowing the ring to
remain in service even if some nodes are
switched off. In addition, as an unpowered
opto-isolator is guaranteed to be in a high
impedance state, it is a simple matter to ensure that an unpowered control section compels
the interface section to enter bypass mode.

In all, each node requires some three dozen
integrated circuits all of which are easily
obtainable and inexpensive. Although the
protocol has been determined in some detail,
implementation has not yet proceeded beyond
simple test routines. These have not revealed any substantial errors and no major
redesign work is envisaged. A doubling of
ring speed is planned at an early date. There
is little chance of pushing ring speed beyond
500,000 bits per second due to the use of firmware control. All transfers are made under
direct control of the 4 MHz processor, so
modest gains are possible using a direct memory
access controller. This raises the
possibility of experimenting with a modified
protocol designed to make better use of the
high inherent bandwidth of the ring cable,

drivers and receivers (1 Mbit per second is
easily achieved, higher bandwidths being at a
cost of lower maximum unrepeated cable runs).
To do this without a hardware-intensive node
redesign seems to require byte level interleaving of transfers around the ring.   As
each byte would have to be packaged in its own
control information, the utilisation would
have to be increased substantially before this
technique becomes appropriate.   Work is continuing in this area to try to define a
protocol which minimises the byte level overheads, even if this increases the cost of
setting up a transfer.   There are no plans to
modify the current design to give higher
intrinsic performance, for reasons already
given, although straightforward technology
advancements such as higher speed versions of
the microprocessor will, of course, be incorporated where beneficial.   Rather we would
seek higher performance by using our present
experience to produce a new design.

8. SUMMARY

A digital communication network based on the
concept of a simple node with all protocol
fully distributed has been designed and built
in prototype.   A protocol to enable transfers
of data blocks has been specified and is
nearing completion.   Early testing has been
encouraging and much assisted by the lack of
complexity in the design.

It is expected that the network will serve the
purpose for which it was originally designed:
accordingly, it will be installed as a service
utility within the School of Mathematics.

ACKNOWLEDGEMENT

I am most grateful to Dr. T.J. King for much
help with aspects of the Cambridge Ring and
with the host to node protocol of the token
ring described here.

REFERENCES

{1} M.V. Wilkes and D.J. Wheeler, The
    Cambridge digital communication ring,
    Proc of the Local Area Communications
    Network Symposium, The Mitre Corporation/
    National Bureau of Standards, May 1979,
    47-61.

{2} R.M. Needham, System aspects of the
    Cambridge ring, Proc of the 7th symposium
    on operating system principles, ACM, 1979,
    82-85.

{3} R.M. Metcalfe and D.R. Boggs, Ethernet:
    Distributed packet switching for local
    computer networks, Commun. of the ACM,
    vol. 19, no. 7, July 1976, 395-404.

{4} The Ethernet: A local area network,
    Digital/Intel/Xerox report, Sept. 1980.

{5} D.D. Clark, K.T. Pogran and D.P. Reed,
    An introduction to local area networks,
    Proc. IEEE, vol 66, no. 11, Nov. 1978,
    1497-1517.

{6} G. Le Lann, Distributed systems - towards
    a formal approach, Proc Information
    Processing 77, Aug. 1977, 155-160.

{7} E. Chang and R. Roberts, An improved
    algorithm for decentralized extrema finding
    in circular configurations of processes,
    Commun. of the ACM, vol. 22, no. 5, May
    1979, 281-283.

Philip Willis graduated
from Sussex University in
1971 and then spent a year
at Essex University
studying for a Computing
Science MSc. He then
moved to ICL where he
worked on telecommuni-
cations and cluster
displays before retur-
ning to Sussex in 1973
as a postgraduate
student. He was
appointed a Research Fellow in 1975 having
completed a D.Phil in real time computer
graphics applied to Flight simulator visual
systems. In 1979 he joined the University of
Bath as a Lecturer in Computing where he now
researches communications systems, multiprocessors, program development environments
and interactive graphics.

An Innovative, Shared Intelligent Network Service

W R Smith, J S Hubley
American Telephone and Telegraph
Company, USA

The expansion of customer communications needs, the convergence of communications and data processing technologies, and the evolving public policy regarding the role of a common carrier have led to the development of a unique intelligent data network concept. The implementation of the concept will require the execution in the network of customer-written programs that are linked together by a communications transmission capability that creates a virtual, distributed intelligent network for communications. This integration of computer functions and services which have not been subject to government regulation, and communications functions and services which have been traditionally subject to government regulation has been the subject of public debate.

1. INTRODUCTION

By the mid-1970's the revolutionary advances in microelectronics had opened new opportunities for meeting the information needs of organizations and individuals. The potential for change challenged conventional thinking regarding the kinds of equipment, systems, organizations and public policies most suitable to realize the advantages offered by the new technology.

Microelectronics technology could be applied to data processing systems and to communications systems. Many large organizations had begun to combine data communications and data processing to create significant information systems that defied easy categorization into the data processing equipment business or the communications services business.

The tradition of governmental provision or economic regulation of communications services and the rapid growth of data processing equipment suppliers as competitive businesses raised questions of public policy regarding information systems. Efforts to resolve these questions have been protracted, and risk has been increased for those considering investments to exploit the new capabilities. At the same time our societies have experienced increasing needs to improve productivity in the broad sense, and new information systems appear to offer great promise in improving the management of resources and the direction of efforts for meeting the complex needs of society.

2. STRATEGIC PLANNING

From the viewpoint of the American Telephone and Telegraph Company (AT&T) a number of strategic questions were raised by the new opportunities and changing conditions. Cost projections for logic and storage sug-gested that customers would find it increasingly attractive to substitute these functions for transmission, where feasible, to reduce the overall cost of information systems. In order to maintain and strengthen its position as a supplier of complete communications systems, it would be necessary to exploit the capabilities of microelectronics to meet customer needs. Three types of considerations drove strategic planning: (1) customer needs, (2) technical and economic factors, and (3) public policy. The inter-relations among these considerations and the rapid rate of change in each required review of all three whenever a variation in any was considered.

3. CUSTOMER NEEDS

A number of problems exist in the complex information systems that dominate the market place. Historically, users have tended to develop and use information systems to solve one business problem or application at a time, thereby creating a multiplicity of single-application networks. These networks are frequently incompatible with each other because the terminals and computers on one network often cannot transmit data to terminals and computers on other networks. Multiple networks also have resulted in substantial under-utilization of resources, including data communications personnel, equipment, and transmission paths, thereby decreasing productivity. In order to improve resource utilization, users require an information system that is able to integrate diverse terminals into a single network for access to multiple business applications.

A second major problem is the relative inflexibility of users' information systems. Today, many users find it difficult to expand or otherwise modify their data communication networks to accommodate changing business requirements, such as changing traffic volumes, new applications or new terminal equipment. In many cases, it is virtually impossible to add technically advanced terminals without substantially redesigning or replacing the user's existing information system.

A third major problem is that users find the task of network management increasingly difficult, expensive, and time-consuming. However, the need to manage the investment represented by these networks and to monitor their performance is growing as the investments and operations take on greater importance to the customer's business.

In order to achieve the desired level of flexibility, users require separation between the functions that control the terminal network and the functions that control the operation of application programs. Further, they need to be able to customize their resources to meet unique requirements. These capabilities are important steps to allowing migration to newer technologies or newer adaptations of current technologies, at the user's own pace, without having to make wholesale changes in the communications equipment and related software.

A fourth major problem is the high start-up costs associated with designing and implementing information systems. This has created barriers particularly for smaller users who have limited volumes of data traffic. Even larger users have concentrated primarily on high payback applications due to the cost and complexity of implementing individual networks.

4. SERVICE CONCEPT

A variety of service concepts were postulated as the basis for the establishment of functional needs upon which technical studies could be made. The concept selected for ongoing effort was that of an intelligent shared network. Within the United States of America the network would consist of a large number of dispersed service points interconnected by transmission capabilities. At the service points the customers would be offered network interconnection, communications processing, data storage, and data transmission. The service points were envisioned as communications processing nodes interconnected by a switched data communications network.

Most previous data communications systems were private networks wherein one or more host computers were connected by dedicated transmission channels to dispersed data terminals. Although public data networks offered some advantages over private networks through efficiencies in sharing channels and operating expenses, they offered limited capability to substitute storage and processing for transmission. By making these capabilities generally available at dispersed locations, it would be possible to limit the interactive communications required to control terminals and support data entry by operators to the local access channels connecting the terminals to the service points.

The conceptual separation of transmission from nodal services would provide flexibility to utilize various transmission capabilities without structural redesign of the overall intelligent network. Studies indicated that packet switching would be economical for a large range of customer needs, including responsive interaction across the network. However, requirements were foreseen where slower response and less costly bulk transfer capabilities would be desirable.

Because of customer needs for a very great variety of terminal types, it was decided that the intelligent shared network should be offered disaggregated from local access channels and terminals. This would enable many vendors to apply their ingenuity in devising ways to exploit the capabilities of the network, making it attractive for use by the maximum number of customers.

It was decided that the intelligent network should emphasize usage pricing so that customers would pay only for capabilities actually used. Moreover, the various functional capabilities of the network would be offered independently to permit customers to select the most advantageous combinations for each application. Thus, charges would be made separately for network termination (ports), communications processing, storage, and transmission.

By supporting many terminal protocols, speed conversion, and code conversion it would be possible for many types of terminals and computer hosts to intercommunicate using the intelligent shared network. However, information systems depend on prearranged data formatting to process information. The number of different formats and the complexity of possible conversions made it unfeasible to offer the necessary conversions as optional selections built into a fixed design. This view led to the conclusion that support for customer programming of the intelligent network would be mandatory.

Many design problems as well as related additional customer needs were introduced by the decision to support customer programming. It would be necessary to avoid undesired interactions among customers. Additional concerns for data protection and resource controls were raised. It would be necessary to establish a logical structure for the service that could be retained over several generations of hardware and system software in order to protect the investment made by customers in preparing programs. Participation by customers in the design of programs to operate on a distributed system required a logical view of the system that would be easy to learn and apply. The logical structure would have to include convenient mechanisms to allow the customer to control use and charging for resources as well as access to his data.

5. LOGICAL RULES

Some of the fundamental logical rules that were adopted for the intelligent shared network follow:

1. Programs are the basic logical entities. They have address identification and reside at service points. They control access to files and ports.

2. All logical communications within the intelligent shared network are by calls between programs.

3. All system capabilities are made available to programs by the execution of system commands expressed as statements in the high-level programming language.

4. No program may make a call to another program anonymously. The handling of call setup by the system identifies the calling program to the called program so that authorization screening cannot be circumvented.

5. Standard authorizations controlled by the customer determine whether a program will accept a call and how execution of the called program will be billed.

6. Standard applications program packages, such as those for the message service, are built upon the fundamental logical structure.

6. CONCLUSIONS

Changing customer needs, technical capabilities, and public policy led to strategic decisions regarding the type of future activities that would be sought by AT&T. One project that has resulted is the development of a new intelligent shared data communications network. The considerations that led to the selection of the specific service concept have been reviewed. The effectiveness of the effort may best be judged by future experience. At this time action by the Federal Communications Commission on a capitalization plan to allow the formation of a separate subsidiary to offer the service in the United States of America is pending. Testing and debugging of hardware and software is in process, and customer needs are being evaluated for initial utilization of the service.

Bill Smith received his B.S. degree in Electrical Engineering in 1947 and his M.A. degree in Mathematics in 1962. Mr. Smith has held numerous positions in marketing, development, manufacturing, and implementing both data processing and data communications products and services. He was founder of Terminal Communications, Inc., a manufacturer of data terminals, and a development engineering manager for IBM. He is a member of IEEE and was the 1980 ICCC Conference Chairman. Presently, he is the Director of Project Implementation for AT&T Long Lines.

Jim Hubley received his B.S. degree in Mathematics in 1968 and his M.B.A. degree in 1974. After joining the Western Electric Corporation in 1968, Mr. Hubley held positions in the fields of computer systems operations and maintenance and software systems development and documentation, at both Western Electric and Bell Laboratories. He has taught courses in data processing engineering and operations and presently is the AT&T Product Manager responsible for all product plans and requirements for AT&T's enhanced network services.

Deployment Considerations for a Shared, Intelligent Network

S J Barbera, D J Sandow
American Telephone and Telegraph
Company, USA

An innovative, shared intelligent network implemented through a network of storage and processing nodes interconnected by a separate packet switched transmission network presents unique deployment considerations. Customers will obtain access at specific geographical locations, known as service points. These service points are provided by a variety of possible implementations. This paper will describe some of the significant attributes of deployment planning including: the selection of service point implementation, the control of service point growth, and the control of service point migrations.

1. INTRODUCTION

Deploying a ubiquitous shared intelligent network where none exists today and having that network attain a high degree of stability within a short period of time are by themselves significant problems. Paralleling these major activities are technological development, evolution of strategic plans and implementation reality. The simultaneous consideration of these issues is addressed in this paper.

The plan for directing and managing this growth must recognize the dynamic nature of the industry and of any new data service. It must therefore acknowledge the inability to predict exactly where customers will be located or to predict customers' community of interest with one another. It must permit the maximum exploitation of all the processing power available in the network at any time. The plan described below has been selected as the model for deployment of this shared intelligent network.

2. OVERVIEW OF THE NETWORK DESIGN

The shared intelligent network service is offered at geographically distributed service points. These service points are of two varieties: nodes and remote front ends.

Each node consists of a number of computer processors and their required peripheral data storage devices. The number of processors at a single node can range from 2 to 10 or more, dependent upon market demand and available hardware configurations. Each node is the service point for its city and serves as host for remote front ends in nearby cities.

Cities which require service points, but do not require the computing capacity of a node, are equipped with remote front ends. Each remote front end has the capacity to handle multiples of 24 lines using different styles of hardware configuration. The early remote front ends are statistical multiplexors. Later implementations of remote front ends include processors which are responsible for all protocol and access line handling functions independent of the nodal processors described above.

Most of the remote service points will grow as the network matures and will be upgraded to a node in subsequent years. This process is described in Section 8.

The remote front end service points are connected to the host node by diversely routed digital data circuits acquired from a common carrier under tariff. The nodes themselves are interconnected by a packet switching network designed to operate using the CCITT X.25 standard. Such a packet switching service is a planned offering of the American Telephone and Telegraph Company in the United States of America. It is acquired at tariff prices for use by the shared intelligent network.

3. PHYSICAL ENVIRONMENT

The successful deployment of the shared intelligent network is dependent upon the availability of suitable physical quarters.

The smallest of the remote front end locations requires about 400 square feet (40 square meters) of space conditioned to ordinary administrative office standards. These spaces are acquired in commercial buildings situated reasonably close to a common carrier wire center.

The larger remote front end service points will require about 2,000 square feet (185 square meters) and will be located in one of two different environments:

- If the service point is not expected to grow to the size of a processing node, the remote front end is located autonomously in quarters described above.

- If the remote front end is expected to be replaced by a node within 24 months of its initial service, then a node site (see description below) is acquired, and the remote front end is installed in that location. This will permit the upgrading of the service point to a node configuration without requiring network customers to rearrange their access lines.

Each node requires 12,000 to 15,000 square feet (1,100 to 1,400 square meters). About 8,000 to 10,000 square feet (750 to 925 square meters) is a computer room with temperature and humidity controlled environment, a raised continuous access floor, and rigorous physical security. This installation always has an uninterruptible power supply with a battery reserve averaging one hour. If it is anticipated that the service point will grow larger than the capacity of one node, then an additional 8,000 to 10,000 square feet are required for a second node at the same location.

Two nodes operating in the same building would consume between 5,000 and 10,000 pairs of distribution wires from the local common carrier. This number is an upper boundary on the number of distribution pairs which can be effectively administered between a wire center and a single data processing center.

Sites suitable for remote front end installations have been readily acquired. Sites suitable for a node are available in many medium size cities. However, the deployment plan described in Section 8 has been modified on several occasions due to the unavailability of suitable space in specific target cities.

4. CHARACTERISTICS OF THE HARDWARE EVOLUTION

A shared intelligent network must grow continuously, even as the available hardware evolves. It is axiomatic that processor technology will evolve at a regular pace. However, the exact availability and compatibility of new hardware types cannot be specifically scheduled.

The shared intelligent network is planned to evolve on the following basis. First, it can be predicted that the price/performance of processors will improve (conservatively) three fold every four years. This expected price/performance improvement will be realized in the network by tripling the capacity of the node processors while assuming that the footprint, power requirement, heat load, and price all remain the same.

Further, it is assumed that node configurations are improved through more efficient interprocessor communications at a rate which will permit an additional three-fold improvement in performance every four years.

These assumptions are smoothed and used to create model aggregate capacity assumptions for each of the next five to eight years. In this manner, it is possible to intelligently plan deployment for the network based on predictable evolution, without having specific architectures defined or developed. Thus, the pragmatic deployment plan becomes a requirement for the developers to meet and challenges the developer to continuously adapt to new technologies in order to improve the capacity of each node.

The plan for deploying these nodes of the evolving capacity in the service point cities is described in Section 8.

5. CHARACTERISTICS OF THE DEMAND

The shared intelligent network must grow to serve a large number of customers in a very short span of years. It is inescapable that deployment planning must take place well in advance of precise demand forecasts. Indeed, equipment representing substantial investment is planned and installed even prior to the product announcement.

To efficiently plan for the growth of a network whose customers are undefined, the following demand assumptions are made:

- A shared intelligent network operating as a utility will attract customers with a demographic distribution comparable to the population of the United States. For example, if a particular geographic region contains 5 percent of the population, then at any time during the growth of the network, 5 percent of its capacity should be dedicated to serving this particular region.

- It is assumed that the distribution of customers will not change because the network grows. Rather, the network growth will be tuned to satisfy measurable variation in customer distribution.

- Because the network will be shared among a number of customers, the demands of no one customer will be permitted to bias the growth of the shared network.

- It is assumed that each terminal connected to the network can be described exactly by standard characteristics of processing, storage and transmission requirements. Even in the early years of growth, it is assumed that the law of large numbers applies.

- It is assumed that the cost or availability of transport links among service points do not enter into the economics of locating service points. Service points are located in those regions where customers are likely to exist. By treating all transport links as infinite in size, it is only necessary to optimize the location of service points within each geographic region. It is not necessary to optimize the location of service points with respect to one another.

- Minimal attempt is made to reduce capital expense by managing the timing of the introduction of additional capacity. This shared intelligent network is planned to double in capacity every six months. Thus, a 40 percent overforecast at any service point will merely lead to overprovisioning which should be absorbed within three months.

During the first four years, it is expected that demand for the service will exceed supply. During this constrained growth period, the availability of the network to customers can be managed in order to maximally exploit capacity as it is installed.

An understanding and acceptance of these simplified demand assumptions permit the creation of a framework for tactical deployment planning which is more adaptable than deployment planning based on precise customer demand forecasts.

6. PERMISSIBLE RATES OF GROWTH

The rate of growth of service points and nodes is keyed to meeting a mature network demand after the fifth year. As currently envisioned, that demand will be satisfied by between 100 and 200 nodes of the technology likely to be available in the fifth year.

The growth of capacity need not be linear, for three reasons. First, the growth of customer demand is likely to be geometric for the first few years. Second, the schedule should be structured so as to deploy the maximum number of nodes with the highest order of technology. In other words, as much of the capacity as possible should be available from those nodes with the best price/performance profile. Third, the organization created to achieve deployment must have adequate time to develop and refine its installation methods in the early years.

For these reasons, the growth of a fixed number of nodes per year is not considered. Instead, deployment is planned to progress at the following rates:

Second year	– 1 node per month
Third year	– 2 nodes per month
Fourth year and beyond	– 3 nodes per month

This rate of deployment satisfies the approximate demand assumption that the network should double in size every six months. In addition, it gives the engineering and maintenance force the opportunity to evolve methods which will permit one node to be installed every 10 days.

Note that the installation of three nodes per month does not imply that three additional service points or physical locations will be constructed for service each month in the fourth year. By the fourth year, it is believed that about half the nodes will be entries into new service points, while the other half represents the subsequent nodes installed in preexisting sites in the very largest cities or remote front end sites converted to nodes.

7. SECTORING

Before proceeding with the specifics of the deployment plan, it is well to discuss the sectoring philosophy which underlies the rapid growth of a shared intelligent network. As described above, the deployment is based on an assumption that demand will follow the demographic characteristics of the total population. Further, it is assumed that service points will be located optimally with regard to customers, not with regard to other service points. Thus, it is reasonable to view the entire served area (the continental United States) as composed of a series of equal sectors. At its simplest, if 100 nodes were deployed, then each would serve a sector containing 1 percent of the population. At one extreme, if New York City and its immediate suburbs comprise 8 percent of the population, then it would have 8 sectors and consequently 8 nodes in a 100 node configuration. At another extreme, a sector could include several states.

The first attempt at sectorization plans for the end of the second year when there will be 10 nodes in service. At that point, each of those nodes must support approximately 10 percent of the population (10 percent of the connected terminals). Each of these 10 nodes must be located near the weighted geographic center of the sector for which it is defined. At the beginning of the third year, each of the 10 sectors is further subdivided, resulting in some 30 sectors each of which serves approximately 3 percent of the network demand. This process is repeated annually.

This deployment approach forces the early nodes into cities which may not be the largest city in their sector, but which are well positioned with regard to serving all the terminals located within their sector.

An example of the sectoring model for the end of the second year is shown in Figure 1.

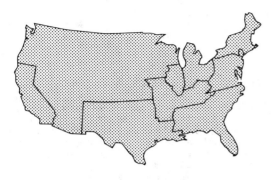

Fig. 1 Network sectors at the end of the second year.

8. A PLAN FOR MAXIMIZING THE OPTIONS

As described in Section 7, the second year network is built on the strategy that the United States is divided into 10 sectors. A node is constructed in a service point city in each of these 10 sectors, and service points equipped with remote front end processors are connected using dedicated data circuits. An example of this configuration appears in Figure 2.

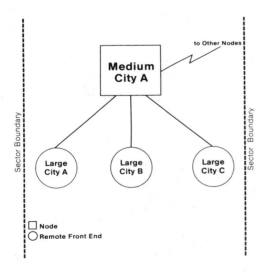

Fig. 2 A second year sector.

The largest cities in the sector are equipped with remote front end service points and are homed on a node constructed in a medium size city near the weighted geographic center of the sector.

During the third year, availability of newer technology nodes is assumed. One of these nodes is placed in the large city which most requires the capacity. This creates spare capacity at the second year node and permits additional service points to be established in additional medium size cities. See Figure 3.

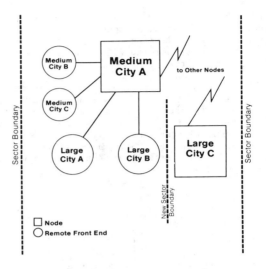

Fig. 3 During the third year, nodes are introduced in large cities.

In subsequent years, this strategy is repeated. Nodes are constructed in large cities as they are required, and additional medium size cities are connected to the original node. See Figure 4.

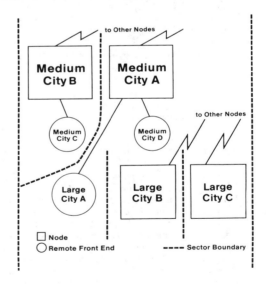

Fig. 4 In each subsequent year the growth pattern is repeated.

Through this deployment sequence, the nodes in the largest cities are never required to serve as host for service points in smaller cities. This permits the nodes in the largest cities

161

to serve primarily the local customer population. This rule stabilizes the growth of demand on the large city node by linking it only to the growth of demand of the large city customers. Placing early nodes in medium size cities permits reaction to demographic dynamics which might dictate a deployment order different from that which was originally assumed. It further maintains the capability for high utilization of deployed equipment. Finally, it makes the nodes in the larger cities immune from the problems of network rearrangement associated with the introduction of subsequent new nodes.

In the final year of this deployment strategy, the node installed in the second year has lived out its usefulness as the host machine for large cities in its sector. As a consequence of the total growth in demand, that node is now fully occupied satisfying the demands of the several medium size cities. See Figure 5.

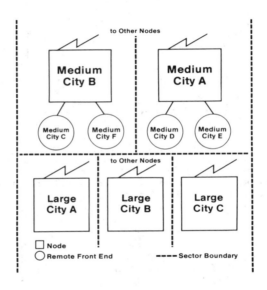

Fig. 5 Sector plan for the mature network.

9. MANAGEMENT OF NETWORK GROWTH

It is apparent that the physical configuration of the network changes continuously. Rather than enlarging each of a multitude of nodes as demand grows, we have chosen to start with a small number of nodes and add to the network. This choice will cause significant internal rearrangement of the shared intelligent network. The majority of these rearrangements will involve the substitution of processing nodes at locations where remote front ends were previously installed. Thus, the management of network rearrangement can be accomplished without involving customers of the network in the rearrangement process.

These rearrangements will be achieved by transporting customer programs and data bases from the old host node to the new node location, reconfiguring the links between the

remote front end and the new host node, and changing the network address tables throughout the network. These activities will be monitored from a central operations location and will be conducted during low traffic periods on the network. See "Operations Strategies for a Shared, Intelligent Network" by R. U. Faust and D. C. Wormley for further details.

10. THE DYNAMIC NATURE OF THIS PLAN

As has been described, this deployment plan is specifically oriented to maximize freedom of choice and reduce the reaction time needed to deploy capacity as the network grows. The growing experience of the engineering and operating forces can be exploited. The developers of this plan are confident that it will provide the greatest opportunity for flexibility and responsiveness to customer needs without affecting the profitability of this service venture.

S. J. Barbera is Assistant Vice President - Director of Major Projects in the Business Marketing Department of AT&T. He holds the Bachelor of Science degree in Physics from Long Island University. Mr. Barbera began his Bell System career in 1947, at New York Telephone Company, where he was named Assistant Vice President - Network Operations in 1971. He joined American Telephone and Telegraph Company as Engineering Director - Switching in 1973. From July 1977 to December 1979, Mr. Barbera was General Manager, Corporate Engineering and Product Planning, in the Corporate Engineering Division of the Western Electric Company. He assumed his present position at AT&T in 1980.

Dennis J. Sandow is Division Manager in AT&T responsible for implementing large shared intelligent networks. He is a 1962 graduate of Rensselaer Polytechnic Institute in Troy, New York, USA, with a degree in electrical engineering. He has worked for AT&T and its Long Lines Department since 1962 in various capacities managing plant operations, engineering, and cost accounting functions. From 1970 to 1972, he directed the fundamental planning for Long Lines overseas service and represented AT&T at CCITT and INTELSAT global planning meetings. He currently directs the deployment planning, engineering and plant operations for a large shared intelligent network within AT&T.

Implementing Applications in an Intelligent Network

L M Cozza
American Telephone and Telegraph
Co., USA

An intelligent data-communication network includes storage and processing that can be programmed by the user. The Bell System has developed such a network, to be managed by a separate subsidiary and used by a large number of customers for both intracompany and intercompany needs. Processing in the network permits data communication to be more efficient, and allows better utilization of user terminals and host computers. Network processing is a new alternative that can be used in conjunction with central and distributed data processing; it is particularly effective in applications that can be constructed in segments for execution on different, cooperating processors.

1. INTRODUCTION

On November 30, 1981, AT&T filed a capitalization plan describing an enhanced network service. The data-communication network for this service contains storage and processing that can be programmed by the user, and therefore is referred to as an intelligent network. The processing capability of the intelligent network provides a new alternative to the central-processing and/or distributed-processing alternatives that are used to solve business problems today. The need for an intelligent network, the characteristics and advantages of network processing, and a number of network-processing applications (including intercompany application) are discussed in this paper.

2. MARKET REQUIREMENTS

The intelligent network is designed to satisfy data-communication needs that have been identified during extensive customer studies over the past several years. Seven principal needs identified were:

. Nationwide Accessibility

The network should be accessible from anywhere in the United States. (International accessibility is highly desirable.)

. Reliability

The network should perform as reliably as the Bell System telephone network, and provide capabilities to easily implement problem-solving measures such as automatic backup, retry, and recovery procedures.

. Resource Utilization

The network should make efficient use of its own data-processing and data-communications equipment, and should allow effective use of the equipment on the customer premises.

. Compatibility

The network should allow communication between terminals and/or hosts with dissimilar protocols, speeds, or codes.

. Increased Terminal Functionality

The network should permit the user to add intelligence to existing terminal sites for improved operator productivity.

. Ease of Implementation

The network should permit reaction to changes, enhancement of existing applications, and addition of new applications, without disruption of ongoing operations.

. Customer Control

The network should let users make changes to their applications quickly. Routine maintenance of the network should be performed by the vendor.

Because no two applications (or customer implementations of applications) are the same, it must be possible to modify or tune the network. Therefore, intelligence (i.e., programmability) is included in the network so that the customer can perform the specific modifications and additions required.

3. NETWORK PROCESSING CHARACTERISTICS

Network processing provides many of the advantages attributable to distributed processing. It permits faster response time by providing processing and storage resources closer to the user, and these resources are shared between fewer users than in centralized solutions.

Network processing also limits some of the disadvantages of distributed processing. In particular, network processing:

- Reduces the need for planning the resources required at distributed processing points, because users utilize network resources at a remote point as much or as little as desired -- and pay for only what they use.

- Reduces the need for upgrading premises hardware resources after an application is installed, because network resources can extend the capabilities of existing premises equipment and/or accommodate extended usage.

- Minimizes the need for personnel at the remote site, because the hardware resources in the network are managed by the vendor of the network, and are not physically located at the customer's site.

- Increases the reliability at the remote site without the need for installing duplicate hardware there, because duplicate resources are provided in the network. Moreover, since the network resources are shared by many users, the cost per user is significantly lower.

The availability of processing and storage in the network allows for new and improved applications. For example, pre-processing and post-processing of input and output data streams might assist in the performance of an application by permitting changes to the input or output form that is presented to the operator without modification of the operating application. This processing might be prohibitively expensive for distributed processing or a private dedicated network because of hardware procurement and lead times, but it is easily implemented in the intelligent network.

Moreover, shared network processing and storage permit implementation in an evolutionary manner. Processing and storage can be distributed without the need to commit capital prior to design. Also, the final design of the application does not need to be committed before the application can be trialed on the network in a low-risk, try-it-and-change-it environment. Using the intelligent network, designs can be implemented, tested, and changed without affecting the applications already installed, and without the need to commit to system changes (hardware or software) specifically for the application until the need for change is demonstrated in the executing software.

In addition to this ability to segment an application for implementation and deployment, intelligence in the network can hide the implementation specificity of network components and devices. Thus, to the programmer, network terminals can be viewed as simple input/output devices; such processing functions as conversion of protocol, code, or speed are hidden from the user, and so are device-specific characteristics such as buffering and multiplexing. This simplified perception of the network reduces special handling of the telecommunications devices by the programmer, and can improve the extensibility of applications by reducing dependencies on specific implementation. Use of processing and storage to hide device specificity also has another advantage: system availability can be extended by automatic duplexing, alternate pathing, or other techniques, independently of the specification and implementation of the application.

4. APPLICATION CHARACTERISTICS

The intelligent network is particularly well suited for applications that are likely to change in function, user performance requirements, or transaction volume, or that make use of the network's versatility and capability for incremental growth. For example, consider the storage of a multi-megabyte date base. Centralized storage may be cost-effective if a large storage device costs less per bit than smaller devices, and if the data base can utilize the large device effectively. But if the data base overflows one device or does not utilize one device completely, or if one small segment of the data is used frequently by many terminals, then parts of the data base should be considered for segmentation and possible deployment near to the using terminals to reduce cost and, more importantly, to improve performance of the application using this data.

The same considerations apply to processing requirements for a user application. That is, segmenting the processing function to permit parallel execution of the processing function on different machines will often improve performance. Moreover, most applications are dynamic; the function, volume, or performance requirements are in a constant state of change. Thus, even if distributed processing and storage are used, new strategies must be continually developed to adapt these changes to the application environment. The capital investments already made in a distributed implementation then become suspect, but they may lock-in the implementation of the application -- resulting in a less-than-desirable application.

If, however, the application is designed for installation on the intelligent network, no capital purchases are required at the time of design. In fact, portions of the application may be moved to centralized or distributed processing elements, if the application is better served. Sections or segments of the application could be moved from the network to dedicated resources whenever the utilization of those resources offers a price/performance improvement.

5. IMPLEMENTING APPLICATIONS IN SEGMENTS

Since the intelligent network extends the range and variety of options -- i.e., the design space -- for data-communications/data-processing applications, it is realistic to investigate implementing parts of business applications in the network, as opposed to looking at implementing the total application in central, distributed, or network solutions. Business applications should be viewed with this segmentation of applications in mind so that the combined application can be implemented in all three of the alternatives if the price/performance is improved.

An example of this segmentation is the use of pre-processing -- that is, the modification of the input data stream in an existing operational data-communication application, without requiring modification of the application. For example, to modify an order-entry function so that a customer address is entered by the network instead of by the terminal operator, the customer name and address file could be placed in the intelligent network. The input data stream would contain the customer name supplied by the operator, and the customer address would be retrieved from the address file and inserted into the output data stream. The operator could then visually validate the total order and send it off to the host computer. The host computer would not have been interrupted until the time that this "validated" order was transmitted.

By this means, the number of transmissions to the host would be reduced. The host application would not have to be modified to handle the new transaction flow, because the record submitted to the host machine for processing would be identical to the record formerly submitted.

The entire input data stream could be validated by using the intelligent network to manage all of the operator-interactive traffic, accumulating the total transaction entry, and then submitting the "error-free" operator entry to the host machine; the operation would closely resemble a batch environment to the host. The efficiency of the central host would be improved, because it would be handling fewer transactions. Also, since the intelligent network is responsible for dealing with the time demands of the on-line operator, the host machine could be modified to schedule its resources more efficiently and not have to be as concerned with user response time.

This segmented treatment of business applications also makes it possible to use specialized programmers in developing the segments of the application. For example, the more user-oriented specialists can deal with the application segments that are in the intelligent network, while the more system-oriented personnel can be applied to the application segments that are implemented in the central host machine. So the intelligent network not only permits this segmentation, but also aids in management of the development process. It thus ensures successful management of the individual segments of the appli-

cation as well as the integration and testing of the whole.

Pre-processing in the network can also be used to let a single terminal access multiple applications that are already implemented in unique systems. A "switching" program can be built into the network to interface with the operator and provide menus and/or prompts to help the operator decide how to attach to the desired application. The program can then switch the operator to the desired system, and remove itself from the communication path. Alternatively, it can stay involved and provide a single interface to the operator while maintaining the interactions required by the applications of the installed systems. This network program must be aware of the interfaces to all of the applications, but can be totally independent of them. This arrangement thus permits the creation of user-friendly interfaces without affecting the application execution and without requiring changes to the applications.

After a telecommunications application is developed (usually not by the end-user organization), the format presented to the operator often requires some modification. The modification may be as simple as changing words that have a data-processing orientation rather than an end-user orientation, or it may be as significant as the need to add data fields to the input record. In either case, by utilizing the intelligent network in the implementation of the application, the user organization can get more involved in the design. It can specify and program the operator interactions in the network, thereby tuning the operator interface, while the data-processing organization specifies and programs the application in the host machine, thereby maintaining the integrity of the host application software. The user organization can trade off operator training costs against interface changes, permitting more timely implementation of these changes since the host application will not be involved. This arrangement eliminates the need for these operator interface changes to be scheduled into the data-processing organization backlog of larger, higher-priority developments.

6. INTERCOMPANY APPLICATIONS

The public nature of the intelligent network allows companies to intercommunicate data for operation of their businesses. It provides data-terminal compatibility, sharing/privacy controls for programs and data, and the ability to use pre- or post- processing in the network to modify the formats of the data communicated between companies with minimal impact on operational intracompany applications.

To fully realize the benefits of intercompany applications, the communicating companies must establish standards for the data to be exchanged and the format for exchanging it. This standardization does not require the companies to change internal procedures and formats, because the network can be used to reformat the input and output data to conform to individual company requirements. The exchange standardization is not a minor task, however, since the content and format must be unambiguous, extensible, and efficient.

After completion of the standards, the file system design -- including segmentation of the file and placement in central, distributed, or network processors -- is of prime importance. It is principally the file system that determines the extent of sharing and protection of exchange data, and ultimately who can join in the intercompany interchange. The intelligent network aids in the design process by providing programs that measure traffic patterns, thus identifying when to off-load data to the central or distributed systems as function and/or costs dictate.

A new company can be added to the data-exchange community without affecting the other companies. Once the new company programs the format translation between itself and the standard, it can exchange data with all of the companies already joined to the community.

7. A FINAL PERFORMANCE CONSIDERATION

In the Bell System implementation of the intelligent network, intelligence is placed at service points near the terminals or processors that access the network. Thus, communicating devices are decoupled by the processing and storage at each service point. The service point polls all of the devices attached to it, and polling between service points within the network is not necessary. This decoupling reduces the number of bits transmitted between service points, thereby providing a more effective utilization of the long-haul transmission facilities. Of course the limited-distance access lines to the service points do require the supervisory signals, and therefore do not experience this improved utilization effectiveness.

8. SUMMARY

The Bell System implementation of a public intelligent network provides a new design space for data-processing/data-communications solutions. It is truly a new alternative for processing, storage, and transmission; it enhances the utility of the other alternatives, and aids by providing a way to develop, test, and measure applications without committing to final hardware investment and deployment. This unique offering of a public intelligent network improves operator productivity by enabling the enhancement of applications without change-out of the application. It can also improve the efficiency of data exchange between companies, and should therefore stimulate the development of new applications in the intercompany marketplace.

Leonard M. Cozza is Manager of Marketing Services in Project Implementation at AT&T. He has worked in product development, architecture, and planning of office automation and data processing systems at Xerox, NCR, RCA, and IBM. His BS(EE) degree is from Carnegie-Mellon University.

Operations Strategies for a Shared Intelligent Network

R U Faust, D C Wormley
American Telephone & Telegraph
Company, USA

The commercial success of a large shared intelligent network depends on the viability of many components; the underlying technology, system architecture, marketing strategy, sales support, network deployment, and operations support. Presented in this paper are some of the philosophies and strategies used in the operation of a shared intelligent network with emphasis on how the initial philosophies affected subsequent network design. Examples highlight the unique nature of the service. For each of the basic operations strategies -- customer service provisioning, customer assistance, billing, engineering, administration and maintenance -- a description of the approach is provided along with the key issues such as the division of responsibility between customer and the network, degree of centralization, and the support of rapid network growth.

INTRODUCTION

The successful development and operation of any large service offering does not happen by chance. The basic operations philosophies or strategies must be determined in the early phases of service definition. Then, specific technical and organizational plans to implement these strategies should be defined and refined through the stages of function and performance definition, systems engineering, architecture, development, deployment, sales, and network operation.

This paper describes only a few of the operations strategies and philosophies adopted in the initial planning of a nationwide, shared intelligent data communications network. Emphasis is placed on how the initial philosophies affected subsequent planning and network design. Examples are used that highlight the unique nature of the service.

From the viewpoint of the network operations personnel, the physical network consists of communications processing nodes interconnected by transparent switched and/or dedicated transmission channels [1]. In the initial version of the network, internode transmission is provided by an X.25 based packet network. Operations planning for the intelligent network was based on the assumption that the packet network would be provided as a separate service, and that no sharing of operations staff, management, or systems could take place.

The intelligence in the service resides in the nodes, which consist of a number of interconnected computers, mass storage devices and front-end processors. Customers' terminals and hosts connect to the intelligent network through geographically dispersed service points. A service point may be implemented with a node, a front-end processor or multiplexor.

Figure 1 illustrates a small (2 node) network topology.

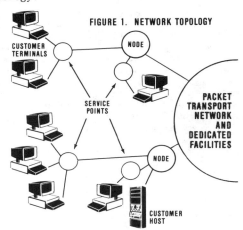

FIGURE 1. NETWORK TOPOLOGY

Independent of this physical topology, private logical subnetworks are implemented on the shared intelligent network, providing communications processing and network management to meet an individual customer's business needs. Communications processing includes not only the more traditional data network functions of code, format and speed translation, transmission, storage, and routing, but also includes an environment for the preparation and execution of customer-written programs.

A number of basic guidelines were established early in the planning process to drive more detailed design requirements.

One guideline was based on the assumption that intelligent network personnel would not have operational control over the access facilities between a customer's premises and the network service point location, since these would be provided by separate corporations.

However, in order to be as responsive as possible to customers' operational needs or difficulties with the network, a single point of operations contact for the customer was considered essential. No matter where a need might arise, or where a customer is located, customers would be provided with a preassigned assistance center for their questions.

Another guideline was that the customer program environment and its associated set of utilities and routines would be operated as a service independent of geographical location. Network operations would assure that customer programs and programs provided by the intelligent network could execute anywhere in the network at the level of performance selected by the customer.

A third guideline was the assumption that the intelligent network would be offered by an affiliate corporation separated from other Bell System affiliates. Because of this assumption, there would be no possibility of sharing an existing broad base of operations personnel. This factor, in addition to increasing expense considerations, contributed to establishing centralized operations centers in carefully selected locations and providing the technical capabilities to remotely operate the hardware and software components.

The final guideline used in planning the operation of the intelligent network was to provide customers with a rich set of network management capabilities that would complement network operations. Surveillance and customization tools were to be available to customers who wished to manage the logical and physical portions of their subnetwork, only involving intelligent network operations personnel where absolutely necessary.

The following sections will illustrate, by example, how the above guidelines were implemented:

SERVICE PROVISIONING

The provisioning or implementation of customer subnetworks on a nationwide shared intelligent network requires the careful coordination of many complex functions. This section deals with a description of functions to be performed and the planning for their support.

The elements to be provided for this service can be divided into two areas of responsibility: those that are customer-provided and those that are provided by the shared network service. Customers are responsible for their premises' terminals and hosts, access channels to the intelligent network service points, customer-developed application programs and customer changeable parameters. Network operations provisions the appropriate network resources, including ports, addresses, storage areas, and access to applications programs, based on customer service requests.

A fundamental philosophy of the intelligent network is that customers are responsible for

requesting the elements they require for their subnetworks, and that they have direct control over them once they have been provisioned by the network. The provisioning activity of the intelligent network operations is limited to the enabling of the basic features, physically installing equipment and assigning unique or security dependent resources consisting of ports, storage, addresses, and access to application programs. Supplemental network features, or feature attributes, are subsequently established and activated directly by the customer. This can be accomplished through customer control facilities interfacing either with a network-provided standard package or a customer-written program.

To provision a given customer's subnetwork, the intelligent network operations may have to assign, schedule, and coordinate the implementation of a large number of tasks at numerous service point locations in the nationwide network. In addition, data bases need to be generated to support ongoing operation of these subnetworks.

To support the provisioning of the shared intelligent network elements, and create the many data bases required, the provisioning process needs:

- an inventory of all assignable basic resources, both physical and logical, assigned and available,

- a task generation system which breaks a service order down to the tasks needed to be performed at every network location effected,

- a scheduler which assigns due dates to the tasks,

- a system which generates the customer specific table updates to be implemented at the service points,

- a means of update distribution to the processors and work centers involved in the above,

- a tracking mechanism for the completion of the above,

- a means of recording and tracking customer actions; e.g., attribute changes, for maintenance reasons, and

- a means of developing customer subnetwork profiles including "non-network;" e.g., access channel and terminal profiles and data to support the maintenance function.

This supports the first major provisioning aspect, the provision of the basic subnetwork.

The second major aspect of provisioning a customer's subnetwork deals with the development and installation of customer-or third party vendor-developed application programs. This is a two step process, one part done by the intelligent network and the "customizing" done by the customer.

A programming facility is provided as part of the intelligent network service. Using this facility, the customer develops an application program, and has that program compiled and linked, thus creating an executable load module ready to be loaded into a service point.

Based on a service order, the intelligent network operations assigns a unique address at every service point at which a customer has requested a program reside. Thus, logical "slots" are created into which the customer's application programs are subsequently loaded and made available for execution at the customer's request.

The system and process described here are initially implemented in a single center, which is responsible for the creation and distribution of all provisioning tasks and updates to the operations locations. Provisioning, implementation tracking and co-ordination, on a per customer basis, is performed by a customer network manager discussed in the following section.

CUSTOMER ASSISTANCE

The intelligent network will play its most comprehensive role supporting customer subnetworks that are characterized by many widespread and different terminal types, interacting with customer-or third party-written software, both in the network and in one or more customer host computers. Customer terminals and hosts will access the network service points using a variety of methods. With this complexity of customer and third party software and access vendor interfaces, it is essential that the points of demarcation between the customer, service point access, programs, and the intelligent network be planned so they are logical, clear, and definable during trouble isolation.

One of the more interesting points of demarcation is the one defining where the customer's responsibility for the application program ends and the intelligent network's responsibility for the communications processing environment begins. Since it is expected that customer application programs in one node will frequently interact with different programs in distant nodes in completing a customer transaction, the job of isolating a trouble to either the intelligent network or customer program is more challenging than in a centralized processing environment. The person responsible for trouble isolation of this sort must have the capability of viewing and understanding the intelligent network's hardware and software as well as the customer's application programs, terminals and hosts, and how these are configured to use the network.

The responsibility for isolating a trouble to the intelligent network, a customer applica-tion program, customer premises' equipment, or customer premises' access to network service points, is assigned to customer network management personnel located in intelligent network customer assistance centers. It is to these locations that customers are asked to report their operating difficulties. Each customer is assigned to a single customer network manager who will be responsible to that customer and interface on behalf of that customer with other intelligent network operations personnel.

Customer assistance centers are provided with surveillance, test, control and reconfigur-ation capabilities, along with customer-specific data to allow the isolation of most troubles. The goal is to complete this isolation while the customer is still on the telephone. If a trouble is identified within the intelligent network, additional capabilities are provided to allow the customer assistance center to isolate the problem and refer it to the repair organization responsible for an individual node, service point location, the packet transport network, or to the service provisioning organization. The customer assistance center will inform the customer of the expected time of resolution. The customer network manager will be responsible for tracking the restoral effort, and referring or escalating it to other work centers, the customer's sales team, or to upper management. In all cases, the customer network manager has the responsibility of keeping the customer informed of progress until the problem has been resolved.

The customer assistance center will also have the ability to track the progress of service provisioning efforts on behalf of the customer. Access to the service provisioning tracking system described earlier will allow the customer network manager to determine the status of a customer's order, the status of related orders, and planned and actual "service ready" dates. Based upon the needs of the customer, the customer network manager can ask that an order be rescheduled or otherwise modified. When an order is completed, the customer network manager's records will be updated by the tracking system.

As mentioned earlier, the intelligent network offers customers the ability to effectively manage their subnetworks, independently of network operations personnel. For those customers who would prefer not to exercise the full repertoire of management and administra-tive capabilities, the customer assistance center will respond to requests for control actions requested by authorized customer personnel. The assistance center has the ability to act as surrogate for customer control facilities.

The key to the level of responsiveness of this center is the range and sophistication of the interactive surveillance, test and control capabilities available to its personnel. The following are the basic categories of capabilities required for maintenance and administration of the intelligent network;

- Network equipment/transmission status reports

- Network operating system status reports

- Global network performance level reports

- Customer control activity audit logging

- Surrogate customer control

- Customer logical network configuration

- Customer logical network resource utilization

- Communications trace, error analysis and test

- Terminal and host access protocol analysis and test

- Customer-written program library access

- Customer program status and error analysis

- Surveillance and control of system recovery activities

- Service provisioning tracking

- Trouble report administration and tracking

These capabilities are then intended to support a highly responsive customer/intelligent network operations interface.

BILLING

The billing function must collect, summarize, and apply current prices to all data to generate a bill. Charges fall into three major categories: fixed monthly charges (e.g., private ports, reserved storage, etc.), non-recurring charges (e.g., installation or consultation), and usage sensitive charges (e.g., data transmission, demand processing and storage, and public dial port usage).

Since the generation of highly detailed bills is an expensive option not wanted by all customers, only summary bills are produced as a standard feature. However, customers will have the ability to inspect and analyze their own detailed usage data using their own programs and storage resident in the intelligent network. For maintenance reasons, the intelligent network operations also has the ability to inspect detailed data as required.

A billing system gathers usage data from the service points, fixed monthly charges from the provisioning system, and non-recurring items from various sources including Sales/Marketing. It then produces the customer bills monthly, retaining data for inquiry, maintenance and auditing purposes.

ENGINEERING AND DEPLOYMENT

The prime objective in the establishment of a shared intelligent network is to deploy sufficient resources to meet market demand in an economically-effective and timely manner.

The major challenge which occurs during the growth period of this network is to accomplish rapid growth while minimizing disruption of customer service. To accomplish this, the timing of the establishment of service points and a robust addressing plan are vital.

It will also be necessary to move customer resources from one location to another, for both network operations and customer reasons. It was imperative that we develop a means to accomplish such changes in minimal time.

The service point concept, which is basic to the network, is defined as that physical location where customers access the service. The customer obtains, from the carrier of his/her choice, access to the service point. To minimize the number of access line moves and the associated outage time required as the network grows, all service points must be equipped. All service point locations will have equipment ranging from multiplexers and remote front-end processers to nodes. When it becomes cost-effective to equip a service point with a physical node, the transmission channel between a multiplexer or remote front-end processor and the node can be removed with no effect on the customer access to that service point. It would also be possible to move the transmission channel between a multiplexer or remote front-end processor and a new node on a "flash cut" basis with no effect on the customer.

So that customers do not have to endure constant numbering addressing changes, there needs to be a addressing plan implemented in such a way that service point IDs become available consistent with primary market needs but independent of network topology. This is accomplished by determining the target number of service points and preassigning addresses to them.

A detailed description of this function and the solutions developed is addressed in [2].

ADMINISTRATION AND MANAGEMENT

To efficiently utilize intelligent network resources and optimize the network's ability to handle customer traffic, four specific functions must be performed. These are:

- System Software Administration
- Data Base Administration
- Node Administration
- Service Management

System Software Administration administers system software implemented at each service point of the intelligent network. In support of maintenance, detailed records of the in-effect software must be available on a real-time basis. Software updates must be planned and controlled so that "flash cuts," which are difficult to implement, are rarely, if ever, required. Mechanisms and procedures need to be available so that when system software changes must be made, they are accomplished in a way that affects service the least.

Data Base Administration is responsible for the efficient relationship between physical storage and logical data base structure.

Node Administration is responsible for three major functions performed on a node specific basis: (1) The Traffic Data Administration function gathers, validates, and distributes processor and communications resource data. (2) The Resource and Performance Administration function monitors utilization levels of all intelligent network components that make up nodes or service points. Based on analysis of such data against expected performance and capacity parameters, requests for maintenance action or additional equipment provision may be originated. (3) The Assignment Administration function is based on '2' above. By providing resource assignment priorities to the service provisioning function described earlier, load balancing can be achieved and maintained without costly service affecting rearrangements. In addition, Node Administration performs a general coordinative function in cases of node or service point equipment additions.

Service Management builds on the function of node administration, in that it performs similar functions for the complex of interconnected nodes, viewing each node as a basic component. Its primary function is to optimize the intelligent network's ability to handle inter-nodal customer traffic. This is accomplished by preventing or controlling congestion in the network that might be caused by overloads or failures. In addition, Service Management performs a control and coordinating function when changes which affect multiple service points are made to the network.

Because of this "global" responsibility, this function must be performed by a single center. The center must receive pertinent data about the performance of each node, and its effect on the communication between service points as well as the status of the transport integrity between nodes and service points. Data reported must be discreet and comprehensive enough to allow isolation of the cause so that appropriate actions, such as flow control, can be initiated or overridden if required. Since, in distributed processing and packet switched networks, corrective actions must often be taken in seconds, automation of much of the analysis and corrective action is required. Further, corrective action must be taken at the lowest level so that higher levels are not affected. Basic service management capabilities must also be resident in each individual node so that control actions can be taken even when the node is isolated from the central management function.

MAINTENANCE

Maintenance has been divided into three areas: customer assistance, node maintenance, and access management. Customer assistance was discussed in an earlier section; the remaining two are explored next.

Node maintenance consists of trouble detection, isolation, restoration, and repair of node and service point hardware and Bell-written software. It is distinct from customer assistance in that customer assistance personnel have a nationwide view of the network for a given set of customers. Node maintenance has a view of only a portion of the network, including all customers that are dependent on that portion. A major emphasis of node maintenance is to centralize a "critical mass" of functions in regional maintenance work centers.

The regional node maintenance centers have administrative and technical control over node and service point components as well as local work forces. The node and service point hardware is configured with redundancy to be automatically and/or remotely reconfigured with minimal or no disruption to active customers. In addition, regional forces have access to both system- and application-level software that duplicates on-site capabilities.

Access maintenance personnel are responsible for service provisioning implementation, trouble isolation, and repair of the intelligent network owned-or operated-portions of customer access and ports at service points. From an equipment standpoint, activities consist of the installation and maintenance of the intelligent network-owned data set and other channel terminating equipment up to the point of demarcation defined by the termination of the customer obtained transmission channel.

Access maintenance personnel are also responsible for the initialization and operation of the customer's terminal or host with intelligent network protocols. Regional centers are provided with the following access maintenance capabilities to realize this goal:

- access line status reporting

- access protocol error logging

- error thresholding and alarming

- remote protocol initialization

- protocol option modification

- network communications equipment(i.e., front-end processors, concentrators, etc.) status logging

- tracing communications through network in progress over an access line

- monitoring line and link level protocol

SUMMARY

Several of the operations philosophies and strategies for a shared intelligent data communications network have been described and their implementation illustrated. The intent was to provide a sample of the operations planning that is required for the development of a responsive and efficient shared, nation-wide customer-programmable data communications network. Figure 2 summarizes the relationship of work functions and centers to the network.

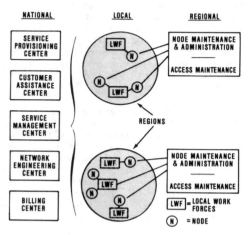

FIGURE 2. OPERATIONS WORK CENTER STRUCTURE

No matter how careful the planning, knowledge gained from continual experience must be used to revise and redefine operations objectives, strategies, and capabilities. In order to ensure this rapid feedback, most of the operations support systems described are implemented on the network in the form of an "operations subnetwork", similar to the subnetwork a customer would use [3]. The operations subnetwork, with its special privileges, can be programmed by field operations personnel independently from the generic or system software. The operations subnetwork approach decouples operations support system revisions from the inherently slower rate of revision of generic software, and places the user of the operations capabilities in a position of responsibility for their development. In addition, the approach requires field operations to be not only one of the first but also a permanent customer of the network. This on-going experience will help ensure that the intelligent network operations personnel are responsive to and aware of the customer's experience.

REFERENCES

[1] B. P. Donohue, III and J. F. McDonald, "An Innovative Architecture for a Programmable Shared Network," ICCC '82.

[2] S. J. Barbera and D. J. Sandow, "Deployment Considerations for a Shared, Intelligent Network," ICCC '82.

[3] O. W. Traber, "Implementation of Operations Support on the Supported Network," ICCC '82.

Rainer U. Faust received his BS in Electrical Engineering from Western Michigan University in 1969 and an MBA from the University of Michigan in 1971. He then joined Michigan Bell Telephone Company and managed the operation of voice switching systems until 1976 when he joined AT&T in Basking Ridge, N. J. There he was responsible for the planning of advanced voice networks including Enhanced Private Switched Communications Service and Electronic Tandem Network. Since 1977 he has directed the development of operations strategies for shared intelligent data networks at AT&T, where he is a District Manager.

Donald C. Wormley received his BS and MS in Electrical and Computer Engineering from Clarkson College in 1973 and 1974 respectively, and the degree of Engineer in Computer Science from Columbia University in 1977. In 1974 he joined Bell Laboratories in Holmdel, NJ, where he helped plan the feature complement of PBX systems. In 1976 he was responsible for aspects of the systems engineering of shared intelligent networks in the areas of architecture, customer features, operations planning and support, and competitive analysis. Since 1981, Mr. Wormley has been responsible for the operations support of shared and private intelligent networks at AT&T, where he is a District Manager.

Systems Engineering for Intelligent Data Network Services

A F Rehert
Bell Telephone Laboratories, USA

In this paper, examples of Systems Engineering for a new intelligent data network service being developed by Bell Laboratories will be presented. These examples include:

- Modeling example customer business data flow scenarios
- Modeling technology to compare customer alternatives
- Applying business flow models and technology models to analyze customer choices
- Validating functional requirements against representative examples
- Applying operations activity models to operations mechanization planning

In addition, by projecting customer needs and technologies into the future, systems concepts offering opportunities for meeting future customer needs are identified.

INTRODUCTION

Systems Engineering for new systems and services at Bell Laboratories has been an evolving discipline. In this paper, examples of System Engineering activities which have contributed to the development of a new Intelligent Data Network Service will be described.

What Is Systems Engineering?

Systems Engineering refers to the functions of system development that result in

1. measurable technical requirements,
2. systems analyses and methods.

The technical requirements are used by system architects, designers and testers to build the needed system capabilities. The analyses and methods are applied to sales, deployment and operations plans as the service is offered. They form the basis for both requirements and economic tradeoff studies and, therefore, support both the planning and implementation phases of a project.

What Is An Intelligent Data Network Service?

To a systems engineer, an Intelligent Data Network Service takes on at least three forms.

First, from a customer point of view, it represents a collection of features and capabilities that can be applied to solve business problems [SH82].

Second, from an engineering point of view, the Intelligent Data Network Service represents a collection of equipment to be placed in locations and quantities to serve customer needs [BS82].

Third, from an operations point of view, the Intelligent Data Network represents a collection of work centers and associated data flows which must meet customer demands for system resources and respond to needs for maintenance actions [FW82].

These three views must be blended by Systems Engineers into a coherent whole serving the many masters of the different viewpoints. In this paper, we look at a few examples of how this was done for an Intelligent Data Network Service under development at Bell Laboratories.

CUSTOMER/MARKETING APPLICATIONS OF SYSTEMS ENGINEERING

Systems Engineering has been applied in the customer/marketing area by:

1. developing models of customer business scenarios expected to benefit from the application of Intelligent Data Network Service capabilities,
2. mapping these business flows onto technology models of customer alternatives,
3. comparing customer alternatives using cost as a decision variable, and
4. applying the resulting cost tradeoffs to the requirements and early design plans to best match market needs.

Business Flow Models

The objective of business flow models is to provide a complete and precise description of target customer business needs. Such a description has been developed using an appropriate language and methodology which is commonly called structured design [GS79].

Because a customer's business flow is generally complex and highly intricate in terms of information flow, we must first aim at understanding WHAT needs to be accomplished in the business flow rather than HOW it is accomplished. In other words, we seek an implementation-free scenario.

To achieve a truly implementation-free description, we must speak only in logical constructs. Four such logical units suffice: (1) a logical source or sink of information [graphically denoted by a cube], (2) a logical process [rectangle], (3) a logical data store [open rectangle] and (4) a logical information flow [arrow]. A source or sink of data identifies a business unit which originates or requires information. A logical process is an activity which transforms the information.

Once we have a logical description of the business flow in diagramatic display, we document the scenario. Processes are precisely described (structured English) and information units are unambiguously defined (data dictionaries).

In Figure 1 we see an example of the use of these techniques. The process begins with a high level, implementation free description of a customer's order fulfillment process. A business unit called a sales office sends information (sales transaction) into the process. The process uses data stores (reference files) to perform its functions. The output of the process is status data returned to the sales office.

BUSINESS FLOW MODELING
STRUCTURED BUSINESS FLOW

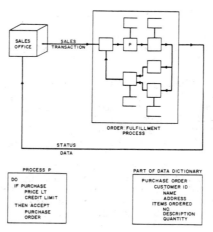

FIGURE 1

We could go top-down through the order fulfillment process identifying its functions in more and more detail. Every process is documented in structured English, every label defined in a data dictionary. With this kind of effort, we have a precise description of a customer's business application.

Technology Models

Technology modeling is intended to capture the essential price/performance characteristics of computer/communications systems so that price/performance can be estimated under a wide variety of customer/application/system configurations.

Price/performance modeling is accomplished by first characterizing the performance (or capacity) of components. The component capacity is determined by relating performance objectives to delays calculated by performance models. Then the system price is estimated for a particular situation.

Processor delay can be estimated through the use of queueing network models which model resources (CPU, disks, etc.) as queues [K76]. For a given application scenario, the capacity of the processor can be estimated by relating the application performance objective to the delay calculated by the model.

Access accounts for the other major component of delay. Well-known formulas exist for the delay for various communications protocols [M72]. Line capacities can then be obtained.

Pricing models take the component capacity information along with specific customer volume and geography input to configure and price-out an end-to-end system. It is important to configure an entire end-to-end system so that the many price/performance trade-offs inherent in each system are included.

Modeling Customer Choices

From a set of computer/communications system alternatives, there is one which offers the best price/performance for a particular customer/application situation. Through use of the models described above, it is possible to outline those customer characteristics most appropriate (in a price/performance sense) for each of the alternatives. For the Intelligent Data Network Service, this approach has been used to set performance objectives relative to customer alternatives, to validate proposed price levels, and to identify target customer/application situations. As an example, we will consider a Central Host solution, a Remote Computing Service solution, and an Intelligent Terminal solution to a customer business scenario.

The Central Host solution is assumed to have the following structure. A host owned or leased by the customer is located at a single location. The customer has a fixed number of remote offices located over some geographical area. Terminals are located at the offices. All processing and storage is done at the central host. Processing for the application is a small part of the host's resources and is charged on a usage sensitive basis.

The Remote Computing Service (RCS) solution is assumed to be similar to the Central Host solution except for processing and storage costs which are typically higher than for customer owned and maintained hosts.

This premium provides customers access to high value software facilities and data bases and system management.

The Intelligent Terminal solution assumes that processing and storage is provided local to the source of data input. Processing charges are not usage sensitive in this solution. A central host is generally included in this solution as a central collection or switching point.

A direct price/performance comparison of these alternatives can be made by configuring each system for a particular set of circumstances and comparing the price. It is useful to calculate the system prices as a function of parameters which characterize the customer. Two such parameters are the area over which the customer's office locations are dispersed normalized to the area of the U. S. (geographical dispersion), and the rate at which an office location performs the application scenario (activity rate).

In order to display results of the comparisons compactly and intuitively, we will take the following approach. Given an application scenario, each pair of values for customer activity rate and geographical dispersion describes a particular kind of customer and a particular set of alternative configurations. There will be one lowest cost alternative for each such pair of values. For certain pairs of values, the cost of two alternatives will be equal. The locus of all such "breakpoints" defines a boundary between two regions in customer parameter space. In one region, one competitive solution offers the lowest cost; and in the other region, another alternative solution offers the lowest cost.

This approach reveals the customer geography and volume characteristics most favorable in a price/performance sense to each system. Figure 2 displays the comparative results on the customer parameter plane for a message preparation function.

EXAMPLE OF SYSTEM TECHNOLOGY COST BREAKPOINTS

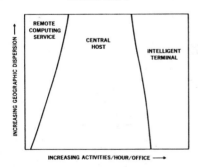

FIGURE 2

The results indicate that the Central Host solution is least costly for many of the assumed customer conditions. Centralized Hosts offer relatively cheap processing but require a relatively expensive communications network for dispersed customers.

The Remote Computing Service solution is similar to the Central Host solution because it uses the same technology. The difference in system prices between an RCS solution and a Central Host solution increases as the processing usage increases. Thus, the RCS solution is least costly for customers who have relatively small processing needs, and do not wish to manage a dedicated central host system. The RCS solution has an advantage over the Central Host solution at higher geographic dispersions because the RCS model assumes that remote service points were provided to customers.

The Intelligent Terminal solution offers the lowest communications costs of any of the alternatives because most of the processing is performed locally. This is the classical advantage of distributed processing. It also potentially offers the lowest processing costs when the processor can be sufficiently utilized. However, an under-utilized processor becomes expensive on a per activity basis. Thus, the Intelligent Terminal solution is least costly at activity rates which are large enough to sufficiently load the processor.

This approach quantifies results which may otherwise be only intuitive. It is useful input for product planning as well as sales support functions.

Requirements Validation

Requirements validation assesses the degree to which the functional and price/performance aspects of the service meet the needs of example applications. Requirements validation builds upon the business flow models and technology models discussed earlier. The functional requirements were validated by applying (on paper) the Intelligent Data Network Service to solve example customer business problems.

The Intelligent Data Network Service solutions were designed using its networking and programming capabilities. Using the business flow models, program modules were written to validate the service. Requirements validation was done to test three areas:

1. The ability of the service capabilities to implement the customer application.
2. Expected ease of use by customer programmers, and
3. Functional capabilities and price/performance characteristics provided by other customer choices.

Several areas of functional enhancements were identified which enabled key requirements and design improvements at early stages of design.

DEPLOYMENT/ENGINEERING APPLICATIONS OF SYSTEMS ENGINEERING

Systems Engineering has been applied in the deployment/engineering area by developing models and applying judgements to the strategic and tactical aspects of network provisioning.

Network Planning

An Intelligent Data Network is a classic example of a distributed network with various functions and associated hardware/software capable of being deployed nationwide. Network planning includes the process of determining the best locations, timing and interconnections of equipment in order to serve the available market at minimal cost, and meet performance, operations and maintenance objectives.

In addition to the obvious need to know when and where to deploy equipment, realistic network designs are also needed to evaluate the project in its formative stages. Business decisions are based on both revenue from the market and the investment and expenses necessary to implement a network to serve the market.

Characteristics Which Affect Network Engineering

There are three areas in which network engineering for an Intelligent Data Network Service offers new challenges. The first arises from the multidimensional characteristics of the service. An Intelligent Data Network supports a large number of port types (speeds, protocols, dial and private line) and provides both a call transport and a store and forward service. The service also provides distributed communications processing and storage. Therefore, the elements of line, packet and message switching networking must be blended with engineering for distributed storage and processing.

The second characteristic is that this is a new service. Its growth will occur rapidly. One of the important tasks of network engineering is to minimize the numbers and cost of rearrangements in the presence of a rapidly growing market and coincident network expansion.

The third area is brought about by evolving technology and capability. Initial architecture nodes will have less choices for engineering than later nodes. Although this later flexibility allows tailoring to reduce costs and enhance growth capabilities, it also increases the complexity of network engineering.

Network Engineering Problem Formulation and Solution

The basic networking problem is to deploy and interconnect network components to meet both strategic and tactical needs. The deployable entities are multiplexers, Remote Front End Processors (RFEP) and nodes.

Multiplexer capacity is generally a function of number of ports and the particular speed mix of ports. The cost/capacity of the RFEP is not only a function of ports, but in addition has processing throughput considerations. The node cost/capacity is more a function of processing and storage requirements.

The market parameters are multi-dimensional. Demand is stated in terms of ports by type and speed, storage and processing needs, and transport requirements. Specific geographical statements on where this demand occurs, and the community of interest between service points also impact the network design.

Cost inputs are a mixture of investment and expense categories. Equipment prices and engineering and installation costs form the basis for the investment calculation. Maintenance and operating expenses are provided as a function of site size and type of equipment deployed. The expense of interconnecting transmission facilities and of carrier supplied transport and switching are also necessary.

The strategic objective is to provide yearly network designs over the project life cycle which meet the market demand and minimize the total network annual costs of investment and expenses. An Integer Linear Program is one of the ways used to study the strategic choices for the network.

Tactical network designs also have the objective of minimizing total network costs. However, the granularity required of the solution allows many more practical aspects of deployment to be considered. Networks are usually designed as a month-by-month growth process. Rearrangements due to growth can be checked, and can affect the design to insure that they are manageable. Solutions to the tactical problem are generally less mathematically formal and more algorithmic in nature.

OPERATIONS APPLICATIONS OF SYSTEMS ENGINEERING

Systems Engineers worked with operations planners to develop overall data flows for the operations functions needed to provide an Intelligent Data Network Service. These flows were mapped into operations functional groupings. For each work function, system capabilities were defined to improve operations responsiveness and reduce expenses. Given a model of deployment and operations plans, judgements were made to determine the rate of mechanized support warranted for the new service.

Operations Objectives

Operations must provide high quality, profitable service. Expenses, which are a significant fraction of revenue requirements, should be minimized within the constraints of the service performance objectives.

Operations must also provide a clean division of responsibility between Bell and its customers. The flexibility offered by an intelligent network carries with it a high degree of customer responsibility. Customers will be responsible for assuring that their part of the service is operating correctly just as Bell Operations is responsible for assuring that the system itself is working. To accomplish this, customers will be provided with a single, responsive operations interface for trouble reporting and system inquiries.

Operations plans must also provide a support environment capable of handling rapid deployment. The network will start with a small number of nodes and a relatively small number of customer terminals. In order to be an economic success, it must be capable of expanding rapidly.

Operations Functions

The major operations functions which must be considered in the planning process are: provisioning, maintenance, administration, and billing.

Provisioning deals with providing resources to meet customer demand. Maintenance is concerned with the sectionalization, isolation and repair of network equipment and service elements in a timely fashion. Administration is concerned with monitoring the network to ensure that performance objectives are being met and that equipment is being utilized efficiently. Billing deals with collecting network usage data in an accurate and timely fashion.

The systems engineering effort in these areas consisted of analyzing the functions to be performed and the personnel charged with performing it, and then determining the system capabilities needed to perform the task. These capabilities were then converted into requirements.

Activity Models

Given the functions to be performed, the persons assigned to perform them, and the capabilities available, the next task is to determine needs for mechanized support. This requires quantitative models of operations activity and costs. To build these models estimates of failure rates, repair times, deployment rates, market quantities, etc., are needed. In some cases the data is readily available as part of the project planning process, e.g., deployment rates. In other cases, the data must be extrapolated from similar services and past experience. This data is used in models ranging in complexity from simple algebraic models of billing quantities to queueing models of the repair process which take into account dispatch times, duplicated components, etc.

Mechanization Phasing

The activity models are used to identify critical activities in terms of operating expenses, deployment constraints, and system availability and performance. The feasibility and impact of mechanizing the activity is then determined.

As an example, consider the service provisioning process. The model gives an estimate of the number of orders which need to be processed under the proposed deployment plan. Experience with other services is then used to determine how long it takes to perform the tasks necessary to complete the process of implementing the order. In this particular example, one finds that without mechanization the number of people needed and associated expense is very large. Moreover, experience with other service provisioning systems has shown that mechanization can provide major improvements in required staff levels. Thus, this clearly becomes a candidate for early mechanization.

FUTURE DIRECTIONS FOR INTELLIGENT DATA NETWORK SERVICES

In addition to initial technical requirements, Systems Engineers also plan the future directions for Intelligent Data Network Services. These directions will be driven by changes in customer needs and by changes in the technologies available to meet those needs. Examples of such changes will be explored here.

Intelligent Data Network Services will be used in a variety of business applications. As these applications expand, it will become very desirable to complete many types of business transactions electronically instead of via paper documents. Verification and authentication of these electronic transactions may be required to gain business user acceptance.

Digital signature technology based on public key cryptography [DH76, RSA78] promises to offer a solution to the transaction authentication problem. The potential application of this technology to an intelligent data network is illustrated in Figure 3.

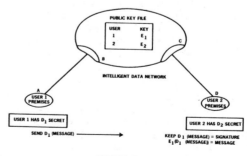

POSSIBLE FUTURE APPLICATION OF DIGITAL SIGNATURES

FIGURE 3

Digital signature systems can be integrated with intelligent data networks in several ways. First, the network could serve as only the public key file storage and end users could provide public key algorithms on their own premises (points A and D in Figure 3). Another option provided by an Intelligent Data Network Service is that the public key algorithms be run in the network (points B and C in Figure 3) with users authenticated to those points via traditional password schemes. By using passwords to authenticate to network end-points and then create digital signatures, it is possible to generate digital signatures without additional customer premises equipment.

The ability to move intelligence in and out of a network is important because of the growing trend towards customer premises intelligence. Future directions for Intelligent Data Networks created by this trend are support for applications that span customer premises intelligence and network intelligence, and better transport support for customer premises intelligence.

An example of an application that could span customer premises and network premises intelligence is electronic message communications. Large user sites would likely be effectively served by a customer premises vehicle, while small user sites would be better served by the network. An intelligent network can be built to effectively tie the large customer premises sites and small user together in such a way that all users receive similar service capabilities.

The increased use of customer premises intelligence will change the transport requirements for data networks. Early value added data networks were designed for time sharing or inquiry response applications. The transport was thus oriented towards low speed access and transport of short character strings. With increased use of intelligent terminals, such terminal interactions will stay local and transport needs will become more machine to machine. Coupled with the availability of higher speed access, this means that it will become useful for an intelligent data network to support integrated high speed circuit switched type transport. This capability would allow better support of customer premises intelligence and also the further integration of data streams from many types of customer devices with similar transport needs.

SUMMARY

The activities reviewed in this paper have illustrated some of the Systems Engineering functions performed during the development of an Intelligent Data Network Service by Bell Laboratories. These activities have illustrated the multifaceted nature of the Systems Engineering function. Systems Engineers have been responsible for unifying the many different viewpoints of the initial development while keeping an ever focused eye on the future.

REFERENCES

[BS82]   S. J. Barbera and D. J. Sandow, "Deployment Considerations for a Shared, Intelligent Network," ICCC82.

[DH76]   W. Diffie and M. E. Hellman," New Directions in Cryptography,: IEEE Trans. Inform. Theory," pp 644-654, November, 1976.

[FW82]   R. U. Faust and D. C. Wormley, "Operations Strategies For A Shared, Intelligent Network," ICCC82.

[GS79]   C. Gane and T. Sarson, "Structured Systems Analysis: Tools and Techniques," Prentice Hall, 1979.

[K76]   Kleinrock, Leonard, "Queueing Systems, Volume 2," Wiley, 1976.

[M72]   Martin, James, "Systems Analysis For Data Transmission," Prentice Hall, 1972.

[RSA78] R. L. Rivest, A. Shamir and L. Adleman, "On Digital Signatures and Public Key Crypto Systems," Commun. Assn. Comput. Mach., pp 120-126, February, 1978.

[SH82]   W. R. Smith and J. S. Hubley, "An Innovative, Shared Intelligent Network Service," ICCC82.

Allen Frank Rehert is Director, Data Network Systems Engineering Center, Bell Laboratories, Lincroft, N.J. His Center is responsible for planning and development of customer services involving data network concepts and technologies.

Dr. Rehert joined Bell Labs in 1962, initially working on the development of switching and operations systems. In 1966, he began supervising studies of the application of technology to local switching systems. In 1970, he headed the studies and planning of systems and technology to address service and operations needs of Bell System telephone companies.

Dr. Rehert received his B.S. degree in Electrical Engineering from the University of Maryland in 1962 and his Masters degree in Electrical Engineering from Rutgers University in 1964. In 1968 he earned his Ph.D. degree in the same field from the University of Pennsylvania.

An Innovative Architecture for a Programmable Shared Network

B P Donohue III, J F McDonald,
H R Liu
Bell Laboratories, USA

The Bell System's intelligent network service is a modern-day marriage of data processing technology and telecommunications technology. It is a data communications service that is fully integrated with a customer-programmable distributed-processing capability. It provides both call service (providing simultaneous, two-way communication between the end points) and message (store and forward) service, interfaces with a wide variety of terminals and hosts, supports data storage within the network, is customer programmable, and provides a stable and secure operating environment. This paper describes and gives the rationale for the architectural strategy that has been followed in developing the intelligent network service. This paper also describes the resulting architecture of the call and message services, and the architectural attributes of its customer-programmable environment.

Introduction

The Bell System's intelligent network service is a modern-day marriage of data processing technology and telecommunications technology. It is a data communications service that is fully integrated with a customer-programmable distributed-processing capability. It provides both call service (providing simultaneous, two-way communication between the end points) and message (store and forward) service, interfaces with a wide variety of terminals and hosts, supports data storage within the network, is customer programmable, and provides a stable and secure operating environment. This paper describes and gives the rationale for the architectural strategy that has been followed in developing the intelligent network service. The paper also describes the resulting architecture of the call and message services, and the architectural attributes of its customer-programmable environment.

Objectives and Requirements

The development of the intelligent network service as it exists today was initiated in the latter part of 1979. The architectural strategy that was established at that time, and that is described in this paper, was aimed at achieving a few critical objectives and at satisfying an explicit set of requirements. A brief summary of these objectives and requirements will help set the stage for a discussion of architectural strategies.

The primary objectives then and now are to: be ready for market entry in 1982; maintain, by continued innovation, a superiority in price/performance attributes over other entries in the marketplace from time of entry through several years of service; support customer programmability through a repertoire of languages and a stable environment that protects the customer's investment in software throughout the life of the service; provide security for customer programs and data; provide high availability of service; and support an ever-increasing functionality throughout the life of the service.

Figure 1 illustrates pictorially some of the key initial requirements. As shown, the intelligent network service is a port-to-port service that provides access to a wide variety of customer-provided terminals and hosts. Customer terminals and hosts are connected to ports at geographically dispersed "service points" via private line or dial access. One or more service points are supported by a node, which is a hardware/software complex at a single location. Because service points are widely dispersed in differing market environments, nodes of different capacities and varying configurations are required by the varying mix of attached customer terminals and hosts. Nodes are interconnected via packet switched networks using 56 kb/s trunks and CCITT X.25 standard protocols.

Key service requirements include:

- compatibility between supported terminals via "common mode", a teleprinter-style virtual-terminal protocol to which all terminals can be mapped;

- support of terminals either in a mode with the features of the appropriate class of terminal or in a common mode;

- call service between terminals and programs in a manner consistent with international standards and with the ISO reference model;

- message service with varying grades of delivery service;

- customer programmability in COBOL initially, to be followed by other languages;

- support of customer-program-callable software "building blocks" that support such things as mnemonic translations, an editor, a menu driver, a command interpreter, forms facilities and the like;

- support of customer data storage at service points on either a reserved or demand basis;

- and support of various grade of processing services at service points, including priority, interactive, and deferred.

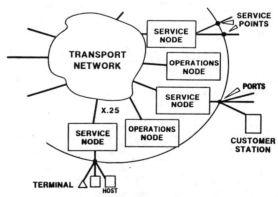

FIGURE 1: INTELLIGENT NETWORK SERVICE STRUCTURE

The Architectural Strategy

The architectural strategy can be separated into three parts: explicit and strict layering of the software; the "day-one" establishment of a migration strategy that supports evolution from an initial configuration using off-the-shelf components to a target configuration that meets long-term objectives with minimum redo of Bell-developed software and no reprogramming of customer software; and the "functional unit level" structuring of the architecture. Each of these strategic concepts will be described.

The Software Layering

The software architecture is strictly layered. The three major layers are the application layer, the control layer, and the operating system or kernel layer, as illustrated in Figure 2.

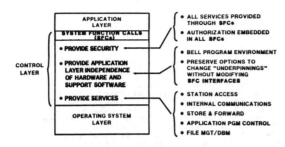

FIGURE 2: THE INTELLIGENT NETWORK SERVICE LAYERED STRUCTURE

The application layer is where applications, both customer- and Bell-provided, execute. All customer-provided software is contained within this layer. Network-wide addressing is available at this layer so that program-to-program communication becomes machine (and node) independent. Also, the required callable building blocks mentioned earlier reside in the application layer. Linkage to these facilities is provided to customer (and Bell) application programs at compile and link time.

The control layer provides customer security, provides customer application-program independence of specific hardware and support software, and provides the application layer with a variety of services through libraries of system function calls. The hardware and software providing the environment in which the application layer operates can and will evolve and change, while the interface seen from the application layer remains stable.

System function calls (SFCs) are subroutines that are callable by application programs. Examples of services provided through control layer SFCs are call service, message service, file management, and program execution control. Application layer programs cannot obtain services from the kernel layer without the execution of a control layer SFC. This structure is necessary both for security reasons and for application-layer independence of the hardware-software underpinning of the system.

Security is imposed principally by performing all privileged functions within control-layer SFCs. When an application layer program invokes a control layer SFC, appropriate authorization checks are made by the control layer to verify that the calling application program has the authority to use the services it is requesting.

The operating system or kernel layer provide the local machine environment and operating system services, including processor scheduling, memory management and I/O device management. In the initial realization of the intelligent network, commercially available operating systems are being employed. Operating system protection mechanisms are used as firewalls to help in bug detection and isolation for Bell-written software and to prevent the bypassing of intelligent network service authorization enforcement, but not to implement that enforcement. The intelligent network service enforcement is provided by control layer mechanisms such as the authorization checking done when a SFC is invoked.

Control layer functions can obtain services from the kernel layer by using operating system services. Control layer functions also make use of other control layer functions whenever possible in order to decouple the control and kernel layer to the degree possible.

The kernel layer provides a uniprocessor environment. The intelligent network, however, utilizes a multiprocessor node and multinode configuration. The control layer provides both multiprocessor and multinode capabilities for the intelligent network, including synchronization and configuration control.

The Strategy of Architecture Evolution

Major emphasis was placed on establishing clear and explicit architectural objectives for an intelligent network target configuration for the mid- to late-eighties time frame. These objectives and the anticipated target architecture configuration were established at the outset. We then selected off-the-shelf components for our initial configuration where the selected components had either a known future upward compatible price performance upgrade, or were candidates for internal Bell System component development where such development was considered viable. Finally, we defined a specific and sequential node architecture migration plan that evolves the node from its initial configuration to its anticipated target configuration with minimum redo of Bell-developed software, and no reprogramming of customer software.

Functional Unit Level Structuring

A multiprocessor configuration was selected for the intelligent network node for a variety of reasons. The most important reasons included: variation in capacity requirements as a function of time and geographical location; the use of specialized front end processors (FEPs) to off-load low-level protocol handling when interfacing with customer terminals and hosts; and the decision to employ a 1-for-n redundancy approach in achieving high availability in a cost-effective manner.

Figure 3 provides a pictorial representation of the initial hardware configuration for the intelligent network node. It depicts the multiprocessor configuration described above. For the initial realization of the intelligent network, VAX 11/780s are being used for the node processors, spares, and data base processors, and the IBM Series/1 is being used to implement the FEPs. For the initial configuration, as shown in Figure 3, FEPs are dedicated to specific processors. Because of this latter dedication, a single data base processor per node is used in this initial configuration in order to simplify reconfiguration mechanisms in the presence of failures of replaceable components, and to keep node data base administration procedures simple. This single data base processor imposes a limitation on the number of active node processors that can be efficiently used in the initial configuration.

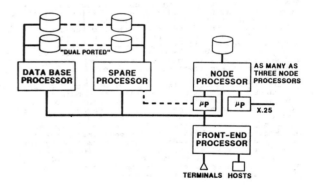

FIGURE 3: INITIAL NODE CONFIGURATION

Our target configuration eliminates the dedication of FEPs to node processors and introduces a robust, modular data base machine that can be configured to support a wide range of capacities. Because of proprietary considerations, an explicit description of the target configuration cannot be given at this time. However, a conceptual picture (see Figure 4) can be given for the purposes of illustrating our strategy of evolving the system component (as opposed to developing a sequence of monolithic systems). This strategy allows evolving services while holding down costs by avoiding unnecessarily short equipment life.

As depicted in Figure 4, a flexible, high-capacity
interconnect structure that eliminates the physical
dedication of components to one another will be
employed in the target configuration. Using this
interconnect and the new, robust data base machine, a
large number of active node-processors can be
supported. In addition, this interconnect structure
allows the incremental addition of specialized
processors that provide cost-effective implementation
of specific functions. For example, the full level-3
X.25 protocol used to interface to a packet switched
network will be implemented in a specialized protocol
processor. Other specialized processors, such as
session or protocol processors, will be introduced at
future times.

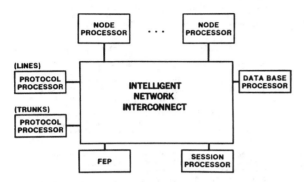

FIGURE 4: TARGET NODE CONFIGURATION

Each component shown in Figure 4 can be replaced at
any time without changing any of the other
components. This elemental component evolution
strategy is simple, straightforward, and exceedingly
effective.

*The Intelligent Network Architecture for Data
Communications*

The two key data communications services that the
intelligent network service provides through its
control layer system function calls (SFCs) are call
service and message service. Both provide
communication between programs. If information is to
be sent from or delivered to a customer terminal, an
intelligent network program called a port facility
serves as a software surrogate for the terminal.
Call service provides simultaneous, two-way
communication between the end points. Message
service allows one program to deliver a message to
one or more programs on a timed schedule. As has
been emphasized here and elsewhere, the intelligent
network service is a data communications service
fully integrated with a distributed data processing
and storage capability. As such, these two data
communications services are the communications
backbone of the intelligent network service. The
architecture of these two facilities is summarized in
the following sections.

Internal Communications (Call Service)

Within the intelligent network, an entity scheduled
for execution is called a *process*. Each process has
a unique, ten-digit address, the Network Standard
Address (NSA), associated with it. Another important
concept is the *port facility*; a port facility is
associated with each and every station (i.e.,
terminal, emulated terminal, or host computer)
attached to the intelligent network. Each port
facility has a unique NSA; thus, each station,
control layer process, and application layer process
is assigned a logical (rather than physical) address
by which it can be reached.

The Internal Communications Subsystem provides
communication facilities that have data transfer
integrity. This subsystem provides uniform
interfaces for inter-node, intra-node, and intra-
processor communications. The *endpoint* for the
Internal Communications Subsystem can be a control
layer process, a port facility, or an application
process.

The Internal Communications Subsystem consists of
layers adopted from the CCITT Recommendations,
specifically, the Session, Transport, Network, Link,
and Physical Layers. Call Service users interface
with the subsystem through Session Level SFCs.

ISO REFERENCE MODEL LAYERS	SOFTWARE STRUCTURE	FUNCTIONS
APPLICATION AND PRESENTATION	APPLICATION PROGRAMS	●ENDPOINT ●ASYNCHROUS INTERFACE
SESSION	LIBRARY OF SYSTEM FUNCTION CALLS (SFCs)	●DIALOGUE MGT ●NEGOTIATION ●INFORMATION UNIT
TRANSPORT	LIBRARY OF SFCs	●CONNECTION INTEGRITY ●FLOW CONTROL
NETWORK	LIBRARY OF SFCs AND NETWORK INTERFACE PROCESSES	●ROUTING ●PACKETIZING
LINK AND PHYSICAL	I/O DRIVERS FIRMWARE (IN OUTBOARDED MICROS) I/O DEVICES	●LINK CONTROL ●PHYSICAL INTERFACE ●ELECTRICAL TRANSMISSION

**FIGURE 5: THE INTELLIGENT NETWORK SERVICE
INTERNAL COMMUNICATIONS STRUCTURE**

Figure 5 provides a high-level diagram of the
software architecture of the Internal Communications
Subsystem. As shown in the figure, this subsystem is
strictly layered into separate libraries for the
session, transport and network levels, separate
processes to control interprocessor and internode
activities, and separate drivers for each I/O device.
This architecture was established for several
reasons. First, it is consistent with the ISO
reference model for open system connection.
Secondly, because of this strict layering, changes
confined to a single level can be accommodated
without changing software in the other layers.
Thirdly, if and when cost savings for one or more
layers can be achieved through outboarded specialized
hardware/software, the outboarding can be achieved
with little impact on the overall structure.

This internal communications capability is one of the
key elements of the intelligent network. It is the
vehicle for data communications between programs and
stations. It is the foundation upon which the
intelligent network's distributed processing
capabilities are built. Because of its criticality,
the attributes of the session, transport and network
layers are described below.

The *Session Layer* provides interfaces for endpoint
processes to set up, disconnect, and accept or reject
a connection.[1] In addition, an endpoint process may
send and receive data and interrupts (out-of-band,
expedited signals) through a connection. Functional
modules in this layer provide asynchronous
interfaces. Most Session Layer SFCs do not wait for
status or confirmation. Instead, status or
confirmation information is returned asynchronously

via an event. The actual status or confirmation of
an event can then be extracted from the data
associated with this event. The unit of data transfer
on the Session Layer and Transport Layer is referred
to as the Information Unit (IU). Information Units
can be several thousand bytes long. The unit of data
transfer on the Network Layer is referred to as the
packet. The intelligent network uses packets sized
at 128 bytes.

The Session Layer at the termination end point
arbitrates the negotiation parameters. These
parameters include such things as end-to-end
assurance options, reconnect options, throughput
class, data mode and IU size for each direction. If
the parameters supplied by the two ends are not
compatible, the connection cannot be set up. When
end-to-end assurance is chosen, the origination
process will be notified when the data is
successfully delivered to the process space of the
destination (a process or a port facility).

The *Transport Layer* acts on setting up connections
between two endpoints, sending data and interrupts
through the connection, and disconnecting a
connection. This layer reacts to Network Layer
inputs as well. Functional modules in this layer
provide connection integrity. During periods of no
traffic, this layer sends probes to assure that the
other end is still functioning. When the connection
is abnormally disconnected due to Network Layer
errors, functional modules in this layer may attempt
to reconnect this circuit.

For purposes of data integrity, functional modules in
this layer generate transport sequence numbers,
conduct purges, and retransmit lost IUs.
Acknowledgement may also be generated after the data
is read into the process space of the destination
process, thereby accomplishing assurance. Window
rotation mechanisms that are normally used for flow
control may be used to generate acknowledgement. In

addition, timers may be used to detect failure to complete the procedure in sending acknowledgements. The resolution of timers is on the order of seconds. Reliability is discussed further in a companion paper by Palframan and Yates.[1]

The *Network Layer* relays data units (typically packets) through one or more Network Level entities until the destination Network Layer is reached. The Network Level entities can be categorized into inter-node (via Packet Network), inter-processor (via inter-cpu bus), and intra-processor modules. Each of these entities multiplexes, demultiplexes, transmits, and receives data through the appropriate communication link.

Routing, a functional module of each entity of this layer, selects the next entity to which an IU is to be transferred. Network Layer entities are chosen at connection setup time. That is, when a process issues a connection setup request, the routing module in the process chooses the next entity based on the address translation tables, the status of the network layer processes, and the status of the hardware associated with the processes. The connection setup request is then forwarded to the chosen entity. Subsequently, an inter-node or an inter-processor entity will invoke the routing function in the chosen entity to decide the next entity, based on the address of the destination, the status of the Network Level connection, and the conditions of the communication links.

On channel failure, a Network Layer entity sends notification to a Transport Layer entity, which will generate a reconnect procedure if so optioned at connection setup time. A new route will be chosen for the reconnected virtual circuit.

The *Link and Physical Layers* actually move data through functional modules .in these two layers. Here again, the implementation varies depending on whether this is an inter-node, intra-node, or intra-processor transfer.

Store and Forward Communication

Store and forward communication in the intelligent network service allows an application program to transfer data (store and forward message) to one or more destination programs according to a specified time schedule. The originating program enters the message after specifying a transfer priority, destination addresses, and an optional confirmation address. The system transports the message to the destination program's node and holds it until the specified delivery time. After notification by the system, the destination program reads and processes the data. If requested, a confirmation report is sent to the specified address when the destination program releases the message.

The transfer of information from one program to another using store and forward communication involves four distinct steps:

1. The originating program enters the data to be transferred.

2. If necessary, the transport of data to the destination program's location takes place.

3. The delivery of the data to the destination program occurs at the appropriate time (after the earliest delivery time, but within the service grade limits).

4. If requested, a confirmation report is sent to a specified program.

The application program interacts with the store and forward service during steps 1 and 3, using a set of system function calls (SFCs) which will be briefly described. The actual transport of store and forward messages and confirmations in steps 2 and 4 is accomplished by a store and forward transfer process contained within the control layer. This process utilizes the capabilities of the Internal Communications Subsystem just described. Indeed, the intelligent network service store and forward capabilities are built directly on this communications foundation.

The originating program initiated the store and forward operation by using an "open" SFC. The arguments to this SFC provide control information such as destination addresses, the priority[3] at which the data is to be transferred, and selection of other options. The originating program then uses a "write" SFC to transfer the message to the intelligent network for delivery. A "close" SFC is used to complete this operation. This operation of entering data can be aborted at any time by the originating program through the use of an "abort" SFC.

Upon notification of a message arrival, the destination program must issue a "check" SFC to receive the message. "Check" performs termination screening as specified for the destination program by the customer. The destination program receives the message by issuing a "read" SFC. The data is placed by the system in a local buffer specified by the destination program. The destination program indicates end of processing by issuing a "release" SFC.

The Intelligent Network Service Customization Support Environment

The Customization Support Subsystem, which provides intelligent network service customer programmability capabilities, is a collection of Bell-supplied programs that provide an environment for the development and installation of customer-provided application programs. The Subsystem includes the following program development and installation services:

- Programming Services - these services provide the customer with the capabilities to create, compile and link application programs.

- Forms Services - these services provide the customer with the capabilities to define and include forms in their application programs.

- Program Library Services - these services enable customers to organize program files (source, object and load) into libraries and manage them at this higher level.

- Program Transport Services - these services, which directly utilize the Internal Communications and Store and Forward capabilities already described, enable customers to transport copies of program files between a service node and the centralized operations node where such activities as compilation and linking are actually performed.

- Job Management Services - these services enable the customer to determine the status of service requests sent to the operations node for execution. This includes the capability to cancel requests waiting to be processed.

- Program Installation Services - these services enable customers to install and remove programs, developed under the customization subsystem, in the network. They also provide customers with the capability to generate reports identifying where the programs are installed.

In order to minimize Bell operations and support cost and to effectively use intelligent network node resources for revenue-producing communications processing, the processing associated with providing the services is distributed between service nodes and an operations node. Highly interactive activities, such as source code creation, editing and forms definition are performed at service nodes. Batch type operations, such as source code compilation, forms translation, and program linking, are performed at the centralized operations node in a background environment.

The following sections provide an overview of the architecture of the Customization Support Subsystem and a description of ech of the services provided.

The major architectural elements of the Customization Support Subsystem include both service node and operations node processes. Some of these will be briefly described.

The Standard Software Support Process (SSSP), which is designed to execute as a multi-image program, is available to customers at each service node in the network under an NSA reserved for intelligent network service operation usage. The SSSP provides customers with a gateway in the form of a command level interface to intelligent network service program development services that are available at both the service node and the operations node. It performs the following functions:

- performs those services that are available at a service node and displays the results at the requester's terminal

- forwards requests for services to the operations node and displays the results returned at the requester's terminal

- upon receiving the results of a background job from the operations node, saves these in customer files at the service node and notifies the requester of the job completion.

The Foreground Process executes at the service node and performs the following functions:

- queues requests for background services at the operations node in a job queue and returns the assigned job number to the originator

- signals the Operations Node Dispatcher when it places a job in the operations node job queue.

The Operations Node Dispatcher Process executes at the operations node and performs the following functions:

- selects jobs (or job steps) eligible for processing from the job queue and passes the job to a Background Process for execution

- removes the job (or job step) from the job queue when all processing associated with it has been completed.

The Background Process executes at the operations node and performs the following functions:

- performs the processing associated with providing background services (compilation, linking, etc.)

- returns the results of providing the service, via Store and Forward, to the originating service node process

- signals the Dispatcher Process upon completion of the processing associated with a job (or a job step).

The communications between the service node and operations node processes use both call and store and forward services. Communications requiring real time interactions between the processes, such as the exchange of the transactions and transaction responses associated with processing commands, use call services. Communications that are less time critical, such as the transport of files and job outputs, are carried out in the background using store and forward services.

All files that are input to or are created by the various Customization Support Subsystem programs reside in customer program libraries at either node. The files are managed by using Program Library Manager SFCs (system function calls). These SFCs implement an authorization scheme that protects against direct customer access and modification of "sacred" files, such as program load and object files.

Summary

This paper has provided a brief description of the intelligent network service architectural strategy and outlined the architecture of some of the key elements of the intelligent network service, namely, Internal Communications, Store and Forward, and Customization Support. The discussion of the latter elements was aimed at illustrating the underlying structure of some of the major software interfaces that are visible to the intelligent network service customer. These interfaces will be maintained throughout the life of the service. At the same time, the price performance of the will keep pace with technology and its functionality will expand. The architectural strategy to achieve these objectives has been outlined in this paper as well. We believe this strategy to be simple, straightforward, and efficient. It will serve both the Bell System and intelligent network service customers well.

FOOTNOTES

1. A *connection* is a Session Layer element. Protocols for a connection have end-to-end significance. A *channel* is a Network Layer concept. Protocols on a channel do *not* have end-to-end significance.

2. J. D. Palframan and G.S. Yates, "Reliable Interprocess Communication in a Distributed Network," ICCC '82.

3. The intelligent network supports three grades of store and forward service. In effect, delivery in seconds, minutes or hours.

B. P. Donohue, III, was named Executive Director of the Data Communications Division at Bell Labs on September 1, 1981. He joined Bell Labs in 1962 and worked on various military projects until 1975, at which time he was named Head of the System Development Department. He became Head of the System Design Department in 1976, and the following year he was appointed Director of the Trunk Operations Engineering Center, transferring in 1979 to become Director of the Data Network Systems Development Lab. He held this position until his current appointment to Executive Director. He holds a B.S. in Mathematics from Monmouth College, and a M.A. in Mathematics from the University of Maine.

J. F. McDonald joined Bell Labs in 1961 as an MTS, working on various assignments on NIKE projects. Between 1967 and 1978, he was Supervisor working on SAFEGUARD software design and development, and later was involved in system engineering studies aimed at identifying OTC manual procedures that could effectively be mechanized by BIS. In 1978, he became Head in charge of development of the Billing Order and Support System. In 1979, he transferred to the Data Network Architecture Department. In October of 1981, he assumed his present position of Director of the Data Network Product Planning and Architecture Center. He holds a B.S. in Electrical Engineering from Kansas University, and a MS. in Electrical Engineering from New York University.

H. R. Liu is a supervisor in the Data Network Architecture Department at Bell Labs. He joined Bell Labs in 1976, involved in various design and implementation aspects of data network experimental work. In 1979, he was assigned to the Architecture Department in ACS. He was appointed to his current position in 1981. Mr. Liu received his B.S. in Electrical Engineering from National Taiwan University in 1969, and his M.S. and Ph.D. in Computer Science from the State University of New York at Stony Brook in 1971 and 1976, respectively.

Reliable Interprocess Communication in a Distributed Network

J D Palframan, G S Yates
Bell Laboratories, USA

The Internal Communications (IC) subsystem for a data network project at Bell Laboratories provides communicating processes with interprocess communications services which correspond to the lower 5 levels defined in ISO's Reference Model of Open Systems Interconnection. Within IC the transport layer provides the session layer with highly reliable connections based on the services provided to the transport layer by the network layer. The transport service may make use of several different types of network layer entities, not all of which are capable of providing the quality of service required between two communicating processes. The transport service provides recovery mechanisms for both data and connection loss. The mechanisms to detect such loss as well as recovery strategies are described. Error detection mechanisms include sanity timers, end to end sequence numbers, probes, and error detection by the network layer (resets, clears, or internally detected problems). Recovery mechanisms include retransmission, resynchronization, and reconnection. Finally the effect of these procedures on the efficiency of data movement is examined.

1. INTRODUCTION

A data communications system being developed at Bell Laboratories consists of a set of multiprocessor nodes connected together by a packet network (see figure 1). Processes communicate via an Internal Communications (IC) subsystem that uses a set of protocols that correspond approximately to the lower five levels defined by the ISO's Reference Model on Open Systems Interconnection. Some of the processes, especially those that monitor and control the network, require a virtually error-free communications capability.

The level 4 portion of IC, the Transport Layer (TL), provides end-to-end connections that meet the stringent reliability requirements. The general error recovery strategy of the TL is to make limited attempts to overcome connection establishment failure since it cannot be known in advance if all network elements required to complete a connection are available. Once a connection exists, however, it will be kept working with complete reliability unless all possible paths between the endpoints become disabled for more than a specified period of time. In addition to receiving error reports from lower layers, the TL discovers that situations requiring recovery action have occurred by such methods as timers, sequence numbers and internal consistency checks. Once an error is detected, progressively more complex

recovery attempts are made until the error is corrected or the connection is deemed irretrievably lost, at which point the TL user is notified. The recovery strategy and the mechanisms used to implement it were designed to minimize the degradation of efficiency while maintaining the desired reliability.

The next section gives an overview of the entire IC subsystem. Section three describes the problems that must be overcome in order to provide reliable connections and the strategy employed by the TL in doing so. Sections four and five present the methods used to detect and recover from errors. Some of the tradeoffs between reliability and efficiency are presented in section six.

2. THE IC SUBSYSTEM

The IC subsystem consists of two logical components:

— upper layer services: This piece is logically contained in all processes. It consists of a Session Layer (SL), TL, and common Network Layer (NL) entity. The common NL manages the intra-processor NL protocol. There are no restrictions on the number of connections an entity can handle, or on the number of processes that can be using IC within a processor.

— underlying Communications Services: The second piece is contained only in special network interface processes. The NL portion of these processes handles both the intra-processor protocol and the various inter-processor network protocols (see figure 2).

2.1 Upper Layer Services

The services provided by the Session Layer and Transport Layer correspond roughly to the services described in the ISO reference model on Open Systems Interconnection. The users of the services need not know whether they are communicating within the same processor, in the same node, or across nodes.

2.1.1 The Session Layer The Session Layer provides a user interface to the connection establishment, data transfer (normal and expedited), and connection termination services provided by the Transport Layer. In addition, it provides the following services:

— negotiation: Each end of a session may specify its needs with regard to several session characteristics such as dialogue type and maximum Session Protocol Data Unit (SPDU) size.

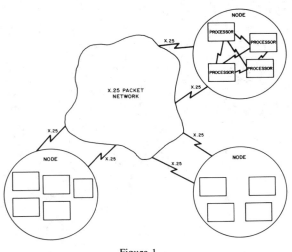

Figure 1
Network Configuration

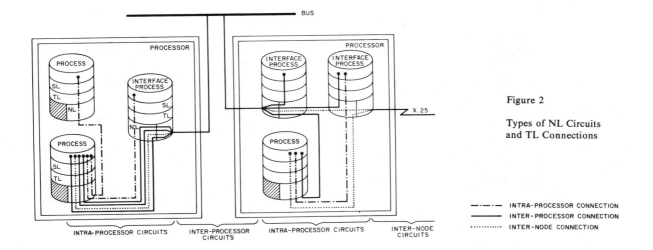

Figure 2

Types of NL Circuits
and TL Connections

INTRA-PROCESSOR CIRCUITS   INTER-PROCESSOR CIRCUITS   INTRA-PROCESSOR CIRCUITS   INTER-NODE CIRCUITS

—·—·— INTRA-PROCESSOR CONNECTION
———— INTER-PROCESSOR CONNECTION
········· INTER-NODE CONNECTION

— dialogue management: The SL manages two way simultaneous, two way alternate, and monologue sessions.

— exception reporting: The SL notifies the SL user of any errors that occur during the session.

— multi-party sessions: The SL allows sessions to be temporarily spliced together or forwarded to another SL user.

2.1.2 The Transport Layer The Transport Layer provides the SL with an interface to the circuit establishment, data transfer (normal and expedited) and circuit termination services of the Network Layer in addition to the following:

— data loss recovery: The TL will lose no data even though some data may be lost by the lower layers. This feature is selected on a per-circuit basis.

— circuit loss recovery: Provided a functioning path exists between TL endpoints, TL will maintain a connection even if one or more circuits used by the connection terminate prematurely. This feature is selected on a per-circuit basis.

— end-to-end flow control: Flow control, using a windowing mechanism, is provided on each connection. The size of the window for each direction of data transfer is independent of the other.

— end-to-end confirmation: A TL user may elect to receive positive confirmation that Transport Protocol Data Units (TPDUs) have been received by the destination TL entity.

2.1.3 The Network Layer The Network Layer provides circuit establishment, data transfer (normal and expedited), purge, and circuit termination services to the TL. As part of the circuit establishment service, the NL uses a network address to determine the appropriate path to the addressed process. The possible types of paths are described below. The design of the TL reliability features was influenced by the following characteristics of the NL services:

— circuit establishment: The NL will not duplicate any circuit establishment requests.

— data transfer: The service is byte oriented, and Network Service Data Units (NSDUs) are delivered in sequence.

— expedited data transfer: Data that is not subject to normal flow control and sequencing may be transmitted, with the restriction that only one such request may be outstanding.

— circuit termination: Once a circuit has been terminated, no NSDUs from that circuit will be delivered to the TL.

— error reporting: All problems detected by the NL will be reported to the TL.

2.2 Underlying Communications Services

Each type of inter-process link shown in figure 2 uses a different protocol although they all provide circuit-based services. The protocols used on the inter-processor links are transformed into the intra-processor protocol by the special interface processes that manage the node processor end of the links. Thus, the TL is unaware of the variety of level 3 protocols and qualities of service. Certain network level circuits, such as those existing between nodes, are highly reliable; however the TL's recovery strategy must handle the least reliable type of circuit.

2.2.1 The Inter-Node Network Layer Protocol This protocol is built on X.25 with the fast select option. A node interface process converts the internal NL protocol to X.25. There exists a sublayer in the NL which handles signaling between the node interface processes across the packet network. This layer envelopes the TL protocol elements. The level 2 protocol used is LAPB.

2.2.2 The Inter-Processor Network Layer Protocol This is a simple circuit protocol. It is able to distinguish only circuit setup and circuit clearing packets. All other packets are taken to be involved in data transfer and are passed transparently to the entities handling the intra-processor protocol. Level 2 is based on a reliable high speed bus.

2.2.3 The Intra-Processor Network Layer Protocol This protocol is functionally similar to level 3 of X.25. The major differences are:

— restarts: There are none since multiplexing between process pairs is done at level 2.

— circuit identification: Each circuit is identified by a pair of reference numbers, one provided by each NL entity.

— formats: The internal packet structures emphasis ease of manipulation rather than minimizing the number of bits to be transmitted.

— flow control: The flow control and acknowledgement mechanisms are not compatible with the X.25 mechanisms.

— control information: There is a greater amount of control information in each protocol element than exists in the X.25 counterparts.

— additional functions: New protocol elements are defined to perform such functions as re-routing during circuit-setup and circuit aborting.

— Level 2: Interactions between level 2 and the NL are different. Level 2 is a buffer passing-mechanism that uses standard operating system services.

3. RELIABLE CONNECTIONS

The network layer provides circuits with low probability of sequence errors, duplication, or loss. TL enhances this service to make connections as error free as possible. Various error recovery procedures are used to accomplish this. The TL attempts the simplest recovery technique first, invoking more drastic measures if these do not succeed. In some cases, such as the termination of one of the communicating processes, the TL will find it impossible to recover the connection.

3.1 Recoverable Situations

Before designing the TL error detection and recovery mechanisms, it was necessary to examine the situations from which TL would need to recover. Most of these, described below, can be attributed to transient failures in the lower layers.

— lost, duplicated, or out-of-sequence data: The TL treats any deviation from the expected NL service of delivering all data in sequence and without duplication as an error requiring recovery action.

— loss or duplication of control information: Protocol elements used by TL to establish, maintain and terminate a connection may become lost or duplicated.

— loss of NL circuit: A TL connection may require the establishment of several Network Layer circuits. If any of these terminates before requested by TL, the TL connection is unusable. As long as the NL circuit can be re-established or perhaps bypassed, the error is recoverable.

— congestion: Due to congestion in the lower layers, TL data or control information may take so long to traverse the connection that it appears to have been lost.

— routing failure: During establishment of an inter-processor TL connection, the NL routing function may select an out-of-service interface processor due to transient conditions. Connection establishment would fail, but as long as the interface process returned to service quickly or another was available, the TL would recover.

— corrupted connection control data structures: The TL entity at each end of a connection maintains a data structure used to control the connection. Recovery action is required if one of these structures becomes corrupted.

3.2 Unrecoverable Situations

Not all errors are recoverable. The loss of key processes or hardware elements for extended periods of time, such as in the situations described below, make recovery impossible.

— endpoint process failure: If one of the endpoint processes in a TL connection terminates, the connection cannot be re-established. This may be caused by the failure of the processor in which the process was running.

— communications isolation of the processor: If all of the hardware communications links to a processor are out of service for longer than the TL recovery period, any connections involving processes in that processor are lost.

— Network Level interface process failure: If one of the interface processes shown in figure 2 fails and no backup is available, any connections using the link controlled by the process are unusable.

— Packet Network failure: If the X.25 transport network is unable to establish or maintain any circuits between two nodes for a time longer than the TL recovery period, for example due to an access line failure, no TL connections can exist between the nodes.

— no inter-process buffers: If the level 2 buffer-passing mechanism used by the intra-processor protocol fails to operate properly, or the buffer pool becomes exhausted, connections cannot be established.

3.3 Recovery Strategy

If an error is detected, usually recovery action is initiated. The primary goal of all recovery actions is to provide error free service on an established connection and to keep the connection in the data transfer state until one of the TL users wants to terminate it. If the connection must be terminated other than by user request, TL tries to keep both ends consistent. It is the user's responsibility to recover if, despite the best efforts of TL, the connection is broken.

The reliability strategy is divided into three phases: connection establishment, data transfer, and connection termination.

3.3.1 Connection Establishment During connection establishment, the calling TL is unaware of the state of either the called process or the portion of the network between the two TL entities. It can make no commitment to its user until the connection is established.

3.3.2 Data Tranfer Once a connection has been established, the TL guarantees that it will keep the connection functioning in an error-free manner until connection termination occurs. Depending on the type of situation encountered while in data transfer state, the TL progresses through up to three distinct stages, each one more complex than the previous one, in its attempt to maintain an error-free connection. In the simplest stage, used on connections that have carried no traffic for a significant period of time, one TL asks the distant TL to confirm the health of the connection. In the next stage, the transmission path between the two TLs is cleared of all data, and the two endpoints are resynchronized. In the last stage, a new TL connection is established, and all control information from the old connection is applied to the new connection. If the last stage fails, the TL user is informed that the connection has been broken.

3.3.3 Connection Termination TL ensures that the two TL entities handling a connection agree that a connection is being terminated for a particular reason. Thus both TL users will be presented with a consistent picture of the connection, and the TL entities will be able to free the resources that the connection used.

4. ERROR DETECTION MECHANISMS

The TL is able to detect all protocol problems on its own. However, the error detection process is hastened if the NL tells TL of errors that occur below the Transport Layer. The TL itself checks fields in both incoming protocol elements and internal data structures for correctness. It employs sanity timers to detect loss and uses a probe technique to determine the operational status of a connection at any time.

4.1 Lower Layer Detection

It is much more efficient for the NL to tell the TL of errors which occurred in the Network Layer or below than to wait for the TL to detect that there is a problem. In addition, the NL can indicate exactly what the problem is, thus helping recovery procedures and later analysis of the problem. The Network Layer notifies the TL by a reset, clear, or abort, depending on the severity of the problem. The characteristics of resets and clears are the same as described in X.25. Across the X.25 interface the abort is mapped to a clear. Within a node these packets contain precise information as to the cause of each error. Using NL to signal errors has the advantage that as the NL is modified the TL need not be changed to detect new types of errors.

4.2 Sequence Numbers and Acknowledgements

In order to detect lost, out-of-sequence, or duplicated data, the TL numbers each TPDU that it sends, and it expects the distant TL to positively acknowledge all received TPDUs. The end-to-end sequence number mechanism is also used to enforce flow control and to keep track of unacknowledged TPDUs that must be saved for possible re-transmission.

For each direction of data transfer, each TL entity maintains a 'window' within the modulo 256 sequence number space that is bounded

— on the bottom by the sequence number of the most recent TPDU that has not been acknowledged, and

— on the top by the first sequence number that cannot be used due to flow control constraints.

The current sequence number lies somewhere within the window. The lower window edge advances as TPDUs are acknowledged, and the upper edge advances when TPDUs are passed up to the TL user. These two operations are independent.

Each TPDU carries a TL data transfer header containing the current sequence number, acknowledgement for all previously received TPDUs, and the upper limit on sequence numbers that will be accepted from the other TL entity. Upon receipt of a TPDU, the TL checks to be sure it carries the next expected sequence number, and if so, it updates its own outgoing window with the acknowledgement and flow control data. The TPDU is considered to be a duplicate if its sequence number is less than the next expected number, but by no more than the maximum allowable number of unacknowledged TPDUs. If the TPDU's sequence number differs in any other way from the expected number, the TPDU is considered out of sequence. If a TPDU needs to be acknowledged, or the upper window edge advances and no TPDUs are available to carry the information, a special acknowledgement TPDU, carrying only the TL data transfer header, is sent.

4.3 Timers

TL timers serve two purposes:

— sanity checks: These timers guard against protocol elements being lost, the remote process not responding, and Network Layer difficulties.

— efficiency: These timers attempt to minimize the number of control TPDUs transmitted.

Each sanity timer is associated with a magnitude which indicates the number of seconds until expiration and a set of instructions to execute should the timer expire. Some of the expiration actions are to repeat the previous operation. This continues until the number of repeats reaches a threshold, at which point separate instructions associated with the threshold being exceeded are invoked. To accommodate the different traffic patterns that processes may have, the magnitude and threshold of each timer can be tailored on a per-process basis.

The TL logically maintains nine sanity timers. These are summarized in tables 1a and 1b. Normal data transfer timers are cancelled if a reset occurs, and these plus the reset timer are cancelled if a disconnect occurs.

4.4 Probes

The probe mechanism, which is a simple request-response exchange, is used to determine the health of a connection. The TL initiates a probe upon expiration of the idle timer, which indicates that there has been no traffic on the connection for a significant time interval. The probe is also used as part of the re-connection recovery mechanism described below.

In order to bypass flow control mechanisms, the TL uses the expedited data service of the NL to implement the probe. Since NL expedited data is used for other purposes as well, the data field is used to indicate that the transaction is a probe request. The proper response to a probe is an expedited data confirmation. If no response is received within the probe timer interval, the reset and resynchronization recovery mechanism is invoked.

4.5 Internal Checks

During the processing of all transactions, the TL checks the validity of the data structures that it references. Each data structure contains a stamp field used to uniquely identify each type of structure. If a structure is found to contain an improper stamp, the entire structure is considered invalid, and recovery action appropriate to the data structure type is invoked. Consistency checks between circuit control data and control data carried with each protocol element are also used to detect errors.

5. METHODS OF ERROR RECOVERY

As mentioned above, the recovery strategy is divided into three phases. If connection establishment fails, the only action TL takes is to retry it.

During data transfer the TL can perform any of:

— reset and resynchronization: The reset indicates that an error occurred, clears the connection of data in transit, and removes flow control conditions within the NL. Resynchronization ensures, by retransmitting unacknowledged TPDUs, that TL user data has not been lost.

— reconnection: This establishes a new NL circuit to service a connection if the NL circuit which was handling the connection is cleared.

If these procedures fail, the TL will terminate the connection.

During termination, the TL requires confirmation that the connection has been completely torn down. If it does not receive confirmation it will retry, until finally it invokes an abort procedure.

5.1 Connection Retry

If connection establishment fails because of a NL originated clear, and if the reason for this is of a temporary nature, TL will periodically retry connection establishment. The number of retries and time between them are parameterized for each process. There is no retry if the connection is terminated by the destination TL or TL user, if the reason for clearing indicates that further attempts at connection establishment would not succeed, or if the connection establishment timer expires. The destination TL disconnects if the destination TL user does not respond to the connection indication.

An example of a connection that is not retried is one that attempts to connect to an entity that does not exist. Retry does not occur if the connection establishment timer expires. This means the NL failed to deliver the connection establishment request. This is taken as an indication that there is a serious problem within the NL. Since the TL has received no information about the destination and questions the health of the network, the connection is not retried.

Although connection requests are retransmitted, they cannot be duplicated by the TL. The connection must be disconnected for retry to occur, ensuring that the previous connection request is no longer in the network.

5.2 Reset

The reset mechanism forces both ends of a connection back into a known state and clears the data transmission path of all protocol elements. The TL uses the NL reset service, which is functionally equivalent to the X.25 reset, to clear the transmission path and to notify the other TL that a reset is being performed. The TL must confirm a reset notification by issuing a NL reset confirmation. In case both ends simultaneously issue reset requests, each end treats the reset notification as confirmation of the reset request. Before returning to normal data transfer state, the resynchronization function is performed.

TL Timers					
Timer	Purpose	Mag*	Expiration Action	Timer Set when:	Timer Cancelled when:
Connection Setup	guards against loss of connect request or confirm	240	disconnect sent	connect sent	accept received, DRC†
Connection Response	ensures TL user responds to connect indication	180	disconnect sent	connect indication received	TL user responds, DRC†
Normal Data	ensures normal data and ack not lost	240	reset sent	data sent & none outstanding, ack received & data still outstanding	No data outstanding, DRC†
Expedited Data	ensures expedited data or confirmation are not lost	45	reset sent	expidited data or confirmation sent	acknowledgment received, DRC†
Reset	ensures reset & confirmation are not lost	90	reset sent	reset sent	reset confirmation received, DRC†
Probe	ensures probe and its confirmation are not lost	45	reset sent	probe sent	probe confirmed, DRC†
Idle	ensures connection still viable during no traffic periods	1000	probe sent	no traffic on connection	reset occurs, traffic received, DRC†
Reconnect/ Retry	defines period between reconnect attempts	120	connect sent	disconnect received in response to connect request	TL user disconnects or incoming reconnect request received
Disconnect	ensures disconnect and its confirmation are not lost	30	disconnect sent	disconnect sent	Confirmation received, DRC†

TABLE 1.a TL TIMERS

TL Timer Repeat Thresholds			
Timer	Threshold	Action	Threshold Count Cleared
Reset	2	disconnect sent	when reset confirmed
Reconnect/ Retry	5	TL user disconnected	Connection (re-)established
Disconnect	3	abort sent	disconnect confirmed, abort received

TABLE 1.b — TL REPEAT TIMERS

* Timer magnitude indicates the default number of seconds.
† DRC: disconnect or abort received, or TL user disconnects.

5.3 Resynchronization

Since previously transmitted data may be lost during a reset operation, unacknowledged data must be re-transmitted following the reset. To indicate which TPDUs require re-transmission, each TL entity sends to its partner a special resynchronization transaction which carries the current acknowledgement and flow control data. Once this is received, all unacknowledged TPDUs are re-transmitted, in their original sequence, and the TL entity returns to normal data transfer state.

5.4 Reconnection

The TL environments describing each end of a connection can be retained for up to ten minutes after the clearing of the NL circuit that supported the connection. To reconnect, one or both TL entities attempt to establish a new TL connection using a new NL circuit. The TL user is not told of this new connection. The normal connection establishment procedures are used with the following changes:

— retry: The number of times reconnect will be attempted (between successful connection establishments) is parameterized. The default is five. The reconnect procedure may be abandoned before this limit is reached.

— format: The connection request is formatted to indicate that reconnection is taking place.

— initial connection environment: Once the connection is established the TL swaps the control blocks that describe the old and new connections. The old connection is then terminated.

During reconnection it appears to the TL user that the TL connection is temporarily congested. Any data received from the TL user will be queued until the connection is re-established. However, the reconnect process will be abandoned if the TL user requests disconnection. Once the connection has been re-established, re-synchronization takes place before normal data transfer resumes.

The reconnect procedure is also abandoned if the connection establishment timer expires. Again this indicates to the TL that the NL is in trouble and should not be given additional work. The only time a reconnect request will be sent is if all of the following occur:

— circuit cleared: The NL circuit was cleared because of an error in the layers below TL. Circuits which are cleared because TL connections are being terminated are not reconnected.

— temporary problem: The cause of the clear indicates a temporary problem. Examples of this include network congestion or the failure of one of the hops used by the Network Layer.

— TL user option: The TL user indicated at connection establishment that reconnection should be attempted if the above occur.

If the number of consecutive reconnect attempts exceeds a reconnect threshold (parameterized for each process) without re-establishing the connection, the TL user is told that the connection terminated. There is no limit on the number of successful reconnections that can occur over the lifetime of a connection.

In order for the TL entity which receives the reconnect indication to identify the connection being reconnected to, each connection must be uniquely identified. This identity is composed of:

— the transport addresses of the two transport-entities,

— the date and time the original connection was established, and

— a reconnect-id.

The addresses identify connections between any pair of processes. The time and reconnect-id then identify a particular connection between the two TL entities. The date and time are used to avoid problems when processors are re-initialized and new processes may re-use transport addresses. The reconnect-id distinguishes connections that were established at the same time.

In order to resolve reconnect collisions, where both ends originate reconnects for the same connection, one end of each connection is designated as reconnect primary. If a collision occurs the reconnect originated by the non-primary end is disconnected. The primary designation also resolves the connection identification problem which occurs when a single TL entity is the endpoint for both ends of a connection being reconnected.

It may be that the TL entity which received a reconnect believes that the original connection is still operational. In this case a probe is sent over the original connection. If the proper response is not received, then the reconnect takes place, otherwise it does not.

It is worth noting that reconnect handles the case where one of the processes, devices, or lines that handles inter-processor/node traffic becomes inoperable. The NL will clear circuits that use the failed component. New NL calls, such as those that handle the TL reconnect, will be routed via a different path.

5.5 Connection Termination

The TL terminates a connection whenever the TL user requests it, the remote TL requests it, or data transfer recovery procedures fail. In addition, the NL may clear the circuit that the connection uses and indicate that reconnection will serve no purpose. The TL attempts to ensure that both ends of a connection agree that the connection is terminating. To accomplish this the TL requires that disconnects be confirmed. If none arrives, it again attempts to contact the remote TL entity issuing a disconnect. If this repeatedly fails, the connection is aborted. This does not require confirmation. The TL user is informed when an abort is sent or received, or if a disconnect confirmation is received, that the connection is gone.

The disconnect may bypass data or acknowledgments. It is assumed that the higher layer protocols have negotiated a termination agreement before the TL user disconnects.

6. EFFICIENCY CONSIDERATIONS

The transport layer was designed to minimize transmitted data while maximizing throughput and reliability. Reliability-efficiency tradeoffs occur when:

— using receipt confirmation services of the Network Layer,

— piggybacking control information, or

— using timers.

A receipt confirmation service is one of these where protocol elements and their confirmations are piggybacked on lower layer protocol elements rather than being transmitted as lower layer data. Examples of this are connections setup, tear down, reset, and expedited data. Using receipt service complicates the TL because during connection establishment and termination there is not a solid circuit upon which to base its actions.

In connection establishment the connection request is piggybacked on the Network Layer fast select call request packet, and the connection response is piggybacked on the network layer accept packet. The IC Session Layer uses a similar method. This reduces the number of X.25 packets required to establish a level 6 connection from 22 to 2 . An example of a problem this can cause occurs if it is possible for the NL to establish circuits, but not transfer data. In this situation the TL may end up reconnecting forever. The TL has to ensure that data is transferred between reconnects to avoid this problem.

Where possible, control information is piggybacked on regular traffic, rather than in separate TPDUs. This involves two timers:

— flow control timer: This timer withholds credits for a fraction of a second. If a TPDU is sent to the other end of the connection during this time, then the timer is cancelled and the window rotation information conveyed in the TPDU.

— acknowledgment timer: This timer causes acknowledgments to be held back until either the timer expires or a TPDU is sent to the other end of the connection.

The timer values must be set so as to not interfere with the normal data transfer sanity timer.

To decrease CPU usage the IC clock ticks very slowly, thus keeping timer management to a minimum. The TL assumes that, because the NL provides a generally reliable service, that protocol errors are rare events. Even rarer should be those occasions where the NL fails to notify the TL of NL errors and the sanity timers actually expire.

7. CONCLUSION

The TL protocol was designed to make efficient use of the features offered by X.25 while recovering from errors that could occur either in accessing the X.25 network or in the local area network connecting to a packet switch. It does not recover from errors resulting from problems in higher layers or from fundamental problems with the operating systems or buffer passing mechanisms.

The design of the TL protocol occurred while ISO was studying the services to be offered by their Transport Layer. The services provided by the TL were chosen to be compatible with those described by ISO. As the ISO services and protocol work evolves the TL protocol will be made compatible. In order to handle additional signaling and error recovery requirements, such as reconnect, the TL protocol will likely be a superset of the ISO work.

ACKNOWLEDGEMENTS

The authors wish to thank A.H. Arastu, G.R. Babecki, C.M. Garnant, G.F. MacLachlan, T.A. Wendt, and M.J. Welt for their contributions to the design of the IC system.

REFERENCES

[1] CCITT Recommendation X.25, CCITT yellow Book vol. VIII-2 (ITU, Geneva, Switzerland 1981).

[2] A.M.Rybczynski, J.D.Palframan, A Common X.25 Interface to Public Data Networks, Computer Networks, Vol 4 number 3 (June 1981).

[3] ISO/TC97/SC16, Reference Model of Open System Interconnection, DP7498 (August 6, 1981).

[4] ISO/TC97/SC16, Draft Connection Oriented Transport Service Definition, Document N697 (June 1981).

John Palframan is a Member of Technical Staff with Bell Telephone Laboratories in Lincroft, N.J. where he works in data network development. He received a Bachelor of Mathematics degree in 1975 and a M. Math in 1977 from the University of Waterloo. Mr. Palframan has worked with the Computer Communications Networks Group at Waterloo and with the Computer Communication Planning group within Bell Canada. At Bell Canada he was responsible for packet protocol specifications(X.25/X.75), gateway development, and automated protocol verification.

Gregory Yates is a Member of Technical Staff at Bell Telephone Laboratories in Lincroft, N.J. He received his AB degree from Dartmouth College in 1976, and his Master of Engineering degree from the Thayer School of Engineering at Dartmouth College in 1978. Mr. Yates initially worked on a message switching system within a data communications network. Currently, he is working on the design and implementation of network protocols. In particular, his recent efforts have concerned the development of reliable end-to-end data transfer mechanisms.

Implementation of Operations Support on the Supported Network

O W Traber III
Bell Laboratories, USA

As an integral part of its development of a programmable data communications service, Bell Laboratories is developing several associated operations support systems. A primary design objective is to provide a network wide scope to operations while permitting unattended node operation. A second goal is to smoothly evolve the support from that of a small service to that of a large service.

To meet these objectives, the operations support systems are integrated with the service, operating as applications in the service itself. This approach eases centralization and evolution while minimizing development and operating cost. This paper will describe operations support for the service, including the benefits of using integrated operations applications, and several examples of those applications.

1. INTRODUCTION

Bell Telephone Laboratories has developed an innovative, programmable, data communications service [1,2] which will provide access support for a wide range of data terminals and host computers; communications between terminals, hosts and programs; processing to manage communications and manipulate data; and storage to support these functions. The service is directed at systematically solving customer communication problems [1] by providing terminal protocol compatibility, networking flexibility, and logical network management. A unique aspect of this service is its ability to be programmed by customers (or third party customer representatives) to fit their application needs through the use of a high level procedure language. Application programs written by the customer will use service facilities to: 1) communicate with each other and terminals, 2) process and store data, and 3), support the users of the applications.

The implementation of this programmable service is based on processor complexes called nodes. Each node is fully functional: each contains the complete set of the service's capabilities including execution of customer developed applications; and operates as an equal in dealing with the other nodes while managing its own resources. The service is provided by a number of these nodes interconnected by a transport facility to form a distributed processing network. The network providing this service will evolve from a single node to many interconnected nodes.

Any service or product, whether a voice switch or a mainframe computer, depends on several activities to enable it to begin and continue operation useful to customers. These activities are defined as operations support for the service or product. [3] While they do not provide service directly to customers, these operations support activities do provide functions vital to the service as exemplified by the following activities. To begin operation, the nodes must be initialized prior to service and re-initialized as part of recovery operations. Once operational, the service must be kept running, with problems affecting service identified and promptly repaired. Given an operating service, one must be able to add customers, and assign to the customers the resources and capabilities needed to perform their applications. Finally, the service must charge the customers for the use of the service; costs both for resources reserved and for those actually used must be recouped.

A key consideration in the design of the service then is the form of the mechanization of this operations support. Operations support for the programmable service is built as a number of applications operating within the service itself. This approach contrasts with the more traditional approach of using external processing capabilities (e.g., minicomputers) to provide operations support. External operations support is the normal form of operations support for existing Bell System networks.

This paper will briefly describe the operations support required by the service and the strategy of providing it on the service itself. This strategy will be contrasted with a more traditional alternative of external operations support systems. The integrated approach will then be characterized in greater detail with descriptions of the designs of several operations support applications.

2. FUNCTIONS OF OPERATIONS SUPPORT

For the programmable data communications service, operations support activities are divided into the following five major internal systems:

1. *Service Provisioning* - accepts and processes customer requests for service (orders). This activity results in the updating of internal data structures and the installation or modification of equipment (primarily equipment involved in access to the service).This activity also provides support for status tracking and control of activities related to each order.

2. *Maintenance* - involves the detection of, diagnosis of, repair of and recovery from service providing system errors. It also includes many day-to-day administrative activities of the node. These include initialization of node elements (e.g., processors) and the control of node resources (e.g., customer database administration).

3. *Customer Trouble Handling* - supports the "single point of customer contact" which handles customer trouble queries. The initial activity is to determine if a malfunction exists or if the query reflects some user lack of information. If the trouble is real, then this activity determines whether or not it is in the service itself. Internal troubles are referred to maintenance and their resolution is tracked; other troubles are returned to the customer for resolution.

4. *Network Management* - collects performance and traffic data for 1) the identification and resolution of congestion problems, and 2) the analysis required to plan the long term evolution of the network.

5. *Billing* - involves the collection and storage of all data required to produce a bill for a customer, the actual calculation and preparation of that bill, and the tracking of customer payment of bills.

The above operations support systems are those considered critical to the effective operation of the programmable service. While each provides a distinct part of the support, they all have similar attributes, as described below:

- Central operation interacting with all local nodes.

  A major goal of the operations of this service is to centralize personnel so as to allow unstaffed local node locations, at least during normal operation. Although the central operation is fully mechanized, some functions still require local processing. Thus, processing required at local and central locations must cooperate and thus requires very interactive communications.

- Support systems interact with each other.

  The support systems are required to interact with each other to accomplish many functions. For example, in response to customer requests, Service Provisioning changes the resources reserved for that customer. This must also cause a change in the customer's monthly bill. Thus, Service Provisioning must pass information about the response to this change to the Billing system to update the monthly bill amount.

- Each operations support system interacts with both remote and on-site operations personnel providing some functions common to both.

  While central operations support is a primary goal, a second goal calls for the independent operation of each local node. In other words, each local node must be able to operate for limited periods without support from the central operations nodes. As a result, both the local and central operations personnel have the same basic set of capabilities.

- Operations personnel perform privileged functions not available to customer users.

  Examples of such capabilities include disabling hardware components of a node and halting the execution of a customer program.

Successful operation of each of these operations support systems is vital to the service itself; effective operation of these systems is critical to the financial success of the service. Therefore, these systems require early mechanization to insure success. The major planning issue was to determine the strategy for mechanizing operations support. There were two major alternatives; one was to develop separate external operations support; the other was to integrate the operations support into the service itself.

3. ALTERNATIVE DESIGN STRATEGIES

3.1 External Operations Support Systems

The more traditional approach to mechanizing operations support is to build it as part of a separate system external to the service. In other words, the service and its operations support systems are independent systems with defined cooperating interfaces. As a result, the service, each operations support system, and the interfaces have essentially independent evolutions. The service itself then contains only those interfaces (e.g., keyboards, tapes, maintenance and communications protocols) and low level mechanisms (e.g., initialization) required by the external operations support system. Each operations support system itself is designed and built as a system that operates at arm's length and communicates with the service through its interfaces to effect changes in the service, activate the service's low level mechanisms, or to collect data from the service. The mechanization plan of the external operations support system is not tied directly to the evolution of the service itself.

An example of this type of external operations support system is the traditional Service Provisioning System. The service itself has an interface that accepts "recent change" requests to update the internal tables. External to the service is the Service Provisioning System which accepts customer requests (orders), and processes them through such steps as resource assignment until a set of recent change requests has been defined. These are then sent to the service which applies the recent changes to its tables.

This alternative of external operations support does allow independent development of the service and each of its support systems. However, the arm's length approach causes additional complexity in several areas. First, the development efforts of the service and the operations support systems are both complicated by problems related to slightly differing definitions of the interface between the systems. Second, the interfaces themselves are more complicated owing to the need to make them robust enough to handle unfriendly inputs and responses and disparate data structures. Third, the communications protocols to support the robust interfaces become more robust themselves (for example, additional acknowledgements). Finally, the overall system, the service and all its operations support, becomes a complex of many cooperating systems rather than one integrated system.

Although this complexity leads to higher overhead which offsets the benefits of flexibility, most communications systems have had no alternative to the approach of external operations support systems. The alternative of integrated operations support was not available since these services could not directly provide the operations support.

3.2 Integrated Operations Support Systems

The new programmable service developed by Bell Laboratories combines customer programmability with communications and storage; this array of capabilities provides an opportunity to carry out the functions of the support systems as well as those of the service's customers. This alternative approach of taking advantage of the service itself to implement integrated operations support considers the operations support systems simply as application systems in the service itself. Conceptually, the operations support applications use the facilities of the service available to the customer to provide the communications oriented functions of operations support.

First and foremost, the integrated approach capitalizes on the match between the features of the service and the needs of operations support. These operations support needs are both communications and storage oriented with a major dependence on communicating with operators and with other components.

Second, this integrated approach takes advantage of existing development facilities and experience to reduce the cost of development. In order to develop the service itself, Bell Labs has built an extensive development laboratory which provides substantial development, testing and manufacturing tools. This development lab can be expanded to support the development of the operations support applications without requiring the construction of a different lab. Further, the development staff has intimate knowledge of and experience with the service itself. Taking advantage of the established staff and facilities is preferable to the development of expertise in another environment simply for operations support.

Third, the ability to integrate the service itself with its operations support systems reduces the cost of development of those systems by reducing the complexity of those systems and the number and complexity of the interfaces between them. Further simplification is achieved through the sharing of similar data structures and common communication capabilities.

Finally, the integrated approach eases the problems of growing with the network (e.g., moving applications between nodes). Built as applications, the operations support applications are structured (as customer systems are) in units appropriate for migration. As the service moves customers, it can move its operations support applications with no changes required beyond those caused by the addition of function.

In summary, the integrated approach of building the operations support as application systems on the service has several major advantages:

1. Closely matched service capabilities and operations support system needs

2. Reduced development overhead

3. Less complex applications

4. Easier evolution

While the integrated approach emphasizes the concept of operations support as applications on the service, the actual implementation calls for some enhanced support from the underlying service-providing system not generally available to customers. The first group of these enhancements includes such things as the usage collection software for billing and the initialization software for maintenance. The second group of enhancements are motivated solely by the integrated approach. This small group includes such features as access to underlying file systems normally hidden from customers and use of extended database capabilities. Overall, these enhancements are not a major fraction of the operations support applications, which remain almost entirely applications in the service.

4. DESIGNS OF SEVERAL OPERATIONS SUPPORT APPLICATIONS

4.1 Common Structural Characteristics

To provide insight into the way the service is used as the vehicle for operations support, the designs of several of the operations support applications are described in more detail. Each of these designs reflects the differences in the functions of each application; however, there are several common structural characteristics.

First, all of the applications have a major central portion in a central operations node; this centralization was a primary operations support goal. Each application also has a local portion in each node of the service. The local portion supports those functions which could not be removed from the node (e.g., internal table update in service provisioning or data collection in billing) or should not be removed for functional design considerations (e.g., local tracking in service provisioning).

The communication between the central and local interfaces is via a set of well defined transactions which are exchanged between the central node and all local nodes. The placement of these interfaces was based on the degree of interaction between the central and local nodes and was designed to minimize that interaction in an effective fashion. For example, in the Service Provisioning Application (see Figure 1), only tasks to be implemented and final completion reports are exchanged; this results in the placement of some tracking and control functions in the local node.

Second, the databases of each of the systems are partitioned according to the likely evolution of the application and its relationship to service providing nodes. For example, the local and central portions of each application do not share databases; they transfer requests for data to the other portion of the applications. A similar transfer of query/update requests also occurs between operations support applications.

Third, most of the operations support terminals are supported by terminal managers which have the primary function of parsing commands and forwarding them to other programs which handle the request. This structure allows a great deal of flexibility in command repertoire for a terminal. Moving a command function from one terminal to another (or having both support it) simply requires changes in command parsing in the terminal managers. Further, the terminal and the command servicing program can now be on different nodes; the communications capabilities of the service allow the command request to be sent to any program in any node.

Finally, wherever one of these applications needs access to underlying system capabilities, a set of interface routines is defined to provide a standard, well defined interface to these facilities. These interfaces also provide protection, allowing only the privileged operations support applications to use them.

The remainder of the section describes the high level designs of three of the service's major operations support applications, Service Provisioning, Maintenance, and Billing. Each of these reflects several of the characteristics described above.

4.2 Service Provisioning

The Service Provisioning Application supports the entry and implementation of customer requests for service. Customer requests for service which require provisioning are those that change some billed quantity (e.g., storage in the service) or require physical work (e.g., adding a line). The customer request becomes an order which is entered via a screen oriented forms interface which uses descriptive English prompts and responses.

The order is decomposed into a set of tasks for tracking and control. A task is the smallest independently scheduled unit of service provisioning work. Each task is individually tracked through the steps required to implement it. In the central portion of the application, the task is scheduled in detail and any required resources are assigned. In the local portion, the task causes the actual updating of the internal tables and any physical work that may be required.

The reporting from the Service Provisioning Application consists primarily of status reports, jeopardy reports, and future work reports.

4.2.1 *The Service Provisioning Design* Figure 1 presents the high level design of the Service Provisioning Application. Orders are accepted through the Order Entry Program which validates the requests against the Customer Account File (CAF). Once the entry is complete, the order is released by the operator and automatically decomposed into its constituent tasks. These are passed to the Coordination and Control Program which places them in the Pending Order File (POF) where they provide a record of the order until it is complete.

The tasks are distributed to the Assignment Program for scheduling and resource assignment automatically or on command entered via the Coordination and Control Terminal Manager. The Assignment Program provides a form-based system for manual entry of assignments. (The Assignment Program will be extended in the future into a complete Inventory Management system.)

The tasks are also distributed from the Pending Order File to the local node, the Local Coordination and Control Program, where they are placed in the Local Pending Order File for actual implementation. The System Update Program actually changes the internal tables on receipt of a task from the Local Coordination and Control Program. The requests for physical work (and the whole local craft interaction) are handled by the Maintenance Terminal Manager. Indeed, this interface supports the complete local control of service provisioning. However, commands for the Local Coordination and Control Program can also be entered though the Coordination and Control Terminal Manager and through the Central Maintenance Terminal Manager. (described in Section 4.3)

After the task is implemented, a completion report is returned to the central portion for posting in its Pending Order File by the Coordination and Control Program. Each of the Pending Order Files (central and local) contains status information related to the corresponding central or local processing steps. The Coordination and Control Programs maintain that information and react to status and due dates to take action. The status and jeopardy reports are derived from this database.

As a final step in processing an order, the Coordination and Control Program distributes the tasks in it to the CAF Update Program for updating of the validation file.

4.3 Maintenance

The Maintenance Application supports the detection of, diagnosis of, repair of and recovery from overall system errors. It further supports day to day administration of the node. All these activities can be performed either locally or centrally; however, a major goal of the maintenance operation is to be able to operate unstaffed nodes during normal operation.

The detection activity depends primarily on self-detection of errors by all system software. All such errors are logged and, if severe, handled immediately. In addition, several watch-dog mechanisms are used to detect the complete failure of a component of a node. Finally, performance and congestion measurements also provide information about current and future problems.

To diagnose a problem, the Maintenance Application provides the operator with the ability to query the status of most parts of the system, review the history of an error by reports from error logs, and finally to request the execution of various levels of diagnostics.

Once an error is understood and the exact problem is defined, the operator can remove offending hardware and software components from service, initialize backups, request repair of the bad component, and then re-initialize it to return to the original configuration. If the error is simply an error in an internal data structure, the operator can directly update the data itself.

The scenario presented above is concerned with the resolution of errors requiring human intervention. While this is the focus of the Maintenance Application, there are transient errors and errors that are automatically fixed by the system. In these instances, the error is recorded for later analysis by operations personnel using mechanisms similar to those used for human fixed errors.

The day to day administrative activities consist of such things as implementing customer orders (see Service Provisioning), adding node equipment, and database administration. These are all performed at operator request from either the central site or the node site.

These activities can in general be performed from either the local node site or the central operations node site. The primary difference between the two interfaces is that the central operators are presented a network-wide view and scope of control. The enhancements made to each central interface simply reflect this more global view of the network.

4.3.1 *The Maintenance Design* The maintenance design (see Figure 2) emphasizes the distinction between the terminal manager programs and the command service programs which provide the requested function in the background.

The terminal managers define various work positions: the local node maintenance terminal, the central maintenance terminal, and the supervisory terminal. Each of these is able to exercise similar command service programs and as such implement similar commands.

The command service programs come in two types. First, much of the function of maintenance is provided by the service through such underlying system processes as Maintenance and Configuration (MAC) and the Applications Control Program. Second, there are a set of support command service programs for the Maintenance Application itself. These command service programs provide storage, retrieval, and processing functions in support of the central operations functions.

An example of such processes is the pair of Trouble Management Programs which log and track all trouble messages. This pair of cooperating programs also maintains the status of each trouble (open, assigned, resolved, etc.) and coordinates the responsibility for the trouble (e.g., assigned locally or centrally).

In addition to the application based operations support, maintenance activities use a number of capabilities in the underlying system which are there for maintenance only. One such capability provides central initialization of nodes as required by the objective of centralized operations. This capability is provided by the Remote Operator's Console (ROC) subsystem. The

initialization of the processors in the node requires the use of each processor's console interface prior to the initialization of the service on that processor. Since the application environment does not yet exist at that point in the initialization sequence, there is no way to use the service's own capabilities to provide remotely controlled initialization. Instead, the console of each processor is remoted to the central maintenance center through the Remote Operator's Console subsystem. This subsystem consists of a two level concentrator network which culminates in a remote processor console that emulates many individual consoles for the central operator. With the Remote Operator's Console subsystem, the central maintenance personnel are able to use a second interface to the node (the first is the central maintenance terminal). This second interface centralizes several functions, not only initialization but also access to low-level system diagnostics and error logs.

4.4 Billing

The Billing Application supports the collection and storage of all data required to produce a customer bill for the service, the actual calculation and printing of the bill, and the tracking of the payment status of the customer. The data that is input into the bill is of two types: usage data corresponding to the per activity rate elements, and fixed data corresponding to the monthly recurring rate elements.

The detailed usage data is collected in real time in the local node. Once a day this per event usage data is reduced to daily totals for each customer and stored in that accumulated form. The detail is not kept for the actual billing function; if a customer desires the detailed usage information, it can be placed in a customer file on customer request for a fee.

The fixed data is maintained in the same customer database and is changed via transactions received from Service Provisioning reflecting completed orders for service. At the end of a billing cycle, the accumulated usage and the fixed data are input to a bill calculation that results in the final bill which is presented to the customer. As payments on past bills are received, the current payment status is updated and printed as part of the next bill.

4.4.1 *Billing Design* In each local node, the Billing Data Collector (see Figure 3) receives detailed usage data from various system programs. It accumulates this data for later billing and it stores the detail in a customer detailed file structured by customer account. Customers may copy their data from this file into their own file through the use of a system capability. At day's end, the Local Billing Program retrieves the accumulated usage and sends it to central billing via store-and-forward transfer. The Local Billing Process also assists in recovery and reporting functions.

In central billing, the Reception Program handles all incoming accumulated data transfers, tracks which nodes have sent data, and aggregates the data further. The Database Update Program adds the usage data to the billing database. It also receives and responds to fixed data update transactions from the Service Provisioning Application.

At the end of a billing cycle, the Bill Maintenance Program retrieves the cycle's information, produces the bill, and clears the usage from the billing database.

The Billing Terminal Manager provides the operator interface to the Billing Application for two major functions. First, it supports the manual override of sequencing of processing for those cases when the automatic mechanisms do not work properly. Second, it supports the controlled updating of various billing files including portions of the billing database.

5. SUMMARY

The operations support for a programmable data communications service is being built and executed as application systems in the service itself. This integrated approach to operations support has several advantages over the more traditional approach of operations support external to a service. Primary among these advantages is a reduction in development effort due to a reduction in complexity of the operations support systems. Other important economic advantages of the integrated operations support approach are that development resources can be shared and personnel experienced in the service can develop the support system.

The functions of the service for the major operations support applications were defined; these included Service Provisioning, Maintenance, Network Management, Customer Trouble Handling and Billing. The common characteristics of these applications were discussed, as well as possible design strategies. Finally, the designs of the operations support applications implemented as part of the service itself were described in detail to illustrate the unique aspects of the approach of developing the operations support of a service on that service itself.

FIGURE 1: SERVICE PROVISIONING

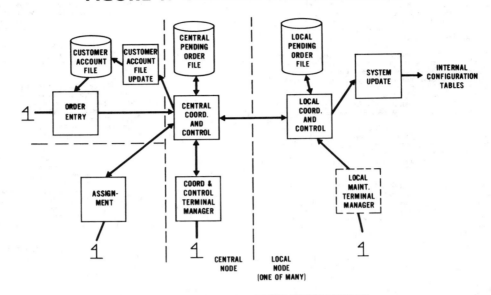

THE SERVICE PROVISIONING APPLICATION IMPLEMENTS CUSTOMER ORDERS FOR
SERVICE THROUGH CHANGING HARDWARE AND UPDATING INTERNAL TABLES
(BOTH IN THE LOCAL NODE). THE TWO COORDINATION AND CONTROL PROGRAMS ARE
CENTRAL TO THE APPLICATION, TRACKING AND CONTROLLING THE PROCESSING OF
ORDERS. AFTER ENTRY, THE COORDINATION AND CONTROL PROGRAMS INITIATE
ALL SUBSEQUENT PROCESSING STEPS (ASSIGNMENT, TESTING, ETC.). THE PENDING
ORDER FILES CONTAIN ALL THE INFORMATION ABOUT THE ORDERS, INCLUDING
STATUS, BETWEEN THEM.

FIGURE 2: MAINTENANCE

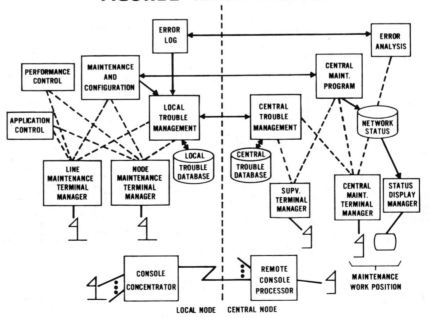

THE PRIMARY FUNCTION OF THE MAINTENANCE APPLICATION IS THE DETECTION OF, DIAGNOSIS OF AND RECOVERY
FROM SYSTEM ERRORS. THE FLOW OF THIS ERROR ACTIVITY BEGINS WITH DETECTION OF ERRORS IN THE LOCAL NODE AND
CONTINUES THROUGH LOGGING OF THE ERRORS IN THE TROUBLE DATABASE, NOTIFYING OPERATIONS PERSONNEL AT THE CENTRAL
(OR NODE) MAINTENANCE TERMINALS, AND UPDATING OF THE NETWORK STATUS. THE DIAGNOSIS AND REPAIR IS HANDLED BY
OPERATIONS PERSONNEL REQUESTING REPORTS, TESTS AND RE-CONFIGURATION THROUGH THE VARIOUS MAINTENANCE
TERMINAL MANAGERS. LOW LEVEL (OPERATING SYSTEM AND EQUIPMENT) ERRORS ALSO FLOW IN THE SAME LOCAL TO
CENTRAL DIRECTION; HOWEVER, THE ERRORS AND REPAIRS GO VIA THE CONSOLE CONCENTRATOR AND REMOTE
CONSOLE PROCESSOR.

FIGURE 3: BILLING

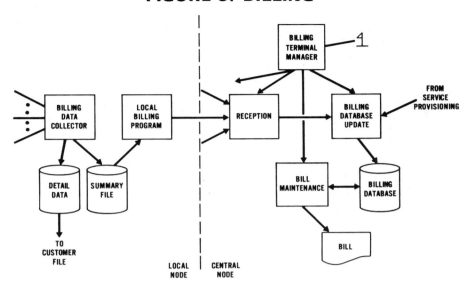

THE BILLING APPLICATION PROCESSING BEGINS WITH COLLECTION OF USAGE DATA IN THE LOCAL NODE WHERE THAT DATA IS IMMEDIATELY SUMMARIZED FOR LATER TRANSFER TO THE CENTRAL BILLING PROCESSING. THERE, THE RECEPTION PROGRAM COLLECTS DATA FROM ALL NODES AND INITIATES THE UPDATE OF THE CUSTOMER'S CUSTOMER BILLING DATABASE (FIXED CHARGES AND USAGE TO DATE). AT THE END OF A BILLING CYCLE, THE CUSTOMER'S BILL IS PRODUCED AND THE BILLING DATABASE IS PURGED.

References

(1) W. R. Smith and J. S. Hubley, "An Innovative, Shared Intelligent Network Service", ICCC82

(2) B. P. Donohue, III, J. F. McDonald and H. R. Liu, "The Architecture of an Innovative Data Communications Network", ICCC82

(3) R. U. Faust and D. C. Wormley, "Operations Strategies for a Shared, Intelligent Network", ICCC82

O. W. Traber, III currently heads the Data Network Product Architecture Department. His work at Bell Laboratories, beginning in 1976, initially focused on defining the features of and specifying the functional requirements for a data programmable data communications network service. In 1979, he moved to the specification of system architecture for customer and operations support applications for that service. Mr. Traber started his current cross product architecture planning job in 1980. Prior to joining Bell Laboratories, Mr. Traber spent several years in system development for a major bank.

Mr. Traber has an AB degree in Computer Science and Applied Math and a MS degree in Operations Research, both from the University of California at Berkeley.

Italian Experiences and Plans in Videotel

D Gagliardi, G Morganti, G Ruzza
SIP, Italy

A short summary on the Videotex activities carried out in Italy has given in order to inform the international forum on the present status of the Italian Videotel pilot trials. The field trials will be officially opened by the end of present year and in order to achieve this goal,different problems have been solved. The lecture takes into account the standard problems and the Prestel attitude to cover the pilot trials exigencies mainly devoted to cover the business needs . Furthermore,information is given on the activities carried out to operate the pilot trials; particular concern is given to the I. Ps and users choice and to the tariffes definition.

1. INTRODUCTION

Videotex experiences started in the world with the pilot trials operation in U. K. in 1974. Before that date research and development activities were carried out in order to verify the feasibility of the new technology which had to introduce a new service in the telecommunication world.

After that date videotex activities blew up in the world and today it is possible to adfirm that, although at different level, Videotex services or initiatives are in progress in a lot of European and extra European Countries. Prestel, Bildshirmtext, Teletel, Viditel, Telidon, Videotex, Videotel are only some names used for national Videotex services.

Videotel is the Italian name for the public Videotex service which SIP under the main guide lines and in agreement with the Italian P. T. Ministry is setting up for the pilot trials. Before introducing Italian experiences and plans in the Videotel framework it is useful to consider and to reflect on the main strategies that is possible to use for implementing the Videotex service.

The different choices that are on the table of the service Operators are relevant to:
- the standard;
- the general strategy;
- the network architecture;
- the tariffes principles.

In the present lecture some considerations concerning the general problem of the Videotex service implementation are reported,af

terwards the Italian situation will be considered dealing with the Videotex plans and experiences in progress in Italy.

2. GENERAL STRATEGY

The main point to be defined before offering any kind of good is the knowledge of the relevant user population. In the Videotex service a great debate exists in some Countries on the "nature" of the Videotex population at least considering the short time. All Operators intend to offer the new information service to the largest subscriber population ,but the main question is: who will be interested to the Videotex service from the out set ?who will be available to pay some fees for having information on the adapted TV set? How is it possible to have some profits?

Two kinds of subscribers may be forecasted:
- business
- residential

Taking into account that new tariffes must be paid for the new service it is very likely that enough time will run before residential user will be familiar with and confident on the new information technology . Information is available at the residential premises in different, competitive and complementary ways: newspapers, magazines, booklets, timetables, TV programs, radio programs, other systems offer enough information to the residential user for his normal life.

In this respect, very likely, residential users will be interested to the Videotex service under two main conditions:
- information availability only through the Videotex service;
- low (or non applied) tariffes.

(*) - Italian P. T. Ministry
(**) - SIP - Italian Telephone Operating Company

In conclusion it is possible to foresee, at least in the Italian environment (cultural, economical aspects must be considered) that the business population will firstly be interested to the Videotex service which may be considered a new "working tool" able to simplify the working procedures, to access remote and essential information, to reach very quickly and simply a large population users.

3. THE STANDARD ARENA

Videotex was developed in the U.K. and a very simple standard was defined able to fullfill the English language needs (no accents are present in the English language). The standard was conceived to cover all English text exigencies and to reproduce simple pictorial information. Alpha mosaic mode was defined where alpha-numeric and other graphic symbols were used for the text information, while a mosaic repertoire with 64 characters was defined for graphic information. The possibility to manage the information presentation on the TV screen was also offered with the "display attributes" able to handle the character presentation at the "string" level.

In France a new standard was developed, able to manage characters with accented letters. Furthermore, display attributes were defined and managed in such a way to be considered independent attributes of each character position.

In Canada the Telidon system was developed. It is characterized by the use of the P.D.I.s (Picture Description Instruction), which are commands relevant to simple geometric configuration (point, line, arc, rectangle, polygon). When they are received by the terminal a microcomputer uses them to reproduce the required geometric draw. The display attributes, including the picture definition (number of pel/line) are transmitted using a coding system completely different from both the U.K. and France proposal. The Canadian standard is able to offer better pictorial information at the expenses of more complicated decoder. Japan, taking into account its language needs (ideograms instead of alphabetic characters) developed the Captain system which is mainly based on the principle of point by point (similar to the fac-simile one) transmission of information.

The memory terminal has a larger capacity if compared with the memory for European standards. Presently 64 K bits are considered sufficient for a complete picture.

DRCS (Dynamical Redifinable Character Sets) have also been studied to "load", from the center to the terminal, pattern relevant to some specific draws which can be defined on the

willingness of the I.Ps. They are very useful to reproduce logos and very small pictures (e.g. chessboard with relevant chess figures).

ATT presented in Toronto (Viewdata 81 Exhibition) a new proposal which is mainly based on the Canadian system with some additional enhancements to offer better and enhanced performances. The cost of the decoder is also in this case higher then those working according to the European proposals.

CEPT in May 81 recommended a new standard which integrates both the UK and the France proposals. Terminals working in conformity with the CEPT Recommendations are able to manage both English and France display attributes and they are compatible with the existing data basis operating in France and in the U.K.

In conclusion it is possible to adfirm that presently for the Videotex operators the standard choice appears to be difficult taking into account the different listed proposal that if considered uncorrelated and independent are uncompatible.

4. ITALIAN CHOICE CONCERNING THE STANDARD FOR THE PILOT TRIALS

The Italian Consultant Committee of the P.T. Ministry decided in November 1980 to use the Prestel know-how to set up and to carry on the pilot trials.

The main reasons for that choice can be summarized as follows:
- Prestel know-how has the experience of a public service and has been developed by a public administration;
- the main purpose of the Italian pilot trials are related to the marketing aspects and to the business area;
- the Prestel facilities and performances (information retrievel, closed user groups management, response frame availability etc...) are considered satisfactory for the pilot trials needs;
- the gateway facility which is available also in the Italian pilot trials-offers the possibility to connect external Host computers enlarging the information framework offered to the user;
- text information is considered the basic one for the pilot trials. In the business area it is thought that pictorial information will have not great importance and that the mosaic performances can be considered satisfactory enough;
- the terminal cost should be strongly taken into account in order to avoid that the Videotex service success is conditioned by high not required performances;
- the decoder availability-VLSI chip are not

yet economically available for solutions different from the Prestel one must be taken into account.

5. ITALIAN POINT OF VIEW AS CONCERNS THE STANDARD FOR THE PUBLIC SERVICE

Italian Administration has been strongly involved to help a unified world wide Videotex standard approval in the international bodies. The Italian point of view is that it is possible to work to facilitate as much as possible the interconnection between Videotex services operating in different countries. A first proposal exists, drafted by CEPT where all performances considered separately by the mentioned existing proposals, are available under the main umbrella of a unified standard.

Italian position is to be in line for the final service, with the international agreement and mainly with the CCITT and CEPT Recommendations.

In any case the final Italian decision will be taken no later than the pilot trials conclusions taking into account the international evolution on the Videotex standard matter.

6. MARKETING ACTIVITIES

Marketing aspects have a paramount importance for the Videotex service. Particular investigations have been carried out in Italy in order to find out the basic characteristics on which the new service should be based. Marketing enquiry have been oriented to explore the users and IPs interest, to define a users and IPs sample from which it could be possible to draw the main guidelines for the service implementation.

As concerns the users a specialized organization on the markeitng investigation had the task to define the procedures to be adopted to identify the users and the IPs that should be involved in the pilot trials. As concerns the users the sample population should be limited roughly to 1000 people; for the IPs no restrictions were put down; it was only intended to avoid overlapping of information.

6.1 USER sample : characteristics and allocation

The acquisition of the users started last April in the city of Milan [1] and is carried out by a special taskforce, created in SIP, that will extend, afterward, such activity also in other cities of the trial.

_____
(1) At the moment, over 60 users have been acquired of the 300 foreseen in Milan

Such sample foresees the acquisition of about 1.000 users (300 in Milan, 220 in Rome and Turin, 90 in Bologna and Naples, 80 in Venice) of which the 80% are in business area and only the 20% in the residential area. The population of business users is divided in 7 economical macrosections foresee 38 categories, chosen with the criteria to identify category groups and homogeneous conduct from the point of view of the availability for the investment in Telecommunications and informatics.

At its time the residential ambit sample will be compounded by families belonging to the middle-high economical classes, with determined availability to the expenses in electronic products and/or of telecommunications.

6.2 IPs Characteristics

From the first contacts with the I.P.s it can be adfirmed that great interest has been shown by Italian Information Providers. Taking into account the main nature of the pilot trials, mainly devoted to the market investigation in the business area it has been decided to set up a bank information able to cover different needs of business people . At the same time also the residential population needs have been considered in order to get together all information useful to set up the public service.

In this area the main result up-dated at June 1^1982) can be summarized as follows:
- I.P.s connected: 59
- Assigned pages
- Edited page

The complete (updated at June 1^1982) IPs list is reported in the Annex 1.

The main covered areas are at the same date the following ones:
- Newspaper agencies
- Tourism
- Air Traffic Timetables
- Mail ordering service
- Stock exchanges
- Pharmaceutical products and health informations.

7. TARIFFES

In order to have real and useful information from the pilot trials it has been decided that suitable tariffes should be adopted both for the users and IPs.

The following tariffes have been established by the Italian P.T. Ministry:

7.1   User tariffes

7.1.1 Residential user

Annual fee: 20.000 lire
Telephone network use: local telephone char
ge
Videotex computer access: 150£/3min. from
8 a.m. to 10p.m.

150£/9min. from
10 p.m. to 8 a.m.
and not on work-
ing days.

Terminal rent : see later
information   : charge for the competence of
the IPs

7.1.2 Business user

Annual fee   :   120.000 Lire
Telephone network use: local telephone char
ge
Videotex computer access: 150£/3min. from
8 a.m. to 10p.m.
150£/9min. from
10p.m. to 8a.m .
and not on working
days.

Terminal rent : see later
information   : charge on the competence of
the IPs

7.1.3 I.P.s

Annual fee for data: 120.000
connection

Videotex subscription : 2.000.000 Lire/year
Computer memory use   :   10.000Lire/year
page
Telephone network use : local telephone char
ge on the property
of the IP

7.1.4 Terminal rent cost

In so far as it concerns the users terminals,
they will be produced by the Italian industry and
will be of the following type and will have the
following fees for rent and maintenance.

Colour TV set with numeric keyboard :L. 37.000
Colour TV set with alpha-numeric keyboard:
L. 47.000 per month
Colour TV set with alpha-numeric keyboard
and prearranged for printing maching:
L. 50.000 per month
Colour Videoterminal with alpha-numeric
keyboard: L. 73.500

All the above-mentioned terminals for the
user for the trial phase will be directly supplied by SIP.

8. CONCLUSIONS

Strong and intensive activities have carried

out in Italy on the Videotex matter. In order
to touch the consistence of such activities it is
advisable to consider the general plans introduced in London at Viewdata 81 Exhibition. To
day the following results have been obtained:
- the complete Videotex Center with two GEC
4082 machines is in operation;
- the gateway facility is available
- the marketing investigation to identify the
user sample have been completed
- the pilot trials are about to be officially ope
rated
- More than 60 IPs are connected
- More than 20,000 pages are available
- the first users both in the business and in
the residential area are connected.

Useful results should be available in a short
time as concerns both the technical and the
marketing aspects; the authors will in the futu
re opportunities present them in the international areas in order to cooperate for a world
wide coordination in the Videotex area.

ANNEX 1

IPs Connected on the Italian VIDEOTEL Pilot
Trials (*)

AGENZIA ANSA

A.G.I.

ALITALIA

ALPITOUR

AMERICAN EXPRESS

A.N.A.S.

ANMCO

ASSICURAZIONI GENERALI

AVIATOUR

BANCA NAZIONALE DEL LAVORO

BANCO DI ROMA

C.D.S. ITALIA

CENTRO TELEVISIVO UNIVERSIT.

C.E.S.A.C.

C.I.T.A.M.

C.I.T.E.

CLINICON ITALIA

COGESPE

CONFIDUSTRIA

C.R.E.I.

C.S.E.L.T.

_____
(*) list updated at June 1^1982

200

DITRON

EDITEL TOSCANA

EDITRAGNO

E.S.A. C

ETAS KOMPASS

EUROPEAN HOTELS'CLUBS

FINTEL

FONDAZIONE MARCONI

GE-DA

IL MESSAGGERO

IL SECOLO XIX

INFORMATICA SHOP

ISDA

I.S.I.S.

ISTITUTO BANCARIO S. PAOLO TORINO

ITAL INFORMATION SYSTEM

LA STAMPA

L'EDITORE

MINISTERO POSTE E TELECOMUNICAZIONE

P. FELLETTI SPADAZZI

PHILIPS T.L.C.

POSTAL MARKET ITALIANA

RADIOCOR

SAINTSEAL

SEAT

S.I.P.

SIPE OPTIMATION

SLAMARK

SWISSAIR

SYSTEM INFORMATICA

TECNETRA

TELEMACO

TELERENT

TORO ASSICURAZIONI

UNIONE NAZIONALE CONSUMATORI

VESTRO

VIDEODATA ITALIA

ZANUSSI ELETTRONICA

BIOGRAPHIES

Professor Diodato GAGLIARDI - is director of the Istituto Superiore delle Poste e Telecomunicazioni of the Italian P.T. Ministry. In this position he is the responsible for research and standardization problems in the Italian P.T. Ministry environment with particular reference to the problems relevant to the networks and to the telecommunication services.

He is also strongly engaged in International activities:
- He is chairman of the CCITT/SG XIV, involved in the analogue and digital transmission systems, and of the CEPT-CCH Committee which has the mandate to coordinate and harmonize the telecommunication activities within the CEPT Administrations.

Ing. Giuseppe MORGANTI is a manager of the R&D Department of the Italian Telephone Operating Company and has been involved in the telecommunications field since 1959.

He is particularly dedicated to the new information services and with this task he is member of various standardization bodies.

Ing. Giancarlo RUZZA was born in Roma where he got his Electrical Engineering degree.

In 1962 he was engaged by STET and here he attended a specialisation course in "Electronic Data Processing"; and in this activity he worked until '65.

In 1966 has joined for SIP (Società Italiana per l'Esercizio Telefonico), where, now, he is responsible of the Department "Sistemi d'utenti" which is also engaged in the implementation of the Videotel activities.

Teletext and Videotex Systems in the USA

J T Armstrong
British Videotex and Teletext,
Logica, USA

Strongly competitive market forces and a firm commercial basis for most services characterized the US market presenting both opportunities and obstacles for teletext and videotex
services. AT&T are attempting to exploit their communication medium (the telephone line) and
protect revenue from 'Yellow Pages'. However, the author believes the low cost of delivering
a mass audience by broadcast and/or cable favours these media. In order to provide more
extensive services than are possible with conventional broadcast teletext, FULL-CHANNEL
TELETEXT and INTERACTIVE TELETEXT systems with multiple levels of service are evolving for
cable and broadcast use. This paper outlines such systems and describes the kinds of
services which are planned for them as well as the more conventional forms of videotex and
teletext.

1. INTRODUCTION

In the UK and other countries two forms of
information delivery (electronic publishing)
via TV screens have developed. Both systems
present pages of information to the user in a
format of 24 rows of 40 characters plus graphics. The two systems are Teletext which was
developed for broadcast use by sending digital
information during the vertical blanking interval of TV signals and Videotex, an interactive
system using telephone lines and modems. Teletext typically delivers a continuously-updated
news magazine of 200-300 pages and is a mass
medium with advertising potential for the
residential market. Videotex, formerly known
as viewdata, permits access to much larger
data bases (100,000 pages or more) and has so
far developed as a medium for services to
specific industries, notably the travel
industry. Because videotex has two-way communications, in addition to seeking specific
information, users may also send messages
including the placing of orders for goods and
services.

Although some 16 countries have established or
emerging teletext and/or videotex services the
USA has yet to see such services implemented
on a commercial basis. This is despite a high
level of interest and numerous trials of competing systems. The presently confused situation will gradually become clearer with new
types of teletext and videotex systems playing a significant role.

2. THE US MARKET

There has been extensive debate on technical
standards in the USA. AT&T supported by CBS
and others has proposed standards considerably
more complex than any existing systems. Indeed
no equipment meeting those standards is known
to exist yet. It is clear that these proposals
are not based solely on technical considerations but arise at least in part from a defensive commercial posture by these organizations.
Many of the paradoxes of the US market are

explained by consideration of the revenue mechanisms concerned. There is no problem with
specialized business services where revenue
flows from the user to the information provider
via a system operator. Such mechanics do not
present a large scale disturbance of revenues
to major corporations. The situation with the
mass residential market predicted for electronic publishing is quite different.

The market is currently based on multi-billion
dollar advertising revenues. AT&T (yellow
pages plus associated telephone revenues),
newspapers and magazines (including classified
advertisements), TV and radio broadcasters all
receive shares of these revenues and all are
concerned with potential redistribution of
advertising revenues as a result of teletext
and videotex services. AT&T in particular
must seek to keep the telephone line as the
prime delivery mechanism for these services
rather than allow TV or cable systems to become
viable alternatives.

Despite AT&T's attempts to delay matters by
proposing new standards, the regulatory
position in the USA is effectively that no
technical standards will be imposed for either
videotex or teletext services. (The Federal
Communications Commission-FCC which regulates
broadcasting has proposed a rulemaking for
teletext which sets no standards and is likely
to take effect during 1982). Thus a 'open-
market' situation exists in which technologies
and services may be expected to compete on a
commercial basis. Services for the residential
market may be considered in a number of levels
based upon system complexity and size of data
base:

Level 1 - News magazine comprising world and
local news, sports, leisure, weather
and travel information (conventional
teletext)

Level 2 - Classified advertisements

Level 3 - <u>Directories</u> <u>and</u> <u>Timetables</u> (e.g. Yellow Pages, airline guides etc.)

Level 4 - <u>Interactive</u> <u>Services</u> (teleshopping, telebanking, etc.)

It is important to recognize that two thresholds must be crossed before the residential market can be a success. Firstly, the price of a decoder/adaptor device must fall to a figure at which significant numbers can be sold or rented to householders and secondly, sufficient devices must be in use to allow advertising rates to be established. In order to achieve these thresholds an information provider must promote attractive services for an extended period of time before advertising revenue will accrue. A competitive unregulated market clearly accentuates the risks involved in attempting to overcome these thresholds and there is understandable interest in various high-priced specialized services to help funding during the early stages of build up of population of decoders/adaptors. Such 'premium' services require that text services be 'tiered' i.e. each subscriber may opt to pay for various grades or levels of service. This is easily achieved on videotex through the billing mechanism for page access or by the operation of closed user groups (CUG's) whose members may be charged a premium. On teletext systems the tiering concept is relatively novel but easy to implement with levels of authorization being transmitted in teletext format to individually-addressed decoders. Such equipment is now available[1] and is expected to play an important role in subscription TV and cable systems applications (see below).

3. NEW COMMUNICATIONS MEDIA

To date teletext and videotex have developed almost exclusively using the broadcast and telephone communications media for which they were designed. However, in the USA, geographic size and competitive markets bring a number of additional communications media into play. These are:

(a) Subscription TV (STV)
Television requiring a descrambler in the subscribers' home is becoming widespread and it is possible to add teletext to these TV signals. This allows user subscription to replace advertising revenue and high-priced services for specific user groups to be created.

(b) Satellite transponders
Nationwide distribution of TV programmes and commercials by satellite is now a reality. This will clearly be an important mechanism for distribution to local TV stations of national teletext services. (Regional information and advertising will be added by the local TV stations). Leased telephone circuits via satellite will also form an important part of the communications needs of videotex systems.

(c) Low power TV
A flood of applications to operate low power TV stations is currently in abeyance at the FCC. Among the many business opportunities offered by use of the whole TV signal for text trans-

mission purposes (full-channel teletext), offering speedy and cheap delivery of several thousand pages of text.

(c) Cable systems
More than half the homes in America are now served or 'passed' by cable TV systems. Competition for the remaining few franchises is fierce and text services are being promised by bidders. Cable systems offer opportunities for development of text services because they often have unused or under-used channels and the ability to establish a user base rapidly. Technically a number of attractive possibilities exist for cable systems.

(d) Data on FM radio
FM side band transmission of data is possible without interference with the existing audio service. Such digital transmission is already in use in some areas for high value data services giving up to the minute stock and commodity prices.

4. SYSTEMS LIKELY TO EMERGE

There are many uncertainties in forecasting what will happen in a confused and competitive situation such as currently exists. The following are strictly personal projections by the author, of the major forms which will be taken by teletext and videotex systems in the USA. I mention only the general characteristics for conventional <u>teletext</u> and <u>videotex</u> and particular points relevant to the US market. For the derivative systems of <u>full channel teletext</u> and <u>interactive teletext</u>, further explanation is given.

A. <u>Teletext</u> (in the vertical blanking interval, VBI) will develop as one or more national services distributed by satellite. Regional and local broadcasters will add to these national services both in 'open' teletext broadcasting and as tiered text services on STV (subscription TV). Cable operators will carry VBI teletext from national and local broadcasting sources and will also put teletext signals of their own onto cable for such purposes as program listing and local advertising.

B. <u>Videotex</u> will develop, as in Europe, as public and private services primarily for business users. 'Gateway' facilities to Data Processing computers (third party hosts) will be of increasing importance allowing videotex to become the principal means for unskilled personnel to access computing systems. Private viewdata systems will have a significant input for the US market performing this role. Large populations of existing computer terminals and home computers will affect the types of videotex terminals used and message transmission via videotex systems will be widely used.

C. <u>Full-channel teletext</u> is the first derivative of videotex/teletext to emerge in response to US market pressures. The perceived requirement is to provide classified ads, and continuously-updated directories and timetables for the residential market. Such services require the capability to deliver thousands of pages to a large section of the population. Cable has the answer in that it serves an increasing

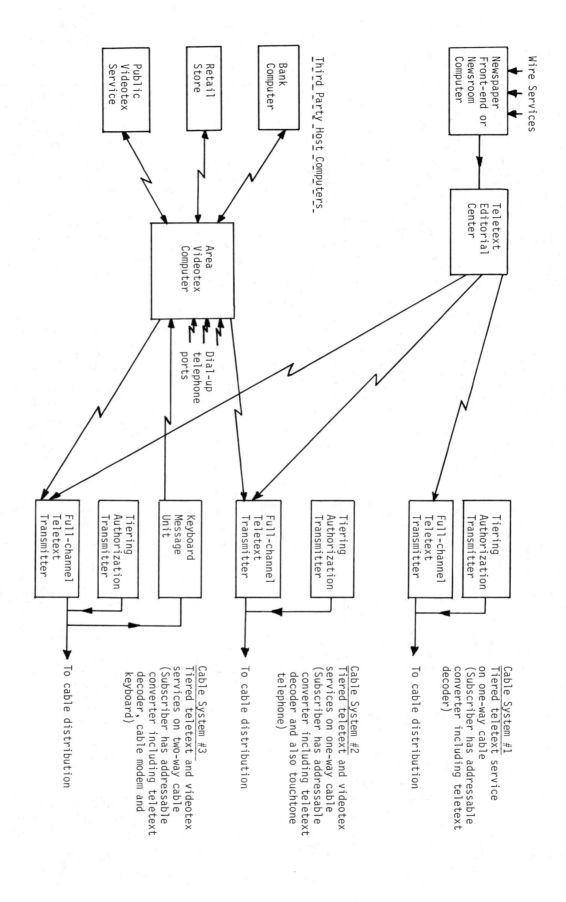

Figure 1.

proportion of the residential market and can generally provide at least one TV channel dedicated to text purposes. Such a channel can provide transmission of several thousand pages with an acceptable access time.

Approximately 2 pages per second my be transmitted per TV scan line used for teletext transmission (in both fields). Typically, about 4 lines are available in the VBI which do not interfere with other functions or with normal receiver operation. Thus, teletext in the VBI has a cycle time of 12½ seconds for a 100 page magazine, or an average access time of 6-7 seconds. The judicious use of rolling pages (pages which cycle through a series of sub pages at predetermined intervals) increase the capacity of such a magazine to between 200 and 300 pages which is normally adequate for a news magazine but not for the additional services desired. A 'full-channel' with around 250 scan lines available transmit at 500 pages per second. A magazine with the same 12½ second cycle time would have a capacity of over 6000 pages. This is the attraction of full-channel teletext, that thousands of pages of information may be distributed to large audiences with low delivery costs. (A teletext service may be likened to a newspaper with no newsprint or delivery costs).

Implementation of full-channel teletext transmission is an extension of existing techniques for the VBI. Editorial functions are largely unaltered by transmission itself requires access to megabytes of memory with stringent timing constraints. Realization of a cost effective transmission device requires carefull design and acceptance of some functional constraints. As well as the transmission cycle, the device must also permit updates from an editorial source, system recovery from disturbances and make provision for transmission of signals to control the tiering of services, which is important for commercial success.

Thus, full-channel teletext may be significantly more expensive than teletext in the VBI alone. Clearly editorial costs could be very much greater in the case of full-channel teletext. Distribution of such a service nationwide via satellite can spread these costs but is itself expensive and this is a partial solution only as much of the information it is desired to transmit will be of a local or regional nature. Another minor problem is that a slightly different form of teletext decoder is required. Despite these difficulties, full-channel teletext services are likely to make their debut within the next year. Low power TV stations are another potential distribution medium for such services.

D. Interactive Teletext is a further extension of conventional teletext providing videotex services with large data-bases as an additional service to conventional teletext. In these systems, videotex pages are delivered to individual subscribers by inserting them momentarily into a teletext magazine. Broadcast (VBI) teletext can support small-scale interactive teletext. A 50-port videotex system with page requests at a rate of 3 per minute would, when fully working, 'slow down' the normal teletext magazine by up to 30%. With full-channel teletext much larger systems could be supported. A 1000-port videotex system with 3 page requests per minute per port would slow a full-channel teletext magazine by about 10%. Implementing such a system requires that a videotex system be closely linked to teletext transmission equipment. This arrangement poses no significant system design problem. As well as all the one-way services desired by the US marketplace, interactive teletext is capable of two-way facilities such as teleshopping and messaging. Fig. 1 is a schematic of the kind of videotex/teletext system expected to emerge for full-channel delivery via cable.

This system may be the 'ultimate' solution for the residential market. It provides a means via broadcasting and cable to deliver videotex services as well as teletext at economically viable prices. Videotex via telephone lines provide a degree of privacy which cannot be fully matched by interactive-teletext but the costs of conventional videotex seem to put it out of reach for most residential markets for some time. Although local telephone calls are still free in parts of the USA, the trend is for increasing charges for local calls. This trend is reinforced by anti-trust legal action against AT&T and by the current administration's 'open market' policies. Unless AT&T can itself introduce videotex facilities at artificially low prices, residential services by telephone line would seem to be a remote prospect, and teletext-based services look considerably more viable.

5. CONCLUSIONS

There is great interest and also great uncertainty regarding the future of videotex in the USA. In the main this centers around the residential market which is largely funded by advertising revenue. Commercial viability is of great concern. The fundamental competition is seen to be between broadcast/cable and telephone lines as the delivery mechanism for the new text services. A wide range of services is likely to develop and these will be 'tiered' to allow differential pricing of the various services. Full-channel teletext and interactive teletext are developments which are seen to favor broadcast and cable establishing comprehensive consumer-oriented services.

REFERENCES

1 William L. Thomas, Full Field Tiered Addressable Teletext, Technical Papers of the National Cable Television Association's 31st Annual Convention, May 1982.

BIOGRAPHY

The author has 20 years experience in communications and other real-time computer applications. He has worked for Logica Ltd. since 1969 and is a director of that company. He is presently assigned to Logica's USA operation working on the application of Videotex and Teletext to that market.

Monitoring the Technical Performance of a National Videotex Network

K E Clarke, B D Cantwell
British Telecom Research
Laboratories, UK
G J Steel
British Telecom, UK

Prestel, the world's first public videotex service, now has some 16,000 customers and is available to 62% of telephone subscribers in the United Kingdom on a local call basis. To provide this service either a computer or a remote multiplexer is provided in the customer's local service area. The computers accessed by customers for information retrieval receive their videotex page "updates" from a national centre, to which they are connected in "star" configuration.

Monitoring the performance of this nationwide, and largely unattended distributed computer network is of prime importance to the operating authority and its customers in order to maximise the throughput of expensive equipment and to guarantee a reliable service. To this end BT have adopted several methods of performance monitoring. Specialist microprocessor equipment known as VAMPIRE automatically monitors the status of computer input ports to detect faulty modems and computer equipment. Hardware monitors have been deployed at selected centres to determine the utilisation of various hardware and software processes. Mini-computers have been programmed to simulate user access to gain quantified information about response times. These specialist techniques are deployed along with more conventional computer and communications fault reporting procedures and the data thus obtained gives a reliable indication of the reliability and efficiency of the network.

INTRODUCTION

Prestel, the world's first public videotex service, now has some 16,000 customers and is available to 62% of telephone subscribers in the United Kingdom on a local call basis. To provide this service either a computer or a remote multiplexer is provided in the customer's local service area. The computers accessed by customers for information retrieval receive their videotex page "updates" from a national centre, to which they are connected in "star" configuration.

Monitoring the performance of this nationwide, and largely unattended, distributed computer network is a prime importance to the operating authority and its customers in order to maximise the throughput of expensive equipment and to guarantee a reliable service. To this end BT have adopted several methods of performance monitoring and these are described below.

VIEWDATA ACCESS MONITOR AND PRIORITY INCIDENT REPORT EQUIPMENT (VAMPIRE)

Early in the operation of the original viewdata pilot trial computer at Martlesham Heath, problems were experienced in maintaining a full service on the data modems used to access the computer ports. Any faults which occurred were only discovered when complaints were received from users accessing the service. It was then necessary to make repeated test calls over the public switched telephone network, busying out each line in turn until the fault was discovered. In addition, due to the possibility of computer software faults, it was necessary to cause the computer to transmit the initial page of data to confirm correct operation. This was usually done by humming at the correct frequency (390Hz) into the handset and listening for the modulated data carrier from the computer!

When Prestel computers were planned with 200 lines in unattended computer rooms, it was realised that maintaining an acceptable service would be impossible, unless an improved fault-finding and clearing method could be found. Proposals were therefore made for the provision of monitoring equipment to carry out the required functions.

The VAMPIRE Hardware

Several standard data communications control systems were investigated to see if they were suitable for the application proposed. This study showed that they were primarily intended for use on high value private wire circuits, such as are provided for banks and airline networks. They provided sophisticated line-switching and fault-monitoring facilities, but required high cost equipment at the operations centre, and on each line being monitored. They also required the use of the manufacturer's proprietary modems to minimise interface problems. It was thus decided to commence construction of a purpose designed microprocessor based system (using a Motorola M6800 microprocessor). Figure 1 shows the mode of use of VAMPIRE, and its components are described below.

Monitor Interface

Four interface lines are monitored on each viewdata computer port. The signals monitored are:
- calling indicator (No 125)
- receive carrier detector (No 109)
- transmitted data (No 103)
- modem telephone circuit busied (added control circuit).

(The numbers in brackets are from CCITT Recommendation V23)

The first three signals are derived directly from the normal computer/modem interface circuits where they terminate on the back wiring and the fourth from a contact of a relay in the modem control unit. Additional circuits enable the telephone line to be busied automatically when faults occur. Figure 2 shows the arrangement.

Output from the VAMPIRE unit is transmitted to the remote operations centre at 1200 bit/s over a BT Datel 600 circuit with a full duplex return speed of 75 bits/s. The normal output will generate a graphic display table of computer access port status using coloured squares to show the different conditions. Figure 3 is a typical example. In addition, the control options available to the operator for busying lines are displayed as a viewdata menu choice. Pressing a numeric key for a valid choice will cause the display to show a request for the port number(s) to be operated upon. Once a correct entry has been made, the action requested is executed and the normal port status display resumed.

Four separate output channels are provided to give access as follows:
- private circuit to Prestel Operations Centre
- private circuit to the local Prestel manager's office, if required
- auto-answer switched telephone circuit for standby access in the event of a failure of the private wires
- direct, modemless circuit for local test purposes.

The main hardware for the VAMPIRE equipment is based on a 19 inch card frame, using 3 shelves. The top shelf contains the microprocessor, random access memory (RAM), read only memory (ROM), serial input/output cards, and the power supply. The second and third shelves contain parallel input/output cards which are used for interfacing to the modem equipment being monitored. All the cards are connected by a common microprocessor bus extension backplane which is terminated to the component side of the printed circuit cards. The non-component side of the parallel input/output cards are brought out to rear panel connectors for linking to the modem racks using four circuits for input monitoring and one circuit as an output to drive a "busy" control circuit.

The VAMPIRE Software

The programs for the VAMPIRE unit are held in non-volatile memory, so that either "power on" restart, or manual reset will initiate full operation of the unit.

Start-up Routine
On initial start-up, all "busy" control outputs are set off (unbusy) state. Each port on the monitor interface is then scanned in turn and any port which shows a busy state is recorded in the status table as not in use. During normal status scanning these ports will be skipped. This enables ports to be busied locally for maintenance purposes. When a port is restored to service, the on site engineer will press the reset switch to cause VAMPIRE to make a new start-up scan.

Status Monitor
The monitor ports are scanned in sequence and the status of each port recorded in the status table, at least once per second. The transmitted data status is latched when a logic 0 is detected at the commencement of transmission. This status is held until the modem on line signal goes to logic 0 at the end of a call.

The calling indicator port status signal has a software delay to prevent the intermittent ringing signal giving a false display indication.

All other status bits follow the transitions of their related input signal.

Display Driver
A graphic display of the complete 196 ports is generated and transmitted to all four display outputs, at a speed of 120 ch/s. The display is updated continuously during normal status display, with a cursor "home" character (from standard IS0646) being sent after each 960-character frame block.

Each port status rectangle in the display will be set to the status colour appropriate to the current state of the port. The colours used are the standard videotex ones, as described in standard CEPT T/CD6-1 (Ref 1).

The display terminal used to receive output from the display interfaces is a standard viewdata receiver as defined in the UK Prestel Service Terminal specification (2) and full details of the transmission standards to be used on the display interfaces are given in that document.

Error Reporter
The error-states that are detected are:
- Modem on line for 20 secs with no received carrier signal
- Received carrier signal "true" and no transmitted data transition within 2 secs.

An independent, real time process checks that status table entry for each port and if an error-state is detected, the busy control output for that port is set to "on". An error-report message will then be transmitted to all the display outputs, with printer control characters to enable a printed record to be made at control centres equipped with printers. This error-message is formatted such that the busy choice display is completely overwritten and the status display is left intact for the period of the error display (see below). ISO 646 characters DC1 (print on) and DC3 (print off) are used for printer control.

Busy Control
Receipt of a busy choice character on any input will cause all other inputs to be inhibited for 20 secs. This time-out is renewed on each subsequent character received from the active input. The received character is tested for validity as a busy choice. Receipt of a valid character will cause a reply message to be sent to all active outputs, using one of six display frames selected by the value of the received

character. This reply overwrites the busy choice display, leaving the status display intact for operator convenience. The status display will not be updated during the busy control time-out period.

Following a valid busy choice, a three-digit character string will be received from the active input and formed into a port number or code number. This number is checked for validity in relation to the chosen busy command, and an error-message sent if the number is incorrect. If the busy choice requires a second number, for the operation chosen, the above operation is repeated. In addition, the two numbers are checked to ensure that the second entry is equal to or greater than the first before proceeding. After all required input has been received the busying operation will be carried out and the normal display of status resumed.

Operator's Console
The display output from VAMPIRE is transmitted over a private circuit to the Prestel control centre. At the control centre a standard Prestel receiver is used to display the status information. The use of colour has been found to be essential in giving a clear indication of the status of the monitored ports.

THE 'PET' PERFORMANCE MONITOR

Early in the public use of the Prestel system, it became apparent that human estimation of response time is highly subjective. Widely varying reports on the acceptability of the speed of the system were received, many of these relating to coincident periods. Additionally, manual attempts at measurement of response were of limited success, due primarily to the short intervals to be measured, the ergonomics of the timing process and the tedium factor.

The need for an autonomous mechanism for the measurement of the performance of the system was thus demonstrated. This mechanism would be required to provide accurate timings of system responses (in an easily digestable format) and should be capable of running unattended for extended periods. It should also relate its findings, at regular intervals, to the overall load on the system.

Hardware

Initial research into the provision of a performance monitor was based on a Commodore PET microcomputer and current implementation remains on this device (8 Kbytes of memory is just sufficient). The program is written in BASIC for ease of maintenance. The PET is interfaced to Prestel via a bi-directional RS232 interface and a standard modem. A spur is taken from the receive side of the modem and used to drive a Prestel terminal as a slave. This permits visual confirmation of the activity of the PET. An interface is also provided to a 30 CPS character printer.

Control Data

The PET process is driven by a data stream of control information to determine the sequence of activities and the data which is sent to Prestel. The latter is timed.

The data which is transmitted to Prestel is logically divided into two basic categories; user facilities (frame retrieval etc) and Information Provider (IP) facilities (frame editing). This latter category is further subdivided into "edit control" (the IP dialogue which establishes a frame's characteristics - number, price etc), "frame construct" (in which the visible part of each frame is established) and "edit ends" (which signify the completion of edit of frames and trigger their inclusion into the database). These four categories are deemed to have potentially differing criteria of acceptability of response and their independent monitoring permits separate results to be produced for each of them.

Time Bands

The interval between the transmission of a character to Prestel and the receipt of the first (or only) character of response is measured by the PET's internal clock. According to the value of each measured interval, one of five time-band counts (for each data subdivision) is incremented by one. The process thus maintains counts of the number of characters within each category whose response times fall within certain prescribed limits.

The predefined time bands, each of which is exclusive of any which precedes it, are up to half a second; up to two seconds; up to five seconds; up to ten seconds and over ten seconds. Of these, the first two encompass by far the majority of the results on live systems, the last three being intended for exception reporting and loading trials.

Because of the coarse nature of the time bands, a separate reporting level may also be specified for each category of data. Any character whose response time exceeds this level is subject to an explicit report which specifies the exact response interval and the time at which the delay occurred.

System Load

The Prestel System Manager function of Prestel owns a page on which certain load characteristics of the system are constantly updated. The monitor is granted access to this page and periodically reads it and extracts information relating to the current occupants of the machine ports and the user and editing systems.

Results

Every thirty minutes, on the hour and half hour, the monitor outputs a cumulative table of results to the character printer. This table is prefixed with the time of day and the last set of load characteristics extracted from the system. The table's columns represent the time bands and a linear total of characters in each row. There are five rows of information; one for each of the four data categories and a totals row for the overall system. Each entry in the table thus indicates the number of

Example:

```
TIME IS 102004 ON TUE 22 SEP 1981

RESULTS SINCE 084543

102803 S/PARMS: 50 PORTS, 0 USERS & 34 I/PS
```

TIME VALUES (SECS)		=0.5	0.5-2	2-5	5-10	10	TOTAL
0-USER SYSTEM							
	NO:	217	2	0	0	0	219
	%:	99	1	0	0	0	
1-EDIT CONTROL							
	NO:	385	15	0	0	0	400
	%:	96	4	0	0	0	
2-FRAME CONSTRUCT							
	NO:	174	0	0	0	0	174
	%:	100	0	0	0	0	
3-EDIT ENDS							
	NO:	4	31	0	0	0	35
	%:	11	89	0	0	0	
TOTALS							
	NO:	780	48	0	0	0	828
	%:	94	6	0	0	0	

characters within the appropriate category (or overall) whose response times fall within the indicated time band. Appended to each count entry is a percentage, these indicating the proportion of the total responses for the category which are contained in the time band.

It can be seen from this example, taken from the live system, that all responses from Prestel over the monitored period were received within two seconds and that 94% were within half a second. All but two of the user system and frame construct inputs (which are of a particularly sensitive nature) were replied to within half a second, this boundary being that which is subjectively satisfying for these categories. Larger proportions of edit controls and edit ends exceed half a second, but these areas are less demanding in their acceptability of response.

For the convenience of interested parties who are not colocated with the monitor, the current table of results may also be written to a frame on the Prestel system, if this is required.

The tabular format of the monitor's reports, together with the allocation of response times to bands, leads to very rapid visual assimilation of each set of results; thus little time is wasted in interpretation when the system is behaving in a satisfactory manner. However, if things go awry the presence of the exception reports (printed above the half-hour period to which they refer) enable rapid identification of the rogue category to be made.

Scope

Prestel's National Operations Centre maintains a constant monitor of the performance of the Update Centre (where all editing is carried out)

during normal office hours; this is the period where any loading problems can be expected.

All output is sent, on a daily basis, to the team responsible for system performance and is used, in conjunction with that from the Hardware Monitor (described below), to enable tuning adjustments to be made to the live system's configuration, if increased load during the life of a system version so demands.

A second configuration may be employed to monitor the performance of information retrieval machines.

Additionally, the development team maintains a further PET system which is used, inter alia, for performance measurement of new system versions as they are produced. Before such a system is released for live use, it is subjected to a flood test during which it is made to experience load levels considerably higher than those it is expected to meet in the public service. This machine also provides back-up for the operational systems.

HARDWARE MONITORING

A hardware performance monitor has been used at the Update Centre (UDC). It recorded the average CPU and selected disc drive usage, as a percentage, during each 15 minute period. This was further averaged to half hour periods to match the PET figures described above. It also carried out a sample, every milli-second, of the current program in use and from this the heaviest CPU usage programs were determined.

The output for a typical month is given below. Note that the figures are illustrative only.

Highest Recorded During Month
These are the highest recorded figures and in which period and date they occurred.

		Half hour period commencing	Date
Port usage	70	9.30	1 Oct 80
IP usage	49	9.00	29 Oct 80
CPU usage	66.05%	11.00	28 Oct 80
Disc usage	22.04%	11.30	27 Oct 80

Top 5 Periods for Port/IP Usage
(Averaged over the month) with corresponding average CPU and system disc usage.

Ports				IPs			
Number	Half hour period	CPU %	Disc %	Number	Half hour period	CPU %	Disc %
45	15.30	66.74	13.34	39	11.00	72.67	14.14
45	10.30	74.92	15.33	34	15.30	66.74	13.34
43	11.30	72.35	16.83	33	11.30	72.35	16.83
43	16.00	62.38	15.89	33	14.30	61.29	13.69
43	15.00	66.61	17.03	33	16.00	62.38	15.89

Top 10 Programs for CPU Usage
(Averaged over the month) this was given as a percentage of the non-idle time.

Program	%Time
TSC	14.56
TIM	12.22
ORG	8.81
TK4	4.43
DDS	3.55
BASO	3.46
OPTM	2.51
TFO	2.54
GATE	2.10
PC	1.95

Idle Time
Average time during month.   37.94%
Overlay Activity
(Average over the month) this is the average number of accesses to the overlay area of the system disc per minute.   476

Although it is not expected that the detail given above will be understandable by readers not familiar with the Prestel system and its program names, it does illustrate the degree of detail that is necessary for performance optimisation and that is available to Prestel system designers.

CONCLUSIONS

The response to VAMPIRE, by the Prestel operational staff, was favourable. Even with a very simple display they have found the equipment useful in detecting Prestel failure before any other indications of error are apparent. The use of colour has proved to be very convenient in highlighting various status conditions. While VAMPIRE was developed specifically for Prestel, it is possible that similar equipment could be used by other operators of large computer bureaux using the public switched telephone network.

The output from both the "PET" and the hardware monitor have proved essential in both monitoring and optimising the performance of the Prestel National network. The operators of national videotex systems go through three phases. The first is the easiest, it is an acquaintance with display technologies. The second is familiarity with "stand alone" computing systems. The last is an appreciation of the true problems of running a national network, and it is this area that the techniques described above are highly relevant.

ACKNOWLEDGEMENTS

Acknowledgement is made to the Director of Research of British Telecom and the Director of Prestel for permission to make use of the information in this paper.

REFERENCES

(1) CEPT Recommendation No T/CD6-1. European Interactive Videotex Service. Display Aspects and Transmission Coding. Available from BTRL, Martlesham Heath.

(2) Prestel Terminal Specification. Edition One. Prestel Liaison Group Technical Sub Committee, Telephone House, Temple Avenue, London, EC4Y OHL.

Figure 3

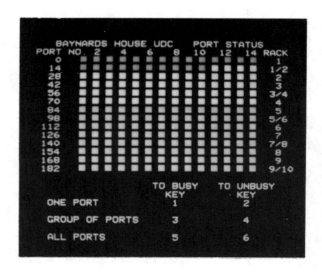

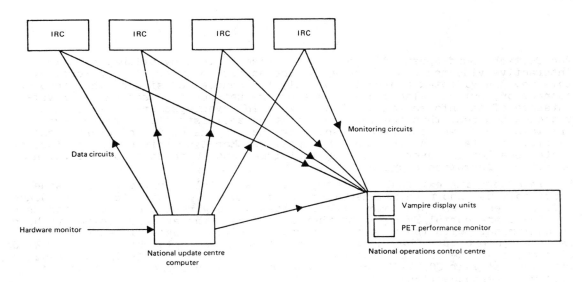

Data circuits

Monitoring circuits

Hardware monitor →

National update centre
computer

Vampire display units

PET performance monitor

National operations control centre

IRC is an Information Retrieval Computer
Figure 1

Figure 2
Vampire/Prestel Interface

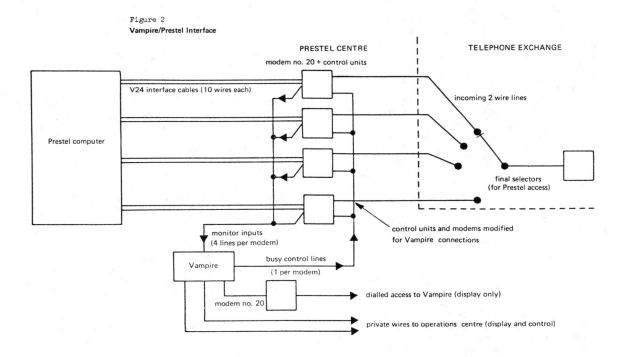

PRESTEL CENTRE

TELEPHONE EXCHANGE

modem no. 20 + control units

Prestel computer

V24 interface cables (10 wires each)

incoming 2 wire lines

final selectors
(for Prestel access)

control units and modems modified
for Vampire connections

monitor inputs
(4 lines per modem)

Vampire

busy control lines
(1 per modem)

modem no. 20

dialled access to Vampire (display only)

private wires to operations centre (display and control)

Videotex – A Gateway to Open Computer Communication

M Hegenbarth
Deutsche Bundespost, Federal
Republic of Germany

The Deutsche Bundespost added a major supplement to conventional existing interactive videotex system concepts: the access to external computers. By this way the videotex centre is not only the source and sink of the videotex connection, but can also operate as a bridge between the user and a private database of an information supplier. Two main advantages are obvious: the videotex centres, thus the telecommunication administration, are relieved of providing less own databases by shifting the responsibility of storing and retrieving data to the information suppliers. Moreover this extended videotex system enables the user to have an individual and up-to-date communication with the information supplier.

So, incorporating external computers into its videotex system the Deutsche Bundespost has shown an immense increase of the videotex service value. Hence a first step to an open computer communication is given to everyone, for user terminals are normal TV sets and therefore cheap. The external computers have to communicate with the videotex centres according to established protocols. In order to preserve the information suppliers from implementing several kinds of protocols, the Deutsche Bundespost is developing protocols in accordance with the relevant CCITT/ISO definitions, e.g. the reference model for open systems interconnection.

1. BILDSCHIRMTEXT INVOLVING THE COMPUTER NETWORKING PRINCIPLE

The Deutsche Bundespost (DBP) started its interactive videotex, called Bildschirmtext (Btx), field trial in Berlin (West) and Düsseldorf with totally 6000 subscribers and information providers (IP's). This new medium was not only highly accepted, but the interest for it increased even more when the existent Btx system was given a major and till then unique supplement in November 1980: the facility for subscribers to get access to private computers. This event was the world opening for the realization of an open system, useful for everyone, because no more than the usual and relatively cheap devices as a TV set with decoder and a telephone set with a modem are needed in order to take part. Figures like 40,000 calls per Btx centre per month (i.e. 0.44 call per subscriber per day) and 20 per cent of those for being connected with external computers (EC's) prove the acceptance of this innovative medium.

After having got the PRESTEL software from the BPO, the DBP realized quite early the future interest for the ability to be connected with computers of IP's. So, its development of this computer networking (CN) was initiated in 1978 in cooperation with the IP's. In 1979 a CN system specification was completed so that CN could be demonstrated first on the occasion of the

VIEWDATA congress in March of 1980. Finally, in October of 1980, 5 EC's began testing in the live system and can be accessed by all subscribers since November of 1980. Meanwhile (May of 1982) there are 24 EC's bound to the Btx live system and more than 30 applications of EC providers for participation in Btx CN are pending.

2. HOW TO OPEN COMMUNICATION AMONG COMPUTERS?

At the starting point of the CN development, it was clear, that CN should provide the feature to be able to get access to computers of any firm by an independent communication protocol. At that time, the first concrete thoughts about open systems interconnection have just been launched by the ISO (TC97/SC16) as a definition of the 7-layer architecture model. A CN protocol development as close to the ISO model as possible was attempted (see figure 1). Based on the lowest three layers defined by the CCITT Rec. X.25, the so called Btx protocol was made, consisting of a protocol handler as layer 4, i.e. a software to process networking commands and handle dialogue exchanges, and of a gateway control as layer 5, i.e. a software to establish and release a logical link with a private computer and finally of the Btx application and presentation functions.

The Btx protocol was kept relatively simple in order to allow a cheap imple-

Btx centre

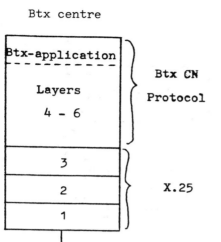

Fig. 1 Btx CN field trial communication model

mentation on EC's. It allows a transparent data transfer and doesn't restrict applications of nearly any kind.
Of course, there are also EC's not
being able to communicate by X.25 rules
but by the BSC protocol. For those, a
front end processor (FEP) was developed
which performs the necessary conversions.

So, a Btx CN system was created, whose
configuration is shown in figure 2.

As the DBP packet switching data network (PSDN) wasn't yet available, the

X.25 software of the Btx centres was
made symmetric in that it can be
applied for connections via PSDN as
well as via leased lines. This means,
till being connected to the PSDN in May
of 1981, the Btx centres were able to
communicate with the EC's by the X.25
protocol via leased lines (see figure
3).

3. DETAILS OF THE BTX CN PROTOCOL

The communication between a subscriber
(SUB) and an EC consists of two parts.
One part contains the dialogue between
the SUB and the Btx centre (Btx C) by
which the latter one comes to know the
SUB's demands on the EC. The second
part is the dialogue between the Btx C
and the EC in this the Btx C has to
match the application protocol elements
sent by the subscriber onto analoguous
ones to be transmitted to the EC. Two
main tasks of the Btx C in this connection are obvious:

- exchange of application demands and
  data
- guiding the SUB and providing intelligence to the SUB terminal for CN

The CN protocol between the SUB and the
Btx C consists of the following
elements:

(digits)	page selection
* (digits) #	direct page selection
#	next page, in gateway-pages: connection establish

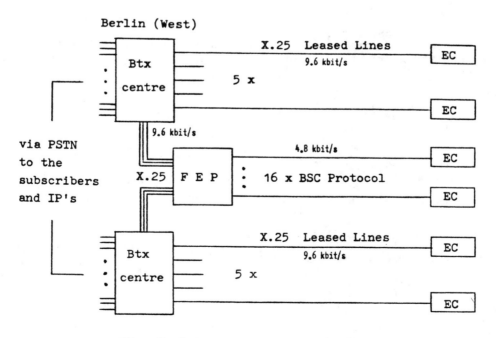

Fig. 2 Initial Btx CN configuration

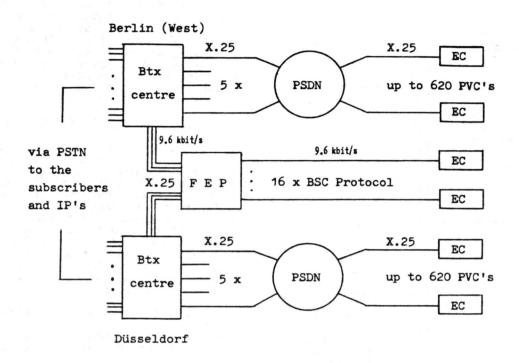

Berlin (West)

via PSTN
to the
subscribers
and IP's

Düsseldorf

Fig. 3 Btx CN configuration after getting connected to the PSDN

00   redisplay page
**   clear user input,
                    in data collection
                    pages: backstep
                    function
* #   last page
* 0 #   get Btx contents
                    page
* 9 #   get EC goodbye page

The establishment of a connection to
an EC is initiated by confirming (#)
the socalled gateway pages, which can
be interpreted as the doors within the
Btx C seeking tree to the EC's. Of
course, depending on the kind of application, an EC provider may store several gateway pages in the Btx C, so that
the SUB gets rather quickly to his
desired dialogue.

The protocol between the Btx C and the
EC has the following features:

- connection establishment is initiated
  only by the Btx C (asymmetric protocol)
- communication by a strict dialogue
  ("handshaking" principle) with the
  exception of a disconnection
  request
- protocol failures result in connection termination (no recovery)
- providing as transparent transmission
  as possible
- protocol is block oriented, each
  block contains a block type identifier and the user number, followed

by variable amounts of data relevant
to the block type

It contains following 10 block types:

Connection Request (CRQ)

   the Btx C attempts to establish a
   session with the EC

Connection Acknowledgement (CAK)

   the EC accepts the session

Connection Refusal (CRF)

   the EC does not accept the session

Disconnection Request (DSR)

   the Btx C or the EC requests the
   termination of the session

Disconnection Acknowledgement (DSA)

   the session is terminated

Frame Selection Block (FSB)

   the Btx C requests a frame from the
   EC

Frame Data Block (FDB)

   the EC transmits a frame to the Btx C

Collected Data Block (CDB)

   the Btx C transmits a data collection
   frame to the EC

L 24 Message Block (L24)

   the EC transmits a short message to

the SUB via the Btx C

Data Acknowledgement Block (DAB)

the EC may acknowledge the received data collection frame

The above mentioned matching of SUB → Btx C protocol elements onto those of Btx C ↔ EC is shown for following communication phases:

Session Establishment

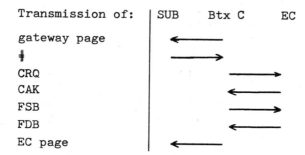

Transmission of:	SUB	Btx C	EC
gateway page	←		
#	→		
CRQ		→	
CAK		←	
FSB		→	
FDB		←	
EC page	←		

Information Retrieval

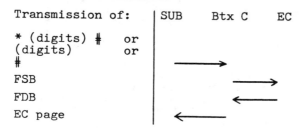

Transmission of:	SUB	Btx C	EC
* (digits) # or (digits) # or #	→		
FSB		→	
FDB		←	
EC page	←		

Data Collection

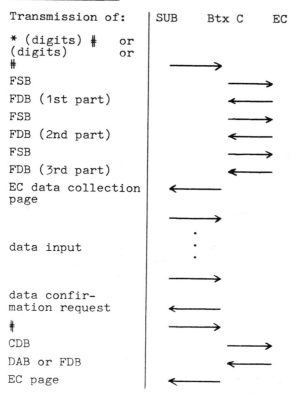

Transmission of:	SUB	Btx C	EC
* (digits) # or (digits) # or #	→		
FSB		→	
FDB (1st part)		←	
FSB		→	
FDB (2nd part)		←	
FSB		→	
FDB (3rd part)		←	
EC data collection page	←		
		→	
data input	⋮		
		→	
data confirmation request	←		
#	→		
CDB		→	
DAB or FDB		←	
EC page	←		

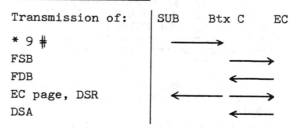

Transmission of:	SUB	Btx C	EC
* 9 #	→		
FSB		→	
FDB		←	
EC page, DSR	←	← — →	
DSA		←	

4. DATA COLLECTION AS THE HIT OF BTX CN

Mainly by the data collection function of CN the Btx system is raised to a level of commercially acceptable data communication. To both the user and information provider the possibility of a direct access to private databases in connection with the data collection indisputably has opened a much wider field of applications.

The EC sends a data collection page to the Btx C, which is displayed on the SUB's TV set screen. Within this page there may be up to 62 fields, whose definitions (length, location, with-/out echo) and additional SUB guiding comments displayable on line 23 are given in 2-4 subsequently transferred pages. After the SUB has filled in these fields and has confirmed his agreement of transfer permission by # , the Btx C sends these data to the EC, which then reacts after processing them.

By this principle that the SUB not only can retrieve informations, leaving out his ability to input control information for page selection, but also can send user data to the EC's, Btx CN is going to become a remote data processing system on a large base with a great variety of applications.

5. BTX CN TODAY'S APPLICATIONS

From the beginning of the CN concept development many EC providers optimistically made efforts to get an effective and much acceptable use of Btx CN. After the start of operation in the live system and being available they were highly confirmed by the unmistakable behaviour of the SUB's. 20 per cent of their calls include the use of Btx CN.

Because of supporting open systems interconnection the DBP has proved the successful cooperating of EC's as DEC, HONEYWELL BULL, IBM, UNIVAC, PHILIPS, SIEMENS. Of course, an EC provider is first faced by some problems. So there are difficulties to learn and understand the special communication procedures for the lower layers and even more for the higher layers. Storage reservation for Btx software and information is not naturally available.

Moreover, there is a uncertainty about development costs. In spite of all these handicaps the EC providers have shown that there are a variety of applications which beyond that are used quite frequently.

50 per cent of the CN calls are directed to the home banking facilities. The Btx SUB's can

- inspect their personal statement of account
- give postal money orders
- order money transfer between accounts
- create, amend or cancel standing orders
- cause display of account information as credit limits, exchange rates, cheque availability, overdraft facilities
- send messages to the bank etc.

A further much accepted application is the mail order business service. Customers can

- get actual catalogue information
- come to know delivery times
- order articles
- be shown alternatives to not available items
- inspect their personal customer accounts
- send and receive messages

Travel agencies enable customers to order actual travel information and to book travels.

Furtheron there are applications of

computer centres, insurance companies, DP manufacturers and tax consulting groups followed by other consultation services as teaching programs etc., tele games, software development and telesoftware in the near future.

The commercial area are looking forward to an increase of Btx CN as there are very promising applications as

- Btx terminal as a terminal for mail order agents
- cheap booking facilities for smaller travel bureaus
- pharmacie orders
- inquiry retrieval system for doctors

The great advantage of Btx CN for the EC providers is the shift of costs for terminals and of the responsibility related to their maintenance etc. to the end users. They even have no charging problems because the DBP thinks itself responsible for that as the provider of this public Btx service. The amazing fact moreover is those advantages on side of the EC providers don't cause disadvantages at all on side of the SUB's. They anyway possess their TV set and a telephone and can be profiteers of the highly interesting EC services with the main features:

- real-time dialogue
- high degree of security
- access to nearly unlimited data bases
- possibility for participation in the data processing area

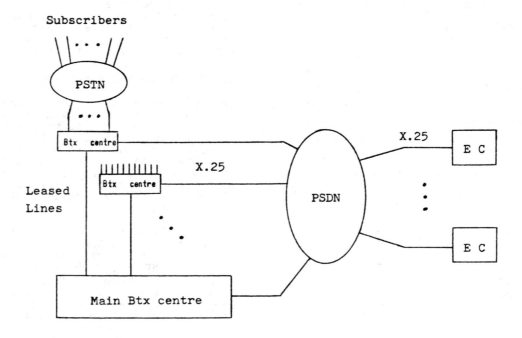

Fig. 4   Btx CN configuration in the future

6. BTX CN IN THE FUTURE BTX SYSTEM

Already, a short time after the Btx field trial had begun it could be foreseen that the interest for and the acceptance of the Btx system would grow up more and more. So as its successful result the DBP decided in May of 1981 to introduce the Btx system into its pallett of provided telecommunication media as a public service in 1983. The order for the Btx C development was given to the firm IBM.

The configuration of the planned Btx system is shown in figure 4. It contains one main Btx C, where all Btx system pages are stored and maintained by updating, editing or canceling them.

The main Btx C is connected with several Btx C's via leased lines. These Btx C's only hold pages being retrieved statistically often, so that in only 2 per cent of the page retrieval a page transfer between the main Btx C and the Btx C will be necessary. Whereas the Btx C's have access to the PSDN in order to reach the EC's for Btx CN applications, the same EC's shall be able to contact the main Btx C for the purpose of bulk updating there pages, which they store there as information providers.

A FEP won't be any longer operated by the DBP, so that the EC provider will have to implement X.25, if not done already. Unfortunately a whole set of internationally standardized protocols for the higher layers is not yet available. So, the DBP decided to use the at least within the FRG uniform version of a transport protocol and a still to be specified version of the layers 5-7. These protocols will be applied in an intermediate period until a set of internationally standardized protocol will be available.

Of course some new features in comparison to the today's Btx presentation capabilities will emerge in the future system.

In any case it will support the new videotex decoder standard according CEPT T/CD 6-1.

Moreover the following features shall be possible:

- area protection (against overwriting)
- area marking (to designate data for the purpose of being specially processed)
- window/box (field reservation for combined operation with television)
- scrolling pages
- redefinable colours (analoguous to DRCS in order to extend the colour range)

7. ABBREVIATIONS

Btx	Bildschirmtext (German name of "Interactive Videotex")
Btx C	Btx centre
Btx CN	Btx computer networking
CN	computer networking
DBP	Deutsche Bundespost
EC	External Computer
FEP	Front End Processor
FTZ	Fernmeldetechnisches Zentralamt
IP	Information Provider
PSDN	Packet Switching Data Network
PSTN	Public Switched Telephone Network
SUB	Subscriber

M. Hegenbarth is a Member of Technical Staff at the Telecommunication Engineering Centre (FTZ) of the Deutsche Bundespost, where he works in the section for Technics of Text and Data Communication Systems. He received his GCE from a science orientated secondary school in Koblenz and his graduate engineer degree for electrical engineering from the Technical University of Berlin West in 1975. After a five year stay at the university as an assistant he changed over to the Deutsche Bundespost in 1980. As a scientific expert he works as well on computer communication protocols, especially for the Teletex and Videotex service, as on protocol validation methods.

Huffman Polling in a Nonuniform Local Network

Jin-Fu Chang, Te-Son Kuo & Chin-Hsen Lin
National Taiwan University, Republic
of China

A polling technique using Huffman algorithm for nonuniform local distribution is presented
in this paper. The objective of the algorithm is to minimize the required overhead in
interrogating all terminals. The optimality of this algorithm is proved by induction on the
number of terminals in the network. Mean value theorem plays an important role in the
proof. The delay performance of the algorithm has been completed in this paper.

INTRODUCTION

In computer communication networks, local distribution [1,2] deals with the techniques for connecting geographically dispersed users to a central facility. Local distribution plays a rather important role in the design of a computer communication network. In [1,2], Hayes gives a complete review of local distribution techniques with an emplasis on basic mathematical models.

One problem in local distribution has been the search for efficient techniques that serve many dispersed users each generating sparse traffic. Conventional polling suffers from the drawback of excessive overhead which leads to the dominance of message delay by the time required to poll all terminals in a system consisting of many lightly loaded users. An information theoretic point-of-view is given in [1]. Through the calculation of entropy, Hayes shows that for lightly loaded systems using polling a large portition of a polling cycle is spent on determining which of the stations have messages with relatively little gain in terms of information.

Motivated by inefficiencies in conventional polling techniques in lightly loaded systems, a modification of the polling techniques named "probing" is then proposed in [1] so as to reduce overhead by polling groups of stations rather than individual stations. (See [pp. 1180-1181, 1] for an illustrative example.) There is a penalty, however, in probing for heavy loading in which the number of inquiries needed to examine all stations turns out to be more than that of polling. In order to guard against paying this penalty an adaptive technique derived from polling and probing is next proposed in [1]. The essence of adaptive polling is simply to first probe groups of stations and then to poll each station in a group which responded positively during the probing stage. In order to adapt to system loading, criteria for deciding the size of the groups are developed in [1]. The delay performance of adaptive local distribution has been completed in [3].

In [1,3], the algorithms are developed and the analysis is carried out only for a system consisting of N identical users. The arrival process at each station is modeled as an independent Poisson process with the same mean rate λ messages per second. In practice the rates could be different at different sites. The well known Huffman algorithm [4] may be valuable in coping with nonuniform users. The optimality of Huffman algorithm for local distribution has been proved in [5]. The purpose of this paper is to carry out the analysis of delay performance of the algorithm.

THE ALGORITHM AND ITS OPTIMALITY

In this paper we are concerned with a group of n stations, denoted by $u_1, \ldots, u_n$, to be polled by a central facility. Let the arrival process at u_i be modeled as an independent Poisson process with mean rate λ_i messages/sec and let $\Lambda = \{\lambda_1, \ldots, \lambda_n\}$.

We shall now use an example to illustrate the polling procedure making use of Huffman algorithm. Suppose n=5 and $\Lambda = \{0.05, 0.05, 0.2, 0.3, 0.4\}$. Notice that in this example we happen to have $\lambda_1 + \ldots + \lambda_5 = 1.0$. However, in practice the condition $\lambda_1 + \ldots + \lambda_5 = 1.0$ is by no means necessary. Due to the fact each polling procedure can be uniquely represented by a tree, we first apply Huffman algorithm [5] to Λ so as to obtain a binary tree with minimum path length as shown in Fig. 1(a). The central processor then uses the binary tree in Fig 1(a) to pursue its message gathering process. The signaling scheme in Fig. 3[1] can still be applied to conduct the polling represented by the tree obtained from Huffman algorithm. Suppose that at the very beginning of some polling cycle only u_3 and u_5 have messages waited in their respective queues then Fig. 1(b) shows the actual polling that takes place in the present cycle. In Fig. 1(b), an intermediate node visited by the central processor represents the situation that all the users rooted at that node will be

*This work is supported by the National Science Council of the Republic of China under Grant NSC71-0201-E-002-07.
**On leave at the Electrical Engineering Department, Naval Postgraduate School, Monterey, CA 93940, USA

questioned simultaneously in a polling signal issued from the central processor. On the other hand, a user will be interrogated individually if its corresponding leaf in Fig. 1(b) is visited by the central processor. The numbers associated with the edges in Fig. 1(b) indicate the order that these edges will be traversed by the central processor in executing the polling cycle represented by the tree. As a comparison, Fig. 2 shows the tree representing the conventional polling technique for = 0.05, 0.05, 0.2, 0.3, 0.4 .

In general, given the set Λ we can always apply Huffman algorithm to construct the binary tree of minimum average path length for the central processor to collect messages from users. Notice that the polling technique represented by Huffman tree reduces to the one proposed by Hayes in [1] if $\lambda_1 = \ldots = \lambda_n$.

In evaluating the performance of Huffman polling we further assmue that each user has a buffer of infinite capacity and all messages arriving during a polling cycle must wait until the next cycle in order to be transmitted. The number of inquiries issued by the central processor in a polling cycle is an important measure of effectiveness of the algorithm. For example, 7 inquiries are needed for the cycle represented by Fig. 1(b). In determining the average number of inquiries per cycle, we denote an intermediate node by $n_{i,j}$

if its corresponding position in a complete binary tree is the jth ($0 < j < 2^i - 1$) node counted from the left at level i. The intermediate nodes and their corresponding labels also appear in Fig. 1(a). For each node $n_{i,j}$, a corresponding random variable $X_{i,j}$ is defined as follows

$$X_{i,j} = \begin{cases} 1, & \text{if } n_{i,j} \text{ is vistied and} \\ & \text{responds positively in a cycle} \\ 0, & \text{otherwise} \end{cases} \quad (1)$$

Let the subtree rooted in $n_{i,j}$ be denoted by $T_{i,j}$. Clearly, $X_{i,j} = 1$ if and only if at least one user in $T_{i,j}$ has messages to be transmitted. We use $\lambda_{i,j}$ to denote the sum of arrival rates for the users in $T_{i,j}$. Due to the fact that the individual arrival processes are independent and Poisson,

$$p(X_{i,j} = 1 | \ell) = 1 - e^{-\lambda_{i,j}\ell} \quad (2)$$

where ℓ is the cycle length of the previous cycle. Notice that nodes $n_{i+1,2i}$ and $n_{i+1,2i+1}$ will both be questioned by the central processor if $X_{i,j} = 1$. If we use I to denote the total number of inquiries needed in the present cycle, then

$$I = 2\Sigma X_{i,j} + 1 \quad (3)$$

Hence

$$E(I | \ell) = 2\Sigma P(X_{i,j} = 1 | \ell) + 1 \quad (4)$$

$$= (2n-1) - 2\Sigma e^{-\lambda_{i,j}\ell} \quad (5)$$

Huffman algorithm is optimal compared to any other binary polling tree in the sense that $E(I | \ell)$ in (5) is minimal. The following theorem guarantees the optimality of Huffman polling.

THEOREM H Given $\Lambda = \{\lambda_1, \ldots, \lambda_n\}$ and $\ell, (I | \ell)$ attains minimal value if and only if the corresponding polling tree is Huffman. This theorem was proved in [5] by induction on n while mean value theorem in elementary calculus [e.g. 6] plays an important role in the proof. We refer to [5] for details of the proof.

DELAY ANALYSIS OF HUFFMAN ALGORITHM

Let the transmission time of a message be expressed in units of the time required for the central processor to issue an inquiry and to hear the response from the group of users being interrogated. We use X to denote the transmission time of a message and assume that X follows geometric distribution, i.e.,

$$P(X = x) = \alpha(1-\alpha)^{x-1}, \quad x = 1, 2, \ldots \quad (6)$$

Next, we use $M_i(z)$ to denote the probability generating function (pgf) of the random variable representing the total transmission time required by u_i conditioning on the previous cycle had length of ℓ inquiry times and u_i has a least one message in queue. Clearly,

$$M_i(z) = [e^{\lambda_i \ell \left(\frac{\alpha z}{1-(1-\alpha)z} - 1\right)} - e^{-\lambda_i \ell}]/p_i \quad (7)$$

where $p_i = 1 - e^{-\lambda_i \ell}$ represents the probability of the event that u_i collected at least one message during the previous cycle and in (7) we have normalized λ_i with respect to an inquiry time.

Let L_k denote the random variable representing the length of the kth cycle and $Q_k(z)$ the pdf of L_k conditioning on $L_{k-1} = \ell$.
In general, given $\Lambda = \{\ell_1, \ldots, \ell_n\}$, let T be the corresponding Huffman tree rooted at $n_{0,0}$ then

$$Q_k(z) = z[A(T_{0,0}) + B(T_{0,0})] \quad (8)$$

where $A(T_{0,0})$ and $B(T_{0,0})$ are defined recursively as follows
Procedure $A(T_{x,y})$; (9)
If $n_{x,y} \notin \{u_1, \ldots, u_n\}$, i.e. if $n_{x,y} \neq$ leaf then $A(T_{x,y}) := A(T_\ell) A(T_r)$
else if $n_{x,y} = u_i$ then
$A(T_{x,y}) = 1 - p_i$;
end;

Procedure $B(T_{x,y})$; (10)
If $n_{x,y} \neq$ leaf then $B(T_{x,y}) :=$
$z^2[A(T_\ell)B(T_r) + B(T_\ell)A(T_r) +$
$B(T_\ell)B(T_r)]$
else if $n_{x,y} = u_i$ then $B(T_{x,y}) := p_i M_i(z)$;
end;

In $A(T_{x,y})$ or $B(T_{x,y})$, T_ℓ and T_r
respectively represent the left and right
subtree of $T_{x,y}$.

Let L_k and Var (L_k) denote the mean and
variance of L_k respectively. Then

$$\overline{L}_k = Q_k{}'(1)$$

$$= A(T_{0,0}) + [B(T_{0,0})]_{z=1} + [\frac{d}{dz} B(T_{0,0})]z=1 \quad (11)$$

where $[B(T_{0,0})]_{z=1}$ can be obtained recursively
from setting $z=1$ and $[\frac{d}{dz} B(T_{0,0})]_{z=1}$ from
$B'(T_{0,0})$ as follows

Procedure $B'(T_{x,y})$; (12)
If $n_{x,y}$ leaf then $B'(T_{x,y}) =$

$2[B(T_{0,0})]_{z=1} + \{A(T_\ell)B'(T_r) + B'(T_\ell)A(T_r) + B'(T_\ell)A(T_y)$

$B'(T_\ell) [B(T_r)]_{z=1} + [B(T_\ell)]_{z=1} B'(T_r)\}$

else if $n_{x,y} = u_i$ then $B'(T_{x,y}) := p_i M_i'(1)$;
end;

As a matter of fact $A(T_{0,0}) + [B(T_{0,0})]_{z=1} =$
$Q_k(1)=1$, thus

$$\overline{L}_k = 1 + B'(T_{0,0}) \quad (13)$$

Similary,
$$Var(L_k) = Q_k''(1) + Q_k'(1) - [Q_k'(1)]^2$$

$$= 2 B'(T_{0,0}) + \frac{d^2}{dz^2} [B(T_{0,0})]_{z=1} + Q_k'(1)$$
$$- [Q_k'(1)]^2 \quad (14)$$

In (14), $\frac{d^2}{dz^2} [B(T_{0,0})]z=1$ can be obtained

recursively from $B''(T_{0,0})$ as follows

Procedure $B''(T_{x,y})$;

If $n_{x,y}$ leaf then $B''(T_{x,y}) := 4B'(T_{x,y})$
$-6[B(T_{x,y})]_{z=1} + \{A(T_\ell)B''(T_r) + B''(T_\ell)A(T_r)$
$+B''(T_\ell) [B(T_r)]_{z=1} + 2B'(T_\ell)B'(T_r)$
$+ [B(T_\ell)]_{z=1} B''(T_r)\}$

else if $n_{x,y} = u_i$ then $B''(T_{x,y}) := p_i M_i''(1)$;
end;

Let $\overline{L}$ be the average cycle length at steady
state, i.e.,

$$\overline{L} = \lim_{k \to \infty} \overline{L}_k \quad (16)$$

then the system throughout S is given by

$$S = (\lambda_1 + \ldots + \lambda_n) \frac{1}{\alpha} \overline{L/L} \quad (17)$$

$$= \frac{\lambda}{\alpha}$$

where $\lambda = \lambda_1 + \ldots + \lambda_n$.

The delay D_i of a message at u_i consists
of the following.

D_r the remaining cycle time of the cycle
during which the message arrives

D_m the total message transmission time of
the users which are interrogated earlier than
u_i by the central processor

D_q the total inquiry time taken so far when
u_i is questioned

D_w the system time of the message which
includes the waiting time of the message in
the queue of u_i and the transmission time
of the message itself

In other words

$$D_i = D_r + D_m + D_q + D_w \quad (18)$$

We use $\overline{X}$ to denote the mean of random variable
X, then at equilibrium

$$\overline{D}_i = \overline{D}_r + \overline{D}_m + \overline{D}_q + \overline{D}_w \quad (19)$$

In (19),

$$\overline{D}_r = \overline{L}/2 , \quad (20)$$

$$\overline{D}_m = \frac{1}{\alpha} \overline{L} \sum_{j=1}^{i} \lambda_i \quad (21)$$

$\overline{D}_q$ = number of branches which have to be
traversed by the central processor in order to
reach u_i ,

and

$$\overline{D}_w = \frac{1}{2} \frac{\alpha \lambda_i \overline{L} - \alpha}{1 - e^{-\lambda_i \overline{L}}} + \frac{\alpha}{1 - e^{-\lambda_i \overline{L}}}$$

$$= \frac{1}{2} [\alpha \lambda_i \overline{L} + \alpha] /(1 - e^{-\lambda_i \overline{L}}) \quad (22)$$

221

The results derived in this section are applicable to any other polling tree. In other words, various polling algorithms can be compared with Huffman polling via these results.

As a closing remark of this section, we observe that the construction of Huffman polling tree indicates that light users suffer longer delays than heavy users. In order not to penalize light users one could always flip the Huffman tree such as that in Fig. 1(a) over or, equivalently, have the central processor traverse the Huffman tree from right to left instead of the converse. We shall in this paper call such scheme the modified Huffman Polling.

EXAMPLES AND DISCUSSIONS

Based on the results obtained in the previous section, many numerical examples have been obtained to demonstrate the significance of Huffman Polling. In these examples Huffman polling are compared via L, Var(L), and D with Hayes probing [1]. The delay performance of the modified Huffman polling is also included in these examples. Part of these numerical examples are shown in Figs. 3-6. The others are not included due to the six-page limit of the paper.

From these examples, we observe the following
1) As far as $\bar{L}$ is concerned, Huffman algorithm always has the best performance. This agrees with Theorem H.

2) Modified Huffman algorithm has the same value of $\bar{L}$ as Huffman algorithm. Furthermore, $\bar{L}$ of the modified algorithm differs little from that of the Huffman algorithms. This shows that the modified algorithm is an attractive alternative.

3) For a small group of nonuniform users or a large group of small users whose traffic do not differ too much from Hayes' method is good enough. Otherwise Huffman algorithm is worthy.

4) In all these examples, each system achieves a maximum throughput 1 when λ approaches α. This result is explainable since $\frac{\lambda}{\alpha}$ (inquiries) represents the input rate and we require $\frac{\lambda}{\alpha} \leq 1$ for the system to have state behavior.

CONCLUSIONS

We have in this paper analyzed the performance of Huffman polling. Results such as the probability generating function of the cycle length, the mean and variance of the cycle length, and message delay have been obtained. Based upon these results Huffman algorithm can be compared with various algorithms. Through examples we have witnessed that unless we are dealing with a small group of users or a large group of small users not differing too much in their traffics, Huffman algorithm is useful.

Several extensions of the present work are possible. First, similar to [1] the adaptivity of the algorithms worths further investigations. Second, contraint could be imposed on how many messages a certain user may deliver when he is interrogated by the central station. Finally, the assumption of infinite buffer at each station may be relaxed. However, the analysis could be difficult.

REFERENCES

[1] J.F. Hayes, "An Adaptive Technique for Local Distribution," IEEE Trans. on Communications, VOL. COM-26, No. 8, pp. 1178-1186, August 1978.

[2] J.F. Hayes, "Local Distribution in Computer Communications," IEEE Communications Magazine, Vol. 19, No. 2, pp. 6-14, March 1981.

[3] A. Grami and J.F. Hayes, "Delay Performance of Adaptive Local Distribution," Proc. International Conference on Communications, pp. 39.4.1-39.4.5, Seattle, June 1980.

[4] D.A. Huffman, "A Method for the Construction of Minimum Redundancy Codes," Proc. IRE, Vol. 40, pp. 251-252, Sept. 1952.

[5] J.F. Chang, K.T. Wu, and S.C. Chen, "The Application of Huffman Algorithm in Local Distribution," Proc. Symposium on Electromagnetic Waves and Communications, pp. 425-442, May, Taipei, 1981.

[6] R.E. Johnson, F.L. Kiolemeister, and E.S. Wolk, "Calculus with Analytic Geometry," 5th ed., Allyn and Becon, Boston, 1974.

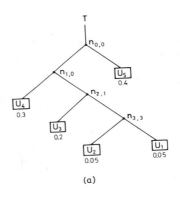

(a)

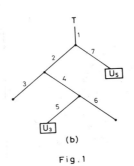

(b)

Fig.1

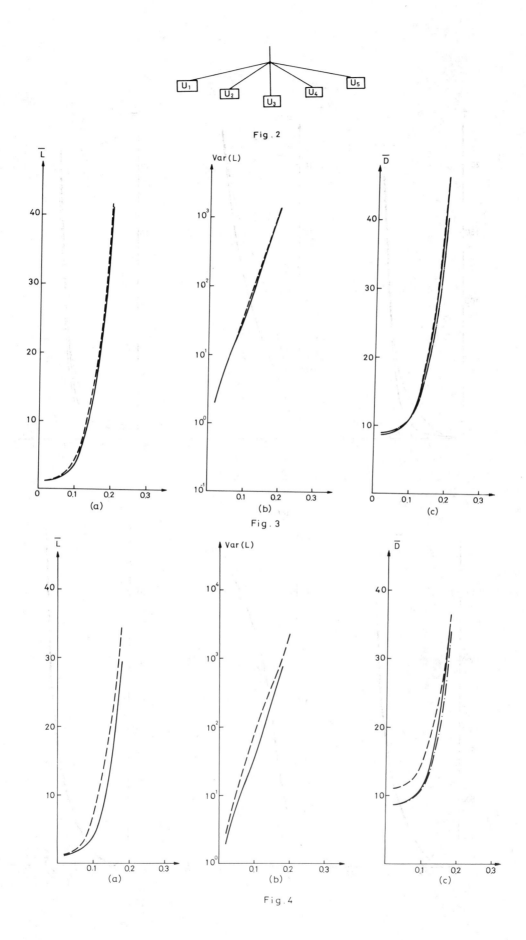

Fig . 2

Fig . 3

Fig . 4

223

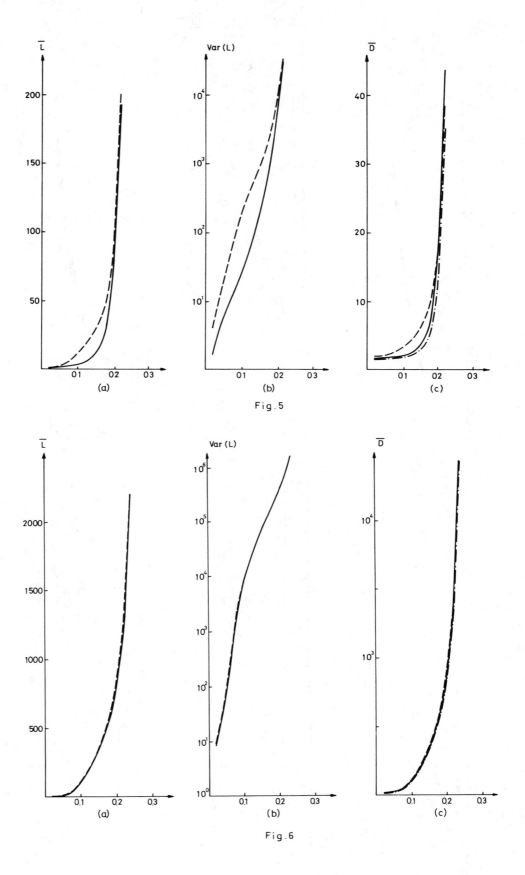

Fig.5

Fig.6

A Local Network Structure in a Flexible Management Framework

H Lorin, B Goldstein
IBM, USA

ABSTRACT

This paper describes a memory based interconnection between computer systems that permits flexible management policy about relations between business units and data processing staffs. We describe the interconnection concepts, systems hardware/software features of a memory interconnected local network. We then describe the management dynamics that might surround such a system. The central concept in the management section is the notion of a **negotiated service level** established between using organizations and the DP complex.

BASIC SYSTEM CONCEPT

In [1] and [2] Lorin discusses the relationship between management and technology issues in distributed processing systems. In [3] and [4] Goldstein and Lorin discuss systems that have extended memory interconnect features.

The heart of the system of this paper is an interconnect mechanism that permits a set of computer systems to make remote memory references within distances commonly associated with local networks assuming high speed wide bandwidth connections.

Figure 1 shows the interconnect facility. The facility includes an interconnect processor and a transportation path. The interconnect processor has the characteristics of a single board computer in power and packaging. The interconnect processor connects, on one side, to the transportation path, and on the other side to the processing units of the system. The connections of the interconnect processor to the computers of the system are (1) through the Storage Control Unit of a processor to its memory access lines and (2) an additional connection to the I/O elements of a processor. There is a set of commands that direct the

movement of data from the memory of one processor to the memory of another.

The movement of information from a computer of the system is by issuance of a transmit command that starts data movement from local memory to the interconnect processor. The interconnect processor puts the data on the transportation path where it arrives at the interconnect processor of the receiving computer. The receiving interconnect processor contends for the memory bus through the storage control unit to place data in the remotely accessed memory.

The notion of a transportation path surrounded by interconnection processors allows the definition of networks of any shape or complexity including those that can be formed by the presence of multiple transportation paths coming from an single interconnect processor and those formable by the presence of more than one interconnect processor for each using computer system. Figure 1 shows a specific configuration of local network that is the base of the systems notion of this paper.

The pictured system is a hierarchy consisting of connections between a large scale computer and a set of smaller computers that exist in business unit locations. Each computer in the structure has local memory and local software support appropriate for its fundamental applications functions. Computers of the system can communicate with each other in three ways:

1. Smaller computers can request the large computer to perform subsystem services. This involves the use of subsystem service requests that are locally transformed into SEND/RECEIVE type functions that enable a smaller processor to enqueue service requests in the memory of the large computer.

2. Smaller computers can use the software at the large computer in a remote paging mode so that pages of an address space can be managed and made available by the auxiliary storage manager of the large computer.

Thus the system has some of the characteristics of a tightly coupled multiprocessor and some of the characteristics of a hierarchically distributed local network. This convergence is natural as we more and more witness the decay of crisp edges between SIMD, MIMD, Loosely-coupled and tightly coupled machine concepts.

SYSTEM INTENT

The particular system organization we describe is intended to provide the functional software capabilities of very large machines to machines of moderate capacity. Thus with software and virtual concepts discussed below a small processor can ask a larger processor to execute a large data manager on its behalf, or can page the data management to itself dynamically for local execution. In the same spirit as [5] McQuilken, the need for multiple copies of program products is reduced, the problems of software product management across multiple installations can be eliminated, and the capacities of large machines can be made available to the users and applications of much smaller machines. An important realization of some notions of **single system image** may be achieved.

CONCEPTUAL EXTENSIONS

A functional model of a hierarchic system can be achieved with the components so far described. An optimum realization of the structural concept, however, might involve an additional component and some computer design modifications.

A number of objections can be raised to the routing of the memory access through the Storage Control Unit of the large processor of Figure 1. Amongst them is that when the large processor goes down the memory associated with it goes down. In addition an almost overwhelming burden for total systems relocate is placed in the large processor. These

objections are addressed by the extension of the interconnect facility using a relocate engine and some redesign of paging and segmentation concepts in the processors. This is suggested by Figure 2 that shows a more elaborate system. In Figure 2 access to the remote memory of the large system is through a relocate engine that handles relocation and access contention for the entire system. It has the virtue of making the remote memory available when the large processor is down, enabling remote computers to continue with those functions that do not require large computer service but only access to the memory in order to enqueue asynchronous service requests.

COMPUTER CLASSES

The system includes a set of complete computer systems of various capability that are physically dispersed within an establishment of an enterprise. These systems are of three classes. A General Services Processor (GSP) of large scale capability that is sited in a data-processing center. Business Unit Processor(s) (BUP) of medium capacity that operate as departmental consolidated workload

systems, and Single User Systems (SUS) available for individual functions in a department. The systems will operate in heterogeneous software environments and may be architecturally heterogeneous. This paper will assume homogeneous processor architectures but the concepts can be expanded to include heterogeneous architectures by additional software effort. As we will later discuss the software of the system includes a kernel operating system for the smaller processors, a set of monitor application environments and a set of interface components that allow the execution of function at various places in the system..

The General Services Processors

The General Services Processors (GSP) are sited at a data processing center. GSPs are machines of large capacity, conceptually the

largest available general purpose processor of its time frame. A rough sizing of the capacity of this machine in the middle years of this decade would make it a 16 to 20 MIPS machine.

The purpose of a GSP is to provide software function and operational services to the business unit systems (BUP AND SUS). The software of the GSP is the large general purpose operating system usually associated with such machines, and a complete set of compilers, utilities, data base management systems, etc., available to systems of this class. Within the context of IBM software, for example, this would be an MVS, IMS, system that would also run whatever network management services the installation deemed appropriate for its local network. This network management service set would naturally include remote maintenance and operator support described in [5].

In pure form, the systems concept precludes interactive application programs from running on the GSP. The function of this unit is to only provide remote operating system, subsystem, batch, and operator services for the BUP and SUS units.

The General Services Processor memory provides, of particular interest to this architecture, a large fast memory to and from which remote processors can make data references and enqueue service request messages and otherwise communicate to the GSP.

The Business Unit Processor

The Business Unit Processor is a departmental level, multifunction machine. It may have a significant population of devices and storage units and will run a kernel operating system capable of providing support to significant programming development subsystems or **surrogate** interfaces that define an application production environment. A surrogate interface is a layer of software that prepares service commands issued by applications programs for transport to the general services processor that is the host system for the referenced subsystem.

The Business Unit Processor is a suitable system for multiuser and even multiapplication timesharing and multiprogramming applications. It may be run standalone with suitable software if the business unit desires. It is a machine with a MIPS rate in the 1 to 3 MIPS category and with appropriately sophisticated I/O.

A Business Unit Processor designed for this system would ideally have some properties that are now not common to intermediate machines of this general class. For the purposes of this system it might be useful to provide a total memory map so that page and segment tables and their management is not locally necessary. The cost of this map might be offset by the possible elimination of cache mechanisms in machines of moderate speed as memory speeds increase.

Single User Stations

This is a computer system with the characteristics of contemporary single user or personal computers. It includes a keyboard, video display of some type, perhaps 256K to 1megs worth of work space for a user, an optional printing device (such as a relatively cheap, slow copier), limited DASD, and an interface to the interconnection processor. These processors may talk to the General Services processor directly in the same manner that the Business Units processors talk, or they may talk to business Unit Processors. In general a business unit processor may be used as a pass thru device or communicated with on a usual processor to processor communications mode. At the moment we do not perceive the Business Unit Processor taking on the role of a General Services Processor for the Single User Systems. This is primarily because the Single User Systems when requiring off-node function will not, in this structure, find those services available at a BUP.

The most significant detail about the Single User station is that, unlike the business unit and general services processors, it is a single virtual memory machine, geared to a single user environment.

SOFTWARE ENVIRONMENTS

AND OPERATIONAL DYNAMICS

We will describe the operational concept of how address spaces are mapped across the family of memories, some mechanisms for supporting remote memory reference of various kinds, and the software that will exist in each class of machine.

Memory to Memory Interaction

Applications in a BUP or SUS run in virtual address spaces. A common occurrence is for an application to issue a macro that calls upon the services of a subsystem like a data base manager (DBMS). A DBMS application running on a business unit processor issuing a data base request will essentially be invoking an interface (surrogate) layer that represents the DBMS in the business unit processor. This surrogate layer processes the service call until it transforms it into a cross virtual memory interaction. The DBMS system, running on the GSP, operates in its own virtual memory on that processor. There is a defined request space supporting cross virtual memory communications. The surrogate layer at the BUP submits the cross memory service request to the interconnection mechanism. The request arrives at the global services processor on an appropriate queue.

In the (preferred) presences of a Relocate Engine, the addresses of shared request space used by the business unit processor that is transmitted to the global services processor is a virtual address. The interconnect processor at the GSP passes it to the Relocate Engine that uses the appropriate memory mapping tables to determine the real addresses to be used at the GSP memory.

An interesting way for requests to be transmitted across memories is for the Relocate engine to modify page tables directly. Thus a request is transmitted to a virtual memory by writing its location in a page table associated with the virtual memory

It is not necessary for a GSP to be interrupted on request receipt, but the concept allows for designers to determine when interrupts should be taken on the arrival of a service request in the virtual memory of the subsystem at the GSP. If no interrupt is taken the subsystem at the GSP will process the request and deliver the service at such time when it inspects queues and finds the request at the top.

The GSP processor uses GSP memory to provide the service. When a response is properly constructed, the GSP issues commands that will send it to the requesting processor. It will follow the path through the relocate engine to the business unit processor memory.

Whatever local functions, paging, I/O, etc., are required at the GSP system do not concern the business unit processor that is continuing with concurrent processing.

A question arises as to how deep the surrogate layer is. Should it do some local processing so that the cross of machine boundaries is beneath the data base request level? The risk of not doing so increases the task switch burden of software in the business unit processor. It is probably better for the surrogate processor to collect the elements of the data base request before transmission to the GSP.

Paging Services

A business unit processor may execute software that is not local by use of the relocate engine and a remote paging scheme. This mode maps all of real storage associated with a virtual memory into the memory of a business unit (or single user) unit. The disk units of the business unit processor, however, are not the repository of the copy of software that is being executed. A single copy of software exists at the GSP. This mode uses a business

unit processor and the auxiliary storage devices of the GSP. It also uses the GSP to execute its auxiliary storage manager on behalf of a requesting processor. If there is no relocate engine in the system the GSP will have additional local relocate function.

When a business unit processor undertakes to execute a non-local program it will experience a page fault. The auxiliary storage manager at the unit will recognize that the program is not mapped into local auxiliary storage. It will then develop a auxiliary storage manager services request to send to the GSP queue of paging requests. Return of the page is through operation of the GSP auxiliary paging manager, through whatever buffers are necessary, through the relocate engine to the memory of the requesting unit, transparent to the user and application.

A word about memory mapping in the small systems. In the presence of a relocate engine it is possible to remove page and segment tables from them. If there is a lookaside buffer that maps all of memory then a page fault can occur when the lookaside buffer has a no find. Instead of inspecting local page and segment tables, the local fault handler goes immediately to the creation of a remote paging request. The address handed to the relocate engine is a virtual address transformed at the relocate engine into a real storage address.

Software Population

The software at the GSP may be changed for some number of reasons.

1. To accommodate the offload of relocate management to the relocate engine

2. To support the notion of queue driven service if the operating system does not have it.

3. To provide for communications with the interconnect processor as a port into and out of the system.

4. To extend the subsystem support of cross memory conversation with applications running remotely.

Essentially, however, the "flavor" of the GSP remains unchanged. It runs a large operating system and a full complement of subsystems very much like it would were it running local applications.

The software at the business unit and personal unit, however, undergoes a considerable functional and structural change. The components of software at a BUP or SUS are -

1. An Operating System kernel or Hypervisor that provides such operating system function as is necessary for basic operation of a BUP or SUS and that provides interface for diverse "guest" operating systems or monitors. Multiple guest operating systems can coexist on a given BUP, while only one can be operative at a time in a SUS. The guest operating system operates with extended privilege in an environment where sharing is minimized between virtual address spaces in a BUP.

2. In the absence of a Relocate Engine the guest operating system will operate its relocation and paging functions in the usual fashion. The auxiliary page manager must be extended to recognize the need for interaction with a remote auxiliary page manager. In the presence of a Relocate Engine, the guest operating system will be relieved of page and segment management.

3. A set of surrogate interfaces that present the service calls of remote subsystems to a local application running in a guest operating system environment. The surrogate interface transforms local service calls into remote cross memory interaction functions.

4. An intercommunication handler process as a service of the kernel operating system.

FINAL COMMENT ON SYSTEMS STRUCTURE

Two observations are still to be made. The Relocate Engine is obviously the nucleus of a Central Systems Control and Global Resource Manager that can provide access to intelligent devices as well as to the GSP. By extension a single systems lock manager and pathways to shared I/O sink/source devices can be made through mapping in the Relocate Engine.

The relocate engine is a processor of some significance with a specialized architecture and sufficient memory to hold paging and segment tables for the entire system.

Not addressed at all in this structure as described is the relationship between multiple BUPs in a single business configuration.

A potential extension to the system concept, under certain technology assumptions about relative memory speeds and postulating interconnect pipes as fast as memory lines, would be to allow certain forms of direct execution and data reference for processors that were physically proximate. Mappings of Virtual Memory across local and remote memories might be accomplished. Remote memory reference delays (6) have been serious when remote and local memories are the same speed. But the availability of memories of high speed remotely may address performance problems in a hierarchic structure.

The technology assumptions of economically effective memories of an order of magnitude difference in speed are not firm.

There are some connected considerations in contention resolution, banking and interleaving methodologies, and the use of caches in intermediate machines. Success for such a system extension would be that the expected time for a response from memory would be the same whether the instruction or operand reference was local or remote. Stability of performance and insensitivity to "local hit ratios" would be an operational plus for such systems if technology allows them.

THE MANAGEMENT ENVIRONMENT

The structure described above intends to provide a system that provides for flexibility in the systems management arena. The Data Processing Complex offers the Business Units where the BUPs and SUSs are located a set of operational and systems services to which they may, optionally subscribe. The degree of optionality is a matter of enterprise policy. Thus it may be mandated by enterprise management that a business unit accept all offered services and run essentially as a dependent node in terms of operator and systems services. If the enterprise style permits more autonomous decision making on the part of business units, then the business unit management may select from a menu of operational services offered by the Data Processing Center either through the GSP or through the operations and systems programming staff associated with the GSP. The services are offered on a priced basis and are formalized in a negotiated "level of services" contract between the business unit and the data processing center.

McQuilken [5] discusses an environment which provides remote operator and remote maintenance support. Such support would be a part of the offering of the D.P. center. In addition to this, however, the business unit should be able to contract for various levels of systems programming support services.

A business unit may desire to maintain special versions of its own software product at its own machine but contract for installation and maintenance services from the GSP staff. Alternatively the business unit may desire to keep its specialized software at the GSP site and contract for space and software services at that sight. Further options include the use of data space at the GSP, and the basic use of software packages on a fee basis, either in remote paging mode, direct execution mode, or on a service macro basis. Accounting may be done on a unit of service basis plus a fee for professional support.

The concept of distributed processing attempts to define a management stylistic that represents a middle position between autonomy and systems management specialization. The variations in desirable sites of competence and function, however, are still vast within the concept of distributed processing. Business units differ considerably in the amount of responsibility and authority they desire. A negotiated service level scheme within the single systems concept presented here allows those issues to be resolved within a single consistent framework based upon perceptions of cost and desired autonomy.

We do not address issues of systems selection and justification. We assume that those processes, rational or otherwise, have already gone forward and that the management issue requiring resolution is the discovery of an intersection between management prerogative and suitable systems structure for accommodating the various styles of management within a business unit.

ACKNOWLEDGEMENTS

The authors would like to thank Irving Wladawsky-Berger, Andy Heller and Gene Trivett for their invaluable insights.

REFERENCES

1. Lorin, H. "Key Decisions In Distributed Processing" Proceedings IEEE COMPCON '80.

2. Lorin, H. **Aspects of Distributed Computer Systems** John Wiley & Son, 1980

3. Lorin, H., B.C. Goldstein, "Operating System Structure for Polymorphic Hardware", Proceedings ACM Pacific '80.

4. Goldstein, B.C., H. Lorin, "An Inversion of Memory Hierarchy", Proceedings ACM Pacific '80.

5. McQuilken, G., "Distributed Machines", Proceedings IEEE COMPCON '80.

6. J.K.Ousterhout, D.A. Scelza, P.S. Sindhu "Medusa: An Experiment in Distributed Operating System Structure" **CACM 23,2** (Feb.1980) pp.92-105

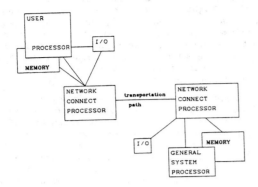

FIGURE 1: NETWORK CONNECTIONS

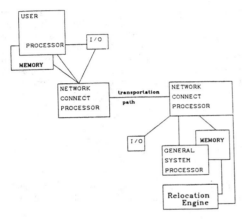

FIGURE 2: NETWORK CONNECTIONS

A Virtual Token Scheme, GBRAM, for Local Data and Voice Distribution

T T Liu
GTE Laboratories, USA

L Li
Gould Inc., USA

Investigating the ability to include real time voice communications as a part of the local area network's applications is the major objective of this paper. We focus on the analysis and simulation of a virtual token media-access scheme, GBRAM (Group Broadcast Recognizing Access Method), and reveal its superiority over random-access schemes in supporting real time voice applications.

GBRAM is a collision-free protocol applicable on bus type of local area networks. It offers a deterministic transmission service, and enables the network to achieve a very high throughput. A series of performance comparisons between GBRAM and CSMA/CD are given in this paper. These studies indicate, among other things, that GBRAM is able to offer 125 voice circuits, while CSMA/CD can offer at most 94 voice circuits on a 10 Mbps channel.

1. INTRODUCTION

Until recently, local area networks have been used primarily for non-real time data communications. But in recent years, more and more people have recognized the need to integrate voice traffic into local networking. As a result, digitized voice transmissions have been proposed to be incorporated into the network traffic [1,2,3,4].

While many communication protocols exist or have been proposed to handle data traffic on the local area networks, there is still an absence of a good technique for handling real time voice traffic, which poses its own unique arrival pattern and transmission requirements.

To date, two major categories of local network protocols for data communications prevail for their performance and reliability: The random access (contention) schemes and the decentralized demand-assignment schemes. The random access schemes are typified by the CSMA/CD (carrier sense multiple access with collision detection) protocol [5,6], which can be characterized as "listen before transmission, listen while transmitting". One well-known implementation of CSMA/CD protocol is the Ethernet [7], which uses a binary-exponential backoff scheme to resolve packet collision. Studies show that, although CSMA/CD is very efficient in light and medium traffic loads, there is no guarantee of packet delivery time due to the undeterministic nature of contention and collision/backoff. Furthermore, when the traffic loads become heavy, the CSMA/CD scheme suffers from large mean and variance of packet-delay.

The decentralized demand assignment schemes, on the other hand, dynamically allocate channel bandwidth to the busy nodes in a decentralized environment. A good example of this type of technique is the virtual token passing protocol BRAM (broadcast recognizing access method) [8]. In this protocol, the channel time is divided into time slots of size a, the end-to-end propagation delay. The

users (nodes) are assigned, by a distributed algorithm, time slots in a "logical ring" fashion. No physical token exists; instead each node senses the carrier and recognizes the source address of the transmitted packets to determine who has the next transmission right. The transition of transmission right by scheduling one single user at a time for transmission is referred to as virtual token passing. Since the time of transmission attempts of different nodes are separated by at least one end-to-end bus delay, transmission collision can be totally avoided in normal operation.

Analysis shows that BRAM performs very well under all traffic loads for small user population, and is able to provide an upper bound to the network response time that the users experience. However, BRAM's performance degrades as the number of nodes and the bus propagation delay increases.

Recently, a modification of BRAM, called Group-BRAM, or GBRAM [9,10], has been proposed, which employs a two-level BRAM scheduling structure on a baseband bus to reduce the control overhead. GBRAM significantly enhances the performance of BRAM, and is able to support a much larger user population. Since GBRAM is also conflict-free, a maximum packet-delivery time can be guaranteed, therefore, making GBRAM a desirable protocol for handling integrated voice/data communications.

In the following section, we briefly review the definition of the GBRAM protocol and outline its performance characteristics. In Section 3, we evaluate the performance of GBRAM under voice traffic, and compare it with the performance of CSMA/CD. In Section 4, the characteristics of GBRAM under integrated voice/data traffic is studied by simulation. Finally, a summary in Section 5 concludes this paper.

2. REVIEW OF GBRAM

2.1 Definition of GBRAM

It has been observed that, in most local area networks, the user terminals have a tendency to form clusters (e.g., a set of nodes located within a room, or on the same floor of a building). Typically, the bus propagation delay within a cluster (group) is just a small fraction of the total bus propagation delay. Therefore, it is advantageous to pass the token between nodes within a group (i.e., intra-group token passing) before the token is passed to another group (i.e., inter-group token passing), as is depicted in Figure 1.

In GBRAM protocol, the N user nodes on the bus are divided into M groups according to their physical locations. Each group g_i will be allocated a group slot $\underline{a}$ for its intra-group token passing. Since the transmission attempts from different nodes of the group must be at least one intra-group propagation delay a_i apart, group g_i can accommodate $\lfloor a/a_i \rfloor + 1$ nodes. Following the group slot, GBRAM allows another $\underline{a}$ (the worst-case propagation delay) for the token to travel to the next group. Figure 2 illustrates the channel scheduling for user node (g_j, n_j) to receive the virtual token, where n_j is the node index within group g_j.

There are at least two basic variants to the GBRAM protocol: the exhaustive GBRAM and the non-exhaustive GBRAM. The former allows a node, upon receiving the token, to transmit all the packets queued in its buffer. The latter permits each node to transmit at most one packet at one channel access. The scheduling function of the exhaustive GBRAM is given as:

$$F((g_j n_j), (g_i n_i)) =$$

$$\begin{cases} 2\underline{a} \ [(g_j - g_i + M)\bmod M] + a_j(n_j - 1) & g_j = g_i \\ a_j \ (n_j - n_i) & g_j = g_i \text{ and } n_j \geq n_i \quad (1) \\ 2\underline{a}M + a_j(n_j - 1) & g_j = g_i \text{ and } n_j < n_i \end{cases}$$

Each node executes a simple algorithm as follows:

STEP 1. If node (g_j, n_j) senses the channel to become idle at time t_n, then the node schedules its transmission at time $t = t_n + F((g_j, n_j), (g_i, n_i))$, where t_n is the end of transmission time of node (g_i, n_i). If the channel is sensed busy on or before this scheduled time t, then Step 2 results; otherwise, node (g_j, n_j) can start its transmission at time t.

STEP 2. If the channel is sensed busy, then node (g_j, n_j) waits for the end of current transmission so that t_{n+1} can be determined. Then go to Step 1.

2.2 Performance of GBRAM

For the purpose of our performance analysis, let us assume a "worst case" configuration where the N nodes are evenly spaced on the bus. Since no physical clusters exist in this case, we partition the entire bus into M segments of equal length, so that each segment captures approximately N/M nodes, and form a group. The intra-group delay (the "subslot") is then $\underline{a}/M$, and the relationship of the throughput S to mean delay D of the exhaustive GBRAM, by applying the polling analysis of [11] can be derived as [9]:

$$E(\text{Delay}) = \frac{a\delta^2}{2rM} + \frac{1}{2}\frac{S}{1-S} + \frac{a}{2M}\ (1 - \frac{S}{N})(1 + \frac{Nr}{1-S}) \quad (2)$$

in units of packet transmission time, where

$$r = \frac{1}{N}\ [(1+S)M^2 + N-M] \text{ Subslots}$$

is the mean of token passing time, and

$$\delta^2 = \frac{1}{N}\left\{ M[(1+S)M-r]^2 + (N-M)[1-r]^2 \right\}$$

is the variance of token passing time.

The analysis of the non-exhaustive GBRAM is considerably more difficult, and will be handled by simulation.

The performance of the exhaustive and non-exhaustive GBRAM for a network with 50 data nodes with a Poisson packet arrival process and at various bus lengths are plotted in Figure 3. Also in this figure are the performance curves of the BRAM protocol, the CSMA/CD protocol, and the M/D/1 perfect scheduling. It shows that, for a small propagation delay (a=0.01), both GBRAM and CSMA/CD perform very close to M/D/1, with CSMA/CD having a shorter delay then GBRAM at low to medium loads. However, in heavy loads GBRAM's performance exceeds that of CSMA/CD due to its collision-free property. As $\underline{a}$ increases to 0.1, the performance of CSMA/CD degrades significantly, while GBRAM remains close to M/D/1. Under such a circumstance, even BRAM performs better than CSMA/CD in medium to high loads. When the propagation delay is extremely large ($\underline{a}$=1.0), GBRAM can still provide an acceptable service, yet CSMA/CD deteriorates to the level of slotted ALOHA at best.

2.3 Control Overheads of GBRAM

The algorithm of GBRAM mentioned so far is based on an assumption that the end-of-transmission can be identified by all nodes with zero time. But the fact is it takes each node a different amount of time in the range from 0 to $\underline{a}$ (due to propagation delay) to realize the occurrence of each end-of-transmission. In view of this phenomenon, an "asynchronous" GBRAM is devised, in the sense that each node will calculate its own time slot based on the time it detected the end-of-frame (EOF) signal, rather than a common time reference. The timing difference between different nodes detecting the EOF signal is known as the "EOF skew". By adding an extra latency into the token passing time between every two nodes (i.e., doubling the sizes of time slots and subslots), we resolve the time skew problem at the cost of degrading system's performance due to this added overhead. For a detailed discussion of this aspect, the reader is referred to [10].

Two other implementation considerations of the GBRAM protocol are the nodes turnaround time and the carrier-sensing/signal-generating time. The turnaround time t is the time a node takes to change its current state of receiving or transmitting to the next state of receiving or transmitting. This is also referred to as interframe time by IEEE-802 and the Ethernet specification. Since this turnaround time is associated with the transmission of each packet, we can imagine the packet as being enlarged by a factor of t (i.e., the new packet transmission time is now $1+t$). The throughput-delay relationship can thus be obtained by substituting S with $S(1+t)$ in equation (2).

The carrier-sensing/signal-generating time d is the time a node takes to detect the absence of a carrier on the channel, and have its signal appear on the bus. To account for this overhead, we simply let the inter-group token passing time be $a+d$ and the intra-group token passing time be $(a/M+d)$, so that a group slot is now $a+(N/M)d$. The throughput-delay formula in (2) now becomes:

$$E(Delay) = \frac{\delta^2}{2r} \left(\frac{a}{M} + d \right) + \frac{1}{2} \frac{S}{1-S} + \frac{1}{2} \left(\frac{a}{M} + d \right) (1 - \frac{S}{N})(1 + \frac{Nr}{1-S}) \qquad (3)$$

in units of packet transmission time, where

$$r = \frac{1}{N} \left\{ M [(a + d) + S(\frac{a}{M} + d) \frac{N}{M}]/(\frac{a}{M} + d) + N-M \right\}$$

and

$$\delta^2 = \frac{M}{N} \left\{ [(a + d) + S(\frac{a}{M} + d) \frac{N}{M}]/(\frac{a}{M} + d) - r \right\}^2 + \frac{N-M}{N} (1-r)^2$$

The analysis of the synchronous GBRAM can also be adjusted accordingly.

The carrier-sensing/signal-generating has an accumulation effect for virtual token passing scheme. This accumulation effect appears greater when the network is lightly loaded then when it is heavily loaded.

3.   REAL TIME VOICE COMMUNICATIONS

3.1   Characteristics of Voice Traffic

Arrivals and departures of phone calls are generally modelled by the Poisson process. The Erlang B and Poisson equations are employed to describe the system service in terms of traffic loads and the call-blocking probability. As an example, for a system to provide services to 400 users, each generating 9 ccs (nine-hundred call seconds per hour) of traffic, with a blocking probability of $P=0.01$, 117 voice circuits are required according to the Erlang B equation.

Our intention in this section is to determine the number of voice circuits a local network can offer. Based on this figure, the user population that a network can support is then defined.

With PCM and silence detection techniques in voice digitization, we assume that the two ends of a voice circuit together generate 64 Kbps of traffic into the system. If the packet generating cycle is determined as 12 milliseconds, then each voice circuit will periodically generate a 102-byte packet, which consists of 96 bytes of actual voice information and 6 bytes of control overhead and synchronization. If a single buffer is provided at each transmitting and receiving port, a constraint of 12 ms packet-lifetime must be imposed. A packet with delay longer than the cycle time results in a packet loss.

However, it is not necessary that 100% of the packets generated be received at the other end in order to maintain an acceptable telephone conversation. Studies show that, a loss rate of less than 2% is barely noticeable to the human ear if the packet size is within the range of 1 ms to 20 ms, and the loss does not occur periodically [4,12]. A larger packet size will result in improved network performance, but the loss of packets, even at a low rate, is very disturbing to human ear. Therefore, it is not considered here.

3.2   Performance Analysis of GBRAM Under Voice Traffic

Since GBRAM is a collision-free protocol, the network can only be in one of the following two states: token passing or packet transmission. Our analysis in this section will be based on this assumption, and will focus on the situation where only voice traffic is offered. As stated earlier, there is a constraint on a voice packet's lifetime in that a packet has to be transmitted within its generating cycle time t_g. A reasonable range for t_g is from 1 ms to 20 ms. Those packets queued in the system longer than t_g are discarded in order to empty the buffer space for the newly generated voice packets. The packet's generating cycle, under the equalibrium conditions that the number of calls remain constant, and that each call generates a fixed size packet every t_g, can be expressed as:

$$t_p + n \frac{B_c + B_g}{B} (1-L) = t_g \qquad (4)$$

t_p = the time network spends in token passing;
n = the number of active phone conversations;
b_c = the control bits for each voice packet;
b_g = the voice information bits;
B = channel bandwidth;
L = the packet loss rate of voice traffic.

For example, a network consisting of 64 Kbps PCM (with silence detection) voice terminal and operating on an 1 Mbps bus, with b_g=96 bytes and b_c=6 bytes, can support up to 14.7 voice circuits with packet loss rate L=0 if the token passing time t_p can be ignored. One can view t_p as a complementing term of $n(b_c+b_g)(1-L)/B$ in expression (4). Its value, depending on the traffic load, ranges from t_g at an extremely light load (i.e., most of the channel time is spent in idle token passing), to some minimum value under an extremely heavy load (i.e., throughput S→1). This lower bound of t_p is the time the token takes to visit each user exactly once, and is what decides the maximum throughput of the system. For the asynchronous GBRAM with carrier-sensing/signal-generating time considered, the worst case of token passing time can be expressed as:

$$t_p(\text{worst case})=M(2(\underline{a}-\frac{a}{M})+\underline{d})+$$

$$(\frac{N}{M}(\frac{2a}{M}+\underline{d})+\frac{3a}{M}-\underline{a})+(N-M)(\frac{2a}{M}+\underline{d})\quad(5)$$

To study the achievable network capacity of GBRAM protocol, let us consider the following two configurations. Both assume $M=2\sqrt{N}$ which will result in a best performance in term of mean delay for asynchronous GBRAM.

Configuration A.

N = number of active users = 64,
M = number of groups = 16,
Bus length = 1 Km,
Bus bandwidth = 1 Mbps,
Bus propagation speed = 0.66 C,
$\underline{d}$ = carrier-sensing/signal-generating time
   = 2 bits = 2 microsec.,
Packet size = 102 bytes.

The calculated maximum lower bound for the token passing time t_p is 0.042 of the network capacity. This implies that the maximum achievable throughput is 0.958 of the channel capacity.

Configuration B.

N = 400,
M = 40,
Bus length = 1 Km,
Bus bandwidth = 10 Mbps,
Bus propagation speed = 0.66 c,
$\underline{d}$ = 2 bits (200 ns),
Packet size = 102 bytes.

The maximum lower bound for t_p is calculated at 0.0434 of the network capacity. This implies that the maximum achievable normalized throughput is 0.9564. The throughput here includes all kinds of transmission.

Although the normalized end-to-end propagation delay $\underline{a}$ (w.r.t. packet transmission time) in Configuration B is 10 times larger than that of Configuration A, the carrier-sensing/signal-generating time $\underline{d}$, on the other hand, is 10 times smaller than that of Configuration

A. This results in a nearly equivalent maximum throughput for the two configurations. If the turnaround time, which is fairly constant, is put into consideration, the maximum throughput of the 10 Mbps case will be affected more significantly than the 1 Mbps case due to the relative larger overhead (as compared with the packet transmission time) involved. In any case, our analysis indicates that, for a network filled with periodic traffic such as voice packets within the maximum throughput loading, the network will provide service to each packet with a delay shorter than the periodic cycle time with little or no packet loss.

3.3 Some Simulation Results

The GPSS simulation language is employed to simulate CSMA/CD and GBRAM for both 1 Mbps and 10 Mbps cases. The same parameters as listed in configurations A and B of the previous section are used in our simulation. As a result, the normalized propagation delay a is 0.00612 for the 1 Mbps case, and is 0.0612 for the 10 Mbps case. For the CSMA/CD simulation, a binary exponential backoff algorithm is used as the backoff algorithm, and a jam-time of 4.8 microseconds is enforced after each collision. Also, a 9.6 microseconds of turnaround time is imposed on both CSMA/CD and GBRAM. During the simulation, the system generates n packets (i.e., n active conversations) periodically every 12 ms, and these packets are uniformly distributed over the period of 12 ms. These settings provide a common ground for the comparison of these two protocols. The carrier sensing/signal generating time is neglected in the simulation for both cases.

The simulation results of the throughput and the packet loss rate for both CSMA/CD and GBRAM in the 1 Mbps case (Configuration A) are plotted in Figures 4 and 5, respectively. The CSMA/CD under the arrival rate of 0.957 can achieve a throughput of 90% at the cost of 6% packet loss. GBRAM, on the other hand, under the arrival rate of 0.99 can achieve a throughput of 95% with only 4% packet loss. If we limit the packet loss rate to be within 2%, then CSMA/CD can roughly support 12.6 voice circuit, while GBRAM can support approximately 14.2 voice circuits, an improvement of 12.5%.

Figure 6 shows the packet delay distribution of both protocols at a traffic load equal to 88% of the channel capacity. Although the majority of the packets experience a lower delay under CSMA/CD, GBRAM guarantees an upper bound to the network delay, which results in no loss of packets. If we impose the 12 ms lifetime constraint, then CSMA/CD will lose 3% of its packets.

Next, we simulate the 10 Mbps case (Configuration B) for both protocols. Their throughput and packet loss rates are depicted in Figures 7 and 8. As shown in Figure 7, CSMA/CD can only achieve a maximum throughput of between 66% to 67%. Increasing the traffic load beyond this point only results in more packet losses. If we consider the constraint of 2% maximum packet-loss, then CSMA/CD can only support 94 phone circuits (see Figure 8). The GBRAM protocol, on the other hand, can achieve a 85% capacity with less than 5% packet loss. Again, under the same constraint of 2% packet-loss, GBRAM is able to support 125 phone circuits. This is a 33% improvement over CSMA/CD's capacity. These figures will be slightly lower for the implementations that require more control bits and longer preamble for each voice packet.

4. THE INTEGRATED DATA/VOICE SERVICE

The traffic pattern of data packets differs from that of voice packets in its non-periodic nature, and is generally modelled as a Poisson arrival process. Due to the probablistic nature of Poisson arrivals, the network, when running with both data and voice traffic, can be overloaded instantaneously even though the mean traffic load is within its capacity. This will result in a mean delay higher than that of when only voice traffic is presented.

To study the effect of the integrated voice/data traffic, we simulate the asynchronous GBRAM with various loadings of data traffic on top of a 100 voice-call background traffic. We will continue to assume that both voice and data packets are of fixed size (102 bytes). Only the voice packets are dropped after their lifetime exceeds 12 ms. Figures 8 and 9 show that the voice packets experience a higher loss rate in the integrated service when compared to the all-voice case of equal overall traffic loads, due to the fact that the data packets will remain in the network until they are successfully transmitted. However, the persistence of these data packets enables the network to achieve a slightly higher overall throughput; our simulation shows that the loss of voice packet does not increase as much as the amount of data packets that would have been lost if data packets had also been allowed to drop. This is explained by the improved overall throughput.

The mean delay of data packets at different loads are also plotted in Figure 9. It clearly points out that, a 10 Mbps local network implemented with the GBRAM protocol can easily support 100 voice circuits with virtually no packet loss and still leaves more than 2 Mbps of channel capacity for data traffic. The mean data packet delays range from 1 ms to 4 ms, depending on the actual data loading.

5. CONCLUSION

In this paper, we first reviewed the definition of GBRAM protocol and its basic analysis and simulation results. Some critical timing considerations that can affect the network's performance were discussed. We then focused on the real time voice application of GBRAM. The maximum achievable throughput of GBRAM was derived. The performance differences between GBRAM and CSMA/CD were compared throughout the paper by a GPSS simulation model. We observed that GBRAM is superior to CSMA/CD for its higher achievable throughput and lower packet loss rate,

which is due to the deterministic nature of GBRAM's algorithm. CSMA/CD may provide a lower averaged delay to the packets at low to medium traffic loads when the normalized propagation delay a is relatively small. But in practice, it does not matter if a voice packet is transmitted in 1 ms or 2 ms. Rather, the guarantee of an upper bound to the packet's delivery time and higher achievable throughput is more of a concern in most applications.

The maximum number of 64 kbps voice circuits that CSMA/CD and GBRAM can support with a reasonable delay performance is investigated. This will provide a basic guideline to those who are interested in integrating voice communication into their local networks. Finally, we concentrated on the performance of GBRAM when both data and voice traffic were presented, and concluded that GBRAM is suitable for real time voice applications, especially in the environment where high utilization on network capacity is required.

REFERENCES

1. Don H. Johnson, Gerald C. O'leary, "A Local Access Network for Packetized Digital Voice Communication", IEEE Trans. Comm. Vol. COM-29 No 5, May 1981.
2. G.J. Nutt, D.L.Bayer, "Performance of CSMA/CD Network under Combined Voiceand Data Loads," IEEE Trans. Comm. Vol. COM-30 No.1, Jan. 1982.
3. F.A. Tobagi, N. Gonzalez-Cawley, "On CSMA/CD Local Networks and VoiceCommunication," Proceedings InforCom '82, Mar. '82.
4. Musser, J.M., T.T. Liu, F.P. Tredeau, "Packet-Voice Performance on a CSMA/CD Local Area Network," The International Symposium on Subscriber Loops and Service, Sep. 1982.
5. Kleinrock, L., F.A. Tobagi, "Packet Switching in Radio Channels: Part I - Carrier Sense Multiple-Access Mode and Their Throughput-Delay Characteristics," IEEE Trans. Comm., Vol. COM-23, No. 12, Dec. 1975, pp. 1400-1416.
6. Tobagi, F.A., V.B. Hunt, "Performance Analysis of Carrier Sense Multiple Access with Collision Detection," Proc. LACN Symp., May 1979, pp. 217-244.
7. Metcalfe, R.M., and D.R. Boggs, Ethernet: "Distributed Packet Switching for Local Computer Networks," Communications of the ACM, Vol. 19, No. 7, pp. 395-403, 1976.
8. Chlamtac, I., W.R. Franta, K.D. Levin, "BRAM: The Broadcast Recognizing Access Method," IEEE Trans. Comm., Vol. COM-27, No. 8, Aug. 1979., pp. 1183-1190.
9. Konheim, A.G., B. Meister, "Waiting Lines and Time in a System with Polling," JACM, Vol. 21, No. 3, July 1974, pp 470-490.
10. Liu, T.T., L. Li, W.R. Franta, "The Analysis of a Conflict-Free Protocol Based on Node Clusters," Sixth Conference on Local Computer Networks, Oct. 1981, Minneapolis, MN, pp. 61-72.
11. Liu, T.T., L. Li, W.R. Franta, "A Decentralized Conflict-Free Protocol, GBRAM for Large Scale Local Networks," Computer Networking Symposium, Dec. 1981, pp. 39-54.
12. Forgie, J.W., "Network Speech System Implications of Packetized Speech," MIT Lincoln Labs., ESD-TR-77-178, Sept. 1976.

Fig. 1 : Virtual Token Passing of GBRAM.

Fig. 2 : Channel Scheduling of GBRAM.

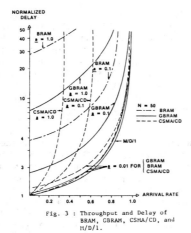

Fig. 3 : Throughput and Delay of BRAM, GBRAM, CSMA/CD, and M/D/1.

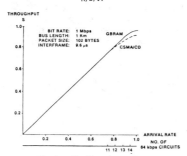

Fig. 4 : The Throughput of CSMA/CD and GBRAM.

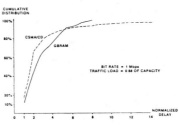

Fig. 6 : The Packet Delay Distribution of CSMA/CD and GBRAM.

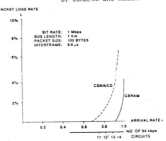

Fig. 5 : Packet Loss Rate of CSMA/CD and GBRAM.

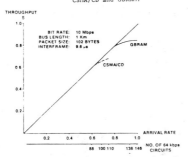

Fig. 7 : The Throughput of CSMA/CD and GBRAM.

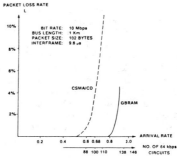

Fig 8 : The Packet Loss Rate of CSMA/CD and GBRAM.

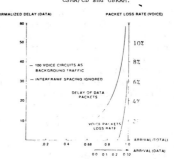

Fig. 9 : The Data Packet Delay and Voice Packet Loss of GBRAM with Mixed Traffic.

Then Tang Liu is a Member of Technical Staff in the GTE Telenet Technology Center. He received the B.S. degree in physics from National Tsing Hua University, Taiwan, and the M.S.E.E. from the University of Massachusetts, Amherst. He joined GTE Laboratories in 1980, where his research interests have included computer networking and communication system performance evaluation. Mr. Liu is a member of IEEE and ACM.

Liang Li is an advanced technology planner at Gould Inc., S.E.L. Computer Systems Division, where he is responsible for technology planning in local area networks, distributed processing, and computer architecture. Before joining Gould-S.E.L., he was a research assistant at Michigan State University where he researched in the areas of computer performance evaluation, computer simulation, capacity planning, and local area networking. He is also the co-author of several research articles.

Li received his B.S. degree in Mathematics from National Central University of the Republic of China in 1973, his M.S. degree in Computer Science from Central Michigan University in 1978, and a Ph.D degree in Computer Science from Michigan State University in 1982. He is a member of ACM and IEEE Computer Society.

Operational and Maintenance Experience of PSS

A C Barnes, J Graves
British Telecom, UK

BT's packet switched service (PSS) started commercial operation in August 1981. This paper reviews the operational and maintenance experience gained in running the network, including the pre-operational phase which started with a pilot network of 3 nodes in Sept 1980.

PSS is controlled from a Network Management Centre (NMC) in London. The standard facilities provided by the NMC minicomputers are described as well as the enhancements which have been implemented by BT in order to optimise performance monitoring and maintenance control of the network. Finally the various categories of PSS statistics produced are outlined.

1   INTRODUCTION

By implementing one of the first public packet switched systems in Europe, the Experimental Packet Switched Service (EPSS), British Telecom gained a great deal of experience in running and maintaining such a system (Ref 1). EPSS came into full service in April 1977 and provided service to customers until it was closed down in July 1981. While EPSS did not reveal a large customer demand for packet switched services it was recognised that such a service with its unique features could act as a stimulus to the development of new applications. This view was strongly endorsed by the government sponsored National Committee on Computer Networks (NCCN) and confirmed by the success of the International Packet Switched Service (IPSS) which opened in December 1978.

While EPSS was being brought into service agreement was reached at CCITT on Recommendations for packet switching principally X25, and later X3, X28, X29 and X75. The EPSS protocols were incompatible with CCITT Recommendations and it was not technically practicable to modify EPSS to X25. It was therefore decided to invite competitive tenders for the supply of a packet switched system. As a result BT placed a contract with Plessey Controls Ltd in February 1979.

Because of contract delays and to enable customers to test their implementations on a 'live' system a pilot network of 3 nodes, London, Reading and Bristol was opened in September 1980. This was under the control of the PSS Operations Group and enabled maintenance staff to gain hands-on experience with the system. The remaining 6 nodes were integrated into the pilot network by December 1980. The pilot network ran on pre-release software while System Acceptance Testing continued in parallel at the factory.

Following the formal schedule of Network Acceptance Tests (NAT) carried out by the PSS Software support group (ref 2) a period of pre-operations commenced on 23 February 1981 during which time customers were progressively connected to the system. Full commercial operations commenced on 20 August 1981.

Concurrent with the pre-operational period work was started on the 1st extension to PSS which introduced 3 new PSEs (packet switching exchanges) and doubled the capacity of the original system. Started in January 1982 the 2nd extension again doubles the system capacity as well as introducing 6 more PSEs. Further extensions are planned in the successive years.

Testing of the X75 link to the IPSS gateway was completed in December 1981 and transfer of the existing customer base of over 1000 dial-up users started in January 1982 (the transfer was arranged in 3 tranches to allow alignment of billing cycles in the 2 systems). A similar exercise to transfer the existing EURONET customer base also started in 1982.

2   BRIEF DESCRIPTION OF THE PSS EQUIPMENT

The planning and choice of equipment for PSS has been described elsewhere (ref 3). Like many modern packet switched systems PSS is controlled centrally from a Network Management Centre (NMC) and therefore minimum maintenance facilities or capabilities need exist at the remote PSEs. On PSS the PSEs are made up of one or more multiprocessor units designated TP4000s which are similar to those used in the GTE-Telenet network in the USA. The TP4000 automatically requests a reload by setting up an X25 call to the NMC. Sufficient information is stored in read only memory (ROM) within the TP4000 to enable an X25 call to be made requesting a reload. This would occur when initially powered up, following a software crash or a scheduled outage when modifications have been made to customer parameters.

The TP4000 equipment is a dual redundant configuration designed for unattended operation (see Fig 1). The

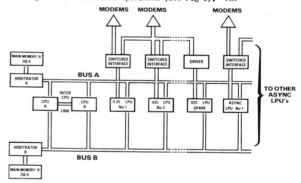

single board central processor unit (CPU) has a microprocessor (MOS Technology 6502), 16 kbytes of parity protected random access memory (RAM) and 1 kbytes of ROM. 47 kbytes of main memory can be uniquely addressed by the CPU. The 2 types of line processing units (LPU) are single board modules containing the same microprocessor as the CPU and 8 kbytes of RAM. The asynchronous LPU performs the packet assembly and disassembly (PAD) function, and the synchronous LPU handles levels 1 and 2 of X25 and X75. The 256 kbytes of main memory is used for packet transfers and call buffering as well as containing a copy of the CPU and LPU code and storage of each user's programmed facilities. The main memory is shared by the CPU and LPUs, the bus transfers being controlled by the arbitrator. LPUs are not duplicated but in the case of a failure a spare LPU is automatically switched in.

The performance of the TP4000 modules is monitored by the standard facilities and using refinements developed by BT (see section 5).

The hardware configuration of the NMC consists of duplicated Prime 750 Minicomputers each with 2 300 Mbyte discs, 2 800 bpi tape decks and a control console. The machines are connected to the London PSE using dupli ated 48 kbit/s links.

In normal operation one machine, NMC 'A', is designated the LOAD machine and is responsible for all on-line network functions. The other machine, NMC 'B', is designated the BUILD machine and handles mainly off-line functions, principally table building of customer parameters. If NMC 'A' fails both functions are handled by NMC 'B'.

The direct connection of customer data terminal equipment (DTE) to the PSE is known as a Dataline and currently uses standard BT modems, in-station and out-station, and analogue leased lines. Packet mode X25 DTE's can operate at 2400, 4800, 9600 and 48000 bit/s. In addition for start-stop DTE's the Datalines can operate at 110, 300 and 1200 bit/s full duplex. Dial-up access is available via the Public Switched Telephone Network (PSTN) to the PAD at 110, 300 bit/s full duplex and 1200/75 bit/s assymmetric duplex. 1200 full duplex dial-up access will be available from mid-1982.

The trunks between PSEs use 48 kbit/s group band modems. From 1983 onward use will be made of digital bearers to provide both trunk and customer Datalines (Ref 4).

3   ORGANISATION OF PSS OPERATIONS

The PSS Operations Group consists of 2 sub-groups, one responsible for maintenance oversight and development of maintenance and monitoring facilities and procedures and the other, the Network Administration Group (NAG) which has the following responsibilities:-

a.   Keeping records of all customers in PSS including all relevant parameters and facilities. This was initially on a paper base but was transferred to a computerised database in January 1982.

b.   Using Dataline access to the NMC, building tables of subscriber parameters. When completed these tables are loaded on to both NMC machines by the site staff who also schedule the updating of PSE software by initiating remote reloads at night when network use is low.

c.   Process customer requests received from the National Sales Office (NSO) part of Marketing Department.

d.   Liaise with the designated PSS Billing duty to aid the resolution of any customer billing disputes.

e.   Resolve service disputes escalated by Datel Customer Service Officers (DCSO) who are available in each Telephone Area to deal with service problems raised by customers using BT data services.

In January 1982 the transfer of the NAG responsibility to field staff was begun. The PSS Operations Group will retain oversight and provide development and software support for the devolved NAG.

The NAG database is run on a Tandem Computer connected to PSS by a 48 kbit/s Dataline. During 1982 an Order/Entry system is being implemented which will be used to input the initial customer requests for service and the subsequent stages including Dataline completion, permission to connect, building of tables and acceptance by the customer. A statistics package will allow system growth, provisioning times and system resources to be closely monitored (see Section 6).

The NMC is staffed 24 hours a day and is the fault reporting point for the whole network. Because of this and as the TP4000 are designed for unattended operation the staff at the smaller PSE's are shared with other services (Radiopaging and Prestel).

Faults on access circuits are passed to the existing customer service organisation which is supported by Regional and Datel support teams. Network faults not cleared by the NMC staff within prescribed time limits are escalated in the first instance to the PSS Operations Group and if still unresolved to Plessey Controls with whom a 2nd Line maintenance contract for hardware and software has been taken out. Faults which may be due to customers violating the X25 protocols are

referred by the NMC staff to the PSS User System Support Team (USST).

The maintenance organisation is shown in Fig 2.

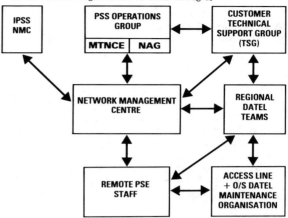

4   STANDARD NMC FACILITIES

The standard facilities supplied rely on the ability of the NMC machine to make and receive virtual calls via the network. This enables control and monitoring to be carried out centrally with the relevant commands and responses being transmitted as data packets over PSS.

An important feature of this approach is that restoration of service after a failure must be automatic, since it is not possible to interrogate a TP which is not already running. TP reloading is initiated automatically by an inactivity detection routine in the TP hardware. Also, a failed module is automatically replaced by a standby after a failure.

The main diagnostic aids are described below.

4.1   TP Diagnostic Tool (TDT)

TDT is a FORTRAN program which runs on the PRIME NMC processors. Its function is to communicate with TPs in the network, using standard PRIME X25 system communication subroutines. A virtual call is established to a 'debug port' which is a simulated port on the TP providing access to internal system status flags. The debug port is password protected for security. User commands cause the appropriate data packets to be transmitted to the TP under examination. Its responses, also in the form of data packets, are then presented to the user in translated form.

TDT can be used to monitor the status of network components and of individual access ports. Ports may be instructed to send test data to a remote loop for line and modem test purposes, and to display the resulting error counts. This enables faulty lines and outstation modems to be identified by looping the line or the data interface. The status of lines can be changed as required, or a back-up module can be switched in to replace a unit which is suspected to be faulty. A further important function of TDT is to force the TP to request a reload from the NMC after changes have been made to configuration data.

TDT is th refore the main method of controlling and monitoring the network. It is initiated as required by NMC staff, and therefore only provides information on request. This means that it is used to investigate suspected problems which have been flagged by other means.

4.2   TP Reporting Facility (TPRF)

TPRF is the system by which alarms are generated by the TPs in response to network events. Unlike TDT, which is invoked only on demand, TPRF runs continuously. It is therefore complementary to TDT, since problems reported by TPRF can then be investigated by TDT.

TPRF alarms are initiated by TPs when an abnormal condition is detected during operation. A simulated X25 port on the TP sets up a virtual call to a process on the NMC. The data packets sent to the NMC contain a code corresponding to the event, plus other relevant information such as the identity of the module or port on the TP which detected the alarm condition. The alarm messages are date and time stamped by the NMC and then stored on disc. Particular categories of alarms, or alarms from particular TPs, can also be sent to nominated terminals anywhere in the network by a further TPRF module which translates the raw data into a text message and queues it for transmission.

In practice, terminals at the NMC have been configured to receive alarms from anywhere in the network, with separate terminals for particular broad alarm categories. A disadvantage of this approach is that the terminals have to be checked regularly for incoming messages, since an important event report can be easily missed if several alarms are received over a short period. However, TPRF reports are an essential aid to fault diagnosis.

The same data collection mechanism is, incidentally, used for collection of raw billing data and for receiving system statistics for subsequent analysis (see section 6).

5 BT ENHANCEMENTS TO ORIGINAL SYSTEM MONITORING FACILITIES

BT experience of the system as supplied showed the testing and monitoring facilities to be powerful in diagnosing faults. However, it became apparent that improvements could be made in the way information was presented, and in collecting specialised statistical information. BT therefore decided to develop enhancements using the standard PRIME system subroutines; all programs have been written in FORTRAN. These enhanced monitoring facilities are described below, and rely on the existence of the debug port.

5.1 TP and Network Availabilities

In the early stages of operation, TP availabilities were calculated from data collected manually by NMC technicians (principally from TPRF). This suffered from a number of disadvantages. Notably, a TP which has failed cannot usually provide information on its own status. Therefor TP failures were deduced from TPRF trunk failure message generated by other TPs, in conjunction with a knowledge of the network topology. However, it was found that this was always a laborious process, and attempts to mechanise it revealed that a TP would only generate a trunk failure message if it happened to need to use the trunk. On the lightly loaded network then in operation, this resulted in messages which were widely spaced in time, and which were often very confusing when multiple failures occurred.

These problems were overcome by setting up an NMC process which performed a network status check every time a trunk line status change was detected by TPRF. To guard against information being lost if TPRF failed, the process also checks network status regularly at preset intervals (currently 10 mins).

The method of status checking in use is to set up a call to each TP's debug port in turn: a successful call is assumed to indicate a working TP. This simple process has been found to result in negligible overheads, and has enabled the whole process of collecting TP availabilities and down times to be automated.

5.2 Crash Vector Recording

Crucial information about software or hardware failures is preserved by the TP in the form of a 'crash vector' for a failed module. The crash vector contains status information and register contents at the time of a failure, and is not over-written when the module is reloaded. However, further failures will result in new crash vectors over-writing earlier ones, and therefore it is important that the vector is read as soon as possible after a failure.

A program has been developed to run on the NMC which examines TPRF messages at regular intervals. In the event that a failure message has been received during the interval, the program calls the debug port of the TP and obtains the crash vector for the failure, which is stored on disc files at the NMC. These files are used subsequently to identify system problems whose details would otherwise be masked by the automatic reloads initiated by the TP. This is a very useful means of identifying hardware faults in an operational

network, and it also provides information to aid the diagnosis of possible software problems.

5.3 Activity Monitor for Dial-up Asynchronous Ports

A process was set up to monitor useage of dial-up ports on TPs throughout the network. It connects to each TP in turn via the debug port, and examines the status indicators for each dial-up line. This information is stored on disc, and the whole process is then repeated at present intervals (currently 15 minutes). The resulting files are processed on demand to yield the following information.

- Call rates and distribution over 24 hours, expressed either per TP or over the whole network. This information is not available from accounting records because charges are raised against a Network User Identifier (NUI) rather than against a physical port for dial-up lines.

- Useage of individual ports on a TP. This is intended in particular to provide a list of ports which have not been used in the period of observation. It is hoped that this will help to point out faulty ports on the TP which can then be routined manually, and therefore reduce the incidence of the 'ringing no reply' class of fault. These faults are notoriously difficult to trace by other means.

5.4 Network Status Display

The system as supplied gives sophisticated failure messages and test facilities but there is no readily available method of monitoring the current status of the network in a single operation. A program has been developed to drive a status monitor from information on port, module and TP status obtained via calls to debug ports of TPs in the network. The program calls each TP in turn, and currently updates a network status display on a standard VDU using cursor control. The display shows the status of trunk links by reference to a map of the network; also, if it is unable to connect to a TP then an appropriate failure message is generated. Other items monitored are module status, bus in use, and number of free buffers (to identify network congestion problems).

The display has proved very useful for network maintenance staff and a more elaborate version is planned, using a colour graphics display. As the network expands, we expect to provide a simplified 'all network' alarm display, with the ability to 'zoom in' on trouble spots for more detailed information.

6 STATISTICS PRODUCED FOR PSS

The following categories of statistics are produced:

A   Maintenance System

B   NAG

C   Billing

D   System Statistics Database

Maintenance and NAG statistics were specified by the PSS Operations Group and a number of items are generated automatically using programs developed by that group. They have been progressively refined and augmented in the light of operational experience.

The Billing and System Database statistics are produced by off-line processing of the tapes produced at the NMC for customer billing and the standard system statistics generated by the PSS System. They are primarily used for planning purposes but also provide inputs to a monthly Operational Report which is produced for BT management.

6.1 Maintenance Statistics

These are produced weekly, and are used by the PSS Operations Group to monitor the availability and reliability of the TP4000s and the NMC and their principal components; to provide an analysis of cleared faults into various categories for each PSE; and to check the operation of the second-line maintenance contract. Statistics are presented in both weekly and cumulative formats.

6.2 NAG Statistics

These are updated weekly and are available on-line to selected users. They not only provide information on system growth, but also allow resources to be closely monitored as the network is expanded. When fully developed, the NAG database will provide access to these statistics for a wide range of users. Figs 3 to 5 show graphs included with the Monthly Operational Report.

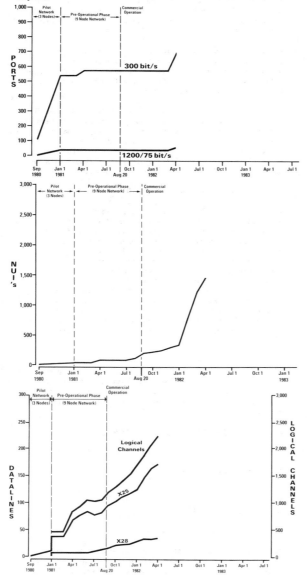

6.3 Billing Statistics (Produced Monthly)

These are produced by DPE by analysing the Billing tapes produced by the NMC. Computer printouts are produced monthly and used for planning and input to the monthly Operational Report. Extensive analyses are provided on successful, unsuccessful and ineffective calls, call volumes and durations, overall and in the busy hour.

6.4 System Statistics Database

As well as collecting billing information, the NMC has standard routines provided for collecting statistics falling into 2 broad categories, Interval and 1 in N. These will be processed by DPE and be available from mid 1982.

The statistics will be displayed as time distributions and distributions about the mean with standard deviations. The

periods displayed will be for the busy-hour, working day, 24-hour day, working week and weekends. The periods can be selected to be displayed.

6.4.1 Interval Stats

The counts are of packets or samples of activity over every 15 minute interval and are recorded within each TP4000. Statistics are recorded on traffic volume, CPU utilisation, and LPU and synchronous line activity.

6.4.2 1 in N Statistics

These stats record all events concerning every Nth call. Two of the uses of this detailed sampling will be to derive call profiles and distributions of length of data fields, lengths of calls, numbers of hops in calls, analysis of routing, and call set-up times.

7 CONCLUSIONS

As has been described PSS is a system which is centrally controlled and was initially provided with a comprehensive range of operational and maintenance facilities. These have been extended by BT to maximise the efficient management of the system. Future developments planned include computerising the fault record system and displaying network status on a colour graphics terminal.

REFERENCES

1 Hadley D E and Sexton B R — The British Post Office Experimental Packet Switched Service (EPSS) — A Review of Development and Operational Experience. ICCC Tokyo 1978.

2 Spiegelhalter B R and Miller C G — Testing of Packet Switched Networks, ICCC82.

3 Adam A R and Lee E J B L — The BPO National Packet Switched Service. Communication 80 IEEE Birmingham.

4 Forster J F S, Green W H and Redburn L — A Digital Data Network for the 80s. ICCC82

Anthony Barnes joined the British Post Office in 1970 having previously been a student apprentice with GEC Ltd at the Hirst Research Centre. He is currently with the Data Network Division and is responsible for PSS Operations and Maintenance.

Formerly he was involved in the planning and implementation of the BPO Experimental Packet Switched Service (EPSS) and the planning and acceptance testing of EURONET.

He has a BSc in Applied Physics, and MSc in Telecommunications System Design and is a member of the Institution of Electrical Engineers.

John Graves joined the BPO as a Student Apprentice in 1965. He worked on maintenance of the Experimental Packet Switched Service (EPSS) and is now also with the Data Networks Division. He is currently responsible for PSS maintenance.

He has BSc (Eng) in Electrical Engineering.

Field Technical Experience in the Use of a Packet Switching Public Network

M. Huet, J. J. Trottin
Transpac, France

Since its commercial opening in 1978, TRANSPAC has grown very quickly, and is one of the largest packet switching networks with 6000 X25 subscribers and a total of probably over 10 000 users including dial access.
A significant experience has been gathered in management, operation and maintenance of a large number of subscriber'accesses with the considerable variety of user DP equipments. This paper gives an overview of the organizing and technical problems encountered in this field, and the relevant solutions and methods chosen .

1/ INFORMATION ON EQUIPMENT THAT CAN BE CONNECTED TO THE NETWORK

1.1/ OBJECTIVES

The packet-switching network constitutes only one part of the service offered to the user, the rest being determined by data processing equipment computers or terminals connected to it. The important thing is that together, they form a whole. It seemed necessary that the supplier of the value-added network have some information about the data processing equipment which can be connected in order to contribute to the design of the users' networks, their installation, and their maintenance, by taking into account the possibilities of the equipment about X25 and higher level protocols which define interfunctionning between different pieces of equipment and between different applications (interactive, file transfers). The 2nd aspect is the great variety of connectable equipment. Table 1 illustrate this diversity in the adaptation modes and in number not to mention asynchronous equipment using PAD access teletype compatible (3) (4).

Type of equipment	Number of manufac- turers	Number of X25 products	
		Announced	Available
Computers	30	43	35
Terminals	23	30	20
Protocol converters	20	33	32

Type of equipment	X25 interface		X28 (PAD)	Direct ac- cesses on operation or ordered at 01/5/82
	Integra- ted	Protocol converter		
Computers	48 %	41 %	11 %	2 508
Terminals	31 %	45 %	24 %	6 994

Table 1

1.2/ ORGANIZATION

Contacts with manufacturers took place from time to time in meeting either with marketing or technical managers.
By the use of different questionnaires, a documentation is set up about :
- the main characteristics of data processing equipments, date of availability of X25, its costs, interfunctionning with other equipment (4)
- subscription parameters allowed by the equipment so that the client's configuration can be checked
- use and maintenance aspects : how communications are established or broken off, what are the different incident menages (for example X25 causes diagnostics) so that to improve maintenance
- how is designed X25 in the equipment.

1.3/ APPROVAL

From the very beginning of the Transpac project (starting in 1975), we studied the problem of approval of data processing equipment and concluded that it wasn't neccessary.

1.3.1. To be able to test equipment systemically requires :
- a large staff supplied with special tools ;
- the availability of test equipment, especially for large systems ;
1.3.2. Systematic tests are not sufficient :
- a certain number of programming errors show up only in special circumstances, and don't appear during a test ;
- software behaviour changes from one version to another, with intermediate patches. In each of these cases, is it necessary to reach a new agreement, with all the administrative complications which would result ?
- they do not help guarantee smooth operation for the user, because operation use cannot be simulated on a test basis. A smooth operation is also conditionned by higher levels which are not relevant of the X25 approval.
1.3.3. The attitude of Transpac on this problem has been :
- to protect the network against irregular

241

behaviour of DTES
- to supply very detailed specifications on the behaviour of the network which is a reference (1) in case of malfunction.

Given this background, the policy of Transpac has been to open access to the network to all manufacturers who desire it, with ordinary subscription contracts. This policy has been in effect for more than 4 years and it seems largely positive. The major consequence has been the very rapid appearance of a variety of X25 equipments adapted to the clients' needs. This has helped play an important role in the fast development of the network.

2/ DESIGN OF THE CONFIGURATION OF USERS' NETWORKS

2.1/ STUDY OF THE CONFIGURATION

The role of Transpac is not of course, to choose the teleprocessing system for the user, but to give him the elements which well permit him to make his own choice.
- For X25, to know what kind of X25 adapters exist (internal or external), those proposed by his supplier or the manufacturers of compatible equipment for example when protocol converters are involved (3) (4).
- For asynchronous terminals, to know if they can use Transpac, especially in a block mode (quite different from purely compatible teletype).

2.1.1. Economic study
This includes the transmission costs, but also the cost of X25 adapters, economizing of modems, couplers on the computer, and intermediate concentrators or multiplexers.

2.1.2. Technical Aspects
Because its tarif system is not based on distance and because of its switching services, TRANSPAC can provide users with choices that are completely different from those of private networks based on dedicated lines where the primary consideration is economizing the costs of telecommunications. This is important in the case of hierarchical systems, or of those with several hosts as well as a back-up organization (6).

2.2/ CHOICE OF SUBSCRIPTION PARAMETERS

This choice must be made when the contract is signed, for reasons of efficient managment, to see if any incompatibilities exist because of the particular type of equipment involved. From the large number of configurations presently managed by TRANSPAC (1100 at the end of 1981) we can give some informations on criteria for choosing and on the values of the parameters retained.

2.2.1. Access speed
This is the most important parameter ; the criterion for choosing depends on the configuration and applications.

2.2.1.1. For file transfers, efficient rates are the most important. Here, the X25 procedure is especially valuable, since it can assure efficient rates of nearly 80 % in both directions.

2.2.1.2. For interactive applications, the criterion for choosing is different for terminals and computers.
- For terminals, the desired response time determines the access speed. Today, because few tarif rates are based on transmission speed, users usually choose 4 800 bits per second. 9 600 bits per second is used only for some double implementations of external adapters (for terminals and computers) or for especially large clusters (15 screens).
- For computers, the criterion is the line load owing the fact the access handles all communications with terminals.

Terminal	No convert.	1convert.	2convert.
Small size cluster	2400 bit/s	4800	4800 9600
Great size cluster	4800	4800 9600	9600

| Computer | Number of terminal accesses | | | |
	10	10-30	10-70	70
Computer handling TTY	4800 bit/s	4800 9600	9600 19200	
Computer handling cluster	4800 9600	9600 19200	19200	48000

Table 2

2.2.2.Permanent and switched virtual circuits :
There are 2 different approaches :
- if Transpac didn't exist, the user's network would have used dedicated lines. Cleanly, the permanent virtual circuit is best suited for this design.
- on the other hand, the real basic service of packet-switching network is the switched virtual circuit which offers all the possibilities of flexibility inherent in this technique.

For example :
. With permanent virtual circuits any add-ons, changes or eliminations from the terminals connections lead to simultaneous changes in the configuration of the computer and the network. The use of switched virtual circuits requires such less modification in the connections to the central computer, which is generally slightly oversized to allow for terminal add-ons without changing the configuration.
. The use of back-up access on the same computer or on another often excludes a permanent virtual circuit.

Only 7 % of logical channels are the mean time used for permanent virtual circuits.

2.2.3. Parameters of window size, packet and frame level, and length of packets :
Here, there is a definite tendancy toward standartization. Both manufacturers and TRANSPAC advise their clients to choose the same subscription parameters for a given type of equipment in order to facilitate maintenance, thanks to the similarity of configurations.
For example
- packet size : a very large majority has chosen 128

- window packet size : the choice is split between 2 (CCITT norm) and 3 (the largest authorized in Transpac)
- frame window size: 4(advised by TRANSPAC)or 7

2.2.4. The facilities offered on TRANSPAC :

They include :
- reverse charges
- throughput class negotiation
- packet and window size negotiation
- closed user groups (CUG).

Some of these facilities are not largely used :
- for a management network within the same
company, reverse charges are not useful ;
- for throughput class, the network itself decides the throughput, taking into considera-
ration access speed and throughput class by
default so that few cases need throughput
class negociation by the equipment.
- packet and window size negociation depending
on the virtual circuit is only justified when
there is very different traffic on the same
access (fast file transfer and low speed
transactional mode, for example). This type
of configuration is still rare.
- the closed user group : the user wants to
protect an internal network from non-autho-
rized calls. In most cases, only one CUG is
sufficient. Today, 35 % of the accesses are
in one CUG but only 8 % of the clients have
one.

2.2.5. PAD parameters.

The diversity of asynchronous terminals, of
computers and applications very often requires
a careful choice of parameters. There are
keyboard printers, screens, ancillary devices
(paper tape reader/puncher, cassettes, mini-
disks), telex, terminals operating in block
mode, micro-computers, and word-processors.
A bad choice of parameters can effect :
- billing
- loss of data (flow-control)
- response times.
Curiously, asynchronous equipment creates more
problems than X25 equipment because PAD is a
conversion service which allows an existing
group of terminals (teletype compatible) to use
the services of a packet network. But what is
possible with dedicated lines or telephone
networks, is not always possible through a
packet network (for example : data entry
software which involving character by character
checks, implies an end to end echo).

3/ INSTALLATION OF USER'S NETWORK

3.1/ ACCESS DELIVERY

The "Direction de l'Exploitation" (Operation
division) is in charge of planning access deliveries. A TRANSPAC technician installs the
modem, and adjusts it, taking into consideration the characteristics of the line. The DTE
is not necessary when the access is put into
service to test if the link is functionning
smoothly, thanks to the digital tests made from
the switching mode with loop-back commands.
This offers flexiblility and efficiency for
both TRANSPAC and the client.

3.2/ STARTING OF USERS' APPLICATIONS

For small networks (with only a few connections), service usually begins simultaneously
in the various locations involved ; on the
other hand, for big networks there is :
- a test stage with the connection to the computer (sometimes with the final sofware generation) and some terminals ;
- a generalization stage often conducted
quickly.
In effect, the connection to various locations
is carried out independantly ; it is done in a
parallel fashion so that the loss of time between the start-up of the computer and the terminals is short. Any problems encountered on the
way are usually local problems, either at the
terminals themselves or on the access line for
which Transpac handles the maintenance. This
independance between different elements of the
system makes logistics and coordination
considerably easier for the client.

4/ MAINTENANCE OF ACCESSES TO THE TRANSPAC NETWORK

4/1. REMEMBER OF THE TOOLS AVAILABLE ON THE TRANSPAC NETWORK

Figure n°1 shows where the different maintenance tools for the accesses are found.

4.1.1. Means available for the subscriber :

For the modem and V24 junction the client can
either look at the display lights or be informed about the state of the junction circuits by
his terminal. If the modem is switched on, if
no manual loops has been turn on the local
level, if the terminal equipment activates
circuit 105, then circuits 106, 107, 109 must
be on and 142 "off". In all other cases, there
is malfunction in the network or in the access,
which would require a call to the TRANSPAC
maintenance service. At the higher levels the
client's terminal can analyse the causes and
diagnostics of the X25 protocol if it is
connected in synchronous mode, or the error
mnaemonics in asynchronous mode. Most often,
this allows it to distinguish local or distant
subscriber's error from malfunctions to the
network. To help the diagnostic, the client
either conducts a loop-back test of his own
terminal by himself, or a local and manual
loop = 2 on his modem, or calls an artificial
on duty TRANSPAC subscriber which will give him
an echo, absorption and traffic generating
service however he is connected.

4.1.2. Means available on the switching node

Here is the greatest number of facilities for
diagnostics.

4.1.2.1. Working level of the access leased line

All the subscriber's access links to the TRANS-
PAC network are connected to the place where
TRANSPAC'S switching node is, first by a
distribution frame then through a switching
cabinet before reaching TRANSPAC'S modems. The
job of the distribution frame is to guarantee
cross connections and in special cases, to
connect test equipment directly to the line.
The switching cabinet is made up of relays with
doubled gold contacts adressed by a matrixed

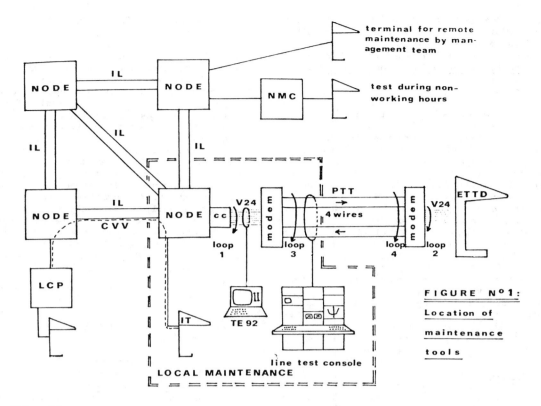

FIGURE N°1:

Location of maintenance tools

LOCAL MAINTENANCE

command. This allows remote control from the operating center of a high impedance connection or an electrically switched connection of tests equipments ordered by the operator in front of a line test console.

There are devices to measure the quality of transmission of the line in loop or in opposition with portable devices brought by technicians to the subscriber.

4.1.2.2. Test on the physical level

Operators rarely use display lights of modems. TRANSPAC nodes constantly watch the junction circuits. TRANSPAC modems, on 4 wires only, are equipped with a system of local or remote loopback operated by the node itself. This system is activated by an operator (see recommendation n°74 made by FRANCE to CCITT in january 1978). It can distinguish the 6 following cases : normal working condition - out of service access due to the fact of the subscriber (circuit 105 off) - No power on the subscriber modem. A breakdown in a subscriber modem - a breakdown in a central office modem - an out of service access link - coupling on the TRANSPAC node unworking.

4.1.2.3. Bit level

Error rate is controlled by using a remote loop-back test at the client's, the transmission of a certain number of frames and the verification of their reception.

4.1.2.4. Procedural level

- Optional tests

The procedural level can be controlled if the operator puts into operation a certain number of optional measures. These optional measures are carried out by the nodes themselves, thank to procedural error counters which are compared to the number of the transmitted frames or packets. The opening of these counters is done during a fixed length of time determined by the

operator ; thus, the duration of the measurement can be very brief or can last several weeks if necessary. The measurements can be grouped in various categories, depending on what defect is being looked for. Each node can carry out 80 tests simultaneously.

- Examination of billing

The operator can request a print out of information on billing processed by the node. This information which includes all the characteristics of the communication are also extremely useful for maintenance.

- Use of an external procedure analyzer TE92

This device is connected to the V24 junction. It shows the display of data on a screen in symbolic and condensed form for frame and packet headers. It allows triggering on events of any type of programmed in advance as well as the recording of relatively long periods of transmission on mini-disks, with a later, detailed analysis. Moreover, this device can be managed at a distance. It is also able to analyse the X25 protocol, as will as those of X3, X28 and X29.

- The role of artificial onduty subscribers (AFS)

Each node has an internal subscriber which can be put in connection with any other subscriber, either at the request of the operator, or at the request of the user himself. This internal subscriber works either in echo absorber or traffic generating service. It works in X25 and can contact an asynchronous subscriber by the PAD function handled by the node. The user chooses the way of operating at the call level.

4.1.3. Distance level

- The role of the local control point (LCP) with the intervention terminal

Operating functions are carried out by a specialized computer called local control point

(LCP). This machine controls several nodes (from 1 to 4). The dialogue between man and machine is obtained either by terminals directly connected to a LCP computer, or by intervention terminals which can be placed anywhere on the network, especially on distant nodes not equiped with LCP. The function of an intervention terminal is primarily to found man machine dialogue everywhere on the network. This is especially useful for the maintenance operations, especially for the maintenance of accesses.
- Possible role of the management center
The management center is not normally in charge of maintenance for subscribers' access line. It may however be considered as an intervention terminal attached to any local control point and so can control all the nodes. Thanks to this possibility it is used to find the location subscribers' malfunctions, outside of the switching centers normal working hours. It is also used for the optional measurements tests (see 4.1.2.4.) of long durations.
- Terminal in the technical or operation departments
With the help of an intervention terminal having access to all the network nodes and with a TE 92, all the observation operations of the procedural level can be made by the engineers of these two departments, a situation which allows the center of operations to transfer immediatly problem which is beyond its levels of competence.

4.2 ORGANIZATION

4.2.1. Role of the operations centers (central offices of TRANSPAC)
Warning of malfunctions are usually made by the client at his access center. As soon as this information is received, the center notes the observations made by the client (modem display lights, condition of interface circuits, diagnostics observed) and immediatly tries to pinpoint the problem. A remote loop back test rapidly is conducted, and has the advantage of finding the most common problems (transmission defect on the modems or the line). It suggests the direction to follow either on the procedural level if a good transmission of frames can be obtained, or on local or distant modems, or on the level of a defect in the access line. Line defects are solved by the competent telecommunications services. The in TRANSPAC'S line test consoles can give a precise indication on the detected defect to these services, and can also verify that in fact the defect has disapeared after being repaired.

4.2.2. The role of engineers in the central operations department
In all the following cases
- the defect cannot be found at the local level
- the defect losts more than 48 hours
- the defect has been found at the local level but due to the client's application or TRANSPAC itself
The department also carries out over-all inspection of this activity and prepares all the statistics about it.

4.2.3. The role of engineers of the technical department, specialized in access procedures
They intervene systematically and almost exclu-

sively when the functioning of the TRANSPAC system itself is called into question.

4.2.4. The role of technical-commercial engineers in the commercial department
It is not unlikely that an unhappy client will notify the commercial department of a defect if he is not satisfied with the local operations. Moreover, the first contact that a potential client has, is with the commercial department. Consequently a special relationship is established right from the beginning. In general, these contacts are made by those people in charge of the clients network and not by local subscribers. If any defects are found later on, this information is then transmitted to the operations department. In the other way the operations departement transmit to the commercial department all problems founded in the client tele-processing application or located in the system delivered by his DP manufacturer

4.3. EXPERIENCE AND RESULTS

4.3.1. General results on the quality of TRANSPAC service
The following average results were noted during the 12 month period ending in april 1982
- availability of TRANSPAC nodes   99,91 %
- average time of unfaulty functionning of a virtual circuit   98 hours
- availability of the distribution network (lines, modems, and multiplexers) 99, 86 %
Commercially, these results may be considered highly satisfactory.

4.3.2. Statistics on complaints
The montly percentage of complaints is 17%. In round numbers, the complaints fall into the following categories :
- 30 % occurs at the client's, and are not TRANSPAC'S fault.
- 25 % are due to defects in access lines.
- 33 % are due to TRANSPAC defects, half in the distribution network(modems and multiplexers) half in the node and the TRANSPAC system (in the case, there is almost always a short halt in service seen by almost all clients and this can lead to several hundred alarms, sometimes in less than five minutes).
- 12 % are not attributed, either because the client's complaint is unfounded, or because it disappeared at the time of surveillance
In so far as the amount time needed to rectify problems :
- 90 % of them (except those at the client's or those non detected) are resolved in less than 24 hours, and 72 % in less than 4 hours. The longest problems to resolve are related to problems of lines ; regarding dedicated access lines supplier to TRANSPAC by the PTT, the following figures reveal :
. rate of alarms : about 4,5 %
. availability (99,88 %). These excellent figures, which are better than the national average for dedicated lines, are in general due to the fact that the access lines to TRANSPAC are relatively short and moreover, have been recently made.
They are never more than 20 complaints per month handled at the central level either by the operations department, or the commercial department, nevertheless, the rate of com-

plaints remains high : the more complex and essential a network's service becomes for a professional client, the higher the rate of complaints.

This high rate is also due to TRANSPAC'S commercial policy, which is to help its clients find their faults as much as possible.

4.3.3. The experience of some cases

- The case of asynchronous terminals connected directly to TRANSPAC

Although the procedure is very simple at this level, on one hand it is not programmed inside the terminal (therefore insensitive to human errors) and on the other hand, since these terminals are very cheap, the after-sales technical service from the supplier is very reduced. The problem is often simply to explain to the client how the terminal works. This has been relatively costly, paradoxically, there are considerably fewer problems to set up a synchronous X25 access.

- Elusive defects

Obviously, these are the most difficult to find. There are two different types :

. asynchronous procedures are not protected against transmission errors. When clients complain, it is difficult to distinguish possible errors due to the complete datatransport chain via TRANSPAC, especially on the case of a PAD to PAD operation, from the normal rate of errors on access lines.

. Certain synchronous accesses seem relativily sensitive to micro-interruptions ;

For example, V29 modem can restart in equalizing the line, this causes circuit 107 going off which can disconnect the line and interrupt the virtual circuit, depending on the type of the client's terminal.

- Quality of service for telephone accesses

The use of the same national number to contact TRANSPAC everywhere in FRANCE has sometimes unreased the number of switched nodes to reach TRANSPAC, compared to the number needed for a direct call. In some cases, the rate of transmission errors has slightly increased, primarily when accoustic couplers were used. The automatic speed recognition system at TRANSPAC (the letter H followed by a carriage return) requires the client to process it a rigourous way.

- Quality of service of accesses to international data banks

In the special case where a terminal located in FRANCE, connected to the telephone network, wants to reach an American data bank via TRANSPAC, it must follow pass through this sequence

. the french telephone network
. the TRANSPAC network
. the french international transit node
. A dedicated line accross the Atlantic
. the gateway of one of 4 international carriers in the U.S.A.
. American packet-switched network on which is connected the data bank.

Certainly, it is difficult to obtain a very high MTBF of virtual circuits, given all these complex elements. In reality, the results are 5 to 6 times less than for the use of TRANSPAC alone.

- Billing errors

Some subscribers have been surprised by their volume tax. It was necessary to show them, with the appropriate instruments, that their packets were barely filled (one character per packet) most clients have very noticable increased the quantity of bits in their packets. Now TRANSPAC has noted an average of 60 octects per packets.

CONCLUSION

The use of a computer service on a public packet-switching network demands a close collaboration between users, manufacturers, and the suppliers of the network, in order to obtain the level of service required by the client. It requires the network's supplier to provide tools and great variety of expertise, as well as familiarity with computer systems, in order to determine the best configurations and to improve efficiency.

If significiant results have already been achieved, efforts must continue especially for clients connected to data banks by the telephone networks, and for users of international services where even greater cooperation is necessary since more people are involved.

REFERENCES

1) Manuel de référence "TRANSPAC".
Spécifications techniques d'utilisation du réseau, environ 500 pages, septembre 1977 doc. TRANSPAC (mise à jour permanente).

2) P. PICARD "The industrial completion of TRANSPAC",
Commutation et transmission, numero special Telecom 79, septembre 79

3) J.F GUILBERT "la connexion des systèmes in-formatiques à TRANSPAC",
Convention informatique 79, Paris, sept. 79, tome 1, p. 25-31.

4) "Equipements informatiques connectables en X25 à TRANSPAC", doc. TRANSPAC réf. TEC/06/05/81 (mise à jour permanente.

5) M. HUET "Managing functions of the TRANSPAC network",
IFIP Teleinformatics 79, Paris 11 - 13 june 79

6) J.J TROTTIN "Impact de TRANSPAC sur les systèmes téléinformatiques",
Convention informatique 80, Paris, septembre 1980, p. 315.321.

J.J. TROTTIN is born in 1950, and is graduated from the Ecole Polytechnique and the Ecole Nationale Superieure des Telecommunications. He is in charge of the new services marketing of TRANSPAC.

M. HUET is born in 1948, and is graduated from the Ecole Polytechnique and the Ecole Nationale Superieure des Telecommunications. He is manager of the "Direction de l'Exploitation of TRANSPAC" (operations and maintenance).

Acceptance Testing of Packet Switched Data Networks. A new Challenge for Telecommunications Organisations

J-J Jaquier, J Pitteloud
Swiss PTT, Switzerland

The introduction of public data networks based on packet switching techniques brings new challenging tasks for telecommunications organisations like the PTT. The paper deals with the particular problem of Acceptance Testing of a PSDN. It describes the approach chosen by the Swiss PTT for introducing the Telepac Network. The initial acceptance was carried out in 3 phases (in-plant acceptance testing, system acceptance testing, and acceptance testing with DTE manufacturers). Conclusions are drawn from experience gained during the tests and are expressed as general guidelines for the planning of future network acceptances. The last part of the paper draws attention to the fact that acceptance testing becomes necessary also during commercial service, e.g. when new software releases are integrated in the network. Procedures and tools planned by the Swiss PTT are described.

1. TELEPAC, THE PUBLIC PSDN OF SWITZERLAND

The Swiss PTT is introducing a public Packet Switched Data Network (PSDN) called Telepac, which will go into commercial service in the second half of 1982.

The network is based on hardware (SL-10) and software produced by Northern Telecom LTD (Canada), which are similar to the products used in Datapac Canada's PSDN.

A Swiss telecommunication equipment supplier (Zellweger Uster AG) has been commissioned as a general contractor to introduce the network in Switzerland and to coordinate all aspects of the project. This decision reflects the PTT aim of a direct, long range partnership in the country itself so as not to be wholly dependant on an oversea contractor. Another objective was to ensure the transfer to Switzerland of sufficient know-how in the domain of packet switching.

DCC : Data Collection Centre
NCC : Network Control Centre

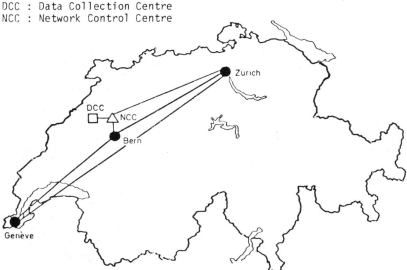

Fig. 1   Initial configuration of the Telepac network

The initial configuration of the Telepac network comprises 3 fully interconnected Packet Switching Exchanges (PSE) in 3 major cities (Bern, Geneva and Zurich).The network is controlled and managed by a single centralized Network Control Centre (NCC) located in Bern. The generation of new software or preparation of network parameters for connecting new customers to the network requires a dedicated system (DEC PDP 11), which communicates with the network as a normal user host. This equipment, named Data Collection Centre (DCC), is also in charge of gathering all statistical information needed for traffic engineering on the one hand and for customer billing on the other hand (Figure 1).

2. TELEPAC INITIAL ACCEPTANCE TESTING CONCEPT

The acceptance testing of Telepac has been devised in order to satisfy the initial acceptance criteria and the ongoing requirements of the users once the network is in commercial operation.

The rationale for devoting so much attention to acceptance testing is the fact that a PSDN is much more then a black box. The basic system elements consisting of nodes, trunks, NCC and DCC, are but a small part of a much larger composite system of hardware, software, facilities, modems, computers, terminals and customer applications. As well, there is a synergistic effect of the system that has a significant impact on the service organisation which must bring all of the system elements together so that a viable customer service can be offered.

The acceptance tests of Telepac have been planned in 3 phases, each with its own objective:

a) **In-plant Test (IPT)** executed in a laboratory environment on the supplier's premises

b) **System Acceptance (SA)** carried out under "clinical" conditions on the network installed in Switzerland

c) **Acceptance with Manufacturers (AM)** of Data Terminating Equipments (DTE) executed in an environment as near as possible to real operation

The main objective of the IPT phase was to demonstrate as a platform test and in a laboratory environment on the manufacturer's premises that the network configuration (the 3 nodes, NCC and DCC, together with the modems used in Switzerland) was working correctly and was ready for shipment to the PTT.

The SA phase goal was to test the functioning of the network with the equipment installed in its definitive locations. The system acceptance was designed in such a way that controlled and "clinical" test conditions were available. This allowed us to gather well defined and reproducable results. Unknown influences, such as those caused by real users, were excluded as far as possible. Data traffic was produced with test equipment only.

The objective of the last phase of the acceptance (AM) was to examine in a near life environment the services and facilities offered to the customers. In order to deal with the practical aspects of the problem as early as possible the PTT planned to execute this phase of the acceptance with the collaboration of real users.

This approach was new for the PTT. It was the first time customers became involved so directly in the acceptance of a new telecommunication system and this in a phase of a project, where the available quality of the new service was yet completely unknown.

When the PTT began looking for potential users ready to assist in the planning and execution of the AM phase, it appeared very quickly that the complexity of packet switching technique and the short time for organising the tests would restrain the search to computer suppliers or highly sophisticated EDP users. In any event 10 partners were found without much difficulty. Most of them were EDP manufacturers already providing computers or other teleprocessing products for PSDN connections, i.e. products with packet oriented CCITT X.25 or character oriented CCITT X.28/X.29 interfaces. IBM, Data General, DEC, NCR, Nixdorf and Borer Electronics belonged to this group. The user companies on the other hand comprised the European Nuclear Research Centre (CERN), Radio Suisse SA, an educational institute in Geneva with a Prime computer, and the PTT itself.

The main objectives of the coordinated tests during the AM phase with real users were the following:

- to check the functions of the X.25 and X.28 interfaces

- to examine the throughput and transit time delay of virtual connections as observed by real customers

- to evaluate the network stability and availibility as measured from the customer's point of view

- to gain experience within the PTT in the planning and managing of PSDN customer connections and in the operation of the network

It was evident that the participation of well-known external companies as partners in the AM phase would produce some major pressure on the project. The images of both the PTT and the supplier were at stake, the first as future network operator and the second as general contractor. For the PTT it was a bet on the quality of service of a not yet opened public PSDN service, because users, most of them experienced EDP manufacturers, would be in contact with a network in its development state. Their criticisms would have a major impact on the initial reputation of

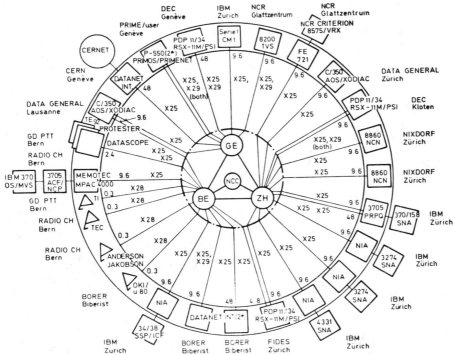

Fig. 2 Configuration of the access network for the Telepac AM Acceptance phase

Telepac. For Zellweger as a general contractor the game was risky, too, because the milestone defining the start of the AM phase became one of the most important deadline in the whole project planning. This milestone had to be reached in time at any price by both the seller and the buyer of the Telepac network.

A countrywide access network to the 3 nodes was set up for the AM phase. It was composed of 30 dedicated access paths to Telepac (four 48 kbit/s and twenty 9.6 kbit/s links) and forty telephone dial up ports. (Figure 2)

3. EXPERIENCE GATHERED DURING THE ACCEPTANCE OF TELEPAC; GUIDELINES FOR FUTURE WORK

The three test phases shortly described above proved to be a very sound concept for the initial acceptance testing of a PSDN. Each phase produced valuable results allowing to evaluate the status and degree of achievement of the network, in order to define the time, if any, for cutover to commercial service. In addition, useful experience was gathered of testing methodology, revealing many deficiencies and producing valuable information for future work.

A detailed description of the Telepac tests, which were carried out in the middle of 1981, is beyond the scope of this paper. One has to consider too that the presented results are a snap-shot of the state of Telepac in 1981. The network and the system on which it is based have been considerably improved since then.

Therefore, the authors prefer to present in the following some conclusions about the organisation and methodology of PSDN Acceptance Testing, trying to draw guidelines of general value for organisations faced in future with the introduction of a PSDN or any new public value added network. In this context some results of the Telepac tests are only mentioned as far as they serve to illustrate the conclusions drawn by the authors. They do not qualify in any kind the actual state of Telepac and of its components.

3.1 Is your know-how sufficient to undertake meaningful acceptance testing ? Know-how transfer is a long time consuming process

One of the biggest problems to be solved by a telecommunication organisation faced with the introduction of a PSDN is the acquisition of training and know-how. Data services based on PSDN are much more complex than the traditional Datel services on the Public Switched Telephone Network. It may be difficult for the network operator to gather sufficient skills at time of delivery of the initial network. To begin meaningful acceptance testing both partners must have more or less the same level of system know-how. If this is not the case, the manufacturers tests and demonstrations will be only a training exercise for the buyer, who is himself unable to detect any malfunctions in the delivered system.

Aside from the knowledge base which must be built within the organisation, one other serious concern exists from an organisational point of view. That is, how does one integrate a complex ressource-demanding system into a large well-structured carrier organisation which traditionally deals with telephony or telephony related technology. The issues here are not trivial. Traditional ordering, installation, trouble report handling, and problem solving methods and procedures may not be able to cope with PSDN requirements. This point was initially underestimated by the Swiss PTT.

The objective of the Swiss PTT to involve a Swiss company in the Telepac project, in order to create know-how in Switzerland in the domain of packet switching technique and development, produced some problems during the initial Acceptance Testing. Packet switching was a new domain for the Swiss partner as well as for the PTT. At the beginning contact with the manufacturer through a third party was more impairment than help to project progress. The transfer of know-how takes time. This statement is valid for both the user company and its industrial partner if both are entering new techniques and technologies. If this problem is not taken into account very early in project planning, the network introduction will be handicapped. Operating errors and lack of firmness in network management are two examples of the possible consequences.

3.2 Ensure that the system you are testing corresponds to the system ordered

It is very important to ensure that the system you are testing in the different test phases corresponds as closely as possible to the system ordered. Otherwise the value of tests must be strongly questioned. If this requirement is easily met for the hardware components, the check can be much more difficult for the software, owing to its "immaterial nature".

In the case of Telepac it first became apparent during the SA and AM tests that the delivered software did not correspond to the one ordered and was a several-year old version no longer used on other networks of the same technology.

3.3 Test all parts of your system

The test results may differ greatly if the test configuration differs from the operational one.

For Telepac an IBM 370 computer instead of the ordered PDP 11 was used as DCC for the IPT phase. The DCC tests carried during the SA and AM with the definitive hardware and software proved that the IPT tests were not significant for the DCC/Network interface. Major data collection errors occured, making the accounting functions unusable.

3.4 Define your performance requirements in such a way that you can measure them

Measurement of transit time delay of PSDN as defined in the contract is no easy task. Elimination of the test equipment's own overhead, synchronisation of time between measurement points, and evaluation of the influence of the number of nodes (PSE) to be crossed are some of the problems to be solved in order to measure precisely transit times.

Performances tests were carried out during the AM period of Telepac. They constituted one of the most complex problems to be solved by the 10 co-testing partners. Quite different and imaginative approaches were used. However the correlation between results was very high and lead to significant conclusions about network performance.

3.5 Be sceptical about results of load demonstrations in a clinical environment

The Telepac load tests carried out during the IPT phase in a laboratory environment were quite successful. In the AM environment with real users the network showed a much degraded performance.

3.6 A meaningful load test is possible only if adequate test tools are available

If you intend to check the capacity of the network, make sure that loading tools are available, and in due time. Meaningful load testing is possible only with highly comfortable and reliable tools .

In the case of Telepac load tests were important not merely to check the network as a whole, but above all to measure the throughput of the 48 kbit/s high speed customer interfaces, which were completly new developments.

3.7 There are more hidden bottlenecks in your network than those you initially think of

Some network limitations will appear only indirectly as side effects of other tests.

Customer interface equipment in the network may be subjected to load and will react in a manner which can be projected. However, this same load condition may propagate its way through the network to other critical links.

3.8 Do not forget to test the overload protection mechanisms

The overload protection mechanisms are an important feature in a PSDN ensuring a good quality of service. Congestion control and overload protection should not be mere theoretical concepts. They need thorough testing too.

3.9 Try to test your system in an testing environment as near as possible to the operational environment

EMC problems or operational limits of the power supply and air conditioning may be very important for the reliability of the switching nodes. The real environment should be simulated if possible for the IPT in order to eliminate unpleasant surprises after installation on the definitive sites.

The Telepac nodes had to cope with such problems on the Swiss sites. Electrical power switching produced minor and sometimes major unexpected and unjustified console alarms.

3.10 Do not underestimate preparation time for the test infrastructure

Setting up a test network can take several months. In the connection of DTE products for testing purposes 3 phases can be defined:

a) test requirements definition and negotiations with the test partners

b) network customization (installation of access lines, modems, etc. and preparation of the customized X.25 and X.28 software parameters)

c) implementation of the connections

For the Telepac AM tests the a), b) and c) phases took up respectively 4 months, 6 months and less than 10 days. The relatively long time needed for phase b) was due to difficulties with high-speed links and shortage of spare modems. This lead to the transmission problems becoming the "critical path" during the preparation of the Telepac AM phase. The ordering procedure for the access links, which was based on standard procedures for ordering leased lines, also proved inadequate on that occasion.

3.11 Simulation and monitoring tools are the wrong items to save on for test budget considerations

It is essential for effective and efficient testing that enough number of simulation and monitoring equipment is available.

Only two DCE/DTE simulators were delivered initially for Telepac. This was insufficient for the 3 nodes and the large number of access lines. Moreover no simulation was possible on the V.35/48 kbit/s interface with this equipment. The PTT had to buy its own additional tools to fulfil the AM requirements.

3.12 Exceptional situations during the testing phases give the more rewarding results

Throughout the test period, and indeed during commercial operation, one must be aware that exception conditions can arise and cause seemingly unrelated side effects in the network operation.

Most of the discrepancy reports discovered during the AM phase were related to exceptional situations.

3.13 High availability is not compatible with large maintenance windows

The user of a public PSDN expects continuous service. The network has to be available 24h/day and 7 days/week. From the user's point of view there is no major difference between system breakdowns and planned interruption of service for maintenance purposes. In this context the procedures for changing the customer's parameters (service data) or integrating new software releases into the network have to be examined carefully and practised during the acceptance phase.

If the duration of a service interruption necessary to change customer parameters in Telepac is more or less acceptable, the time to introduce a new software release has proved too long and was one of the most important points to be improved in the network.

3.14 The delivery of a PSDN as a turn-key system is something more complex than the delivery of black boxes

The introduction of a PSDN is a very complex undertaking for a telecommunications organisation. The task has more similarity with a large teleprocessing EDP project than with the introduction of traditional telephone or telex exchanges. Installing the hardware of the switching node is only a small part of the job. Software management, planning of operational procedures and user documentation, and integration of all network components are but some of the problems to be solved. It is particularly on these items that the strength or weakness of the partners will be put to the test.

3.15 "State of the art" gap between telecommunications and EDP technologies ?

As a basic data communication infrastructure, public PSDNs have to provide a quality and stability of service equal to EDP user systems.

One of the facts revealed by the Telepac acceptance tests is that PSDN technology has yet to be improved to reach the state of the art obtained with advanced EDP teleprocessing systems.

Three key points must be noted to improve the introduction and operation of packet networks:

- in a public network the software release production management is an essential key point. It has been improved for Telepac since initial acceptance.

- documentation management, especially matching between software releases and operational documentation has to be strengthened in a PSDN

- testing tools are vital and should be designed concurrently with the PSDN products, in order to optimize their integration for system and acceptance testing

3.16 Unity means strength: You need a buyers' interest group

Dissemination of information and exchange of experience are essential between PSDN operating companies, especially between those using the same products. The situation is similar to that of the EDP community where users' interest groups have an important lobby function in relation to the manufacturers.

In this context the Swiss PTT is pleased that an SL-10-Network Operators Group has been founded to discuss experiences and to influence the development of new products and facilities.

4. ACCEPTANCE TESTING IS NEEDED ALSO AFTER COMMERCIAL OPERATION HAS STARTED

4.1 Testing in commercial operation

The three steps of the acceptance procedure for Telepac (IPT, SA, AM) proved to be valuable and yielded good results. They can be recommended for initial acceptance of future PSDN.

However this way of testing is not appropriate for further acceptance tests as needed on introducting configuration extensions or new software releases in a network already in commercial operation. The PTT therefore required the general contractor to build a representative test network in Switzerland, including its own NCC and DCC, in order to allow exhaustive tests without interference to the Telepac users.

It is an important goal for the PTT to minimize the integration time (maintenance windows) of modifications to the operational network. An essential means is to use the totally independant test network as far as possible for the following tasks:

- Acceptance testing of new software releases

- Acceptance testing of new generations of hardware components

- Routing tests under as near life conditions as possible for any extension of the number of nodes of Telepac

4.2 User oriented testing tools

4.2.1 Tools for qualitative testing of services and facilities

In order to facilitate future acceptance testing and give effective support to the Telepac customers, supplementary test systems are under study at the Swiss PTT. The first system is quality oriented. Its goal is to check functions as automatically as possible at the customer interface. It can be seen as a test cases data base used either against the network or against a new EDP product wanting support before introduction on the Telepac nework.

4.2.2 Tools for quantitative testing of services and facilities

An important task of the regression tests of future releases is to check that no degradation of performance is caused by modifications.

The PTT is designing small microprocessor controlled boxes running up to 64 kbit/s and able to generate, to echo and to drop traffic.

With an appropriate number of these simple testing tools gradual test loading of the network will be possible, starting from small load up to overload situations.

The load boxes are also intended for use on the real Telepac network. They will provide go / no go test facilities and transit delay degradation control features to the customers.

4.2.3 Other tools under study for testing support

The following additional features are under study for testing support:

- An information data base connected to Telepac as a normal user host and giving customers, on inquiry, information about the network status.

- A telediagnostic system. This feature has been planned as an aid to troubleshooting on non-EDP oriented ("naive") X.28 users. The system will try to diagnose the user's problems by means of the echo functions of the network, by analysing the PAD parameters, etc.

- A support tool for interworking. Successful connection to Telepac does not by itself solve the problem of interworking between different DTE products. The PTT plans to introduce a programmable monitoring tool, able to analyse the higher-level protocols in accordance with parameters defined by the testing parties (manufacturers, users). Such a feature will be useful both for testing private applications and for debugging value added public services like Videotex or Teletex.

5. CONCLUSIONS

This paper has shown that the introduction of a public PSDN is not an easy task, even if a network is based on apparently well known and proven off-the-shelf systems.

The task has more similarity with a large teleprocessing EDP project than with the introduction of traditional telephone or telex exchanges. Setting up the hardware is only a small part of the job. Managing of software, planning of operational procedures and user documentation, integrating of all components are some of the problems to be solved. It is particularly on these items that the strength or weakness of the organisations involved will be put to the test.

The experiences gained with the introduction of Switzerland's Telepac network could be useful for the acceptance of other networks and also large EDP systems.

ACKNOWLEDGEMENTS

We thank all PTT and suppliers' staff involved in the Telepac project who contributed to the preparation of this paper.

Remark:

The views presented in this paper are those of the authors. They should not be interpreted as necessarily representing the official opinion of the Swiss PTT.

REFERENCES

[1] J.-J Jaquier, Acceptance Tests of Computer Based Communication and Teleprocessing Systems, Bulletin Technique PTT, July 81.

[2] J. Pitteloud, Principes de la commutation par paquet. Output, September 80 to May 81.

J.-J. Jaquier received his degree in electronic engineering from the Swiss Institute of Technology in Lausanne.

In 1964, he joined the Swiss PTT where he worked first on various projects in data communications.

From 1969 to 1972 he had responsabilities in the planning and testing of the ATECO Telegraph Message Switching System. From 1973 to 1978 he was mainly involved in the planning of the TERCO project, a large teleprocessing system for Telephone Directory Assistance. Finally he was the PTT manager for the acceptance tests of the whole system.

Since 1978, he is in charge of the Informatic Section of the Research and Development Division of the Swiss PTT, whose main activity is currently related with the introduction of the Telepac data network and other added value services like Videotex, Teletex and Message Switching.

J. Pitteloud received his degree in electronic engineering from the Swiss Institute of Technology in Zurich.

After activities in the telecommunication industry he joined the Swiss PTT in 1974 where he worked first on diverse planning and engineering activities in relation with the TERCO project. He was successively involved in the hardware planning, the development of the teleprocessing software and finally the acceptance tests. Following the starting in operation, he was responsible for the system software group of TERCO.

J. Pitteloud joined the Research and Development Division of the PTT in 1979. He is in charge of the Teleinformatic group and is mainly involved in the Telepac project team. He was the test manager for the final phase of the acceptance carried out by the PTT with the collaboration with DTE manufacturers.

Experience with and Performance Measurements of the Packet Switching Network in the Federal Republic of Germany

D Runkel
Deutsche Bundespost, Federal
Republic of Germany

This paper reviews the first year of experience with the packet switching network of the Deutsche Bundespost, called DATEX-P. As a basic information the existing technology is explained, followed by some statements to the actual capabilities of the different modules. First experiences from the network providers point of view and the reaction of the customers, their experience and their problems from the first touch with this new service through the period of field trials to the actual use are illustrated. The second part describes first measurements in the field of network performance parameters especially throughput and network delay. Detailed investigations have been made as to node capabilities, particularly with high speed transmission rates.

1. INTRODUCTION

On August 26th,1981, the Deutsche Bundespost (DBP) opened their public packet switching service called DATEX-P. The system is a product of Northern Telecom Canada Ltd. in SL-10 technology. The present network consists of 17 nodes, planned to handle up to 13,000 ports, a network control centre (NCC) and a data collecting centre (DCC) for traffic data processing purposes. The different nodes are linked via 64 kbps PCM trunks.

The services offered are the X.25 service (1978 LAP B version) with transmission rates ranging from 2400 up to 48000 bps and the asynchronous PAD service according to CCITT Rec. X.28 for 300 and 1200 bps devices. PAD service terminals can be connected to the network either directly, via the PSTN,or via the DATEX-L circuit switched network.

The DBP provides a tariff based on a time of day accounting algorithm using five different periods during a normal working day. The charges themselves are distance independent but usage sensitive with volume discount after 200,000 segments transmitted.

The switches employ a multiprocessor architecture. A common bus enables communication between the different modules. It works on a 2 Mbps basis, which corresponds approximately to a capability of handling 1000 packets per second (pps). It permits physically interconnection of 15 processors and one common memory.

The common control equipment includes a common memory and two control processors to handle nodal administration and call processing. Each control processor is able to handle call set-up for 10 calls/sec. The line control equipment consists of trunk and line processor modules. The transmission speed of a trunk processor may vary between 9.6 and 72 kbps. The line processor exists in three basic configurations; either with up to four 64 kbps HDLC lines, or with a mixture of two of these lines and up to 62 medium speed lines (async and sync connections operating at 110 to 1200 bps and 1.2 to 9.6 kbps, respectively), or with up to 124 of these medium speed connections.

The throughput of a line processor is dependant on service type and speed of connections and is typically 80 to 120 pps. The subscriber lines are terminated by line cards. The maximum number of processors that may be connected to the central bus is generally planned as six trunk and seven line processors.

2. EXPERIENCE WITH THE NETWORK

2.1 From the Network Providers (DBP's) Point of View

Since installation the network has grown to 1200 connections (May 1982). The distribution of these connections in terms of transmission rates is shown in Fig. 1. Contrary to experience made in other countries (e.g. DATAPAC) the number of async connections are very low. But there is a very high usage of 9.6 kbps ports.

At the moment, it is quite difficult to provide guidelines for the planning of the DATEX-P network because of its short history and the lack of information in which way the packet switching service is going to develop. It is therefore assumed that the customer growth is proportional to time only and an application of linear extrapolation is possible.

Utilizing projected customer connections and initial performance standards, it comes out that DATEX-P will likely grow to 27 nodes interconnected by more than 80 trunks by the end of 1982. It should be pointed out that both the popularity of X.25 connections and the use of higher speeds (9.6 and 48 kbps) are the major contributing factors to the growth in switching capacity. In fact, in major centres 20 to 30 trunks are planned to distribute the traffic, and in some cases as many as 4 trunks between centres are anticipated.

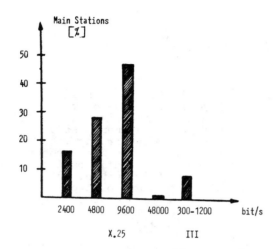

Fig. 1   USAGE OF THE DATEX-P NETWORK

(April 1982)

2.2 Experience with the network from the customers point of view

In order to be in close touch with the customer, a forum has been arranged - the DATEX-P User Group - were manufacturers and potential customers could express their ideas, demands and plans to the DBP planning and marketing staff. After the installation of the network and the first year of experience, an adhoc group was formed to deal with technical questions and difficulties being observed.

The responses during the testing period and the input from this adhoc group can be divided into two categories. The first relates to actual problems with the packet switching technique (hardware as well as software), and the second with peripheral techniques (e.g. transmission), administrative and maintenance problems.

In the very beginning the customer was confronted with the fact that the switch-over from leased lines to DATEX-P affected generally the performance of his data transmission application.

These difficulties are being overcome with the closer matching of applications using a packet switch transport media. For example a batch application with a packet size of 1024 bytes used a level 4 window size of only 1 in the DTE. These circumstances caused a big delay in the sending DTE, because the application program had always to wait for the acknowledgement from each packet.

On the other hand the customers had to take into account that packet switching is more suitable for short time response oriented switched data transmission such as dialogue sessions rather than for file transfer. Long calls with high data volume as for example file transfer do not take optimum advantage of the merits of the packet switching principle. These are more a domain for circuit switching techniques. Packet switching should not be used as a cheap straight forward replacement for leased point to point lines as may happen.

Since opening of the service, connections have increased steadily and in general it appears that the customers are satisfied with the service. It can be observed that initial euphorism for packet switching has calmed down to normal and stable usage of the service. It is regarded now as a necessary addition to existing data services of the Deutsche Bundespost. As our customers have the choice between packet switching and circuit switching data networks they can decide which network is appropriate and gives the most advantageous service for their specific application.

3. PERFORMANCE MEASUREMENTS

Performance characteristics of a network address only one part of the big area of service quality, however, it can be mathematically described and measured. All other factors which form service quality such as the general provision of services, new features, operation and maintenance, customer's advise, and documentation are more or less administrative issues which can hardly be qualified by figures.

Today one tries to standardize features related to service quality on a national as well as on an international basis. The aim is to enable the providers of a network to publish comparable values. In the present discussions availability, reliability, delay, throughput, and data integrity are the most relevant items in this area.

For the time being the DBP have only made specific measurements in the area of throughput and delay times.

3.1 Throughput of Node Modules

On the node the throughputs of line cards, line processors, and the common bus were tested. Of special interest for the DBP was the provision of 48,000 bps. The initial purpose for offering this speed was to provide the customer with a means to achieve very short response times in the network, and only a secondary consideration was to provide a high throughput switched transmission path. However, actual high usage of 48 kbps ports for file transfer became apparent during the test period and consequently detailed measurements were made, which also apply to the fast response, lower volume applications.

Fig. 2 shows the results obtained by loading the line processor with a full duplex data stream via one and more line cards over 56 kbps access lines. It can be seen that the throughput from the customers point of view is 48 data pps in both directions with 100 % piggybacking. Hence, this limitation is due to the 56 kbps access line. The number of data packets handled in the line card was 96. Fig. 2 also shows the line processor capability; it indicates that there is a limit of about 116 pps. Consequently when connecting up to four line cards to a line processor, the average line card throughput goes down to 15 pps in both directions. This is an important mark for the network planner when measuring actual usage to attempt to engineer additional high speed ports to that line processor.

The next test should show the throughput of a line card as a function of window sizes and the number of logical channels using a fixed packet size of 128 octets (see Fig. 3). It can be seen that the maximum throughput increases with more logical channels if the packet level window size is small, however, there is a small decrease if the packet level window size is large to begin. In a test made with 256 octets, the maximum is not affected with more logical channels.

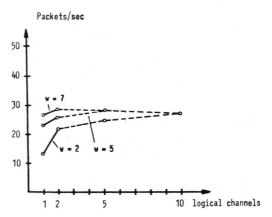

Fig. 3 THROUGHPUT OF LINE CARDS AS A FUNCTION OF WINDOW SIZE AND NO. OF LOGICAL CHANNELS

Parameters: packet length: 128 octets; no. of packets transmitted: 8192 full duplex; line processor throughput 115 packets/sec max.; 2 line cards per line processor

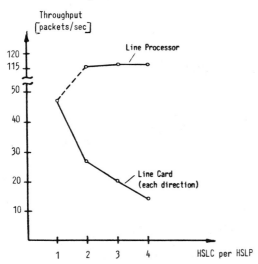

Fig. 2 THROUGHPUT MEASUREMENTS ON HIGH SPEED LINE CARDS (HSLC) AND HIGH SPEED LINE PROCESSORS (HSLP)

Parameters: packet length: 128 octets; no. of logical channels: 2; window size: K = w = 7; full duplex transmission

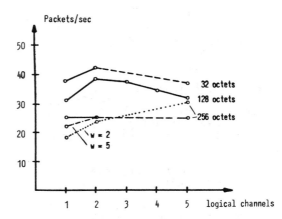

Fig. 4 THROUGHPUT OF LINE CARDS AS A FUNCTION OF NO. OF LOGICAL CHANNELS AND PACKET SIZE

Parameters: packets length: 32/128/256 octets; window size K = w = 7; no. of packets transmitted: 8192; unidirectional transmission; line processor throughput 115 packets/sec max.; 2 line cards per line processor

Further tests were made with unidirectional traffic, i.e. with no piggy-backing. Variables were both window size and packet length as a function of the number of logical channels (Fig. 4). It was generally found that the number of packets transmitted was less than in the first case (taking into account full duplex transmission), because no piggy-backing was used and all acknowledgements had to be sent and handled as separate packets. They are not counted in the data flow but have an impact on the processor load.

When packet lengths of 256 octets and w = 7 were used the maximum throughput is already reached with one logical channel. When the window size w is reduced to two, a better throughput can be reached with a higher number of logical channels.

3.2 Network Performance

For network performance both delay time and throughput measurements were made. First of all it is important to define what is understood by network delay. It is necessary to distinguish between three different values

- Round trip delay time which includes processing times in the DTEs

- Round trip transmission delay time which excludes DTE processing

- Network transit delay which excludes DTEs processing and propagation delay of the access line.

Delay in packet switching networks depends on different factors such as transmision rates on the access lines and trunks, node capability, network load, routing principles and the number of hops.

The values obtained are round trip delay times, and in the case of dialogue sessions round trip response times (i.e. including processing delay in the DTEs in both cases). Tests were made for two applications:

- Dialogue, where very short response times are of importance

- File transfer with high throughput demand and short transit delay

File transfer

In addition to the measuring of delay, it was an aim to evaluate the capacity of a logical channel. In order to exclude all influences originated by data storage devices, the data transmitted in the file mode test was procuded by the program of the source DTE and was discarded at the receiving station. Variable parameters were

packet length and the number of hops. The window sizes were kept constant (K = 7, w = 2). Also the influence of higher level protocols (level 4) was observed.

The results for round trip delay show (Fig. 5) that with one hop and a packet size of 128 octets the highest throughput was approximately 67 % of the access line capacity. The throughput decreased slightly to 57 % when 3 hops (or 4 nodes) were included in the transmission path. One should note that these results stand as an example and are to some extent dependent of the measuring equipment. There is for instance a DTE delay of approximately 12,5 ms from the application program down to the V.24 interface.

a)

	packet size [octets]	network delay including DTE [sec]	effective data rates	
			DATEX-P [bits/sec]	leased lines [bits/sec]
without level 4	1	518.76	158	
	16	42.10	1946	
	32	26.22	3124	
	64	16.46	4977	
	128	12.69	6456	
with level 4	256 *	37.49	2185	5358
	512 *	20.28	4040	6559
	1024 *	17.50	4681	7374
	2048 *	15.30	5354	8039

b)

No. of hops	network delay including DTE [sec]	data rates achieved DATEX-P [bits/sec]
1	12.69	6456
2	14.32	5721
3	15.05	5443

Fig. 5 THROUGHPUT AND NETWORK DELAY MEASUREMENTS IN THE DATEX-P NETWORK (file transfer 10240 octets)

   a) access line 9.6 kbit/sec, 1 hop
      * block size in level 4

   b) access line 9.6 kbit/sec, packet size 128 octets

Dialogue session

Two different dialogues with request packets of 16 and 64 bytes data and 128 bytes response packets in both cases were run. Again in this test all data was generated by program, then sent down to the destination DTE where the request packets were filled up to 128 octets and retransmitted to the source DTE. Time measuring was started before WRITE and was stopped after READ was finished. The results contain average values out of 80 measurements each (see Fig. 6).

Packet size Request/Response [octets]	TEST 1				TEST 2				TEST 3			
	call set-up [ms]		dialogue [ms]		call set-up [ms]		dialogue [ms]		call set-up [ms]		dialogue [ms]	
	av.	95 %	av.	95 %	av.	95 %	av.	95 %	av.	95 %	av.	95 %
16/128	334	≤370	381	≤410	361	≤380	427	≤460	380	≤400	452	≤490
64/128			463	≤480			503	≤510			545	≤550

Fig. 6   ROUND TRIP RESPONSE TIME MEASUREMENTS IN THE DATEX-P NETWORK

Test 1, 2, 3 with 1, 2, and 3 hops; no level 4 protocol

CONCLUSION

High throughput and short delay times can be reached by using high speed access lines and trunks with transmission rates up to 48 kbps, and 64 kbps respectively (on trunks). As a result and as an advice to the customer it can be summarized that users with mainly dialogue applications have more advantages in using high speed access lines and those who make use of file transfer will benefit more out of a bigger window size. It should also be noted that a good matching of the higher level protocols over X.25, especially on level 4, is very essential for high throughput communication between two DTEs. From the network providers point of view appropriate activities are already underway to provide enhancements in the switching devices themselves. Additional features such as the use of priority, fast select, closed user groups, window size, and throughput class negotiations are planned.

Dieter Runkel studied telecommunication engineering at the Technical High School in Darmstadt and graduated as a Diplom-Ingenieur. He joined the Deutsche Bundespost, Research Department, in 1968 were he worked in the field of character recognition. From 1971 he was involved in transmission techniques - specifically new telecommunication services - and the international standardization of interactive Videotex systems in the Telecommunication Engineering Centre of the Deutsche Bundespost. Since 1979 he is head of the packet switching development section.

An Information Communication Strategy

I G Dewis
BL Systems, UK

BLSL has recently adopted an "Information Communication Strategy" which, together with "Data" and "Processing" strategies, forms the basis of an "Information Utility" to meet the business needs of its customers. The strategy covers all types of information that need to be transmitted between BLSL and its customers' sites, including data, text, image and speech. It is assumed that the current use of analogue transmission will continue for a number of years until it is replaced by digital transmission. The strategy addresses the issue of communication standards by adopting the use of ISO "Open Systems Interconnection" recommendations as appropriate ones become available.

1. INTRODUCTION

Communications in the information systems context can be broken down into three categories:-

(i) The simple electrical medium used to transmit signals. In the case of BLSL, this includes twisted pairs of wire as provided by British Telecom or as used in the office, coaxial cables as used in the Metro factory and BLSL's own microwave system.

(ii) Once the connection medium is available, there is a need for standards to enable simple electrical linking to be implemented. This is termed "interlinking".

(iii) Once devices are connected and interlinked, it is necessary for them to be able to communicate in a meaningful way. This is termed "interworking".

The problem in the information systems world is that interlinking and interworking standards tend to be set by manufacturers to cover their own products.

There is little natural compatibility on interlinking between manufacturers (except in the case of one or two interlinking standards or where some manufacturers have decided to exploit a large market created by another).

Standards for interworking are even less generally accepted. The issue is being addressed internationally through various standards organisations and the BLSL strategy addresses the issue by following the route being established by ISO (the International Standards Organisation) with its Open Systems Interconnection (OSI) recommendations.

BLSL has a sub-set of the total problem. Equipment compatible with the communication standards set by IBM and Digital Equipment Corporation represent 90% of the installed base of information systems equipment.

Providing there is a similar standardisation on future office systems and providing users follow the BLSL Procurement Policy, this sub-set will continue and it is this that the strategy is designed to cope with.

2. THE NEED FOR A STRATEGY

Every company, whatever its size, should develop a communication strategy to address its business needs and to be in a position to make maximum use of appropriate technological developments.

They should not be tempted, however, to exploit technology for technology's sake, but to make use of technology only where it can be seen to support their business aims. An example of such a temptation is in office systems, where many companies are currently installing individual modules which do not form a consistent whole. Indeed there are many examples where the use of word processors and copying machines has led to a greater inefficiency in an office environment.

3. BL SYSTEMS LIMITED

BL Systems Limited (BLSL) is a wholly-owned subsidiary of BL Public Limited Company. It offers systems services (systems analysis, programming, bureau services, consultancy and Operational Research) to the parent company which is its major customer and to external companies. BLSL employs some 1100 people, some of whom work in a small Research and Development department called Advanced Systems.

Advanced Systems' main function is to develop and maintain strategies in key areas. It also evaluates new technologies and methods, backing these up with pilot projects where necessary.

BLSL operates a large data centre in Redditch, near Birmingham, comprising mainly IBM and IBM-like equipment, for example an IBM 3033, an Amdahl V7, several IBM 4300s, etc. The second area where computers are exploited is in production and process control at plant level, where equipment from Digital Equipment

Corporation or its equivalent is used. A
sophisticated microwave network is operated,
giving access to over fifty sites.

4. INFORMATION COMMUNICATION

"Information" is a global phrase used to
encompass various traffic types including
data (ie. a structured format), text
(i.e. unstructured, for example as passed
between communicating word processors),
image and speech. The importance here is
not a precise definition of what is meant by
information but rather an indication of the
wide scope of the traffic to be carried.
The bringing together of these various types
of information is recognised in the company by
having one communications group with overall
responsibility for all such communication,
and not separate data transmission and speech
transmission groups.

"Communication" is defined as being composed
of two parts - interlinking and interworking.
Interlinking is the transport of information
from the output of a source device to the
input of a destination device, whereas
interworking applies to the useful dialogue
taking place between the two parties so
connected.

5. THREE KEY STRATEGIES

The information technology strategies of the
company depend on three key strategies -
data, processing and communications. These
in turn lead to other strategies as
illustrated in Fig 1.

Supportive strategies enable the company to
enact the three key strategies and these
include Procurement, Development, Training
and Organisation.

Technical sub-strategies are more detailed
statements of those elements that comprise
the relevant key strategies. Examples in
communications are the use of ISO's "Open
Systems Interconnection" protocols, IBM's
Systems Network Architecture, Local Area
Networks, Wide Area Networks, the use of
satellite capacity, etc.

As far as the user is concerned, all of these
produce what is seen by him as being the most
important set of strategies - Application
Strategies which, as applied to the business
environment, include factory, office,
engineering and administration strategies.

6. INFORMATION COMMUNICATION STRATEGY

The Communication Strategy is divided into
two phases - Phase One where analogue transmission is used (from now until some time in
the 1990s) and Phase Two where digital
techniques are exploited (beginning in about
1984 and being adopted increasingly). It
will be seen that each are further broken
down into the elements of interlinking and
interworking, (Fig 2).

The key elements of the strategy for each
phase are :-

6.1. Phase One - Interlinking

(i)   remain analogue,
(ii)   make better use of existing
       facilities, having a period of
       consolidation in order to maximise
       the use of existing resources,
(iii) no integration of speech and non-
       speech traffic,
(iv)   a minimal integration of non-speech
       traffic (data, text, image),
(v)   gradually adopt the International
       Standards Organisation's "Open Systems
       Interconnection" (OSI) interlinking
       protocols in place of proprietary
       ones.

6.2 Phase One - Interworking

(i)   gradually adopt ISO OSI interworking
       protocols in place of proprietary
       ones,
(ii)   a three stage approach to be adopted
       to achieve this, (Fig 3):-

Stage One, which will last until the
end of 1982/middle of 1983, will use
existing IBM protocols (eg. 2780,
3780, HASP, 3270) to link the three
generic types of system - IBM, DEC
and X, where X is the yet-to-be
appointed office systems supplier.

Stage Two, from about 1983 to 1986,
will still exploit IBM protocols from
IBM to DEC and from IBM to X, but will
gradually introduce OSI protocols
between DEC and X.

Stage Three, from about 1986 onwards,
will gradually replace all
communications protocols with OSI
ones.

6.3 Phase Two - Interlinking (Fig 4)

(i)   gradually change from analogue to
       digital transmission as each such
       implementation becomes cost effective,
(ii)   develop a wide area digital network
       to offer a cost effective inter-site
       facility,
(iii) develop local area networks at
       selected sites to provide cost effect-
       ive intra-site facilities,
(iv)   provide service networks on top of
       the digital network which each user
       or application will see, so that the
       basic digital infrastructure is
       hidden from him.

6.4 Phase Two - Interworking

(i)   applications to use the most
       appropriate service network,
(ii)   a continuation of implementation of
       OSI protocols,
(iii) emphasis placed on supporting
       internal users when interworking
       with external services and external
       users accessing the company's
       services.

7.   RESULTANT SUB-STRATEGIES

The following technical sub-strategies
need to be developed in order to
further enhance and enact the key
Information Communication Strategy and
these areas are currently being
investigated:-

(i)   IBM's Systems Network Architecture
       (SNA),
(ii)   Local Area Networking (analogue and
       then digital),
(iii) Microwave conversion (analogue to
       digital),
(iv)   exploitation of satellite capacity,
(v)   speech communication,
(vi)   facsimile,
(vii) conferencing.

8.   CONCLUSIONS

Phase One has an emphasis on efficient
interworking, utilising today's
communication facilities, whereas
Phase Two is a gradual move towards
digital transmission as this becomes
cost effective, together with the
associated integration of the various
types of information.

FIGURE 1 STRATEGIES FOR INFORMATION TECHNOLOGY

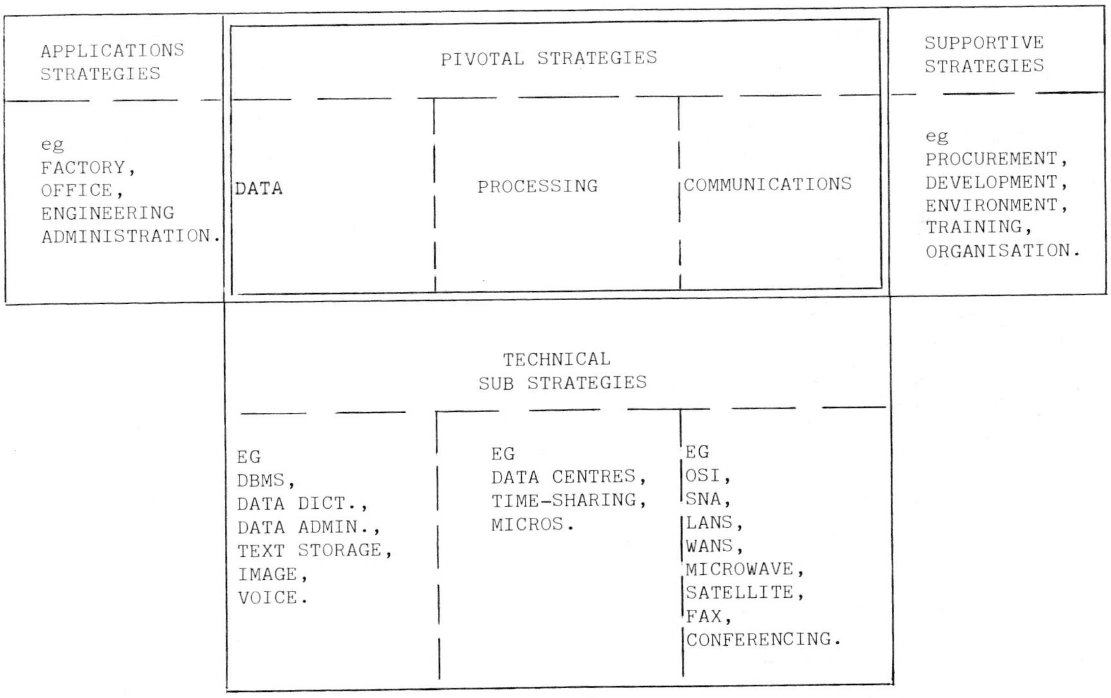

APPLICATIONS STRATEGIES	PIVOTAL STRATEGIES			SUPPORTIVE STRATEGIES
eg FACTORY, OFFICE, ENGINEERING ADMINISTRATION.	DATA	PROCESSING	COMMUNICATIONS	eg PROCUREMENT, DEVELOPMENT, ENVIRONMENT, TRAINING, ORGANISATION.

	TECHNICAL SUB STRATEGIES		
	EG DBMS, DATA DICT., DATA ADMIN., TEXT STORAGE, IMAGE, VOICE.	EG DATA CENTRES, TIME-SHARING, MICROS.	EG OSI, SNA, LANS, WANS, MICROWAVE, SATELLITE, FAX, CONFERENCING.

FIGURE 2 STRATEGY - KEY POINTS

TIMING

PHASE ONE - ANALOGUE

1981   1990

PHASE TWO - DIGITAL

1984

RECOMMENDATIONS

A. PHASE ONE - INTERLINKING

B.   INTERWORKING

C. PHASE TWO - INTERLINKING

D.   - INTERWORKING

FIGURE 3 THREE STAGE APPROACH

(a) Stage 1 (until end 1982/mid 1983)

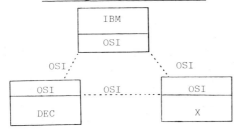

(b) Stage 2 (1983-86)

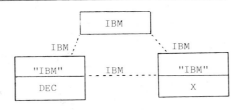

(c) Stage 3 (1986 onwards)

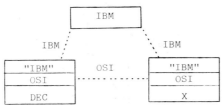

X = To-be-appointed supplier of office
     systems

FIGURE 4 DIGITAL HIERARCHY

SERVICE
NETWORKS   EG. DATA, SPEECH, VIDEO

DIGITAL
NETWORKS

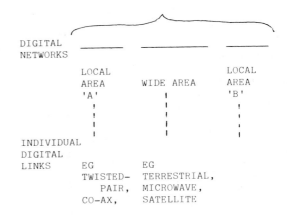

LOCAL   LOCAL
AREA   WIDE AREA   AREA
'A'   'B'

INDIVIDUAL
DIGITAL
LINKS   EG   EG
            TWISTED-   TERRESTRIAL,
            PAIR,   MICROWAVE,
            CO-AX,   SATELLITE

IAN DEWIS

 Ian Dewis graduated in Electrical Engineering in 1967 and a year later gained an MSc in Information and Systems Engineering at the University of Birmingham. He continued his research in the field of Information Communic- ation by studying inter- computer links, gaining a PhD in 1971.

His next four years were spent as Senior Scientific Officer at the Division of Computer Science, UK National Physical Laboratory, where his responsibilities included the development of a pilot link between the NPL Data Communications Network and the Post Office Experimental Packet Switched Service. In 1975, he joined the British Steel Corporation as Chief Technical Officer, Data Communications, where he project managed the design and development of the BSC Data Communications Network and its subsequent enhancements.

Dr. Dewis joined BL Systems in 1979 as Manager, Advanced Communication Systems, where his responsibilities included the development of long term strategies for BL in the field of information communication. He also managed pilot projects in areas such as networking, Viewdata and electronic messaging. He is currently Manager, Communications Development, where he is responsible for strategic and business planning of, and technical and project management of, communications facilities and value added network services.

He is author of about 50 published papers on computer networks, packet switching software and information communication and has written chapters of two books on computer networks. He is a Chartered Engineer, a Member of the Institution of Electrical Engineers and of the British Computer Society. He is a Director of the Telecommunications Managers Association, a member of the International Telecommunications Users' Group (INTUG), a past Chairman of the British Computer Society's Specialist Group on Data Commun- ication and a member of the Focus Advisory Committee on Local Area Networks.

He is married with two children and his hobbies include sailing and violin playing.

The New Keywords in Communications Technology and Office Automation

S Schindler
Technische Universität Berlin,
Federal Republic of Germany

The new products for computer communications and office automation are introduced by their manufacturers by means of a confusing variety and almost deliberate use of new keywords, such as OFFICE TEXT, TELETEX, VIDEOTEX, TELEFAX, BUS/RING SYSTEM, VALUE ADDED NETWORK (VAN), LOCAL AREA NETWORK (LAN), WIDE AREA NETWORK (WAN), GATEWAY, RELAY, BRIDGE, PRIVATE AUTOMATIC BRANCH EXCHANGE (PABX), INTERNETTING, NETWORK INTEGRATION, INTEGRATED SERVICES DATA NETWORK (ISDN), SPEECH INTEGRATION, SATELLITE COMMUNICATION, BROAD-BAND COMMUNICATION, TELECONFERENCING, OPEN SYSTEM, FUTURE OFFICE-SYSTEM, MULTI-FUNCTIONAL WORKSTATION, ...

All these new keywords either refer to the lower three layers (i.e. to the area of transmission and switching issues) or to the highest layer (i.e., to the area of application issues) of the ISO 7-layer model. The structurally very important layers 4, 5, and 6 either are only implicitly affected by these keywords or they are not touched at all. The organization of this paper follows this simple insight, clearly emphasizing the office automation aspects.

1. Introduction

The new products for computer communications and office automation are introduced by their manufacturers by means of a confusing variety and almost deliberate use of new keywords, such as OFFICE TEXT, TELETEX, VIDEOTEX, TELEFAX, BUS/RING SYSTEM, VALUE ADDED NETWORK (VAN), LOCAL AREA NETWORK (LAN), WIDE AREA NETWORK (WAN), GATEWAY, RELAY, BRIDGE, PRIVATE AUTOMATIC BRANCH EXCHANGE (PABX), INTERNETTING, NETWORK INTEGRATION, INTEGRATED SERVICES DATA NETWORK (ISDN), SPEECH INTEGRATION, SATELLITE COMMUNICATION, BROAD-BAND COMMUNICATION, TELECONFERENCING, OPEN SYSTEM, FUTURE OFFICE-SYSTEM, MULTI-FUNCTIONAL WORKSTATION, ...

It is unfortunate but understandable that the manufacturers' explanations of these keywords do not mention the interrelations between these terms nor the concepts they have in common. This simply mirrors the actual state of knowlegde in this market. As a consequence, the area of new communications and office automation technologies looks like an ocean of incommensurable technical details, requirements, properties, etc. The debacle of software incompatibility of the last fifteen years seems to continue in a pronounced manner in this area. This could signal the early end of any economically reasonable progress in this originally very promising branch of new information technology.

When this problem had been recognized, a couple of years ago, a considerable effort was undertaken to work out the fundamental concepts of computer communications and to make the insights so obtained operational by developing international standards - in short, the development of the architecture of "Open Systems" was initiated, /1/. Today, this process has achieved various far-reaching results, which have been accepted willingly by the decision-makers in almost all large enterprises and administrations. This paper simply states that and where the above-mentioned keywords fit into this architecture. /2,3/ give sufficient references to the recent literature containing the technical details

*) The paper was supported by the BMFT, FRG, under contract No. TK05020 7: 'System Management In Offenen Kommunikationssystemen'.

omitted here.

A basic understanding of these keywords is sufficient to recognize, in reading this paper, the interrelations between them and the architecture of Open Systems. Also, some knowledge about the Open Systems communications architecture and terminology (as stabelized with /1,4/) is assumed.

All these new keywords either refer to the lower three layers (i.e. to the area of transmission and switching issues) or to the highest layer (i.e., to the area of application issues) of the ISO 7-layer model. The structurally very important layers 4, 5, and 6 either are only implicitly affected by these keywords or they are not touched at all. The organization of the rest of this paper follows this simple insight, clearly emphasizing the office automation aspects.

2. Transmission and Switching Issues, Internetting and Network Integration

In this chapter we will order in the usual keywords of the lower layers, such as the terms BROADBAND COMMUNICATION, SATELLITE COMMUNICATION, WIDE AREA NETWORK (WAN), BUS/RING SYSTEM, LOCAL AREA NETWORK (LAN), GATEWAY, RELAY, BRIDGE, and PABX (= Private Automatic Branch Exchange). Going above the INTERNETTING issues we continue this chapter by a discussion about NETWORK INTEGRATION as required for SPEECH INTEGRATION and more generally for ISDNs (= Integrated Services Digital Networks).

Let us start with clarifying the common basis for the discussions in this chapter, namely the functionality of layers 1 and 2 of the OSI communications architecture and related implementation questions. Important current work suffers from uncertainties how to understand the Reference Model with respect to these issues.

2.1. The Physical Layer

The satellite or terrestrial radio link, the ring or bus (see Section 2.3) is considered as the "physical transmission medium" in the sense of the OSI communications architecture. These physical transmission media have a higher transmission capacity than the ordinary telephone cables, which conventionally are used as the physical transmission medium. For the rest, no matter which of these different physical transmission media is taken, above the layer 1 nothing is known about the individual physical embodimentations of the transmission media it uses, but only the quality of the bit transmission services it provides.

Thus, the services of layer 1 provide for transmission of sequences of bits in a simple way over a physical connection, and these services hide all the technical implementation details of the physical transmission medium and equipment that must be used for its realization.

2.2. The Data Link Layer

The services of layer 2 are still concerned with transmitting sequences of bits, just as the services of layer 1. But the services of layer 2 have higher qualities than the services of layer 1: they have compensated for the qualitative shortcomings of the transmission technology used by the Physical layer. For obvious reasons, this compensation should be performed individually per data link connection.

Thus, the services of layer 2 (i.e. the Data Link layer services) are further abstractions from the technical properties of the actual physical transmission medium and devices used, than the services of layer 1 (i.e. than the Physical layer services). In order to emphasize this "logical" nature of a Data Link connection (for the realization of which a part of a single Physical connection or several Physical connections may be used, depending on the quality of these Physical layer services) they sometimes are called "logical link connections".

2.3. Implement Layers versus Standard Layers

The layering of services just discussed must not be misunderstood as ultimate guideline for layering implements. Probably the best known implement design, demonstrating that implement layers may legitimately differ from standard layers, is also the cause of most of the confusion. (Note, that the we use the term "implement" to refer to the product resulting from the process of "implementation"; in addition, the term "standard layer" refers to the notion of layer as defined in the OSI Reference Model.

This implement shall provide the Data Link layer services. Its design consists of two parts. The first part is a board or a chip providing the Physical layer services (i.e. bit-sequence transmission services), but also performing "framing", "bit insertions/deletions", and/or "FCS generation/checking". The second part is a software package using the board or chip, resp., and providing the Data Link layer services. Usually these two parts would be considered as two (implement) layers within a particular computer organization.

One easily sees that these two implement layers differ from their corresponding standard layers of the Reference Model. The three activities of the lower implement layer mentioned above, improve the

quality of the bit-sequence transmission service provided by the Physical layer. Namely, it allows to identify the beginning/end of a frame, to transmit arbitrary bit-sequences and to reduce the bit error rate in the bit-sequences transmitted. Therefore these activities performed by the implement layer 1 clearly belong to the standard layer 2 of the Reference Model.

Without regard of its design this implementation of the Data Link layer services is considered to be completely legitimate, if it only provides the Data Link layer services as specified in the corresponding layer standard for layer 2. Note, that this implement may be unable to expose also the Physical layer services. This were the case if there were no way to prevent the board/chip from performing framing and/or bit insertion/deletion and/or FCS generation/checking (but in most commercial boards/chips these activities may be switched off/on by appropriate bit settings).

2.4. Local Area Networks

Let us consider a net of physical links, i.e. a net consisting of physical transmission media interconnected by physical switching devices. If the physical links are either "twisted shielded pair" or "coax/triax" or "fiber optic" cables and if they are used for transmitting only over short distances, i.e. a couple of hundred meters, then this net may serve as the "physical transmission medium" in a "local area network" (LAN).

This physical medium in a LAN may have either physical bus or physical ring topology, /5/, and accordingly this LAN would be called a "bus system" or a "ring system". For arbitrating simultaneous accesses to this physical medium two classes of mechanisms are being discussed: "csma/cd" (carrier sense multiple access with collision detection) mechanisms and "token" mechanisms, where both kinds of arbitration mechnisms may be based on a large variety of different algorithms, /5/. Busses as well as rings may be arbitrated by csma/cd or token mechanisms.

There is a whole plethora of additional keywords characterizing the technical functioning of the physical media of LANs. For example, the terms "broadcast/sequential" medium would express that on a bus/ring an information signal transmitted is available simultaneously/sequentially at all receivers, respectively (in both cases any signal is transmitted to all receivers on the medium). The terms "broadband/baseband" cable would express that several/only one information signal can be present on the cable at one time without disruption, respectively. There are many more the physics (in a LAN) describing important terms, but none of them has any meaning in layer 3 or above, i.e. for users of LANs. There the Data Link services are characterized in terms of quality of service, but not in physical terms.

2.5. The Network Layer and Internetting

Most networks will be accessible from other networks. "Gateway" or "relay" or "bridge" are the equivalent terms for the mechanism which provides for internetwork communications; this mechanism must be located within a switching node having Data Link connections to the several networks to be interconnected.

Local networks with a gateway to wide area networks have always existed, namely on the technological basis of the normal private telephone subnetwork and a private (automatic) branch exchange (PBX or PABX, resp.). Note, that the terminus technicus "local area networks" presently does not include these conventional local networks, even if the PABX used is particularly sophisticated (communications technology has advanced dramatically here also). But it can be expected that this distinction will soon disappear, namely as sonn as sufficiently powerful PABXs are on the market - at present they are still in the laboratories.

In any case, in WANs as well as in LANs, the services of layer 3 of the OSI communications architecture abtract from performing switching (based on possibly several switching techniques) for realizing a Network connection between two end systems by means of several Data Link connections; in particular, they abstract completely from gateways (which ultimately are required, if these end systems belong to different networks). With respect to a LAN, the task of the Network layer is particular simple as follows from the previous section.

2.6. Network Integration and ISDN-interface

It remains to be clarified that the networks for data communications need a close integration with telephone networks. More generally stated, what we actually need are "integrated networks", and not just gateways between networks.

The CCITT term for these integrated networks is "integrated services digital network", ISDN. This term is somewhat misleading because of two reasons. Firstly, it talks of integrated services, whereas we are concerned with providing an integrated network access. Secondly, it talks of digital networks, whereas we do not care about a network's internal implementation: Only the interface need to be digital. In spite of this terminological problem we, too, shall use the term ISDN-interface for referring to this universal network interface to come, hopefully.

The need for the ISDN-interface becomes obvious when considering the present situation. For accessing the different existing networks or their services (telephone, telefax, telex, teletex, line switching/packet switching data, cable-TV networks) we usually would have to use completely different network interfaces, have to maintain separate inhouse lines supporting these interfaces, use separate devices obeying completely different network access protocols in using these services, have to pay separate network subscription fees and account for different network tariff structures.

This surely is not what the users want to have: Users want to have a single network interface, or a simple hierarchy of interfaces, through which they can access all networks (and the application services they are providing) in a uniform way. The "external" network integration achieved by an ISDN-interface, i.e. the uniform access mechanism for all networks and the services they provide, is even more important from the point of view of designing new equipment for users to effectively organize their

work (as discussed in the next chapter). Finally, the ISDN-interface would make the internetting problem obsolete!

Except for extremely high bit rates (above 10 Megabit/sec) one can get along with a simple extension of the X.21 interface. Thus, presently the X.21 is a most prominent candidate for this universal interface, /6/.

Although there is no major technical obstacle, it may be hard to achieve a common agreement between the parties involved in the ISDN-interface standardization, due to political and tariff structure reasons as far as the carriers (i.e. the PTTs and RPOAs, /8/) are concerned and due to market defending measures, as far as the major vendors are concerned.

But, there is an enormous pressure to solve this ISDN-interface problem, because of the push of technological innovation and commercial benefits in the applications area which would result from being able to replace, where needed, the many different present network interfaces by a single ISDN-interface (and by providing this interface in LANs, right from the beginning). Therefore, the further technical development in this area seems to be certain, even if this may cause some political complications between network administrations or with major vendors.

2.7. Summary

The discussion in this chapter about the technological progress indicated by the keywords initially quoted and about the communications architecture of Open Systems may be summarized in two simple statements:

- In developing and learning about the new transmission and switching technologies and in filing their keywords the Open Systems communications architecture has proved to be extremely helpful by providing a clear and technology-independent understanding of the semantics of transmission and switching services (i.e. of the services of the three lower layers),

and

- all higher layers are not affected at all by this technological progress. It does not change anything, but it adds new applications to layer 7, which become realizable by means of the broader transmission capacity of the new transmission techniques and their multicast/broadcast capabilities within local area networks.

3. Applications and Office Systems

Here we consider the keywords OFFICE TEXT, TELETEX, VIDEOTEX, TELEFAX, TELECONFERENCING, OPEN SYSTEM, VAN, MULTI-FUNCTIONAL WORKSTATION, and FUTURE OFFICE SYSTEM. As soon as one tries to go into detail, one finds out that presently there is quite a terminological mess; nevertheless there is a pretty broad common understanding of the essential meanings of these terms and their commonalities.

3.1. VANs and CCITT Regulated Application Services

From a structural point of view teletex, interactive videotex, broadcast videotex and telefax are considered to be Application services, i.e. to be provided on layer 7 of the ISO Reference Model, just as the future teleconferencing services. Thus, in publicly providing these services the PTTs in many European countries do not just run networks for exchanging information "absolutely transparently" (i.e. without asking for what and for whom these informations are being transferred), but they also run "value added networks" (VANs); more precisely, they have the monopole for any kind of public networks and services which these networks provide. Note that this does not mean that a company cannot run a private VAN (exclusively for its own use) using the PTT's public network services. In countries not restricting the commercial use of network services (namely not to be used for third parties' information exchange), such as the USA, a publicly accessible VAN may be run by one company using the network service of another company. In particular the first company may publicly provide a powerful set of LAN application services in n distant areas and integrate these n LANs by means of leased lines of the second company.

A VAN is implemented on top of one or several appropriate network(s). Typical examples would be that the teletex service or the telefax service is provided on a line-switching or packet-switching data network or on the telephone network; the interactive videotex service on some data communication network and telephone network or on some LAN; teleconferencing services on some LAN. Note that a user would not have to care about the question on what network the application service he wants to access is implemented, if there were ISDN interfaces which he could use and where his Application can access the service it needs.

The Application services mentioned so far differ from other Application services (such as the standardized Virtual Terminal service or from user defined Application services) solely with respect to administrative aspects: these four services are (or are going to be) "CCITT-regulated", i.e. presently the specification of their technical details is not performed by the ISO, but primarily by the CCITT *). In distributed applications these CCITT-regulated services may be used (e.g., teletex for text transfer, telefax for document transfer), but this is not required. That is, there will be distributed applications which will not use any one of the standardized Application services. They will be designed to use only the ISO standardized Presentation services for their communication purposes, /7/.

Today, no reliable figures are available saying how many distributed applications, in particular from the large area of future office systems, will be based on the CCITT-regulated text-, document-, videotext-transfer services, exclusively, and how many of them will design their (additional or

---

*) This is indicated by the artificial names "teletex", "telefax", "videotex" given to them in the corresponding CCITT recommendations specifying these standard text/facsimile/TV-set communications services. By the way, the terminal "x" in these names stands for "exchange", i.e. for a term sometimes used as synonym for "communications".

alternative) own individual office communications services. All we know reliably is that the above CCITT-regulated office communications services will offer substantial technical support and probably will be used exclusively in all those areas in which there is no manpower or time or money for new investigations or developments or products, i.e., in many smaller and medium sized companies.

3.2. Open Systems and Office End Systems

A distributed application, such as an office system, may not only get along without standard Application services (and their protocols) - it can be designed such as to avoid any use of ISO standards for the layers 6 and 5, and even for layer 4 (under certain special circumstances); and, nevertheless, it may be realized on top of the ISO Network service. After a moment of thinking, one sees that there may be good reasons for particular applications to take this approach, but that, in general, all end systems should ideally offer to their users all standard services and protocols of the communications architecture of Open Systems: i.e. ideally all end systems, including office end systems, should be Open Systems. In a "partially open" end system (where some of the standardized layer services are not available), an implementor of distributed applications may face the same kind of unsurmountable difficulties as he would have to face, if some conventional local operating system functions were not available (such as the functions of a file system, of an I/O system, of a virtual memory system).

But, as a strong diversification of the standardized Application services/protocols will take place, and as one obviously cannot insist on having all these standards available in all end systems, it is foreseeable that an end system will be termed Open System already,

- if it meets all requirements of the ISO standards for the layers 1 - 6 (and in addition, some management ISO standards on layer 7), and

- if it is a mere routine activity to "download" a missing standard Application service/protocol to this end system (given it has the appropriate devices for this standard Application service).

This would imply, then, that there would be Open Office Systems for which it is not known, a priori, whether they can provide the teletex, telefax, videotex, teleconferencing services or the future ISO standardized Application services and their protocols, or whether an initially missing standard Application service must be downloaded first, before it can be used.

Devices which allow the realization of several Application services (without any regard to whether these Application services are CCITT-regulated, standardized, or individually designed) are termed "multi-functional" devices, and a "multi-functional workstation" is a workplace (based on one or several end system(s)) equipped with devices of this kind. On their users future Open multi-functional office workstations are not expected to impose any restrictions. Quite the contrary, they would neither be restricted to a uniform functionality nor a uniform man/machine interface, but they will (more precisely, they should) be adaptable to the task profile of the workplace and, if people are working there, to their individual capabilities and needs.

3.3. Service Integration in Office Systems

It took some time until it was commonly accepted that office text systems (see /11/ for examples) must be much more flexible and powerful than the usual word processing systems and that teletex and telefax services meet only some very basic requirements of office communications. It probably will take some more time until it will be commonly accepted that the requirements of office communications also include the need for a flexible and powerful videotext communications service (even of typesetting quality, if required and the appropriate devices are available) and some teleconferencing service. Without these latter kinds of services the management/organizatorial/public-relations activities of an enterprise were not integrated into its office systems. An office system of this restricted kind would provide the communications services needed for the clerical works but not those needed for integrating, in an enterprise, its offices and its control/neural/information system.

The extent to which the various services for office automation would make use of the underlying Presentation services may be quite different in different office applications; it may be high in typesetting Application services, it would be low in teletex Application services, for example. Nevertheless, none of these Application services requires something qualitatively new from the Presentation service. This means that the interactive videotex device (with or without some restricted capabilities for moving picture and speech transmission as they are needed for teleconferencing, based on a transmission capacity of about 50 Kbits/sec and highly compressing picture encoding), as well as the teletex device, some standardized or non-standardized virtual terminal device, an individual office text device conceptually can "communicate with each other". I.e., any two of these devices conceptually can be used for realizing a single communication activity, if only the capabilities of the weaker one of them are used (more precisely, if only those capabilities of both devices are used, which may be mapped onto each other in a unique way); these two devices may be both with one of the communicating two partners or any partner may have one device. It is the task of the Presentation service to provide to the communicating partners the appropriate means for reconciliation of the different presentations/representations of informations (exchanged or shared between them) due to the use of different devices, /7,9/. Thus, the Presentation service plays a crucial role in achieving a far reaching service integration.

In the past, this universal approach has hardly been considered. In spite of the fact that, in the office automation area, we are dealing with a class of devices for pretty similar applications, for which the values of the technical parameters typically are harmless (no unexpected high volume traffic, no unexpected real-time requirements), these devices and their protocols are designed and implemented so differently, that their integration into a single communication activity frequently is considered as unrealistic, today and tomorrow. For today, i.e. for the current devices, this assumption would hold in most cases, and this is a bad

technical misdevelopment! But, to predict that this will remain so in the future – that is to claim that there are fundamental differences between office text, videotex, teletex, telefax, office graphics, typesetting, or similar services – is nothing else but documenting a pretty restricted knowledge of the actual technical problems and the current state of developments.

The recovery from this misdevelopment is already well advanced:

- manufacturers of devices are marketing the first multi-functional terminal devices (which are able to provide office text, teletex, telex, telefax, videotex, graphics and typesetting), /10/,

- branch leaders of office organization are reporting publicly about their text systems that are designed so device-independent as to allow the integration of all these Application services, /11/,

- the ISO is designing its Presentation service, /7/, such that it is really suitable as the general basis for office communications,

- the CCITT is modifying its relevant recommendations (for example, teletex, videotex, message exchange) in a stepwise but clearly goal-directed fashion so as to make them consistent with the Open Systems communications architecture.

3.4. The State and Perspective of Standardization in Office Automation

In the context of this paper, office automation is understood to be "text preparation and interchange", so the new slogan. The notion of text here is understood in an extremely general sense, including graphic or other picture elements and all kinds of presentation attributes, up to what is required for typesetting quality. Similarly, the notions of "preparation" and "interchange" are to be interpreted. Thus, the process of text preparation includes editing, modifying, filing it; interchange includes the use of communications technology as well as the exchange of storage media for office systems (i.e. of floppies, today anyway).

Working group 5 of ISO/TC97/SC16 is responsible for the technical verification of application issues pertinent to the OSI communications architecture, a particular issue of this kind being office communications. But other subcommittees of ISO/TC97 have the primary responsibility for this particular application area, namely SC18 (office automation) and SC19 (devices for office automation). At the moment the situation is somewhat unbalanced: As a result of several years of work WG5 of SC16 arrived at a clear understanding of the information presentation/representation problems to be solved in any communication between users located in heterogeneous end systems (and is not concerned with the users' local activities, at all) and proposes an appropriate Presentation service, while SC18/SC19 are primarily concerned with the users' local issues and are so young that they are still busy structuring their work on these local user issues and therefore could not yet care so much for coordinating their activities with what has been done, already, elsewhere. But, based on individuals working in SC16 and SC18 simultaneously, the beginning of a cooperation has already clearly been marked at the last plenary meetings of SC18 and SC16 (April in London and June in Tokyo, resp.). As SC18 started working at an extremely ambitious time schedule, one expect a consistent set of documents in SCs by the end of '82, /3/.

The reason for this unfortunate delay of ISO's work in the office automation areas is that until last year, their standardization work took place in TC95, which did not consider information technologies. Last year, TC95 was dismissed and appropriate subcommittees were established within TC97.

In the office automation area, this past partial blackout of the ISO led to a remarkable situation: the CCITT was left completely on its own in designing Application services for these areas such as Teletex, Fax, or Videotex. As a consequence, it presently is not clear how these services of the CCITT can be used within more complex distributed applications, or what their user interfaces are in detail. But it is no questions that SC18 started the serious attempt to completely integrate these services into the future services for text preparation and interchange. As the urgency of this work has been clearly recognized by SC18, the first series of "draft proposals for international standards" on text preparation and interchange may be expected by the end of 1983 - early enough for the CCITT to take them into account when elaborating on their working documents for these Application services. The corresponding CCITT recommendations then are expected by the middle of '84. Also the first (DPs for) ISO standards on devices for text preparation and interchange may be expected to be issued by SC19 about a year, after the corresponding functional specifications (which they would turn into implementation specifications) are approved by SC18.

It remains to hope that this process of consolidation will proceed fast enough, before a broad publicity gets the impression that any far-reaching office automation had to built on the present chaos in the area of standard Application services. Indeed, office automation then surely would become much more expensive/complicated/confusing/restricting/incapacitating/unreliable than expected and tolerable. In total, it then had to be considered as of questionable social value.

4. Conclusions

There has been an increased public discussion about various new transmission techniques (primarily LAN and satellite techniques) and various seemingly unrelated Application services with mass basis (e.g. videotex and office text). These developments in communications technology and office automation raised the question whether other communications architectures were evolving besides the Open Systems communications architecture and whether these new communications architectures would require communications standards of their own. Due to technical considerations as briefly outlined in this paper (and also, in order to keep the area of communications standards as manageable as possible) the answer to this question is a clear "No" in probably all expert committees, and this reply is considered as being definitive in the international steering organizations, ISO and CCITT. Therefore, the new and frequently used keywords in communications technology and office automation do indicate those parts w i t h i n the Open Systems communications architecture deserving particular attention and even standards of their own. They do not indicate one/two/many new communications architectures!

This implies that the Open Systems communications architecture is going to be the central ordering principle in those application areas, which are headed towards considerable restructuring because of new communications technologies, such as the office/administration areas. It is this ordering principle that allows one to understand, also in these areas, the overall structure of progress, i.e., in particular, the impact of new communication technologies on office automation. Without this ordering principle this progress seemingly is a jungle of communications-technological developments, completely isolated from each other or interrelated in some obscure way, articulating itself only in a flood of incomprehensive keywords.

References

/1/ ISO DIS 7498, Information Processing Systems - Open Systems Interconnection - Basic Reference Model, January 1982.

/2/ Schindler: Keywords in Communications Technology, Computer Communications, June 1982.

/3/ Schindler: Handbook of Structured Distributed Systems/Applications and their International Standards, to be published by Springer-Verlag, autumn 1982.

/4/ ISO/TC97/SC16/N919: Draft Connection Oriented Presentation Service Definition, Florence, March 1982.

/5/ Tanenbaum: Computer Networks, Prentice Hall, 1981.

/6/ Schindler, Luckenbach, Steinacker: X.21 - The Universal Interface to Distributed Systems Implementations, Proceedings of the "ICCC '82", London, 1982.

/7/ Schindler, Bormann, Wilke: Open Systems Interconnections - Towards a Presentation Service Standard, Proceedings of the "ICCC '82", London, 1982.

/8/ Sunshine, Schindler: Working Title "Standards for Communication Services and Protocols", appears in Computers and Standards (1982).

/9/ Schindler, Flasche, Bormann: Open Systems Interconnection - The Presentation Service Model, Computer Communications, Vol. 4 No. 5, October 1981.

/10/ For example, the manufacturers: Barco, Three Rivers, Apollo.

/11/ BRAVO/ALTO (RANK XEROX), JANUS (IBM), KAJAK (INRIA), SCRIBE (CMU), ...

How to Determine your Organization's Telecommunications Potential (and how to get there)

W H Peters
Woods Gordon-Arthur Young, Canada

Management of organizations at all levels face a bewildering array of options in utilizing the explosive growth in telecommunication capabilities and services. This paper presents, in non-technical terms, what is now available and what is likely to become available through the 80's. The paper then suggests what the senior management of an organization should do to determine which of these practical capabilities should be utilized and how.

INTRODUCTION

Telecommunications is emerging as the dominant force linking all aspects of the information needs of organizations. Despite this growth, there remains a serious shortage of people with a broad enough perspective to direct the efforts needed in organizations to deal fully with all telecommunication needs. Staff gain traditional telecommunication expertise in one of three areas: voice, data communications or administration where services such as teleconferencing and facsimile are handled. These staff still generally lack a full understanding of the broad scope of telecommunication needs and often are not equipped by training or experience to deal with the organizational and senior management challenges now faced.

This paper provides a perspective from which senior management can view total organizational telecommunication needs. The forces contributing to the explosive growth in telecommunication potential are presented first, followed by the key market offerings, including both products and services. A recommended overall strategic and detailed planning approach is then developed which can dramatically improve the degree to which your organization identifies and achieves its telecommunication potential.

The number and variety of telecommunication hardware and service options available is accelerating rapidly. The main reasons for this are:

o the continuing decline in cost and increase in reliability and robustness of the silicon chip (exhibit 1);

o the convergence of telecommunications, computer and office equipment technologies;

o the explosive growth in public offerings available either as interim solutions or as part of your overall approach to meeting your telecommunication needs;

o the continuing scarcity and increasing costs of staff; and

o the increasing cost and decreasing reliability of conventional communications systems.

Minicomputer suppliers are increasingly marketing word processing and other office system capabilities on their minis. Office equipment vendors are adding many computer capabilities to their word processing products. The computer is used extensively to support and manage both local and national telecommunication networks. Many vendors are offering products and/or services that are part computer, part telecommunication and part office equipment. Examples are electronic filing, linkage of word processors to photocopiers and packet switching networks.

There has been a serious lag in the amount of attention generally given telecommunication matters by senior management. Like it or not, senior management face a number of new challenges:

o substantial pressure to adopt "integrated office" systems now available;

o as data processing systems migrate deeper into the day-to-day conduct of your business, they demand increased commitment to telecommunication services;

Effect of Increased Chip Storage Capability Based on a 4 Megabyte Capacity

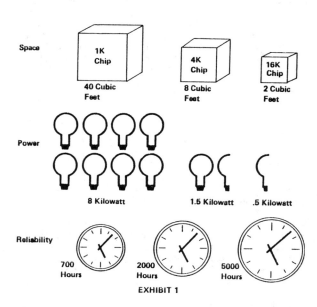

EXHIBIT 1

o vendors produce office equipment increasingly capable of communicating but incompatible with those of other vendors, making careful organization-wide planning and acquisition fundamental to realizing the benefits of these new capabilities;

o telecommunication vendors that are absorbing many vendor incompatibility problems into their value-added network service offerings. A good example of this is CN-CP's INFOTEX, an electronic messaging and mailbox service that can be used by a wide range of word processing vendor equipment; and

o the advent of these new services and capabilities is bringing many units of your organization into direct competition and conflict. The office management staff are trying to claim office automation, the data processing department tries to claim telecommunications and both run headlong into administration, where traditional messaging services such as TWX, Telex and Facsimile are handled.

As the technology has merged, the list of participants in the marketplace has begun to change. Exhibit 2 illustrates these changes. Traditional data processing suppliers are set out inside the dashed line. Clearly, a major challenge exists in simply remaining current with service and product offerings as competition among these diverse participants heats up.

Exhibit 3 summarizes the key types of participants in the telecommunication marketplace. It is a strange mixture of free enterprise and government; of data processing firms and of much enlightened office equipment suppliers.

MAIN PRODUCTS AND SERVICES

The explosive growth has led to an incredible array of products and services. Underlying most of these is a local, regional, national or international networking capability. These networks can be constructed on a leased line basis from the traditional common carriers or through special services obtained through value added networks. An example of a value added network in Canada is Datapac, a national packet switching network. In this case, the value added carrier leases the lines from the common carrier and delivers a specific network based product to the user organization.

Packet Networks

These value added carriers offer intelligent packet switched networks connecting combinations of subscriber terminals and computers. An added advantage is that the value added carrier service usually reduces user concern about network optimization and eliminates user concern about network maintenance and operation.

In Canada, Datapac is now a national network with improved penetration into many smaller centres. It also has interconnect gateways into Telenet and Tymnet in the United States. Links to packet switched networks in several other countries are either planned or in place by now.

Participants in the Marketplace
(Canada)

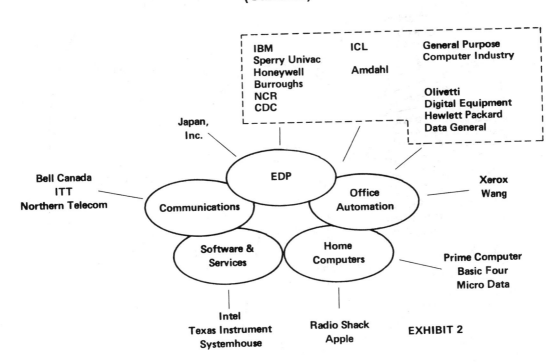

EXHIBIT 2

271

Many clients experienced initial patterns of very high cost due to attempts to bring up older applications with inappropriate terminals. The basic problem has been the tendency to send relatively empty packets, increasing costs considerably. This was particularly true, for example, of poled networks - they could not utilize packet switching networks. Much effort has been directed at modification of the application software and the replacement of terminal equipment to reduce packet switching costs to acceptable levels. Many users have been able to realize dramatically reduced communication costs for certain configurations and certain applications. At present, the packet switching networks are not transparent to the user. There is, however, a small but growing interface support capability in Canada. Some modest additional network response time delays (about 1 to 2 seconds) are experienced in going through the gateway interconnections to the USA packet switching networks. This is reportedly due to the differing packet sizes and the consequent need to restructure the packets in the gateway. Datapac normally uses a packet allowing up to 256 characters in the data portion of the packet while the USA networks only allow 128 characters. Thus each packet going from Canada to the USA must be split into two Telenet or Tynmet packets. Despite adoption of X.25, the gateway interface is not simple.

In the early packet switching network days, the uses tended to be replacements for existing leased lines. Now, however, many users are structuring applications and hardware configurations for the packet network. Thus it is an integral part of the available telecommunications options that organizations should consider. Organizations will continue to find a rapidly increasing number of circumstances where a packet switching network hookup makes good sense as an integral part of the organization's telecommunication resource.

Local Networks

Local networks currently consist mainly of the links between multiple computer and/or terminal sites for use on fairly standard arrays of applications and timesharing. However, looming large are the uses of local networks to link intelligent office equipment in the "integrated office". These are now being installed at a fast clip all over North America. Some, such as Xerox's Ethernet, are designed and built with the linking of electronic office equipment primarily in mind. They will, however, face strong competition from local networks built around the electronic private branch exchange (PBX/CBX).

Market Participants

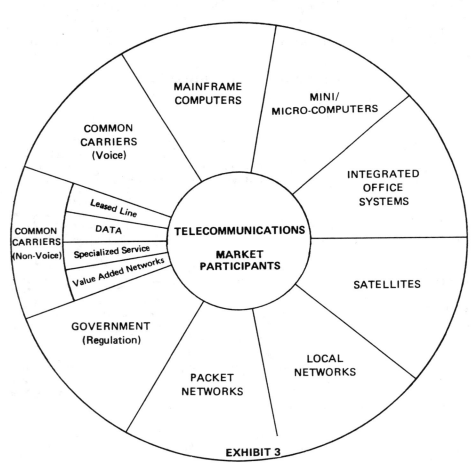

EXHIBIT 3

The key advantages of local networks are:

o reduction in the number of times text/data must be keyboarded;

o speed and accuracy in communications;

o sharing of device capability; and

o facilitation of multi-unit tasks such as linking a word processor to a photocopier unit for ease of production of copies.

o the average cost of installed networks is now about $1.2 million each in current Canadian dollars. This is expected to rise to about $2.0 million each by 1984.

The end uses of telecommunication resources required by various elements of your organization are clearly diversifying and growing rapidly. They represent substantial cost and could affect your competitive position or service levels. Thus senior management must ensure that the planning, design, acquisition and management of the telecommunication resources are carried out on an organization-wide basis.

Several other implications are also clear:

o much senior management attention must be directed at reconciling and managing the various groups in the organization that are competing for the telecommunication resources;

o the telecommunication analyst is a key player in the planning, design, acquisition and management of all telecommunication services and products. These people are beginning to play a coordinating role among the various users of the telecommunication resources. They are also very scarce resources and the ones currently in your

Typical End-User Services

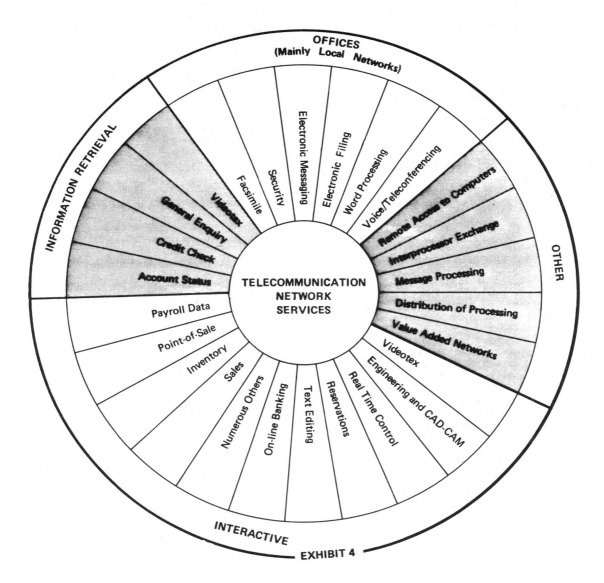

EXHIBIT 4

273

organization often have limited
exposure to only a part of the area,
e.g. a voice analyst or a data
communication analyst;

o   the trend toward integration of voice,
message, data and facsimile
telecommunication needs on a single
network within medium to larger
organizations will accelerate. The
main arguments in favour of this are
very persuasive:

Manufacturers are continuing to deliver ·
electronic equipment with the capability to
communicate. It has been estimated that 11
million pieces of equipment that could
communicate will be installed in North America
by 1985. While less than 2% of these will
actually be communicating, sales of local
networks are expected to be $225 million in
1985 and $900 million in 1990, a growth of over
30% per year.

Organizations are now devoting considerable
senior management attention to strategic
planning for "integrated office" systems. A
key element in that planning is clearly the
telecommunication people resources needed to
plan, design, acquire and implement the chosen
local networks and terminal devices.

End Uses

Typical end uses of telecommunication resources
are shown in exhibit 4. This list is intended
to be illustrative and is by no means
exhaustive.

Recent surveys that we have conducted on
telecommunications in Canada indicate that:

o   the average installed network in 1982
carries about 3.8 applications or
uses and this is expected to rise to
about 4.5 by the end of 1983;

o   the average company with networks
operates about 1.9 separate networks
and expects this to rise to about 2.6
by the end of 1983;

o   most installed networks (about 75%)
utilize leased common carrier long
haul lines;

o   most network users project extremely
rapid growth in the number of
terminals connected to the networks:
about 20%-25% annual growth rate; and
    -   Voice circuits currently not
        utilized after business hours
        will be available for data,
        message and facsimile traffic.

    -   Integration allows a reduced total
        number of circuits to provide
        adequate service levels hence
        reducing overall costs to your
        organization.

    -   An integrated network will support
        integrated functions which might
        combine voice, data facsimile
        and video in a single exchange.

Exhibit 5 is a schematic of what the
telecommunication network resource needed in
your organization might look like. This
schematic also illustrates:

o   the number and diversity of
organizational units that must be
involved;

o   the all-pervasive nature of these
networks in the organization;

Integrated Information Services

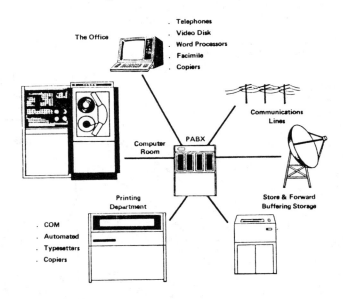

EXHIBIT 6

o   the substantial investment that will
likely be required; and

o   the major challenge now faced to do the
initial feasibility and planning work
for your organization.

RESOLVE STRATEGIC ISSUES FIRST

Management at the Chief Executive Officer or
Chief Operating Officer level must be involved
in establishing the strategic telecommunication
plan for your organization. Examples of
strategic plan elements are:

o   the key end uses for the network(s) and
other telecommunication resources
that may be acquired;

o   the degree of integration desired for
data, voice, office systems and
messaging;

o   the basic architecture of the network
(e.g. mainframe host or multiple
minicomputer hosts);

o the organizational units that must participate in the feasibility and planning;

o other design concepts desired for the telecommunication resources such as the extent to which value added or packet networks should be considered instead of leased line facilities; and

o the organization structure and staffing needed at the feasibility and planning stages. This is particularly challenging due to the competing jurisdictions and the extreme difficulty of finding staff with the appropriate <u>demonstrated</u> skills (rather than just an interest).

The strategic issues review should lead to explicit senior management commitment. If it does not, then the organization faces a substantially reduced telecommunication potential and this should be reflected by scaling down planned end uses, scope and level of integration anticipated in the organization's telecommunication resources. A fragmented approach that works, is supported and is cost-effective should be preferred to a comprehensive approach that fails due to lack of adequate senior management commitment.

DEVELOP A COMPREHENSIVE PLAN

Once the strategy is settled and an interim project organization in place, work can commence on the comprehensive telecommunication plan for the organization. This work should be carefully monitored and controlled by a senior management Project Committee. Each element in the plan should be tested carefully through a cost/benefit analysis and the project team given regular direction on the resulting desired options. Care should be taken to avoid going into detailed design work at this stage - a conceptual design is generally enough. Major challenges to those involved are progress monitoring, ongoing determination of the appropriate level of detail and the integration with the organization's overall business plan.

Once the conceptual design and plan are complete, a brief Request for Proposal document should be prepared. Typical content of this document is shown in exhibit 6. The main objective of this document is to shift some of the telecommunication design work to where it can best be done - to the ultimate suppliers of the networks and services.

GET THE RIGHT ORGANIZATION IN PLACE

At this point you will have a clear picture of:

o the strengths and weaknesses of your staff in this area;

o the strategic objectives and end uses your telecommunication resources;

TYPICAL REQUEST FOR PROPOSAL CONTENT

1. **INTRODUCTION**
   - **Present Situation**
   - **Network Objectives**
   - **Network Applications**

2. **NETWORK DESCRIPTION**
   - **Terminating Equipment**
   - **Communication Terminating Equipment**
   - **Intercommunications**
   - **Network Operations**

3. **TRAFFIC**
   - **Volumes**
   - **Patterns**
   - **Traffic Assumptions**

4. **NETWORK SECURITY**
   - **protection of information**
   - **point-of-access security**

5. **PERFORMANCE**
   - **Outages**   **— Test**
   - **Serviceability**   **— Audit**
   - **Errors**   **— Control**
   - **Back-up**

6. **IMPLEMENTATION**
   - **Tasks**   **— Customer Role**
   - **Schedule**   **— Sign-up**
   - **Vendor Role**

7. **ACCEPTANCE**
   - **Network Performance Tests**
   - **Notification of Acceptance**

8. **PROPOSALS**
   - **Format**
   - **Questions**
   - **Delivery**

EXHIBIT 6

o the probable design of the telecommunication networks and other resources that you will acquire; and

o the tasks and schedule that are faced by the telecommunication resources.

In other words, you now have all the information needed to put an appropriate organization in place. Many clients have responded at this point by establishing a new Senior Vice-President of Information (Chief Information Officer). Exhibit 7 shows the main elements that might be assigned in a typical organization. This will require considerable work to develop, implement and staff. Staffing is particularly critical to the achievement of your goals since existing staff may not possess the perspective needed. Thus they must be replaced or exposed early to carefully structured training and development programs.

A Possible Organization Structure

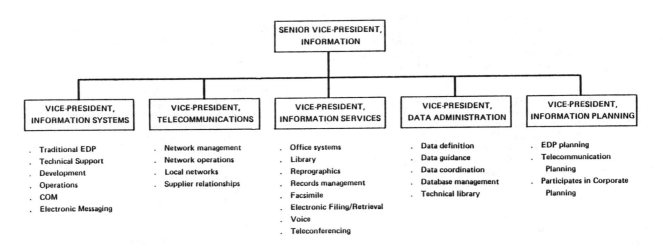

SENIOR VICE-PRESIDENT, INFORMATION				
VICE-PRESIDENT, INFORMATION SYSTEMS	**VICE-PRESIDENT, TELECOMMUNICATIONS**	**VICE-PRESIDENT, INFORMATION SERVICES**	**VICE-PRESIDENT, DATA ADMINISTRATION**	**VICE-PRESIDENT, INFORMATION PLANNING**
. Traditional EDP	. Network management	. Office systems	. Data definition	. EDP planning
. Technical Support	. Network operations	. Library	. Data guidance	. Telecommunication
. Development	. Local networks	. Reprographics	. Data coordination	Planning
. Operations	. Supplier relationships	. Records management	. Database management	. Participates in Corporate
. COM		. Facsimile	. Technical library	Planning
. Electronic Messaging		. Electronic Filing/Retrieval		
		. Voice		
		. Teleconferencing		

EXHIBIT 7

THE ASSIGNMENT OF THESE INTERRELATED RESPONSIBILITIES NEEDS CAREFUL THOUGHT FOR YOUR ORGANIZATION SIZE AND COMPLEXITY

There is always a great deal of difficulty deciding who should head up the organization's telecommunications function. Data processing staff are usually into data communications. Traditional administration may have the voice network experience. The introduction of local networks for the integration (linkage) of electronic office equipment (and perhaps combined usage for data) adds a new element that neither group usually fully grasps. Then, as the question of who should head it up emerges, conflict can result which often requires a firm hand from senior management to resolve.

SUMMARY

The substantial changes in perspective and patterns of thought essential to successful determination of your organization's telecommunication potential have been presented. Proven practical methods of reaching the telecommunication potential were discussed, followed by the main organizational and staffing concerns. Easily the greatest challenges faced in this area are the shifts in organization, in staffing and in the level of senior management commitment needed for success.

Reference

(1). Peters, W.H., Alternatives to Building Your Own Application Software (when and how to use them), Canadian Datasystems, June 1980.

Wayne H.Peters, B.Sc. M.Sc.

Mr. Peters is a Partner with the Canadian Management Consulting firm of Woods Gordon. He has more than 15 years experience in information systems and tele-communications. Mr. Peters is well known in industry and government in Canada through publications, work with the Canadian Information Processing Society and his extensive consulting experience. He has also taught at universities and has spoken extensively in industry and government.

Adding Value to Value Added Services

R A Clark
Joan de Smith (Systems) & Computex
Systems, UK

Current office automation processes are often dedicated to only one aspect of handling electronic information. As more and more information becomes available in electronic form, so standards will emerge which allow users to capture and process such information on their own systems before passing it to other users. This paper looks at some of the issues raised by such activities, and how they relate to the development of genuinely productive and acceptable office automation systems.

1. INTRODUCTION

Looking up the definition of information in Chambers dictionary one finds it to be defined as either 'knowledge' or 'an accusation given to a magistrate'. Assuming the former to be more likely, looking up knowledge, one finds 'assured belief' - or 'information'. Such a rapidly circuitous definition is hardly likely to benefit those of us whose job it is to differentiate between information and data - and hardly helps define products which are going to lead to the information revolution.

When Shannon developed the concepts of information theory in the 1940s, he was almost entirely concerned with the rate at which meaningful data could be carried through a communications channel of limited capacity. He specifically did not address questions of semantics, of understanding and of availability in defining his formulae - and it is precisely these questions which cause the most problem to the information system designer.

Until the last few years, the emphasis in providing an information source was based on rapid availability of information - its presentation and dissemination were rather secondary issues. Wire services broadcast continual text to recipients on a small variety of topics, leaving problems of filing and distribution to the recipient.

Currently however, technology has cracked most major obstacles in speed and flexibility of distribution until now only the weakest link remains - we humans. Consider, for the UK:

- public telephone access is available to probably every business in the country.

- deregulation is likely to mean users have almost a free hand in deciding end to end forms of communication.

- an A4 page can be transmitted over the telephone network in 1 or 2 seconds.

- a document can now be described fully in electronic form in terms of the diagrams, special letters and colours which it consists of.

- databases can generate in a few seconds, hundreds of responses to a simple query for information.

The major point about these is that at long last we can generate, manipulate and retrieve vast quantities of information faster than we are able to read and understand it. Until now, we could always blame poor decision making on 'a lack of information', 'delays in finding out relevant facts' or 'poor communications'. One aspect of the information society is that these excuses are no longer any more valid than claiming that a journey was too arduous or far, after adequate means of transport were developed. Now we suffer from a dearth of information, far too many relevant facts and over elaborate communications.

Designers of all aspects of communication systems must take note that is no longer adequate to prove a concept technically feasible, but that it must add value to an existing way of working. This paper is concerned with how the concept of adding value to an information service can be developed - even though the information services themselves are often referred to as value added, since they add value to raw data. Now what we need are ways of adding value to raw information.

2. CHARACTERISTICS OF INFORMATION SERVICES

A child is educated in the UK in the three 'R's - reading, writing and arithmetic (although clearly not spelling'.). Although there have been moves to make subjects relate to future career expectations a little more closely , the three 'R's have long formed the foundations of school curricula. Our actual needs in the information society are very unlikely to have a high content of any of these subjects. Voice recognition or keyboard entry takes away the need for good writing skills, calculators and computers perform arithmetic, and few of us need to start with page 1 of a book and continue to the end.

Perhaps the three 'D's could be introduced to the curriculum - Discover, Diagnosis and Dispersal. These certainly cover far more efficiently the normal tasks we concern ourselves with from day to day. They also describe the way in which current information services normally work - information retrieval, processing and transfer.

Information retrieval services are now fairly effective for those items of information where a person has some idea of what they are looking for. Most on-line database services have ways of searching indices via a wide variety of keys - either singly or in combination. Even general purpose database services such as videotex are now demonstrating methods by which such multi-keyed access can be applied to simple menu driven software.

A more difficult question is posed by those users who are either sufficiently expert (or perhaps sufficiently naive!) to not know what they are looking for. It has long been understood that the more scarce the information, the more valuable it is. If what is being sought is capable of some formal definition, then much of the current work on expert systems should prove rewarding. If on the other hand, only a vague outline exists of the required information, then the problem comes fully into the area of artificial intelligence, and we must look to rather longer timescales.

While current electronic information retrieval services help in the discovery of factual evidence, there are very few tools which effectively link to this information to help in dissemination. Many of the problems presented to todays analysts consist of redefining retrieved data in such a form that it can be automatically analysed. Almost by definition it is in this process that the human operator is most required, and an element of judgement is needed. In requiring human analysis and decision making, information processing can thus be distinguished from data processing.

Many methods exist for information transfer - facsimile, teletex, videotex telex, communicating word processors, computer mailbox, voice mailbox, wire broadcast, even television techniques can all be used. Each has its own characteristics, and can be shown to be viable or best suited for specific applications. These services mostly developed before electronic information retrieval and processing techniques, and so reflect the way in which we currently operate, rather than how we might like to work. Many organisations are working on integrating two or more of these services - indeed the International Standards Organisation has set up a committee with these specific objectives - and it is in this area that most confusion reigns.

Office automation - or 'the office of the future' has always been difficult to describe. Some organisations would claim that just one of the above facilities fell into this category - others that a merging of two or three into a single workstation was sufficient. What is needed is not just a clever method of connecting together some dissimilar devices. A properly conceived office automation system must integrate retrieval, processing, and transfer of information into a single entity which can be used with ease by expert and non-expert alike. Perhaps it is useful to consider how this can be done - and what work still needs to be carried out before such systems can be designed to work effectively.

3. DESIGN IN AN OFFICE AUTOMATION SYSTEM

In the real world, few 'giant steps for mankind' are recorded. Certainly individuals get merited acclaim (sometimes) for major improvements. Sometimes major breakthroughs are made in technology. When these are balanced against commercial, economic, and even chance criteria, these 'quantum leaps' are often shown to be just another way of looking at an old problem, or an expected development.

So it is with office automation. Videotex is either the great public information revolution - or a very limited and poor application of data processing, according to on which side of the fence you are seated. Fascimile is a 'new method of document transfer' and was invented in 1842. Teletex is a very clever and sophisticated method of text transfer - or an obvious development from quill pens and messenger boys.

In a practical sense, office automation must come gradually. Few really think that the problems in it are at the expert end. The real difficulties are in developing a system which is sufficiently universal that it can meet many conflicting criteria.

- it is cheap to use – or at least cost savings over a manual operation can be proven.

- it is economic to purchase – it will not require vast capital expenditure only to find that new technology will replace it in a few years, to add insult to injury, the replacement cost becomes so low that it calls serious doubts on the original decision to purchase.

- it does not cause an upheaval – acceptability to staff is essential and a lack of interference with the way they work. It should not replace, but augment and steer existing operations.

- it must interface to existing systems – handling sophisticated data is not enough; most organisations need to integrate office automation with existing information resources without the need to totally rekey information.

- it must link to other systems – no one wants to be caught with the only such device, and information will be passed between systems. After this transfer, the information must be technically, and more importantly legally preserved.

- it must match an organisations needs – not the reverse. It is difficult to contemplate a society in which all processes concerned with a particular application or vocation are carried out identically. Each organisation has their own idea of their needs – what is need is not software, but software tools.

- It must have other characteristics than office computerisation – currently offices have rest rooms, noticeboards, internal magazines, clocks sometimes even gamesrooms and even bars for outside working hours. For some strange reason, these 'entertainment' features are the last to be candidates for an office automation system – yet they are the very functions which if implemented are likely to persuade passive or hostile users to experiment.

- it must have accessability – no-one likes to share clerical support. or stationery or telephones. Equally, for office automation, there must be a per station cost which is comparable with current expenditure on office furniture,

to allow sufficient penetration.

- it must support alternative configurations – no two offices are the same, equally individual personalisation of workstations must be possible – without preventing occasional use by other users.

There are just a few of the criteria which users will use to judge the potential and success of office automation technology. At the heart of the problem is the way in which the user interacts with the system. In some ways, perhaps, the seven level model proposed for ISO standardisation and along which many office automation systems are being developed, could be called the 'seven obstacle' model. Each link in the connection requires its own protocol to establish – so often becoming another interaction for the user. The network can sometimes be defined as the thing which comes between a user and the information he requires. A current dialogue with a US database can require battles with the UK public telephone service, a packet assembler, a packet network in the UK, transatlantic communications, a packet network in the US, a host site, a host machine, a DBMS, and even the translation from American to English. Office automation should surely make these tasks easier – not more complex.

In a better scenario, a user might interact purely with local intelligence in his workstation – that could then translate his commands and interact on his behalf with a variety of remote information sources. Having extracted all the information available, he could then process it locally (his terminal calling on extra resources if required) before forwarding his results to another user or group of users.

The major problem in all these cases is defining a dialogue which is consistent from initial sign on, through retrieval, processing and despatch of information. Few people want to learn two languages to carry out their everyday tasks (although perhaps Canada has had limited success) – no-one wants to learn four or five for this purpose. Yet this is precisely what many vendors of office automation services expect of users.

How can this objective be met ? It requires design to be coordinated over all aspects of an office automation system – from user interactions with his terminal through to how and what information is communicated between systems. To some extent the Star and Perq workstations, for example, attempt to improve user/terminal interaction. Developments such as videotex gateway services or computer mailbox services look at the inter system interactions. The challenge is to link all these systems and approaches together to form a cohesive and integrated system.

It can be done now - some vendors of videotex systems or of computer message services have products meeting these criteria, and these can be linked to produce a user service with the sort of features outlined above.

4.   POSSIBLE APPROACHES

Current work in international standardisation is concentrating on defining an electronic document as a whole, rather than just specifying individual characters which form a part of it.   This specification calls on format definition, allows mixed graphical and character coded text, and most importantly adds additional addressing and filing information to the document definition.   Having defined a document in this way, it can be readily transferred to a similar (or even a dissimilar) remote device.   The next stage is to allow documents created in this way to be divided, processing and manipulated so as to form new documents, before their transmission to another user. The flexibility and ease with which a user can pull together information, reprocess it and finally present it are important criteria in office automation systems.

Most computer message services (CMS) are moving in this direction.   In one of the more advanced services it is already possible to use the computer as a message switch and communications device in order to extract information from remote databases.   The information so captured becomes part of a text file, which can then be edited using the same tools that a user would use if he had created the information online by keyboard entry.   At this stage the full power of the computer message service can be applied to forward a document created in this way to its intended recipients - either of the mailbox service, or via Telex, TWX, Mailgram - or even via the postal service.

In a similar way, a user of a private videotex system could use a gateway protocol to extract information from a variety of remote computers.   Using a standard videotex protocol, he could then change those information frames to become messages, to which he might append his own frames of comments. A videotex mailbox service would then forward his requests to one or many other users, or by interworking to users of Telex or Teletex.

These two approaches, using rather different terminals and services end up with the same result - with the CMS, a sophisticated process, requires some expert knowledge while with the simple videotex dialogue a more rudimentary process is performed. There is of course, no reason why such services could not be combined - allowing both naive and expert users to use the same system.   Not suprisingly, the designer of the CMS described above is working on simplifying control procedures for naive users, while the videotex designer is looking to increasing sophistication within the videotex framework.

What then are the problems presented by these 'solutions' to a system designer ?   perhaps these can be categorised under four headings:

- user acceptance and use
- cost
- integration with external sources of information
- technological advance

There are clearly other issues, such as security, interfacing to existing systems and ergonomic or physical constraints - but these are often specific or individual organisations, and often of less importance.

On user acceptance and usage, evidence shows that perhaps two out of every three users are essentially passive - and that providing extensive online help messages is not necessarily the best approach.   Passive users may destroy the effectiveness of a system unless they can be persuaded to participate - particularly in mailbox activities.   Some options exist for designers to try - suggestions include: keeping terminals permanently on with received message indication; providing background information like commuting details, dining room menus, vacancies and the time; printing out undelivered messages for alternate delivery; or providing on-line internal telephone directory information - each either cajoling or forcing users to interact with the system - preferably on a frequent but short time basis.

Cost is another challenge, as conventionally office workers could be expected to require only a few hundred pounds each for recognisably individual equipment, other than perhaps accommodation or desks.   Given the difficulty in persuading management to purchase even such limited technical sophistication as automatic dialling equipment, it would appear difficult to sell such systems unless their purchase is viewed in total by comparison with such costs as a new telephone exchange, main-frame com-

puter, or new office building.
Perhaps the best answers here are left
to the marketing departments of system
suppliers.

Integration is still difficult to
achieve in practice. Although
there are moves to adopt universal
protocols and languages for database
enquiry, these still seem some way
off. Very often the information
requested is formatted making some
assumptions about terminal type which
are incorrect, and occasionally
undesirable. Until suitable standards for a virtual terminal exist
which are usable, with the current
level of sophistication, it may be
much better to use multi-function
terminals and wherever possible to
transmit data and formatting
instructions separately.

The final challenge is that of
technological advance. In part,
office automation systems and value
added services have grown up through
technical excellence. Now, the
cost and abilities of new generations
of microprocessors and their
peripherals allow more and more
sophistication to be located at a
users terminal. Designing equipment
which can still form a basis for a
good office automation system can be
difficult when a designer knows that
within a few months improvements in
circuitry will allow a competitor to
produce a rival machine with superior
facilities, or at a reduced cost.
The temptation is to produce equipment
which is difficult to duplicate,
reducing the user benefits of low
costs and standardisation, which
office automation surely requires.

Richard Clark is joint
managing director of Joan
de Smith Systems, a spec-
ialist telecommunications
and office automation
systems consultancy based
in London. His career has
included an initial period
with British Telecom where
he was active in the
development of new services
such as facsimile, viewdata
and teletex, and where he
represented the UK on various international
standards bodies.

As a consultant he has been responsible for
many major projects including the remote printing of the Financial Times in Frankfurt,
advice to Bell Canada on new videotex services,
advice to British Telecom on the introduction
of Teletex, and new Computer Message Services
(in association with Dialcom), and the European Commission on suitable keyboard designs
for multi-lingual text. He is widely regarded
as a leading expert on viewdata systems, and
was instrumental in the formation and strategic
development of the Computex private viewdata
system.

In May 1981 he gave the keynote address to the
Society for Information Display in New York on
developments in viewdata technology, and he has
given many other major presentations in this
area.

An Approach to Strategy for Office Systems

C Tristram
BL Systems, UK

The foundation of this approach to strategy for office systems is to define the purpose of office systems and all the assumptions on which the strategy is based. An important consideration in this approach is the type, health and objectives of the company and the industry of which it forms a part. The cultural attitudes of the company's staff have to be examined. Detailed examples are drawn from the author's experience.

The title of this paper includes three of the most misused phrases in computing. I will, therefore, start by giving my definition for each. These definitions are not put forward as absolute, but rather as a common point of reference between us; you, the reader and I, the author.

1. Definitions

1.1 Strategy

a. 'An attempt to organise my own forces so that they can exert their influence cohesively and achieve the maximum effect on the objective of the strategy'.

b. 'An attempt to influence a selected part of the world so that the objective of the strategy is more easily achieved'.

It thus becomes immediately clear that an item of major importance precedes the production of a strategy and that is the statement of what I am trying to achieve - the objective.

1.2 Office

'a. The ROLE of the office is to acquire, analyse, create and disseminate data, for use both inside and outside the organisation.

b. The ACTIVITIES which take place in an office are generally executed in parallel. They are frequently subject to changed priorities and interruption.

c. The OBJECTIVES of a particular office are achieved by the interaction of several persons and equipment.

d. The NATURE OF WORK UNDERTAKEN in an office is related to the level of the participants in the organisation. This varies from routine to non-routine and the level from clerical to executive.

e. The DATA FLOWS through an office comprise many forms including voice, numeric and textual data as well as pictures.

f. DATA STORAGE is predominantly textual'.

It is, thus, clear that an office is a complex place in which simple answers will most probably have little or a negative effect.

1.3 Office Systems

'Systems Which Take Place In Offices'

The portmanteau phrase 'Office Automation' is used in a more rigorous way and refers exclusively to use of systems in which there are clearly defined inputs, processes and outputs in a way analogous to factory automation. It does not cover those systems in which there is a significant element of discretion.

2. Why Should We Have A Strategy?

Now that we have a common foundation we can progress towards a rational argument (though you will not be able to respond in an interactive fashion to my statements. This is but one of the limitations of paper!).

Office Systems are developing rapidly as manufacturers leap frog each other with the offerings they bring to the market place. The pace of change and its direction leave many with a feeling of helplessness:

How can they ally this technology to their needs?

Many, therefore, feel that some sort of framework in which to progress will benefit them. Others take an opposite view and change their direction with every new offering. The approach taken will be heavily influenced by the type of organisation, whether it is strongly centralised or a loose federation of companies with a common shareholding. It has been suggested that the effect of each course can be illustrated as in Fig. 1.

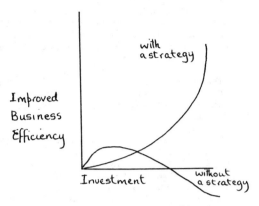

Fig 1. Investment Effectiveness

The first results from an organisation not having a strategy are likely to be substantially better than for one with a strategy. However, these benefits do not carry over to the remainder of the investment program. These results come from the following causes:-

a. Enthusiasm for the product results in immediate application and benefits.

b. Little or no carry over of ideas between functions.

c. Each new implementation requires a start at the bottom of the learning curve.

d. Little integration between implementations resulting in the same or, worse, similar data being entered in a number of discrete systems.

The 'with strategy' results come more slowly as it is necessary to get the strategy accepted, prove the results and generate enthusiasm. Thus when they do start to come they are cumulative and beneficially affect the organisation as a whole. The benefits can also be directed towards those areas which exert maximum effect on the company's performance.

Successful office systems are fundamental to the ultimate success of the organisation. It cannot, therefore, be left to the whims of individuals and the vicissitudes of the market, with the implications of continually restarting and throwing away learning. The creation of a strategy will have a significant effect on the success in harnessing the potential benefits of the technology.

The reasons for having an office systems strategy are :-

a. To get the most benefit from the office systems
b. Additional investment gives a cumulative benefit
c. To achieve the best integration of all systems
d. To prevent multiple starts at the bottom of the learning curve.
e. To concentrate the energies of individuals in the organisation on common goals
f. Can quickly get to the stage where there is a critical mass of users per system and systems per user.
g. Facts learnt can be quickly applied across the whole organisation.

3. What Type Of Strategy

If you are still reading you will have followed my arguments about why we need a strategy, but will still not know what objective I am going to propose.

There seem to be two basic types of strategy

  * A strategy expressed in terms of needs
  * A strategy expressed in technological terms

The former concentrates on the organisational individual needs, whereas the latter concentrates on how to do it.

It is my contention that a strategy in which everything is related to the needs of people will be successful and point clearly to the equipment which is required. It will also help to prevent progressing up blind alleys as the thing which ultimately influences the success of a product is its relevance. It also helps to avoid time spent on technological niceties and exotica.

A technological emphasis is likely to result in reams of paper devoted to keyboard layout, communications etc. instead of what they are to be used for and how they will benefit the organisation. It will, however, make it much easier to talk to manufacturers. Because of this it is a very good idea to express the strategy in terms of needs, but the plan, how you will implement it in terms of technology. Few people apart from paper manufacturers would be impressed with regurgitations of storage costs by type and mountains of other interesting, but irrelevant facts - facts which make no contribution to solving one office problem.

4. The Objective Of The Strategy

We now move on to examine what should be the objective of the strategy.

The objective is heavily dependent on four factors.

* The type of industry
* The profitability of the company
* The attitude of the company to technological change
* The geographical location and size of the offices

4.1 The Influence Of The Industry Type

All industry may be considered to operate as in Fig. 2.

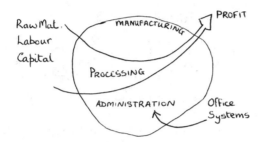

Fig 2 Industrial Operation

From the diagram (Fig 2) it can be clearly seen that the Administrative processes are heavily dependent on the processing activities. It comes as no surprise then to note that the objectives defined for office systems in a car manufacturer differ very significantly from an insurance company.

In the former case the source of much of the data is the operations which take place on the shop floor, whereas, in the latter there is no shop floor.

The result of an examination of a manufacturing industry is likely to be concerned with:

* Keeping stocks to a minimum
* Maintaining a positive cash flow
* Highlighting any unbalanced loading of facilities or under utilisation etc.

and these can be seen to be those traditionally associated with the administrative processes of any manufacturing company.

4.2 The Influence of Company Profitability

This really dictates how much room a company has for manoeuvre.

If a company is unprofitable it is almost inevitable that objectives will be geared towards reducing the cost of administrative services. In this case increased productivity equals less people. It is also likely that greater emphasis will be placed on computerising deterministic tasks so that measurable improvements can be made.

If a company is profitable it is likely that the emphasis will be placed on improved decision making and better communications.

The results will be evidenced by where money is spent. In the case of the unprofitable company it is highly likely that it will be spent on equipment in clerical and secretarial areas in an attempt to reduce easily identifiable costs, whereas in the profitable company it will be spent on equipment for professionals and managers.

The most effective way of spending money is to improve the effectiveness of managers and professionals. This group comprise 60-70% of the payroll costs of many companies and make decisions which intimately effect the performance of the company.

4.3 The Influence of the Attitude to Change

The past history of the company and its attitude to change will be the most significant factor in determining how successful office systems will be introduced.

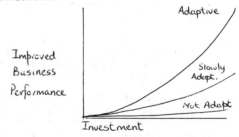

Fig 3 Influence of Attitude

If a company has not been used to change then the first objective must be to change that so that later investment will be productive. Otherwise, so much effort will be put in resisting that change that business performance will be adversely effected and the whole programme could be aborted.

4.4 Geographical Spread and Size of Offices

Whilst the predominant effect of these factors will be on the implementation of any strategy, they also contribute to the setting of objectives.

It may be that a prime objective of the systems is to coordinate and standardise the work of widely spread offices. Or, it may be that another objective is to use the technology to create more smaller offices that will be more responsive to the needs of the companies' customers.

4.5 My Own Case

By now the reader may wonder what is my own situation.

I have distilled the analysis of each of these factors to a statement in which both productivity and effectiveness are given equal status, but my own case is complicated by a further factor. This is

Who are you preparing a strategy for?

The two main options are:-

* A Systems department or
  company which is looking
        to implement these systems
* A user who is looking to his
  own organisation.

The main difference here is that in the first case the objectives will be more loosely or generally stated whereas in the second case they are likely to be quite specific. For example, I was looking at the first situation and I concluded that there were several subsidiary objectives, which include.

*To provide tools which
 enable better job performance
*To encourage integration of
 data types
*To increase communication
 efficiency
*To improve data accessibility
*To reduce data movement

All of which are generalised statements but capable of tailoring to specific customers requirements.

This enabled us to construct a strategy relationship diagram

In a client study this has resulted in us being able to:

* Identify the main objective to be
  achieved by the strategy
* Identify the way in which the
  problems need to be tackled
* Produce a plan over time, so that
  the expenditure curve is closely
  followed by the benefits.

The main objective could be:

'To improve by 10% the productivity of purchasing staff measured in terms of the value of processed orders whilst maintaining the increasing cost of goods purchased at half the rate of inflation recorded for that class of goods'.

The important thing is that the objective is quantified and can therefore be monitored.

· 5. The Requirements for Office Systems

In the construction of a strategy this is the big question, when the objectives have been produced. This is the justification for the construction of a strategy.

Dependent on your position and degree of cynicism this can range from

'To extend the scope of the DP department and increase the sales of vendors of office systems equipment

to

'To reconcile the conflict between the desire to decrease office costs (which are rising in most companies) and gather more data for government and the company'.

I think the requirements are

* To use data already captured more
  effectively within the company

* To control office costs by increasing
  productivity

* To enable data to be available
            * more quickly
            * more accurately
        * in a more usable form

* To free the organisation from the
  constraints imposed by the existing
  media used to hold data (which is
  predominantly paper). These
  constraints are often seen as

    - centralised bureaucracy due to
      problems of accessing papers

- slow data flow caused by the need to copy paper and send it by slow postal services
- difficulty in re-analysing data and presenting in more attractive graphical forms
- too much paper circulating, as it is not possible to create and up-date reference files for every potential user.

* To ensure that everyone who needs data has it in a form which is up-to-date and meaningful to the individual.

* To improve the communication of data between individuals in the organisation.

It was felt useful to apply a rider to all the above. This was, that any changes had to consider the ecology of the administrative organisation. If this is not done the whole functioning of this organisation could be adversely affected and only the adaptability of the humans involved could prevent it from total collapse.

6. The Requirements of Office Systems

These are in contradistinction to those 'for Office Systems'. This section is concerned with the identification of those factors which will significantly affect the likely success of any implemented system. They are, therefore, an important part in developing a strategy.

As office systems will be used by people who can refuse to change their work methods, they have to be designed in a way which ensures that they will want to use them.

They will need to have the following characteristics:

* High reliability
* Excellent human factors
* Easy to learn
* Easy to use
* Good fit into the existing and changed office system, both computerised and paper
* Capable of personalisation by the user
* High transparency to changed equipment.

These general statements will, of course, require additional detail for application to a user of the system, but they will provide a good basis for structuring a systems department's strategy for the implementation of office systems.

This section is best summed up by Amy Wohl of Integrated Technologies.

'Systems that replicate familiar, comfortable, human activities are at an immediate advantage'.

7. Basic Assumptions

Now that we have worked out where we are going to go and the reason for going, as well as considering some of the things we will need along the way, we now need to sit down and think about the route. Here, many assumptions and forecasts will have to be made otherwise we will never get started or stand little chance of getting to our destination.

These assumptions fall into three areas

* Technology projections
* People assumptions
* Cost projections

7.1 Technology Projections

The ones I used are shown below. They are generally given without comment.

* The vendor produced distinction between office systems and DP systems will disappear in mid to late 80s.

* Office Systems will develop from text based systems and move towards DP systems and vice versa.

* Hardware will be increasingly reliable.

* Costs for good quality software will comprise an increasingly large share of system costs.

* Software production will still remain expensive and long winded.

* Software package use will increase in the mid 80s.

* Analysis techniques will only slowly evolve over the 80s or 90s.

* The user interface will improve in the mid 80s.

* Communication costs will rise dramatically in the early 80s.

* Capture of existing data (or paper) will provide a major stumbling block for most of the 80s.

* Cost effective distributed databases will be difficult to implement until the mid to late 80s.

* Equipment design and cost/performance will be subject to revolutionary change with leapfrogging vendors. The market is unlikely to settle until the mid 80s.

* Standards will only slowly be defined and accepted.

These give the broad outlines of technology development.

7.2 People Assumptions

The magic ingredient; without them office systems will not work.

* There are no inherent objections to the use of computer equipment - it is just that a lot of it is either not worth using or unusable!

* Few people will be prepared to do programming - they do not have the time.

* The opposition to the installation of computerised equipment comes because of its effect on the organisational power balance.

* There will be a gradual move towards more structured work patterns.

* Take up of office systems will be patchy.

* Many redundant data paths will be maintained by office workers.

The easiest company in which to install systems will be those which are growing. They will be able to realise the benefits without affecting the employment prospects of the staff. Insensitive handling of staff affected by technology will be a major cause of resistance to change and the introduction of office systems.

7.3 Cost Forecasts

These are important in indicating the likely success in implementing systems.

* The historic low investment in office areas will cause high investment office systems to be resisted.

* The investment in training people in paper based systems will have to be written off.

* The equipment cost per employee will increase over the next ten years.

* Calculation of benefits will become clearer over the next ten years.

8. Creation of the Strategy

The picture painted above is of a rapidly developing technology which could be applied with disasterous consequences. Any strategy to be successful will, therefore, need to be evolutionary and have an in-built learning mechanism.

The key points I feel it is essential to include are:

* Progress from today's base in an evolutionary manner.

* Identify who is going to do the changing.

* Identify where it is going to be easiest to implement office systems.

* Identify where it is going to achieve greatest success.

* Identify those areas which are critical to the success of the company.

* Produce an implementation plan for the identified areas and state how this will be spread to other areas.

* Plan to use technology widely when it is at its most cost effective, not when it is first introduced.

* Take the danger out of leap frogging technology by running small pilots on new products in an area where they can be stopped.

* Encourage the organisation to learn from its experience and continually reflect on the ecological framework within which work is being done.

The strategy may be stated as:

'Pick the areas which are most likely to be succesful and impact the success of the company and apply office systems here in an evolutionary manner and CAREFULLY".

9. Summary

It only remains to say thank you for reading this far and I wish you the best of luck in working towards a strategy for your organisation.

I have included below some books you might find interesting.

W O Gallitz., Human Factors in Office Automation (Loma).

Various., IBM Systems Journal (IBM).

Uhlig, Farber & Bair., The Office of the Future (North Holland, Amsterdam, 1980).

Naffah., Integrated Office Systems (North Holland, Amsterdam).

National Bureau of Standards Computer Based Message Systems Standards Efforts: a Status Report

S W Watkins
National Bureau of Standards, USA

The Institute for Computer Sciences and Technology (ICST) at the National Bureau of Standards (NBS) is developing standards and guidelines for Computer Based Message Systems (CBMS) as part of its Computer Based Office Systems program. A CBMS allows communication among entities using computers. The computer's role in this messaging process is threefold: assistance to the user for message creation, assistance to the user for message reading and storage, and mediation of the actual communications.

This paper provides an overview of the ICST program for CBMS standards, discusses the technical specifications of the first proposed standard out of this program which is for message format for CBMS, and introduces ICST work on a message transfer protocol.

Introduction

The Institute for Computer Sciences and Technology at the National Bureau of Standards has a program aimed at providing interconnection of different manufacturer's equipment through network protocol, local networking and computer based office systems standards [1]. The computer network protocols program develops high-level network protocols to enable the effective exchange of information among computers as well as between terminals and computers. The local area networking program produces standards and guidelines for the selection of local area data networks, for the connection of devices to local area networks, and for the interconnection of local area networks to national and international global networks. The computer based office systems program develops standards and guidelines to enable the effective transfer of documents among systems through electronic and media interchange of information; this paper will describe the initial products from this program.

The term "computer based office systems" refers to computer based techniques applied to the information processing requirements of office workers to help them do their jobs more efficiently and effectively. For the purposes of the ICST program the term "office workers" refers not only to administrative and clerical personnel but also to managerial and technical staff. In fact, it has become evident that the major area of productivity gains for the office worker is related to managerial and technical staff (sometimes, referred to as knowledge workers) where the majority of organizational dollars are required to pay salaries and benefits [2]. History shows us that the original office automation equipment was developed for administrative staff and was synonymous with word processors. However, true office automation encompasses communication processors, utility processors, advanced peripheral devices, local networks, and user processors. One well publicized pilot study conducted by Bell Northern Software Research, Incorporated, in Canada found that a major

problem in office automation is the lack of standard communication protocols for terminals, communicating word processors, microcomputers, or small business systems [3].

The scope of the ICST Computer Based Office Systems (CBOS) program recognizes this broader view of office automation, and in fact, due to the recognition that communication is such a major problem in office systems, the ICST CBOS program has prioritized its products for computer based message systems (CBMS). A CBMS allows communication among entities using computers. The computer's role in this messaging process is threefold: assistance to the user for message creation, assistance to the user for message reading and storage, and mediation of the actual communications between systems.

ICST participates in international and national activities to identify and develop standards required to ensure information interchange among heterogeneous CBMSs. Since 1979, the International Federation of Information Processing (IFIP) Wg 6.5 has been discussing services to be provided by a CBMS; a major accomplishment of this group was the development of a model for messaging. This pioneer work has provided the foundation for the more recent work by the International Telephone and Telegraph Consultative Committee (CCITT). CCITT is investigating CBMS standards within Question 5 (Message Handling Facilities) of Study Group VII. Over the last year both the American National Standards Institute (ANSI) under X3V1 and the International Organization for Standardization (ISO) have begun work on CBMS standards.

Based on its work with these groups, ICST has identified several standards required for the full utilization of CBMSs including message format, message protocol, message presentation, control codes embedded in text, and the user interface. The first proposed standard from the ICST program is message format; the second is a message protocol. The remainder of this paper describes the technical specification for message format which is part of a proposed Federal Information Processing Standard, and introduces the initial findings from the development of a message protocol. In its efforts, ICST is using the logical model of a CBMS developed by IFIP Working Group 6.5 which is essentially identical to one being used by CCITT Study Group VII, Question 5 [4].

CBMS MODEL

The CBMS model consists of a message transfer system (MTS) and a number of User Agents (UA). In this model a message flows from an originator's UA into the MTS to the recipient's UA. (See Figure 1.)

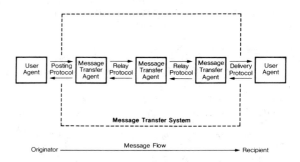

Figure 1 Logical Model of A Computer Based Message System

A UA is a functional entity that acts on behalf of a user, assisting with creating and processing messages and communicating with the MTS. The MTS which may be composed of one or more Message Transfer Agents (MTA) accepts a message from its originator's UA and ultimately passes it to each of its recipients' UAs. Transferring a message from an originator's UA to the MTS is called Posting; transferring a message from the MTS to a recipient's UA is called Delivery. The point at which responsibility for a message is transferred is called a Slot; therefore, there are Posting and Delivery slots associated with these responsibility transfers.

The model divides a message into the message content and the message envelope. The message content is the information that the originator wishes to send to the recipient; the ICST message format specification deals solely with the message content. The message envelope consists of all the information necessary for the MTS to do its job; the ICST message format specification does not specify the message envelope. Some of the data appearing on the message envelope could be redundant with some data found in the message content. The MTS is not expected to examine the message content unless it is explicitly told to do so by the originator's or recipient's UA.

MESSAGE FORMAT

The ICST message format specification addresses the form and meaning of messages at the points in time when they are sent from one

CBMS and received by another [5]. Thus, the contents of a message posted by one CBMS can be received and interpreted by a different CBMS. Messages are composed of fields, containing different classes of information. These fields contain information about the message originator, message recipient, subject matter, precedence, and references to previous messages, as well as the text of the message. Standard structures (syntax) for messages ensure that the contents of messages generated by one CBMS can be processed by another CBMS. Standard meanings (semantics) for the components of a message facilitate standard interpretation of a message, so that everyone receiving a message is able to understand the meaning intended by the originator.

Originators and recipients can be people, roles, or processes. People as originators and recipients are specific individuals. Roles identify functions within organizations as opposed to the specific individuals who perform them. Finally, a process in a computer can serve as either an orginator or recipient.

When the message format specification refers to the identity of a message originator or recipient, it means "that information which uniquely identifies the message originator or recipient within the domain of the given message system". While the syntax and semantics of message addressing are not within the scope of the message format specification, ICST is currently designing a naming and addressing specification which will be ready for initial distribution in 1982.

The ICST message format specification places no restrictions on the MTS itself, except that it reliably transfer the contents of messages. In addition, the message format specification does not dictate the form or nature of any protocol used by the MTS. Finally, the message format specification does not specify the content or form of the message envelope. That is, the message format specification defines the format for the contents of messages, not the manner in which they are transmitted.

Semantics

There are seven categories of message fields: originator, date, recipient, cross-reference, message-handling, message-content and extension. There are three compliance categories: required, basic and optional. Required fields must be present in all messages and must be processed by message receiving programs as defined by the ICST specification; there are three required fields. Basic fields need not be present in all messages, but when they do appear they must be processed by message receiving programs as defined by the ICST specification; there are four basic fields. Optional fields need not be present in all messages and may be ignored by message receiving programs; there are seventy-two optional fields.

Originator fields identify a message's author(s), who is responsible for the message, who or what sent it, and where replies should be directed; these four pieces of information may all refer to the same entity or to distinct entities. There is one required field (From), one basic field (Reply-To) and two optional fields (Author, Sender). The From field contains the identity of the originator(s) taking formal responsiblity for the message. The contents of the From field are to be used for replies when no Reply-To field appears in a message. The Reply-To field identifies any recipients of replies to the message.

Date fields are provided for two types of usage. Dates can be associated with some event in the history of a message, and dates can delimit the span of time during which the message is meaningful. There is one required field (Posted-Date), no basic fields, and five optional fields (Date, End-Date, Received-Date, Start-Date, Warning-Date). The Posted-Date field contains the time at which a message passes through the posting slot into the MTS.

Cross reference fields can be used to identify a message and to provide cross references to other messages. There are no required or basic fields in this category. There are five optional fields (In-Reply-To, Message-ID, Obsoletes, Originator-Serial-Number, References.)

Message-handling fields describe aspects of how a message is to be handled or categorized. There are no required or basic fields in this category, and four optional fields (Precedence, Message-Class, Reissue-Type, Received-From).

Message-Content fields contain the particular information which the originator wished to communicate to the recipient. There are no required fields in this category, two basic fields (Subject, Text), and three optional fields (Attachments, Comments, Keywords). The Subject field contains any information the originator provided to summarize or indicate the nature of the message. The Text field contains the primary content of the message.

Extension fields include both vendor-defined and as-yet-undefined (extension) fields which represent extension to the ICST specification. By their nature, both of these fields are optional.

Syntax

Fields in a message are composed of syntactic elements called data elements. Each field defined by the ICST specification is assigned a unique message identifier, there are no required field names or labels which must be used by a CBMS in presenting a message to a user. Message presentation is outside the scope of this specification but will be addressed by ICST in 1983.

There are two types of data elements; primitive and constructor. Primitive data elements are basic building blocks, and contructor data elements contain one or more primitive or constructor data elements. Some constructors may be composed of any other data

elements, while others are restricted to only certain data elements.

There are two compliance categories for data elements: basic and optional. The meaning of these categories is the same as for fields. There are five basic data elements (ASCII-String, Date, End-of-Constructor, Field, Message) and fourteen optional (Bit-String, Boolean, Compressed, Encrypted, Extension, Integer, No-Op, Padding, Property, Property-List, Sequence, Set, Unique-Id, Vendor-Defined). This paper will discuss the basic data elements; the reader is referred to the ICST Specification [4] for discussion of the optional data elements.

Data elements consist of a series of components; a component contains 8-bit groups called octets. The ICST specification uses a right to left (low to high) order numbering scheme. The low order (least significant) bit is labelled "bit 0" and the high order (most significant) bit is labelled "bit 7".

There are five data element components: identifier octet, length code, qualifier, property-list, and data element contents. While not all components are present in every data element, the components which are present must appear in the order given.

The identifier octet is a numeric code which identifies the data element; it is always the first component. This octet contains a one-bit flag (bit 7) to indicate the presence of a property list and a one-bit flag (bit 6) to indicate the presence of a qualifier.

The length code indicates the number of octets following it in a data element and is formatted as either short, long, or indefinite. A short length code is one octet long. A long length code is at least two octets long. An indefinite length code is one octet long and may appear only as part of a constructor data element. A constructor data element with an indefinite length code is terminated by an End-of-Constructor data element.

The qualifier component is used to provide information essential to the interpretation of the data element contents that is beyond that encoded in the identifier octet or length code. For example, in the Bit-String data element, it indicates the number of unused bits in the final octet of the contents.

The length code and qualifier are both normally one octet in length; however, there exists an encoding scheme which permits extending the component to the size necessary to present the required length or value of the qualifier. The most significant bit of the length code and qualifier components determines the length; if this bit is zero, the component is one octet in length; if it is one, the remaining seven bits encode the number of octets in the rest of the component. The actual value begins in the next octet and is interpreted as an unsigned integer.

A property list component contains property data elements. This component allows an attribute(s) to be associated with a data element.

Recipient fields identify who or what is to receive a message. There is one required field (To), one basic field (Cc), and three optional fields (Bcc, Circulate-Next, Circulate-To). The To field identifies the primary recipients of a message and the Cc field identifies the secondary recipients (a "carbon copies" list).

There are two primitive data elements classified as basic: ASCII-String and End-of-Constructor. ASCII-String contains a series of ASCII characters, each character right-justified in one octet. End-of-Constructor terminates the "data element contents" in a constructor data elements of indefinite length.

There are three constructor data elements classified as basic: Date, Field and Message. Date contains an ASCII-String data element which is a representation of date and time. Field uses a qualifier data element to indicate the specific field being represented. Message contains a field or message data element; the qualifier component indicates the message type.

Message Construction

The type of a field in a message determines both its meaning and the form for its contents. Using the required and basic fields, this section presents the meaning and form for those fields. The reader is reminded that the ICST specification does not indicate the forms of originator or recipient identifiers, these must be agreed upon by sending and receiving CBMSs in advance.

The minimal message which can be constructed contains From, To, and Posted-Date fields. Additional information may be added to messages with the use of the Basic and Optional fields. Figure 2 provides an example of the encoding of a field containing "Watkins" and a Posted-Date field with the value of 11:00 A.M., April 9, 1982.

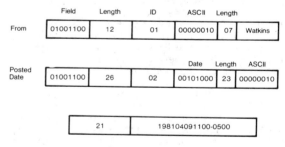

Figure 2. Sample Encoding

MESSAGE PROTOCOL

ICST has begun development of a message protocol which draws upon the current efforts in IFIP Wg 6.5 and CCITT Study Group VII, Question 5. Prior to the development of the design specification, a feature analysis of a message protocol and a service specification

were circulated for comment; an implementation of the protocol will follow. In parallel with this effort is the development of a naming and addressing design. This paper will overview the initial findings of the feature analysis; the information contained herein reflects the December, 1981, version of ICST Report CBOS-81-5, Features of a Message Transfer Protocol [6].

Message transfer protocols govern how a message is moved from the originator's CBMS to the recipient's CBMS. Message transfer protocols exist above the session layer of the ISO reference model for Open Systems Interconnection [7]. At the current time no presentation layer features have been identified; therefore, the protocol is strictly an application layer protocol. The application layer is subdivided into three sublayers: the user agent sublayer (UASL), the message transfer sublayer (MTSL) and the reliable transfer sublayer (RTSL). The UASL is concerned with the processing that UAs perform on message contents. The MTSL is concerned with moving the message from the originator's UA to the destination UA(s). The RTSL is a thin sublayer which deals strictly with checkpointing and recovery from errors not detected by lower layers of the model.

The next two sections discuss the service features and the protocol features of a message transfer protocol. Features are categorized as either kernel or value-added. The kernel is that part of a protocol that is required in every implementation. As such, it is sufficient and complete; and provides all of the essential services. Value-added portions of a protocol are optional to implement. Value-added features are enhancements; however, if implemented they must operate as defined by the protocol. This paper will only discuss details of the kernel features; value-added are described in the ICST feature analysis [6].

Service Features

The service features of a message protocol are the features which are provided to the users of the message transfer protocol. There are nine message protocol services: message posting, message delivery, delivery cancellation, message trace, subscriber directory, interworking, permanent storage, message history, and message transfer system status information.

Posting is the transfer of responsibility for a message from an originator's UA to an MTA. The UA gives the MTA a copy of the message content and instructions about what to do with it including the destination(s), handling for the message en route, and delivery options (that is nondelivery notification and return receipt). As part of posting, the MTA verifies that the instructions are feasible. When the MTA accepts responsibility for the message, it gives the UA an acknowledgement and may give the UA some identifying information that the UA can use in future references to this transaction. The kernel posting features are: an originating UA requests message delivery to a single receiving UA, and upon delivery failure the originating UA is notified.

Delivery is the transfer of responsibility for a message from an MTA to a recipient's UA. The MTA gives the UA a copy of the message content; it also gives the UA all or part of the message envelope. There are a number of options associated with this service; however, the kernel for message delivery includes: an MTA transfers message content to a receiving UA; initiation of the service is by the MTA.

Delivery cancellation is a service which can be requested by the UA that has posted a particular message. The service aborts delivery of the message to its recipient's UA. There is no delivery cancellation in the kernel due to the logistics of attempting to "catch" a message and the associated costs.

Message trace is a service which locates a message in the MTS. It may be used to find the location of a message which has been posted but has not been delivered. Message trace may also be used by the providers of the MTS for diagnostic purposes. There is no message trace in the kernel because it is not necessary for operation of the MTS and because no known systems support this feature.

Subscriber directory services help identify and locate CBMS users. Message originators and recipients may be idenfified by name or by address. The name does not necessarily indicate where a message should be sent; "where" is determined by the address which is obtained by looking up the name in a directory. The kernel includes a directory (either on-line or on a physical medium, as paper) listing all registered subscribers.

Interworking services are transformation services relative to message content format and the media in the message content which provide compatibility between UAs. Message content format reflects the capability of a message transfer system to support types of messaging other than CBMS, such as Teletex. The media concern results from the variety of data types that may be found in a CBMS message, such as text and facsimile. The kernel includes: a receiving UA can reject the delivery of a message expressed in a format or containing data it cannot handle.

Permanent storage is a service used to provide backup or archival storage beyond the usual storage facilities that are offered by a recipient's UA. There is no permanent storage in the kernel because it is not necessary in a message transfer protocol in general.

Message history is a record of what has happened to a message while in the message transfer system; this service is used to determine message authenticity and integrity. It also serves as a basis for customer billing and account settlement among administrations that provide the MTS. The kernel includes: MTS maintains a record of each operation on a message in the MTS; the record identifies the operation, the entity that performed it, and when it took place; at delivery, a receiving UA can determine where a message originated; timestamps for these events are included.

MTS status information contains details on MTS operation. UAs query the MTS for this information; in emergencies, the MTS can initiate this service in order to send alarms to UAs concerning resource shortages or MTS failures. This feature is not in the kernel because only rarely do CBMSs support it.

Protocol Features

Protocol features are features that the message transfer protocol must provide for its own use. There are ten such features; negotiation mechanism, error recovery, timestamping, unique identifiers, MTS addressing, message routing, message buffering and storage, accounting, acknowledgements and security.

A negotiation mechanism is used by message transfer protocol participants when there is no prior agreement on which features will be used and how. The use of parameters to the protocol and the use of features not in the protocol kernel are two items which must be agreed upon. The kernel includes: simple true/false negotiations.

High-level error recovery features are required for the orderly recovery from errors not normally detected by lower level protocols, such as file system and operating system errors. Checkpointing is a common method to accomplish such error recovery; since checkpointing is not provided by the session layer, it must be accomplished by the message transfer protocol. The kernel includes: checkpoint and restart features.

A timestamp indicates when a given operation or transaction takes place. The MTS provides timestamps at posting, relay, and delivery and whenever an interworking service is performed. The kernel includes: universal date and time used for marking events in the MTS; resolution and accuracy fall within some defined range.

Unique identifiers provide a means of referring to messages in an unambiguous manner. Both UAs and MTAs need to use unique identifiers. The kernel includes: MTAs must be able to generate identifiers which are unique in their domain.

An MTS address is used to identify where messages should be routed for delivery. This address specifies a location relative to the MTS. The kernel includes: the address of an

MTA is the concatenation of a network-wide host identifier with a locally allocated identifier; the address of a UA or of an entity other than an MTA is the concatenation of an MTA address with an additional identifier known to that MTA.

Given an initial location and the address of a CBMS entity, the MTS must be able to determine a route joining those two points. A route is a series of MTAs through which a message passes in reaching the destination UA. The kernel includes: an MTA determines the next step in the route a message must take to cross the MTS and be delivered to its recipient's UA.

Each MTA must be able to buffer the messages in its possession. Typically, a message resides in an MTA for seconds or minutes, however, for timed delivery, longer periods of storage may be necessary. In the kernel, the MTS buffers messages reliably while they are in transit between UAs.

The MTS performs accounting functions in order to enable customer billing and settlement between different CBMS administrations. In the kernel, the MTS makes information available about its uses for accounting purposes.

Acknowledgements are required to indicate success or failure for various operations. There are two kinds of MTS acknowledgement: between two MTAs within an MTS and between a UA and an entity in the MTS. In the kernel, MTAs must be able to generate positive and negative acknowledgements to MTS transaction.

The MTS must be able to positively identify UAs to protect against unauthorized use of services. Security issues include passwords, permanent connections, information segregation, and message routes through secure MTAs. In the kernel: messages can be delivered to the UA only at the address specified on the message envelope.

SUMMARY

This paper has presented an overview of the Computer Based Office Systems Program of the Institute for Computer Sciences and Technology at the National Bureau of Standards and two of the products from this program. In order to ensure information interchange among heterogeneous office systems, a number of different types of standards are required. Protocols for the physical, link, network, transport and session layers for local area and global networks are required. Protocols for the presentation and application layers are required for specific applications. Standard codes must be supported so that information exchanged is understood.

ICST has been cooperating both nationally and internationally in the design of its standards program and in the development of individual standards. Computer Based Message Systems have been identified as a high priority for standardization; the Computer Based Office Systems Program has finalized the technical specifications for message format for Computer Based Message Systems and has begun development

of a message protocol. This paper described the message format specification and gave an overview of the initial version of the feature analysis for the message protocol. The feature analysis is the first step in the development of a message transfer protocol; it will be followed by a service specification, a design specification and an implementation.

REFERENCES

[1]   Blanc, R., J. Heafner, R. Rosenthal, and S. Watkins, The ICST Computer Networking Program, ICSTIR, 80-2154, p 16.

[2]   Rhodes, Wayne L., Jr., "How to Boost Your Office Productivity," InfoSystems, August, 1980, pp. 38-40, 42.

[3]   Bleackley, Beverley, "Tying It All Together," Datamation International, September, 1980, p. 218-20..

[4]   CCITT Study Group VII/5. Message Handling Systems: Interrelationships and Control Procedures Draft Recommendation X.___, Version 2, CCITT, November, 1981.

[5]   National Bureau of Standards, Specification for Message Format for Computer Based Message Systems, September, 1981.

[6]   Institute for Computer Sciences and Technology, CBOS 81-5, Features of a Message Transfer Protocol, Draft Report, November, 1981.

[7]   Information Processing Systems -Open Systems Interconnection -Basic Reference Model, International Organization for Standardization; Draft Proposal, ISO/DP 7498. (ISO/TC97/SC16 N 890) February 4, 1982.

BIOGRAPHY

Shirley Ward Watkins manages the Computer Based Office Systems program of the Institute for Computer Sciences and Technology at the National Bureau of Standards. She is responsible for the identification and development of Federal Information Processing Standards to ensure information interchange among automated offices; a key component of this program relates to Computer Based Message Systems. Mrs. Watkins' responsibilities also include management of in-house developmental projects for computer based office systems applications. Prior to assuming her management role in office systems, Mrs. Watkins worked in the areas of network measurement, and automating network user assistance, for which she received the Department of Commerce Silver Medal.

Mrs. Watkins joined the National Bureau of Standards in 1968 after obtaining her B.A. in Mathematics from Hood College. Mrs. Watkins performed her graduate work in Computer Science at the American University.

iNet: the Intelligent Network

R Begbie
TransCanada Telephone System, Canada

I M Cunningham, H Williamson
Bell-Northern Research, Canada

This paper describes research and development work on a new set of value added network services. This work is being done by Bell-Northern Research (BNR) and the Computer Communications Group (CCG) of the TransCanada Telephone System. iNet*, the Intelligent Network, offers a set of user functions which include directories, information access, messaging and filing. The paper describes these features and outlines the system architecture and administrative issues. The service is being implemented as a network based set of value added services with a limited service set currently undergoing user trials.

1. INTRODUCTION

The Computer Communications Group of the TransCanada Telephone System with the support of Bell-Northern Research has been investigating the implementation of network based value added services.

It is postulated that enormous advances in computer technology will stimulate an Information revolution, which may have an effect on this century's society as profound as the Industrial revolution. In the same way as the transportation system was vital to the distribution of goods during the Industrial revolution, the communication network will transport information from databases to users in the Information revolution. [1]

In Canada, the network has been the catalyst in connecting the information and computational service providers with their geographically distributed users. The introduction of digital time-division multiplexing technology (Dataroute (TM) 1973) and packet switched technology (Datapac (TM) 1977) and digital data on the digital voice network (Datalink (TM) 1982) have aided in reducing the distance barriers inherent in Canadian geography.

The next logical step in this evolution is to add additional features to the network in order to stimulate greater network usage by lowering barriers to information services. This has resulted in the decision to explore a new service called the intelligent network - iNet*.

Market research indicates that obstacles currently perceived by users are:

- Difficulties in rapidly identifying resources and services available to assist in performing a job function.

----

* iNet - Trademark Pending

- The need to remember network connection commands, and logon procedures to access the desired services.

- Difficulties in remembering the dialogue required for interaction with each service.

- Lack of the means to deal effectively with information obtained, e.g. store, retrieve and reformat for further use.

- Barriers in communicating information to others.

The lowering of these barriers will allow users to more easily access a growing set of network connected services. A result predicted by market research is that many potential users, for example middle managers who today do not use terminals, will consider their use.

Section 2 of this paper describes a set of functions designed to address these user problems. The architecture of the service is described in section 3. Finally, section 4 provides a summary of current status and trials.

2. iNET USER FUNCTIONS

2.1 User Community

iNet provides capability to its users who wish to access services, and information service providers who wish to offer them to a broad user community. Within this general population, it is expected that common interest groups of information service providers and users will form to create specific applications aimed at, or even restricted to, a particular subset of users.

Four main classes of users have been considered in feature and user interface design [2]: the information specialist, who is conversant with multiple information services, the information "go-for" who assists his colleagues in acquiring information, the direct regular and the direct casual user who use iNet to meet their ongoing job requirements.

2.2 User Environment

The user community is structured into "organizations", where an organization is an administrative grouping for subscription to the service, for example members of a business corporation. An organization consists of individual "users". The organization can assume a degree of self-administration, by assigning one of its users to be an "organization co-ordinator". This person creates and maintains an organizational environment of shared information, and controls use of iNet by members of his organization. Each individual user may also maintain a personal environment which he can tailor to meet his individual needs.

The user's environment has been defined using a desktop analogy (see Figure 1). This electronic desktop provides a consistent environment from which the user can interact with a variety of information services.

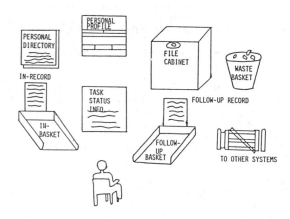

FIGURE 1 - User's Personal iNet Environment

Those elements that exist in the user's environment depend on what his organization has initially defined. How he uses those elements depends on how he tailors the environment to suit his own preferences.

The user can have a set of indexed file folders, containing documents of various types, such as messages, or text reports obtained from an information service. Associated with this filing space is an electronic wastebasket.

The user can create a personal directory using his own mnemonics for people with whom he communicates, and information services that he accesses frequently. He has an in-basket to which the system delivers incoming electronic mail, and a follow-up basket in which he places outgoing mail whose status he wishes to monitor. He can tailor this environment by

setting a profile of options.

In addition to use of his personal environment, the user has shared access to an organizational environment, which contains organizational files, bulletin boards and an organizational directory.

iNet provides the user with a gateway from his personal environment to different information services, each with its own user interface. This paper describes some approaches that alleviate this transition for the user and assist him in interacting with each service in its own dialogue. However, the functionality is designed to allow the user to continue to work with his own environment, rather than having to keep track of multiple electronic desktops, each with its own set of procedures.

2.3 Directories

iNet directories, like existing paper directories, provide a capability to keep up-to-date records of people and services. Unlike existing directories, the services listed can either be provided by people, or by computer systems on the network.

There are three types of iNet directories: the Gateway directory, Organizational directories and Personal directories.

The Gateway directory supports casual use, allowing users to obtain information on people, organizations and services. The Gateway directory contains a generalized electronic version of white and yellow pages in the telephone directory. However, a more extensive set of standard fields is provided including electronic mail addresses.

Listings may be scanned in different orders including alphabetic. Boolean search on keywords from a controlled vocabulary is backed up by a general thesaurus. Listings may be displayed at different levels of detail, the most detailed being equivalent to the yellow pages advertisement, with full descriptive information on a service in mixed text and (videotex) graphics. This may include tutorial information to give the user an understanding in advance of how to interact with a service new to him.

The Organization directory is analogous to a company's internal telephone directory. This lists members of the iNet organization and the services that they access on a regular basis. It essentially defines the organization's application in iNet. It is administered by the organization co-ordinator if he chooses to use this capability. Search is again by scan and keyword combinations.

A Personal directory, on the other hand, is more like a notebook in which the user jots down his own mnemonics for people and services. He can scan it in order of entry or alphabetic order. The user can also invoke a cross-reference to a directory with more detailed information, that is from a Personal directory entry to an associated Organizational directory listing.

2.4 Access

The user obtains information on people and services in his iNet directories. Using this information he can communicate with people via text messaging or conventional means. He can also gain access to services provided by computer systems (hosts) on the network. iNet supports an automatic access facility to services via a single user command. This provides the link between user and information service provider.

This function is achieved by creation of an "access procedure" for each service. The access procedure defines a dialogue which iNet carries out with the host and service on the user's behalf. A general access procedure simply creates a connection to the host, invokes a service on that host, and then hands over control to the user for interaction. In addition to the connection, a specific access procedure may also invoke a particular function for the user, for example displaying a page of information to him. Specific access procedures, while restrictive, have the advantage of shielding the user from differences in dialogue between services.

Information service providers may restrict access to their services; for example to users in a particular common interest group.

2.5 User Activities and Information Transfer

The user can interact with his personal environment and also access a wide variety of information services, within any interactive session with iNet. That is, he can perform a variety of activities to satisfy a goal. As in his existing office environment, a user can deal with multiple activities, in sequence or in parallel. A activity can be interrupted and resumed later, or it can be finished.

At any one time in a user's session, he has one current activity presented on his screen but may have others which are either active or inactive. He can review status of activities at any time, and may also be alerted by the system of a change in status.

To facilitate use of information services to perform activities, the user can transfer information between his personal environment and a service to which he has gained access. He can transfer information into his environment by recording selectively or automatically his dialogue with a service. He can transfer information out of his environment by specifying a file or parts thereof to be sent to the service. In the case of automatic transfer of a volume of information to or from a service, the user can continue with another parallel activity.

The capability to deal with multiple activities and to transfer information between the user environment and information services,

allows a user to deal with information effectively and according to his own preferences, to work in a sequential or parallel fashion.

2.6 Messaging

The above describes facilities to locate, access and deal with information. iNet messaging gives the user a means to communicate information, by extending the capabilities of CCG's existing message service, ENVOY 100 (TM) [6], to iNet users. The user's in-basket and mail functions are integrated with his personal environment in iNet, in order to avoid multiple electronic desktops.

iNet messaging assists the user in preparation and sending of messages and in dealing with incoming mail. The user starts by filling in a form, either in the standard memo format, or in a special format defined by his organization, for example a purchase order.

The form can be filled by copying from a document in a file folder, and also by information transfer from another service. The user can review and edit before sending the final version. Some fields express the intent of the message to a recipient, e.g. "urgent", "private" or "please acknowledge".

iNet provides a number of supporting features including a "follow-up" folder for outstanding messages and a means of relating replies back to previous correspondence [3].

The integration of messaging into the user's environment simplifies transfer of information between iNet functions and provides a unified interface for the user.

2.7 Personalization

Personalization features are provided to allow tailoring of iNet to meet the needs of individual users and of the organizations to which they belong. This is the key to support of a variety of user classes, and of the individuals within those classes, interacting on different terminals.

There are two general sorts of personalization: personalization of a user environment, e.g. amount of file space or use of messaging; and personalization of interaction, e.g. French/English dialogue. Personalization is achieved by such mechanisms as a user profile of options, templates, distribution lists and Personal directories.

Thus iNet provides the user with a personalized environment, access, information transfer and messaging functions backed up by directories, and means of using these functions effectively in sequence or in parallel.

3. iNet ARCHITECTURE

This section identifies the major iNet systems
and their respective functionality. In
addition, the administrative structure is
outlined and the data communications
architecture and protocol strategy described.

The need for a range of security features in
iNet has been recognized from the beginning.
The types of mechanisms provided include
multiple and redundant processors, duplicated
storage media, system level controls,
exception monitoring and the ability for
organizational co-ordinators to enforce
adherence to security policies and procedures
by their members.

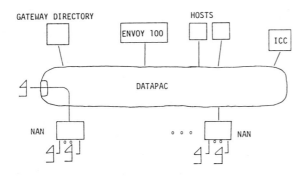

NAN   Network Access Node
ICC   iNet Control Centre

FIGURE 2 - iNet System Configuration

3.1 iNet Systems and Associated Functions

The major iNet systems and communciations
networks are shown in Figure 2.

3.1.1 Network Access Nodes

Network Access Nodes (or NANs) are the systems
that provide the individual user environments
described in the previous section. The exact
functionality in a particular user environment
is determined at subscription time. The needs
of a large base of users are met through the
deployment of multiple NANs with users being
served by their "home" NAN.

NANs will normally be accessed through the
switched telephone network but a user who is
distant from his home NAN can also access his
individual environment via Datapac.

3.1.2 Gateway Directory

The Gateway Directory is a separate system
providing an electronic directory of people
and services, and is available across Canada.
Initially, only one Gateway Directory will be
required to serve all iNet NANs.

Both iNet subscribers and general Datapac
users are permitted to browse through the
Gateway Directory to identify services and
electronic mail addresses. iNet subscribers,
however, can also request automated access to
a service.

3.1.3 Electronic Mail/Messaging

The iNet messaging architecture follows the
guidelines developed in recent CCITT work
aimed at developing communication protocols
for sophisticated store and forward message
services [4,5]. Two key functional objects
defined in the CCITT work are the User Agent
(UA) and Message Transfer Agent (MTA). The UA
provides an environment for composing,
storing, retrieving and editing messages.
Normally each recipient (i.e. subscriber) has
his own UA tailored to his needs. The MTA
provides the store and forward services and
interacts with a set of UA's via a
submission/delivery protocol.

In iNet, NANs provide User Agent functions
integrated with the user environment. When a
message is completed and ready to be sent, the
User Agent in the NAN initiates a dialogue
with ENVOY 100 which contains the MTA
function. ENVOY 100, which is a separate
system, provides Canada-wide distribution and
eventually interconnection to similar message
systems in other countries.

The use of the Gateway Directory for recipient
address validation permits both ENVOY 100 and
iNet users to perceive a single messaging
community.

3.1.4 Service Hosts and Information Service Providers

iNet supports the notion of Information
Service Providers (who develop information for
sale) and Hosts (systems which sell computing
and storage facilities). For example, a user
can access information by using a service name
and not be aware of the address/name of the
serving Host which may support many different
Information Service Providers. These can
include any organization that wishes to
provide (alphanumeric or videotex) services
via the network.

Lowering barriers to information access,
particularly for the casual user, is a basic
iNet objective. One of the significant
barriers mentioned in the introduction is the
difference in user-system dialogue between
services. Although descriptive and tutorial
information is available in the directory
users do not have detailed documentation on
all services available to them. It would be
desirable for all services to offer common
dialogues. Standards work is progressing, for
example, on information retrieval dialogues
[7,8]. However, it will be some time before
this work impacts existing systems.

iNet is investigating the possibility of
providing a limited translation capability
oriented to the information retrieval

languages. It will consist of translating ANSI Z89G like user commands [8] to the native format of the particular service being accessed. In addition, general help facilities for the "standard" command language plus service specific help features will be provided. Initially, no translation of host responses will be performed.

In the long term, translation in the Host rather than in the NAN is seen as the most effective solution. Pressure to achieve this can be expected, as more users experience the difficulties that differences in service dialogues place on their ability to effectively use information services.

3.2 Administration

A well defined administrative structure and set of supporting tools is key to the success of any sophisticated service or product. In determining the administrative structure for iNet, the cost of the day-to-day operations and the responsiveness to service change requests and trouble reports were key criteria.

Administration is structured into three hierarchical levels: user, organization and CCG.

3.2.1 Administration Structure

Each user has a personal profile and set of commands to tailor his iNet environment.

Each organization may be served by multiple NANs and one user can serve as organization co-ordinator. The Organization Co-ordinator can add and delete users and define individual user allowances, e.g. ability to access services, or resource limits. The existence of the Organization Co-ordinator decreases CCG administrative tasks and provides users with faster responses to change requests.

Customer Services Administration functions are provided by CCG staff and include the ability to add/delete organizations, to assign basic iNet resources to an Organization Co-ordinator for distribution to individual users and to interface with organizations and other CCG administrative groups to resolve subscriber problems.

3.2.2 CCG Administrative Tools

CCG administrators are iNet subscribers and hence can use all the communication services offered by iNet. The iNet Control Centre (ICC) shown in Figure 2 provides a real-time database of alarms, statistics and usage data, which is available to the Customer Services Administrators. The ICC also prepares specific data files which are transferred to other systems for preparation of customers bills and other related processing.

3.3 The iNet Data Communications Architecture

iNet requries a variety of protocols to support the various services. These include terminal protocols for user-to-NAN communications, electronic mail/messaging protocols between iNet and ENVOY 100, administrative protocols between NANs and the ICC and finally file access protocols to permit file sharing between users served by different NANs.

Work is proceeding in both ISO and CCITT to develop a standard architecture (Reference Model for Open Systems Interconnection) and associated protocols. As this work has not progressed sufficiently to define all the protocols required by iNet, a mixture of standard, internal, and other protocols are used.

LAYER

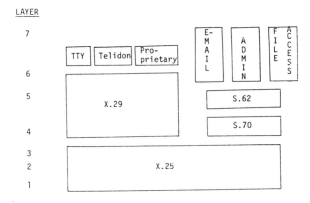

FIGURE 3 - iNet Protocol Structure

The iNet protocol structure and its relationship to the 7 layers of the Reference Model is shown in Figure 3. Where possible, existing standards are used. Thus, for example, all communications between systems will use X.25 levels 1, 2 and 3. Recommendations S.70 and S.62 which were developed for Teletex, will be used to provide Transport and Session. iNet administration, file and message submission/delivery protocols align with developing standards where appropriate.

Recommendation X.29 is used to control asynchronous terminal communication. iNet will support three classes of asynchronous terminals: ASCII, Videotex (Telidon picture description instructions) and Screen. In the latter case the protocols defined for the more common terminals will be supported.

4. SUMMARY

In 1980, a multi-disciplinary team was formed and began research on the services outlined above. This team was made up of behavioural scientists, network planners, computer scientists and market researchers. A number of service hypotheses were formulated and comparatively evaluated. This was coupled with exploratory research to evaluate functionality and technological implementation alternatives. Progress to date has resulted in the specification of initial service and the trial implementation of a limited set of services in 1982.

The iNet trial currently in progress is aimed at supporting 400 users and 25-30 host computer systems on a Canada-wide basis. The trial provides Gateway, Organizational and personal directories, automatic access services and interfaces to the ENVOY 100 messaging service. The trial supports both ASCII and Videotex (Telidon) type terminals in the business environment.

The results of trial applications are being examined through organizational impact studies before, during and after the trial period. Information obtained from operating the trials is being incorporated into the service development and ongoing market research activity.

In summary, this paper has outlined barriers to the growth of the "Information Market Place". These include difficulties in the identification of available services, in access to services, and in effective communication and use of information obtained from services. The paper has described service features intended to lower these barriers, the system architecture of iNet and the status of ongoing market trials.

5. ACKNOWLEDGEMENTS

The authors wish to acknowledge colleagues at BNR and CCG who contributed to the evolution of iNet, in particular R.P. Uhlig, G.E. Edwards and B.A. Parsons. Specific acknowledgement goes to J. Raiswell, S. Rohlfs, I. Kerr, D. Steedman and G. Ghetler for contributions to the service and architectural definitions.

REFERENCES

[1] R.P. Uhlig, "Text Processing, Computer Messaging and the Information Revolution", Proceedings of Comnet 81, Budapest, Hungary, May 1981, North Holland Publishing Co.

[2] H. Williamson and S. Rohlfs, "The User Interface Design Process", Computer Message Systems, North Holland Publishing, Ottawa, April 1981.

[3] First Report of the European User Environment Subgroup of IFIP WG 6.5, Bonn, July 1981.

[4] I. Kerr and D.J. Rhynas, "The Interconnection of Public Electronic Mail Systems", ICCC 1982.

[5] "Message Handling Systems: Inter-relationships and Control Procedures", CCITT SGVII Com No. , March 1982.

[6] "ENVOY 100 Users Guide" Computer Communications Group of the TransCanada Telephone System, October 1981.

[7] Project Diane, "Common Command Language".

[8] American National Standard Terms, Abbreviations, and Symbols for use in Interactive Retrieval Systems, ANSI Z39-G, March 1981.

Ron Begbie graduated from Concordia University (Montreal) with a B.Sc. in Math and Physics. He has been involved in various transmission system developments within Bell Canada. He is currently Section Manager responsible for the definition and implementation of CCG's data oriented value-added network services.

Ian Cunningham is responsible for defining iNet services and architecture. He has extensive experience in data communication architectures and is currently the CCITT special rapporteur on Message Handling Facilities. He holds a B.A.Sc. from University of Waterloo and an MS from the University of Illinois.

Hilary Williamson has a B.Sc. from McGill University and an M. Math from University of Waterloo. While at BNR she has worked on both definition and implementation of computer aided design, computer conferencing, messaging and videotex systems, with emphasis on their user interfaces. Hilary is currently responsible for iNet trial development.

Document Processing & the Integration of Relevant Public Services

P T Kirstein, S W Treadwell
University College London, UK

This paper outlines some of the developments in the Public Document Transmission service standards. It defines a model of multi-media documents - which includes text, line graphics, bit- map graphics and voice. It then discusses how the present service standards, e.g. for Teletex and Videotex, could be extended to cater for multi-media document processing, especially in local networks such as office systems.

Within a multi-media system there will be several domains, each consisting of devices and processes that share the same data type. Devices within the same domain can interact easily, devices in different domains require special procedures being necessary to map the data from one standard to another.

1. INTRODUCTION

There is considerable discussion, in the International Consultative Committee on Telephone and Telegraph (CCITT), the International Standards Organisation (ISO), elsewhere and about the "Integration of Public Services" like Teletex [1], Videotex [2] and Telefax [3]. Many other organisations are concerned with Computer Standards, but less with document standards. There is sometimes a particular difficulty in reconciling the activities of the different bodies, though the liaison is improving. The considerations on Standards are usually either very general or very specific. When general, they centre around the desirability of using common terminals and reducing the number and variation of Standards recommendations. When specific, they usually home onto a specific recommendation - e.g. for Teletex [1] - and say it should be extended in a particular way to deal with another service (e.g. Videotex codes [2]).

This paper starts from another viewpoint. It tries to analyse what is meant by a "Multi-media Document", and the types of operation required in its composition, storage, transmission, filing and subsequent retrieval.

We consider first, in Section 2, what facilities are important in multi-media documents (which include alphanumeric text, graphics and voice). In Section 3 the Standards for various informaton services are considered - in particular Teletex, Videotex and Computer Based Message Systems (CBMS). We show how these services fit into the framework of the Open Systems Interconnection architecture of the International Standards Organisation (ISO).

Clear data structures are one of the most significant differences in these services. Section 4 suggests a general data structure which would be appropriate to multi-media documents. A key problem is the tradeoff between providing for the types of facilities users might wish to have, and these which are essential for a viable service. Section 5 discusses the questions of multi-media data entry in some detail, and introduces the concept of domains of services. In Section 6 the questions of storage and retrieval of information in one domain, and of protocol conversion between services are discussed. Finally, some conclusions are drawn in Section 7.

2. OFFICE FUNCTIONS

While we will not try to analyse all office functions, some examples will illustrate the requirements in terminals and communication services. We assume that there is some sort of local network, so that managers, secretaries and others can access data from data bases and outside resources; they can also enter data when required. In such a network, we can classify the users of the network into groups depending on their use of the network.

For document preparation, e.g. by secretaries, a word processing facility is needed. The input keypad will have to be a complete Latin keyboard with additional keys to perform editing functions. As well as the written word, it is often convenient to use voice dictation or annotation as a mode of communication; this type of function could be integrated into our system by having the terminal equipped with the ability to digitise and playback voice data, and synchronise the voice with text. No interpretation of the data by the computer is implied here; it is purely a recording technique. Better is the ability to associate the voicegram with a specific piece of text. At least voicegram deletion, but possibly voicegram generation, would be useful attributes. It should be possible to submit a message to Computer Based Message Systems; these may well have service interfaces which are Teletex compatible. For information retrieval, ability to access Videotex datebases - local or elsewhere - would be useful. The ability to receive or initiate normal facsimile would help. Often this is required to associate illustrations with specific pieces of text.

The manager would want to have data presented with extensive graphic capabilities, colour double-sized characters, and perhaps the ability to draw lines and curves. His terminal should be designed primarily to present statistics and data in a very effective format. It would also be expected that this terminal would be used for outputing data rather than for the manager to enter much data. The keyboard for this terminal could be a simple, alphanumeric keyboard. While dictaphones are much cheaper than terminals, the ability to annotate specific parts of a documents is very useful. One purpose is in document correction, another is in filing instructions. In a similar way to voice, graphics or facsimile output can be important. There may be just a brief sketch, but it should be associated with a place in a document or a voice instruction. The choice of which work stations to equip with such facilities will be complex. However clear requirements are the following:

a. Ability to enter information by keyboard, voice or facsimile

b. Ability to ouput information as text, graphics (in colour) or voice

c. Access to retrieval services in standard form (e.g. Videotex), with single keyboard, Querty keyboard, or

d. Access to facilities which can offer transmission and reception of standard services, e.g. Teletex and other computer based message services

e. Ability of systems to store, retrieve and transfer data irrespective of their content. Only when the data arrives at terminals, need the nature of the digital stream be understood.

While procedure translations might be performed automatically, media transformation may be manual. Thus a drawing may be entered via a Telewriter, and appear as a crude drawing. This may be redrawn accurately by hand (or with CAD facilities), thus replacing the crude sketch. Voice annotation to a document may require complex editing functions, but these could be done by standard word processing techniques.

3. DOCUMENT TRANSMISSION SERVICES

3.1 Introduction

A key to the rapid penetration of electronic office services is an ability to communicate widely. 80-90% of communication in typical offices is internal to the organisation. However if completely different facilities to the internal ones are required for communication between organisations, many of the benefits of office automation are either unused or become uneconomic.

There are three different functions of such standards for communication: Conventions on the presentation of data, instructions on what to do with the data, and conventions on how to transfer the data. The distinction between the three will be considered below for three

services: Teletex, Videotex and Computer Based Message Services. Because current designs of such services are attempting to model their functions on the Open Systems Interconnection (OSI, [4]) model of the International Standards Organisation (ISO), we will use the OSI notation here.

3.2 The Teletex Service

The Teletex service, as envisioned by the PTTs [1], is a memory-to-memory service. Its basic operation is simply to transfer a document from the memory of one terminal to that of another, in such a way that the document can be universally displayed and understood. To achieve this aim, the protocol levels have been defined largely according to the OSI architecture.

The Data Presentation layer (S61, [5]) is essentially textual in its present formal specification. It allows for a much larger range of character sets, to cater for most Western (as distinct from ideographic) text. A data structure is provided, to allow for later addition of graphic or facsimile data segments. However, little detail has been decided on the relevant data formats. Several countries, e.g. France, are already extending the specifications to allow for facsimile formats at their introduction of Teletex. There are still problems in these procedures as related to the Open Systems Interconnection (OSI) model – mainly because many session control functions and transport level are still somewhat confused. The data structure is linear. Different types of data can be concatenated (e.g. facsimile and text can be mixed). However the present structure envisages a hardcopy, monocolour, terminal. Thus there are no functions for colour, multiple size characters, or flashing characters.

There are no processing instructions in the data; the data structure so far defined assumes the document is meant for the addressee terminal in the address. Consideration is being given to providing storage in the network, and multiple addressees. Interworking with the Teletex network is being provided from the beginning. Interworking with Telefax and Videotex is for further study [1]. These aspects will imply processing instructions.

The transfer function are well defined. The formal definition of the Transport Layer (S70, [5]) is deliberately designed to sit above the Public Switched Telephone, Public Data, and Public Circuit Switched Data networks according to these lower ISO levels. The OSI Session layer (S62, [5]) encourages unidirectional document transfer; it allows, however, for negotiation of the features available at the receiving end.

3.3 Interactive Videotex Services

The interactive Videotex services [2] are quite different from the Teletex ones. Fundamentally they are designed for information retrieval, with cheap but attractive terminals. For this reason it is an asymmetric service, with Information Providers and Users. An elaborate set of conventions for data transfer between information providers has been specified by different administrations (e.g. [6]). However, for pure data access, the transfer conventions are minimal, and processing instructions are not standardised (if they exist).

The presentation levels have been completely defined - even though several incompatible specifications exist [7], [8]. The aim of the Videotex standard is to provide a uniform meaning to data reaching a Videotex terminal. There are difficulties in this, since there are at least four different systems. These terminals should be simple, interactive, capable of colour, and have some features specific to displays (e.g. ability to flash, ability to conceal, cursor addressing). The fundamental unit of Videotex is a page; in the European proposals a page contains 24 rows of 40 characters with graphics being simulated with special characters (alpha-mosaic). In the North American proposals, a normal page contains 20 rows of 40 characters, with graphics being defined by geometric constraints. The proposals make provision for a photographic mode, akin to the facsimile mode, but there are no standards yet for this.

3.4 Computer Based Message System

Computer Based Message Systems (CBMS) have many of the attributes of the other services of this section. Although many such services now exist, even in some cases run by PTTs, no standards have yet been set. However, standardisation in this area is only just starting. In the ARPA network standards for Message Headers were defined many years ago.

Now the processing instructions need careful specification. These refer to the information implied in the Header. Transfer features are still under study, these will presumably eventually be a derivation of the Teletex procedures. However, because the source and final destination systems may not be available simultaneously these systems must use relaying techniques. Here they may adopt procedures similar to the Store and Forward Teletex, which have not yet been defined.

There is little real reason why CBMS must define the data representation. Certainly most current systems are restricted to alphanumeric text - but this is because of the way control procedures are embedded in the data structure. Several systems do not have this limitation, and any bit stream can be carried. It is almost always possible to scan the data and arrange for data to be inserted at source and removed at destination to ensure the data will pass through correctly yet transparently. While multi-media messages could be sent by common agreement, no standards yet exist for a universal structure of such data.

3.5 Commonality of Facilities

Any attempt to integrate services must build on common features of the services to be integrated. Here it is important to distinguish between the local operations on documents and files, and the activities in their transmission. Many of the services are now being defined with the OSI model in mind. Thus Teletex, Videotex database update, CBMS message transfer, and even Videotex access via packet switched network, can all use X25 at levels 1-3. There is no reason why Teletex and Videotex update activities cannot use the same transport service - but the latter have not yet been standardised; because CBMS message transfer may need relaying, there may have to be some variation at this level (Level 4). At present Teletex uses some control procedures inside the Level 5 for page acknowledgement, and assumes character coded text. Provided the control is so embedded that aribitrary binary streams can be sent, the same control procedure could be valid for Teletex and CBMS (even with multi-media messages). It may be necessary to use the convention that the current page boundary only represents a logical boundary.

The presentation levels will show strong variation dependent on the type of data inside one service (eg the different types in Teletex or the different types in a multi-media CBMS). It will also have differences for the same sort of information in different services (eg bit-map graphics in Teletex and Videotex). However these differences are discussed more fully in the following sections.

4. DATA STRUCTURES

4.1 Introduction

While it is tempting to make the document structure complex, it is more important that at least the data structures used for transmission become accepted universally. We discuss in Section 4.2 the types of data to be considered. In Section 4.3 we consider data segments, and in Section 4.4 document description. It is important that these descriptions contain the right information that standard structures, e.g. Teletex, could be derived by simple transformation.

4.2 Data Types

The data encoding methods could be used to represent any graphic symbol or audio, but most encoding methods fall into roughly five different categories:

a. Extended Character Sets. Often these extensions of the Latin character set include simple graphic forms such as horizontal and vertical lines.

b. Line-Described Graphics. These are special encoding methods, usually more complex than the coding of the Latin text, that describe the length and slopes of lines, arcs and other line-oriented graphics.

c. Bit-Map Graphics. This includes all forms of encoding that use a simple dot technique to encode an image. Included in this is facsimile.

d. Presentation Functions. These do not convey a graphic image in themselves, but indicate how subsequent text is to be presented. They may indicate the size of the symbols, the colour, the length of the lines, the number of lines to a page, and many other attributes.

e. Voice Functions. Here there are a wide variety, depending again on the technology used to digitise and compress the voice.

4.3 Data Segments

In order to express the data of the preceding types, it is necessary to make up the data as Data Segments. Each segment has a Descriptor followed by Text. It must contain the following:

An identification indicating the segment is a data segment.

An identification defining the type - this includes information on how the rest of the segment is to be interpreted. Thus, for example, the bit-map type may have several variants.

An identification defining the name of the data text.

Parameters required by this type (e.g. data compression, data encryption, pixel width)

Pointer to Data Text.

There may be a document descriptor as described in Section 4.4. If not, there needs to be extra information to indicate the location and size of the data text. It is preferable that general relationships between Data segments should also be a function of the Document Descriptor. For a linear structure, like the present Teletex, pointers should be given to one or more other data segments. The Data Text need then contain only the following:

An Identifier, Data, End of Record.

4.4 Document Descriptor

Just as there are several Data Segments, so there are several Document Segments. These are parameters concerning the whole document:
Name, author, date, references, title, pointer to Connectivity Descriptor.
The Document Descriptor must contain a Domain Descriptor, which gives information on all the types of data used in the document, and the sort of coding used (see Section 5.2). It should also indicate whether the type is essential or optional; e.g. a document with text and Teletex facsimile (for illustrations) may still be worth viewing on an alphanumeric terminal.

4.5 Processing Instructions

Finally, there should, in some cases, be processing segments associated with a document. These will include instructions about where to distribute the document, and often a Connectivity Descriptor to provide a set of pointers to data segments. The latter will often include some pointers and scaling information; in the case of voice-annotated

text, or movie pictures, timing information may also be necessary. These parameters are best in the Connectivity Descriptor for multimedia documents; this facilitates later document manipulation and editing.

5. MIXED DATA TYPE SUPPORT

5.1 Introduction

In this Section we discuss the different types of data, and introduce the concept of domain. A domain is associated not only with the presentation of the data (e.g. ASCII text or line graphics), but also with its application area (e.g. Teletex, Videotex).

We introduce the notion of domain in Section 5.2, and support for multiple domains in Section 5.3.

5.2 Multiple Domain Storage

In Section 4.2 we introduced the notion of "Data type". There we discussed different types of data (e.g. alphanumeric, bit-map graphics, voice), but did not comment on the exact representation of each type. In fact, data may belong to different "domains", where a domain is the data presentation structure associated with specific types of service. All elements that share this data structure are members of the domain. Clearly, these domain members may exchange information freely without the need to convert the data from one form to another. Thus it is possible to define domains for each of Videotex, Teletex, and Datafax data types. Inside one domain, the data structure will usually have been defined logically. Thus it is straightforward to distinguish between characters, mosaic graphics and picture graphics in European Videotex, and between text and facsimile in the French Teletex. However to translate between Videotex and Teletex may be impossible; the relevant features in Videotex like colour or flashing are just not supported.

It would be possible, but could be become very cumbersome, to define a generalised data representation, so that all data types can be perfectly mapped onto this data representation. However the conversion may be costly, and the specification very difficult. Alternatively data may be generated in a fashion appropriate to a particular domain, and data from different domains could be intermixed in some data base. As long as data is output from terminals in the same domain as they were input, no problem would arise. This form of storage can be very useful - particularly if the data transmission functions are well separated from the data representation ones. Only if they are retrieved from a terminal designed for a domain different from the data domain may difficulties occur.

The conversion of data, in the case where it has to cross domain boundaries, can take place either centrally, or at preassigned points about the network. This will have to be performed by a processor previously programmed for the task. Not all conversions need be supported by the network, as some may be too complex to perform; some of the data in a message may be either omitted from the converted text or only partially translated.

For instance, ASCII text can be translated into facsimile by mapping the ASCII codes into the set of dots that represent the character; the reverse conversion requires image processing and character recognition, which may be beyond the scope of any resources available on the network. As a further example, ASCII text can be converted to Videotex, but due to the restricted 40 character line in Videotex, the format of the message will vary slightly from the original. However, a graphic Videotex page would have a lot of information omitted when being converted to ASCII; the colour and most of the graphic symbols would be stripped - only the text would survive.

5.3 Displaying and Entering Data

The way in which the information can be recorded and displayed is dictated by the terminals being used. Graphic symbols cannot be portrayed if the terminal is unable to generate the required symbol. Usually, terminals are developed for certain applications so that they can generate and display all the symbols required for that one application. Most commonly in use is the ASCII terminal which displays the Latin alphabet and understands some rudimentary presentation functions such as carriage-returns and linefeeds. Terminals have also been developed for Videotex that permit the Latin alphabet as well as a large Extended Character set and an impressive set of presentation functions.

Clearly, data intended for an 80 column ASCII terminal will not be displayed correctly on a Videotex terminal, and vice versa. This is true even though both terminals display Latin text, and both use the same encoding for this text. It is the presentation functions, both implicit and explicit, that make the mutual exchange of data impossible.

It is often possible to modify the data descriptor or connectivity descriptor from a terminal of a different type, where the modification of the text is impractical. Thus, for example, it is possible to change the point in text with which a voicegram is associated by a display cursor; the variation of the voice itself needs a voice terminal.

The domain concept can refer to the complexity of a terminal function as well as to its application area. Thus, for example, a European Videotex terminal may not have bit-map graphics support. This can be indicated by the domain - and bit-map data structures may have to be crudely converted to alphamosaic form for such a terminal. A group 3 facsimile device may be said to belong to the same domain as Teletex - but the characters would need to be converted to Teletex bit patterns.

6. MULTI-MEDIA SERVICES

6.1 Introduction

Even if multi-media documents have the appropriate structure and data formats, it is not obvious what service support is of interest. Eventually very complex transformation of documents will be possible. In this Section we concentrate on a few specific aspects. In Section 6.2 we stress the need to work with instances of portions of a document when editing or dispatching. In Section 6.3 we show that in many cases the data transfer aspect of a service can be quite divorced from the data representation aspect. We discuss in Section 5.2 how documents arising from different single domains can be stored together - and accessed by conventional terminals belonging to that domain. Alternatively terminals may be designed to operate with alternate domains - merely changing the appropriate control program. Finally, we discuss in Section 6.4, that the rich data structure of Section 3, can be transferred into the linear streams required in the current series of data structures.

6.2 Master Element and Instance

The document structure introduced in this section would allow documentation to be sent to many addressees, while keeping only one copy of the document. The document itself could be contructed from different terminals, and could have its different components edited separately. Facilities can be provided for fragmenting segments. It is clear how a text segment could be divided into smaller ones; a facsimile segment could be similarly split - or its scale might be changed. Because of the richness of the structure, not only could these operations be performed during document creation, but they could also be performed on the transmitted document. Anyone performing such editing would need to operate with a so-called Instance of the document. An "Instance" is another copy, at least of the structure segments of the document, and possibly also of any data segments that may need to be modified. He would have to create new data segments and connection segments by modifying an instance of the appropriate master segment. A new document would then be formed automatically (possibly with its history of creation.)

6.3 Multi-media Document Transfer

If all the services were developed from scratch, a common layering system might be devised. In practice, various Data terminal standards, Teletex service standards, Videotex Gateway standards etc. have all developed in parallel. This is reflected not only in different data representations, but also in different data transfer procedures. Thus for many purposes, it is possible for a local network to support traffic in several domains, using the technology of Section 5.2. There must then be appropriate control procedures to support the relevant domains.

Both Teletex and Prestel Gateway can be services above X25. Pages can therefore be transfered either from Teletex Hosts or Prestel, via a single X25 gateway to a local network. Different processors on the local network could provide the relevant support for the transport, in view of the discussion of Section 5.3. Terminals can be connected to an appropriate terminal concentrator (TC). If we are concerned with messages arising from a computer based message service on a public Videotex system, such messages can easily be stored in a file system also on the local network. No conversion is needed to access such messages from a Videotex terminal; if such messages arrive via Teletex, they could be transfered to the file system via a Teletex service convertor and the X25 gateway. Reading these with a Teletex format terminal would be trivial.

There are, therefore, several methods of multi-media terminal support. It may be that documents on the filing system belong to different domains - but each document to only one domain. By choosing a terminal of the same domain, the document is easily displayed. A second approach capitalises on the programmable nature of many modern terminals. The appropriate code can be loaded into the terminal so that it could display the relevant document - to whichever domain it belongs. Another, and often conceptually difficult approach, is to try to transform the relevant data segments to run in one domain when it was designed for another. Which approach is the best in a given instance, is strongly dependent on the application.

6.4 Domain Transformation

It is to be hoped that as the standards for multi-media documents develop, the document structure of Section 3 becomes accepted. However it would also be an ongoing requirement for terminals obeying current standards to interwork with those supporting a more complex structure. While transformation of the data text segments can be difficult, complex and unsatisfactory, removing structure is much simpler. Suppose, for example, a multi-media document had the structure of Section 3, but the individual data segments were consistent with the French Teletex standards for text and facsimile. It would be comparatively simple to traverse the data structure, and produce a sequential data file exactly Teletex compatible. By a different scan though, a Videotex file, with appropriate structure, can be produced.

7. CONCLUSIONS

We have shown that variations of the Standards for document and interactive information services fit into a common frame- work. It is possible to set up levels of protocol which separate out clearly the transport, control, presentation and application areas. By suitable modification of the current presentation functions, a common presentation data structure can be defined. This structure would require enrichment of the current public Standards. Alternatively, the richer standards could be used for multi-media documents, which are beyond the range of applications of the current

service standards; preprocessing can transform a document with the richer structure to that used in the public standards.

The concept of domain was discussed in some detail. The Data entry, and storage resulting in one domain would be much simpler than the protocol conversions needed to transform document between domains. This approach may well lead to a full set of user capabilities, with only a small number of physically different terminal types.

The concepts would work well, the resulting services would have broad appeal, and the variety of terminals could be kept low. It is more questionable whether there really exists an organisation which could force acceptability of the more elaborate data structures and protocols which might result. Hopefully the current strong interest in multi-media facilities will lead to a standardisation of functions and facilities on the lines suggested here.

The approach suggested in this paper will permit the absorption of new techniques in the future, so that new concepts can be added to the system as they become available.

ACKNOWLEDGEMENT

The authors acknowledge the support of the Science and Engineering Research Council, under grant B/RG/A/75695 and the British Library for Grant SI/G/294, who supported the practical work on which this paper is based.

REFERENCES

1. CCITT: "Teletex Service". Final Report to the 7th Plenary Assembly (Part III), F200, Document No 91, ITU, Geneva, 42-79, 1980

2. CCITT: "Videotex Service", Draft Recommendation F300, ibid, 80 - 96

3. CCITT: "Standardisation of Group 3 facsimile apparatus for document transmission", ibid Draft Recommendation T4, Document No. 79, 34 - 51.

4. ---: "Reference Model on Open System Interconnection", ISO TC 97/SC16 N230, Paris, 1979.

5. CCITT: "Draft Recommendation S60, S61, S62, S70 for Teletex", Document No. 88, ITU, Geneva.

6. ---: "Prestel Gateway Technical Interface Specification", British Telecom, 1981.

7. CEPT: "Draft Recommendation for European Interactive Videotex Service, Display aspects and transmission coding", Recommendation T/CD6-1, CEPT, Paris, 1981.

8. ---: "Videotex Standard Presentation Level Protocol", Bell Laboratories, Parsippany, NJ, 1981.

An Electronic Mail Based Integrated Business System

P Drake
British Telecom, UK

A major growth area during the 1980's will be systems which allow business managers to access both information systems and electronic mail systems. This paper outlines the design of a two tier information service based on store and forward principles. Tier 1 describes a universal communication service equivalent to existing mail services and initially based on the Teletex service. Tier 2 describes a document distribution and information interchange service for integrated business systems. The key to information interchange is through the development of document structures, naming conventions and presentation rules. The paper then describes British Telecom's current CCITT working papers.

1. INTRODUCTION

The term electronic mail has many different meanings. Within this paper electronic mail is defined as a service which an originator uses to post a document via a postbox over one or more local or wide area networks (LAN/WANs) to a mailbox owned by the recipient. A document represents any piece of information, of any length, in any form, eg. narrative text, graphics, image, voice, and obeying the structure governed by the electronic mail service, eg. envelope, parcel sizes, addressing rules. Once posted a document may not be changed and will be delivered as far as possible in its original display form. Using this definition it is possible to provide a public universal service which is as ubiquitious as the existing mail or telephone services.

The term integrated business system has also been used in many ways, depending on the users, computer or communication supplier's viewpoint. Within this paper an integrated business system is defined from the user's viewpoint and provides document creation, eg. word and graphics processing, document filing, electronic mail (as defined above), and multi-retrieval techniques. Successful integrated business systems are designed to aid specific business staff perform specific office functions. Users require a combination of both of the above, eg. intra-company they would like an integrated information service, whilst globally subscribing to a universal electronic mail service.

This paper thus proposes a two tier information service (see fig 1), consisting of a first tier electronic mail service and a second tier, information interchange service.

The justification for a two tier information service is to improve the customer's information handling capabilities and hence his ability to make timely and accurate decisions. These factors cannot be justified with direct manpower savings, but like the telephone, provide inter and intra organisational savings if used correctly. The key is the ability to send readable information to all recipients.

2. THE TWO TIER INFORMATION SERVICE

The first tier service is a vehicle for the input, transport and display of data, and not an information service. The launching of the British Telecom Teletex Service (ref 1) is the first step in the universal implementation and use of international communication standards (ref 2).

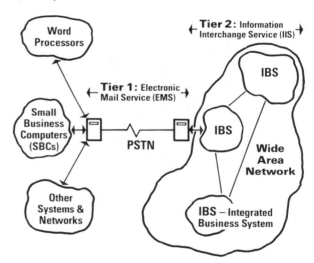

Fig 1: The Two Tier Service

The correct creation, retrieval and presentation of information is the responsibility of the second tier service. This service provides closely coupled information interchange in accordance with the user's distributed information systems requirements.

2.1. The Electronic Mail Service (EMS)

The British Telecom Teletex service allows any user with an approved terminal to be registered in a directory. Communication is either via the public switched telephone network (PSTN) or via the packet switched service (PSS), and when available, between each other and the telex network via gateways. The service provides a memory to memory transfer using a series of defined images, eg. page size, character set, etc. However, it makes no demands on how the user "posts" or "collects" mail from the memory. These functions are left to terminal implementors.

2.1.1. EMS Functions

An electronic mail service has three basic functions: posting, mail transport and collection by the recipient. The Teletex Service guarantees to provide only the mail transport, whilst EMS guarantees successful posting and collecting to one of a number of user interface options.

EMS is likely to support interfaces to word processors, small business computers using simple and readily available interfaces eg. teletype CCITT V24 with XON,XOFF type control, and batch transfer protocols eg IBM 2780.

EMS should also be upward compatible to future enhancements to Teletex to allow for text, graphics, image or facsimile mixed mode representation of mail.

2.1.2. EMS Facilities

A number of optional facilities could be supported:

    a. Document Intray
    b. Document Outtray
    c. Continous 24 hours operation
    d. Unattended operation
    e. Confirmation delivery
    f. Priority mail
    h. Mail logging
    i. Mail interception to remove junkmail
    j. Multi-addressing for mailshots
    k. Subscription from poster addresses
    l. Re-routing to new mailbox address
    m. Directory service
    n. Mailbox service.

Options h to n may be performed by special computer centres with a role analogous to that of a general post office.

2.2 The Information Interchange Service

Whilst EMS is a pure communication service, the primary aim of the information interchange service (IIS) is to improve information quality and user productivity in information creation, handling and retrieval. From the user's viewpoint IIS is supported by one or more integrated business systems (IBSs) which provide an environment to support a wide range of office tools and inter- and intra-office electronic mail. The key element is an information concept known as the Universal Standard Document (USD) (ref 3) which provides the structure for IIS to allow data interchange between the various IBS products such as word processors, multi-functional workstations, printers, and databases, etc. USD is supportable within each IBS and between IBS sites.

2.2.1. IBS Architecture

Each integrated business system consists optionally of a number of multi-functional workstations, multiplexers for non-intelligent (teletype compatible) devices, file, printer, reprographics units and gateway servers (see fig 2). These are interconnected via a transport service based on the concepts of open systems interconnection. Which local area network is used is of no consequence to the user except with regards to performance criteria and quality of service. Hence IBS could assume to support circuit switched PABX connections, or Ethernet and Cambridge Ring connections. Using this philosophy allows a user to tailor his cloth to his needs and yet evolve from circuit switched connections to other network configurations by adding the appropriate level 3/4 access interface.

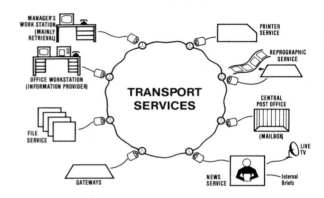

Fig 2: An Integrated Business System (IBS)

The trend in the electronic office is towards multifunctional systems which support a wide range of applications and provide a common interface for the user via a single workstation (ref 4). IBS provides this multifunctionality within each site by presenting the user with a common user image stored in USD form and generated and retrieved by all application packages.

2.2.2 User Image

The user image is based on simulating the top of an office desk. Hence the full image provides multiple windows, each representing a document or part of one, to allow the user to move between them in the same way as paper documents on a normal desktop. Some windows represent sets of user interaction tools eg menu lists, action keys, and are akin to pens, rulers etc placed on the desk. The number of windows or the types of interaction tool a particular workstation can support are implementation dependent.

To meet the real user requirements the user image must be as close to the human senses as possible ie colour, text, graphics, images and voice. The image must provide a structure to allow random access and pointing devices to select and manipulate any field within the image. The image must be capable of being pre-defined and storable.

The user image must also support <u>multiple context working</u>. This means that users can leave working on a particular image eg page of a document, store all the tools and status of the job and perform a completely different activity. Later they may return to the document without loss of control and resume where they left off. This reflects most office work patterns which result in several partially finished jobs on an office desk during the course of a day.

The man-machine interaction of the user image is based on a hierarchy of images. Each image displayed represents the job from the workspace currently being worked upon and may consist of documents, menus and user tools. All images provide status keys to allow an "UNDO" action. Menus represent the full range of options available within a working job and thus guide the user to successful use of the system. This approach is ideal for new users and requires little formal training. Experienced users override menus by issuing multi-functional commands that lead straight to the desired action in one operation.

2.2.3 <u>IBS Functions</u>

Functions which IBS support are:-

a. Electronic Desk - an intray, outtray, a workspace area and document files.

b. Word Processing - full editing and format sets based on USD. It also optionally handles the full teletex character set.

c. Graphics Processing - full line and symbol graphics creation, movement, positional identification based on the use of individual pixel addressing eg bitmap graphics (ref 5).

d. Image Processing - limited image creation, manipulation facilities using encoded bitmap graphic techniques.

e. Voice Processing - supports a voice messaging system stored in USD format.

f. Mixed Mode Processing - the USD structure allows multiple windows for intermixing graphics, images, text and voice . This allows unique identification of fields for the underlying application processes.

g. Electronic Mail - functionally the same as for the EMS 1st tier service, but with the addition that graphics, images and voice mail can be sent in USD form.

h. Document and Record Filing- the USD structure allows hierarchical filing at a level determined by the user.

i. End User Programming - supports high level languages and functional programming, eg config packages, for users to add their own facilities.

2.2.4 <u>IBS External Services</u>

IBS users communicate either by IIS(tier 2) or via gateways to external services. Gateways supported include both store and forward and interactive versions.

a. Tier 2 Network Only Gateway - each IBS site supports LAN/WAN network gateways to allow inter IBS transparent network communications. The IIS tier 2 protocols mask these gateways from the users.

b. Store and Forward Gateways - the following gateways can be envisaged which allow upto level 6 OSI translation from the USD structure into the form of the external electronic mail service:-

Telex gateway - USD to telex interworking.

Teletex gateway - USD to teletex interworking eg tier 1 product range.

Mailbox gateways - USD to central mailbox interworking eg Telecom Gold.

Other gateways - USD to proprietary file transfer protocols eg IBM 2780/3780.

c. Interactive Gateways - these include terminal access gateways such as:-

Prestel gateway - IBS workstation interworking with Prestel Information Retrieval Centres and Information Provider Centres.

X28,X29,X3 gateway - IBS workstation interworking with computer systems supporting X28,X29,X3 protocols.

Other gateways - IBS workstation interworking with IBM/ICL mainframes and systems through proprietary interactive terminal protocols.

3. UNIVERSAL STANDARD DOCUMENT (USD)

The successful interchange of data between two cooperating sites requires a common data structure representation between them, which with local transformations can be mapped onto the local hardware. This can be best explained by describing the interchange of data between two workstations.

3.1 <u>Information Interchange Model</u>

Fig 3 shows that the information interchange model consists of a number of workstations through which the user interacts with a number of information databases. The databases are defined in USD structure and provide total information interchange as and when necessary depending on the application. Workstations can support USD structures either at the file access (option A) or application level (option B).

Option A requires that the application data structure is translated into USD structure by a file access process. This option is valid where existing workstations, eg word processors, are interfaced to an IBS.

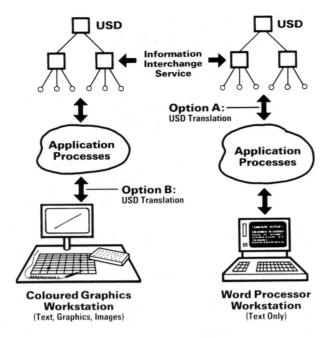

Fig 3: Information Interchange Model

Option B assumes the USD structure is an integral part of the application and thus allows the full facilities of mixed text, graphics, image mode working. Each workstation consists of four main components: input, USD generator, USD interpreter and display output devices. The workstations are connected to the USD databases at the operating system level, which may reside in each workstations or centrally for dumb terminals.

This leads to the requirement of forward and backward compatability between terminals and the USD structures. The former means that future workstations must be able to access existing USD data, and latter means that existing terminals must be able to display and manipulate new USD data created by advanced workstations (ref 5). For example, data generated by a high resolution (4000*4000 points) coloured graphics display terminal with multi-windowing and using keyboards and positioning devices (light pens, tracking balls etc) must be displayable on a simple text only 80*24 line VDU. In this case only the text portion of the USD data will be converted by the VDU interpretor (or intelligent concentrator interpreter for dumb VDUs). Similiar text only data should be displayable on the coloured graphics display. The important point is that the data in the USD database is in a form to meet whatever technology of display and manipulation is used.

3.2 USD Structure

Using the interchange model, the Universal Standard Document (USD) structure (ref 6) is British Telecom's current contribution to the evolution to total information interchange (ref 7).

When a document is created it contains three types of information:-

- Structure
- Presentation (Display and Control)
- Manipulation (Edit)

The proposed USD provides a document structure which includes the basic presentation standards and manipulation information to allow subsequent editing, record processing, and display at the destination site.

In order to make USD a universal information interchange format it has been assumed that the structure should not:-

a.   inhibit individual vendors from offering a variety of   user interface and editing facilities

b.   impose any particular filing and retrieval scheme on the   local system (for non-IBS systems).

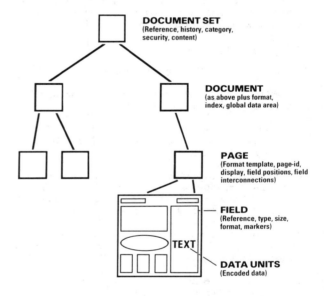

Fig 4:USD Structure

USD is a hierachical structure consisting of document sets, documents within each set, pages within documents, fields within pages, and data units within fields (see fig 4). Presentation information is primarily found in data units which contain display data plus embedded presentation control data. Manipulation information is primarily at the field level when concerned with display editing and at the page level for document "cut and paste" editing. Record processing can occur at any level of the structure.

3.3 Presentation Standards

The basic data units of USD consist of sequences of 8 bit bytes which are only meaningful when associated with presentation control information. The control data describes the display media and coding scheme for the data stream. A different control set will be used depending on whether text, graphics, images or voice is presented. The basic default set is ISO 646 text only. A number of sets can be identified as described below.

Text Sets - can be based on the teletex standard with the addition of colour, character sizes, and word processing control parameters.

Graphic Sets - can be based on the picture description instructions (PDI) concept for alphamosaic, alphageometric graphics. These include picture shapes (predefined icons, lines, circles, polygons, rectangles etc) and control information giving greyscale/colour setting, line texture, thickness, graphic sets (special DRCSs), resolution, absolute or relative drawing.

Image Sets - can be based on facsimilie standards (group 4) and provide various data compression techniques.

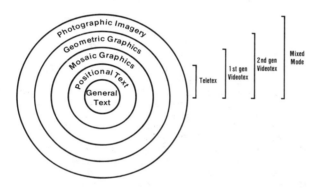

Fig 5: Presentation Standards

Each of these sets can be intermixed within the USD structure because they are all invoked through the same control mechanism as defined in ISO2022. Fig 5 represents this upward compatibility between sets.

3.4 Manipulation Standards

There are two forms of manipulation tools required: those that provide access to individual data items; and those that change such items. Within USD the former is implemented by providing markers within each field which can be directly addressed by application programs. The latter is best explained in terms of the standard input functions to which all input devices must convert in order to manipulate the USD data. The USD generator has not yet been fully defined but should include menu and item picking with the identification of the USD level picked, eg field, data item etc, keyboard standardisation, function button identification, and N display locators. These locators can be directly controlled by one or more input positioning devices.

4. POSSIBLE IMPLEMENTATIONS

4.1 EMS Products - Tier 1

A possible EMS product requires three capabilities: a communication interface, a store and forward management unit and a user interface acting as an inexpensive post/mailbox.As the storage system and mail transport requirements are the same for all users, this part of the box can be standardised and cost reduced. Differences only arise in how users post and retrieve mail to and from the box.

Communication Interface - supports both a PSTN and PSS interface for Teletex. A PSTN interface requires a CCITT V22.bis 1200/2400 FDX modem connection with auto calling/answering capability and CCITT X75 level 2 support. A PSS packet interface requires o dataline 2400/4800/9600/48K modem connection with CCITT X25 level 2 support. Both interfaces require software to support CCITT X25 levels 3, and CCITT S series teletex levels 4/5/6 communication protocols. In addition the PSTN connection requires software to drive the auto-calling and answering capability.

Management Unit - this provides hardware and software to store mail, maintain incoming and outgoing status logs, implement the facilities outlined in chapter 2.1.2 and provide general housekeeping.

User Interface - these interfaces will vary from simple adaptors to full terminal interfaces. Adaptors will allow existing word processors and small business computers (SBCs) to use the BT Teletex Service. Full terminal interfaces will be incorporated into either multifunctional workstations or word processors, and support Teletex interfaces based on the EMS functionality .

Telecom Gold, a British Telecom Enterprise company, plan to link their Dialcom Electronic Mailbox Service to Teletex terminals. Using this facility teletype compatible terminals and VDUs operating at various speeds (300/300, 1200/75 and 1200/1200) can interwork with customer based EMS products operating at 1200 or 2400 bits/sec speed and using the Teletex Service. The combination of the Dialcom Mailbox Service and customer based EMS products potentially offers electronic mail to all types of users for a capital outlay of £20 to £2000 depending on whether a simple VDU access or a full Teletex gateway is required.

4.2 IBS Products - Tier 2

IBS systems consist of workstations and resource servers supporting either a local network operating system with closely coupled interactions or a local electronic mail system with loosely coupled interactions.

Workstations can be further categorised into those that support the full electronic desk user image and those that provide only specialist subsets.

The full user image requires the combination of

text, graphics, image and voice presentation devices with appropriate processing and software support. The new generation of professional workstations, such as the Perq, Star, Domain, Imp, B20, provide some of these facilities and when combined with USD structure provide a mixed mode environment for an information interchange service.

As hardware costs continue to fall then the full user image supported workstation will be available at every desk. However, in the medium term, the casual users and specifically limited user will require a low cost workstation which provides standalone or cluster capabilities and interworks with a subset of IIS Tier 2. It may also provide a full EMS Tier 1 interface. Examples of these workstations are CP/M based systems, communicating word processors, VDU/telephones, special graphics terminals, and simple terminal to minicomputer clusters.

The aim of IBS is to provide each user via his workstation with resources as and when he requires them. For the full user image supported workstation, such resources will consist of connections to file, print, reprographic and additional processing services. The interconnection of these resources will in general be closely coupled to the workstation because of their high usage and dynamic resource allocation. Hence the local area network operating system requires high connectivity, equal access to all stations, high speed and non-blocking throughput.

Where either workstations are primarily standalone or are very simple and permanently connected to a terminal server, then the closely coupled local network system may be inappropriate. A loosely coupled network based on lower speed, lower connectivity and including store and forward capabilities may suffice.

User requirements consist of both types of systems and when combined with the requirement for voice processing and communications one possible solution is hybrid LAN (Ethernet/Cambridge Ring) and digital PABX network on to which the IIS is mapped.

As an initial starting point the use of digital PABX switching is attractive because of it's current availability. For example, Monarch, British Telecom's digital PABX , has a customer base of approx. 2500 systems and can be adapted to act as a terminal concentrator and network gateway to Ethernet/Cambridge type LANs.

The development of resource servers can be based on the same microprocessor technology in one or more multiple units for reliability and performance.

5. FUTURE

The evolution from existing office, ADP and communication systems to electronic mail based integrated business systems is still at an early stage. However, the continuing fall in hardware costs and rising complexity of distributed processing costs provides a favourable climate for the growth of document creation, distribution and retrieval by electronic mail store and forward principles. The development of a standard structure and representation of information, requires the cooperation of all of the international committees from CCITT, CEPT, ISO, ECMA, IEEE,IFIP etc.

6. ACKNOWLEDGEMENT

Acknowledgement is made to the Chief Executive, Business Products and Systems, British Telecom Enterprises, for permission to publish this paper.

References

{1} British Telecom, Teletex Service Guides
{2} Teletex Protocol Recommendations S60, S61, S62, S70. CCITT Vol VII - Fascicle VII.2 VIIth Plenary Assembly, Geneva Nov 1980.
{3} British Telecom Contribution. A Standard Document Structure for Enhanced Teletex (for discussion). CCITT Study Group VIII
{4} W M Newman. Office Systems and People. Office Automation, Infotech State of the Art, 1979.
{5} H G Bown, C D O'Brien, W Sawchuk, J R Storey. Picture Description Instruction - PDI - for the Telidon Videotex System. CRC Technical Note No 699-E, Department of Communications, Ottawa, Nov 1979.
{6} British Telecom contribution. A Standard Document Structure for Enhanced Teletex - Further Thoughts. CEPT CD/SE Teletex Rapporteurs Group Working Document TD2, Oslo 2-6 Nov 1981.
{7} M R Desouza. Electronic Information Interchange in the Office Environment. IBM System Journal, Vol 20, No 1, 1981.
{8} P Drake, M J Norton. Integrated Non-Voice Services in the Electronic Office. New Advances in Distributed Computer Systems, NATO Advanced Study Institutes Series C: Mathematical and Physical Sciences, published D Reidel,1981.

P Drake BSc, MSc joined British Telecom in 1968 and promoted early work on interactive computer graphics and computer aided design, and followed this by 5 years in the design of the packet switching networks and terminals. From 1977 to 1980 he was principle designer of the current SHAPE military command and control information system. He is currently the design manager of BTE 's new office systems. P Drake has written several conference papers on packet switching, open systems interconnection, videotex and non-voice services.

Experimental Results of Satellite Aided Computer Network with CS

Y Kakinuma, A Ito, H Takahashi,
K Uchida, K Matsumoto
Ministry of Posts and
Telecommunications, Japan

The experimental system is essentially a computer network which exchanges packets in lower protocols. A large number low traffics users' computer with small earth station is able to communicate with one central computer, through the satellite for experimental usage of the Japanese domestic communication (CS). Packets are exchanged through CS, sharing one or two SCPC channel. The implemented protocols are based on transmitting packets at random from users'terminal to center. Each station has only a function to receive the packets own destined. The purpose of the experiment is to investigate the influence of the link control protocols and multiplex transmission algorithm, on the achievable the impact via a satellite packet-switching system.

1. INTRODUCTION

The satellite aided packet switching computer network system uses mechanically smaller earth stations, utilizing wave-length of K-BAND (30/20 GHz). The communication satellite (CS) for experimental usage was launched on the geostationary orbit (135 deg.E), in Dec. 1977. The experiment is one of a digital communication activity using smaller stations, for example, roof to roof business service links. To evaluate a performance of protocols used in the computer network with CS, the experiment is operational since Jan. 1981. Many small geographycally scattered user stations can communicate with a central large computer system by transmitting their packets through the CS K-BAND transponder, sharing an SCPC (Single Channel per Carrier) channel (A-channel). The central station transssmits packets to user stations through another SCPC channel in a TDM mode (B-channel). The channel data rate is 64kbits/sec with QPSK.

The lower protocols have two levels. One is access schemes and the other is link-level. The channel access schemes implemented is three kinds, based on random transmission technique.
(1) Slotted ALOHA scheme.
(2) Reservation scheme.
(3) Composite scheme.
The packet-error recovery is such as function of being informed by the oposite link, namely the link-level control satisfies ISO-HDLC.
This paper describes the performance of protocols regarding the experimented results.

2. OBJECTIVES AND METHOD

The experimental system was described in detail in previous reports {1} and {2}. Let us say briefly the model. The experimental system is schematized in Fig. 1. The model is centralized type (star network) which consists one center station and two user stations having up to 30 light capacity fake user stations. The sub-network protocol has structure of two levels. One is the SCPC channel usage technique of which the many user can send packets at random and the other is

the link control procedure. Fig. 2 shows schematically the interface and that of queues. The packets in the queues are sent by the following order: the first; supervisor, the next; retransmission and the third; new packets. The table 1 shows the experimental parameters used.

The experimental measurments allow us to gain valuable insight regarding the network usage and behavior. They provide a means to evaluate the performance of protocols of the system. Some types of statistics are employed as the measurments and the artificial traffic generaters.
(1) Cumulative statistics; cumulative statistics consist of the data regarding a variety of events, accumulated a pre-given period. These are in the form of sums and frequencies.
(2) Snap shot methods; this is instantaneous look at the queue length and sending probability.
(3) Packet-trace methods; the trace mechanism allows one packet flow in each event of flowing through. Its packet is stamped with time.
(4) Trafic generator; the traffic generation is clearly a requirments of this system. This generates a fixed length data-packet which consists of any length message. The generating message rate is assumed as Poisson arrival.

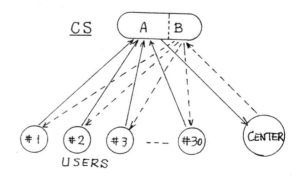

Fig. 1 EXPERIMENTAL SYSTEM

The overhead of HDLC procedure is investigated in the link level characteristics. On increasing in the packet error rate, the supervisor-packets augment to sending the data. In the experiment we choose one channel reservation scheme.

3. CHARACTERISTICS OF ACCESS SCHEMES

The experimental data was collected under a error-free condition. Each user station/terminal generates messages according to the Poisson arrival. They are two types of messages; one is file-transfer and another is inquiry/responce. An approximate analysis of the performance has been done in the reference {2}. Fig. 3 - Fig. 6 show the throughput vs delay and the throughput vs channel traffics (included new-packet, retransmission and supervisor packet) respectively.

3.1 Slotted ALOHA scheme

The slotted ALOHA scheme {3} is well known. In this scheme, as the channel load increases, the probability of collisions among different user's packets increases, and the throughput of the total system rather decreases and finally falls into zero. The user stations are informed failures of transmiting from the central station through B-channel. In the case of the error recovery of packets at link-level, the channel throughput was analized in reference {2}.

When the throughput is a few percent, the average delay is nealy equal to a one hop propagation time, in the case of file-transfer. Channel traffic is a good agreement with the analysis {4}. In the inquiry/responce message type, the delay is very long, due to increasing channel traffic to center. The problem may exist in a timing of sending supervisor-packets. No control to them has been made.

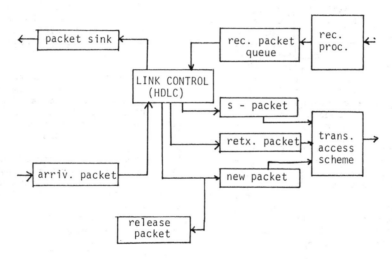

Fig. 2 sub-network structure

Table 1   Experimental parameter

System parameter	Access			
	Slotted ALOHA	1ch. Reserv.	2ch. Reserv.	Composite
max.outst.	10	64	64	64
error recov.	srej/rej	rej	rej	srej/rej
p/f timer	50	150	150	100
time out rec.	RR	RR	RR	RR
No. users	30	30	30	30
message	file inquiry	file inquiry	file inquiry	file inquiry
mesg.length	1	1	1	1

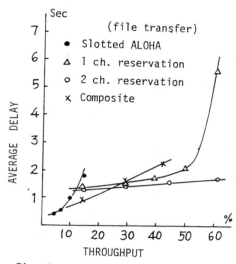

Fig. 3 Throughput vs delay

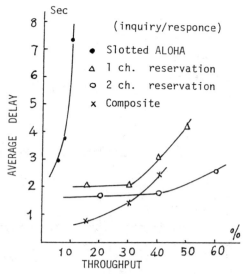

Fig. 5 Throughput vs delay

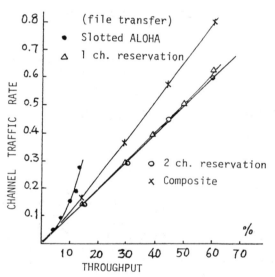

Fig. 4 Channel traffic

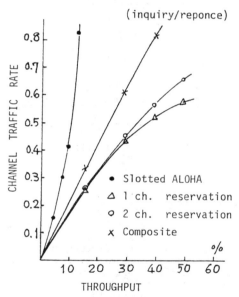

Fig. 6 Channel traffic

3.2 Reservation scheme

In case of one channel slot reservation scheme, the channel(A-channel) is devided into fixed length cycles. Furthermore each cycle is devided into two regions which are data slots and reservation slots devided into some small slots (eg. four small slots). The user station starts to send a reservation burst contained the information of a number of necessary slots for sending data and of their priority , with a slotted ALOHA-mode. The central station allocates the necessary slots according to the requests from users and broadcasts the slot allocation burst for every cycle through the B-channel. The B-channel has at least one broadcast slot. In two channel reservation case, data sending channel and reservation request channel are used. A transmitting algolism is the same as the one channel.

In case of one channel reservation, the packets reach at the center, only one time reservation, if those of input do not exceeded about 50%. The input rate being over 50%, the reservation-region is going to decrease. This means that the reservation-packets collide frequently. Fig. 7 shows the histogram of packets delay and the throughput. When the throughput is greater than 60%, packets are sent through all of data-slots in one cycle.

In the two channel reservation, the delay is fairly short, most of packets are sent only one time reservation. The channel traffics are almost data-packets in the case of the file-transfer. On the other hand, in the inquiry/responce, it crooks right in excess of throughput 30% in Fig. 6.

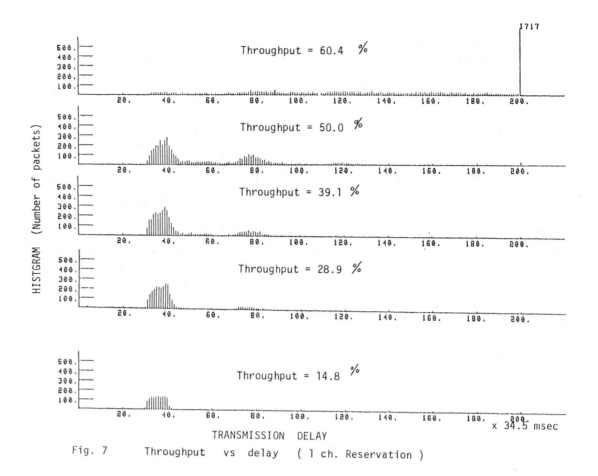

Fig. 7   Throughput   vs   delay   (1 ch. Reservation)

3.3 Composite scheme

In the composite scheme, user stations can use two channels. The one channel sends new data packets with pre-setting probability by the slotted ALOHA mode. Retransmitted packets and supervisor packets are transmitted by exclusively preassigned TDMA mode. If there occured more excess packets to sent, the user station sends 'HELP' burst through preassigned slot. After that the user is informed the allocated slots, then the retransmission can start.

In the composite scheme, the performance of delay shows the Slotted ALOHA, when the throughput is less than 30% shown in Fig. 8. It is supposed that the scheme will make one of effective network under an adequate channel control.

4. CHARACTERISTICS OF HDLC

The presence of the 0.27-second one way propagation delay has an important impact on the performance of error control techniques by HDLC. Being used HDLC procedure, the throughput efficency can be made virtually sensitive to propagation delay. It is observed the performance of HDLC in the satellite link in a condition of noisy channel. In this case there are some problem;-

(a) After requesting to send packet, a large and random transmission delay exists.
(b) A packet is vulnerable by noise, which causes long transmission delay.
The experimental run was characterized by focussing the one channel reservation. The message type is 10-packets of Poisson distribution.

4.1 Overhead

Fig. 9 shows the relation of throughput vs traffic under some burst error rate respectively. The overhead of HDLC is the kinds of packets as follows:
(1) Discarded packets which are detected sequence error at the the received link.

(2) Supervisor packets (RR, RNR, REJ and so on).

Now It could be considered that the overhead is in directly proportion to the throughput except a heavy loading input rate, from Fig. 9. Fig. 10 shows the overhead vs burst error rate curves, regarding the supervisor and discarded packets. This curves are modified from fig. 9. When the burst error rate increases, the maximum throughput decreases in the cause of increasing the overhead.

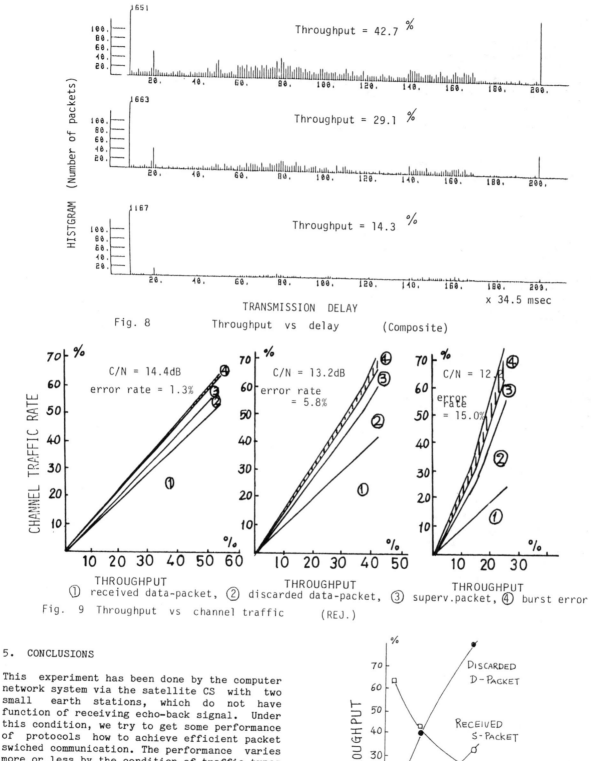

HISTGRAM (Number of packets)

|651

Throughput = 42.7 %

|663

Throughput = 29.1 %

|167

Throughput = 14.3 %

TRANSMISSION DELAY

x 34.5 msec

Fig. 8   Throughput vs delay   (Composite)

C/N = 14.4dB
error rate = 1.3%

C/N = 13.2dB
error rate = 5.8%

C/N = 12.
error rate = 15.0%

CHANNEL TRAFFIC RATE

THROUGHPUT

① received data-packet, ② discarded data-packet, ③ superv.packet, ④ burst error

Fig. 9 Throughput vs channel traffic   (REJ.)

5. CONCLUSIONS

This experiment has been done by the computer network system via the satellite CS with two small earth stations, which do not have function of receiving echo-back signal. Under this condition, we try to get some performance of protocols how to achieve efficient packet swiched communication. The performance varies more or less by the condition of traffic types or the quality of its channel. Authors try to integrate burst and link protocols a suitable one.

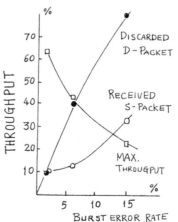

THROUGHPUT

DISCARDED
D-PACKET

RECEIVED
S-PACKET

MAX.
THROUGPUT

BURST ERROR RATE

FIG. 10   HDLC OVERHEAD

REFERENCES

{1} H. Takahashi, et al,. Experimental system for satellite computer network via CS. 5th. ICCC, 1980 Atlanta, 451-456

{2} H. Takahashi, et al., Experimental packet communication system via K-band japanese communication satellite, 5th Int. conf. on Digit. Sat. Commun. in Genoa, March 1981.

{3} N. Abramson, Packet swiching with satellite. AFIPS Conf. Proc. NCC,42. 1973. 695-702

{4} H. Matsunaga, et al., The performance of protocols in the satellite channel. 5th. ICCC, 1980 Atlanta, 445-450

Y. Kakinuma joined in the Radio research laboratories (RRL) in 1964. He engaged in the NASDA to launch the CS & BSE from 1976 to 1979. Since 1980 he has engaged in the division of information processing of RRL.

A. Ito received ph.D in physics from Kyoto University in 1974. He joined in Radio research laboratories in 1974. His present work is on communication protocols' design & experiment.

H. Takahashi joined in Radio research laboratories (RRL), MOPT, in 1957. Since 1976 she has engaged in the research on computer communications. She is the Chief of Information process-ing Section.

K. Uchida was born in Hokkaido, in 1943. He has worked in RRL since 1965 on information process-ing.

K. Matsumoto was born in Yamaguchi, in 1952. He entered RRL in 1975, His research interests are system analysis, simulation and computer communications.

Bulk Broadcasting with High Speed Satellite Links

J P Hilsz
Projet NADIR, France

Satellite Communication Systems, such as TELECOM 1, provide high data transmission rates (several Megabits per second) and broadcasting facilities. To support new distributed applications using satellite links, fast Bulk Broadcasting and Switching form a convenient tool. This paper presents general principles for a protocol allowing to quickly broadcast bulks of data, e.g. 10 Megabytes in less than one minute. First, the Multidestination Bulk Transfer Service between one sender and several receivers is defined. Then, in order to achieve a realistic design, satellite links characteristics are reviewed. Specific key points are examined : multi-receiver transmission control, sender processing load, behaviour of transport entities during recovery procedures. Main protocol mechanisms are discussed before summary : distributed error control and alternate recovery strategies, loose control flow policy, packet structure and connection monitoring. Finally, the methodology used for validation and performance measurement is presented.

INTRODUCTION

Satellite Communication Networks are a versatile tool for transfering bulk files and high throughput stream traffic. In France, the satellite TELECOM 1 will be launched in 1983. In order to study and implement new applications for distributed information systems taking advantage of satellite networks such as TELECOM 1, the NADIR project was started by French Ministries of PTT and Industry.

First applications developed by NADIR include high speed file transfer. TELECOM 1 broadcasting services offer high data rate links, but unfortunately involve long propagation delays and fluctuating error rates. Because of such parameters and the multidestination aspect, available protocols do not fit efficiently. So appropriate solutions are discussed and defined.

BULK TRANSFER OBJECTIVES

Bulk Broadcasting using high speed satellite links performs the multiple copy of a bulk data file from one sending station (broadcaster) to several receiving stations (receivers). Each copy is globally available only after the complete reception on a bulk device.

This service is equivalent to usual physical carrying of magnetic tapes between distant informatic centres. It uses the broadcasting properties of a communication satellite network.

Satellite Network Characteristics

TELECOM 1 [1] provides high speed broadcasting X21 circuits, including :
A - simple broadcasting without return channels,
B - broadcasting with return channels.

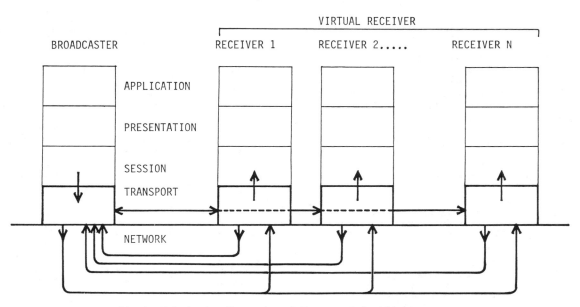

Fig.1. Multipoint Network and Transport Architecture

The service A can be used in conjunction with terrestrial packet switching circuits (e.g. TRANSPAC) in order to support reception acknowledgment and control.

With the service B, return channels are merged within a total throughput equal to broadcasting throughput.

Since it involves only one homogeneous network, the service B will be used for first bulk broadcasting implementation.

The Multidestination Transport layer assumes that the Multipoint Network provides :
- one broadcasting channel such that each packet transmitted by the broadcaster is received by each receiver,
- several return channels (one for each receiver) such that a packet transmitted by a receiver is received only by the broadcaster.

TELECOM 1 broadcasting circuit throughput ranges from 2400 bit/s to 2 Mbit/s. Bit error rate is guaranteed to be less than 10E-6 during 99 % of time or 10E-10 using forward error correction (FEC). Propagation delay per circuit is about 300 ms and remains constant once the connection is established.

Error distributions and propagation delays are roughly independent for each circuit.

Transport Architecture

Data to be transmitted are viewed as a string of bytes recorded on a bulk device. Efficient access is assumed for any substring (data blocks) such that bulk device input/outputs do not slow the transfer process.

Multidestination Transport software resides in the layer 4 (Transport Layer) of the ISO Open Systems Architecture (Fig.1). The end-to-end transport uses layer 3 (Network) Services, which are only required to deliver the error-free packets, keeping their sequence. The bulk file is a Transport Service Data Unit (TSDU), it is transferred using network packets carrying bulk blocks or Transport Protocol Data Units (TPDUs).

A PROTOCOL COPING WITH SATELLITE MULTIDESTINATION ENVIRONMENT

To cope with network characteristics (throughput, delays, errors, multidestination), no standard protocol is available {2, 3} and existing link procedures such as HDLC cannot be simply adapted {4}. Because of on-the-air storage induced by propagation delay (up to hundreds of kiloBytes), full efficiency can be reached only if any well transmitted message is considered as well received by any destination - even when it is out of sequence and follows not received ones.

New schemes must be designed to achieve :
- safe data transmission, with error correction,
- multidestination control (flow control and reception monitoring).

Error correction

The network service discards packets in error. Retransmission mechanisms must be used. They are distinguished by :

- their triggering conditions and semantics: positive acknowledgments (ACKs) or negative ones (NAKs), reject from some packet number or selective reject,
- their retransmission order : immediate or deferred for convenience (optimising bulk storage access).

The common principle is that the broadcaster segments the bulk into a stream of unambiguously identified packets. Numbering allows each receiver to build its own bulk copy.

Using ACKs a good efficiency can be obtained only if a receiver can acknowledge and accept packets out of sequence {4}, thus only packets not acknowledged by all receivers need to be retransmitted. Moreover, with many receivers, ACK management tends to be complex. To be reliable, ACKs must be identified, and so corresponding tasks are performed as many times as there are receivers. This applies also to the case of acknowledging rejects such as HDLC's REJ or SREJ.

Using Selective Retransmission Requests or NAKS, receivers control explicitly the retransmission process, optimisation is achieved if the broadcaster retransmits only negative acknowledged packets. NAKs may not acknowledge previous receptions and therefore can be anonymous : broadcaster is only required to retransmit the referenced packet. But this mechanism must be completed by a global positive acknowledgment for the whole bulk to prevent any deadlock resulting from a last packet loss.

Retransmissions can take place following two strategies:
- instant correction, where the broadcaster is committed to retransmit lost packets as soon as possible,
- deferred correction, where the broadcaster corrects errors with sequential passes on the bulk.

Flow Control

A 2 Mbit/s satellite circuit stores about 75 kBytes. So, if the broadcaster takes account of receivers current capacity, instant throughput control is impossible. Even if such a mechanism was effective, its extension to multidestination would not be obvious.

Throughput tuning will be done first by previous negociation of a maximum broadcasting throughput.

Another concern is resource freeing. Usually main core buffers containing transmitted packets are released when receiving ACKs. Because of channel storage (150 kBytes/round trip), asynchronous corrections and specific bulk device access, the basic resource management principle is that bulk blocks are available via some kind of direct virtual storage access.

Packet Length and Numbering

Short packets tend to minimise the amount of retransmissions - in the worst case, the number of lost packets equals the number of bit errors. But short packets tend to increase the communication devices processing load, and multidestination increases the broadcaster load.

As a trade-off, a constant packet length is chosen according to the number of receivers and the class of channels quality (using F.E.C. or not).

Normal transmission and retransmission on error are quite independent (deferred correction), so an infinite numbering scheme (say 32 bit field) assigns a unique number for each packet of the bulk.

PROPOSED PROTOCOL SUMMARY

The broadcaster sends the bulk as a sequence of packets and retransmits only those requested by NAKs.
Each receiver detects missing packets on receiving out-of-sequence packets, and then sends corresponding selective NAKs without waiting for previous error correction. Negative acknowledgments are not identified : correction is global. The last packet is signalled by an End-of-TSDU mark and permits the receiver to state its complete bulk reception or ask for correction of residual missing blocks.

Correction is either instant or deferred.

Instant Correction

When the broadcaster receives NAKs, it retransmits the referenced packets as soon as possible. To protect against multiple NAKs for the same packet lost by several receivers, NAKs for one retransmitted packet are ignored until some time interval has elapsed.

A receiver repeats any NAK periodically while the corresponding packet is still missing, and ignores any replicated packet. When the last data packet is reached, the broadcaster repeats it periodically until each receiver has acknowledged the whole bulk file.

Deferred Correction

The broadcaster sends the whole bulk and collects the NAKs. Retransmissions take place in successive correction phases. Each phase includes :
- retransmission of NAKed packets following their sequence order, plus the last packet (to signal a new phase),
- collection of received NAKs, for next phase.

Successive phases are entered until each receiver acknowledges the whole bulk file, indicating there is no more correction left.

Each receiver sends NAKs for missing packets, once per phase. Phase changing is detected upon last packet reception or when the last received packet number decreases.

Monitoring

In any correction mode, to allow reception monitoring :
- each receiver sends periodically a presence acknowledgment indicating its name and its reception progression,
- the broadcaster checks with a greater period the reception of at least such one presence indication from each receiver.

PLANNED EXPERIMENTATION

Bulk Broadcasting will be experimented on NADIR experimental network with 3 CII Honeywell Bull Level 6 computers interconnected by ANIS, a TELECOM 1 simulator.

The measurement plan makes service parameters to vary in order to determine performance and field of application of the Bulk Transport Service.

CONCLUSION

A new class of Multidestination Bulk Transport Protocol is defined coping with high throughput and other characteristics of satellite broadcasting services.

Such a transport service is the base for High Speed File Transfer, a versatile tool to complement terrestrial packet networks.

REFERENCES

{1} J.P.Guénin, B.Ghillebaert, C.Funtowicz. "Towards the Integrated Service Digital Network: TELECOM 1". 5th Int. Conf. on Digital Satellite Communication. GENOA 81.

{2} "HDLC/Checkpoint Mode - Elements of Procedure". ECMA Working Paper. April 1981.

{3} "Connection - Oriented Transport Protocol Specification". Draft ISO/TC 97/SC16 N698. June 1981.

{4} Ch.Huitema, I.Valet. "An Experiment on High Speed File transfer using Satellite Links". DATACOM 81 Conference Proceedings, Mexico. October 1981.

J.Philippe HILSZ received the Civil Engineer Degree in Communications and Software Engineering from the Ecole Nationale Supérieure des Télécommunications in Paris, France.

After serving the avionics industry, he has been involved in communication network projects. Currently consultant at TECSI, an ALCATEL company subsidiary of CGE, he is now working with the NADIR project at INRIA. His main concerns are High Speed Data Transfering and Message Systems using Satellite Networks.

He is an AFCET member and contributes to IFIP Working Group 6.5 on Message Systems.

A New Type of Communication Satellite needed for Computer Based Messaging

S Ramani
National Centre for Software
Development & Computing Techniques,
India
R Miller
Infomedia, USA

It is difficult to implement electronic mail and computer conferencing in areas where no public data networks exist. Even where the PDNs do exist, these systems can benefit from the use of more appropriate communication techniques. The use of an inexpensive communication satellite in a low level orbit (100-5000 kms high), operating a relatively narrow band transceiver (offering 64 KBPS to 256 KBPS of throughput) is proposed. It would employ a frequency below 3000 MHz to enable the use of antennas with low directivity and low cost direct reception equipment on the ground. The satellite would carry an on-board computer. Polling ground stations, it would collect and store messages which it would distribute around the world. The proposed satellite is promising for use in modern forms of telegraphy particularly relevant to developing countries [1].

1. INTRODUCTION

The essence of computer mediated communication, both in messaging and in computer conferencing, is asynchronicity and the automation of filing, indexing, copying and notification aspects. By buffering messages, such systems eliminate the need for communicants to be on-line simultaneously. Offering written (and automatically filed) records of all messages, they facilitate a reliable, convenient mode of communication in which there is time to create responses after deliberation, unlike the case in telephony. Requiring an effective throughput of only a hundred bits per second (BPS) to carry all that a person could dictate at full speed, they offer a tremendous economy in/transmission requirements. It is worth noting that a keyboard operator working at full speed produces a net output of only 40 BPS. An electronic teleprinter receiving messages at 100 BPS can print out one 100-word message every minute. The contrast with voice communication is best illustrated by considering the current annual telegraph throughput of a typical country, of the order of a few hundred million telegrams per year. If all these telegrams were to be transmitted through a single channel, a transmission capacity of 64 KBPS, normally used to carry one voice channel in the PCM format, would be more than adequate for the purpose.

But, traditionally, message systems have had to suffer all the problems and overheads of voice communication. In most areas of the world, access to computer conferencing systems involves the use of an analog telephone network through modems, even though key segments of such a network may be employing PCM transmission at 64 KBPS, two way, but delivering only an effective throughput of 100 BPS, one way (limited by the key-boarding speed at the terminal, and the reading speed of user). An undue dependence on interfacing to a telephone network not originally designed with this application in mind creates a variety of problems. Local access arrangements based on good quality local cables, switching equipment, modems, etc. become essential. The user usually has to cope with an immoderate tariff for long distance transmission (up to 4 US $ per minute over long distances).

2. SUB-SYNCHRONOUS SATELLITES

Communication satellites have not so far eliminated these problems in messaging, mainly because they have been designed, again, without this applicaton in mind. Because of this, it is necessary to investigate new types of communication satellites.

Consider a message switch in a sub-synchronous orbit. With its on-board memories, it can store and forward messages. Instead of using a transponder, it will use a transceiver, communicating purely in digital format. Signals will then do only a one way trip at a time, either up-link or down-link before the signal is regenerated. This feature, and those covered below in Sec. 2.2, vastly simplify communication design problems, permitting the use of low power transmitters and simple antenna systems.

2.1 Global distribution: The very fact that such a satellite will not be stationary at any longitude will become its strength. Orbiting the earth every few hours, it would be able to distribute messages globally without extensive inter-network connections otherwise required.

2.2 Narrow bandwidth and power requirements: Since the information to be communicated is very compact, a few thousand bits per message, a single 64 KBPS transceiver seems adequate to meet the needs of thousands of small earth stations. Earth stations would serve a range of computer installations: from one terminal micro or mini computers equipped with individual transceivers, to larger computer systems with an average of 20 to 30 terminals per transceiver. Each earth station computer would support message preparation and handle relevant communication protocols. Assuming net throughput through the satellite to be 100 BPS per active terminal, it is clear that several thousand terminals could use a single satellite

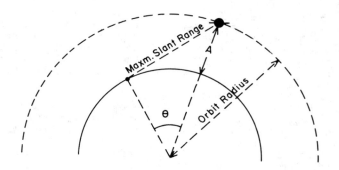

Fig.1 Orbit Size and Visibility

Formulas used to compute parameters in Fig. 2:

$$\text{Real Period} = 84.49 \left(\frac{A+R}{R}\right)^{3/2} \text{Minutes [3]}.$$

Theta, the highest latitude at which the satellite is visible,

$$= \cos^{-1}\left(\frac{R}{R+A}\right)$$

R being the earth's radius, taken as 6378 kms.

Fig.2 Altitude vs Visiblity

Alti-tude A	Orbit Radius R	Maxm Slant Range	Theta in de-grees	Visible Time	Real Period	Visible Time for Pass
300	6678	1979	17.2	9.6%	90.5 mts	8.7 mts
500	6878	2574	22.0	12.2%	94.6 mts	11.4 mts
1000	7378	3708	30.2	16.8%	105 mts	17.5 mts
1500	7878	4624	35.9	19.9%	116 mts	23.1 mts
2000	8378	5432	40.4	22.4%	127 mts	28.3 mts
2500	8878	6175	44.1	24.5%	139 mts	33.9 mts
3000	9378	6875	47.1	26.2%	151 mts	39.6 mts
4000	10378	8186	52.1	28.9%	175 mts	50.7 mts

Notes

1. Distances are in kilometers.
2. Visible time given in the last column holds only for locations on the equator. However, 'visible time' does <u>not</u> fall sharply with latitude till limiting latitudes are reached.

323

of the type envisaged.

The narrow bandwidth required will make it possible for the satellite and earth stations to use low power transmission and to use relatively low (possibly VHF or UHF) frequencies. The earth stations will need only to use inexpensive transceivers. The fact that the satelite will be ten times nearer, at the moment of communication, than a geosynchronous satellite will also contribute significantly to the reduction in power requirements.

Earth stations would be able to use directional antennae, pointed due south (in the Northern hemisphere) or in a direction west of south. With a lobe 10 to 30 degrees wide between 3 dB points, such antennae will reduce power requirements further, without unduly restricting communication. Transmitted power of the proposed satellites could be in the range from 1 to 20 watts. The transmitter need not be continuously on and would be kept completely off, for instance, during major ocean crossings, and over all territory where there are no participating earth stations.

2.3 Direct reception from satellite: The greatest benefit to be conferred by the proposed system will be the nature of the communication access offered: direct reception from satellite, making it possible to reach, at very low cost, remote areas and other areas where traditional data communication is difficult or impossible.

2.4 Attitude control: If non-directional antennae are employed in the satellite, attitude control requirements would be vastly simplified, leaving only the requirements of pointing the solar panels properly. On the other hand, attitude control could be helpful, enabling the use of directional antennae, reducing power requirements further. In any case, the beams would not be narrow beams and only coarse attitude control would be required.

2.5 Control and security aspects: The large number of earth stations in the proposed system poses new, but not intractable, problems. How does one prevent unauthorized access? How does one safeguard against a transceiver on the ground getting stuck in the 'on' position?

Apart from usual telemetry and telecommand channels, there is need for a communication control channel. A control station, using a highly directive antenna, would use this channel to pass on control information to the on-board computer. For instance, such transmission would carry individual keys to be used in encrypting the up-link and down-link for each transceiver on the ground. Using any simple encryption scheme, the system could easily attain a high degree of protection from individuals, though not from professional cryptanalytic attacks by major agencies.

The satellite would poll earth stations in the order of their longitude as it passes, to collect messages and repeat this polling a few times during the visible period each pass over a station. It would use an internal clock and

its own longitude counter maintained by the on-board computer, corrected once each orbit by the control station. At each polling time, the satellite should report to each earth station, as a security measure, the last message number received from that station and the time of last contact. If unauthorized access does occur, this arrangement will facilitate prompt discovery. Routine statistical reports concerning all earth stations should be sent by the satellite to the control station each time it passes over it, to help in monitoring and management.

Special design features could be incorporated into the earth station transceivers to make it impossible for them to be stuck 'on'. An output monitoring arrangement, in hardware or software, which automatically detects this condition and triggers an isolator is worth considering.

In applications requiring more than routine precautions against unauthorized access, techniques such as spread spectrum communication may be considered.

2.6 Orbit size: The orbiting altitude will have a major effect on the performance of the satellite proposed (see Figs. 1 and 2). At a higher altitude, the satellite would be visible for a longer period each pass, but the passes would be separated by many hours.

Within a small or medium sized country, a visible period half an hour long or more would confer special benefits. All messages transmitted during this period for delivery within the same country or region would be delivered with almost no delay. On the other hand, a low orbit reduces the guaranteed delivery time, making it as low as a hundred minutes. Figs. 1 and 2 illustrate the relationship between satellite altitude and delivery time. They also provide other information, such as visibility of satellites at different latitudes away from the equator. Theta, in the figures, indicates the latitude upto which equatorial satellites are visible for a given altitude. Minimum elevation angles necessary for good reception and refraction effects need to be taken into account in discussing high latitude stations.

An interesting possibility is the use of two or more satellites. This will require the software on the ground (see Section 3) to be a bit more complex, to take different message sequence numbers into account. Inter-satellite communication would be the next feature to be considered in such a design. The narrow bandwidth links necessary can be established with great ease compared to high bandwidth links between geo-stationary satellites handling voice bandwidth signals. A satellite moving east to west, if possible, would complement a conventional satellite very well for delivery of international messages [4].

With multiple satellites, it may also be worth considering the use of relay stations on the ground meant to facilitate inter-satellite traffic of messages. They could reduce on-board storage requirements and act as intelligent intermediaries in inter-satellite communication.

3. GROUND EQUIPMENT

Each earth station will have a transceiver connected to a microprocessor which would run special software to control the equipment. Possibly using a yagi antenna, the transceivers would transmit on a specified up-link frequency, different from the down-link frequency, offering the usual benefits of isolating signals going up from those going down. Transmission would be rigidly controlled by polling commands from the satellite asking a station to send at a strictly specified time. Using a programmable real-time clock synchronized by software to time signals from the satellite, the microprocessor would carry out these commands, thereby adopting a reservations technique [2] for time assignment. After sending a message segment, a few hundred characters long, an earth station would indicate if it had anything more to transmit, further segments of the same message or those of another message. The microprocessor would also be carrying out monitoring and diagnostic functions to ensure trouble-free operation of the whole earth station, giving suitable indications to the control station or to the local user as appropriate.

The use of a reservations technique will make it possible to obtain a high throughput. The microprocessor could also implement text compression algorithms, possibly offering an increase of 30% to 50% greater throughput and on-board message storage using the same hardware configuration (shortening of messages by text compression would actually save storage both on ground and on the satellite).

3.1 User facilities: The user would need message preparation facilities, on-line filing and indexing facilities, conferencing facilities and would require hardcopy output facilities, frequently on office quality output devices. It seems ideal that these functions be separated from those of a communication control microprocessor which would be identical in all user installations. Messaging and conferencing facilities could be provided in a variety of ways by employing one-user micro computers or multi-user computers of different sizes. The interfacing between the microprocessor and the user computer should ideally be a simple standard 25 pin interface that is used between data terminal equipment and modems. However, no modems would be required on these links which would operate under a standard hand-shake arrangement.

Interface speeds of 300, 600, 1200, 2400, 4800 and 9600 BPS seem ideal, with a speed selection arrangement to suit the needs at each location. An additional current loop interface at 50/75/100/200 BPS seems profitable to have, to connect teleprinters using the 5 bit alphabet. The microprocessor should also be able to accept messages, prepared in a standard format, directly from a terminal or a teleprinter and should not make a messaging system computer essential at all locations.

4. THE ON-BOARD COMPUTER

The computer on-board the satellite should ideally be capable of storing all the messages it receives in one orbit period. At 64 KBPS, 50% duty factor, this would be 15 or 20 megabytes. This is not, however, a rigid requirement. Depending upon the traffic expected, altitude, distribution of earth stations on the ground, nature of traffic, etc., an on-board storage in the range of 1 to 5 megabytes could be chosen. Note that traffic within a region need not be stored over an orbit, as it can be switched more or less instantaneously. On-board storage should be in the form of a semiconductor memory built out of RAMS, or be a bubble memory system. In view of the small physical size involved, radiation shielding seems to pose no problems.

The on-board computer would handle communication with the control station, communication protocols and polling, message reception, storage and transmission. It will also generate periodic statistical reports.

5. OTHER CONSIDERATIONS

A number of questions need to be examined: for instance, the choice between a single channel and multiple channels for ground to satellite communication. Multiple channels could help in increasing traffic handling capacity and in reducing impacts of equipment failure. But, increase in traffic handling capacity would have to be matched by an increase in the size of on-board memory.

The question of choice of orbit is also interesting. An orbit inclined to the equator can facilitate a low orbit satellite to reach farther north and south, but there will be no guarantee that each earth station would be able to access it once per revolution; but these orbits are attractive when a multiple satellite scheme is visualised. Polar orbits have their advantages, but the cost/benefit ratios may not be all that attractive. Fig. 3 illustrates the

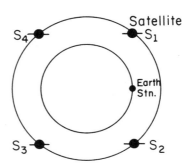

Fig.3 Four Equatorial Satellites

effect of having four equatorial satellites. For stations at low latitudes, at least one of the four satellites will be visible at any given time. With inter-satellite relay, it will then be possible to provide for no-delay communication between any pair of locations at low latitudes. Similar configurations may even permit on-line data communication between remote locations, in a packet-switching mode.

Being in low orbits, the proposed satellites will be in earth shadow for several hours a day. But, because of low power requirements, this is not expected to pose a major problem. Further, it should be noted exposure to Sun and shade alternate regularly every two or three hours; the period in shade per revolution is half an hour or less. Satellite design from the point of view of power to be used and from that of cost is a critical area which needs attention.

6. APPLICATIONS

The technology proposed here could revolutionize telegraphy and create modern forms for it. Its impact should be particularly high in the developing world, not too far from the equator. New forms of telegraphy, offering transmission in 7 bit alphabets and in local scripts can be created. Extension to facsimile transmission is a clear possibility, subject to on-board storage limitations. By making possible several thousand low cost earth stations per satellite, remote and rural areas can be brought the benefits of low cost communication. Message relay in Telex and in similar systems is another possibility. In industrialized economies, this low cost technology may hasten the arrival of the office of the future, vastly reducing the use of paper and lowering the significance of distance as a factor in communications.

A major application of the proposed satellite could be to offer a "broadcast videotex" service. A hundred pages of information, possibly incorporating graphics, could be transmitted simultaneously to all users in a region in 5 to 10 seconds. Special techniques relevant to broadcast videotex, such as selective updates of part of the stored information, economic encoding of graphic primitives etc., could be used with profit.

Common interest groups who might be interested in adopting this technology would include airlines, banks, shipping and oil companies, international bodies in science, education and culture, scientific cooperation groups, inter-university groups, etc. Defence applications are obvious, but it should be noted that this proposal offers an opportunity to redirect what is partly a military technology to peaceful applications.

ACKNOWLEDGEMENTS

The authors thank the International Development Research Centre, Canada, which organized a workshop on "Computer Message Systems for Developing Nations" in Ottawa, October 1981. This proposal was conceived and developed during the workshop, stimulated and supported by the vigorous discussions it triggered. The authors are indebted to the participants at this Workshop for their comments and observations.

S. Ramani thanks the Space Applications Centre (SAC), Ahmedabad, India, and the Telecommunications Research Centre (TRC), New Delhi, for collaborative arrangements under which he gained valuable learning and work experiences in the area of data communication via satellite channels.

REFERENCES

1. Gupta, P.P. and Ramani, S.
   Computer Message Systems for Developing Nations:
   A Design Exercise
   in (Ed.) Uhlig, R.
   Computer Message Systems,
   North Holland, 1981
2. Roberts, L.,
   Dynamic Allocation of Satellite Capacity through Packet Reservation,
   AFIPS Proceedings, NCC, 1973

3. David Fishlock,
   A Guide to Earth Satellites,
   Macdonald/American Elsevier, 1971

4. Vinod Kumar, K.,
   Private Communication

Dr S. Ramani studied at the Indian Institute of Technology, Bombay, and works at the National Centre for Software Development (NCSDCT), Bombay. He is the Editor of the Journal 'Computer Science and Informatics'. He has led a team in the development of packet broadcasting software currently used in an experiment run in collaboration by SAC, TRC (see Acknowledgement) and the NCSDCT through the satellite APPLE.

Dr Richard Miller studied at the Stanford University and is a co-founder of the Infomedia Corporation which specialises in computer message systems and computer based conferencing. He has been a consultant to NASA. He works at the Telematics International Corporation at Menlo Park, California.

Teletex in Sweden

C E Gustawson
The Swedish Administration of
Telecommunication (Televerket)

The public service Teletex

Telegraph from the middle of the eighteen
hundreds, the telephone from around the turn
of the century, radio from the 20's, telex
from the 40's and television from the 50's.
All are taken for granted in our daily lives.

None of these Breakthroughs in Telecommunications could have happened had it not been
for the vigorous work done by international
standardisation committees. In no other area
has standardisation work started so early nor
come as far as it has in the field of telecommunications and the Swedish Televerket are
internationally one of the most active
bodies.

Let's talk a bit about the origins of
Teletex. The Telex technique available up to
now and with its roots in the 30's had, when
the whole thing started in 1976, 40 years
behind it. Telex was the only technique we
had for communicating text within an ordered,
generally distributable form. It's hardly
suprising that people in various places
started to think about the possibilities of a
new, common, word's embrasing communications
system based upon the technologies of the
80's. A basis for such a system emerged after
agreement was reaced within CCITT
international working group for telecommunications in November 1980. That's slightly
less than 2 years ago!

Now back to the communications service
Teletex. The enormous potential of Teletex is
hidden in the words "world standard".
What makes Televerket's Teletex different to
other text processing systems is that Teletex
will become a public service within the
community. And that ladies and gentlemen is a
very big difference!

With Teletex it will be possible from day 1
to communicate in a completely uniform and
carefully standardised manner with absolutely
anyone else connected to the Teletex network.
Now this must sound like music in the ears of
those who have become hot under the collar
due to the never ending battle of the systems
currently raging in other areas such as video
and data processing.

This will not be the case in this area I can
assure you. As a result of an international
agreement the whole of the western world will
link into the Teletex system. This in turn
means that Teletex is obliged to provide
reception and transmission services 24 hours
a day, 7 days a week, throughout the world.

Right from the start Teletex will link itself
up with the already enormous Telex network.

All this means that Teletex has prospects of
becoming the system that everyone dare invest
their money in very early on.

An advanced textprocessor but at the same
time a public service.

You must agree that it all sounds fantastic.
The result of all this is Teletex.

This of course will have some unique
consequences. Teletex will be sold with an
official, world wide numbersystem as an
important component. A reliable, fully up to
date, number directory covering Teletex and
Telex terminals throughout the world.

The background to our current endeavours

In order to have a better understanding of
Televerket's investment and Teletex's role in
Sweden I'd like to breafly go over some of
the parameters that we're using as a basis
for our current direction.

Telecommunications has become an area of
fervent activity for most companies in the
industrial world. Thousands of millions have
already been allocated for investment during
the 80's. New media and methods of communication can radically change both our working
and private lives.

In other words the scene is set for one of
the biggest controversies yet, when computer
and telecommunication technologies converge.
The telecommunications branch has come into
contact with the clamorous and aggressively
energetic computer branch. Companies from
both areas are now trying to expand into each
others territory. At the same time the
national telecommunications monopolies are
creaking at the joints due to the pressure of
the frontier war currently being waged with
the computer and business system companies.

In this connection it is important to have a
company gool. In our case it is to become the
leaders within the fields of telecommunications and information management i.e.

Telematic.

"If there's information there and it moves,
then were interested in it" is a slogan that
we can justifiably place on our buisness
cards. We've been involved in the four areas
of image, voice, text and data for a long
time and have the ambition to invest further
in these areas in the future.

Taken together, our role in both business and
community affairs place us in a unique and
responsible position that we have to consider
in all our future developments.

In summary one can say that a product introduced in the area of text processing cannot
be sean in isolation but as an integral part
of a total system and communications
framework.

Teletex`common elements

All of Televerket's Teletex systems have at
least 4 common elements, independent of the
level of sophistication enjoyed.

They are as a minimum word and text
processors, obviously with widely varying
functionality but all are capable of
producing and editing text.

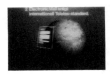

All of course will be capable of sending
electronic mail according to at least the
basic Teletex standard but in most cases
higher, and communicate with all the Telex
equipment already installed in the world. In
our case it is also thought to use the equipment for internal communication based on
local area networks and also for
communicating with computers using for
example 3780 and 3270 protocols.

Another function, common in all the products,
will be the ability for storing and
retrieving text. Examples of the storage
media used for this purpose are RAM memory,
floppy diskettes and harddisks. Taken
together these give the user maximum flexibility when chosing equipment that best suits
his particular volumes and requirements for
archiving.

Naturally the systems will also be equipped
with functions for printing. The minimum
standard for a Teletex printer is that it
should be capable of 308 characters but it
our case it can reach as high as 417
characters. The latter figure implies that
some types of printers are disqualified
immediately from consideration which will be
seeing later on. In order to avoid the need
to tend a printer during printout we will be
offering as an option an automatic paper
feeding unit.

A fingerprint is the way in which one identifies a particular individual. It is this
method that shows people are different from
each other. In so much as we are all
different, so must we as suppliers adapt our
products to this fact by resolutely
concentrating on ergonomy. Fortunately equipment dynamically adapted to the individual

leads to increased productivity.

In our current plans we see 4 different
levels of Teletex products. From the simple
typewriter orientated systems, sometimes
referred to as supertelex, to the very
advanced totally graphical system for
tomorrow's office comprising extremely
advanced word and text processing, search
techniques, sorting, arithmetic etc. Between
these two systems we find configurations of
varying character depending upon the hardware
and software alternatives chosen. But as
exponents for these systems we could equally
find a Wangwriter and an IBM displaywriter
-80 on one side and the new Philips 5900 on
the other.

TELETEX 6000

And this, ladies and gentlemen, is what our
Teletex 6000 looks like. This particular
equipment represents level 3 of our range.
Here we have the keyboard. Moveable, sufficiently heavy, it comprises the usual Swedish
keys together with a handful of function
keys.

This is the numeric keypad on which one can
type in large quantities of numeric information. This is the screen with in-built diskette unit. Here we have the printer.

One of the unusual aspects of the Teletex
6000 is its compact size.

A new technique has made it possible to build
the diskette stations, electronics and screen
into a single compact unit.

In this way we have one box less to bash our
elbows against and at the same time a comfortable handling of diskettes of the right
working height.

An important factor for one who types is the
possibility to adjust the display screen to a
comfortable height and angle.

The base we see here offers just these advantages. The base support can vary in height
some 8 inches which ought to be adequate for
most people.

The problem with window reflection on the
screen can be reduced by one being able to
adjust the angle of the screen 5' forwards
and 15' backwards.

Sitting in front of the 15 inch screen one
can enjoy black text on a white background.
According to most experts, this is the most
easily readable form.

One can say that the screen imitates normal
writing paper. It's easily readable and more
natural because the eye is not obliged to
adjust between the two media; screen and
paper.

As can be seen here, there's room for 25 rows
on the screen and for 88 characters on each
row. That's equivalent to 1/2 of an A4 page.

There are however two aspects that makes the
Teletex screen more easily read than most
others. A particularly tight character matrix
made up of 9 x 17 points in combination with
a newly invented sharpness accentuator known
as half-dot shift.

Look at these two enlargements of the letter
"Aa". The picture on the right is taken from
a Teletex screen, the one on the left from
another suppliers screen.

One can see clearly, with the closeness of
the points and the higher definition of the
Teletex screen, how we are able to form
letters in a more realistic way.

Notice the sharp angles in the A's. The other
reason why the Teletex screen is more easily
readable and flicker free is because of the
exceptionally high refresh rate of the video-
signals. 70 Hz.

Flicker and instability, apparent on other
screens, is normally due to the low scanning
rate. Most of them are around 50 Hz, just
like on the television at home.

We demanded 70 Hz. Teletex has therefore a
picture quality that is 40 % better than the
average word and text processing equipment or
display screens.

Now, we'll go over and have a look at the
small and unbelievable printer.

This is what it looks like. It can be obtained with a table or on it's own stand.
However, the most important is not its impressive design but it's unique capabilities.
Characters are built up of densely packed
points ingeniously placed in various combinations on the paper by the pins of the
writehead. Because each pin combination is
programmed in electronically it means that we
are free to build up any kind of character we
choose.

In this enlargement you can see quite clearly
the difference between a normal matrix printer and the Teletex printer. The "S" on the
left consists of 11 sparsely positioned
points and the one on the right consists of
50 densely packed points.

Now for something so amazing that I sometimes
have trouble in believing it myself' The
Teletex printer contains 417 basic characters
in 12 different styles. Now if I can do my
maths correctly that represents around 5000
character variations. I have no hesitation in
saying that this is slightly more than you'll
find on a normal typewriter.

One can also vary the speed of printing from
40 or 80 c.p.s. to 300 c.p.s. One would
choose 40 c.p.s. if one required output of
particularly high quality such as in business
letters or contracts. 300 c.p.s. can be
choosen when one is not interested in quality
at all.

In a national system there must also exist a
practical and simple way to deal with the
different types of paper and envelopes that
have to be written upon.

The Teletex printer is therefore equipped
with a number of different paper feed units
for varying requirements.

Here in the picture we can see an A4 paper
feeder unit. While you are working away at
the display screen it will keep the printer
busy by automatically feeding it with paper
as required. This particular unit can be obtained with one or two paper magazines, e.g.
for first page and second page or perhaps for
C5 envelopes.

Now you're looking at the tractor feed. This
is used for continuous forms printout.

We can also complement this unit with a front
feeder, In the picture you can clearly see
how the paper is loaded in order for it to be
automatically fed downwards for printout when
required.

We've also tried to make the Teletex 6000
easy to use for all classes of user.

It's not just possible to operate the Teletex
equipment in one way but two. Well in fact
almost 3 ways.

On the one hand one can work in an advanced,
skilful way, e.g. one can go directly into
the word/text editing process.

Secondly, there's a middle of the road, half
advanced way to operate the machine.

Finally, there's the third level, suitable
for the casual user or less skilled operator. Here the system provides help and advice
in a friendly non technical manner that even
the most untrained operator can understand.

Primarily there are two types of word and
text processing solutions. They differ in the
1 man machine dialogue used in carrying out
operations.

On the one hand there's the plain language
based dialogue and on the other there's the
menu driven dialogue.

Here you can see the learning curve for a
typical plain language system which most
suppliers offer. The learning period is
normally difficult, taking a long time and
one tends to use only a few of the finesse's
offered. We've placed 3 categories of user
out along the curve, the beginner, average
user and professional user.

The equivalent curve for a menu based system
looks something like this. With these types
of systems the initial starting point is
better, the learning time shorter, however a
professional never comes up to the same speed
as with the other system.
The point about Televerket's Teletex system
is that it allows both types of operation
i.e. it has plain language commands, menu
techniques and as we mentioned earlier a
number of function keys.

As a consequence Teletex will be easy and
quick to learn. One can reach a high level of
competence within a relatively short period
of time and the office will aquire a fast and
effective work station.

An electronically maintained archive is much more dependable than one kept manually. Especially if one uses Teletex's advanced system with so called search words and master index lists in combination. In this way one can feed documents into the archive without worrying about where they end up being stored.

Later on one may retrieve them again without having to aimlessly look through all documents stored. Here's an example of how it works.

One goes in and has a look at the master index. This contains entries for every single document stored on all ones diskettes, together with a description of what the documents contain.

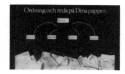

The picture roughly illustrates how the whole system is organized. At the top you have the Teletex Master Index. It keeps a check on an unlimited amount of diskettes containing your working documents which in turn are themselves linked back to the master index. At the end of the working day one updates the Master Index by running the working diskettes used during that day against it.

Now we'll go over and consider some possible ways of configuring or building up a Teletexsystem.

Alt.1 One station installation

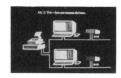

Perfect for the productive small business, the lauyers office, the consultant, the doctor, the contractor, the wholesaler, the shop etc. etc. That is to say for all those business that have lots of typing work or are dependent upon the Telex system.

Alt.2 Several people sharing the same printer

An economical alternative. Two, three or four writers have access to a centrally places printing resource. Adequate enough in most cases if ones not interested in an extremely high output rate.

Alt.3 The cluster configuration

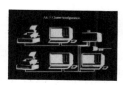

The organization that acquires a Teletex cluster controller can achieve an effectively rationalised Teletex traffic internally and externally. At the same time one reduces the need to have separate D.C.E.'s in so much as one C.C. can serve up to 4 workstations.

Teletex 10

The system representing level 1 of the 4 Teletex levels envisaged goes under the name of Teletex 10. It's a typewriter based system which combines the advantages of the electronic typewriter with textprocessing and communications.

Teletex 10 communicates in accordance with CCITT's basic requirement 308 characters which means that it can transmit, receive and store Teletex and Telex messages. It will also be capable of communicating with other terminals in the family. It also works as a text processor with functions such as printing, editing and storing of text.

Teletex 10 has four types of main memory:

The line memory which is always in operation will be cleared when the carriage returns. When the text memory is engaged the contents of the line memory is transferred to the text memory.

The format memory is used to store formats for margens, tabs and first writing line.

The phrase memory can be used as a storage for often used phrases such as addresses, Teletex numbers, typical phrases. The phrase can then be types automatically into the document.

The text memory has a capacity of 42 000 characters that is 20-25 pages. It can be used for store and edit funchins as well as automatic storage for Teletex and Telex documents.

As an option a dual disc station may be provided with 2x600 000 characters capacity.

Printing is done by a daisy wheel at a rate of 16 c.p.s. Eight different forts are available including a special Teletex typewheel. Pitches of 10, 12, 15 and proportional are obtainable. An automatic pin feeder handling A4 and A4 landscape and a pin tractor feeder can be provided as optional extras.

Policy

Televerkets´s Teletex — Private suppliers — CF — DATEX — Telex

The Swedish policy is formulated in such a way as to on the one hand create a state of competition between private supplier and Televerket whilst on the other hand not hinder competitors product development with respect to local functions and other technical designs.

As we are responsible for Swedens interaction communications we have chosen only to have views on and approve signalling procedures, leaving the individual suppliers free to design their products and product characteristics as they like.

Technically this will be achieved by Televerket setting up the public Teletex network within Norden's circuit switching data communication network, DATEX, as a CUG (closed user group). The remaining part of the "DATEX" network will be available for use by private suppliers. In order that Televerket can guarantee correct Teletex Traffic internationally, equipment called an Interworking Facility (IF) will be installed. The functions of this equipment is to check that traffic wishing to access the public Teletex network complies with CCITT's recommdations before being passed across. A part from this the I.F. also performs a store and foreward function for messages that are unable to be delivered immediately.

To allow for the integration of the Teletex and Telex services a conversion facility (CF) will be installed that charges the speed of messages between the two systems and generally controls the dialogue.

Time scedule

The CF equipment came into operation during May 1982, and the IF equipment is planned for introduction in November 1983 at the latest. With regard to Televerkets terminals, we plan to run some pilot projects during the summer and autumn, of, 1982. Orders for the system 6000 are already being taken and sales of the System 10 will start in September.

Official deliveries of both models will commerce in November 1982 but volume deliveries cannot be aspected before the start of the new year.

Circuit-Switching Versus Message-Switching at a Teletex PABX

R Lehnert, G Jaskulke
TE KA DE, Philips Kommunikations
Industrie, Federal Republic of
Germany

In this paper traffic models of Teletex PABX's of the circuit-switching and the message-switching type are analysed and compared. The analysis has been done in order to prove that PABX's which collect and concentrate text communication directly at the message source better meet the requirements of the grade of service for Teletex than heavy-duty Teletex terminals used in typewriting pools. Furthermore it is meant to point out the advantages of message-switching compared with circuit-switching in Teletex-PABX's. The analysis is based on traffic parameters which were internationally agreed on for the Teletex service. Above that internal duplicates of external messages and pure internal traffic is also taken into account. As the different features of the PABX's are modelled in detail, the traffic models often become rather complex. Consequently analysis is done mostly by extensive simulation runs. Finally, the analysed PABX's are compared with respect to the grade of service and the total memory space needed.

1. INTRODUCTION

The new Teletex service is about to be introduced in some countries, e.g. the F.R.G. or Sweden. This new service offers some important improvements over the well established international Telex service:
Firstly, in this service it is possible to use the same office typewriter to prepare a text document as well as to transmit and receive such kind of documents via the Teletex network. Transmission is done on a memory to memory basis, therefore the typewriters are continously ready to receive messages while preparing new text documents in a local mode.
Secondly, Teletex messages may be composed of the full character set of the typewriter, including capital and small-case letters, figures and various graphic symbols.
Thirdly, the Teletex service offers an transmission speed about 40 times higher than the Telex service. This results in a typical interval of 11.5 seconds to transmit a Teletex message with a typical length of 2250 characters.
Fourthly, Teletex guarantees a grade of service defined and controlled by the national PTT's.
In Germany, it is ensured that the probability of unsuccessful calls to a Teletex number will not exceed 5.5%. In this probability of blocking is included (1) the call rejection probability due to a busy line and (2) the rejection probability due to memory overload.

Terminals may be connected to the Teletex network directly or via PABX's. Being private extensions of the public networks these PABX's allow the profitable use of the Teletex service and beyond that, the charge-free inhouse text communication with additional facilities.
In this paper different techniques of switching are compared with respect to the grade of service of the PABX.
Section 2 presents the types of traffic and the traffic parameters on which the analysis is based. In section 3 the switching principles are described.
Models of traffic theory are derived in section 4. In section 5 some analytical but approximate calculations are presented.

Section 6 give some simulation results and a comparison of the switching techniques with respect to the PABX's traffic handling efficiency.

2. TYPES OF TRAFFIC IN A PABX

In this paper we distinguish between four types of traffic flow in a PABX:
The external traffic can be subdivided into
- incoming external traffic with traffic intensity λ_{ic},
- outgoing external traffic with intensity λ_{og}.
The intra-office traffic is subdivided into
- internal traffic with traffic intensity λ_i,
- duplicate traffic.

External traffic consists of messages which are transported between an external and an internal subscriber.
Internal traffic means internally originated new messages which are independent of the external traffic and are transported to another subscriber at this PABX. Duplicate traffic consists of duplicates of messages of the incoming external traffic, the outgoing external traffic and the internal traffic. The number of duplicates is named D_{ic}, D_{og}, and D_i resp. For instance, duplicates are generated by a multi-address call.

In this paper the following random variables are assumed to be negative exponentially distributed:
- the interval between arriving messages (interarrival time),
- the message length and, derived from this, the holding time of a line for the transmission of a message,
- the interval between local modes,
- the duration of local modes.

3. THE INVESTIGATED SWITCHING TECHNIQUES

Messages between Teletex terminals are transported on a store to store basis. Thus eventual local activities at the receiver's terminal do not disturb a transmission and new messages can be created at a terminal while keeping it in an uninterrupted receiving condition.
When a message is sent to a stand-alone Teletex

terminal (a terminal with its communication line connected directly to the public network) the grade of service is determined by two different blocking probabilities:

(1) the probability B_1 that the communication line is busy -- occupied by an incoming or outgoing call; situation "line blocking",

(2) the probability B_s that the receiver's memory is full due to an excessive arrival rate in the local mode interval; situation "memory blocking".

Both conditions lead to a call rejection. As mentioned in sec. 1, for an acceptable grade of service this sum B of B_1 and B_s must be limited. In the F.R.G. the total blocking probability B at the network line is limited to $B \leqslant 5.5\%$.
Although not yet fixed, it is assumed that these grade-of-service parameters are valid for PABX's as well.
In a PABX the total blocking probability B_{tot} is composed of the terms B_1 and B_s and another additive term, the probability B_{in} of internal blocking. This means that blocking may occur because a terminal line is busy due to an internal transfer. Internal blocking due to limited accessibility in the switching matrix is neglected. It will be shown that this internal blocking probability alone may bring B_{tot} beyond the threshold value of 5.5%.

The following five switching techniques are investigated and compared with respect to the grade of service and the amount of memory space necessary:
Circuit-switching PABX's: three configurations

C1 A PABX with direct addressing of a terminal, if it is busy, a situation of "blocking" occurs (fig. 1.1),
C2 a PABX same as above, but equipped with extra terminals to which the overflow traffic is rerouted (fig. 1.2),
C3 a PABX same as above, but overflow traffic is rerouted to another terminal which is not busy (fig. 1.3).

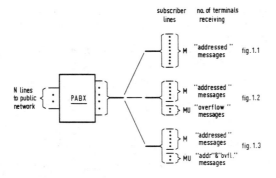

Fig. 1: Configuration types of a PABX with circuit-switching

In case C1 incoming external messages addressed to a terminal which is busy due to an internal message are blocked.
In case C2 this kind of blocking is avoided by installing extra terminals, to which incoming messages are routed if an addressed terminal is busy.
In case C3 this overflow traffic is rerouted to an idle "normal" terminal instead of routing it to one of the extra terminals of case C2.

A configuration, where overflow traffic is written into a buffer memory inside the PABX, is not considered. This case can be easily analysed by calculating the amount of storage needed from the blocking probability multiplied by the traffic intensity at the subscriber line group.
At a circuit-switching PABX the subscriber terminals must be equipped with a receiver memory, whose size is sufficient to buffer the incoming messages during the local mode.

Message-switching PABX's: two configurations

M1 A PABX with direct transmission of text to the addressed terminal if the requested data path is idle, otherwise messages may wait in distinct queues (fig. 2),
M2 a PABX with "pure" message-switching (store-and-forward, fig. 2).

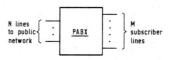

Fig. 2: Configuration of a PABX with message-switching

In case M2 a message is at first written into the memory inside the PABX and then transmitted to the receiver regardless of the state of the data path. Therefore in fig. 2 we cannot distinguish between the two models, because the functional difference is hidden inside the PABX.
At a message-switching PABX the memory to buffer incoming messages during the local period of the subscribers' terminals is centralized in the exchange. Only a small memory inside each terminal is necessary in order to buffer one message during editing or printing phases.

4. TRAFFIC MODELS

From the configuration figures and the involved types of traffic models of congestion theory can be derived. In principle, we can give a general traffic model for the circuit-switching PABX and for the message-switching PABX each.

Inside a circuit-switching PABX there is no buffer storage, therefore the corresponding traffic model represents a pure loss system (fig. 3).

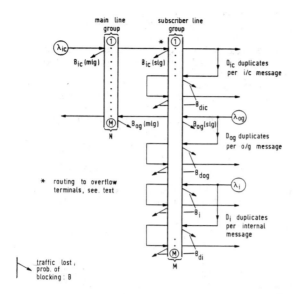

Fig. 3: Traffic model of a PABX with circuit-switching

An incoming message generated with traffic intensity λ_{ic} seizes an idle line in the main line group. If there is no idle line, blocking occurs with probability $B_{ic}(mlg)$. After that the message tries to seize the addressee's line. If this line is busy, the following occurs depending on the type of configuration of the PABX:

In a model of type fig. 1.1 the message is blocked and lost. In a model of type fig. 1.2 the message is rerouted to one of the MU extra overflow terminals. If all of them are busy, blocking occurs with probability $B_{ic}(ovf)$. In a model of type fig. 1.3 in the case of the addressed terminal's line being busy the message is rerouted to one of the MU terminals with overflow function. If all of them are busy (with original or overflow traffic) the message is blocked and lost.

After the transmission of a successful message, the first of D_{ic} duplicate messages is generated. It tries to seize its source and destination line. If one of these is busy, blocking occurs with probability B_{dic}. The duplicates are transferred one after another.

Outgoing traffic with intensity λ_{og} takes the opposite way. There are blocking probabilities $B_{og}(slg)$ and $B_{og}(mlg)$ resp. Here the first of D_{og} duplicates is generated together with the original message. The duplicates are transferred one after another, too.

Internal traffic (traffic intensity λ_i) touches only the subscriber line group. The corresponding blocking probabilities are B_i (original traffic) and B_{di} (duplicate traffic).

The message-switching PABX allows messages to wait in different queues, therefore the corresponding traffic model is a queueing system (fig. 4). Waiting times occur due to a receiver's line being busy or a receiver being in the local mode. Because of the possibility of waiting, blocking probabilities appear only where

messages from the network arrive at the PABX; the probabilities are B_{ic}, B_{dic}, B_{og}, and B_i resp.

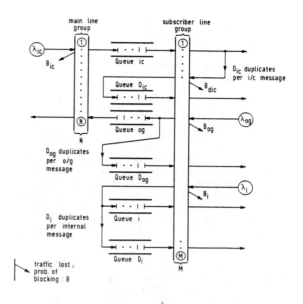

Fig. 4: Traffic model of a PABX with message-switching

The six queues of the traffic model are located and handled in the central memory of the exchange. In the investigation the storage is assumed to be infinite. The necessary memory size is then determined from the complementary distribution function of blocking of the sum of the lengths of all queues.

5. SOME APPROXIMATE CALCULATIONS

As stated in sec. 3 the grade of service namely the total blocking probability B_{ic} for the incoming traffic comprises three terms:

$$B_{ic} = B_{ic}(mlg) + B_{in} + B_s \qquad (1)$$

With the traffic parameters set to pure chance traffic type 1 (exponentially distributed interarrival and holding times), some approximate calculations are possible:

5.1 Blocking probability B_{ic}

Assuming that one is able to lower B_{in} to a value near to zero by appropriate arrangements, the behaviour at the main line group with respect to blocking of incoming messages is decoupled from the behaviour at the subscriber line group. Thus we can calculate the blocking probability $B_{ic}(mlg)$ by ERLANG's loss formula [KLEI75]:

$$B_{ic}(mlg) = \frac{\frac{A^N}{N!}}{\sum\limits_{i=0}^{N} \frac{A^i}{i!}} \qquad (2)$$

A : total traffic offered at the m.l.g., sum of
    i/c and o/g traffic
N : number of main lines

By eq. 2 we can approximately dimension the main line group.

5.2 Probability of Overflow at a Terminal's Memory (Circuit-Switching PABX)

At a circuit-switching PABX each subscriber terminal is equipped with its own memory to buffer incoming messages during local periods. Because of the extra internal and duplicate traffic, the intensity λ_t of traffic terminating at a subscriber terminal is much higher than the incoming traffic alone. And due to the in serial transmission of duplicates right after or in parallel with the original message, the arrival process is no longer Poissonian as the original traffic is. Thus the amount n of memory places (multiples of mean message lenghts) needed to buffer messages with a given probability of loss for a constant duration T_ℓ of local periods can only be approximately calculated by means of the Poisson probability distribution function (P.D.F.), see [RUEG80].

$$B_s = \sum\limits_{i=n+1}^{\infty} \frac{(\lambda_t \cdot T_\ell)^i}{i!} e^{-\lambda_t \cdot T_\ell} \qquad (3)$$

T_ℓ : duration of local period
λ_t : intensity of traffic terminating at a subscriber's terminal
n : number of messages arriving in interval T_ℓ

From eq. 3 we get the memory size needed by multiplying n with the mean length of a message. In practice, the duration of local periods is a random variable itself. In this case, the probability of loss must be computed from the total probability

$$P(n) = \int\limits_{\tau=0}^{\infty} P(n,\tau) \cdot f(\tau) \, d\tau \qquad (4)$$

$P(n,\tau)$: P.D.F. of the arrival process
$f(\tau)$: p.d.f. of the duration of local periods
$P(n)$: P.D.F. of n arrivals in T_ℓ

With negative exponentially distributed duration of local periods, we get from eq. 4

$$B_s = 1 - \sum\limits_{i=0}^{n} \frac{r^i}{(1+r)^{i+1}} \qquad (5)$$

r : $\lambda_t \cdot E\{T_\ell\}$
$E\{T_\ell\}$: mean duration of a local period

5.3 Probability of Overflow of the Central Memory in a Message-Switching PABX

In a message-switching PABX there is no internal blocking; conflicts of access are solved by the possibility of waiting in a queue.
Under the following assumptions we can calculate the memory size needed approximately [LEHN81]:
  - memory space needed due to waiting on a busy line may be neglected,
  - arrival process at the memory input of type NEGEXPO,
  - duration T_ℓ of local periods constant.

With a time T_u of a terminal being in use, the probability p_ℓ of a terminal being in the local mode is

$$p_\ell = \frac{T_\ell}{T_u} \qquad (6)$$

The traffic intensity λ_t of the arrival process at a terminal can be calculated from the intensities λ_{ic}, λ_{og}, λ_i and the number of duplicates

$$\lambda_t = \lambda_{ic} \cdot (1+D_{ic}) + \lambda_{og} \cdot D_{og} + \lambda_i \cdot (1+D_i) \qquad (7)$$

With the number M of terminals connected to the PABX we get the total traffic λ_{tot} to be buffered by the central memory from eqs. 6 and 7

$$\lambda_{tot} = p_\ell \cdot \lambda_t \cdot M \qquad (8)$$

Now we may compute n from eq. 3.

6. SIMULATION RESULTS

Simulation programs [SCHB78], [LEMY81] have been written in order to
  - avoid restrictions in traffic parameters necessary to do approximate calculations,
  - get complete information on all blocking probabilities, queue lengths, and waiting times.
Extensive simulation runs have been made in order to investigate the behaviour and the traffic handling capability of the different PABX's.

Table 1 presents a comparison of the switching techniques at a level of traffic intensity in accordance to [CCIT80].
From this two main conclusions can be drawn:
• In a message-switching PABX there is no internal blocking, therefore no precautions against it, such as overflow terminals, are to be taken.
• In a message-switching PABX the total memory space required is about 3 to 10 times smaller than in a circuit-switching PABX. In addition, the subscriber terminals are simpler and therefore less expensive.

M	Conf	MU	N	B_{ic} %	S kByte
10	C1	O	np.	8.77	374.0
	C2	1	2	0.21	312.4
		2	2	0.17	312.4
		5	2	0.17	319.0
	C3	1	2	2.36	310.2
		2	2	0.87	312.4
		5	2	0.17	308.0
	M1	–	2	0.26	72.6
	M2	–	2	0.14	72.6
30	C1	O	np.	8.76	1122.0
	C2	1	2	1.54	932.8
		2	2	1.49	937.2
		5	2	1.49	946.0
	C3	1	2	2.76	928.4
		2	2	1.84	928.4
		5	2	1.50	924.0
	M1	–	2	1.40	134.2
	M2	–	2	1.53	138.6
100	C1	O	np.	8.46	3740.0
	C2	1	3	2.24	3099.8
		2	3	2.05	3102.0
		5	3	2.05	3113.0
	C3	1	3	3.07	3093.2
		2	3	2.32	3097.6
		5	3	2.05	3091.0
	M1	–	3	2.45	312.4
	M2	–	3	2.58	321.4

Table 1: Grade of service and memory requirements in Teletex PABX's with configurations described in sec. 3

Traffic parameters in the busy hour (in accordance to [CCIT80]):

$\lambda_{ic} = \lambda_{og}$ = 1 message/h $\quad \lambda_i$ = 2 messages/h
$D_{ic} = D_{og} = D_i$ = 2 duplicates/message

Mean duration of a local period $E\{T_\ell\}$=10 min

Mean interval between local periods $E\{TI_\ell\}$ = 60 min

Mean time to transfer a message (holding time of a line) $E\{TH\}$ = 11.5 sec

M   no. of subscriber terminals
Conf   Configuration (described in sec. 3)
MU   no. of overflow terminals
N   no. of main lines
S   total memory required in the PABX (in kBytes)
np.   not possible, because internal blocking probability alone exceeds given limit

REFERENCES

[CCIT80] CCITT: Revised Draft Recommendation F.200, 6 March 1980
[KLEI75] Kleinrock,L.: Queueing Systems Vol.1. John Wiley, New York 1975
[LEHN81] Lehnert,R.: Traffic-Dependent Di-
mensioning of the Central Memory in a Teletex PABX with Message-
Switching, (in german)
TE KA DE, internal report LG-1981-11-17
[LEMY81] Lehnert,R.; Meyer,L.: New Modules for the Simulator GPSS-FORTRAN, (in german) TE KA DE, internal report, LG-1981-03-16
[RUEG80] Rüggeberg,R.: Teletex - ein neuer in-
ternationaler Textkommunikationsdienst der Fernmeldeverwaltungen (Teletex -
A New International Text-Communication Service of the PTT's, in german).
Der Fernmeldeingenieur no. 10, 1980
[SCHB78] Schmidt,B.: GPSS-FORTRAN Version II (in german).
Informatik Fachberichte 6, Springer, Berlin, 1978

Ralf Lehnert received the graduate degree and the Ph.D. degree in electrical engineer from the Technical University of Aachen, Germany in 1972 and 1979, respectively.
In 1972 he joined the In-
stitute for General Elec-
trical Engineering and Teleprocessing, Technical University of Aachen, where he worked as a Research Assistant on simulation of queueing networks.
Since 1980 he is with the applied research de-
partment of TE KA DE, a division of Philips Kommunikations Industrie AG, Nuernberg, F.R.G., as the head of a research group in traffic theory.

Gerhard Jaskulke received his "Engineer Degree" in electrical engineering in 1964 from the polytechnic of Munich, Germany.
From 1964 to 1971 he has been on the staff of the Siemens Central Laboratory for Communications in Munich, where he worked on the development of the EDS.
In 1974 he received his "Diplom" in electrical engineering from the Technical University in West Berlin.
From 1974 to 1978 he was Research Assistant with the "Lehrstuhl für Nachrichtensysteme" at the Technical University of Braunschweig, Germany, where he was engaged in the field of local telephone network problems and received the doctor's degree in 1979.
In 1979 he joined TE KA DE in Nuernberg, where he is now the head of the department for Private Text and Voice Switching Systems.

The Development of the Teletex Service in the Federal Republic of Germany

R Rüggeberg
Deutsche Bundespost, Federal
Republic of Germany

SUMMARY

The Teletex service as it is defined by CCITT is described in its main features. The facilities offered by the Deutsche Bundespost to the customer are presented. Some national aspects, e.g. use of PABXs and a possible impact on existing services like Telex and Telefax are shown briefly.

The presentation will include the experience with the new service during the first year after the introduction (available autumn 82). The charges the customer has to pay and a cost comparison between different textcommunication services show the efficiency of this new service.

The conditions and the strategy of the Teletex field trials are presented, too, in particular
- the objective of these trials
- acceptance of the new service by users and operators
- impact on office organization
- economic efficiency including qualitative and structural aspects.

1 INTRODUCTION

From the beginning, the Deutsche Bundespost has attached great importance to the fact that the new Teletex service will be an internationally compatible textcommunication service.

A new Study Question was adopted by the CCITT, and since 1977 Study Groups I (Recommendation for the Teletex service) and VIII (Recommendation for the Teletex terminal) have been engaged in laying down the conditions for the international Teletex service.

The work in these bodies was concluded in June 1980, and the Draft Recommendations were adopted by the Plenary Assembly at its last meeting in November 1980 in Geneva.

For the Teletex sector the following Recommendations have been worked out:

F.200   Teletex Service

S.60   Terminal Equipment for Use in the Teletex Service

S.61   Character Repertoire and Coded Character Sets for the International Teletex Service

S.62   Control Procedures for the Teletex Service

S.70   Network Independent Basic Transport Service for Teletex.

2 BASIC DEFINITIONS

2.1 Definition by CCITT

- The Teletex service allows the exchange of information between the subscribers in an automatic memory-to-memory system.

- Basically it should be possible that the Teletex terminal is operated like a normal office typewriter.

- Operation of the keyboard and text production shall not be subject to any restrictions and be possible in the same way as it is usual with office machines.

A first definition of the Teletex service was given in 1976 by the "Commission for the Development of the Technical Communication System":

The new telecommunication service Teletex is feasible in the existing telecommunication network and is characterized by a novel terminal which serves for both the production and the transmission of texts using the full character repertoire of the typewriter.

2.2 Delimination to Telex

The Teletex terminals are located at the work places in the secretariats and will be used for textproduction as well as for transmission and receiving of texts. In most cases the Telex terminals are located in separate parts of the organization. The texts to be transmitted are already produced by the typing staff in the secretariats.

The Teletex terminal has the whole capability of either an office typewriter or up to a word processor while the Telex terminal is based on the International Telegraph Alphabet No. 2.

The texts (office correspondence) is transmitted via the telecommunication networks using the transmission rate of 2.400 bit/s. That is about 20 - 30 times faster than Telex.

The main difference between Teletex and Telex is that the Teletex terminal is used at the work places within the organization of secretariats for textproduction and transmission. Teletex is not "improved Telex". Teletex terminals cover the whole range of terminals from a typewriteroriented basic terminal up to high sophisticated word processors.

2.3 Teletex is a subscriber service

The Teletex service is a communication service between subscribers to exchange office correspondence. The essential characteristics of a public subscriber service are as follows:

1. Compatibility between terminals
2. Guaranteed quality of service
3. Subscriber directory
4. Adequate charges.

The first item is within the responsibility of CCITT, the other items of the national administrations or RPOAs (Recognized Private Operating Agencies).

3 FEATURES OF THE TELETEX SERVICE OFFERED BY THE DEUTSCHE BUNDESPOST

3.1 The Teletex service in the F. R. of Germany is based upon the CCITT recommendations. In addition some facilities which belong to the responsibility of a national administration are described below.

3.2 The Teletex service is provided in the circuit switched data network (Fig. 1). A Teletex/Telex Conversion Unit allows communication between Teletex terminals and Telex terminals. The procedure used for the interworking service is defined in CCITT Recommendation F.200.

3.3 Each Teletex terminal must be equipped with a receiving memory. The capacity depends on the amount of traffic and will be determined by the individual subscriber where the criteria described in CCITT Recommendation F.200 will be taken into account.,

3.4 All Teletex terminals are able to receive and present the whole Teletex Basic Graphic Character Repertoire.

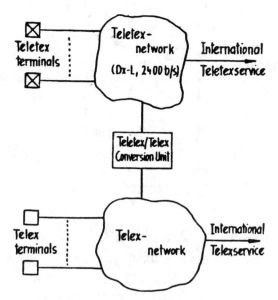

Fig. 1

3.5 The terminal identification consists of the data country code, national subscriber number and a mnemonic abbreviation.

Example: 2627-6151913=FTZ

On each page the first printable line is reserved for an optional print out of the call identification line which consists of

- the terminal identification of the called terminal
- the terminal identification of the calling terminal
- date and time
- additional reference information.

3.6 Use of PABX

3.6.1 Telephone PABXs may be used for Teletex. In this case a PABX has to be equipped with a conversion unit which gives access to the circuit switched data network (Fig. 2).

3.6.2 Existing Telex PABX may also be used for Teletex. A Teletex module is added to the Telex system including an internal Teletex/Telex conversion unit (Fig. 3).

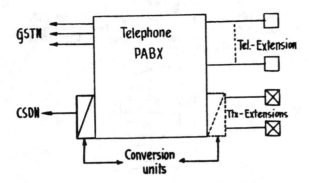

Use of Telephone PABX for Teletex

First step to the so called "K-System" (communication system) on customer's premises with access to different networks, eg. GSTN, PSDN, CSDN, Telex. (under study)

Fig. 2

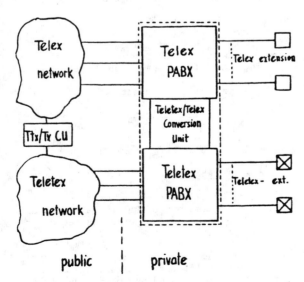

Use of Telex PABX

Fig. 3

4 TELETEX AND TELEX

Fig. 4 shows the basic configuration for Telex/Teletex interworking, the international link being a 50-baud Telex circuit. The operational procedures have already largely been defined taking account of the above requirements.

According to them the Teletex terminal works in a so-called Telex mode of operation where the Teletex terminal is allowed to use only characters of the International Telegraph Alphabet No. 2 and to print a maximum of 69 characters on one line (= Telex format). All other conversions such as

- code conversion
  (7 bit code ⟶ 5 bit code)
- rate conversion
  (2.4 kbit/s ⟶ 50 bit/s)
- procedure conversion
  (Teletex procedure in Telex procedure)

are performed by the conversion unit in the network. The same applies to the opposite direction (Telex – Teletex).

The rate conversion necessitates that the conversion unit has to be equipped with a store for buffering the messages. By that it is guaranteed that the Teletex subscriber line is not occupied longer than in the case of a normal Teletex connection.

An exact analysis of the future effects of the Teletex service on the Telex service is not possible yet at the time being, as some factors and parameters are still unknown, e.g.

- the cost of the Teletex terminal,

- the development of the costs of the Telex terminal after introduction of the Teletex service.

On the assumption that the number of Teletex terminals will be about 40 000 in 1985 and increase to about 130 000 in 1990, it is expected that

- the Telex service will not be affected noticeably in the first years following the introduction of the Teletex service,

- from 1985 the number of Telex terminals will decrease by 10 000 annually (Fig. 5).

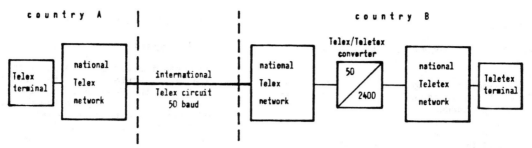

Fig. 4   Basic configuration for interworking with Telex

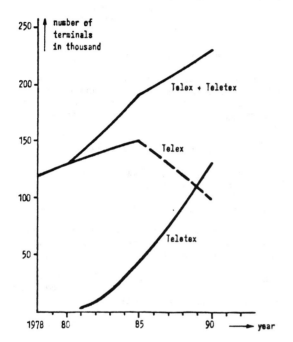

Fig. 5   Estimate effect of Teletex
          on Telex

5   TELETEX AND FACSIMILE

Interworking between Facsimile and Teletex
equipment will only then be possible when
the standardization of group-4 equipment
(digital transmission, use of data networks)
has been completed.

The problem involved in interworking between
the two services is whether a Teletex terminal can, in addition to character-coded,
receive and represent also facsimile-coded
information and thus is suitable for a mixed
mode of operation.

Here a wide field of applications opens up,
which are at present being investigated and
probed with regard to their effects and
consequences. There are not precise concep-
tions yet in which way character- and
facsimile-coded information can be used in
"the office of the future" and how the
demand and costs situations will develop.

But it can already be foreseen that

- for the phase of text production a mixed
  mode of operation will not be necessary
  (character- and facsimile-coded information will be generated separately)

- for the phase of transmission and thus
  also for the phase of reception there will
  be a demand for mixed modes of operation.

As an example it may be mentioned that fair-·
ly often there is the need

- to insert texts into drawings or to in-
  scribe them,
- to write texts on forms
- to enclose texts already existing as
  annexes.

In the CCITT a possible future mixed operating mode was taken into account such a way
that, as far as possible, common transmission procedures were defined for character-
and facsimile-coded transmissions.

6   TELETEX AND BILDSCHIRMTEXT

Type and extent of interworking with the
Bildschirmtext service (provisional CCITT
term: Videotex) is yet to be determined. A
new Study Question was formulated at the
Final Meeting of Study Group I in Montreal
(June 1980), and it can be expected that
the basis for interworking between the two
services will be provided during the next
Study period.

One thing is certain - interworking between
the Teletex and Bildschirmtext services will
be confined to that part which is common to
both services: the transmission of texts.

It is to be expected that the future Teletex
subscriber will be supplier (and also receiver) of information in the Bildschirmtext
service and will have access to the Bildschirmtext centres. The prerequisites that
the character repertoire in the Bildschirmtext service corresponds to that of the
Teletex service and that an unambiguous
assignment of the character repertoires
exists have already been created.

7 CHARGES

The following charges the customer has to pay:

1. installation charge   400.- DM
2. monthly access charge   170.- DM
3. traffic charges

    a) area < 50 km
      daytime   0.76 Pfennig/sec
      nighttime   0.36 Pfennig/sec

    b) area > 50 km
      daytime   1.40 Pfennig/sec
      nighttime I   0.72 Pfennig/sec
      nighttime II   0.36 Pfennig/sec.

8 COMPARISON OF TRANSMISSION TIME AND CHARGES

Fig. 6 shows the cost advantage of the Teletex service compared with letter mail, Telex and Telefax. In all cases a two page message with 2000 characters is taken into account.

Service	time	charges		
		daytime	nighttime	
			I	II
Letter Mail	1 day	0,60 DM		
Telefax	6 min	6,90 DM	2,15 DM	
Telex	5 min	3,00 DM	0,67 DM	
Teletex	15 sec	0,26 DM	0,16 DM	0,11 DM

Fig. 6

9 INTRODUCTION OF THE TELETEX SERVICE

Since March 10th 1981 the service is opened on the basis of the national technique (Hanover Fair Protocol).

The service was without charges for one year. Only for the traffic to Telex terminals the subscriber had to pay for. Since March 82 the subscribers have to pay full charges.

The Teletex service was interrupted for about one week in June 82 in order to implement the final CCITT protocol in the switching centres. During that time the terminals had to be changed by the suppliers.

10 TELETEX FIELD TRIALS

10.1 General

At present several large-scale field trials are being carried out by the industry (supported by the Federal Minister for Research and Technology) in which the possibilities of improving office organization including qualitative and structural aspects are investigated. The following projects are under way:

Field trial textcommunication Allianz
User: Allianz Insurance Comp.
Manufacturers: AEG-Telefunken, TN, Olympia AG

TEKOM field trial (Siemens AG).

The objective of these trials is, in addition to testing the equipment under operational conditions, to obtain above all the following information on the following points:

- acceptance of the new service

- economic benefit including structural and qualitative aspects,

- repercussions on existing organization

- effects on the individual and chances for the utilization of a wide range of communications offered.

The socio-scientific side of these projects is handled by the Hanover University and the Bundeswehr Academy in Munich.

10.2 First results

The procedure for the Teletex field trials was divided into three phases:

Phase I

Investigation of the existing organization before the implementation of the new technique. After that installation of Teletex terminals and instruction of the operators about the local functions.

Phase II

Examination of the local functions by the operators. After that starting with the communication.

Phase III

Examination of the technique used for the communication and the operation. Investigation of the impact on office organization.

Phase I and II were finished at the end of
1980, phase III has begun in January 1981
and was finished at the end of 1981.

The results of the investigation carried out
in phase I and II allow some basic statements about future expectations in conjunction with the introduction of the Teletex
service:

- The relation between internal and external
  communication of the enterprises concerned
  is about 6 : 1. Consequently big organizations will use the Teletex service first
  to handle the internal communication.

- There is a demand for an increasing usage
  of technical communication facilities such
  as Telex and Telefax. This existing demand
  will facilitate the application of the
  Teletex service in future.

- A dezentralized location of the Teletex
  terminals will offer good chances to make
  office organization more effective and
  improve the working situation of the
  typing staff considerably.

A first presentation of the results of the
Teletex field trials was at 25. March 82.
These results will be available at ICCC 82
in London.

Rolf Rüggeberg, study at
Technical University
Aachen, diploma 1969,
1971 to Telecommunication
Engineering Centre Darm-
stadt (FTZ), section
Telegraph and Datel
services, 1977 Special
Rapporteur on Teletex
service in Study Group I,
CCITT, 1979 Head of
section Textcommunica-
tion services (Telegram,
Telex, Telefax and Teletex
service) since 1980 Vice Chairman of Study
Group I (CCITT) and Chairman of Working Party
3/I (Teletex service).

A Modular Integrated EPABX for the Office of the Future

S Yoshida, T Nakayama, Y Hashida
NTT, Japan

In the office of the future, an electronic private automatic branch exchange (EPABX) should accommodate non-voice terminals and should connect them to other terminals through public data networks. An extension number, which is necessary to identify a particular terminal in an EPABX, needs to be transferred from a calling terminal to a destination EPABX. An example of enhanced X.21 sequences is proposed in this paper.

An integrated EPABX, which controls both voice and non-voice communications, should be constructed without any excess cost being incurred for the voice communications. A functional modular structure is the optimal technology for such an integrated EPABX. Based on these considerations, an experimental system is briefly outlined in this paper.

1. INTRODUCTION

Recently various terminals, such as facsimile, wordprocessor, telex and small business computer, have been emerging for improving information production, storage and transmission efficiency in the office. They are developing as communications workstations for the office of the future.

As these non-ovice terminals increase in an office, in-house switching service for non-voice communications is required. An electronic private automatic branch exchange (EPABX) has been offering telephone services in the office. Therefore, an integrated EPABX is expected to play this role for non-voice as well as voice communications. The integrated EPABX should interface with public data networks to utilize the network facilities. However, an extension number is necessary to identify a particular terminal in an EPABX, and the extension number should be transferred from a calling terminal to a destination EPABX and the existing interface condition should be enhanced.

Though an integrated EPABX should handle both voice and non-voice communications so as to manage all communication facilities in an office, voice communications would still take up most of it. Therefore, the prime requirement for economically designing such an integrated EPABX is common control processor and switching network application without any excess cost for voice communications.

This paper presents some considerations concerning the necessary interface conditions among digital data terminals, an integrated EPABX and public data networks (PDNs), as well as also proposing an integrated EPABX structure for the office of the future.

2. PUBLIC DATA NETWORK INTERFACE

It is important for each data terminal in an office to have access to terminals in public data networks, as well as to terminals in the office. An EPABX would be able to provide this ability to the office terminals in a manner similar to the present telephone services. An EPABX would concentrate traffic onto a public data network. As a result, the subscriber lines could be used in common, and their usage rate be remarkably improved.

(1) Subaddressing

With connection between an EPABX and a public network, an extension number would be used to identify a particular terminal in an EPABX. With this extension number, a public network would identify a calling EPABX terminal when it called a terminal in a public network, and a destination EPABX would identify a called EPABX terminal. Therefore, the extension number needs to be transmitted through the public network.

In the case of circuit switching services, there are two possible methods by which a destination EPABX would identify the called terminal (Fig.1):

(i) Phase 1 method, in which the EPABX receives the extension number as a subaddress in a connecting phase (phase 1) from a public network exchange.

(ii) Phase 3 method, in which the EPABX receives the extension number at the beginning of a data transfer phase (phase 3) from a calling terminal.

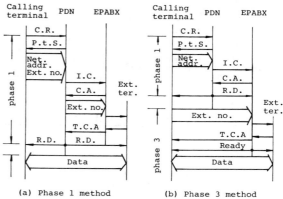

(a) Phase 1 method   (b) Phase 3 method

C.R.: Call Request,   C.A.: Call Accepted
P.t.S.: Proceed to Select,   R.D.: Ready for Data
I.C.: Incoming Call,   T.C.A.: Ter. Call
                                       .ccepted

Figure 1 Extension Number Transmission Method

Table 1 shows a comparison of these method.

The phase 1 method is preferable, because various kinds of terminals would be accommodated in an EPABX and not all of them could have a character transmission facility in a data transfer phase. Also, the extension number transmission protocol would be standardized.

(2) X.21 enhancement

A subaddress preceeded by a delimiter would be signalled by a calling terminal following the network address. A destination EPABX would be called by the network address. After returning the 'call accepted' signal, it would receive the subaddress.

Figure 2 shows an example of enhanced X.21 sequences for EPABX-EPABX connection via circuit switched network. In these sequences, end to end call setup time would be longer than the time required for setting up existing services for several reasons. The added subaddress would increase the number of transmitted digits by some 20 digits, when a 4 digit subaddress is used. Also, the call processing time would increase at the EPABXs and PDN exchange systems. The former increase is estimated at some 70 ms (for the 2.4 Kb/s class). The latter still needs to be estimated after some pertinent experiments.

(3) X.25 enhancement

In X.25 sequences, a subaddress can be indicated in a call request packet and in an incoming call packet. There are two possible fields in those packet formats for carrying a subaddress: call user data field and facility field. The facility field is more appropriate for indicating a subaddress.

3. DIGITAL DATA TERMINAL ACCOMODATION

In Japan, DDX (digital data exchange) circuit switched network and DDX packet switched network have been in service since 1979 and 1980, respectively. The DDX networks provide high quality and high speed data transmission services. Their service area has been expanded and their service facilities are expected to be enhanced in the near fugure.[1]

Table 1 Comparison of Extension Number Transmission Method

Method \ Item	Phase 1	Phase 3
Required function at calling terminal	Enhanced network control in phase 1	Digit transmission in phase 3
Calling terminal class recognition at EPABX	Not necessary	Necessary
Existing data network enhancement	Necessary	Not necessary

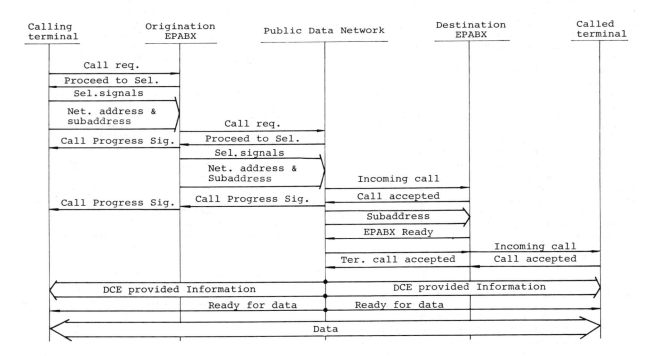

Figure 2   Enhanced X.21 Signal Sequences

A lot of terminals with CCITT X-series standard interfaces have been developed in Japan. These include computers, data terminals and digital facsimile equipment. Figure 3 shows proportional customer usage of the DDX circuit switched network.

An EPABX should accommodate these terminals with the same interface conditions as with the DDX. In an EPABX, an in-house cable distribution system would be based on a star layout to utilize existing wiring. Figure 4 shows an example of in-house cable distributions.

There are two ways in which an EPABX could accommodate terminals having an X.20 or an X.21 standard interface (Fig.5). The standard interface electrical characteristic makes it possible for signals to be transmitted over some 500 meters of in-house cable. Figure 5(a) shows an economical structure for a small office, where in-house cables are not long or the number of data terminals is small. Figure 5(b) shows the preferable set up for large offices, where in-house cables are long enough for a DSU (digital service unit) to be set up. The DSU decreases the number of in-house cables or transmits signals over a longer distance.

Some computers have many channels for time sharing services. A multiplexed interface, such as an X.22 interface, is simpler than many X.21 interfaces. In this case, it is preferable to use one of the multiplexed channels as a data link between an EPABX and a computer. When an integrated EPABX has a packet switching facility, X.25 interfaces can be adopted for the computer interface.

4. MODULAR STRUTURE FOR AN INTEGRATED EPABX

An EPABX has been improved to accommodate high level feature telephones which have function keys and display. [2] An integrated EPABX would accommodate such high level feature telephones and various kinds of data terminals, in addition to regular telephones, and would

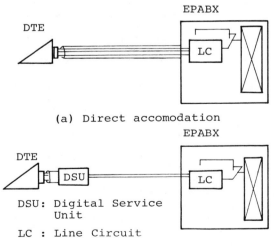

(a) Direct accomodation

DSU: Digital Service Unit

LC : Line Circuit

(b) Indirect accomodation

Figure 5 Digital Data Terminal Accommodation

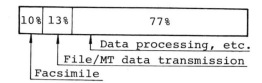

Figure 3 Customer Usage of Portions of DDX Circuit Switched Network

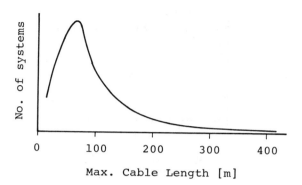

Figure 4 In-House Cable Length Distribution (for telephone sets)

offer communication services according to each terminal condition. If an integrated EPABX is designed under the most severe conditions for all of the services to be offered, it would give excessive quality of service and would become very expensive. Especially, an integrated EPABX should not cause any burden on voice communications, because voice communications would continue to play a major role in office communications.

Therefore, an integrated EPABX should be set up in the following modular configuration to satisfy various customer needs.

An integrated EPABX modules should be divided into two blocks, a system common block (SCB), and a peripheral interface block (PIB). The SCB has a common service function for all the services, such as a system operation and maintenance function, and a switching network and control function. The PIB is subdivided into line terminal interface modules (LIMs), trunk interface modules (TIMs) and communication processing service modules (CPMs).

These PIB modules can be constructed using the most suitable conditions for each module. As a result, the integrated EPABX can accommodate non-voice terminals without imposing any burden on voice communication by separating the LIMs from each other. It can accordingly cope with the various communication requirements in an office rather economically.

These modules would have their own control processors, and communicate with each other while following the call set up progress in a call control. For this communication, a bus communication system can be applied. It transmits control data at high speed. The queueing delay depends on its usage rate. The delay will be short enough for the system to be efficient, when the usage rate is under about 1/6 at the most (Fig.6).

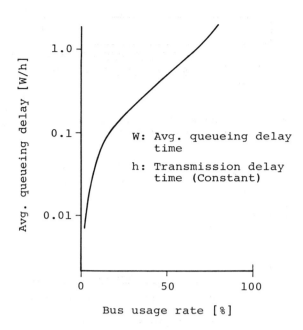

Figure 6   Bus Communication Queueing Delay

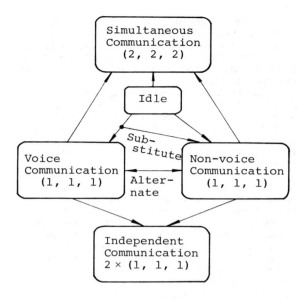

Figure 7   Transition between Integrated
Communication States

5.   VOICE AND NON-VOICE INTEGRATED COMMUNICA-
TION SERVICES

The integrated EPABX would offer voice
and non-voice integrated communication services because it could control both kinds of
terminals. Voice/non-voice integrated communication services can be classified by several
factors, described below under (A, B and C)
category headings.
   They are;
    (A) The number of media, such as voice,
       still picture, telewriter, facsimile
       and data code, used for the communica-
       tion.
    (B) The number of bands, or channels, used
       for the communication.
    (C) The number of calls which are proces-
       sed in a switching system for the com-
       munication.
For instance, an alternate facsimile and
telephone communication could be represented as
(2,2,1), a simultaneous facsimile and telephone
communication as (2,2,2), and a simultaneous
communication with a channel divided into two
bands as (2,2,1).
An effective integrated communication
service is a substitute communication service.
[3] When a called party is busy, or does not
answer on a voice channel, a calling party can
change the channel to a non-voice channel with
the assistance of a switching system. In this
way, the calling party could send a message to
the called party over a non-voice channel.
Figure 7 shows a possible transmission pattern
for integrated communication states.
An integrated terminal plays an important
role in realizing these services. It would be
desirable that an integrated terminal have a
telephone set for voice communication, a keyboard for data input, a cathode-ray-tube display for softcopy output, a facsimile for hardcopy input/output, and/or a dot printer for
hardcopy output.

6.   EXPERIMENTAL SYSTEM OUTLINE

An experimental, integrated EPABX was
manufactured to help in comprehending important
technical points, as well as to help in estimating traffic and other characteristics. The
experimental system, called a Time Division
Switching System with Digital Interface (TDD),
accommodates telephones, voice/data integrated
terminals, synchronous data terminals (X.21),
and start-stop terminals (X.20 bis). It can
connect a synchronous data terminal to the DDX
circuit switching system with an enhanced X.21
interface.
It can also offer integrated communication
services.
Figure 8 shows a blockdiagram of the TDD
system. The D 30 processor, which had been
developed for small telephone switching offices,
was adopted for the central processor, and the
switching network was structured in a single
stage time switch, which is a 64 Kb/s transparent network, with a 1024 multiplexity.
For the bus communication system, a general
purpose interface bus (GPIB), or an IEEE-488
standard bus communication system, was adopted
after it was slightly modified. The service
request control line was separated from the bus
management lines, so that an originating module
could be found without a polling sequence. The
bus control processor (system bus interface:
SBI) was separated from the module processors
to simplify the call control program.
Figure 9 shows the TDD program structure.
The SCB and PIB programs are structured in a
mono-level configuration. The PIB programs
sequentially supervise line states for the
terminals, execute a call control task and
send a control command to SCB programs. Accessed from the PIB programs, the SCB program
excutes such processes as network control or
call control data base management, according
to the input command.
An integrated terminal provided integrated
communication services using voice and 1200 b/s
data channels. It was composed of a personal

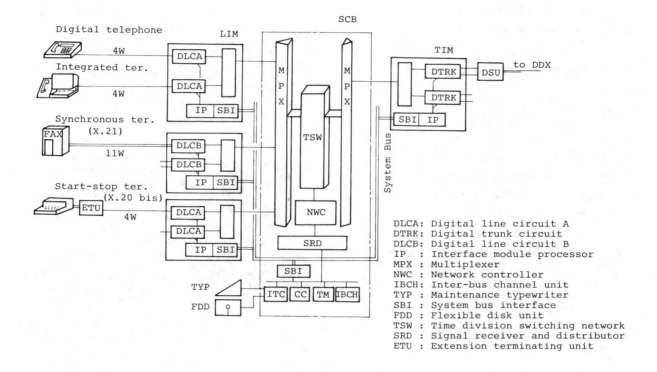

DLCA: Digital line circuit A
DTRK: Digital trunk circuit
DLCB: Digital line circuit B
IP : Interface module processor
MPX : Multiplexer
NWC : Network controller
IBCH: Inter-bus channel unit
TYP : Maintenance typewriter
SBI : System bus interface
FDD : Flexible disk unit
TSW : Time division switching network
SRD : Signal receiver and distributor
ETU : Extension terminating unit

Figure 8 TDD System Blockdiagram

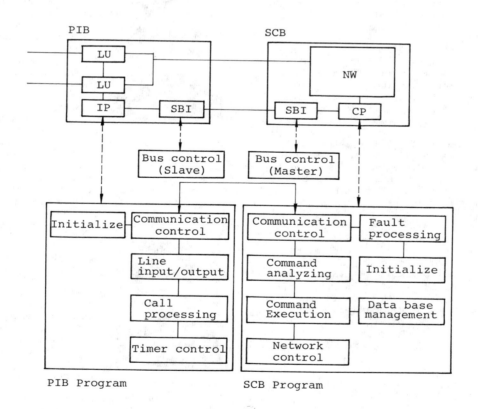

Figure 9 TDD Program Structure

Table 2 Integrated Terminal Interface
for the EPABX

Item	Description
Transmission format	F V D S *
No. of wires	4 wire
Transmission code	CMI
Bit rate	88 kbps
Signalling	Fixed length (8 bit) code

* F: Framing, V: Voice, D: Data,
  S: Signalling

computer and an adaptor. The personal computer was used as an intelligent data terminal and network control unit. The adaptor converted analog voices into PCM coded voices and multiplexed the digital information into the transmission format. Interface characteristics are shown in Table 2.

7. CONCLUSION

In order for an in-house switching system to identify the called terminal at the terminating end of a public data network, enhanced X.21 sequences, which include subaddressing sequences, have been proposed. In these sequences, a subaddress is transferred in a connecting phase.

A modular integrated EPABX structure has been proposed, which can accommodate digital data terminals, while putting little burden on voice communication. The integrated EPABX could offer voice/non-voice integrated communication services. NTT has also proposed integrated terminal construction using a personal computer.

Technical points concerning integrated services expansion for a closed network, which connects integrated EPABXs, need to be studied. Considering the application of a subscriber optical fiber system, it will also be necessary to study multiplexed interfacing to an ISDN.

ACKNOWLEDGMENT

The authors wish to express deep appreciation to Dr. M. Kato, Director of the Switching Systems Development Division in Musashino ECL and to Mr. I. Shimizu, Chief of the Telephone Switching Systems Section in Musashino ECL, who furnished guidance in advancing this study.

REFERENCES

[1] T. Takatsuki, S. Tomita and T. Shinozaki.: DDX (Digital Data Exchange) A Review of Development and Operational Experience, ISS '81, 31C4.
[2] T. Ishizuki and I. Nishikado.: A System Architecture for EPABX with Functional Telephones, ISS '81, 33C1.
[3] N. Kuroyanagi, M. Kajiwara, T. Nakayama and H. Yamamoto.: Enhanced Telephone Services Provided with Graphic Facility, NTC '80, 23.7.

Shinichiro Yoshida
Staff engineer, Integrated Communication Division, Yokosuka Electrical Communication Laboratory (ECL), is presently engaged in fundamental developmental studies on integrated EPABX.

Since joining ECL in 1971, Mr. Yoshida has been engaged in the development of a DDX circuit switching system and research on digital switching systems and digital EPABXs.

He received B.S. and M.S. degrees in electrical engineering from Waseda University in 1969 and 1971, respectively.

He is a member of the Institute of Electronics and Communication Engineers of Japan.

Toshihiko Nakayama
Staff engineer, Switching Development Division, Musashino Electrical Communication Laboratory (ECL), is presently engaged in research on message communications systems in DDX networks.

Since joining ECL in 1968, Mr. Nakayama has been engaged in the development of electronic telephone switching systems and research on digital EPABXs.

He received B.S. and M.S. degrees in electrical engineering from the University of Tokyo in 1966 and 1968, respectively.

He is a member of IEEE and of the Institute of Electronics and Communication Engineers of Japan.

Yukio Hashida
Staff engineer, Switching Systems Development Division, Musashino Electrical Communication Laboratory (ECL), is presently engaged in research on integrated switching systems.

Since joining ECL in 1970, Mr. Hashida has been engaged in development of a D20 electronic switching systems and research on digital EPABXs.

He received his B.S. degree in electrical engineering from Kyushu University in 1970.

He is a member of the Institute of Electronics and Communication Engineers of Japan.

Alternatives in the Use of Circuit Switching for Local-area Data Networks

D A Pitt
IBM, USA

The evolution of private branch exchanges (PBXs) for circuit switching has been toward the augmentation of voice features with capabilities for handling data. While most PBXs are still installed and optimized for voice, with data being of secondary importance, the recent interest in multiple-access, high-speed, local data networks has stimulated greater consideration of the ability of the switch to satisfy the requirements of these networks. This paper examines the possible means of integrating PBXs and in-plant data facilities. The particularly interesting case of including both a PBX and a high-speed data-only medium in the same establishment is discussed.

1.0 INTRODUCTION

Three simultaneous trends are causing increased scrutiny of the possible uses of circuit switching, in the form of private branch exchanges (PBXs), for the handling of data. The first trend is the growth in customer demand for PBXs, which in the U.S. has been stimulated by deregulation allowing customers to purchase and install telephone equipment from suppliers other than the private monopolies. The number of suppliers of PBXs worldwide is now over 40 (reference [1] lists 35 of them).

The second trend is the increased application of digital design and implementation to PBX hardware, traditionally an analog domain. The distinction between voice and data therefore becomes less significant when they are both in digital form.

The third trend is the profusion of local-area data networks intended to connect a growing number of data processing and electronic office system products in a business establishment. Interest in the hardware, topology, and architecture of local-area data networks has drawn attention to PBXs, which are being examined for their possible contribution to the solution of the data device interconnection problem.

To address this contribution, this paper discusses the fundamental characteristics of local data networks, the structure, properties, and features of digital PBXs, and options for consolidating the two. A simple model of a digital PBX is used to illustrate the ideas; this model does not represent the product of any particular manufacturer.

2.0 FUNDAMENTAL CHARACTERISTICS OF LOCAL DATA NETWORKS

2.1 ATTRIBUTES OF THE NETWORK ITSELF

For the purposes of this paper, the term local means strictly within a customer's premises. Any circuits that cross a public right-of-way are excluded from this discussion. The implications of this legal and geographical restriction include the following

- single ownership of all resources, allowing the owner the freedom to optimize the network without the usual constraints of line speeds, installation schedules, and tariffs.

- potentially high bit rate, on the order of 1 to 100 Mbit/s (or Gbit/s for optical fibers).

- short transmission propagation delay (often <1 ms) resulting from the short distance.

- low error rates, potentially better than the public switched network by two to four decimal orders of magnitude.

2.2 REQUIREMENTS IMPOSED ON THE NETWORK BY ITS OWNERS

When actually faced with the task of designing and implementing a local network, network planners must satisfy the particular needs of both the network users and providers. These requirements can vary widely, but most networks have the following ones in common. In the ensuing discussion, we assume that these requirements are satisfied by the high-speed cable portion of a customer's local network and evaluate the PBX portion of the data network against these same requirements.

Throughout the paper, the term high-speed cable network is used as a general term for local data networks comprised of any of a wide choice of media (including but not limited to coax, twinax, triax, quadrax, twisted pair, shielded twisted pair, and optical fiber) and configured in a bus, ring, loop, or star topology. The distinctions among these are better addressed in [2,3].

The essential requirements are:

- full connectivity, allowing a physical path to exist between any two nodes in the network.

- simple rearrangement, allowing the moving of devices from one physical location to another. This requirement applies not only to the physical attachment of a device to the network but also to the addressability of the device so that connections with it may be established.

- reliability, and the integration of the management of the transport network with the management of the devices that attach to it.

- smooth growth in size for both the addition of physical space to that already served by a local network and the addition of users within the original space. Inherent in this requirement is the elimination of overcrowded raceways, even as the number of users grows.

- eventual integration of voice, data, and video to the point that they are all carried on the same medium.

3.0 AN OVERVIEW OF THE DIGITAL PBX

3.1 COMPONENTS OF A DIGITAL PBX

Consider the model of the digital PBX shown in Figure 1. It is useful to partition the PBX into four major subsystem components - a controller, a switch matrix, and analog and digital interface modules.

The controller is a stored program control processor that runs software routines for real-time voice traffic and trunk signaling, for administrative and maintenance applications, for internal directories and maps, and for customized features for specific users. As a programmable processor, it may also be made to communicate with other processors in the data network, as we will see later. An administrative operator console (not a telephone switchboard) may provide local programmer access to the software.

The switch matrix furnishes a transparent path for digital traffic between attached stations, and may be implemented completely in hardware or as a combination of hardware and software. Its fundamental characteristic is that it provides a digital path through the PBX; this property distinguishes the digital PBX from its analog counterparts.

The digital interface modules provide attachment capability for data devices and digital telephones. Their two main functions are to separate the digital information (whatever its source - data terminal, digital telephone, or other) from the signaling information (routing the former to the switch matrix and the latter to the controller) and to implement full-duplex transmission over the 2-wire half-duplex link to the data or voice station. For a discussion of some proposed implementation schemes refer to [4,5]. In addition, they can be adapted to interface to the integrated services digital network (ISDN), which is an all-digital voice and data network concept that is currently undergoing development in various countries.

As the digital interface modules do, the analog ones separate the signaling from the voice traffic and control the transfer of information to and from analog stations and trunks. The voice traffic is digitized to be compatible with both the switch matrix and the digital telephones and is sent transparently through the switch. Very often, the architecture of the PBX reflects the nature of the digitized voice signal, the latter having been standardized by the telephone companies and telecommunication administrations for their interoffice trunking.

3.2 THE VOICE MODEL FOR PBX ARCHITECTURE

The widely accepted technique of digitizing speech using pulse code modulation (PCM) results in a continuous bit rate of 64 kbit/s [6]. More sophisticated digitization techniques have recently been developed [7,8] that allow transmission of speech at significantly lower bit rates, but this compression has not been standardized, and it is the full bandwidth representation that underlies the design of many PBXs and the ISDN. Bit rates higher than 64 kbit/s are, of course, possible but are not used except in applications requiring very high fidelity.

The 125 microsecond sampling period (1/8000 s) and the 64 kbit/s signal bit rate pervade the architecture of digital PBXs in two major ways. First, the switch matrix (especially for a switch employing time-division multiplexing) is designed to switch, in a manner transparent to the data stream, 64 kbit/s full-duplex channels, by transmitting a byte (representing an 8-bit sample) in each direction every 125 microseconds for each channel. Second, the link between the digital stations and the digital interface module is designed to support a 64 kbit/s full-duplex conversation plus some amount of signaling (usually 8 to 32 kbit/s), again by

transmitting one byte of voice or data traffic plus 1 to 4 bits of signaling every 125 microseconds.

For the PBX to carry digital information transparently at bit rates greater than 64 kbit/s, an integral number of voice channels must be multiplexed together. For the PBX to carry data at bit rates less than 64 kbit/s, either the unused bandwidth can be wasted by filling it with idle or repeated bits, or the 64 kbit/s channel can be submultiplexed to carry an integral number of low-speed data channels. In the case of submultiplexing, again the PBX may or may not provide the service, and a restriction that all the subchannels must enter and leave the PBX by the same path applies. Clearly, the advantage of having the full bit rate, or any fraction thereof, of a high-speed medium available at every access port is not achievable.

3.3 PBX FEATURES THAT APPLY TO THE DATA NETWORK

While most features of PBXs exist to enhance the usability of the PBX on behalf of the voice user, many can be used to similar advantage by the data user. Still others can be provided that apply only to the data user. These two categories are summarized below.

3.3.1 Features for Both Voice and Data

*   Least-cost routing of long-distance calls

*   Classes of service

*   Call-back queuing when a station is busy

*   Abbreviated dialing

*   Call detail recording

*   Automatic call distribution within a service group, such as a group of dial-in ports on a communication controller

*   Call forwarding

*   Security code screening

*   PBX-owned autocall units (ACUs) (rather than one per line)

*   Conference calling for internal multipoint configurations

*   Very high availability (to meet telecommunication administration regulations for voice)

3.3.2 Data-only Features

*   Pooling of modems

*   Pooling of protocol converters

*   Pooling of encryption devices

These features can be extended to voice transmission when digitized voice is carried outside the establishment. They are also most liable to constraints in their design because they interface closely to the public networks.

4.0 IMPLEMENTATIONS OF LOCAL DATA NETWORKS WITH PBXS

The existence of a PBX in an establishment offers three broad categories of its application to data services: it can provide only voice services, leaving the responsibility for data to a high-speed data-only network; it can provide connection services for voice and data devices; or it can provide the voice services itself but share the responsibility for data with a high-speed data-carrying cable. In this final major section of the paper we examine the last two options, studying first local data networks based solely on a PBX and then those that include both a PBX and a separate high-speed data-only system. Throughout the discussion, the user requirements outlined in section 2.2 are employed as benchmarks by which we can evaluate the different approaches.

4.1 THE PBX AS THE HUB OF THE DATA NETWORK

Refer again to Figure 1 for a depiction of a PBX that by itself controls the local data network. Implicit but not shown are adapters on the data devices, either natively or separately attached, that make the devices appear as digital telephones, using the same two-wire interface. The PBX is capable of connecting any data device to any other data device (as it would two telephones), any data device to the digital side of any modem in a pool, and the analog side of any modem in a pool to any line to the public switched network. The other pooled services can also be interposed in any link connection through the switch.

As in most local data networks that provide only connection between devices, little device compatibility is provided by the PBX. Modems can be set or chosen to match the speeds of certain devices, and protocol converters can be used only between certain classes of devices, but beyond that the delivery of bits is the main function of the switch; any two devices that do not understand each other's data stream when they are directly connected will not understand each other any better when they are connected through the PBX. The open systems interconnection (OSI) reference model of the International Organization for Standardization (ISO) would place the switch's functions in the 2 or 3 bottom layers only, except for network management applications running in the controller, which would be in the top layer.

Another important limitation is that end-to-end bit integrity is the responsibility of the data devices. The subjective nature of voice allows occasional bit errors without greatly disturbing the speakers, and so PBXs have had no motivation

for detecting or correcting bit errors. Data devices must treat the PBX as part of any vulnerable link.

4.1.1 Connection Establishment

The protocols for the establishment of connections between devices can take many forms. Connections of long duration can be effectively hardwired by the PBX administrative operator; this usually requires written or verbal communication between the user and the operator. Connections of shorter duration may be automated or may require human intervention. These options are worth exploring.

Connections that require human intervention for their establishment are considered to be manual dial calls. Existing terminals with dial capability usually connect directly to an analog line (using a modem) and so are not of interest here. For terminals without built in dialing three options remain.

1. The adapter between the data device and the digital interface module may possess a facility for specifying the extension number, or public switched network number, of the station to be called. This facility may be implemented strictly within the adapter or in conjunction with the terminal.

2. A separate telephone may be used to effect the connection by dialing a service processor and a series of digits specifying both the calling station and the called station. Disconnection can be accomplished in a similar way (except that only one of the numbers need be specified) or by turning the power off, provided that the switch can recognize that as a return to an on-hook condition.

3. Both the terminal and the PBX can implement an in-line signaling technique, of which CCITT Recommendation X.21 is a good example; call establishment, data transmission, and call takedown phases are clearly defined, and neither separate equipment nor an extra pair of wires is required.

For all of these cases, control signals that flow over the data device interface, which is normally a modem interface (such as RS-232-C, V.24, or V.35, for example), must be passed through the switch along with the actual data traffic, whether or not the call actually requires a modem. This task is usually the job of the adapter, and reflects the continuing influence of today's analog world in which communicating terminals send digital data over modulated analog lines.

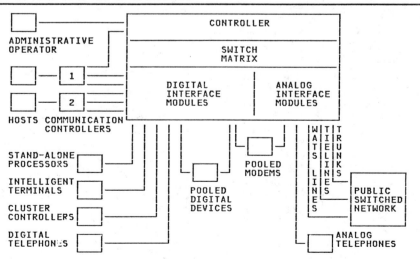

Figure 1. The Digital PBX as the Hub of the Data Network

Automated dialing under program control has fewer possibilities. As in the discussion of manual dial, autocall units (ACUs) are not considered here, because one of the advantages of the digital PBX is that having dialing capability into the public switched network obviates the need for line-by-line ACUs on communication controllers and the separate ports they require. Eliminating that, two options remain. One is digital in-line signaling, as in the above description of X.21, and the other is common-channel signaling.

Common-channel signaling requires communication between the central processing unit (CPU) in the calling device and the controller of the PBX. This is represented in Figure 1 by the line between communication controller number 1 and the PBX controller, and should not be confused with the common-channel interoffice signalling (CCIS) system of American Telephone and Telegraph (ATT). This is the first time we have seen the advantage of the similarity between the PBX controller and the other data devices in the network. If the CPU and the controller implement the same communication protocols and have running software to implement the required tasks, then the CPU can send call requests not only for itself, but for other hosts in the network as well. These requests, being limited only by their driving software, can take on a more general nature, and may include requests for the establishment of permanent connections, configuration of existing or new connections into point-to-point, multipoint (the data equivalent of a conference call), or even loop arrangements, or the imposition of changes to a station's profile.

4.1.2 Evaluation against the Requirements

FULL CONNECTIVITY: The PBX scores well in meeting the demands for long-term (call duration) connectivity but not well for short-term (packet duration) connectivity. It is true that any device can be attached to any other device, but it may exchange data with only that device during the connection. While some devices do not have sufficient processing capability to sustain conversations or sessions [12] with more than one device at a time, and so are not constrained by having a transparent path to only one device at a time, other devices that can maintain sessions with several devices at a time must rely on multiple lines, even if they have the capability of interleaving packets with addresses of different destinations together into one stream. One result of this is that attached CPUs must still be relied upon for packet routing, even when that forces the traffic from certain sessions to traverse the switch matrix multiple times.

SIMPLE REARRANGEMENT: Since devices are known by their telephone number (or an alias that is resolved by the abbreviated dialing function), moving a device is as simple as moving a person's telephone number: all that is required is an operator command. Changing a configuration, such as adding a terminal to a multipoint line, is also done by software.

RELIABILITY: The reliability of the basic PBX is very high because of the duplication of all its essential components, including the controller, that is necessary to meet the requirements of the common carriers or telecommunication administrations. Failures on individual lines are not likely to affect other lines (unless a high-speed multiplexed line is used to carry traffic from the PBX to multiple stations). Rapid recovery through the use of pooled services allows gradual rather than catastrophic degradation of service. Incorporation of the PBX into the management scheme of the data network depends largely on the ability of the management applications in the data network to interact with the PBX controller, using the same path as common-channel signaling.

SMOOTH GROWTH IN SIZE: The difficulty here is not in exceeding the line capacity of the PBX, which can usually be increased in a modular fashion, but rather of requiring a separate line for each station-PBX link. This follows directly from the radial wiring topology dictated by the PBX (and is a property that is shared by star-wired high-speed data networks as well). If surplus lines are installed between the PBX and the wiring closets in different parts of the building, and if multiple lines are run to each office, then this problem can be reduced.

EVENTUAL INTEGRATION OF VOICE, DATA, AND VIDEO: In a sense, voice and data are integrated in a PBX because the switch matrix treats all channels, be they voice or data, the same, and because they are carried on the same type of medium. In a different sense, however, they are not, and this is based on the notion that the integration of voice and data means that voice will be considered as simply another form of digital information. The asynchronous packetized nature of data is not ideally served by a system designed around the synchronous fixed-bit-rate nature of voice channels. In concrete terms, voice and data are separated by space (separate links) outside the PBX and by time within it.

The integration of video with voice and data is much more difficult to imagine. It is not likely that real-time video will ever be carried through a PBX because there are no 4-6 MHz analog paths through the switch. Furthermore, the multiplexing of digitized video would not only consume at least twenty-four 64 kbit/s voice channels through the switch but would also require imposing multiplexer of the same ratio.

4.2 COEXISTENCE OF A PBX AND A HIGH-SPEED CABLE SYSTEM

For those establishments with needs not satisfied by a PBX alone, the combination of a PBX and a high-speed cable system can often provide a more comprehensive and varied solution, although most cable systems take little account of PBXs or voice traffic. The publicity surrounding high-speed local data networks has been widespread, and standards bodies, IEEE 802 for example, are attempting to codify acceptable procedures.

Again, this discussion will not distinguish among the various types of high-speed cable systems, except in the section regarding the integration of video. Rather, cable systems possessing any of the following (not necessarily mutually exclusive) attributes - bus, ring, loop, optical, baseband, or broadband - will be considered only as variations of a generic system that has the following properties:

• megabit speeds

• packet delivery based on header addresses

• linear (either open or closed) rather than radial topology

The form of integration of the PBX with the high-speed cable network that will be investigated in this section places the PBX in the role of a gateway to the public switched network, as Figure 2 below illustrates. All telephones, digital or analog, attach to the PBX, and all data devices attach to the cable. It is assumed that ports on the cable are furnished with adapters to handle the megabit speeds, cable access, and physical transmission protocols of the particular cable design. The transfer of data between devices attached to the cable does not involve the PBX in any way. Only when a device on the cable needs to access a device in the public switched network does the PBX assume an active role. The advantageous features of the PBX listed in section 3.3 still apply, although the set of calls they apply to is reduced to only those that go outside the establishment. The next section describes some potential mechanisms for effecting public switched network access using the PBX.

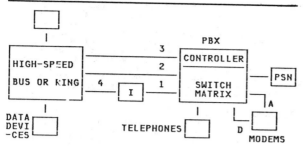

Figure 2. The PBX: Gateway to the PSN

4.2.1 Connection Establishment

Consider first the case of dial-in calls from the public switched network. When the PBX has a direct inward dial facility, it seeks to ring an autoanswer port on a communication controller, small host, or autoanswer terminal. The simplest implementation of this employs an interconnection node, labeled I in the figure, that connects directly to both the PBX (via line 1, which may be multiple) and the cable (via line 4). Such a node could take the form of a communication controller with multiple lines and intermediate routing [13] logic. A more complex implementation requires, instead of the interconnection node, an autoanswer port (on a device attached only to the cable) that has a PBX adapter (to serialize the modem signals) and a cable adapter. It is doubtful that this arrangement could satisfy the timing regimen of the two-wire signaling scheme discussed in [5], however, and the direct connection between the switch matrix and the cable (line 2) must have some intelligent device that passes the address of the destination to the physical-level cable adapter so that it can build the packets.

Devices that make dial-out calls can also employ the interconnection node but have greater flexibility in using it. If advantage is to be taken of the PBX dialing capability, then none of the data devices will have ACUs on their own ports. The passing of dial requests to the PBX must then follow one of the methods described in section 4.1.1, except that the lack of direct attachment of the data devices to the PBX and the difficulty of cascading the PBX and cable adapters (using line 2 in Figure 2) leave only in-line digital signaling and common-channel signaling, both of which require the interconnection node.

With in-line signaling, call requests are sent to the interconnection node as part of the contents of a data stream _above_ the link level. Thus the interconnection node must contain a processor of its own, and cannot implement just a physical level passthrough. In this capacity, the interconnection node could be a logical description of a communication controller and a CPU, even though only one box is shown in the figure.

Common-channel signaling involves not only the interconnection node but also the PBX controller. With this arrangement, call requests are passed to the controller on line 3 from any capable device, including the interconnection node (which uses line 4 to reach line 3). Any number of devices can communicate directly with the controller but only one link to the controller, from the cable, is needed; the PBX-only solution requires one link per device that needs to attach directly.

Upon receiving the request through its controller, the PBX makes the call and rings an autoanswer port on the interconnection node, which can be instructed by the requesting station to pass data sent on that call to the calling station; there is no restriction that the requesting station and the calling station be the same. Alternatively, the interconnection node can perform intermediate routing based on information in the incoming data stream.

4.2.2 Evaluation Against the Requirements

FULL CONNECTIVITY: The any-to-any connectivity of local data devices is provided by the cable portion of the network, and the connection to remote devices is provided by the PBX. In contrast to the PBX-only solution, short-term (packet duration) connectivity _is_ a property of this scheme. Speeds are limited only for traffic that passes through the PBX into the public switched network.

SIMPLE REARRANGEMENT: Any devices that are directly attached to the PBX can be moved as easily as described in section 4.1.2. The simplicity of rearrangement on the cable depends on the particulars of the cable network, but recall that we assumed that these requirements are satisfied by the cable-only network.

RELIABILITY: The PBX has less effect on reliability when it is coupled with a cable network because no permanent connections are established through it. When a failure occurs on a switched connection, most recovery schemes merely redial. Even so, the PBX's participation in data connections implies that, as in the PBX-only case, communication between the PBX controller and the other data devices be supported, not only for common-channel signaling but for the exchange of network management information as well.

SMOOTH GROWTH IN SIZE: As the data network grows, undoubtedly more switched connections will be required. The number of ports on the cable will not have to be increased, however, as lines 3 and 4 can carry packets from any number of different stations. The only increase will be in the number of lines between the interconnection node and the switch matrix. The growth in the number of telephones will prompt the same difficulties stated in section 4.1.2, but the number of telephones in an existing worker population will not grow nearly as fast as the number of data terminals, so this telephone growth should be easy to manage, and will occur regardless of the activities of the data network.

EVENTUAL INTEGRATION OF VOICE, DATA, AND VIDEO: The full integration of voice and data implies the uniform treatment of both as digital information, and includes the placement of digital telephones on the cable and the shrinking of PBX functions to those involving only public switched network trunks and modems. This arrangement seems eminently feasible if the cable access and transmission schemes allow the carrying of synchronous voice traffic, and if the digitized voice signal can be compressed in each telephone to a more reasonable bit rate (considering the number of telephones there will be), such as 9.6 kbit/s.

The integration of video could be accomplished in stages, all of which involve its being carried on the cable. Separate channels on a broadband frequency-modulated cable could be allotted to analog video signals, much the way cable TV is carried today. With extremely high bandwidth cables, such as optical fibers, full bandwidth digital video could conceivably be interleaved by time with the other signals on a cable, but not many video channels could be carried at once. When simple video compression techniques are employed, bringing the bit rate down to the order of a few Mbit/s, then video traffic will hardly seem different from high-speed facsimile and will be readily integrated. The problems of synchronous transmission for both voice and video are partly ameliorated, by the way, when the signals are compressed, for the compression usually involves the extraction and transmission of slowly varying parameters whose updating period is generally much larger than the typical variance in access time of an asynchronous cable-access protocol.

5.0 CONCLUSIONS

We have examined two very different ways of
incorporating PBXs into local data networks, as
the central controller hub of the data network
and as a gateway to the public switched network.
Solutions intermediate between these extremes
may also be chosen, in which some data devices
are connected to the PBX and others to a cable.
We have seen that hub solution is restricted to
longer term connectivity than the cable-gateway
solution, and it serves permanent connections,
long sessions, single-session devices, and
hierarchical configurations (in which packet
routing is done by higher architectural layers)
well. The cable-gateway solution not only
serves these applications well also, but is in
addition capable of supporting short sessions
(as short as datagrams [14]),
multiple-destination data streams, and
peer-to-peer configurations.

If a customer requires a PBX to provide voice
services regardless of the needs of data, then
having a cable network in addition means having
two separate networks. When the future
requirements for the integration of voice, data,
and video are considered, however, the
high-speed cable network seems indispensable.

As long as both a PBX and a data network (of any
type) coexist and interconnect, one outstanding
notion remains. The treatment of the PBX
controller as another data device, and the
subsequent provision of compatible software
allowing the controller and the data devices to
communicate, is not only desirable for enhanced
usability of the PBX but is also required for
effective maintenance of aggregate system
integrity.

A.0 ACKNOWLEDGMENTS

The author wishes to thank Philippe DeBacker and
Art Potocki of the IBM Centre d'Etudes et
Recherches in La Gaude, France, for many
fruitful discussions.

B.0 REFERENCES AND NOTES

1. "PBX Buyers Guide," Communications News,
   Vol. 18, No. 7, p. 45, July 1981.

2. Markov, J. D., "The Taxonomy of Local
   Computer Networks," Proc. Intl. Conf. Local
   Networks and Distributed Office Systems,
   London, May 1981.

3. Bux, W., "Local-Area Subnetworks: A
   Performance Comparison," IEEE Transactions
   on Communications, Vol. COM-29, No. 10, pp.
   1465-1473, October 1981.

4. Meyer, J., T. Roste, and R. Torbergsen, "A
   Digital Subscriber Set," IEEE Transactions
   on Communications, Vol. COM-27, No. 7, pp.
   1096-1103, July 1979.

5. Inoue, N., R. Komiya, and Y. Inoue,
   "Time-Shared Two-Wire Digital Subscriber
   Transmission System and Its Application to
   the Digital Telephone Set," IEEE
   Transactions on Communications, Vol.
   COM-29, No. 11, pp. 1565-1572, November
   1981.

6. The study of human speech [9,10] has
   determined that speech contains frequency
   components throughout the audible range,
   which extends up to 20 kHz in exceptional
   individuals, and beyond that to around 100
   kHz for unvoiced fricatives such as /s/.

Most of the energy, however, is at
frequencies below 10 kHz, and the telephone
companies and telecommunication
administrations have established standards
for lowpass-filtered and bandpass-filtered
speech in the frequency ranges of 0-3400 Hz
and 300-3400 Hz respectively [11]. Sampling
this nominal 4 kHz signal at the Nyquist
rate of 8000/s and digitizing to 8
bits/sample yield the resultant 64 kbit/s
bit rate.

7. Atal, B. S., and S. L. Hanauer, "Speech
   Analysis and Synthesis by Linear Prediction
   of the Speech Wave," J. Acoust. Soc. Am.,
   Vol. 50, No. 2, pp. 637-655, 1971.

8. Makhoul, J., "Linear Prediction - A Tutorial
   Review," Proc. IEEE, Vol. 63, No. 4, pp.
   561-580, April 1975.

9. Dudley, H., "The Carrier Nature of Speech,"
   Bell Syst. Tech. J., Vol. 19, pp. 495-515,
   1940.

10. Fant, G., Acoustic Theory of Speech
    Production, The Hague, Mouton, 1960.

11. Jayant, N. S., "Digital Coding of Speech
    Waveforms: PCM, DPCM, and DM Quantizers,"
    Proc. IEEE, Vol. 62, No. 5, pp. 611-632, May
    1974.

12. A session is a conversation between two
    logical entities, such as programs, that are
    usually in two different machines.

13. Intermediate routing is the routing of
    messages, based on packet headers, by a node
    that is neither the origin nor the
    destination of the messages.

14. Datagrams are self-contained packets that
    are not part of a continuous conversation
    and that are sent once without the need for
    an acknowledgment.

Daniel Avery Pitt was born in
Madison, Wisconsin in 1949.
He received a B.S. in
mathematics (magna cum
laude) from Duke University,
Durham, NC, in 1971 and the
M.S. and Ph.D. degrees in
computer science (hardware
emphasis) from the
University of Illinois,
Urbana, in 1973 and 1978,
respectively.

In 1979 he joined IBM in
Research Triangle Park, NC,
in the advanced technology
group, where he was engaged in the development
and analysis of satellite data communication
facilities and in data compression techniques
for video. Since 1980 he has worked in the
Systems Network Architecture (SNA) development
group, pursuing topics in switching,
multiplexing, and routing. Dr. Pitt is also an
Adjunct Assistant Professor of Computer Science
and Electrical Engineering at Duke University,
and is a book reviewer for the AAAS publication
Science Books and Films.

Information Management and the Automated Office

R C Hawk, F R Zitzmann
American Telephone & Telegraph Co.,
USA

The automated office has the potential for achieving substantial productivity improvements for most businesses. However, the introduction of new technology in the office has been less than revolutionary so far. Customers and office product vendors alike have learned that making a transition from conventional office practices that have evolved over many years is much more complex than originally assumed. This paper discusses the major role of voice-based products and services, such as the PBX, in the modern office. It is shown that evolutionary enhancements of one major premises product, DIMENSION® PBX, have already enabled business customers to improve the way that they manage information in the office. Criteria are described for the next generation of Bell System premises systems that will enable customers to enter the age of the automated office incrementally and with minimum business risks.

1. INTRODUCTION

For nearly a decade, the automated office has been called the answer to problems of business productivity. Today, the full potential of office automation is still more a promise than a reality - an ill-defined Shangrila located somewhere on a distant planning horizon.

Equipment vendors and customers alike have been frustrated as they have sought to move successfully into the era of the office of the future. In a recent Fortune Magazine article [1] vendors are described as "far from giving up," while customers are said to be "showing signs of exhaustion." The article goes on to say that "one leading edge user speaks for most customers when he protests: 'We don't need any more technology; we need to find out how to use what we've got.'"

Information consultants also are trying to focus on the underlying issues in this area. For instance, David L. Holzman, in the abstract to his paper, "The Elusive Office Automation Benefits," observes:

> American management is ill-prepared to enter the information age. Utilizing information technology to cut costs and improve decision making requires a great deal more knowledge about administrative activities than top management currently possesses . . . Recently recognizing the problem, management turned to office automation as a solution. The rub is you cannot automate what you can't structurally represent . . . [2]

Even widely quoted data that have been the underpinnings for much office automation activity are coming under attack. The belief that low productivity in the office is due to too little capital investment per office worker (only $1,500 to $2,500) may be flawed, according to one of the originators of that theory:

> Michael D. Zisman . . . now says, . . . "Investment looks low because companies expense their office-related costs instead of capitalizing them. If you capitalize actual expense streams for the office, you'll find companies have already invested $15,000 to $20,000 per office worker . . ." [3]

It is apparent that the automated office will become a reality in an evolutionary, rather than revolutionary, way. This situation is of profound importance to designers of next generation information management systems as well as to business customers who will be investing their capital and betting the future of their companies on those systems.

2. THE OPPORTUNITY

While experts may differ on reasons why the automated office is still more promise than reality, there is general agreement that a productivity opportunity exists. In the United States, the white collar worker force has experienced a productivity gain of only about ten percent since 1965. During the same period, the gain for farm workers was sixty percent and for blue collar workers, thirty percent.

The disparity is bad enough now, in and of itself, but it is cause for even greater concern when one realizes that the white collar work force also is growing more rapidly than the other segments. In 1965, blue collar workers accounted for 55 percent of the work force in American industry. By 1988, that percentage is expected to drop to 45 percent; the other 55 percent will be comprised of white collar workers. Even today, the salaries of white collar workers represent the largest single component of corporate operating expenses.

It is instructive to examine how this large, growing and costly segment of white collar workers spends its time in the office. Figure 1 shows that about 95 percent of the work-day of a business executive is devoted to some form of communications. Figure 2 summarizes how a typical secretary's work-day is occupied; again, communications is a large part (75%) of the worker's activities. AT&T studies have shown that knowledge workers and middle managers spend 82% and 85% of their work days, respectively, on communications related activities. United States businesses are spending $667 billion on office communications today, of which 80 to 85 percent is related to salaries. It is clear from these data that communications systems must play a central role in improving white collar productivity in the automated office of the future.

**WHITE COLLAR WORKERS
TIME DISTRIBUTION
EXECUTIVES**

Source: AT&T Customer Studies

Figure 1

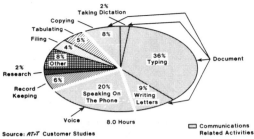

WHITE COLLAR WORKERS TIME DISTRIBUTION
SECRETARIES

Source: AT&T Customer Studies

Figure 2

3. CURRENT OFFICE SYSTEMS

One way or another, most business customers have incorporated products such as word processing and management information systems using computer mainframes as initial steps towards breaking the productivity bottleneck in the office. There is much debate today about how successful such steps have been. For instance, a recent study by SRI International that was reported in the previously referenced Fortune Magazine article concluded:

> After surveying 4,000 offices to find out which activities could be automated at a profit, SRI discovered that in all but special cases, such as legal departments, there were few direct cost savings from current form of office automation, including word processing. [4]

The Bell System with one million employees, one of the largest corporations in the world, has had extensive experience in the use of current office systems in business operations. Barbara Thompson, AT&T District Manager-Administrative Services, who has been involved in the area of word processing since 1970, was recently asked for her perspective of the automated office of the future as an experienced user:

> As to the office of the future, I've yet to see a complete office of the future system that will elevate my productivity. I can hang on devices to current offerings that will provide me electronic mail capabilities, do electronic calendaring, file and sort, but they're not all tied together. I'm looking for a system that is multifunctional, that will do more than just the creation of text, that will afford me the opportunity to telecommunicate, do more sophisticated filing, access my host computer and even facilitate phototypesetting. I see some of this in a few products but they haven't yet been brought together. [5]

One of the more ambitious efforts in office automation in the Bell System is being pursued by the Advanced Office Systems group in the Long Lines Department of AT&T[6]. With help from Bell Laboratories, the group is conducting seven "trials" among several hundred Long Lines middle managers. The term "trial" can be misleading because the mission of the group is to demonstrate the feasibility of the automated office. Systems of state-of-the-art products have been assembled for use in real, day-to-day operating situations, and data are being carefully evaluated to address a variety of concerns that include how to measure managerial productivity, how to evaluate office systems and how automation influences group and individual behavior and output.

The Long Lines group is testing software features such as electronic messaging, information storage and retrieval, computer-aided conferencing, personal support, decision support and text management. Most of these are based on

the UNIX™ operating system developed at the Bell Laboratories that is rapidly becoming a standard in the industry because of its inherent flexibility of use and its ease of portability among processor mainframes. The hardware being used in the study by the Long Lines group includes products from many vendors and comprises a variety of text terminals (CRT, printing, portable and pocket), voice-based terminals, laser printers, OCR devices, networking and processors.

™ UNIX is a trademark of Bell Laboratories.

4. VOICE COMMUNICATIONS IN THE OFFICE

The experiences gained from conducting customer studies, from internal Bell System trials and from day-to-day operations of a business using contemporary office products, have also shown us the importance of voice in the office environment. For example, the same AT&T studies that produced the data in Figures 1 and 2 on how time is spent in the office have produced the data in Figure 3 that summarizes how customers spend money in the office. The second largest expenditure category in the office today is for voice communications, and 80 percent of that figure can be traced to salaries of people who now spend a lot of time on the telephone.

USER EXPENDITURES

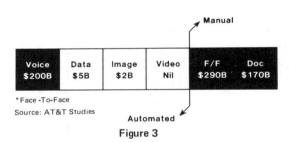

* Face -To-Face
Source: AT&T Studies

Figure 3

Our customers tell us that their voice communications systems are vital to the way they conduct business. For that reason, they have come to demand a level of reliability that substantially exceeds what they expect other office products to provide. Yet, if a business customer is asked to name office products used in his or her business, the telephone rarely comes to mind. The obvious reason is that the telephone has become such a commonplace part of our daily lives that we automatically think of it as always being available; in fact, we depend on it. The ubiquitous telephone - there are 46.5 million business phones in the USA [7] - is the largest conveyor of information messages in the office today and offers enormous opportunities for productivity improvements through new information management methods.

Recognizing the ubiquity of the telephone in the office and its centrality to office functions, the Bell Laboratories conducted a five-year research project on experimental telecommunications services and terminals. The experimental "teleterminal," a combined voice and data telephone which was discussed at the 1981 National Telecommunications Conference in New Orleans, Louisiana, showed considerable promise as a basis for designs of future interface equipment for use by managers in the automated office. The experimental teleterminal delivered several services that were studied, including enhanced calling, electronic messaging, information and news retrieval and calendaring. Most of the software for this research was based on the UNIX operating system.

In spite of the overall encouraging results of the research, the concluding remarks of one researcher (R. A. Thompson) underscored essentially the same point about the state-of-the-art in the automated office that was made earlier in this paper:

> (The experimental work) was a valuable experience and significant genuine learning occurred in human-machine interaction. The experimenters are now tempted to call themselves experts: two phenomena detract from this.
>
> (1) Many users still complain about items which appear to us to be "trivial." The number of people with the same complaints suggests that we don't understand the significant underlying concept. (2) Almost every change that was made to the system was met with virtually unanimous approval or dissent. This suggests that we know so little about the human-machine interface, that we are still dealing in the gross areas of general human behavior and have not reached the finer points which are separated by individual personal taste.
>
> As in so many other areas of science, the more one learns, the more one discovers what he does not know. [8]

5. THE ROLE OF THE PBX

Experiences and study data such as those previously mentioned have led the Bell System to conclude that the PBX is not only a central element in the automated office, but it is the logical starting point that allows customers to evolve into the office of the future at minimum risk while reaping early productivity benefits.

It is widely agreed that PBXs will continue to be used by more and more businesses. For instance, one consulting firm, The Eastern Management Group, was recently reported as expecting a 45 percent increase in installed PBXs in the United States over the next ten years [9]. In addition to a steady growth in volume, the PBX has changed substantially in terms of the feature/function capabilities that newer systems now offer to the user. For instance, DIMENSION PBX, a widely successful Bell System PBX, now offers over 150 different features to customers that greatly enhance the ability of the customer to control costs and to improve the productivity of office workers. The PBX has major advantages as the central element of the automated office: it is already a part of most businesses; it provides an opportunity to improve the information management associated with the voice segment of office systems, already a large factor in how business managers spend time and money; and, in its more modern designs, it allows for non-disruptive incremental additions of non-voice office automation functions as such products become available.

Earlier this year, the Bell System announced five new functional capabilities for DIMENSION PBX that illustrate the PBX's advantages:

(1) Distributed Communications System (DCS) - permits up to twelve DIMENSION PBX (Feature Package 8) to be linked together over large distances into a unified transparent communications system. This extends the benefits of DIMENSION PBX to as many as 25,000 users.

(2) Data Switching - provides for the integrated switching of voice and data in a single DIMENSION PBX system at rates up to 9.6kbps without the use of modems.

(3) Message Center Service - allows customers to route calls automatically to message center attendants, thereby reducing "telephone tag" problems and enhancing the image of the customer's organization. Several levels of sophistication are offered, including electronic messages and Electronic Directory.

(4) Energy Communications Service Adjunct - permits automatic on and off cycling of equipment, scheduled control of lighting and air conditioning, monitoring and reporting of energy consumption - all using existing telephone cables.

(5) Call Management Systems - integrates automatic call distribution functions with sophisticated management report capabilities into the DIMENSION PBX system.

The DIMENSION Prelude PBX, which also was announced earlier this year, illustrates the impact of technological progress on systems of modest size. Among the more than 150 features available on Prelude are some new features that were introduced for the first time on a DIMENSION PBX designed for the below 100 line category (Six-Way Station Conference, Priority Queuing, etc.).

All told, these announcements are illustrative of capabilities recently made available to customers of DIMENSION PBX that enhance the handling of office messages, enable tighter control of operating costs and provide for the management of information vital to business; and, all evolved naturally from the concept and role of the basic PBX.

6. THE NEXT GENERATION OF PREMISES PRODUCTS

Let us summarize. We have established that the automated office is in the process of evolving. Customers and vendors alike are still learning how to employ new technology to improve office productivity in a way that will substantially improve the bottom line of the business balance sheet. Voice-related communications have remained a major element of office processes and represent a large part of today's office costs. The PBX has established itself as the key means for improving voice communications in the business environment. Furthermore, by reference to recently announced enhancements to the DIMENSION PBX, we have shown that the PBX offers customers the opportunity to incrementally move forward into information management for both voice and data-oriented applications. What then are the implications for future systems?

7. MEETING CUSTOMER NEEDS IN THE '80s

The Bell System has identified ten factors and criteria that its next generation premises product line must satisfy in order to meet customer's needs as they move into the automated office of the future. The choice of words, "next generation premises product line" is an appropriate one, since the next generation must be much more than the conventional PBX of previous generations. It must be a communications and information management system that will satisfy increasingly complex applications of information in the office.

7.1 Evolution

The system must ensure customers of clear evolution paths from current Bell System premises products such as DIMENSION PBX and HORIZON® Communications System. Customers must be able to enter into a next generation system at varying degrees of sophistication, with minimal impact on current operations and as part of an evolutionary change. This means, for example, that the next generation system should interface with current generation Bell-provided systems that form part of existing customer communications networks such as an Electronic Tandem Network (ETN), main/satellite, DCS, or centralized attendant service configurations — in a way that is essentially transparent to the customer. As another example, customers who have system management capability for current DIMENSION PBX systems should be able to move to a next generation system without significant changes at the system management interface, or without the need for fully retraining personnel.

7.2 Multi-function Capabilities

The next generation must be more than a conventional

PBX; it must provide much more than integrated voice and data switching. The future system must have the capability of supporting incrementally the full range of emerging information management functions that will be required for the office of the future. These include call management functions, document mail, personal office services such as calendar, high speed host-to-host and terminal-to-host data communications, sensor services such as life safety and energy control, message storage and retrieval, text editing and advanced system management capabilities.

7.3 Connectivity

A major requirement for a next generation system is that it accommodate the hundreds and thousands of terminals that will need to be connected together in various ways in the automated office. This must be achieved economically and with minimum impact on business activities, and that means that the next generation system must accommodate existing building telephone wiring (twisted pairs). This flexible and economical approach to connectivity is essential in a field as dynamic as office automation. For example, if a customer guesses wrong on where high-speed terminals, or even standard station sets, are to be located, the system must permit the customer to make simple changes by unplugging the terminals and reconnecting them to other system ports using the telephone wiring that is already in place.

7.4 Human Interface

The next generation system must provide a common user interface across all multi-function applications. If the customer is to get maximum price/performance benefit from advanced office products, interfaces must be easy to use and uniform and require a minimum of specialized training. Evidence is strong that many experimental office systems fail because of complexities involved in integrating new technology into long-established office procedures and underlying organizational cultures. It is essential that the next generation system facilitate the introduction of automated functions by providing the most consistent, user friendly interface possible.

7.5 Build From Voice

One Bell System strength over the years has been its ability to manage customers' voice communications. As we contemplate the requirements of the automated office over the next decade, it can be expected that significant customer needs will still depend on the ability to enhance and improve human-to-human communication using voice. The studies discussed previously in this paper support that view; a large percentage of executive time is spent in such communications. Executives will tend to rely increasingly on this kind of communication for decision making; and, although the Bell System also intends to place emphasis on non-interactive document forms of communication and mail, it seems obvious that messaging and communications systems that utilize voice will soon become the significant factors in the next generation of office systems. The Bell System has been a leader in this area as evidenced by its early introduction of a public voice mail system in Philadelphia, Pa., and will continue to play a large role. The ongoing research in this area at Bell Laboratories continues to receive wide international publication. An added objective should be the ability to offer voice mail as part of a continuum that starts with call coverage and call forwarding, progresses through the ability to leave "pink slip" messages electronically, the centralization of messaging systems and, ultimately, voice mail — continuing on through electronic document communications. Customers must be able to evolve easily along this continuum, starting at any level in the evolutionary path while keeping the same, consistent, friendly user interface all the way.

7.6 Distributed Architecture

The next generation system should have a distributed architecture so that processing capabilities can be located in the departments and office locations where the requirements exist. This criterion also means that as customers move to campus environments or multi-building locations, the system should allow the provision of current and future capabilities to users as if the users were located in a single building. In many instances, parts of the system configuration will have to be interconnected over distances (using tariffed facilities as well as private microwave and fiber optic links) in order to provide the most economical configuration for the customer. The Distributed Communications System (DCS), recently announced for DIMENSION PBX and discussed in a companion paper for ICCC 82 [10] illustrates how a distributed architecture can be implemented and designed for evolution into next generation systems.

7.7 Modularity

This criterion has two dimensions. First, the next generation system must be able to grow economically and be upgradable with minimum disruption to the customer's business. Secondly, it should be possible to add new office system applications on an incremental basis, without the need for reconfiguration of the underlying premises system.

7.8 Customer Participation

In recent years, business customers have expressed increased interest in system capabilities that enable them to participate actively in a variety of system administration and management functions. Options such as the customer administration panel for DIMENSION PBX and similar options for HORIZON CS have been well received by the marketplace. Customers of the 1980s will want to be able to perform their own station translations, make physical moves and changes (including associated distribution-panel cross-connects), become active participants in maintenance procedures that may include replacement of defective terminals, and participate in a host of other activities that formerly were performed only by Bell System personnel. Not only can the customer often reduce operating costs by participating in such activities, but many customers find that they can provide more rapid response to day-to-day needs of office users when their own personnel are able to participate. The next generation system must facilitate more and more customer participation, leading ultimately to a supporting software environment that will enable customers to program the system for new or customized business applications.

7.9 Digital, Integrated Voice/Data (from terminal to terminal)

It is clear that emerging office applications will require a next generation system that has the architectural foundation and associated protocols that will support integrated digital voice and data among all ports (and terminals) in the system. Moreover, this integration must be accomplished economically, while providing for very high data rates, compared to today's typical speeds. At a minimum, the system must provide rates in the 56 or 64 kbps range. These data rate requirements reflect growing customer needs for rapid response time in office applications involving large volumes of information, for high speed facsimile transmission over packet and circuit-switched digital networks, for high speed graphics terminals, and for computer-to-computer communication. The Digital Communications Protocol (DCP) described in a companion paper for ICCC 82, will enable the next generation system to meet these digital, integrated voice/data needs [11]. A requirement for new business premises products of the Bell System is that they be compatible with DCP.

7.10 Networking

Next generation premises systems must be capable of functioning synergistically in a variety of network arrangements. They must be compatible with the planned Integrated Services Digital Network (ISDN) which the Bell System is implementing, along with many other countries in the international community; full digital communications, user to user, on a network basis across great distance will soon be available to business customers in most major cities. The next generation system must interface efficiently and compatibly with other digital transport systems also, including DATAPHONE® Digital Service, the Bell System packet switching network and the Circuit Switched Digital Capability (CSDC). On premises, the next generation system must be capable of compatible interconnection and cooperative operation with local area networks (LANs). One authority [12] does not expect a standardization of LANs for the next five years. Yet, during that period he expects the number of LANs in use to grow from 5,700 to nearly 20,000. The next generation premises system must be capable of enhancing the value of a LAN to the customer who requires one. Finally, the next generation system must operate synergistically with intelligent network services such as those described in sessions A8 and A9 at this conference. Customers ought to be able to use such network-based services for certain, perhaps lower usage, applications while using the premises system for applications that are more heavily utilized. As needs grow, or otherwise change, the customer ought to be able to switch from the intelligent network solution to a premises solution, and vice versa, as appropriate — and in a way that is as transparent to the end user as possible.

8. CONCLUSION

Though the automated office is yet to realize its full potential for improving business productivity, the tools are at hand to enable business customers to reap enormous benefits during the next decade. The PBX has evolved continuously over the years, to the point where it is a principal element of modern communications and information management systems for the office. The next generation PBX is well positioned to be the mechanism that will enable the business customer to evolve gracefully from current systems and procedures in the office and to evolve his operations into the full "office of the future" at minimum risk. The next generation "PBX" will truly become the premises communications and information management system of the automated office for the next decade.

REFERENCES

[1] "What's Detaining the Office of the Future," Fortune Magazine, NYC, USA, May 3, 1982

[2] D.L. Holzman, "The Elusive Office Automation Benefits," Information Society, Crane Russak & Co, NYC, USA, Volume IV, 1982

[3] pg. 178, Ref. 1, op. cit.

[4] pg. 182, Ref. 1, op. cit.

[5] "Office of the Future - A User's Perspective," Business Focus, AT&T Internal Publication, Morris Plains, NJ, USA, January, 1981

[6] R. Epstein, "An Approach to Introducing and Evaluating Automated Office Systems," Electronic Office: Management and Technology, Vol. 005.0001.013, Auerbach Publishers, Inc, 1981

[7] The World's Telephones, AT&T Long Lines, Morris Plains, NJ, USA, January, 1980

[8] R.A. Thompson, "Users' Perceptions with Experimental Services and Terminals," conference paper, National Telecommunications Conference, New Orleans, La, 1981

[9] J.F. Malone, "What's the Outlook for PBXs in the Next 10 Years?" Telephone Engineer and Management, Geneva, Ill, USA, March 15, 1982

[10] R.S. Divakaruni, et al, "New Directions in Enhanced Voice Networking," ICCC 82

[11] G.M. Anderson, et al, "A Communications Protocol for Integrated Digital Voice and Data," ICCC 82

[12] Statement attributed to Dr. Mirek J. Stevenson, Quantum Science Corp., in Telephone Engineer and Management, Geneva, Ill, USA, March 15, 1982, page 95.

R.C. Hawk is Marketing Director of Advanced Systems Development for American Telephone and Telegraph Company. He began his Bell System career in 1964 with the Long Lines Department as a Sales Supervisor for large accounts in Omaha, Nebraska. For the following ten years, he held a variety of sales, technical and marketing assignments with Long Lines, culminating in his appointment in October, 1975 to Marketing Manager - Complex Network Switching Systems at AT&T Headquarters. He was appointed to Marketing Director - Product Development, October 1978 with responsibilities for the development and introduction of all data and voice products located on the customer premises and to his current position in August, 1979. Mr. Hawk has a BA degree in Business Administration from the University of Iowa and an MA in Business Administration from the University of San Francisco.

F. R. Zitzmann is Division Manager of System Requirements and Strategy for American Telephone and Telegraph Company's Advanced Systems Development Department. Mr. Zitzmann holds BEE and MEE degrees from the Polytechnic Institute of New York. Prior to joining AT&T, he held engineering and operations management positions in the Bell Telephone Laboratories, IBM, Comsat, and Satellite Business Systems; he was a founder of a private engineering consulting firm and several CATV operating companies. Mr. Zitzmann is a registered Professional Engineer, a senior member of the IEEE and a member of the Programme Advisory Committee for ICCC 82.

New Directions in Enhanced Voice Networking

R S Divakaruni, G E Saltus,
B R Savage
Bell Laboratories, USA

This paper describes an architecture for interconnecting a group of stored program controlled Private Branch Exchanges (PBX), so that they work together in an integrated fashion, appearing much like a single system to the user. In this paper, such a complex of interconnected PBX systems is referred to as a Distributed Communications System (DCS).

The DCS can be treated as an intelligent sub-network within an Electronic Tandem Network[1] (ETN) which provides a means of offering advanced voice networking capabilities. The DCS architecture provides a mechanism to share control and intelligence among interconnected and autonomous PBXs by the use of a Data Communications Interface Unit (DCIU), which operates like a packet switch controller supporting X.25 protocol and permanent virtual circuits. The DCS provides feature transparency[2] between the interconnected PBX systems. This intelligent network architecture increases the potential for new customer applications by supporting larger line-sizes and functionality.

1. INTRODUCTION

In general, customers require communications systems which are continually providing higher levels of functionality to increase employee productivity and price to performance ratios, thereby, maximizing the return on investment of the communications systems. Current Bell System PBXs are implemented in one of the configurations described below:

(i) Stand-alone operation:

This is a single-PBX system which supports intra-premises customer communications needs and provides access to other communications networks via DDD network, WATS trunks and/or FX trunks.

(ii) Main/Satellite operation:

These are multiple-PBX systems installed on multiple premises which provide integrated, inter-premises station-to-station communications. Main/Satellite operation provides a limited feature transparency between the PBXs. Interaction with other networks is usually provided via the trunking arrangement from the Main PBX switch.

(iii) Electronic Tandem Network (ETN) operation:

These are multiple-PBX systems that can be installed at separate geographic locations and connected by private line tie-trunks [1]. These systems operate as independent nodes in the network for providing intra-premises service and they co-operate with each other for routing inter-premises calls. Interaction with external networks is handled locally at each node. Customers have the flexibility of controlling inter-location call routing.

The internal implementation and operation of these configurations to certain extent are transparent to the users (for example, the call routing functions of ETN where the route selection is transparent to the caller based upon customer pre-selected least cost routing patterns). The DCS represents another evolutionary step towards providing multiple-PBX communications systems without requiring users to be aware of the networking and engineering of the DCS arrangement. Thus, for certain applications, the DCS appears to be a single PBX arrangement to the users. The DCS features also work in a uniform and consistent fashion across multiple-PBX systems when the PBXs are installed at multiple premises, so that inter-premises communications can be enhanced.

This paper describes the DCS architecture for interconnecting a group of PBXs, so that they work together in an integrated fashion, and appear as a single system to the user. The following capabilities are incorporated in PBXs to provide feature transparency in the DCS complex.

1.1 A Data Link Between Processors

This is used to provide communications among the control processors of the individual PBXs. Several approaches were considered for providing this capability:

(i) Use of TOUCH-TONE®[3] sender and receiver arrangements utilizing the trunk tip and ring pair. The trunk connection between the switches of communicating PBXs can be established on a dynamic basis, or a dedicated connection can be used to eliminate call set up times. In either case, this approach has limitations due to trunk signaling characteristics and slow data transfer rates, besides being real-time intensive for the processors during data transfers.

(ii) Use of a direct link from the output port of a control processor to each of the other control processors in the DCS complex. This approach requires a dedicated link between each communicating pair of PBXs for providing transparency in the DCS. Thus, if there are "n" PBXs in a DCS, each PBX needs (n-1) output ports, and n(n-1)/2 data links are required in the system. As "n" becomes large, this approach becomes impractical due to the port requirements at each PBX and due to the cost of data links. This approach also has a severe real-time impact on the control processor.

(iii) Use of an intelligent unit associated with the PBX control processor having a Direct Memory Access (DMA) to the PBX processor memory, and thus having a minimal real-time impact on the PBX capacity. This unit can support multiple X.25 data links, and data cannot only be packet-switched between these links, but also between the PBX processor and the links. Using this packet switching capability, a data network for the purpose of transferring control information can be established between the PBXs of a DCS complex without having to interconnect them directly.

The third approach, which does not have the disadvantages of the other alternatives, was chosen to be implemented in the DCS. This intelligent peripheral unit is called a Data Communications Interface Unit (DCIU).

1.2 Co-operation Between PBXs

This is required to establish calls and to respond to feature activations, such that the response time criteria is met. This capability is provided by designing the call processing software so that call control information can be shared between the participating PBXs of a DCS to provide transparency.

2. SYSTEM ARCHITECTURE

Each PBX system in the DCS complex has a DCIU associated with it. The DCIU is a microprocessor based unit which provides a highly efficient I/O capability. It is an integral part of the PBX control processor and cannot operate in a stand-alone mode. The output links of a DCIU associated with a control processor can be used to connect to the DCIUs associated with other processors for establishing inter-communications between control processors. Other adjunct processors connected directly to the output links of a DCIU can also communicate with each other via the DCIU. The DCIU links can be used with modems for longer distances between individual PBXs.

The basic architectural concept is illustrated in Fig. 1 which depicts three PBXs connected together. The switches are linked with voice trunks like an ETN, and the control processor of each of the PBXs has a DCIU associated with it.

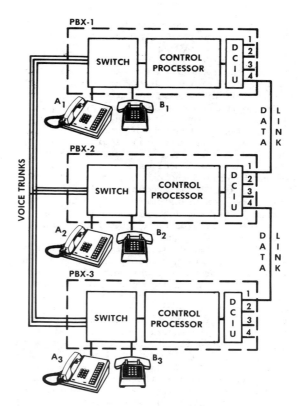

Fig.-1: Basic DCS Architecture

The control processor of PBX-1 can communicate with the control processor of PBX-2 in the arrangement shown in Fig. 1. This connection between the two DCIUs of the two PBXs is used as the data link to exchange information. Currently, this information does not include signaling. In this arrangement, the in-band signaling is done as susual via the voice trunks.

In Fig. 1, for total transparency in the DCS, the user of station A1 should not perceive any difference whether A1 is talking to stations B1, A2, B2, A3 or B3.

There is no direct association between the voice trunks and data links as in the case of the Common Channel Interoffice Signaling (CCIS) scheme [2]. The data required to augment inter-PBX feature operation is transmitted over the data link and is associated with a call on a particular trunk. The transmitting PBX control processor sends the message by using the trunk group number (p) and the trunk number (q) within the trunk group between the switches as an identifier for the data message. The receiving processor uses this identifier (p,q) for associating the received data with the call on trunk "q" of trunk group "p". This means that the trunk group numbers and trunk numbers within that group linking two PBX switches in a DCS, must be the same. However, there are data messages between processors for implementing certain features for which this association is not required.

The DCIU operates like a packet switch supporting X.25 protocol by using permanent virtual circuits. It has Direct Memory Access (DMA) to the communications memory of the control processor; the memory is segmented into mail-boxes that can be associated directly with the processor logical channels. The DCIU pairs a processor logical channel with a logical channel on the output links by an entity called the "network channel" and thereby establishes a communications path. Similarly, for transferring data between two output links, the logical channels on the links are paired using a network channel. Thus, a network channel is always used to establish a communications path. While using a DCIU in permanent virtual circuit mode, the association of logical channels for establishing a communications path (mapping) is defined at the system configuration time. Data from one link can be switched to another link without involving the mail-boxes of the host control processor. This provides the capability of using the DCIU as an intermediate node (relay point) to switch control messages. In case of an output link failure, the DCIU can route the data to the specified destination via an alternate route. Message acknowledgement and retransmission capabilities are provided in the system.

Voice paths between the individual PBXs in the DCS are provided by establishing tie-trunks between each PBX pair, and the data paths are established via the DCIU. If the DCIU is implemented with four output links, and if all four output links at each PBX are used to connect directly to other PBXs for communications, then a maximum of five PBXs can be connected in the DCS complex, as shown in Fig. 2A.

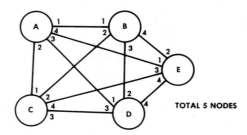

Fig.-2A: Directly Connected DCS Configuration

Inasmuch as the DCIU has the capability of switching data to a destination using logical communications paths, there is no need to connect all DCIUs of the PBXs directly. However to keep the message transmission delays within an acceptable range of call processing handling times, the message routing is restricted to at most one intermediate DCIU before reaching the destination. This is called the "one-hop" constraint and is imposed only for call processing messages. The link

and channel allocation for message routing at each PBX is done by using configuration algorithms. An example of a DCS configuration to meet the "one-hop" constraint by utilizing four output links of a DCIU, is shown in Fig. 2B.

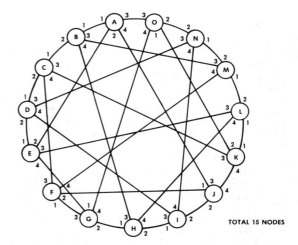

FIG.-2B: A Theoretical Maximum DCS Configuration Using 4-Link DCIUs and 1-hop Constraint

As shown, this configuration, derived using one of the available algorithms, theoretically allows a maximum of fifteen PBXs to be interconnected in the DCS complex. However, when the call traffic requirements of a given DCS are considered, the practical limitation may be less than the theoretical maximum.

A 9.6 Kilo-bit data link used between systems as the transmission medium can support any DCS configuration. However, for smaller DCS complexes, lower bit-rate data facilities will be sufficient.

3. SYSTEM THROUGHPUT ANALYSIS

Connecting PBX systems together to work like a single system has an impact on each PBX control processor in the DCS complex. This interconnection will reduce their ability to support the load (stations and terminals) per PBX as compared to a stand-alone PBX, and therefore, the DCS throughput is affected. The impact on each PBX in the DCS complex due to this proposed arrangement is modeled and quantified for estimating the call throughput of a DCS complex. The additional real-time penalty on the control processors in a DCS arrangement over a single PBX is primarily due to (1) DCIU support and (2) overhead from realizing transparency of features.

The DCIU support has a minimal impact under normal operating conditions. The call processing overhead for realizing transparency of features is a function of the call type and calling rate. Referring to Fig. 1, the intent of the DCS arrangement is to mask the differences, whether A1 is talking to B1 or to any other station on other PBXs. This implies that inter-PBX calls within a DCS complex should be perceived by the user as intra-PBX station-to-station calls. For the purpose of this analysis, the calls originating in one PBX and terminating in another PBX of a DCS complex are called "cross-over" calls.

Within PBX-1, Calls between A1 and B1 are truly intra-PBX station-to-station calls; but calls going to A2 are handled as station to tie-trunk calls. The analysis of a single PBX shows that tie-trunk calls use more real-time in each PBX than station-to-station calls. Thus, there is an additional real-time expense in treating inter-PBX calls as intra-PBX station-to-station calls. This additional expense within a PBX of a DCS is termed the "penalty factor"[4] and is designated by "α". Because of this additional expense involved in handling cross-over calls, the throughput of a DCS can be improved by minimizing the number of cross-over calls. It is known that, in a multi-processor environment, the net throughput of two processors is less than the sum of the two individual processor throughputs. Due to the above facts, each DCS node has a net throughput which is less than the throughput of a stand-alone single PBX node. This reduction in PBX throughput is called the "reduction factor" in the DCS arrangement.

3.1 DCS Operational Model

The results of a basic operational model of DCS based on the following assumptions is presented in this section.

- All PBX nodes in the DCS complex are identical.

- The traffic is equally distributed among all nodes. The total traffic constitutes an equal distribution of incoming, outgoing and intra-system station-to-station calls.

- The penalty factor is the same for calls going over to other nodes and for calls coming from other nodes of a DCS. It is also assumed to be the same for all types of calls.

This DCS model consists of "n" independent, autonomous and identical PBX nodes. The fraction of total calls handled locally within any node is designated as "f", and therefore, the fraction of calls which cross over to other nodes is (1-f). The total call handling capacity of a DCS complex is designated as "C", and "K" represents the capacity of each individual PBX node. The cross-over calls are associated with a penalty factor "α". Basically, three cases are considered for throughput evaluation of a DCS.

Case 1: Only station-to-station calls are allowed to cross-over between PBXs of a DCS. The outgoing calls are handled locally at each PBX by assigning individual outgoing trunk groups at each switch. The incoming calls are engineered to go to separate PBXs by pre-switching them to separate trunk groups at the central office. It can be

shown that the total call handling capacity of a DCS in this case is

$$C1 = \frac{3Kn}{[2+f+(1-f)2\alpha]}$$

CASE 2: Both station-to-station calls and incoming calls are allowed to cross-over between PBXs of a DCS. The outgoing calls are handled locally as in the previous case. The total call handling capacity of a DCS in this case can be shown to be

$$C2 = \frac{3Kn}{[1+2f+(1-f)4\alpha]}$$

CASE 3: All types of calls (station-to-station, incoming and outgoing) are allowed to cross-over between PBXs of a DCS. The total call handling capacity of a DCS in this case is

$$C3 = \frac{nK}{[f+(1-f)2\alpha]}$$

In general, the capacity of a DCS can be expressed as

$$C = nK\gamma \text{ where "}\gamma\text{" is the reduction factor.}$$

Fig. 3 illustrates the relationship of reduction factor for the above cases as a function of calls handled locally within each PBX node of a DCS complex.

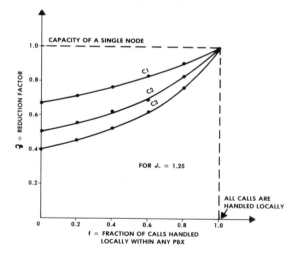

Fig.-3: Capacity Reduction For A PBX In A DCS Complex As A Function of Cross-Over Calls

4. SUMMARY

The DCS architecture provides a PBX based communications system to multiple premises, and large single location customers by providing a means of sharing intelligence among the PBX nodes.

The cost effectiveness of DCS interconnection schemes for providing data links between PBX nodes increases as the size of the complex increases. It takes $n(n-1)/2$ links to interconnect "n" nodes directly; however, using a DCIU and interconnecting them logically with at most one intermediate relay point, it takes only $nL/2$ data links where "L" is the number of links used on the DCIU. For example, to connect 15 nodes directly, 105 data links are required while it takes only 30 links when a DCIU is used.

As PBXs are added to the DCS complex, the capacity of the system keeps growing. By identifying communities of interest, crossover calls can be minimized, and therefore, the throughput can be optimized.

Unlike out-of-band signalling schemes, calls can be established in spite of data link failures, with only a loss of feature transparency.

FOOTNOTES:

1   A private network offering from Bell System using customer premises and central office stored program controlled switching exchanges.

2   Definition: If the operation of a feature, when invoked by a user, is perceived to be the same when that user is talking to a station within the same PBX or a different PBX, then transparency is said to exist for that particular feature across the two PBXs.

3   Registered trademark of AT&T.

4   The penalty factor is defined as the ratio of PBX processor occupancy for call processing for handling a station to tie-trunk call to that required for handling a station-to-station call.

REFERENCES:

[1] Bush, S. E., et. al., Expanding the Role of Private Switching Systems, Bell Laboratories Record, Vol. 57, October 1979, 243-248.

[2] A special issue on "Common Channel Interoffice Signaling", The Bell System Technical Journal, Vol. 57, No. 2, February 1978.

R. S. Divakaruni received his bachelors and masters degrees in Electronics and Telecommunications from the University of Madras, India in 1969 and 1971, respectively. He also received a masters degree from the University of Iowa, Iowa City, Iowa, in Electrical Engineering in 1972. He worked with Rockwell International and McDonnell Douglas Automation Company before joining Bell Laboratories in 1978. He is currently a Member of Technical Staff in the Systems Planning Group in Denver, Colorado.

G. E. Saltus received his bachelors and masters degrees from Worcester Polytechnic Institute, Worcester, Massachusetts, in Electrical Engineering, in 1953 and 1954, respectively. He joined Bell Laboratories in 1953 and is currently the director of the Customer Switching Laboratory in Denver, Colorado

B. R. Savage received his bachelors and masters degrees from Utah State University, Logan, Utah, in Electrical Engineering, in 1964 and 1965, respectively. He joined Bell Laboratories in 1967 and is currently the supervisor of the Systems Planning Group in Denver, Colorado.

A Communications Protocol for Integrated Digital Voice and Data Services in the Business Office

G M Anderson, J F Day, L A Spindel
Bell Laboratories, USA

The general work station communications needs of businesses in the eighties will extend beyond traditional voice to include data, text, image, and sensor information. While there are several approaches to serving these needs, the most promising is a star topology, using standard telephone building wiring and a single communications controller. In this paper we describe a protocol to provide these information channels and the control channel to the communications controller via a single digitally multiplexed communications link. This protocol is the basis for digital systems and voice/data terminals, interconnected over a single in-house wiring system based on ordinary telephone cabling.

INTRODUCTION

It is widely anticipated that business office communications needs in the 80's will go beyond the traditional voice and data needs to include text or document communications, image communications and even sensor/activator communications. The text and document communication needs are expected to result from the rapidly expanding word processing market as well as broad efforts to automate many business office functions. Image communication needs will result from improvements in the areas of facsimile, graphics and video workstations, as well as the office automation push and the need to reduce mail and travel expense. Sensor/activator communication needs will result from the continuing pressure to control heating and cooling systems to keep energy costs manageable. While there are several approaches to providing office communications, we believe the most attractive is to integrate the new services with the traditional voice PBX and utilize common twisted pairs for all building communications to the work station. In the future, as the need to widen bandwidth proliferates, optical fibers can be added. The Bell System's Digital Communications Protocol (DCP) for intrapremises communications provides this integrated office communications capability via a layered protocol which is intended to be upward compatible with emerging CCITT (International voice and data) standards. This paper describes the motivation behind this decision.

BACKGROUND

The cost of providing office communications is affected by the bandwidth requirements of the services, the number of workstations needing them, and the degree of cost sharing of workstation equipment, centralized processing/control equipment, as well as the interconnecting building communications transmission media itself (see Figure 1). We will concentrate in this paper on the bandwidth requirements and building communications media.

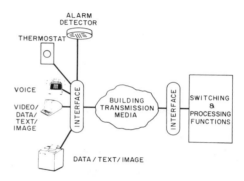

FIGURE 1   BUILDING COMMUNICATION COST ELEMENTS

Ubiquitous voice communications has been achieved by transmitting voice in analog form over inexpensive copper wire pairs from telephone instruments to switching arrangements such as PBXs. The bandwidth required for analog voice is 4 kilohertz; however, the cables serving these connections are capable of carrying megabit bandwidth signals. In recent years, the use of digital circuit switching principles in PBXs has become common. Digitally encoded voice requires 64 kilobits per second (Kbps) for toll-grade PCM transmission; however, lower speed transmission through a variety of encoding schemes is achievable.

Low speed data communication for asynchronous terminals can be carried over this same wiring; however, most customer locations require some transmission modulation scheme such as data sets to achieve acceptable error performance over typical building distances. While data rates of 300 to 1200 bps are most common, rates up to 19.2 Kbps should be planned for.

The other common data terminal arrangement is synchronous operation; IBM 3270 terminals are the prime example. Speeds up to 4.8 Kbps are common; however, higher speeds such as 56 Kbps are possible and should be considered in planning. Cabling for these terminals can also make use of the telephone wiring.

Image communication needs vary widely. Low speed facsimile can be carried at speeds in the kilobit per second range, while high speed facsimile operates in the tens of kilobits per second range. Graphics workstations can require on the order of 100 kilobit per second bandwidth. Video workstation needs vary from the kilobit per second range for still pictures to the megabit per second range for moving pictures. All can be carried on the building telephone wiring.

Sensor/activator communication needs are in the low speed range, i.e., kilobit per second range and can also be carried on the telephone wiring plant. (See Figure 2 for a summary of these workstation bandwidth requirements.)

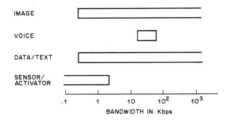

FIGURE 2   BUSINESS WORK STATION COMMUNICATION NEEDS IN THE 80's

Proponents of office automation envision service and workstation concepts that integrate all of these areas of office communications. Some examples of this integration include:

* Integrated voice/data workstations –

  a) The workstation receives an incoming voice call and displays the identity of the calling party, or

  b) a workstation user returns after an absence and obtains a display of names and telephone numbers and even short messages, and can request a return call, or

  c) a workstation user accesses word processing document storage via his integrated voice/data terminal, yet can interrupt this to display the identity of incoming calling party, and resume after completing the call.

* Simultaneous voice/data operations –

  a) two or more parties on a voice connection simultaneously view a text document, edit it and transmit it to other parties,

  b) a user reviews a text document, annotates it with voice information and transmits it to someone.

* Simultaneous voice/data/image – all the above plus the ability to include graphics in the documents.

* Simultaneous voice/data/image/sensor – all the above plus the ability to monitor temperature and fire alarm sensors near the workstation, without requiring any additional wiring to the workstation.

* Simultaneous voice/data/video/sensor – all the above plus the ability to see the other party or receive graphic information from the other party.

COMMUNICATIONS TOPOLOGY

The question is, how best to provide these integrated services in the office environment. There are several practical approaches to interconnecting the system control and the terminal or workstation, including bus networks, ring networks, and star networks. (See Figure 3.)

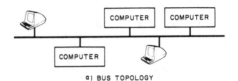

a) BUS TOPOLOGY

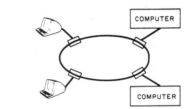

b) RING TOPOLOGY

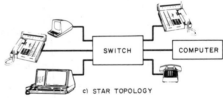

c) STAR TOPOLOGY

FIGURE 3   BUILDING COMMUNICATION TOPOLOGIES

Many dedicated terminals today are connected to a specific host computer over multidropped private line telephone wiring. In this case, the host typically controls the communications by polling the terminals in turn. This approach is a type of bus network as shown in Figure 3a.

Other types of bus networks are currently attracting considerable attention for applications involving the data communications needs of office automation systems. They usually involve a wide bandwidth media (megabits per second), such as coaxial cable, that is shared by multiple users. This arrangement has the advantage of providing wide bandwidth for short periods of time which matches the needs of increasingly intelligent terminals. Different approaches have been taken on the control of such networks. Some designs avoid the need for a centralized controller but substitute complex interface controllers which detect the presence or absence of transmission on the medium, determine when a collision with another terminal's transmission occurs and carry out the subsequent retransmission algorithm. Other designs involve the idea of token passing to assure each terminal equal access opportunity to the bus. At present, no commercial bus system offers voice service. Proponents argue that they can carry packetized, digital voice and indeed such implementations are possible.[1] However, the economics of speech packetizing and bandwidth compression as well as the high sensitivity of people to impairments in voice communications, such as syllabic clipping, lead us to conclude that packetizing on a bus system is not the optimum approach for mainstream voice communications. Further, these systems require the installation of a separate communications medium, and are vulnerable to service interruptions to many workstations when the bus loses integrity.

Ring networks share many similarities with bus networks in media used, control approaches, and switching techniques. Interfaces communicate with adjacent interfaces, which means that the loop is interrupted when an interface is added. Since rings are closed, installation and ongoing growth administration are complicated. However, they can be configured in a duplicated (bidirectional) mode to improve reliability.

Star networks are used in all buildings to connect telephones to PBXs over twisted copper pairs. Virtually all buildings are wired in a pattern that interconnects work stations on a floor with centralized equipment rooms or closets on that same floor. The floors in the building are interconnected via riser cables. Multipair cables are usually employed. The primary advantage of basing integrated office communications on this wiring is economy because it avoids the need for installing additional communications media. The savings occur not only at the time of installation but continue over the life of the system due to having only one building communication system to grow and administer. As mentioned earlier, this wiring is capable of carrying megabit per second bandwidths. It has the additional advantages of terminal usage independence, i.e., no information blockage occurs in transmission over the wiring (blockage in the switch is a controllable factor which can be reduced to virtually zero) and ease of terminal growth and rearrangement. This makes the star network approach ideal for voice and with the Bell System's Digital Communications Protocol (DCP) for intrapremises communications described below, it becomes the ideal approach for providing fully integrated office communications services to the workstation.

PLANNING FOR INTEGRATED NETWORK SERVICES

Telephone administrations around the world are planning to provide integrated digital networks capable of offering voice, data and image network services. This is referred to as the Integrated Services Digital Network, ISDN.[2,3] Preparation of standards for the ISDN is under way in several Study Groups of CCITT (i.e., 7, 11, 18), the international body for voice and data communications standards involving services provided by telecommunications carriers.

Extending the ISDN to the customer's premises for digital PBXs or digital voice and data terminals is an integral part of the plans. This extension will employ and build on digital transmission and switching systems already widely deployed. These systems employ a channel of 64 Kbps capacity as the basic element. Multiples of this unit are assembled for specific transmission systems.

As previously discussed, integrated office services will be best provided by an integrated voice and data workstation. ISDN planners anticipate this need also and have proposed a generalized digital station format of nI + mJ + pK where n represents some number, usually one or two, of 64 Kbps I (Information) channels capable of carrying voice or data; m represents some number, again usually one or two, 16 Kbps channels capable of carrying slow speed data or network signaling, and p represents some number of wider bandwidth channels. Two 64 Kbps channels plus a 16 Kbps channel for low speed data and network signaling has been proposed as the common access format.

The ISDN offers the promise of public network capabilities that will be attractive to business communications planners in addition to their private network options. Clearly, selecting an office communications architecture well matched to ISDN can be expected to result in minimizing network interface device cost and maximizing the network service options. The Bell System's Digital Communications Protocol (DCP) will offer communications planners a smooth and cost effective transition to this exciting network of the future.

DIGITAL COMMUNICATIONS PROTOCOL

The Digital Communications Protocol (DCP) has been designed to meet the needs for integrated intrapremises voice/data services and will be provided in future customer premises products. The architecture is intended to be upward compatible with the emerging International Organization for Standardization (ISO) and CCITT standards. Information is sent in frames (see Figure 4). There are four fields within a frame. The first is a unique pattern (framing) to define the frame boundary. The second is a one bit Signaling (S) channel for call related and control functions. The third and fourth fields are two independent Information (I) channels, each with eight bits of user information. These I fields are used to carry voice or customer data. There are 8000 of these frames each second. Therefore, the bit rate available is 8 Kbps (1 bit/frame x 8000 frames/sec.) for the S channel and 64 Kbps for each I channel. The format can be extended in the future to include additional fields which could be wider bandwidth.

FIGURE 4   DCP FRAME

Physical Layer - Transmission Characteristics

ISO has defined a multi-layer architecture with particular functions assigned to each layer. The physical layer (level 1) is concerned with the mechanical, electrical, functional and procedural functions to establish, maintain, and terminate physical connections.[4]

Regarding the first layer of DCP, it uses four wires (two for transmission in each direction), and Alternate Mark Inversion (AMI) coding (also known as alternate bipolar) to encode the information for transmission. This is the same approach used successfully in the Bell System for many years in digital transmission systems (e.g., T1 lines). The transmission distance requirement is up to 1500 meters on 24 gauge wire. Power to the work station sufficient for voice telephony functions can be provided on the DCP 4 wires.

A variety of terminals can be connected to DCP, as shown in Figure 5. Voice only (telephones), data only (CRTs, hosts, printers, etc.), and combined voice/data terminals can be provided with direct 4 wire DCP interfaces. In addition, converter boxes provide the necessary translation between common existing terminals interfaces (e.g., Electronic Industries Association RS 232-C) and DCP.

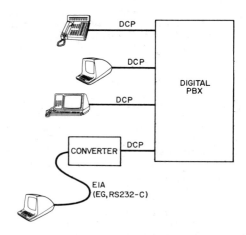

FIGURE 5   DCP TERMINAL INTERFACES

Physical Layer - Information Channel

Each 64 Kbps Information (I) channel can contain digitized voice or data. They are routed independently so that simultaneous voice and data calls can be made to different destinations. Three different modes of operation have been defined to perform the

level 1 function of moving bits in the Information channel and will be discussed below.

The repetition rate of 8000 per second and the eight bits per frame per I channel is consistent with other systems in the telephone network that digitize voice, such as T1 carrier. As discussed earlier, this consistency minimizes conversions when the digital PBX interfaces digital network facilities. Either the North American standard, mu 255 voice encoding, or A law voice encoding can be carried by DCP.

The 64 Kbps available for data provides sufficient bandwidth to handle a wide variety of data needs. The first mode of operation, mode A, provides the full channel for transparent use by a 64 Kbps source. Digital voice, high speed facsimile or graphics terminals, batch communications between computers, or file download are examples of typical applications. This mode is depicted in Figure 6.

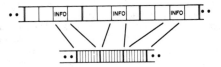

FIGURE 6   DCP MODE A: VOICE OR 64 Kbps DATA TRANSMISSION

A second alternative, mode B, is to use seven of the eight bits per frame to derive a 56 Kbps speed. This approach is the same as that used in 56 Kbps Bell System DATAPHONE® Digital Service (DDS). The eighth bit can be used to carry a limited amount of control information. This mode, shown in Figure 7, has similar applications to the first mode as well as offering compatibility with DDS for calls between locations.

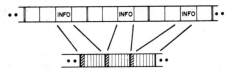

FIGURE 7   DCP MODE B: DDS COMPATIBLE 56 Kbps DATA COMMUNICATION

The vast majority of existing terminals and hosts operate at speeds of below 300 bps up to 19.2 Kbps, asynchronous or synchronous. In DCP mode C, an approach was defined which maps any such terminal into the 64 Kbps channel. These terminals and hosts will also have need to occasionally call off premises. To do so, a function equivalent to that provided by a conventional analog modem (modulator/demodulator) is needed to convert the DCP format to the analog format of existing telephone networks. DCP must also transport the control information necessary for proper terminal and modem operation. The approach used to meet these needs makes use of some of the same techniques as HDLC (High-Level Data Link Control), the data link layer ISO standard protocol[5], and the CCITT Link Access Procedure B (LAPB) used as level 2 of the X.25 protocol. These are international standard protocols with procedures worked out to reliably transport blocks of data. The approach provides a basis for compatibility with standards as higher layer functions are added as well as meeting the above needs now. Within the 64 Kbps channel, Information channel frames are defined by means of a unique flag character. (NOTE: Until this point, the term "frame" has been used for one repetition of the pattern that makes up DCP. The remainder of this section will use "frame" as it applies in HDLC: a delimited block of information found within the Information channel.) Extra flag characters are added to fill voids between frames containing useful information. (Figure 8).

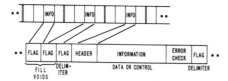

FIGURE 8   DCP MODE C: DATA COMMUNICATION
TO 50 Kbps AND CONTROL

The first non-flag field, typically the address field in HDLC, contains a new type character for DCP. This header character indicates that the next field holds either actual data or control information. It can also include timing information for synchronization to external networks. The data or control information follows. Next comes an error checking field. It is needed when control information is sent. For existing EIA terminals, error checking of the user's data may be provided by the user in his data field. For terminals that connect directly to DCP, the error checking field can also be used to check the user's data. Another flag delimits the end of the information. This approach supports data to about 50 Kbps, synchronous or asynchronous.

Link Layer - Information Channel

DCP can be used as purely a level 1 function, transparently carrying any higher level protocol. However, it has also been designed to be easily extended to particular standard higher level functions. For example, the second layer of the ISO model is the data link layer. The main function of this layer is to insure that the information flows essentially error free.[4] As discussed earlier, the Information channel frame described in Figure 8 has used a number of concepts from HDLC and LAPB and has a similar frame format. The header definition can be extended to include other standard link layer functions such as flow control and error recovery. The header can be further extended to provide logical channel capability at the link layer.

Signaling Channel

The Signaling (S) Channel supports basic

switched circuit connection setup procedures among telephones, terminals, data processing systems and transmission facilities. It is used between the communications system controller and the terminating units. The S channel must carry signaling data and related information for connections on either I channel. For reliability, a robust protocol with error control and flow control is appropriate. To meet these objectives a variant of HDLC was selected.

ADMINISTRATION

With the DCP approach, the communications manager planning for office information automation will have a much simplified task. Data communications can be provided to any workstation along with voice, at any time, via a universal wall jack and standard building wiring without any special wiring or cabling construction. Users will be able to perform their own distribution panel cross connections and system control translations to initiate data communications at any workstations at speeds up to 19.2 Kbps asynchronous or 64 Kbps synchronous. In this way, office information automation can grow in response to the user's needs and not in response to major building wiring decisions.

SUMMARY

The Digital Communication Protocol (DCP) is designed to meet the office communications needs of the 80's for integrated voice, data, image and sensor services. It does this economically by providing work stations with digital transmission over ordinary telephone wiring. The flexible digital format of the DCP will interface smoothly with emerging international standards, will provide sufficient bandwidth to workstations for the foreseeable future and has the capacity to grow to wider bandwidth when the market needs it.

REFERENCES

[1]   D. Cohen, On Packet Speech Communication, in Proceedings of the Fifth International Conference on Computer Communication, October 1980.
[2]   I. Dorros, Challenge and Opportunity of the 1980s: the ISDN, Telephony, January 26, 1981, pp 43-46.
[3]   R. Kennedi, Plotting a Strategy for the Emerging ISDN, Telephony, June 22, 1981.
[4]   Open Systems Interconnection, ISO/TC97/SC16, Draft Paper 7498, International Organization for Standardization.
[5]   High Level Data Link Control (HDLC) Procedures of the International Organization for Standardization, Document Numbers 3309 (Frame Structure), 4335 (Elements of Procedures), and 6256 (Balanced Class of Procedures).

George Anderson is the Head of the Business Communications Systems Analysis Department at Bell Telephone Laboratories. His Bell System career spans 17 years and includes experience with Bellcomm on the Skylab program. Prior to joining the Bell System, Mr. Anderson was an Assistant Professor at Carnegie Mellon University. Mr. Anderson is a graduate of Carnegie Mellon with a PhD in Electrical Engineering.

Jim Day is the Director of the Business Communications Systems Engineering Center at Bell Telephone Laboratories. His Bell System career spans 21 years and includes assignments in electronic switching at Bell Labs and A.T.&T. Engineering. Mr. Day has degrees in MSEE and BSEE from New York University and the New Jersey Institute of Technology and is a Licensed Professional Engineer.

Les Spindel is the Supervisor of Business Communications Systems Data Group at Bell Telephone Laboratories. His 15-year career with the Bell System includes assignments at A.T.&T. as well as Bell Labs in the area of data communications. Mr. Spindel has degrees in MSEE, MSBA and BSEE from Rutgers, Pace and Lehigh Universities.

Local Area Networks in a PABX Dominated Environment

W P Bain
ITT Business Systems, UK

The author examines the emergence of local area networks, and suggests some reasons for the LAN phenomenon. Although local area network technology is seen as the major contender for the office automation market, an assessment of its suitability in the two phases of an organisation's involvement with office automation indicates that this is not necessarily the most suitable medium in every case. An analysis of traffic within companies then shows where LAN topology is most suitable, and where PABX technology is superior. An indication of the way in which most user organisations will build and enhance their communications systems over the next few years is then given.

1. DEFINITION

Local area networks, in the context of the title of this paper, and in comparison with PABX, are defined as transmission and switching systems that provide high speed communication between devices located on a single site. In other words, communications systems designed to link computers and other devices over a restricted area, such as in a building or a group of buildings, up to typically one kilometre radius. The essential elements of this definition of LAN are the restricted geographic area of coverage, the speed of transmission - typically 0.2 to 20 Mbps -, the low error rate - typically 1 in 10^8 -, and the ring or bus, rather than a star topology.

In other words, LANs do not possess central switches or nodes through which all communications must pass.

2. THE LAN PHENOMENON

Local area networks of the type just defined have emerged as the major contender in the office automation marketplace. Office automation can be loosely defined as anything electronic found in an office which is not used exclusively to communicate with mainframes or allowing direct verbal communication between people. It is the emergence of interest in the "automated office" which provides the first answer to the question 'Why do LANs arouse so much interest?'

In this respect we should ask ourselves whether it is the transmission medium itself which we find desirable, or the fact that the sort of features needed for the automated office are associated with LANs rather than with PABXs or traditional data processing equipment. It could be argued that the LAN

LOCAL AREA NETWORKS
○ Why so much interest?

— LAN features are aimed at office automation
— PTT control
— PTT liberalisation
— Fashion
— Vociferous marketing
— User management structures

Fig. 1. The LAN phenomenon.

Suppliers, by offering different technology, by not supplying traditional star networks, but mainly by concentrating exclusively on the emerging OA market, have been seen as providing the technological breakthrough needed to help users towards office automation. In contrast, PABX suppliers have been so busy replacing electromechanical systems with modern electronic PABXs, where the customers' requirements have been almost exclusively for voice-only systems, that their later entry into the OA market is perceived by many as the chasing of a new, expanding market with second-best technology.

Figure 1 gives other reasons why there is interest in local area network technology.

In most countries the PTT retains some form of control over PABXs and their suppliers. This could take the form of monopoly marketing to all or part of the PABX market, or subsequent maintenance of the PABX. Almost certainly the PTT will insist on some form of approvals procedure before PABXs, and their telephones and terminals, can be connected to the public network. Under these conditions, the PABX becomes a heavily controlled, heavily defined, restricted product, which does not lend itself naturally to a new, fast moving market. Under these circumstances, suppliers will look for a way round the problem. LANs are not licensed or controlled by the PTT. On the other hand,

For the PABX

— Ease of use; users comfortable with PABX concept.
— Low risk because equipment already justified for Voice.
— Easy to upgrade local comms since system in one unit.
— Easy migration to office of the future through software upgrades.
— Single wire connectivity, and cabling already runs from PABX to all personnel locations.
— Voice/data integration in central controllers avoids duplication of comms processors.
— Users have limited budgets & voice will remain the dominant form of traffic.
— Modern PABX gives data users features such as least cost routing, call detail recording.
— Full access to PTT carrier and information services.

Against the PABX

— May not be electronic, but not ready for replacement.
— Will never be able to handle large enough volumes and high enough speed of data.
— Vested interests: controlled by telecomms manager.
— Not fashionable.

For the LAN

— Too much complexity in one single switch.
— Too much dependence on one device.
— Distribute control and risk: gives resilience, greater power, greater cost engineering.
— Use of a ring or bus topology requires less cabling than Star PABX.
— Easier sharing of specialised resources.
— Economic connection of terminals.
— Frees PABX for other functions.
— Vested interests: attractive to DP manager, departmental managers.
— Fashionable.

Against the LAN

— Lack of standards, and connectivity with outside world.
— Lack of reliability, redundancy, fragility.
— Lack of privacy.
— Limited bandwidth.
— Limited no. of terminals.
— Limited distance.
— High interface costs.
— High installation costs.

Fig. 2. PABX or LAN ?

where the market has been liberalised or deregulated, market interest has been aroused by the offering of choice in communications. Major changes induce new thought in associated areas and LANs, being new and different, are ideal products to demonstrate an organisation's commitment to technological innovation and ability to take advantage of changes in legislation.

That last statement touches on another reason why local area networks arouse so much interest. LANs with all their new technology are fashionable, and fashion influences people more than most would care to admit.

Local area network suppliers have marketed their products most effectively. They have quite rightly made full use of the opportunities available to them, for instance to write articles and give interviews to the industry press. As the subject is so newsworthy, and the potential benefits of the products are so great, local area networks are constantly in the electronics and computing press. This high level of activity in them stimulates further interest in the technology.

Finally, there are now more managers in an organisation with a legitimate interest in its communications systems. The Telecommunications Manager and the Data Processing Manager, who often share different views on who is responsible for non-voice communications within an organisation, are now joined in the debate, by an Office Systems Manager and Managers of large departments. The fact that a local area network is not a PABX, only transmits data, and can operate almost exclusively within a single department, is seen as an advantage by some parties.

Having looked at the LAN phenomenon in a somewhat critical manner, perhaps it is

appropriate to state that local area networks represent the most significant improvement in in-house communications since the electronic PABX was introduced in the 1970's.

3. ASSOCIATION WITH OFFICE AUTOMATION

Local area networks are generally associated with office systems and office automation. PABXs, in contrast, are generally associated with voice-only communications, and in many cases quite correctly. Electronic PABXs, however, have high bandwidth and can set up switching paths quickly and accurately. This means that they can transfer information quickly and accurately - certainly quicker than most terminals can operate. If an organisation has an electronic PABX, or is about to replace an old system with a new electronic PABX, then that system could represent the best option for an office systems strategy, particularly in the evaluation phase.

4. TWO PHASES OF OFFICE AUTOMATION

There are basically two phases to an organisation's involvement with office automation. In the first phase, it is evaluated, paper studies carried out and a pilot system is installed. At this stage, cost is important. Because it is a trial, costs have to be kept down. However, some functions, such as electronic mail and inter-office memos, need the participation of a number of people in the organisation to make the trial effective. In this evaluation phase, LANs and the sorts of terminals associated with LANs are unlikely to be cost-effective. An added complication is that organisations which install LANs in this phase can end up evaluating LAN technology rather than the suitability of OA functions to their own operation. Using the existing PABX to perform the switching is invariably less expensive.

The second phase is the installation and use of a production office automation system. In this phase, cost is not as important as the suitability of the system to the pattern of work within the organisation. In this phase, PABXs and LANs both have advantages and disadvantages, as shown in Figure 2. Basically, a PABX has the advantage that it and its block wiring is already installed, and extends to every part of the organisation. It also provides access to the carrier services, and it can provide data switching at minimal cost. Against the PABX approach is the fact that many companies still have electromechanical systems that give a good level of voice communications service, and will do so for many years. However, they are not really suitable for switching data, because they take a long time to set up a call, they cannot carry the extra traffic caused by office automation, and they do not have sufficient bandwidth to allow accurate, fast transmission. The main attraction of local area networks is that they usually have office automation features provided with the system, whereas PABXs do not have such features as 'standard.' The disadvantages of LANs are claimed to be mainly those of reliability and cost effectiveness, or the difference between theory and practice. This is not surprising considering the newness of the technology, though conversely it would be surprising if these disadvantages were still valid in the next generation of systems.

5. LOCALITY OF COMMUNICATIONS.

Looking at office systems, there are basically four levels of communication. These are communication within a group, with other local groups, with other inter-company groups and with the outside world.

The major volume of traffic occurs within a group of the same interest, such as a department within a company. Most, though usually not all, people in such a group are located within the same geographic area. The next levels of communication occur between groups which are in the same building or on the same site. The third level occurs within the organisation, but between geographic locations, e.g. branch offices. The fourth level is with customers, suppliers and administrations outside the organisation.

Many studies have been carried out analysing information from within offices. Typically, they find that 50% of all communication circulates within one site, and that 70% of all communication circulates within the organisation. Only 30% reaches the outside world.

Local area network topology and architecture are more suitable for the first two levels of communication than those of PABXs, especially when very high data rates, high occupancy and transaction levels are involved.

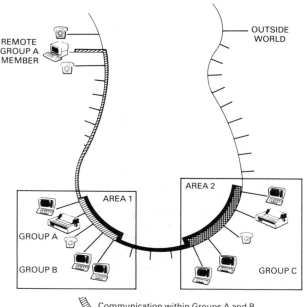

Fig. 3. The LAN solution.

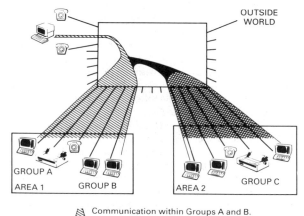

Fig. 4. The PABX solution.

However, PABXs are more suitable for the third and fourth levels of communication. Figure 3 shows the sort of environment proposed by LAN suppliers for non-voice communications, and Figure 4 shows that suggested by PABX suppliers. Most organisations will see that both systems offer their own advantages and disadvantages in the particular situation the organisation is in at the time of evaluation. For this reason, companies will tend to employ a mixture of LAN and PABX systems, one to provide high bandwidth data transfers in geographically close communities of interest, the other to provide access to a much wider environment of people and equipment. Provided interworking between PABX and LAN attached devices is available, this represents the ideal solution.

6. HOW COMMUNICATIONS SYSTEMS WILL EVOLVE

The following is a view of how company communications will evolve. It is based on what is now technically possible and will soon be commercially feasible. Full account has been taken of the requirements stated by users.

Figure 5(a) shows the communications networks most organisations currently possess. Voice, data and text communications are separate, with a variety of different terminals and cabling, all performing separate functions and all separately managed. Figure 5(b) shows the introduction of information transfer modules between the three primary switches for voice, data and text. These processors enable any terminal to interwork with any other terminal, or computer or service, regardless of speed or protocol. For instance, the generation and reception of telexes can now be made available on any terminal in the company, rather than just those directly connected to the message switch. Modules are also available to enhance the operation of the system, for example to automate communications between word processors. The essential element of this strategy is that it protects the user's investment in equipment, both switches and terminals, and is relatively easy and inexpensive to implement. All 'cross-boundary' traffic is carried on PABX block wiring and is switched through the PABX in the normal way. Figure 5(c) shows local area networks replacing star networks in local groups, such as word processors in the typing pool or data terminals in the accounts department. LANs have been substituted to reflect the anticipated reduction in wiring, and interfacing costs, but mainly to recognise the fact that office systems will be coming along which use embedded LANs.

The fourth phase, Figure 5(d), will see users continuing to use PABX block wiring to carry data, but allowing concurrent voice and data along the same tail. The new services from the PTTs and other carriers will require interfaces or gateways to handle their multiplexing, addressing and protocols. Organisations will therefore tend to provide access points to these services to reduce costs and pool resources rather than give direct connection to all equipment likely to use the service. These gateways will be separate units in some cases, and PABX interface cards in others. Figure 5(e) shows schematically how PABXs will develop as the PTT's high speed digital services are expanded. These carrier services, which will be available for voice, data and text, will become increasingly faster and more complex. LAN switching techniques are ideal for distributing the very high speed, 'bursty' data traffic,

whereas PABX circuit switching techniques will continue to offer the most cost effective solution to voice and low volume, low speed data/text switching. The 'ring' will be on printed circuit boards within the PABX cabinet.

Figures 5(f) and 5(g) show what may occur when LAN wiring and interfacing costs are less than PABX wiring and port costs, and LANs have sufficient bandwidth to handle the unique immediacy of voice traffic. The next generation of PABXs will almost certainly use embedded LAN technology. Whether they are described as LANs or PABXs or as something else will be decided by how many boxes make up the system, where they are located, and who manufactures and markets them, rather than by the technology employed.

7. CONCLUSIONS

Local area networks have an important role now in an organisation's communications system. In most cases they will be employed because they are part of a chosen communications or office system, rather than for the technology itself. There are circumstances where general purpose LANs can complement an existing PABX, although often the choosing of a LAN will not be for pricing or technical reasons. Organisations should as a general rule choose LAN systems which are able to inter-work with equipment and services available through the PABX.

In the future, LANs, PABXs and the differences between them, will become more difficult to define. PABXs will make increasing use of LAN switching technology. LANs will also become more deeply embedded as transport mechanisms in information systems, rather than developing as a communications product in its own right.

Bill Bain is Business Development Manager for ITT Business Systems. His responsibilities include identifying new business opportunities and proposing and evaluating product developments for the company. He joined ITT in 1975 as a systems analyst supporting sales of IBM compatible equipment, and progressed to manager of sales support for the data, voice and text communications equipment sold by the company.

He obtained a B.Sc. in Mechanical Engineering at Nottingham University in 1968, and received a Ph.D. in 1972 for research into design of operating systems.

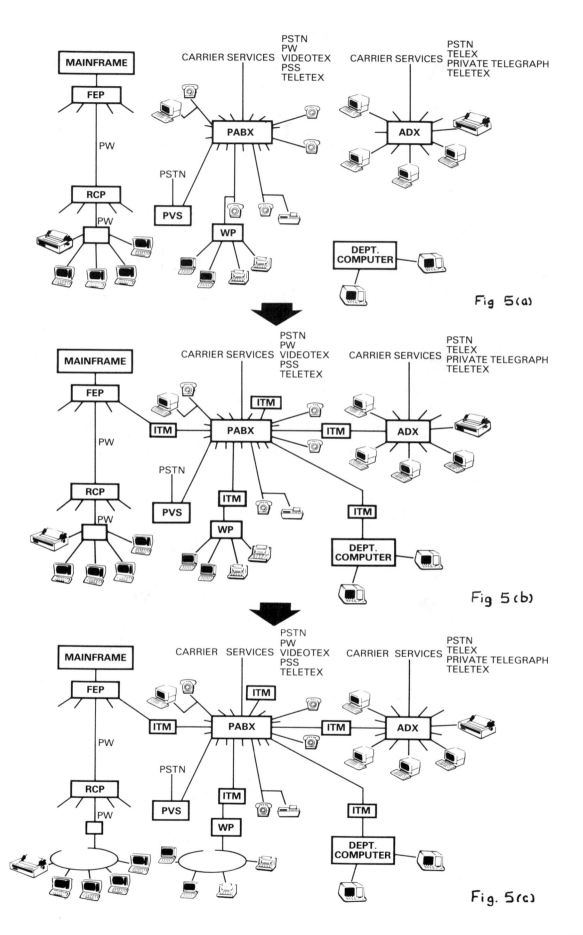

Fig 5(a)

Fig 5(b)

Fig. 5(c)

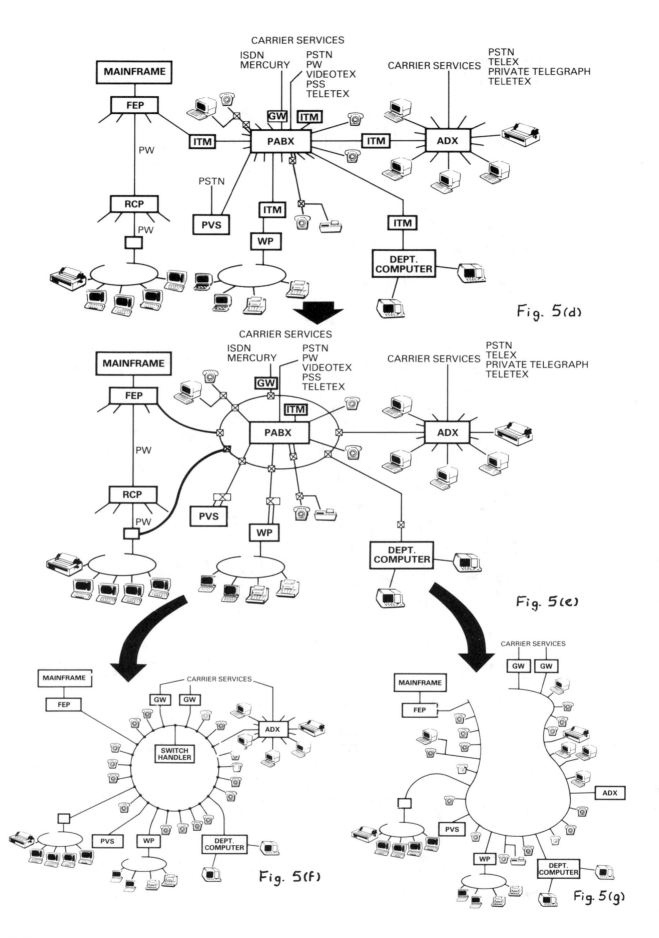

Fig. 5(d)

Fig. 5(e)

Fig. 5(f)

Fig. 5(g)

Protocol Architecture of the UNIVERSE Project

C J Adams, G C Adams, A G Waters
Rutherford Appleton Laboratory, UK

I Leslie
Cambridge University, UK

P Kirk
Marconi Research Centre, UK

The UNIVERSE Network consists of a number of Local Area Networks connected together by a broadcast satellite communications channel. This paper describes, in general, the protocols and services which define the basic network, and how these are accessed by hosts. This network is different from many in not providing error correction and flow control in the network; instead this is left as options to the end-to-end procedures. "Lightweight Virtual Circuits" and "Single Shot Protocols" as well as "Broadcast Facilities" are available to users. The range of application of this protocol structure will be investigated experimentally and theoretically in the context of this experiment.

1. INTRODUCTION

Project UNIVERSE is a combined initiative by the SERC, DOI and several UK companies to develop Local Area Networks and their interconnections by high speed links, especially satellite links. The project uses the OTS satellite for this purpose [1].

The protocols described in this paper assume an environment where the error rates are very low and that retransmission due to error may be left as an exception condition. The user, in fact, may prefer to ignore errors and only rely on the good BER of the system. The BER of the satellite link should be around $10^{**}-9$ and that of the ring $10^{**}-12$.

Local Area Networks based on the Cambridge Ring contain a number of clients and services which support a distributed computing environment. Some of these services, e.g. the name-server, are important elements in the functioning of the network, and are described here. Other services such as the file-servers and print-servers perform only as client services and are not part of the network description, these are best left to a description of the experimental programme of the project [2].

A Transport Service, which conforms to the OSI model and the UK Interim standard "A Network Independant Transport Service" is defined as an end-to-end procedure for those applications requiring such an interface. A broadcast service is also defined which utilises the true broadcast facilities of the satellite.

The topology of the network:-

Six widely separated sites are connected by a satellite network

- Each site has one ring connected to the satellite network through a bridge (the link driving computer).

- Several sites have additional rings connected to the first ring through ring-ring bridges.

- One site has other types of local area network which will also be connected through bridges.

- Six sites have these rings linked to X25 Networks at medium speeds (9.6 to 48Kbps)

The functions of the bridges are described later.

It is intended that it should be as easy to use the UNIVERSE network as to use a single ring, so after a brief introduction to the protocols a description of single ring working is given. We discuss here the network described by Ring Bridges, Satellite Bridges and Name-Servers. The high speed terrestrial bridges and possible bridges based on the X25 networks are not described here as these are still under design (The X25 networks are used , in a support role, for mail, file transfer, terminal access and many other uses).

2. PROTOCOLS

The unit of communication is the Basic Block (Fig 1). A basic block contains up to 2048 bytes of data preceded by a 'route' field; this contains a port number (8 bit source and destination ring addresses are carried by the mini-packets making up the block). The port number indicates the destination within a machine connected to a particular ring station. It may correspond to a process, or have a similar meaning to the X25 logical channel number. There is no acknowledgment associated with a Basic Block, although it does carry a checksum allowing the receiver to check for errors. On detection of an error, a receiver usually discards the block. It is assumed that higher level protocols will detect this event by timing out. All hops in the network must transfer data reliably, that is sequentiality is maintained and the bit error rate (BER) should be below $10^{**}-9$

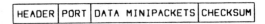

| HEADER | PORT | DATA MINIPACKETS | CHECKSUM |

FIG. 1   BASIC BLOCK. TYPE O

The Single Shot Protocol (SSP) consists of a request block (SSPREQ) to a host eliciting a reply (SSPRPLY), no state information being held by the two ends. It is used for simple transactions such as name lookup on a name-server and requesting the time of day from a timeserver. The Single Shot Protocol sets up a single path from the receiver to the sender of the SSPREQ.

The Initial Connection Protocol (OPEN and OPENACK) is similar to SSP but is used to set up connections to remote services, it is described more fully below. Such remote services may employ higher level protocols such as BSP for further communication. The Initial Connection Protocol sets up two paths, one in each direction, between the sender of the OPEN and the receiver.

The Byte Stream Protocol (BSP) is an example of a higher level protocol which may be built on top of Basic Blocks and provides error correction and flow control with a window of one. It is used over the UNIVERSE network in an end to end manner, that is the bridges have no knowledge of BSP states. TSBSP [3] is a version of BSP providing transport service facilities. An extended version of BSP and TSBSP has also been designed which is compatible with them but may use larger (<= 16) window sizes. This protocol should allow much higher throughput on single links when satellite delays of up to 1 sec will delay acknowledgements.

3. SINGLE RING WORKING

We will consider three sorts of object connected to the Ring; clients[5], servers and name-servers[4].

A client is a machine which wants to make use of a service provided by another machine, a server. A machine which is a client in one context may be a server in another context. Clients are usually computers with people attached to them. Servers include such things as file-servers, time-servers and compiler-servers.

Of course a name-server is a type of server; it is considered separately since it is the means by which clients find the addresses of other services (the other servers). A client only knows about services in terms of symbolic names (strings), for example, "FILE-SERVER", "CMS". To find the corresponding station and port the client sends a name lookup request (Fig 2) containing the name as a string to its local name-server. The name-server replies with the service's address. [It is apparent that it is both necessary and sufficient for a client to know initially only one ring address, that of the local name-server's name lookup service.]

The client proceeds to contact the service by sending an OPEN request block to the supplied address, the OPEN quotes a port on the client to be used for the reply. The

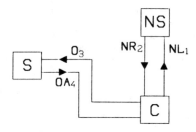

FIG. 2   SINGLE RING SERVICE REQUEST

NS = NAMESERVER
C = CLIENT
S = SERVER

NL = NAME LOOKUP REQUEST
NR = NAME LOOKUP REPLY
O = OPEN REQUEST
OA = OPEN ACK

server determines a port which the client should use for the rest of the conversation. This port number is returned to the client in an OPENACK block. If the OPEN fails then the name-server lookup and OPEN transaction are retried a few times before finally giving up. The protocol used between the service itself and the client may be specified by the name-server in its reply to the lookup request. The client will know the protocol associated with the service and may use the extra information, if available, for checking.

The client is at liberty to send any Basic Blocks on this opened route using the port number returned in the OPENACK. Many procedures use flow-controlled protocols such as BSP, but this is _not_ imposed by the network.

The name-server keeps its name lookup table in high speed memory for obvious reasons; this is copied from some updateable non-volatile storage, probably a file on another machine. A reserve table is kept in read only memory in case the 'real' table cannot be found and to provide a means by which the real table can be found.

4. MULTIPLE RING WORKING

A client may wish to use a service provided on another ring, possibly on another site of the satellite network. As far as the client is concerned there is hardly any difference from the single ring case [5] The name sent to the name-server may be prefixed with a site identifier giving for example "CAMBRIDGE*CAP". The client may notice some differences in the network behaviour, mostly extra delays before transactions (request – acknowledgement pairs) are completed. OPEN transactions are marginally more likely to fail the first time they are attempted (this depends on the

likelihood of the local name-server having invalid global information, see below).

Contact is established in the following way:

Let us first assume that the name-server knows the global address of a requested service, but does not believe a path exists to that address. The global address contains site number, ring number, host and port. It passes this to a bridge (Fig 3) in an Address Insertion request, causing the bridge to allocate a port dynamically and associate it with the given address. The bridge passes the port back to the name-server in an Address Insertion reply. The name-server passes this port along with the ring address of the bridge back to the client in its normal reply to a name lookup. The client now sends its OPEN request to this port on the bridge (because it thinks it is talking to the initial connection port for the desired service). The port has the property that an OPEN sent to it is transformed into a BRIDGEOPEN block by inserting the global address supplied previously by the name-server.
The BRIDGEOPEN is now passed between bridges each inspecting the address to find the next Bridge. Each bridge remembers the reply port number given in the OPEN (in the case of the first bridge) or BRIDGEOPEN, then replaces it with a port number which it allocates on its outgoing side. Thus a return path is set up ready for the OPENACK. The last bridge before

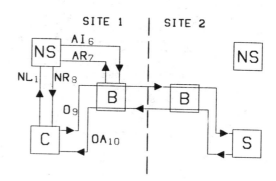

FIG 3   MULTIPLE RING SERVICE REQUEST (2 SITES)

NS = NAMESERVER
C = CLIENT
S = SERVER
B = BRIDGE

NL = NAME LOOKUP REQUEST
NR = NAME LOOKUP REPLY
AI = ADDRESS INSERTION REQUEST
AR = ADDRESS INSERTION REPLY
O = OPEN REQUEST
OA = OPEN ACK

the destination changes the BRIDGEOPEN back to an OPEN so that the server need not deal with blocks containing global addresses. The OPENACK

is now sent by the server back to this bridge which changes the destination port number and reply port number. The destination port is changed to that for the next bridge in the backward path. The reply number is changed to that of another dynamically allocated port on the current bridge, now forming part of a forward path. This is repeated at each bridge so that by the time the OPENACK reaches the client a complete forward path has been created. The paths through the bridges may now be used transparently, the route field of each block travelling down a path being mapped in each bridge. The paths may be thought of as forming a skeletal virtual circuit with no flow control or error correction. (An analogy which has been used to describe the path set up process is that of an arrow (the BRIDGEOPEN) pulling a string (the path) through bridges to the destination.)

We now consider the case where the name-server does not know the global address of an off-site service (Fig 4). It must find the global address by asking a name-server on the remote site. It can do this by performing an Address Insertion request to the satellite bridge quoting the global address of the remote name-server. Addresses for each remote site must be known by every name-server. An SSP transaction with the remote name-server may then be performed in order to acquire the global address of the service. This address will be remembered (cached) so that it may be returned immediately to a client making subsequent name lookup requests; in this case the name-server - remote name-server transaction still takes place afterwards because the cached information may be wrong. It is assumed that the client will retry and eventually get to the right place. The whole question of the assignment and maintainance of Names in this type of distributed system is under study in this experiment. We are adopting the principle that naming areas (domains) are each responsible for the maintainance of their own Name Tables.

5. DATAGRAMS

A datagram service is provided by the bridges which is largely independent of the path setup mechanism already described. Datagrams are carried as a version of type 3 Basic Blocks. They contain source and destination global addresses. They are provided to allow experiments with other ways of using the UNIVERSE network and are an important part of the policy of providing flexibility to network users.

A datagram user may use a name-server but would do so in order to obtain global addresses, not to cause a port to be allocated on a local bridge.

Datagram blocks have been defined as a special type 3 Basic Block in order that they will be rejected by clients who do not expect or are unwilling to receive datagram traffic.

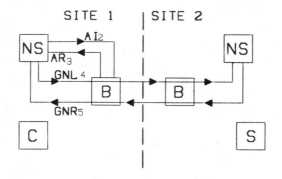

FIG. 4 NAMESERVER - NAMESERVER LOOKUP

```
NS  =  NAMESERVER
C   =  CLIENT
S   =  SERVER
B   =  BRIDGE

AI   =  ADDRESS INSERTION REQUEST
AR   =  ADDRESS INSERTION REPLY
GNL  =  GLOBAL NAME LOOKUP REQUEST
GNR  =  GLOBAL NAME LOOKUP REPLY
```

6. SATELLITE CHANNEL

The use of the satellite channel is not apparent to the user and serves only as a subnetwork to support the UNIVERSE internet. The satellite channel is organised as a TDMA system (Time Division Multiple Access). A MASTER station establishes a Time-frame by repeatedly broadcasting a reference burst with a fixed time interval; this interval s likely to be between 100msec to 200msec. All other stations lock on to this burst to estasblish Time-frames which are in exact synchronism with the MASTER's, this is achieved by implementing a "phase lock loop" using the received reference bursts.

Each site has one or more distinct windows in which he can transmit data packets; each packet consists of a Basic Block encapsulated in an HDLC frame. Many packets may be transmitted in each window and these may be addressed to different sites. A site is open to receive all the time but only receives those packets addressed to him or broadcast packets.

The size and number of transmission windows for a particular site are determined by the MASTER station according to the amount of throughput on a particular site and these allocations are broadcast in the reference burst. Further details are given in [6]. All sites keep the MASTER updated on their requirements via control messages sent on the

satellite channel.

7. BRIDGES

Most bridges connect a ring to the satellite network or join two rings. Some sites will have bridges to other types of local area networks (ethernets for example). A broad outline of the bridges' functions has been given in Section 4. Generally, bridges should impede the progress of Basic Blocks as little as possible; they should be fast and reliable. The ring to satellite bridges are GEC 4065 computers with 'intelligent' interfaces on both the ring and satellite sides. The ring-ring bridges are based on the 68000 microprocessor, the ring interfaces being controlled by 6809s.

A possible method of choosing which blocks to discard in the case of congestion is based on the use of virtual circuits. Blocks may be queued for transmission on each path separately, when congestion occurs the longest queue is found and its contents discarded. It is also possible to stop receiving completely from the ring by becoming unselected for any source. (This sets the ring interface to a state such that hosts sending to the bridge are informed that their transmission has been rejected.)

8. SUMMARY

- Both virtual circuit (Cambridge style) and datagram modes of working are provided.

- The virtual circuit mode may be used almost identically whether one or many rings are being crossed.

- The de facto Basic Block protocol is used (types 0, 1 and 3).

- The sequence of events involved in setting up outward and return paths is as follows (* items do not always occur):
  - {client -> name-server} NAME LOOKUP REQUEST
  -* {name-server -> bridge} ADDRESS INSERTION REQUEST for remote name-server
  -* {bridge -> name-server} ADDRESS INSERTION REPLY
  -* {name-server -> remote name-server} (via bridges) GLOBAL NAME LOOKUP REQUEST
  -* {remote name-server -> name-server} (via bridges) GLOBAL NAME LOOKUP REPLY
  - {name-server -> bridge} ADDRESS INSERTION REQUEST for remote service
  - {bridge -> name-server}

    ADDRESS INSERTION REPLY
  - {name-server -> client} NAME LOOKUP REPLY
  - {client -> remote service} (via bridges) OPEN
  - {remote service -> client} (via bridges) OPENACK

ACKNOWLEDGEMENTS

This work is carried out with the generous support of the Science and Engineering Research Coucil, the Department of Industry, British Telecom, the General Electric Company and Logica Ltd. The material presented in this paper has resulted from the discussions in the Protocols Working Group of the UNIVERSE project, whose contributions are gratefully acknowledged.

REFERENCES

[1]   P T Kirstein et al: "The UNIVERSE project", ICCC '82

[2]   J Burren: "The Experimental programme of the UNIVERSE project", UP 196

[3]   I Dallas et al : "Transport Service Byte Stream Protocol",UKC 1

[4]   I   Leslie,   N   Ody: "UNIVERSE Name-servers",UP 126

[5]   G C Adams et al: "Client Protocols", UP 94

[6]   A G Waters, C Adams: "Satellite Transmission Protocols", UP 125

[7]   A G Waters,I Leslie: "UNIVERSE Bridges",UP 95

Design of an Encryption System for Project UNIVERSE

W B Newman
James Cook University of North
Queensland, Australia

This paper discusses the design of an encryption system over the UNIVERSE satellite/terrestrial communications network. The encryption system uses RSA Public Key Cryptography to exchange keys and signatures and then uses the Data Encryption Algorithm (DEA) in software or the DES chip in hardware to perform encryption. The system will be implemented using both mini and micro computers. In addition to the standard mode of operating the DEA, a mode called Stream Cipher Mode will be introduced which allows parallel processing to achieve higher data rates in software encryption.

1. INTRODUCTION

As part of project UNIVERSE, an experiment in implementing an encryption system over a terrestrial/ satellite network is being carried out. This paper outlines the encryption system being used, and the reasons why this particular system was chosen.

The need for security and privacy in transmission of sensitive data through a communications network has been recognised for some time. There has not yet been established a widespread commercial cryptosystem. Such a system would need to be of low cost, with low error rates, and automatic to the extent that a minimum of human intervention is required. The technology to achieve this is available. All that is needed is a widespread acceptance of some standard encryption and key management service. As a step towards exploring these problems, and gaining experience of how such systems will work under real conditions, it was decided to perform an encryption experiment within project UNIVERSE.

Project UNIVERSE (UNIVersities Expanded Ring and Satellite Experiment) is a major experimental facility designed to explore and develop the state of the art in communication between computers via local area networks and a satellite [1]. Those involved in this project are British Telecom, Cambridge University, the Department of Industry, GEC-Marconi Electrics Ltd, Logica Ltd, Loughborough University of Technology, SERC, and University College of London. The cost of the project over three years will be approximately £3 million, shared between DoI, SERC, British Telecom, GEC-Marconi and Logica.

Each site contains one or more high speed earth station. The combination of ground based Cambridge Rings and the high technology of satellites makes this project of special interest, and will be of increasing importance to industry, business, and scientific research. There are six earth stations, each equipped with a 3m diameter dish aerial, 14 GHz radio transmitters and 11 GHz receivers, providing communication between each site via the Orbital Test Satellite (OTS) operated by the European Space Agency.

A model for the security system [2] of project UNIVERSE identified vulnerabilities in the system as represented on a communication channel diagram in Fig 1.

The security of the system was based on a joint authentication system [3] and an encryption system. A system of security tests and spy games are to be developed in order to measure the degree of security.

In order to achieve some standardisation in encryption, the US National Bureau of Standards has issued a Data Encryption Standard (DES) [4]. This federal Information Processing Standard requires the encryption algorithm to be implemented in hardware within certain standards (FED STD 1027 [5]) specifying the security requirements for key storage, status and fault indications, tamper proofing of enclosures, and protocols for manual key loading.

It seems almost certain that this DES will become the defacto standard throughout the commercial and business world. As project UNIVERSE is seeking

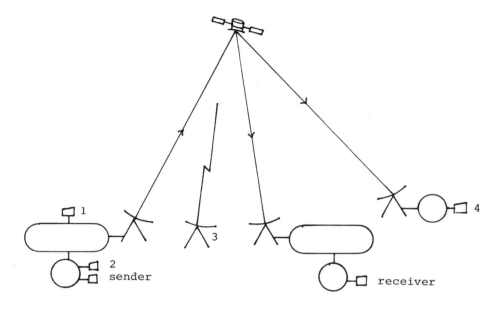

Fig 1. Vulnerability Modes in project UNIVERSE

Intruders

(1) Eavesdropping and insertion of false messages on senders/receivers ring
(2) Another user on sender's host

(3) Another transmitter jamming or sending false messages breaks computer security
(4) Eavesdropping through the broadcast nature of satellite communication

---

to develop a system with applications to the future commercial and industrial environment, this standard was, therefore, a natural choice.

This encryption algorithm has become well known and chips to perform this algorithm have been produced. The US government has, however, placed an embargo on their export, causing their implementation to be restricted. The Standards Planning and Requirements Committee (SPARC) of the American National Standards has proposed a Data Encryption Algorithm (DEA) identical to the Federal DES, except that it will be implemented in software.

The encryption algorithm has been well documented [4], [6]. Briefly, it takes a 64 bit block of data and scrambles it together with a 56 bit key. Both sender and receiver require the same 56 bit key. The task of communicating this key before a session commences is part of the Key Management Service (KMS). To solve this communication problem, a system of Public Key Cryptography (PKC) [7] has been adopted.

2. DATA ENCRYPTION ALGORITHM

The encryption experiment for project UNIVERSE is being carried out by Logica Ltd, and the Marconi Research Laboratories. Logica is developing the software to implement the DEA, PKC and KMS. This will be implemented in the first instance on a PDP 11/44 mini-computer and an Intel 8086 micro-processor operating under Xenix (a UNIX like system). This software will also be interfaced to an Intel 86/05 SBC which Marconi Research Laboratories will use to drive an Advanced Micro Device AMZ8068 encryption chip.

There is a timeout factor applying through bridges so that if a message is not transmitted within one or two seconds after opening a virtual channel between sender and receiver, the connection is broken. The encryption speeds achieved will be sufficiently fast that timeout will not be a real constraint. Nevertheless, in order to experiment with DES hardware communicating with DEA software and gain experience of the limitations, an

385

attempt will be made to squeeze the encryption time to a minimum.

To this end, various modes of operating the encryption system will be implemented (two are shown in Fig 2). In particular, a new mode, Cypher Stream Mode (SCM) [8], seems to hold some interesting possibilities. This mode, like Output Feedback Mode (OFM), does not need the plain-text to begin the DEA operation, and so allows a sender or receiver to precalculate an auxiliary encryption file, and then encrypt the plain-text at rates exceeding 130 kb/s. This speed is achieved, of course, at the expense of memory space.

Examples of the speed of operation are shown in Table 1.

Speeds of Operation in k bits/sec

Mode	PDP 11/44
DEA encryption alone	2.1
DEA with I/O	1.87
Output Feedback Mode*	125
Cipherblock Chaining Mode	1.8
Stream Cypher Mode	125

* file of DEA previously created

TABLE 1 Speeds of operation of DEA implemented in software using a PDP 11/44 computer

SCM has two advantages over OFM. Firstly, the period before the output of the DEA begins recycling is known and is very large for SCM, whereas it is unknown for OFM. Secondly, SCM allows the possibility of parallel processing, replacing bit manipulation within the DEA by 16 bit word manipulation, and thereby achieving higher encryption speeds.

3. POSSIBLE LOCATIONS OF ENCRYPTION PROCESS

One of the early questions faced in the design of the system was where the encryption process should take place. Some of the possibilities are shown in Fig 3. These are:

(1) End to end with encryption device on terminal
(2) End to end with encryption performed by host computers
(3) Black box on back of host
(4) Bridge encryption
(5) Earth station encryption

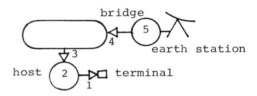

Fig 3. Possible Location of Encryption Devices in project UNIVERSE

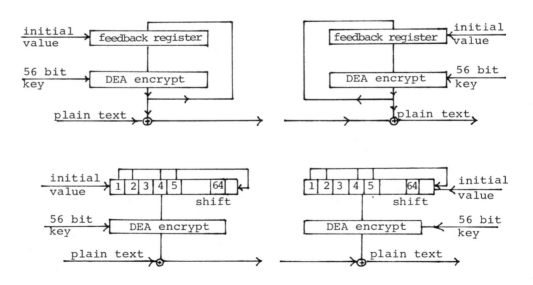

Fig 2. Modes of Operating DEA

Because of the experimental nature of project UNIVERSE, options (2), (3) were chosen. If (3) can be implemented satisfactorily in a transparent fashion, then (4), (5) could be implemented without much further effort. Option (2) is a less transparent mode and gives the user more scope for control and experimentation of encryption.

4. PUBLIC KEY SYSTEM

The public key cryptography (PKC) in this project is based on the Factorisation Problem originally suggested by Rivest, Shamir and Adlemen (RSA system) [8]. Reasons for choosing this system rather than other well known PKC are:

1 It offers an authentication and signature system not offered by the other systems.

2 The PKC based on the Exponential Problem is no faster than the RSA system, and in addition requires a dialogue between sender and receiver before messages can be transmitted. It is, therefore, not suitable for electronic mail where the receiver may be absent.

3 The PKC based on the Knapsack Problem has the advantage that it is fast, but it requires a very large file of numbers to be used in the knapsack. It was felt that such an unwieldly set of public keys made this system untidy. Since the PKC is to be used only to transfer keys and authentication messages, the slowness of the RSA system did not seem to be a handicap.

4 The problem of setting up the parameters for the RSA system is difficult, and may require a high speed computer. But as these calculations only need to be performed once per user, they can be done independently of the machines performing the encryption and the programs were written with this in mind.

An early task was to decide on the size of the large primes p,q, used in the public key N. A lower bound for the bit length of these primes is forced on one by the requirement that there should be no easy factorisation of N (=pq). If p,q are about 200 bits long, then the factorisation of N is extremely difficult and the encryption system is secure. For fuller security $(p-1)/2$, $(q-1)/2$ should also be prime, but for this experiment we are leaving this requirement to individual users, since it will mean a trade-off between security and cost.

A choice of bit lengths of 256 for p,q was made. The time to initialise RSA is shown in Table 2.

In order that all encryption using the RSA system has the same block length, we require N to be 512 bits long. This can be achieved by choosing the most significant bits of p,q to be 11.

The number e will be made public, and therefore has no secrecy attached to it. We can, therefore, see no reason why the value of e should not be fixed for all users. In order for the encryption to be performed fast, an ideal choice of e is

$$e = 2^{16} + 1 = 65537$$

since this particular power can be calculated efficiently. If it should happen that the value of d for which

$$e.d = 1 \bmod (p-1)(q-1)$$

is small, then it will be necessary for security to select another value of N. By fixing on a particular value of e, we reduce the amount of information required in the public file.

The relationship between the bit length of n and the speed of encryption and decryption is shown in Table 3.

Production of n,d for PKC

average number of trials before two primes found	232
average user time (including testing primes)	2 hr 13 min
average real time (including testing primes)	2 hr 47 min
maximum real time	4 hr 51 min

TABLE 2   Measures of the difficulty of producing n,d for PKC on PDP 11/44

5. SUMMARY

The encryption experiment planned as part of project UNIVERSE will implement the data encryption standard algorithm in both software and hardware in end to end encryption. The key distribution problem will be handled using RSA public key cryptography. The software system, DEA, should work at speeds significantly slower than the hardware, but sufficiently fast to be acceptable over the terrestrial/ satellite link. The PKC algorithm is slow, but as it is used only to perform key exchanges and authentication, this is considered to be not too great an overhead in time.

The problems and advantages of locating the encryption devices at different places in the system, and the whole problem of setting up and operating a complete public key cryptosystem are being investigated as part of this project.

REFERENCES

[1] Kirstein, P T, et al, The UNIVERSE Project, companion ICCC paper.

[2] Newman, B B, Modelling and Measuring a Security System, Logica report (1982).

[3] Girling, G, Authentication and Access Control, companion ICCC paper.

[4] Data Encryption Standard, FIPS PUB 46, US National Bureau of Standards (1977).

[5] Telecommunications: Security requirements for use of the data encryption standard (draft), FIPS PUB 1027, US National Bureau of Standards.

[6] Katzan, H, The Standard Data Encryption Algorithm, (Petrocelli Books Inc, New York, 1977).

[7] Diffie, W, and Hellman, M, New Directions in Cryptography, lEEE Trans Infor Th IT22 (1976).

[8] Davies, D, et al, A mode of Encipherment entitled 'Additive Stream Cipher', NPL, Teddington UK (1981).

[9] Rivest, R, Shamir, A, and Adleman, L, A Method for obtaining Digital Signatures and Public Key Cryptosystems, Comm ACM, 21 (1978).

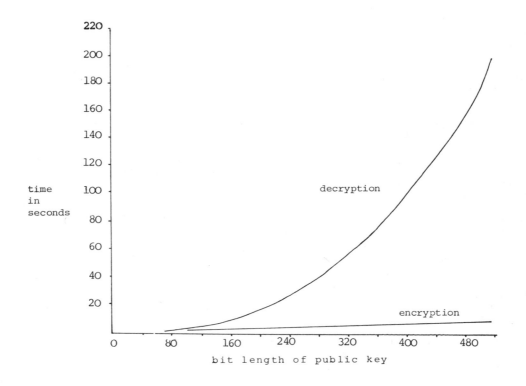

Table 3. Time to encrypt and decrypt as a function of bit length

 Bill Newman is a senior lecturer in mathematics at James Cook University of North Queensland, and is at present on special study leave at Logica Ltd London. His speciality is coding theory and he has acted as consultant to British Aerospace on the error correcting code to be used on the GIOTTO spacecraft to Halley's Comet, manager of the encryption experiment on Project UNIVERSE, and consultant on source coding of satellite imagery and image processing.

An Outline of Network Measurements in Project UNIVERSE

S R Wilbur, Z Ma
University College London, UK

The UNIVERSE network consists of many local networks linked by both satellite and X25 wide area networks. Lightweight protocols are used throughout to capitalise on the high performance offered by the hardware. Three broad areas of network measurement are proposed: reliability, traffic patterns and performance. Reliability is being studied to determine the practical needs for redundancy, to ascertain the most vulnerable parts of the system and to understand the needs for routing control in such networks. The traffic patterns are important not only in understanding where bottlenecks and congestion occur, but also in seeing how they vary between organisations, and applications, and are affected by network load and time of day. Finally, the performance under controlled loads will be examined and contrasted with that of high reliability protocols found in conventional wide-area networks.

1. INTRODUCTION

The UNIVERSE network is based on high speed local area networks (Cambridge Rings) operating at megabit/sec (Mbps) data rates, connected by a satellite network running at similar data rates but with very much longer transmission delays. In the present configuration six sites are directly connected to satellite ground stations, and one site (Logica) has a high speed terrestrial link to UCL. The satellite link will not be continuously available; however each site (except Logica) is also connected to an X25 network, albeit at low speed (2.4kbps – 9.6kbps). This will allow advance preparation to be made for experiments, documents and messages to be transferred while the satellite is unavailable, and data from measurement experiments to be passed through an independent channel from the one being studied, if necessary. The configuration is described in more detail in section 2 and in [1].

The measurement activities in UNIVERSE are split broadly into three areas: hardware component availability, network traffic patterns and protocol performance. A number of claims for local network reliability have been made, but very few cases are well documented. In UNIVERSE we hope to be able to document the availability of individual local networks, complexes of local networks, the total system and key services and hosts. Thus the availability of all network layer components, including rings, bridges and name servers must be monitored. Based on these observations, the necessity for and feasibility of network reconfiguration will be assessed.

The second measurement activity will be concerned with the collection of traffic patterns, including traffic density, inter-connectivity, and packet sizes. This will be done at several sites, intermittently over the project lifetime. Such information is useful for identification of heavily used services, and some protocol optimisations. Seven organisations, four academic and three industrial, are participating in Project UNIVERSE. Each has its own areas of interest and each is involved in some joint experiments. These experiments include protocol design and analysis, distributed system design and analysis, distributed system development and maintenance, access control and data security, and high speed text, graphics and voice distribution. In addition, the network will be used to support these experiments by providing both local and remote access to program development services. The various sites will exhibit very different traffic patterns, and a study of these will provide insight into the requirements for future networks.

One of the aims of the project is to investigate whether the inherent high throughput of the constituent parts can be preserved in the wider context by using lightweight protocols [2]. The final aspect of measurement is to measure the actual protocol performance under both normal and induced loads. This will allow a proper assessment of the protocol design to be made, and will identify bottlenecks.

There are several interesting constraints to measurement on UNIVERSE. First, it is known that the satellite channel will be unavailable for significant periods, and the alternative path is very slow. Therefore a measurement hierarchy is proposed. Secondly, if network control is added to organise re-routing in cases of bridge failure or congestion, a network control centre at any single site will be unattractive because it is of the order of 3/4 sec. away from the incident, but the alternative of local control mechanisms in bridges may seriously affect bridge performance under normal conditions. Finally, only the minimum of additional code can be incorporated in components such as bridges to provide measurement data, before their own performance is affected. Thus great care has to be taken in designing measurement tools.

2. NETWORK COMPONENTS

The part of the UNIVERSE network at UCL is shown in Figure 1. This has been chosen because it is the most general at present. Only the network components are shown, service machines and terminals are omitted for clarity. At present all the local networks in use in the project are Cambridge Rings, and three are shown here. However, the protocols have been designed such that other local network technologies could also be used. One ring at a given site is connected to the satellite bridge (SB) which is described in [1]. Inter-ring bridges based on a Motorola 68000 processor with two 6809 processors for data management, connect the three rings (B).

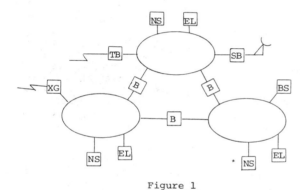

Figure 1

Network Components at UCL

The architecture of the network [2] relies on there being a name-server (NS) on each local network. This translates symbolic names containing domain and service names into network addresses consisting of site, subnet, node and port fields. An embryo mapping table is kept in PROM in each name-server, but to allow for moderately frequent changes, a more comprehensive reference table is kept in the boot-server (BS), and is copied to each name server on demand, normally only at power up or after a table change. The main role of the boot-server is to provide local storage and management of program images for the network components. In a production system such a service might not be important as the code would be changed infrequently and could be held in PROM. In an experiment such as UNIVERSE, the code for network components will change periodically, and a common place for storage of code for specific experiments is

envisaged. Hence, each site has one boot-server with some 10 Mbytes of disk storage which will also be used for filing of monitoring and measurement data. As mentioned above, each site except Logica has a gateway to an X25 network; this is shown as XG. Logica is connected directly to UCL via the terrestrial half-bridge shown as TB. Finally, most rings include an error-logger (EL).

Inherent in the design of the Cambridge Ring is a fault reporting mechanism which reports data transmission and ring break faults. One function of the error-logger is to collect such reports. Since a specific network address is used for such reporting, it is possible for protocol software (or firmware) to use this mechanism too, and a proprietary intelligent ring interface which is used in the satellite bridge and boot-server takes advantage of this.

3. NETWORK RELIABILITY

This part of the measurement activity is concerned with determining the availability of the various network components, and assessing whether connections to specific parts of the network and services within it are possible. It is also concerned with assessing whether any components are so weak or so critical to proper network functioning as to require improvements in the architecture.

Collection of fault reports is organised on a hierarchical basis. The error-logger on each ring collects the initial reports and filters them. The filtration is necessary in the case of faults of finite duration such as ring reset, when tens of thousands of fault messages might be received in the matter of a second; filtering compresses these to one event. The error-logger has 64 kbytes of local memory and so can store several thousand events before needing to offload them to some more permanent, larger storage. The second level in the hierarchy is provided by the boot server. This has a large amount of storage, and is only infrequently used for its other (booting) functions. Suitably tagged blocks of fault reports can thus be sent by each error-logger at predetermined intervals or when their internal buffers are nearly full. Finally, a network monitoring centre at one site on the network can retrieve all or parts of the record kept in each boot-server, and produce an overall picture of network reliability.

There may, on occasion, be a need to correlate events on different sites. In order to obtain an accuracy of the order of 5 msec between sites, the radio clock transmissions from Rugby will be used as the reference clock, and the error-logger will also provide a standard time-of-day service to any network user. Minimal time distortion should occur on rings with an error-logger, but variable delays through bridges will reduce the accuracy of the time service on rings without error-loggers.

The fault collection procedure outlined above is primarily oriented to faults notified by hardware or firmware. Such reports are contained in isolated mini packets (38 bits long, 16 data bits), and are sent to node zero on the ring in question. It is generally necessary to correlate such reports not only with time but also other network events, of which the most significant are the powering up or down of hosts or network components. For this reason, each error-logger will probe each node on its ring at regular intervals. Probing with a single mini-packet provides sufficient information to record whether the node is powered or not without involving the attached device in any CPU load. This is because two response bits in the mini-packet get modified if the node is powered and enabled.

Such probing of bridges does not indicate whether remote rings can be accessed. For example, the bridge may be powered up but may not be loaded with software. It is valuable therefore to do probing at a higher protocol level, such that probe packets pass through bridges. The simplest approach would be for each error-logger to probe all others periodically. There are two objections to this. First the number of probe packets increases approximately as the square of the number of subnets. Secondly, no single network component has a complete picture of the network topology, as it is distributed among the name servers at the several sites. The approach which will be explored initially is to use a hierarchical approach again, such that error loggers at a given site probe each other and report to the boot- server, while the boot-server probes its peers. Quantitative information such as delay may be gathered by such probing, but if probes are infrequent (e.g. 1 minute intervals) such information may rapidly grow stale.

Within the terrestrial part of the network, broadcast transmission has to be performed by the transmission of multiple copies of data. However, over the satellite hop, broadcast addressing can be used, so that the inter-bootserver probing could use such a service to reduce the number of outgoing probe packets. A broadcast service is currently under discussion within the project team.

Finally, functional probing of services and hosts at suitable protocol levels will be included in the future. However, because this probing relies on additions to protocol software and firmware, it will not be included initially. The statistics gathering mechanisms described below will provide some relevant information. This aspect of reliability measurements is intended to monitor the availability of network and host services. For network services, such as bridges, gateways, terminal concentrators, print servers etc, a "crash" service exists which allows a record to be taken of software failures, allows memory in the machine to be probed and for software to be reloaded. The

records from the functional probe will be compared with the crash server record to determine the incidence of partial and transient failures.

4. TRAFFIC PATTERNS

Measurement of traffic patterns is concerned with determining the major sources and sinks within the network, determining the distribution of packet sizes, determining network load and identifying both short and long term congestion. Most of these characteristics are of particular value to network and system designers, providing information which confirms their initial design assumptions or allows them to reconfigure the system to provide improved performance. In the UNIVERSE context, these measurements are difficult to perform.

It is possible to design a "promiscuous" node for many local networks which records important details from the packets passing by. By this means, packet length, source, and destination address can be extracted. Such promiscuous nodes are only of limited use on the Cambridge Ring because each packet is broken down into a suitable number of fixed size mini-packets. Each mini-packet may be transmitted several times if the receiver is slow, and although response bits in the mini-packet indicate to the transmitter whether the receiver accepted the mini-packet or was busy, in general the promiscuous node will not be able to distinguish accepted mini-packets from retry attempts. (For n active nodes, n promiscuous nodes would be needed if correct reconstitution of traffic between all parties is to be performed).

However, in order to get an accurate picture of inter-ring and inter-site traffic without adding additional code to the bridges, an experiment may be carried out using a pair of promiscuous nodes, one on either side of the bridge. These allow a true picture of transferred blocks to be obtained without code changes in either services or bridges.

On the whole, traffic patterns must be collected by software at each node. This is far from ideal, since a logging overhead is associated with each packet, which may be of the order of 50-100 usec, and each implementation must include code to perform logging, and to disseminate this information when asked. It is currently proposed only to monitor the number of packets sent to a given destination, and to form a histogram of the logarithm (to base 2) of the packet size. Initially no attempt will be made to record the number of retry attempts at any level of protocol but at a later stage retransmissions will be monitored in selected hosts. In some cases even these measurements will not be gathered since proprietary firmware is used for packet transmission, and this code cannot be easily changed.

Periodically the error-logger will request each node to unburden its statistics and these will be forwarded to the boot- server for filing. Control of such statistics gathering will be done either through the boot-server or through a network monitoring centre. Unlike network reliability reports, which will be gathered continuously, these traffic patterns will be sampled intermittently, as they are expected to be of most value in showing long term trends or in relation to specific experiments.

5. PERFORMANCE

The UNIVERSE network architecture relies on simple protocols in order to draw the maximum performance from the high speed network components. Measurements to determine the actual performance of network components need to be done both with "normal" loads and under controlled applied loads.

Normal loads depend heavily on site, time of day and the applicaions being used. Hence, it is important to gather the traffic patterns as described above so that controlled performance measurements can be interpolated for projected mixes of traffic. However, it will be important in the early stages of the project to quickly assess the performance of the network. The routing architecture is based on the use of name servers which make requests of each other via bridges, including the satellite bridge. To reduce the latency when the satellite is involved, some caching of information may take place. At a very early stage it will be necessary to establish how much the name server interactions cost, whether caching is working adequately and whether cache hold times are correct. Additionally, early measurements will be made to establish the spread of delay through the bridges under light loading, and to establish data rates for isolated blocks, and for streams of data with a range of block sizes.

To facilitate a number of experiments, several Z80 processors are provided at each site, which can be loaded from the bootserver with software relevant to a given experiment. To aid in gathering performance measurements, software to provide "echo", "sink" and "traffic generator" functions is being developed. It will be possible to control traffic generators remotely and to synchronise them within the limitations of the standard clock, ie. about 5 msec. Such tools will be used to determine the throughput of components such as the terrestrial and satellite bridges under controlled load conditions. For example, the satellite TDMA scheme allows for a mix of short and long packets to be sent in a single frame. By varying the packet length distribution from the traffic generator it will be possible to examine its effect on the performance of the satellite hop.

The use of lightweight protocols has meant that bridges are designed with a large amount of buffer storage and a throw-away policy when buffers are exhausted. This eliminates the normal hop-by-hop flow control found in other networks, and provided congestion does not occur there are no adverse effects. In the presence of congestion, the strategy is to throw away the whole of the longest channel buffer queue. It will be important to determine with normal and applied loads, what is the effect of such a strategy. For example, some end-to-end transmission strategies may assume that loss of blocks in transit is rare. It will be important to discover the incidence of such losses and hence determine the practical volume of data which can be transmitted with such strategy.

In particular, with Mbps data rates, and very low error rates, it may be faster to throw away the whole of an incorrectly received transfer (e.g. file) and retransmit, than to build in error detection and block retransmission mechanisms. For some applications this protocol approach will be tried, and measurements of data rates and error rates will be carried out to determine its viability.

Consideration has been given to whether and how congestion reporting should be handled. For transient congestion reporting to the local error-loggers at each end of the bridge will be adequate. For persistent congestion, reports should be processed rapidly so that reconfiguration of name tables can be performed if necessary. Initially congestion reports will be sent to error-loggers until the extent of congestion under various loads has been observed.

The measurements performed will be compared with those taken from more conventional wide area networks, to establish whether the lightweight protocol approach provides significant benefits.

6. NETWORK CONTROL

Many large-scale wide-area networks (e.g. ARPANET) have a network control centre [3]. The UNIVERSE network differs from these in that the network has the satellite as the focal point, and most of the network is in one or other participants' premises. The local networks are under the control of the individual organisations, as is name table management. Software for specific network components is at present in the charge of the implementing institution, and distribution of software through the network to bootservers will soon be available. Thus the need for a network control centre is not clear.

In the context of a small scale experiment there appears to be no real need for a control centre at present, although in a service environment it would provide a vital software quality control function. It is not clear yet that any useful centralised routing table maintenance is possible because of the long satellite delays, although if the satellite were replaced by fibre optic links it may be more attractive. Consequently, although centralised monitoring will take place, control will remain distributed, and probably manual, at present.

A fixed routing scheme is part of the current UNIVERSE architecture, and this is a sensible initial strategy since most sites have a very limited topology. Early measurements should show the degree to which congestion occurs, and later experiments can be made with more dynamic routing. Such dynamic routing will need new forms of interaction between bridges and name servers to inform of congestion.

7. SUMMARY

Network measurement is UNIVERSE will be organised as a hierarchy with three levels: individual subnet, site, and whole network. The components and their functions are:

Error-Logger

Responsible for collection of both fault and measurement reports on a single ring, for probing nodes on its ring to determine their state, for probing other error-loggers on its site and periodically reporting to the boot machine.

Boot-Machine

Site monitoring centre. Responsible for storage of reports from error-loggers, probing of other boot machines in the network and responding to network monitor centre requests for information. Name-table maintenance for a given site is also dealt with here.

Network Monitoring Centre

Responsible for collection of relevant reports from boot machines, and presentation of collated reports. Presentation of total network topology by collection of name tables from boot machines.

In addition to this hierarchy, performance measurements will use various test boxes to provide artificial loads and measure delays. Parts of the above collection heirarchy will be used to gather the measurements.

8. ACKNOWLEDGEMENT

This work is being carried out with the generous support of the Science and Engineering Research Council, with financial support from the Department of Industry, British Telecom, GEC/Marconi, and Logica. The material presented in this paper is a result of discussions in the Distributed Computing and Protocol Working Groups of the UNIVERSE Project. The authors also wish to acknowledge the assistance of members of the UCL networks group.

REFERENCES

[1] Kirstein, PT et al, The UNIVERSE Project, ICCC '82 (North Holland, Amsterdam, 1982)

[2] Adams, CJ et al, Protocol Architecture of the UNIVERSE Project, ICCC '82 (North Holland, Amsterdam, 1982)

[3] Santos, PJ et al, Architecture of a Network Monitoring, Control and Management System, (Bolt, Beranek and Newman)

BIOGRAPHIES

Steve Wilbur graduated in Electrical Engineering and went on to gain an M.Sc. in Computer Science. Since then he has worked mainly in London University both in research and teaching. His interests have been in systems software, computer networks, computer graphics. More recently he has been heavily involved in loosely coupled distributed systems and the local area network technology to support them. Currently he is a Senior Research Fellow at University College London, leading the Project UNIVERSE team.

Zonghou Ma graduated in 1967 from Chinese University of Science and Technology. He is now a research student in the Department of Computer Science of University College London, and is a member of the INDRA research group. His areas of research interest include Cambridge Ring Protocols, Network Interconnection and Network Service.

Authentication in Project UNIVERSE

C G Girling
Cambridge University Computer
Laboratory, UK

The provision of a standard method of naming and accessing abstract objects is essential to the construction of any uniform operating system. The paper outlines such a method that is specifically designed for a distributed environment, such as the UNIVERSE project for which it is being adopted, in which many autonomous and heterogeneous systems must interact. The system, which has been implemented on a ring at Cambridge University, is both simple and practical. It provides verifiable, unforgeable tokens for the representation of objects which may be considered to be "network capabilities". The paper draws a distinction between secure communication and secure object representation. An experiment to extend the facility to the UNIVERSE system is outlined.

1. INTRODUCTION

When a human user first starts using a computer, it is very often necessary for him to prove who he is by giving both some kind of name for himself and his password. Each time he uses another computer system this type of authentication usually has to be repeated – probably with a different password, and possibly with a slightly different form of identification as well. This is not normally a problem, because the number of systems to which a user has access is commonly quite small. However in a network such as that provided by the UNIVERSE project [1], each user may have access to a great number of computers: some large, offering long duration terminal connections, and some smaller, providing only comparatively simple services for a short duration. It would be inconvenient to operate a system in which users had to remember different names and passwords for every large computer they could use, and it would be totally impractical to have to log on to every small service they might use (or which might be used on their behalf).

Since people may not be the only clients of a network's facilities, this identification problem is not confined to them alone. Other computer systems or services might also be numbered amongst the general population of clients. In this case authentication by changeable password may not be at all suitable (e.g. a small server might be unable to "remember" a password in the same way that a human client can). As a hypothetical example, consider two fileservers that give access to a distributed filing system; when a file is updated on one of them, it may be necessary for one fileserver to pass data to the other so that the two banks of information can be kept up to date. Obviously the recipient will want to authenticate the originator of this update since it will only be willing to accept requests from other fileservers. Note that it is the identity of a client that a fileserver will want to verify – not its address. The actual position of the client is irrelevant to its authentication: it might even be variable!

Nor is authentication necessary for the principal* of a communication alone. Because some servers have procedure-like interfaces (in which a particular function is performed on a set of parameters which are provided by the user) they may need to identify their parameters. To use another example consider a document printing service that guarantees to print the document's name at the top of each sheet. Apart from the principal (an operating system perhaps) and the document to print, this server will require the document's identity as a "parameter"; it must subsequently be able to check that this parameter is correct before using it at the top of each sheet printed.

In these examples authentication is used for people, servers and operating systems, and files (at least) all of which may show themselves to be "authentic" in different ways (a user because his password matches his name, a document because its name refers to a file containing it, and so on). Moreover, some of these forms of authentication (e.g. reading in a whole file to see if it corresponds to a document on hand) may be very expensive. In general it would be desirable to do this authentication only once, then to generate some sort of 'ticket' which says "this is to introduce such-and-such: which is a valid something-or-other", and then pass it around with the object, so that it would not have to be authenticated again. Such a ticket constitutes a representation for the authenticated object and is similar to a card of introduction, a bank card or even a pound note. A representation, although it is not actually the object it represents, will very often do instead (e.g. a pound note). This is very important in a computer network, because it is often impossible to move the actual object (e.g. a person or a computer) from one place to another.

It would be possible to operate a system in which representations were different for each object

---

* The principal of a communication, put simply, is the thing which, if there is accounting, will pay for the service being provided.

(e.g. a name and password for people, a document name and the contents of a file for documents), but such anarchy would be rather inconvenient for recipients; they would have to cope with a potentially large number of ways of verifying representations. A better idea would be to have some standard format for a representation; e.g. the statement "this is so-and-so", and something to prove that proposition. The statement "this is so-and-so" admits only a single authority, since either this can be proved (and so has been universally authenticated) or not - there is no question about the recipient of the representation discriminating about who says "this is so-and-so"; it must either be accepted absolutely or ignored. A more general statement would be "such-and-such says that this is so-and-so", so that there may be many authorities that authenticate objects; each recipient of a representation could decide exactly which authorities it is prepared to believe.

A system based on these lines has been developed at Cambridge University, and is in experimental operation. The system, and its extension to the UNIVERSE project, are discussed in this paper.

2. OBJECT REPRESENTATION

We may isolate two components of a representation system:

    i)   Propositions of the form: "X says that this is Y"

    ii)   Things which prove the propositions in i)

It is easy to see how a proposition can be passed around a network; the two names, X and Y (in some standard format) would be sufficient. X here is the identity of the authority under which the proposition was made. It will be referred to as the authentity (from authority identity) of the representation. A key that is related to a proposition in such a way that its holder can see that they are associated would do as proof. This demonstrates the need for the third component of a representation system which is:

    iii) A relation between the propositions in i) and the proofs in ii).

The two names, X and Y, and the key are kinds of name (Unique IDentifiers or UIDs for short) associated with an object's representation. X and Y, each object names, are permanent and so are called PUIDs (Permanent UIDs). The key, which is the essence of a representation, only exists when the object is being represented* and so is called a TUID (Temporary UID).

In order to be able to name uniquely all the objects that a network is likely to encounter

----

* A user, for example, has a name (PUID) which always refers to him but there need only be a key representing him on a network when he is actually logged on.

during its lifetime, PUIDs must have a large number of bits; 64 are used in the Cambridge implementation. This does not, in any way, imply that PUIDs should be difficult to guess. Indeed, since a PUID will always refer to a single object and never be used for another, it is quite acceptable to "write them into" the code of programs etc. in the same way that one might a file name, or the name of a user.

In the same way that a pound note enables its holder to use the thing that it represents (some gold), the holder of a key is granted access to the object that it represents. Naturally, if 'the holder' of a key is to be distinguishable from all other potential holders it must possess that key uniquely. It is therefore important that a potential key holder cannot steal or guess keys belonging to a genuine key holder.

2.1 Stealing Keys

It is useful to group together all the things that communicate (the potential key holders) on a network under the single term "service" (there being a small distinction between "service" and "server" which is a service that serves something). If services are constrained to communicate only through the network (i.e. not through shared memory etc.), then it becomes impossible for one service to steal another's TUID (since the initiative must be taken by the giver).

2.2 Guessing Keys

A key can be made arbitrarily difficult (but not impossible) to guess simply by extracting it from a sufficiently large name space. That keys cannot be made absolutely impossible to guess is unimportant, because the chances of a key being guessed at random can be made smaller than the chances of any other part of the network failing. In particular a state can always be obtained in which the probability that a key will be guessed is smaller than the probability that the security of the network's communications will be compromised. In the Cambridge implementation TUIDs are effectively 48 bit random numbers.

Having decided on the attributes of PUIDs for propositions and TUIDs for keys the design of some relationship between authentities, PUIDs and keys is all that is necessary before a full object representation system can be produced.

3. ACTIVE OBJECT TABLES

One way to provide the relation between propositions and proofs referred to above it is to use the one that an encryption function creates between plain text and encrypted data. The relation between a key and the proposition "X says this is Y" can be set up by choosing the key to be the one for which <X,Y> will be its encrypted form. Thus a key will prove the

proposition if its encrypted form is <X,Y>*. Note
that <X,Y> cannot be "decrypted" to reveal its
key.

While this method is being investigated in the
context of the UNIVERSE project [2] it suffers
several disadvantages not the least of which is
that (expensive) encryption and decryption are
involved. In addition, it is impossible to have
more than one key for an object (a user could not
log on twice and have his two instances
distinguished, for example), it is impossible for
a key to represent more than one object (so a
user's representation could not simultaneously
be valid under more than one authentity), and
representations cannot be revoked (e.g. users
cannot log off). A better method implements the
relation in the same way that a relational data
base does: as a table.

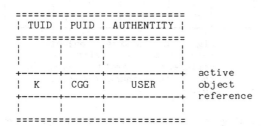

Fig. 1. An active object
reference for the object CGG
has been created by the USER
authority.

Each object active on the network will have a
proposition involving its name and authentity
associated with a key representing it in one of
the tuples of a central table (called an Active
Object Table or AOT for short). For example Fig.
1 shows an AOT in which an authority called USER
has authenticated (i.e. logged on) user CGG and
given him representation key K.

The key, K, can be used to prove that "USER says
that this is CGG" simply by checking that K, CGG
and USER constitute one of the tuples (or active
object references) in the AOT. When the
representation is to be invalidated the active
object reference is simply removed from the
table, whereupon such a check would fail (an
operation similar to revoking a capability).

A server (called an AOT service), which supports
a number of procedure like entries, is used to
manage an AOT. These entries are now discussed in
detail.

----

* Naturally, assuming private key encryption,
  both the encryption and decryption would be
  done in some central service(s) to prevent
  misappropriation of the encryption key.

3.1 Creating Active Object References

It is clear that there must be some control over
the creation of active object references in the
AOT. Otherwise it would be possible for any
arbitrary service to be able to gain a
representation for any object simply by creating
a new tuple for it in an AOT.

To solve this problem, a request to create a new
active object reference must include the
representation of an authority. The AOT service
will check this association before allowing a
new active object reference to be created, making
it impossible for an authority to create any
active object references except those marked
with its name.

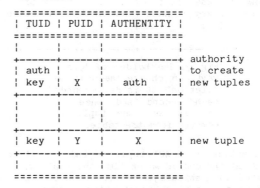

Fig. 2. A tuple for the
object 'Y' has been created.
'auth key' and 'X' were given
to allow the creation.

3.2 Deleting Active Object References

Deletion, in terms of AOT tuples, is trivial: the
tuple corresponding to a particular active
object reference is removed from the table so
that the key will no longer be able to prove the
proposition indicated by the corresponding PUID
and authentity.

As with creation, some control over the deletion
of tuples from an AOT is desirable. If deletion
of an active object reference merely required
its TUID, PUID and authentity to be quoted, then
any service passed the TUID of an object could
potentially delete it behind the original
owner's back, since the PUID and authentity are
not "secret". In a sense the active object
reference is itself an object for which a
representation is necessary in order to
manipulate it (in this case to delete it).
Requiring a representation for a representation
is, at first, somewhat alarming, because it seems
to point to a hopeless case of recursion; it
implies the creation of a new active object
reference for each active object reference that
is created. However the generality implied by
allowing representations of representations of
representations ... etc. is of very little
practical use. The problem is best avoided by
making the representation of an active object
reference part of the same tuple in an AOT. In
effect this representation is a key which proves

the proposition 'This AOT says that this is the proof of "X says this is Y" by the key Z'. For historical reasons it is called a TPUID. In general the possessor of this key will be the object's owner, and the holder of its TUID will be one of its users. When deleting an object's representation both its active object reference (including the TUID) and TPUID must be quoted.

```
+-------+------+------+-----------+---------+
| TPUID | TUID | PUID | AUTHENTITY | TIMEOUT |
+-------+------+------+-----------+---------+
|       |      |      |           |         |
|   :   |  :   |  :   |     :     |    :    |
|   :   |  :   |  :   |     :     | seconds |
| owner | use  |  :   |     :     |   to    |
|  key  | key  | name | authority | deletion|
|   :   |  :   |  :   |     :     |    :    |
|       |      |      |           |         |
+-------+------+------+-----------+---------+
```

Fig. 3. The holder of 'owner key' can change 'seconds to deletion'. It is decremented each second and when it reaches zero the tuple is removed from the table.

In practice each AOT tuple includes a timeout value, at the end of which time the tuple will be deleted automatically. Only the possessor of the TPUID for an active object reference can update this timeout value. Thus it is the TPUID's holder that is responsible for either maintaining the existence of the active object reference or (either implicitly or explicitly) deleting it. Explicit deletion is achieved by setting a tuple's timeout to zero.

3.3 Verifying Active Object References

An AOT service must provide an entry for checking that a particular key is a valid reference to an active object under a given authority. Indeed the AOT exists principally to fulfil this function.

Two forms of tuple verification are provided: the first verifies that a given TUID represents a given PUID under a given authenticity, and the second verifies that a TPUID represents a particular active object reference (given by its TUID, PUID and authenticity). The former verifies permission to "use" an object, and the latter verifies ownership of its representation.

3.4 Enhancing Active Object References

By repeatedly creating active object references to just one object, many TUIDs can be associated with a single PUID and authenticity. In contrast, enhancing an active object reference enables several PUIDs to be associated with a single TUID under more than one authenticity. This last type of entry to an AOT service is equivalent to creating a new active object reference except that the key (TUID) for the new tuple is specified in advance. This can sometimes have practical advantages when a large number of

references to different objects need to be passed about a network simultaneously since it can be accomplished using only one TUID. The owner of such a multi-attributed key can control the "power" associated with it by using the TPUIDs for each of the active object references that the TUID forms to individually control their existence.

```
+-------+------+--------+-----------+--------+
|TPUID  | TUID | PUID   |AUTHENTITY |TIMEOUT |
+-------+------+--------+-----------+--------+
|       |      |        |           |        |
1) |tpuid1| tuid | CGG    |   USER    | time1  |
2) |tpuid2| tuid | CGG    |  NETUSER  | time2  |
3) |tpuid3| tuid | GRAY   |   USER    | time3  |
4) |tpuid4| tuid |LABUSER |PRIVILEGE  | time4  |
   |      |      |        |           |        |
5) |tpuid5|bitrep| BIT1   | FACTORY1  | time5  |
6) |tpuid6|bitrep| BIT2   | FACTORY2  | time6  |
   |      |      |        |           |        |
+-------+------+--------+-----------+--------+
```

Fig. 4. Active object references can refer to different objects, even though they share the same TUID.

Enhancing an active object reference has several uses: by varying the name and the authenticity associated with the TUID it can be used as a combined reference to several different objects — e.g. 1) and 4) in Fig. 4; by varying just the name the active object can be given synonyms — e.g. 1) and 3); and by varying only the authenticity an authority (i.e. the possessor of an authenticity TUID) can "confirm" an existing TUID and PUID association (to give something analogous to an unforgeable signature of approval to an active object reference) — e.g. 1) and 2). An alternative view of enhancement is that it enables compound active objects to be created – the single TUID being the representation of a complex object consisting of several different parts, each with different names and authenticities. In order to verify such an object it is necessary to verify each of its component parts — e.g. 5) and 6).

4. AOT SERVICE ENTRY SUMMARY

The different functions outlined above constitute the entries that an AOT service must support. In summary they are as follows:

```
Entry              Send                Receive

gettuid  * P,a.t,a.tp,A,timeout          T,TP
verify     T,P,A                       <nothing>
identify   T,TP,P,A                    <nothing>
refresh    T,TP,P,A,timeout            <nothing>
enhance  * T,P,a.t,a.tp,A,timeout         TP
```

In which:
P   = a PUID   A   = an authenticity
T   = a TUID   TP = a TPUID

In addition to whatever appears under "receive" in the above a return code is given indicating the success or otherwise of the operation. A, a.t, and a.tp are related in the above by the fact that identify(a.t, a.tp, A, 'auth') must succeed.

GETTUID is used to create new active object references.

VERIFY is used to prove that a key represents a particular active object.

IDENTIFY is used to prove that a key represents a particular active object representation.

REFRESH is used to maintain or delete an active object reference.

ENHANCE is used to enhance an active object reference that already exists.

5. AUTHORITY REPRESENTATION

To initially obtain a representation for the authority that it needs in order to create representations, a service could apply to a server. Such a server would itself need to obtain a representation for a particular authority (call it 'auth') in order to create active object references for authorities. That is, this service needs a greater authority in order to create lesser ones. Indeed <u>any</u> particular level of authority must be delegated from a higher level. Eventually these higher levels will not be found in the network itself; and must continue in hierarchies outside it (e.g. line management). Within the network there need be only one place from which all authority can be delegated. This point is the <u>Source Of All Power</u> (SOAP) for the network and can be arbitrarily protected by its immediate superiors (e.g. with stone walls, iron bars etc.). The details of the way in which a service might actually obtain an active object reference for an authentity from the kind of server (provided by SOAP) outlined above rely upon service identification methods (a discussion of which is beyond the scope of this paper).

If all objects created under a particular authentity have the same 'type' then that authentity can be taken to denote the type of the represented object. The representations that authorities use to create new representations are themselves active object references distinguished by a common authentity ('auth') so that 'auth' could be thought of as their type. The possessor of a representation for the 'auth' authority can create arbitrary authority representations and hence can create and manage 'types' in the above sense. Thus 'auth' could be considered as a the name of the type 'type'.

----

* An entry in which an authority representation is necessary.

6. SECURITY

The topic of this paper (i.e. object representation) should not be confused with those concerning the characteristics of network communications - the two issues are independent. This paper is concerned with what should be sent where, and not with how it is to get there. Obviously the mechanics and reliability of any particular underlying communications system will greatly influence the reliance that can be put on the mechanisms given above. No attempt, however, is being made to increase a network's security, only to provide a way of utilizing it.

The mechanisms given can be likened to a bolt on a door that represents a network's data communication system. The bolt does not make the door any stronger (even though it may be stronger than the door) it only keeps it shut: without it the door, no matter how strong it is, would provide no security at all.

Object Representation can be thought of as a network facility which can be built on top of a layer in which secure communication (e.g. using encryption or well protected hardware) has been provided. In the UNIVERSE Project plans for achieving a secure communications layer include the development of fast hardware to implement both link encryption over the satellite and an end-to-end encryption option.

7. PRACTICABILITY

An initial system consisting of an AOT service, a PUID server, a user authenticator, an authentity server, SOAP and a privilege manager has been built on the Ring at Cambridge. Virtual terminal connection and file transport protocols which make use of the representation system have been designed and implemented. A revision of an existing processor allocation mechanism is under way which will use it to represent network resources. However, it is not yet in a state in which heavy regular use is made of it.

The service itself runs on a Z80 microprocessor (along with the other related services just mentioned) with no peripherals other than the Ring. The AOT resides in store for fast access. Since the maximum timeout for a representation (about six months) is large in comparison with the likely mean time between failures of the service it has proved necessary to automatically backup the table to a secret file on the Ring's file server every now and again. This has proved successful and, at the time of writing, at least one representation has been valid for a period of one and a half years.

The interface to AOT services and the structure of PUIDs and TUIDs has been chosen so that multiple AOT services can be provided on a network — each with a portion of the total number of representations.

8. EXTENSION TO THE UNIVERSE PROJECT

As part of an experiment in this project the Cambridge representation system is to be used over the UNIVERSE network. There is to be an AOT at each site holding locally produced representations. The TUIDs used in this system include a small field which identifies its home AOT in which it resides, so that, given a representation, it is possible for a local AOT to identify at which global AOT the representation must be verified. Thus, for example, if user CGG logs on at Rutherford, obtaining a representation for himself in Rutherford's AOT, and sent it to a Cambridge machine called X, X would verify CGG's representation in the following way:

- X would send it for verification at the Cambridge AOT

- This AOT would recognise it as a Rutherford representation

- It would be sent to the Rutherford AOT for verification

- The result of the verification would be sent back to the Cambridge AOT and thence back to X

Note that since the representations are always held in an AOT local to the represented object the severance of the network will cause relatively few problems. Services which hold representations remotely, and which consequently are unable to verify them, will find that the objects represented are also unavailable - being located at the disconnected site.

Making the representation system essentially global to all sites does not threaten their autonomy. It is still possible, for example, for a computer at Rutherford to be prepared to accept only Rutherford users, simply by accepting no representations other than those with the "Rutherford user" authenticator uniquely creates representations under that authenticator (assuming that the Rutherford user authenticator uniquely creates representations under that authenticity).

When an object is physically moved from one site to another as for example, a file, its representation will no longer be held at the same site as the object itself. In consequence the holder of a representation for such an object may be unable to use it when the network is severed, even though the object is physically at the same site as its user. Moving a representation away from its site of creation to the same site as that of the object it represents is not simply a matter of moving an entry from one AOT to another. There are problems which accrue from the maintenance of multiple or cached AOT entries, on the one hand, and problems stemming from the location of a single mobile AOT entry (since its TUID will no longer point to the relevent AOT) on the other. Solutions to these issues constitute a research topic that will be addressed as the project progresses.

REFERENCES

[1] PT Kirstein et al., "The UNIVERSE Project", ICCC '82.

[2] BB Newman, "Design of an Encryption System for Project UNIVERSE", ICCC '82.

[3] ____, Study Group Three of The Post Office PSS User Forum, "A Network Independent Transport Service", February '80.

Gray Girling is a member of the research staff at Cambridge Univesity Computer Laboratory currently completing a thesis on identification, authentication and representation in computer networks. He obtained his B.Sc.(Eng) and A.C.G.I. from the Imperial College of Science and Technology in London University. Mr Girling is now a member of the Universe Project team at Cambridge.

Encipherment and Signature in Teletex

D W Davies
National Physical Laboratory, UK
I K Hirst
British Telecom Research Laboratory,
UK

Teletex will become widely available in the next few years.   The character repertoire,
coding, format and procedure have already been adopted by office system manufacturers for
compatibility in the exchange of documents.   There is a need for extra security and/or
authentication in handling certain documents which can be met by modern methods of encipherment and digital signature.   This paper describes how encipherment and signature
can be fitted into Teletex procedures.   It also proposes key distribution methods for use
in an open network.

INTRODUCTION

Teletex has been defined by CCITT in a series
of documents which describe the service, the
terminal equipment, the character repertoire
and its coding, the control procedures and the
network independent basic transport service on
which the Teletex procedures depend.

The Teletex recommendations may come to have a
wider significance than the service itself.
Office equipment for handling text information
is being manufactured and supplied to users on
a large scale but without standards which would
enable these equipments to exchange documents
through telecommunication networks. Many of
the manufacturers will be persuaded to provide
a Teletex interface to their systems and this
could lead to the adoption of the Teletex
character repertoire, coding, format and
control procedures as a standard method for
communication between office systems. It is
generally believed that computer-based message
services will be very important to the future
of business and commerce. Probably these
systems will offer services going beyond those
of Teletex but the Teletex 'standards' can form
the basis on which these additional message
services are built.

Wherever messages carry valuable information or
perform valuable transactions, there is a
danger that interference with telecommunicaton
systems by criminals will result in the loss of
confidential information, forgery of
transmitted documents or other undesirable
things. The wide use of Teletex for office
correspondence and transactions will make the
system a target for illegal activities.

Technology now exists which can provide all the
security which is necessary and is not
inherently expensive. When Teletex terminals
and Teletex gateways are in large scale
manufacture the necessary additions for
encipherment and signature could be cheap in
the sense that they add no more than, say, 10%
to the cost of the terminal.

For this to happen there must be an agreed
method for employing encipherment and signature
in Teletex and this preferably should take the
form of a CCITT-standardised optional function.

There are many technological possibilities for
encipherment, signature and key distribution.
In proposing methods in this paper we make a
choice wherever there seem to be good arguments
for one course of action, otherwise we present
alternatives. The choices made available to
the user must be minimized because users will
not usually understand the technology involved.
There should be user alternatives only where
this is demanded by their different
requirements.

In this paper we describe proposals for the
enhancement of Teletex procedures to
incorporate encipherment from terminal to
terminal, including the procedure for
distributing keys from a central service. The
use of a digital signature is mentioned
briefly, having been described elsewhere
(Reference 5).

THE STRUCTURE OF TELETEX PROCEDURES

Fortunately, the Teletex procedures are
transparent to the bit patterns contained in
the data units which carry the documents.
Therefore these can be replaced by enciphered
data without problems.

Teletex procedures are organised in three
layers, document, session and transport. The
document layer is special to Teletex. The
session layer corresponds approximately to the
session layer of open systems interconnection
architecture. It uses the services of a
transport layer which has been defined by CCITT
for this purpose. The transport layer is
network-independent so that the administration
operating a Teletex service can choose a
suitable telecommunication service as the
carrier.

At any instant one terminal is the information
source and the other the information sink. The
source/sink relationship may be changed by the
sending and receiving of 'command session
change control' (CSCC) and 'response session
change control positive' (RSCCP). This
changeover allows documents to be sent in
either direction once a session is established.

Presentation information and the actual text are contained in commands and responses at the document level. The text is carried from source to sink in a command called 'command document user information' (CDUI). Control of document transfer begins with 'command document start' (CDS) and ceases with 'command document end' (CDE) and its positive response 'response document end positive' (RDEP). Other elements of document procedure deal with linking, page boundaries, capabilities, recovery points and rejects.

The task of the Teletex procedures is to complete the transmission of a document. Any document that is not complete will not be passed on to the user. Error recovery mechanisms are provided so that partly sent documents can be aborted or communication can be restarted at some intermediate point.

For encipherment and signature purposes it seems best to treat the document as a whole. If the user wishes to encipher or sign small parts of the document he can do this by some higher level procedure. When Teletex is responsible for encipherment or signature it is best to adopt the simplest convention. The cost of employing encipherment or signature for the whole document is no more than a small extra computer load. The user can lose nothing by enciphering or signing documents as a whole.

The Teletex document procedure recognises the division of documents into separate pages. At the end of each page a 'command document page boundary' (CDPB) is sent which contains the page reference number. This requires a 'response document page boundary positive' (RDPBP) or else it may receive a negative response. For the last page, the corresponding function is carried out by 'command document end' (CDE) and 'response document end positive' (RDEP).

The page may be transmitted as a number of CDUI but the internal structure of the page is not the concern of these procedures. In order to deal with the future possibility of adding facsimile to the Teletex page which would make the page carry a lot of data, a commitment unit smaller than the page is possible, but not in the basic Teletex service. For this purpose a recovery point reference number is used so that recovery can take place starting from these smaller units than a page. We shall need to recognise these optional commitment units in the encipherment procedures. Normally, the recovery and commitment unit is the page and the document and page numbers form a sufficient reference for recovery purposes.

Encipherment could be carried out either at the session or the document level. At the session level, it would be applied to the user data in each session command or response . This would encipher all the commands and responses at the document level and conceal not only the contents of the document but also the various commands and responses needed to control the document procedure.

Encipherment applied at the document level results in enciphering only the message data in the commands CDUI. The additional security obtained by enciphering all the document commands and responses seems very small since the nature of these items can probably be deduced from their lengths. Encipherment at the document level has the advantage that it is similar to the effect of enciphering just the document contents, which can be done at a higher level of protocol when enciphering off-line. For these reasons we recommend encipherment at the document level.

ENCIPHERMENT METHODS

We propose the use of the 64-bit block cipher known as the Data Encryption Standard or DES. First adopted for US government non-classified purposes (reference 1) the DES went on to become an ANSI Data Encryption Algorithm (DEA) standard and is under consideration by ISO as an international standard. It is widely adopted in banking and a range of hardware implementations is available.

Four modes of use for the Data Encryption Algorithm have been defined (reference 2) and there are two of these which are suitable for our purpose. These are 'Cipher Block Chaining' (CBC) which operates on 64 bit blocks and 'Cipher Feedback' (CFB) which, for our purpose, would be used with a 'character size' of 8 bits. There is very little difference in their properties but CBC would be more effective if very high speed operation was needed and CFB has the advantage of working in octet units which are natural to Teletex. The choice between them is evenly balanced and so we shall consider both possibilities here.

Public key cryptosystems have great potential advantages (reference 3) in two respects. They avoid the need for transporting an encipherment key in secret and they provide a convenient form of electronic signature. Two forms of public key cipher have been widely discussed, the RSA cipher, due to Rivest, Shamir and Adleman (reference 4) and the Knapsack cipher, with several variants, due initially to Merkle and Hellman. We propose the optional use of the RSA cipher for key distribution and its use for signature. Its advantages over the Knapsack method are greater certainty about its level of security and a more conveniently short key. We believe, nevertheless that a key length of nearly 512 bits (with a 512 bit maximum) should be chosen to give adequate security. In order to carry out RSA encipherment rapidly enough, special hardware is needed, but at the present time even this is too slow for normal encipherment purposes, though adequate for key distribution and signature. Therefore we propose that where the RSA algorithm is used for encipherment it should be used to transmit a 64 bit key block for the purpose of DES encipherment. The coding of parameters which specify the method of encipherment and key distribution should allow for other possibilities in the future.

Electronic signature is a method of authenticating a message which is proof against forgery by the receiver of a message, even though the receiver is able to check the authenticity, using the sender's public key.

We propose that the RSA algorithm should be used for forming the signature and that the same public keys should serve for both key distribution and signature.

In order to sign the whole of a document with one RSA operation (since the RSA operation takes approximately 1 second) a hash function of the whole document must be formed for signature. The method for forming this hash has been proposed (reference 5) after examining the weaknesses of several methods and altering them accordingly. The result of this procedure is to produce a 512 bit (maximum) signature which can be appended to the document.

THE ENCIPHERMENT AND SIGNATURE SERVICES

When two Teletex terminals are engaged in a session, they can encipher and decipher documents on-line. That is to say, plaintext documents at one terminal can be enciphered, transmitted, deciphered at the other terminal and presented as plaintext automatically. During this procedure, both terminals must possess the session key used for encipherment. The procedures for distributing a session key will be described later. The acknowledgement for each page can contain a cryptographic response which ensures that the page has been received by the authorised terminal, one which possesses the session key. The authentication procedure is such that an attempt by a third terminal to repeat an earlier message which it had intercepted would be foiled. On-line operation with cryptographic sum check reassures the sender that the message is getting to its destination. We can call this method 'terminal-to-terminal' encipherment because it depends on keys possessed by the terminals themselves.

When a user prepares a document for sending by Teletex but does not trust the security of the Teletex terminal (at the sender or the receiver's end) a different method of operation will be appropriate. The sender would like to encipher the message in a system over which he has control, using a key which identifies him. (The system which carries out this encipherment might be a Teletex terminal.) In any case, the user would leave the enciphered document in the transmitting terminal, which would send it using normal Teletex procedures. At the receiving terminal, the enciphered document would be stored until the intended reader either copied the document to decipher elsewhere or supplied his personal key to enable decipherment, after which the user would remove the cleartext version from the terminal. This is 'author-to-reader' encipherment.

Author to reader encipherment has no effect on the Teletex procedure and it can be regarded as taking place at a higher level, using the document level to transmit its enciphered documents. But in practice the encipherment and decipherment will often, for convenience, take place in Teletex terminals. It makes sense to integrate as far as possible the two modes of Teletex encipherment.

This paper will describe terminal to terminal (that is: on-line) encipherment.

The method of signature has been mentioned above. The sender of a document uses a secret key to sign it and may not wish to trust this key to a Teletex terminal unless this terminal is strictly under his control. Signature is therefore also a higher level function than Teletex. Although signature could be applied to the enciphered form of the document, signature of the plaintext is preferable because the signature then remains valid after the document has been deciphered. Reference 5 gives more information.

ALTERNATIVES FOR KEY DISTRIBUTION

The session key will be transmitted immediately after the session begins, or at least before the first enciphered document in the session. To encipher the session key, a master key is used. We propose that this arrangement of master and session key should be used in all calls, for example when a terminal is calling a key distribution centre. It is easier to adopt one method uniformly and it adds to the security.

The simplest way to provide master keys is for two users to exchange these keys outside the system. Users with a frequent need to exchange enciphered documents would keep a 'bilateral master key' for the purpose.

Where Teletex terminals are used to make calls to any other terminal in an 'open network' situation the proliferation of bilateral keys would be excessive. A group of such users can avoid this by employing a key distribution centre which they all trust. Each terminal establishes a bilateral master key with the centre. Before beginning a session, the calling terminal first makes a call to the KDC to obtain a session key.

When the RSA algorithm is used for key distribution, a terminal may have available, in a cache, the public key of the called terminal. Otherwise, it must make a call to a key registry to obtain the public key, then check the signature which the key registry has added to its reply. For this purpose, the public key of the registry is held in such terminals.

DETAILS OF THE PROPOSED ENCIPHERMENT METHODS

We can summarise the characteristics of the encipherment method which have already been described.

(a) Encipherment is applied to the CDUIs carrying a designated document.
(b) The Data Encryption Standard Algorithm will be used, either in the CBC or the CFB mode.
(c) The unit for encipherment is the document.
(d) The chains for the encipherment method will consist of one page of Teletex or, if smaller recovery units are employed, one such recovery unit.

The proposed chain format is shown in Figure 1. It begins with a chain identifier which is the document number followed the page number and optionally the recovery point reference number. This identifier is not allowed to repeat during

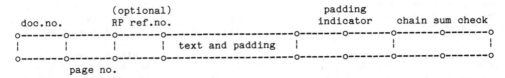

```
                 (optional)                                 padding
doc.no.          RP ref.no.                                 indicator    chain sum check
o-------o-------o-------o----------------------o-------o-------o-------o-------o
|       |       |       |  text and padding    |       |       |       |       |
o-------o-------o-------o----------------------o-------o-------o-------o-------o
                page no.
```

Figure 1. Format of a chain

the lifetime of a session key, therefore it ensures that pages (or recovery units) cannot be interchanged. The last two octets of a chain consist of a chain sum check formed from the exclusive-or function of the even and odd octets of plaintext. This sum check detects with high probability any changes to the ciphertext which might have been made by an enemy.

The possibility of padding and the use of a padding indicator is also shown in this format. When cipher block chaining is used, the total length of the chain must be a multiple of 8 octets, so padding may be necessary. For cipher feedback, this padding is not essential. A padding indicator of 2 octets is shown because it might be useful to employ extensive padding to prevent an enemy from making deductions from the size of pages.

In formulating definitive recommendations for encipherment in Teletex a choice should be made between CBC and CFB encipherment. This is not a choice which should be offered to the user because the properties of the two modes are very similar. Whichever mode of operation is used each chain is started with the help of an initialising variable (IV) of 64 bits. The same IV can be used for the duration of a session key. It can be transferred (using the session key for encipherment) at the same time as the session key is established. Although this is not the customary method of initialisation in cipher feedback, we propose it here because it avoids the need for transferring an IV at the beginning of each chain.

Security is improved by having the receiver respond to each page or recovery unit, for which it finds a correct chain identifier and chain sum check, with a 'cryptographic response'. This response is a parameter in the 'response document page boundary positive'. There is no provision in the Teletex protocols for a positive response to the 'command document recovery point'. To form this cryptographic response, the chain to which it responds must be deciphered and the last 8 octets are added, modulo 2, to the initialisation variable then enciphered. The The source of the data is able to check this response and will continue to send data only if the response is correct. This is possible only for on-line (terminal to terminal) encipherment.

KEY TRANSFER

Key transfer means the setting up of the session key before enciphered documents are transferred. With terminal-to-terminal (on-line) encipherment, the key transfer

procedure can authenticate the two terminals with the aid of data provided by the key distribution centre. The necessary exchange consists of two commands followed by their responses. As one possibility for this procedure, we propose that an existing feature of the Teletex procedures might be employed, the 'command document capability list' (CDCL) and the 'response document capability list positive' (RDCLP). The parameters contained in these commands and responses are shown in Figure 2a.

Key Transfer A - B

CDCL (1) or special document

encipherment method   - DEA1
key distribution method   - key distribution
                             centre
key transfer chain *   - enciphered by kbx
initialisation variable   - ekab (I)
test pattern   - ekab (S)

*format of key transfer chain in Figure 2 (b). If a bilateral key ekmab is used, this parameter is replaced by the enciphered session key ekmab (kab)

RDCLP(1) or special document

returned test pattern   - ekab (I + S)
new test pattern   - ekab (S')

CDCL(2) or special document

returned test pattern   - ekab (I + S')

RDCLP(2) or special document

key accepted / rejected

USER DOCUMENTS

chain enciphered with key kab and initialising variable I

Figure 2a

In Figures 2a and 2b, the notation for the enciphered value of variable X using key k is ek (X). Where the + sign appears, this means modulo 2 addition of each bit of the 64 bit variables to form a 64 bit result.

A CDCLP/RDCLP exchange can be initiated by the source terminal whenever a document is not being transferred. Normally the calling terminal would carry out this exchange immediately after session start.

Figure 2a shows the key transfer for the case of a session key provided by a key distribution centre (KDC). The key distribution centre has earlier provided the key transfer chain to the calling terminal which now transfers it as a parameter to the called terminal. The contents of that key transfer chain are the session key (kab), an identifier of the calling terminal and the date and time. The date and time can be checked by the called terminal to ensure that a recently obtained session key is being offered. The key transfer chain is enciphered with a zero IV, using the master key of the called terminal, which is known to the KDC.

If a bilateral master key is being used, the enciphered key transfer chain is replaced by the enciphered session key.

At the end of this exchange of four messages the calling terminal examines the second response and, if the called terminal has accepted the key, it can go ahead with the transfer of the users' documents, enciphered or not, though some are expected to be enciphered.

Obtaining the session key from a key distribution centre, shown in Figure 2b, is carried out by a normal Teletex session transferring two enciphered documents, one a request from the caller to the KDC and the other a reply from the KDC. A session key is used for this purpose and its transfer, using the CDCL/RDCLP exchange that we have described, employs a bilateral master key.

The document received from the KDC, as a chain enciphered with the session key of this session, contains two items, the session key for the forthcoming call and the enciphered key transfer chain which we mentioned earlier, intended for passing to the called terminal.

This procedure for key acquisition and key transfer uses authentication at each stage to prevent the replay of a previous session key or the impersonation of either a caller or the key distribution centre.

AN ALTERNATIVE TO CAPABILITY LISTS FOR KEY DISTRIBUTION

The use of CDCL to transfer enciphered keys in 'capability lists' is a distortion of the original intention for this facility in the Teletex procedure. An alternative would be to carry out the key exchange procedure of Figure 2 entirely in specially formatted documents. This can be regarded as carrying out key distribution at a level above the Teletex procedure. It is a more natural use of Teletex procedure but it requires many more commands and responses to carry it out. These key exchange documents can be given a special 'document type' which, according to the Teletex specification, indicates to the operating system of the receiving terminal that a special action is required. The choice between

Key Acquisition A - X

CDCL(1) or special document

encipherment method	- DEA1
key distribution method	- bilateral key
session key	- ekax (ks)
initialisation variable	- eks (I')
test pattern	- eks (R)

RDCLP(1) or special document

returned test pattern	- eks (I' + R)
new test pattern	- eks (R')

CDCL(2) or special document

returned test pattern	- eks (I' + R')

RDCLP(2) or special document

key accepted / rejected

KEY REQUEST DOCUMENT - chain enciphered with key ks and initialising variable I'

command	- key request
target terminal identifier	- B

KEY REPLY DOCUMENT - chain enciphered with key ks and initialising variable I'

session key for A-B	- kab
key transfer chain	chain enciphered with key kbx and initialising variable zero
48 bit random number	- R''
session key for A-B	- kab
calling terminal identifier	- A
time stamp	- date, time

Figure 2b

CDCL/RDCLP and special documents for key transfer is still under discussion.

ERROR RECOVERY IN ENCIPHERED DOCUMENT TRANSFER

There is no change in the method of error recovery. Recovery always starts from the beginning of a recovery unit and the re-transmission of the enciphered chain uses the same IV as before and the same chain identifier. Consequently, exactly the same data are transferred and the re-transmission does not weaken the security in any way. The transmission of a document must be completed within one session. If it cannot be completed, the document must be discarded and transmitted in a subsequent session.

MASTER KEY DISTRIBUTION

In order to provide a low cost terminal with encryption facilities, there should be an agreement on the method of loading master keys, such as from magnetic striped cards with a swipe reader. For terminals intended for on-line use, the KDC-based master key will be loaded in this way. A card may also be used to load a bilateral master key. The magnetic data on the card should also indicate the type of key it holds and the address of the destination terminal with which this key is intended to operate, so that the key cannot be misused by accident. This method of carrying the key is convenient, but provides no security for secret keys, which must be safeguarded by the users taking precautions.

When microcircuit cards (like credit cards in appearance) become more widely available and cheaper, they can be used as key carriers and give some physical protection to their keys. A password can be used to authorise the release of a key, so that a lost carrier cannot easily be exploited.

Magnetic striped cards can carry RSA public keys for session key distribution, together with the address of the terminal or the name of the person with whom they can be used. A stock of these cards can be kept for giving, like name cards, to business associates. Much greater precautions are needed for handling bilateral DES keys as compared with RSA public keys, where the main precaution is to prevent an enemy tampering with the card.

CONCLUSIONS

A Teletex terminal, or any system which uses Teletex protocols, can employ simple enhancements of these protocols to give encipherment and signature facilities. The design of the protocols allows these features to be added conveniently. In this paper, proposals have been made for the handling of encipherment and the associated key management.

By incorporating such services in the terminal or system in association with the Teletex protocol, the cost should be minimised, since the processing, storage, power supply and physical structure can be shared. Extra physical protection may be needed in sensitive applications and if master keys are to be stored. It is important to find convenient methods of key distribution. Two promising developments are the RSA public key cipher and microcircuit cards.

In this way, extra security can be given to electronic mail in the future, while signature will open up many new applications in commerce.

Acknowledgement is made to the Director of Research of British Telecommunications and to the Director of National Physical Laboratory for permission to publish this paper.

References

1. 'Data Encryption Standard,' Federal Information Processing Standards Publication No.46, U.S. Department of Commerce, National Bureau of Standards, Gaithersburg, MD. Jan. 1977.

2. 'DES Modes of operation,' Federal Information Pricessing Standards Publication No.81, U.S. Department of Commerce, National Bureau of Standards, Gaithersburg, MD, Dec. 1980.

3. An evaluation of public key cryptosystems; Davies, D.W., Price, W.L. and Parkin, G.I. Information Privacy, Vol.2, No.4, July 1980, pp 137-154.

4. A method of obtaining digital signatures and public-key cryptosystems; Rivest, R.L., Shamir, A. and Adleman, L., Comm. ACM, Vol.21, No.2, February 1978, pp 120-126.

5. The application of digital signatures based on public key cryptosystems; Davies, D.W. and Price, W. L., Proc. Int. Conference on Computer Communications, Atlanta, Oct. 1980, pp 525-530.

D.W.Davies

Born in Treorchy, Rhondda Graduated at Imperial College in Physics in 1943 and Mathematics in 1947. Joined NPL in 1947 to assist in building the ACE Pilot Model and continued in computer applications. Specialised in network design in 1965. Author and co-author of three books. At present engaged on research and consultancy in the fields of data security and authentication.

I.K.Hirst

Born in Huddersfield, West Yorkshire. Joined PO Tele-communications in 1973 and received the BSc degree in Electronic Communication from the University of Salford in 1980. In 1980 he joined the Office Systems group at British Telecom Research Laboratories and is currently working on the implementation and assessment of high level communication protocols, including Teletex procedures.

The GILT Project – connecting Computer-based Message Systems via Public Data Networks

E Fergus
AERE Harwell, UK

GILT is the name of a collaborative research project where several European institutes co-operate in developing techniques and protocols to interconnect computer based message systems (CBMS) via public data networks. GILT protocols are developed in accordance with the principles of Open System Interconnection (OSI), and full use is made of existing relevant standards: X25 and Teletex.

The essential features of a real CBMS are expressed by an abstract model called an "open CBMS" (OCBMS), which is the manifestation of the real CBMS within the OSI environment. GILT protocols are specified in terms of OCBMS.

The GILT CBMSs are interconnected in an "open" manner, and each CBMS obtains services from other CBMSs on behalf of its local users. The results of the GILT work will increase the usefulness of existing (but isolated) CBMSs, lead to a better understanding of the upper 3 OSI layers, and demonstrate the use of Teletex in applications more general than document transfer.

1. ABOUT THE GILT PROJECT

GILT (Get Interconnected Local Text systems) is the title of an international research project in which several European institutes co-operate to develop standards for advanced electronic mail. GILT is a subproject of the COST-11-bis project, a four year informatics research program ending in September 1983. COST-11-bis is sponsored by the European community, plus Finland, Sweden, Norway and Yugoslavia. The purpose of COST-11-bis is to create an environment which will encourage international collaboration in teleinformatics; to promote standardisation by advising the appropriate standards bodies; to transfer acquired expertise to European industry. COST-11-bis finances suitable pilot projects, and covers the international element in the costs of co-ordinating nationally funded projects.

One of the COST-11-bis projects is GILT. The aim of GILT is to define and implement experimental message exchange protocols to enable existing (but as yet isolated from each other) computer based message systems (CBMSs to interwork via public data networks. The institutes taking part in GILT are listed in Appendix 1.

2. STATEMENT OF THE PROBLEM

A CBMS is a store-and-retrieve message switch which uses the processing power of a computer to provide comfortable user functions for generating and handling messages. Different CBMSs vary greatly in sophistication, but the defining characteristic is that every CBMS supports one or more mailboxes. A mailbox is an abstraction of "user" and is the source of destination of a message. A mailbox may represent a human user, a group of users, a conference, a computer program, or any other entity which can sensibly exchange messages.

Few CBMSs are designed for interworking with other CBMSs. A particular CBMS serves a set of mailboxes which may therefore be termed "local", and the CBMS may be called their "home system". All local users see the functional interface peculiar to their home system, irrespective of whether they are truly local or access the system via a communications network.

Increasingly, it is necessary for CBMS users to have to deal with more than one CBMS in order to collaborate with other users. This trend is encouraged by the growing popularity and availability of robust data networks. At present the several home systems are isolated from each other, and such users must be local to every system.

It would clearly be valuable to interconnect the isolated systems in the "open" manner prescribed by the OSI principles [reference 1]. Then, a local user would effectively have access to a distributed system where the functions of his home CBMS are (transparently) augmented by functions and services obtained from remote CBMSs via the OSI environment. A user would then need to be familiar with only the services and set of operating conventions of his hom CBMS. Users of different home systems would be able to interact transparently via the OSI environment.

The problem is that at present there is no generally agreed method of passing messages between mailboxes of different home systems and (more generally) of making the facilities of one CBMS available to the local user of another CBMS. Ad-hoc schemes have been advanced from time to time, but what is required is a well considered and general purpose standard solution. This solution requires two elements. First, a method of physically interconnecting the isolated systems. Second, an agreement on how to interpret the data exchanged by the connected systems. The first element is provided by the available public data networks, and the second by the GILT message exchange protocols.

3. THE GILT APPROACH

Each of the GILT participants has locally implemented a CBMS. The variety of these systems ensures that the essential features of the majority of existing CBMSs are catered for in the GILT message standard. The local CBMS may be centrally implemented, or may be locally distributed over a local network: only its external appearance to a remote CBMS is important (see section 4).

Each GILT CBMS has access to a public data network, typically the national X25 network supplied by the PTT. These national networks are themselves interconnected by appropriate gateways. The networks relevant to GILT are already (or will shortly be) interconnected. A GILT CBMS is directly linked to every other CBMS. For expediency, the GILT standard at present excludes the relay problem.

The physically connected CBMSs now need an agreement on how to interpret data from each other. The GILT message standard provides this necessary common understanding and permits communicating CBMSs to exchange structured data of pre-agreed syntax and semantics. (In OSI terms, the message standard is concerned with the "communication" protocols of the upper levels rather than with the "connection" protocols of the lower levels).

The GILT message standard is based on an abstract model of a CBMS. This model defines the external appearance of a real CBMS and is in effect a virtual CBMS. The standard defines: (1) a message, in terms of globally significant attributes; (2) a set of service primitives to operate on messages with reference to the logical structure of the abstract CBMS model; (3) a protocol which lays down rules for the use of service primitives. An attribute is globally significant if its meaning is agreed by all CBMSs and is independent of its local representation by any simple CBMS.

The GILT service primitives are chosen to provide the function of CBMS/CBMS message exchange at several levels of sophstication (e.g. simple mail, conferencing, remote access) but not necessarily to express the full capability of any particular system. The correspondence between local user operations and GILT primitives, and the mapping between global message attributes and the local message format, are matters of purely local concern and are outside the scope of the GILT standard.

The net effect of two CBMSs adopting the GILT standard is that users local to each can exchange messages in a transparent manner using the conventions of their home systems. In effect, the interconnected GILT systems form a distributed CBMS.

4. THE ROLE OF OSI

All GILT work proceeds within the framework of the ISO Open Systems Interconnection reference model [reference 1]. It is important to note that the OSI specification (and OSI "layering" in general) describes the external appearance that a GILT system must present, but says nothing about how that appearance is to be achieved. It is purely local decision how to program the CBMS to meet the GILT standard, and the standard imposes no specific implementation constraints.

Thus, each CBMS is interfaced to the OSI environment by a functional entity called the "open CBMS" or OSI, which maps the real characteristics of the system (e.g. user functions, message attributes) on to the virtual characteristics of the GILT standard in a manner consistent with OSI principles. It is the OCBMS which contains the abstract model of a CBMS, and therefore may be thought of as the virtual CBMS augmented with OSI-compatible communication protocols. The structure and semantics of the abstract model guide the design of the protocols. Note again that OSI describes communication but not implementation: the OCBMS is not necessarily a "CBMS agent" or a "front-end", although a particular CBMS may choose to implement it thus.

The GILT task now becomes one of selecting from existing OSI-compatible protocols, and extending these where necessary to accommodate GILT requirements.

5. SELECTION OF PROTOCOLS

GILT does not intend to develop completely new protocols, but aims to make use of existing standards where possible. A suitable protocol must meet two conditions. First, it must be adequate for the purpose, or require a realistically small amount of extension. Second, it must be technically stable and have strong commercial relevance.

5.1 Levels 1 to 3

The natural choice for the Levels 1 to 3 protocol was X25. X25 has gained widespread acceptance as a network access protocol and is available from most European PTTs. X75 gateways exist to interconnect the national networks. Further, most GILT participants already have working X25 implementations.

5.2 The role of Teletex

The choice of protocol for OSI levels 4-5 was less obvious, but the Teletex standard emerged as eminently suitable [reference 2]. This group of protocols has been devised for maximum compatibility with existing international standards; observes OSI principles; is rapidly acquiring commercial importance; is inherently flexible and powerful enough to support major extensions if necessary.

5.2.1 The Transport Protocol, Level 4

GILT has adopted the Teletex network-independent transport service S70, [reference 2]. S70 defines a basic set of services which appears to be adequate for GILT purposes. The use of distinct classes provides for clean extension should future GILT developments require it. Further, this standard has received considerable support from industry.

5.2.2 The Session Protocol, Level 5

Teletext recommendation S62 defines procedures for the secure transfer of documents. GILT requires a more general purpose session service that does standard Teletex. Some early GILT work [reference 3] established that the S62 procedures were capable of a more general interpretation while retaining as a subset the unchanged document transfer application. GILT has a session service [reference 4] which extends the S62 service, principally to give more comfortable synchronisation. Advantage has been taken of the "private use" codes to introduce a new S62 element RDUI for use in two way simultaneous operation, and to carry the GILT-specific parameters in S62 protocol elements.

The session entity provides: both confirmed and unconfirmed services; connection establishment and termination; data exchange and "turn" management; (major and minor) synchronisation; error reporting; capability negotiation. The design has been guided both by S62 and by the ISO work [reference 5], although certain ISO Session Service primitives are not required: expedited data, data quarantining, tokens. Appendix 2 lists the GILT session services and their corresponding S62 protocol elements. The GILT session standard is defined in reference 4.

5.3 The Message Exchange Protocol, Levels 6 and 7

The functions up to and including session level are essentially in support of the mainstream GILT work, which is to define a CBMS/CBMS message exchange protocol. In OSI terms, GILT CBMSs are application entities and the message protocol is therefore at level 7. The Application level functions include: naming of local and remote objects; capability establishment; data integrity, including checkpointing and error recovery; authentication; accounting.

The description of the Application layer is kept independent of any syntactical aspects of object naming, data value representation, etc. These aspects are handled by the Presentation layer, whose function is to maintain a set of application oriented data structures. The Presentation layer allows transparent interaction of Application and Session layers for all cases other than session user data.

The GILT message protocol is defined in reference 6 in terms of the OCBMS structure and operations. The OCBMS provides an abstract model of the real CBMS in terms of application oriented data types and the operations legally permitted on them. GILT uses three principal data types: an OCBMS is a "store", which contains one or more "mailboxes", each containing a set of "documents". Each type of object has an associated set of attributes to regulate the operations carried out on it, both by its "owner" OCBMS and by a remote OCBMS. Operations permitted on "store" are: create mailbox; delete mailbox; select mailbox; deselect store. Operations on "mailbox": add member; delete mamber; list members; deselect mailbox. Operations on "document": read document; write document.

6. IMPLEMENTATION PLANS

The current definition of OCBMS services emphasises simplicity rather than efficiency of operation. This facilitates early implementation in order to gain experience of programming the GILT standard and to assess its functional suitability. All GILT participants are at an advanced stage of implementing the Transport and Session protocols. The Message standard is expected to be ready for public demonstration and preliminary testing by the end of 1982.

7. ACKNOWLEDGEMENT

This paper is a summary of the major working papers produced in the GILT project. The author acknowledges the contribution of the GILT participants in producing this paper, which he submits on their behalf.

8. REFERENCES

[1] "Data processing - open systems interconnection - basic reference model", ISO/TC97/SC16/N719.

[2] "Final report to the 8th plenary assembly (part 3) - new and revised recommendations", CCITT/SG8/N195.

[3] "Is the Teletex session and document level a basis for a general purpose session service?", GILT internal working paper, February 1981.

[4] "The GILT session description" GILT internal working paper, March 1982.

[5] "Draft basic session service specification, version 4", ISO/TC97/SC16/N200.

[6] "The GILT Message Standard, Blue Version", GILT internal working paper, December 1981.

APPENDIX 1: member institutes of the GILT project

The following research institutes participate in the GILT project:

Country	Institute
European Community	JRC-ISPRA (Euratom Joint Research Centre)
Finland	Helsinki University
France	INRIA (Institut National de Recherche en
Informatique et en automatique)	

Germany (Federal Republic)	University of Duesseldorf
	GMD (Gesellschaft Mathematik und Datenverarbeitung):
	    GMD-IFV Darmstadt
	    GMD-IPES Birlinghoven

Italy	CSATA, Bari

Norway	Uninett project
	    Oslo University
	    Norwegian Computer Center
	    Televerkets forskningsinstitutt
	    Tromso University

Sweden	Swedish National Defense Research Institute Stockholm University Computing Center SUNET project Chalmers University of Technology Karolinska Institutet
United Kingdom	AERE Harwell
Yugoslavia	Stefan-Josef Institute

APPENDIX 2: GILT session services and corresponding S62 elements

GILT	S62
S_CONNECT.request	CSS
S_CONNECT.response	RSSP
	RSSN
S_CONNECT.final-response	CSUI+CDS
	CSUI+CDC
	CSE,CSUI+CDCL,CSCC
S_RELEASE.request	CSE
S_RELEASE.response	RSEP
S_U_ABORT.request	CSA
S_DATA.request	CSUI+CDUI
	RSUI+RDUI
S_SYNC_MAJOR.request	CSUI+CDE
S_SYNC_MAJOR.response	RSUI+RDEP
S_SYNC_MAJOR.final-resp.	same as S_CONNECT.final-resp.
S_SYNC_MINOR.request	CSUI+CDPB
	RSUI+RDPBP
S_SYNC_MINOR.resp.	CSUI+CDPB
	RSUI+RDPBP
S-RESYNC.request	CSUI+CDD
S_RESYNC.response	CSUI+CDR
	RSUI+RDDP or RSUI+RDRP
S_RESYNC.final-resp.	same as S_CONNECT.final-resp.
S_ERROR.request	RSUI+RDPBN
S_CHANGE_DU_CONTROL.request	CSCC
S_CHANGE_DU-CONTROL.resp.	same as S_CONNECT.final-resp.
S_PLEASE_DU_CONTROL.request	RSUI / RSSP
S_PLEASE_SEND_TURN.request	RSUI+RDUI
S_RESELECT.request	CSUI+CDCL
S_RESELECT.response	RSUI+RDCLP
S_RESELECT.final-resp	same as S_SYNC_MAJOR.final-resp.

Edward Fergus is a member of
the Networks Group in the Computer
Science and Systems Division at
AERE Harwell. He received a B.Sc
from Keele University in 1976,
and an M.Sc from Manchester
University in 1980.

At Harwell he is concerned with the development
of high level data protocols within the ISO Open
Systems environment, and the development of
computer based message systems.

A Powerful Teletex Workstation: Design and Facilities

A H Ithell
British Telecom Research
Laboratories, UK

Teletex is a new service which makes possible the fast transfer of character based messages on a worldwide basis. In order to achieve this a high degree of standardisation first had to be agreed so that compatible terminals could be built, this Paper describes the design of the Teletex workstation developed at BTRL. Advantage has been taken in the design to incorporate a level of flexibility which will allow further developments to be made readily. The software is modular and has been extended to include testing facilities. The hardware will handle the large (300+) Teletex character set via a special, ergonomically designed keyboard, printer and VDU.

1. INTRODUCTION

Teletex (not to be confused with Telex or Teletext) is a CCITT agreed text communication system offering a user the facilities of

* document creation to A4 size, either upright or "landscape".

* document storage and optional local printing.

* automatic high speed transmission of documents with inbuilt checks on the recipient's authenticity.

* corresponding receipt and storage of incoming documents for later display and printing.

It might be thought that Teletex is no more than a set of communicating word processors but that would overlook many features, not least the tremendous advantages which derive from Standardisation. Since the subject of standardisation attracts many different shades of opinion it is worthwhile briefly to look at the way in which it affects a new service such as Teletex. Considering that Teletex offers a future worldwide text message transference it is instructive to make some comparisons with the way in which telephony has arrived at providing a similar facility for speech. In the UK alone there are over 26 million telephones connected to the BT network and it is possible to establish a transmission path between any two of them and then conduct a conversation. The achievement of this situation has depended upon the careful application of unified signalling and transmission planning rules. This National scene may be extended to a huge worldwide network of some 430 million telephones of which some 92% (in a hundred countries) may be dialled directly from 99% of UK exchange lines. This vast machine has been referred to on many previous occasions but I submit, in the present context, it particularly well illustrates the tremendous potential which is opened up when agreed standards for interworking exist and are implemented. Of course that potential extends right across the size of the market in one dimension and, in another dimension, includes the usefulness of the service as seen by the user (eg the number of locations to which he can communicate).

As an example of how the lack of interworking standards can inhibit the growth of a service one only has to look at facsimile. In this case the basic technique has been around for well over 100 years and many different varieties of machine have been available. In fact most of the difficulties associated with fax interworking have derived from that very variety represented in the machines themselves; the expansion of facsimile in to a worldwide communications service had to await the fairly recent agreement (about 5 years ago) of Group I, II and III standards.

2. SERVICE

As might be expected from the fact that Teletex (TTX) is a recent innovation it exemplifies the trend towards smaller units of processing power, it is a terminal-to-terminal text communication service which does not require the involvement of a central computer. That is not to say that mainframes or minis are incapable of supporting TTX but that it is quite possible to implement it at the microprocessor level.

The implementor of a TTX terminal is free to chose how the user will see the service and what range of local facilities are to be provided as long as the terminal conforms to the service standards for document interchange between terminals. Messages may be composed from a character set of over 300 characters, covering 40 Latin-based languages, to a page size of A4 orientated to either the upright "portrait" or horizontal "landscape" formats and with a choice of character pitches and line spacings. Insofar as the basic TTX service requirements are concerned the receiving terminal must be capable of storing all characters received but not necessarily to display or print every one accurately. However, indications have to be given if "approximate" or "fall-back" renditions are made of some characters.

The networks used for supporting the service are determined at National level; in the UK the PSTN will be the main bearer with facilities also being provided on PSS. Gateway exchanges will enable international working and provide connection to Telex. The setting up and answering of calls, the transmission and reception of documents, together with error recovery are all required to be fully automatic. The full set of requirements for the TTX service and terminals form a significant set of documentation and in this Paper I now wish to move on to the TTX workstation which has been built at BTRL.

3. TERMINAL DESIGN

Designers of Teletex terminals are faced with a number of key issues:

(i) Providing peripheral devices capable of handling the large graphics character set.

(ii) Determining the number and sophistication of the local document manipulation facilities to be provided.

(iii) Reconciling the simple external document structures defined for the Teletex service with any more complex data structures provided internally for sophisticated document handling facilities.

(iv) Providing a human interface capable of controlling efficiently an environment of simultaneous document preparation, transmission, reception and printing.

(v) Designing a suitable software architecture to support all the above.

Special features built into this particular design include automatic, microprocessor controlled, call set-up procedures with "intelligent" interpretation of the network tones encountered. A clock is built into the terminal both to provide date and time stamping of events logged in a system file and to enable the transmission of documents to take place at pre-selected times.

In considering these issues, and bearing in mind the requirement for concurrent operations, it was recognised that the software environment provided by a real-time operating system offered many advantages including the ability to demonstrate ultimately the more advanced facilities which would become available as enhancements to the basic service. The bulk of the processing is performed by a single 16-bit microprocessor using a commercial real-time operating system to provide multitasking and file management.

Any terminal must allow for document preparation and in the workstation being described this is facilitated by the use of a keyboard, VDU, floppy disc stores and associated software. Although these are similar to those found in a conventional wordprocessor, all have been specifically developed to handle the full TTX set of graphics characters. After preparation, documents are stored in the terminal for either immediate or delayed transmission and two removable floppy discs (user discs) are provided for this purpose. A separate terminal store will also receive and hold, on a non-volatile medium, incoming documents for subsequent display and printing by the user. An important requirement of the service is that local mode operation should not be disturbed by incoming calls so that local message preparation, or any other facility which is offered by the chosen terminal in use, may continue independently. In a similar fashion the despatch of messages has also been made independent of local operation thus, once a document has been given a priority or time for sending, it is passed into a file and the operator may get on with the next job. Hitherto, not much has been made of the concurrency feature described above but we consider it to be a very attractive facility. In effect it provides electronic "in" and "out" trays which can automatically receive and send documents at any time without operator intervention. Furthermore, the documents may be examined on screen without printing and, if required, forwarded to another address for attention. Any such forwarding would be logged in the system file.

4. USERS INTERFACE

It should by now be clear that the workstation being described offers to the user a comprehensive and powerful set of facilities. Therefore, there is a great need to present these facilities to the user in such a manner that he can control and utilise them in the most efficient way (indeed it would be quite easy to present them so that no one but the most experienced could use them at all!) The level of efficiency attained will obviously depend upon the individual user's own skills and past experience; a wide range may be expected.

Menus have been used successfully on many systems but care must be taken in their design. It is generally agreed that a menu is a good method for naive or infrequent users to communicate with with a computer but can be irritatingly slow for experienced users. In order to overcome this, an over-ride facility has been provided so that experienced users can enter the commands they require in a concise form.

Because of the limitations of short term memory in humans, it is thought that people prefer completing several small individual tasks rather than one large complex task and this requirement may be met rather neatly by providing a series of short menus. Some recovery mechanism must be provided for dealing with input errors hence a "previous menu" key is provided which returns the user to the previous menu or cancels the previous directly entered command.

In general, all the menus are made up of three parts namely the verb or command area, the directory or document list area, and the command line. Two cursors have been provided, one for the verb and the other for the document, and they can be moved around by special keys provided for the purpose on the keyboard. The command line contains the name of the menu on the left hand side and the date and time on the right. This leaves a 42 character gap for commands or messages from the system.

As an example of the menu system provided the following brief description of just the Master Menu will serve as an indication of how the system is operated. The main menu in the system is the Master Menu from which all others are initiated. The Master Menu is slightly different from the others in that it has a fourth area which gives the user a limited amount of information about the work station. It tells the user which of the two user discs is the active one by highlighting and also records the names of the discs (which can be used for filing). The other line in this area tells the user how many documents

(i)   are on the active work disc,

(ii) have been received from other Teletex terminals,

(iii) are waiting to be printed,

(iv) are waiting to be transmitted to other Teletex terminals.

The grouping of the verbs in the command area has been arranged so that the word processing functions (Edit and Create) are adjacent, as are the communications functions (Transmit, Receive and Print).

The other functions are mainly for housekeeping and are in the middle of the command area.

The commands or verbs can work in one of three ways:

(i)   as verb plus object (eg "Transmit" "Doc 5");

(ii) as a verb plus input (eg "Create" "Doc 5");

(iii) as just a verb (eg (run) RIGHT DISC).

When a command which requires input is highlighted, a prompt is given to the user in the form of an extended length to the verb. This is intended to act as a positive indication to the user that the system expects something to be keyed in and also shows how many characters are allowed.

The experienced user can enter commands without making use of the command cursor, this is especially useful on the Master menu where there are 13 functions available. The command line is the top line of each menu and the space doubles as the message area which the work station uses to keep the user informed.

For those commands which require a document name, the user can either key in the name with the command or make use of the directory cursor. As a reminder of which command was keyed in, a marker is attached to the left hand side of the appropriate verb in the command area.

Whenever command line mode is active then naturally the user can make use of the backspace key to correct the input.

5.   SOFTWARE ARCHITECTURE

5.1 Operating System Environment

The software is organised as a number of jobs running under a real-time operating system, each job being a set of concurrently executing tasks. The operating system co-ordinates the running of the tasks and manages the environment of operating system objects which are manipulated by the tasks. To ease the development process the work station software is composed of a fixed number of tasks and operating system objects, there being no dynamic creation or deletion of tasks and objects after system initiallisation. Furthermore, job interactions have been restricted to message passing so that the work station is controlled by a set of loosely coupled message driven jobs.

5.2 Application Jobs

Figure 1 shows the component application jobs of the work station and their interaction paths.

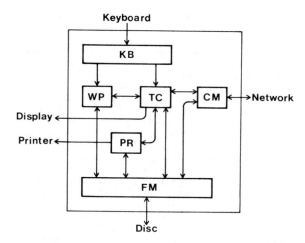

Figure 1 Component Software Jobs

User interaction with the terminal is managed by job TC using keyboard and screen. User commands are checked by TC and can result in control messages being sent to other application jobs to initiate or monitor background activities.

Word processing facilities are provided by job WP which is invoked from TC in response to a user request to create or edit a document. Either TC or WP is active at any one time, never both.

The communications facilities are managed by a number of tasks running within job CM. The functions of CM include scheduling document transmission according to the contents of the transmit queue and responding to status requests from TC. The job is composed of six concurrent tasks which interact by passing messages, actions within tasks being determined by state/message transition tables. Simple user messages and system primitives are interpreted by two (send and receive) front end tasks which then provide control messages to two corresponding Teletex protocol specific tasks. The Teletex high level procedures use the Teletex transport service to transfer the data in, or out, over the network.

Job FM provides document manipulation facilities for the other application jobs. Each document is stored on disc as a number of variable length pages and FM provides page-level services such as read-page(n), overwrite-page(n), insert-newpage(n), delete-page(n).

5.3 Diagnostic Facilities

The applications jobs all run as subordinates to a monitor job (MO not shown). The monitor job is responsible for creating the required environment of operating system objects and then firing up the application jobs. Development engineers can interact with MO via a separate "debug VDU" to monitor and diagnose the behaviour of the system at any time.

The specification of the environment (tasks and passive objects) to be created is held by MO in a number of local data structures. When the environment needs to be changed then only the contents of these data structures need be changed. Within limits these changes can be made interactively so that, for example, jobs can be fired up, suspended, resumed, killed and created as and when specified.

These debug facilities allow the prototype terminal to act also as a tester by observing the interactions between the layered communications software levels during the actual transmission and reception of documents.

6. HARDWARE

Within the space now left to me I would like to pay attention to just one item of hardware, the keyboard. Although it is not mandatory for a TTX keyboard to generate all of the 300 elements defined in the full character set, we in BTRL decided that we should demonstrate how that full set could be catered for on a keyboard which is not excessively larger than a conventional one.

There are three ways in which this may be achieved:

(i) the extra characters could be assigned to a separate key pad just to one side of the main keyboard layout,

(ii) the extra characters could be incorporated as new rows added to the main layout,

(iii) the extra characters could be overlayed onto the existing keys and accessed by different shift modes.

The first method was rejected because the wordprocessing function of a work station would need several keys of its own and would probably be assigned to the separate key pad. Also, the cursor control keys for the Menu part of the work station could be assigned to a small key pad at the side of the main layout. The second method is feasible but the number of extra characters that are specified would mean that more than one row would have to be added making the keyboard unacceptably deep. The third method was therefore adopted as being the most practical and the keyboard was designed with four modes of operation ie one unshifted mode and three shifted modes.

The following assumptions were made in the design. Firstly, although the positions of alphas and numerals on conventional keyboards are standardised, the symbols on the right hand side are not. These symbols can therefore be joined with the remainder of the Teletex character set when the content of the various overlays are considered but the typist would have to "hunt and peck" for them. Secondly, it was thought unacceptable to force the operation of a shift key whenever a diacritical mark was required but, at the same time, it was considered quite acceptable to hunt and peck for non-English alphabetic characters such as D. Therefore the main criteria used in the design of the keyboard can be summarised as follows:

(i) a typist must be allowed to touch-type on the alphas which implies the provision of a conventional alpha layout,

(ii) the keyboard must be easy to use when typing in any one of a range of foreign languages,

(iii) the keyboard must not be too big,

(iv) the number of key depressions necessary for a word ought to be kept to a minimum,

(v) complex keying operations such as holding down two shift modes and then striking a character, ie three simultaneous depressions, must not be required.

To achieve these design criteria two shift modes have been adopted in addition to the conventional "Capitals Shift" action. They have been arranged to facilitate the typing of the English language in a conventional manner with the simple addition of diacritical marks and supplementary characters as independent shifts. With four modes of operation allowed, some of the keys could produce four different characters. A keycap can show clearly only two characters on its top face and, as the capital of an alphabetic on a keycap has always implied the lower case of the character as well, this leaves just one of the sumbols to be assigned. The only place where this fourth symbol could possibly go without any loss of clarity would be on the front face of the keycap. This arrangement would make it essential that the characters on the keycaps be colour coded according to which of the shifted modes were current. The effect of light colour on a dark background was the most satisfactory for this purpose.

One other feature of the keyboard is the provision of coloured LED's to indicate to the user when the keyboard is locked into one of its shifted modes. The keyboard without the WP and cursor control pads is shown in Fig 2. The Modes of Operation are

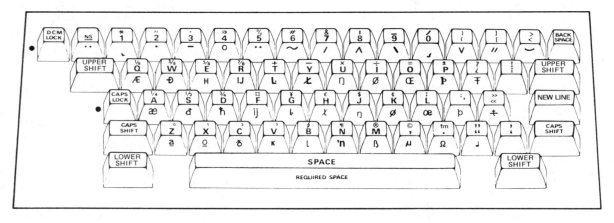

Figure 2   BTRL Teletex Keyboard
(shown without auxiliary keypads)

416

A. Unshifted mode giving:-

    (i)   lower case alphas

    (ii) numerals

    (iii) punctuation marks , . and '

    (iv) non-spacing underline

B. Upper Case Mode (CAPS SHIFT operated)

As (A) except that uppercase alphas are substituted for lower case versions.

C. Symbol Mode (SYMBOL SHIFT operated)

This is non-locking and makes the following characters available.

    Top Row   —   the symbols which normally appear above the numerals eg * " ' etc

    Other Rows — all other symbols excluding the diacritical marks.

D. Supplementary Character and Diacritical Mark Mode

Used as single shift this gives the diacritical marks and all the alphabetic characters that are not English. This shift is fitted with a lock which operates only on the top row so making available the diacritical marks to the unshifted and CAPS SHIFT mode. Thus words such as péché, would be keyed in directly as p´ech´e.

7. CONCLUSION

Teletex terminals may appear to the customer in a number of forms, each compatible with the basic service but offering different levels of enhancement. The workstation described here is towards the top end of that range and could form the basis of an international "Electronic Office" by virtue of offering WP, filing, in and out tray, multiple languages etc all backed by automatic communications. With proposals now being made to include graphics and converge with DP the future for Teletex looks most interesting.

8. ACKNOWLEDGEMENTS

I take this opportunity to recognise the number of original contributions from my team which, from pressure on space, have been condensed into this one Paper. Acknowledgement is also made to the Director of Research British Telecom Research Laboratories for permission to publish this paper.

Since Mr A H Ithell first entered Research Dept. as an apprentice he has worked in various fields and is now Deputy Director. He obtained his first degree in Engineering at London University and is a Corporate Member of both IEE and I.Mech.E.

Dateline 1985 – a User's Experience with Teletex

G Taylor
Langton Information Systems, UK

During the period 1982 to 1985, teletex services will be introduced in most of Western Europe carried by a number of networks. This will be the critical time for the service. Any disharmonies and limitations in the standards and their implementations will be evident. Rival systems for text interchange and electronic mail will be available. Some mixed private networking will be needed until the service is generally available. This paper will describe experiences in becoming a teletex user of this period.

1. INTRODUCTION

During the period 1982 to 1985, teletex services will be introduced in most of Western Europe, carried by a number of networks. This will be the critical period for the development of this service since in this period the service must establish itself amongst a host of competing systems including various electronic mail systems and the existing telex network. The factors which will affect the market share between the various systems are cost (capital cost of equipment and running costs); the size of the market itself and functionality of the service. However, it must be borne in mind that this is a public service and as such is subject to the strengths and weaknesses of any public service.

This paper describes the experiences of a user of the service in the period 1982-1985. The circumstances are true and based on the author's personal experiences as manager of a project funded by the Commission of the European Communities which investigated the likely nature and status of teletex over the next few years.

2. THE TELETEX PROJECT

The project to investigate teletex was performed by a consortium of systems houses of which Langton was the prime contractor. The other systems houses were located in France, Belgium, Germany, Sweden and two others in Great Britain. The task set was relatively straightforward and consisted of an investigation into the teletex standard itself; research among the PTTs of the member states of the EEC plus Sweden and Switzerland; research among manufacturers and potential manufacturers of teletex equipment; together with a number of smaller tasks. The deliverable from the project was to be a major report which would form the basis for public dissemination of information on teletex in Europe.

The project timescales were fairly tight. In order to meet the deadlines it was important to be able to schedule interviews carefully, draft the results and send them to London for integration into the final draft. Whereas some sections of the report were written by a single company, others, particularly those containing the research, were built from the investigations of the team into the various PTTs. This meant that each section had to be re-edited in London and the combined copy sent back to the consortium partners to agree a common text. The report itself (25 copies) was then produced and bound in London and shipped to Brussels.

The working language was English so that more than half of the project team were working in a foreign language. Although their standard of English was very high, the joint sections did not read smoothly. A second editing process to deal with this problem was performed once the text was established as factually correct.

Towards the end of the project, during the proof reading of the final report, several of the people who had been interviewed volunteered additional information. Although the team made every effort to incorporate these changes some could not be put into the report.

3. DIFFICULTIES EXPERIENCED DURING THE PROJECT

The major problems experienced by the team during the project were all due to our need to cycle papers amongst ourselves (the multisite drafting problem). Delays to this process were caused by:

- incompatible word processors;
- time taken to make copies of drafts;
- time taken by the postal service;
- documents 'lost in the post';
- Christmas.

The first problem resulted in a lot of rekeying and hence wasted effort and time. Since the consortium was specially set up for this project, rather than as a permanent institution, it was not thought practical for each company to invest in a new word-processor. We expected to run other

FIG. 1

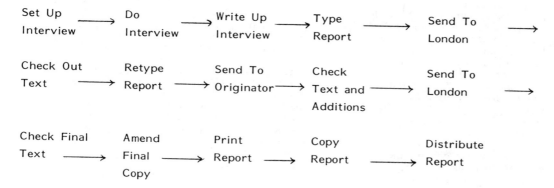

projects with different consortia, so a general solution along these lines was not practical. Given the information circuit for this project the amount of rekeying is very high indeed. A simplified version of the circuit is shown in Fig. 1.

Copying the report was a second problem. Drafts and intermediate reports needed to be turned round to the consortium members fairly quickly. Interim and final reports – 25 copies – had to be copied, bound and transported to the Commission in Brussels. Our copiers were less than perfect and the automatically collated copies had to be checked for shuffling, tilted image and missing pages. It takes a long time to check twenty five copies of a 200 page report for miscollation.

Posting reports around Europe is a risky process. Several documents went astray. At least, the sender claimed to have posted a document which never arrived. I decided that our 'session level protocol' was inadequate and consequently it was agreed that either a telephone call or a telex would be sent to London or from London whenever a document was put in the post.

This at least gave us a retry procedure but only with at least a week's delay. Eventually we switched to air couriers.

Christmas was a problem we had not expected. Not only did the postal service slow down but we were also faced with holidays. It is arguable that New Year's Eve is a bad time to complete projects; but it fits perfectly into the Commission's financial year which is the same as the Calendar Year.

4. REQUIREMENTS FOR A CONSORTIUM INFORMATION SYSTEM

Several new consortium projects were started in 1982 each using a different consortium. We decided very early in that year to improve the information system of the consortium. Indeed, we felt that we could hardly convince others of our commitment to information technology without using it ourselves. The requirements followed directly from the problems of the teletex project:

- the system must get over the problem of incompatible word processors.

- it must eliminate the paper transfer; that it must cut out the copying and the posting.

- it must ensure delivery of documents.

- it must work in unattended mode.

The first requirement was crucial. Either we could build a telecommunications link using a 'black-box' which would change the coding of one or other of the word processors and so build compatibility, or we could find a standard and migrate towards it. We had already rejected the idea of imposing a buying policy on the consortium partners as impractical.

We also rejected the idea of posting floppy disks to each other since incompatibilities in disk formats were a worse problem than setting up the telecommunications link.

You will remember that in 1982 a general 'black-box' which would convert any word processor's text to any other word processor's text was not available; and many pundits claimed that the problem would not be solved in the near future.

The natural standard for us to think of was Teletex.

We knew that the teletex service would eliminate the paper transfer and the copying, would guarantee delivery of the documents and would operate in unattended mode. Teletex had the added advantage that as a public service it would be easy to set up extra links whenever a new consortium partner came along.

There were, however, one or two problems with choosing teletex. Firstly, the system was in its infancy. A few national services were starting but we expected that full coverage would take some time to achieve. It is only now, in 1985, that something like a reasonable coverage of Europe exists.

The second problem concerned the diagrams in the reports. The teletex standards cover the character sets in almost all Latin based alphabets. (Esperanto, Latvian and Lithuanian being the exceptions) but they do not cover graphic symbols. Even in 1982, enhancements to the standards to include a provision for graphics were being considered. The French thought this was an essential component of the standard and should be implemented fairly rapidly. We are just starting to see the results of this extra standardisation work.

5. THE INITIAL NETWORK

The first step was to convince consortium partners that they should have a Teletex terminal and connection. Teletex terminals were costing from £5,000 each and this sum could not be justified in terms of the consortium projects alone. Accordingly we decided to try for agreement on a terminal which had good word processing capability and would interface to the telex network.

In this way the teletex terminal would become a fundamental office automation device. The smaller companies (British) found it relatively easy to integrate teletex into their buying policy. Our Continental partners were large companies who were tied into many other contracts. Being large they could more easily afford the device but were not able to make the policy decision to standardise on an untried technology.

Investigations with the relevant PTTs had shown some discrepancies in the intended services and one PTT was not considering introducing its service until 1984. We were therefore faced with the problem that even if we had the terminals they could not be used.

The initial solution was to invest in the terminals and connect them with a private network. We had already done some work on connecting teletex terminals back-to-back directly and using a telephone line for compatibility testing. The terminals were already in existence and we had some experience with them. The larger companies agreed to acquire a single machine for test purposes. The smaller companies made an act of faith.

Towards the end of 1982 the consortium was able to send out an invitation to tender for the equipment. The main points of the specification were:

- full word processing.
- implementation of the CCITT teletex standard.
- telecommunications interface using public switched telephone network (PSTN).
- enhanced character set giving some graphics capability and the printer to produce hard copy.

Using the replies to the request for tender and our experience with teletex equipment we found that:

- No British company had a production machine although several were about to have such machines.
- At least three different PSTN connection standards were proposed.
- Each implementation was not quite standard and so a single choice of manufacturer had to be made.

On the last point it is interesting to note that the Swedish PTT had felt it necessary to add to the standard in their request for machinery. The additional characters which they asked to be added to the basic character set included a full Greek alphabet and 'box elements'. The box elements included vertical and horizontal rules together with corners. These allowed the construction of tables and certain other line diagrams which was a decided advantage.

In 1983, the equipment was installed (See Fig. 2).

FIG. 2

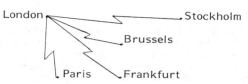

6. EXPERIENCE WITH THE INITIAL NETWORK

The international telephone system in North Western Europe is very good and the network worked well except at peak times when lines were crossed or jammed. Using the PSTN system had limitations in that the machines had to be attended at all times. The software did not include autodialout so that each call was preceded by a telephone call. This ensured that the receiving terminal was ready and alerted consortium members that a document was on its way. Difficulties did occur with projects run over greater distances. The telephone system in Greece was not developed to take teletex traffic and trunk lines to Greece were often engaged. This led to delays with document transfer compared with transfer around North Europe. However, it was still very much faster than either post or an air-courier. It did indicate to us that for projects requiring a wider geographic span, especially with developing or third world countries, we would need a better system.

The single supplier policy necessary for the initial network and agreed to by the original consortium would not work in general. Companies wanted to buy more advanced terminals, terminals manufactured locally and those with the best local support. Any network with a mixture of terminals would need the standard to be applied rigorously. At the time, the end of 1983, there was still no standard test rig which could be used to verify the implementation of the standard. It was therefore essential to enforce the single machine network until such a test centre was ready.

As soon as the public teletex system started in each country it was hoped to transfer the work onto it progressively. Unfortunately the PSTN connection we were using could only be connected to a single country's system. The temporary solution adopted was to have dual connectivity – one form for private use and the other for the public system. This not only resulted in a complicated system of hardware and software – a veritable lash-up – but also increased deviation from the standard. Since other companies were also suffering the same difficulties, a number of products appeared each promising to solve the problem. The public teletex system integrated telex traffic within a single service. Throughout 1983 and 1984 the telex back-up proved invaluable. We even developed software which allowed limited reformatting of input telexes so that an intelligent word processing operator could produce decent copy from them, even if rather slowly.

We were still sending most diagrams by other means. Some were posted and some sent by facsimile. We had been experimenting with integrating a facsimile machine with the teletex kit and transmitting a page as a set of coded characters. This was a distinctly non standard approach but it did work. It was very slow. Full integration of diagrams would, of course mean new equipment with a bit-mapped screen, but these were now reasonably cheap. Our original printer would do the job but several manufacturers were having to improve their printer technology.

7. THE NEW NETWORK

By late 1984, the problems being experienced in the initial network were capable of solution. New invitations to tender were sent out separately by members of the consortium. It was expected that each would choose a different machine reflecting the greater choice available and the increased standardisation. The emphasis in the request was now :

- the terminal must be capable of connection to the publicly available networks.
- the terminal must have been certified by the European Teletex Terminal Test Centre.
- the screen must be of graphics quality (black and white only) and the printer must be able to give a high quality copy of a screen image.
- the terminal must connect to local area networks and private branch exchanges.
- the terminal must be capable of composing and modifying documents including text and diagrams.

The requirement was for a terminal which integrated text and graphics using the new CCITT standard agreed in 1984. The adherence to the new standard had to be assured by reference to the European Teletex Terminal Test Centre, but this was not fully operational. The other notable feature was the requirement for local area network connection. We could have had this in the first network but the larger companies had preferred to keep the terminal separate from the rest of their equipment. By 1984 the situation had changed radically and those companies were now seeking to integrate teletex into their internal systems. For some companies their system was built using a true local area network and for others by means of a teletex extension attached to a private telephone exchange.

We were heavily in favour of using the public system since most of the countries involved in the projects had introduced them. However some private networking was still going to be needed for full coverage (See Fig. 3)

8. THE CURRENT SITUATION – 1985

The second network is now implemented and running. The public networks have been harmonised by the PTTs so there is no fundamental incompatibility problem at the transport level. We have learned to work around the other limitations.

DIAGRAM 3

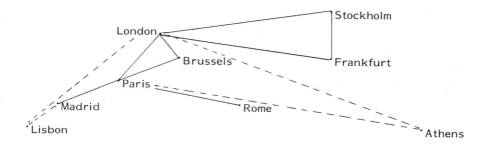

_____ Public Teletex Links
- - - - - Private Teletex Links
SECOND NETWORK

Since the text version of teletex has been running for three years it gives us no real problem, but we have still not yet sorted out all the problems of graphics. There is still not a rigid adherence to the standard caused both by holes in the standard itself and by the lack of certifying test beds.

Local area network connections give some problems especially as the software for session and presentation protocols are not yet fully stabilised. The difficulties will disappear when all the terminals involved are teletex compatible so that the local area network connection problem is then merely a transport one.

Our main desire, at the moment, is to convert all our private teletex attachments to public ones as soon as the standard reaches each country. We expect it to be worldwide Standard, with a capital S, by 1990.

9. CONCLUSIONS

The two networks implemented in 1983 and 1985 have given great advantages over the previous document transfer systems used by our consortium. Development of terminal facilities and functions continue, so that we prefer leasing to buying. In a developing market which has not yet answered all our needs, it is important to be able to upgrade regularly. The PTTs have introduced services and are being persuaded to improve harmonisation - or at least provide a buffer against disharmony. The standard is being developed without changing the initial basic standard. This will enable us to pick-and-mix without becoming non-standard. We have not yet found a good reason for utilising the videotex component of teletex but our clients have shown great interest in it.

We believe that the Test Centre has improved the adherence to the standard but this has only been possible because of user pressure (See Fig. 4).

The Commission of the European Communities has been a prime mover in ensuring that user needs are answered by PTTs and manufacturers. We hope that they will ensure the completeness of the Test Centre procedure.

By 1990 we will use teletex with as little difficulty and incompatibility as we used the telephone in 1982. It fills such a real business need that it cannot be allowed to fail.

FIG. 4

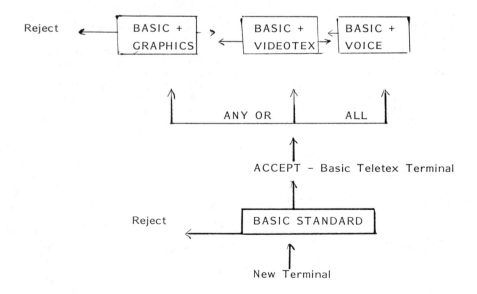

European Teletex Test Centre Procedure

Graham Taylor is a graduate of Oxford University and was a Ferranti prize winner in the British Computer Society examinations in 1975. After some years with Burroughs he joined the Civil Service in 1973 as lecturer in computing and acted as a consultant to a number of departments. Since 1978 he has been a consultant with Langton Information Systems Ltd and has specialised in establishing user requirements, database systems and Government Information Systems. In 1981 he managed a team which produced a major report on the future of Teletex for the Commission of the European Communities and is now project manager of the team which is investigating the needs of the European Community Institutions for IT.

STELLA – Satellite Interconnection of Local Area Networks: Present State and Future Trends

N Celandroni, E Ferro, L Lenzini
CNUCE-Institute, Italy
B M Segal, K S Olofsson
European Organization for Nuclear
Research, Switzerland

STELLA (Satellite Transmission Experiment Linking LAboratories) is the first operational European wide-band data transmission experiment. The STELLA project is first described. The environment in which the STELLA project operates and the institutes collaborating in the project are presented. The hardware and software employed is then illustrated. The major results obtained from the experiment are commented. The more important design characteristics of an improved version of STELLA are emphasized. Collaboration between STELLA and UNIVERSE projects in the framework of COST-11Bis is then outlined.

1. INTRODUCTION

In western Europe, there are approximately 2,000 high energy physicists working in about 100 different centers. Experiments are normally conducted at CERN in Geneva, in collaborations between several Universities, and the heavy computing effort frequently necessary is made particularly difficult by the absence of a fast data transmission service between CERN and centers in different countries. This leads to much travelling, duplication of data and programs, and delay in the communication of the results of data analyses. Consequently, CERN and four major European high energy physics Institutions, INFN (Pisa) in Italy, Saclay in France, Rutherford Appleton Laboratory (RAL) in the U.K. and Desy in the Federal Republic of Germany, were immediately interested in a suggestion by the European Space Agency (ESA) to utilize the Orbital Test Satellite (OTS) to provide an experimental high speed service (approx. 1Mbps) to transmit large quantities of data between small stand-alone computers at CERN and the other 4 centers. This project is named STELLA (Satellite Transmission Experiment Linking LAboratories). By the end of 1979 the University College (UC) of Dublin (EIRE) and the Technical University (TU) of Graz (Austria) had also joined the experiment; they are mainly involved in the area of measurements related to the satellite data channel. By the end of 1980 another INFN section, located in Frascati (near Rome) joined STELLA and during 1981 the Joint Research Center (EURATOM) located in Ispra (near Milan) joined the experiment too. Because of financial problems the joint Research Center gave up the idea of installing an antenna and decided to get connected with CNUCE through an X.25 virtual circuit provided by a Public Data Network. On the other hand, the French PTT refused to give permission for Saclay participa-

tion in STELLA. The nature of STELLA leads naturally to three interest groups among the participants: those primarily concerned with the earth stations and the space segment (PTTs, ESA, UC Dublin, TU Graz), those responsible for the informatics aspects (CERN, CNUCE, RAL), and the high energy physicists, who are attached in various ways to CERN and the national laboratories. These groups have taken on responsibility for different aspects of the STELLA program.

2. SYSTEM CONFIGURATION

The main components at each STELLA site are shown in Figure 2.1. Details about each component can be found in [1]. In the rest of the paragraph emphasis will be put on LDC and CIM.

2.1 Link Driving Computer

There is one LDC in each laboratory (or computing center) participating in the STELLA experiment. The basic function of the LDC is to provide communication between user programs (from now on called Applications), by means of a very simple end-to-end protocol. In the present version of STELLA, each LDC runs only one Application specialized for bulk tape/disk file transfers. There is therefore no routing problem towards the Application, even if Application identification is required because different Applications can run at different times. The LDCs used in STELLA are shown in Table 2.1. Link Driving Computers at each installation are connected to the earth station via the Communication Interface Module. During present STELLA operation, one station is master, and this transmits its bulk data to one (or more) slave station(s) which ACK/NAK the blocks received according to a simple unbalanced protocol. The fixed TDMA scheme used for satellite access is controlled by the CIM. The choice of master station is made before each run; it is not dynamic. Each station is allocated one fixed transmission window relative to the operating cycle (typically 75 msec.) and may transmit only one HDLC frame in each window. The master performs the bulk data transmission, and is allocated most of the bandwidth (e.g. 40 msec.); the slave(s) divide the rest.

2.2 Communications Interface Module

The CIM is a full-duplex data communication interface between the LDC and its earth station. It provides standard CCITT signals to the modem, and offers automatic serialization/deserialization, HDLC framing/deframing, bit insertion/deletion, CRC generation/ checking the data blocks for transmitted or received, and offers status information for error recovery. It also provides selective reception based on HDLC address byte and full timing functions for the TDMA satellite link access scheme.

		**	LDC	LDC Software
CERN	operating	GEC 4080	O.K.
CNUCE	operating	PDP 11/70	O.K.
RAL	operating	GEC 4080	O.K.
DESY	operating	AEG 8060	adapted CERN version
DUBLIN	installed	PDP 11/45	have got CNUCE version
GRAZ	operating	PDP 11/44	have got CNUCE version
INFN Fra-scati	*	PDP 11/34	have got CNUCE version

* The RF/System and Modem/Codec are those used by ESRIN in the framework of the SPINE project
** Antenna RF/system, Modem/Codec and CIM

Table 2.1

The CIM contains a Motorola M6800 microprocessor, and two LSI special-purpose chips for the HDLC function (SMC COM5025 Synchronous Receiver-Transmitters). CIM circuitry provides a 16-bit wide full-duplex interface to the LDC PIO (Programmed Input-Output) channel, used for exchange of control/status information, and two high-speed parallel channels connecting the LDC DMA interface to the COM chips via a FIFO (First-In-First-Out) buffer of 32 bytes, to carry the data flow (see Figure 2.2). The microprocessor

connects itself to the data channels only to control the setup of block transfers and to retrieve status information, but is isolated during the transfers. All microprocessor software (5 Kbytes) normally resides in EPROM. The Timer section has two operating modes in a slave station: 'Starting Mode' and 'Running Mode', while the master station is always in Running Mode. A slave station is in Starting Mode after initialization, and waits for transmitted bursts from the master station to synchronize its Timer basic cycle to them. Master burst content is irrelevant to the CIM, provided that the first byte (HDLC Address Byte) has a correct address and the burst length is within the expected limits. Once synchronized, the CIM enters Running Mode and keeps track of any small phase drift between the master's data bursts and its own Timer basic cycle, updating the latter to keep precisely synchronized with the master. This 'tuning' is done by software; if it should fail, the CIM returns to Starting Mode. Until it is in running mode, a slave station in inhibited from transmitting.

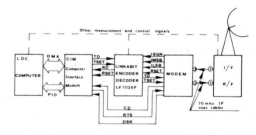

FIG 2.1 Equipment block diagram

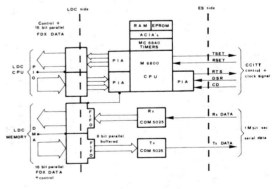

FIG 2.2 STELLA CIM Communication Interface Module

3. LDC SOFTWARE AND SERVICES

The STELLA LDC software was designed to be portable between all types of LDC's in the project. It comprises:

- a set of 7 cooperating asynchronous processes written as independent modules in the BCPL high-level programming language;
- a set of system primitives to imple-

ment the environment for the process modules, providing inter-process communication, resource sharing semaphores, buffer management and I/O functions. These are in BCPL, or BCPL-callable library routines.

In principle the modules are machine-independent, and are ported to each LDC by simply installing BCPL on that LDC; the environment is of course machine-dependent, and its mapping onto each LDC involves detailed knowledge of the LDC operating system. The latter required much more effort on the PDP-11 and Nord-10 machines than on the GEC or AEG machines whose operating systems already contained most of the necessary primitives; in general 1-3 man-months were needed to port the environment to a system already running BCPL. The STELLA experience has shown that porting of such a system is perfectly practical using the above scheme, but in order to guarantee functional equivalence of the various LDC versions, the interface between modules and environment must be scrupulously defined and adhered to.

4. OPERATIONS

After an initial period of technical tests, operation of the system for transmission of physicists' tapes between CERN, RAL and CNUCE started in the Autumn of 1980, and has continued in a more or less regular way since then. Some 500 tapes in total have been sent so far, for six physics groups and a few individuals. The rate of transmission was 4-5 1600 bpi tapes per hour when the system was set up and running smoothly, which is the design rate. The set-up time could however be very variable, since system changes and new features were added during the year, and there were problems of organization of operators at some sites and of pre-run communications. The time scheduled on OTS started with one three-hour run every other day at the start, building up during 1980 to two two-hour runs and then two three-hour runs later in 1981. Runs were very occasionally made at weekend time; once 40 tapes were sent to CNUCE in an overnight session with physicist operators. Technically, when the systems at either end of a link were working correctly, the tapes were transmitted smoothly, with typically 1-10 block retransmissions per tape, each taking only about one second. The average throughput thus corresponded to the specifications. The error detection and recovery mechanisms worked as planned: no cases occured of received tapes later found to contain errors which could not be traced definitely to other causes such as user failure to add end of tape marks or out of adjustment tape units. A further development at CERN, made at the request of the Swiss PTT and with their own resources, was to design and build two interfaces

to the standard PTT 2.048 Mbps PCM transmission system, for connection to the LDC and to the earth station. These interfaces, after a period of testing, allowed a demonstration that the earth station could be run at a distance from the LDC, after which the PTT transferred the station to their Intelsat site at Leuk, 180 km. away in the Valais, in December 1981, where it has since been running without special problems.

Measurement results of the STELLA system can be found in [2].

5. FUTURE TRENDS

The aims of STELLA as designed and now implemented were to try out in practice a potentially useful Application of satellite data transmission using small earth stations, in the simplest and most economical way. The resulting design was limited to the transfer of big files stored on magnetic tapes or disks, using simple but appropriate transmission protocols. It was clear to everyone after the project was well under way that many of its limitations could be removed, and that it could be extended to handle a variety of Applications, as well as allowing testing of more complex protocols which could be relevant to future public systems. In addition, a new technical element appeared in the form of high-speed Local Area Networks (LANs) in several of the laboratories, with the result that the natural use of a satellite broadcasting channel would be to interconnect such LANs, rather than individual computers. The studies in 1980 evolved, therefore, towards a design for upgrading STELLA whose aims are:

- to function simultaneously both as a transit network with attached internetwork gateways and as a network per se supporting directly Applications of differing capabilities and requirements;
- to accomodate packets with a wide range of lengths, allowing a short packet containing a message with a small number of characters to coexist efficiently with a packet containing a long message or perhaps several host-multiplexed messages;
- to evaluate the impact of satellite technology on the Open Systems Interconnection/Reference Model both from the services and protocol viewpoints;
- to demonstrate the feasibility of a so-called Remote Control Room; i.e. by extending CERN's existing LAN (CERNET) via a satellite broadcasting channel into the remote physics institutes, to allow physicists there the same access to a CERN physics experiment as they have via CERNET at CERN,
- to implement the improvements so as to allow practical use and operation-

al testing by:
. high energy physicists in several laboratories;
. those interested in system and protocol design.

For the rest of the paper, the STELLA version presently running will be referred to as STELLA/I and the improved version as STELLA/II.

5.1 STELLA/II Architecture

The STELLA/II architecture has already been specified [3]. It reflects the current understanding of the architectural aspects of the Network Layer, as defined in the Reference model for Open Systems Interconnection. The STELLA architecture was designed to accomodate a diverse assortment of underlying subnetworks (X.25, Satellite and Local Area Network subnetworks) according to the "Local Network Independence" principle [4].

The STELLA/II architecture includes the interconnection of subnetworks via Network Layer relays (also referred to as internet gateways). Two types of gateways are distinguished:

- Inter Subnetwork Gateways which are placed between subnetworks to perform the necessary adaptations;
- End-System Gateways which are placed between (End-System) transport entities and subnetwork(s). End-System Gateways mask for the transport entities in End-Systems the existence of the individual subnetwork and Inter Subnetwork Gateways

In the rest of the paragraph the major design characteristics of STELLA/II are outlined.

A) TDMA Scheme for STELLA/II

For STELLA/II, it was decided to generalize the original fixed-TDMA unbalanced satellite access protocol [1] to a dynamic-TDMA symmetrical scheme [6] as proposed for the UK UNIVERSE project 5]. This represents a more flexible and efficient test-bed for research into protocols related to layers on top of the Network Layer. There are two principal extensions involved: the dynamic allocation of transmission windows for all stations (mediated by one master station, which also provides reference synchronization as in STELLA/I), and the ability to pack multiple HDLC frames into a single window, with a different address possible on a frame-by-frame basis. The dynamic window allocation is received in the master burst by each station, and is immediately activated in each CIM for the current and later cycles, until a new allocation arrives. This was implemented easily in the CIM by invoking the programmable timer features already incorporated. The typical operating cycle of STELLA/II is

as shown in Figure 5.1; a Reference burst (transmitted by the master) begins the cycle, containing allocations for the succeeding cycle(s). A small fixed data window is then allocated permanently to each station for control and special purposes. (Provision has also been made to combine these small windows into one for which all stations must contend). Finally a large data window may be allocated dynamically to each station, in which multiple HDLC frames may be put; the reference and small-data windows are by convention limited to a single HDLC frame each. All stations, including the master, adjust allocations simultaneously upon (correct) reception of each master burst; in case of a missed or bad master burst, the station is inhibited by the CIM from any transmission in the current cycle, to avoid possible allocation clashes. The multiple frames/burst feature required hardware modifications to each STELLA/I CIM. The major work in going to the newer TDMA scheme was, however, not the hardware redesign, but a considerable amount of LDC and CIM reprogramming to deal with this more complex and intensive burst and frame traffic.

B) Network Layer Structure for STELLA/II

Current work within ECMA, NBS, and ISO defines, for the purpose of interconnecting subnetworks, a sublayering within the ·Network Layer. The STELLA/II architecture includes only the internetwork sublayer, which is referred to, within ECMA, as sublayer 3c [7]. Figure 5.2 illustrates the layering for communication over two LAN subnetworks. Layers 1, 2 and sublayer 3a are subnetwork specific and exist to implement the different subnetwork access protocols. CERNET [8], and INET [9] are the LANs (subnetworks of the Global Network) considered within STELLA/II. Connectionless is the type of service available to sublayer 3c for internetworking. In addition, sublayer 3c provides to the transport layer a connectionless type of service. The STELLA/II internet protocol implemented in sublayer 3c is adaptable to fit features or special needs not originally foreseen. The internet protocol is also such that features not actually used in a particular case do not add to the amount of data-unit overhead in terms of processing and of internet control information [3]. The internet protocol features are managed by the "Optional Control Functions" module (see Figure 5.5 and 5.6). The transport protocols envisaged for layer 4 are CERNET [10]; STELLA/I [1] and ISO [11].

C) Gateway Structure

In STELLA/II each subnetwork can implement its gateway on a fully owned and controlled machine, or even as additional code on an existing End-System. Gateways can be connected together (see Figure 5.3) via the broadcasting satellite channel provided by OTS or by means of an X.25 Virtual Circuit provided by EURONET (see Figure 5.4). The internal structure of an Inter Subnetwork Gateway (Figure 5.5) closely resembles that of an End-System Gateway (Figure 5.6).

D) Protocol Headers and Addressing

A protocol header structure like that illustrated in Figure 5.7 is used in STELLA/II. The Subnetwork-Access-Protocol Headers (from now on called Local Header (LH)) would be added as the message enters each subnetwork, and stripped off as it leaves. These functions are carried out by the "Subnetwork Embedder" and "Subnetwork Stripper" respectively (Figures 5.5 and 5.6). The Internet Protocol Header (IPH) would be added when the message enters the Global Network, and stripped off when it leaves. These functions are carried out by the "Internet Embedder" and "Internet Stripper" respectively (Figures 5.5 and 5.6). The Transport and higher level protocol headers would be truly end-to-end, in fact they are added at source and stripped off at the ultimate destination, without any intermediate operations. This layered protocol header structure complies fully with the local net independence principle because no changes at all are required in subnetwork addressing and routing strategies. Subnetworks are completely unaware that they are carrying internet traffic. The IPH, in STELLA/II, includes a two level internet address of the form <subnet, local address>. These internet addresses are operated on by sublayer 3c functions and are carried "over the top of" each subnetwork involved (encoded as data for the subnetwork's network-access-protocol) (see Figure 5.2).

E) Routing

On each subnetwork, gateways are given addresses consistent with the addressing conventions of the subnetwork they are attached to. Each gateway contains a Routing Table to perform internet routing. Within STELLA/II, routing is provided by fixed table lookup.

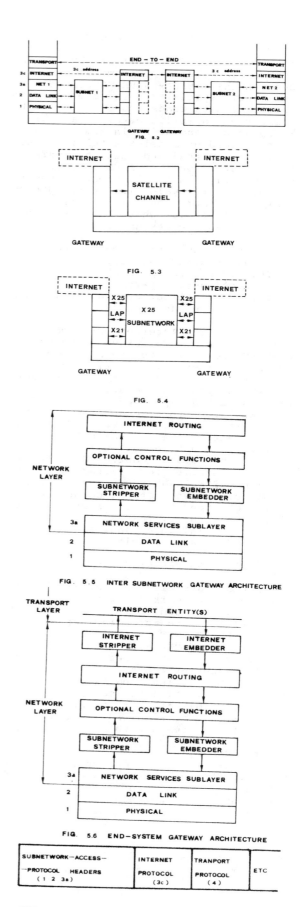

FIG. 5.2

FIG. 5.3

FIG. 5.4

FIG. 5.5 INTER SUBNETWORK GATEWAY ARCHITECTURE

FIG. 5.6 END-SYSTEM GATEWAY ARCHITECTURE

SUBNETWORK—ACCESS— —PROTOCOL HEADERS (1 2 3a)	INTERNET PROTOCOL (3c)	TRANPORT PROTOCOL (4)	ETC

FIG. 5.7 LAYERED PROTOCOL HEADER STRUCTURE

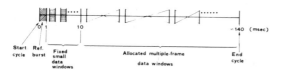

Fig. 5.1 STELLA II Operating cycle

429

6. STELLA-UNIVERSE COLLABORATION

In the second half of 1981 the COST-11bis management promoted meetings between the STELLA-UNIVERSE communities and other specialists in the area of satellite data transmission in order to discuss possibilities of a wider European collaboration in some projects in the field of satellite teleinformatics. It was realised that the work on STELLA and on UNIVERSE overlapped considerably, and could produce results of more general value if the two groups worked together with this in mind. The particular topic which looked most suitable was the design of:

a) a common channel access scheme to allow sharing of satellite time. This is already a reality, as shown in section 5.1, part A.
b) a common Internet Protocol which has already been defined [12].

With a common Internet Protocol, it will be feasible to extend some of the UNIVERSE experiments to CERN and to CNUCE by installing small Cambridge Rings [13] on their sites. This would allow independent comparisons of the Ring and a high speed packet net and of the satellite interconnections in the three laboratories in very different environments. A common Internet Protocol would also allow experimentation of the Remote Control Room Application, conceived for STELLA/II, in the combined STELLA-UNIVERSE environment. It was also seen that the connection of such high speed LANs via X.25 networks should be tested. This is feasible by using the INET interconnection to the CNUCE LDC located in Pisa.

7. OPERATIONAL PLANNING

It seems possible and desirable to carry out the work in two phases: the first would be limited to using the OTS broadcasting channel for connection between the CERNET users in CERN and on small stubs of CERNET installed in the Pisa area, Frascati area, and possibly at RAL. The interconnection of INET to STELLA, by using an X.25 virtual circuit, will also be carried out in parallel. This first phase program has the advantage of allowing a quick start of practical tests both of the system and of a limited form of the Remote Control Room, while the more refined system is still being developed. In the second phase, which can be carried out at the end of the first one, the interconnection between STELLA/II and UNIVERSE will be experimented.

Acknowledgements

The STELLA project has necessitated the collaboration of many people. The authors would like to thank everybody involved for their assistance, in particular Prof. G. Pierazzini (INFN-Pisa), Dr J. Burren (RAL), and Dr M.G.N. Hine (CERN), as well as the Directors of the Laboratories concerned, of the European Space Agency, and of the Commission of the European Community who provided resources and much help in setting up the experiment. Particular thanks are to be given to C.J. Adams (RAL) and B.W. Evershed (CERN) for their major contributions respectively in the area of channel access schemes and in that of measurements.

References:

[1] A.B.Bonito, N.Celandroni, E.Ferro, L.Lenzini, E.Perotto, B.M.Segal, K.S.Olofsson, C.J.Adams, STELLA: Status and Trends, Fifteenth Hawaii International Conference on System Sciences 1982 (Volume I), Honolulu, Hawaii, January, 6-8, 1982.

[2] B.W.Evershed, STELLA System - BER Analysis, STELLA/CERN/81/9, November 1981.

[3] N.Celandroni, E.Ferro and L.Lenzini, Gateway Architecture and Internet Protocol for STELLA, STELLA/CNUCE/82/01, March 1982.

[4] Carl A.Sunshine, Interconnection of Computer Networks, Computer Networks, 1 (1977) 175-179.

[5] P.T.Kirstein, the UNIVERSE Project, this issue.

[6] A.G.Waters and C.J.Adams, Satellite Transmission Protocol: implementation protocol, Universe Paper UP/48, November 1981.

[7] Network Layer Principles, Final Draft, ECMA/TC24/92/18.

[8] J.M. Gerard, The development and use of a high speed packet switching network in a high-energy physics laboratories, EURO IFIP Proceedings, 1979, December 1981.

[9] A.Endrizzi, L.Lenzini, J. Loquet and M.Mannocci, INET Interconnection to STELLA, STELLA/CNUCE/82/02, March 1982.

[10] C. Adams et al, Network Project Note 16, Version 3, CERN, Geneva, 01/08/80.

[11] Draft Connection-Oriented Basic Transport Protocol Specification, Version 1,2, ISO TC97/SC16/WG6, New Port Beach.

[12] N.Celandroni, E.Ferro, L.Lenzini, C.J.Adams, I.Barely, J.Burren, R.Cole and I.Leslie, Internetwork Architecture Proposal for STELLA and UNIVERSE, INDRA Note 1201, Universe paper 74.3, April 1982.

[13] M.V.Wilkes and D.J.Wheeler, The Cambridge Communication Ring, Proceedings of the LACN symposium, May 1979.

Interconnecting Local Area Networks through Satellite Links

C Huitema, J Radureau
Projet Pilote NADIR, France

Local area networks (LAN) allow high speed communication and broadcasting. Satellite communication systems will also offer high bandwidth transmission and broadcasting. interconnection of LAN's using satellite links looks promising. In order to gain experience in that field, the NADIR project studies and experiments the interconnection of LAN's of the DANUBE type, through satellite links, similar to those to be provided by the TELECOM 1 network. Two types of experiments are to be conducted using a satellite system simulator (ANIS). The first type of experiments uses dedicated satellite links (both point to point and multipoint) to interconnect LAN's. In a second type of experiment, high speed data transmission is performed (e.g. file transfer) between two computers communicating through a switched satellite link and a LAN interconnected by a gateway.

1. INTRODUCTION

Local area networks (LAN) characteristics include high bandwidth, broadcasting, and total connectivity. But they are only local networks, while users may wish to communicate with the same facility although they are located in the same area. Satellite communication system, such as TELECOM1, will offer high bandwidth and broadcast links between distant users.

The NADIR pilot project was launched by the end of 1980 by the French PTT and the Ministry of Industry. It aims at investigating new types of computer applications made feasible by taking advantage of new satellite communications systems. Among these applications, interconnection of LAN's through satellite links is being studied.

Within the TELECOM1 satellite, five transponders will be shared for business communications. The TDMA system will provide numeric links either on a call per call basis, or in a semi-permanent fashion. Multipoints and point-to-point links will be available, at data-rates from 2400 bit/s to 2 Mbit/s. Point to point links will be either duplex, either simplex.

The ANIS satellite simulator was developped by the NADIR team to emulate TELECOM1 links; it offers the same interfaces (x21 or V35), and enables us to establish various link configurations between computers within the NADIR laboratory, with various data-rates, bit-error-rates, and propagation delays. Several type of LAN's are available now; among those we have choosem to experiment first with DANUBE, a LAN developped at INRIA by the KAYAK project. Like many other (e.g.Ethernet) DANUBE is based on a coaxial cable, shared between up to 256 stations via a CSMA-CD access method. It offers a "datagram" service, each frame carrying a destination and a source indentification; connection, error recovery and flow control are available on a end-to-end basis, at the "transport" level.

Two types of experiments are to be conducted, using DANUBE's network (1) and the ANIS simulator: building an internal network for a large organization and interconnecting DANUBE and TELECOM1 network.

2. BUILDING AN INTERNAL NETWORK FOR A LARGE ORGANIZATION

Large organizations are usually not located at a single place. Large companies have different factories. National administrations have regional headquarters. Within one site, LAN's will provide for data communications. Unexpensive internets could be built by using dedicated satellite links.

A goal for the internet designers is that the whole net appears like a "long range local network". The interconnection should not introduce any restrictions on such services as datagrams or broadcast messages which are already available on existing LAN's. No tricky connection procedure should be mandatory; the internet should have the same degree of transparency as the LAN's.

Keeping this goal in mind, we first studied the interconnection of two LAN's of the DANUBE type through a medium data-rate (64 kbit/s or 128 kbit/s) point to point link. Then, we studied the way to interconnect several DANUBE's through multipoint links.

2.1. Interconnecting two DANUBES: through a point link:

Figure 1 shows the interconnection experimented. End-users on Network 1 wish to communicate with other end-users on Network 2, through gateways 1 and 2.

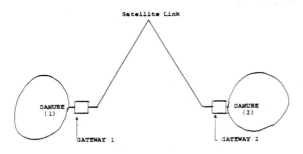

Satellite Link

Figure 1. Interconnecting two DANUBE's through a point
to point link

CII-HB "Mini6" minicomputers will be used as
gateways during the first experiments; taking
advantage of the experience obtained, special
gateways will then be designed.

ISO's Open Systems Architecture is a useful
tool for analyzing interconnections problems.
Question marks on figure 2 show the big questions to be solved: what link and network
protocols shall be used on the satellite link;
how shall routing, error control and flow
control be performed?

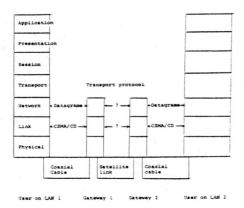

Figure 2. OSI representation of the interconnection

2.1.1. Routing

Each packet transmitted on the DANUBE network
carries a destination address and a source
address. Our goal being to design an internet
for a single organization, we assume that an
address corresponds to only one destination on
the whole network.(i,e,the address scheme is
global). Routing is then easily performed by the
gateway: it receives all packets travelling on
the local network. If so, the packet is transmitted on the satellite link, and forwarded to
the distant LAN by the distant gateway.

Routing decisions are made easier if addresses
are composed of two fields, one designating the
local network, and the other one designating the
user within the network.

A specific problem arises with DANUBE's "Broadcast" address. A packet carrying this address
should be delivered to every user on the network,
and thus should be transmitted by the gateway
on the satellite link. To prevent those packets
to be sent back by the distant gateways (thus
creating an end-less loop) the gateway will look
not only at the "broadcast" destination address
but also at the source address. Broadcast packets
originated from the local network only will be
transmitted over the satellite link.

2.1.2. Error control:

The propagation delay over satellite links
such as those provided by TELECOM1 is about 300ms
The bit error rate (BER) is lower than 1 in 10^6
in 99% of the cases. A 4/5 forward error correction could be provided as a value added service
lowering the BER to about 1 in 10^{10}.

Error rate on a short distance (1 km) coaxial,
operated like DANUBE with base-band modulation
at 1 or 2 M bit/s is generally said to be very
low. A question then arises: should we run a link
protocol, including an error detection.correction
mechanism between the gateways, in order to
improve the "link quality" ?

We decided not to do so for two reasons: first,
error correction is made available on the DANUBE
network by the end to end protocol, no error
correction being done on DANUBE at the link
level.

Second, an error correction mechanism applied to
the satellite link would deteriorate the network
"reponse time": a link level protocol generally
assume that packets should be delivered at the
other end of the link without error, and in the
same order they were first transmitted. If an
error occurs, the erroneous packets would have
to be retransmitted; this retransmission would
last 300 ms for a negative acknowledgement to be
carried to the sender, and another 300 ms for
the repeated packet to be carried to the receiver. During those 600 ms, incoming packet would
be either ignored (HDLC "Reject" mode, GO-BACK N
stategies), or queued (HDLC "Selective Reject"
mode). Multiple independent dataflows will reasonably be multiplexed on the satellite link;
thus a link-level error connection strategy
would lead to slow down all data flows when an
error occurs on one of them!

Computations (4) have shown that this phenomenon increases proportionally to the link bit
error rate, throughput, and propagation delay.
Figure 3 shows the mean delivery delay on a
satellite link (propagation delay: 300 ms), as
a function of the product BER times throughput.
A possible solution would be to execute a separate error control protocol for each separate
data-flow (which could be differentiated by the
source address and destination address), but
this would seriously increase the complexity of
the gateway.

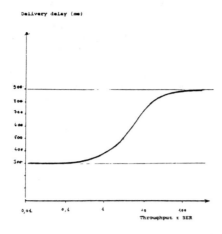

Figure 3 Mean delivery delay of a packet, as a function of the product throughput times bit error rate (i.e., the mean number of error per unit of time).

2.1.3. Flow control:

Various studies have been conducted on the Ethernet. In (3), for a typical 3 M bit/s Ethernet configuration, the following figures are quoted;
- Average load 0.8%
- Average load during the busiest hours 2%
- Max load over a 6 minute interval = 7.9%
- Max load over a 1 second interval = 32.4%
- 72% Intranet traffic versus 28% Internet traffic.

Indeed interconnecting LANs through satellite links implies that a satellite link data-rate is to be chosen. It can be computed from Network utilization statistics. With the above figures, the satellite data-rate could be as low as:
3 Magabit/s x 2% x 28%   16 800 bit/s
Of course, a greater capacity will generally be chosen in order to minimize queuing problems typically a compromise between quality of service and cost.

Still, flow control problems can very likely arise during peak periods. Two approaches can be proposed to cope with this problem. One could be called deterministic, the other undeterministic. The deterministic approach is based on an X25-like step-by-step flow control mechanism. This implies a call set-up procedure not existing in the DANUBE local network. It also involves a step-by-step error control mechanism. It could not be operated for a datagram traffic, neither for a broadcast traffic. A much simpler undeterministic scheme can be designed. When a packet is to be transmitted on a busy satellite link, the gateway queues it; if the queue is full, it simply discards the packet. Retransmission of discarded packets will be triggered on an end-to-end basis by transport protocols. It is also to be noted that this protocol will cause the traffic to be eventually slowed down.
This simple scheme will be experimented. It is

believed it leads to a very simple and "transparent" system structure. Two IM bit/s DANUBE networks will be interconnected through a 64 Kbit/s "satellite" link, provided by the ANIS simulator.

2.2. Interconnecting several DANUBEs through multipoint links:

Figure 4 shows the interconnection experimented

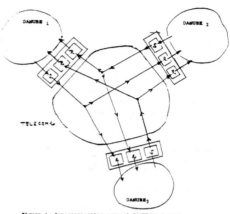

Figure 4. Interconnecting several DANUBEs through multipoint Links.

On each Network, a gateway is connected to the emitting end of a TELECOM1 broadcast circuit, and to the receiving ends of several broadcast circuits: one for each distant LAN. We can assume that this gateway is made of "half gateway" : a unique "sending" half gateway, and several "receiving" half gateways.

Routing is very simple. Each "sending" half gateway receives all packets travelling on the Local Network; it decides which of them are not destined only to the local network, and transmits them over the satellite link. Each "receiving" half gateway receives all packets emitted over the satellite link; it decides which of them are destined to the LAN to which it is connected, and forward them on it.

Problems shown in the point-to-point interconnection also arise in multipoint interconnection. The same simple solutions can be applied, i.e. only end-to-end and no step-by-step error control and flow control. Moreover, it should be noted that step-by-step solutions would become very difficult to implement in a multipoint environment.

3. INTERCONNECTING DANUBE AND TELECOM1 NETWORKS

It was assumed in previous sections that it was possible to build a common addressing scheme for the various LAN to build an organization internal network. This of course might not be always true. Users connected to various LAN, with incompatible addressing scheme, may wish to exchange data through a Public Network such as TELECOM1. For example, they may wish to transfer a file from a computer connected to DANUBE to a computer connected to TELECOM1.

Question marks on figure 5 show main problems to be solved for this particular interconnection: what link protocols shall be used on the satellite link. What network protocols shall be used on the LAN and on TELECOM1?

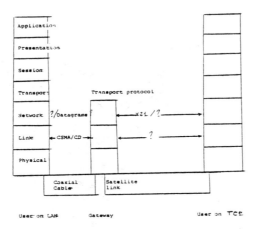

Figure 5 OSI representation of the interconnection

It should be noted that, for the typical usage considered (file transfer) there is no need to multiplex several network connections over the satellite link.

3.1. Establishing a circuit:

Danube can be considered as a datagram network. A user connected to it can, at any time, send a packet to any other user. TELECOM1 is a circuit switched network; before exchanging data, a call must be set-up. Thus, there is a need for a network protocol on DANUBE, to enable a user connected to DANUBE to place a call on TELECOM1 or to receive a call from it.

We have chosen to experiment on explicit call set-up procedure. This has two advantages: it enables us to use any of TELECOM1 facilities, and the gateway can be completely transparent in the transfer phase.

The gateway from DANUBE to TELECOM1 has several addresses: one for the gateway itself, and one for each X21 interface (i.e., for each possible circuit).

When a user on DANUBE wants to place call, he sends a "call request" message to the gateway. This message indicates the TELECOM1 number of the TELECOM1 user to be connected, and also the facilities to be requested: link data-rate, forward error correction, etc. After he has received such a message, the gateway chose an interface, performs X21 signalling on it, and, when the call is established, sends a message to the caller (i.e., the user on DANUBE). This message indicates that the interface is "ready for data", it also indicates the DANUBE address of the interface.

The same procedure is applied on incoming calls. When a call request is received through an X21 interface, the gateway sends a call request message to the called user; this message indicates the number of the TELECOM1 user requesting the connection, and the DANUBE address of the interface. This implies that the X21 call request message carries an identification of the requested DANUBE user the "user data" field.

When the user on DANUBE wants to clear the call, he sends a "liberation request" message to the gateway and the gateway liberates the circuit through the X21 interface. When the user on TELECOM1 clears the call, this is indicated on the gateway's X21 interface, and the gateway transmits a "liberation indication" message to the DANUBE's user.

3.2. Error and flow control during the transfer phase:

If the user connected to the local network sends packets faster than the gateway can forward them over the satellite link, the gateway's buffer will become full. This will cause incoming packets to be discarded. Since the user knows the satellite link's data-rate, it should be very easy to prevent this situation without setting up a complex credit mechanism.

The LAN bandwidth (1 or 2 Mbit/s) will be, during our experiments, much higher than the satellite link data-rate (64 or 128 Kbit/s). So we assume that the gateway will be almost always able to forward incoming packet from the satellite link to the LAN.

The LAN bit error rate being assumed very low (see 2.1.2. above), we decided to experiment a very simple procedure during the transfer phase. The user on DANUBE sends packets to the gateway; these packets include (see figure 6) a destination address and a source address. When the gateway receives such a packet, he removes the destination address and the source address, and transmits it over the satellite link corresponding to the destination address.

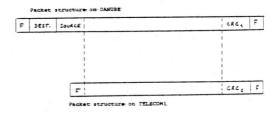

Figure 6. Structure of the packets during the transfer phase.

When the gateway receives a packet from the satellite link, it adds to this packet the destination and source addresses corresponding to the circuit, and forwards it on DANUBE.

4. CONCLUSION

Satellite telecommunication systems will offer high speed links at relatively low cost. These links can be dedicated to build a large organization's internal network by interconnecting various LANs. These links can also be set-up on demand to exchange data between an LAN and a public network.

We have designed very simple protocols, leading to a highly transparent gateway design. Experiments will learn us if this protocols were oversimplificated or not.

REFERENCES

[1] Naffah N./Scheurer B. et al. Description fonctionnelle du réseau expérimental DANUBE Jul.80 - Projet Kayak - Rel 2.514.2

[2] Huitema C./Cartianu I. Spécifications fonctionnelles du simulateur de satellite Anis . Mar. 81 - Projet Nadir- Spe 3500

[3] J.F. Shoch/J.A. Hupp. Measured Performances of an Ethernet local network.Feb.80 - Xeros Corporation

[4] Huitema C. Why usual transmission protocols are not appropriate for high speed satellite transmission. Jul 81 - Projet Nadir - Pro 3 501

Christian Huitema was born in 1953 in Nantes (France). He graduated from the Ecole Polytechnique de Paris in 1975.

He was with SEMA as a consultant in informatics from 1975 to 1980. Then he joined the Centre National d'Etudes des Télécommunications where he worked first on specifications of the control center for the TELECOM1 Network, and now with the NADIR project. He is presently focusing, within the NADIR project, on file transfer and Local Area Network interconnection through satellite links.

Joëlle Radureau was born in 1952 in France. She gratuated from University of Paris (DEA in Computer Sciences - Paris VI) in 1976. She was with Cap Sogeti, as a consultant in informatics from 1977 to 1981, on telephone and data processing projects. Then she joined Cogintel,.. nd she is presently within the NADIR project where she works on the local Area Networks interconnection through satellite links.

Christian Huitema was born in 1953 in Nantes, (France). He gratueted from the Ecole Polytech nique de Paris in 1975.

He was with SEMA as a consultant in informatics from 1975 to 1980. Then he joined the Centre National d'Etudes des Télécommunications where he worked first on specifications of the control center for the TELECOM1 Network, and now with the NADIR project. He is presently focusing, within the NADIR project, on file transfer and Local Area Network interconnection through satellite links.

Joëlle Radureau was born in 1952 in France. She gratuated from University of Paris (DEA in Computer Scien- ces - Paris VI) in 1976. She was with Cap Sogeti as a consultant in informatics from 1977 to 1981, on telephone and data processing projects. Then she joined Cogintel,... she is presently within the NADIR project where she works on the local Area Networks interconnection through satellite links.

Small Dish Satellite Systems for Business Use

G P Jones
British Telecom International, UK

The degree to which the novel aspects of small dish satellite systems will be exploited depends in part on the 're-useability' of the satellite resource and the extent to which manufacturers explore the emerging customer terminal market.

The particular facilities of a small dish satellite system , wide bandwidths, multipoint, occasional use, can only be enjoyed by the customer provided that the local network of the earth station can support them too. The paper illustrates how British Telecom International will connect customers to small earth stations using special independent networks.

1. THE CURRENT SCENE, TERRESTRIAL AND SATELLITE

The rapid growth in digital communications has stimulated the introduction of new data networks and the harmonisation of networks supporting telephony and data traffic. British Telecom is currently modernising the Public Switched Telephone Network (PSTN) by introducing digital switching and digital transmission equipment creating an Integrated Digital Network (IDN). Extension of the digital connection to the customers premises and the ability to carry a variety of services will result in the formation of an Integrated Services Digital Network (ISDN) (1) which is the subject of much discussion within the International Telegraph and Telephone Consultative Committee (CCITT) Study Groups. International connections via the ISDN, however, depend on the relative progress made by administrations towards the digitalisation of their networks and inevitably not all networks will be at the same state of evolution at any one time. Satellite systems using small dishes of typically between 3-5m in diameter are seen as a way of offering new services in advance of the development of the terrestrial network. It is also recognised that satellite systems can offer facilities difficult to reproduce terrestrially.

To lay the foundations for a European small dish satellite network, EUTELSAT, comprising 19 member European countries, is currently defining the characteristics of the special multi-services transponders added to the European Communications Satellite (ECS) and has agreed in principle with the French PTT Administration for the lease of about one transponder's worth of capacity in the Telecom 1 Satellite System. The satellites are due to become operational in early 1984. The facilities offered by the two satellite systems will differ since Telecom 1 will operate in a Time Division Multiple Access (TDMA) mode working at 25Mbit/s (2) and ECS will be operating in a Frequency Division Multiple Access (FDMA) mode using typically a Single Channel Per Carrier (SCPC) system. (Ref. 3).

2. THE SMALL DISH SYSTEM

Small dish satellite systems may be operated either as a network resource and as such would be fully integrated into the terrestrial network or be used to establish a private overlay network with terminals on or close to customers premises with permanent leased lines from the customer to the earth station. The two approaches are fundamentally opposite in objectives since the network resource would be designed around shared use and could absorb the cost of a relatively large diameter aerial and complex access system whereas the objectives of the private overlay network are to utilise a small low cost terminal.

An attractive system would be one which utilises dishes of around 1m in diameter with transmit and receive facilities. Such systems, however, require a relatively high satellite transmit power for good quality reception, around 25 times greater than a similar system using 5m diameter dishes, and the restrictions on off axis radiation patterns plus the requirement for transmitter powers of several hundreds of watts if high capacity channels are to be supported, make small dual transmit and receive dishes impracticable. Nevertheless small receive only dishes of around 1.8m diameter are feasible and these systems would only utilise around 8 times more satellite power than an equivalent 5m diameter dish. Hence flexibility does exist for designing systems around specific applications but the penalty is a reduction in the space segment capacity. The customer of course would see this as a higher space segment charge.

The ECS and Telecom 1 compromise these design features to the extent that the ECS system defined for standard SCPC operation employs a relatively simple access system but requires a standard antenna of around 5m diameter whereas Telecom 1 employs a complex access system but only requires a 3.5m diameter antenna. This results from the larger coverage area of ECS relative to Telecom 1. Although ECS has been designed to support approximately 400-64kbit/s channels requiring a 5m diameter antenna it is recognised that other systems using smaller or larger dishes and demanding differing power requirements may be accommodated in the same transponder.

Within the UK it is envisaged that Telecom 1 will be more suitable for shared use where the customer service area is fairly large whereas ECS will be suitable for large businesses with dedicated or shared terminals on or near their premises.

The consequence of moving the terminal away from customers premises is the need for a terrestrial extension and it is this aspect which the author believes will present most difficulties to administrations. The options open to British Telecom are discussed in later paragraphs.

3. EARTH TERMINALS & SITES

Not all buildings are suitable for terminals either because they would need extensive modification to withstand the point loads imposed by high winds (Fig.1) or because there is no clear view of the satellite. Furthermore, it is usually more cost effective to share terminals in which case the best location may not even be on the premises of the participants. Each earth terminal site must be suitably engineered to accommodate the aerial and mount and the necessary transmission equipment in addition to the provision of suitable power supplies and signal cables. Before installation can take place local authority planning permission and Home Office frequency and site clearance will be required.

The transmission equipment typically comprises a transmitter of about 250 watts, or less in the case of SCPC, a low noise receiver having

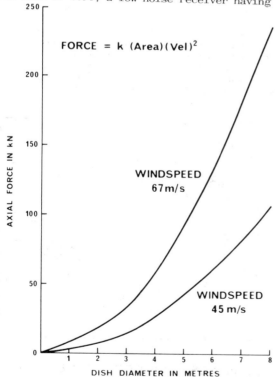

$$FORCE = k \ (Area)(Vel)^2$$

WINDSPEED 67 m/s

WINDSPEED 45 m/s

FIG. 1

a noise figure of around 2 dB, frequency up and down converters for transmission at 14GHz and reception at 12GHz, 4 phase shift keyed modulators and demodulators and SCPC or TDMA equipment (see Figure 2). This equipment may be fully redundant depending on the availability required and can either be housed in accommodation specially provided or in a convenient office. It is important, however, that the transmitter should be located relatively close to the antenna eg no more than 5m away to avoid excessive waveguide attenuation and hence loss of output power. The low noise amplifier is usually mounted at the back of the antenna to minimise the system thermal noise contribution.

It is usual to specify the performance of earth stations in such a way that the required characteristics can be calculated for any location. The sizes of aerials usually quoted, however, assume operation within the -3dB contour of the satellite coverage beam and hence some countries may need standard aerials in excess of the 3.5m to 5m diameters previously mentioned (see Fig. 3).

4. PERFORMANCE

The bit error rate (BER) specified for the satellite link is 1in 10^6 for 99% of the year. As an option a bit error rate of 1in 10^{10} can be offered but the method of achieving this performance in the two satellite systems is slightly different. In ECS the satellite carrier to noise ratio link budget is based on a BER performance of 1in 10^3 but a forward error correction (FEC) technique using a rate 1/2 convolutional codec with a soft decision Viterbi (maximum likelihood) decoder improves the overall performance to a BER of less than 1in 10^6. The high grade circuit having the better performance of a 1in 10^{10} BER is achieved by increasing the transmitted power and hence carrier to noise ratio.

In Telecom 1 the performance of 1in 10^6 BER is based on a circuit without FEC whereas the performance of 1in 10^{10} assumes a 5/4 block code system.

5. NETWORK CONFIGURATIONS.

Terrestrial Networks have characteristic configurations namely stars, rings, partially connected nodes or fully connected nodes (see Fig. 4). Each connection is formed by the establishment of a link between two nodes usually on a full time basis. A satellite system can replace such terrestrial configurations if so desired but the real potential of a satellite system lies in its ability to broadcast to all nodes simultaneously. Clearly it would be uneconomic in a satellite system to establish 45 separate dedicated channels for a ten node network requiring full interconnection when 10 broadcast channels might suffice.

A technique which can be easily implemented in satellite systems is the ability to share high capacity circuits in the time domain on demand, and yet still retain the multi-destination capability. No longer is it necessary for

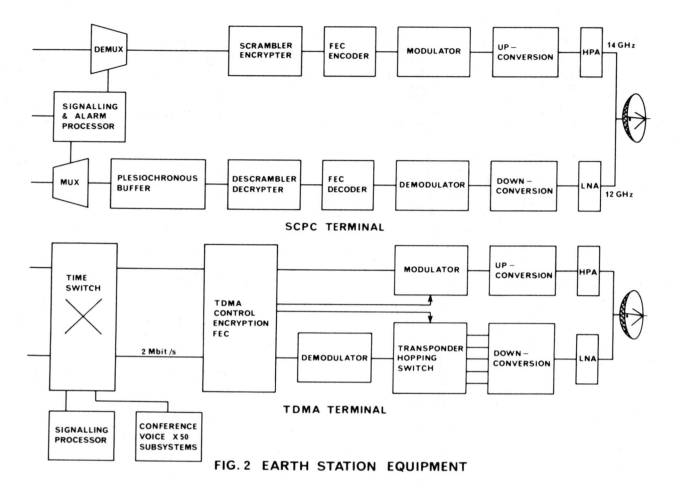

SCPC TERMINAL

TDMA TERMINAL

FIG. 2 EARTH STATION EQUIPMENT

customers to permanently lease high capacity circuits to each destination if the link is not required 24 hours a day. Furthermore the same capacity can be shared between their different premises. Perhaps the greatest advantage with satellite systems is the ability of the network to grow with relatively little capital expenditure and little modification to the existing network. This potential is being exploited in North America by the newspaper industry to aid the distribution of daily newspapers. Page-facsimile terminals transmit via satellite a page of text and pictures in 2-3 minutes to remote printing centres. The distribution of bulk printed paper is then confined to relatively small areas thus speeding up the delivery time and also allowing the source material to be formatted as late as possible to ensure the most up-to-date news.

6. CUSTOMER TERMINAL

There are several technical reasons why an aerial co-sited with the customers terminal equipment is advantageous:

- the high bit rates that can be supported by satellite systems are not so easily provided on terrestrial tails.

- elimination of a terrestrial tail improves the overall availability and performance of the circuit.

- growth in circuit requirements is relatively easy to implement.

Offsetting these advantages is the cost of providing a dedicated terminal. Nevertheless some large companies and corporations will not only see these advantages but will also have a sufficiently large traffic base to justify a dedicated terminal.

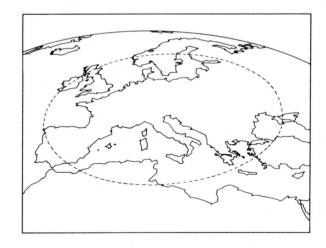

FIG. 3a ECS (-3dB) COVERAGE ZONE

FIG. 3b TELECOM 1(-3dB) COVERAGE ZONE

7. SHARED LOCAL TERMINAL

Since the earth terminal could represent a major portion of the overall cost of the small dish network it makes economic sense to share terminals. One of the principle aims of the network operator is to provide service quickly and any activity which requires lengthy planning is undesirable. British Telecom is proposing to use 2Mbit/s digital radio links where line of sight is possible as the initial connection. These links would operate in high frequency bands which hitherto have not been exploited to a great extent. The 2Mbit/s bearer can support a mixture of voice, low and high speed data which will be demultiplexed, if necessary, at the earth station. Alternatively laser links could be used if the distance is limited to a few hundred metres. As soon as high capacity cable links are installed the radio equipment could be removed and utilised elsewhere. Point to multipoint local radio systems employing TDMA/TDM techniques are also being investigated which could provide both leased circuit facilities and on demand facilities for customers with circuit switched access. Where line of sight links are not possible, dedicated terminals on a temporary basis might be possible using transportable terminals.

Apart from radio systems there are a number of options based on cable technology namely:-

- using components employed in British Telecom's Kilostream network (4) utilising 4 wire - WAL$_2$ transmission systems and PCDDS multiplexers which assemble 30 low speed (2.4, 4.8, 9.6 and 48kbit/s) circuits onto 2Mbit/s bearers.

- analogue circuits for voice may be used which interface standard 30 ch PCM multiplexers.

- using components employed in British Telecom's ISDN utilising 2 wire burst mode transmission systems supporting a 64kbit/s and 8 kbit/s data channel with out-of-band

signalling, and ISDN multiplexers with 2Mbit/s outputs.

- use of optical fibre techniques.

8. CIRCUIT SWITCHED ACCESS

In addition to a leased line facility, it is possible that customers on the ISDN could gain access to an earth terminal by means of a switched connection probably in the form of a two stage 'dial up' procedure. Since in theory any customer on the ISDN will have this facility, a signalling protocol will be required to indicate various customer terminal features such as terminal identity, bit rate, close user group code (possibly) and service type. This type of access is under study.

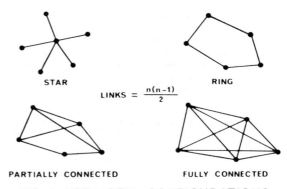

STAR

$$\text{LINKS} = \frac{n(n-1)}{2}$$

RING

PARTIALLY CONNECTED

FULLY CONNECTED

FIG. 4 NETWORK CONFIGURATIONS

9. MESSAGE BASED ACCESS

The trend towards message based systems has encouraged the development of packet switched networks (5) (6) and in particular local rings (7) for communications within organisations. A feature attributed to local ring networks is the ability to share resources between a number of terminals as well as the basic ability to inter-communicate. There are situations, however, where the resources are not on the

439

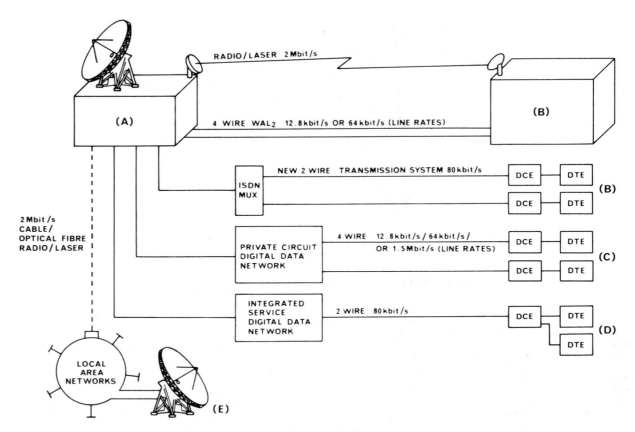

FIG. 5 EARTH STATION ACCESS

same premises and hence there is a need to interconnect rings. This may be established by means of virtual circuit such as is used between two nodes of a packet network. Alternatively the broadcast facility of satellite systems can be exploited thereby improving the connectivity. Broadcast systems, however, need to be designed around the architecture of the local ring since the modulators and demodulators operate in burst mode, either transmitting uncoordinated short messages such as in the ALOHA system (8) or transmitting blocks of messages in a structured time frame.

Project Universe (9), in which British Telecom is participating both in the experiment and in the supply of terminals, is designed amongst other objectives, to develop a suitable protocol for interconnecting local rings.

10. FACILITIES ON SATSTREAM

British Telecom's small dish satellite service, SATSTREAM, will offer a number of options namely:-

- full time leased line

- part time leased line

- hot line (leased line to the earth station, but on demand over the satellite links to a pre-determined destination).

- circuit switched (leased line to the earth station but circuit switched over the satellite link).

Hence a customer is able to design and optimise his system in terms of connectivity requirements, bit rates, and the time periods when the links are required.

Full time leased line service is aimed at customers who either have conventional machines operating at low speeds or who have equipment which can exploit a higher speed channel on a long term basis. A typical installation might comprise a single primary customer satellite terminal interface and several secondary internal interfaces supporting data terminal equipment and connections to a PABX.

Full time leased lines are also essential for those communications links where end-to-end connections must be permanently available and where the chance of congestion is an unacceptable risk.

Part time leased line service would offer similar facilities as the full time service but would be more suitable for customers generating traffic having specific operating patterns such as the bulk transfer of data. This service therefore permits the satellite capacity to be re-used. Satellite capacity might typically be used for PABX voice and real time low speed data during the day whereas the same capacity might be used for electronic overnight mail.

Part time leased line service constitutes a contract between customer and administration for capacity made available on a regular long-term basis. Such capacity would be guaranteed and would have a service priority commensurate with a full time leased line.

The hot line service enables the same facilities as full time and part time leased lines to be enjoyed except that the circuit is only established at exactly the moment it is demanded. Hence if the call cannot be established due to congestion, a second seizure attempt will be required after a short time period. This type of service is therefore attractive to customers who are not inconvenienced by the occasional delay in establishing an end-to-end link. The benefit is of course a reduced tariff. A typical application might be for a voice link or even the bulk transfer of data.

All the three previous services relate to links established to predetermined destinations. The Circuit Switched service, however, offers greater connectivity where the selection is made by the customer. This type of service is therefore most attractive to multi-national companies having centres throughout Europe or even businesses requiring access to data banks, geographically located over a wide area. Since high speed links are available, customers may transmit stored data quickly thereby minimising the circuit holding time.

11. FUTURE

ECS and Telecom 1 will be the first satellites available to European businesses. The degree to which they are exploited will not only depend on the tariffs but also the extent to which businesses are willing to consider new approaches to their telecommunications needs and the initiative taken by manufacturers to produce terminal equipment for novel applications. Furthermore, the introduction of new services, such as video conferencing, may well result in businesses making radical changes to the way in which they operate. Small dish satellite systems are likely, therefore, to revolutionise the communications systems of those companies with significant communications requirements permitting full connectivity, simple expansion and high bit rate data exchange.

12. ACKNOWLEDGEMENTS

Acknowledgement is made to the Director of International Networks, British Telecom International, for permission to publish the information contained in this article.

13. REFERENCES

(1) A G Orbell. Preparations for Evolution Towards and Integrated Services Digital Network - International Communications Conference, Boston 1979.

(2) J P Buenin and B Ghillebaert, Telecom 1: A Multiservices Satellite Network - ICCC 1980.

(3) D McGovern and K Hodson, The ECS multi-services Transponder - IEE Communications Conference 1982.

(4) M Smith - A New Network for Digital Data - IEE Communications Conference 1982.

(5) W Neil, Experimental Packet Switched Service, Procedures and Protocols - POEEJ Vol67 p332 Jan 1975.

(6) P T F Kelly and E J B Lee, The Telecommunications Network for Euronet - POEEJ Vol70 p208 Jan 78.

(7) M Fowler, Personnal computer networks - Electronics and Power Nov/Dec 1981.

(8) R Binder, N Abramson, F Kuo, A Okinaka and D Wax: ALOHA Packet Broadcasting, A retrospect - University of Hawaii.

(9) J W Burren, Universe Experiment - IEE Colloquium on Small Dish Satellite systems for Specialised Services 28 Sep 1981.

Godfrey Jones joined British Telecom in 1960 and in 1969 he gained a degree in Electrical and Electronic Engineering at City University in London. From 1969-1979 he was responsible for the procurement of satellite earth stations and equipment for INTELSAT Systems and after a short period in Network Strategy Division he rejoined satellites and is now responsible for the procurement of small dish terminals.

The UNIVERSE Project

P T Kirstein
University College London, UK
J Burren
Rutherford & Appleton Laboratory, UK
R Daniels
British Telecom, UK
J W R Griffiths
Loughborough University, UK

D King
GEC/Marconi, UK
C McDowell
Logica, UK
R Needham
Cambridge University, UK

This paper gives the motivation and progress of a project to investigate the use of concatenated Cambridge rings and small dish satellite earth stations accessing the OTS satellite. Both metropolitan transmission at Mbps speeds and Wide Area terrestrial transmission at Kbps speeds are also incorporated. The basic components of the system are described, and the planned applications discussed. Some indications are given of the scope of the applications for business communication and for computer communications.

1. INTRODUCTION

With the introduction of small dish satellite services, the development of techniques for their exploitation is becoming an important area of investigation. Many projects have started looking at this problem. Three such projects are the DARPA wide-band satellite project in the US, the NADIR project in France, and the UNIVERSE project in the UK. This paper gives a brief introduction of the last.

The UNIVersites Extended Ring and Satellite Experiment (UNIVERSE) has participants from four academic establishments (The Rutherford and Appleton Laboratories (RAL), Cambridge U (CU), Loughborough U (LU), and University College London (UCL)), Industry (GEC-Marconi Research (MRL) and Logica Ltd) and from British Telecom (BT). It is being funded by the Department of Industry, the Science and Engineering Research Council, British Telecom, GEC-Marconi and Logica. The total expenditure is budgeted at £3M over the period 1981-1984, with about 70 man-years effort.

The aim of the project is to investigate the facilities which must be developed for allowing business communication over a concatenation of terrestrial and satellite networks – with particular emphasis on the use of Cambridge Rings for the local distribution inside single establishments.

In order to carry out this investigation experimentally, it was decided to site a number of small earth stations in most of the participants' premises, which can communicate at 1 Mbps via the OTS Research Satellite (though the equipment is compatible with the future service satellite ECS [1]). At each site there will be one or more Cambridge Rings [2], capable of a local user data bandwidth of 4Mbps. The Rings are connected to various service hosts, local servers, computers driving the earth stations, and computers containing gateways to other networks. At least one alternative ring technology will also be connected to show the generality of the end-to-end communication protocols.

From the beginning it was decided to enrich the experiments by putting several Rings at many of the sites, and have high speed Mbps terrestrial links between certain locations. The access to the satellite will be intermittent, possibly only 3 hours/day. Moreover it was decided to task each participant with specific subsystems, and then to replicate these at many (or all) sites. This decision increased the need for methods of software and documentation dissemination. To ease problems of intercommunications, and to allow monitoring and control while the satellite system was being developed, it was decided to connect the relevant sites also by X25 networks.

This basic configuration is discussed in Section 2, and some of the components needed in Section 3-5.

From the beginning, utilisation of the system was considered vital. For this reason, the project was set up in such a way that many service computers at several of the sites were encouraged to consider using the system for real service. Moreover, the use of relevant communication services (e.g. Teletex, Videotex, graphics, facsimile) slow-scan TV and voice were proposed. The participants in the project plan to use these facilities heavily for communication amongst each other, experiment coordination, program distribution and measurement data organisation. In Section 6 we discuss

442

'the modes of use being studied. A good indication of the progress can be obtained from the Technical Working Groups, which have been set up (Section 7).

We are conscious that OTS will not be up for long, so that tight timescales are essential. We expect to have the complete system operational by the third quarter of 1982, so that computer-computer applications should be possible before the end of that year, and Teletex experimentation should be possible during 1982, with slow-scan TV and voice a few months later.

Both system and equipment design for the project draws heavily on the previous experience of the partners, which covers satellite networking in the SATNET and STELLA projects, local area network design, distributed computing systems and communications equipment design including speech and video processing.

2. THE BASIC CONFIGURATION

The components of the communication system are four:

(i)   The Satellite System (SS)

(ii)   The Cambridge Rings (CR)

(iii)   The High Speed Terrestrial Links (HTS)

(iv)   The X25 Networks

Each of these will be mentioned in turn.

A Schematic of the total configuration is shown in Fig 1. Six sites have satellite earth stations. British Telecom Research Laboratory (BTR), Cambridge U (CU), Loughborough U (LU), Marconi Research Laboratory (MRL), the Rutherford and Appleton Laboratories (RAL) and University College London (UCL). In addition there are a number of Mbps links between UCL and Logica as the High Speed Terrestrial System (HTS); (there may later be others). Each site has one or more Cambridge Rings (CR). Finally, to allow down-line loading, connectivity when the SS is not available, and control, all the sites with earth Stations are connected to one or both of two X25 networks – SERCNET or PSS.

Clearly the various networks must also be connected together. For this reason four types of Gateway or Bridge are under development or in use:

(i)   Satellite Bridge SB, (between Earth Station and Ring)

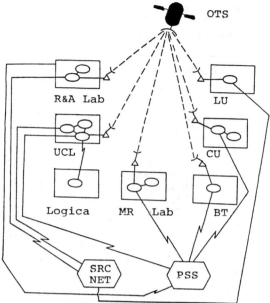

Fig 1.   General Configuration for UNIVERSE

(ii)   Ring Bridge RB, (between Rings)

(iii)   X25 Gateway XG, (between X25 net and Ring)

(iv)   Terrestrial Half-Bridge THB, (between Ring and high speed terrestrial link)

The first three are required at most sites. The terrestrial half-bridge, which is discussed in Section 4 is peculiar to UCL and Logica.

A more detailed diagram of the network interconnections is exemplified by exploding the UCL portion of the diagram in Fig 2. This shows all the constituent bridges and gateways in position. Details of the protocols used are given in [3].

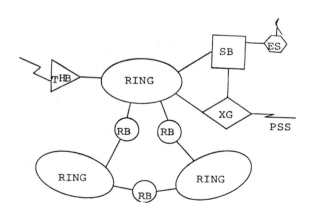

Fig 2.   More Detailed View of UCL Configuration

3. THE NETWORKS

The Satellite Network

This network is built up from four basic components:

    The OTS Satellite
    The Earth Station
    The Station Interface Module (SIM)
    The Satellite Bridge Computer

The OTS satellite has been described extensively in the literature. For this experiment we may use both the wideband Module A, taking a 5MHz frequency share of the channel with other experiments using different parts of the band or the narrow band Module B, with its 5MHz circularly polarised channels. The rest of the earth station and SIM equipment is compatible with that of the STELLA project.

The earth stations, which are supplied by Marconi, have 3m dishes and can operate with both linearly and circularly polarised beams. They have a maximum EIRP of 71 dBW and a G/T of 22.5dB/K. Data is transmitted using a 2 Mbps BPSK modem with half-rate Viterbi encoding to give a 1 Mbps data rate.

The SIM is a Motorola 6800-based device, which does the framing, timing, multiplexing and demultiplexing and synchronisation of the data stream to the Earth.

The data is packetised by the Link Driving Computer (LDC). This is a 512 Kbyte GEC 4065 computer, with a 2 x 4.8 Mbyte disc, and interfaces to the Cambridge Ring, SIM and X25 networks. It is discussed further in Section 4. On a computer-computer link, using only the LDC, SIM, earth station and OTS portions of the system, a full 1 Mbps data rate is achieved. By mid-1982 we will have information on the data rate achievable by a single LDC in its current more demanding role.

The data is packetised in the SIM into HDLC format packets. There is a Master earth station, which allocates slots in a frame for each transmitting earth station. The frame size is currently 125ms (125 Kb), and the maximum data packet size is 2K bytes (16 Kb). The HDLC address can be designated for one or all destinations. There is a slot for short resource request packets from each earth station on each frame. The data slot allocation is made by the Master station. It is possible to multiplex HDLC packets for several destinations in one transmission slot. At present there is no provision for flow or congestion control, or error reporting, between LDCs. It is assumed that the low error rate on the satellite hop and the substant buffers in the LDC, together with e₁ to-end transport level acknowledgement procedures, will suffice to ensure efficient data communication.

The Cambridge Rings

The Cambridge Ring has been described extensively in the literature. The implementation currently used on UNIVERSE operates at 10Mbps, with 38 bit minipackets (mp) containing two data bytes, a source and a destination data byte, and six control bits. The intrinsic minipacket error rate is low (2×10^{-9}), and a simple parity error check is adequate to protect this data. Unlike most networks, the transmitter compares the transmitted minipacket with that received on the next revolution. Therefore the transmitter knows if the mp has been corrupted.

The minipacket can be used in many different ways. For the purposes of UNIVERSE, all data is sent in Basic Blocks (BB). One type of BB has a 2 mp header consisting of a single mp which describes the type of mb and the length (i.e. upto 1Kmps); a second mp has a 12 bit port header. After the data, there is a sumcheck.

A second type of BB is sent as a complete datagram, and has 2 mps for each of source and destination in addition to the route.

The High Speed Terrestrial Links

The project is looking at several types of Mbps terrestrial links. Loughborough U is tasked with investigating the use of optical fibres. Here the initial task is the replacement of lengths of Cambridge Ring, of up to 1 km, by optical fibres. Since the ring transmission uses two pairs of balanced transmission lines, the electronics must be designed to multiplex and demultiplex the signals onto single fibres (this is different from the current position of Cambridge U, where four fibres are used (2 in each direction) for a ring spur).

Logica/UCL are investigating three methods of using transverse-screened cables. In one method several pairs would be used, in order to make a node at Logica part of a UCL Ring. In a second method, existing proprietary hardware, with special modems, will connect Ring bridges at UCL and Logica. In the third method, special hardware will be developed which interfaces between a standard Computer interface (probably X21 [4]), and the HDB3 [5] form of pcm used in digital pcm telephone transmission. The last activity will not begin seriously before the fourth quarter of 1982.

The X25 Nets

Here two conventional Packet Switched networks are being used; these are PSS, the Public Network run by British Telecom (BT), and SERCNET, the network operated by the UK Science and Engineering Research Council.

The connections to the sites are at medium speeds of 2.4 - 9.6 kbps. For simplicity, the BBs used on the local Cambridge Rings are sent across the X25 nets. This allows complete testing of end-to-end protocols and other software facilities with very simple gateways.

4.   THE GATEWAYS

General

The four types of Gateways or Bridges operate largely in similar ways, and are discussed below. In each one a Client machine makes a connection to a remote service, via a local name server. The name server either recognises the remote service, or has to initiate a dialogue with a remote name server (whose address is known) to determine the current address. It then sets up the appropriate routing information in the bridge, and sends a return address to the client system. By concatenating this procedure, it is possible to set up Virtual Routes with return paths; this requires some status information to be held in each bridge. Alternatively, it is possible to send single datagrams across these routes. All the bridges (and half bridges) use this principle. Flow control on a single ring can be exercised by appropriate connections in Basic Block and refusing minipackets at particular parts of the cycle. Flow control in Bridges is discussed below.

Ring Bridges

These are based on a Motorola 68000 with Motorola 6809s as intelligent interfaces to each Ring; CU is responsible for this development. Across the Bridge, Basic Blocks are used as the unit of data transport. Because of this transmit speed of BBs, multiplexing at a Ring bridge is not supported. Congestion control in one Ring can (but will not initially) be implemented between the two sides of a Bridge. The response speeds are sufficiently fast that such signalling would be effective. In general, congestion control will operate by not accepting further BBs if the Bridge is holding too many, and discarding blocks if they cannot be delivered fairly fast.

Satellite Bridges

These are based on a GEC 4065, with a Motorola 6800 as intelligent interface (SIM), to the Earth Station, and an Intel 8086 as intelligent interface to the Ring. Two satellite bridges, separated by a satellite hop, act identically like a Ring Bridge - except the transit time is so long that flow control between the bridges is very difficult. For this reason large buffers (several hundred kilobytes) are being provided in the GEC 4065, and it is hoped that end-to-end flow control will reduce the build-up of queues in the GEC to acceptable limits. The GEC 4065 also has a X25 interface to allow program loading across SRCNET or PSS.

Terrestrial Half-Bridges

These are based on HDLC-type block structures, with conventional acknowledgements. The signalling between the bridges is fast, and the individual blocks are not multiplexed. For this reason, the operation is very similar to that of the Ring Bridge. Variants based on cable transmission between half-bridges, and proprietary modems, with PDP 11/24 computers, are the responsibility of Logica.

The other aspect of the conventional half-bridges (using the pcm transmission with an X21 interface to PDP 11/24) will be a UCL responsibility; the bridge operation will not, however, be different.

X25 Bridges

Several sites, including RAL and UCL, have implemented proper transport level X25 gateways to Cambridge Rings. For this purpose of the project, however, the X25 bridges should act as similarly as possible to the Satellite and Ring bridges. Cambridge U and RAL have the responsibility for this development, which is based on INTEL 8086 computers. The bridge must manage X25 call set-up and close-down, and act as a switch to the GEC 4065 (for blocks diverted to that machine) or to the Ring (for blocks diverted to other Hosts on the Ring).

5.   COMMON SERVERS

It is essential to have sufficient standardisation in several of the services available on each ring to allow a minimum of important services to be standardised. The services in this category include the Satellite bridge, ring bridge, and X25 bridge discussed in the previous section; they also include error-logger, the name-server, time-server, boot-server, exerciser/echoer. These are discussed below. In addition common protocols are being defined, which must be implemented on the Hosts on UNIVERSE; these include transport protocols, bulk transfer protocols, terminal protocols and file servers.

The exact host to be used for the common services is still under discussion, but will probably be a Z80. The responsibility of the provision of the hardware will be RAL's; the exact allocation of responsibility for each individual server is still to be determined. The five versions of each of the above should be completed by mid-1982. In most cases the specifications are based on devices already in existence. thus CU already has implemented a version of all the above servers on a Ring except the echoer/exerciser - which has been implemented on a different network by UCL [6].

In addition to programming the Common servers, we are developing a common set of methods for loading the programs (hence the common boot-server) or cross loading from a central site (hence the X25 bridge).

The functions of name-serving are so entwined with the bridge functions, that a single implementation is essential. Much effort has been wasted in STELLA in making different implementations compatible to the same specifications. This is the type of problem we are trying to avoid.

6. PROGRAMME OF UTILISATION

So far we have considered the basic constituents of the system; of greater import is the utilisation. There are several aims of the project:

(i)   Measure the performance of the system for the types of traffic likely to be encountered in practice.

(ii)   Develop procedures to ensure the utility of the system for computer-computer and terminal-computer interaction.

(iii) Investigate the utility of the concatenation of Mbps satellite links and local networks for business communications.

(iv)   Develop more appropriate components and bridges for optimising a system of this type.

Clearly each of these depends on the prior commissioning of the system itself - hence our emphasis on that activity.

(i)   Performance Measurement and monitoring
One reason for the extensive implementations of common servers on each ring is to ease the problems of performance measurements and monitoring. We are building the exercisers/echoers in such a way that we will simulate the types of traffic we expect to encounter in the different applications. The aim is to superpose specific traffic patterns as traffic already developed for other applications - but in a way that the data generation and acquisition can be controlled remotely. At present the appropriate infrastructure is under design [7].

(ii)   Computer-Computer Service Traffic
We aim to connect, by early 1983, a number of Hosts which already have a substantial traffic on leased lines. It is premature to discuss the exact mode of connection. However, many UK academic groups use the IBM 360/195 - 3032 complex at RAL. This will be attached during 1982 to the RAL ring.

Another computer to be attached is the PRIME 750 at RAL; which is the centre of the Computer Aided Design and Mask making system at RAL. Another is the VAX 780, which is one of the STARLINK astronomy systems. At CU, LU and UCL, other VAX and PRIME computers will be attached for CAD, electronic engineering, physics and astronomy purposes. A key aim of the project is to investigate the utility of the system for these applications. Here job submission, file transfer, data base update, and data base access will be the principal requirement.

(iii) Business Communications
Many projects are looking at business communications over small earth station satellite systems. Comparatively few are looking at the concatenation of local networks with such satellite systems.

We are expecting to develop pilot implementations in this area, using minimal modification of state-of-the-art equipment; this is expected to make possible a demonstration of the system by the end of 1982. Examples of application areas to be investigated include Teletex [8], Viewdata database up-date, and image transfer. These will help identify limitations of equipment, procedures and performance - which would be rectified in later iterations. A clear problem here is access control. Our activities in this area have been described elsewhere [9].

446

(iv) Component Development

The present equipment is being assembled specifically with the aim of using off-the-shelf components where possible. As a result of monitoring of the applications (i) - (iii), we expect to identify many areas where the existing components and procedures are inadequate. In parallel with the short-term aims of utilisation and demonstration, we expect to mount a long-term component development programme.

Examples of where we already see need for such development are the following:

(a) Earth station monitoring and control
(b) Flexible use of the Satellite channel with impact on SIM and Earth Station design
(c) Better coding of the digital stream - making bit error rate depend on the application requirement
(d) Ring monitoring and control
(e) Multi-mode terminal for these applications
(f) Procedures for voice and teleconferencing
(g) Generalised name servers
(h) An economic technology for intra-city distribution

Clearly the participants in the experiment will themselves be major users of the systems. We plan to use it heavily for document and message traffic, multimedia conferencing, cross network loading of programs, data acquisition of measurements, and experiment coordination. A wide variety of the services to be investigated will be used for communication between the participants during the project.

7.   PROJECT ORGANISATION

Working Group Structure

In a project of this size there are several administrative committees; their composition is immaterial for this paper. However, a more informative indication of the technical interests are the composition of the Technical Working Groups. These are currently the following:

System Construction
Equipment installation, Protocols and Servers, Intra-urban Communication, Host Attachment

Experiments
Network Performance, Distributed Computing, Long Term Voice and Image, experimentation, encryption and authentication

Demonstrations
Voice, Teletex, Videotex and Graphic Messages

ACKNOWLEDGEMENT

It is clear that a project of this sort involves many people in each establishment. The names of the authors, merely record the team leader at each site; the work has already involved at least 30 people directly, and many others indirectly. It is essential to acknowledge however, the generous support of the Science and Engineering Research Council under this specially promoted project, the Department of Industry for their financial contribution, and British Telecom, both for their financial contribution and their extremely helpful technical and administrative assistance. Both General Electric-Marconi and Logica are making substantial financial contributions to the project.

REFERENCES

1. S Hannel: "The European communications satellite", Proc. Conf. on Satellite Communications, Online, London, 71-82, 1980
2. A Hopper: "Data Ring at the Computer Laboratory, University of Cambridge", Proc. Conf. Local Area Networking, NBS Special Pub., 500-531, 11-16, 1978
3. C Adams and I Leslie; "Protocols for the UNIVERSE network", Companion ICCC paper
4. CCITT: "Recommendation X21: General purpose interface between data terminal equipment (DTE) and data circuit terminating equipment (DCE) for synchronous operation on data public networks", Public Data Networks Orange Book, Vol VIII.2 6th Plenary Assembly, Int. Telecom Union, Geneva, 38-56, 1977
5. DW Davies et al: "Communication Networks for Computers", John Wiley, 170-173, 1973
6. SW Treadwell, "Measurement methods in packet switched networks", TR 63, University College London, 1980
7. SR Wilbur and Z Ma: "Measurement and Monitoring on the UNIVERSE Project", Companion ICCC paper
8. CCITT: "Teletex Service", Final Report to the 7th Plenary Assembly, (Part III), F200, Document No 91, Int. Telecom Union, Geneva, 42-99, 1980
9. Girling: "Authentication and Access Control", Companion ICCC paper

Perfect Scheduling in Multi-hop Broadcast Networks

J A Silvester
University of Southern California,
USA

Broadcast Networks have been proposed for use in local access networks and general mobile communications. Various random access protocols have been suggested for use in these networks due to their efficiency in bursty data traffic environments. Some studies exist on the performance of these protocols in distributed multi-hop environments, but these results are difficult to interpret since the maximum throughput that could be achieved with perfect scheduling is unknown. For fully-connected networks, perfect scheduling allows a maximum throughput of 1 and we thus have a measure against which to compare other access protocols, such as Slotted ALOHA which has a 'capacity' of $1/e$. In this paper, we present an algorithm for determining the maximum throughput of multi-hop broadcast networks, present some simple examples and compare the perfect scheduling results against those of Slotted ALOHA.

1 INTRODUCTION

In recent years there has been much interest in the use of broadcast radio for computer communication networks. The first such network was the ALOHAnet at the University of Hawaii [1]. This network concept has been generalised to include multi-hop networks which allow arbitrary point-to-point communication without the use of a central station in the packet radio network (PRnet) [4, 5].

Much work has been done to determine the performance of such networks. In particular the maximum achievable throughput of the ALOHAnet was determined to be $1/2e$, or 18% of the throughput that could be achieved if perfect scheduling were used [1]. By using a Slotted version of ALOHA, the capacity can be increased to $1/e$ (36%) [9]. These results have been generalised to two-hop centralised networks in [3, 13, 14]. For the arbitrary multi-hop non-centralised network, however, much less is known. In [6, 11] we developed a simple model for multi-hop networks with random structure operating under the Slotted ALOHA access protocol and evaluated the network capacity as a function of the network average degree. We found that a tradeoff between the number of hops and the amount of interference existed, and that for an appropriate choice of the average degree, a throughput proportional to the square root of the number of nodes in the network could be achieved by spatial reuse of the channel. We have also studied networks with regular structure in [12] and were able to gain some insight into the routing problems. In [8], we present an algorithm for determining the capacity of a distributed multi-hop Slotted ALOHA network satisfying an arbitrary traffic matrix, using a non-linear optimisation technique.

In fully-connected networks it is easy to interpret these capacity results by comparing them to the performance that can be obtained with perfect scheduling (TDMA or FDMA). For a multi-hop network, such comparisons are not as straightforward since the corresponding perfect scheduling results are not available. In this paper we present an algorithm based on a generalised graph colouring technique to determine the network capacity if perfect scheduling is used. We are not proposing that these fixed assignment techniques be used for a channel access protocol, since their inefficiency and complexity for data traffic in networks with many nodes are well known. Rather we are interested in determining performance bounds against which to measure the various different access protocols that would be used in a real implementation, (such as ALOHA or CSMA). We find that for certain network configurations, the problem is harder than a straightforward graph colouring problem, so we introduce the notion of fractional colouring. We then give some preliminary results of our studies of the capacity of perfectly scheduled networks and make comparisons to Slotted ALOHA for some simple configurations.

2 NETWORK MODEL

In [10, 11] we give a general formulation of the network model. We reproduce part of that here as a basis for the development of our algorithm. We consider a network to be characterised by the following matrices:

The Adjacency Matrix This specifies the hearing patterns of the network. If node i can hear the transmission of node j, then $a_{ij}=1$. (Note that we are considering reception to be a discrete process.)

The Traffic Matrix This specifies the amount of end-to-end traffic carried between node pairs. It could be measured in number of fixed bandwidth channels required (for FDMA) or in packets or slots per unit time (for packet switching or TDMA). If the traffic requirement from node i to node j is t then $t_{ij}=t$. The network traffic (total throughput), γ, is given by:

$$\gamma = \sum_i \sum_j t_{ij} \qquad (1)$$

The <u>Routing Matrix</u> This defines the paths that traffic follows from source to destination. In many situations this would be a design variable. For the purpose of this paper we consider the routes to be fixed and given, however. For simplicity we consider the special case of single path routing, although the results are readily generalised.

From these matrices we can determine the flow required on each link of the network to be:

$$f_{ij} = \sum_s \sum_d t_{ij}\, d_{ij}^{sd} \qquad (2)$$

Where d_{ij}^{sd} is a path selector such that $d_{ij}^{sd} = 1$ if link (i,j) is on the path $[s,d]$ as defined by the routing matrix.

Perfect scheduling requires the allocation of frequencies or time slots to each link such that these flows can be satisfied with no interference from neighbouring channels. We can then proceed to compute the network capacity.

2.1 FDMA

In FDMA the numbers obtained in Equation (2) correspond to the number of frequencies that must be assigned to each link. We can thus use a colouring algorithm which assigns a number of colours equal to the f_{ij}'s found above to the links of the network such that those links that would interfere with each other have no colours in common. We give a more precise formulation of this colouring problem in the following section. Suppose that the colouring algorithm determines that k colours are required, then if the total bandwidth available is B with corresponding data rate C (bits per second), each channel will have bandwidth B/k and the total traffic carried by the network is channels or C/k bits per second.

2.2 TDMA or Perfectly Scheduled Packet Switching

For TDMA or perfectly scheduled packet switching the formulation of the problem is a little more complex. Since the traffic matrix entries may in general not be integers, we first scale the traffic matrix by multiplying by some scale factor so that all entries are integers. For the purpose of this paper we can assume that this scaling is done before we proceed to colouring. With integer values for the f_{ij} we can proceed to the colouring algorithm as was described above for FDMA. Assuming that we need k colours, we see that the throughput is given by C/k, (from the analogy with FDMA where the subchannels are now derived by time splitting rather than

frequency splitting).

2.3 Note on Improving Performance

Before proceeding to give the colouring algorithm, we note that we could double (triple, etc.) the f_{ij}'s (and the corresponding value for) and then solve the colouring problem. This corresponds to splitting the frequency assignment for a particular channel into two (three, etc.) subchannels. In general, the modified colouring problem will require less than 2k colours (and certainly no more), which allows us to obtain a higher maximum throughput. We discuss this issue in more detail in a later section and present some results on whether this splitting and the use of "fractional colours" is beneficial.

3 THE CORRESPONDING COLORING PROBLEM

The algorithm presented here was proposed in [10] and a similar approach can be found in [2], where they are concerned with frequency assignment for non-broadcast networks.

Let the original network be represented by the graph $G=(V,E)$, where V is the vertex set corresponding to the nodes of the original network, and E is the edge set, where the edge (i,j) E iff $a_{ij}=1$, i.e., node j hears i's transmission. We construct a derived edge graph, $H=(V',E')$, where the vertex set of H corresponds to the edge set of G, i.e.,

$$V' = \{ \, x=[i,j] : (i,j) \in E \, \}$$

The edges of H correspond to the channels that can interfere with each other (i.e., cannot be assigned the same frequency or time slot), and are defined as follows:

$$E' = \{ \, (x,y)=([i_1,j_1],[i_2,j_2]) :$$
$$i_1 = i_2 \;\; (A) \;\;|\;\; i_1 = j_2 \;\; (B) \;\;|$$
$$j_1 = i_2 \;\; (C) \;\;|\;\; (i_1,j_2) \in E \;\; (D) \;\;|$$
$$(i_2,j_1) \in E \;\; (E) \, \}$$

Case A corresponds to two channels having the same source; case B is where the source of one channel is the destination of the other; case C is the same as case B but the channel roles are reversed; case D is where the destination of the second channel is within range of the source of the first channel; and case E is the same as case D with the channel roles reversed.

The algorithm now proceeds to colour this resulting graph, assigning f_{ij} colours to vertex $x=[i,j]$ such that adjacent vertices in H have no colours in common, which is the traditional graph colouring problem generalised to assign multiple colours to a vertex.

4 IMPLEMENTATION CONSIDERATIONS

In order to increase the efficiency of this algorithm we use the following technique [7]. The vertices of the modified graph are first sorted in order of decreasing degree, where the degree of a vertex now corresponds to the total amount of traffic that it handles, i.e., the degree of the vertex $x=(i,j)$ is given by:

$$\sum_{([i,j],[k,l]) \in E'} f_{kl}$$

In addition, the vertices are also sorted by affinities, i.e., we first select the vertex with the highest degree and increment a count for all vertices that have an edge to this node. The vertex with the highest count is now selected and the counts of those vertices adjacent to this one are incremented. This process is repeated until the whole graph is ordered.

This sorted list defines the order in which the vertices are scanned by the colouring algorithm. The running time is greatly reduced since we are very likely to find a large clique at the beginning of the colouring process. This clique never has to be recoloured and for many networks the number of colours required by the clique will be sufficient for the whole graph.

4.1 The Algorithm

The following is a high level description of the algorithm used to generate the modified graph and colour it as outlined above. The algorithm was coded in Pascal and run on a PDP-20.

```
1)  Read in the network (adjacencies, flows);
2)  Create the derived edge graph;
3)  Sort the vertices of the graph by degrees
       and affinities;
4)  Colour the clique (first few vertices of
       sorted graph);
    i=cliquesize+1;
    maxcolor=sum of flows for all vertices;
5)  while (cliquesize < i < #vertices+1) do
       attempt to colour vertex i;
       if #colors used < maxcolor
           then i=i+1
           else i=i-1;
       od
6)  at the end of this loop either:
    i=#vertices + 1 => we have coloured graph,
       set maxcolor=#colors_used-1;
       set i=index of first vertex coloured
       with #colors_used;
       return to step 5;
                      or:
    i=cliquesize => previous pass was the best
    colouring,
    stop;
```

Although the worst case complexity of this algorithm is exponential we expect that the average case will be fast since we will commonly encounter a large clique which determines the colouring for the whole graph. This has been found to be the case in runs that we have made on many experimental networks. An analytical study of the complexity of the algorithm is currently in progress.

5 FRACTIONAL COLORING

As mentioned above, we could consider doubling each of the f_{ij} and then using the colouring algorithm, where now each colour assigned is in reality a "half-colour". We define k^n to be the number of (fractional) colours needed to colour G when the load on link (i,j) is nf_{ij}. We are interested in finding:

$$k^* = \lim_{n \to \infty} \frac{k^n}{n}$$

which we define to be the fractional chromatic number of the graph. We then assign the f_{ij} frequencies (time-slots etc.) as the set of n sub-frequencies determined by the fractional colours. (We are ignoring overhead due to guard bands to allow separation of the sub-channels.)

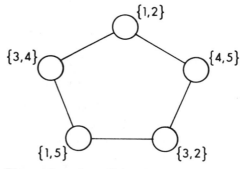

Figure 1:   Loop Network Simple Coloring

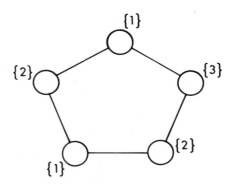

Figure 2:   Loop Network with Fractional
Coloring (Half Colors)

To see that this may result in fewer (whole) colours being needed, consider the loop of Figure 1, if we assign single colours to each vertex we note that 3 colours are needed, whereas with fractional colouring only 5 half-colours are required (see Figure 2). The capacity resulting from the single colour assignment is C/3, compared to 2C/5 for the half-colouring. For this particular network we can in fact prove that the fractional chromatic number is 5/2 (i.e., using third-colours is not beneficial). For arbitrary graphs it is not easy to determine when this colour splitting process should be terminated, but for certain simple topologies we can find the fractional chromatic number:

Theorem 1: For a m-vertex fully connected graph $k^*=m$ i.e., fractional colouring is of no benefit.

Theorem 2: For a m-vertex line network $k^*=2$

Theorem 3: For a m-vertex loop $k^*=2$ if m is even, and $k^*=2m/m-1$ if m is odd.

Much work remains to be done to extend these results to general graphs and in particular to the types of graph that we encounter as a result of the broadcast nature of the underlying networks. We do note that the graphs that we encounter typically have large cliques which define the colouring for the whole graph, (in which case no advantage is gained from fractional colouring).

6 EXAMPLES

In this section we consider some simple network examples and determine the perfect scheduling capacity.

6.1 A Very Simple Network

Consider the simple network shown in Figure 3, with the obvious routing matrix and a uniform traffic requirement of 1 unit for each source destination pair (the units here are msgs/time). The corresponding flow matrix is given by:

$$F = \begin{bmatrix} 0 & 1 & 2 & 0 \\ 1 & 0 & 2 & 0 \\ 2 & 2 & 0 & 3 \\ 0 & 0 & 3 & 0 \end{bmatrix}$$

In Figure 4, we show the derived edge graph, which is a fully-connected graph of 8 vertices and thus requires a number of colours equal to the total flow carried by the network, i.e., 16 colours, to handle 4*3=12 traffic units. Thus the capacity of this network is 0.75 (times the bandwidth available). The program output for this example can be found in the appendix.

The maximum throughput that could be achieved in this network if the access protocol were Slotted ALOHA can be found by solving the following optimisation problem:

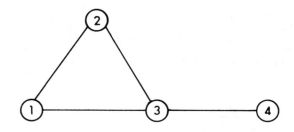

Figure 3:   A Simple Network

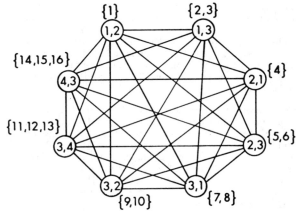

Figure 4:   The Derived Edge Graph

maximise γ

subject to:

$$\gamma f_{ij} = p_{ij} \prod_{\substack{(k,j)\in E \\ k\neq i}} (1 - \sum_{l} p_{kl}) \quad \forall i,j$$

$$p_{ij} \geq 0 \qquad \forall i,j$$

$$\sum_{j} p_{ij} \leq 1 \qquad \forall i$$

Where p_{ij} is the probability that node i transmits to node j in any slot and can be adjusted to optimise the throughput. For this particular network we find that the maximum achievable throughput is 0.39.

Thus for a fully-connected network of 4 nodes the Slotted ALOHA throughput is 27/64 (0.42) as compared to 1 for TDMA, whereas for the configuration of Figure 3, the ALOHA throughput is 0.39 compared to 0.75 for TDMA.

6.2 A More Complex Network

Figure 5 shows a more complex example. The traffic matrix used was:

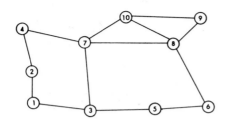

Figure 5: A More Complex Network

$$T = \begin{bmatrix} 0 & 0 & 0 & 0 & 0 & 0 & 0 & 0 & 1 & 0 \\ 0 & 0 & 0 & 0 & 1 & 0 & 0 & 1 & 0 & 0 \\ 0 & 0 & 0 & 0 & 0 & 0 & 1 & 0 & 0 & 0 \\ 0 & 0 & 0 & 0 & 0 & 1 & 0 & 0 & 0 & 0 \\ 0 & 1 & 0 & 0 & 0 & 0 & 0 & 0 & 0 & 1 \\ 0 & 0 & 0 & 1 & 0 & 0 & 0 & 0 & 0 & 0 \\ 0 & 0 & 1 & 0 & 0 & 0 & 0 & 0 & 0 & 0 \\ 0 & 1 & 0 & 0 & 0 & 0 & 0 & 0 & 0 & 0 \\ 1 & 0 & 0 & 0 & 0 & 0 & 0 & 0 & 0 & 1 \\ 0 & 0 & 0 & 0 & 1 & 0 & 0 & 0 & 1 & 0 \end{bmatrix}$$

Using a shortest path routing algorithm, the flow matrix becomes:

$$F = \begin{bmatrix} 0 & 1 & 2 & 0 & 0 & 0 & 0 & 0 & 0 & 0 \\ 1 & 0 & 0 & 1 & 0 & 0 & 0 & 0 & 0 & 0 \\ 2 & 0 & 0 & 0 & 2 & 0 & 3 & 0 & 0 & 0 \\ 0 & 1 & 0 & 0 & 0 & 0 & 2 & 0 & 0 & 0 \\ 0 & 0 & 2 & 0 & 0 & 0 & 0 & 0 & 0 & 0 \\ 0 & 0 & 0 & 0 & 0 & 0 & 0 & 1 & 0 & 0 \\ 0 & 0 & 3 & 2 & 0 & 0 & 0 & 3 & 0 & 1 \\ 0 & 0 & 0 & 0 & 0 & 1 & 3 & 0 & 1 & 0 \\ 0 & 0 & 0 & 0 & 0 & 0 & 0 & 0 & 1 & 0 \\ 0 & 0 & 0 & 0 & 0 & 0 & 1 & 0 & 1 & 0 \end{bmatrix}$$

From the listing in the appendix we see that this network requires a total of 18 colours for a throughput of 14 traffic units (the sum of the traffic matrix entries). The capacity of the network is therefore 14/18 = .78 of the bandwidth.

We note that no backtracking was required for either case since the coloring determined by the large clique is sufficient to color the rest of the network.

7 CONCLUSIONS

We have presented a simple algorithm for computation of the maximum throughput that can be achieved using perfect scheduling in an arbitrary multi-hop network. The technique used is an extension of graph colouring to include assignment of multiple colours to a vertex. We find that we must also consider the assignment of fractional colours to find the

truly optimal assignment (although in many practical examples this is unnecessary). Finally we present the output generated by our algorithm for some simple networks.

A.1 Computer Output for the Simple Network

We now give the computer output for the simple example network.

nodes =   4

adjacency matrix of original graph

```
0  1  1  0
1  0  1  0
1  1  0  1
0  0  1  0
```

Link #		Flows		Link #		Flow
1 = [1, 2]	1			5 = [3, 1]	2	
2 = [1, 3]	2			6 = [3, 2]	2	
3 = [2, 1]	1			7 = [3, 4]	3	
4 = [2, 3]	2			8 = [4, 3]	3	

Total Flow =   16

Sorted index by degrees
   1 2 3 4 5 6 7 8

Sorted index by proximities
   1 2 3 4 5 6 7 8

Max clique size = 8
Upper bound = 16 (Total Flow)
Lower bound = 16 (Clique)

Successful Coloring

[1, 2]	1		[3, 1]	7 8	
[1, 3]	2 3		[3, 2]	9 10	
[2, 1]	4		[3, 4]	11 12 13	
[2, 3]	5 6		[4, 3]	14 15 16	

using   16 colours

Throughput is   0.750000

Computer Output for the More Complex Example

What follows is the computer printout for the more complex network.

nodes = 10

adjacency matrix of original graph

```
0  1  1  0  0  0  0  0  0  0
1  0  0  1  0  0  0  0  0  0
1  0  0  0  1  0  1  0  0  0
0  1  0  0  0  0  1  0  0  0
0  0  1  0  0  1  0  0  0  0
0  0  0  0  1  0  0  1  0  0
0  0  1  1  0  0  0  1  0  0
0  0  0  0  0  1  1  0  1  1
0  0  0  0  0  0  0  1  0  1

0  0  0  0  0  0  1  1  1  0
```

Link #		Flows		Link #		Flows
1 =	[1, 2]	1		14 =	[7, 3]	3
2 =	[1, 3]	2		15 =	[7, 4]	2
3 =	[2, 1]	1		16 =	[7, 8]	3
4 =	[2, 4]	1		17 =	[7,10]	1
5 =	[3, 1]	2		18 =	[8, 6]	1
6 =	[3, 5]	2		19 =	[8, 7]	3
7 =	[3, 7]	3		20 =	[8, 9]	1
8 =	[4, 2]	1		21 =	[8,10]	0
9 =	[4, 7]	2		22 =	[9, 8]	1
10 =	[5, 3]	2		23 =	[9,10]	1
11 =	[5, 6]	0		24 =	[10, 7]	1
12 =	[6, 5]	0		25 =	[10, 8]	0
13 =	[6, 8]	1		26 =	[10, 9]	1

Total Flow = 36

Sorted index by degrees
7 14 16 17 19 24 9 15 21 25 2 5 6 10
13 18 20 22 23 26 4 8 1 3 11 12

Sorted index by proximities
7 14 16 17 19 24 9 15 21 25 13 18 20 22
23 26 6 10 11 12 2 5 4 8 1 3

Max clique size = 10
Upper bound = 36 (Total Flow)
Lower bound = 18 (Clique)

Successful Coloring

[1, 2]	2			[1, 3]	13 14		
[2, 1]	5			[2, 4]	1		
[3, 1]	9 10			[3, 5]	7 8		
[3, 7]	1 2 3			[4, 2]	4		
[4, 7]	15 16			[5, 3]	11 12		
[5, 6]				[6, 5]			
[6, 8]	1			[7, 3]	4 5 6		
[7, 4]	17 18			[7, 8]	7 8 9		
[7,10]	10			[8, 6]	4		
[8, 7]	11 12 13			[8, 9]	5		
[8,10]				[9, 8]	2		
[9,10]	3			[10, 7]	14		
[10, 8]	.			[10, 9]	6		

using 18 colours

Throughput is 0.777778

REFERENCES

[1] The ALOHA System - Another Alternative for Computer Communications, N. Abramson, AFIPS Conference Proceedings, 1970 Fall Joint Computer Conference, Vol. 37, pp 281-285, 1970.

[2] Application of Network Optimisation Algorithms to Radio Frequency Assignment Problems, G. Barberis and V. Zingarelli, Conference Record of the International Conference on Communications, Vol. 3, pp 66.6.1-66.6.5, June 1981.

[3] On the Capacity of Slotted ALOHA Networks and some Design Problems, I. Gitman, IEEE Transactions on Communications, Vol. COM-23, pp 305-317, March 1975.

[4] The Organization of Computer Resources into a Packet Radio Network, R.E. Kahn, IEEE Transactions on Communications, Vol. COM-25, pp 169-178, Jan. 1977.

[5] Advances in Packet Radio Technology, R.E. Kahn et al, Proceedings of the IEEE, Vol. 66, No. 11, Nov. 1978.

[6] Optimum Transmission Radii for Packet Radio Networks or Why Six is a Magic Number, L. Kleinrock and J.A. Silvester, NTC Conference Record, Dec. 1978.

[7] The Graph-Colouring Problem, S.M. Korman, in Combinatorial Optimization, chapter 8, editors: N. Christofides, A. Mingozzi, P. Toth, and C. Sandi, Wiley, 1979.

[8] Optimal Retransmission Probabilities for Multihop Slotted ALOHA Networks, I. Lee and J.A. Silvester, in preparation.

[9] ALOHA Packet System with and without Slots and Capture, L. Roberts, Computer Communication Review, Vol 5., No. 2, pp 28-42, April 1975.

[10] Capacity Issues for Multi-Hop Broadcast Networks, J. A. Silvester, Proceedings of the 3rd MIT/ONR Workshop on Distributed Information and Decision Systems motivated by Command Control Communication (C3) Problems, Vol. 5, 1980.

[11] On the Spatial Capacity of Packet Radio Networks, J.A. Silvester, UCLA Modelling and Analysis Group, UCLA-ENG-8021, May 1980.

[12] On the Capacity of Multi-Hop Slotted ALOHA Networks with Regular Structure, J.A. Silvester and L. Kleinrock, to appear in IEEE Transactions on Communications.

[13] Analysis of a Two-Hop Centralised Packet Radio Network - Part I: Slotted ALOHA, F.A. Tobagi, IEEE Transactions on Communications, Vol. COM-28, No. 2, pp 196-207, February 1980.

[14] Analysis of a Two-Hop Centralised Packet Radio Network - Part II: Carrier Sense Multiple Access, F.A. Tobagi, IEEE Transactions on Communications, Vol. COM-28, No. 2, pp 208-216, February 1980.

John Silvester was born in Kent, England in 1950. He received the B.A. (M.A.) degree in Mathematics and Operations Research from Cambridge University in 1971 (1975); the M.S. in Statistics and Computer Science from West Virginia University in 1973; and the Ph.D. in Computer Science from the University of California at Los Angeles in 1980. The dissertation for his Ph.D.,supervised by Professor L. Kleinrock,was related to performance studies of packet radio networks. In January 1979 he joined the University of Southern California as an Assistant Professor of Electrical Engineering, where he teaches courses in Computer Architecture,Queueing Theory and Computer Networks and is actively engaged in research in broadcast communication networks. He also consults for several companies and government agencies on related topics.

Interference Considerations on a Local Area Radio Network

G K Chan, J B deMercado,
J S daSilva
Department of Communications, Canada

S A Mahmoud
Carleton University, Canada

As a result of the increasing demand for person to computer and computer to computer communications, data communications over local radio networks is expected to grow in the next decade. Some of the main problems associated with the use of radio channels are the effects of fading and co-channel interference on the channel throughput. In this paper, a local area radio mobile system model implemented on a cellular structure is described and a mathematical analysis of the degradation of system performance due to fading and co-channel interference is presented.

1. INTRODUCTION

As a result of the increasing demand for person to computer and computer to computer communications, data communications over local radio networks is expected to grow in the next decade. The decreasing cost of digital equipment has provided end users with many desirable distributed processing capabilities over local networks such as communications with a central computer from a mobile vehicle via a digital mobile channel.

One important concern associated with this growing use of local area mobile radio systems is the scarcity of the radio spectrum. As the number of users increases, the same radio channel has to be reused more and more often and assigned to users separated from each other by a certain reuse distance. This reuse distance is largely determined by the level of co-channel interference that can be tolerated at the radio receiver.

In addition, the radio channel is further affected by the occurrences of shadowing and fading. Fading is caused by multipath propagation and wave interference. The received signal amplitude can be approximated very closely by the Rayleigh distribution over short distances. Over larger areas, the mean value of the Rayleigh distribution has a lognormal distribution. This variation of the mean is due to shadowing by features of the terrain as the vehicle moves along.

Several authors {1,2,3,4} have discussed the effects of shadowing and fading on a mobile channel and in {1}, a mathematical expression has been derived to describe the probability of receiving a packet of data successfully in a Rayleigh fading channel. Using this expression, we further investigate in this paper the combined effects of Rayleigh fading and co-channel interference on the digital mobile channel.

2. SYSTEM MODEL

Consider a local area mobile radio system, predicated on a cellular architecture, in which a base station of a given cell communicates with a number of mobile stations on a downlink channel and the mobiles communicate with the base station on an uplink channel. Both channels are reused at a certain distance away from the given cell. The frequencies of the two channels are spaced sufficiently far apart from each other so that interference would not exist between them.

Packets of equal lengths are transmitted on both downlink and uplink channels. It is assumed that the base station transmits continuously to the mobiles in its own cell in frames with each frame divided into a number of packet slots. This number is determined by the amount of traffic in the cell and more than one slot may be used consecutively for transmission to a single mobile. The mobiles transmit to the base station using the random access slotted ALOHA scheme. Both base and mobile transmissions are synchronized and propagation delays are accounted for as part of the packet transmission time. It is further assumed that the base station transmitter powers are equal in all the cells and the mobile transmitter powers are also equal over the entire system.

3. CO-CHANNEL INTERFERENCE TO A DOWNLINK CHANNEL

Since the amplitude of the signal at the mobile receiver is Rayleigh distributed, the power of the received signal is given by the probability density function:

$$P(X) = 1/Xm \cdot \exp(-X/Xm) \tag{1}$$

where X = instantaneous received signal power level
Xm = mean received signal power level

and

$$P(X \geq X_T) = \exp(-X_T/Xm) \tag{2}$$

gives the probability of receiving a signal above the threshold power level X_T to ensure reliable reception.

As the mobile receiver moves, say, with speed v, it traverses a series of fades during which the received signal would dip below X_T. The probability P_{SM} that a packet can be received successfully by the mobile within a time period where no fading occurs is given by {1}:

$$P_{SM} = \exp\left[-\frac{X_T}{Xm} - fdT\sqrt{\frac{2\pi X_T}{Xm}}\right] \tag{3}$$

where fd = Doppler frequency = v/λ_c

λ_G = wavelength of the carrier frequency of the base station

T = packet transmission time

Now consider the case when the packet transmission is interfered by a co-channel base station with received power level Xi. Co-channel interference would occur if the desired signal X is less than or equal to rXi where r is the protection ratio.

Since the interfering signal also suffers from fading, the probability that the interfering signal power level would exceed X/r for a given X is:

$$P(X_i \geq \frac{X}{r} /X) = \exp\left[-X/rX_{im}\right] \tag{4}$$

where X_{im} = mean power level of the undesired signal.

Hence, the probability of interference is obtained by integrating the above conditional probability over all values of X:

$$P_I = \int_o^\infty P\,(X_i \geq \frac{X}{r} /\,X).P(X).dX$$

$$= \int_o^\infty e^{-X/rXim}.\frac{1}{Xm}.\,e^{-X/Xm}.dX$$

$$= \frac{rXim}{Xm+rXim} \tag{5}$$

In the case when there is more than one co-channel interferor, it is necessary to find the cummulative effect of all the co-channel interferences. In a cellular structure, considering only the six co-channel interfering base stations on the first 'ring' around the given base station, the mean power level of each of these interfering signals at the receiver is approximately the same. Furthermore, it is assumed that each of the six interfering power levels is independent and identically distributed. Hence if Z is a random variable denoting the sum of the interfering power levels at the receiver, its probability density function $f(z)$ is given by the convolution of the six probability density functions. A general expression for n co-channel base stations is therefore given by:

$$f(Z) = P_1\,(Xi_1)\,{}^*P_2\,(Xi_2)^*\ldots.P_n\,(Xi_n)$$

$$= P\,(Xi_1)\,{}^*P(Xi_2)^*\ldots\ldots P(Xi_n) \tag{6}$$

Taking the Laplace Transform,

$$f(s) = P(s).P(s)\ldots\ldots\ldots P(s)$$

$$= \frac{1}{X_{im}^n} \cdot \frac{1}{(S+\frac{1}{X_{im}})^n} \quad . \quad \text{Hence,}$$

$$f(z) = \left(\frac{1}{Xim}\right)^n \cdot \frac{Z^{n-1}.e^{-Z/Xim}}{(n-1)!} \tag{7}$$

The probability that Z would exceed X/r given X is

$$\text{Prob}\left[Z \geq \frac{X}{r} /X\right] = \frac{e^{-\frac{X}{rXim}}}{Xim^n} \quad .$$

$$\sum_{k=0}^{n-1} \left(\frac{X}{r}\right)^{n-1-k} \cdot \frac{Xim^{k+1}}{(n-1-k)!} \tag{8}$$

Hence the probability P_{IM} of getting co-channel interference from the n^{IM} stations would be

$$P_{IM} = \int_o^\infty P(X).\text{Prob}\left[Z \geq \frac{X}{r} /\,X\right] dX$$

$$= \int_o^\infty \frac{1}{Xm} \cdot e^{-X/Xm} \cdot e^{-X/rXim} \quad .$$

$$\sum_{k=0}^{n-1} \left(\frac{X}{rXim}\right)^{n-1-k} \cdot \frac{1}{(n-1-k)!} \cdot dX$$

$$= \sum_{k=o}^{n-1} \frac{r(\frac{Xim}{Xm})}{(1+r\frac{Xim}{Xm})^{n-k}} \tag{9}$$

According to the inverse 4th power law which states that the received power level is inversely proportional to the 4th power of distance,

$$Xim = \frac{\epsilon}{D^4} \quad ; \quad Xm = \frac{\epsilon}{d^4}$$

where ϵ is a propagation constant common to both the desired and undesired signals, D is the distance between the undesired base station and the mobile station and d is the cell radius as shown in fig. 1.

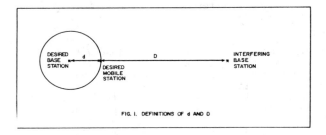

FIG. I. DEFINITIONS OF d AND D

$$\therefore \quad \frac{Xim}{Xm} = \left(\frac{d}{D}\right)^4$$

If $\quad R = \left(\frac{D}{d}\right)^4 = \frac{Xm}{Xim}$

then $P_{IM} = \displaystyle\sum_{k=o}^{n-1} \frac{\frac{r}{R}}{(1+\frac{r}{R})^{n-k}}$ $\tag{10}$

For $r/R \ll 1$,

$$P_{IM} = \frac{nr}{R} \tag{11}$$

Expressions (10) and (11) show that the probability of co-channel interference depends only on the number of interfering stations, the protection ratio and R which is related to the co-channel reuse distance U since

$$U = \frac{d + D}{d} = 1 + R^{\frac{1}{4}} \tag{12}$$

The relationship between P_{IM}/n which is the probability of co-channel interference divided by the number of interferors and U for different values of r is plotted in fig. 2.

Since the desired and undesired signal levels are assumed to be independent, the probability P_{SM}' of successful reception of a desired packet at the mobile receiver is therefore given by the product of P_{SM} and $(1-P_{IM})$. Hence,

$$P_{SM}' = P_{SM} \cdot (1-P_{IM}) \tag{13}$$

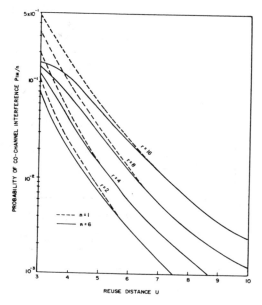

FIG. 2 PROBABILITY OF CO-CHANNEL INTERFERENCE P_{IM}/n AS A FUNCTION OF REUSE DISTANCE U AND PROTECTION RATIO r

4. CO-CHANNEL INTERFERENCE TO AN UPLINK CHANNEL

Mobiles transmit packets to the base station using a random access slotted ALOHA scheme. If G is the average rate of packet transmissions per slot in a given cell including transmissions, repeated transmissions and acknowledgements, and the mobiles generate equal amounts of traffic, each mobile station would be transmitting packets at an average rate of G/M packets per slot where M is the number of mobiles in any given cell. Since packets are transmitted randomly, there exists a probability that they would collide with each other. It is assumed that whenever collision takes place, the transmissions would not be received successfully. The probability that no packet collision occurs within a given cell is given

by {6,7}:

$$P_{nc} = (1-\frac{G}{M})^{M-1} \tag{14}$$

Since the uplink channel suffers the same kind of Rayleigh fading as the downlink channel, the probability that a packet can be successfully received by its own cell base station in the absence of any other transmissions within the same cell is given by:

$$P_{SB} = P_B \cdot P_{nc} \tag{15}$$

where $P_B = \exp\left[-\frac{Y_T}{Ym} - f_d' T \left(\frac{2\pi Y_T}{Ym}\right)^{\frac{1}{2}} \right]$ (16)

Y_T = threshold power level for the desired signal at the base receiver

Ym = mean power level of the mobile signal

f_d' = Doppler frequency = v/λ_c'

λ_c' = wavelength of the carrier frequency from the mobile

Denoting by H the average rate of successful packet transmissions per slot per mobile within a cell, then in the absence of interference.

$$H = \frac{G}{M} \cdot P_{SB} \tag{17}$$

and the system throughput S is:

$$S = G \cdot P_{SB} \tag{18}$$

In considering co-channel interference to the packet reception at the base station, it is assumed that there are approximately the same number of mobiles in each cell and also the same amount of traffic carried by each mobile. Hence the probability that a mobile in any one cell would transmit is G/M.

We further assume that the mobiles are at about the same distance from the base station so that the mean mobile signal power levels at the base station receiver are about the same. Now, for a given number, m, of mobiles transmitting at the same time, the probability of receiving co-channel interference at the base station may be obtained from (11):

$$\text{Prob (co-channel interference / m)} = \frac{m.r}{R} \tag{19}$$

It is also necessary to find the probability that m mobiles would be transmitting at the same time. This is given by:

$$P(m) = \binom{nM}{m} \left(\frac{G}{M}\right)^m \left(1-\frac{G}{M}\right)^{nM-m} \tag{20}$$

From (19) and (20), the probability of interference P_{IB} at the base station receiver is given by:

$$P_{IB} = \sum_{m=1}^{nM} \frac{mr}{R} \cdot P(m) = \frac{nGr}{R} \tag{21}$$

457

The probability P'_{SB} that a mobile packet
transmission may be successfully received
at the base station under co-channel interference in the Rayleigh fading channel can therefore be obtained from (15) and (21):

$$P'_{SB} = P_{SB} \cdot \left[1 - P_{IB} \right] \tag{22}$$

The new average rate of successful packet
transmissions per slot per mobile within a cell,
H' and the system throughput S' now become:

$$H' = G/M . P'_{SB} \tag{23}$$

$$S' = G . P'_{SB} \tag{24}$$

5. RESULTS AND DISCUSSIONS

We have presented above a number of mathematical expressions to evaluate the probabilities
of successful packet reception in a downlink
and uplink channel under the effects of
Rayleigh fading and co-channel interference.
In this section, by using some numerical
examples, we attempt to investigate the
significance of these effects.

In order to calculate the received signal
power levels, the path loss model proposed by
EGLI {5} is used. If the average effective
transmission heights for the base and mobile
stations are 45 metres and 2 metres respectively, the path loss, P (in dB) is:

$$P = 44.6 + 40 \log d + 20 \log f \tag{25}$$

where d = distance in Km
and   f = carrier frequency in MHz.

We then assume that X_T = -145 dBW, Y_T =-145 dBW,
T = 0.01 sec. v = 50 k m/hr, and the carrier
frequencies on the downlink and uplink channels
are 850 MHz and 870 MHz respectively. Also,
the line losses and antenna gains are equal.

With these assumptions, the probability P_{SM} of
successful reception of a packet
transmitted by the base station in the absence
of co-channel interference is a function of the
base station EIRP (equivalent isotropically
radiated power in dBW) and distance. Fig. 3
gives the values of P_{SM} for different values of
distance and base EIRP. It can be seen
that a large coverage distance or a low EIRP
could result in less than desirable values of
P_{SM}.

The probability P_{SB} of successful reception of
a packet transmitted by the mobile in the
absence of interference from other mobiles in
the surrounding co-channel cells may also be
calculated in a similar manner. For G = 0.65
and M = 65, we obtain from (14), (15), (16) and
(18), the values of P_B, P_{SB} and the system
throughput S for different values of d and
mobile EIRP and the results are presented
in fig. 4 and fig. 5.

By comparing P_{SB} in fig. 4 with P_{SM} in fig. 3
for the same values of d, it can be seen
that a mobile station has a lower probability
of successful packet transmission than a base

station. This is indeed one of the limiting
factors that have to be considered in
determining the most desirable radius of the
cell.

In order to demonstrate the impact of reuse
distance on the probability of co-channel
interference and system throughput, cellular
structures with different reuse distances U are
compared. As the reuse distance U is related to
N which is the number of cells per cluster in
a cellular structure by the expression,
U = $\sqrt{3N}$ {8}, cellular structures with 3-
cell, 7-cell, 12-cell and 19-cell clusters
correspond to reuse distances of 3, 4.58, 6 and

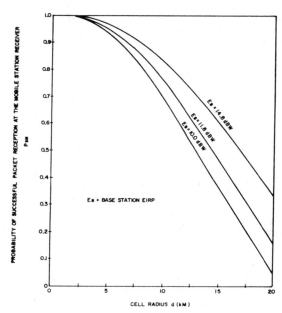

FIG. 3. PROBABILITY P_{SM} OF SUCCESSFUL PACKET RECEPTION AT THE MOBILE
STATION RECEIVER AS A FUNCTION OF CELL RADIUS d AND BASE
STATION EIRP IN THE ABSENCE OF CO-CHANNEL INTERFERENCE

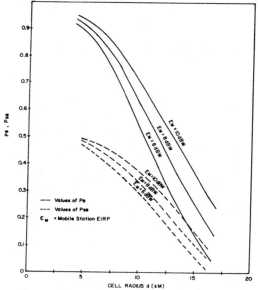

FIG. 4. PROBABILITY OF SUCCESSFUL PACKET RECEPTION AT THE BASE STATION
RECEIVER WITH AND WITHOUT CONSIDERATION OF PACKET COLLISIONS AS A
FUNCTION OF CELL RADIUS d AND MOBILE STATION EIRP IN THE ABSENCE
OF CO-CHANNEL INTERFERENCE.

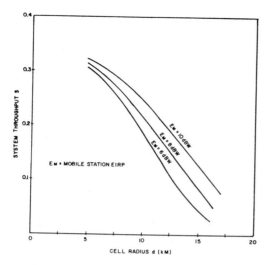

FIG. 5. SYSTEM THROUGHPUT S AS A FUNCTION OF CELL RADIUS d AND THE MOBILE STATION E I R P IN THE ABSENCE OF CO-CHANNEL INTERFERENCE

7.5 respectively. In the comparison, a cell radius of 6 Km., a base station EIRP of 10 dBW and a mobile station EIRP of 6 dBW are assumed. Values of P_{IM}, P'_{SM}, P_{IB}, P'_{SB} and S' are evaluated using fig. 2, 3 and 4 for the different cellular structures and the results are shown in table 1. It can be seen that by using a 19-cell structure instead of a 3-cell structure, the system throughput has increased from 0.13 to 0.28, the probability of successful packet reception at the mobile receiver has increased from 0.14 to 0.87 and the corresponding probability at the base receiver has increased from 0.195 to 0.42.

TABLE I

COMPARISON OF SYSTEM PERFORMANCE FOR DIFFERENT CELLULAR STRUCTURES

CLUSTER SIZE	U	P_{IM}	P'_{SM}	P_{IB}	P'_{SB}	S
3 CELL	3	0.84	0.14	0.546	0.195	0.13
7-CELL	4.58	0.14	0.77	0.094	0.39	0.25
12-CELL	6	0.08	0.82	0.051	0.41	0.26
19-CELL	7.5	0.024	0.87	0.016	0.42	0.28

6. CONCLUSION

In this paper, we have explored the possibility of using a radio channel as the link between a fixed base station and a mobile vehicle in a local area data communications network. We have also described the fading and co-channel interference problems associated with the use of such digital mobile radio channels. A number of mathematical expressions giving the probabilities of receiving a packet successfully in a downlink and uplink Rayleigh fading channel in the presence of co-channel interference have been described. All parameters other than the base and mobile EIRP's, the cell radius and the reuse distance have been kept constant. We have shown graphically how the cell radius and

the transmitted powers of the base and mobile stations affect the probabilities of successful packet transmission in the downlink and uplink fading channels. We found that in the absence of co-channel interference a mobile station has lower probability of successful packet transmission than a base station. However, both base and mobile station transmissions suffer a degradation of performance due to co-channel interference. We have also shown graphically how the probability of receiving co-channel interference varies with different values of reuse distance U and the protection ratio r. Finally, a comparison of the impacts made by the different cellular structure configurations on the system performance with different values of reuse distance is presented.

It must be noted that the above analysis does not include the effects of shadowing on the transmission of packets on the digital radio channel and work is currently being done in this area. Also, different diversity techniques that may be applied to combat the effects of Rayleigh fading are presently being investigated.

REFERENCES

{1} J. S. DaSilva and S. Mahmoud, "Capacity Degradation of Packet Radio Fading Channels" Sixth Data Communications Symposium -- 1979, Pacific Grove, Calif.

{2} R.C. French "The Effect of Fading and Shadowing on Channel Reuse in Mobile Radio" IEEE Transactions on Vehicular Technology, Vol. VT-28, No. 3, August 1979.

{3} W. Gosling "A Simple Mathematical Model of Co-channel and Adjacent Channel Interference in Land Mobile Radio", IEEE Transactions on Vehicular Technology, Vol VT-29, No. 4, November 1980.

{4} F. Hansen and F.I. Meno "Mobile Fading-Rayleigh and Lognormal Superimposed", IEEE Transactions on Vehicular Technology, Vol. VT-26, No. 4 November 1977.

{5} J. Egli "Radio propagation above 40 MC over Irregular Terrain", Proceedings of the IRE October 1957.

{6} N. Abramson "The Throughput of Packet Broadcasting Channels" IEEE Trans. on Communications, Vol. COM-25, No. 1, pg. 117-128, January 1977.

{7} I. Gitman "On the Capacity of Slotted Aloha Networks and Some Design Problems", IEEE Transactions on Communications, Vol COM-23, No. 3, March 1975.

{8} V.H. MacDonald "The Cellular Concept", The Bell System Technical Journal, January 1979.

Gerald K. Chan received his B.A. SC. and M. Eng. in Electrical Engineering from Queen's University and Carleton University in 1972 and 1977 respectively. He has been with the Canadian Department of Communications since 1976 and as project leader, he has developed a computer-assisted Land Mobile Electromagnetic Compatability Analysis System for spectrum management purposes in Canada. He is currently a consultant in systems engineering with the Telecommunication Regulatory Service and is working towards a Ph.D degree in Systems Engineering at Carleton University.

Dr. John deMercado obtained his Ph.D. (Magna Cum Laude) in electrical engineering from the University of Ottawa. He has been Director General of the Telecommunication Regulatory Service of the Department of Communications since 1975. He also holds an appointment as (adjunct) Professor of Systems Engineering and Computing Science at Carleton University in Ottawa. As Director General, he is responsible for the management of the radio spectrum in Canada and for spectrum coordination between Canada and the United States and other countries.

Dr. deMercado joined the federal government in May 1966 and came to the Department of Communications on its inception in 1968. He has worked in the Policy and Research Sector of the Department and was Director General of the Educational Technology Program from 1973 to 1975. A Canadian citizen, Dr. deMercado was born in Jamaica and came to Canada in 1962.

S. A. Mahmoud received the B.E.E. degree from Ain Shams University, Cairo, Egypt, in 1968, and the M. Eng. and Ph.D degrees from Carleton University, Ottawa, Canada, in 1971 and 1974, respectively. In 1975, he joined the staff of the Systems Engineering and Computing Science Department, Carleton University. His current research interests include distributed database systems, distributed computing and packet radio networks.

J. Schwarz daSilva received his B.Sc. and M.Sc. degrees in Electrical Engineering from the Ecole Polytechnique of the University of Montreal in 1970 and 1971 respectively and his Ph.D degree from Carleton University in 1979. He has been with the Canadian Department of Communications since 1971 where he was a consultant in systems engineering with the Telecommunication Regulatory Service working in areas related to Spectrum Management and local area network studies. He is currently with the International Telecommunication Union in Geneva, Switzerland.

Two Interfering Queues in Packet -Radio Networks

M Sidi, A Segall
Israel Institute of Technology,
Israel

We consider several classes of interfering queues that appear in packet-radio networks. We analyse the class of systems where one of the queues is given full priority and obtain an expression for the joint probability distribution of the queue lengths. For ALOHA-type systems with two symmetric queues we calculate the average packet waiting time and queue length.

1. INTRODUCTION

The present study was motivated by the problem of investigating the behavior of random-multiple-access systems and of packet-radio networks. These systems are characterized by the fact that a number of radio stations exchange digital information by using a distributed random access algorithm on a common radio channel. In such situations, whenever a given station attempts transmission of a packet to another station, the attempt may be unsuccessful, in which case the packet must be retransmitted. In addition to channel noise, unsuccessful transmissions occur because of interference from another station trying to send a packet over the common channel at the same time or by the fact that the intended receiver is itself in transmission mode, in which case it is not able to detect incoming packets. The fact that the activity at one node affects the behavior of the queue at other nearby stations gives rise to statistical dependence between the queues at the nodes.

In most cases, the queue length statistical dependence is quite complicated and there is little hope to obtain explicit analytical results for general topology networks and general access schemes. The purpose of this paper is to present several analytic as well as approximate results for certain classes of interfering queues. We assume throughout the paper that all packets have equal length and that the time is divided into slots corresponding to the transmission time of a packet. A station may start packet transmissions only at the beginning of a slot and the distances between stations are assumed to be such that propagation delay is negligible. Also, we neglect channel noise and assume no channel errors.

Because of the difficulty in the analysis of dependent queues of the type introduced above, even the case of two queues cannot be treated analytically in the general case. However, we consider here two classes of systems with two dependent queues where such results can be

obtained. The first is the case when the length of one of the two queues is not allowed to decrease, unless the other queue is empty. A packet radio network consisting of two nodes that transmit their packets over a common channel to a central station and one of the nodes is given full access capability, is an example for such a situation; other examples are given in Section 2. No other restrictions are necessary in order to allow for analytical solution of this class; in particular, the input streams to the queues may have arbitrary distributions and they need not be independent processes. For this class of problems we present a general method for deriving the generating functions of the queue lengths and of the average delay times. Then these general results are applied to three special cases of packet-radio networks that can be shown to belong to the considered class of systems.

The second class of problems for which we can obtain explicit analytical results is the case of a two-node symmetric multiple access system. For this situation we cannot obtain the queue length probability distribution (or generating function), but we give a method for calculating the average queue length and hence the average time delay. The results are given in Section 3.

2. ANALYTICAL RESULTS

Here we consider a class of discrete-time queueing systems consisting of two queues with the following properties: packets arrive randomly at the queues from two sources, that in general may be correlated. Let $A_1(t)$ and $A_2(t)$ be the number of packets entering node 1 and node 2 from their corresponding sources in the time interval $(t, t+1]$. The input process $[(A_1(t), A_2(t)]$ is assumed to be a sequence of independent and identically distributed random vectors with integer-valued elements. Let

$$a(i,j) = \text{Prob}(A_1(t) = i, A_2(t) = j) ;$$

$$\sum_{i=o}^{\infty} \sum_{j=o}^{\infty} a(i,j) = 1 . \qquad (1)$$

*The work of A. Segall was conducted as part of a consulting agreement with the Laboratory for Information and Decision Systems at MIT, Cambridge, Mass., U.S.A., with partial support provided by the Advanced Research Project Agency of the US Department of Defense (monitored by ONR) under Contract No. N00014-75-C-1183.

and

$$F(x,y) = E[x^{A_1(t)}y^{A_2(t)}] = \sum_{i=o}^{\infty} \sum_{j=o}^{\infty} a(i,j)x^i y^i \quad (2)$$

We assume that $F(x,y)$ cannot be x-independent and that the queues have infinite buffers.

Next, we describe the departure processes. It is assumed that no more than one packet may leave each queue in any given time slot and the combined departure process is taken to be as follows: When both queues are empty, no departures may occur (packets arriving during a given slot may depart only in the next one). When only one of the queues is nonempty, a departure from that queue may occur and the packet may be transferred either to the outside of the system or to the other queue. We denote by p_{01}^0, p_{01}^1 the respective probabilities when the nonempty queue is queue 2, and by p_{10}^0, p_{10}^1 the corresponding probabilities when the nonempty queue is queue 1. When both queues are nonempty, it is assumed that a departure may occur only from queue 2. We denote by p_{11}^0 p_{11}^1 the probabilities that the departing packet leaves the system or joins the other queue, respectively. Consider the steady state joint generating function of the queue lengths:

$$G(x,y) = \lim_{t \to \infty} E[x^{L_1(t)}y^{L_2(t)}] \quad (3)$$

where $L_1(t), L_2(t)$ are the queue lengths at time t at nodes 1 and 2 respectively, and where we assume that the Markov chain $[L_1(t), L_2(t)]$ is ergodic, namely $G(0,0) > 0$. For this class we compute the function $G(x,y)$ and in the Appendix we show that:

$$G(x,y) =$$

$$F(x,y) \frac{b(x,y)G(x,0)+c(x,y)G(0,y)+d(x,y)G(0,0)}{x \cdot e(x,y)} \quad (4)$$

where functions $b(x,y)$, $c(x,y)$, $d(x,y)$, $e(x,y)$, $G(x,0)$, $G(0,y)$ and the constant $G(0,0)$ are defined in the Appendix.

We next consider several examples of two-node packet networks, where it turns out that the general assumptions characterizing the class of two dependent queues indeed hold. The networks are given in Fig. 1. In all cases the nodes share a common radio channel and are equipped with radio transmitter devices and in systems 2 and 3, node 2 has also a receiving device. Node 2 can either transmit or receive, but not both simultaneously. The circle in Fig. 1 is a station that receives packets correctly provided that there is no interference. Finally, we assume that a transmitter knows instantaneously at the end of a slot if the packet has been received correctly. In all three systems of Fig. 1 node 2 is assumed to have full access capability to the common channel. This means that it always transmits a packet when its buffer is not empty. Node 1 has only partial access capability to the channel and its transmission policy is randomized as follows: at the beginning of each slot for which its own buffer is nonempty, node 1 tosses a coin with probability of success p, independently of any other event, and in case of success the node attempts to transmit the packet at the head of the queue. At any node, if the transmission is not successful, the transmitter repeats the procedure described above. Since node 2 has full access capability to the channel and node 2 cannot receive and transmit packets at the same time, it is clear that in all cases no packets can leave node 1 whenever the queue at node 2 is nonempty and therefore all cases of Fig. 1 belong to the class of queues considered earlier.

We now calculate the parameters $\{p_{ij}^k, 0 \le i,j,k \le 1, i+j>0\}$ in each of these systems. System 1 in Fig. 1a is a two-node non-symmetric packet-radio network, where both nodes send their packets to the station. Since no packets are sent from one node to the other, $p_{10}^1 = p_{01}^1 = p_{11}^1 = 0$. When one of the nodes has packets to transmit while the other is empty, any attempted transmission is successful. Since node 2 transmits with probability 1 and node 1 with probability p, $p_{10}^0 = p$; $p_{01}^0 = 1$. When both nodes have nonempty queues, successful transmission occurs at node 2 whenever node 1 does not attempt transmission, so $p_{11}^0 = \bar{p}$, where $\bar{p}$ denotes $(1-p)$. System 2 in Fig. 1b is a network of two tandem nodes where the station that is the "sink" for the packets transmitted by node 2, is out of the transmission range of node 1. Therefore node 1 cannot interfere with the transmissions of node 2. However node 2 does interfere with the transmissions of node 1 since when it is transmitting, it does not accept packets transmitted by node 1. Consequently $p_{10}^1 = p$; $p_{01}^0 = p_{11}^1 = 1$; $p_{10}^0 = p_{01}^1 = p_{11}^0 = 0$. System 3 in Fig. 1c differs from system 2 only in that the station is in the transmission range of node 1, therefore node 1 does interfere with the transmissions of node 2 and therefore $p_{10}^1 = p$; $p_{01}^0 = 1$; $p_{11}^1 = \bar{p}$; $p_{10}^0 = p_{01}^1 = p_{11}^0 = 0$.

Special Cases

Although the results of this section hold for general input processes, the equations become much simpler when one considers independent Bernoulli processes. In this case we have

$$F(x,y) = (xr_1+\bar{r}_1)(yr_2+\bar{r}_2) \quad (5)$$

where r_1, r_2 are the input rates. For this example we give for each of the three systems the average delays (in unit of slots) T_1, T_2 at nodes 1 and 2 respectively and the total average delay T in the network. This is done by first calculating the average queue lengths at the nodes and then applying Little's Theorem {7}.

System 1   (Fig. 1a)

$$T_1 = 1 + \frac{(\bar{p})^2 + r_2 p}{p(\bar{p}-r_2)-r_1\bar{p}} + \frac{r_1 r_2 p \bar{p}}{(\bar{p}-r_2)^2[p(\bar{p}-r_2)-r_1\bar{p}]}$$

$$(6)$$

$$T_2 = 1 + \frac{r_1\bar{p}}{(\bar{p}-r_2)^2} \quad (7)$$

$$T = \frac{r_1 T_1 + r_2 T_2}{r_1 + r_2} \quad (8)$$

where these equations hold for $p(\bar{p}-r_2) > r_1\bar{p}$ which is the ergodicity condition in this system.

In Fig. 2 we plot T versus p, the transmission probability at node 1, for $r_1 = 0.1$ and r_2 ranges from 0.01 to 0.4. It is interesting to see that for given r_1, r_2, the average delay T is minimized at a certain value of p. The reason is that when p becomes small, node 1 attempts to transmit relatively rarely, so its queue increases. When p becomes large, then node 1 attempts to transmit more frequently, thus interfering with the transmissions of node 2, and the queue lengths at both nodes are large. As we see from Fig. 2, the parameter p is a very critical design parameter of this system and for given values for r_1 and r_2, there exists an optimal p that minimizes the total average delay in the network. In Fig. 3, T_{min}, the <u>minimum</u> total average delay is plotted versus γ the total throughput of the system, when $r_1 = r_2 = r$ (clearly $\gamma = 2r$).

<u>System 2</u> (Fig. 1b)

The average delays are:

$$T_1 = 1 + \frac{r_1 p + \bar{r}_2 (1 - p\bar{r}_2)}{\bar{r}_2 [p(1 - r_1 - r_2) - r_1]} \tag{9}$$

$$T_2 = \frac{1}{r_1 + r_2} \left\{ r_2 + \frac{r_1}{1 - r_2} \right\} \tag{10}$$

$$T_3 = \frac{r_1}{r_1 + r_2} T_1 + T_2 \tag{11}$$

where these equations hold for $p(1 - r_1 - r_2) > r_1$ which is the ergodicity condition. In this system node 1 does not interfere with the transmissions of node 2. Therefore, it is optimal to always attempt transmission at node 1 as well, namely to take $p = 1$.

<u>System 3</u> (Fig. 1c)

$$T_1 = 1 + \frac{p(r_1 + r_2 \bar{r}_2) + (\bar{p} - r_2)(\bar{p})^2}{[p(\bar{p} - r_2) - r_1](\bar{p} - r_2)} -$$

$$- \frac{p[r_1 + r_2(r_1 + \bar{r}_1 r_2)]}{[\bar{r}_1 (\bar{r}_2)^2 - p(1 - \bar{r}_1 r_2)](\bar{p} - r_2)} \tag{12}$$

$$T_2 = \frac{1}{r_1 + r_2} \left\{ \frac{r_1 + r_2 \bar{r}_2}{\bar{p} - r_2} - \right.$$

$$\left. - \frac{p[r_1 + r_2(r_1 + \bar{r}_1 r_2)][p(\bar{p} - r_2) - r_1]}{(\bar{p} - r_2)[\bar{r}_1(\bar{r}_2)^2 - p(1 - \bar{r}_1 r_2)]} \right\} \tag{13}$$

$$T = \frac{r_1}{r_1 + r_2} T_1 + T_2 \tag{14}$$

where these equations hold for $p(\bar{p} - r) - r_1 > 0$, which is the ergodicity condition for this system. The behavior of the average delays in this system is very similar to that of System 1.

3. SYMMETRIC TWO-NODE 'ALOHA' NETWORK DELAY ANALYSIS

In this section a two-node symmetric ALOHA network is considered. This network is similar to System 1 with the following modifications. Here node 2 uses the same channel access scheme as node 1, i.e. at the beginning of each slot, if its buffer is not empty, node 2 tosses a coin, independently from any other event in the system, with probability of success p. According to the outcome, the node

either transmits or remains silent during the current slot. In addition, it is assumed that the arrival processes to the nodes are independent Bernoulli processes with equal rates, denoted by r, where, as we will see shortly, $0 < r < 1/4$. Therefore we have for this system $F(x,y) = (xr + \bar{r})(yr + \bar{r})$. In this case we cannot obtain an explicit form for $G(x,y)$. However, we can exploit the symmetry to obtain a closed expression for the average delay in the system. The details of our method appear in [2]. The result is

$$T = \frac{G_1(1,1)}{r} = 1 + \frac{(\bar{p})^2 + \frac{1}{2} rp}{p\bar{p} - r}$$

$$\text{for } p\bar{p} > r . \tag{15}$$

From (15) it is found that $p^* = 1 - \{0.5r + [0.5r(1 - r + 0.5r^2)]^{1/2}\}/(1 - 0.5r)$ minimizes T for $0 < r < 0.25$. In Fig. 3 the minimum total average delay T_{min} is plotted versus γ, the total throughput of this system. Comparing the curves in Fig. 3 it is clear that the non-symmetric access scheme used in system 1 provides only slightly better performance than the symmetric access scheme, when the arrival rates into the nodes are equal.

APPENDIX

Using a standard technique we obtain for our system described in Section 2 that

$$b(x,y) = y(p_{10}^0 + y p_{10}^1) - x(p_{11}^0 + x p_{11}^1)$$
$$+ xy(p_{11}^0 + p_{11}^1 - p_{10}^0 - p_{10}^1) \tag{A.1}$$

$$c(x,y) = x[p_{01}^0 - p_{11}^0 + x(p_{01}^1 - p_{11}^1)] +$$
$$+ xy(p_{11}^0 + p_{11}^1 - p_{01}^0 - p_{01}^1) \tag{A.2}$$

$$d(x,y) = -y(p_{10}^0 + y p_{10}^1) +$$
$$+ x[p_{11}^0 - p_{01}^0 + x(p_{11}^1 - p_{01}^1)] +$$
$$+ xy(p_{10}^0 + p_{10}^1 + p_{01}^0 + p_{01}^1 - p_{11}^0 - p_{11}^1) \tag{A.3}$$

$$e(x,y) = y - F(x,y)[p_{11}^0 + x p_{11}^1 + y\overline{(p_{11}^0 + p_{11}^1)}] \tag{A.4}$$

The problem is now to determine the boundary functions $G(x,0)$, $G(0,y)$ and the constant $G(0,0)$ in (4). Before proceeding we claim that for $|x| < 1$ the equation $e(x,y) = 0$ has a unique solution $y = f(x)$ in the unit circle $|y| < 1$. The correctness of the claim follows from a direct application of Rouché's theorem [8] to the equation $e(x,y) = 0$. To find $G(0,y)$ let $x = 0$ in (4). Then after simple algebra we obtain:

$$G(0,y) =$$
$$= F(0,y) \frac{(p_{01}^0 + p_{01}^1 - y^{-1} p_{01}^0) G(0,0) + (p_{10}^0 + y p_{10}^1) G_1(0,0)}{1 - F(0,y)[y^{-1} p_{01}^0 + \overline{(p_{01}^0 + p_{01}^1)}]} \tag{A.5}$$

where $G_1(x,y)$ is the derivative of $G(x,y)$ with respect to x.

Now from the analyticity of $G(0,y)$ for $|y| < 1$ it follows that

$$G_1(0,0) = \frac{t^{-1}p_{01}^0 - p_{01}^0 - p_{01}^1}{p_{10}^0 + tp_{10}^1} G(0,0) \qquad (A.6)$$

where t is the unique point within the unit circle where the denominator of (A.5) vanishes. Substituting (A.6) in (A.5), $G(0,y)$ is determined up to the constant $G(0,0)$.

To find $G(x,0)$, we use the analyticity of $G(x,y)$ for $|y| < 1$, $|x| < 1$ and find that

$$G(x,0) = -\frac{c(x,f(x))G(0,f(x)) + d(x,f(x))G(0,0)}{b(x,f(x))}$$
$$(A.7)$$

Substituting (A.5) in (A.7), the function $G(x,0)$ is determined up to the constant $G(0,0)$. Finally, $G(0,0)$ is obtained from the normalization condition $G(1,1) = 1$, and we find that

$$G(0,0) = [e_1(1,1)b_2(1,1) - e_2(1,1)b_1(1,1)]/K$$
$$(A.8)$$

where

$$K = d_1(1,1)b_2(1,1) - d_2(1,1)b_1(1,1) +$$

$$+ \frac{[c_1(1,1)b_2(1,1) - c_2(1,1)b_1(1,1)]F(0,1)}{1 - F(0,1)p_{01}^1}$$

$$\left[p_{01}^1 + \frac{(p_{10}^0 + p_{10}^1)(t^{-1}p_{01}^0 - p_{01}^0 - p_{01}^1)}{p_{10}^0 + tp_{10}^1} \right] \qquad (A.9)$$

and the subscripts 1 and 2 correspond to the derivative of the function with respect to the first and second variables, respectively.

REFERENCES

[1] Kobayashi, H. and Konheim, A.G., Queueing models for computer communications system analysis, IEEE Trans. Communications, COM-25 (1977) 2-28.

[2] Sidi, M. and Segall, A., Two interfering queues in packet-radio networks, submitted for publication to IEEE Trans. on Communications.

[3] Morrison, J.A., Two discrete-time queues in tandem, IEEE Trans. Communications, COM-27 (1979) 563-573.

[4] Kleinrock, L. and Yemini, Y., Interfering queueing processes in packet-switched broadcast communication, IFIP Congress, Tokyo, 1980.

[5] Saadawi, T.N. and Ephremides, A., Analysis, stability and optimization of slotted ALOHA with finite number of buffered users, IEEE Trans. on Automatic Control, AC-26 (1981) 680-689.

[6] Tobagi, F.A. and Kleinrock, L., On the analysis and simulation of buffered packet radio systems, Proceedings of the 9th Hawaii International Conference on System Sciences, Honolulu, Hawaii, Jan. 1976, pp. 42-45.

[7] Little, J.D.C., A proof for the queueing formula $L = \lambda W$, Operations Research 9 (1961) 383-387.

[8] Copson, Theory of Functions of a Complex Variable (Oxford University Press, London, 1948).

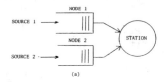

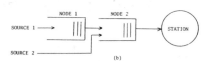

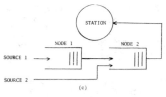

Fig. 1 - Two-node network.

(a) System 1: non-symmetric ALOHA network.
(b) System 2: tandem network; no interference at the station.
(c) System 3: tandem network; interference at the station.

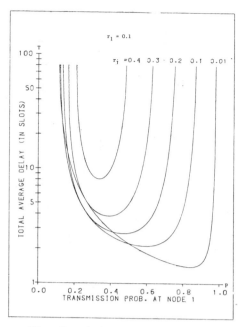

Fig. 2 - System 1: T versus p.

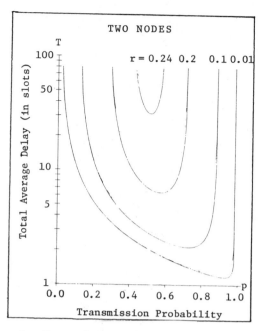

Fig. 4 - Two node symmetric ALOHA network.

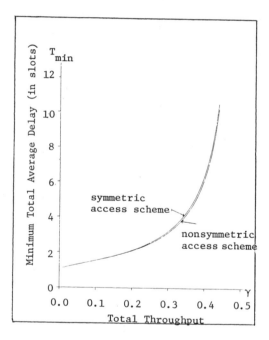

Fig. 3 - T_min versus γ for non-symmetric and symmetric access schemes.

MOSEH SIDI was born in Israel on April 11, 1953. He received the B.Sc. and M.Sc. degrees from the Technion in 1975 and 1978 respectively, both in electrical engineering. He is currently working towards the Ph.D. degree at the Technion in the area of packet-radio networks.

From 1975 to 1976 he worked at the Israel Water Company as a Communication Engineer. Since 1976 he has been a Teaching Assistant at the Technion in communication and data networks courses. He received the 1981-1982 IEEE Communications Society Scholarship Award and the 1981-1982 Gutwirth Scholarship Award.

ADRIAN SEGALL, Dept. of Electrical Engineering, Technion. B.Sc. 1965, M.Sc. 1971 both at Technion, Ph.D. 1973 Stanford Univ., 1965-1968 Israel Defense Army, 1968-1971 Research Engineer, Israel Armament Development Authority, 1973-1974 Research Engineer, Systems Control Inc., Palo Alto, Calif., 1974-1976, Assistant Professor, MIT, 1976 - present Dept. of Electr. Eng., Technion, 1975 - IEEE delegate to the IEEE-USSR Information Theory Workshop, 1981 - Miriam and Ray Klein award for outstanding research.

Reuters Monitor Dealing System

R Etherington
Reuters, UK

G Seel
CAP Group, UK

The paper describes the Reuters Monitor Dealing System. This system allows foreign exchange dealers throughout the world to contact each other and complete deals using special purpose terminals. Additionally the system provides access to a number of Reuter databases containing current foreign exchange rates and important news items.

The system is described in terms of the particular requirements of the foreign exchange market and the techniques used to meet these requirements. Due to the large amounts of money involved in deals and the speed at which rates may move it is vital for the system to be very secure, provide a very fast response and be simple to use.

1. THE MARKET AND THE MONITOR DEALING SYSTEM

On 23 February 1981 Reuters launched the fastest, the most versatile and efficient dealing service in the world'. From day one, some 251 foreign exchange dealers in 17 major business centres in nine countries were able to contact each other within four seconds.

By the end of 1981, nearly 400 dealers in 25 cities enjoyed this facility.

***

Foreign exchange and money markets are truly international; foreign exchange dealing goes on between cities and continents 24 hours a day. Direct dealing has traditionally been conducted by international telephone and telex. However, in foreign exchange dealing rates now move with such rapidity that every extra second a dealer spends to get through to another bank can cost a large amount of money.

An international telex calls takes 15 to 20 seconds to establish a connection - even longer when public circuits are engaged. In fast moving market, these seconds can be a very long and costly time-lag.

There has been a long felt need in the foreign exchange and money markets for a very fast direct interbank dealing service. The Reuter Monitor Dealing Service was designed specifically to meet this need.

Reuters pioneered the use of modern technology in the foreign exchange market with the introduction of the Reuter Monitor Money Rates Service in June 1973. This computerised information service provides continuously updated rates, and is now available to over 10,000 subscribers in 56 countries. The development of the Reuter Monitor Dealing Service was a logical extension after a detailed study of market

requirements and took five years to launch at a cost of over £8 million.

The most important requirement of the new service was fast direct contact between banks, to eliminate the problems of overcrowded international circuits. Today the Reuter Monitor Dealing Service offers bank-to-bank contact in four seconds, sometimes even less. As the service uses a dedicated Reuter packet-switched network, it is not exposed to engaged international circuits. The service gives dealers the confidence that not only are they able to get through to other banks to obtain a price and deal; but that they can do so much faster than was previously possible. This assurance is extremely valuable to dealers, particularly in volatile markets.

In addition, having in mind the importance of personal contact in the foreign exchange market, the service is designed so that a dealer can direct his call to a particular contact. There is also a facility to transfer calls between dealers.

The Dealing Service is suitable for use either by dealers themselves or by telex operators. It is up to individual banks to decide how they can best utilise the service. However, many banks prefer the dealer-to-dealer contact.

A dealer wishing to make a call on the system keys a four character code which relates to the name and geographical location of the bank he is calling. The incoming call is displayed in a dedicated area of the screen and flashed to attract attention. The identity of an incoming call is shown by the four-character code of the calling bank. Once the call has been accepted and contact established, the dealing conversation takes place on the screen on a line-by-line basis and is in free format.

Dealers can use their own shorthand which they have developed over the years, and deal in the sam way as they have traditionally done by telex. There is an automatic print-out of the whole video conversation.

While simple to operate, the Reuter Monitor Dealing Service uses the power of the computer to assist the dealer. It is thus possible for the dealers to abbreviate standard parts of a dealing conversation, such as payment instructions, to a single character. The computer recognises these abbreviations and displays them in fully expanded form on the screen. This facility makes the dealing service quicker and easier for the dealer to use.

The dealing system has a built-in security function, a password, so that no unauthorised person can use the service. Every subscriber bank has its own password which it alone knows and can change.

The Reuter Monitor Dealing Service meets the requirements of the market by providing a fast, easy-to-use, secure, direct-dealing system.

2. THE EQUIPMENT

The system as seen by a dealer consists of a desk-unit, i.e. a VDU screen and a separate keyboard. The screen is split into a number of areas by software. The layout of the screen is shown in Figure 1. The two main areas of the screen are used to display dealing conversations. Two different conversations can be held simultaneously, one in the lower area and one in the upper area. The right hand side of the screen is again divided into two areas. One of these shows alert messages providing general system information and the other provides a list of incoming calls awaiting servicing. The bottom two lines of the screen are reserved for data insertion by the user and for error or status messages from the system.

The keyboard has been specifically designed for the Monitor Dealing system to assist fast error free usage. It also has a set of keys which can be used for accessing a subscriber in-house computer system. Any individual key position can be programmed to transmit a code of the subscriber choice. The layout of the keyboard is shown in Figure 2.

Up to six desk units may be connected to a terminal controller, which is a Digital Equipment PDP-8 computer, installed on the client's premises. Associated with each terminal controller are two printers that automatically print the text of conversations when the conversation terminates and any messages left by other subscribers. Additionally, the current contents of the page area of any screen may be printed on request from the associated keyboard.

The remainder of the system is a hierarchy of PDP-11 computers acting as concentrators for the terminal controllers, nodes of the packet switching network and central computers providing the user services.

3. CONDUCT OF A CONVERSATION

The use of the system can best be illustrated by a description of the course of a typical conversation.

Each subscriber is assigned a four character mnemonic to be used by other subscribers when requesting a conversation. Thus if the subscriber with mnemonic ABCD wishes to contact the subscriber with mnemonic WXYZ he will initiate the contact by use of the CONTACT key followed by the mnemonic WXYZ. If he knows that he wishes to converse with a particular dealer at subscriber WXYZ he may add a two character dealer identifier, e.g. inputting WXYZJB instead of WXYZ to specify dealer John Brown. Alternatively, he may describe his interest, that is the currency and date he wishes to deal, in a short message, e.g. SPOT DM PLSE. This again will allow the correct dealer to take the call. On completion of this input the TRANSMIT key is pressed.

The system then analyses the contact request, determines the condition of the subscriber being called, reports on this to the calling subscriber and if possible adds the call to the list of incoming calls for the called subscriber. In the majority of cases, i.e. when a call can be established or a message may be left, the dealer at subscriber ABCD will have the conversations area of the screen cleared and a heading line set up showing the called party and his status. This is either FREE (desk units are available to accept the call), QUEUED (all the subscribers desk units are busy, but the calling party is in a short waiting list) or BUSY (all the subscriber's desk units are busy, and the waiting list is full).

The called party (WXYZ) will have the call displayed in the incoming call queue of all screens. The entry will consist of a single letter, used to identify the call when it is accepted, the mnemonic of the calling subscriber (ABCD) and any dealer indentifier or interest message provided by ABCD. When a dealer is ready to accept the call, he uses the ACCEPT key followed by the letter identifying the call and the TRANSMIT key. This causes the removal of the call from the queue on all screens, the setting-up of the conversation area on the dealer's screen with a heading line and the updating of the heading line on the calling dealer's screen. The heading lines will now contain the exact identity of the other party (i.e mnemonic plus answerback and desk unit number) and the time the call was established.

The actual conversation can now commence. One or other party is always in control of the conversation, which means that they are the party currently able to input. Initially control will reside with the calling party unless he originally input an interest message, in which case this is considered his first contribution to the conversation and the called party is in control to reply. Control is maintained until the controlling party uses the TRANSMIT key or other party interrupts (see below). The system transfers the input text normally in blocks of 10 to 15 characters although smaller blocks will be transmitted if there is a period of no input. The lines input by each dealer are marked on his own screen by a hash sign in the first position. The conversation continues until the contact is ended by one party pressing the END CONTACT key. This causes a printout of the conversation at his controller and frees the conversation area of his screen. The conversation remains on the other party's screen, with an indication that it has ended until END CONTACT is pressed when the conversation is printed and the area freed.

There are a number of additional facilities available during the course of the conversation. Either party may gain control of the conversation using the INTERRUPT key which interrupts the current input of the counterparty. This was designed to enable a dealer who has quoted a price to interrupt and change the price if the market begins moving.

If a dealer is awaiting a response during the conversation he may 'alert' the counterparty using the BELL key. This causes a short audible alarm at the counterparty's desk unit and flashes a bell symbol on the screen until input is begun.

If a deal has been made, the dealer may receive automatic acknowledgement that the other counterparty has received the dealing instruction and also highlight it on the print out of the conversation using the DEAL key. The acknowledgement takes the form of returning an asterisk to the sender's screen, and the printout is marked with a string of asterisks.

Abbreviations may be used by pressing the ABBREVIATION key followed by a sequence of characters which define one or more abbreviations. Certain common abbreviations are system wide (e.g S for I SELL and B for I BUY), others are defined for individual use by the subscriber. The system automatically expands the abbreviations for display on both screens involved in the conversation.

4. DESIGN OBJECTIVES

During the initial design of the Monitor Dealing system, four major requirements were identified that had to be satisfied to produce a system that would be acceptable to the technically sophisticated foreign exchange market. These were:

- speed
- ease of use
- reliability
- security.

Speed is an obvious requirement both due to the volatility of the market and to the alternative dealing methods with which the system is competing. It is not possible to compete directly with the spoken word once the conversation has started so it is necessary to provide a quicker method of establishing the connection and then to allow the information to be exchanged with the minimum number of keystrokes.

Ease of use by the dealer is essential as he will frequently be listening to prices being called out by other dealers in the room, observing rates from an in-house computer system and even holding a telephone conversation with a broker at the time as conducting a conversation on the system. Thus the dialogue between the dealer and the system must be informative but concise and the keyboard must be laid-out in such a way that functions can be requested simply with a low probability of error.

As the alternative dealing methods will continue to be available, it is vital that the Monitor Dealing system is functioning correctly when the dealer needs it. One or two failures during the initial period of use can easily turn enthusiasm into contempt and a determination to use the system only as a last resort.

Security is clearly a vital consideration in a market where a typical deal will involve millions of dollars. There will normally be tight physical security in terms of access to the bank's dealing rooms, but in addition the chief dealer will wish to control access to systems by means of passwords and to have a hard copy of the activity on the systems.

These four requirements were thus paramount during the design of the system, although there were also a number of more technical objectives which were of major importance. These were mostly associated with the need to produce a flexible system that could be extended easily both in terms of the number of subscribers and the range of functions and services.

The remainder of the paper describes how the requirements were addressed in the design of the system. A brief overview of the architecture of the system is first necessary.

5. TECHNICAL OVERVIEW

The system is built round a packet switching network developed within Reuters and known as SWM (Software Multiplexing). This network was designed as a general purpose network although its development was closely tied to that of the Monitor Dealing system. The network connects the parts of the system and provides a reliable means of transferring data packets.

In addition to the general purpose nodes of the SWM network, the system contains a number of computers specific to the Monitor Dealing system. These comprise three types: central service machines, concentrators and terminal controllers.

The central service machines were designed as specialised nodes of the network to make full use of the logical connection facilities. However they do not carry through traffic for the network. The central service machines provide the processing power and secondary storage used to support the services provided by the Monitor Dealing system.

Concentrators act as a point of connection to the network for a number of terminal controllers. They are not nodes of the network as the memory size restrictions of the computers used (Digital Equipment Corporation PDP 11/34) made it impossible to hold the node and concentrator software in a single computer.

Terminal Controllers are installed on clients' premises and support up to six desk units each, as described earlier. They have no secondary storage and can thus be left unattended for considerable periods of time.

6. SPEED

As mentioned previously, there are a number of areas to be considered in providing a fast service. The major aims were to provide an extremely fast initial contact establishment, to minimise the transit time through the system for blocks of conversational text and to minimise the number of keystrokes by provision of abbreviation facilities. However, it was also necessary to adopt an approach that allowed for continuing expansion of the number of subscribers without significantly affecting the response times.

The two major processing components of establishing the initial contact are the directory function of converting the mnemonic into a system address for the terminal controller(s) of the called party and determining the status of the called party.

These functions are performed by a central service machine with a back-up processor. The directory is held in memory and contacts can be established with no disk access, thus the limit on performance is the power of the central processing unit.

In order to minimise the transit time of conversational text, the most direct path through the system must be used. For this reason the central service machine is not involved in a conversation, once the initial contact has been established. All the system addresses needed to establish the logical connection between the two terminal controllers are provided in the responses to the controllers from the initial contact request. As the Monitor Dealing system is based on a packet switching network the size of the text packets affects the transit time as each packet carried an envelope which absorbs network capacity. The ideal from the system point of view would be character by character transmission, matching the circuit switched characteristics of the telex system. This would involve unacceptable protocol overheads so a figure of 10 to 15 characters per block was adopted and the protocol designed to minimise the overhead on each packet.

7. EASE OF USE

Making the system simple to use is achieved by the careful design of all aspects of the man-machine dialogue. This covers subjects ranging from the shape and layout of the keyboard and screen to the meaningfulness of error messages output by the system.

Dealers' desks, in most banks, incorporate a large amount of equipment in a relatively small area. The dealer may need access to up to three screens, one or more keyboards and a small telephone switchboard of direct telephone lines to brokers and other banks in addition to writing space, calculator and so on. The Monitor Dealing desk unit was therefore designed around a 9 inch screen with a separate keyboard.

The keyboard incorporates a large number of functions keys to minimise the number of keystrokes necessary. The keyboard has been laid out with the keys in logical groups and using different colour key tops to distinguish between various functions.

All user input to the system, other than conversational text which is free format, is echoed onto a reserved insert line on the screen. This enables the dealer to observe his input clearly. Error or informational messages in response to input are displayed on a message line immediately beneath the insert line. The messages are carefully designed to be meaningful and explicit.

8. RELIABILITY

Reliability is provided by duplication of hardware, automated error detection and hardware switching, software monitoring and the provision of fast response to faults in hardware on users' premises.

All computers within the system, except
Terminal Controllers, are configured in pairs.
Each pair is connected by a Reuters developed
watch-dog controller. This polls both
machines regularly and if there is no response
from the currently live machine within a
specified time window, all relevant
communication lines will be switched to the
stand-by machine which will then become the
live machine.

Communication lines between Terminal
Controllers and Concentrators and between
Concentrators and Nodes are duplicated
and where these are PTT lines they are
routed over different paths. The
computers will detect line failure and
will switch to the back-up line, which
will also be tested at regular intervals
to ensure it is maintained in working
order. Between nodes of the SWM network,
lines are duplicated and in addition the
software provides alternative routing
capabilities to overcome a total direct
communications loss between two nodes.

At the software level, in the event of a
computer switch, affected conversations
will be closed with a suitable warning
message as it was considered that the
complexity involved in providing total
protection from loss of text could not
be justified. Thus for concentrators
and nodes the new machine can take up
the load of the system through normal
activity without having had to monitor
the actions of the failed machine. For
service machines, it would not be
acceptable to work on this principle as
large amounts of information concerning
the subscribers are maintained upon these
machines. Thus a pair of service
machines will have a communications link
and the stand-by will be kept up to date
with all transactions performed by the
live machine thus providing a warm stand-
by facility.

The cost of duplicating terminal
controller hardware cannot be justified,
so instead it is modularized and in the
event of a failure, the failed component
can be replaced by Reuters in a short
period of time. This period naturally
varies with the location of the
subscriber but within the City of London,
the normal response time to a call is
less than an hour.

9. SECURITY

Security facilities are built into the system
at all levels. The major concerns are that
only authorized users should have access to
the system and that conversations between two
subscribers are transmitted fully and
accurately.

Access is controlled by the use of passwords.
Before any services can be accessed, a
password must be entered. If the password
matches that stored by the control software,
the relevant services will be supplied to
the subscriber.

Additional security is available in that
particular services may be supplied to only
a subset of desk units. A facility to change
passwords is provided,this requires the input
of the old password and two identical inputs
of the new password.

The logical connection facilities of SWM
provides a guarantee of sequenced delivery
of packets between nodes. In order to extend
this to controller to controller connections,
each text packet contains a conversation
sequence number to enable the receiving
controller to detect any lost or mis-ordered
packets. Additionally the special features
such as "Interrupt" and "Bell" incorporate
a positive acknowledgement to ensure that the
text is in agreement.

The DEAL key, provides for positive
acknowledgement of the text status after a
deal has been agreed.

10. IMPLEMENTATION

The Monitor Dealing system was developed
at the London Technical Centre of Reuters
Ltd by a team composed of Reuter's own
staff, consultants from Computer Analysts
and Programmers (CAP) and Hoskyns with a
small number of other contractors.

The Reuter Monitor Dealing Service was
launched with 145 subscribers in nine
countries in Western Europe and North
America. The UK, USA, Canada, Holland,
Belgium, Luxembourg, Italy, France,
Switzerland, Germany, Austria, Finland,
Ireland, Norway, Spain, Bahrain, Kuwait
U.A.E., Hong Kong and Singapore are now
on the network. Further expansion in
Europe, the Middle East and Far East,
and into Africa and Latin America will
follow soon.

The system has already been well received
by the market, with the usage up by
approximately 500% on the immediate post-
launch period.

The major design objectives have been
met as shown by the average contact time
of less than four seconds, the high level
of availability of the system and the
positive response from the users.

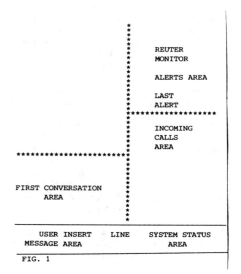

```
                    *
                    *
                    *
                    *       REUTER
                    *       MONITOR
                    *
                    *       ALERTS  AREA
                    *
                    *       LAST
                    *       ALERT
                    ************************
                    *
                    *       INCOMING
                    *       CALLS
                    *       AREA
                    *
  ***********************************
                    *
                    *
   FIRST CONVERSATION*
        AREA         *
                    *
                    *
                    *
                    *
                    *
  ─────────────────────────────────────
       USER  INSERT     LINE   SYSTEM STATUS
      MESSAGE  AREA             AREA
```

FIG. 1

SCREEN LAYOUT

SYS		OVERVIEW	LINE BACK	ALRTS	LINE FWD		RESET	CANCL	PRINT	END CONT					
RON		CONV	←	HOME	→		RCALL	CHGE CONV		PASS WORD					
COMP		REUTER	PAGE BACK	TAG	PAGE FWD		VIEW	TRFER		INTPT					

HIGH LIGHT	!	Q	W	E	R	T	Y	U	I	O	P	)		7	8	9	.
ACCPT	:	A	S	D	F	G	H	J	K	L	END LINE		4	5	6	/
CONTACT	BELL	Z	X	C	V	B	N	M	.	SHIFT		1	2	3	.
ABBRV	%	?	SPACE						INSERT		DEAL	TRANSMIT			

PROGRAMMABLE KEYBOARD VERSION D: DEALING, IN-HOUSE

KEY COLOUR CODES: PLAIN   =   GREY
                         *   =   BLACK
                         :   =   RED
                         *   =   BLUE WITH CLIP-ON COVER
                         *   =   BLUE
                         ▼   =   GREEN

FIG. 2

A Worldwide Integrated Service Communication System for The Sanwa Bank

Y Kudo
The Sanwa Bank, Japan
T Hyodo, M Seto
Hitachi, Japan

ABSTRACT

Sanwa Bank has constructed an international network system with distributed data processing computers to meet the rapid growth of overseas activity. This new advanced system, which was developed in Tokyo and is in operation in overseas branches, uses Hitachi Packet Network System (HIPA-NET), Hitachi computer system HITAC L-340 and Hitachi facsimile equipment as major components.

This paper describes the design philosophy, system structure, technologies, etc. of the new system.

1. INTRODUCTION

The remarkable progress of computer and communication technology has changed the business world. An increasing number of computer network systems have been developed for various applications. Recently, facsimile facilities have been added to the conventional telephone and telex systems.

Each type of communication system, however, is usually based on different networks or circuits. From an economical point of view, it is desirable to use the same transmission system and switching system for the various kinds of communications. Particularly a company with international operations wants to use international communication lines efficiently for multiple purposes among its overseas branches because the lines are expensive.

Sanwa Bank, which has played a major role in developing advanced banking systems, constructed an international network system with distributed data processing computers installed in remote locations. The system, which is called new Sanwa Overseas Banking Automation System (SOBAS), uses Hitachi Packet Network System (HIPA-NET), HITAC L-340 computer systems and Hitachi facsimile equipment. This article describes the SOBAS system.

2. NEED FOR THE SYSTEM

Sanwa Bank has its head office in Tokyo and many overseas branches. In the past, the major communication media among them were the telephone and telex. Each branch used a small computer for business batch processing. However, conventional communication systems did not have sufficient capability to handle the increasing flow of information, and the small computer did not meet the diversified requirements of the overseas branches. So a new network and computer system were planned and developed to meet the following requirements.

2.1 SOBAS network system

(1) Efficient use of communication lines
The system must efficiently utilize leased lines for various kinds of communication, such as telephone, telex, facsimile and computer.

(2) Time difference adjustment function
The system must have a function to store data temporarily, so that the local staff in overseas branches can use it during their local work hours.

(3) High reliability feature
All transmitted data should be checked and, if necessary, retransmitted between any of the nodes to insure high reliability.

The system design should include stand-by components for the main components of the system.

2.2 SOBAS computer system

(1) Business data processing improvements

Routine clerical work is rationalized in various applications such as foreign exchange, loans and deposits.

(2) Efficient network system connections

(3) Easy operation and maintenance
The system software must be developed in Tokyo head office, but the system is to be operated in the branches by the local staff. No special engineer is required to operate the system. If there is any system trouble, the Tokyo staff must be able to fix it by using maintenance facilities that report the trouble to the Tokyo system and send corrected data or programs to the branch system through the network.

3. OUTLINE OF THE SYSTEM

To meet the above requirements, the new SOBAS comprises HIPA-NET, HITAC L-340, Hitachi facsimile equipment, teletypewriters, telephones and other equipment. The system diagram is shown in Fig. 1.

HIPA-NET node processors which handle data exchange and data storage have been installed in Tokyo, London, New York and Hong Kong. HIPA-NET uses international voice grade leased lines which are capable of transmitting both voice and data. The line is used by voice or data alternately, according to the fixed time schedule plan. HIPA-NET operates 24 hours a day, while the local computer systems operate during their local office hours.

An example of transmitting computer data from Tokyo to New York is shown in Fig. 2.

(1) The computer data is transmitted to the HIPA-NET node processor in Tokyo.

(2) The data is stored on disks and waits if the line is occupied with telephone communications.

(3) When the line is free, the data is sent to the node processor in New York.

(4) The data is stored on disks and waits until the L-340 in New York starts its operations.

(5) The L-340 in New York starts its operations.

(6) The response message is sent to Tokyo in the same way as described above.

Since facsimile equipment (FAX) and teletype-writers (TTY), operate 24 hours a day, they can receive the messages even at night in the branches.

4. HIPA-NET

HIPA-NET has been developed as a packet switching system capable of handling data, facsimile, and voice.[1]-[4] A packet is block of data 256 bytes long. The features of HIPA-NET are as follows.

(1) Communication between different types of terminals
The packet switching equipment can convert the message of the transmitting terminal and send it to the receiving terminal so that even terminals which differ in transmission speed, coding, synchronization, etc. can communicate with each other.

(2) Packet multiplexing communication
With the packet multiplexing facility, the system allows many terminals to communicate with each other at the same time using only one subscriber line.

(3) Temporary storage
HIPA-NET includes a function which temporarily stores transmitted data on disks of node processors to adjust for time differences between overseas branches.

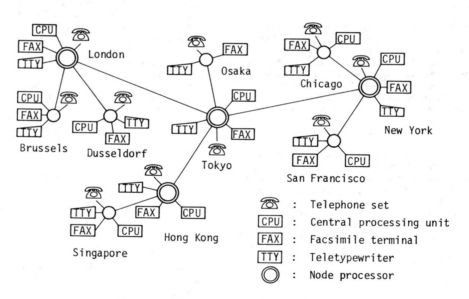

Fig. 1 SOBAS System Configuration

Eight overseas branches are connected by the international network.

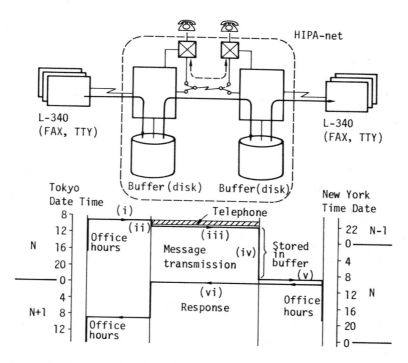

Fig. 2 Message Transmission Flow

The computer data is transmitted
through HIPA-NET.

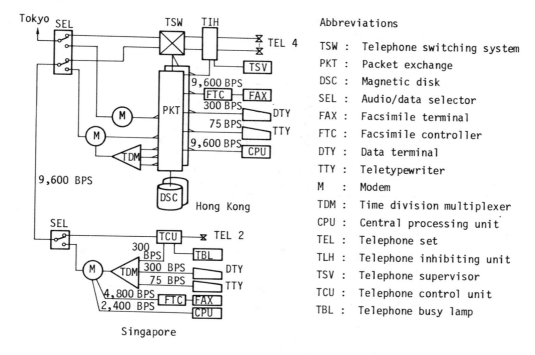

Abbreviations

TSW : Telephone switching system
PKT : Packet exchange
DSC : Magnetic disk
SEL : Audio/data selector
FAX : Facsimile terminal
FTC : Facsimile controller
DTY : Data terminal
TTY : Teletypewriter
M   : Modem
TDM : Time division multiplexer
CPU : Central processing unit
TEL : Telephone set
TLH : Telephone inhibiting unit
TSV : Telephone supervisor
TCU : Telephone control unit
TBL : Telephone busy lamp

Fig. 3 Configuration of HIPA-NET

Shown are examples of Hong Kong and
Singapore branch systems.

(4) High transmission quality
Packets containing errors caused by transmission line noise are checked and corrected by retransmission of the packets.

The transmission quality of packet switching networks has been greatly improved, as composed with that of existing public networks.

(5) High reliability feature
All processors of HIPA-NET have stand-by processors and dual disk files. The system configuration of the network in Hong Kong and Singapore is shown in Fig. 3. The Hong Kong branch has a node processor which exchanges data among Tokyo, Singapore and Hong Kong. The Singapore branch has no node processor but only network terminals such as a facsimile, equipment teletypewriters and a computer.

The international leased line between Hong Kong and Singapore is divided into five transmission lines by multiplexer modems. Each transmission line is attached to a terminal in Singapore. The type of communication between the terminals is shown in Table 1.

5. MAIL SERVICE PROTOCOL (MSP)

HIPA-NET offers two types of data transmission. One transmits the data directly in packets; the other assembles the data in a message format which consists of several packets and stores it on disks at each node of the network and then transmits it forward to the receiving location. The former type is used when real time data transmission is required, while the latter type

Table 1. Telecommunication Classification

Type of communication allowed between terminals.

Receive / Send	L-340	Facsimile	Teletypewriter	Telephone
L-340	o	–	o	–
Facsimile	–	o	–	–
Teletypewriter	–	–	o	–
Telephone	–	–	–	o

o : Supported
– : Not supported

is used when the data storage function is required. The latter type was chosen for SOBAS because the Bank required the ability to adjust for time differences in the network and did not require real time data transmission.

Thus MSP was developed to support this type of transmission. The message format of MSP is shown in Fig. 4. As with a letterhead, there is a message header which identifies the address, priority, and characteristics of the message. The message that follows is controlled by this message header in HIPA-NET. For facsimile data transmission, the information on a sheet of paper forms one message unit made up of several hundred packets.

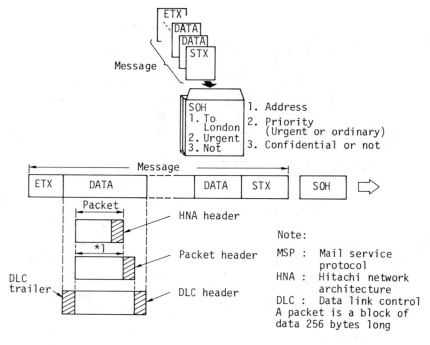

Fig. 4 Concept of Mail Service Protocol (MSP)
The computer data is transmitted in message form.

Each element of data in the packets has a
Hitachi Network Architecture (HNA) header so
that the data is handled in the computer system
under HNA, which has a standard network architecture of HITAC computer communication.

6. DISTRIBUTED DATA PROCESSING

To improve the business processing capability
of the overseas branches, the distributed data
processing system was adopted for the following
reasons.

(1) Each branch requires special functions to
comply with local regulations in addition to
the standard banking system functions.

(2) Most of the transactions are processed in
the local branch, but a few transactions must
be transmitted to other branches or to the head
office.

(3) Bank holidays vary from branch to branch.
Therefore, because it would be difficult for a
centralized system to cover all branches, a
distributed data processing system was adopted.
L-340, which was developed as a distributed
computer, is used for the system,[5],[6] and
the schematic diagram of the L-340 system is
shown in Fig. 5. The L-340 system is controlled by the operating system VOS1-S.[7] It has
three partitions which handle on-line data
processing, data exchange on-line processing
and batch data processing.

6.1 On-line data processing

Application software "SOBAS-DP" was developed
to handle various kinds of data processing;
such as foreign exchange, loans and deposits.
SOBAS-DP is controlled by the program "TSM-1"
under VOS1-S. The messages enter the system by
using video data terminals. SOBAS-DP receives
messages from the terminals and updates the
files of disks, then sends response messages to
the terminals, the response message varies
depending on the application.

6.2 Data exchange processing

SOBAS-DX was developed to control data exchange
between the overseas branches. SOBAS-DX reads
the data from the file in which the data was
stored by SOBAS-DP, and transfers it to HIPA-
NET. HIPA-NET transmits the data to the
designated branch, where another L-340 receives
and stores the data in a file.

TMS-1 and SOBAS-DX support MSP, while Hitachi
Network Architecture Subhost Communication Program (HICOP) supports HNA in the L-340 system.
In addition to the normal messages, programs
and memory dump information of the L-340 can be
transmitted between the branches by using
SOBAS-DX.

6.3 Batch processing

File copy for back up files, daily account
transactions and printing are examples of daily
batch processing. Some of these are executed
after on-line processing, but all are designed
to be processed easily by the local staff.

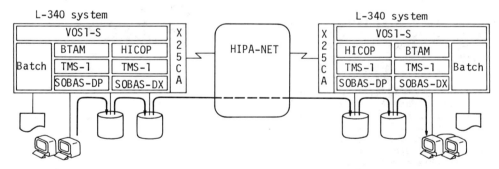

(Hardware)

X25CA   : X25 Communication control feature

(Software)

SOBAS-DX : Sanwa Overseas Banking Automation System-Data Exchange

SOBAS-DP : Sanwa Overseas Banking Automation System-Data Processing

TMS-1   : Transaction Management System-1

HICOP   : Hitachi Network Architecture Subhost Communication Program

BTAM   : Basic Telecommunication Access Method

VOS1-S   : Virtual Operating System 1-S

Fig. 5 Configuration of L-340 System

The L-340 system uses three partitions for three
functions such as on-line, data exchange and
batch data processing.

7. CONCLUSIONS

The first stage of the network system became operational in April, 1981. The L-340 in the Hong Kong branch has been operating since June and the system is now being expanded in scale on a planned time schedule. Highlights of this project are summarized as follows.

(1) International integrated network system has been constructed successfully.

(2) Communication among overseas branches has been greatly facilitated. Facsimile equipment is being used much more frequently than was expected.

(3) The L-340 computer system has improved the business processing and rationalized clerical work in branches as expected.

(4) The maintenance facility which transmits programs or computer information through the network is very useful. This facility is also a necessary maintenance function for a system that is domestically developed and operates in overseas offices.

(5) The new SOBAS has proved very effective in reducing the costs of communication and business processing.

(6) The experience and technologies resulting from this project are applicable to other advanced systems in many companies with international operations.

REFERENCES

(1) T. Hyodo et al.: "Packet Data Switching and Its Application to Corporate Communication System," HITACHI REVIEW 28, pp. 291-294(1979)

(2) T. Kato et al.: "Hitachi Packet Switched Network (HIPA-NET), "HITACHI HYORON 60, pp. 25-28 (December 1978, in Japanese)

(3) CCITT, "Sixth Plenary Assembly, Data Transmission over the Telephone Network," Series V Recommendations V. 24 and V. 28 Orange Book Volume VIII. 1, Geneva, 27 September to 8 October 1976

(4) CCITT, "Sixth Plenary Assembly, Public Data Networks," Series X Recommendations X. 25 Orange Book Volume VIII. 2, Geneva, 27 September to 8 October 1976

(5) M. Hino, et al.: "Outline of HITAC L Series Computers," HITACHI REVIEW 28, pp. 127-132 (June 1979)

(6) T. Uraki, "Development Philosophy and Characteristics of HITAC L Series Computer System," HITACHI REVIEW 28, 117-121 (June 1979)

(7) T. Ikeda, et al.: "Operating Systems of HITAC M/L Series Computers," HITACHI REVIEW 28, pp. 122-126 (June 1979)

Yoshiharu Kudo graduated from Osaka City University with B.C. in 1960. Since 1956 he has been working for the Sanwa Bank Ltd. Since 1973, after having got the diversified knowledge and experience of a domestic and international banking business, he has been engaged in the development of SOBAS (Sanwa Overseas Banking Automation System).

Takashi Hyodo graduated from University of Tokyo in 1966, and received M.S. of Electrical Engineering of Stanford University in 1973. Since 1966, he has been working for Hitachi, Ltd. in the development of audio response system and data.

Misao Seto graduated from University of Tokyo in 1964. Since 1964, he has been working for Hitachi, Ltd. in design of computer and data communication.

A View of Banks as Interconnected Open Systems

D A Sheppard
Canadian Imperial Bank of Commerce,
Canada
H C Dickson
LGS Consultants, Canada

The processing and communications (telematic) requirements of banks and the banking industry are examined using concepts and terminology drawn from the Reference Model of Open Systems Interconnection. A concept of the banking function in society is presented, along with scenarios for future banking systems. The objectives and goals of the Reference Model of Open Systems Interconnection are reviewed briefly and compared to the emerging needs of bank systems. Open Systems Interconnection is shown to be a potentially valuable aid for banking evolution into a global financial infrastructure. Some observations are drawn from the material presented, and examples are given based on existing systems to illustrate.

1. INTRODUCTION

Banks are presently undergoing, often subconsciously, a dramatic transformation that will position them as key information brokers of the Telematic Society (1). The banking industry will become a global enterprise consisting of loosely-coupled but cooperative institutions. Their role will be to organize and manage the storage and movement of the world's "electronic money".

Alvin Toffler, author of The Third Wave (2), has described the approach of the Information Age. A change as significant as the industrial revolution will occur as society moves into the age of information and communications. Banks, without doubt, must adapt to and exploit the tools of this new era if they are to survive and function meaningfully and profitably.

Bankers are realizing, also, that their survival as financial intermediaries even now depends upon the availability of timely, accurate financial function and information in electronic form. Lenders and users of money are increasingly linked to computerization, not only for primary operational activities such as teller transactions but also for connections to Point-of-Sale terminals, customer terminals, company computers, etc. This shift away from paper-intensive operations is resulting in a dependency on telematics that industry planners have only now begun to recognize and understand.

This paper develops a simplified conceptual model of a bank's function, examines requirements for the systems that must implement it, and discusses the application of Open Systems Interconnection (OSI) to the structuring of banking communications. Observations are provided to stimulate further discussion among industry standardization groups and corporate planners. The ultimate goal of such efforts would be a unified, integrated systems direction for the banking industry.

It is not intended that this paper be either an authoritative description of the banking industry or of OSI. The opinions contained herein are entirely those of the authors and do not necessarily represent currently approved policy or direction within any bank or the banking industry.

2. BACKGROUND

Today, less than two decades after the pioneering days of computing, almost every new information system requires a network and terminals. Indeed, the terminals are often other computers (perhaps microcomputers) and are outside the direct control of the systems developer. In general, society is heading towards an era of mass information transfer among large numbers of computers, just as the telephone is now providing voice interconnection for many millions of people all over the world. Banking, while not the only driving force in this scenario, is expected to play a significant role due to the universal use of "money messages" for the exchange of society's goods and services. The conversion of paper-based money messages (i.e., dollars) into electronic form is a result of the creation of Electronic Funds Transfer Systems. Such systems require a sophisticated and widely available transport capability to reliably move the information between users anywhere in the world.

Large networks of computers now appear to be in the entrepreneurial stage of growth, much as Nolan (3) has described for computing and databases. Most existing networks use techniques developed by communications carriers or equipment manufacturers, and are geared to specific, limited environments (or sets of equipment). A lack of commonly agreed standards is beginning to hinder the development of generalized inter-organizational communications and the unrestricted interworking of diverse species of equipments. These capabilities, however, are precisely what the banking industry needs to successfully create a "global" banking infrastructure for funds storage, movement and management.

In the past few years considerable emphasis has been placed on "architectures" for systems. In this paper we consider an architecture to be a set of implementation rules which define functional modularity, protocols, and interfaces. Two architectural views are presented: firstly, a simplified view of the functional architecture of a bank; and, secondly, a structural view of interconnected Open Banking Systems.

3. THE PURPOSE AND GOALS OF OPEN SYSTEMS INTERCONNECTION

The Reference Model of Open Systems Interconnection (4) is a standard being developed by the International Organization for Standardization (specifically, Technical Committee 97/ Subcommittee 16). Its overall purpose is the following:

- to provide a common basis for the co-ordination of standards development for the purpose of systems interconnection;
- to allow existing standards to be placed into perspective within the overall reference model;
- to identify areas for developing or improving standards;
- to provide a common reference for maintaining consistency of all related standards; and
- to provide a conceptual and functional framework for development of layer services and protocols.

The banking industry has also developed, for its own use, standards and practices which are currently used for payment message transfer. The SWIFT (Society for Worldwide Interbank Financial Transactions) network, for example, has proven effective and useful to many banks. Another committee of the International Organization for Standard-ization (TC68/SC5-Banking Telecommunications Messages) is currently developing a standard message format for Telex payment messages(5).

The OSI Architecture is stated as being applicable to:

- the exchange of information among systems that are "open" to one another for this purpose; and
- systems comprising terminals, computers and associated devices, and the means for transferring information between such systems.

Thus, Open Systems Interconnection can apply to all information systems that must communicate, including those of the banking industry.

From a banker's perspective it is important to recognize that "openness" does not imply that all information stored in a system is freely accessible or that there is any degradation of the security, accuracy or privacy of banking operations. On the contrary, OSI creates an environment in which data accessibility can be even more

strictly controlled and managed. The standardization of well-defined layers permits connections to be managed in each layer and ensures that interworking occurs only when authorized.

The elements of OSI (application-entities, physical media, connections, and open systems) are illustrated in Figure 1. The Reference Model is based on the concept of co-operating application users (called application-processes). An application-process can be one or a cluster of elements performing a specific set of activities designed to satisfy defined needs. Fundamental to OSI are the assumptions that multiple application-processes exist in more than one physical system, that they must interact to achieve their purposes, that the interactions are definable as messages, and that the messages must be transported between systems.

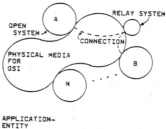

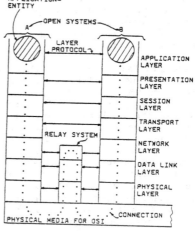

Figure 1: Interconnected Open Systems

The Reference Model of OSI provides for a layered decomposition of the various functions. Seven distinct layers have been identified and are presently being standardized, as follows:

```
LAYER 7: APPLICATION LAYER ] - processes,
                                 management
       6: PRESENTATION LAYER] - information
                                 representation

       5: SESSION LAYER     ]
       4: TRANSPORT LAYER    ] -interprocess
       3: NETWORK LAYER      ] communication
       2: DATA LINK LAYER    ]
       1: PHYSICAL LAYER     ]
```

Standards for the Application and Presentation Layers are designed to provide generic, commonly required services such as system management and file transfer. They are not intended to eliminate innovation or creativity from the systems development process. With concerns for interprocess communications eliminated, more effort can be devoted to the design of application-processes specific to the bank or the customer. The expansion and evolution of services in a controlled, planned manner would then be more feasible.

4. MONEY: A FORM OF INFORMATION

Before the invention of money, exchanges of goods and services occurred through a process of bartering. Later, methods of exchange were developed that used commodities of standardized value to represent the goods or services, with gold and currency notes being the most recent. Cheques are presently widely used as a convenient representation for currency, and credit cards are beginning to have a similar impact. The next step is what may be the ultimate payment mechanism - electronic messages flowing between computers. Electronic Funds Transfer (EFT) Systems, which is the popular name for computerized money transfer, are based on the assumption that it is the information represented by the cheque or currency note that is important to the exchange, not the physical paper itself.

Electronic Funds Transfer, in its most general sense, occurs whenever financial information is stored, transported, transmitted, or otherwise processed in electronic form (6). Many of a bank's interactions with its customers and correspondents therefore involve EFT, including such services as:

- transfers between customer accounts using Telidon;
- a teller reconciling transactions to a database;
- transmission of payment messages via SWIFT or Telex;
- paying a bill using an automatic teller machine;
- automatic deposit of a corporate payroll; and
- withdrawal of funds for storage on a chip card.

Electronic Funds Transfer Systems and their associated money messages will become the infrastructure for bank processing and funds movement in the future. Standards for both

the transport structure and the representation of money messages are clearly needed to achieve the most cost-effective interconnection. These standards must be accepted by a large number of institutions, including not only the banks themselves but also their customers.

An illustration of the banking role in society in "layered" terms is given in Figure 2. This diagram places the bank in the role of financial intermediary, and shows how independent customers form associations for exchange of goods and services using the funds access and transfer facilities of a bank. Physical dollars are one form of the "media" for a paper-based exchange and the bank manages the "interconnection" between the parties involved in the exchange. Banks earn a profit by charging for this service and by investing money that customers store at the bank when not in use.

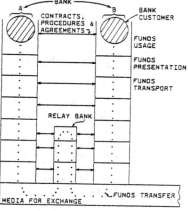

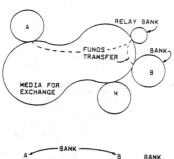

Figure 2: Layers of Financial Function

A macro-view of a banking system is shown in Figure 3. Figure 4 gives a similar view drawn in "OSI format". It can be seen that bank's in the future will be heavily dependent on their ability both to access the systems of

481

other banks and customers, and also to deliver information to widely dispersed terminals. Significant savings in the implementation and operation could accrue from the simplification and standardization of the interfaces needed for providing such accesses.

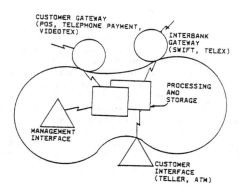

Figure 3: A Conceptual Banking System

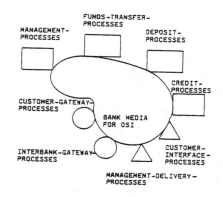

Figure 4: An OSI View of a Banking System

5. CURRENT BANKING SYSTEMS

Most large banks have substantially completed the computerization of basic internal operations, including deposit accounting, loan accounting, teller support, automated teller machine support, etc. Additionally, banks have developed sophisticated processes to assist in such services as the clearing of cheques, the authorization of credit card purchases, and the transfer of international payments. Each bank has created systems that are unique to its own environment, thus resulting in a variety of approaches that differ at the corporate, national and international levels.

For bank systems planners the search for ways to permit an orderly evolution of diverse, incompatible systems into an integrated, interconnected, worldwide banking architecture is the current challenge.

For example, the Canadian Imperial Bank of Commerce, which is one of the largest banks in Canada with over $65 billion in assets, currently has more than 5000 terminals located in over 1600 branches across Canada (that is, distributed across 4000 miles)(7). These are connected to a pair of IBM 3033 computers in Toronto for on-line banking processing. IBM 4300 series computers, located in six data centres across Canada, control IBM 3890 cheque reader/sorters and are linked to other computers in Toronto for cheque processing. More than 300 million cheques per year are processed with overnight return to any bank branch in Canada.

The banks in Canada that offer Visa services are presently implementing a co-operative system to route merchant enquiries to the appropriate bank's authorization centre. This relieves the merchant of any concern over which bank to call for credit verification. Computers in each bank are being linked using Tandem computers and Bell Canada's Datapac packet network in what may be the forerunner of a more generalized Canadian Interbank Communications Architecture.

A number of national and international networks exist for the transfer of payment messages, including SWIFT, CHIPS (Clearing House Interbank Payments System), Fedwire and Bankwire (8). SWIFT, for example, is a bank owned co-operative society that has approximately 1000 participants in more than 30 countries. It provides a secure networking vehicle for international payments transfer. Additionally, SWIFT has designed and implemented message formats to ensure that each bank correctly interprets the intended meaning of messages despite varying languages and procedures. Thus, both transport and presentation facilities are provided. As noted previously, similar money message standards are being drafted for use on Telex transport systems.

Clearly, many vendors are involved in the banking systems market and configurations will continue to proliferate. While innovation and experimentation is desirable and to be encouraged initially, a means to ensure that the variety of applications, computers, terminals, and networks does not make the achievement of global interconnection a prohibitively expensive undertaking will be needed. Open Systems Interconnection is expected to provide an appropriate set of standards for this purpose.

6. INTERCONNECTED OPEN BANKING SYSTEMS

Financial institutions are generally in business to be profitable for their shareholders. High level goals for a bank, of concern to the developers of its systems, are:

- market share increase, which is an indicator of capacity growth and customer connectivity;
- cost control, which results from efficient and effective operational systems;

- customer service, which relates to the accessibility of the systems and the richness of functionality provided; and
- management information, which involves making information available to decision makers relating to the state of the business, the economy and the customer.

To a large extent, these goals can be netted down to: increased customer convenience through more access points and more flexible arrangements for accounts and statements/passbooks; reduction in the volume of paper through conversion to EFT and on-line databases; and, increased productivity of both personnel and resources through the provision of user-friendly decision support systems and uniform terminal control procedures.

Most bank customers, for example, will eventually want to perform their financial transactions at locations of their choice, including at any branch of any bank, at ATM's located in public areas anywhere in the world, via a merchant's computer in a store, or at their home or office. The customer will want his accounts to be available 24 hours a day (especially when time zones are involved), 7 days a week, and to be continuously up-to-date. One step further, the customer will want to submit transactions to the bank for later processing at a convenient time and location, either repetitively or on a once-only basis. Ultimately, the customer will expect comprehensive financial management facilities under his personal control and tailored to suit his unique combination of needs, including budget planning, investment analysis, interest optimization, and tax accounting.

If the above service directions are valid, it is not hard to see that flexible, standardized facilities for the interconnection of computers, terminals, and customers would be consistent with the objectives of the banks. This leads to the proposition that a business case exists for the adoption of Open Systems Interconnection as a banking industry direction.

A conceptual model for a global banking system based upon OSI is given in Figure 5. The model recognizes three levels: corporate systems, national links between banks, and international interconnection. OSI at the corporate level is suggested but would not be necessary if gateways are provided to interface existing systems. Such a gateway would also be suitable for connection to other systems such as Point-of-Sale, government reporting, videotex, etc. if they are also "open". At the national level OSI is proposed to ensure optimal use of carrier networks and diverse manufacturers equipments with a minimum of unique interface development. National concerns are magnified at the international level, where different legal and social environments result in even greater diversity.

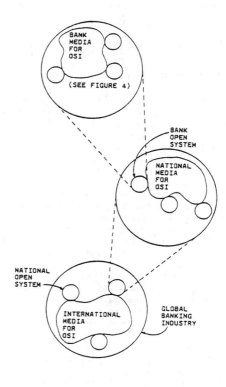

Figure 5: Interconnected Open Banking Systems

A most valuable aspect of OSI relevant to banks is the way that the layers define a sphere of influence for a particular function, and therefore for its vendor. OSI provides a methodology for making vendor and function boundary decisions. This will enable functions to have different vendors and undergo change at different times. It will make clear which design features must be common and which features can express the local business climate (i.e., national options for application and presentation functions). In this way, the design process for new systems will be considerably simplified.

OSI provides a design model for computer interworking that includes multiple peer and/or subordinate networks to any number of levels. The banking industry exhibits a large number of peer relationships in its exchange of electronic and other forms of money messages. Internally, most banks have traditionally been organized hierarchically and their computer systems reflect this.

These hierarchical structures must now permit peer relationships for independent areas within a single bank, for exchanges among banks in each area, and for interconnection to customer systems for paperless transactions. If competitive service, security and control are to be offered, these networks must have a consistent, well-defined set of network modelling standards. OSI provides this.

7. CONCLUDING REMARKS

In this paper we have reviewed the principles of Open Systems Interconnection and shown them to be generally in line with the telematic requirements of banks and the banking industry. A view of banking in OSI terms was presented, and a conceptual structure for globally interconnected Open Banking Systems was derived. Existing networks were used to illustrate trends and developments in banking networks. Adoption of OSI as a direction for the banking industry was proposed, based on the identified need for mass interconnection among financial computer applications.

A general observation is that standards will become more and more important as a means of managing systems change. In an environment where diversity in equipment is the rule, where detailed requirements can vary significantly for equivalent services, and where all users are at a peer level, it will be essential to have general agreement on principles and practices if a truly global banking infrastructure is to evolve.

Our discussion here has been confined to architectural considerations since standards developments are the most advanced at this level. It is suggested that the resulting layer services and protocols will fall into two categories, from a bankers point of view. These are:

- essential services required to "stay in business"; and
- services of an entrepreneurial nature which result in competitive edge for their implementors.

The initiation of standards projects in those areas generally considered to be competitive (Layers 6 and 7) should be carefully reviewed to ensure that concensus among competing parties is attainable. Standards in Layers 1–5 should be adopted and implemented as quickly as possible.

The various layers proposed by OSI should be implemented as they are needed or are incorporated into products that are purchased by banks. Transport networks representing Layers 1 through 5 can become inter- and intra-bank standards as well as inter-industry standards. Networks such as SWIFT should be considered as their forerunners.

The following further observations are provided as a stimulus for further study and research:

- Banking systems must be able to use all available transport subsystems as long as qualities of service such as security, accuracy, privacy, and reliability can be maintained. Bankers should be prepared to agree upon their needs in this respect.
- Bankers should consider standardizing "Virtual Banking Terminals" and similar Presentation Layer services to ensure that true interworking (as opposed to data transmission) can occur.
- Money message standards must be expanded to be generally applicable both to banks internally (such as SWIFT and Telex) and to associated customer systems (such as Point-of-Sale). Completion of overall banking transaction protocols at the Application Layer is also required. The international forum for such an effort, to a large extent, already exists in the ISO.
- Another important area is the standardization of management aspects of bank interconnection.
- OSI service standards must permit different manufacturers to supply equipment for different layers, and yet also minimize overhead in homogenoeus systems.

ACKNOWLEDGMENT

The authors gratefully acknowledge the assistance of Linda Taylor in the typing of this paper.

REFERENCES

[1] Martin, J., Telematic Society: A Challenge for Tomorrow, Prentice-Hall Inc. Englewood Cliffs, New Jersey 1981

[2] Toffler,A., The Third Wave Bantum Books Inc. 1981

[3] Nolan,R.L., Managing the Four Stages of EDP Growth, Harvard Business Review, Jan./Feb.1974

[4] -- ISO DP7498 -Reference Model of Open Systems Inter-connection, Feb. 1982

[5] -- ISO DP7746-Standard Telex Formats for Inter-bank Payment, Messages, Nov. 1981

[6] Clark,R., The Growth of Electronic Funds Transfer and Automated Banking in the Next Ten Years, Teleinformatics 79, North-Holland Publishing Co.

[7] Fistell,L., Rising Volume, Costs Pave the Way for Self-Serve Banking., Canadian Datasystems, Nov. 1981

[8] Meir,E.E., Bank Data Networks: Moving Millions Electronically, Data Communications, April 1981

High-speed and Large-cross-section Data Links on Fiber

S S Austin, S S Cheng, J S Cook,
P H Krawarik
Bell Laboratories, USA

Following the implementation of the fiber link between N. Y. Telephone's computers in lower Manhattan, other needs for 1) high-speed and 2) large-cross-section data links began to appear. The Lightwave Data Transmission Interface originally designed for the lower Manhattan link was further developed to meet the high-speed data needs. The equipment accommodates the V.35 standard interface protocol, to provide synchronous data transmission at pre-selected rates of 56 kb/sec to 10 Mb/sec. Certain maintenance and trouble-shooting features were included in the new design. Large-cross-section needs can be met using some of the new standard telephone transmission system equipments operating at the North American standard 6.3 Mb/s, DS2 and 44.7 Mb/s, DS3 digital rates that utilize the optical fiber medium. One such system has been implemented for a large industrial user, R. J. Reynolds in Winston-Salem, NC. Initially installed as a FT2 facility, it will use eventually the DS3 rate to interconnect two buildings about 5km apart. Similar solutions have been proposed for a large commercial customer of Pacific Telephone and others. In most cases, central offices would provide distribution points to the customer locations. Efforts are underway to offer such wide band access as a tariffed service. Multiplex and terminating equipment normally located only in central offices would be located on customer premises.

INTRODUCTION

In April of 1980, New York Telephone began operating four 50 kb/s data links on a pair of fibers between two computers, one at 50 Varick Street and the other at 375 Pearl Street in downtown Manhattan. The pair of computers takes care of the Loop Maintenance Operating System (LMOS) for New York City. The fiber line has been literally error-free since its installation.

SYSTEM CONFIGURATION

The four 50 kb/s copper lines are combined in a General DataComm Model 1253 Time Division Multiplexer to provide a single 256 kb/s data stream. This data stream drives a modem called a Lightwave Data Interface (LDI) which is connected through fiber to a corresponding modem at the other computer location, 3.7 km distant (Figure 1).

The fiber run is in three parts: 1) inter-bay, 2) riser, and 3) outside plant. Single-fiber cable and WE standard molded connectors connect the LDI to the Lightwave Cable Interface Equipment (LCIE). Here the fibers fan into eight-fiber ribbons. The fiber ribbons are housed in a steel reinforced sheath which carries the fibers down to a splice case in the building cable vault. Steel-reinforced, PVC-sheathed cable carries the fiber through ducts to an intermediate building (where some fibers are accessed for telephone service), and thence to the building where the host computers reside. Like the preponderance of ducted (under-ground) telephone cables, the outside plant fiber cables are pressurized.

Cable ducts under the streets of lower Manhattan are old and crowded. There were no available ducts along the required fiber route.

There are, however, a number of unused cable-pressurization air pipes that exist in the area. WE standard lightwave cable carries fibers in 12-fiber ribbons in a sheath of about 1.5 cm outer diameter,--too large to pull easily through the 1.9 cm ID air pipes. Special cable of about 1 cm OD was fabricated by WE for this application; and was easily installed.

CLOCK

Dipulse coding of the 256 kb/s data stream that comes into the LDI translates the information onto a 512 kb/s transition-rich data stream on the fiber. Clock is easily recovered from the data stream by an integrated phase-frequency locked loop in the receiving modem.

LIGHTWAVE DATA TRANSMISSION INTERFACE

The success of these data links and growing interest in fast data lines on fiber led to further development of the lightwave modem used in Manhattan. Designated now as the Lightwave Data Transmission Interface (LDTI), it is able to handle data rates from 56 kb/s to 10 Mb/s. The frequency at which it operates is built into each unit by appropriate selection of a few passive components. As in the case of LDI, it can accept digital inputs from data sources through a variety of interfaces. New features have been added: local and remote loop-back, self-testing, internal and slave clock options, full handshaking, half or full duplex operation, asynchronous transmission capability, and improved physical design.

The present design can accommodate TTL or V.35 type inputs. Other interfaces can be accommodated by redesigning a simple circuit pack. In some cases this redesign is trivial.

485

So far, the LDTI has been configured to operate synchronously at discrete data rates in the range from 56 kb/s to 6.3 Mb/s. Since it transmits and processes information at the dipulse-coded rate, a 10 Mb/s input rate results in 20 Mb/s switching speeds in the LDTI circuitry. This is near the design limit of several of the TTL integrated circuits.

The low end of its range is constrained by the limitations of the phase-frequency-locked-loop timing recovery circuit. The WECo 555R PFLL, used for clock recovery, was originally intended for 44.7 MHz operation in the FT3 system. However, by proper selection of a few external passive components, other frequencies are possible. From a design standpoint, the 555R should be able to operate down to very low speed. It has been found, however, that lower frequency operation can lead to various locking problems in the presence of high frequency spectral components in the pulse stream (sharp rising and falling edges). This problem has been overcome by suitable low pass filtering at the PFLL input for input rates down to 56 kb/s (i.e., 112 kb/s input to the PFLL) and can be expected to work at yet lower rates. However, these locking problems are accentuated at lower frequencies and it is uncertain as to the precise lower limit of operation.

The LDTI can also transmit data from asynchronous sources by using INTERNAL timing. Since the clock to the dipulse coder is then provided by an internal crystal oscillator, the input data is simply sampled by the coder. These samples are coded in the usual fashion, transmitted, and reconstructed as samples by the receiving LDTI. There is edge jitter, of course, whose magnitude is given by the ratio of the INTERNAL clock to the asynchronous data rate.

The upper frequency limit of asynchronous transmission is determined, then, by the jitter tolerance of the data user and the upper design limit for the INTERNAL clock.

The maximum span between LDTIs is determined as follows:

The 1250A optical transmitter subassembly, which is used independent of the transmission rate, is specified to couple at least -20 dBm average power into the optical fiber.

Two WE APD receivers and one PIN receiver are available. The APD receivers (WECo 1350B and 1351B) have an average power sensitivity (for a 10^{-9} BER) of about -47 dBm. For the 1351A PIN receiver the sensitivity is about -37 dBm. The receiver sensitivity is essentially independent of data rate because of the way the packages are designed. Any of these receiver packages can be mounted in the LDTI.

If one allows 3 dB system margin and assumes a spliced fiber loss of 5 dB/km (conservative), there results a maximum span length of 4.8 km with an APD receiver

and 2.8 km with a PIN receiver.

Dynamic range constraints in the optical receivers prevent them from operating over too short a span length without an optical attenuator. Attenuators are available which can be inserted directly into the receiver optical connector socket.

The LDTI incorporates four circuit boards (Fig. 2): The LOGIC Board performs dipulse coding, decoding, and clock recovery operations. It also houses the lightwave receiver and transmitter subassemblies, as well as the oscillator circuit which generates the low frequency clock (LFC) signal used to initiate remote loopback. The LOOPBACK Board contains the digital discriminator designed to perform carrier detection and recognize an incoming LFC. It also contains most of the logic required to initiate a remote loopback and, along with the discriminator, distinguish between a loopback command and a loopback confirmation signal. The INTERFACE Board contains both the TTL and V.35 interfaces. The TTL interface consists essentially of line drivers and receivers as well as the handshaking logic. A number of options switches are provided to control and set various modes of operation. In addition, the board houses the crystal clock used for "internal clock" and "test mode" operation. The POWER SUPPLY Board (not shown in Figure 2) houses AC-DC and DC-DC converters required to power the other three circuit boards and front-panel LED's. (Figure 3)

A number of these LDTI units have been manufactured to satisfy requirements that resulted from exploratory marketing by Western Electric Company.

LARGE CROSS-SECTION SYSTEMS

The success of the lower Manhattan data links, among other things, has led to reevaluation of the 5-year cable growth plan for New York City. Much more emphasis is now being placed on fiber, than on copper wire cables. The flexibility of digital transmission, particularly over a noise-free medium, allows its use for data as well as for quality voice. The demand for large-cross-section lines between business locations is growing; and New York Telephone is positioning itself to handle that demand.

A system has been implemented for R. J. Reynolds in Winston-Salem, NC. In a phased build-out, over 50 data circuits on 9.6 kb/s and 56 kb/s will eventually be provided between the computer center in the Plaza Building and the World Headquarters approximately 5 km apart. (A number of voice frequency circuits are provided over the same facility.) While the initial installation makes use of the DS2 data rate, scheduled growth calls for ultimate use of FT3 technology. Only certain plug-ins need to be exchanged, and more equipment added, in order to upgrade.

Like in New York, similar forces exist across the United States. A proposal for a large commercial customer of Pacific Tel and Tel suggests the use of FT3 transmission systems to link several of the customers downtown locations. Standard digital phone circuits would be used.

Figure 4 shows the arrangement. For each two-way 44.7 Mb/s FT3 transmission link there is a two-way back-up link that automatically takes over service if the primary link should fail. Note that the DPC may be connected to two telephone switching offices along separate routes by separate systems. In each case the back-up links are routed through the alternate office and along the alternate route, to optimize the protection.

Each FT3 system is designed to carry 28, 1.544 Mb/s systems, or 672 telephone circuits. Multiplexing of the T1 systems to the DS3 rate takes place in an MX3 Line Terminating Multiplex in the switching offices and in the DPC at the other end. Each T1 is designed to carry 24, 64 kb/s digital voice circuits. The T1 lines terminate in D-banks that normally do D/A conversion on a single channel unit insert for each telephone circuit.

In a D4 Terminal Bay (D-bank), these Telephone Channel Units can be replaced by Dataport Channel Units that allow any of four standard data signals to be carried in place of a telephone circuit.

D4 DATAPORT CHANNEL UNITS

D4 Dataport Channel Units provide direct digital access to and from T1, T1C, and T2 systems via the D4 Channel Bank. They avoid analog-to-digital conversion of data signals; and provide inexpensive access to the Digital Data system network.

There are currently 7 different Dataport Channel Units. Four of the units, intended for use in end office or business premises applications, provide the electrical interface to the subscriber loop, and convert the incoming data to the 64 kb/s, DS0 Rate, Digital Format. These units are called Office Channel Units, and are available in subrates of 2.4 kb/s, 4.8 kb/s, 9.6 kb/s and 56 kb/s. Two of the 7 units are primarily intended to be used in hub office applications and allow 64 kb/s, DS0 Rate, Direct Digital Access to and from T1, T1C, and T2 lines. These units are called Data Speed Zero Channel Units and one of them may be used with OCUs whose subrates are 2.4 kb/s, 4.8 kb/s, and 9.6 kb/s, while the other is associated only with the 56 kb/s office channel units. There is one Dataport Channel Unit that provides an EIA Standard Interface (RS449) where the distance between a data terminal and a channel bank is within 200 meters. This unit is called the Data Service Unit Dataport, and is primarily used for intra Bell Central Office to Central Office Data Communications.

All of these Dataport Channel Units have error-correction circuitry.

The Office Channel Unit and the Data Speed Zero Channel Units have a front panel test connector which provides test access for local testing of remote dataports.

The Data Service Unit Dataport features:

Data rate selection using a coded rotary switch mounted on a printed wiring board, four test switches for local loopback, self test, remote loopback, and remote terminal loopback; in addition, there are several light-emitting diodes to indicate that certain operating conditions of the DSUDP have been activated.

INTERMEDIATE-CROSS-SECTION LINKS

Often the high-quality/low error characteristics of fiber transmission justify their extra cost where the data load does not (or not yet) require a full FT3 link. In those cases, the customer may be connected to the CO's by fiber carrying a 6.3 Mb/s T2 bit stream.

A terminating multiplex called the MX2L is capable of multiplexing either 4 T1 or 2 T1C lines onto a single fiber. Automatic 1x1 protection of the fiber link is possible with this equipment, too. Full standard transmission test and maintenance features are included.

CONCLUSION

Quality, capacity, and reliability of digital transmission are the hallmarks of the fiber medium.

A family of data lightwave transmission interfaces emerges to provide adaptive solutions for High Speed and Large Cross Section data communication needs.

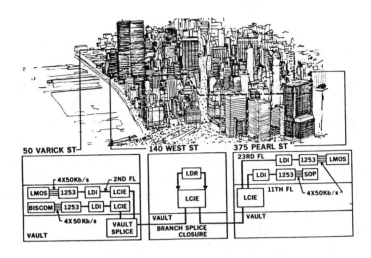

50 VARICK ST
140 WEST ST
375 PEARL ST

FIGURE 1   LOWER MANHATTAN DATA ROUTING COMPUTER
DATA LINK

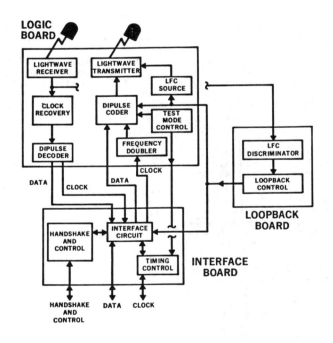

FIGURE 2   BLOCK DIAGRAM OF LDTI (EXCLUDING POWER
SUPPLY BOARD)

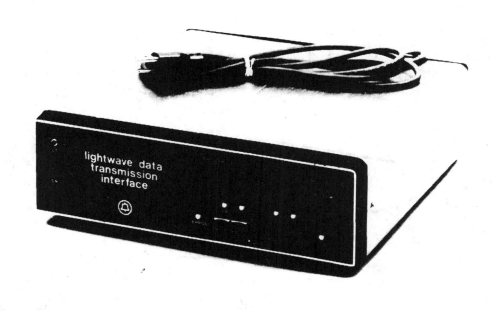

FIGURE 3   LIGHTWAVE DATA TRANSMISSION INTERFACE

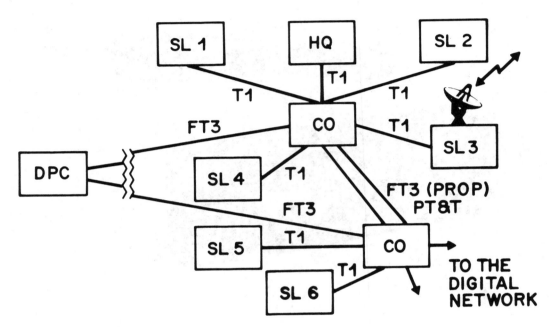

CO   CENTRAL OFFICE, TEL CO.
HQ   CUSTOMER HEADQUARTERS
DPC CUSTOMER DATA PROCESSING CENTER
SL   CUSTOMER SATELLITE LOCATIONS

FIGURE 4

NASA Goddard Space Flight Center Fiber Optic Demonstration System

E F Boose, C R Husbands
The MITRE Corporation, USA

NASA Goddard Space Flight Center (GSFC) initiated a development program in 1979 for a fiber optic communications system to support the Spaceflight Tracking and Data Network. A brassboard of a slotted, time division multiple access (TDMA), fiber optic bus was delivered to Goddard Space Flight Center in September 1980. The bit rate of the bus is 100 Mb/s. This paper reviews the NASA requirements that led to the choice of a slotted, TDMA, fiber optic system; describes the bus architecture and protocol that satisfied these requirements; and discusses the final optical configuration and the concerns about available components.

INTRODUCTION

The NASA fiber optic system was designed to demonstrate a method of meeting the communication needs of the Spaceflight Tracking and Data Network. This network provides telemetry, command, and tracking services for satellite and other spaceflight operations. In particular, it will be required to support improved ground stations, the Tracking and Data Relay Satellite System, and other mission control centers.

In May 1979, NASA Goddard Space Flight Center initiated a program to demonstrate the practicality of a fiber optic bus for the Spaceflight Tracking and Data Network and to produce plans for a fiber plant that could expand to interconnect all technical centers at Goddard. This report reviews the NASA requirements, describes the slotted, TDMA bus that evolved, discusses the recommended fiber plant, and examines some concerns about component performance.

REQUIREMENTS

Major features of the preliminary requirements that emerged, after many discussions with potential users, were:

- Initial Installation. The initial system should connect six buildings: 3, 13, 14, 23, 25, and 28. (The demonstration system however, has just three terminal units to provide proof of concept.) Later, the fiber optic system could be extended to all technical centers at Goddard Space Flight Center.

- Repeaters. The system should take advantage of low fiber losses to span the maximum distance of 1.6 km from building 14 to building 25 without requiring repeaters.

- Universal Connectivity. Every user on the system should be able to transmit and receive data from every other user.

- Number of Users. Two to eight users should be accommodated by each terminal device.

- User I/O. Simplex communication lines should be used for transmitting and receiving between each user and the terminal device. User rates from 10 b/s to 10 Mb/s should be accommodated. The electrical interface should be RS-422, and the encoding, non return to zero. Information is to be introduced into the system in blocks of 4800 bits, including header and trailer.

- Maximum Traffic. The maximum traffic rate is determined by the rate at which telemetry sources can deliver data to Goddard Space Flight Center. With everything operating simultaneously, the traffic rate is estimated to be 70 Mb/s. Command and operations traffic do not add significantly to this.

- Bit Error Rate. An error rate of 10^{-9} or less is needed so that the bus does not add significantly to the errors of long haul communications circuits.

SYSTEM ARCHITECTURE

Although most developmental fiber optic communications systems are point to point, the requirements for the NASA system clearly indicate that a bus should be considered. A slotted, TDMA system was proposed with slots assigned by a Network Control Processor to meet scheduled telemetry requirements and to assure that a communications channel is always available when needed. The bus provides the universal connectivity that is required, as well as a

* This work was carried out by the MITRE Corporation under contract to the National Aeronautics and Space Administration (Contract Number F 19628-81-C-0001).

means of interfacing users with widely different I/O rates.

To avoid bidirectional traffic, inbound and outbound fibers are used. Each terminal is connected to each of the fibers, transmitting onto the inbound fiber and receiving messages on the outbound fiber as shown in figure 1. The terminals that interface to the users are called Channel Interface Units (CIUs). A Channel Control Unit (CCU) is located at the head end of the bus. It receives all incoming messages, checks their timing and the correctness of the header, and then places correct messages on the outgoing line for distribution to all CIUs. The CCU also acts as an interface for the Network Control Processor (NCP), permitting it to send status requests and receive status messages, allocate slots, and activate user interfaces.

The bit rate of the fiber transmission is 100 Mb/s. This rate is a careful compromise between requirements and the state-of-the-art of commercially available transmitters and receivers. Greater bit rates in 1979 and 1980 would have created cost penalties and increased the technical risk.

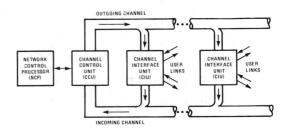

Figure 1. CONCEPTUAL SYSTEM DIAGRAM

Each message on the fiber has a header that provides synchronization and the desired routing information. The header is added by the CIU that receives the 4800 bit block from a user. This brings the block size on the fiber up to 5120 bits.

The algorithm that avoids conflict on the bus is very simple: each block must arrive at the CCU in its proper time slot. A guard band, equivalent to 32 bits, is used between blocks to avoid interference. Figure 2 shows the timing. A frame consists of 65536 blocks.

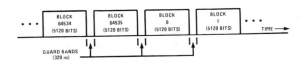

Figure 2. TIMING DIAGRAM

A block diagram of the CIU is shown in figure 3. The Channel Interface Section (on the left) receives messages from the outbound channel while message disposition is determined. The bit slice microcontroller reads the channel message header and determines whether it is intended for the users connected to the CIU. When a match occurs, the message is passed to the appropriate output buffer in the Link Interface Section where the message is transmitted. The Channel Interface Section also transmits over the inbound channel messages that are received through the Link Interface Section from users. Control messages, including slot assignment, output link assignment, on-line/off-line commands, and status requests, are received and appropriate responses made. Most of the Channel Interface Section of the CIU is designed with ECL to accommodate the high bit rates.

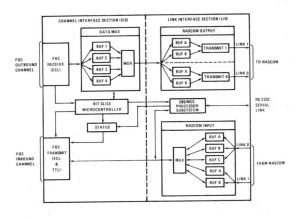

Figure 3. CHANNEL INTERFACE UNIT BLOCK DIAGRAM

The CCU is similar to the CIU except that its only user is the Network Control Processor and its incoming messages are received on the inbound line and repeated over the outbound line.

The fiber optic demonstration system differed from the concept described above in three principal respects. An active star configuration (shown in figure 4) was used because suitable tee couplers were not obtained in time. To minimize construction cost and technical risk, fiber optic links that were available from prior development efforts were used. These components were limited to 50 Mb/s rates, so parallel fibers were run to accommodate the 100 Mb/s line rate. Finally, and again to minimize the cost and development time, a separate fiber carried the clock from the CCU to each CIU.

The demonstration system was delivered to Goddard Space Flight Center in September 1980 for testing.

492

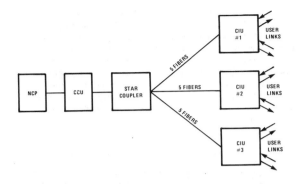

Figure 4. DEMONSTRATION SYSTEM

FIBER OPTIC NETWORK DESIGN

In designing a high data rate distribution network for the Goddard Space Flight Center, several factors have been considered. The first factor is the requirement to develop a cable plant that would permit graceful expansion of the network. Initially the network was designated to service a small number of buildings with the network head end in building 14. Figure 5 is a map of the Goddard Space Flight Center main site that shows the location of buildings, distances, and relative directions that the cable network design must consider. By adding a few more couplers and additional cabling to the initial installation, the data distribution network can be extended to service nine other buildings. If additional couplers are installed initially, units can be added without disturbing operation of the original

communications channels. With the addition of three more cable paths, all remaining buildings in the GSFC complex, scheduled for service, can be accommodated. All cable plans developed in this study are constrained to the use of existing duct work.

A second major factor in establishing the architecture of the network is cost. The most desirable cable plan would require minimum cost in terms of materials and components, and would be inexpensive to install and maintain. In this paper, two architectural plans are discussed and priced on the basis of material and components. However, installation cost, also a primary factor in the systems implementation, is not included.

To satisfy both the initial installation requirements and the expanded network configuration, the entire cable plant consists of six optical legs. Each leg has an inbound and outbound cable, but for simplicity, only one of these cables is discussed. In establishing the power loss and cost associated with the fiber optic network design, several assumptions are made. These assumptions cover the losses expected in fibers, splices, the access couplers and connectors. For a baseline, a glass-on-glass, 50-micron core/125-micron clad, graded index cable with a 400-MHzkm bandwidth-distance product is chosen. With this cable, having a conservative 6-dB/km optical loss, the system is power limited and not dispersion limited. To conservatively estimate power budgets and to allow for the problem of splicing in a manhole environment, 0.5 dB is established as the maximum attenuation value of a splice. A value of 2 dB is chosen as a realistic connector loss for the environment in which the connectors

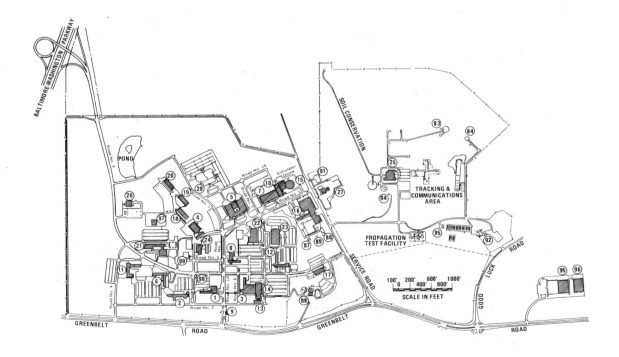

Figure 5. GODDARD SPACE FLIGHT CENTER MAIN SITE

will operate.

Both the tee and star couplers used in this analysis are of the fused, biconical type. The tee couplers are available in three tap ratios of 40/40, 60/20, and 75/5. (In this type of coupler it is normally assumed that 20 percent of input optical energy is lost and appears at neither designated output port.) In the analysis, a six-legged transmissive star is used in all cases. The power at each of six legs is 7.78 dB below the applied input power. In addition to the power splitting loss, 2 dB of loss are added to account for excess power loss and workmanship factors.

The final cable plant design using tee couplers is shown in figure 6. The figure notes the loss seen at each of the buildings being served on the Goddard Space Flight Center complex. As a rule of thumb, the allowable optical power budget is limited to 32 dB. Commercial optical transmitter/receiver systems are available which can provide 35 dB of optical power margin at 150 Mb/s with a bit error rate of 10^{-9}. From the loss values given in figure 6, it can be seen that this system can be supported by commercially available components.

As part of the study, the buildings serviced in figure 6 are interconnected using the same leg designations but replacing the tee couplers with a series of centralized transmissive star couplers. A comparison of the networks shows that the maximum optical power variation from terminal to terminal using a tapered and balanced tee network is less than that of a star network. Table 1 shows the optical power variation on a leg-to-leg basis and a cost comparison of the two networks. From the data, it can be seen that the tee configuration is most cost effective and requires the system receivers to support a smaller range of optical power variations. Based on this information the tee configuration shown in figure 6 is recommended for system implementation.

TABLE 1

COMPARISON OF COST AND OPTICAL POWER VARIATIONS FOR A TEE AND STAR NETWORK CONFIGURATION

LEG	OPTICAL POWER VARIATION (DB) (Terminal-Terminal)		MECHANIZATION COST	
	Tee Network	Star Network	Tee Network	Star Network
A	3.63	5.95	$6,970	$10,913
B	3.76	3.46	5,764	10,904
C	0.07	3.20	5,445	15,326
D	3.6	3.4	5,144	10,574
E	0.4	0.2	3,680	8,165

CONCERNS ABOUT COMPONENTS

During the development of the Goddard Space Flight Center Network, a number of

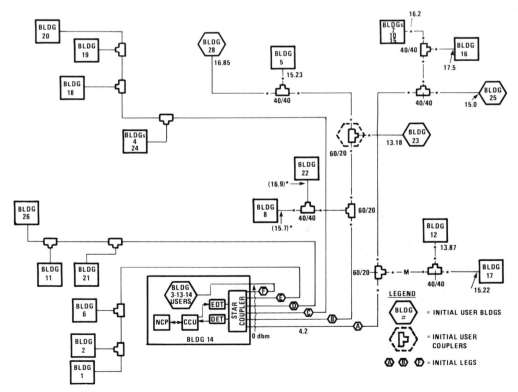

Figure 6. CABLE PLANT DIAGRAM AND LOSS BUDGET

technical issues have caused concern. One of the major issues is whether commercially available optical transmitter and receiver modules could operate as bus components at the chosen data rates. Because no information about the bit pattern of the data is available prior to transmission, some form of encoding must be imposed on the data stream. The encoding technique must insure transitions on a periodic basis to comply with low frequency limitations of the receiver and to permit clock recovery at the receiving terminal. If a technique such as Manchester encoding is employed, both of these goals can be realized at the expense of doubling the bandwidth. The ability of commercially available components to support a 200-Mb/s transmission rate is the subject of one of a series of tests run in the laboratory.[1] These tests include examining the effects of selected bit patterns on the optical transmitter and receiver performance, the effects of intermessage gaps on receiver operations, degradation in receiver performance due to threshold biasing of laser transmitters and transient response of the receivers. In addition to the active component testing, a series of tests has been performed to determine the effects of high data rates through fused, biconical couplers. Coupler linarity and mode sensitivity are examined. The results of these tests are reported in reference 1.

These tests demonstrate that care must be taken in the selection of active components for high data rate applications. Even though some of these devices are advertised as bus network components, they have limitations that can degrade their performance in network implementations. The passive components have proved most effective in this test series, indicating that the concerns over linarity, dispersion effects, and modal sensitivity are not warranted.

CONCLUSIONS

The brassboard built and tested for this NASA program demonstrates that a slotted, TDMA, fiber optic bus can meet future needs of the Spaceflight Tracking and Data Network. The analysis and design of an initial fiber plant has been completed, and an extended fiber plant, serving all technical centers at Goddard, is recommended.

Although there were many concerns about the capability of available components at high data rates in a bus configuration, a test program answered most of these. The test program results, the fiber plant design, and the demonstration system provide a solid basis for future implementation of a high-speed, fiber optic bus network at NASA Goddard.

REFERENCES

{1} R. Cresswell, M. Drake and C. Husbands, Fiber optic component test in high speed data bus applications, SPIE Conference Proceedings, April 1982.

Emery F. Boose received the Bachelor of Electrical Engineering Degree from Cornell University, Ithaca, New York, in 1950. As an undergraduate, he was elected to Tau Beta Pi and Eta Kappa Nu. He received the Degree of Master of Science in Electrical Engineering from Northeastern University, Boston, Massachusetts, in 1966. Until 1958, Mr. Boose was employed in the design of compass controlled directional gyro systems at General Electric Company, Lynn, Massachusetts. From 1958 until 1966, Mr. Boose was engaged in the design of R&D telecommunications systems for missile reentry vehicles at Avco, Incorporated, Wilmington, Massachusetts. In 1966, Mr. Boose joined the MITRE Corporation at Bedford, Massachusetts. At MITRE he has worked on a variety of tasks in the aerospace, digital communications and radar areas. He is currently a Group Leader in the Jam Resistant Communications Department.

Mr. Boose is a Registered Professional Engineer in the State of Massachusetts and a Senior Member of the IEEE.

Charles R. Husbands received the Bachelor of Science Degree in Electrical Engineering from the Milwaukee School of Engineering, Milwaukee, Wisconsin in 1960. He received the Degree of Master of Science in Electrical Engineering from Newark College of Engineering in 1964 and a Master of Science in Engineering Management from Northeastern University in 1973. In 1973, Mr. Husbands joined the MITRE Corporation where he has worked on a variety of communications system design tasks. Over the past several years one of his principle areas of interest has been the application of fiber optics to local area networks. He is currently Project Leader on the Army's Fiber Optic Local Distribution Program.

Mr. Husbands is a Member of the IEEE and Chairman of the SAE A2K Fiber Optic Task Group.

High Throughput Optical Fiber Loop Network with Effective Detection Mechanism of Lost or Duplicated Token

K Yagyu, J Kashio, S Nakayashiki,
H Nakase, M Kida
Hitachi, Japan

ABSTRACT:
An optical fiber token ring network with a transmission speed of 32 Mbps has been developed to be applied to production control, laboratory automation and office automation. The network services variable length packet switching functions with a compatible CCITT X.25 interface. In order to obtain high throughput, the token is released before the acknowlegement is returned from the destination node. Since this mechanism indicates that multiple frames exist on the loop, serious consideration is required in sequence control of the frame and in detection of duplicated or lost token. The sequence is controlled by the comparison between the send sequence number of the transmitted frame and that of the circulated frame with the loop answer appended at the destination node. Token error is detected by pairing the token with the specific string which is transmitted from the supervising node just before the token, and is returned to the supervising node with only the transmission delay of the loop.

1. INTRODUCTION

Awareness of the need for local area communications has made it one of the most exciting growing markets in the information industry. The market has been approached from two directions. One is the extention of private branch exchange(PBX) to handle digital data as well as voice. The other is a separate local area network with bus, ring or loop topology to handle mainly data traffic. The pros and cons of these two approches are described in several documents[1]. In order to handle a large volume of high speed data traffic, the separate local area network is preferable.

The bus topology, coupled with Carrier Sense Multiple Access with Collision Detection technology[2] is popular and simple to implement. However, this type of network is restricted to application area in which traffic rate is moderately low and propagation delay time vs a packet transmission time is comparatively small[3]. The loop network with token access is less restrictive [4], and thus it can be used in wider areas of application, i.e. factory automation, production control, laboratory automation, and office automation. In this paper the term loop is used synonimously with the term ring.

Total length of loop network required in factory automation, such as iron and steel production may amount to as much as several tens of km. The network for factory automation should be high speed to provide short response time, e.g. order of hundreds of milli seconds to control production processes, and should also be highly reliable to meet continuous operation of production, e.g. 24 hours/day.

The network for laboratory automation requires throughput as high as several Megabits/sec. to transfer to a host computer a large volume of experimental data accumulated at minicomputers. At the same time, the network is used for time sharing services where moderately short response time is required.

The network for office automation requires a large number of terminals or small business computers which are logically connected to multiples of server hosts. The network should provide the standard packet interface, and CCITT X.25 is a strong candidate for this interface. Futhermore the network should be flexible and should be able to easily accomodate terminals with various interfaces.

Hitachi has ten years experience in loop type networks called "Data Free Way (DFW)" which are applied in distributed process computer control of factory production, water works, and laboratory experiments. In 1976, the shipment of 2 Mbps coaxial cable DFW [5], and in 1980, the shipment of 10 Mbps optical fiber DFW [6][7] were started. So far the total number of DFW networks is about 100.

In order to satisfy the wider market requirements stated above, a 32 Mbps optical fiber loop network, H-8644 has been developed. The system configuration and its characteristics are described in section 2. Protocols which aim at high throughput and short response time are described in section 3.

2. SYSTEM CONFIGURATION

The system configuration of the optical fiber loop network, H-8644, is shown in Fig.1. Characteristics of the system configuration are as follows.
(1) Nodes (Maximum 125 Field Service Nodes ----FSN, and a Loop Service Nodes----LSN) are connected by transmission lines (optical fibers). The data is transmitted in one direction with a speed of 32 Mbps.
(2) The node consists of a loop control and terminal interface. The latter is composed of multiples of link control features (LCFs) each of which consists of a micro-computer and a dedicated memory. The number of LCFs is determined by the required throughput and terminal interface variations. Thus a new required

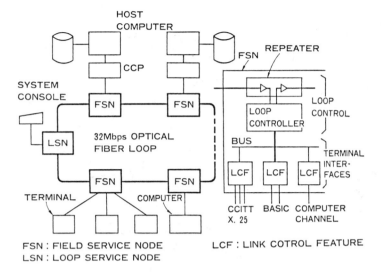

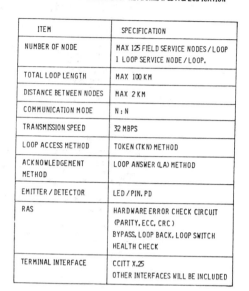

TABLE 1 OPTICAL FIBER LOOP NETWORK, H-8644 SPECIFICATION

ITEM	SPECIFICATION
NUMBER OF NODE	MAX 125 FIELD SERVICE NODES / LOOP 1 LOOP SERVICE NODE / LOOP.
TOTAL LOOP LENGTH	MAX 100 KM
DISTANCE BETWEEN NODES	MAX 2 KM
COMMUNICATION MODE	N : N
TRANSMISSION SPEED	32 MBPS
LOOP ACCESS METHOD	TOKEN (TKN) METHOD
ACKNOWLEDGEMENT METHOD	LOOP ANSWER (LA) METHOD
EMITTER / DETECTOR	LED / PIN. PD
RAS	HARDWARE ERROR CHECK CIRCUIT (PARITY, ECC, CRC) BYPASS, LOOP BACK, LOOP SWITCH HEALTH CHECK
TERMINAL INTERFACE	CCITT X.25 OTHER INTERFACES WILL BE INCLUDED

FIG. 1 CONFIGURATION IN H-8644 LOOP NETWORK

FSN : FIELD SERVICE NODE
LSN : LOOP SERVICE NODE
LCF : LINK COTROL FEATURE

interface such as computer channel interfaces and basic mode or HDLC mode of terminal interfaces can be satisfied by adding corresponding LCFs. The loop control is made up of a repeater and the loop controller. The repeater repeats the incoming frames to the outgoing line with a few microseconds delay. The loop controller examines the destination address of the incoming frame, and, if the address matches its own, receives the frame in its buffer storage. The received frame is then transfered to the LCF through the bus. Note that circulated frames are eliminated at the source node.

(3) The minimum functions of the LSN are as follows;

— processing bit timing signal, i.e., loop timing (LTM) and sending it to FSNs.
— generating a initial token.

These minimum functions are also installed in one of the FSNs to overcome system failure due to the failure of the LSN. Other functions of LSN are patrolling FSNs and accumulating error statistics. Each node has a node control portion which manages the LCFs in the same node. LSN communicates with the node control portions to manage the entire network.

(4) In order to avoid a total system failure, the transmission lines and repeaters are duplicated to form the dual loops, where one is active and the other is a back-up. On the detection of the active loop failure, the data path is switched to the back-up loop. If failure is detected in both of the loops, the loop back operation is attempted, in which the active and back-up loops are connected in such a way that a complete data path can be formed by avoiding the failure portion of the loop.

The specification of the H-8644 Loop Network is summarized in Table 1.

3. LOOP CONTROL PROTOCOL

3.1 Loop Access Control

The token access method is widely applied in a message (variable length packet) multiplexing loop network. A control token is a stream of unique bit pattern which circulates around the ring in one direction. A node with frames (packets with loop control headers) in its output buffer to be transmitted must wait until it detects and traps the token before sending its frames over the transmission line. In ILLINET [8] and DCS [9], the transmitting node waits for an acknowledgment response to a frame. If a positive response is returned it can transmit the next ready packet or release the token. If a negative response is returned, retransmission of the frame continues until a positive response is received or until a maximum allowable number of retransmissions are made. During this period, the token is held up in the transmitting node.

In such a network, there exists only one frame circulating on the loop at a given time. Thus, the longer the loop length (the round trip delay in the loop is large compared to average packet transmission time), the more the average throughput tends to decrease as shown in Fig.2.

497

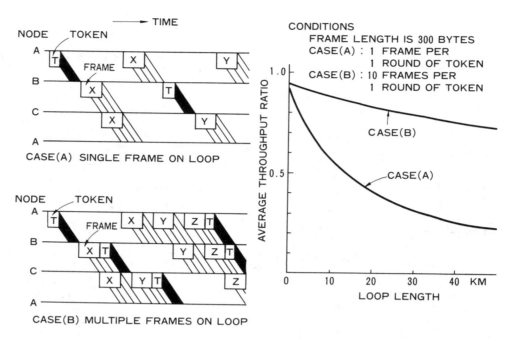

FIG. 2 THROUGHPUT VS LOOP LENGTH

When a node with ready frames traps the token, it will transmit all the ready frames within the maximum allowable number. The transmitting node releases the token immediately after the last bit of the last frame is transmitted, that is, neither the returned frame nor acknowledgement is waited for. High throughput is maintained in long loop length as shown in Fig.2.

Note that, the design of this method requires particular care in the following respects:

(1) When errors occur in transmitting or receiving frames, they affect multiple frames thus, elaborate sequence contol is required for error recovery.

(2) Since a token is not expected after every frame, the technique adopted in ILLINET or DCS, is not applicable for detecting lost or duplicated tokens. Thus, a new technique is required for controlling the tokens.

3.2 Frame Format and Loop Answer

The frame format on the loop is shown in Fig.3. The loop header consists of source and destination addresses and a sequence number. The address uniquely distinguishes the node and the Link Control Feature (LCF) within it. The independent frame sequence number is assigned at the source LCF for each distinct destination LCF.

The acknowlegment to the frame is piggy backed on the loop answer portion of the frame as it returns to the source node. More precisely, the initial value of a loop answer is given at the source node and the destination (loop controller) rewrites the value while it repeats the incoming frame to the output transmission line.

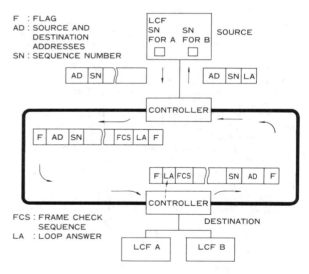

FIG. 3 FRAME FORMAT AND LOOP ANSWER

When the frame is circulated and returned to the source node, the loop controller subtracts the loop header and loop answer and then stacks this information in the dedicated memory of the source LCF. The subtracted loop header is used to identify the corresponding frame sent from the LCF. The loop answer returned to the source LCF indicates one of the three following conditions:

(1) Positive loop answer : The error free frame is accepted at the destination node.

(2) Negative loop answer : The frame is not accepted at the destination node because an address error or receive buffer busy condition is encountered. When the initial value of the loop answer is returned, it is interpreted as an address error because no destination node accepted the frame.

(3) Lost loop answer : An FCS (Frame Check Sequence) error, frame aborted, or frame lost are the cause of a lost loop answer. This condition is detected by the time out of the loop answer, or by receiving the next loop answer. The loop header and the loop answers are used in the sequence control of the frame which is described next.

3.3 Sequence Control

The sequence number N(S) in the loop header is assigned independently by the source LCF to each distinct destination LCF.

(1) The Sequence Control at Source LCF

The source LCF maintains the following two state variables SN and AN and constant M for each destination LCF.

SN : The latest send sequence number

AN : The latest acknowledged sequence number (AN < SN)

M : Maximum outstanding frame number

The source LCF transmits frames according to the following algorithm ;

(a) If SN $\leq$ AN + M, then the source LCF transmits the frame whose sequence number N(S) = SN, increases SN by 1 (SN = SN + 1), and restarts the loop answer timer.

(b) If SN > AN + M, then the source LCF refrains from transmiting the frame until the loop answer is returned and AN is increased. The transmitted frames are moved to the end of the acknowledgment (loop answer) waiting queue. The control of this queue is described next in conjunction with loop answer.

(2) Acknowledgment Waiting Queue

Observation of the characteristic of the loop answer indicates that the acknowledgment waiting queue should be a single queue irrespective of the number of destination LCFs.

Note, that unless the loop answer is lost, the loop answers are returned to the source LCF in the same order as that of the transmitted frames. For example, if the source LCF sends frames FA(1), FA(2) and FB(1) to the destination LCFs A and B in this order, then the loop answers are returned in the same order. If the loop answer for FA(1) and FA(2) are lost and positive loop answer for FB(1) is returned, then the frames FA(1) and FA(2) should be retransmitted, but FB(1) should not be retransmitted, because the destination LCF B is receiving the frames in the correct order.

On the other hand, if the loop answer for FA(1) is lost and a positive loop answer for FA(2) is returned, not only FA(1) but also FA(2) should be retransmitted, because the destination LCF is expecting the retransmission of all the consecutive frames once the frame is lost.

More precisely, at the receipt of a positive loop answer, the following algorithm clarifies the necessity of retransmission. Let N(S) be the sequence number of the frame returned with the loop answer. Then, if N(S) = AN + 1 (i.e. all the previous frames destined to the LCF are acknowledged), no retransmission is required. However, if N(S) $\neq$ AN + 1, retransmission is required.

The control algorithm of the acknowledgment waiting queue is summarized as follows:

(a) Identification of Acknowledged Frame;

The relation between the frame in the queue and the sequence number is found by keying them with the returned loop header accompanied with the loop answer. The queue is searched from the top.

(b) Retransmission of the Previous Frame;

Unless the identified frame is at the top of the queue, all the frames in the queue prior to that frame are subject to retransmission.

(c) Release the Identified Frame;

If the loop answer is positive and N(S) = AN + 1, the identified frame is correctly accepted at the destination. The frame is released from the queue and AN is inceased by one.

(d) Retransmission of the Identified Frame;

If the loop answer is negative or N(S) $\neq$ AN + 1, the identified frame should be retransmitted.

(e) Loop Answer Time Out;

Each time the frame is transmitted, the loop answer timer is restarted. Thus loop answer time out occurs on the last frame in the continuous transmission of the frames. When the time out is detected, all the frames in the queue are subject to retransmission.

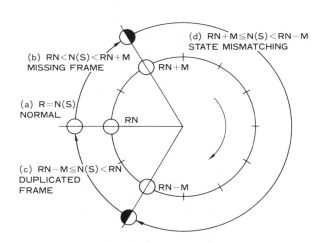

N(S) : SEQUENCE NUMBER IN RECEIVED FRAME

RN : EXPECTED SEQUENCE NUMBER FOR RECEIVED FRAME

M : MAXIMUM OUTSTANDING NUMBER

FIG. 4 SEQUENCE CONTROL AT DESTINATION LCF

(3) Sequence Control at Destination LCF

The destination LCF maintains a state variable RN and a constant M for each source, where

RN : The expected sequence number for the received frame

M : The maximum outstanding frame number.

The sequence number in the received frame N(S) is tested with the following algorithm (shown in Fig.4) where the calculation is modulo;

(a) N(S) = RN indicates a normal situation, then RN is increased by one, and the received frame is handed to the terminal interface.

(b) RN < N(S) < RN + M indicates the missing frame, then the received frame is deleted and it is necessary to wait for the retransmission of the expected frame. The source can be aware of this situation by the loop answer.

(c) RN - M $\leq$ N(S) < RN indicates the duplicated frame, then the frame is deleted.

(d) RN + M $\leq$ N(S) < RN - M indicates state mismatching between the source and destination channel, then the state variable RN is forced to become N(S) + 1 and the communication is continued.

Situation (d) occurs for the following reasons:

— The loop answer is returned by the loop controller prior to transferring the frame to the destination LCF.

— The destination LCF does not report sequence errors to the source LCF.

Thus, if the error occurs while transmitting the frame from the loop controller to the LCF (e.g. bus transmission error and LCF overrun), a mismatching state which cannot be recovered by the loop answer is caused. The occurrence of this situation is extremely rare, but if it occurs, the technique stated in (d) is useful in avoiding deadlock. However, it does not guarantee the recovery of the missing frame. The consistent recovery is required in the higher level (e.g. network level), for highly reliable applications.

3.4 Token Supervision

If the control of a token is such that nodes do not release the token until the response to a frame is returned, then a frame followed by a token is the correct cycle. In other words, by monitoring the violation of this cycle we can detect lost or duplicate tokens. However, if the node releases the token immediately after the transmission of frames, then multiple frames followed by a token is the normal cycle. Thus an additional erroneous token inserted among frames, still results in a normal cycle, frames followed by a token. This token, however, can not be distinguished from the correct one.

The above observation, however, gives us the hint to consider the following ingenious technique to detect the duplicated or lost token.

——The Loop Service Node (LSN) inserts a specific signal S before the token distinguishable from the frames, so that a signal S followed by a token is a correct sequence. In other words, a violation of the cycle, e.g. a token followed by another token, indicates the lost or duplicated token.

——S should be returned to the issuer, LSN, within the predetermined time, so that the lost or duplication of S can be detected easily.

In H-8644 Loop Network the above idea is implemented as follows (See Fig.5).

(1) Whenever a token arrives at the LSN, LSN transmits the specific bit string S just before the token.

(2) FSNs do not trap the S and the S is returned to the LSN with only the propagation delay of the loop. LSN eliminates the returned S and keeps monitoring the cycle until the token is detected.

(3) S , frames (optional) and token is the correct cycle handled by LSN. A violation of this cycle results in lost or duplicated tokens (See Fig.6).

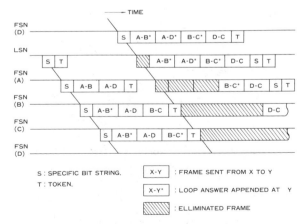

S : SPECIFIC BIT STRING.

T : TOKEN.

X-Y : FRAME SENT FROM X TO Y

X-Y* : LOOP ANSWER APPENDED AT Y

: ELLIMINATED FRAME

FIG. 5 TRANSMISSION SEQUENCE CHART

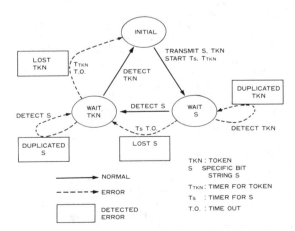

NORMAL

ERROR

DETECTED ERROR

TKN : TOKEN

S : SPECIFIC BIT STRING S

T$_{TKN}$: TIMER FOR TOKEN

T$_S$: TIMER FOR S

T.O. : TIME OUT

FIG. 6 TOKEN ERROR DETECTION ALGORITHM

4. CONCLUSION

An optical fiber token loop network with the transmission speed of 32 Mbps has been developed to be applied to production control, laboratory automation and office automation.

In order to handle a large volume of high speed data traffic, H-8644 Loop Network is designed to allow multiple frames circulating on the loop at given instance of time. When a node with ready frames traps the token, it will transmit all the ready frames within the maximum allowable number. The transmitting node releases the token immediately after the last bit of the last frame is transmitted, that is neither the return of the frame nor the acknowledgement is waited for. The acknowledgement scheme and token supervision which meet in this environment were proposed.

5. ACKNOWLEDGEMENT

The authors would like to thank Dr. Takeo Miura, general manager of Systems Development Laboratory, and Dr. Kisaburo Nakazawa, general manager of Kanagawa Works, Hitachi, Ltd., for their direction and encouragement. The authors also wish to thank Toyokazu Hashimoto, Takeaki Matsuoka, Isao Nakata, Takeshi Harakawa and Hisashi Matsumura in Kanagawa Works, and Susumu Matsui in Systems Development Laboratory, Hitachi, Ltd.,for their creative suggestions and assistance related to this research.

6. REFERENCES

[1]"Intra-Office Communications Vendors,", Gartner Groupe, Inc., Jan., 1981.
[2]"The Ethernet, A Local Area Network Data Link Layer and Physical Layer Specifications, version 1.0", Sep., 1980.
[3]Werner Bux,"Local-Area Subnetworks: A Performance Comparison", IEEE Trans. on Com. vol. COM-29, No.10, Oct. 1981, pp.1468-1473.
[4]G.J.Clancy,Jr.,"A Status Report on The IEEE Project 802 Local Network Standard", Proc. of Local Networks and Distributed Office Systems", May 1981, Published by Online Publications Ltd., pp.591-609.
[5]M.Yanaka, M.Takahashi, M.Fushimi, and S.Yasumoto, "An In-House Data Communication System for Distributed Computer Control", IEEE Tokyo Section, Denshi Tokyo, 1979, pp.20-23.
[6]M.Takahashi, M.Yanaka, H.Fushimi, M.Maeda, J.Kashio, and H.Mitsuoka,"Optical Data Free Way System--- A Local Network for Distributed Computer Control", COMPCON '81 Spring, pp.458-463.
[7]M.Terada, J.Kashio, K. Yokota, Y.Mori, and H.Fushimi, "Network Operating System for High Speed Optical Fiber Loop Transmission System", ICCC '80, pp.641-646.
[8] W.Y.Cheng, S.Ray, and R.Kodstad,"ILLINET---A 32 Mbits/sec. Local-Area Network",Conf. of NCC 1981,AFIPS Press,Montvale,NJ:(1981), pp.209-214.
[9] P.V.Mockapetris, M.R.Lyle, and D.J.Farber,"On the Design of Local Network Interface", Proc. of IFIP Congress 1977, pp.427-430.

Kazuo Yagyu, researcher at Systems Development Laboratory, Hitachi, Ltd.. Since joining Hitachi in 1974, he has been engaged in research and development of computer communication network and network architecture. His current interest is in local area network. He received B.S. and M.E. degrees from Fukui University in 1972 and 1974, respectively.

Jiro Kashio, senior researcher at Systems Development Laboratory, Hitachi, Ltd.. Since joining Hitachi in 1970, he has been engaged in research and development of data communication software and related protocols. He received B.S. and M.S. from Kyoto University in 1964 and 1966, respectively and Ph.D. from Rice University in 1970.

Susumu Nakayashiki, graduated from Tadotsu techinical high school in 1974, and Hitachi Technical College in 1977. He joined Hitachi Ltd. in 1974. Since then, he has been working on reliability design and development of computer networks.

Hiroshi Nakase, graduated from Kobe University in 1968. After joining Hitachi in 1968, he has been working on development of design automation system and data communication system. He is a senior engineer at Kanagawa works and manages the local area network projects.

Masahiko Kida,graduated from Waseda University in 1968. After joining Hitachi, he has been working on the development of general purpose computers and packet switching network. In 1974, he was a visiting researcher at Carnegie-Mellon University and engaged in Computer Module Project.

Introducing Lightwave Technology to Customers' Premises

G A Petritsch
New York Telephone Company, USA

The author proposes, for large metropolitan office buildings, a getting started strategy to introduce lightwave technology in the local loop. This strategy utilizes a ring architecture to provide a network that is failsafe, maintenance insensitive and easily reconfigured.

This network is established by connecting three central offices with fiber optic cable that routes through 27 customer locations. Each customer location is served by two of the three central offices and contains A/D conversion, lightwave terminating and multiplex equipment. This scheme allows any customer location access to any of the other 26 locations and provides a backup path (FT3) from any customer location to the serving central office in a completely independent path.

Initially this arrangement will provide 20,000 special circuits. This capacity can be expanded to nearly 100,000 circuits of which 50,000 are fully protected special service circuits and the rest partially protected dial tone circuits such as digital PBX trunks, DID lines, WATS, etc.

It is no longer a question of whether to deploy lightwave technology in the local loop. It's become a question of when, where and how to introduce this technology in the local loop. While I am convince convinced that now is the time to introduce lightwave technology in the loop, care must be taken to reduce the risk of using a new technology before we fully understand the advantages, disadvantages and the direction this technology will take. With this in mind; I propose a strategy to minimize the risk. I call it, "a getting started strategy to introduce lightwave technology in the local loop".

Before discussing this strategy, let us examine some of the conditions that enhance the use of fiber in the local loop:

- New office building growth
- Building codes that require emergency power
- Architects who want the latest technology
- Industries that require continuous service
- Regulatory controls that dictate downtown intervals
- Digital central offices (public switching centers)
- Digital customer premises equipment
- Large concentration of special service circuits
- Main frame and underground duct congestion
- Rising labor costs
- Churn, an American slang word for turn over

In the United States, most of these conditions are found in Metropolitan areas. One such area is downtown Manhattan in New York City. The area has all the conditions for making fiber economical in the local loop. It also has a mix of markets that can hasten the development of a communications architecture to handle the integrated services envisioned in the future.

The getting started strategy introduces this technology in such a manner as to create a special service network that is failsafe, maintenance insensitive and easily reconfigured. I define failsafe as a network that continues to function during a cable failure. Centralized alarms identify the failure which is then scheduled to be fixed at some future date. Maintenance insensitive describes a passive (electronic free) local loop that seldom has to be touched after installation. This network is easily reconfigured by the choice of a family of terminal equipment that is both modular and interchangeable.

To establish this network we begin by connecting three central offices with a fiber optic cable ring. This cable routes through customer locations with a large number of circuit requirements. The cable consists of a sheath containing twelve fiber ribbons. Each ribbon has twelve fibers. Figure 1 depicts one ribbon of fiber going from one central office to another through a manhole outside of a customer location.

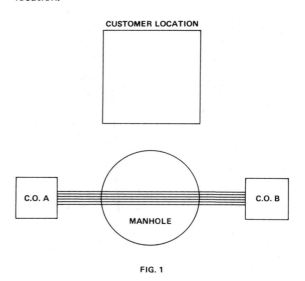

FIG. 1

Two fiber ribbons are obtained from this ribbon by cutting the ribbon in half, in the manhole, and splicing each end to one ribbon of a two fiber ribbon entrance cable (see figure 2). One ribbon originates on the left side of the customer location and terminates in Central Office A on the left. The other ribbon originates on the right side of the customer location and terminates in Central Office B on the right.

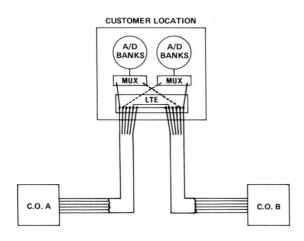

FIG. 2

The customer location has now been divided in half, each with its own Analog to Digital (A/D) converters and multiplex equipment. One Lightwave Terminating Equipment (LTE) serves both sides. The A/D converters are supplied in banks that combine 24 analog circuits onto one T1 line. The multiplexers combine 28 T1 lines onto one fiber pair. These multiplexers include one by one protection devices that will automatically switch from the operating pair of fibers (solid line) to the backup pair of fibers (dashed line) during cable failures.

Each line terminating in the LTE represents a pair of fibers. Notice that each side has:

- One pair for service (solid line to MUX)
- One pair for backup (dashed line to MUX)
- Two pairs are spare
- Two "Through" fiber pairs (patched to other side)

The "through" fiber pairs provide protection for other customer locations. This arrangement allows for future growth and the transfer of spare capacity from one customer location to another.

Figure 3 depicts nine customer locations connected between two central offices. Each line represents a ribbon of fiber. This arrangement provides a ribbon of fiber for each side of a customer location. The left side terminates at the central office to the left and the right side terminates at the central office to the right. The bottom three dashed lines represent three ribbons that route directly from one central office

to the other. These will be used for backup fiber pair protection and future enhancements to this network.

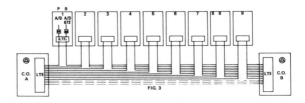

Figure 4 shows 27 customer locations connected to the three central offices. The three central offices must be connected in a fiber ring before using the network. While this looks like a bus arrangement, it really is a point to point "star" configuration that connects T1 lines between customer locations. I intend to clarify this in the next few figures.

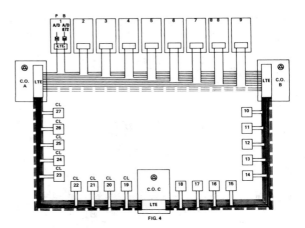

Figure 5 shows the initial fully automatic completely redundant special service network. The solid line represents the primary FT3 system (fiber pair) that carries 28 T1 lines from a customer location to Central Office A on the left. The 28 T1 lines are hard wired from the multiplex equipment to a DSX1. The DSX1 is a manual T1 cross connect (patching) bay. The dotted lines represent the loop around or secondary path. The originating multiplex equipment transmits simultaneously over the primary and secondary path. In event of a failure in the primary path, the terminating multiplex equipment will automatically transfer to the secondary path. The secondary path consists of a backup fiber pair from the customer location to Central Office B which is cross connected to a "through" fiber pair in the adjacent cable run. The "through" fiber path is cross connected there to the multiplexer which completes the path to the same 28 T1 lines that are hard wired to the DSX1. All cross connections are accomplished via fiber optic patch "cords".

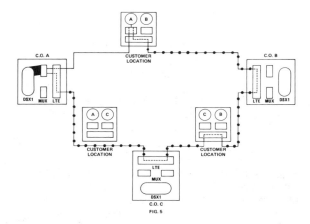

FIG. 5

Figure 6 shows only the primary FT3 (fiber) systems. The loop around or backup fiber pairs are not shown here. For simplicity, only two customer locations are shown between the central offices. Notice that Central Office A serves the A side of customer locations 1 through 9 and 19 through 27. Central Office A does not connect to customer locations 10 through 18. Similarly Central Office B serves the B side of customer locations 1 through 18 and Central Office C the C side of customer locations 10 through 27.

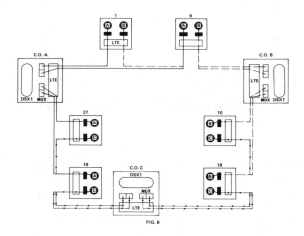

FIG. 6

The A/D converters in each customer location are assigned in the same manner. The first bank of 24 analog circuits in any customer location will be assigned to circuits that terminate in customer location #1. The 9th bank is used for 24 circuits to customer location #9 and the 27th bank to the 27th customer location, etc.

Once a customer is assigned to a particular circuit pack number (1 through 24) in an A/D converter,

that circuit number (in the analog mode or time slot number in the digital mode) remains constant throughout the entire circuit. For example, circuit (pack) #1 of any A/D converter becomes and remains time slot #1 in the digital mode and will eventually terminate in circuit (pack) #1 at the terminating customer location.

Before I explain how a circuit is established between any two customer locations, I must point out three items. The first is, there are two ways a circuit can be established between customer locations in the same cable run, since both central offices connect to these locations. The second is, there is only one way a circuit can be established between customer locations in adjacent cable runs, since only one Central Office has connectivity to both runs. Finally, special service circuits within the same customer location will be established via local networks and not via this network. I will now explain how a circuit is established between any two customer locations. I will not mention circuit (pack) number or time slots since they remain constant.

If a customer in location #1 wants a circuit to customer location #9, he can be assigned in 2 ways (same cable run). The first via Central Office A using the 9th bank of A/D converters on the A side of customer location #1. This becomes the 9th T1 line multiplexed on to the FT3 system to Central Office A. The circuit is then demultiplexed on to the 9th T1 line hardwired from the multiplexer to the DSX1. The DSX1 cross connects this T1 line to the first T1 line to customer location #9 which is multiplexed with 28 other T1 lines to customer location #9. Here it is demultiplexed to the first T1 line which terminates in the first bank of A/D connectors on the A or left side. The path is similar via Central Office B using the 9th bank of A/D converters on the right side (B path).

If, however, the customer wants a circuit to customer location #27 in the adjacent cable run he must go via Central Office A. He must use the A path and is assigned on the 27th A/D bank which cross-connects in the DSX1 at Central Office A to the first T1 line to customer location #27 and terminates in the first A/D bank on the A side. Finally, if this customer wants a circuit to customer location #19, he must use the B path. He is assigned on the 10th A/D bank on the B side of customer location #1. This will cross-connect in DSX1 at Central Office B to the first T1 line to customer location #10 and terminates in the first A/D bank. In this manner, every customer location can reach all the other customer locations.

Note that every customer location has 28 T1 lines (24 circuits a T1 line) on each side. Seventeen of them will be preassigned to each of the other locations served by the central office. The remaining 11 T1 lines can be assigned to any other T1 line that terminates in the DSX1. See figure 7 for an internal view of the DSX1. Figure 7 shows only 4 of the 18 customer locations terminating on the DSX1 in Central Office A. Notice the algorithm used to cross connect the Customer Locations (CL). The algorithm exchanges the CL# with the T1 line #. For example;

CL#1-T1 line 9 to CL#9-T1 line 1, CL#1-T1 line 19 to CL#19-T1 line 1, CL#1-T1 line 27 to CL#27-T1 line 1, etc. The only T1 lines not preassigned (pre-wired) are T1 lines 10 to 18 from each customer location. These can be cross connected (using 4 wire T1 patching cords) to long haul T1 lines (SS in figure 7) or provide additional T1 lines between the customer locations served by the central office. At the start, a second set of T1 lines will be preassigned between customer locations in adjacent cable runs. Furthermore, T1 line #28 and the T1 line # of the customer location number will be used for long haul special service.

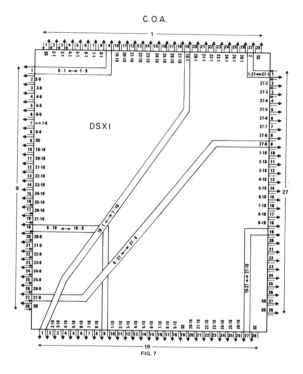

FIG. 7

Initially this arrangement will provide 20,000 special service circuits. Embedded, however, is enough fiber pairs in each customer location to double this amount almost immediately. This could easily be expanded, within a few years, to nearly 100,000 circuits, of which 50,000 are fully protected special service circuits and the rest partially protected dial tone circuits such as digital PBX trunks, DID lines, WATS, etc.

The capacity of this network could be increased extensively through the use of wavelength division multiplexing; which is a technique of combining optical signals of different wavelengths for transmission on a single fiber. The beauty of this new technology is that it can be upgraded or downsized to suit our needs.

Let's look at some of the future uses for protected networks:

- Large PBX's
- WATS
- DID Lines
- Trunk Network
- Riser Cable
- Data Services
- CCITT Network
- Extending Central Office functions to the customer's premise. This will permit the sharing and reuse of access to the "public" network for any service; special or otherwise.

To summarize what I have said; I believe now is the time to deploy lightwave technology in the local loop. I recommend a getting started strategy that minimizes the risk and utilizes the cost trends and modular design of this new technology. The fiber represents a very small cost (less than 10%) of the network. The multiplexers cost about 25% and are coming down in price. The largest portion of the cost (about 70%) is the A/D conversion equipment which should disappear altogether as digital technology permeates the terminal equipment.

I further propose a continuous special service network that is failsafe, maintenance insensitive and easily reconfigured.

A network that takes advantage of the enormous circuit capacity inherent in lightwave technology.

A network that will easily include the plain ordinary telephone services such as subscriber lines, PBX trunks, Direct Inward Dialing, etc.

A network that will eventually allow a customer to reuse as much of "his" network as he can, for whatever use he wants, while sharing as much of the "public" network as possible.

BIOGRAPHY

George A. Petritsch graduated from one of the City Colleges of New York with honors in Physics. He is a member of Alpha Sigma Lambda and Sigma Xi. His technical experience in telecommunications spans 26 years with the Bell System. George worked 5 years with Western Electric on the ADES Air Defense Project before accepting a position with the New York Telephone Company. His experience includes special service design, network design, redesign and implementation of a sector tandem plan that established and rerouted over 10,000 trunks in the metropolitan area to a sector tandem arrangement, design of the initial 911 emergency network in N.Y.C., design of the first choke network for telethons, and is presently working within the Conceptual Planning Organization evaluating new technology and future network architecture.

Computer Communications for Rural Subscribers using a Fibre Optic Transmission System

K B Harris
Canadian Telecommunications Carriers
Association & Canadian Department of
Communications, Canada

A fibre optic trial system was installed in the rural communities of Elie and St. Eustache, Manitoba to bring a variety of integrated telecommunications services to 150 subscribers. Each subscriber receives individual line telephone service, Telidon the video-tex service developed by the Canadian Department of Communications, 9 television channels and 6 FM stereo radio stations. The purpose of the trial is to learn how well a fibre optic system operates in an environment in which there is a wide range of temperature extremes and which is installed by regular telephone craftsmen using regular construction tools. The trial is being conducted as a joint venture by the Canadian Telecommunications Carriers Association, the Federal Department of Communications, and the Manitoba Telephone System in cooperation with Northern Telecom Canada and Infomart.

INTRODUCTION

In the home of tomorrow there will be an increasing demand for a variety of tele-communications services. Many of these are being provided today such as telephone, Telidon and other computer communication services, fire and burglar alarms, remote meter reading, and cable television. No doubt there will be many additional services that have not been dreamed of yet. The Government of Canada and the Telecommun-ications Carriers have a common desire to ensure that all Canadians, no matter where they may live, are able to receive the tele-communications services they need when they need them.

TELEPHONE SERVICE

In Canada the basic charge for telephone service includes free local calling within the base rate area with the result that call-ing rates and holding times are high. Additional computer communications services such as videotex will increase calling rates and holding times which will make it essential for the subscriber to have individual instead of party-line service.

In the urban areas individual and two-party service is provided and there has been a steady reduction in the number of two-party telephones in Canada from 17.5% in 1962 to 2.5% in 1980.

In rural areas the customers are offered multi-party service. In the early days of this century there were 10 or more sub-scribers on one line. Over the years line loading has been reduced so that there are less than four parties per line today. In addition, the telephone companies have extended the base rate boundaries, establish-ed additional small offices, and used new technology to provide urban type service to a large percentage of Canadians living in rural areas. This has resulted in a steady reduction of multi-party telephones from about 10.5% to 4% during the past 20 years. In view of the fact that 25% of Canadians live in rural areas and many of them may live 50 miles from the nearest telephone office, the telephone companies have reason to be proud of this achievement, and are continuing to try new technology with the expectation that a way will be found to offer all Canadians a choice of the full range of tele-communications services that will be avail-able in the world of the future.

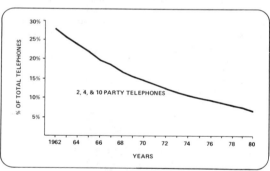

FIG. 1   PARTY LINE TELEPHONES IN CANADA

The effect of this steady trend from party line service to individual line service is illustrated by Figure 1 which shows a reduction from about 28% to about 6% of total telephones using party line service.

COMPUTER COMMUNICATIONS SERVICES

Electrical data transmission started when Samuel Morse invented the first practical telegraph system about 150 years ago and transmission speeds of less than 100 bits per second (bps) were used until the 1950's. It then became apparent that com-puters were going to be used extensively in business and there would be a growing need for computer communications. The telephone network was an obvious choice and data sets were developed for converting the digital data signals into a form suitable for transmission over the analogue voice network. The early data sets operated at 1200 bps on the public telephone network and at 1600 bps on private line facilities. A major breakthrough was made during the 1960's with the development of the phase quadrature data set. This set operating at 2000 bps on the switched network or 2400 bps on a private line was found to have a lower error rate than previous sets operating at 1200 bps. In response to the demand for even higher transmission speeds, data sets with adaptive equalizers were introduced about 1970. These data sets can operate satisfactorily on the public telephone network at 4800 bps and at 9600 bps on private lines. This difference in transmission speed between a switched connection and a private line is due to the fact that switching of circuits provides a wide variety of possible combinations of circuits many of which are beyond the self equalizing capability of the data set. Much of this variation occurs in the loop connecting the subscriber to the central office. If both of the subscribers involved in a connection are close to the central office there is a good probability that the data set will equalize the connection so that 9600 bps transmission can be used. For this reason many Canadian subscribers in the downtown section of large cities will establish a switched connection and transmit a test tape at 9600 bps. If the error rate is satisfactory, they will continue to transmit at 9600 bps, but if the error rate is too high, they will then switch to 4800 bps. The subscribers in rural areas are less fortunate. Some of the rural loops are many miles in length and it is difficult for adaptive equalizers to have sufficient range to compensate for the variations that may be encountered. These factors make it difficult to achieve the transmission speeds on switched connections involving rural lines that are common for connections involving only urban loops.

When considering computer communications for the home it should be recognized that the high cost of adaptive equalizers may make it more attractive to use simpler data sets with the lower speeds of 2000 or 2400 bps.

CABLE TV

A large percentage of Canadians live within 100 miles of the border with U.S.A. Canadians living close to the border can use an antenna on the roof to pick up three to five local television stations and five or six American stations. In the larger cities cable television will deliver these stations and a number of other channels. In the rural areas the problem is more difficult. A cable television system requires an off the air pick-up for each distant station, transmission facilities from the pick-up point to the distribution studio, and a network of distribution facilities to the individual subscribers. In order to install a cable television system that can be provided at rates that customers are prepared to pay the population density must be high and there must be a large number of customers. As a result, most of the cable television systems operate in the cities and very few in rural areas.

WHY FIBRE OPTICS

When telecommunications carriers have a demand for a number of different types of circuits in a given cross section, particularly on backbone routes, it is customary to integrate the circuits and multiplex then on a broadband system. For example, microwave systems usually carry a variety of integrated circuits such as telephone, teletype, data transmission, alarm and signalling, television, radio broadcast, etc. When fibre optic systems were introduced it was found that they can carry a variety of integrated circuits and could be installed economically in many cases in comparison with microwave and copper systems. Most of the Canadian Telecommunications Carriers are already using fibre optic systems as part of the regular network.

The use of optical fibre has a number of advantages and disadvantages as compared with the use of copper pairs for distribution to individual customers. Optical fibre cable is smaller and lighter than the equivalent copper pair cable. This reduces the strength requirement for supporting structures and conserves duct space under streets and in buildings. Optical fibres are not subject to electro-magnetic induction from electric power lines which causes hazardous voltages and noise on copper pairs particularly in rural areas. An optical fibre can carry integrated signals requiring wide bandwidth that can be used for a very large number of circuits.

As might be expected, optical fibre systems have a number of disadvantages. An optical fibre, a strand of glass about the thickness of a human hair, has the tensile strength of a steel fibre of the same dimension, but it is brittle and cracks and chips easily. If stress is applied to an optical fibre, the axis can be distorted which will result in microbending loss. Stresses can be caused by mechanical pressure on the fibre or by tensile forces tending to stretch it. A variety of things can cause this such as mechanical pressure on the cable from tools or winches, contraction of the fibre as the temperature drops etc. Around Winnipeg the ground freezes to a depth of three or four feet and the ground heaves unevenly as it thaws in the spring. This can apply very severe pressure on cables buried within this frost zone. Aerial cables expand and contract as the temperature goes up and down and this can cause stresses on the individual fibres.

Figure 2 shows a cross section of the cable supplied by NTC for this trial. Six fibres are laid loosely in a slot along with a powder designed to reduce friction so that

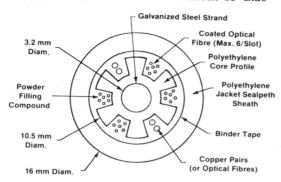

FIG.2 Cross-Section of NTC Optical Fibre Cable

the fibre can slide easily as it contracts and expands. The construction of the cable minimizes the possibility of stresses being applied to the fibres when the cables are being handled by contruction equipment.

One of the hazards that threatens buried cables is the danger that someone digging in the vicinity will cut the cable. In the case of a copper cable the pairs can be spliced without impairment. When optical fibres are spliced, a loss is introduced at the splice that can be as high as 0.5 db and, if a fibre operating at its limiting value for loss is accidently cut, the increased loss at the splice may make it necessary to replace the cable. Optical fibres can be spliced as illustrated in Figure 3. The ends of the two fibres are cut cleanly without chipping, then butted together in a special jig in the splicing set. An electrical spark fired between the two electrodes softens the fibres and welds them together.

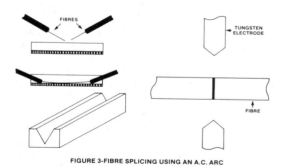

FIGURE 3-FIBRE SPLICING USING AN A.C. ARC

Another disadvantage is the fact that a fibre optic system includes a considerable amount of electronic equipment which requires maintenance to correct faults that may occur, whereas most subscriber copper loops for telephone service use only a pair of copper wires that have few troubles.

FIBRE OPTIC FIELD TRIAL IN ELIE MANITOBA

When looking towards the future, the question arises as to what is the best means of carrying a full range of telecommunications services to Canadians living on the farms and in the rural communities.

Although the potential bandwidth offered by a fibre optic system is substantially more than needed for the individual home, it was believed that a field trial should be undertaken to assess this new technology to learn how it could be used to provide the full range of services that will be required in the future and to assess the response of the subscribers to some of the urban services that they do not have today.

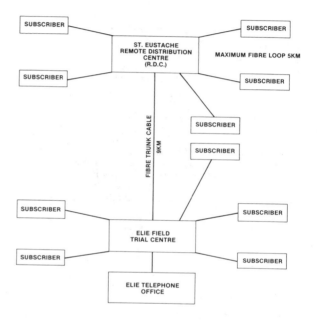

FIGURE 4 — SYSTEM LAYOUT

With this in mind the Canadian Telecommunications Carriers Association, the Canadian Department of Communications and the Manitoba Telephone System in cooperation with Northern Telecom Canada, and Infomart, Canada's largest electronic publisher, undertook a fibre optic field trial about 30 kilometres west of Winnipeg, Manitoba. In this trial, a fibre optic system is being used to bring to 150 subscribers in the rural communities of Elie and St. Eustache and the surrounding farming area four basic telecommunications services:

- individual line telephone service

- Telidon - the videotex service developed by the Canadian Department of Communications

- a choice of 9 television channels

- 6 stereo FM stations.

As shown in Figure 4, two centres are established; the Field Trial Centre (FTC) to serve the subscribers in and around the town of Elie and the Remote Distribution Centre (RDC) for the subscribers in and around St. Eustache.

The four services are integrated to produce an electrical signal with the spectrum distribution shown in Figure 5.

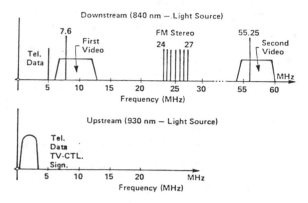

Figure 5 Loop Transmission Plan

This signal is used to modulate the intensity of a laser or light emitting diode (LED) light source for transmission over the fibre loop to the subscriber's premises as shown in Figure 6. The subscriber entrance unit (SEU)

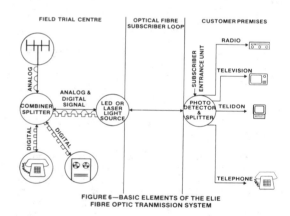

FIGURE 6—BASIC ELEMENTS OF THE ELIE FIBRE OPTIC TRANMISSION SYSTEM

detects and splits the signal and converts it back to the four original electrical signals for transmission over the house wiring to the respective terminals.

The subscriber uses the telephone and FM radio in the usual way. He is provided with a remote control unit to select the required television station. When he keys the appropriate code, the data switch in the telephone office connects his circuit to the appropriate data base as shown in Figure 7.

Figure 8 illustrates the connection of the Telidon terminal to the fibre optic system. The SEU is connected to a data set

using an EIA RS-422 interface and the data set is connected to the decoder and display generator using the EIA RS-232 interface. Coaxial cables connect the decoder to the Telidon Terminal which includes a modified television receiver and a keyboard.

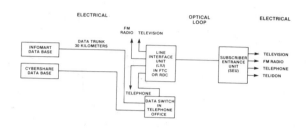

FIGURE 7 — CUSTOMER SELECTION OF DATA BASE

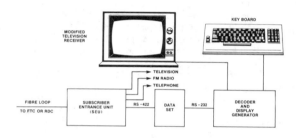

FIGURE 8 — TELIDON CONNECTION TO FIBRE OPTIC SYSTEM

TELIDON SERVICE

Telidon, the videotex system developed by the Canadian Department of Communications, is used by the customer in this trial as an interactive video terminal to access a choice of two data bases located in Winnipeg, thirty kilometers away. Telidon is a highly flexible alpha-geometric system that can display alpha-numeric characters or graphic images. The alpha-numeric characters are transmitted by the ASCII code at 4800 bps. The system uses Picture Description Instructions (PDI) to describe graphic images by defining them in terms of geometric shapes: point, rectangle, arc, polygon and line, and a control command for functions such as colour change. A line is specified by its end points and it is the responsibility of the terminal to decode the PDI and to draw the best line possible between the two end points. Similarly, the PDI includes enough information to define and locate the other geometric shapes and the terminal interprets this and reproduces it to the best of its ability.

This system has the advantage of being independent of terminal resolution. If an arc instruction is sent to a 60 X 80 resolution terminal it will be produced as a stepped curve. In the Telidon Terminal used in this trial, the arc will be much smoother, but the minute steps will still be discern-

510

able. If a subscriber buys a terminal with greater resolution he can receive a curve that appears smooth. This means that a subscriber can select a receiver to provide the resolution he requires and use it to access the same data base as his neighbour who has an inexpensive low resolution receiver.

ALARM SYSTEM

An alarm system monitors a variety of functions which are displayed on a video terminal in Elie and remotely in the toll office in Winnipeg. Functions that affect a large number of subscribers usually give a major alarm indication and those that affect only one subscriber give a minor alarm. A remote monitoring interface allows remote interrogation of the system status by a 300 baud dial-up data channel. The video monitor provides an up-to-date report on the status of irregularities in the distribution centres or on the customer premises.

INFORMATION PROVIDERS

The development of the technology is the first step towards making an interactive video system available. In order to be a useful service, there must be a data base that will provide the information that a customer needs, in a form that he can use readily. This introduces a whole new field of electronic information providers. The preparation of a data base is labour intensive and a great deal of time must be spent to determine what subjects are of interest to the subscriber, how he will use the data, and in what form should it be in order to be most useful. Graphics can be useful, but care must be taken to ensure that they are not so complex that the time required to display the picture is out of proportion to its usefulness. Dialogue and feedback between the subscriber and the information provider is useful for developing an effective data base. Trials such as this create an excellent opportunity to develop this dialogue.

Infomart has developed a data base of about 10,000 pages related to the interests of a farming community and is continuing to prepare additional pages. This data base covers a wide range of subjects as illustrated by the following:

Commodity reports   - Grain and special crops
                        - Street prices
                        - Market analysis

Live stock reports - Prices
                        - Market trends

Fertilizers and chemicals

Regulatory agencies - Wheat board

Farm equipment and repairs
                      -Dealers
                      -New product announcements

Farm Management	-Directory of services -Least cost feed -Formulation for live-stock
Life style	- News and sports - Community news - Travel - Consumer service - Real Estate - Financial and business
Weather reports	- Local - Province of Manitoba - Western Canada - Canada - North America - Other continents

Cybershare, another information provider, offers the subscribers computer aided education courses. The following seven courses are available now and others are being prepared:

Integers and rationals
Intermediate arithmetic
Math Pro - (in French)
Prerequisite mathematics skills
Mathematics of Finance
Technology Mathematics
Electricity

Some of these are at the high school level and others provide university credits. In classroom instruction, the teacher interacts with the students and can modify his presentation to respond to the needs and learning ability of the students. Some of the Canadian telephone companies have done some pioneering development on self-paced audio visual training and have found this procedure superior to classroom training for technical subjects. However, preparation of these self-paced courses requires much more extensive study and careful development with resulting higher costs, because the student is working alone and does not have a teacher to sense the student's grasp of the subject and to modify or repeat his presentation as required. When preparing courses for home study using Telidon, it is important that the courses be structured so that effective use is made of graphic images and that "on line" time is used effectively.

SUBSCRIBER REACTION TO THE TRIAL

The subscribers are displaying keen interest in the trial and are experimenting extensively, particularly with the Telidon, to become familiar with the information that is available and to learn what Telidon will do. This is part of the subscriber learning process. When the novelty has worn off, the usage will settle down to a steady state usage pattern and that will be the time to analyse the usage data and to draw some conclusions.

CONCLUSION

The Canadian Telecommunications Carriers and the Federal Government are determined to continue to provide a full range of telecommunication services to meet the demand of all Canadians wherever they may live. This joint resolve is illustrated by this trial which is shared by the telecommunications Carriers, the Government, and Industry. It is not known what the role of fibre optics will be in bringing a variety of services to individual homes, but trials such as this will help to provide background information needed to make sound decisions that will keep Canada in the forefront as we move into the Information Age.

Kenneth B. Harris graduated from the University of Western Ontario in Mathematics and Physics in 1947.

He has been employed by British Marconi, the Canadian Department of Transport, Bell Canada, the TransCanada Telephone System, and the Canadian Telecommunications Carriers Association (CTCA).

On one of his assignments with Bell Canada he was in charge of a group which was responsible for the design and engineering of all toll computer communications services.

He represented CTCA at meetings of seven CCITT Study Groups on transmission and maintenance.

In 1981 he formed a consulting company and has been retained by CTCA and the Canadian Department of Communications as Program Manager for the Elie Fibre Optic Trial System.

Mr. Harris is a member of the Association of Professional Engineers of Ontario, a Senior Member of IEEE, and a Governor of ICCC. He is the IEEE representative on the Canadian Radio Technical Planning Board.

Application of Optical Fibres to the Cambridge Ring System

G W Litchfield
Oxford University Computing Service,
UK
P Hensel, D J Hunkin
British Telecom, UK

A Cambridge Ring System which includes a 500 meter optical fibre section has been installed at Oxford University. The paper outlines a program to develop the use of optical fibres as a transmission medium for the Cambridge Ring.

1. INTRODUCTION

Most of the activities outlined in this paper will take place over the first half of 1982. Hence at this stage the paper is more of an outline of the intended development than a report on work carried out.

The development program outlined in the paper is a joint effort between Oxford University Computing Service and the British Telecom Research Laboratories, Martlesham Heath. The Optical Databus Group at Martlesham are providing the opto-electronic development effort and the Computing Service at Oxford the effort to integrate these developments into an operational Cambridge Ring, and monitor performance. Funding for the installation and development at Oxford has been provided by a Joint Network Team development grant.

2. THE CAMBRIDGE RING SYSTEM

The Cambridge Ring system [1] is one of the methods of implementing a local area network. It works on the principle of one or more packets circulating serially in a closed-loop, which physically covers the area to be served by the network. Each packet contains source and destination addresses, data and various control and status bits. Attached systems access the ring via station and repeater units. Information is transmitted by inserting address and data on the fly into an empty packet circulating on the ring. Corresponding information is received by an attached system when its associated station unit recognises its own address in the packets which are constantly circulating on the ring. A repeater unit may be installed on its own in order to regenerate the transmitted signal. There is a special unit refered to as the monitor station which is responsible for framing packets during the initialising process and monitoring the integrity of the ring during normal running. Figure 1 shows a diagramatic representation of the Cambridge Ring system.

The above description serves to provide a simplified outline of the way in which the Cambridge Ring functions. Since the activities in this paper are solely concerned with providing an alternative transmission mechanism for the Cambridge Ring it is worth describing the conventional Cambridge Ring transmission system.

The transmission rate is 10Mbit/s and is transformer coupled. A four wire coding scheme is employed which is illustrated in Figure 2. A change on both pairs indicates a one and a change on only one pair indicates a zero each pair used alternatively. The maximum distance allowed between repeaters is usually quoted as 200 metres.

FIG.1 DIAGRAMATIC REPRESENTATION OF THE CAMBRIDGE RING SYSTEM

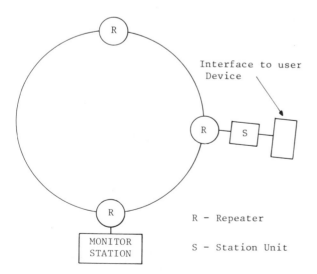

Interface to user Device

R - Repeater

S - Station Unit

FIG.2 CAMBRIDGE RING CODING SCHEME

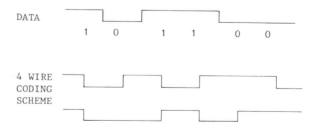

3. THE INSTALLATION AT OXFORD UNIVERSITY

At Oxford University an in-house Cambridge Ring was installed at the Computing Service and this has since been extended to cover connections in the University Science Area where, as the name implies, the majority of Science based departments in the University are located. The extension includes a section of approximately 500 metres over which it would be impractical to install repeaters. A decision was made to solve the problem by employing optical fibres for this section. Figure 3 illustrates the physical layout of the ring.

In extending the Cambridge Ring to other buildings it became evident that the problem experienced in installing a network covering several buildings are different to those of installing an in-house system. At Oxford we have found that using existing ducting between buildings typically results in entry to a building via a basement or ground floor electrical sub station. Onward routing to the next building uses the same entry point.

Connection to systems within a building form a loop from this point. It became clear that a Cambridge Ring 'distribution' box was required for wall mounting close to the entry/exit point. This would be capable of cutting off the loop within the building in the event of failure and re-routing the ring to the next building. In many cases optical fibres will be used for connection between buildings and twisted pair

for internal connections. Thus, a need for an optical fibre module for the Cambridge Ring which would be suitable for incorporation in the above mentioned 'distribution' box. A development plan has been laid down which should produce a suitable optical fibre module.

Figure 4 illustrates a typical route of the Cambridge Ring through a building.

4. DEVELOPMENT STAGES

4.1 Stage 1 - The Basic Installation

As shown in Figure 3, the optical fibre link provides the transmission path between Engineering Science and the University Science Area. The type of fibre employed is a double crucible fibre 160/200 µm core/ cladding diameter supplied by GEC Teloptic Ltd., who also supplied the optical transmitters and receivers.

The cable is made up from six fibres contained in 2.24 mm PVDF tubes, a central strength member, moisture barrier and outer sheath. Initially the optical fibre section has been incorporated into the Cambridge Ring by employing the existing Cambridge Ring coding scheme which is described earlier. Two fibres are required in each direction to provide the outgoing and incoming transmission paths for the ring. This leaves two remaining fibres which will be used for further development stages.

FIGURE 3   SCHEMATIC OF THE CAMBRIDGE RING AT OXFORD UNIVERSITY

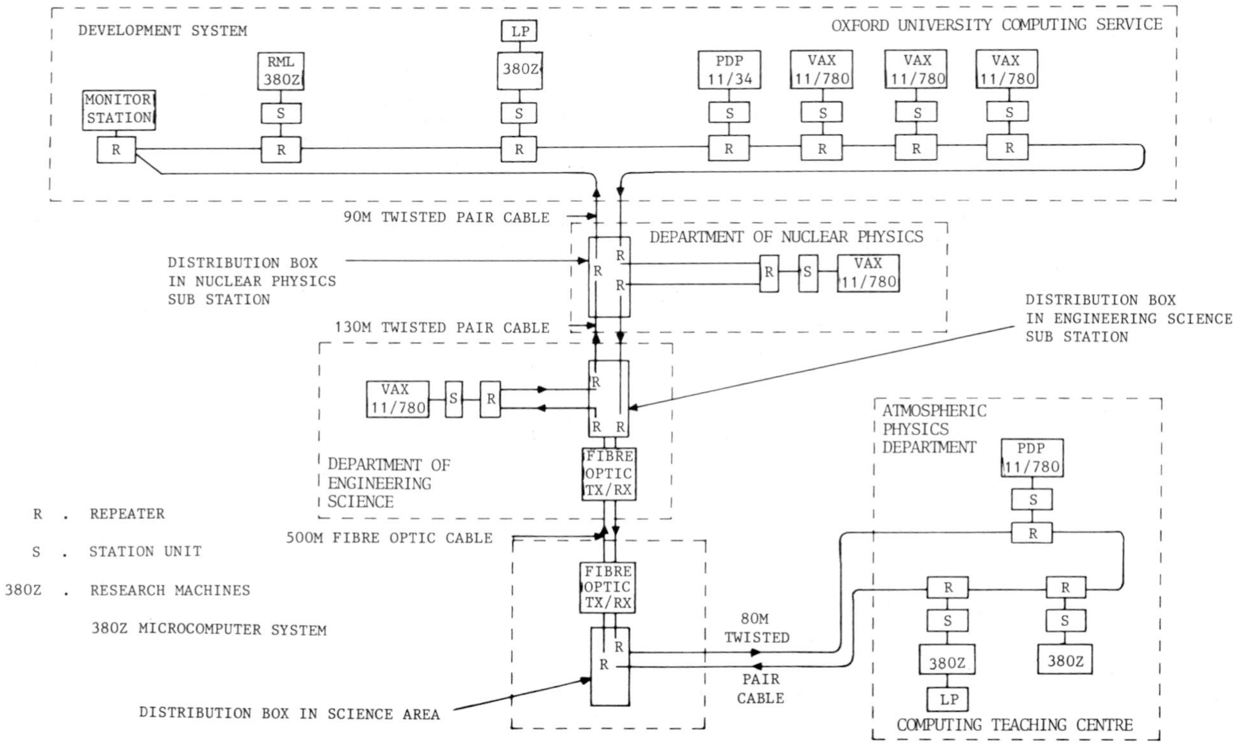

514

FIG. 4   TYPICAL ROUTE OF THE CAMBRIDGE RING
           THROUGH A BUILDING

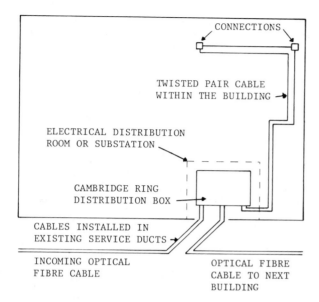

CONNECTIONS

TWISTED PAIR CABLE
WITHIN THE BUILDING

ELECTRICAL DISTRIBUTION
ROOM OR SUBSTATION

CAMBRIDGE RING
DISTRIBUTION BOX

CABLES INSTALLED IN
EXISTING SERVICE DUCTS

INCOMING OPTICAL
FIBRE CABLE

OPTICAL FIBRE
CABLE TO NEXT
BUILDING

Prior to undertaking this basic installation,
a test optical fibre section was installed
within the Computing Service building,
employing identical components to those of the
main installation. This operated without
making any measurable change to the overall
error characteristics of the ring. At present
it is too early to make any comment on the
performance of the main optical fibre link in
this respect.

4.2 Stage 2 - Transmitting Data Down a Single Fibre

As mentioned earlier, the standard Cambridge
coding scheme requires two fibres. In
addition it is necessary to ensure that there
is no differential delay between the two
transmission paths since the coding scheme
relies upon the two separate signals arriving
at the same time. For operational installations where interchangeability of components
would be required, this factor could pose
problems if the delay characteristics of the
opto-electronic components are likely to vary.
There may also be variations in the speed of
propagation determined by the material
composition of the fibre which may vary from
batch to batch.

It was concluded that development of data
transmission down a single fibre would be
worthwhile both from the economic point of
requiring only half the components and the
removal of potential operational problems due
to differential delay.

At Martlesham a test ring has been set up to
carry out the developments for this stage. The
configuration of this is shown in Figure 5.
The single fibre section employs code conversion to Manchester line code at the transmitting repeater and reconversion at the receiving
repeater.

FIG.5   SCHEMATIC OF TEST RING AT MARTLESHAM

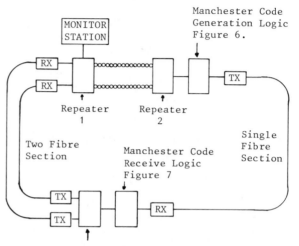

Manchester Code
Generation Logic
Figure 6.

MONITOR
STATION

RX

RX

TX

Repeater
1

Repeater
2

Two Fibre
Section

Manchester Code
Receive Logic
Figure 7

Single
Fibre
Section

TX

TX

RX

Repeater 3

At the transmitting repeater, the serial data
stream is synchronised with the repeater clock
using a D-type flip-flop and the Manchester
code generated using an exclusive - OR operation as shown in Figure 6. It was found
necessary to reform the clock at this stage to
ensure an equal mark to space ratio which is
required for the Manchester coding.

FIG.6   BLOCK DIAGRAM OF MANCHESTER CODE
          GENERATION

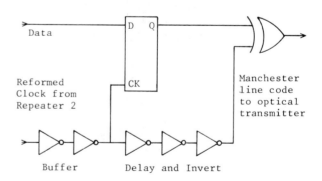

Data

D   Q

CK

Reformed
Clock from
Repeater 2

Manchester
line code
to optical
transmitter

Buffer   Delay and Invert

Re-conversion at the receive repeater is more
difficult since it involves clock recovery and
synchronisation with the repeater's phase lock
loop. Since TTL monostables are not fast
enough, it was necessary to use ECL for the
clock recovery circuit. A block diagram is
shown in Figure 7 and a timing diagram for
transmit and receive is shown in Figure 8.

FIG.7 MANCHESTER CODE RECEIVE

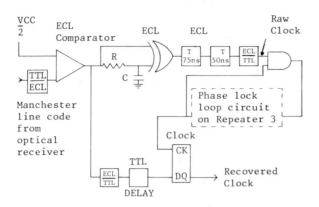

FIG.8 TIMING DIAGRAM OF MANCHESTER CODE

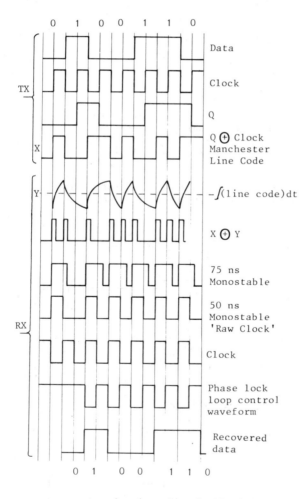

At present the circuitry for the Manchester coding is working solely on the test ring. The intention is to incorporate it in the optical fibre link at Oxford in order to check the operation of the circuitry in an operational Cambridge Ring System.

4.3 Stage 3 - Optical Fibre Repeater Module

A further stage of development will be to design an optical fibre repeater module for the Cambridge Ring. The elements which will go into this development will be the Manchester code circuitry described in Stage 2 and the utilisation of Cambridge Ring LSI repeater chips which are becoming available. The module will be packaged such that it will be suitable for incorporation into a Cambridge Ring 'distribution' box described earlier.

It is thought a simplification of the optical fibre module can be achieved by employing dual-in-line optical fibre transmitter and receiver modules which have internal Manchester bi-phase coding/de-coding. An important aspect of this development will be to ensure that using these components in the transmission path of the Cambridge Ring does not introduce instability in the ring of phase locked loops which are a fundamental part of the existing system. These modules are presently being developed by Plessey Optoelectronics and Microwave Limited, with funding provided by British Telecom Research Laboratories.

4.4 Stage 4 - Transmitting Cambridge Ring Data in two directions on a Single Fibre

A further development proposed is to transmit Cambridge Ring data in two directions on a single fibre. This would involve coupling transmitters and receivers, possibly at different wavelengths into the same fibre.

REFERENCES

1. Data Ring at Computer Laboratory, University of Cambridge.

    A. Hopper.

ACKNOWLEDGEMENT

P.C. Hensel and D.J. Hunkin thank the Director of Research of British Telecom for permission to present this paper.

G.W. Litchfield thanks the Director of Oxford University Computing Service for his permission to present this paper.

The authors wish to thank A.R. Cash of the Rutherford and Appleton Laboratories for his help in solving some of the technical problems.

Gavin Litchfield was awarded a BSc in Physics from the University College of North Wales, Bangor in 1966. After graduating he joined International Computers Ltd working as a Computer Development Engineer. In 1971 he joined the Computing Service at Oxford University and is now the Hardware Manager.

Paul Hensel received his BA degree in Physics from the University of Oxford in 1968. He remained in Oxford to carry out research in cryogenics at the Clarendon Laboratory and was awarded the degree of Doctor of Philosophy in 1972. He sub-seqently joined the Post Office Research Centre to work in the Optical Communications Division. He is now Head of the Optical Fibre Databus Studies Group at the British Telecom Research Laboratories at Martlesham Heath.

David Hunkin spent 10 years in a telephone area before embarking on an Honours degree course in Electrical and Electronic Engineering at the University of Bath. Upon graduation in 1980 he transferred to British Telecom Research Laboratories at Martlesham Heath where he has worked in the field of optical databus systems.

Optical Networks for Integrated Broadband Communication

H Schaeffner, H J Matt, K Fussgaenger
Standard Elektrik Lorenz AG
Federal Republic of Germany

I. INTRODUCTION

For applications of fibre optics there are today three main areas to be seen:

1) Low cost fibre optic links to interconnect local systems with remote units at moderate bit rates ($<$ 1 Mbit/s/fibre) and distances ($<$ 100 m) /1-6/. Such applications include optical links within computer systems (e.g. where terminals, memories and other I/O units are connected to a main-frame), and optical links for remote measurements and control (e.g. in high power plants, vessels and airplanes).

2) Fibre optic links for medium bit rates ($<$ 20 Mbit/s) and medium distances ($<$ 1 km) which are especially of interest for integrated local communication systems which handle telephone and data communication services simultaneously by means of time-division-multiplex switching /7-10/.

These optical links are also well suited for interconnecting local computers to form a computer network. However, if several arbitrary connections have to be handled simultaneously, the need for an integrated switched network becomes obvious.

3) Fibre optic links for bit rates ($>$ 20 Mbit/s and distances ($>$ 1 km) are of particular importance for the PTTs with respect to the national and international communication networks, especially since new services will be introduced. The high performance of optical links

finally makes it possible to realize 'Integrated Broadband Communication Networks' /11-13/ economically. Such networks transmit and handle all communication services known today and can be designed to be so flexible that new services can be easily integrated and existing ones can evolve.

II. BASIC PROPERTIES OF FIBRE OPTIC SYSTEMS

Fibre optic transmission systems allow one to transmit both analog and digital signals. However, due to the nonlinearities of the light sources, non-stationary and modal noise effects, linear light-amplitude modulation requires more careful design than FM with respect to signal quality and transmission distance. Therefore, known optical analog transmission systems mostly use FM modulated signals and PFM (pulse frequency modulation) techniques /14-15/.

Furthermore, fibre optic systems appear to be particularly well suited for digital transmission; a large variety of system components has been developed for this purpose and is available on the market /1-6/.

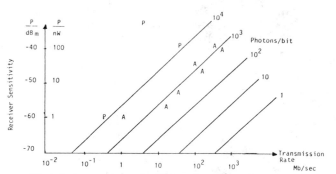

Fig. 1 Performance of several optical receivers being realized at 850 nm
A denotes systems with Avalanche photodiodes
P denotes systems with PIN photodiodes

From electromagnetic quantum theory, it has been estimated /16/ that any practical optical receiver, in order to achieve an output bit error probability of 10^{-9} will need at least an average of 10.5 photons/bit.

However, due to imperfect optical detectors (dark current noise, thermal noise) and noise in preamplifiers (thermal noise, FET channel noise) this bound is rather optimistic with respect to practical systems /16-19/. In Fig. 1 the average received light power for optical receivers being realized to achieve 10^{-9} bit error probability is shown as a function of the transmission rate. From this diagram one can see that optical receivers at 850 nm using APDs which provide a considerable avalanche gain will need about 600-1300 photons/bit, whereas systems with PIN photodiodes need about 10000 photons/bit which is a factor of 10 less in sensitivity; systems with PIN-FET detectors need 800-8000 photons/bit. This shows /20/ that PIN photodiode receivers using a GaAs FET at the preamplifier input achieve similar sensitivities compared with APD receivers and a high dynamic range. However, PIN-FET receivers are usually much simpler in design and cost so that this technique is mostly suited for practical applications.

II.2 Optical Transmitters

Practical optical sources being mostly used in fibre optic systems are light emitting diodes (LEDs) and laser diodes (LDs). Both elements emit light stimulated by the drive current at a rather large bandwidth, compared with conventional radio oscillators. Since the LED light radiation is much similar to a broadband noise source (also for many lasers due to phase, frequency, mode and amplitude instabilities) comprising many spatial modes, it is only possible to modulate the output power of the source; for simplicity this is done by modulation of the drive current. From these properties it becomes apparent that the randomness of the light source already limits the signal-to-noise ratio of the transmitted signal.

Fortunately, for many practical situations where many output modes reach the receiver these 'modal noise' effects are reduced by averaging; then quantum effects at the receiver again dominate the transmitter noise and limit the performance of the link.

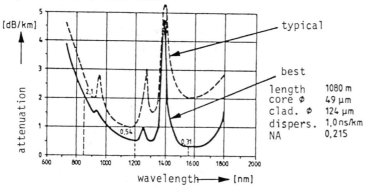

Fig. 2 SEL graded-index fibre

length   1080 m
core ⌀   49 μm
clad. ⌀   124 μm
dispers.   1.0 ns/km
NA   0.215

The above mentioned properties of optical links suggest digital modulation schemes to be superior compared with analog light amplitude modulation techniques. The light power of LDs

launched into the fibre usually ranges between 0.5 mW - 5 mW and for LEDs between 15 μW - 150 μW.

II.3 Optical Fibres

Optical Fibres exist in a rather large variety covering a spectrum of many possible applications.

For low cost systems covering short distances at moderate bit rates, it is common to use multimode step-index fibres with a rather large core diameter (200 μm) and large numerical aperture (~ 0.35) to increase the coupling efficiency to the LED light source. For cost effectiveness such fibres have been made of a silica core and a plastic cladding which yields an attenuation of ~ 50 dB/km. Such fibres are effectively combined with LEDs, since enough light power can be launched into the fibre.

For medium bit rates and distances to be covered, multimode graded index fibres are mostly used. The core diameter of these fibres is 50 μm, the cladding 125 μm, and its numerical aperture about 0.2 which needs more effort for efficient coupling. However, the big advantage of these fibres is that small values for attenuation (depending on wavelength) can be achieved (Fig. 2), together with relatively high values for the bandwidth (several 100 MHz·km).

On long-distance trunks and for transmission rates beyond 1 Gbit/s only monomode fibres are suitable. In particular, these fibres have very low dispersion at the wavelength 1.3 μm which makes them very promising for broadband applications. A laboratory system has been realized /21/ to demonstrate that 1 Gbit/s can be transmitted at 1.3 μm over 25 km monomode fibre. The monomode fibre for this experiment had a similar attenuation as shown for the fibre in Fig. 2. The main disadvantage of these fibres is the small core diameter of 7-9 μm which makes handling and coupling of these fibres difficult. For a specific application one first should make an appropriate light power estimation for the link. More detailed computations to find the optimum parameters can then be made

as shown in /19/.

III. SYSTEM STRUCTURES USING OPTICAL LINKS

III.1 Bus Structures

For the interconnection of local systems bus type structures are mostly used which offer a simple and reliable way to exchange information between arbitrary units.. Parallel transmission of messages by words allows each line of the bus to be operated at a relatively modest bit rate and with very simple synchronization circuitry, but at the expense of many parallel lines. Therefore, this bus technique has been realized by copper wires only for very short distances of a few meters.

At greater lengths, the attenuation and risk of electromagnetic interferences disturbing the message strongly suggest the use of optical fibres /22-25/. The question whether optical fibres shall be used in parallel (one per bus line) or as a single fibre to carry all information is only one of economics. The use of one fibre reduces the total length, the number of light sources and detectors, but requires a parallel-to-serial converter (multiplexer) at the transmitter and a corresponding unit (demultiplexer) at the receiver /25/. In addition, the link must operate at n times the transmission rate and requires some additional word synchronisation.

Optical bus structures as shown in Fig. 3 can be realized with the aid of optical couplers /22-25/. There are basically two different structures, the T-type bus and the star-type bus which use T-type and star-type couplers, respectively. Both structures can also be combined to yield more complicated architectures. The T-type coupler simply splits the light from one or two entering ports on the two output ports. By appropriate design, the light power ratio between the two output ports can be choosen in a wide range /24/. The T-type bus structure seems to be well suited for realizing some well known 'open communication systems' using polling or ethernet techniques /26/.

However, the T-type couplers used in straight-line or ring type systems require the optical receivers to operate in a rather wide dynamic range due to the light power ratio between the light generated by a nearby transmitter and the light from far-end user.

The star-type coupler equally distributes the light of each entering port onto each of its output ports. Since each user generates the same light power, the receivers do require a much less dynamic because only differences in fibre lengths can cause variations in attenuation. However, the star-type networks in general do require an increase (by a factor of N) in total fibre length compared with ring-type networks (N being the number of users) /27/.

519

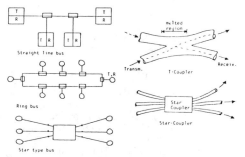

Fig. 3 Basic bus structures and corresponding optical couplers

III.2 Switched Structures

Communication in bus structures usually is governed by some controlling device which assigns the bus to a single pair of transmitter and receiver during the time necessary to transmit a specific message. Meanwhile, other units have to wait until they are allowed to use the bus. The bus thus allocates its total channel capacity during subsequent time intervals to the users. If the number of users increases, this soon leads to queuing problems, since the response time of the system (the time a unit waits until it gets access to the bus) grows rapidly.

This problem can be overcome by the use of switched architectures where simultaneous communication between many pairs of users is possible. Again there are two basic structures, a star-type network and a ring (or loop)-type network which look much similar to the bus structures of Fig. 3.

However, in the star-type network the central unit is a switch (and not a coupler) which allows every input signal to be switched to arbitrary output ports. Here, queuing can only occur when a user is called by two or more other users.

The ring-type network (Fig. 3) uses, in addition to the electrical (or optical) T-couplers, small switching modules, one for each subscriber station. The transmission medium itself is required to offer multiple-access techniques and to carry the maximum average traffic generated by the users; this usually is accomplished by TDM transmission. If the number of users is large enough, the actual traffic in the system will have little deviations from its mean value.

IV. INTEGRATED BROADBAND NETWORKS

The large bandwidth, long repeater distances and low cost, offered by fibre optics in conjunction with large scale integrated circuits (allowing low cost mass production of signal processing and switching units) makes it possible to apply new design concepts for future communication networks. Thus these new technologies will enable the introduction of 'Integrated Broadband Communication Systems' in this decade /11-13/.

The next step to introduce an Integrated Services Digital Broadband Communication Network (ISDBN) will be the realization of several field trial systems called BIGFON (Broadband Integrated Glass Fibre Optic Network) which has been initiated by the Deutsche Bundespost /28/.

IV.1 Experimental System for Integrated Broadband Communication Using Optical Channels

This system, described in detail in /12/, consists of

- an all-digital integrated broadband network including data, telephone, audio, videotelephone, broadcast and cable-TV services, and

- a conventional network for analog transmission and switching of telephone channels whose bandwidth capability has been extended to accomodate the same set of broadband services; it is compatibly interconnected to the digital network.

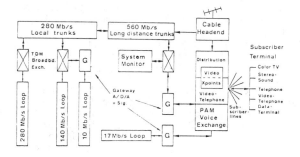

Fig. 4 Block Diagram of Experimental System

The system architecture of the digital network consists of four different local distribution loops - one at 280 Mbit/s, one at 140 Mbit/s, one using twin 17 Mbit/s channels, and one at 10 Mbit/s. These local distribution loop systems connect the subscribers via a time-division-multiplex switch to a trunking section which comprises a 280 Mbit/s local trunk and a 560 Mbit/s long-haul system (Fig. 4). Thus the whole PCM hierarchy is involved in the system. The subscriber stations realize multiple access to the many TDM channels. Its basic structure (Fig. 5) consists of a special HF unit, two busses, several interfaces being connected to the busses and a central control unit. The HF unit performs the necessary synchronization at 280 Mbit/s and a serial-to-parallel conversion of the high speed data on the 34-digits-wide busses. The control unit and interfaces then perform well known word processing at moderate speeds (34 times lower) and power consumption. All necessary funtions, e.g. channel assignment, signaling, etc. is done by the control unit and the interface, one for each service or terminal. The bus structure of the station offers great flexibility, since it can easily be extended for implementation of additional services or to serve other subscribers too. Since the busses of the station contain all information on the fibres, the station may serve many subscribers and operate as a TDM concentrator without penalty.

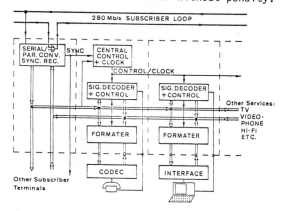

Fig. 5 Subscriber terminal

The bus structure of the station allows the service modules and interfaces to be realized in a high-density, low-power and low-cost technology by using modest operating frequencies and parallel processing.

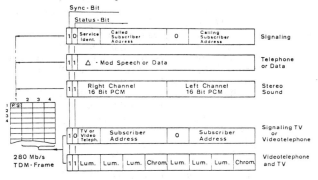

Fig. 6 Time slot formats

The integration of all services into one network demands that new operational algorithms be well-matched to the requirements of signal characteristics, bit rates, A/D conversion methods, signal standards, signaling, switching, multiplexing, transmission and synchronization. Therefore, a new TDM frame has been designed that matches both, the bus structure of the subscriber station by its word structure (Fig. 6) and the bit rate of existing PCM systems. As basic elements, it uses time slots containing 34 digits where 32 digits carry arbitrary user information. This word structure meets particularly well the word or byte structure of many computers and also the needs of the subscriber station design.

Since the telephone channel is the most widely-spread channel now and in future, the 64 kbit/s channel was chosen as the basic unit of channel capacity throughout the system. Services that today require $\leq$ 64 kbit/s are easily transmitted via this channel, leaving enough space for the further evolution of these services. Services requiring bit rates > 64 kbit/s then use multiples (favorably powers of 2) of this basic unit. The experimental system thus uses for

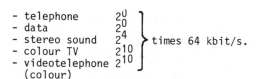

- telephone $\quad 2^0$
- data $\quad 2^0$
- stereo sound $\quad 2^4$ } times 64 kbit/s.
- colour TV $\quad 2^{10}$
- videotelephone 2^{10}
  (colour)

This technique also allows line switching and packet switching to be used simultaneously and offers a wide range of channel capacity being selectable for a service.

The TDM channels of the loop can be assigned in a fixed or variable mode to the services by appropriate modification of the station's control software. Thus the station can be used in a star-shaped network with a central exchange as well as in a multiple-user loop applying decentralized exchange techniques. In a multiple-user loop system, the station operates as some special type of concentrator without penalty, since each bus has unlimited access to the TDM frame. The bus can be easily extended for other service modules (new services) and/or to serve more than one subscriber at a time.

IV.2 BIGFON Field Trial

In 1983 ten BIGFON systems, to be delivered by six German telecommunication companies, will be installed in seven German cities. The SEL BIGFON system employs an all-digital solution. Its basic structure is shown in Fig. 7. The optical channels transmit bit rates of 140 Mbit/s at wavelengths of 850 nm and 1200 nm, respectively, over a single graded-index fibre. The bit rate of 140 Mbit/s allows the transmission of one broadband channel for either colour-TV or videotelephone and several narrowband channels for stereo-sound, telephone, data, etc. /31/.

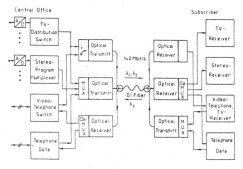

Fig. 7 SEL BIGFON field trial

IV.3 Integration of Computer Communication Services

The integrated broadband communication networks mentioned above will open new possibilities for improved computer communication compared with today's data transfer techniques in packet- or circuit-switched networks /32/. Besides an extended use of 2.4 kbit/s up to 64 kbit/s transmission rates, the transfer of larger data files for fast real time computer applications will be desirable. Higher transmission rates will allow one to cut unacceptable long transfer times to reasonable values. Therefore, new transmission rates for computer communications are being considered in ISDN concepts. At present, there are three main classes of transmission rates to be distinguished. The first class includes all applications which can be satisfied with a 64 kbit/s channel. The second class would require a channel capacity similar to the capacity for stereo sound transmission ($2^m \cdot 64$ kbit/s; $m \sim 4$) and would be desirable for bulk memory I/O traffic. The third class includes future applications such as data transfer between data banks containing very large bulk memories where data transmission channels of about 8 Mbit/s ($m \sim 7$) may be required.

In integrated broadband networks such channels (type 1, 2 and 3) can easily be provided for. Moreover, such a network would fulfill some additional constraints set by the class 2 and 3 communication. Once a connection is established, there is no time varying delay in the link (usually involved with packet switching), since it is circuit-switched.

The integration of fast computer communication into broadband networks requires a standard interface unit between the individual computer equipment and the network. This interface unit has to meet the standard operational algorithms with respect to signaling and data transfer on the network side and the operations required from the computer side.

The procedure to establish the connection should follow the proposal of the OSI model /33, 34/ which includes the X.25 recommendations. Since at present there exist only recommendations for a virtual terminal and class 1 communication channels, it seems to be an important goal to define similary a virtual disk or bulk memory for future high speed communication between computers in integrated networks.

V. CONCLUSIONS

Optical fibre technology has developed to such a mature level that many useful applications are allowed in closed local systems (to interconnect remotely located units to a data collecting and processing centre), in private integrated communication systems and in the evolution of public networks towards integrated broadband communication networks. For the future, the integration of all telecommunication services into one broadband network seems to be the most economical solution for public telecommunication networks. Considerations about the market for the new services being offered, look very promising and justify the efforts being made for BIGFON. Also the price trends indicate that such systems including fibre-optics can be produced at economical cost if the market will be as large as expected. Furthermore, for the low-cost realization of future broadband systems the improvement of microelectronics (VLSI) will become very important.

VI. REFERENCES

/1/ Lemme, H., Im Blickpunkt Lichtleitertechnik, Elektronik 14, 1980.
/2/ Mirtich, V.L., Designer's guide to fibre optic data links - part I, EDN vol. 25, no. 12, June 1980, 133-140.
/3/ Mirtich, V.L., Fibre optics offer promise in data-network design, EDN vol. 26, no. 5, March 1981, 93-100.
/4/ Roworth, D.A.A., Fibre optics for industrial applications, Optics and Laser Technology vol. 12, no. 5, Oct. 1980, 255-259.
/5/ Bates, C. and Tassell, C., Low cost fibre optic data links, Comm. Int. vol. 7, no. 7, July 1980, 35-36.
/6/ Lombaerde, R., Fibre optic data link snaps in place, Electronics vol. 53, no. 27, Dec. 1980.
/7/ Crow, J.D. and Sachs, M.W., Fibre optics for local data networks, SPIE Fibre Optic for Comm. & Control vol. 224, 1980, 53-56.
/8/ Neff, R. and Senzig, D., A local network design using fibre optics, Proc. Spring Comp. Conf. on 'VLSI in the laboratory, office, factory, home', Febr. 1981, San Francisco, 64-69.
/9/ AEG-Telefunken, Backnang, 'DIKOS-System', 1981.
/10/ 'SILK-System für integrierte lokale Kommunikation', Hasler Mitteilungen vol. 40, March 1981, 1-40.
/11/ Haller, U., Herold, W. and Ohnsorge, H., Problems arising in the development of optical communication systems, Appl.Phys. vol. 17, no. 2, 1978, 115-122.
/12/ Matt, H.J. and Fussgaenger, K., Integrated broad-band communication using optical networks - results of an experimental study, IEEE Trans. Comm. vol. COM-29, no. 6, June 1981, 868-885.
/13/ Dupieux, J., Kao, C., Ohnsorge, H. and Radley, P., Optical fibre technology: application to broadband networks, Electrical Communication vol. 56, no. 4, 1981.
/14/ Powell, W.H. and Allsop, B.E., Versatile optical fibre transmission system, 2 nd IEE Conf. on Telecom. Transm., March 1981, London, IEE Conf. Proc. no. 193, 85-90.
/15/ Fox, J.R. and Dalgoutte, D.C., Cable TV using optical fibre transmission to the customer - the Milton Keynes trial, 2 nd European Fiber Optics & Com. Exposition (EFOC'81), Nov. 1981, Cologne, Proc. 35-37
/16/ Smith, R.G. and Personick, S.D., Receiver design for optical fiber communication systems, in 'Topics in Applied Physics' vol. 39, Springer Verlag, Berlin 1980, 89-160.
/17/ Personick, St.D., Fundamental limits in optical communication, IEEE Proc. vol. 69, no. 2, Febr. 1981, 262-266.
/18/ Levitin, L.B. and Ihlenburg, L., A theoretical model of a binary PCM optical communication channel, Faculty for Mathematics, University Bielefeld, W. Germany, 1981.
/19/ Tanaka, T.P., Maeda, M. and Tanaka, M., Optimization of fibre optic data way systems, Proc. of 1980 IEEE Int. Symp. on Circuits and Systems, 931-934.
/20/ Chown, D.P.M., Dynamic range extention for PIN-FET optical receivers, 7th ECOC, Sept. 1981, Copenhagen, Conf. Proc. 14.5-1 till 14.5-3.
/21/ Bludau, W., Kaiser, N. and Stephan, W., Fibre-optic transmission at 1 Gbps, 25 km without repeaters, Telecommunications vol. 16, no. 4, April 1982, 88.1 - 100.2.

/22/ Witte, H.H., Optische Datenbusse fuer
Mess- und Regelaufgaben, Elektronik
April 1981, 63-70.

/23/ Winzer, G. and Witte, H.H., Comparison of
fibre optic data bus networks, Siemens
Forsch. & Entw. Ber. Bd. 10, No. 1, 1981,
9-15.

/24/ Weidel, E. and Wengel, J., T-Koppler fuer
die optische Datenuebertragung, Wiss. Ber.
AEG-Telef. 53, 1980, 17-22.

/25/ Seinecke, S., Fritzsche, H. and Lobkowicz,
J., High-speed optical data transmission,
in 'From Electronics to Microelectronics',
Kaiser, W.A. and Proebster, W.E. (eds.),
North-Holland Publish. Comp.,1980.

/26/ Xerox Corp., The Ethernet, a local area
network, data link layer and physical
layer specifications, Sept. 1980.

/27/ Herold, W., Mrozynski, G. and Weber, J.,
Components, structure and operation of
integrated digital networks based on an
experimental system, Proc. Int. Zurich
Seminar, 1978, B7.1-B7.6.

/28/ Haist, W., Fiber optics in the Federal
Republic of Germany, integrated-service
local networks, 2 nd European Fiber Optics
& Com. Exposition (EFOC'81), Nov. 1981,
Cologne, W. Germany, Proc. 3-7.

/29/ Arkat, S., et al., Teilnehmerstation in
einem dienste-integrierten digitalen
Nachrichtennetz, NTZ vol. 32, no. 9, 1979,
598-602.

/30/ Ballering, H. and Thielmann, H., Digitale
Teilnehmerschleife mit dezentraler Ver-
mittlung, Techn. Mitteilungen TEKADE,
1978, 36-41.

/31/ Ljungstroem, P.A., Matt, H.J. and Ohnsorge,
H., Experimental study and field-trial
system for broad-band communications in
Germany, Proc. of IEE Int. Conf. on Com.,
April 1982, Birmingham, England.

/32/ Hillebrand, F., DATEX, Infrastruktur der
Daten- und Textkommunikation, R.V. Decker
Verlag, 1981, ISBN 3-7685-3081-7.

/33/ Zimmermann, H., OSI reference model - the
ISO model of architecture for open systems
interconnection, IEEE Trans. Comm. vol.
COM-28, no. 4, April 1980.

/34/ Data communication networks, CCITT Yellow
Book vol. VIII, Rec. X.1-X.29, Genf 1981.

A Low Cost Transparent Fibre Optic Link for Inter-Rack Communication

G W Sumerling, P J Morgan
Plessey Research, UK

The concentration of electronic processing allowed by microelectronics has demanded minimisa-
tion of the inter-card interconnection to cope with the increased information density. One
solution is to multiplex the data up to higher bit rates and use a fibre optic link. A low
cost transmitter and receiver module has been designed for up to 50 MBit data. Each module
is of the form of a dual-in-line integrated circuit package and has a fibre pigtail with
attached field connector. The transmitter contains a Zn-diffused GaAs LED and a silicon
bipolar integrated circuit which encodes clock and data and provides the drive for the LED.
The receiver contains a silicon PIN-diode and a silicon bipolar integrated circuit which amplifies, digitises and decodes the received bit stream to give a clock and a data stream.

1. INTRODUCTION

Continuous advances in integrated circuit technology have enabled a greater number of functions to be realised in a single I.C. package.
In addition, the functional operations can be
carried out at a higher speed. This implies a
far larger processing capability for each
printed circuit board - a trend which will
eventually lead to interconnection problems
because of the number of inputs and outputs
per board, each of which could be passing a
high data rate. A great deal can be done by
multiplexing the data streams but this solution
is less attractive when the power required to
drive the high speed multiplexed wire interconnections becomes significant in comparison with
the total power consumption of the board.

Fibre optic links can offer very high data
rates with reasonable power consumption and
give the added bonus of electromagnetically
insensitive, secure optical coupling with no
earth loop problems. To date, most fibre optic
products have been aimed at long distance, high
capacity links, commanding a high price, or low
price modules for short distances and low
capacity.

This paper describes a link which is economic
for the transmission of data streams of up
to 50 MBits/sec. over distances from 1m to
500m (or up to 4,000m at the lower data rates).
This has been achieved by making use of the
same advanced integrated circuit technology
which caused the interconnection bottleneck
and by an early consideration of high volume
production costs for the link modules.

Each link consists of two modules - a transmitter and receiver (Figure 1), each with a
short optical fibre pigtail and fibre connector
for joining the main optical fibre cable run.
Each module is no bigger than a 16-pin dual-in-
line (DIL) IC package and requires no external
components or trimming on installation. The
link is transparent to the user; binary data
and a synchronous clock are input at the
transmitter end and output at the receiver end,
using standard ECL or TTL interfaces.

If a synchronous clock is not present, a simple
oscillator at the transmitter can provide an
asynchronous clock. Its properties are not
critical; all that is needed is a frequency
fast enough (depending on timing accuracy
required) to clock the data into the transmitter and to be compatible with the link operating frequency of 2-50 MHz.

2. OVERALL SYSTEM

A schematic illustration of the optical link
carrying 50 MBits/sec. is shown in Figure 2.
The same link will operate with clock rates down
to 25 MHz and, by adding capacitors
within the receiver module, physically identical
links will operate down to 2 MHz. The
transmitter module takes in a binary data
stream at conventional ECL interfaces (TTL for
low frequencies) and encodes the data with the
clock to incorporate timing information. A
Light Emitting Diode (LED) converts the coded
stream into a pulsed infra-red beam which is
focussed through a microlens onto the end of
the fibre optic pigtail. The pigtail is joined
to the main optical fibre cable run by a connector which can be attached and mated in the
field. The core dimension of the main cable
is larger than that of the transmitter fibre
pigtail to ease alignment of the fibre ends and
thus reduce transfer losses. For the same
reason, at the second (receiver) connector, the
pigtail core diameter is larger than that of
the main fibre. No lens is required to focus
the infra-red beam emitted from the end of the
fibre pigtail onto the PIN diode because the
diode has a larger diameter than the fibre.
The diode converts the optical power incident
upon it into an electrical current which is
amplified up to standard binary logic levels
thus recovering the coded data stream. Decoding follows and the original data and clock are
output through conventional ECL interfaces
(TTL for lower frequencies).

The data is encoded before transmission by combining the data with its synchronous clock.
This has several advantages; the most important is that both can be transmitted together
and recovered separately so that at the receiver

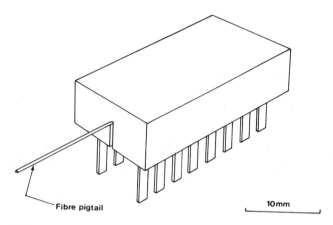

Fibre pigtail

10mm

FIGURE 1   PHYSICAL ASPECT OF A TRANSMITTER OR RECEIVER MODULE

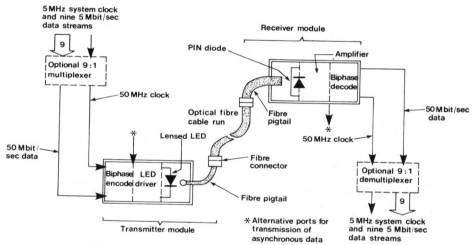

5 MHz system clock
and nine 5 Mbit/sec
data streams

9

Optional 9:1
multiplexer

50 MHz clock

Receiver module

PIN diode

Amplifier

Biphase
decode

Optical fibre
cable run

Fibre
pigtail

50 Mbit/sec
data

50 Mbit/
sec data

✳

Lensed LED

50 MHz clock

✳

Biphase LED
encode driver

Fibre
connector

Fibre pigtail

Optional 9:1
demultiplexer

9

Transmitter module

✳ Alternative ports for
transmission of
asynchronous data

5 MHz system clock
and nine 5 Mbit/sec
data streams

FIGURE 2   SCHEMATIC ILLUSTRATION OF A SYNCHRONOUS OPTICAL LINK
CARRYING 50 MBits/sec. OF DATA AND A 50 MHz CLOCK

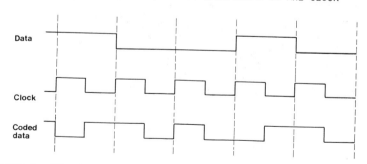

Data

Clock

Coded
data

FIGURE 3   MANCHESTER BIPHASE CODING

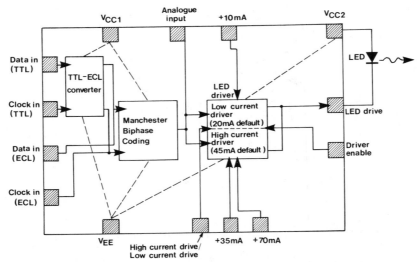

FIGURE 4   BLOCK DIAGRAM OF THE TRANSMITTER INTEGRATED CIRCUIT

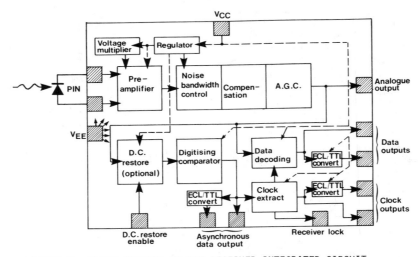

FIGURE 5   BLOCK DIAGRAM OF THE RECEIVER INTEGRATED CIRCUIT

all the timing information for the data is contained in the synchronous recovered clock. This means that no external clock has to be provided for synchronisation of the received data, nor does any timing information have to be extracted from the uncoded data. The latter implies that the transmitted data is unrestricted; for instance, the data can remain in one state for hundreds of bit periods and the receiver can still recover that data and the associated clock.

The coding chosen for transmission was Manchester Biphase, otherwise known as WAL 1 (Figure 3) which has significant advantages for receiver design. It has a constant mean d.c. level and contains a great deal of clock information, necessary for clock recovery and, in addition, inter-symbol interference is minimised because the coded data can remain in one state for no more than two half clock periods. The defined nature of the code means that the receiver can be optimised for minimum bit error rate. The design provides for other codes, even NRZ data, to be transmitted without an accompanying synchronous clock by bypassing the transmitter coding and receiver decoding sections but the sensitivity at the receiver will be degraded leading to a lower maximum bit rate and/or physically shorter receiver to transmitter spacings.

If data multiplexing/demultiplexing is required custom integrated circuits can be designed to provide elegant one-chip solutions for these functions. Under development is a multiplexer and corresponding demultiplexer, which serialises nine 5 MBit/sec. parallel inputs and a 5 MBit/sec. synchronisation code (generated internally) into a 50 MBit/sec. data stream. In addition, the associated 5 MHz system clock is multiplied up to 50 MHz. The tenth channel containing the synchronisation code is used by the demultiplexer to route the 5 MBit/sec. data streams to the correct outputs. The demultiplexer also divides down the 50 MHz clock to the 5 MHz system clock. These chips can also operate with system clocks down to 2.5 MHz or lower with one or two external passive components.

3.   MODULE CONSTRUCTION

The internal package structure consists of an extended single-layer chip carrier board with a sub-packaged LED (Tx module) or PIN diode (Rx module) attached to the ceramic board. On-board interconnections, die pads, wire bond pads, resistors and capacitors (for low frequency modules) and access to the outside world are printed onto the ceramic chip carrier board using conventional hybrid circuit technology.

To achieve the degree of reliability necessary for telecommunications and military applications, each active component (IC, LED and PIN diode) is individually hermetically sealed. The modular approach to the package construction permits the burn-in and test/select operations of the active components after hermetic enclosure, and prior to assembly. Thus only verified components are assembled together.

For the Rx module, protection against Electro-Magnetic Interference (EMI) for the sensitive PIN diode to IC interconnections is afforded by applying shielding metallisation. The PIN diode is protected by the metal sheath of its own package.

Electrical access to the module is via clip-on lead frames soldered to the ceramic chip carrier, to produce a package of the DIL format (0.1 inch lead pitch x 0.3; 0.6 or 0.9 inch lead row space). An alternative flat-pack format can be produced by using a suitable clip-on lead frame.

Package construction is completed by adding a plastic cover, either by sealing on a pre-formed lid, or by including a cover around the ceramic chip carrier board, encapsulating the on-board components. The package height of the plastic cover is $\frac{1}{4}$ inch (6.35 mm) for both Tx and Rx modules. The number of package pins (16) is significantly greater than the number required for the module (9 pins for the transmitter, 7 for the receiver) because the package length has to be extended to accommodate the LED or PIN diode subpackage.

4.   INTEGRATED CIRCUIT DESIGN

A block diagram of the integrated circuit within the transmitter is illustrated in Figure 4. The LED current (and hence optical output power) can be programmed for various values between 20 mA and 150 mA by connecting the various current select pins to ground. The driver enable can enable or disable the drive to the LED within a clock cycle. Externally, the transmitter module will have nine live pins: two power pins, ECL clock in (doubles as asynchronous data in) and data in (TTL for lower data rate modules), driver enable and four current select pins.

A block diagram of the integrated circuit within the receiver is illustrated in Figure 5. The d.c. restore enable is used if asynchronous uncoded NRZ data is received. The receiver lock signal is generated when a biphase signal is received and the decoding circuitry has locked onto the signal correctly. There is an on-chip voltage regulator which, together with an all differential preamplifier design, enables proper processing of low level received signals in the presence of up to 0.5v spikes on the power supply. Externally the receiver module will have seven live pins: two power pins, ECL clock out and data out (TTL for lower data rate modules), asynchronous data out, d.c. restore enable and receiver lock.

5.   LINK PERFORMANCE

The performance of the transmitter and receiver is summarised in Tables 1 and 2 respectively. The modules have been combined with relatively cheap 160 micron core cable which is joined to the fibre pigtails by connectors which can be attached to the fibre ends in the field (Table 3). Longer ranges can be achieved by using a low loss, high bandwidth cable 100 micron core) and low loss connectors (Table 4). Fitting of the low loss connectors needs fairly sophisticated aids and is difficult to do in the field.

Table 1
Summary of Transmitter Performance

Data Rate   D.C. - 70 MBit/sec.
Clock Rate   D.C. - 70 MBit/sec.
Temperature Range 0-70°C

LED Current	Typical Power Consumption	Mean Optical Output Power (minimum)
20 mA	180 mW	15 μW
30 mA	240 mW	22 μW
45 mA	460 mW	34 μW
80 mA	680 mW	60 μW
115 mA	890 mW	87 μW
150 mA	1110 mW	112 μW

Table 2
Summary of Receiver Performance

	High Data Rate Module*	Low Data Rate Module*
Data Rate	D.C. - 50 MBits/sec.	D.C. - 4 MBits/sec.
Clock Rate	25-50 MHz	2-4 MHz
Bit Error Rate	1 in 10^{10}	1 in 10^{10}
Sensitivity	-35 dBm	-41 dBm
Dynamic Range	21 dB	27 dB
Power Consumption	400 mW	400 mW

*Two other modules cover intermediate clock rates.

Table 3
Range of Transmission using 160 micron Core Fibre Optic Cable
(Attenuation 10 dB/km, Optical Bandwidth 20 MHz km) and Field
Terminated Connectors.   A System Margin of 5 dB is assumed.

		Transmitter Power Consumption (mW)		
		180	680	1110
Bit Rate (MBit/sec.)	4	1.2 Km	1.7 Km	2.0 Km
	10	0.9 Km	1.4 Km	1.7 Km
	50	0.15 Km	0.35 Km	0.5 Km

Table 4
Range of Transmission using 100 micron Core Fibre Optic Cable
(Attenuation 5 dB/Km, Optical Bandwidth 200 MHz Km) and Low
Loss Connectors. A System Margin of 5 dB is assumed.

		Transmitter Power Consumption (mW)		
		180	680	1110
Bit Rate (MBit/sec.)	4	2.6 Km	3.6 Km	4.0 Km
	10	2.0 Km	3.0 Km	3.5 Km
	50	0.7 Km	1.7 Km	2.0 Km

6. CONCLUSIONS

A complete low cost fibre optic link has been described consisting only of a transmitter module, the fibre cable and a receiver module. The module construction utilises well established hybrid microelectronic techniques to produce a low cost package with hermetically sealed active components which is as good as an equivalent expensive metal package.

The link can be used as a transparent replacement of existing bulky and power-dissipating electrical interconnections or indeed where electrical interconnections are not practicable. Possible data rates are from 50 MBits/sec. to 2 MBit/sec. or down to d.c. if an asynchronous clock is provided. The maximum range is 0.5 Km increasing to 2 Km at lower frequencies. These transmission distances can be increased significantly by using more expensive fibre optic cable and connectors with the two modules.

7. ACKNOWLEDGEMENT

This work has been carried out with the support of British Telecom. The development of this link has been made possible by the active help and guidance of the following:

P. Hensel and R.C. Hooper - British Telecom, Martlesham
M. Edmonds - Plessey Opto & Microwave Limited, Towcester
A.V. Flatman and N. Baker - ICL, Kidsgrove

N. Batty and J.S. Arnold - Plessey Telecom-munications Research Limited, Taplow

B.J. Prior, D.N. Lee, D.J. McCabe, J.B. Mason, A. Mabbitt, M. Faultless and D. Jenkins - Plessey Research (Caswell) Limited, Caswell

The development of a suitable cable and field terminated connector has been carried out by GEC Optical Fibres and ITT Cannon, respectively.

P J Morgan graduated Queen Mary College, University of London, with honours degree in Physics in 1973. He joined the Wolfson Centre for Magnetics Technology (University of Wales Institute of Science and Technology) where he worked on thin film magnetic recording heads. He received the degree of MSc from the University of Wales in 1977. During 1978 he worked for National Semiconductors Ltd, Montreal Canada, on stability problems in CdS photocells. On returning to the UK in 1979 he took up the post of Research Fellow in Advanced Recording Heads at Plymouth Polytechnic. Since 1981 he has worked at the Plessey Research (Caswell) Centre, where he is currently engaged on packaging problems of optical fibre components.

Geoffrey Sumerling graduated in Physics from the University College of North Wales, Bangor, in 1971 where he also gained a Ph.D. in 1975 for work on Lateral PNP Transistors in Integrated Circuits. Since 1975 he has been employed by Plessey Research (Caswell) on a variety of topics associated with the design of Silicon Integrated Circuits. These topics include process and circuit design for Integrated Injection Logic (I^2L); cell based semi-custom design techniques; and a comparison of processes for VLSI. Currently he is heading a small team designing integrated circuits for fibre optic applications.

Problems in Man-machine Dialogue Design

A L Kidd
British Telecom Research
Laboratories, UK

If interactive computer systems are to be easy and efficient to communicate with then their dialogue design must be compatible with the information processing characteristics of the human mind. This paper aims to illustrate this point by considering the problem of designing auditorally presented menus for interactive voice information systems. The problem is analysed in terms of the information processing constraints imposed by human short term memory. It is proposed that the critical factor in successful user performance is the degree of problem solving required to select the appropriate option from an auditory menu list. User performance on two different auditory menu tasks supports this proposal.

1. INTRODUCTION

Although the use of interactive computing systems is continually expanding in a wide range of applications, the effectiveness of these systems is often markedly reduced because users experience such difficulties in communicating with them. In order to overcome this communications problem, it is necessary to develop systems which are 'user-friendly' i.e. which enable users to interact naturally and effectively with them. The basic principle in designing user-friendly computer systems is to create interactive dialogues which are compatible with the particular cognitive attributes of the human user. This is because the use of a computing system is primarily an information processing task and therefore the user's speed of processing information, the constraints imposed by his limited attention span and short term memory capacity, his communication skills etc. all need to be taken into account in the design of a system [1].

The aim of the present paper is to illustrate this point by considering a particular dialogue design problem i.e. the use of auditory menus in voice information systems. The first section of the paper provides background information on the nature of human short term memory. The problem of auditory menus is then introduced and it is shown how this problem can be analysed in terms of the information processing constraints imposed by short term memory. Two observational studies of user performance on different auditory menu tasks are described and implications for the design of future voice interaction systems are discussed.

2. CHARACTERISTICS OF SHORT TERM MEMORY

Despite the fact that experimental research into human memory has been going on for over a century, there is still much that we do not understand about this topic. As a result, current theories of memory and interpretations of experimental data are still subject to a rapid rate of change. This makes it very difficult to sum up what we know, or think we know about memory in a section as short as this. However, I will attempt to provide a basic outline of those salient features of current thinking on the topic which I see as most relevant to the problems of interactive dialogue design.

One of the most influential models of human memory in recent years was devised by Atkinson and Shiffrin in 1968 [2]. On this model, information from the environment first enters a series of sensory registers (temporary buffers) which hold information in a relatively raw unprocessed state. The channel from the senses to short term memory (STM) is of limited bandwidth which means that more information is available to our senses at any one time than we are able to pay attention to. STM processes the sensations and can hold interpreted units of information for up to about 20-30 seconds [3,4].

STM, however, is not merely a repository for new information but also includes a working memory responsible for decision making, problem solving and the general flow of information within the memory system. These functions are governed by a set of control processes, one of which is rehearsal, the overt or covert repetition of information. Rehearsal is used to maintain information within STM. For example, a telephone number, a stranger's face or a melody will quickly fade from STM unless purposely repeated or reviewed. However, even with rehearsal, there is still a limit to the amount of information which can be held in STM. The capacity limits of STM have been much discussed ever since Miller's classic paper "The Magical Number Seven Plus or Minus Two" [5]. Miller demonstrated that in a wide variety of situations, people can remember only approximately seven items - digits, unrelated words, different tones or whatever. He showed moreover that combining items into 'chunks' (e.g. a string of letters into a meaningful word or a string of digits into a meaningful date) increased the number of items which could be recalled. Miller therefore distinguished between 'bits' of information and 'chunks' of information. Each separate item of information held in STM he referred to as a 'chunk' but the number of 'bits' of information making up one chunk could vary. He concluded that the span of STM is limited to approximately seven chunks of information almost independent of the number of bits of information per chunk. This view is still held as being broadly correct, although it has been shown that memory span is also influenced by such additional factors as acoustic similarity [6] and word length [7].

Because STM incorporates a working memory as well as a storage buffer, a certain amount of interference between the two functions can occur. For example, Baddeley and Hitch [8] reported a consistent impairment of performance on a number of problem solving/decision making tasks when the subject was simultaneously required to remember more than about three items. With less than three items, there was little decrement in working memory performance.

For man-computer interaction, the short term memory limitations described above imply that the processing capacity of computer users is extremely small and is therefore constantly vulnerable to overload [9]. It seems that to make the most effective use of STM we must maximise our ability to recode a number of bits of information as one chunk and we must also take into account the fact that meaningful or familiar chunks are more easily recalled. Also, the Baddeley and Hitch results imply that requiring users to hold more than a small amount of new information in STM severely restricts their capacity for processing other information.

It should be noted here that from STM, information is transferred into long term memory (LTM) either consciously, by using control processes to relate its contents to those of LTM, or unconsciously [2]. It appears that the capacity of LTM is virtually unlimited although information may sometimes become very difficult to retrieve and it is also subject to decay or interference by more recent information.

The function of LTM is to store information and rules for its processing when these are not actually in use. This sort of storage need not be conscious because we do not use all of our knowledge nor all of our cognitive subroutines all of the time. But this information needs to be maintained so that it can be called up into working memory when it is required [10]. The organisation of information in LTM is only poorly understood, but its apparently unlimited storage capacity, its durability of knowledge and rapid recall capabilities enable us to perform a variety of information processing tasks.

3. USE OF AUDITORY MENUS - A DIALOGUE DESIGN PROBLEM

The purpose of this section of the paper is to consider in detail a recently-encountered man-machine dialogue problem in order to illustrate how the information processing characteristics, discussed above, must be taken into account in the design of interactive computer dialogues. The problem considered here is that of auditory presentation of menus in dialogues employing computer speech output of the sort which might be encountered in the development of interactive information systems for use over the telephone. Such systems are constrained, at the present time, to pushbutton entry of data (and therefore to a set of only 12 possible entries) and synthetic speech output. If users are going to be able to freely interact with these information systems without the need for written documentation, then as there are no alphanumeric characters available to them for data entry, it seems that the dialogue will have to be conducted in menu mode.

3.1 Use of menus as an information processing task

In classic man-machine dialogues, where the user is interacting with the computer via a visual display terminal, displayed menus are considered the most easy-to-use and therefore most suitable form of computer-initiated dialogue for inexperienced and/or unsophisticated users. A typical example of the use of menu mode for a hypothetical train timetable information system is shown below:-

WHAT IS YOUR DESTINATION?

```
    1   LONDON
    2   IPSWICH
    3   NORWICH
    4   HARWICH
    5   COLCHESTER
```

ENTER CHOICE>

Some of the main advantages of using displayed menus of this kind are as follows:-

(i)   Ideal for untrained or infrequent computer users - no specialised knowledge or training is required for successful entry of data.

(ii)   Low memory load for user - user does not need to learn command words, parameter names etc. but can select menu item simply by typing a single key.

(iii) Users can still perform effectively even if they are frequently distracted or interrupted [see 1].

In the case of auditory menus, the user's task is a very different one with none of the advantages listed above. The crucial difference is that in contrast to visually displayed menus, auditory menus present a real information processing problem because of their intrinsic incompatibility with the memory and processing limitations of the human user as discussed in the previous section of this paper, namely:-

(i)   A user's short term memory is severely limited in storage capacity and any new input to STM will decay rapidly unless constantly rehearsed.

(ii) If a user is involved in any problem solving, decision making or other information processing, then this will severely restrict his ability to carry out the necessary rehearsal of new information.

The use of auditory menus is also made more difficult by the following:-

- Synthetic speech (in its current state at least) requires more effort to process than human speech.
- The user cannot control the rate at which he receives the information.
- The user does not know how many menu items he is going to have to remember. This may lead to panic.
- The user is not able rapidly to scan the menu list in search of a target item. Each item has to be heard individually.
- Digits paired with words is a difficult combination for people to remember.

How then do the processing limitations of short term memory actually affect user performance on auditory menus? It seems that selecting the appropriate option from an auditory menu list involves both a memory component ("what are the options I'm choosing between?" and "what number do I have to dial for a particular option?") and a problem solving component ("which option best matches my requirements?"). Because of the known interference effect between the storage capacity of STM and its problem solving activities [8], it is proposed that the critical factor in successful user performance on any auditory menu task will be the degree of problem solving required to select the appropriate option from the menu list. For example:-

(a) If the task is such that minimal problem solving is involved (i.e. the 'correct' option is immediately obvious), then the user will be able to reject 'wrong' options as he hears them (and therefore will not need to retain these in STM) and he will recognise the 'correct' option as he hears that. If this is the case then all the user has to hold in STM is the number to dial for the 'correct' option and therefore he should be able to perform the task successfully irrespective of the overall number of options on the menu list.

(b) If, on the other hand, the task involves a much higher degree of problem solving (i.e. the 'correct' option is not immediately obvious for some reason) then the user may not be able to reject 'wrong' options as he hears them (and so will need to retain these in STM) nor may he recognise the 'correct' option as hears that. If this is the case, then the user will have to hold in STM his whole set of possible options and the appropriate numbers to be dialled for each one, and make a decision between them at the end of the list. A strong interference effect will occur between the problem solving activities of this decision making process and the storage capacity of STM [8]. It is very likely

therefore that in this case, the overall number of options on the menu list will be a critical factor in successful user performance.

In order then to identify the degree of problem solving involved in any auditory menu task, it is important to understand something of the nature of the problem solving required to select the correct option from any menu list.

3.1.1 Problem solving in menu selection tasks

Answering any type of simple question is a problem solving task but as long as listeners have the right information i.e. a proposition in memory that matches the given information, then giving the right answer should be relatively easy. However, when the match between the question and the propositions in memory is poor, the listener will experience much greater difficulty in providing the right answer [11]. In other words, the match between a question and the relevant stored information in memory is critical to the speed and success with which that question can be answered. In the case of responding to menus, the problem becomes one of how well the options given match the stored possibilities in the user's head. Recent work by Young and Hull [12] on the use of displayed menus in Prestel suggests that users come to Prestel with some plan in their heads of how to find a particular item of information. As a result they have certain expectations about both the contents and format of any menu before it is displayed. Whether or not the displayed menu matches these expectations will strongly affect the users' ability to select the appropriate option from that menu.

Young and Hull also show that different lists of menu options have different classification structures. Users may again have problems selecting the appropriate menu option for their needs if the classification structure of the menu is not clear to them or if the classification categories used divide up the topic in a different way from what they expect or if the categories overlap and they are not sure which option category is most appropriate for what they want. If any of these situations arise, then the users may be unable to select an appropriate option until they have read through all the options at least once [12].

Obviously, menu selections demanding this type of problem solving/decision making task on the part of the user will create even more severe problems if the menus are presented auditorally rather than visually. This is because:-

(i) There are no visual cues to make the structure of the menu explicit i.e. when the menu options are presented auditorally, the user cannot 'scan' the format and contents of the display before hearing it, to see if the classification structure of the menu matches his expectation. If, therefore, the structure does not match his expectation then he may find it difficult to interpret the individual options as he hears them. Indeed, he may need to hear all the menu options before he is able to work out the classification structure of the menu and therefore before he is able to recognise which option is most appropriate for his requirements.

(ii)   If the user is unable to recognise the option he wants the first time he hears it read, then he must either remember all the possible options and numbers to be dialled and make a decision between them at the end of the list (a very difficult task given the limitations of short term memory); or he must opt to hear the complete menu read through again (a lengthy process).

3.1 User performance on two types of auditory menu task

Having examined the kind of problem solving/decision making requirements of an auditory menu which may most affect user performance; this section describes two studies set up to examine user performance on two different information systems both requiring the use of auditory menus. The purpose of the studies was to test the validity of the proposal that the critical factor in successful user performance on any auditory menu task is the degree of problem solving required to select the appropriate option from the menu list. The first study was designed to minimise the degree of problem solving involved in using auditory menus on an information system whereas the second study (which has only been carried out in pilot form so far) was designed to present the users with a reasonably high degree of problem solving (of the type described by Young and Hull). In both cases, we were interested in seeing how quickly and successfully users could select the correct options from the menu lists presented and whether their performance was affected by the number of options in the menu list.

3.2.1 Study 1 : Recipe Advice System

The system was designed as an example of the kind of interactive information system which could be provided over an ordinary telephone.

Twenty-six members of the public were used as subjects. Each subject was presented with a short written scenario e.g. "You've been asked by your boss to put on a dinner for him and two business associates. There are no limitations as far as the money's concerned ...... etc.". Their task was to familiarise themselves with this scenario and then ring up the service and find a suitable recipe for their requirements. Each subject carried out the task three times with three different scenarios. A vocoded human voice was used in the experiment to simulate synthetic speech.

Once accessed, the system gave a short introduction and told the subject that to repeat any question he should dial 'star' and to get help on any question he should dial 'square'. He was also told that he must not dial his response until the end of the menu

list (a constraint of this particular system). The subject was then presented with eight successive menus of which the one shown below is a typical example:-

HOW EXPENSIVE DO YOU WISH THE MEAL TO BE? ECONOMICAL DIAL 1 / MODERATE DIAL 2 / LAVISH DIAL 3.

The menus varied in length between two and six options. The response times to the different menus were recorded. Also, at the end of each task, the subject was asked to complete a questionnaire about the system.

On the following grounds, it was predicted that the use of this recipe advice system would demand minimal problem solving effort on the part of the subjects:-

(i)   The system covered a very restricted problem domain - that of recipes.
(ii)   Although the written scenario did not explicitly state the answer to each menu question, the information provided implicit clues as to the sort of questions the system would require the answers to and the responses were all readily deducible from the script.
(iii)   Each menu had clear, non-overlapping response categories.
(iv)   Each menu question was independent of every other - i.e. there was no hierarchical tree structure of menus (cf. Prestel).

Results

(i)   All subjects successfully completed the tasks and reported on the questionnaires that they found the system easy to use and had no memory problems.
(ii)   There was no effect of increasing response time with increasing length of menu list. In fact the menu with 6 options had the shortest mean response time (!) but it is suspected that this was due to subjects finding it an 'easy' question to answer for some arbitrary reason.
(iii)   There was no effect of the serial position of the 'correct' menu option in the list.

The results of this study will be discussed in conjunction with those of the study 2.

3.2.2 Study 2 : An Interactive Auditory Database

The idea of carrying out a study on a large interactive auditory database came from a system currently under development at Southampton University which aims to provide a Prestel service for blind users using synthetic speech output and keyed input. Also, the study was intended to explore the feasibility of developing interactive auditory systems which could provide direct access to a range of large databases over the telephone.

Unfortunately, the study reported here has only been carried out in pilot form so far. Prestel was used as the database in the study and several relatively experienced users acted as pilot subjects. These subjects were given the task of retrieving specific items of information from Prestel, e.g. information about the weekly child benefit amount or the temperature in a particular holiday resort. Each subject was then presented auditorally with the standard series of Prestel menu frames (a human voice was used in this pilot study). These menus progressively break down the subject information into categories and on each menu the subject must select the category which best matches the information he is looking for until the specific page of information he requires is reached. The menus covered varied in length between two and ten options. Response times were not recorded on this pilot study. The purpose was to carry out a preliminary observation of how well subjects could perform on this task.

In contrast to Study 1, it was predicted that the auditory Prestel system would demand a high degree of problem solving effort on the part of the subjects. This prediction was made on the following grounds:-

(i)   Prestel consists of a very large database; within this subjects are trying to find highly specific items of information.
(ii) Subjects were given no clues as to how to find the information they required or what menus they would be presented with.
(iii) The classification structure of some of the menus accessed was unclear and in many cases the option categories overlapped.
(iv) The hierarchical tree structure of menus is known to cause problems with the use of Prestel [13].

Results

(i)   Subjects found the task very difficult but always succeeded ultimately in retrieving the information required.
(ii) Subjects often cycled round the same menu several times before they selected the 'correct' option.
(iii) Subjects reported having severe memory problems, particularly with the longer menu lists.
(iv) Subjects independently reported that the absence of visual cues made it (a) difficult to "get a feeling for" the structure of a menu e.g. what the range of choices were etc. and (b) difficult to 'visualise' where they were in the tree structure at any point in time thus making it difficult to decide where to go next.
(v)   On some menus, the option numbers did not start at 1 and included double figure numbers (e.g. 11 - 18). Subjects found these more difficult to remember.

3.2.3 Discussion and implications for future development of voice information systems

The results of these two observational studies support the proposal that the

critical factor in successful user performance on any auditory menu task, is the degree of problem solving required to select the appropriate option from the menu list. If the problem solving required by the task is minimal as in Study 1, then it seems that the auditory menus pose no particular difficulties and users can retrieve the information they require quickly and successfully. The results of this study imply that the development of carefully-designed limited information systems for use by the general public is a feasible proposition. In fact, we are currently testing a train timetable information system based on similar lines. However, it is not clear whether user performance on such systems would be as successful in a real life situation where users would be coming to the system with their own 'scenario' in mind which would be unlikely to match so exactly onto the questions being asked by the system as the artificial scenarios presented to the subjects in Study 1.

In the case of Study 2, where a much higher degree of problem solving was required by the task, the subjects experienced serious difficulties in retrieving information successfully from Prestel. Again this result supports the ideas set out in section 3.1. However, the fact that the subjects on this experiment did ultimately manage to retrieve the information they required from the system implies that the development of large interactive auditory databases may be a feasible consideration for the future. It is critical to the success of such future systems, however, that the problem solving requirements of the auditory menus are reduced to a minimum. It is possible that this could be acheived by implementing some of the following design strategies. The effect of these is currently being explored.

(i)   Incorporating a brief introductory 'blurb' to each menu question which provides the user with some clues about the classification structure of the menu so that he is more likely to be able to recognise the 'correct' option the first time he hears it. This would need to be combined with a 'skip the blurb' option for experienced users.

(ii) Using auditory cues to give the user some information about the structure of the menu and to help him keep track of where he is in the interaction. This could be done by using tones or by using different voices to distinguish between different classes of information e.g. question vs options etc. [14].

(iii) Giving the user some control over the pacing of the synthetic speech output [14].

(iv) Equipping the user with the right set of 'dialogue control acts' [15] (e.g. 'star' to repeat the question; 'square' for help etc.) so that he can always be in control of the interaction and need never get stuck.

4. CONCLUSION

This paper has considered in some detail the problem of using auditory menus in interactive voice information systems. The problem was first analysed in terms of the information processing constraints imposed by human short term memory. On the basis of this analysis, it was proposed that the critical factor in successful user performance on any auditory menu task is the degree of problem solving required to select the appropriate option from a menu list. The validity of this proposal was supported by the results from two observational studies of user performance on two different auditory menu tasks. The results implied that interactive information systems using auditory menus are a viable proposition as long as they are designed in such a way that any problem solving demands on the user are reduced to a minimum.

In conclusion then, this paper has clearly illustrated the point that interacting with a computer is a complex information processing task and therefore to be truly usable, an interactive system must always be designed to take into account the relevant information processing characteristics of the human mind.

ACKNOWLEDGEMENTS

I would like to thank my colleagues in British Telecom Human Factors Division and Dr Richard Young of the Applied Psychology Unit, Cambridge, for helpful discussions on the contents of this paper.
Acknowledgement is made to the Director of Research, British Telecom Research Laboratories for permission to publish this paper.

REFERENCES

[1] A. L. Kidd, Man-machine dialogue design, British Telecom Research Laboratories, Research study no. 1, 1981.

[2] R. C. Atkinson and R. M. Shiffrin, Human memory : a proposed system and its control processes, In K. W. Spence and J. T. Spence (Eds.) Advances in the psychology of learning and motivation research and theory, vol. 2, Academic Press, New York, 1968.

[3] J. Brown, Some tests of the decay theory of immediate memory, Quarterly journal of experimental psychology, vol. 10, 1958, 12-21.

[4] L. R. Peterson and M. J. Peterson, Short-term retention of individual items, Journal of experimental psychology, vol. 58, 1959, 193-198.

[5] G. A. Miller, The magical number seven, plus or minus two: some limits on our capacity for processing information, Psychological review, vol. 63, 1956, 81-97.

[6] R. Conrad and A. J. Hull, Information, acoustic confusion and memory span, British journal of psychology, vol. 55, 1964, 429-432.

[7] A. D. Baddeley, H. Thomson and M. Buchanan, Word length and the structure of short-term memory, Journal of verbal learning and verbal behaviour, vol. 14, 1975, 575-589.

[8] A. D. Baddeley and G. Hitch, Working memory, In G. H. Bower (Ed.) The psychology of learning and motivation, vol. 8, 1974, 47-90.

[9] B. Shneiderman, Software psychology: human factors in computer and information systems, Winthrop Publishers, Inc. Cambridge Mass., 1980.

[10] R. Lachman, J. L. Lachman and E. C. Butterfield, Cognitive psychology and information processing: an introduction, Lawrence Erlbaum Associates, Publishers, Inc. New Jersey, 1979.

[11] H. H. Clark and E. V. Clark, Psychology and language: an introduction to psycholinguistics, Harcourt Brace Jovanovich, Inc., 1977.

[12] R. M. Young and A. Hull, Cognitive aspects of the selection of viewdata options by casual users, Proceedings of the 6th international conference on computer communication, 1982 (in press).

[13] N. S. Sutherland, Prestel and the user, Report commissioned by the Central Office of Information, 1980.

[14] S. L. Smith and N. C. Goodwin, Computer-generated speech and man-computer interaction, Human factors, vol. 12, no. 2, 1970, 215-223.

[15] H. C. Bunt, F. F. Leopold, H. F. Muller and A. F. V. van Katwijk, In search of pragmatic principles in man-machine dialogues, IPO Annual progress report, vol. 13, 1978, 94-98.

BIOGRAPHY

Alison Kidd obtained an MA in Psychology from St Andrews University in 1977 and a PhD in human stereoscopic vision from Sheffield University in 1981. She joined the Human Factors division at British Telecom in January 1981 where her main research interests include computer dialogue design, interactive voice systems and the development of expert systems.

Basic User Engineering Principles for Display Editors

H Thimbleby
University of London, UK

Based on a small set of straight-forward principles, this paper gives a preliminary set of user interface guidelines (for text editing type tasks) and their rationales. The purpose of this paper is to present reasoned guidelines, and hopefully stimulate research, or argument, both to check premises and to improve the reasoning and its scope.

OVERVIEW   "Like all Vogon ships it looked as if it had been not so much designed as congealed." {1}

There is still great diversity in the design (read congealing) of the low level aspects of interactive systems, even within the same application area. Although there are recognised and accepted methods specifically for interactive text editing (e.g. scrolling, cursor motion, overwriting etc.) there is little agreement on the best way in which to implement them for particular classes of user and task. This is partly because

- display technology no longer places overriding restrictions on text representation and manipulation.

- with the increase in processor capability per user, there is no need to buffer user input simply to achieve acceptable efficiency.

- programming standards have improved.

- negligible _relevant_ human criteria.

User interfaces are therefore idiosyncratic at best, and at worst they are unpredictable (because they are designed without conceptual constraint in lieu of implementation constraints) -- this is most noticeable in error and boundary situations, unfortunately also being where the user needs most support.

Thus guidelines are required for designers; especially designers who are constructing systems for users who do not wish to become system experts but who are nonetheless skilled in their own task domain.

This paper examines some design decisions in screen based text editing in order to relate them back to more abstract design principles. A distinction must be drawn between necessary and merely attractive features or attributes (e.g. 'power') -- many so-called desirable features are detrimental to user acceptability. Most systems are designed on a vague combination of prejudice and principle -- prejudice for proscriptive design and principle for retrospective epigrams.

On the whole, I derive principles here by laying emphasis on predictability and skill acquisition (both in the mechanics of typing and with a computer based system -- which may also involve learning new typing conventions).

Systems can improve predictability by better use of feedback and by more consistent behaviour. A number of low level principles suggested here are contentious (and might thereby be classified as prejudices): keystroke count is not a good design guideline; overwriting is bad (and can be avoided); there should be no 'blank spaces'; repeat keys are bad; etc.

INTRODUCTION

Many systems appear to be designed around <u>ad hoc</u> principles or within entirely local paradigms. Interactive systems are frequently designed personally for (say) 1.2 actual users, and may be imposed on a user community running into thousands: interactive systems standards reflect parochial prejudices, rather than serious attempts to meet the needs of most final users. The worse the paradigms are, the more work users have had to expend in acquiring skill with their systems, and the less likely they are to accept 'objective' improvements. Thus designers, as experienced users themselves, are often confused between power and ease-of-use; the more powerful their system is, the harder it <u>used to be</u> to use (which is soon forgotten), and in contrast (having learnt an awkward system) other systems do not give a better results-capability to learning-cost payoff.

A common question a designer asks of a proposed system is, "can it do such-and-such (which takes 2 keystrokes on my system)?" -- and the implied rejoinder, "if it can't then it's no use." This ignores the concept of usage strategies: slightly different interfaces may encourage the user to operate in radically different fashions, and it is possible that certain facilities will be a hindrance if provided in one context. **A system ought not be designed as a collection of "good ideas", but must be an integrated, coherent whole.** Discussion in this paper may be incompatible with the reader's favourite interface for this reason.

It is important in any discussion of interactive systems design not to get into defending extreme points of view. Some people may prefer certain styles of interaction and that is their right; but in this paper I am discussing the design of interactive systems for others who will often not be computer specialists. Indeed, few computer scientists are skilled typists, and 'short cuts' (e.g. command completion) in dialogue may be heavily biased for wrong requirements if the final users are professional typists.

Finally, I exclude from this paper task organisation (and social) aspects of man-machine interaction and very specific details of interaction (including hardware issues), such as which key does what (not implying these issues are trivial). We may assume, subject to superordinate considerations, that system response should be minimised and need not be discussed further.

With this brief discussion as background, I can give a few concise principles and discuss their implications for text processing system design.

BASIC PRINCIPLES

1. Evaluate -- adopt user experience
Interactive systems are inevitably out of step with user requirements. This is either because they are badly designed or because their use has suggested new possibilities to users. Although rigorous evaluation is certainly tedious, and likely to have results of strictly restricted applicability, this is not to say that informal evaluation is without its value. Monitoring user commands and errors (where this is not intrusive), gathering user feedback and watching users on-line, can help indicate potential improvements. In particular, any "improvements" can be evaluated by comparing with previous results. Using evaluation is an example of 'engineering out the errors'.

On the other hand, users may be reluctant to adapt to an 'improved' interface. Moral -- give the prototypes substantive user exposure.

2. Ensure predictability
First, note that any functioning computer system is presumably self-consistent but not necessarily predictable to the user! And it is not true that the more a user knows about the system state, the easier it will be to predict how to interact with the system; there is some optimum window onto the state set which facilitates use -- the user can be overcome by clutter (although what degree constitutes unacceptable clutter varies according to the user).

There are two levels of predictability: cognitive and ballistic. Humans tend to plan task performance ahead, and gather sequences of actions into "response units". The more practised a user, the longer will response units become -- if the skill is acquired by rote learning it is likely that the response

units become inflexible, however it is a characteristic of skill (as opposed to habit) that response becomes more flexible. There is evidence that humans perform remarkably well if response sequences in progress are adjusted infrequently[*]; such responses may be called ballistic. For example, little use is made of visual feedback once a response unit is enacted. Thus, if the response is to be successful, the interface must be sufficiently predictable for the pre-planned response to be valid throughout its utterance. It is asserted that an interface is preferable if it encourages the steady acquisition of increasingly long response units: this is only possible when there is requisite compatability between the user's model and the perceived interface behaviour. (It is clear that such a system would provide positive reinforcement to the user, since practice will develop the user's skill and hence job satisfaction.) The more skilled the user then, the larger the area of dialogue which is covered by ballistic considerations. Corollary: the more unpredictable a dialogue at the ballistic level the harder it will be to use, and the less "user friendly".

At a cognitive level of predictability we are concerned with determining strategies of anticipated task execution: the main influences on cognitive predictability are obvious, and include training, documentation, attention-getting diagnostics, social determinants (e.g. how accessible the local expert is). Although there are systems which are exceptional, we may assume, for the purposes of this paper, that routine text editing can be performed without involving specialised problem solving skills, for users with sufficient training and experience. Indeed, it is clear that text editing in a non-computerised environment is entirely routine and is functionally almost equivalent -- it has a clear "user model".

3. Ensure congruence -- avoid task interference
The user wishes to perform tasks with minimum interference from the system as a system per se, as opposed to using it as a tool for the task in hand. This is simply an extension of point 2, and has been termed passivity elsewhere {7}.

SUMMARY (so far)

These points may be summarised with reference to the user model:

1 refine/find/create/define a user model
2 use it emphatically
3 do not elaborate on it (Occam's razor)
   -- subject to 1

The user model
These three stages are iterated until an acceptable implementation emerges. The user model is partly defined by designer, partly brought to the system by the user (as influenced by training and documentation) and partly acquired from the operation of the

---

[*] On slow systems, users may type ahead of system feedback anyway.

system -- it may not be wholly conscious or verbal but may be quite complex and sophisticated♦. Most problems, certainly all complaints, stem from a mismatch between the user's model and the model embedded in the system. Thus the designer should have a clear notion of user model and implement it faithfully -- and completely. The user rarely knows what areas are hard to implement and would be surprised by (to him) inexplicable omissions. Even noble maxims like "what you see is what you get" go a long way towards helping the designer express user-related concepts in a which may be reflected in the implementation: such notions form the basis of a user model and all development should be with respect to them. Any common ground between designer and user, even such as this type of maxim, should be utilised.

SOME IMPLICATIONS

4. Fast -- 'reactive' (from 2, 3)
Speed is of course critical for initial skill acquisition; skilled typists can correct typing errors using motor responses and it would unnecessarily restrain users if feedback was delayed in excess of their own response times.

The importance of immediate feedback to the use of display manipulating functions cannot be over emphasised. There is, of course, now considerable evidence that interactive systems must respond to [routine] user requests as fast as possible and preferably be perceived as instantaneous -- especially for initial skill acquisition; user satisfaction and effectiveness are often inversely correlated with feedback time. A delay in visual feedback disrupts error checking, although skilled typists adapt to delays after several minutes of normal typing (it is not clear that they would under the complex feedback conditions typical of iteractive systems).

5. Feedback -- Diagnostic support (from 2)
Prompts and clear status indicators should always be used♦, and displayed in conventional (or otherwise expected) screen locations. A point which is often overlooked is that a command (or key) which does nothing still requires feedback, and a command which takes a noticeable time to start generating results should give some feedback to indicate that processing has already commenced.

Error conditions, which occur either due to a mistake in the user's understanding or in enacting an intended response (e.g. typing errors, but including consequences of reaching system limitations) are the main restriction on ballistic predictability. It is important that the user is informed as rapidly as possible when the system detects unexpected input: and any diagnostic must attract attention. Sound

---

♦ Contrast the complex nonverbal model a pilot has of his aircraft.

♦ Assuming the display is large enough and has sufficient resolution. (They are less important on hardcopy terminals.)

should always be used as an attention getting device (possibly supplemented by explicit displayed text if the sound is non-specific).

Note that loud sounds may be socially unacceptable -- colleagues may be aware, for example, of a user's "error" rate. This problem may be avoided by: volume controls and directional transducers (or headphones), user selected sound, and by making noises after errors and in certain other well defined situations.

6. Recoverable (from 3)
Reversibility is difficult to implement for any non-trivial system (impossible if there is communication with other systems or isolated subsystems), but the user is going to make mistakes and should be provided with reasonable means to recover from their consequences. It is not feasible to provide an "undo" operation for all eventualities, but it certainly increases interface acceptability if a well defined subset of actions is reversible. Reversibility can be applied to the smallest detail -- e.g. if the user can move the cursor right there should be an analogous function to move the cursor left etc. To recover at higher levels the user should be able to alter previously issued commands and resubmit them. Undo facilities (when available) have to be learnt, and this imposes an avoidable burden on the user: having lost text, it is equally easy to get into an emotional state which makes correct use of typical undo systems unlikely.

Three techniques simplify uniform application of recoverability:

- textual commands   } or equivalent
- text editing   } combinations
- use of windows
    (so text may be edited independently)

Various, clear, techniques can enable command operands to be reused without retyping {6}. Even conventional command processors may be interfaced with text editors (or, equivalently, terminals with editing capability).

7. Mode-free (from 2)
Modes are sets of states (in a state automaton model of the user interface) with no more than one transition for each lexime. For example, if "d" means variously delete or duplicate, then the meanings (state transitions) occur in different modes.

A problem occurs when the system changes modes but the user is unaware of this, or the user is aware but is stressed by keeping track of mode changes.

Modeless operation may be achieved by immediate evaluation of postfix commands.

COMMENTS

8. When copy typing (and interviewing, say, with computer-aided form filling etc.) the user cannot pay undivided attention to the display, so it is crucial that interactive systems are extremely predictable. It is worth emphasising again that consistency does not of itself imply predictability.

9. If the user issues an editing command which cannot be obeyed for some reason, such as <**move left**> at the left hand side of a line, then the system should respond with an <u>audible</u> diagnostic (or indeed, any stimulus in a non-visual mode), such as a bell. This will enable the user to type without paying undivided attention to the system's visual feedback: without sound it would be extremely risky attempting to copy type/edit, or make any alterations to text whilst looking at a (paper) document. Again, this feedback should be effectively synchronised with user typing.

10. The facilities should encourage confidence in using similar sequences of keystrokes to do similar sorts of edits. The facilities should allow the same sorts of edits to be performed in the same sort of way irrespective of context. Thus the user will be able to learn generalisable habits. The facilities should not have subtle variations depending on the type of text being edited. **The user interface is a (conceptually) separate software module and does not interact semantically with the application.**

One important thread in the ideas suggested throughout this paper is that they not only form a coherent whole, but there is, in fact, no need to distinguish between entering new text (including commands) and editing existing text.

11. It is disruptive to use a mixture of computer-selected command protocols, especially at times guided and occasionally unguided; e.g. menus and positional commands.

12. Since the user is generally unaware of implementational issues, their intrusion into the interface significantly reduces predictability (although usually eases the task of implementation). Records, buffers, backing-up, conversions and so on should be handled transparently.

13. Read the literature {2,3,4...}.

SOME SPECIFIC GUIDELINES

14. The user should be able to edit what is displayed, rather than the underlying data representation. Thus tabs (and other layout directives) are transparent to the user.
  > <u>Rationale</u>. Tabs are at best an archaic form of data compression, and should not concern the user. (I am not discouraging use of tab-like editing functions on the keyboard.) See point 12.

15. Editing functions should not be displayable and this implies per-key responses (at least for these functions).
  > <u>Rationale</u>. If editing functions <u>are</u> displayed they mess up textual layout, and can be ambiguous when mixed with text. If they are not displayed, the user can only be aware of their intended effect if it occurs immediately on typing.

16. All blanks should be treated as 'written spaces', records should be transparent... all parts of the screen should be "equal" (equally editable).
  > <u>Rationale</u>. If editing capabilities are position dependent (e.g. trailing blanks on lines "don't exist" and can't be edited) the user will first have to construct a model of the text which is not <u>quite</u> what can be seen. This does not preclude a separate representation for written spaces (e.g. small dots). Many systems treat typed and unlit parts of a screen (which looks like spaces) differently, and thereby confuse the screen editing user model.

17. Both replacement and 'expand/closeup' tend to lead to overlapping modes (e.g. erase and delete, written and blank spaces). In addition, the expand technique for insertion does not nest, and a situation like "<insert> A C <**move left**> <insert> B (between A and C) <**move right**> <insert> D" to achieve ABCD is awkward.
  > <u>Rationale</u>. Expand/closeup methods for insertion rely on a special "insert blanks and then overwrite them" philosophy. This confuses the rôle of blanks. The introduction of additional modes is detrimental, and the screen does not show at <u>all</u> times what the user is editing.

18. Replacement is by itself inadequate -- but offering replacement <u>and</u> insertion is confusing.
  > <u>Rationale (a)</u>. Replacement is inadequate because there is no means to lengthen text, which is sometimes necessary. Providing both insertion and replacement facilities opens up the possibility that the user may accidentally assume the system is in the other mode; since no diagnostics are implicit in replacement mode, it is possible for users (e.g. copy typists) to lose arbitrary amounts of work.
  > <u>Rationale (b)</u>. Diehards may be reassured that if sufficiently long <u>continuous</u> replacements are required*, or indeed if there are sufficiently long insertions adjacent to deletions, a sensible interface with both insert and replace modes will always require fewer keystrokes for the same final effect. But the probability of mode related user error is doubled. The only justification for providing a replace mode is to reduce system (or communications line) overheads. On small personal systems (that is, ones with limited address space) the extra program space required if both insertion and replacement are supported should be a further argument not to support replacement as well; in fact, per-character insert/delete will have <u>less</u> code overheads than any other complete and sufficient method.

---

* Thereby excluding on-line composition or review: i.e. pure copy editing.

19. The clearest method of text editing uses per-character insert/delete, by "shuffling", without an 'expand/closeup' operation. Display editing by per-character shuffling for insertion and deletion, with no supplementary methods, is the ideal way, given the resources and an adequate response time, for typing and editing documents.

> Rationale. Primarily because at all times, the display shows exactly what the form of the text is and, in particular, this makes the layout of text, tables and diagrams very simple. (The fact that there is no mode change between insertion and deletion is also important when wraparound is supported.)

20. Reversible highlighting gives the user incremental control over defining large pieces of text and can be a basis for generalised commands.

> Rationale. Highlighting provides a direct way of specifying textual operands, e.g. for copying, movement or deletion. If the boundary of the highlighted area can be moved under cursor control, this provides a direct -and visible- user model.

21. Repetition factors (e.g. n in: do command n times) are not useful -- except in specialist applications where the extra learning burden is acceptable.

> Rationale. Most of their advantages are achieved in a more user-oriented way by defaulting command parameters and providing <repeat>. Immediate feedback can drastically alter the user's needs: step keys can be used more easily and accurately than a step command which requires prior counting.

22. Auto-repeat keys are never useful: if an equivalent facility is required it should be achieved with a separate repeat key (which need not operate on "dangerous" keys). The situation is improved if keys click when repeated.

> Rationale. Resting ones' fingers on the keyboard inadvertently can have disastrous consequences. Whatever the appeal of repeating keys they are rarely implemented correctly: holding down a key until it repeats (or hitting it and a separate <repeat> key) then releasing it should immediately stop the repetition.

23. Minimising user keystrokes (on a per-subtask basis) is not a useful predicate alone. However it is definitely worth getting a preliminary system operational and monitoring usage to find, for example, frequently used command sequences which might be condensed.

> Rationale. Minimising keystrokes loses redundancy. It is clear that a replace mode provides for minimal editing of replacements, insert mode for minimal editing of insertions (and so on) but although keystrokes per subtask (for replacement, insertion respectively) are minimised, keystrokes per task may not be affected sufficiently to warrant the inclusion of specialised keystroke-reducing features if each additional feature increases interface ambiguity (and learning time etc.)

CONCLUSION

The discussion above is a small step towards designing better text editors and hence word processors. It is not suggested that the guidelines are complete, sufficient nor necessary for every application. Indeed, it may be that you disagree with specifics -- if this leads you to reason about the user interface, so much the better. There is certainly more work required in this area, and it is hoped that the manner of presentation -- namely, background reasoning and airing the author's marginally enlightened prejudices -- will stimulate further work!

The user interface should:

- be faithful to the user model
- provide current feedback
- be context independent
- respond to each user action immediately

Being faithful to the user model implies that the system is sufficiently predictable so that it may be used effectively without requiring the user's undivided attention -- few actual systems meet even this minimal criterion.

By "current feedback" I mean that the system not only gives feedback, but keeps the feedback up-to-date. As mentioned (e.g. most recently under point **19**), the display should provide current feedback on the state of the text being edited.

The latter two points indicate that the user interface can be effectively implemented separately from the application, essentially as a structured peripheral handler, possibly in the workstation or terminal.

BIBLIOGRAPHY

{1} D. N. Adams, <u>The Restaurant at the End of the Universe,</u> Pan Books Ltd., London (1980). [Worth reading, if irrelevant.]

{2} A. Cakir, D. J. Hart & T. F. M. Stewart, <u>The VDT manual,</u> IFRA, Darmstadt, FDR (1979). [Review of hardware ergonomics for video terminals.]

{3} B. R. Gaines, The technology of interaction -- dialogue programming rules, <u>International Journal of Man-Machine Studies,</u> **14** (1981), 133-150. [A systematic development of general interactive programming rules.]

{4} M. Maguire, An evaluation of published recommendations on the design of man-computer dialogues, <u>International Journal of Man-Machine Studies,</u> **16** (1982), 237-261. [A brief but clear review.]

{5} H. Ledgard, J. A. Whiteside, A. Singer & W. Seymour, The natural language of interactive systems, <u>Communications ACM,</u> **23** (1980), 556-563. [A "natural" editing interface is demonstrated to be more successful than <u>functionally equivalent</u> stereotypical computerese: this is a controversial paper which deserves attention.]

{6} H. W. Thimbleby, Text editing interface -- definition and use, In press. <u>Journal of Computer Languages</u> (1982). [Defines and discusses a complete editing interface based on ideas of this paper.]

{7} H. W. Thimbleby, Character level ambiguity: consequences for user interface design, <u>International Journal of Man-Machine Studies,</u> **16** (1982), 211-225. [Gives a relevant analysis of some low-level interface issues.]

Harold Thimbleby is a lecturer in Computer Science at Queen Mary College. His main area of research is in developing applicable criteria for interactive systems design. He is married and has two children.

Usability and its Multiple Determination for the Occasional User of Interactive Systems

P Barnard, N Hammond
MRC Applied Psychology Unit, UK

For occasional users of interactive packages, factors such as choice of vocabulary, dialogue style and its structure are critical determinants of ease of use. However, these explicit factors are not the only important considerations. Many implicit factors also influence performance:- the general cognitive demands imposed on the user by the system; the context in which a dialogue exchange occurs; the particular problem the user is trying to resolve; and the cognitive strategies adopted by the user himself. Examples of the multiple determination of user-system performance will be drawn from laboratory studies of interactive communication. The wider "user-friendliness" of human-computer dialogues is best viewed as multiply determined by dialogue, task and user variables which influence performance as a result of subtle interactions rather than as simple main effects.

The computer industry is now placing considerable emphasis on the development of forms of human-computer communication that are usable or "user-friendly". This emphasis reflects a growing acknowledgement of the requirements of a whole range of actual and potential users who have little or no expert knowledge of the mechanics of computing. There is now considerable evidence, (e.g. [3]), that such users all too often experience difficulties in understanding what a system is doing or how they should operate it.

The difficulties are particularly marked for occasional users whose occupation imposes only intermittent requirements to interact with one or more software packages. Applications in information retrieval, text processing, decision support, electronic mail, etc., offer substantial potential benefits for occasional users. However, such users will only benefit if they can learn and remember how to operate a variety of systems without too many demands being placed on their intellectual resources and on their patience.

One of the more frequently reported types of difficulty concerns the nature of the "language" employed in human-computer dialogues and in associated documentation. Occasional users often identify computer "jargon" and unfamiliar usage of terminology as important contributors to their lack of understanding [3]. They also report difficulties in being able to remember, from one occasion to the next, the details of dialogue transactions required to complete a particular operation. One of the reasons for these types of difficulty has been that the process of software design has been "computer-centric" (e.g. see [4]). Software designers have, for one reason or another, assumed that end-users share their specialist experience and knowledge or that users would have to learn or adapt to it.

There can be little doubt that many of the problems faced by occasional users of specific systems could have been avoided or substantially reduced had more attention been paid to the nature and requirements of end-users. However, it is relatively easy to identify the problems in human-computer communication and to trace their origins in the process of software development. It is far more difficult to analyse these problems in a way that provides clear recommendations for the development of truly usable dialogues. One reason for this is that problems in communication are fundamentally of a cognitive nature. Difficulties arise because of an incompatibility between system dialogue and the users' cognitive skills in communication, in mobilising their knowledge from memory or during problem solving. From a human factors point of view these skills are themselves poorly understood. This general lack of understanding of the nature and functioning of human cognitive skills means that we must approach the problems of producing firm recommendations for usable dialogues only with considerable caution. There are numerous claims that one form of dialogue is more usable or "natural" than another. However, as we hope to illustrate, many of the detailed issues underlying these claims will be resolvable only if we develop our basic understanding of the ways in which human cognitive skills function in the kind of constrained communicative context of human-computer dialogues. It is the purpose of this paper to discuss these issues.

One approach to providing an initial analysis of potential issues has been outlined by Morton et al. [4]. This analysis points out than an "ideal" occasional user would, amongst other things, possess perfect knowledge of the task he is required to perform, the command language used, aspects of the particular computing procedures and devices (terminals etc.) that are relevant to his task, and a perfect grasp of the properties of the particular software version of the application (e.g. a relational database) together with knowledge of the information it can provide and manipulations it can perform. Obviously, most occasional users will possess less than ideal knowledge concerning each of these areas. Furthermore, amongst the "other things" possessed by this type of user are knowledge of natural language, knowledge of other procedures and devices as well as knowledge and experience of non-computer means of achieving the same ends (e.g. a filing cabinet).

Any lack of correspondence between "ideal" knowledge of a system and the normal functioning of the user's cognitive skills could lead to <u>cognitive incompatibility</u> between the user and the system. Conversely, correspondence between the "ideal" and the "actual" might be expected, via cognitive compatibility, to enhance the learning, use and retention of system requirements. Since human-computer communication implicates a variety of cognitive skills and types of knowledge, we expect the overall usability or cognitive compatibility of a system to be multiply determined. The evidence furnished by research in cognitive psychology also suggests that human performance in communication depends not so much on individual factors operating independently of each other (e.g. syntax, vocabulary, meaning etc.) but rather upon their interrelationships in particular environments and task contexts.

The remainder of this paper will review some of the major points which have emerged from a series of studies designed to investigate the multiple determination of the usability of dialogues. The first two studies focus on keyboard entry of pidgin command languages and the second two focus on simple menu selection of command elements.

Consistency and Compatibility in Command-Argument Sequences

The first of our series of studies focussed on three aspects of the relationships between command verbs and their arguments. These are best introduced by reference to examples. A command such as DELETE might require two arguments, an entity to be deleted, X, and some location or context, Y, from which it is to be deleted. Thus, the command sequence might be DELETE ⟨X⟩⟨Y⟩. The corresponding "natural language" version of this command would usually be "Delete entry X from file Y". It would be rather less usual to state "Delete from file Y, entry X". Except in special circumstances the direct object of an imperative verb comes before its indirect object in the structure of an English sentence. Thus, one way of structuring command strings in a manner compatible with natural language would involve mapping argument identities onto the simple ordering principle COMMAND VERB ⟨ DIRECT OBJECT⟩⟨INDIRECT OBJECT⟩. On this basis a command set for file handling and editing might include DELETE ⟨ENTRY X⟩(from)⟨FILE Y⟩; MOVE ⟨FILE Y⟩(to)⟨LOCATION P⟩; INSERT ⟨ENTRY X⟩(into)⟨FILE Y⟩; RENAME ⟨FILE Y⟩(with)⟨NEW

NAME Q⟩; etc.

In this particular example one of the arguments, "the filename", is common to several commands, as might also be the case with, for example, line numbers in a text editor. Use of the natural language principle ⟨DIRECT OBJECT⟩⟨INDIRECT OBJECT⟩ has the consequence that the position of the common argument varies from command verb to command verb. In this respect the command set is positionally inconsistent in relation to the common argument. It could be argued that this positional inconsistency is undesirable and that the command set would be easier to learn and remember if the common argument occupied a consistent position. In this case, the user would simply have to learn and remember the identity of the variable argument for each command, plus the positional rule. Thus, the set might be organised COMMAND VERB ⟨VARIABLE ARGUMENT⟩⟨COMMON ARGUMENT⟩. This principle would yield the following set DELETE ⟨ENTRY X⟩(from)⟨FILE Y⟩; MOVE (to) ⟨LOCATION P⟩⟨FILE Y⟩; INSERT ⟨ENTRY X⟩(into)⟨FILE Y⟩; RENAME (with) ⟨NEWNAME Q⟩⟨FILE Y⟩; etc. The disadvantage would be that for a subset of commands the positional rule would be incompatible with the ⟨DIRECT OBJECT⟩⟨INDIRECT OBJECT⟩ principle discussed in the context of natural language.

Compatibility with natural language and positional consistency/memory considerations might also conflict with a third cognitive component: perceptual strategies in reading. For example, the values of a number of variables may be displayed on the screen. If a pair of these were in a different order from the order required in command entry, users would have to reorder the arguments in their own heads. This is because the normal reading strategy would lead to an order of encountering argument information which was incompatible with their required order of entry. We will refer to this factor as display compatibility.

The relationships among these linguistic, memory and perceptual forms of consistency and compatibility were investigated in a task where naive users learned how to operate a system for deciphering "secret" messages (see [1]). One group of users learned a command set based on natural language compatibility (COMMAND VERB ⟨DIRECT OBJECT⟩⟨INDIRECT OBJECT⟩); another group learned a set involving an inverse natural language order (i.e. COMMAND VERB ⟨INDIRECT OBJECT⟩⟨DIRECT OBJECT⟩; and two further groups learned positionally consistent command sets (either COMMAND VERB ⟨COMMON ARGUMENT⟩⟨VARIABLE ARGUMENT⟩ or COMMAND VERB ⟨VARIABLE ARGUMENT⟩⟨COMMON ARGUMENT⟩). The command set consisted of six operations all of which were required to find, decode and store a message. A "message identifier" was the argument common to all commands. An example of the task is shown in Figure 1 for an INVERT operation. The operation to be performed next was always indicated by a command being high-lighted in the uppermost field of the display. Thus, a user's task simply involved learning argument identities and their order.

```
                    *** ATHENE DECODER ***
----------------------------------------------------------------
  Search      Trim        Replace    Invert    Delete     Save
----------------------------------------------------------------
Invert groups of characters in the message
(Specify group size and message identifier)
--) invert group size, message identifier (ENTER)
----------------------------------------------------------------
Message identifier: 33   Code number: 19   File number: 5   Groupsize: 3
----------------------------------------------------------------
                    Current message state
     GEPUSA :S5A5EHT SNO5T5R EMO5A UGU5T5R* FE5ERE5CN 5E4
----------------------------------------------------------------
invert 3 33
----------------------------------------------------------------
----------------------------------------------------------------
----------------------------------------------------------------
```

Fig. 1. Study I. Sample display
during task solution.

The second field in the display contains
instructions. This information was present
during the decoding of the first two messages,
but could be optionally called upon during
later learning if the user remained unsure of
what to do. The third field specifies values
for a subset of arguments. For all groups of
users display compatibility was manipulated by
systematically rearranging this field. In the
case of the command current in this display,
the required order of argument entry (group
size, message identifier) is incompatible with
their displayed order in the argument field.
The fourth field shows the current message
state and the fifth field shows the actual
command in the course of entry. Illustrative
data are reproduced in Figure 2. These data
show the number of times additional
instructional information was required during
the decoding of the eight messages. The
findings on both errors and times showed a
similar pattern.

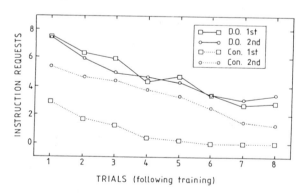

Fig. 2. Study I: Mean referral to
instructions across the 8 post-training
trials for the 4 groups.

Essentially there was no overall difference
between the command sets involving the natural
language "principle" of placing the direct
object first (DO1) and the inverse order where
the direct object occurred as the second
argument (DO2). In this case natural language
compatibility did not appear overall to
enhance learning relative to its inverse.
However, there was some evidence of

interfering effects attributable to this same
principle. Where a command required its
arguments to be specified in the inverse of the
natural language order, then the number of
argument reversals was found to correlate
reliably with an independent measure of user
preferences.

Performance with the positionally consistent
command structures was generally superior on
all measures where the position of the common
argument varied. However, this superiority was
almost entirely due to the positionally
consistent command structure (CON1) where the
common argument preceded the variable argument.
On most performance measures the alternative
(CON2) positional arrangement was not
significantly different from the two
positionally variable command structures (DO1
and DO2). Only in the case of the frequency of
reversed argument errors were both positionally
consistent command structures superior to the
positionally variable ones. In fact, both
positionally consistent command structures
virtually eliminated reversed argument errors.
This absence indicated that the positional rule
was adequately represented in the user's memory
from very early on in the learning process.
However, the absence of a clear superiority on
the other measures when the common argument
occupied the second argument position suggests
that the simple existence of a positional rule
did not generally enhance the learning of the
identity of the variable argument. This
advantage apparently only accrued to the
command structure where the variable argument
was the last element in the command string.
Accordingly simple accounts concerning a
reduction in overall "memory load" must be
superseded by a more subtle and a more complex
interpretation (see [1]).

The effects of display compatibility were
relatively straightforward. For commands where
the order of arguments in the appropriate field
on the display was incompatible with their
required order of entry, then users experienced
more difficulty. This was reflected in
increased time, more errors and greater
recourse to the instructional information.

The Influence of the User's Task and the
Command Vocabulary

Our second study, followed up the strong
effects of positional consistency (see [2]).
The user's task was made more complex in three
respects. First, the user was required
actively to select and enter commands rather
than being prompted by the system. Second, the
command set was expanded from six to twelve so
that the total set could involve two "common"
arguments referring to different classes of
objects (Tables and Messages). Third, to
decode a message users were required to perform
four mandatory operations on tables followed by
four operations to decode a message. The four
decoding operations had to be chosen from among
eight possible options. It was assumed that
these changes would force users to understand
the nature of the operations more fully than in
the previous task. In addition the type of

command vocabulary was varied. Users were either faced with a command vocabulary derived from "general" verbs (e.g. USE, EDIT, CHANGE) or from more specific equivalents (e.g. LIST, ERASE, REPLACE) which implicitly provide more semantic information concerning the nature of the operations they perform. As such the general terms were expected to be more confusable than the specific ones and to be more difficult to interpret. Thus, this second investigation compared four types of command sets derived from the combination of general or specific vocabularies with the two alternative realisations of positional consistency (CON1 and CON2). An example of the table manipulating phase of the task (to establish "codes" for subsequent message decyphering) is shown in Figure 3. This illustrates the different class of object to be manipulated and the larger menu from which all commands had to be selected.

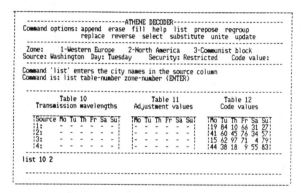

```
----------------------------ATHENE DECODER----------------------------
Command options: append erase fill help list prepose regroup
                 replace reverse select substitute unite update

Zone:   1-Western Europe   2-North America   3-Communist block
Source: Washington Day: Tuesday    Security: Restricted   Code value:

Command 'list' enters the city names in the source column
Command is: list table-number zone-number (ENTER)

     Table 10                Table 11               Table 12
Transmission wavelengths   Adjustment values       Code values

|Source Mo Tu Th Fr Sa Su|  |Mo Tu Th Fr Sa Su|  |Mo Tu Th Fr Sa Su|
|1:     -  -  -  -  -  - |  |-  -  -  -  -  - |  |19 84 10 66 31 27|
|2:     -  -  -  -  -  - |  |-  -  -  -  -  - |  |41 60 45 76 34 57|
|3:     -  -  -  -  -  - |  |-  -  -  -  -  - |  |15 62 97 71  4 79|
|4:     -  -  -  -  -  - |  |-  -  -  -  -  - |  |44 38 18  9 55 83|

list 10 2
```

Fig. 3. Study II: Sample display during task solution.

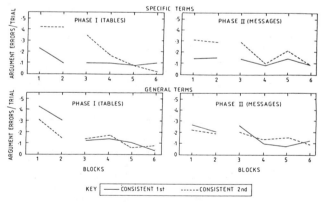

Fig. 4. Study II: Mean argument errors across the 6 blocks (pairs of trials) during table and message manipulation phases for the 4 groups.

Figure 4 illustrates the main findings as a function of experience with the four types of command sets investigated. With the "specific" commands, there is an advantage for placing the common argument first. This confirms the finding in the first experiment, where the commands were also specific. There is, however, an important qualification to

this result. Unlike the previous study the relative advantage of placing the common argument first declines rapidly with increasing experience of operating the system. In fact, the advantage is clearest during the training phase (blocks 1 and 2 of Figure 4), when users were explicitly informed what the next command should be. A more dramatic contrast is found with the "general" commands (lower panel of Figure 4). There were no reliable differences between the two alternative realisations of positional consistency for either table manipulations or message manipulations. Thus, the advantage of placing the common argument first is obtained when the task conditions most closely approximate those of the previous study. With specific commands, as soon as the users must utilise their own judgment in the selection of commands, the effects of the structure of the command string rapidly diminish for both table and message manipulations. On the other hand, when general command terms are used, the user is forced to think about the system operation rather than being able to rely on the semantics of the command.

The fact that the findings of the first experiment do not generalise across all task conditions should not be taken to mean that users' behaviour is unsystematic or un-principled. It simply means that any coherent analysis of the usability of different forms of dialogue must take into account an analysis of the cognitive demands imposed by the task conditions and those imposed by the type of command vocabulary. The full reports of these investigations consider the cognitive under-pinnings of these results in greater detail ([1] and [2]).

Consistency and Compatibility in Menu-Oriented Communication

The first two studies involve keyboard entry of complete command strings. Two further studies involved simple menu selection. Since they involved comparable tasks and command structures they will be summarised together.

For both experiments the basic task required users to answer a sequence of preset questions on the basis of information stored in a data base. The information was structured into a set of objects (FILES, LISTS, TABLES, STATE-MENTS, ITEMS) which could be manipulated by an equal number of functions (DISPLAY, COMPARE, DELETE, INSERT, REPLACE). Using these functions and objects, users were asked questions such as "Display the file for agent Aquarius. Does it contain a list called travel?" The question could be answered by selecting a function (e.g. DISPLAY) and an object (e.g. FILE) from command menus. In addition, instructional information could be obtained via a HELP function. For the first ten questions, the answer could be derived after a single transaction (DISPLAY FILE). The last four questions were more complex and required two such transactions (e.g. DISPLAY FILE; COMPARE LIST).

The two experiments differed in terms of a dialogue constraint. In one experiment (FREE ORDER) both functions and objects were displayed in a single menu. To answer a question users had to select one function and one object but they were free to choose these in either order. The full menu is illustrated in Figure 5. The position of the functions and objects in that menu was also varied. For one group of users the functions were displayed above the objects and for the other group the objects were above the functions (as in Figure 5).

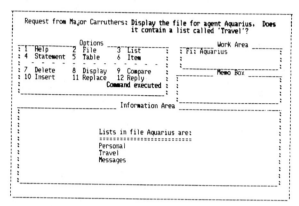

Fig. 5. Study III: Sample display during task solution

In the second experiment (FIXED ORDER) the functions and objects were presented in separate menus. Users were either first shown the menu of functions and then the menu of objects or vice versa. Thus, these users were forced to use a fixed order of entry. The fixed sequence either reflects the usual ordering in an imperative in natural language "Open the door" or the less usual form "The door should be opened" which conveys a rather different meaning.

In both experiments one further structural variable was manipulated concerning task relevant information. This concerned the structure of the question asked. The questions either mentioned function information first (Display the file for agent Acquarius...) or object information first (The file for agent Aquarius should be displayed...). The variation in the structure of the question mirrors the display compatibility variable in the case of the pidgin command language of the earlier studies. Finally a "semantic" variable was manipulated in relation to functions and objects by initially providing different instructions concerning the individual terms in the vocabulary. For half the users the function terms were fully defined and the object terms simply listed in context. For the other half, the object terms were fully defined and the function terms simply listed. In certain respects this variation in initial instruction mirrors the use of general and specific verbs. Specific terms were assumed to provide the user with more implicit semantic information than the general terms. Formal definition of objects

or functions provided additional information for one set explicitly.

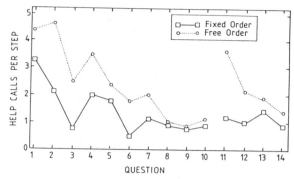

Fig. 6. Study III: Use of "help" across questions for fixed and free dialogue

Figure 6 shows some representative data for the comparison between conditions of free and fixed order of entering objects and functions. Two points emerge from these data. First, users under the "free" condition required more "help" than those under the fixed order of entry.Second, although this effect disappears over the course of the first ten questions (single transactions), it dramatically reappears when the more complex two-transaction questions are encountered (questions 11-14). Even though performance levels had become equivalent, only in the fixed condition did this performance level transfer directly to the more complex questions. Apparently the "free choice" users had actually learned less about the system which would generalise to new types of problem. The parallel here with the pidgin command language is that order uncertainty is present in the "free" condition and in the positionally inconsistent arguments of the first study where positional consistency provided one condition for enhancing learning.

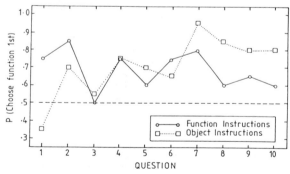

Fig. 7. Study III: Effects of initial instructions on order of entry in free dialogues

Another parallel with the pidgin command languages emerges from the difference in performance between the free order of selection and the fixed order. As with the positionally variable arguments of pidgin command structures, there is order uncertainty in free selection. In both cases natural language predispositions biased performance. With pidgin command languages it was related to reversals in argument order and with menus it was related to order of selection. Figure 7 shows the probabilities of users selecting a function first, dependent upon the provision of initial definition of functions or objects. Overall there is a bias in the "natural language" direction of specifying a function prior to the object. However, for the first question dealt, initial instruction overrules this general bias. Users given object definitions tend to select objects first. As learning progresses the bias rapidly switches towards selecting functions first.

This does not mean that natural language predispositions will invariably exert an influence. When the order of selection was fixed by sequential presentation of two menus, the "natural" order (FUNCTION-OBJECT) and the "unnatural" one (OBJECT-FUNCTION) gave rise to the same levels of performance throughout the course of learning. As with the pidgin command languages, when there is no order uncertainty, structuring the dialogue according to a natural language principle apparently did not enhance overall learning.

Again, as with the influence of display incompatibilities on pidgin command entry, menu selection was biased by other forms of information available to the user. In the "free" condition there was a significant bias towards selecting the term which corresponded to the first mentioned item in the question posed. Likewise in the free order of entry more errors were precipitated when a selection was being made from those terms in the lower half of the menu.

Discussion

The studies which have been summarised reveal aspects of the multiple determination of the usability of human-computer dialogue. The fact that there are parallel findings for keyboard command entry and straightforward menu selection could be seen as encouraging for the development of guidelines such as "natural language characteristics do not necessarily enhance learning", "display incompatibilities may lead to error", or even "fixed principles can enhance learning and performance". However, to do so would be essentially misleading and would miss the principal implication of the findings.

Such summary statements serve only to capture limited aspects of the data. The findings also indicate that user performance is highly task dependent. This applies both for continuous and transient task demands. The continuous demands may be provided by the need to select commands rather than the simpler need to follow prompts; by the type of command vocabulary; or by the presence of order uncertainty. Transient task demands may be provided by a current display of information; or by the exact form of question which the user wants to answer.

The important implication is that the structure and content of the dialogue itself would never provide a sufficient or complete analysis of usability. A more appropriate form of analysis would involve a consideration of the way in which the user's cognitive strategies for learning and using the system recruit a variety of sources of information which can be used to fulfill the objectives of those strategies. Some of these sources will be external - as with displays of information, others will be represented in the user's own memory - as with an ordering rule, knowledge of the natural language meaning of terms, system knowledge etc. The experimental evidence demonstrates that users actually recruit these sources of information in different ways as a function of the task demands. For example, where there is order uncertainty, we find that natural language orderings, menu structures or the order of items in a parameter field may be strategically recruited to govern actual order of entry. Where there is no order uncertainty different sources of information may be recruited with other consequences for user performance. For example, absence of order uncertainty may have provided better conditions for the encoding in memory of detailed information concerning the nature of functions and objects. Subsequently, this information is more readily available to cope with the change to more complex questions . Apparently such information was not so readily available to users who had learned the system with free ordering of functions and objects.

In sum, a major implication of this research is that our analyses of human-computer dialogue should not solely focus on the formal properties of dialogues. Rather it should take the form of an integrated analysis of the cognitive skills underlying user performance and the different sources of information and knowledge which these skills draw upon. Guidelines or recommendations which avoid these issues are unlikely to prove fruitful.

REFERENCES
[1] Barnard,P., Hammond,N., Morton,J. & Long,J. Consistency and compatibility in human-computer dialogue, Int. J. Man-Machine Studies, 15, (1981) 87-134.

[2] Hammond,N., Barnard,P., Clark,I., Morton,J. & Long,J. Structure and content in interactive dialogue. Paper presented at Annual Convention of the Amer. Psych. Assoc., Montreal (1980).

[3] Hammond,N., Long,J., Morton,J., Barnard,P. & Clark,I. Documenting human-computer mismatch at the individual and organizational levels, in Mitchell,P., Nassau,S. & Struk,S. (eds.), Improving Individual and Organizational Productivity: How Can Human Factors Help? New York: Human Factors Society (1980) 34-56.

[4] Morton,J., Barnard,P., Hammond,N. & Long,J. Interacting with the computer: A framework, in Boutmy,E. & Danthine,A. (eds.), Teleinformatics '79, Amsterdam: N. Holland (1979) 201-208.

User/Programmable-device Communication: an Informational Simulation Approach

W R Feeney
San Diego State University, USA

A microprocessor supported device requires a well designed user/device interface. The interface design activity needs to precede the hardware and software design, however this is impossible without the physical device to test user/device communication dialogues. This paper describes an approach, called informational simulation, which was used to simulate the communication dialogue between a user and a medical instrument prior to designing the device hardware. This concept is applicable to the design of user interfaces for computers and other logic supported devices.

BACKGROUND

Since the advent of the microprocessor, entirely new types of scientific and medical instruments have been created. These are microprocessor supported devices which make use of the internal program execution capabilities of micro-processors to perform complex tests requiring highly sophisticated control of scientific or medical processes. These devices have a common trait with most programmable systems, general purpose computers included; they have a need to acquire operational information and data from their users. Designing an efficient communication interface between the user (who both uses and operates the device) and the programmable device is the focus of this paper.

PROBLEMS OF INTERFACE DESIGN

Sizable problems exist in designing the interface between user and device. First, there seems to be a reluctance of some instrument designers to recognize the user as an essential part of the entire system.(1) Without a user, most programmable devices are little more than expensive collections of parts. It may seem obvious that user functions are required for programmable devices to work, but because two widely different areas of designer expertise are involved in producing a well designed interface the area of electrical and mechanical hardware, and the area of user psychology, the user interface can become a neglected part of the design process.

Even when the user is considered part of the system, there is a tendency in the design process of a microprocessor supported system to get the hardware working successfully before formulating the way the user will communicate with the hardware. Then, when the successfully operating hardware allows the leisure to think about user communication, hardware oriented designers tend to resolve user/instrument interface problems by concentrating on making hardware changes without looking closely at user functions. It is understandable that engineers feel more comfortable working with hardware, but the result of this lack of attention to user functions produces, at best, a makeshift method of communication with the instrument. At worst, the interface of the user and instrument is inefficient and unnatural to use.

Still another user/instrument design problem is the lack of a well developed theoretical basis for designing a communication dialogue. Although rules of thumb have been formulated through experience, researchers and phychologists are just beginning to understand how to communicate effectively with computers and computer supported devices. (2) With no theoretical foundation from which to start, the communication guidelines for the dialogue between user and instrument must be developed by trial and error. Without overall theoretical guidance, decisions sometimes are made which adversely affect the interface design. These design decisions are frequently made without benefit of input from the type of people who will, typically, be using and operating the device.

A SOLUTION TO INTERFACE DESIGN PROBLEMS

This paper suggests a method by which system designers can determine how users will want to communicate with a programmable device, specifically a medical instrument. It tells about an approach used to design a user/device interface well before the hardware design for the instrument was frozen. A method of informational simulation was used to design the communication interface. This interface information then contributed to completing the hardware design.

This method of designing the user/instrument interface was a definite improvement over the more traditional "wait until later for the user-instrument interface" approach. The method basically consists of writing computer programs to simulate display screens produced by an instrument. Other programs received the user's input, edited them for appropriateness and took simulated action based on the input. Typical users from the population of potential users were asked to operate the simulation in exactly the same way they would operate the instrument itself. Based on their reactions, the interface design was changed and refined. This system allowed the testing of otherwise untested user-device dialogue before freezing the instrument hardware designs.

Informational simulation of the user/instrument interface is highly visual rather than mathematically analytic. It displays CRT screens with which the user works instead of modelling the mathematical dynamics of the system. The informational simulation program we produced used standard data processing techniques. Although the BASIC programming language was used, any compiler or interpreter language which supports string handling could have been used. An inexpensive micro-computer with modest memory and storage capacity was used to run the simulation.

The approach taken to develop a simulation of a user/instrument interface involved five steps:

1. Requirements Definition

2. Instrument Test Sequence Description

3. Static Display Screen Design

4. Informational Simulation

5. Refining The Interface Design

STEP 1. REQUIREMENTS DEFINITION

Here the expected performance of the micro-processor supported instrument is defined in terms of what tests it will perform, what information it will output, what information it must be supplied, how this input information will be supplied (automatically from sensor input or by the user), and what functions the user will perform (both informational and operational). A narrative description usually comes first. As the expected performance of the instrument becomes clearer, qualitative and quantitative performance definitions become possible. It is in this step that major requirements can be defined, and, when desirable, the requirements can be easily changed since they are still in an early planning stage. For example, early in the requirements definition it was thought that the name of the test to be performed by the instrument should be keyed in by the user. Later, it was decided that the name (40 alphanumeric characters in length) should be input by a sensor mechanism reading it from the label of a "kit" of reagents inserted into the instrument.

Operational requirements are defined in a similar manner. For example, it was decided, after an early brief analysis of the informational requirements of the instrument, that a keypad with decimal digits and some special keys would be preferred to a full typewriter keyboard. Later, the actual functions of the special keys were determined.

STEP 2. INSTRUMENT SEQUENCE DESCRIPTION

Using the requirments definition, flow charts (or some other detailed description technique) are prepared to show the functioning of the hardware. Figure 1 illustrates one page of 17 pages which completely described how the hardware would sequence through a single test. The test sequence description consisted of 13 separate modules of which this page was module number six. The flowcharts follow the standard data processing conventions for flowchart symbols: rectangles represent program routines, diamond shaped symbols are decisions, asymmetrical symbols with pointed left sides represent a single CRT screen display, etc. The dashed boxes represent tables in the micro-processor RAM memory. Coded designations adjacent to some of the flowchart symbols tie these symbols to other more detailed explanations. The budget for test sequence description did not permit a finished graphics representation of the flowcharts. They were judged, and correctly so, to be working documents only, and as such hand lettering was satisfactory.

It can be noted that this flowchart representation of the test sequence worked well, but it is not the only representation possible. Everything in this flowchart could be replaced with other equally satisfactory representations.

STEP 3. STATIC DISPLAY SCREEN DESIGN

For every CRT display symbol in the hardware sequence description it is necessary to develop a static screen design. Each such screen is coded to tie it to a particular symbol in the flowchart. The 30 or so screens produced for this design effort, of which Figure 2 is an example, were printed using a custom written microcomputer program. This approach was used to produce static display screens so each display could easily be changed and reprinted. We found the need for a number of changes at this step in the design of the communication interface. Changes were required because of hardware design considerations, and as a result of comments from people posing as users of the instrument.

The four determinants of rational human behavior (3) proved useful at this stage of interface development. The four determinants in equation form state:

User's goal +
Task structure +
User's knowledge +
User's processing limits
= User's behavior.

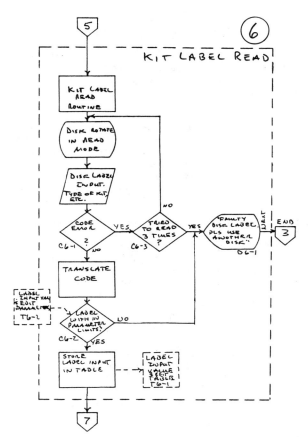

Figure 1. One of thirteen pages of
flowcharts which made up
the Test Sequence Description.

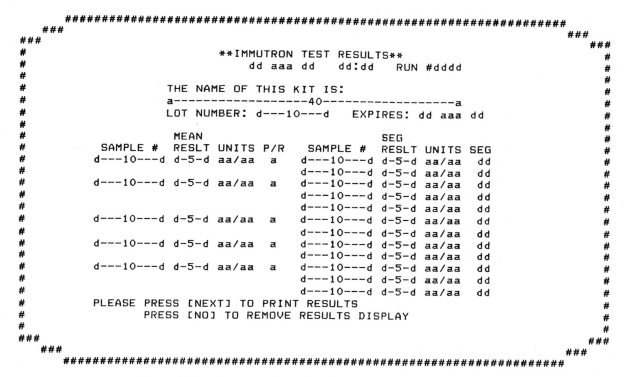

Figure 2. An example of a Static Display Screen.

This equation states that when the user is engaged in goal-oriented activity he attempts to accomplish his goal as effortlessly as possible, within the constraints imposed upon him by the structure of the task, by what he knows, and by his own information processing limits.

Three of the four determinants are outside the designer's control. The user's goal, knowledge and processing limits must be assumed to be at certain levels. These assumed levels subsequently become the definition of the user's personal characteristics.

The single remaining determinant, task structure, is the only one directly under the designer's control. It should be noted that the assumptions of the other three determinants, user's goal, knowledge and processing limits will indicate the structure and level of detail necessary in the interface design. Specifically, the assumptions will indicate the amount of user explanation required, the amount of motivational dialogue necessary and the need for simplicity of moving between display screens.

In the detailed design of the screens, several excellent sources of practical guidance are available. Although no theoretical basis for why these rules work exists at this time, they were found to be helpful as design suggestions. A comprehensive discussion of man/computer interface design is found in Martin's book.(4) Two topics were particularly helpful: alphanumeric dialogues and psychological considerations of users. Another source of helpful interface design information is the discussion of screen design guidelines. (5) Here, practical advice on menus, prompts, information presentation, messages and replies are given.

STEP 4. INFORMATIONAL SIMULATION

The instrument's interface with the user is realistically simulated in this step. A computer program was written similar to the one written to produce the static displays. This simulation program presents displays on a CRT while accepting user responses. Using the program, it is possible to interact with the simulated instrument in the same manner as with the completed instrument. For our instrument, user/instrument communication was to be through response buttons and a CRT with permanent output information being printed on paper. Since the micro-computer used to run the simulation had a CRT with the same capacity the instrument CRT was to have, the informational simulation was realistic looking indeed.

```
################################################################

                 **ENTRY FROM KEYPAD**

  IS THIS A PATIENT SAMPLE NUMBER?

  PLEASE PRESS [YES] OR [NO]

  ------------------------------------------------------------
          ***CURRENT INFORMATION AND MESSAGES***



  ------------------------------------------------------------
  SAMPLE NUMBER ENTRIES
                  PAT/  SGL/                          PAT/  SGL/
     SG,SAMPLE-NUM REF   REP          SG,SAMPLE-NUM   REF   REP
      1,                               7,
      2,                               8,
      3,9224003    P                   9,
      4,                              10,
      5,                              11,
      6,                              12,

################################################################
```

```
################################################################

                 **ENTRY FROM KEYPAD**

  IS THIS A PATIENT SAMPLE NUMBER?

  PLEASE PRESS [YES] OR [NO]

  ------------------------------------------------------------
          ***CURRENT INFORMATION AND MESSAGES***



  ------------------------------------------------------------
  SAMPLE NUMBER ENTRIES
                  PAT/  SGL/                          PAT/  SGL/
     SG,SAMPLE-NUM REF   REP          SG,SAMPLE-NUM   REF   REP
      1,                               7,8248007      P
      2,                               8,
      3,9224003    P     1             9,
      4,                              10,
      5,                              11,
      6,                              12,

################################################################
```

```
################################################################

                 **ENTRY FROM KEYPAD**

  IS THIS A PATIENT SAMPLE NUMBER?

  PLEASE PRESS [YES] OR [NO]

  ------------------------------------------------------------
          ***CURRENT INFORMATION AND MESSAGES***



  ------------------------------------------------------------
  SAMPLE NUMBER ENTRIES
                  PAT/  SGL/                          PAT/  SGL/
     SG,SAMPLE-NUM REF   REP          SG,SAMPLE-NUM   REF   REP
      1,                               7,8248007      P     1
      2,                               8,
      3,9224003    P     1             9,
      4,                              10,4762010      P
      5,                              11,
      6,                              12,

################################################################
```

Figure 3. An example of a sequence of Display Screens which appeared during a simulation run.

Figure 3 shows a sequence of display screens which appeared during a simulation run. Normally the screens would appear on a CRT display one at a time as needed, but they are shown here to illustrate a sequence of a few screens. Data was entered by the user at a position specified on the CRT by a cursor (◆ symbol). Although very little change can be noticed here from one screen to the next, the effect of data characters appearing on the face of the CRT as they are entered by the user is much more attention holding.

The sequence of screens in Figure 3 represents less than four percent of the screens for a typical cycle of the instrument. The actual informational simulation presented all of the potentially possible screens and permitted movement from one screen to another just as the finished device would permit.

It should be noted that for purposes of information simulation other types of simulated output, not conforming to a standard CRT, can still use a standard CRT. An instrument display of five lines and 40 characters per line can be programmed on only a portion of a CRT, ignoring the remaining unused space on the simulation tube.

STEP 5. REFINING THE INTERFACE DESIGN

It is during this step that the interface design produced thus far is checked by having typical users, chosen from the population of those who will use the new instrument, work with it as if it were the finished instrument. This exercising of the simulation program will point out dialogue deficiencies of the user/instrument interface. Once the deficiencies have been isolated, they can be corrected and the improved interface can be tested by further simulation. I found the temporal patterns generated by dynamic simulation produced a realistic feel for communicating with the instrument in a manner not possible with just the static display screens. It was similar to the difference betweeen seeing pictures of an automobile and actually driving the automobile.

The use of informational simulation by typical users produces comments which were quite helpful in finalizing the user/instrument interface design. This final design remained unchanged in all essential elements when it was incorporated in the actual medical instrument. It was rewarding to see the final workable interface design plugged into the developing instrument design just like another well designed hardware or software module. We experienced no need for the quick fixes and design compromises usually associated with last minute interface design.

CONCLUSIONS

The informational simulation approach was used to design the user/instrument interface for a new micro-processor based medical instrument called the IMMUTRON being produced by Immutron, Inc., Newport Beach, California. The instrument is an immunoassay device which performs tests on extremely small concentrations of various substances in blood and other biological samples. The instrument uses specially manufactured disk shaped kits to run small numbers of samples inexpensively and quickly.

A sophisticated yet straight forward user/instrument interface was required for the instrument to communicate with occasional users. The interface was designed, tested and successfully implemented using the informational simulation approach. This approach can be used on any kind of design effort of a computer or device supported by a programmable processor which requires a user interface.

REFERENCES

(1) T.P. Moran, An applied psychology of the user, ACM Computing Surverys, vol.13, March 1981, 1-11.
(2) G. Robertson, D. McCracken and A. Newell, The ZOG approach to man-machine communication, Int. J. Man-Machine Studies, vol. 14, 1981, 1981.
(3) A. Newell and H.A. Simon, Human problem solving, Prentice Hall, Englewood Cliffs, N.J., 1972.
(4) J. Martin, Design of Man-Computer Dialogues, Prentice Hall, Englewood Cliffs, N.J., 1973.
(5) D.E. Peterson, Screen design guidelines, Small Systems World, February 1979, 18-37.

 Dr. Feeney has a B.A. in Physics and Mathematics from Winona, Minn. and a Ph.D. from University of California, Irvine. He has held positions in the computer industry with Remington Rand Univac and General Electric, in aerospace research with McDonnell Douglas. Presently he is an associate professor in the Department of Information Systems at San Diego State University.

Information, Computer and Communications Policy at the OECD

H P Gassmann
Organisation for Economic
Co-operation and Development, France

In October, 1980, a High Level Conference on the theme "ICC Policies for the 80s" was held at the OECD. It covered four main themes:

- Information Technology and the Economy

- The Management of Information Infrastructures

- Information Technology and Society

- International Information Flows

These four themes now constitute the medium-term programme headings of OECD's Working Party on Information, Computer and Communications Policy (ICCP), which on April 1st, 1982 was elevated to Committee status.

Some issues of current concern forming part of this medium-term programme which touch more directly on ICCC interests will be discussed in the following.

1. OECD PRIVACY GUIDELINES

Adopted by the OECD Council in September 1980, they constitute a by now well-known international Recommendation. Of the 24 Member countries of OECD, only Australia, Canada and Ireland have abstained from being part of this Recommendation. The OECD Guidelines consist of five parts:

(i) Definitions and Scope of Guidelines.

(ii) Basic Principles of national application (Collection Limitation; Data Quality; Purpose Specification; Use Limitation; Security Safeguards; Openness; Individual Participation; Accountability)

(iii) Basic Principles of International Application: Free Flow and Legitimate Restrictions.

(iv) National Implementation.

(v) International Co-operation.

Since the adoption of these Guidelines, annual meetings of government officials with responsibility in this field provide the opportunity to discuss the implementation of the Guidelines as well as new emerging issues. Countries which have already enacted general data protection laws consider that they fully comply with the Guidelines. These countries are: Austria, Denmark, France, Germany, Iceland, Luxembourg, Norway and Sweden. Canada and the United States have enacted partial privacy protection laws relevant to data stored by federal agencies or departments. In the United States, the Department of Commerce has vigorously promoted the OECD Guidelines and invited private companies and associations to voluntarily adhere to them. So far, 141 large U.S. firms and banks, and 12 trade associations have adhered to the OECD Guidelines, which means that they will implement their principles in corporate policy.(1)(2)

Another group of countries such as Italy, Japan, the Netherlands and the United Kingdom are at present actively considering what form privacy legislation should take. In these countries, the OECD Privacy Guidelines constitute reference documents. Finally, in the OECD Member countries where so far privacy legislation concerns have not surfaced, the Guidelines have the function of raising the general awareness level of the issue.

2. TRANSBORDER DATA FLOWS

In some countries especially private enterprises doing business abroad tend to consider privacy legislation as a barrier to data flows across borders. It is true that some privacy protection laws contain clauses which inhibit the transfer of personal data abroad if the receiving country does not provide an equivalent data protection. This may pose problems to firms, banks, airlines, travel agencies etc.; in practice so far there have not been many cases of data being stopped from being transferred abroad purely on grounds of privacy protection violation. But increasingly attention focuses on the treatment of "non-personal" transborder data flows.

*The views expressed in this paper are those of the author and not necessarily those of the OECD.

There are some questions raised, and concern expressed, over the effects of the rapidly increasing data communications on multinational firms, the domestic employment situation, the trade balance and on liability issues, to name just a few.

Multinational companies increasingly rely on computer-to-computer (or terminal) data communication, as part of their nervous system. Generally, most of the traffic is between headquarters and branches, but increasingly spider-web networks are created, where the main radial traffic is supplemented with circular or horizontal lines. The question arises whether the existence and use of data communications increases the centralisation of the decision-making process in such firms. Some say it does; others argue that overall planning by objective had already been centralised before the massive use of data communications, whereas day-to-day management of branches as profit centres will always remain decentralised.

In some countries a loss of data processing jobs in branches of multinational companies with headquarters outside the country is feared. It is argued that the growing centralisation of company-wide data processing gives headquarters the main role in overall systems development, maintenance, software standards etc., and reduces highly skilled computer jobs in branches. All these cases concern data processing *within* a company, where no market transactions take place.

A different situation exists when market transactions occur, as in the case of sales of computer services, data bank services (including videotex services), and combinations thereof. Here the services carry a price tag, and can be compared to physical goods which can be imported and exported. To date it is difficult to evaluate the money value of these "commercial" transborder data flows, because of the poor quality of statistics. Most international trade data rely on customs documents as source. However, information services are still badly defined in statistical terms and are often not even measured. For instance, how can the value of a package of a data base with modelling capability accessed in difference countries over telecommunications circuits be evaluated?

Another issue of a more legal character is the question of liability in data communications. This normally refers to situations where errors in data bases, or data transmission leads to an economic loss of the data user. Who is responsible for such losses? The present contractual relations

between data providers, data transmitters and data users often are not clear, and have been frequently established on an ad hoc basis. This is understandable given the newness of this type of business. The rapid generalisation of data communications on an international scale however make a better definition of these liabilities necessary.

An OECD Expert Group on Transborder Data Flows is at present investigating the economic and legal dimensions of these issues. In co-operation with the Business and Industry Advisory Committee of the OECD (BIAC), a survey has been launched in order to arrive at a more factual description of what is occurring, and to analyse the policy implications of these development trends.

3. INTERNATIONAL TELECOMMUNICATIONS SERVICES

The continuing rapid innovations in computer and communications technologies also affect the market structures in telecommunications services. In real terms, the productivity of telecommunication services has increased over the past decades, and has partly been reflected in a relative reduction of costs. In order to further reduce costs to the user, in some countries competition is introduced in what was until recently basically a monopoly. In other countries it is argued that a monopoly situation is still justified because of the public service nature of these services. Internationally, there are diverging views especially concerning "value added" services, where a service provider leases communications lines from a carrier, and provides specialised services such as data communications.

Many users do not understand why there are sometimes substantial cost differences in international telecommunication services for the same distance, depending from which country a line is used. Nobody claims that the price should be exactly the same (as in airlines, where small price differentials are common due to fluctuation of exchange rates and other technical factors). But too large cost differentials are noticed and criticised, because large users (industrial firms and banks for example) nowadays have the means to compare these tariffs internationally. Some users even argue that too high communications costs or unavailability of leased lines are barriers to transborder data flows.

While this view may be exaggerated, telecommunications carriers or administrations nevertheless have to adjust to the fact that these comparisons are made, and that communications cost factors may have an increasing weight in decisions of multinational firms on where to locate branches or manufacturing facilities. Telecommunications tariff differences between countries should be reduced in order to avoid a too great distortion of cost conditions in an increasingly competitive and international environment. Modern telecommunications infrastructures providing low cost services, nationally internationally, will increasingly form the backbone of modern information industries, and may have significant effects on overall productivity and the competitiveness of a country. In December 1982 a meeting will be held at the OECD to discuss policy issues in this field.

4. VULNERABILITY OF COMPUTERISED SOCIETY

Precisely because of the growing importance of these information infrastructures, it is necessary to plan them in such a way as to avoid a too great potential vulnerability. Computer and telecommunications systems are highly complex, especially if they work in network situations. Hence they are potentially vulnerable to sabotage and espionage, lack of spare parts, natural disasters such as earthquakes, but also to industrial action. This vulnerability can be decreased (at a cost) through improving their robustness by systematically developing redundancy, introducing encryption, increasing physical security and availability of back-up systems, and training for emergencies.

Private corporations do of course have the desire to protect themselves against computer/communications vulnerability, and many are actively pursuing such objectives. Gone are the days where computer centres were proudly displayed in ground floor windows as a sign of modernity of a company; today such centres operate in more concealed places. But for cost reasons there are limits to what an individual firm can do; rather, it becomes a matter of collective action, either at an industrial branch level or even at national level. Sweden has been in the forefront in investigating computer vulnerability issues; and proposing recommendations at government level. But increasingly it is reported that for example bank associations finance a common back-up computer centre to enable its members to switch to it should an emergency occur; or that different companies situated geographically in the same area do the same. In May 1981, the OECD held a seminar in Sigüenza (Spain) where policy issues in this field were discussed. More recently, attention has focused on telecommunications exchanges. In November 1981, a fire destroyed the main telephone exchange in Lyon (France); the population of this city suddenly found that it relied quite heavily on the telephone in its day-to-day business and private life. But also more than 50 per cent of the international telephone traffic between Paris and Italy was interrupted for some days.

A major effort was undertaken by the French PTT administration to prevent this sudden loss of a major telephone exchange to paralyse its entire telephone traffic. It is encouraging that the "healing rate" was rapid in this case, but the event points to the need for telecommunications carriers to train for such emergencies. The most recent case of damage to a telephone exchange occurred in Madrid (Spain), when in March 1982 a brand new, super modern telephone exchange was destroyed by bombing. It would seem important that in the future policies be developed to increase the robustness of computer and communications networks. They should be designed in ways so as to minimise damage in the event of fire, sabotage or natural disasters. Employees using computerised work stations should be trained to retain a "paper-capability" so that in the event of a loss of computer power, minimum vital operations can still be carried out, if more slowly. This may be relevant even to electronic mail: it may be too dangerous in the medium-term if society would rely exclusively on an electronic mail system; a redundancy with paper-based mail may need to be maintained because of requirements of societal survival interests.

*   *   *

Without doubt the coming years will see a continuation of the rapid innovations in the computer-communications field. There is no need any more - as during the 70s - to argue that they will have important implications on the citizen and economic activity in general - this is accepted by most people. The crucial question will be how we use these technologies, and how we can insert them in our daily lifes in such a way as to be sure that they bring maximum economic and social benefits to everybody. This is a continuing challenge in all countries. It will be the role of the OECD's Committee for Information, Computer and Communications Policy to assist countries through effective international co-operation in meeting this objective by exchanging experience, analysing development trends, developing international agreements, in short, having an early warning function.

FOOTNOTES:

(1) "Respecting Employee Privacy" in
    Business Week, 11.1.1982.

(2) "U.S. Business comes clean on
    personal files" The Times,
    13.1.1982.

 Hans-Peter Gassmann is
Head of the Information,
Computer and Communica-
tions Policy Programme
of the Organisation for
Economic Co-operation
and Development (OECD)
in Paris. Since 1969, he
has developed the Organ-
isation's work on com-
puter and telecommunica-
tions policy, social
dimensions of information technology,
protection of privacy, and transborder
data flows. His background is in
economics and engineering.

Regulation and Monopoly in Public Telecommunications: Theory and International Experience

M Tyler
Communications Studies & Planning
International, USA

In many areas of the world, the established "European model" of industry structure for telecommunications is under challenge. The rapid evolution of a competitive marketplace for telecommunications services in the USA has stimulated consideration of an alternative, market-based competitive model for the organization of telecommunications in many countries. This paper reviews the issues involved in deregulation from an analytical point of view, defines broad policy alternatives, assesses the advantages and disadvantages of each, and discusses what can be learnt from recent experience in the USA and elsewhere.

I. INTRODUCTION

The purpose of this paper is to review three fundamental questions about competition policy:

o What are the broad alternatives for the structure of the industry?

o What trends can be discerned in that structure?

o What are the arguments, from a public-interest point of view, for and against such a trend?

In considering these questions, it is useful to classify broadly the industry-structure for the telecommunication carrier industry of each country into one of three broad categories:

o The Government Monopoly ("European PTT") Model. In this model a government department has an extensive monopoly of the carrier business. Examples include France, Japan and until recently the UK.

o The Regulated Private Monopoly Model. Here a private company is given a carrier monopoly, which may be general or limited to particular services or geographic region. Until recently this was the prevalent model in the USA. It is also the primary model followed in Canada, Spain, Italy and several other countries.

o The Competitive Model calls for either almost unrestricted entry into the communications carrier business, as in the USA, or at least the licensing of some number of competitive entrants.

TRENDS IN INDUSTRY STRUCTURE FOR TELECOMMUNICATIONS

USA

The traditional monopoly in the USA first came under challenge in the area of interconnection of "customers' premises equipment" (mainly terminals and PBX installations), setting a pattern that has been reproduced in many other countries. In 1968, the FCC made its landmark "Carterphone" decision, allowing a device that interconnected non-AT&T mobile radio-telephone systems to the public telephone network. This was followed by a complex series of decisions

tending towards the opening up of terminal equipment markets: in 1969, new suppliers of PBXs and key systems in the USA (the "interconnect vendors") had a market share of only 0.03%; by 1974, this had risen to 3.7%.

In the early 1970's, after a protracted legal and regulatory battle, the FCC began to include carrier services as well as terminals in its pro-competitive policy, by allowing the construction of a microwave system by Microwave Communications Inc. (MCI), to compete with AT&T's leased-line services on a common-carrier basis and this was followed by the entry into the carrier business of several competitors, including Southern Pacific Communications (SPCC) and USTS (owned by ITT). Over the same period, "value-added" carriers such as Graphnet, Telenet and Tymnet were allowed to set up advanced public networks using transmission links leased from AT&T.

In 1977-78 in a complex series of court and FCC decisions, the competing voice carriers were allowed to offer switched services as well as leased-line services and to interconnect with the AT&T network in order to reach customers for all of these services. This, together with the FCC's decision to permit freely the resale and shared use of telecommunications services, firmly established the competitive model as the industry structure for the USA. A summary of some "milestone" regulatory decisions involved is given in Exhibit 1.

The "competitive model" was so established in the USA by the late 1970s that the entire policy debate began to swing away from the process of opening up competitive entry, towards establishing the framework for coexistence between the dominant carriers (AT&T and GTE) and their competitors. It was argued, for example, that the opening up of their primary markets to competition invalidated the logic underlying some aspects of the Consent Decree of 1956, which settled an earlier antitrust (anti-monopoly law) case against AT&T, with AT&T agreeing to stay out of unregulated activities such as the provision of data processing services. The FCC, in its Computer Inquiry II decision, ruled that AT&T could provide "enhanced services" involved data processing, provided it did so through a separate subsidiary; but this was challenged in the courts. At the same

EXHIBIT 1

SOME MILESTONES IN THE TRANSITION TO A COMPETITIVE INDUSTRY IN THE USA

Event	Year	Explanation	Comment
Private microwave decisions	1960	Private microwave networks	---
Carterphone decision (FCC)	1968	Acoustic coupler (non-electrical) connection of private radio-telephone systems to AT&T	began trend to competition
MCI decision (FCC)	1971	Rival long distance public networking	MCI began operations in 1972
FCC "Open Skies" decision	1972 (first actual entry, RCA, 1974)	Licensed entry into domestic satellite communications	AT&T required to postpone launching system
FCC certification program	1977	Electrical connection of FCC-approved equipment	Elimination of "protective devices"
FCC Second Computer Inquiry (Computer II)	Decision 1980 under challenge.	Separates "basic" transport of signal from "enhanced" service	AT&T may participate in "enhanced" services through arm's-length subsidiary.
Settlement of AT&T antitrust suit	Current	See text	Attempts to impose further restrictions.

time, a long-standing antitrust case brought by the Justice Department against AT&T continued to go (slowly) forward. The time appeared to be ripe for some form of comprehensive resolution of the issues. The two possibilities were legislation by Congress, re-writing the 1934 Communications Act -- which remains a possibility -- or a settlement of the AT&T antitrust suit. On January 8, 1982, when AT&T and the Justice Department announced their proposed antitrust settlement, it became clear that the latter possibility --perhaps modified by legislation and the FCC action, would set the future pattern. AT&T would continue to provide long-distance service, including non-local "interexchange" service within the States, and to control Bell Laboratories and Western Electric, but would divest itself of local Operating Companies. In return, AT&T would be free -- perhaps with a few subsequent restrictions -- to offer a wide range of "enhanced" services.

At the time of this writing, the Federal District Court is considering this proposed settlement and a decisive battle is being fought in the US Congress over legislation.

EUROPE

Since 1979, developments in several other countries have begun to follow the US model to varying degrees at varying speeds. The overall pattern is exceedingly complex, but the details for a few countries are given in Exhibit 2, conveying the general picture and conveying at least an outline impression of the pattern of change. Notable "milestones"

are:

o The "defacto" growth of international telex refiling and of interconnection of privately supplied terminals in the UK over the period of 1977=81

o The Telecommunications Act in the UK and the subsequent licensing of Mercury, a competing carrier operating its own transmission facilities, as well as a number of less spectacular examples such as the hybrid electronic mail ("mailgram") operation being run by Western Union and English China Clays

o The studies being carried out by the Monopolies Commission in the Federal Republic of Germany on the question of relaxing the Deutsche Bundespost's telecommunications monopoly

o The decision of the French PTT in the mid-1970s to head off pressure for more flexible provision of advanced telecommunication services -- especially data services -- by creating separated subsidiaries, notably Transpac, a subsidiary company with private participation, set up to operate packet switching.

JAPAN

Current events in Japan in this field are of particular interest. Over the period of 1976-80, opposition to the monopoly enjoyed by Nippon Telephone and Telegraph Public Corporation (NTT), the inland carrier, and Kokusai Denshin Denwa (KDD), the international carrier, built up rapidly. This was partly a result of

EXHIBIT 2 A TREND TOWARDS COMPETITION?

OUTLINE OF CURRENT STATUS OF COMPETITION POLICY FOR TELECOMMUNICATIONS IN SIX COUNTRIES

POLICY TOPICS	DOMESTIC				INTER-NATIONAL
	terminal and PBX interconnection	resale/shared use value-added carriers	competing carriers with own transmission plan	interconnection of smaller carriers with dominant carrier(s)	
Canada	relatively free	none	only CNCP	CNCP's interconnection required since 1979	monopoly (Teleglobe)
France	major restrictions	none except Transpac	none	none except Transpac	monopoly (DGT)
FRG	relatively free	none	none	none	monopoly (Bundespost)
Japan	major restrictions	none	none	none	
United States	open	yes	yes	yes	legislation favors competition
United Kingdom	relatively open	1981 legislation allows licensing	1981 legislation allows licensing	yes	"gateway" monopoly of BT continues

internal user pressure about services (especially data services) and tariffs, and partly a result of the involvement of US computer-bureau networks (notable Control Data) in the overall pattern of US/Japanese tensions and negotiations over trade issues.

In August 1981, an advisory group to the Ministry of Post and Telecommunications (MPT), which supervises NTT and KDD, advocated a major move in the direction of competition (1). In December, MPT produced its own draft "Value-Added Communications Act." This would allow value-added (resale) data carriers — similar to Tymnet or Telenet in the US — to be established, but would retain strict licensing control by MPT, while extending MPT control over data processing. In response, the Ministry of International Trade and Industry - MTI - one of Japan's most powerful institutions, has criticized the MPT draft

(1) Telecommunications Policy Advisory Group, _Proposal for the 1980's_, Aug. 24, 1981.

and argued that a much more pro-competitive policy, with essentially open entry into the telecommunications carrier business, at least on a resale basis, would be economically beneficial. At the time of writing, the argument continues, but the result seems certain to be some degree of pro-competitive legislation and the licensing of one or several competing carriers. These carriers may or may not be allowed to build their own transmission facilities as well as operate on a resale or "valued-added" basis.

EVALUATING COMPETITIVE AND MONOPOLY INDUSTRY STRUCTURES

What can be said about the relative merits of the rival industry structures, and hence about the advantages or disadvantages of the trend towards a competitive industry structure? This once-theoretical argument is obviously now a matter of great practical importance. Here we briefly consider the issues under a series of topic headings.

Economic Efficiency

Text-book economic argue that resources are
used more productively in a competitive market
than by a monopoly, unless there is a "natural
monopoly" situation – that is, where the
economies of scale are so marked that any subdivision of the market between more than one
firm would greatly increase unit costs. Until
recently, it was widely believed that this was
true of telecommunications. There is, however,
increasing evidence that this is only true of
the local network. Even there the "natural
monopoly" may break down with the growth of
cable television and advanced radio-based local
distribution technologies such as cellular
radio and the DTS (digital termination system)
operations now being licensed in the USA. On
longer distance routes, provided the traffic
density is high enough that the economies of
scale in transmission equipment can be fully
exploited by each competing carrier, the
natural monopoly argument fails.

The economic case for monopoly in basic transmission and switching facilities may be valid
for the local network — though it is likely
to be less so in the future — and for long
distance service in regions and countries
where traffic densities are low. Otherwise,
the efficiency and productivity gains associated with competition are likely to appear
increasingly attractive.

Where competitive operation of the basic network infrastructure is not required (as in
liberalized terminal interconnection or
value-added carriers) the economic efficiency
use for the competitive model appears overwhelming.

TECHNOLOGICAL AND SERVICE INNOVATION

The effect of competition on innovation is a
difficult and controversial topic. On the one
hand, the monopoly Bell System (notably Bell
Laboratories) is the source of many of the
world's key technological innovations — the
transistor, for example. On the other hand,
the competitive entrants in the USA
pioneered many advanced services — notably
packet-switched data transmission. Overall,
competition appears to be more favorable for
service innovation, with a marketing orientation, than for innovation in basic
techniques.

DISTRIBUTIONAL ISSUES

Existing telecommunications monopolies' pricing in effect taxes long distance traffic,
business and urban areas to hold down prices
charged to local calls, residential users and
rural areas. To the extent that these are
considered desirable redistributive objectives
of public policy, they are undoubtedly threatened by a policy of competitive entry which
allows entrants to "cream skim" the more profitable routes. Some sceptics would reply,
however, that not all the redistributive
activity is desirable (in current economic
conditions, should we tax business to

subsidize a consumer luxury?), and that telecommunications carriers should not be an agency
for redistributing income.

In practice, some aspects of this redistributive role — especially the urban/rural and
regional aspect — no doubt should and will be
retained. This does not necessarily require a
limit on competitive entry, but it does require
a financial transfer from the new competitive
carriers to support the subsidized services.
In the USA this is likely to be achieved
through the new unified scheme of charges for
interconnection with the local network, paid by
all long-distance carriers, which forms part of
the proposed AT&T antitrust settlement.

Similar considerations apply internationally
where Intelsat rates cross-subsidize users with
small volumes of traffic: satellite systems
serving only the North Atlantic route using
spot beams, for example, would have lower unit
costs, but would not serve many low-traffic
countries, especially developing countries.

OPERATIONAL AND ADMINISTRATIVE ISSUES

It is often argued that a network built and
operated by a variety of entities will be
technically unsound or will incur excessive
administrative problems and costs. This has
proved not to be the case in the USA. The
establishment of appropriate technical interface standards (for example for signalling)
and the use of computer-based traffic measurement and accounting systems for financial
settlements between the different entities
both help minimize the problem. In smaller
countries, or especially in developing
countries where technical and administrative
expertise is scarce, these considerations
may nevertheless indicate a cost penalty on the
competitive option that is significant compared
with total costs and revenues, and thus argues
for retaining a carrier monopoly.

SERVICE QUALITY

There appears to be no inherent reason why the
entry of competition into the telecommunications carrier industry should prejudice the
quality of service. It is true that the new
US voice carriers such as MCI offer lower
quality (though also lower prices) than AT&T.
This is in part because MCI is deliberately
offering a low quality/low price option —
widening the consumer's range of choice and
thus, one can reasonably argue, creating an
economic benefit. It is also in part because
the present restricted arrangements for physical interconnection into the Bell System local
network require the call to traverse many
more switching and transmission links than the
equivalent call carried by the Bell System
alone. This handicap will be removed, over a
period of (theoretically) six years, by the
equal access provisions of the proposed AT&T
antitrust settlement.

CONCLUSIONS

It now seems clear beyond reasonable doubt
that there is a general trend toward a competitive industry structure for the telecommunications carrier industry throughout the
industrialized market-economy countries of
the world. - a group of countries defined by
the membership of the Organization for
Economic Cooperation and Development (OECD).
This trend is much more pronounced in some
countries than in others, and will sometimes
be reversed as a result of political changes.

The reasons for the trend are less clear. One
reason is perhaps increasingly widespread
criticism of the economic performance of
monopolies, whether in the public or private
sector. A second may simply be the increasingly pervasive role of telecommunications in
the national economy as a whole. As the advanced industrial economies become "information economies," with information workers
becoming the largest component of the labor
force, telecommunications rapidly becomes
arguably the most important, and certainly the
fastest growing, infrastructure sector of the
economy, and the one with by far the largest
potential to transform domestic and business
life. In the light of this, it was perhaps
inevitable that general political will of
society would not allow such an activity to
continue to be wholly controlled by a single
business entity, even though that arrangement
was thought acceptable when only the "plain
old telephone system" was being considered.

Will a more competitive structure be beneficial or not? The arguments reviewed in
this paper are inevitably inconclusive: only
highly detailed analyses of the specific situations in individual countries could hope to
give an answer and even then firm answers are
difficult to obtain. There are, however,
some general conclusions. Some of the
traditional objections to the competitive
model, such as the alleged threat to the network from competitive terminal or carrier
interconnection, have largely been discarded: technical certification safeguards
can take care of the problem. The economic
issues remain more substantial. In some
smaller countries, there may be a considerable case to be made for retaining a unified
control of the basic transmission network,
though not for refusing terminal interconnection or the resale and shared use of services.
Alternatively, open entry could be allowed
subject to a tax designed to support unprofitable but socially desirable services.

BIOGRAPHY

Michael Tyler is President of CSP International, a research and consulting organization based in New York and London; an
economist and business analyst trained at
Cambridge University, Harvard and the London
School of Economics, he. has been active in
telecommunications policy and planning and
in the development of innovative telecommunications services since 1970. Before
joining CSP International, he was head of
Long Range Economic Studies at Post Office
Telecommunications (now British Telecom) in the
UK and Chairman of the Business Communications
Studies and Demand for New Services program of
CEPT, the association of PTT administrations in
urope.

Monopoly – do the Advantages Outweigh the Disadvantages?

P Hughes
Logica Holdings Limited, UK

Considerable changes are challenging the traditional monopoly role of the main telecommunications carriers. Strong arguments are being deployed to show how increased competition will provide great benefit. This paper, whilst not taking sides, puts some of the advantages of the monopoly supply of the main carrier and switching network, and some of the problems that may flow from deregulation.

BACKGROUND

There is a ferment of activity in challenging the traditional monopoly role of the PTTs (For convenience the term PTT is used throughout for major telecommunications carriers. In doing so it is also intended to include in such consideration primary carriers such as AT & T in the USA which have a majority but not a 100% position). Two events of major importance this year have occurred whose effects will be wide spread. The first is the out of court settlement in the USA between the U.S. Government and AT & T. The second is the new Telecommunications Act in the UK passed by Parliament in 1981 and the subsequent licensing of an alternative carrier, Mercury.

The AT & T settlement is the bigger event given the size of the organization. It is likely to have major effects on the supply industries, not only in telecommunications but also in computing. To the extent that this now frees and encourages AT & T to operate internationally, it adds a huge new competitor to that scene. In terms of the monopoly role of the carrier, the earlier cases in the USA courts such as the historic Carterfone case and the rulings that have allowed MCI to develop so successfully, have already had a great influence.

The new Telecommunications Act in the UK legislates for a much smaller market than the USA. But in the UK we have a state owned PTT with, until now, full monopoly powers. This is the traditional world model; it is the USA that is one of the few exceptions. For this reason a great deal of attention is being paid to events here - by Governments, PTT's and Unions of various countries.

The USA and the UK are singled out because of the specific events that have occurred. Other countries are going through a period of investigation of the traditional monopoly role. Examples include Germany and particularly Australia, where a consortium of major companies is attempting to get a part of the carrier business.

THE POLITICAL ENVIRONMENT

One cannot really examine the role of the monopoly without consideration of the political environment. The monopoly carrier is nearly always state owned, either 100% or at least majority owned. It follows that the attack on the monopoly powers is often motivated at least in part as an attack on state ownership. This is certainly the case in the UK where the policy of the current government, clearly stated, is to sell in part or in whole state owned enterprises. This has been carried through with British Aerospace, Cable and Wireless (who are a partner in the Mercury Project), and is planned with the British National Oil Corporation, British Airways and possibly British Telecommunications.

There is a wider political question. The wish on the part of governments to break down monopoly situations and open telecommunications to competition usually goes hand in hand with strong beliefs in advantages of a free market economy and the role of private enterprise. This paper is not the place to make statements of political beliefs either to the right or the left. However, it is not possible to address the subject without clearly stating that arguments dressed up as economic, either in defence or against the monopoly role of the PTT, are more often than not also political. But then this pervades economics as a subject. Economic theory and political beliefs so often go hand in hand. One only has to look at the present arguments on the role of monetarism to see this.

Looking specifically at the deregulation in the UK as already stated, the radical changes that have been made are a part, a central part, of a political programme. The Minister for Information Technology, Mr. Kenneth Baker, in introducing the bill said that he believed the Act to be the single most important piece of legislation likely to be introduced in the life of the current government. The act was intensely debated in parliament along traditional party lines. To say that the deregulation was politically inspired does not mean that when and if its opponents form the UK government the process will be reversed.

It might in part but it is not likely that the clock will be completely turned back. A breakdown of the monopoly role of the PTT in the UK has been set in motion: its effects are likely to spread to other European administrations and wider afield.

THE ROLE OF THE NATURAL MONOPOLY

In a paper[1] published in 1975 I asked the question whether or not telecommunications is a "natural monopoly". By that I meant that the total cost to the community of telecommunications should be the lowest when its provision is undertaken by a single authority or organisation. I did not then, and would not now, extend that argument to cover a restrictive attachments policy, nor to the provision of value added services. The argument applied to the basic carrier network and its associated central switching. Have the technological developments of the past seven years altered the argument? I believe they have, but only to a limited extent.

The technological/economic arguments rest on the economies to be gained from an integrated system. Some of these can be measured as such - for example the costs associated with replicating local feeder distribution. Other costs such as those associated with interfaces and the possible extra need for gateway functions, are more difficult to quantify. The crucial developments in technology include, satellite communications, optical fibres, the greatly reduced costs of microwave, the impact of micro electronics in parts of the system and packet radio.

These developments and others do impact the argument. Clearly the advent of satellite communications direct to and from the end subscriber obviates the need for replication of the local end connections. But the economic arguments for not replicating satellites serving the same markets are powerful. Likewise the development of low cost of micro electronics greatly facilitates building in to the system 'translation' to allow the interconnection of separate networks. But the costs are still there and the software problems in particular still very real.

THE ARGUMENTS IN FAVOUR OF REMOVING THE MONOPOLY

The arguments in favour of the breakdown of the monopoly are loudly and well expressed. They are put by the users, the supply industry (though in many countries the traditional large suppliers are anxious about a change to the status quo) and by politicians and sometimes governments. They have at times been joined by the academic community. For example in the U.K. the report commissioned by the Government from Professor Beesley[2] argues persuasively for the most radical deregulation. It argues without doubting that benefits will flow all round from complete deregulation.

The substantive main argument is in favour of competition, with benefits expected to flow accordingly. In the UK we are already in a position to observe some of these effects.

The relevant act and its effects are examined in another paper in this session by J.P. Compton [3] so I shall not go into detail. The main changes within British Telecom have been a major re-organization aimed at 'going competitive', an effective attack on the low end PABX market with the Monarch exchange, the acquiring from the USA of an electronic mail system and its launch on the market, the rapid provision of overlay point to point digital circuits, and many other moves. The most important specific moves other than the general changed managerial environment, relate to pricing. It is worth examining these.

Successive tariff reductions have been announced, one suspects rather in advance of when these might otherwise have occurred. The table below shows some of the changes since 1981. Quite clearly there is a move away from cross-subsidisation. The loss makers for British Telecom have been rentals, payphones and leased circuits; the profit makers, undoubtedly, international and trunk calls. Mercury, the alternate carrier, will clearly attack the heavily used trunk routes and will completely ignore the rural subscriber. It is bound to. British Telecom will under this pressure, and in advance, move away from the de facto cross subsidising of local by trunk revenues that has occurred before.

Recent British Telecom Tariff Charges 1981 to 1982

Service	Percent Change
Telephone Calls:	
Local	+ 60%
Trunk:	
up to 56km	+ 7%
over 56km (dense routes)	- 20%
over 56km (other routes)	0
International:	
Europe	- 10%
USA	- 33%
Rental:	+ 27%
Leased Circuit:	
5km	+ 50%
100km	+ 15%

One wonders just what in the USA will be the effect of AT & T getting out of local telephone operations? Is the deregularization of the Airlines in the USA any guide? The subsequent price wars have lead to cut tariffs on the trunk routes but in a number of cases reduced service at higher prices on the local feed airline routes. There is reason to believe that with AT & T taking the long lines revenues, the new local telephone companies are bound to put up their charges.

In summary, judged by the UK, changes in the telecommunications legislation lead to quick and substantial response from the traditional monopoly carrier which can give short run benefits to the user, both in pricing and in the earlier provision of new services and facilities.

THE ARGUMENTS AGAINST REMOVING THE MONOPOLY

The arguments in favour have been dealt with in most cursory form as these are well covered by others. The arguments against are far less often covered. It is left in the main to the PTTs and to the unions to put forward these arguments. They are thus treated as special pleading and discounted as such. Some of these arguments now are examined in turn.

Cream Skimming

'Cream skimming'is the main argument of the PTTs. This argument is particularly put against alternative carriers like MCI or the proposed Mercury. It also applies to the resale of trunk capacity on a shared basis either by a third party or within a group of co-operating users. For full alternative carriers it does have substance. One can argue that no form of inherent cross subsidy should occur in the network and that rural users should pay the going rate, or even not expect to be served at all (cf. public transport policy). In that case the cream skimming argument falls away over time. It does not immediately because of the equipment in place, but in the future a true laissez faire policy will naturally lead to pricing and service patterns based on serving competitively the dense routes, and not the rest. As already referred to, British Telecom have taken pricing moves accordingly.

In a study carried out for the Post Office Engineering Union, Logica examined the cream skimming argument for resale of leased circuits {4}. The study assumed that British Telecom would not respond by changing tariffs to remove cross-subsidisation - and therefore the opportunity of cream-skimming - but by recovering the lost revenues from users who could not benefit from the alternative service, i.e. the small business and domestic user. The study estimated that these users would have to pay an extra 25% in charges. This is not an attractive prospect and it is not surprising to see British Telecom move in such a way as to avoid the threat of cream skimming.

The Role of Regulation

The provision of a monopoly service by the State obviates the need for a separate regulatory authority. For better or worse issues are dealt with direct between the appropriate Minister and Ministry of the Government and the PTT. The USA is the main counter example. There the Federal Communications Commission (FCC) is established to regulate or decide in certain areas to deregulate. The USA similarly has numerous bodies to regulate other public utilities on a state and nationwide basis. It works after a fashion. It is a particularly good system for the legal profession who man both sides of any argument as well as holding the ring. Whilst the FCC in the past has instigated important change, it can act as a terrible break on quick action.

From the closely related field of broadcasting comes the example of teletext. The technology was first developed in the UK by the broadcast authorities (BBC and IBA) and first transmitted in 1975. Like all consumer product revolutions it took time to get established but it is expected that in 1982 some half a million new teletext receivers will be supplied in the UK alone. Other countries such as Austria are quickly moving to a high penetration of the use of this technology. Contrast this with the scene in the USA. The FCC have to license the transmission of text by over the air broadcasting. So far they have authorised only limited experiments of a few hundred sets each whilst they examine the question of standards and whether or not to deregulate. In this instance it is clear that the USA , which leads in applying so much new technology, is lagging because of the supply and regulatory environment.

Returning to the UK, it is clear that an equivalent of the FCC will need to be established to replace the breakdown of the current order. This necessary prospect must be viewed with concern even when weighed against the advantages. It may well in certain areas introduce delays to more than match the effects of free competition in bringing new services to the market. The introduction of Mercury competing with British Telecom may also introduce a particularly American phenomenon to the UK anti-trust proceedings. The recent AT & T vs. Justice Department case took 8 years before being settled out of court at a reported cost of $150m to AT & T. There are already possibilities of British Telecom being investigated by the Monopolies Commission.

Long Term Investment

The PTTs are probably the single largest investors in any developed economy. The investment is necessary to plan for an efficient telecommunications network. Furthermore the investments have to be planned carefully to ensure that an acceptable return is made over the period of the investment. The large switching exchanges have a lifetime which is very long indeed, measured in timescales of technological development. Some exchanges have lasted 50 years.

New technology is introduced into the network in a progressive fashion and it is clear that those parts of the network served by new technology have lower costs than the others. Yet one cannot conceive of taking the cost pricing principle to that extent. It is possible for a competitor to offer a limited service based on, say, new microwave technology which would be cheaper than the PTTs average price, based on a mix of microwave and cable. Once the PTT had 'modernised' the network to be competitive, perhaps a new gap would appear as a new opportunity.

It follows that the opening up of the basic network to competition could lead to the primary carrier adopting a more cautious approach to long term network investments. That is precisely what would damage the long term development of the network and not at all what the proponents of competition suppose will happen.

Scale of Venture

The creation of radically new consumer services in telecommunications usually requires both substantial investment and a long wait before achieving pay off. These characteristics make it easier for a national PTT with its scale and monopoly position to undertake rather than a smaller private company with no entrenched position in the market. Take for example the development of videotex.

Videotex (then named Viewdata, a better name which was unfortunately dropped) was invented by Sam Fedida at the research laboratories of British Telecom. It was first launched by British Telecom as Prestel. From this start a number of services generally known as videotex are in development and use in various countries. Other papers at this conference deal with this expanding area.

British Telecom have to date invested tens of millions of pounds in the development and exploitation of Prestel. They did so with the security of their huge installed base of business behind them, and with a preparedness to work at a long time horizon for the eventual returns. In retrospect, as a business venture, they may regret both the scale of the investment (losses) to date as well as the length of time to projected positive cash flow. But because of their initiative the rest of the world has been able to benefit. Few now doubt that videotex is a major new development. The returns will flow to the providers of private systems, of terminals, of chips and above all of information. The PTT's may not get commensurate benefit but without them, in this case British Telecom, it is unlikely that the venture would have started at all.

Australia has suffered from exactly the reverse in the same field. Telecom Australia planned to launch a public videotex service. They did their analysis, worked out their financial case and were satisfied that it was an attractive investment. Because of the size of the investment, though modest by PTT standards, it nevertheless had to be approved by the Minister. Then, because of political pressure by private companies who wanted to set up such a service, the matter became a cabinet issue. In October 1981 the Australian cabinet ruled against Telecom Australia and forbad them to provide the service. Whilst it is too early to analyse the full effects of that decision, the initial effect was certainly to delay the availability of videotex as a public service in Australia.

Another outstanding example is the development of Transpac in France. At the last ICCC meeting in Atlanta in 1980, Philippe Picard [5] described the dramatic success of Transpac. Since then its growth has continued to exceed plans. France has the most developed data transmission service in the world. Without the adventurous scale of investment by the French PTT, again with a longterm time horizon for pay back, this would not have occurred. The French PTT would not have justified this investment unless they had a monopoly of the market which they did. A side benefit for the French is the strength of their supply industry developed out of Transpac. SESA, who designed and provided the packet switches, led the world last year in successfully bidding to provide other national services including Australia and Brazil.

User Interaction

A monopoly supplier of a service can enter into full and open discussion with users about plans for new services. A competitive supplier cannot if he fears that commercially valuable information can pass to others. The effects of the new Telecommunications Act in the UK were immediate in this respect. British Telecom started to quote competitive reasons for not disclosing future commercial plans and not being prepared to discuss these plans with users. Cynics might say that this is just an excuse for secrecy and lack of co-operation. This cannot really be the case because such a marked change has occurred since the earlier environment.

British Telecom has moved away from considering its public service image to a competitive commercial image and as a consequence is naturally not about to gratuitously help its future competitors.

Frequency/Spectrum Allocation

The radio frequency spectrum is a finite resource, so is the geostationary orbit. Technology developments are creating increasing demands for these scarce resources. Discussion, debate, argument and acrimony between the developed countries and the developing countries is likely to increase, as can be seen from examining the complexities of the World Administrative Radio Conference (WARC) in 1977.

Take for example the allocation of geostationary slots for communications and broadcasting satellites. This is now leading to major disagreement between the developed and developing world. The USA has an immediate demand for a large number of satellites providing competing communications services. There are already about 15 satellites in place and the FCC has allocated positions for another 24 to be launched over the next two or three years. South America is less ready to take up these positions even though the value of communications satellites is inherently greater to large, sparsely populated, less developed countries that can less easily justify the huge costs of terrestrial networks. They see North America as making a pre-emptive take up of the positions that may rule out options for them downstream. The Europe v. Africa argument is similar.

Within developing countries the provision of telecommunications is virtually always a state monopoly. These countries point to the USA for example and say that the free competitive environment leads to the grabbing of an unnecessary and wasteful proportion of this finite world resource. They say that if all states operated monopoly systems then the world could better allocate this resource because it is then at least an argument between nations. Even this is not enough and groupings of nations for services are going to be required. The breakdown of the monopoly positions of the PTTs in Europe for example would greatly aggravate this allocation problem.

National Procurement

In the developed world nearly all countries have linked the monopoly position of the PTT with strong national procurement policies to support local industry. This has been particularly marked on the purchase of central switching systems. Indeed it is now spreading to developing countries where they are often insisting on local manufacture as a condition of contract. The Commission have tried to breakdown these conditions within the European Community with no marked success. The USA has put great pressure on Japan to open access to NTT, also with limited success.

Deregulation strongly works against national procurement policy at all levels. The licensing of alternative carriers like Mercury in the UK immediately introduces a new private sector customer for basic transmission and switching equipment, not tied in any formal way to national procurement.

The opening of value added services not only introduces new customers but also means that the traditional monopoly supplier, faced with competition, is far less likely to get systems developed in his country if he can buy an existing system elsehwere. An example was the immediate purchase of an electronic mail system from the USA by British Telecom, an action uncharacteristic of them in the past.

The greatest effect however is likely to flow from the deregulation of attachment policy. Indeed, so concerned were the traditional suppliers in the UK to British Telecom that they persuaded the Government to take this part of the deregulation by stages. The Government also showed concern for the influx of imports that would follow.

Arguments for or against advisability or desirability of national procurement policy for high technology goods and services are as intense as those for or against PTT monopolies. It is not the intent to rehearse them in this paper but to point out that they are linked. As already stated the investment by the PTTs is now becoming the single largest investment programme in many countries. In high technology investment these programmes are only matched by defence procurement. Most European governments are concerned by the worsening trade balance in electronics, computing and communications with the USA and now particularly with Japan. A deregulation of their communications could seriously lead to an influx of systems from these two countries where the industry has developed by supplying the huge and advanced markets.

Instead of a defensive strategy, the large scale procurement of PTTs on major new initiatives can be used to assist national industry in an attacking strategy. An outstanding example is the on-line directory project of the French PTT. Though notionally justified in its own right, it was, and is a thinly veiled case of national industrial strategy. By placing huge (one million plus) orders for small black and white display terminals it has allowed French manufacturers to produce at costs far lower than any competitor and hence obtain major export orders. This is one example of a French way of life. The National Economic Plan in 1976 stated as an objective the modernisation of the French Telephone Network based on Electronic Switching [6]. The objective was however not based purely on the need for a better network, but the need to support French Industry as a means of increasing employment and exports. CIT-Alcatel are now one of the major forces in switching systems contracts in the developing world.

Network Incompatibility

A monopoly supplier can ensure absolute compatibility throughout the main network. This simple condition breaks down if there are a number of competing main carriers. The point is obvious and hardly needs amplification. Of course any competing carrier is likely to seek to remain compatible with the primary national carrier. He needs the co-operation of the main PTT for interconnection, and such co-operation is unlikely to be willingly forthcoming and has to be forced either through the courts, such as in the USA, or by government decree as has been done in the UK.

A clear example of this danger is seen with the development of telex. The USA did not have a national telex network but a variety of competitive services - AT & T teletypewriter exchange services, TWX, and Western Union's telex service. It was only in 1970 that Western Union bought TWX and a few years later introduced interworking between TWX and telex.

The table below shows how telex has fared in the USA and UK.

Telex Penetration in U.K. and U.S.A.
(Connections per 10,000 population)

	1960	1970	1980
UK	1.0	5.2	16.1
USA	1.7	4.2	6.9

Any move away from a unified system has to show that a clear advantage arises from the competitive environment that more than offsets the necessary costs and other difficulties incurred in ensuring full interconnection with competing carriers.

International Interconnection

The problems of international interconnection can greatly increase with multiple competing carriers. Nearly all countries have a single national carrier that acts for all international traffic. Sometimes it is a part of the PTT such as France, Holland, UK. Sometimes it is a separate but single organization such as for Canada, Italy, Australia. In the United States there are competing international carriers. It is not at all clear that this has led to any benefit and it has certainly lead to greater expense in network interconnection and greater customer inconvenience at times. If for example a European national administration wishes to interconnect its data network with the USA it first has to deal with the various international lisenced carriers and then with the main domestic data carriers of Telenet and Tymnet. The extra equipment costs in this form of interconnect are obvious.

The problems are especially marked when establishing new international public services. Teletex is a most important new service being pushed ahead by the main national administrations in close co-operation. Its value as a high quality public service for text interchange will greatly depend on it achieving the kind of universality of telex.

To get this universality requires the closest co-operation on standards, network carrier, numbering and end to end message responsibility. It is unlikely that such universality can be achieved beween a whole range of private electronic mail systems that may spring up in the years ahead.

Facsimile is a good example of how this can fail to happen. For years the suppliers,

heralded this product as major development. Private industry was unable to agree the necessary standards which would allow interworking and fuel its growth. The recent standardisation has been pushed strongly by the French and Japanese PTTs and now the growth is coming.

CONCLUSIONS

This paper has dealt with a number of disadvantages that can and often will flow from a breakdown of the basic PTT monopolies. It does so to provide a counter to the powerful political and commercial arguments have been and are being deployed on the other side. The arguments for and against are complex and a total analysis extremely difficult to prove. Finally it should be pointed out again that however neutral the economic and social analysis, at heart lie political questions of belief in the structure of economic activity and the role of governments.

References

[1] Philip A. B. Hughes, The Future of Forms of Data Communications, OMEGA, The Int. Jl of Mgmt Sci., Vol. 3, No.1, 1975.

[2] Michael E. Beesley, Liberalisation of the use of British Telecommunications Network, HMSO London, 1981.

[3] J.P. Compton, Programme of Liberalisation Policy, Proceedings of the Sixth International Conference on Computer Communication, London, 7-10 September 1982

[4] Logica Ltd., Telecommunications and Competition, Logica, 1981.

[5] Philippe Picard, Business Planning for a Data Network: The Transpac Example, Proceedings of the Fifth International Conference on Computer Communication, Atlanta, 27-30 October, 1980.

[6] Commissariat du Plan, Transports et Communications, Preparation du 7e Plan, La Documentation Française, Paris 1976.

Philip Hughes is Chairman of Logica which he and colleagues set up thirteen years ago. Prior to that he worked in computer consulting and software for CEIR Limited (now Scicon) from 1961 to 1969. He has degrees in Engineering and Economics from the University of Cambridge. His many external industry activities include Governor of the Board of the International Council for Computer Communications and Visiting Professor to the University College of London.

Cognitive Aspects of the Selection of Viewdata Options by Casual Users

R M Young, A Hull
MRC Applied Psychology Unit, UK

An analysis is made of the information needed by casual users of a viewdata system to choose among the options presented on a frame. One factor that can cause difficulty is a "cognitive mismatch" between the designer of the frame and the user, and shows itself as a way of dividing the options that cuts across the user's own categories. Another is that some questions employ unfamiliar jargon or require real-world knowledge that the user may not have. Several different decision strategies are possible, the adoption of which depends on (a) whereabouts the user is in her problem-solving plan, (b) the user's expectations about the form and content of the frame, and (c) the wording and arrangement of the options. This last especially is a potent source of confusion for the unwary user or designer. Given that the total set of possibilities can be divided in different ways, the user may have to rely on the first few alternatives to infer the basis of the classification and adopt an appropriate decision strategy. If the alternatives are inconsistent or misleading, the strategy chosen can prove to be unsuitable.

Probably the best-known viewdata system is the public Prestel service offered by British Telecom and introduced in 1979. In Prestel and similar viewdata systems, the user trying to locate information on a particular topic is first confronted with a series of frames (i.e. TV-screensful of information) which ask the user to specify the topic by choosing one of a handful of options which sub-divide the set of possibilities covered by the frame. Each option is labelled with one of the digits 0-9, and the user communicates his selection by pressing the corresponding button on a numeric keypad similar in arrangement to a push-button telephone. A user trying to find some legal advice on a particular issue, for example, after a couple of appropriate choices would be presented with the frame shown in Figure 1. The option labelled "4 Legal Advice" clearly seems relevant, so the user would press the key 4 on the keypad in order to see the next frame, which would in turn offer a choice among various categories of legal advice.

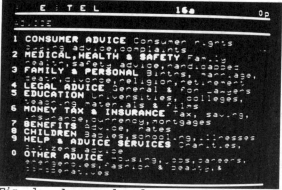

Fig. 1. An example of a Prestel frame. It contains overlapping options.

Despite the existence on Prestel of about 160,000 pages of potentially useful data, it seems clear that the difficulty of accessing

relevant information is a major obstacle to its use and may well be one of the factors preventing its more widespread acceptance (Sutherland, 1980). A recent ASLIB report on its possibilities in public libraries, for instance, comments on "the lengthy and circuitous nature of routing" in Prestel (ASLIB, 1981).

This paper presents an analysis of certain aspects of the problem. In the sections that follow we will first introduce and illustrate the idea of a "cognitive mismatch" between the designer of a viewdata frame and the user, then examine more closely certain factors that affect how users make their choices, and finally offer an outline of an information processing model that ties these various threads together.

DIFFICULTIES DUE TO "COGNITIVE MISMATCH"

Not all the difficulties in accessing information on Prestel are caused by the cognitive factors discussed in this paper. Some, for example, are due to organisational features of the system as a whole. One such problem arises when, after tracking down a particular topic, the user is faced with a choice between a number of "Information Providers" (IPs) without being given any guidance to their relative merits. Similarly, there is the phenomenon of then being "locked in" to the IP chosen, without being offered any cross-links to the other IPs who might be able to supply information on the same topic better suited to the user's needs.

However, many of the problems are caused by the content and layout of individual frames. For these our approach has been to analyse the usability of the viewdata system in terms of its "cognitive compatibility" for the casual user, in other words the extent to which the systems respects the user's prior knowledge, habits, and cognitive limitations. In particular, certain difficulties are to be explained by a "cognitive mismatch" between the designer's decisions embodied in the frame and the expectations of the user. This mismatch can make its presence felt in a number of ways, sometimes occurring in the guise of jargon unfamiliar to the user, sometimes as a way of dividing up the options that cuts across the user's existing categories.

In order to gain a better understanding of the problem, we ran an observational study in which people who had never used Prestel before were asked to retrieve specific items of information, such as "the times of trains from Cambridge to London on a weekday afternoon". Some of the problems that arose through cognitive mismatch were as follows.

Unfamiliar jargon

A number of problems are caused by the use of private jargon unfamiliar to the user. One of our subjects asked to find recommendations for choosing a small-screen colour TV decided to look for Consumers Association (CA: the publishers of Which? magazine) in the alphabetic list of IPs. On the crucial page, much of which is filled with information about how to subscribe to CA and so on, she rejected the option called TeleWhich? which is in fact the name CA uses for its buying guide information on Prestel, although no indication of this is given. Instead she chose to examine the index of recent issues of Which? magazine, month by month, in the hope of spotting an entry about colour TVs. Apparently the designers of the Which? index page expect the user to know what the term "TeleWhich?" means.

Some of the more esoteric terms used on Prestel, especially among the names of IP organisations, although not known to the user are nevertheless assumed to be meaningful, and a wrong guess at their significance can be positively misleading. One subject assumed, not unreasonably, that Promotel is concerned with motels and hotels. Another subject became quite upset with the idea that Social Security information should be provided by the National Consumer Council, and several hours later was still protesting that "NCC are there to give advice on buying things, not information about unemployment pay".

Specialist knowledge

Closely related to the use of private jargon is the fact that some of the frames assume knowledge that the user simply may not have. One of our subjects, in trying to find a list of Cabinet ministers, followed a route which led her to information about Parliament, presumably because she, like many of us, is not altogether clear about the distinctions and relationships between Parliament, the Government, and the Cabinet. Similarly some of the subjects were unsure whether "unemployment pay" would be included under "Social Security benefits", and were unaware of the distinctions between Unemployment and Supplementary benefits — a well known difficulty not confined to Prestel.

Alien classification

Some of the problems are due to the fact that the classification presented on the Prestel frame is incompatible with the user's own mental categories. One example, where the mismatch is with our own rather than with the user's expectations, comes from the question about colour TVs. One of the subjects chose to look for the information under the heading of Goods for Sale. By following an alphabetic breakdown on the term "television", she reached the buffer page for televisions, where she was confronted with a list of about 15 organisations who sell or rent TVs, in the middle of which was a reference to the Which? buying advice. This route caught us completely by surprise, since it is one that would never have occurred to us. On reflection, this is because we ourselves make a clear distinction between information about products (buying advice, comparative reviews, and suchlike) and their purchase (classified ads and so on). Evidently our subject did not enforce as sharp a distinction, and neither does Prestel.

Fig. 2. London rail index. The disruption of the screen is caused by noise on the telephone line.

A related notion is the idea that the user may not share some of the assumptions held by the frame designer. An example from our study concerns a subject trying to find the times of trains from Cambridge to London. By choosing an option for "Rail Travel To/From London", she reached a frame (Figure 2) headed "London: Rail Index" which contains an alphabetic breakdown of towns under the rubric "train services to station required", although that description is not quite accurate. The correct move from this position is to key the "C" option for Cambridge But our subject, by interpreting the rubric too literally, instead selected "L" for London. However, since this was already a London index, there was no entry for London in the subsequent alphabetic listing, a fact that puzzled and frustrated the subject. The trouble seems to be that for the designers, once a journey is known to be between London and another town, the London end is taken as a "given" leaving just the other town to be specified. The subject does not adopt this position, instead treating London as a city that one can travel to just like any other. The problem is in this case exacerbated by some minor inconsistencies in the wording of the frames.

CLASSIFICATION STRUCTURE OF OPTIONS

So far we have been implicitly assuming that subjects deal with each frame independently by reading the rubric, perusing the options, and selecting the one which best fits their query. But on closer examination, and for a variety of reasons, that assumption is not tenable. The problems that our subjects encountered in using Prestel led us to analyse the process by which options are chosen, by asking: What _information_ must the user have, and what _mental procedures_ must she follow, in order to make the correct choice?

In trying to answer that question, it becomes clear that subjects make their choices in the context of a (perhaps loosely formulated) _plan_ for finding the information. In consequence the user will often have an _expectation_, either vague or definite, about the contents and format of the next frame. After making the last choice in an alphabetic breakdown of towns about which "local information" is wanted, for example, the user expects to see on the next frame an alphabetic list of town names, arranged in one or more columns. If that expectation is satisfied by the overall "shape" of the next frame, then she can scan specifically for the target name without having to "read through" the other options. Of course the expectation may be inaccurate, in which case the user may be led astray. One of our subjects attempted to find information about an industrial company by following an alphabetic path based on its name. Unfortunately, the frame happened to present an alphabetic routing by _industrial sector_, and the subject had not noticed.

The second point to become apparent is that the set of options on a frame usually contains an implicit structure (which we call its "classification structure"), and that such structures can be of _several different kinds_. The significance of these different organisations is that _correspondingly different decision strategies_ are needed to respond to them properly. The use of an inappropriate strategy will almost always cause problems. To see this clearly, it is worth discussing briefly some of the possible classification structures and their associated decision methods. Some of the ways the possibilities covered by the frame can be divided up are as follows:

Explicit partitioning

The simplest organisation is for the set of possibilities to be divided into a collection of disjoint (i.e. non-overlapping) sets, particularly if these are all at the same "level", i.e. if none of the options is more finely divided than the others. The commonest example is an alphabetically ordered list. Another example would be where the user is asked to specify her age has falling into one of a number of ranges: "under 18", "from 18 to 35", and "over 35", perhaps. In either case, it is clear that an appropriate strategy is for the user to consider the options in any order, and to accept immediately the first one which fits.

N-plus-other

Figure 3 shows a frame where six of the subtopics under "Agriculture and Farming" have been allocated as explicit options and all the rest have been grouped together as "other". This is like a partitioning, except that a number of the classes have been combined to form the "other" category. It can be handled by a similar decision method, with the difference that it is important to read all the explicit choices before selecting the "other" since the only safe way to know that the "other" is needed is to be sure that the query is not covered by any of the explicit options.

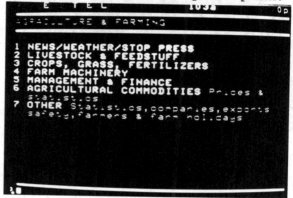

Fig. 3. A frame with classification structure "N plus other".

Overlapping categories

In contrast to the two preceding classifications, many frames contain sets of options which partially overlap. Figure 1 shows a frame where someone seeking advice about claiming Child Benefits may well consider all of options 3, 7, 8, and 9 to be relevant. The decision technique for coping with overlapping categories involves being willing to consider all the options, applying some kind of quasi-quantitative _evaluation_ to them, and finally choosing the _option_ with the highest rating. In practice, this technique is likely to be (a) elaborated by the initial selection of a small set of candidate options, but also (b) to be simplified by allowing any sufficiently good match to terminate the decision immediately.

Multiple biases

A single frame may offer two or more sets of options which carve up the topic along different lines. Sometimes this cross-classification is clearly signalled by the layout and subheadings on the frame ("Restaurants by nationality" vs "Restaurants by price"), but other times not. In Figure 4 (taken from near the top of the Prestel tree), the _layout_ suggests a straightforward choice between five categories. It takes a while to realise that option 1 covers the same ground (literally!) as options 2-5 together, but on an alphabetic rather than geographical basis. For a multiple-basis frame whose structure is reflected in its layout, the decision is appropriately made by a two-stage method, the first stage being to pick the appropriate basis and the second to select within it. For a frame like Figure 4 whose structure is "hidden", decision methods are hard to specify. It is likely that most users of such frames never actually grasp their structure, but instead assume that they are faced with a bad case of Overlapping Categories (of which such frames are certainly an extreme form) and remain confused.

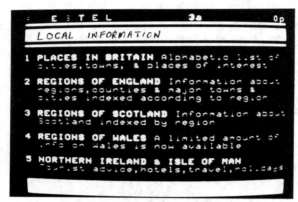

Fig. 4. A frame containing multiple classifications.

Modify interpretation later

Among the more bizarre classification structures are those used in which the user's initial understanding of an option has to be modified when she reads the subsequent ones. The structure is not easy to illustrate out of context, but the flavour is conveyed by the Prestel frame on "News and Weather". One of the options offers "UK Weather", and a later one "Historical Weather Stats", the implication being that the historical information can not be found under the first heading. Someone looking for historical weather information about the UK would have to modify her plausible initial interpretation of the first option, that it covers all UK weather, by later adding the rider "except historical". The crucial features of the decision strategy for these frames are, firstly, that what would normally be a fully justified early decision made without reading the later options may turn out to be incorrect; and secondly, as for the "N plus other" frames, the order in which the options are considered is important.

And so on. There are of course many other possible structures, and indeed one of the difficulties with this research is that we have no satisfactory theory of the space of possible classifications. Nevertheless the analysis has uncovered an important but subtle factor affecting the intelligibility of a Prestel frame. If the user guesses the wrong classification structure, or for any other reason adopts an inappropriate decision method, then she is likely to become confused and have difficulty making a correct choice. It should be noted that the sample of classifications just presented is unrealistically "pure". In practice, classifications occur which contain mixtures and variants of the type described, as well as others not mentioned.

Several of the questions raised by this approach we are not yet in a position to answer. We do not have a good understanding of what happens, for example, when the subject tries to apply a wrong decision strategy. Nor can we say much about how the user confronted with a new frame discovers its classification structure, except that her expectations from the previous choice probably play a role, as do the nature, layout, and wording of the first one or two options. This is just one of the many questions needing more research.

OUTLINE OF A PROCESS MODEL

Underlying this analysis is an informal model of the procedure a viewdata user adopts to retrieve a piece of information. First she is assumed to formulate a plan, which might be qutie detailed but more likely will be rather vague, not much more than a general approach. As the user progresses through the task, the details of the plan become elaborated (and the plan itself gets modified) as necessary: at each stage the current subgoal must be specific enough to guide the selection of the next option. The selection itself depends, as we have just seen, upon recognising the classification structure of the frame and then using an appropriate decision method. As each selection is made the user forms an expectation (again, either vague or detailed) about the content and possibly format of the next frame. A superficial confirmation of these expectations provides a check that the plan is proceeding as intended.

Although this formulation of the model is itself extremely vague, it is nonetheless sufficient to provide a useful understanding of certain aspects of our subjects' behaviour. It is worthwhile "talking through" the execution of the model on the "trains from Cambridge" problem. Initially the user formulates the plan of locating information about travelling by train, expecting later to have to specify the relevant cities. (Notice that this already involves a commitment, since looking first for information about Cambridge and only then specifiying "trains" provides another potentially successful route to the information. Looking first for information about London, it turns out, does not.) The subgoal of finding train information is sufficient to guide the user through the first few choices. An option labelled "Rail Travel" — which sets up the expectation that subsequent information will indeed be about trains — leads to a frame which clearly confirms that expectation, and thereby satisfies the first subgoal. The active subgoal becomes that of specifying the Cambridge to London journey. The first option on the frame offers "To/From London", an obviously good match, so that option can be taken without any further reading of the frame, and an expectation set up that the "London" part of the second subgoal has been met. The next frame, with a large heading "London: Rail Index", again confirms the expectation, and the current subgoal becomes that of specifying "Cambridge". The frame offers an alphabetic breakdown, which fits well with the new subgoal, and the "C" choice is taken. Following down an alphabetic index leads to an offer of "Cambridge", which of course creates an expectation that the user is at last about to be given information about trains between London and Cambridge. Accepting the offer leads to the frame shown as Figure 6, which adequately confirms the expectation. At this point our model would probably halt and claim success, or else remember that it was asked for train times "on a weekday afternoon" and pursue that as a new subgoal. In fact, some of our subjects did precisely that: they assumed they had found the information they wanted without realising that it was for the wrong direction.

One of the outcomes of this imaginary protocol is to explain an observation that is otherwise very puzzling, namely that users often appear not to <u>read</u> what is on the frame, either the rubric or the information being presented. We have already mentioned the user who tried to find the name of a firm in an alphabetic breakdown by industrial sector. Evidently he (it was a "he" in this case) did not "read" (in some sense) the instructions on the frame (just as people notoriously fail to read instructions for equipment they have to operate: Wright, 1981). We have also seen that, quite correctly, most subjects appear to ignore the fact that the alphabetic options from the London Rail Index are labelled as "trains <u>to</u> station required". The model indicates that where a frame meets the user's general expectations and offers information which meshes properly with the next step in the plan, the user is unlikely to distract herself by trying to read and interpret instructions for which she feels she has no need.

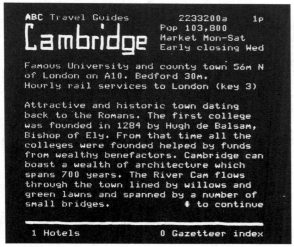

Fig. 5. Local information about Cambridge [reconstruction]: is there any travel information?

A striking example of "not reading the frame" arises when the user attempts to answer the train question by first finding "Local Information" about Cambridge. The information is found easily enough (Figure 5). The trouble is that the frame appears not to offer any information about trains. In addition to the several subjects who got this far along the route and then abandoned it, the <u>experimenters</u> also believed there was no travel information.

The first subject to spot the "Hourly rail service" took us by surprise, and we at first assumed that the information must have only recently been added to the frame. Fortunately the recordings of earlier sessions existed to prove us wrong.

The analysis being suggested here, in terms of the planning model and the classification structures, has a number of noteworthy characteristics. One is that it encourages an integrated approach to the design of the layout and content of a frame, and implicitly argues <u>against</u> any attempt to separate off one as a question of "graphic design", the other as "provision of information". According to the model the <u>physical</u> aspects of a frame play a role in the processing of its contents, for example by indicating to the user that "this frame is indeed an alphabetic list" [true], or (for Figure 5) "this frame consists of two paragraphs of tourist blurb" [untrue]. The analysis shows that the global (format and content) features of the frame combine intimately with the detailed information being presented in guiding the user's decisions.

Fig. 6. Times of trains to Cambridge: how does one find the times <u>from</u> Cambridge?

A dramatic illustration of this interaction between layout and content is provided by the most consistent observation in the whole study, which arises with the "trains from Cambridge" question. Without too much difficulty the user normally reaches a frame (Figure 6) offering times of trains <u>to</u> Cambridge, and the question is, how to find the trains in the direction asked for? None of the three subjects analysed in detail, and only one of the several other people we have tried on this task, picked the right move. It turns out that the "return 0", tucked away with the notes and fares, is British Rail shorthand for "travel in the opposite direction". Not surprisingly, our subjects fail to appreciate its significance.

A further example of the value of the analysis is the following, rather unconventional view of the role of a certain kind of <u>redundancy</u> in the design of Prestel. Many frames have a certain degree of "option redundancy" in the sense that a particular sub-topic can be reached through either of two or more options. The frame on "Entertainment", for example, allows the user to reach information about concerts under either "What's On" or "Music". The provision of this redundancy — as opposed to forcing the options to be strictly disjoint, so that the user has only a single correct choice — must seem like a good idea on general grounds, in so far as it gives the user more freedom in picking her route, enables her to use different facets of the item to be found, demands less careful consideration of the options and allows for a certain amount of carelessness. But it also has the effect of making the categories overlap, and thereby possibly obscuring the classification structure of the frame. This can have the effect of forcing the user to make an apparently difficult and confusing decision (i.e., between overlapping options whose relationship is unclear) which is in fact entirely unnecessary. Each case would have to be judged on its merits, but it may well be that this kind of redundancy is in many cases more harmful than helpful. Note that the present analysis distinguishes sharply between this "option redundancy" and the kind of "order redundancy" which permits the user to focus on different parts of the requirements in any order: "Television" first or "Buying Advice" first, "Cambridge" first or "Trains" first.

CONCLUSIONS

This paper has offered a perspective on the cognitive processes employed by a user when trying to retrieve specific items of information from a viewdata system. Its key features are that:

(1) The user adopts a plan for finding the information.
(2) Different frames have different classification structures.
(3) Different decision methods are needed for different frames.

Once this viewpoint is adopted, certain classes of difficulties that users experience and errors that they make become more understandable. The reasons why certain frames are consistently difficult to respond to, for example, becomes clear, whether because their physical layout is a misleading clue to their content (Figures 5 and 6), or because their classification structure is obscure (Figure 4). The fact that users often appear not to <u>read</u> the frame also begins to make sense.

The kind of analysis presented here is almost certainly needed if in the long term we are to have a sound basis for designing usable viewdata systems. It has definite consequences for the way that frames ought to be written. If, for example, the characterisation of different implicit classification structures is accepted, then it becomes important for information designers to be aware of the different possible structures, to decide clearly which structure a particular frame is meant to have, and to follow agreed practices (or at least good exemplars) for the presentation of each kind.

Acknowledgements. The work reported here was funded by a consultancy agreement between British Telecom and the Medical Research Council. We would like to thank Phil Barnard for comments on an earlier draft.

REFERENCES

ASLIB (1981): Impact of Prestel on public library branch services. Aslib report.

Sutherland, N. S. (1980): Prestel and the user. Report commissioned by the Central Office of Information.

Wright, P. A. M. (1981): "The instructions clearly state ...": Can't people read?, Applied Ergonomics, 12, 131-141.

Richard Young dabbled in Engineering, Computer Science, and Artificial Intelligence before getting his Ph.D. in Psychology from Carnegie-Mellon University in 1973. Most of his research has been on information processing models of the cognitive processes used by adults and children in thinking, problem solving, and mathematical skills. More recently he has become interested in the "cognitive ergonomics" of interactive systems such as computer command languages and pocket calculators, particularly in the question of the conceptual model adopted by the user.

Audrey Hull, (M.A. Hons., St. Andrews University, Scotland) has worked at the Medical Research Council's Applied Psychology Unit since 1961. She has been particularly associated with research on human performance with alphanumeric coding systems, and is now concerned with research on the understanding of instructions and the user's approach to viewdata systems.

Impact of a Computerized Conferencing System upon use of other Communication Modes

S R Hiltz
Upsala College & New Jersey
Institute of Technology, USA

Three models are tested with data from the operational trials of the Electronic Information Exchange System (EIES), and some comparative data for PLANET. The "ADD-ON" model posits that on-line communication is simply added to other, established modes and patterns of communication; the system has "no effect" on the use of other media. The "SUBSTITUTION" model posits that the use of other media will decrease, as the computer network is used to replace mail, telephone, travel, and even the reading of books and journals. The "EXPANSION" model hypothesizes that the expanded number of persons with whom one may communicate because of the network increases the time devoted to communication activities and stimulates communication in other modes to supplement the on-line communication.

1. INTRODUCTION

A computer network can be used to support communication among geographically dispersed groups as well as to share computing power and data bases or programs. A variety of systems have emerged during the past decade and there are several overviews of the characteristics and potentials of this new form of communication (see, in particular, Hiltz and Turoff, 1978; Johansen, Vallee, and Spangler, 1979; Kerr and Hiltz, 1982). One potential is to enable users to save time and money by substituting computer-mediated communication for travel, telephone, and other media that are more expensive or slower.

This paper reviews empirical evidence from a two year longitudinal study of users of the Electronic Information Exchange System related to the effects of the use of the system on other modes of communication: mail, telephone, travel, reading, and informal communication with co-located colleagues.

2. BACKGROUND: A DESCRIPTION OF EIES

Generalizations of the findings to be reported are of course limited by the fact that the data are based on one system and one type of user, scientific research communities.

The Electronic Information Exchange System is designed to support a variety of types of computer-mediated communication among dispersed groups of people. EIES has had more than 2,000 users and 200,000 hours of use since late 1976. It currently has a user population of about 600. Its purpose is to serve as a field trial testbed for utilizing the computer to facilitate human communications. It operates on a dedicated mini computer, and is accessible through Telenet.

EIES provides four general purpose structures for all its users:

o   MESSAGES: The delivery of messages to individuals and/or defined groups. This facility includes confirmations of delivery, a central message file, editing, retrieval, searching and resending.

o   CONFERENCES: Linear time sequential transcripts of group discussions on a particular topic with status information on readership. This facility includes voting, text searches, automatic delivery of new material to individual conferees and other communication support functions. Descriptions of open conferences are listed in a public conference, and an individual may join any number of conferences.

o   NOTEBOOKS: A text composition and word processing space that may be private to an individual or jointly shared among a group of users. It provides features for organizing and distributing documents as well as automatic notification to users of edits and modifications.

o   DIRECTORY: A membership directory containing both individuals and defined groups with self entered interest descriptions and numerous search options. A defined group may be treated as a single individual for purposes such as sending a message.

In addition to the above, EIES has a general purpose language (INTERACT) that can be used to tailor specialized subsystems for specific applications (see, for instance, Johnson-Lenz, 1981).

3. THE STUDY: SUBJECTS AND DATA SOURCES

The Division of Science Information (now the Division of Information Science and Technology) of the National Science Foundation issued a program announcement in 1976 inviting proposals for scientific research communities to participate in "operational trials" of the EIES system. Four groups of scientists were chosen to participate beginning in late 1977; a final three groups were chosen in 1978. The user groups included in this study consisted of scientists studying futures research methodology, general systems theory, social networks, devices for the disabled, and "mental workload" in complex man-machine systems. Note that the cost of using the system was not borne by the individual scientist, and that each participant could reach a significant number of her or his colleagues through the system (20 to 50), but had to rely on traditional communications means to reach others.

Some key aspects of the study affecting generalizability are:
-- Use was entirely voluntary. Participants were neither required to use the system by their employer, nor charged for such use. EIES was like the telephone sitting on the desk, a communications tool available for discretionary use. This is likely to be the most general situation for the use of such systems in the future.
--Since there were generally only one or two scientists at any particular location with access to the system, it could not be used to support communication with co-located colleagues. Future implementations of such systems are likely to frequently involve putting whole organizational units or organizations "on line," which would greatly increase the potential for communications media substitution.
--The subjects in this study were highly educated professionals, who often had some administrative duties but were not primarily managers. Generalizability to managerial and support workers is not possible.
The Division of Mathematical and Computer Research of NSF funded a study to conduct a cross-group assessment of the impact of the use of EIES. The data in this paper are drawn from the final report on this evaluation of the EIES operational trials (Hiltz, 1981).
The main source of quantitative data is a series of three questionnaires, mailed before use, at three to six months after first sign on (the "follow-up" questionnaire), and after approximately eighteen months of use of the system (the "post-use"

questionnaire). Several other sources of data, including monitor statistics on amount and type of use and participant observation of the groups' activities, were used to supplement the questionnaire data. Response rates were generally quite good for the questionnaires, even though they were fairly long and detailed, since the participants felt some obligation to cooperate with the evaluation in exchange for the subsidized use of the system. Thus, the strong point of the study is that it provides a large amount of data over a relatively long period of time. It can provide a comparison point for empirically examining the question of the effects of a computer-mediated communication system on the use of other media. A previous study of the effects of the use of PLANET on energy researchers (Johansen, DeGrasse, and Wilson, 1978) can be used to make some preliminary estimates of the generalizability of the findings to other computerized conferencing systems. Subsequent studies on other types of users and other specific systems will be necessary to determine the overall generalizability of the findings.

4. ALTERNATE HYPOTHESES

One possible expectation is that a computerized conferencing system can SUBSTITUTE for communication via other media, taking the place of mail, telephone, or face-to-face meetings. In the case of scientific communities, information exchanges on line might conceivably even substitute for book or journal reading, in the sense that the time invested in reading papers and conferences on line might be subtracted from some fixed total amount of time available for "keeping up" with the professional literature in one's field. Under the substitution model, one would expect a decrease in the use of other media. Some of the greatest hopes for economic viability of computer-based communication systems stem from the idea that it may replace more expensive means of communication. Nilles et al. (1976) focus on the ability to telecommute to work rather than waste time and petroleum resources on daily commutation to an office. Kollen's (1975) study looks at "travel/communication tradeoffs" mainly in terms of substitution for business trips at which face-to-face meetings take place. Certainly, one of the stated objectives for the use of message systems is usually to replace the letter or the internal memo or the telephone call, in order to displace costs and economically justify the system.

On the other hand, one could speculate that perhaps computer-based communication may be ADDED ON to other communications rather than substituting a new mode. This may be particularly true with a system that includes only a relatively small number of addressees or members, with most of the people whom one communicates not available on line. One might under these circumstances maintain one's usual communications channels, but add on to them new communications with people who have not previously been easily accessible. Under the add-on model one would expect to see use of other communication modes remain constant ("no effect").

A third hypothesis might be termed communication EXPANSION. This model pictures the computer-based communication being added on to existing communications; and then stimulating more communications via other media. This might take the form of telephone, travel, or mails to supplement computerized communications with people met on EIES, increased reading of books or journals due to discussions and references encountered on line, or increased communication with off-line colleagues that is stimulated by system use. Under the expansion model, one would expect to see that use of other media actually increases.

Whether substitution, add-on, or expansion phenomena are observed should vary by the total amount of use made of a system. At low levels of use, one would not expect it to affect other communications very much one way or the other. It is probably the EIES users who spent a relatively high amount of time on line (100 hours or more over eighteen to twenty-four months) who are most predictive of the potential media substitution effects, should such systems become widely used within an organization or interest community. Thus, we will look at reported effects cross-tabulated by amount of time on line. To the extent that significant differences are observed among the user groups on EIES, it indicates that media substitution effects are also dependent on application (task, size and social cohesion of the group, etc, are all bound up in differences among the groups on the EIES system).

In Tables 1 and 2, we see that there is generally an "add on" effect in relation to mail and telephone, but as system use increases, the "substitution" effect becomes more prominant. Overall, one-quarter of all members and half of the heavy users report a decrease in the amount of use of the telephone, as a result of using EIES. However, a minority demonstrate an "expansion" effect: fourteen percent overall report an increase in the use of the telephone attributable to using EIES, and this increase is also directly related to amount of use of the system.

The pattern for mail is similar, but stronger. That is, at all levels of system use, there is most likely to be "no change" in the use of mail as a result. But the likelihood of both reported decreases (substitution of computerized communications for mail) and of reported increases (more mail as a result of system use) varies directly as a function of the amount of use of the system. Among medium to heavy users, substitution of computerized communications for mail is the modal pattern; but expansion also increases to approximate equality in frequency with the "add on" pattern.

A probable explanation is that on-line communication substitutes for some mail or telephone but stimulates other contacts that might not take place otherwise. For instance, users may apprise one other of available preprints or other documents, which are then sent by mail. If a subject of mutual interest is likely to take a great deal of discussion, participants who find themselves on line at the same time frequently seem to decide to talk it over on the telephone to resolve an issue or to get another set of cues about each other's feelings. In other words, qualitative observations suggest that dyads resort to the telephone as a supplementary means of communication for fairly long (ten minute or more) conversations, particularly if they find each other on line at the same time and are thus obviously available to take a call. It is the heaviest users and those who make the most new contacts who are most likely to expand their use of mail and telephone as a result of computerized communications.

The findings of the PLANET study are comparable in the sense the they observe that "there is no simple relationship between computer conferencing and use of conventional media" (Johansen, DeGrasse and Wilson:69). In most cases, however, the frequency of the reported use of mail decreased during the period of observation. On the other hand, telephone use was as likely to increase as to decrease. In both the EIES and PLANET studies, there were some differences in observed patterns among user groups. Looking at the two sets of results, one can project that substantial use fof such systems is likely to result in substitution for the mails, but that the

579

substitution of computerized communication for some telephone calls is likely to be balanced by the stimulation of other telephone communication as a result of new contacts and/or unresolved issues that emerge through communication on the system. In any case, there is likely to be considerable variability among user groups, so that one cannot make predictions for a specific group with any degree of confidence.

Table 1

Impact on Amount of Use of Telephone, by Hours on Line

hrs.	Incr.	No effect	Decr.	#
1-19	11%	71%	18%	28
20-49	6%	81%	13%	32
50-99	24%	52%	24%	25
100+	17%	33%	50%	18
All	14%	63%	23%	103

Source: Post Use Questionnaire
Chi square=16 p= .01
Gamma= .14

Question: Has the use of EIES changed the amount of your use of other media in the last year? (Media checklist with increased-no effect-decreased as choices)

Table 2

Impact on Amount of Use of Mail, by Hours on Line

hrs.	Incr.	No effect	Decr.	#
1-19	11%	68%	21%	28
20-49	19%	47%	34%	32
50-99	32%	28%	40%	25
100+	22%	28%	50%	18
All	20%	45%	35%	

Source: Post Use Questionnaire
Chi square= 11.9 p= .06
Contingency Coefficient= .32

Question: Has the use of EIES changed the amount of your use of other media in the last year? (Media checklist with increased-No effect-decreased as choices)

4.1 Travel/Communication Tradeoffs?

Turning to travel substitution, attendance at professional meetings was separated from travel to make a personal visit with a colleague. Table 3 indicates that system use does not have any significant impact on attendance at professional society meetings. Eighty percent report "no effect", and those who do perceive an effect are almost as likely to report an increase as a decrease, at all levels of system use. In terms of travel for a personal visit (see Table 4), there is more likely to be a perceived impact, and once again, such travel is about as likely to increase as to decrease. Among the heaviest users of the system, almost a quarter report an increase in travel for this purpose. It would seem, therefore, that as long as travel budgets are not cut, contact with colleagues on line is about as likely to stimulate travel as to substitute for it. Anecdotal evidence suggests that among those who interact a great deal on line but have never met in person, there is a tendency for curiosity to prompt extensions to business or personal trips made for other purposes, in order to meet with one's on-line acquaintances.

The PLANET study showed mixed results on travel substitution, just as this study did. Two of their groups showed some increase in travel for communication with other researchers over the period of the study and two showed a decrease (Ibid,: 74-75). They also conclude that a computerized conferencing system has the potential to substitute for travel to face-to-face conferences, if researchers feel overburdened by "too much" travel or have insufficient travel funds to make all the trips that might be useful; but that the new communications channels opened up by such a system when it is on an international network may also actually stimulate travel for meetings that otherwise would not have taken place.

4.2 Reading

The reading of professional books and journals is much more likely to increase rather than decrease as a result of using EIES (Table 5). Apparently the discussions with one's colleagues lead to more interest in reading journals, since the greater the amount of time spent on line, the more likely it is that such reading increases.

However, this effect was found to be group dependent. And for the PLANET study, two of the four groups showed a definite decrease in the reported frequency of reading work-related books and articles (Ibid:76-77).

4.3 Communication with Co-Located Colleagues

In Table 6, we observe the perhaps surprising phenomenon that use of EIES is more likely to increase than decrease communication with one's co-located (off-line) colleagues. It is surprising that even the lowest level users are likely to report an increase in communication with colleagues within their own organization as a result of using EIES. Practically noone reports a decrease in communication with co-located colleagues as a result of using the system. Perhaps the large proportion of low level users who report an increase in local communication can be explained by their use of the system as a kind of toy which they occasionally demonstrated to colleagues as a curiosity or status symbol. Since we did not ask about the content of off-line communications that were increasing for any of the modes, however, we can only speculate about the nature of it.

Table 3

Impact on Amount of Travel to Professional Meetings, by Hours on Line

hrs.	Incr.	No effect	Decr.	#
1-19	7%	83%	10%	29
20-49	7%	81%	13%	31
50-99	12%	88%	0	25
100+	17%	61%	22%	18
All	10%	80%	11%	103

Source: Post Use Questionnaire
Chi square= 7.7, p= .26
Contingency Coefficient= .26

Question: Has the use of EIES changed the amount of your use of other media in the last year? (Media checklist with increased-No effect-decreased as choices)

Table 4

Impact on Visits with Researchers in Other Locations, by Hours on Line

hrs.	Incr.	No effect	Decr.	#
1-19	11%	82%	7%	28
20-49	13%	69%	19%	32
50-99	8%	88%	4%	25
100+	22%	50%	28%	18
All	13%	74%	14%	103

Source: Post Use Questionnaire
Chi square= 10.1, p= .12
Contingency Coefficient= .30

Question: Has the use of EIES changed the amount of your use of other media in the last year? (Media checklist with increased-No effect-decreased as choices)

Table 5

Impact on Reading Journals or Books by Hours On Line

hrs.	Incr.	No effect	Decr.	#
1-19	17%	75%	7%	29
20-49	25%	63%	13%	32
50-99	32%	64%	4%	25
100+	44%	39%	17%	18
All	28%	62%	10%	104

Source: Post Use Questionnaire
Chi square= 7.9, p= .24
Contingency Coefficient= .27

Question: Has the use of EIES changed the amount of your use of other media in the last year? (Media checklist with increased-No effect-decreased as choices)

Table 6

Impact on Communication with Colleagues in One's Own Organization By Hours On Line

hrs.	Incr.	No effect	Decr.	#
1-19	43%	58%	0	28
20-49	15%	79%	6%	133
50-99	20%	72%	8%	25
100+	16%	84%	0	19
All	24%	72%	4%	105

Source: Post Use Questionnaire
Chi square=10.8, p= .09
Contingency Coefficient= .30

Question: Has the use of EIES affected your communication with any of the following? Colleagues at your institution or organization.

5. SUMMARY AND CONCLUSIONS

In terms of effects on media use, EIES communication is most likely to be added onto other communications; but those who use the system the most are likely to also expand their use of other communications modes. There is some replacement of telephone and mails by computer-mediated communication. Travel to professional meetings and visits with other researchers are not affected for most people. Although the majority report no effect on the reading of professional books and journals, a significant minority (28% overall and 44% of heavy system users) report an increase. Communication with colleagues at one's own location is more likely to increase than to decrease.

Of course, subjective reports about the frequency of use of various media are likely to be quite unreliable. However, we did not ask for accurate counts, but only for gross changes: up, down, or about the same. Overall, there is a tendency for the media to add on to other modes and channels of communication, rather than to substitute for them. Previously established scientific and professional networks, maintained by other forms of communication, persist along side of the new, larger, more widespread computer-mediated network. Our results correspond fairly well with a previous study of PLANET users. Impacts on communications might be quite different for a computer-mediated communication system that is implemented on an organization-wide basis, rather than including a few users from many different oraganizations, as in the EIES case. It is probable that an intra-organizational system would show more simple substitution for mail and telephone, and less tendency to stimulate additional communication in other modes. However, our results for the EIES users were unexpected; we anticipated that media substitution would be the dominant pattern. If comparable data were collected for intra-organizational systems, they might also show that a simple substitution model does not fit the observed effects of a computer-mediated communication system on the total flow of communications.

6. ACKNOWLEDGEMENTS

This study was partially supported by a grant from the National Science Foundation (MCS-77-27813). The opinions and conclusions in this paper are solely those of the author and do not necessarily represent those of the National Science Foundation.

This paper is adapted from a portion of a chapter of a forthcoming book (Hiltz, 1982), to be published in late 1982 by ABLEX.

The author is particularly indebted to Murray Turoff, Elaine Kerr, Robert Johansen, and Mary Solimine for their contributions to the research process which led to this paper.

REFERENCES

1. Starr Roxanne Hiltz, The Impact of a Computerized Conferencing System on Scientific Research Communities, Research Report No. 15, Computerized Conferencing and Communications Center, New Jersey Institute of Technology, 1981.
2. Starr Roxanne Hiltz, On Line Scientific Communities: A Case Study of the Office of the Future. ABLEX, forthcoming, 1982.
3. Starr Roxanne Hiltz and Murray Turoff, The Network Nation: Human Communication via Computer. Addison-Wesley Advanced Book Program, Reading, Mass., 1978.
4. Robert Johansen, Robert DeGrass Jr. and Thaddeus Wilson, Group Communication through Computers, Vol. 5: Effects on Working Patterns. Report R-41, Institute for the Future, Menlo Park, Calif., 1978.
5. Robert Johansen, Jacques Vallee and Kathleen Spangler, Electronic Meetings: Technical Alternatives and Social Choices. Addison-Wesley, Reading, Mass., 1979.
Peter and Trudy Johnson-Lenz, The Evolution of a Tailored Communications Structure: The Topics System. Research Report No. 14, Computerized Coinferencing and Communications Center, New Jersey Institute of Technology, 1981.
7. Elaine B. Kerr and Starr Roxanne Hiltz, Computer-Mediated Communication Systems: Status and Evaluation. Academic Press (forthcoming) 1982.
8. James Kollen and John Garwood, Travel/Communication Tradeoffs: The Potential for Substitution among Business Travellers. Bell Canada Business Planning Group, 1975.
9. Jack M. Nilles, F.R. Carlson Jr., P. Gray and G. Hanneman, The Telecommunications-Transportation Tradeoff: Options for Tomorrow. Wiley, New York, 1976.

STARR ROXANNE HILTZ is Professor and Chairperson, Dept. of Sociology and Anthropology, Upsala College, East Orange, New Jersey. She is also Associate Director, Computerized Conferencing and Communications Center, New Jersey Institute of Technology; and President of Computerized Conferencing, Inc., a consulting firm. Present research interests center upon the development and application of social science methodologies to the study of the impacts of computer and information systems.

Voice I/O System Design

A R Willis
British Telecom Research
Laboratories, UK

Until comparatively recently users of the Public Telephone Network, the world's largest and
most complex man-machine system, had only eleven different input signals and five different
output signals with which to control and interpret its operation. This is changing thanks
to the rapid introduction of Stored Program Controlled Telephone Exchanges, such as British
Telecom's System X family of switching systems, in which an automatic voice response unit
assists customers to use the exchange facilities. Now a whole new range of telephone services that exploit Voice I/O technology are being developed. The basis of all these services
is man-computer communication using voice, and the application of Large Scale Integration to
speech processing techniques is making speech a practical man-computer communications medium.

Particular characteristics of speech as a communications medium must be reflected in the system design if Voice I/O services are to be attractive and comfortable for people to use.
These factors are discussed in relation to their impact on system design, and an outline
voice-response system design is developed.

1   INTRODUCTION

Computer controlled telephone exchanges are now
being introduced worldwide, progressively creating the world's largest interactive computer
system. Considering the sophisticated technology used to create this system it is perhaps
surprising that its interface with the user has
remained so crude. For input the user can signal only 10 or in some cases 12 different digits, for output he must interpret 5 or 6 different tones.

System X, British Telecom's range of Stored
Program Controlled (SPC) telephone exchanges
/1/, employs automatic voice guidance to improve the user interface. The announcements guide
a user in the control of telephone services,
confirm to him that his actions have been successful, and inform him of the services which
are in operation on his line.

Work at the British Telecom Research Laboratories (BTRL) to provide voice guidance on System
X exchanges has revealed the power of automatic
voice output, and the potential of voice input
to enhance the man-computer interface, particularly for inexperienced users. It has also
revealed the importance of the human factors of
voice-based interaction, and stimulated a design approach that combines ergonomic requirements with the practicalities of system design.

The object of this paper is to discuss some of
the important human factors, and show how they
are supported by a design of automatic voice
response unit being used at BTRL for experiments
with interactive voice services. Consideration
of the human factors is preceded by a brief
description of application areas being addressed by work at BTRL.

2   APPLICATIONS OF VOICE INPUT-OUTPUT

Progress in the field of speech processing has
been characterised by slow but steady advances

in basic techniques, taking place against a
background of dramatic advances in technology.
Consequently, speech is increasingly being employed at the man-machine interface.

2.1 Voice Guidance

An early application of automatic voice response is to guide and instruct the user of a machine. An example is the voice guidance available on British Telecom's System X telephone
exchanges /2/.

A device called the Automatic Announcement Subsystem can be connected to a call at any stage
and used by the computer that controls the exchange to report information relating to the
status of the call or give guidance in the use
of the supplementary services provided by
System X. The customer signals his requirements to the exchange using a standard keypad
with twelve push buttons labelled 0 to 9 and
"star" and "square".

For example, when a customer wishes to use the
Code Calling Service to store a commonly-used
telephone number against a personal short-code,
the following interaction takes place:

Customer: Lifts receiver, dials "*55".

Exchange: "Code Calling Service. Dial a code
followed by star".

Customer: Dials 7.

Exchange: "Dial the telephone number followed
by square".

Customer: Dials 01 246 8091 .

Exchange: "Telephone number oh one two four
six eight oh nine one has been
stored against code seven".

Used in this way voice guidance can enhance the

man-machine interface in many applications, from vending machines to computer terminals. Voice is particularly useful for guiding untrained users through complicated operations, and where printed instructions may not be suitable or cannot be provided.

Several techniques may be used to reproduce spoken announcements for this class of application. Generally, the speech is stored in digitally encoded form and reconstituted in real-time. If high speech quality is not required then a Formant /3/ or a Linear Predictive Coding (LPC) /4/ synthesiser may be used, at a data-rate of around 2kb/s. This type of synthesiser is available in single chip form, but analysis of speech to produce the data on which the synthesiser operates requires the skilled operation of complex equipment.

To achieve high quality speech the System X Automatic Announcement Subsystem uses Pulse Code Modulation (PCM), at 48kb/s, to encode the speech. In addition to high quality this offers the advantage of readily available single chip encoder/decoders.

In order to reduce the amount of speech data stored and to allow variable data such as telephone numbers or sums of money to be spoken, a technique called utterance concatenation is employed, whereby an announcement is built-up from utterances (typically words) stored separately and brought together in real-time. A frequently used word, therefore, need only be stored once, but may be used in several announcements. However, to achieve natural sounding speech using utterance concatenation it is necessary to pay close attention to utterance boundaries, and the pitch and speed of delivery of each utterance.

2.2 Information Services

From voice guidance it is but a short step to offering information from computer databases over the telephone network using automatic voice response. The user is first guided through a question and answer dialogue to establish what information is required, then the information is delivered.

An advantage of voice-based information services is that they can be used from ordinary telephones, so the service provider has 23 million terminals already installed in the UK alone. The techniques employed are the same as for voice guidance, with greater emphasis on the information delivery phase.

2.3 Voice Messaging

The ability to digitally encode speech, store it in a computer system and reproduce it at will is being exploited to provide Voice Message services within the electronic office, for voice annotation of text for example, and for passing messages over the public telephone network /5/.

Speech encoding techniques that preserve high audio quality, such as Adaptive Differential Pulse Code Modulation (ADPCM) at 32kb/s, are used so that the speaker is recognisable to the recipient of the message.

2.4 Voice Command

The man-machine interface may be further improved by permitting users to control the services described by spoken command. Practical Automatic Speech Recognition equipment cannot yet cope with the range of speakers likely to be encountered by a public service. Indeed, in Britain at least, not enough is known about the range of speaker characteristics that might be expected.

An advantage of Voice Command is that it reduces the need for a user to "re-code" his input. For example, the keypad-based service requires the user to dial "star five five" for the Code Calling service, whereas when Voice Command is implemented he will merely recite the name of the service required. However, the absence of the discipline imposed by a keypad will create its own problems in controlling the dialogue.

3 USER REQUIREMENTS

It is taken as a premise that for successful man-machine communication the machine should accommodate the needs of the user. Consequently the system design function becomes one of accommodating those needs within the constraints of practical technology and cost. But what are the needs of the user of a man-machine interface based on speech? The following sections present features that have been found to be important in telecommunications applications, and consider their influence on system design.

3.1 Meaning

Words are a poor representation of meaning. Science has long recognised this and used precisely defined meta-languages in order to express meaning unambiguously. This approach is applicable to voice-based man-machine dialogues to a limited extent. A study of the first draft of some telephonic announcements revealed three different expressions intended to be used when an invalid entry was received to cause the customer to end his call and check his instruction booklet:

a) "... please check your instructions".

b) "... please consult your user instructions".

c) "... please replace your receiver and consult your instructions".

If a single form of words can be used whenever it is required to elicit this action, instead of the different forms listed above, the customer unconsciously learns a term with a precisely defined meaning, to which may be added other terms to build up a specialised language. Similarly for Voice Command, the expressions used to elicit inputs can encourage users to employ precisely defined terms for input. In telecommunications applications, however, the degree to which this approach may be exploited is limited by the degree of familiarity, and hence learning, that may be assumed of the user.

Given, then, that it is desirable to form a set

of expressions, one for each user action it is required to elicit, how should the wording of these expressions be chosen? Several experiments have demonstrated how user reaction is sensitive to announcement wording. In an experiment conducted by Bell Laboratories /6/ a change of wording from

"If you need a Directory Assistance Operator, please stay on the line."

to

"If you have further questions, an operator will return."

reduced the proportion of customers that stayed on the line from 15 percent to 9 percent. It was surmised that customers interpreted the latter part of the first announcement as an instruction to stay on the line.

However, customers do not always interpret announcement wording so literally. In a Radio Paging experiment performed by British Telecom Research Laboratories (BTRL) staff customers heard one of three different announcements used to indicate that a paging request had been accepted:

"Paging call accepted."

"Paging."

"Your Paging call has been accepted, please replace your receiver now."

The time from the end of the announcement to when the customer cleared-down was measured and taken as an indication of how readily the customer understood the message. Surprisingly, customers hearing the first announcement cleared most quickly.

Further dimensions of meaning are added to the wording of an announcement by the pitch, speed, volume and pronunciation used when it is actually spoken. There is no satisfactory notation by which to describe these variables, and as with announcement wording, judgement of them can only be subjective.

Clearly, then, it is necessary to carefully select the words used in an announcement. The criterion for a satisfactory announcement is that it should elicit the required response from the recipient. The system designer must accept that he will not always get it right first time and that the announcement set will require tuning to suit the particular service, and even the particular set of users which that service attracts. Consequently a voice I/O system must permit user reaction to announcements to be measured, and system components and interfaces must be designed to support flexibility of announcement wording and delivery.

3.2 Speech Quality

The designer of an automatic voice response system has to choose the speech encoding or synthesis technique to be used, and thereby fix the quality (in terms of acoustic fidelity, naturalness or intelligibility) of the resulting speech. A satisfactory measure of quality has defied definition principally because the judgement is application dependent. The complexity of speech and adaptability of the ear-brain receiving apparatus invalidate conventional audio quality measures. However, some guidelines can be drawn. Obviously a Voice Store and Forward service requires a speech coding technique that permits the original speaker to be recognised, whereas this is not an essential attribute for, say, an automatic train timetable information service.

It has been argued that some artificiality is desirable to remind the user that he is interacting with a machine and encourage a realistic user "model" of the system's capabilities. In a Bell Laboratories experiment /7/ 71 percent of customers using an automatic voice response unit that employed "natural quality speech" detected they were being served by a machine. When speech quality was intentionally degraded by using announcements with no pitch variation, this figure increased by only 8 percent. This result suggests that there is some characteristic other than naturalness of the speech that alerts a user to the fact that he is listening to an automatic voice response unit. To underline the caution with which such results should be interpreted, in the same experiment 28 percent of customers who were served by a genuine human operator, who used the same announcements as the automatic unit, thought they had been listening to a machine.

As regards users' preferences between male and female speakers for voice response announcements a recent trial of telephone guidance announcements at BTRL /8/, in which subjects were asked to rank speakers in order of preference, showed that both male and female speakers could be highly rated. Furthermore there was good agreement between male and female subjects. However, the tests did not investigate the effects of distortion resulting from encoding, a matter of some importance, particularly if one of the analysis/synthesis techniques that are themselves sensitive to the sex-related characteristics of the voice is employed.

3.3 Catering for Experienced and
   Inexperienced Users

A significant advantage of voice based man-machine interaction is that the voice response announcement can be explanatory in order to assist the inexperienced user. Explanatory announcements are long-winded, and deter the experienced user. Consider, for example, an announcement used to invite entry of the time-of-day. The following announcements could be used:

a) "Please enter the time."

b) "Please enter the time using the 24 hour clock."

c) "Please enter the time using the 24 hour clock, enter two digits for hours and two digits for minutes."

d) "Please enter the time using the 24 hour clock, enter two digits for hours and two digits for minutes. For example for 4.30

in the afternoon enter 1-6-3-0."

Clearly version a) would suit an experienced user, whilst version d) would be very helpful to someone inexperienced in the concept of entering time using the 24 hour clock. How does the system designer satisfy both types of user?

This problem was identified and solved for telephone guidance announcements by allowing the user to stop an announcement by keying-in his response when ready /9/. This overridable mode of guidance was the most successful of those tested at BTRL, but it is not without technical problems associated with differentiating between the announcement signal and the tone signalling used by the customer /10/. The best solution to this problem requires close coupling of the voice response unit and the signalling receiver via a single dedicated control element that can determine whether an announcement is being delivered and briefly interrupt the announcement in order to verify the received signal.

When Voice Command supersedes tone signalling the problem of differentiating between transmitted and received signals, if they are permitted to occur simultaneously, will be exacerbated.

Notwithstanding the feasibility of overriding an announcement if its content is known, it is desirable that an appropriate level of guidance is offered by a voice response system. Many systems will know the user's identity and can therefore apply a pre-specified experience level and select announcements accordingly. If this is not feasible then the system can always ask! An experimental voice based information system at BTRL follows its introductory phrase with "Do you need advice in using this service? If yes dial one, if no dial oh", and adjusts its presentation according to the answer. Alternatively the system could build its own experience model of the user by measuring parameters such as error rate and whether announcements are being overridden.

3.4 Coping with User Error

Probably the most demanding area of voice response system design is coping with user error in an acceptable manner. No human listener would respond to an incorrectly specified time with the unhelpful statement "You have entered the time incorrectly, please try again", and then continue to repeat that as another and another invalid time was entered by a confused user, yet this is a common strategy in man-machine systems.

To be more helpful the system must learn something from person-to-person interaction. If I have asked you a question and you have revealed by your answer that you did not understand what I asked, I would be unlikely to repeat the question in precisely the same way. Instead I would speak more slowly or enlarge upon the original question, and perhaps give an example. Similarly, user-friendly voice response systems must incorporate fall-back announcements of a more explanatory nature, must record the user's progress through fall-back announcements to

avoid the endless loop situation described above, and must finally default to a human operator when all else fails.

Another impact of the considerations of the last two sections on system design manifests itself as an explosion in the vocabulary required. It is common for more words in the vocabulary to be devoted to error correction and recovery, than to normal operation.

4 SYSTEM DESIGN

Having considered some of the important human factors that affect a man-machine dialogue using speech, and noted their impact on system design in passing, a design for an interactive voice response system will be presented which is structured to accommodate user requirements whilst presenting logical system interfaces that permit economical realisation.

4.1 The Application

The application to be considered is an interactive information search of the type that it is practical to conduct over the telephone, employing an automatic voice response unit to guide the user through the search and present the information, with the user specifying his requirements using a 12-button tone signalling telephone. At BTRL a train timetable information service is being used in experiments, because it is a representative example of this class of application.

4.2 System Outline

The proposed design of the train timetable service is shown schematically in Fig 1. At the top level is the Dialogue Controller which directs lower level units in an interactive dialogue to establish the parameters for a search on the database, and passes down the results of that search.

It is intended that this design should form the model for many interactive information services, and that it should evolve to incorporate advances in the technology employed.

4.3 Database Manager

This unit contains the database of the system together with the ability to undertake searches on the data as requested by Dialogue Control. Naive users would be disturbed by a long silence whilst the data is being searched, so a fast response is desirable. However, it must be recognised that this requirement is likely to conflict with the practicalities of providing voice output from existing databases structured around conventional means of access, and so an appropriate "comfort" message may be essential to compensate.

4.4 Dialogue Control

Dialogue Control is the heart of the system and uses its model of the information available in the database to conduct a dialogue with the user to establish parameters for a search by the Database Manager. It controls the dialogue by instructing Kernel Control to undertake standard "dialogue kernels"; that is self-contained goal-oriented question and answer sequences designed to guide the user through a part of the total dialogue, such as the entry of a time of day, or a menu choice or the entry of a number. Kernel Control responds to Dialogue Control with the user's input, or a failure indication. Kernel Control ensures that the data is valid for the class of input required but it will often be necessary for Dialogue Control to apply further checks, for example to ensure the time is valid given its context in the interaction.

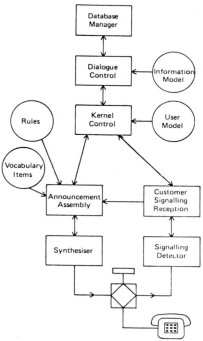

Fig.1   Interactive voice system structure

4.5   Kernel Control

Kernel Control expands the standard dialogue kernels requested by Dialogue Control giving guidance and controlling repair-loops to correct invalid entries, using its own "User Model", built up from measurement of error rates and reaction times, to select a level of presentation appropriate to the experience of the user. In addition to the kernel type, Dialogue Control specifies the set of messages to be used since this is itself application dependent. For example the "Get Time" kernel, which controls the entry of a time-of-day, uses a sub-set of five messages, current versions of which are shown in Table 1.

Table 1. SUB-SET OF MESSAGES USED FOR THE "GET TIME" KERNEL

Message	Announcement
M1	Using the 24 hour clock, please enter the time you wish to depart from Ipswich.
M2	The time must always be entered as a four digit number. Enter two digits for the hour followed by two digits for the minutes.
M3	For example to enter nine AM dial 0900, to enter five thirty PM dial 1730.
M4	Sorry, you have entered the time incorrectly. For Advice dial square.
M5	To repeat the question dial star, for advice dial square.

Fig 2 shows the operation of the "Get Time" kernel; several points may be noted.

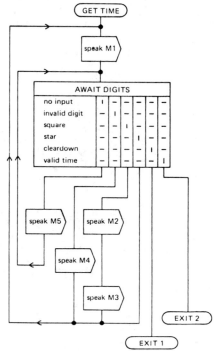

Fig. 2   Operation of the 'Get Time' kernel.

The current implementation does not record the experience level of the user, but instead assumes a competent user until mistakes are made. However the components of the message sub-set have been defined to permit a more explanatory approach to be adopted for inexperienced users.

At all stages of the dialogue the user may have a question repeated by pressing the "star" button of the telephone keypad, or seek further advice by pressing "square". The implementation described requires the user to actively request assistance in this way rather than giving further advice automatically when a mistake is made. It is hoped that success in the relatively simple task of requesting advice will build-up the novice's confidence.

The kernel at present allows the unsuccessful user to loop continuously until he gives up and clears-down. It is thought to be more satisfactory to forcibly terminate the interaction with an appropriate announcement when an excessive number of mistakes are made, or, if possible, fall-back to a human operator.

To implement the kernels, Kernel Control interacts with two lower level units; Announcement Assembly, which arranges for specified announcements to be spoken, and Customer Signalling Reception which receives signalling from the customer.

4.6   Announcement Assembly

Kernel Control specifies a message to Announcement Assembly in the form of a message number, together with any variable parameters and mode of speech controls. Announcement Assembly selects synthesiser parameters for each utterance needed in the announcement from the vocabulary and modifies them according to its utterance concatenation rules. Several utterance concatenation formats are built in to deal with variable parameters such as times of day, telephone numbers and quantities. A telephone number, for example, is specified by Kernel Control as "TO14328091" and Announcement Assembly takes the necessary utterance parameters, imposes the appropriate pitch and speed contour, and outputs the modified string to the Synthesiser.

It should be noted that it is at this level that precise wordings are defined; until now the speech has been considered in terms of abstract "messages" with a meaning that could be expressed by various wordings. This permits precise wording to be refined to suit experience gained, with the minimum of impact on the rest of the system.

At this level synthesis technique becomes relevant, because Announcement Assembly processes parameters before passing them to the Synthesiser. Consequently the choice of synthesis technique can be made to suit the application need, without affecting the higher level system design.

4.7 Synthesiser

The final link in the speech output chain is the Synthesiser which converts parameters passed by Announcement Assembly into the speech signal in a form suitable for transmission to the listener via a loudspeaker, or an analogue or digital transmission link. It is at this level any of the many available synthesiser chips may be employed.

4.8 Customer Signalling Reception

Receives characters (in the system described 0-9, "star" and "square") signalled by users and detected by the Signalling Detector. Kernel Control specifies the format of the expected character string in terms of number of characters, the valid set of input characters and the time-out to be applied. Customer Signalling Reception times the arrival of characters, measures inter-digit pauses and passes the data to Kernel Control at the end of the string. Invalid characters, and any of the "special function" characters (in this case "star" for repeat or "square" for advice) are passed immediately to Kernel Control. Customer Signalling Reception has a direct link to Announcement Assembly by which it can request a short pause in the announcement in order to verify the Signalling Detector output and thereby permit customer signalling to override announcements in the manner described in section 3.3.

4.9 Signalling Detector

Translates customer signalling into characters of the permitted signalling repertoire and passes them to Customer Signalling Reception. In the application described this was a standard decoder circuit for the tone signalling system internationally standardised as Signalling System Multi-Frequency No 4 (MF4).

6 CONCLUSIONS

Developments in speech processing technology mean that voice input and output will be used increasingly at the man-machine interface. Successful applications are those that are comfortable and rewarding for people to use, and to achieve this it is necessary to pay close attention to human factors. Some of the more important considerations have been discussed above.

ACKNOWLEDGEMENTS

Acknowledgements are made to the Director of System Evolution and Standards and Director of Research of British Telecom for permission to publish this paper. The practical work on speech synthesis used an experimental synthesiser which was supplied by International Computers Limited.

REFERENCES

/1/ Martin, J, System X, The Post Office Electrical Engineers Journal, Vol 71, p 221, January 1979.

/2/ Frame, P B and Cheeseman, D S, Customer Controlled Supplementary Services Using a Voice Guidance System, ISS 79, Paris, May 1979.

/3/ Holmes, J N, Parallel Formant Vocoders, Proc IEEE EASCON Conference, Washington DC, 1978.

/4/ Markel, J D and Gray, A H, Linear Prediction of Speech, Springer-Verlag, 1976.

/5/ Hanson, B L, Nacon, R J and Worrall, D P, New Custom Calling Services, Bell Laboratories Record, June 1980.

/6/ Lively, B L and Holinka, H, Automating Number Report in Directory Assistance, Ninth International Symposium on Human Factors in Telecommunication.

/7/ Youngs, E A, Bushnell, W J and Barchone-Wing, A, Automated Coin Toll Service: Human Factors Studies, Bell System Technical Journal, Vol 58, No 6.

/8/ Cox, A C and Cooper, M B, Selecting a Voice for a Specified Task: The Example of Telephone Announcements, Language and Speech, Vol 24, part 3, 1981.

/9/ Cox, A C, Why Your Telephone Will Need to Talk to You, IEE Communications '80, pp 122-124.

/10/ Clapham, W J, The Measured Error Rate of Multi-Tone Telephone Signalling in the Presence of Announcements, British Telecommunications Research Department Report No 921.

A Proposal for Improving Access to Heterogeneous Computer Networks

B A Huckle
The Hatfield Polytechnic, UK

Heterogeneous computer networks commonly present very complex interfaces to their users. We believe that the typical computer network interface acts as a deterrent to potential users who lack confidence in their ability to communicate effectively with machines, and to those who do not have the time to learn such complicated and often exacting procedures. We have designed a system that allows the user to view the network in a uniform manner, providing a user-tailorable communication medium and a network-wide filing system. This paper discusses the requirements for a unified interface and describes the system that we have designed to satisfy the needs.

1. INTRODUCTION

Much progress has been made in the development of facilities in heterogeneous computer networks. It is now possible to access many computer services using only a terminal and a telephone, or a direct connection to a computer network. Thus many users may potentially access many different computer systems offering a wide variety of services.

However, a major obstacle still exists in the form of the user interface. Users must learn to interact with many different environments: the network protocols, a number of different operating system command and response languages where the services required reside, and the services themselves (such as database management systems, special purpose packages, file editors and programming language environments). The amount of time and effort that users are required to invest before receiving the benefits of the services may be enormous. Far from encouraging the use of computer networks, the man-machine interface seems designed to put users off!

In addition there are a number of problems related to the storage of information in a network. Few, if any, networks have a comprehensive filing system that maintains directories of users' files, and allows automatic access to files. Thus users are required to remember where their files are stored and the conventions necessary to access and manipulate their files on each of the different filing systems to be used. Special protocols must be used to transfer files to computer systems where they are needed if they are not already there.

2. USER REQUIREMENTS

We have studied the problems of people communicating with time-sharing computer systems on a casual basis [1], and have identified a major cause of error as being the presence of a number of different environments. Thus the typical heterogeneous computer network can be seen to provide ample opportunity for user error.

We have researched the requirements of a specific group of users, students of disciplines other than computer science [2], but we believe that the findings are relevant for a wide range of potential computer network users, including scientists, managers and professionals.

The users need to view the network as a single entity with a consistent user interface. The users should be required to identify themselves (or log in) to the network only once per session, the connections and log in sequences to the individual hosts being carried out automatically where necessary.

The network facilities should be available to the users in a uniform manner, regardless of which host is being accessed. It is not possible or necessary, to provide all of the facilities of operating systems. A subset of facilities which will provide for the majority of applications is discussed in [2]. This includes the ability to create, delete, edit and manipulate files, execute user-written and system owned programs, set up batch jobs to run later, and invoke command language macros. All of the necessary translations between the command language of the user and those of the host operating systems should be carried out automatically. System and error messages should also be translated into a host independent form.

It should be possible for the user and his programs to access and manipulate files without having to specify where they are stored. Files should be transferred automatically to hosts where they are needed. An on-line explanation system to provide assistance to users experiencing difficulties is required. It is also desirable to provide the ability to communicate directly with a given host computer system, using its operating system command and

*This work supported by the UK SERC, Grant ref. GR/A 38601

response language (that is, a 'transparent' mode of working).

Finally, we have researched the recent developments in man-computer communication in general, and in more detail, the developments in operating systems command languages [3]. This has led us to believe that no single interface can be developed that will satisfy the requirements of the majority of potential users. What is needed is an interface that can be tailored to each individual user's requirements, such as that proposed by the British Computer Society's Working Party on Job Control Language [4].

The Unix operating system [5] is an example, since it is possible for users to reprogram the user interfacing software, the Shell [6]. However, reprogramming the Unix Shell is a major undertaking, that is normally only attempted by an experienced programmer with considerable time at his disposal. We would like to see a system that is much easier to modify and that requires no previous knowledge of programming. After all, the user who merely accesses a database once a month does not need to master programming skills, yet would like his interface with the network to be tailored to suit his needs, assist his memory, and to improve the efficiency of his interaction with the system.

3. A SOLUTION

The networks under consideration are composed of a number of host computer systems and a communications sub-network, which could be anything from a local area network to a public data service.

The hosts might be dedicated to network users, but in many situations (such as in the educational environment) they are more likely to be available for both local and remote use, the network users often being of less consequence to the systems' administrators than the local ones. In this situation, it is desirable that if a network link fails, the hosts should be capable of continuing to provide a service for their local users. In order to facilitate this and because of political considerations, we decided that no modifications to the hosts' operating systems should be required to accommodate the service that we propose, over and above the connection of the hosts to the communications sub-network. Thus the network software that we propose will be implemented either as user processes with no special privileges running on the hosts, or in dedicated processors acting as front-ends to the host computer systems, see fig. 1.

As a consequence, the system that we propose differs from a number of related projects.

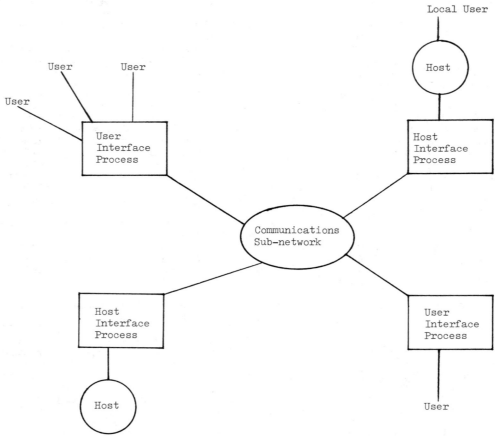

Fig. 1 Elements of the network, including HIPs and UIPs.

590

RSEXEC [7] attempted to implement a network-wide filing system, but required the use of a particular operating system (Tenex) by each of the host computer systems. The National Software Works [8] project also attempts to provide a global filing system, but again the host computer systems have no independently accessible file store.

The KIWINET/NICOLA Project [9] intends to provide a user-tailorable interface through which users may access a heterogeneous computer network. However, special operating systems must be developed for each host in the network, involving enormous effort.

The CONSUL project [10] attempts to provide a user-tailorable interface to any software, using the Unix reprogrammable Shell principle. However, the project requires all of the software to be redeveloped in a particular manner, so that it may be accessed via the user-tailored interface.

We believe that these types of approach are not suitable, due to the work involved and the effect on the operation of the host computer systems and their software.

There will be a number of processes active in the system that we envisage; one set providing the interface between the users and the network, which we shall call the User Interface Processes (UIPs), and another set of processes concerned with providing the interface between the hosts and the network, which we shall call the Host Interface Processes (HIPs).

There will be one HIP active for each host in the network, dealing with the host-dependent actions. Each process will consist of a common core, with host-dependent information being provided as data. Thus the work involved in adding a new host to the network may be minimised.

Any number of UIPs may be active, each servicing a group of users. Each UIP will maintain details of its users, including information about their file stores and their user profiles.

This approach differs from other attempts to solve the same problem, in that it distributes the processing around the network. This provides for rapid processing of host-dependent functions in dedicated processors.

The National Bureau of Standards' Network Access Machine [11] and Network Operating System [12] attempt to carry out all of the processing in a single processor, storing the macros necessary to process four different hosts on backing store [13]. Thus excessive overheads are incurred when accessing the macros, which has an adverse effect on response times.

Other attempts, such as the University of Rochester's Intelligent Gateway [14] have suffered from similar problems.

3.1 The Host Interface Process

A HIP modifies the interactions between the UIPs and its host computer system. The communication between the UIPs and the HIPs will be in a network standard form. UIPs will send commands to the HIPs in a Network Command Language, and responses will be sent from the HIPs to the UIPs in a Network Response Language. The communication between the HIPs and their hosts will be in the appropriate host operating system command and response language, see fig.2.

The HIP will receive commands from the UIPs in the Network Command Language. It will generate the appropriate commands in the host's command language, and send them to a user process running on the host. When the HIP receives a response either from the process initiated or from the host's operating system, it will generate the corresponding Network Response Language, and send it to the UIP.

The HIP may also process file names, transforming them from a network standard form into the format required by the host. The converse translation will also be necessary for file names appearing in systems and error messages.

When the user is communicating with a host in the transparent mode, the HIP will not perform any transformations. The HIP may continue to pass information between the UIP and the host. It will receive a command from the UIP when the transparent mode of working ends, thus signalling the HIP to commence the transformation again.

3.2 The User Interface Process

The UIP will allow access to the network's facilities for legal users in a uniform manner. It maintains profiles for each of its users which allow it to communicate with each user in their personally tailored command and response language. It will interpret commands given by the users and initiate the appropriate actions by sending commands in the Network Command Language to the HIPs, see fig. 2. The responses are translated into the users' tailored response languages by the UIP before being transmitted to the users' terminals.

The UIP will administer its users' network-wide file stores. It will maintain a directory of files for each user, recording where each file is stored (that is, on which host computer system) and implementing a uniform protection scheme. The directories may become out of date if host computer systems are not available or if files are removed by some means other than through the network system. Thus some of the UIP's processing will be concerned with updating its file directories by communicating with hosts where the files should be stored.

Since the users are not required to view the computer network as a series of independent hosts, they are not responsible for specifying where files should be stored. Therefore the UIP must decide which host should be used when

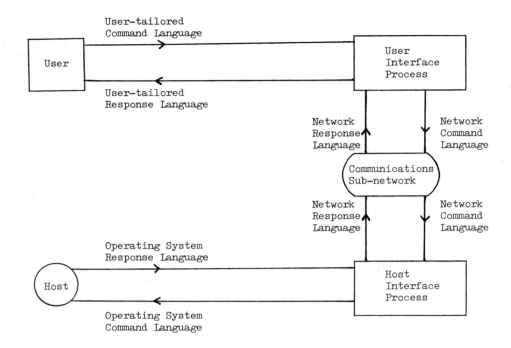

Fig. 2 Languages used for communication between the users, UIPs, HIPs and hosts.

a file is created, copied, etc. The decision will be based on such factors as the loading on the hosts (an attempt may be made at load sharing), user permissions (some hosts may restrict access to specified users), cost and the resources with which the file will be used, such as programming language compilers, and database management systems.

The UIPs will ensure that a given source program is always compiled using the same computer and compiler. It will also ensure that a given object program is always executed on the same host computer system, since even computers of the same model may have slight differences in their configuration that may give rise to inconsistencies. Furthermore, a given user's programs written in a particular language will always be compiled using the same compiler. Thus inconsistencies between different versions of the same programming language may be avoided.

Provision may be made for users to override this system and specify which host and compiler are to be used with a given source program.

The UIPs will be responsible for ensuring that files are present on the correct host computer system when they are needed. If files are located on a different host, the UIPs may transfer or copy them using a file transfer protocol.

4. IMPLEMENTATION

We have implemented the functions of the HIP for the DECsystem-10, and some of the functions of the UIP, including the ability of the user to tailor his own interface in a limited way, see fig. 3. The software runs as a normal user process on the DECsystem-10 at The Hatfield Polytechnic. A pseudo-teletype device is used

to process the commands transformed by the HIP software. A file of transformation information is input to the software, from which tables of commands and responses are initialised, together with their DECsystem-10 equivalents. The software is then ready to accept commands, process them and generate the appropriate responses.

It has been shown that for the set of facilities described above, a variety of different command and response languages may be translated into the TOPS-10 command and response language for the DECsystem-10. Experiments have been carried out using a variety of existing languages (such as the standard Unix Shell [5] and DTSS [15]), user tailored versions of these languages, and some newly devised command and response languages.

The software is not as flexible as we would like it to be, and does not allow for the variety of different types of interface that we would like. For example, it cannot easily provide a menu selection system. However, the software does allow command names to be redefined, and new composite commands to be implemented via the transformations or by the preparation and invocation of programs. In effect, any function that can be carried out using the DECsystem-10's TOPS-10 operating system or a program that exists or that the user is prepared to develop may be initiated via the transformations.

The 'transparent' mode of operation has also been implemented, so that the user may communicate directly with the DECsystem-10's operating system. A corresponding command to reverse the 'transparent' command is also available.

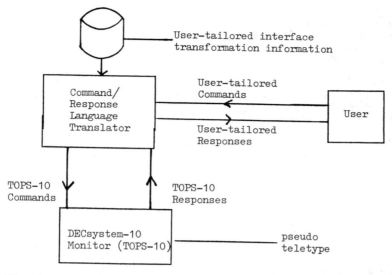

Fig. 3 Representation of software implemented

5. CONCLUSIONS

It has been shown that there is a requirement for a unified user interface to provide access to facilities in a heterogeneous computer network. A user tailorable interface is needed, which allows the user to define his own command and response languages. A network-wide filing system is also needed, which will provide information about files throughout the network in a uniform manner, and provide controlled access to the files.

A distributed software system has been designed to provide such an interface. This provides the potential for greater efficiency and faster response time than a centralised system.

Some of the software has been implemented, which proves the feasibility of the principles upon which the system is founded.

ACKNOWLEDGEMENT

The author would like to acknowledge the support of members of staff at the Hatfield Polytechnic, in particular the contributions to this research made by Dr G M Bull and Dr A .V stokes, and the software developed by Mr C Stephenson.

REFERENCES

[1] B.A. Huckle, Designing a command language for inexperienced computer users, Beech (ed), Command Language Directions, (North Holland, 1980), 201-212.

[2] G.M. Bull and B.A. Huckle, An interface for interactive users within a heterogeneous computer network, Proc. EuroIFIP 79, Samet (ed), (North Holland, 1979), 405-409.

[3] B.A. Huckle, The man-machine interface: Guidelines for the design of the end-user/system conversation, Savant Inst, 2 New Street, Carnforth, Lancs, UK. January 1981.

[4] K. Hopper (ed), A user-oriented command language: requirements and designs for a standard job control language, Heyden and Son Ltd., 1981.

[5] D. Ritchie and K. Thompson, the UNIX time sharing system, Communications of the ACM, Vol. 17, no. 7, 1974, 365-375.

[6] S R. Bourne, The UNIX Shell, Bell System Technical Journal, Vol. 57, no. 6, July 1978, 1971-1990.

[7] R.H. Thomas, A resource sharing executive for the ARPAnet, Proc. NCC, AFIPS Vol. 42, 1973, 155-163.

[8] R.E. Millstein, The National Software Works: A distributed processing system, Proc. ACM Annual Conference, 1977, 53-58.

[9] Three papers on KIWINET/NICOLA in D. Beech (ed), Command Language Directions, (North Holland, 1980).

[10] W. Mark, et. al., ISI research into cooperative interaction systems, University of Southern California, Information Sciences Institute, March 1980.

[11] S.W. Watkins and S.R. Kimbleton, Network access technology: a perspective, Proc. NCC, AFIPS Vol. 47, 1978, 495-503.

[12] S.R. Kimbleton, et. al., Network operating systems – an implementation approach, Proc. NCC, AFIPS Vol. 47, 1978, 773-782.

[13] R. Rosenthal and B.D. Lucas, The design and implementation of the National Bureau of Standards' Network Access Machine, NBS Special Publication, 500-35, 1978.

[14] J.E. Ball, et. al., RIG - Rochester's Intelligent Gateway: System Overview, IEEE Trans. Software Engineering, Vol. SE-2, no. 4, Dec. 1976, 321-328.

[15] S. Hardy and D. Mather, DTSS User's Primer, TM022, Dartmouth College, New Hampshire, USA, Aug. 1977.

Dr. Barbara Huckle obtained a BSc in Computer Science from The Hatfield Polytechnic in 1975. She then undertook research on the user interface to heterogeneous computer networks obtaining her PhD in April 1979 and publishing two papers as a result of this work.

During 1979-80 Dr. Huckle undertook a survey of man-machine interface research and development, sponsored by Savant Research Studies, which resulted in the publication of a technical report.

Dr. Huckle is currently engaged in research at The Hatfield Polytechnic on the improvement of the user interface to command-based software systems.

Dr. Huckle has participated in the development of standards for job control and command languages.

Use of the Video Response System in Education

J Magara, M Takei, J Tamura
Nippon Telegraph and Telephone
Public Corporation, Japan

The Video Response System provides remote users with various service courses by presenting audio-visual information, for example, color photographs, sound and movies, through 4MHz bandwidth transmission lines. The flow of the service course is easily programmed in a high level program language specially designed for this interactive video information system. These make the system adaptable to wide applications including information retrieval, entertainment and CAI. Some educational training courses for internal NTT utilization are provided by the system now. One titled "Fundamental Telephone Network Planning" is used for foreign trainee education.

1. INTRODUCTION

The Video Response System(VRS) is one of the interactive visual information systems developed by Nippon Telegraph and Telephone Public Corporation(NTT).

The VRS presents various kinds of information, such as color photographs, movies and sound, to the user individually and instantly upon request. The system effectively provides various services. One of the impressive applications is computer assisted video/audio instruction. The VRS serves some educational courses to the public and some training courses to engineers engaged in the telecommunications industry.

This paper describes the outline of the VRS and its applications in educational field.

2. System Outline

The VRS is composed of a center, terminals and transmission lines. The center consists of central processing units, audio-visual information files and exchange equipment. A terminal consists of an ordinary color television set and a pushbutton telephone or a keyboard. Individual transmission lines connect the center with individual terminals to transfer audio-visual information. This information may be transmitted from the center to distant terminals via a subscriber relay station, which is installed for economical expansion of the service area.

The VRS center and the subscriber relay station are located in Tokyo, in Ginza and in Shibuya respectively. About 120 terminals are set in telephone offices and exhibition spots in Tokyo and one in Osaka.

2.1 Hardware

The VRS hardware structure is illustrated in fig. 1.

2.1.1 Center
In the VRS center, the central processing units control various kinds of audio-visual file equipment to present information to terminals.

(1) central processing units
Three mini-computers named MCP, IOC and DFC control the system by sharing the system functions.
The main control processor(MCP) supervises the whole system by giving commands and accepting responses to and from the other two processors in the center and the subscriber-relay-station controller. The MCP also communicates with other information systems to use their high computational abilities or databases.
The input/output control processor(IOC) interfaces with terminals by controlling switching equipment.
The IOC also accesses analog movie equipment.
The digital file control processor(DFC) controls digital audio-visual file equipment.
The DFC not also accesses file equipment but generates visual information, such as character messages and statistical graphs, on demand.

(2) information file equipment
There are various kinds of information files, as listed in table 1, according to the type and characteristics of the information stored in them.

The digital video file equipment(DVF) is used for storing color still pictures such as photographs and paintings.
The pattern and character file equipment(PCF) is used for storing or generating color illustrations and characters.

The random access movie equipment(RME) is used for movies in the still-picture and the movie-on-request services. It consists of a video-cassette cell, a mechanical hand and VTR sets.
The time prescheduled movie equipment(TME) is used for moves in the time-prescheduled-movie service. It is a 16mm film automatic setting projecter.

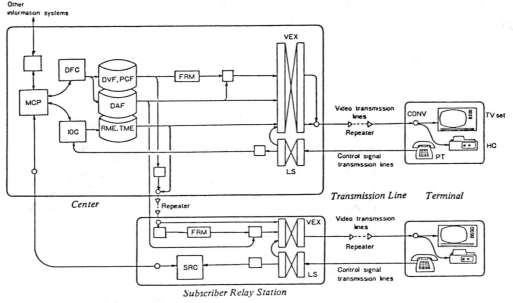

MCP · Main Control Processor
DFC · Digital File Control Precessor
IOC · Input/Output Control Precessor

DVF,PCF · Digital Video Files
DAF · Digital Audio File
RME,TME · Movie Files

FRM · Frame Refresh Memory
SRC · Subscriber-Relay-Station Controler

CONV· Converter
PT · Pushbutton Telephone or Keyboard
HC · Hard Copy equipment

LS · Local Switch
VX · Video Exchange equipment

Fig. 1. Hardware structure

The digital audio file equipment(DAF) is for narration and sound.

(3) information entry equipment
Audio-visual information is easily stored in digital information files by video cameras and magnetic tape recorders during service time.

Color pictures such as photographs and paintings are registered in the digital video file(DVF) through the video camera or the video tape recorder of the video/audi information input equipment(VAI).

Color illustrations and characters are generated by the entry equipment called PAC. Illustrations are inputted by the facsimile part of the PAC. Characters are inputted by tablet. Using the word processing, picture zooming and synthesizing functions of the PAC,

color pictures are easily generated and stored into the pattern and character file(PCF). Sound such as voices and music entered into the digital audio file(DAF) through the audio tape recorder of the VAI. Analog audio signals from the VAI are coded into digital signals by the DAF.

2.1.2 Subscriber Relay Station
The subscriber relay station is located between the center and distant terminals. It is introduced for economical expansion of the service area. The economization is performed by two methods; subscriber line concentration through the exchange equipment in the station, and multiplex transmission of still pictures from the center to the station.

Table 1. Information file equipment

Category		File Equipment		Information	Capacity	Average Access Time	Note
Video	Still Picture	DVF	(Digital video file equipment)	Color still picture	4,000 frames/ 400 MB disk pack	0.2 sec.	
		PCF	(Pattern and character file equipment)	Character, Figure	100,000 ~ 150,000 frames/ 200 MB disk pack	0.1 sec.	5,000 characters, 60 colors
	Movie	RME	(Random access movie equipment)	Movie	120 video cassette tapes, 12 VTRs	11 sec.	Request movie or composite still picture
		TME	(Time scheduled movie equipment)	Movie	10 reels, ~70 min./reel	—	Time scheduled movie
Audio		DAF	(Digital audio file equipment)	Explanatory comment on each picture	4,000 messages/ 200 MB disk pack (10 sec./message)	0.2 sec.	

2.1.3 Exchange Equipment

The exchange equipment in the center and the station consists of local switch and video exchange equipment. This enables the existing telephone network to be used economically as a part of the system.

2.1.4 Transmission Lines

The video transmission lines are ordinary telephone pair cables or low-loss broadband pair cables with IC video band repeaters inserted. The lines transmit video and audio signals simultaneously by modulating audio signals with 4.5MHz carriers. A control signal from a terminal is transmitted as multi-frequency signal through another ordinary telephone line.

2.1.5 Terminals

The terminal consists of an ordinary color television set, a pushbutton telephone or a keyboard, a converter and optional hardcopy equipment.
The pushbutton telephone or the keyboard is for selecting and requesting information. The converter equalizes and amplifies video and audio signals in the baseband frequency and converts them to VHF TV signals for presentation. The hardcopy equipment is for recording pictures displayed on the TV screen.

2.2 Software

The VRS software consists of a control program and service programs, as illustrated in fig. 2.

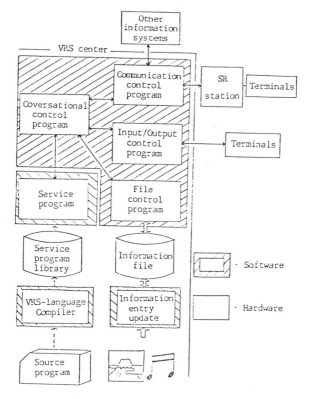

Fig. 2. Software structure

2.2.1 Control Program

A control program consists mainly of a conversational control program, a communications control program and an information entry/update program.

The conversational control program controls data exchanges between the center and terminals by analyzing request signals from terminals, executing service programs and sending various kinds of information back to the terminals.
The communication control program controls the communication between the VRS center and other information systems or the subscriber relay station. With the help of this program, the center communicates with a DEMOS-E system* in the basic mode transmission control procedure and with the station in the HDLC procedure.
The information entry/update program inputs or deletes audio-visual information into or from information files during service time.

(*)   NTT's scientific and engineering calculation time-sharing system.

2.2.2 Service Programs

Service programs define how and what information to present for still-picture service courses. They are coded in a high level language specially designed for this system, a VRS-language. The VRS-language has not only usual data processing instrustions but also various input/output and communication instructions, which present the service functions listed below.

(a)   Presentation of various information patterns, characters, color photographs, animations, movies, voices, music and so forth.

    animations :   successive presentation of series of still pictures at short intervals.

    movies   :   scenes in video cassette tapes may be inserted among still pictures.

    voices   :   any sounds may be added to
    and music   each picture as explanatory comment or effective sounds.

(b)   Various ways of presentation superimposing, flashing, monitoring of terminal input, generating of graphs and figures.

(c)   Free process of service courses Processes of service courses are freely defined by service programs in VRS-language. As the system functions, a user may go backward to see the previous pictures on the way. Moreover, he can restart service courses at the point at which he stopped looking earlier.

(d)   Communication with other information systems This is for obtaining data from the databases of other systems or requesting special or high-load processing.

(e)   E-C-E service(end-to-end via center) In this new kind of video communication service, a terminal communicates with another terminal with the help of the VRS center. At the center, input signals from a terminal are visualized as pictures to be displayed on the other terminal.

(f)   Data File

Each service course may have its own data files as well as audio-visual information files. This makes it much easier to provide information retrieval and to construct a small image database because the procedural part and the data/information part of service programs are made individual.

3. SERVICES

3.1 Service Mode

According to the type of pictures and method of presentation, VRS services are classified into three modes: still-picture service, movie-on-request service and time-prescheduled-movie service.

In the still-picture service, still pictures, such as characters, drawings and photographs, and sounds, such as voices and music are offered to the user upon request. Also, insertion of movies between still pictures, superimposing and animation are possible. Fig. 3 shows examples of still pictures.

In the movie-on-request service, the movie program requested by a user is furnished to him at once. In the time-prescheduled-movie service, movie programs are offered at regularly scheduled times. Any user may enjoy this during the service time.

3.2 Service Courses

The VRS has been providing various service courses. Table 2 shows some examples of them. Still-picture service courses are classified into "home service" and "business service".

Home service is for use in daily life and has three kinds of applications: guidance, education and entertainment. Business service is for use by enterprises and has three kinds of appications: information retrieval, guidance and training.

Fig. 3. Still picture

The service course provided now is limited in number because the service is experimental. A wider range of applications is considered to be appropriate for the VRS service. For example:

(a)   Information retrieval/Information service
* information on various commodities in sales activities,
* marketing, inventory control, manufacturing processes, parts control
* medical information(e.g. remote diagnosis)
* life information service(e.g. shopping, leisure)

(b)   Computer Assisted Instruction(CAI)
* employee training in enterprises
* audio-visual education in educational organizations
* adult education, linguistic education at home

(c)   entertainment
* Quizzes, games

4. APPLICATIONS IN EDUCATIONAL FIELDS

4.1 Computer Assisted Instruction

One of the most effective VRS applications is "CAI"-computer assisted instruction. The CAI service courses provided by the VRS have made full use of the system functions and the VRS-language mentioned before.

Table 2. Service courses

Service			Example of Courses
Still-pictures	Home Service	Guidance	Visiting the museum in Tokyo area
		Education	English study, ABC's of micro-computers
		Entertainment	Othello game, Quiz corner
	Business Service	Information Retrieval	Geographic information, Order entry of car parts
		Guidance	Various NTT products, Real Estate
		Trainning	Fundamental planning for telephone network (English version) Electronics switching equipment
Movie-on-request			VRS introduction Education --- science, sports, arts, musics
Time-prescheduled-movie			Daily life information Entertainment --- hobbies, animation

They are suitable for individual study. The advantage is:
- (a) No time restriction
  Learners can study the desired subject any time they like.
- (b) Free selection of subjects
  Learners can choose any subject among many service courses.
- (c) Study at learners' own pace.

Learners receive educational information and respond to it in CAI courses, whose processes are defined by service programs in VRS-language. So, the CAIs are audio-visual instructions having immediate feedback functions. For example, a CAI course can estimate quickly how well learners have comprehended the contents and verify the teaching process according to the estimation.

The service courses of the VRS are easily and efficiently produced by utilizing the various system functions, so the system can serve CAI courses rich in quantity and quality to many people.

4.2 Actual Educational Courses

The VRS has been providing the various CAI courses;"English Study(Introduction)","English Conversation for Traveling Abroad","Drill in Mathematics","The ABC's of Micro-computer","Table Manners","How to Play GO", etc. for general users and "Electronic Switching Equipment", "Engineering Standards in Fundamental Telephone Network Planning", "Various NTT Products", etc. for internal NTT training.

In these courses, various CAI techniques are found using the VRS functions. "English Conversation for Traveling Abroad" shows several movie scenes after explanations by still pictures. In "How to Play GO", flashing is used to notify viewers of important points on the GO-board and animation is used to show the smooth process of the games . These are realized easily by utilizing rich expression of the VRS-language.

Not only CAI courses, the VRS offers educational movies also, such as "Honorific Expression in Daily Life","Introduction to Oceanography" and "Heredity" in the movie-on-request and the time-prescheduled-movie services.

4.3 Effect in training courses

(1) outline of training courses
Every year, NTT provides engineering group training courses to foreign trainees in telecommunications subjects. One of these courses has been successfully utilizing the VRS service course, "Engineering Standards in Fundamental Telephone Network Planning".

Trainees are college graduates, working in the telecommunications organization or the administrations in developing countries. At the beginning of the course, all of them are assigned to self-paced study in accordance with the VRS training course to uniform their knowledge in the field of telecommunications.

With five terminals provided in the classroom, trainees may use the VRS whenever they like. This enables them to compensate for defect of group training.

This VRS training course consists of five sections: introduction, engineering standards of traffic, transmission, stability and summary. The length of each section is arranged to keep learners' attention, 20-40 minutes for each course.

The trainee can select a proper section at the beginning of the course. If he dose not have enough time to complete the section, he can restart the training course later at the point at which he was stopped.

Explanations, and questions are combined appropriately so as not to bore the trainee. If he thinks the explanation is easy, he may skip to the next question. If he makes a mistake or thinks a question is too hard to answer, he may get a hint or more detailed explanation. By answering questions and getting proper explanations or estimations quickly, he can continue to learn with confidence.

(2) result on courses
According to questionaires after the course, most of the trainees find the following points attractive in the VRS training course:
- (a) The same program can be repeated.
- (b) Information is given both in the form of pictures and sound.
- (c) The system can be used whenever desired.
- (d) Each learner can work at his or her own pace.
- (e) The terminal is easy to operate.

And required improvements are:
- (f) function to designate any specific picture frame required
- (g) indication of the time spent on completing the program at the end.

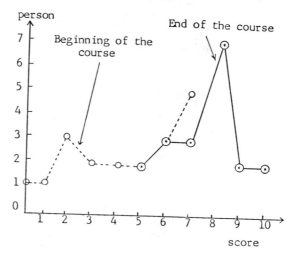

	Beginning		End
mean score	4.4	→	7.5
deviation	2.2	→	1.4

when full score is 10

Fig. 4. Comparison of scores

So, when this system is applied parallel with a group training course, uniformity of the training of the individuals is noticeably improved. It should be noted that scores obtained at the end of the course were not only higher but the deviation was smaller than the one at the beginning of the course, as shown in fig. 4.

5. CONCLUSION AND FURTHER INVESTIGATION

The VRS is a new communication system which can provide various versatile services. Education, especially CAI, is expected to be one of the most useful applications.

Through experimental service, fundamental technologies have been established. For general education service, however, technology for further economy should be developed, considering the public willingness to pay for it. For special education such as training in business, system techniques and service software need to be investigated to meet demands for higher definition and more sofisticated facilities.

Important subjects to be developed are as follows:
(a) Optical fiber transmission technology
    This will enable the VRS network to be constructed economically and also will allow other telecommunications services, such as video telephones and high-speed facsimile, to be provided sharing a single subscriber line.

(b) Optical beam accessed memory technology
    To prepare various teaching materials, low cost and high capacity random access audio-visual information file equipment is necessary.
(c) Devices and techniques for high definition pictures
    In business enterprises or laboratories, it is often necessary to examine detailed figures, such as blueprints and internal organs.

References

(1) K.Haji, "Video Response System-VRS", ICC'78 Conference Record, Vol.3, pp38.3.1-38.3.4

(2) J.Magara et al., "Enhanced Video Response System", ICC'81 Conference Record, Vol.2, pp24.4.2-24.4.5

(1) Joichi MAGARA

Joichi Magara was born in 1944. He graduated Tohoku University, Sendai, Japan and received B.E.E. in 1967. After graduation, he joined Nippon Telegraph and Telephone Public Corporation (NTT) as a carrier transmission engineer and engaged in the development on coaxial transmission line switching systems, and high-speed data transmission system. He was the chief of Plant Engineering section, Tohoku Telecommunication Bureau, 1976. He is now a staff engineer of Visual Communications Division, Engineering Bureau and a project leader of Video Response System (VRS).

(2) Makoto TAKEI

Makoto Takei was born in Tokyo, in 1947. He studied at Waseda University, Tokyo and received Master of Engineering degree in E.E. in 1973. He has been working for Nippon Telegraph and Telephone Public Corporation (NTT) since graduation and joined microwave systems design and microwave PCM systems development. He was the chief of Plant Engineering section, Kitakyusyu Urban Telecommunication Division, 1978. He is now a staff engineer of Visual Communications Division, Engineering Bureau and engaged in the development of Video Response System (VRS). He also received Master Science in Engineering Economic Systems from Stanford University, California, U.S.A. in 1977.

(3) Jun'ichi TAMURA

Jun'ichi Tamura was born in 1949. He graduated Yamanashi Univeersity, Kofu, Japan and received B.E.E. in 1971. After graduation, he joined Nippon Telegraph and Telephone Public Corporation (NTT) as an information system engineer and engaged in the development of online data communication systems and evaluation of system performance. He in now a staff engineer of Visual Communications Division, Engineering Bureau and engaged in the development of Video Response System (VRS).

Status and Evolution of the RPCNET Network in an Operational Environment

F Caneschi, L Lenzini, C Menchi
CNUCE, Italy

RPCNET is the italian computer network which connects several computing centers belonging to the Italian National Research Council, Universities and no-profit organizations, and was described in several papers from the technical point of view. Here we explain the necessity of an evolution in the RPCNET implementation, caused both by political decisions and by the problems that we found in RPCNET version I. This evolution, as a first step, led to RPCNET version II. The future of RPCNET is dealt with in the last part of the paper: in particular, the next-to-come introduction of a public, X-25 based, data network in Italy led us to start a new project, whose deadlines are sketched in the last part of the paper.

1.0 INTRODUCTION

RPCNET is the italian computer network which connects several computing centers belonging to the Italian National Research Council, Universities and no-profit organizations.
The RPCNET architecture and basic services were deeply described in several previous papers, which mainly dealt with network's technical aspects (ICCC78, IAA78 and others).
During the first three years of RPCNET operation, the RPCNET managing team encountered both political and technical problems; some of them were solved, others still need a complete solution. We can cite, among the above mentioned problems, items such as user access control, maintenance, contacts with the Italian PTTs, user assistance, network control and so on.
In the next sections, the choices which based the policy followed by the General Informatics Committee (Commissione Generale per l'informatica - CGI) of the Italian National Research Council (CNR) in the last few years on the distribution of computer facilities to scientific/technical users in Italy are explained.

1.1 Computing Power Distribution

The growing demand by national scientific/technical users for computer facilities has made the institution of CNR computer centers indispensable in areas where users exceed a certain critical threshold. In recent years, different CNR computer centers have been established in Torino, Milano, Bologna, Genova, Firenze and Frascati in addition to the already existing CNUCE Institute in Pisa. Other centers will be instituted in the near future (in Padova, for example). In some areas where computer structures supported by Universities or private bodies already exist, the CGI has, apart from the proposal for the equalization of the tariff duties for

researchers of both organisations, also stipulated conventions (in Roma, Napoli, Palermo - this last center is within the RPCNET network) so as to optimize the use of existing public computing resources.

1.2 Networking

The extensive, always growing and diversifying demands from the field of research, the scantiness of professionally well-prepared staff, the limitations of financial resources and the cost of software and hardware make it difficult for one single computer center to provide the extensive range of facilities required by the different fields of research. The interworking of different computers through a network allows the integration of facilities offered by the individual computing centers, with a consequent qualitative and quantitative enlargement of the overall computing facilities which would otherwise be impossible in the case of individual centers.

1.3 Differentiation of hardware

Up to now, the CGI has maintained a position of equidistance in its relationship with computer manufacturers, encouraging in this way differentiated choices for different areas. The present situation, as far as mainframes are concerned, is as in the table here

Site	Manufacturer(s)
Bologna	DIGITAL
Firenze	OLIVETTI
Frascati	IBM
Genova	CDC
Milano	SIEMENS, IBM
Pisa	IBM, IBM
Torino	IBM

depicted, and it can be foreseen that within a short time, an equilibrium will be achieved on the computing power supplied by the different manufacturers. In addition to the above mentioned main centers, several mini and micro computers from different manufacturers are running within CNR institutions.

2.0 MANAGEMENT EXPERIMENTATION OF RPCNET - ADVANTAGES AND CONSTRAINTS

Right from 1979, the CGI has been experimenting on the proposal mentioned in 1.2. For reasons of practicalness and prudence, a number of computing centers using IBM machines were chosen and through RPCNET, an experimental management project was started (January '80 - December '82), and is still underway. This experiment is already showing how it is possible, through RPCNET, not only to integrate the hardware/software resources of the participating centers, but also, and above all, to transfer precious cultural and professional benefits to recently instituted computing centers from centers which, like CNUCE, are provided with highly skilled staff.

Although RPCNET characteristics and services were already described in a number of papers (ICCC78 and IIA78 among others), it is worthwhile to recall here the three main services that some Applications built on top of RPCNET provide:

* Interactive Terminal Access

* Bulk File Transfer (often referred to as Spool File Transfer)

* Remote Data Access

The above mentioned services were used intensively by the RPCNET users' community, as we already pointed out in BUD181 and BUD281. Generally speaking, we can say that at a first moment RPCNET was used for the same services the users were used to have with standard tools, like hardware terminal concentrators, or bulk terminals. Only after some time, the users recognized the benefits of having some "intelligence in loco", instead of always requesting services to a centralized entity.
A useful example of this may be found in BUD181.

The testing of a certain number of managerial structures, the rationalization of terminal linking within the network, of languages, and of application software, etc. are other objectives which appear to be attainable when the experiment will be completed around December 1982 (see also BUD181);

On the other hand, RPCNET was the result of a research project, and as such, it inevitably presents limitations, namely:

a. given the limited man-power available, the implementation of RPCNET was limited to the operating system VM/370 working on IBM or IBM compatible machines. This fact prevented other computer centers which did not have IBM machines to be connected to RPCNET.

b. for problems of an economic nature, it has not been possible to use front-ends which would have permitted the separation, both physical and managerial, of the communication system from the EDP structure. Infact, in the RPCNET implementation, the communication system is implemented in the EDP structure. This fact implies that, when the system is overloaded, errors may arise, which require re-transmission of packets and, consequently, increasing delay times (see also BUD281);

c. since the present implementation of RPCNET calls for heavy modifications to the operating system VM/370, the maintenance of RPCNET, apart from being extremely complex in nature, has to be done frequently so as to keep pace with the evolution of the VM/370. This requires the part-time work (50%) of 5 persons highly qualified both in the VM/370 and in RPCNET. This also slowed down the development of new Applications, such as an efficient Mail system, for example, and the promotions of the existing ones.

However, it is believed that this constraint will be greatly reduced in a few months time, with the operation of a new network software already designed and at present under implementation.

d. as the RPCNET was designed in the first half of the 70's (see IIA78), the related protocols do not conform to the CCITT and ISO standards (see OSI80).

The constraint of point b) can be eliminated by the next-to-come activation (1982/83) of the Italian public data network. The "Communication System" of the public network will in fact be acquired and managed by the Italian PTT.

The constraints of points a) and b) could be overcome by the CGI with the help of the network architectures that the various supplying companies have recently made available to their customers, as the SNA (Systems Network Architecture) of IBM, the DNA (Digital Network Architecture) of DIGITAL, etc.

These different types of network architecture, even if they have the advantage of working on top of public networks, are normally limited to the use of the hardware/software designed by their producers. The user is thus obliged to have only one supplier and to adapt the applications to the facilities provided by that system. This inevitably leads to the impossibility of selecting, for a certain application, the most adequate and most economical products.

Adopting in this way a certain network architecture, SNA, DNA, etc., it can be envisaged that within the public networks, "clubs" of IBM users, DIGITAL users, etc. will be formed, without being able to take benefit from 'resource sharing' between heterogeneous machines.

3.0 RPCNET VERSION 2

When RPCNET was implemented under the VM/370 Operating System, no "standard" tools were available which could be used for inserting such a system in a computer network. The implementors were so obliged to modify the standard operating system in order to introduce supports like Virtual Terminal and Spool File Transfer (see also ICCC78), just to cite the two most heavily used Applications. RPCNET Version 2 will makes of standard tools for implementing network applications, in order to avoid modifications to the operating system. In the following, a brief description of our approach for the two Applications quoted above will be given.

3.1 Interactive Terminal Support

A new feature in the VM/370 operating system, the Logical Device Support (see also IBMVM), allows a user program to emulate a terminal to the system. In RPCNET Version 2, the Interactive Terminal Support makes use of this feature, so eliminating the need of modifications to the operating system. It should be stressed that the communication part of RPCNET is independent on the evolution of the operating system under which it runs. The Terminal support, as it is implemented under RPCNET Version 1, is shown in Fig. 1. Two modules were added to the VM/370 operating system, which performed the interface between the operating system itself and the Terminal Application. Moreover, some standard modules were modified, in order for the operating system to be aware both of "fake" terminals created due to requests coming from the network, and of real

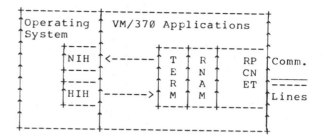

Legenda:
RPCNET - RPCNET network software
RNAM - Network Access Method
TERM - Terminal Application
NIH   - Network Interface Handler
HIH   - Hypervisor Interface Handler

Figure 1:
Terminal Support in RPCNET Version 1

terminals requests which had to be addressed to another operating system. In RPCNET Version 2, the Terminal Application was substituted by a Pass-Through-like (see IBMVM) Application, and the two modules which have been added to the operating system were removed, as well as all other modifica-

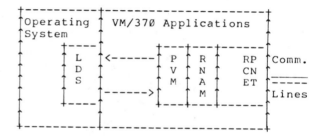

Legenda:
RPCNET - RPCNET network software
RNAM - Network Access Method
PVM   - Pass-Through-like Application
LDS   - Standard Logical Device Support

Figure 2:
Terminal Support in RPCNET Version 2

tions (see Fig. 2).

3.2 Spool File Transfer Support

Up till now, the Spool File Transfer under RPCNET was performed by a set of programs which were extentions of the standard VM/370 operating system: this fact allowed a good performance, but the cost was that of a modification of the operating system. In RPCNET Version 2, the Spool File Transfer is integrated with the RSCS Networking facility, which allows the operator:

1. to issue the same commands for both "standard" file transmissions and RPCNET ones,

2. to reduce the time when a new release of the operating system has to be put into service.

A module was added to the standard operating system for RPCNET Version 1 Spool File Transfer support, which has been removed in RPCNET Version 2.

3.3 Electronic Mail

We decided to give the RPCNET community a reasonable "electronic mail" function, by using the Spool File Transfer Support (see Sect. 3.2). This function should make part of a prototype office automation application which addressess to the various text-processing requirements of technical professionals, secretaries and managers. The text-processing needs of this group of people include the internal correspondence and documentation, ranging from short informal notes to working papers. The office automation application we are considering should address all the various aspects of "document" creation, filing, storage, retrieval and distribution.

3.4 Drawbacks of RPCNET Version 2

With RPCNET Version 2, almost all the troubles coming from the continous evolution of the operating system are solved: only two limitations remain, which can not be solved in a "evolutionary" manner, but rather with a completely different approach:

1. The implicit homogeneity of RPCNET (only the VM/370 implementation is currently running) does not allow an integrated network of different manufacturer's computers;

2. The RPCNET protocols (see IIA78) are not up-to-date with the proposed international standards, and cannot support an X-25 interface.

The drawbacks so far described could be eliminated with a considerable effort of re-programming RPCNET both with new protocols and under different operating systems: this would lead to tenths of men-years dedicated to such a project. On the other hand, the growing demand of a national computer network requires that this problem be solved: our solution is dealt with in the next sections.

4.0 THE END OF RPCNET: THE BEGINNING OF OSIRIDE

In order to obviate fully the constraints of RPCNET without loosing the experience we gained in designing, implementing and managing RPCNET, CNR intends to start a project called OSIRIDE (*) (OSI su Rete Italiana Dati Eterogenea - OSI on Heterogeneous Italian Data Network), articulated as follows:

1. Designing of a network architecture (OSIRIDE) which complies fully with OSI and which, in particular, follows the X.25 specifications of the Italian Data Network (The first three layers of the OSI Reference Model);

2. Identification of a limited number of basic applications, namely the Remote file Access (on top of which the file transfer and the Remote Job Entry are to be constructed), the Access to Interactive Terminals, and the definition of related protocols;

3. Implementation of the above-mentioned architecture and basic applications on different computer manufacturers by means of contracts with either the manufacturers themselves, or highly specialized software houses in that field;

4. Maintenance of the above mentioned software by the companies which have implemented the software.

5.0 OSIRIDE IMPLEMENTATION CHARACTERISTICS

The implementation of the OSIRIDE architecture in the various heterogeneous computers shall:

(*) Osiride (Osiris) was the God of the Syrian Cult, the son of Earth (Geb), the father, and Sky (Nut), the mother; husband and brother of Iside (Isis) and father of Oro. In the myth, Osiris (Summer) was cut to pieces by his brother Seth (Winter) and recomposed and reanimated by Isis and became the God of the Underworld. He was later avenged by Oro who killed Seth. He was worshipped by the Syrians and the Egyptians by a constant cult and was the God of Fertility (in fact, he impersonates Nile), of Summer and of the Underworld, representing in this last case the personal salvation of every dying man.

- not require modifications to the operating systems;

    this implies that up-dating and maintenance of the OSIRIDE software are independent from those of the operating systems under which the network software will work.

- be easily up-datable

    this implies that implementation shall keep pace with the evolution undergone by the protocols in the different working groups of ISO (this process will stop when these protocols are declared standard).

- be easily comprehensible

    this implies that implementation shall be fully documented according to specifications supplied by CNR.

- co-exist with the implementation of the network architecture provided by the manufacturers;

    this implies that the OSIRIDE shall work parallel to SNA, DNA, etc.

6.0   FORESEEN OPERATIONAL PLAN

The OSI/Reference Model architecture may be implemented either on each mainframe or in an "OSI" dedicated processor (OSI Front-End). At the moment we are analyzing the following possibilities:

1. OSIRIDE implemented in the mainframe. Even if we do believe that this be the most logical solution it may require a strong co-operation with the manufacturers. This may cause problems during the test phase, because technical people working for different manufacturers have to interact and collaborate.

2. OSIRIDE implemented on a Front-End processor. This approach has the advantage of requiring only a single implementation, and, consequently, of reducing the needed man-power. The main disadvantages of this solution may be summarized as follows:

    a. In a Direct Memory Acccess (DMA) type of connection, the hardware interface between the mini and the mainframe depends on the structure of the mainframe itself. The implementation of a specialized hardware may require more time

and a considerable amount of co-operation between the two manufactirers involved.

    b. A TP type of connection, even if more easily available, would give rise to problems of throughput and flow-control.

    c. Addressing problems may arise if OSIRIDE is to coexist with the architecture of the manufacturer.

3. Alternative implementations. It is possible, generally speaking, to insert into the network gateways which carry out the transformation between a manufaturer's architecture and OSI. By using this approach, the gateways can use OSI structure and protocols between them, and converse with the mainframes according to the manufacturer's architecture. A gateway of this kind is very complex and would require an additional available man-power.

A decision will, anyway, be taken by the end of this year. The implementation of the OSIRIDE will be articulated in the following phases:

    a.   selection of pilot computing centers where a first experiment will be carried out;

    b.   installation of hardware and software for X25 and PAD (Packet Assembly/Disassembly) in the centers mentioned above;

    c.   test of the hardware and software;

    d.   definition of OSIRIDE in the different computer manufacturers operating systems;

    e.   definition of implementation specifications for the transport layer;

    f.   definition of implementation specifications for the session layer;

    g.   definition of implementation specifications for the Remote File Access protocol;

    h.   definition of implementation specifications for mapping functions between real and virtual file systems;

    i.   definition of implementation specifications for management functions;

j. implementation of OSIRIDE on different computers;

k. final test of OSIRIDE.

At the end of phase c), the software/hardware supplied by the different producers will be extensively tested. In particular, a TTY terminal linked to a public network node (and not to the transmission control unit of the computer) will be able to "log-in" an application on any OSIRIDE subscriber.

7.0 CONCLUSIONS

The RPCNET experiment has shown once more the usefulness of a networking support in a research environment; moreover, it is also showing that such a support should be as much as possible independent of the evolution of the manufacturer's operating systems, and should be flexible enough as to remain up to date with the evolution of the international standards, in order to easily allow the interconnection of different systems. The experience we gained (and are still gaining) on RPCNET led us to the design of OSIRIDE, which is going to be the CNR's computer network for the '80s.

REFERENCES

BUD181: F. Caneschi, G. Cresci, D. Lari, L. Lenzini, F. Naldi, C. Menchi "Tools and organisational structures for managing RPCNET", Working Papers of COMNET'81, Statistical Publishing House, Budapest 1981, pp 5-78:5-91

BUD281: F. Caneschi, L. Lenzini, C. Menchi: "The behaviour of a packet switching network running under a time-sharing operating system", Proceedings of COMNET '81, North Holland Publishing Company 1981.

OSI80: ISO DP 7498 "Data Processing - Open Systems Interconnection - Basic Reference Model".

ICCC78: F. Caneschi, E. Ferro, L. Lenzini, M. Martelli, C. Menchi, M. Sommani, F. Tarini: "The architecture of and the Service Facilities provided by RPCNET- An Italian Computer Network for Educational and Research Institutions." Proceedings of ICCC '78 Kyoto.

IIA78: F. Caneschi: "A computer network: structure and protocols of the RPCNET" IIASA PP-78-12, December 1978.

IBMVM: IBM Virtual Machine/System Product: "Systems Programmer's Guide", Order Number SC19-6203-0.

AUTHORS

Fausto Caneschi was born in Arezzo (Italy) in 1950. He received the Dr. degree in Electronic Engineering from the University of Pisa in 1975. He joined CNUCE in 1977, working for the RPCNET project. In 1978 he joined IIASA (International Institute for Applied Systems Analysis) where worked on high-level protocols. Since 1979, Dr. Caneschi is back at CNUCE, where he has the resposibility of RPCNET R&D, and also works in the field of high-level protocols, partecipating to the WG6 (Ad-Hoc Group on Session Layer) of TC/97/SC16 of ISO.

Luciano Lenzini was born in Lucca (Italy) in 1944. He obtained his Dr. degree in Phisics at the University of Pisa in 1969, and for the whole of that year was assistant Professor of Phisics at the same University. In 1973, he spent a year at th IBM Scientific Center of Cambridge, Mass. (United States), where he worked on computer communication networks design and techniques for distributed computing, with reference to the RPCNET design. Since 1974, he has been the manager of the Distributed Systems Division of CNUCE. Since 1978, he has been leading the Italian part of the international STELLA (Satellite Transmission Experiment Linking Laboratories) project. He is involved in the work of WG6 (Ad-Hoc Group on Transport Layer) of TC97/SC16 of ISO.

Claudio Menchi was born in Sorengo (Switzerland) in 1947. He joined CNUCE in 1970 as system analyst and worked initially in the field of computational linguistics. Since 1975 he has been working on the RPCNET project

Towards OSI among UK Universities

R A Rosner
Joint Network Team of the Computer
Board and Research Councils, UK

A project is underway to establish a unified network and a homogeneous set of protocols so that UK university workers can access computing resources regardless of their location. The paper describes the background to this work, the choice of protocols and the methods being used to implement them. It also indicates some of the benefits already being achieved.

1. INTRODUCTION

Data communications are playing an increasingly important role in the provision of computing facilities to users in the academic community. The original purpose of data links was to give access to expensive computer systems located remotely. Nowadays, the objectives are considerably wider and the emergence of appropriate techniques has led not only to cheaper and more convenient ways of accomplishing conventional tasks but also to many possibilities for new applications.

Over the years, a bewildering array of communications arrangements has grown up among UK universities and research institutes, ranging in complexity from simple point-to-point leased lines, interconnections among sets of similar computers and proprietary or (more recently) X25 packet-switched networks. Most of the protocols used have been manufacturer-specific depending on the nature of the destination system.

Changes in the nature of computing and in the user population as well as the emergence of advanced data communication techniques have led to the setting up of a project now in progress to offer more flexible interconnection facilities at an economic cost. The mechanisms being used to achieve these objectives are twofold. Firstly, connectivity is being secured by constructing a nationwide hierarchy consisting of local communications arrangements connected to a unified wide-area network service. Secondly, capabilities for interworking among the very diverse sets of terminals, micros, mini-computers and mainframes in the community are being developed according to Open Systems Interconnection principles.

2. ACADEMIC COMPUTING AND THE GROWTH OF COMMUNICATIONS

Since the mid-1960s, computing in UK universities has been carried out through two funding agencies. One of these provides mainframes at university computer centres (of which there are about 50) serving the majority of users' needs and these facilities are backed up by a handful of major national centres to which the more demanding jobs or those requiring special facilities are submitted for execution. Within the constraints of normal allocation mechanisms, users may access these local and remote resources as of right. The second funding body supports research projects in selected disciplines and provides the requisite computing both by supplying computers to university reseach workers in their own departments and by authorising them to access large computers located at its own research laboratories. Thus, from the outset, data communications have been crucial to the funding bodies' support of computing services.

The goal of providing remote access to the major computing resources at the national centres and the research laboratories was initially achieved by means of star "networks" with the mainframes at their hubs. The protocols used were either the batch remote job entry (RJE) procedures specified by the mainframe manufacturers (such as CDC UT200, ICL 7020, IBM HASP) or variants to provide enhanced facilities such as mixed batch and interactive traffic.

Following the success of the ARPA network in the early seventies, a number of university computer centres in geographic regions established their own packet-switched networks. These served both to pool their mainframe resources (with each centre being accessible throughout such a region) and to concentrate regional traffic to national centres. The research laboratories also set up a network so that university users could access mainframes at either of them. Some of these networks were formed by connecting the mainframes to a central packet-switch. Others interlinked the front-end processors of all the mainframes in the region and one network used a dedicated minicomputer at each site to combine packet-switching with interfacing to the local mainframe. Most of the networks comprised mainframes from a single supplier and the low and high level protocols were either defined by such a supplier or specified locally.

By the mid-seventies, the links included those of the conventional star topologies onto national centre mainframes as well as the packet-switched regional and research community networks. Thus each network was not only physically disjoint from all the others but also had its own protocols. Not surprisingly, there was considerable duplication and underutilisation of links, many of them following similar paths for much of their length. The arrangements were therefore costly and offered little flexibility to users, who inevitably found themselves locked into one or other scheme.

The initial impetus for a more coordinated approach to data communications was the financial incentive which a reduction in leased lines would represent. However, it soon transpired that such a rationalisation offered an important opportunity to create an environment in which Open Systems Interconnection principles could be put into practice. This would lead to greater convenience for users, access to a wider range of computing resources and possibilities for new applications requiring advanced data communications facilities.

3.   PROTOCOL EVOLUTION

While the academic community was beginning its involvement with packet-switched networks, the UK Post Office (now British Telecom) was establishing its experimental public service EPSS. University participation in EPSS was extensive and rapidly led to recognition of the need for standard non-proprietary data communications protocols. This awareness stemmed partly from the limitations of the academics' own networks where the protocols, although conceptually advanced, had been defined locally.

Those networks which served to interconnect machines supplied by just one manufacturer had resulted in almost complete loss of protocol generality.

The protocol work on EPSS exerted considerable influence on the UK standards body BSI. This in turn was crucial in bringing the topic of Open Systems Interconnection (OSI) into the forefront as a subject for standardisation in ISO/CCITT forums. Also significant was the establishment of a small unit funded by the Department of Industry to coordinate UK activity on the definition of protocols. As befits their role as breakers of new ground, academics participated extensively in all this work.

An important catalyst to the protocol definition activities has been the very real need to implement OSI concepts among computer centres in the academic community where at least 20 different operating systems proliferate. This has meant that progress has had to be more rapid then the emergence of formally ratified national or international standards which could be delayed by several years.

A set of protocols has been defined and is enshrined in the so-called Rainbow Books of references (1) to (4). These may be regarded as interim UK standards and have been adopted as such by the academic community. Despite resistance from some manufacturers, it is felt that the route chosen is the only practicable one given the likely timescale of the standardisation process. It is recognised that international standards, when eventually agreed, will in all probability differ significantly from the present UK definitions. A close watch is therefore being kept on developments within the standards organisations. The concepts described in the UK Rainbow Books are being submitted for debate in ISO and members of the academic community participate in ISO committees.

The structure and definition of the UK protocols have been described elsewhere and other papers at this conference include coverage of the details.

4.   THE IMPLEMENTATION OF PROTOCOLS

Ideally, it should be possible to rely on computer manufacturers to offer support for standard data communications protocols just as they do for compilers. However, in a climate where OSI activity has only just begun in earnest, such a desirable state of affairs is hardly to be expected. This is especially true for protocols such as the UK's, which are relatively new and lack the imprimatur of official standards bodies. The choice is therefore to wait for international standards or to find means of securing the implementation of interim standards.

Free from the constraints of commercial pressures, the UK academic community is following the latter course. This fits well with its role and duty to undertake pioneering activities which could later become accepted practice in other sectors. This decision has contributed to a widespread enthusiasm for data communications as a discipline in its own right and a consequential growth in the reservoir of relevant expertise.

It is expected that attempts to implement the protocols will be limited to those machines which still have a significant lease of life and which are installed at a number of sites. The aim is to build a catalogue of software packages with each protocol being implemented just once for each operating system. The packages would then be mounted at all the relevant installations.

The methods by which the packages are created are twofold. Firstly, when a new computer system is being purchased, the operational requirement now includes a statement of networking capabilities. Manufacturers are asked to indicate how they intend to support the listed protocols and preference is given to those who indicate the stronger commitment. Initially, this procedure was of limited value as suppliers could not be seriously penalised for paying too little attention to the networking aspects. However, as the overall strategy starts to take shape, the community's progress towards an Open Systems environment is becoming more visible and adherence to the standards is being taken more seriously by manufacturers.

The second method is adopted for those systems where little leverage with manufacturers is possible. This covers previously installed systems where the supplier cannot be pressurised or where the networking deficiencies of a leading candidate in a procurement exercise are outweighed by its other capabilities. In these cases, implementations of the protocols have to be carried out under development contracts placed either within the community or with systems houses. There are also examples of joint projects between computer manufacturers and university staff. All such contracts, whether carried out externally or internally, operate on a commercial basis with staged payments against milestones, monitoring procedures and negotiated maintenance arrangements to cover the installation and enhancement of packages at all the subsequent user sites.

In many respects, reliance on university staff for some of the protocol packages is a new departure and has meant the adoption of stricter discipline than is customary in this environment for the design, coding and documentation of software. The architecture of the protocols and their susceptibility to eventual replacement by international standards have reinforced the need for modularity in the implementations.

5. TRANSITION TOWARDS OSI

The move towards OSI using the chosen protocols is being undertaken by a large number of computer centres each of which has to continue to offer a service to its customers. In addition, not all centres will be in a position to move simultaneously towards the new protocols. Some overlap of the old and the new regimes is therefore inevitable.

The major centres are taking the lead in the process. They have numerous users at remote sites whose modes of access include use of their local computer centres as pseudo-RJE stations or genuine RJE stations/terminal concentrators based on small computers. These are at present connected to the major centres by a variety of arrangements, predominantly point-to-point leased lines. The move towards their attachment to a packet-switched wide-area network and their conversion to operate according to the standard protocols are being accomplished gradually. Meanwhile, the major centres have to offer both modes of access in parallel.

Transition arrangements consist of two main elements. Firstly, multi-mode modems are being deployed to split the bandwidth available on point-to-point links. This "hard" multiplexing allows concurrent sharing of a single leased line which can then be used to support old and new styles of access simultaneously. Of course, the price to be paid is a reduction in bandwidth for each mode. The second feature is the development of protocol converters. These are being introduced principally at the major centres so that those of their attached sites which are at present unable to support the modern protocols do not remain isolated. Conversion between old and new regimes means that such sites not only retain access to the major centre but, by virtue of packet-switched networking facilities, can also reach other destinations via the new protocols.

6. EFFECTS OF THE OSI PROGRAMME

6.1 Users

For those wishing to access computing facilities, the position hitherto has been a diversity of disjoint communications arrangements which has meant that different terminals have had to be employed to access different resources. Gradually, a growing number of terminals are becoming "networked" in the sense that each of them can access a variety of computing facilities. As the move towards the standard job transfer protocol takes place, enhanced access will be available for job submission and output retrieval.

Networking has also created major opportunities for collaboration among geographically dispersed workers who can all access their data or software stored at a single site. Programs can be developed cooperatively and either run on the original computer or transmitted over the network to another machine. Examples of such usage can be found in fields such as High Energy Physics where experiments always involve workers from a large number of universities and are carried out at laboratories remote from any of them.

6.2 Service Providers

For computer centres, networking offers the opportunity for site specialisation, whereby a group of institutions agrees that, to reduce duplication, each will offer a particular set of software packages. This means that sites are not obliged to cater for the full requirements of their local users but can offer those packages best suited to the locally available systems or expertise. Groups of UK universities have reached such agreements and work has been done on the provision of remote advisory services as an essential feature.

Networking also allows systems and applications software support to be carried out centrally for a large number of machines scattered in different locations. Several UK research projects have relied on this mechanism as a means of standardising on particular types of computer for which software is developed at a designated site and then shipped to target machines all over the country. The requirement for local support at each site is thereby reduced significantly.

OSI and networking are arriving at a time of rapid change in the price/performance ratio of computing hardware. Taken together, these factors must have a significant influence on the role of the university computer centre. Hitherto, the emphasis has been on running and enhancing a "mainframe" system and providing associated advisory services. There are strong arguments for believing that this aspect will become less significant as more and more users purchase cheap (and increasingly powerful) systems of their own.

There will be a need for a strong operations team to run a university's local data network and its connections to the outside world. The advisory role will shift towards support for systems distributed across the site. Relatively expensive peripherals will still have to be provided centrally for shared usage. The range of skills required to carry out these tasks may be different from those of today's conventional computer centre and adjustments will be needed to cope with the evolution which is taking place.

6.3 Funding Bodies

An important consequence of the OSI programme is the flexibility it gives in the location of major or specialised computing resources and examples may be cited. In one case, two major centres have been equipped with very powerful processing systems which are different but complementary. The availability of standard access mechanisms will mean that users will be able to use whichever processor best meets their needs regardless of their location. A second example concerns the move for political reasons of a sizeable computer system from one centre to another. This could only be accomplished without a major break in service for established users by virtue of uniform access arrangements.

6.4 New Applications

The examples cited above are essentially extensions of conventional computing activities. The real breakthrough which networks and OSI are bringing about is in the general area of Information Technology. The list of potential applications is, of course, large. In the academic sector, the areas include library services, administration, publishing, communicating word processors, electronic mail and teleconferencing. The principle obstacle to rapid progress is the lack of protocols and agreement among equipment manufacturers to a common approach.

Local area networks are seen as an essential part of the infrastructure to support microprocessor systems on university sites. As well as allowing centralisation of support services (thereby reducing duplication), they will also permit the shared use of expensive peripherals (such as printers) and filestores. Moreover, software development and documentation will be significantly simplified by the use of cross-software facilities on more powerful systems.

The widespread publicity given to Information Technology is leading to immense pressure from users for some of these facilities to be provided as soon as possible. Unfortunately, for a variety of reasons, the appropriate products are not appearing on the market as quickly as originally anticipated. For example, the promises made about high bandwidth local networks have not yet resulted in a great choice for customers partly because the specification of standards has been delayed and partly because of production difficulties. Experience has also shown that insufficient attention has been paid to higher level protocols with the result that, for the moment, only centres able to inject considerable expertise from their own resources are able to embark on major local network projects. The availability of intelligent interfaces currently being developed will improve the position significantly.

7. CONCLUSIONS

UK universities and research institutes have embarked on a programme to implement standard protocols on their computer systems in conformity with the principles of OSI. A communications hierarchy is being established comprising local (on-site) campus networks interlinked by means of gateways to a unified X25 wide-area network. The resultant integrated scheme will allow users to take advantage of those local or remote resources most appropriate for their tasks. In addition, it will allow the overall planning of future computing provision to be carried out largely free from the constraint of where resources should be located.

This programme has been made possible essentially because academic computing is centrally funded through a relatively small number of agencies who have agreed to cooperate. The work is probably more ambitious than any comparable project and, if successful, will hold important lessons for other potential beneficiaries of OSI.

ACKNOWLEDGEMENTS

The work described is a collaboration among a group of people too numerous for all to be mentioned individually. The author is particularly grateful to his colleagues in the Joint Network Team without whose efforts the project would not have been possible.

REFERENCES

(1) A Network Independent Transport Service (Yellow Book), SG3/CP(80)2, Study Group 3 of British Telecom PSS User Forum, February 1980.

(2) A Network Independent File Transfer Protocol (Blue Book), FTP-B(80)2, File Transfer Implementors' Group of the Data Communication Protocols Unit, February 1981.

(3) A Network Independent Job Transfer and Manipulation Protocol (Red Book), DCPU/JTMP(81), The JTMP Working Party of the Data Communication Protocols Unit, September 1981.

(4) Character Terminal Protocols on PSS (Green Book) Revision 1, SG3/CP(81)6.

ROLAND ROSNER obtained his PhD in 1969 at University College London and then joined the Science and Engineering Research Council's Rutherford Appleton Laboratory where he led a group developing online computer systems for experiments in High Energy Physics. In 1976, he became a member of a unit studying data communications arrangements among UK universities and Research Council institutes and planning for their evolution. The Joint Network Team, which he heads, was formed in 1979 to coordinate the implementation of this overall strategy.

Radiotext

P Smith, P I Zorkoczy
The Open University, UK

In an effort to enhance the way in which the Open University is able to communicate with
its students learning at a distance, this project has involved the design of a system which
will allow material in the form of computer coded text and graphics to be transmitted over
an unmodified V.H.F. radio broadcast network. In addition to providing a rapid method of
communication for course management, the system can be used for delivery of material such
as audio-visual packages and computer software for appropriate courses.

The Radiotext system is described together with an example of the proposed method of operation. The major technical difficulties and the solutions adopted for them are discussed.

1. INTRODUCTION

The Open University was established in 1969 to
enable adults to pursue courses leading to a
first or higher degree. In 1981 it had some
60,000 undergraduate students and a further
20,000 associate students taking courses in
the continuing education programme.

Students study at home mainly through printed
material in the form of specially prepared
correspondence texts, set books and recommended
reading. Facilities for practical work are
provided at residential summer schools, and by
experimental equipment supplied on loan to the
student for the duration of the course. In
addition use is made of open-circuit radio and
television broadcasts and recorded audio-
visual material. Tuition and counselling is
provided by part-time staff at 269 study
centres throughout the country. Computer
terminals and audio-visual replay facilities
are also provided at these study centres.

At present the University communicates with its
students primarily using the postal service.
The system of operation is well tried and in
general works satisfactorily. However the
time involved in the preparation of printed
material and its distribution through the
postal system is such that rapid communication
between University and student is not possible.
As pressure on resources such as paper
increases and postal charges rise, the cost-
effectiveness of the present method of communication is increasingly in doubt.

In an effort to improve the communication
process the Radiotext system allows material
in the form of computer-coded text and graphics
to be transmitted over a V.H.F. radio broadcast
network. Computer-aided communication may
provide a cost-effective alternative to the
current methods of preparation and mailing of
printed correspondence texts, particularly in
rapidly changing topic areas where information
committed to print becomes out of date in a
short space of time.

In addition to serving as an alternative
delivery system for text, Radiotext needs
to be:

(1) low cost,

(2) highly reliable,

(3) multi-functional, e.g. usable for the
     delivery of computer software and audio-
     visual teaching material,

(4) simple and convenient to use.

Existing electronic information services do not
satisfy all of these requirements. Teletext
systems provide simple text and graphic facilities at moderate cost. However the limited
number of 'pages' available for use imposes a
severe constraint on the volume of data transmitted. Videotext systems have no such limitation on the volume of data together with the
considerable advantage of use in the interactive mode. However for large numbers of
students the cost of operation would be high ,
with separate telephone charges for each student
accessing the videotext computer. The transmission of audio-visual material is not convenient with these existing electronic information
systems.

2. RADIOTEXT - THE USER'S VIEW

It is intended that Radiotext transmissions will
take place at the end of the normal transmission schedule of the broadcast service. This
will enable the unmodified broadcast network to
be used with radio receivers of conventional
design. Overnight transmissions imply that
Radiotext should be capable of unattended operation in the student's home. This is achieved
by the use of a time-switched radio receiver
and interface unit together with an audio
cassette recorder for storage of the received
data.

Prior to receiving Radiotext transmissions, the student is required to set a time clock and select an identifier code on the interface. The audio cassette recorder is set to record although it will remain remotely switched off by the interface.

At the scheduled time for transmission, the radio receiver and interface are switched on by the time clock. The interface compares the header code of each item in the transmission with the identifier code previously entered by the student. Selected items are then automatically recorded onto audio cassette by switching the recorder on and off as required.

At a convenient time the student may play back the recording through the interface unit. Text and graphic material are displayed on a conventional television receiver or printed out on a low-cost printer. Computer software is provided in serial format with a clock signal if necessary.

3. RADIOTEXT - SYSTEM DESCRIPTION

3.1 Data Preparation

A system diagram of Radiotext is shown in Figure 1. In order to keep the cost of implementation to a minimum and ensure that the system is compatible with existing broadcasting standards, material is prepared on magnetic tape and handled for broadcasting in a similar manner to conventionally recorded audio material.

Text and graphic material is either prepared directly at the Radiotext data preparation terminal or taken from the Open University's in-house videotex system, 'Optel'. Computer software is directly downloaded from the appropriate computer into the data preparation terminal. Each item is given a header code to identify the content of the material and indicate for which group of students it is intended. Error correction coding is applied during recording of the material onto magnetic tape. The completed magnetic tape is

then passed to the broadcasting authority for transmission.

3.2 Radio Broadcast

For V.H.F. broadcasts the available signal bandwidth is 15 kHz per audio channel and the signal-to-noise ratio is in excess of 60 dB.

The necessity of recording the data signal on magnetic tape prior to transmission means that the modulation method used for the broadcast link must also be suitable for magnetic recording. If low redundancy pulse code techniques are used, the phase characteristics of the components of the system must be predictable. Tests showed these phase characteristics to be insufficiently consistent to be predictable in the general case. Therefore frequency shift keying was used because its reliability is independent of the phase response of the system. Frequency shift keying proved to be suitable for data recording on studio-quality tape recorders.

The main causes of signal quality deterioration on the broadcast path are noise and multipath propagation.

(i) Noise

The high signal-to-noise ratio of the broadcast channel ensures a very small probability of data error. However in urban areas man-made noise sources produce high levels of impulse-type noise in their immediate environment, [1]. Further impulse-type noise is caused by electrical appliances such as refrigerators, washing machines and the like within the student's home.

The effect and extent of this impulse noise became apparent in a survey carried out with the help of 30 Open University students spread across the country. The most commonly occuring noise appeared to arise from electrical appliances within the home. The effect was to cause the error burst distribution shown in Figure 2. The probability of any burst occuring is

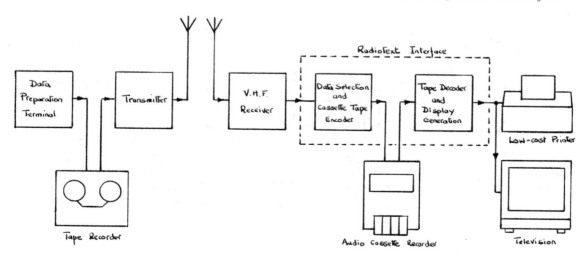

Fig. 1 The Radiotext System

3×10^{-6} per data bit at a data rate of 2400 baud. These results were used to aid the design of error correction techniques to be described later.

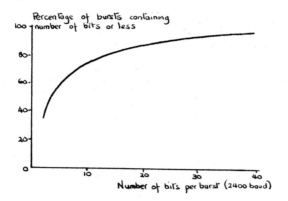

Fig. 2   Error burst length distribution

(ii)   Multipath Propagation

Large obstructions such as tall buildings, mountains and the like reflect V.H.F. radio broadcast waves. Multipath propagation is caused by the simultaneous reception of the direct and reflected signals. The reflected signals are time delayed and attenuated versions of the direct signal, {2},{3}.

The result of multipath propagation is to introduce harmonics of the signalling frequencies present in the data signal. The extent and effect of these harmonic signals were investigated with the use of a simulator which was able to simulate multiple delays up to 87.5 µs at various phase and injection levels. It was found that with even low injection levels and especially with long delay times, multipath propagation caused spurious and inaccurate zero crossings of the incoming modulated data signal making accurate detection difficult.

For stereophonic transmission the harmonic distortion produced in the sum channel moves into the difference channel and affects both the upper and lower sidebands. Additionally intermodulation products between the pilot tone and the signalling frequencies and harmonics will be produced. The distortion effects are thus more severe than those of a monophonic transmission and are coupled with crosstalk between the channels.

The effects of multipath propagation were countered in Radiotext by use of phase continuous sine wave signalling coupled with sharply tuned band-pass filters at the signalling frequencies. The degree of multipath propagation likely to be experienced in practice is not well investigated in the literature. However, our simulation tests show that, with sine wave signalling and the use of suitable band-pass filters, the most severe practical levels of multipath propagation can be tolerated (e.g. even those which would render normal audio broadcast reception impossible).

3.3   Broadcast Channel Encoder and Decoder

The frequency shift keyed signal is produced by using the data stream to switch between two sine wave oscillators at the signalling frequencies of 4.8 kHz and 9.6 kHz. The oscillators are locked in frequency and phase by being included in a phase locked loop circuit fed from accurate frequencies produced by division from a stable clock. In this way phase continuity of the output signal is assured when switching from one signalling frequency to the other.

The decoder is shown in Figure 3. Decoding is achieved by timing the zero crossing intervals of the incoming frequency shift keyed signal. The resulting data stream is retimed before being applied to the audio cassette recorder.

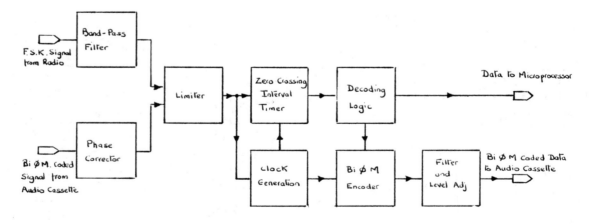

Fig.3   Broadcast Channel Decoder

3.4 Data Storage on Audio Cassette

Open University students make use of audio cassette recorders in their conventional study programme. In order to keep the cost of implementation of Radiotext as low as possible a design aim was to make use of these recorders for data storage.

For some time audio cassette recorders have been used as storage devices for microcomputers with varying degrees of success. In this application reliable data storage has only been achieved at low data rates {4},{5}. In general higher data rates require the use of good quality and so more expensive recorders {6}. The option of specifying suitable quality recorders to enable the higher data rates to be achieved was not open to Radiotext since students already possess the recorders to be used.

Low data rates could impose a severe constraint on the amount and type of data that can be handled, and an effort was made to maximise the data rates obtainable. This meant having to select a suitable channel code and provide an interface design which would enable reliable recording at high data rates to be made with any low-cost audio cassette recorder.

(i) Channel Code

The audio cassette recorder is essentially a band-pass channel which suffers amplitude instability particularly at higher frequencies with 'time jitter' due to short and long term tape speed variation. The channel code should therefore be d.c. free, be self clocking and have a frequency spectrum for a chosen data rate which avoids the higher end of the bandwidth available. A code which satisfies these requirements is Bi Ø M or Manchester-Coding as shown in Figure 4. A transition occurs in the code at every bit edge with an extra transition midway through the bit period to distinguish data '1' from data '0' {7}.

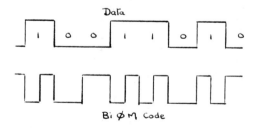

Fig. 4   Bi Ø M Coding

Unlike the other well used bi-phase code Bi Ø L, Bi Ø M is unaffected by the signal inversion which occurs in some makes of audio cassette recorder and the lack of need for synchronisation ensures that recovery is rapid should signal loss occur.

For this application Bi Ø M is preferred to more efficient codes because of the simplicity of implementation and its robustness in the presence of quite severe 'time jitter' produced

by some recorders.

When Bi Ø M is recorded using a digital recorder the playback waveform consists of well defined peaks coincident with transitions in the recorded waveform. The peaks are used to decode the waveform. In audio cassette recording the effect of the amplitude equalisation filter, provided to give an overall flat amplitude-frequency response, is to cause the peaks to be less well defined and not necessarily coincident with the recorded transitions. Consequently most audio cassette interfaces for data recording rely on timing the intervals between zero crossings of the playback signal to detect this type of code.

(ii)   Phase Equalisation

In order to preserve the waveform of the Bi Ø M coded signal and so enable zero crossing timing detection to be used, phase linearity is essential. Because the human ear is fairly insensitive to the relative phases of the frequency components within a signal, no attempt is made by the manufacturers of low-cost audio cassette recorders to linearise the phase response.

A simple yet extremely effective way of providing phase linearity, without influencing the amplitude response of the recorder in any way, was found in the use of a suitably designed active all-pass filter. The effect of the filter is shown in Figure 5. The phase response of a typical audio cassette recorder is shown as curve A (neglecting the time displacement between record and playback). The response results from the combined effect of the +90° phase shift independent of frequency produced at the playback head and the phase response of the amplitude equalisation filter. The phase response of the active all-pass filter is shown in curve B and the suitably linear combined response of recorder and filter is shown in curve C.

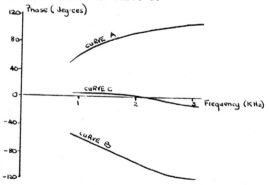

Fig. 5   Phase Response of (A) recorder,(B) all-pass filter,(C) recorder and filter

Photograph 1 shows the effect of the all-pass filter on the playback signal. The phase corrected waveform is very close to that of the original Bi Ø M coded waveform. The difference is due to the band-limiting effect of the recorder. Zero crossing intervals are highly accurate and remain accurate in the presence of severe amplitude instability.

With the designed encoder and decoder it is possible to reliably store Radiotext data at 2400 baud on any low-cost audio cassette recorder, and 4800 baud on any but the lowest quality recorders {8}. With a modified clock frequency, the decoder used for the radio broadcast link may be used to decode the Bi Ø M code from the audio cassette recorder. Duplication of the purpose of this circuit is reflected in a valuable reduction in cost.

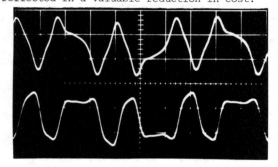

Photo 1.　　　　　Timebase ≃ 250μs/div

Top.　Playback Signal from Tape

Bottom.　Phase Equalised Signal

3.5 Display

The display facilities provided in the Radiotext interface are comparable with those found in many microcomputers. Text and graphics displays are available at low and high resolution. Sufficient memory capacity is available within the interface to allow a second item or 'page' to be loaded during the time the first is being displayed. This ensures a minimum delay when switching from one item to the next.

It is intended that the interface will also be available in a form suitable for use as a microcomputer 'add-on' device. In this form the microcomputer memory and display generation facilities will replace those of the 'stand-alone' Radiotext interface.

4. ERROR CORRECTION

It is highly desirable that students should have confidence in the accuracy of the educational material presented to them. While there is likely to be some tolerance to errors in material of an administrative nature, other items such as names, formulae and numerical information in text display and computer software is rightly expected to be free of error.

The error profile during data storage on audio cassette was observed to be similar to that of the broadcast channel. Errors occur in bursts due to signal 'drop out'. Between these bursts the storage channel has a low probability of data error due to the high signal to noise ratio. It is possible, therefore, to use a common error protection regime throughout the system.

Radiotext makes use of a 'geometric' or 'block parity' code {9} in which the burst detecting capabilities of a cyclic code are incorporated.

In this coding technique information bits are arranged in a rectangular array of V rows of L bits per row. Both longitudinal and vertical check bits are formed. The vertical check bits generated as the modulo 2 sum of each of the L columns within the array. Horizontal check bits are formed using a cyclic code for each of the V+1 rows as shown in Figure 6. The block is transmitted row by row, each row consisting of L information bits followed by C cyclic check bits. The block size is (V+1) x(L+C) bits of which VL are information bits.

Code redundancy is therefore $\frac{C(V+1)+L}{(V+1)(L+C)}$.

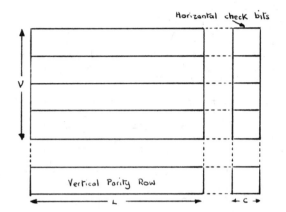

Fig. 6.　Block Code Construction

On reception each row is checked for errors using the cyclic row check bits. The cyclic code chosen has the generator polynomial $x^{16}+x^{12}+x^5+1$ (CCITT Recommendation V41). This generator polynomial produces 16 parity check bits. Therefore a burst of 16 bits or less will be detected. The fraction of bursts of length b>17 remaining undetected is 2^{-16}, (2^{-15} for b = 17) {10}.

If an error in any of the V information rows is indicated the block can be corrected by replacement of the row in error with the modulo 2 sum of the (V-1) remaining information rows and the parity row.

Should two rows of the same block be in error then correction cannot take place. Therefore the possibility of a single error burst causing errors in two rows of the same block has to be avoided. This is achieved by interleaving rows of any single block with rows of other blocks. This will result in a long error burst covering two or more rows influencing only a single row of any one block and so being correctable.

The correction parameters used in Radiotext are row length L = 128 bits and rows of information bits per block V = 4. This gives a block size of 512 bits and a maximum correctable error burst length in a total of 8192 bits of 2048 bits. The residual probability of error resulting from two or more error bursts occurring within a single 'page' is less than 10^{-8} per transmitted bit achieved with a code redundancy of 29%.

5. CONCLUSION

Tests have shown that Radiotext promises to be a highly reliable method of transmission of text and graphic material and computer software. Use of an unmodified broadcast system ensures that it will be simple and cheap to implement and should not affect the normal broadcast service in any significant way.

In the student's home the cost of the Radiotext interface is kept low by utilising the radio receiver, audio cassette recorder, television and in some cases microcomputer already used by students for their existing studies. The provision of a reliable method of data storage by audio cassette allows material received by the Radiotext system to be studied at any desired rate with repetition as often as required.

The cost to the Open University of the 'stand-alone' Radiotext interface is estimated to be £65 (May 1982), or as a microcomputer 'add-on' in the region of £15. The operating cost of such a system is dependent to a large extent on the charges imposed by the broadcasting authority. On a 'per student' basis these are expected to be small.

The Radiotext system is seen as a low-cost method of distributing large volumes of educational material. Its development is part of a sustained effort by the Open University to improve its teaching and communication methods.

6. ACKNOWLEDGEMENT

The Radiotext project is supported by the Faculty of Technology of the Open University. The authors wish to thank members of staff of the Electronics Discipline for helpful discussions throughout the duration of the project.

REFERENCES

{1} Skomal E.N., Man-Made Radio Noise (Van Nostrand Reinhold, New York, 1978).

{2} Ohara M., Distortion and Crosstalk caused by Multipath Propagation in Frequency-Modulated Sound Broadcasting, I.E.E.E. Transactions on Broadcasting, Vol. BC-26, No. 3, September 1980, 70-81.

{3} Corrington M.S., Frequency-Modulation Distortion caused by Multipath Transmission, Proceedings I.R.E., Vol. 33, December 1945, 878-891.

{4} Mauch H., Digital Data on Cassette Recorders, Byte, Vol. 1, No. 7, March 1976 40-45.

{5} Kinsner W., Seiler D., and Britt R., FSK Digital Data Converter for Cassette Tape Recorder, Proceedings of the International Symposium of Mini and Micro Computers, Toronto Canada, 8-11 November 1976, (I.E.E.E., New York, 1977).

{6} Koanantakool T., 4800 Baud Cassette Interface, New Electronics, Vol. 12, No. 21, 30 October 1979, 36.

{7} Mallinson J.C., and Miller J.W., On Optimal Codes for Digital Magnetic Recording, Proceedings of the Conference on Video and Data Recording, Birmingham, England, 20-22 July 1976, (I.E.R.E., 1976) 161-169.

{8} Smith P., and Zorkoczy P.I., Data Recording on Audio Cassette, Wireless World, Vol. 88, No. 1553, February 1982, 50-52,63.

{9} Morris D.J., Introduction to Communication Command and Control Systems, (Pergamon, Oxford, 1977.).

{10} Peterson W.W., and Weldon E.J., Error Correcting Codes (2nd Edition) (M.I.T. Press, Cambridge, Massachusetts, 1972), 228-230.

Dr. Peter Zorkoczy is Senior Lecturer in Electronic Design and Communication at The Open University. He joined the OU in 1970, and has participated in the production of a wide range of courses in Technology, primarily, in the area of digital systems. He is the author of a forthcoming book on 'Information Technology'. Dr. Zorkoczy holds a B.Sc. in Applied Physics from Strathclyde University, an M.Sc. in Electrical Engineering from Birmingham University, and Ph.D. in Cybernetics from Loughborough University.

Peter Smith is a postgraduate student in the Faculty of Technology of The Open University. His research effort has concentrated on the use of computer and communication systems in distance teaching. Prior to commencing postgraduate study, he was Senior Lecturer in Electronic and Radio Engineering at The Nautical College, Fleetwood. He holds a B.A. (Hons) degree from The Open University.

Information Network Architecture: an Introduction

P K Verma
American Telephone & Telegraph Co.,
USA

These remarks are intended to introduce the subject matter of this session and the different aspects of information network architecture addressed by the four papers in the session.

1. WHAT IS AN INFORMATION NETWORK?

An information network is a collection of nodes and interconnecting transmission channels. Nodes are responsible for signal processing, and include sources and sinks of information. Transmission channels convey information from one node to another and are characterized by channel capacity, a finite (but usually constant) delay and a distribution function for errors. An element of distance between nodes is implicit in the definition of a network: in fact this is what distinguishes a network from a system. As a general rule, a transmission line employed within a system to interconnect two devices is considered to be a tight coupling device. Should the performance of the transmission line fall short of that of the devices it interconnects, or start influencing the overall performance to a significant degree, it can no longer be considered to be a tight coupling device. Under these conditions, the system, however small physically, starts behaving like a network. In summary, then, the nodes of an information network are somewhat loosely interconnected through imperfect transmission channels of specified (and constant) capacity, (usually constant) delay and a distribution function for errors. The overall behavior of a network is strongly influenced by the interconnecting transmission channels, usually in a statistically predictable way. The main advantage of networks arises from the sharing of resources they provide. No network need have a capacity to meet the peak demands, imposed simultaneously, from all of its subscribers. This requires every network to have a discipline to allocate its resources to demands and a mechanism to resolve contention should it occur.

2. FUNCTIONS OF AN INFORMATION NETWORK

An information network is an organized structure. Sources and sinks of information are the end points of this structure. Examples of sources and sinks of information are: human beings, terminals - simple and sophisticated, host computers, etc. An information network provides for the communication of information among the netities that can access the network. It will be appropriate to define communication in a generalized sense so that we can characterize the functions of an information network from a relatively abstract point of view. We define communication between two or more entities as (a) programmed response(s) to a stimulus or stimuli originating from one or more entities and conveyed to appropriate destination(s). Note that communication is not necessarily just a bilateral association, it could in general be many to many. Further, the vector of stimuli has not merely combinational but also sequential significance.

3. RESOURCES OF AN INFORMATION NETWORK

The resources of an information network are physically distributed and could be broadly characterized under (i) processing, (ii) storage, and (iii) transport. Processing involves manipulating the bits with or without changing the semantic content of the original stream(s). Storage provides explicit control over information insofar as introducing deliberate delay at any point during its residence within the network is concerned.

4. ARCHITECTURE OF AN INFORMATION NETWORK

Even though physically distributed, the resources of an information network can work cooperatively in accomplishing a single function. This flexibility gives a network solution an advantage in terms of handling localized peak demands relative to non-network solutions where a fixed assignment of resources to tasks exists. Network architecture deals with the overall framework under which resources of the network are organized and managed in order to meet the demands imposed on it. One may think of network architectures in which one or more of its resources are either highly centralized or fully distributed, or where the processing resources are either all functionally identical or are segregated in groups to perform specific tasks.

Network architecture is driven not only by the anticipated demand to which the network will be subjected, but also by the trade-off between its fundamental resources - processing, storage and transport. Further, for any network, particularly for a common user network, user demand profiles evolve and change over time. Similarly, the network's primary constituents (i.e., resources) evolve in terms of their price-performance characteristics. These two sets of variables make it necessary that the network architect not only understand customers' current usage patterns and the price-performance characteristics of the network building blocks, but also anticipate how these variables are likely to evolve over a period of time.

A procedure to synthesize an information network architecture is well beyond our present reach. In practice, one starts with one or more hypothetical architectures. These architectures are then realized using available components and systems. The best of these, using some criteria, then becomes the chosen architecture. Flexibility in meeting unpredictable future need is one key criterion.

5. THE SESSION

This session has four papers addressing different aspects of information network architecture. The paper by P. Pawlita and H. W. Strack-Zimmermann entitled, "Public Services and the TRANSDATA Network Architecture," presents a formal framework for the interworking of a broad line of Siemens TRANSDATA software and hardware products for teleprocessing. It discusses the influence of public services and communication standards on the TRANSDATA network architecture and compares the functional layers of the TRANSDATA and the ISO reference models. The paper provides an illustration of how a teleprocessing network architecture is developed to take advantage of existing PTT transport services as well as standard communication interfaces and protocols.

The paper by B. C. Housel entitled, "On the Design and Formal Description of Messages in Distributed Architectures", presents techniques for defining complex messages in distributed processing architectures. Today's information networks are based on loosely coupled systems, disparate processor architectures and widely dispersed groups of workers implementing a common network architecture. Rigorous rules for defining complex messages in order to facilitate effective communication among network entities are thus a key component of the overall information network architecture and form the subject matter for this paper.

The paper by A. G. Fraser entitled, "The Architecture of a Byte Stream Network," presents a critical assessment of architectures of the emerging data communication networks, most of which are based on the CCITT X-series of recommendations. Citing a requirement for data communication networks to meet an evolving need, be built over an evolving base of technology and keep terminal to terminal communications relatively simple, the author proposes a byte oriented transport structure. The system described uses synchronous time division techniques in an asynchronous environment. The proposed system is capable of realizing a high transmission efficiency and is highly modular.

The final paper by R. Aubin and D. E. Sproule entitled, "SL-10 Network Architecture and Availability Considerations," addresses performance related questions in information networks. It presents specific strategies used for achieving high availability and reliability in Northern Telecom's SL-10 based packet switching

networks. A network management and diagnostic system to identify and locate potential faults before they become critical to users' applications is also discussed.

Information network architecture is and will continue to be a topic for continuing debate and discussion. On the one hand it is driven by what the technology could do in its continuing thrust toward better price-performance at the device, sub-system and system levels. Equally well on the other, it is also driven by ways business is conducted. And the latter - the ways we conduct our business - are a reflection of our social infrastructure, which is continuously evolving.

BIOGRAPHY

Pramode K. Verma is currently District Manager in the Business Marketing Department of American Telephone and Telegraph Co., in Basking Ridge, New Jersey, USA. Prior to joining AT&T, he has worked with Bell Laboratories in Holmdel in the areas of Data Communications Planning and Data Network Architecture. He has previously (1971-78) worked with the Bell Canada group of Companies and was associated with Canada's nationwide data networks, Dataroute and Datapac. He has also served as an Assistant Professor on the Faculty of Engineering at Concordia University, Montreal, during the academic years 1970-71, after getting his doctorate from the same university in Electrical Engineering. Dr. Verma was program chairman of the Third International Conference on Computer Communication, held in Toronto in 1976.

Public Services and the Transdata Network Architecture

P F Pawlita, H W Strack-Zimmermann
Siemens, Federal Republic of Germany

One reason for positive user acceptance of TRANSDATA® is its strong emphasis on cooperation with public services for transmission and switching. The paper describes influences of public services and communication standards on the TRANSDATA network architecture. The support of new services and standards by the communication system is explained, e.g., X.21, X.25, X.29 and Euronet. The incorporation of "Bildschirmtext" and teletex support into TRANSDATA is outlined. A support of ISDN services is suggested. The importance of PTT role and PTT-oriented standards like interactive videotex and teletex for opening of private network architectures is emphasized.

1. INTRODUCTION

The presence of public telecommunication services has become a well-established fact in everyday life of telecommunication users. The present situation is characterized by

- growing spectrum of services
- transition to digital networks
- a challenging but still fluctuating standardization scenario
- growing user uncertainty of advantages, cost and consequences of different services
- discussions on value added services.

In this situation computer manufacturers have to provide facilities for effective usage of those services most beneficial to the user. More, users want computer manufactures and service providers to offer solutions complementing each other. This idea is governed by the "subsidiary principle" of teleprocessing [1]. Roughly spoken, users require optimum solutions for total systems including transmission service and support by the DTE environment. From this overall system point of view requirements can be derived for services [2] and for service support by the DTE manufacturers.

Good solutions are especially required in teleprocessing application areas like
- improved "classical" telecommunication applications, e.g. transactions applications
- distributed data processing applications
- open systems communication
- office communication (via PTT network).

TRANSDATA in cooperation with PTT services offers useful solutions in these main application areas (cf.sect.4).

2. PUBLIC TELECOMMUNICATION SERVICES

The provision of lines and/or switching facilities for interconnection of remote end-user environments is usually the domain of common carriers or a state-controlled monopoly (PTT). Carriers and PTTs can take quite contrary positions. In the USA, for example, about 2000 providers of telecommunication services exist; frequently equivalent services are not governed by the same specifications. On the other hand, technological improvements and new value added services appear very fast on the market. In Europe, the situation in general is as follows:
- one provider (PTT) per country
- rather unified service specifications
- nation-wide service provision
- user certainty for long-time planning.

The strong and unique position of PTTs in Europe is the basis for a considerable influence on user decisions and DTE developments. Comparatively, the influence of users on PTT decisions for services is smaller.
From now, we will concentrate on the European situation. First, we discuss influences of both public services and communication standards on network architectures. Public services mainly influence architectures by

(1) communication standards
(2) service spectrum
(3) level of service
(4) service specifications and performance characteristics
(5) tariffs
(6) permission conditions for DTEs.

On (1): Standardization and public services are strongly interrelated. At least the depth of influence of public services standardization on network architectures has increased. In the past CCITT Recommendations including X.21 and X.25 concerned only lower layers of network architectures. Standardization for

teletex and interactive videotex, however, refers to all ISO model layers.
We rate this tendency mainly positive,
especially in the sense of advance of
open communication.
On (2): The introduction of several
additional services creates expenditure
problems, if new interfaces are introduced (and old ones are not cancelled),
if different PTTs provide different
services, or if the value of a service
or a tariff evolution is unclear.
On (3): Protocols for services like interactive videotex or teletex influence
all protocol layers. This possibly
means an expensive incorporation of a
complete additional protocol "tower"
into an architecture.

3. TRANSDATA NETWORK ARCHITECTURE: OVERVIEW

TRANSDATA is one of the most widely accepted network architectures for design
of private computer and terminal networks in Europe; several hundred installations of networks exist. They range
from networks with one central computer
and few remote terminals to large meshed
networks with several thousand terminals.
One reason for positive user acceptance
of TRANSDATA is the traditionally strong
emphasis on cooperation with public services for transmission and switching.
The TRANSDATA network architecture (NEA)
is the formal framework for interworking
of the broad line of the Siemens TRANS-
DATA software and hardware products for
teleprocessing [3,4]. Especially it is
the basis for interconnection of Siemens
System 7.500/7.700 mainframes and TRANS-
DATA communication computers.
The architecture is based on NEA protocols which are internally standardized
by Siemens (Tab.1). These are published
for inspection by customers to facilitate gateway forms of open communication.
The architecture is well layered and its
functional layers show a good correspondence with the ISO reference model [5].
Siemens essentially agrees to the present functional contents of the layers
of the ISO reference model.
Strictly speaking, the functions of
TRANSDATA layers 1 to 4 are the same as
in the ISO model. On the layers 5 to 7
the ISO standardization is not yet stable; the final delimitation of functions
between layers 5, 6 and 7 is not totally
clear.
On the other hand, many traditional and
approved telecommunication software products exist covering essential functions
of these layers. Until the ISO standardization for layers 5, 6 and 7 is finished, virtually no influence on existing
telecommunication methods can be expected. More, it is our goal to keep existing access method interfaces invariable
and at the same time to take the advantage of using high level services by
these interfaces.

The most important TRANSDATA telecommunication access method interfaces are:

IDCAM   Interface to DCAM (Data Communi-
        cation Access Method; similar
        to VTAM)
IKDCS   Compatible Data Communication
        Interface ≙ Interface to UTM
        (Universal Transaction Monitor)
IRTIO   Interface to TIAM (Terminal
        Interactive Access Method).

Application, presentation and session layer	
NEABD	Virtual file protocol
NEABF	Session protocol for file and job transfer
NEABT	TIAM (time sharing appli- cation) protocol
NEABR	RBAM (RJE appl.) protocol
RSPOOL2	RSPOOL2 (spool appl.) protocol
NEABV	NEA application selection protocol
Transport layer	
NEATE	NEA transport protocol
Network layer	
NEAN	NEA network protocol
Data link layer	
HDLC	High level data link control
NEALK	NEA link protocol for channel coupling
Physical layer	
CCITT-V.-and X.-interfaces, e.g. V.24, X.21	

Tab. 1   Important TRANSDATA protocols

A complete set of higher level protocols
based on the ISO reference model is not
expected to be standardized before 1984.
Siemens is interested in early standardization and supports the ISO standardization actively. In the case of successful standardization Siemens intends to
introduce modules for open communication
using internationally standardized protocols. The structural conformity of
TRANSDATA and ISO model will facilitate
an early implementation. Until completion of international standardization
the users can interconnect via Siemens-
supplied gateways for open communication.

4. INTEGRATION OF SERVICES AND STANDARDS INTO TRANSDATA

To provide really beneficial support of
public services to the users, Siemens
follows these development goals:
(1) to provide support for all PTT com-
    munication services that are impor-
    tant to telecommunication users
(2) to support international standards,
    especially by CCITT and ISO
(3) to provide telecommunication user
    interfaces independent of PTT net-
    work characteristics (the network
    characteristics are hidden); this
    means a clear separation of users
    and applications from the underlying

transport via public data networks
(4) to provide facilities for open
systems communication by implementation of standards and by gateways.

Integration of standardized protocols
The Siemens current effort to integrate
further protocols according to international standardization into TRANSDATA
comprises
(1) new transport protocol NEATE
(2) objective for adaptation of higher
level protocols to international
standards
(3) integration of X.21 and X.25 interfaces
(4) support of teletex protocols
(5) support of interactive videotex.

The support of new services indicated
by (3) to (5) will be described below.

Transport protocol
The transport protocol (NEATE) will be
functionally equivalent to the ECMA 72
level 4 class 3 protocol. The proposed
ISO level 4 protocol can be expected to
be functionally consistent with the ECMA
transport protocol.
NEATE covers all transport functions
currently proposed in the ISO model. The
transport service is network-independent.
NEATE supports, among others, the following functions
- end-to-end flow control
- end-to-end recovery
- multiplexing of transport connections
onto one network connection
- segmenting/reassembly
- transport priorities.

Higher level protocols
With respect to the unfinished standardization scene our efforts are:
- to improve the network architecture
by introduction of application-dedi-
cated protocols for file and job-
transfer (NEABF, NEABD)
- to support protocols for teletex and
interactive videotex as forms of open
communication
- to adapt higher level protocols according to international standards as
soon as possible
- in applications where no standardized
protocols are expected, selected
protocols according to the industry
standard will be implemented.

Support of public services
Taking the services of the German PTT,
the Deutsche Bundespost (DBP), as an
example, the integration into TRANSDATA
is described. This spectrum of services
is rather broad and particular services
like "Datex-L" and "Teletex" are quite
innovative.
TRANSDATA is intended to support the
following DBP data/text transmission
services besides traditional telephone,
leased line (HfD) and telex transmission.
● Circuit (line) switching service.
A modern line switching service like
the DBP's "Datex-L" requires the sup-

port of the general purpose interface
according to CCITT Recommendation X.21
● Packet switching service.
Its use (e.g. "Datex-P") requires an
X.25 interface for packet-oriented terminals or an X.28 interface for asynchronous character-oriented terminals.
● Interactive videotex.
The European PTTs seem to follow principally the Prestel (Viewdata) or Teletel approach. Corresponding "standards" were adopted by CEPT. The DBP
decided to realize a modified Viewda-
ta-oriented service (Bildschirmtext).
● Teletex.
At present the CCITT Recommendations
S.70, S.62, S.61 and S.60 for teletex
represent the only completely standardized set of protocols throughout
all ISO layers.

Integration of X.21
The support of X.21 by the TRANSDATA
communication computers for "Datex-L"
follows a stepwise approach shown in
Fig. 1.

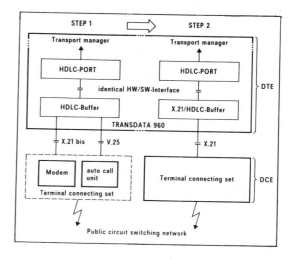

Fig. 1.   TRANSDATA support for X.21

Step 1 of the X.21 support comprises an
HDLC buffer (usually a block-type buffer) and an HDLC software port. The interface X.21bis enables the use of V
type modems. Automatic dialling is carried out according to Rec. V.25.
Functions of this solution:
- automatic dialling by the DTE
- direct dialling
- abbreviated dialling
- data transmission up to 9600 bit/s
- user classes of service
- option for physical connection set-up
for each dialog cycle while holding
the logical connection.

In step 2 the interfaces X.21bis and
V.25 are substituted by the X.21 interface itself, retaining de facto the
same hardware/software interface between HDLC port and buffer.
Functions (in addition to step 1):
- dialling using signalling speed
- support of service signals.

It should also be mentioned that the corresponding X.21 support within the display terminal TRANSDATA 9750 will shortly be available.

Integration of X.25

The packet switching service "Datex-P" of the DBP provides (switched) virtual and permanent virtual circuits according to CCITT Rec. X.25. Siemens provides an X.25 interface completely integrated into the network architecture. We prefer an integrated solution contrary to a black-box solution due to our opinion of X.25 being an elementary communication service. The integrated solution comes in two steps:

step 1) X.25 interface provided on the telecommunication access method level using the packet switching network merely as an X.25 backbone network. Higher level protocols are user-supplied.

step 2) X.25 service provided as a basis for the higher level NEA protocols. The X.25 protocol is used like a network protocol.

For both steps, the functions of X.25 level 3 are located in the software module X.25PORT in the communication computers TRANSDATA 960.

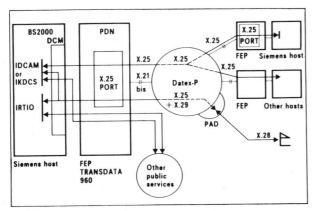

Fig. 2. X.25 step 1: typical communication relations

Fig. 2 shows typical X.25 communication relations of step 1. Mainframes 7.500/ 7.700 with operating system BS2000 use TRANSDATA 960 front-end processors (FEPs) containing X.25PORT. The X.25 service interface of X.25PORT is reflected to the IDCAM and IKDCS (cf.sect.3) telecommunication access method interfaces; within X.25PORT data and commands are transformed into NEA data and commands and vice-versa.
In addition, Rec. X.29 for character-oriented terminals is supported using the access methods TIAM, DCAM resp. UTM (via user interfaces IRTIO, IDCAM or IKDCS, respectively).
X.25PORT realizes functions like
- input to/ output from higher level software module
- transformation of data exchanged bet-

ween host access methods and X.25PORT; fragmentation, reassembly
- transformation of NEA commands
- individual packet processing (connection establishment/disconnect, restart, etc.)
- packet input to/ output from HDLC (LAPB) port.

Fig.3 shows a basic interconnection example for step 2.

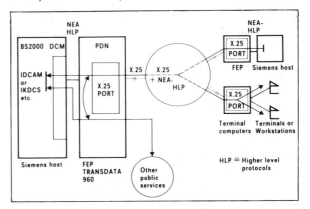

Fig. 3. X.25 step 2: typical communication relations

Siemens computers gained first access to packet switching networks in 1979 by a solution for EURONET (including X.29 access) and for a packet network called "DVS North-Rhine-Westphalia" operated by German state authorities.

Integration of X.29

Fig. 4 shows the interconnection of a Siemens host computer and a PAD with attached start-stop mode data terminals using the X.29 protocol.

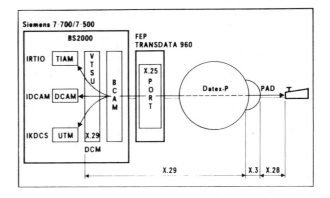

Fig. 4. X.29 support: interworking with the host

The Virtual Terminal Support VTSU-X.29 can be used via the access methods TIAM, DCAM and UTM. From the host point of view the X.28 terminal appears like a line mode terminal: VTSU converts the X.29 protocol into the protocol NEABT. The X.29 support enables host access via Datex-P and EURONET. In both cases the module X.25PORT is obligatory.

Support of interactive videotex

The Eurodata 79 study forecasts that by the end of the decade interactive videotex and teletex will be the most widespread telecommunication services in Europe. The concept of DBP for the interactive videotex service called "Bildschirmtext" (BTX) follows the Prestel (Viewdata) development. However, the Prestel idea was extended by allowing access to external computers of private information providers. In this case the BTX centers act only as a transparent gateway. Siemens is convinced that BTX using this extension will be a very popular form of telecommunication, especially for commercial usage. For communication between BTX centers and external computers BTX protocols defined by the DBP are used. Fig.5 shows the current interconnection of an external Siemens mainframe with a BTX center during the BTX field trial.

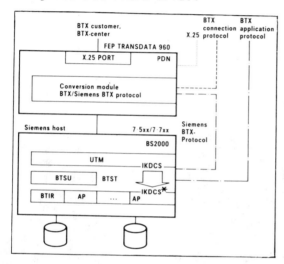

Fig. 5. Bildschirmtext support and protocols

External computer and BTX center are connected via X.25/Datex-P. X.25 and BTX connection protocol are supported in the Siemens FEP. The following host software components running under control of the Universal Transaction Monitor UTM are provided to support BTX:

- BTST (BTX Control). Functions:
  - protocol handling
  - support for creation and management of the menu-driven BTX search tree files
  - support of logical search methods using alphanumeric key words linked by boolean operators
  - control of user programs
  - BTSU calling for support of format-aided dialog
- BTSU (BTX Terminal Support):
  - formatting support for BTX messages using the format handling system FHS
  - format preparation using the interactive format generator IFG
- BTX applications:
  The BTX field trial implies two stand-dard dialog applications with dedicated standard application protocols:
  - information retrieval (access for informations stored in the host)
  - data collection (a type of transaction-oriented format-aided dialog).

Siemens provides application programs using these protocols, for example, the software module BTIR (BTX Information Retrieval).
Functions:
- analysis of BTX page requests
- record processing of user files
- preparation of variable display data fields.

Additional host applications AP used in the BTX service are a basic message system, customer-supplied applications for home banking, etc.
Very useful is the recursive reflection of the functions of the IKDCS interface up to the user level (IKDCS*). Thus, existing UTM applications can be used as BTX applications and vice-versa. Siemens provides the same access possibilities and applications available via the public BTX services also for inhouse use (Siemens inhouse system). Furthermore, conventional display stations can be employed for alphanumeric BTX applications instead of standard BTX terminals.

Support of teletex

Teletex protocols will be widely used and will provide a cooperation basis for teletex terminals, workstations, hosts and word-processing machines.
Siemens intends to support the teletex protocols for Siemens System 7.500/ 7.700/BS2000 host computers. It is suggested that host and attached FEP must behave like a standard teletex machine from the DBP point of view. Thus, teletex messages can be exchanged between teletex machines and a host. The final Siemens solution is a subject for further study; among others the permission of the DBP for host connection to teletex is currently restricted.

Future services

As a forerunner of an Integrated Services Digital Network (ISDN) the DBP plans to introduce a prototype 64 kbit/s digital network called "Model Network" based on the EDS network by 1983. Siemens is highly interested in ISDN and the model network and plans to provide interfaces for Siemens computers in time. An early popularity of these networks for data communication can be expected if existing applications can use the service without modifications, e.g. by an X.21 interface.

5. CONCLUSIONS AND REMARKS

We feel that one essential function of an "information network architecture" is the ability to build up arbitrary communication relations between partners via suitable public services. This can only happen if suppliers take advantage of

public services and standards.
In this connection we briefly try to
rate the special nature of standards
initialized by CCITT/CEPT. We feel that
the contribution of PTT authorities to
standardization of open networks has
been very positive:

- The international standardization in
  telephony cannot be rated high enough.
  World-wide uniform signalling and
  dialling conditions ensure that two
  arbitrary partners around the world
  can be connected within a few seconds
- similarly favourable conditions exist
  for world-wide telex communication
- the teletex standard is de facto a
  first complete open communication
  standard
- among others the influence of PTTs has
  brought about essentially more encouraging conditions for open communication in Europe compared with the USA.

Thus, the monopoly role of the PTTs has
helped to enforce standards.
On the other hand, a monopoly role
implies a serious obligation:

- to establish true international compatibility. Users will be discouraged if
  actual implementations of standardized
  protocols and interfaces vary from
  country to country with respect to
  options, parameters and different interpretation of recommendations (for
  example: X.25) /6/,
- to avoid different standards for similar applications
- to avoid different protocol towers for
  different service areas
- to create nation-independent permission conditions for DTE's
- to concede an appropriate. influence
  of users on PTT decision processes.

These factors would propitiously influence open communication (e.g., relevant
services like teletex and interactive
videotex) and the further opening of
private network architectures.

In the preceding sections was shown that
- TRANSDATA supports all important PTT
  services
- current efforts are just concentrated
  on support for open communication-
  furthering services like teletex and
  interactive videotex
- the influence of public services and
  standards on TRANSDATA is noteworthy
- the same existing user interfaces are
  provided for use of different services.

Thus, a great flexibility in telecommunication solutions is achieved. It is up
to the user's choice to configure an optimum system using public services and
TRANSDATA components and build up its
own tailored information network architecture.

REFERENCES

/1/ W. von Pattay, Incorporation of
    public telecommunication services
    in TRANSDATA communication systems,
    Telcom report 2(1979), 232-239
/2/ P. Pawlita, Anforderungen an künfti-
    ge Kommunikationsdienste für ver-
    teilte Verarbeitungssysteme, in:
    Schindler,S., Schröder,J.C.W.(eds.)
    Kommunikation in verteilten Syste-
    men, Berlin 1981,9-37
/3/ W. Bäker, Transdata 960 - a modular
    system of communication computers,
    Proc.5th ICCC, Atlanta 1980, 499-504
/4/ J. Feldmann, P. Jilek, R. Nowak, Sie-
    mens' teleprocessing system- TRANSDA-
    TA, Telcom report 1(1978), 112-118
/5/ J. Gonschorek, Die Architektur des
    Siemens Datenfernverarbeitungs-
    systems TRANSDATA im Vergleich zum
    ISO-Referenzmodell (in German), in:
    S. Schindler, J.C.W. Schröder (eds),
    Kommunikation in verteilten Syste-
    men, Berlin 1979, 238-254
/6/ L. Pouzin, Computer communications-
    problems and solutions, Computer
    communications 4(1981), 211-214

Peter F. Pawlita received the grad. and
Ph.D. degree in electrical engineering
from Techn. Univ., Aachen, FRG, in 1971
and 1977, respectively. From 1971 he
worked as a Research Assistant on traffic measurements and teleprocessing
problems at Inst. for General Electr.
Engin. and Teleprocessing, Aachen. Since
1979 he has been with Data Processing
Div. of Siemens AG, Munich, working on
product planning for computer communications and computer networks. He has published several papers on teleprocessing.

Hans W. Strack-Zimmermann received his
univ. diploma in theoretical physics
from the Technical Univ. Munich, in 1967.
He has been with Siemens, RCA, the European Nuclear Research Establishment
(CERN) and Hahn-Meitner Institute working on software for operating systems
and computer networks. Since 1979 he has
been leader of product planning for hardware systems and telecommunication products at Data Processing Division of
Siemens AG, Munich, and is currently
working on development of intelligent
terminal systems.

626

On the Design and Formal Description of Messages in Distributed Architectures

B C Housel
IBM, USA

The development of an architecture for network communications or distributed-processing services consists of rigorously defining a set of formats and protocols. It has been widely recognized that formal methods are necessary to produce an unambiguous architectural definition that is useful to product designers and implementers. Current formal description techniques for network architectures have focused on modeling protocols and system structures. On the other hand, there has been a lack of high-level techniques for describing complex messages that have developed in different architectures used in the distributed processing arena. This paper focuses on a formal, high-level data-description technique that has been found useful in defining complex messages that occur in distributed processing architectures. For specificity, the above is discussed with respect to distributed data processing architectures developed by IBM.

1.0 INTRODUCTION

The development of an architecture for network communications or distributed-processing services consists of rigorously defining a set of formats and protocols so that diverse products (hardware, firmware, and software) can successfully communicate to accomplish desired functions. It has been widely recognized [1] that, because of the complex nature of communications and distributed processing technology, formal methods are necessary to produce an unambiguous architectural definition that is useful to product designers and implementers. Current formal description techniques for network architectures have focused on modeling protocols and system structures. For example, the Format and Protocol Language (FAPL) [1,2] used to define IBM's Systems Network Architecture (SNA) has high-level constructs for defining finite-state machines and concurrent processes.

On the other hand, there has been a lack of high-level techniques for describing complex messages that have developed in different architectures used in the distributed processing arena. The description of messages has been limited by conventional programming language data definition facilities, in conjunction with textual descriptions. To fully understand an encoding structure, it is necessary to analyze the encoding/decoding procedures for processing various types of messages. Textual descriptions are often ambiguous and confusing.

In this paper we present a formal, high-level data-description technique that has been found useful in defining complex messages that occur in distributed processing architectures. Section 2 defines terminology and concepts with respect to the design and definition of messages used in distributed data processing. For specificity, the above is discussed with respect to distributed data processing architectures developed by IBM. Section 3 describes DEFINE [5], a general data-description language for formally defining messages. Section 4 states our conclusions.

2.0 CONCEPTS AND TERMINOLOGY

The term MESSAGE is used generically in this paper to refer to a data entity that is transmitted between two distributed processes. A message consists of a sequence of COMPONENTS, where a component is either a FIELD[1] or a GROUP. A field is an atomic unit of information that consists of one or more bits defining a value. A group is recursively defined as a sequence of fields or groups. Each message conforms to a MESSAGE CLASS. Examples of different message classes are path information units (PIU's) defined in SNA [2], and document interchange units (DIU's) defined for IBM's Document Interchange Architecture (DIA) [3]. A MESSAGE ENCODING STRUCTURE (i.e., the message syntax) defines the defined bit-sequences that can occur in messages of a given message class.

A message consists of control information and data. The control information is used by the receiving process to determine what processing is to be done on the data. Some examples of cooperative distributed processing include message routing, state management, distributed file access, device/media formatting, and transaction scheduling. In layered architectures (e.g., SNA, ISO's OSI Reference Model), what is viewed as data in one functional layer (e.g., data flow control) may be a message for a higher layer (e.g., presentation services).

Encoding requirements. Encoding requirements vary greatly, depending on the functional requirements of a given distributed service. However, the following general factors must be considered in the design of encoding structures:

- Efficiency: Encodings should be efficient to conserve on communications costs.

  Encoding techniques for reducing message size include: using variable-length fields to avoid unnecessary field padding, factoring common fields toward the "front" of the message (i.e., compression), and specifying field widths to contain the minimal number of bits to accommodate the required range of values.

- Extendability: Architectures evolve as new functions are required; thus, it should be possible to modify the encoding structure without major rewriting of code.

  The concept of "self-defining" data (components) has contributed significantly in this regard. That is, each component is prefixed with an identifier that identifies the particular component. One of the principal advantages of self-defining components is that the meaning (semantics) of a component is not solely determined by its position within a message; thus, a degree of freedom is possible with respect to the ordering of components within a message. This allows the encoding structure to be extended and modified with minimal impact. However, this conflicts to some degree with the efficiency objective because the identifiers add to the control information.

- Consistency: In order to minimize the number of "parsing rules," generic message structures should be designed so that new messages can be accommodated with minimal changes to the encoding/decoding procedures. Two examples of generic message structures are the function management (FM) headers in SNA, and the Document Interchange Units defined for Document Interchange Architecture.

- Variability: For a given message class, there is usually a number of possible variations that can occur, depending on the possible options. Thus, the definition of some of the control information is data-dependent (i.e., dependent on the values of other components in the message). For example, the fields that may occur in the transmission header (TH) of SNA are dependent on the "FID type." Message contents may also vary depending on the presence or absence of optional components defined for the message class.

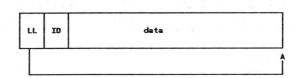

Figure 1. Structured-field encoding structure

Within IBM, structured fields have served as a basis for self-defining encoding structures. The term structured field has been defined in SNA to mean the encoding structure depicted in Figure 1. The use of structured fields in SNA's different logical unit (LU) types is described in [4]. The "LL" field is a two-byte length field that gives the total length of the structured field (including the LL), and the "ID" is a two-byte identifier (sometimes called a "code point") that identifies the genre (e.g., a data stream of the structured field.

Initially, structured fields were introduced to define extended 3270 data streams. Since then, because of the flexibility offered by the self-defining data concept, structured fields have become the basis for encoding structures in a number of IBM architectures. Structured fields are used in SNA device support architecture (logical unit types 2 and 3), SNA function management services (e.g., distributed data management, remote transaction scheduling), and distributed process architectures such as DIA and the various Document Content Architectures (DCAs) [3].

Structured fields can be combined in a variety of ways to produce rich encoding structures. This is exemplified in the various DIUs defined in DIA[2].
While the use of structured-fields is prevalent across different architectures within IBM, various self-defining data constructs have been developed that are architecture specific. These self-defining constructs have been defined in order to efficiently encode components (fields or groups) within a structured field. Figure 2 shows subordinate structured fields used in DIA, where "L" is a one-byte length field, and "T" is a one-byte identification field.

Figure 2. Subordinate self-defining fields

Self-defining data concepts. Because of the advantages described above, self-defining encodings are widely used in message encoding structures. While this technique offers the advantages discussed above, it also yields additional complexity, making the descriptions of encodings difficult. This has led to the possible application of the DEFINE language as shown in this paper.

3.0   THE DEFINE DATA DESCRIPTION LANGUAGE

The DEFINE language was originally developed [5,6,7] by IBM Research to described arbitrary sequential files for the purpose of data base restructuring and conversion. DEFINE is implemented as part of the EXPRESS system, which has been distributed by IBM as an Installed User Program [8]. Here, we present only the features required for describing message encoding structures.

3.1 THE DEFINE MODEL

In order to explain the semantics of DEFINE, we describe the processing model depicted in Figure 3. The DEFINE process model will be discussed with respect to decoding (parsing) a message. The DEFINE interpreter reads the input message bit stream, and parses (decodes) it according to the DEFINE description . A DEFINE description serves as a "template" for the message bit stream. The DEFINE interpreter processes the bit stream according to the sequence of component descriptors (or simply "descriptors") in the DD. In order to explain the various processing states, we introduce the concept of the message bit-stream cursor (or simply the "bit-stream cursor"). Initially, the bit-stream cursor is positioned before the first bit of the message bit stream. The DEFINE interpreter begins processing the DEFINE description with the first descriptor. As each item (field) is decoded, the cursor is positioned between the last bit (or the item) processed and prior to the next undecoded bit in the bit stream. The message decoding is complete when the termination criterion is met for the main (or outer-most) group component.

The output of the parsing process is a sequence of component occurrences (i.e., groups and fields) as prescribed by the descriptors in the DEFINE description. In general, the parsing of a message results in a tree data structure; this follows from the fact that a group may contain items or other groups. The functions of the DEFINE interpreter include:

- Determining and validating component lengths
- Determining and validating the component sequence
- Validating component values
- Evaluating termination criteria for repeating groups

- Determining the existence of optional components
- Mapping the message to a processable, internal form

In general, any of the above tasks may be data dependent. For example, the length of a component may be specified as an expression in terms of other components. Group components may be repeating. Determining the number of repeating group occurrences may involve computing a repetition count or scanning for a delimiter in the message. Components may be conditional. The existence of a component occurrence is determined by evaluating a Boolean expression. When evaluating expressions, it is sometimes necessary to "look-ahead" in the bit stream. For example, the termination of a group with optional components may depend on looking ahead to see if a particular code point value is present. The syntax and semantics for expressing these concepts are described in the following sections.

3.2 DEFINE SYNTAX

The DEFINE syntax for groups and items is shown in Figures 4 and 5. Here, we show only a subset of the full DEFINE language. The full language is described in [6]; the implemented version in the EXPRESS system is described in [8]. The constructs shown here can be used for describing messages in various IBM architectures and architectural layers.

Optional phrases are enclosed by brackets (i.e., [...]). Keywords are capitalized and user-specified entities are in lower case. The abbreviations "ae" and "be" denote "arithmetic expression," and "Boolean expression," respectively. Alternative constructs are enclosed by braces, and separated by a vertical bar (i.e., {...|...|...|...}). Descriptive clauses for groups and items are delimited by semicolons. Although not explicitly indicated, descriptive clauses may occur in any order.

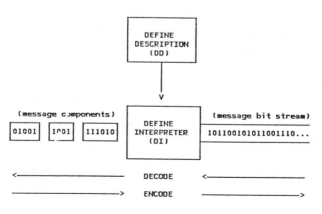

Figure 3. The DEFINE process model

629

```
GROUP group_name [ ( be ) ] :
[ LENGTH IS ae { BITS | BYTES } ]

   ┌ OCCURS                                          ┐
   │  ae TIMES ;                                      │
   │ < FROM ae [ TO ae ] TIMES, DEPENDING ON ae ; >  │
   │  FROM ae [ TO ae ] TIMES, WHILE be ;            │
   │  FROM ae [ TO ae ] TIMES, UNTIL be ;            │
   └                                                 ┘

   (sequence of group and item components)

END group_name;


NOTE:
                                    "┌ .. ┐"
      brackets of the form: <  ..  >   denote
                                    └ .. ┘
      big braces (i.e., {}) and means select
      one of the contained options.
```

Figure 4. Summary of syntax for GROUP Components

```
[ITEM] item_name [ ( be ) ] :

       ┌ BIT ( integer ) ;                    ┐
       │ BIT ( LENGTH IS ae [BITS] ) ;        │
       < CHAR( integer )                      >
       │ CHAR( LENGTH IS ae [BYTES] ) ;       │
       └ BINARY( integer ) ;                  ┘

       [ VALUE IS value_expression ; ]
       [ LENGTH RANGES
         FROM ae TO ae { BITS | BYTES } ; ]
       [END [item_name] ] ;


NOTE:   the abbreviated form is:
   "item_name [(be)]: clause; ... clause;;"
```

Figure 5. Syntax summary for ITEMs

```
GROUP REQUEST_DISTRIBUTION_DIU:
  GROUP DIU_PREFIX:
      .
      .
  END DIU_PREFIX;
  GROUP REQ_DIST_COMMAND:
      .
      .
  END REQ_DIST_COMMAND;
  GROUP DOCUMENT_UNIT:
      .
      .
  END DOCUMENT_UNIT;
END REQUEST_DISTRIBUTION_DIU;
```

Figure 6. Skeleton of 5520 Request Distribution DIU

```
1.  GROUP REQ_DIST_COMMAND:
2.     LENGTH IS REQ_DIST_LL BYTES;

3.     REQ_DIST_LL:   BINARY(15);;
4.     REQ_DIST_IDF:  CHAR(3); VALUE IS EQ HEX'CD1C01';;

5.     GROUP IDENTIFIED_DATA:
6.        IDD_LL:    BINARY(15); VALUE IS EQ 6;;
7.        IDD_IDF:   CHAR(3); VALUE IS EQ HEX'C32301';;
8.        IDD_DATA:  BIT(8); VALUE IS EQ HEX'C1';;
9.     END IDENTIFIED_DATA;

10.    GROUP ORIGINATOR_ID:
11.       ORIG_ID_LL:    BINARY(15); VALUE IS EQ 21;;
12.       ORIG_ID_IDF:   CHAR(3); VALUE IS EQ HEX'C32301';;
13.       ORIG_ID_DATA:  CHAR(LENGTH IS ORIG_ID_LL-5);;
14.    END ORIGINATOR_ID;

15.    GROUP ATTRIBUTE_LIST:
16.       ATTR_LIST_LL:    BINARY(15);;
17.       ATTR_LIST_IDF:   CHAR(3); VALUE IS EQ HEX'C30501';;
18.       ATTR_LIST_DATA: CHAR(LENGTH IS ATTR_LIST_LL - 5);
19.                        LENGTH RANGES FROM 5 TO 12 BYTES;;
20.    END ATTRIBUTE_LIST;

21.    GROUP DESTINATION_LIST:
22.       OCCURS FROM 1 TIMES, WHILE DEST_ID_IDF = HEX'C32F01';

23.       GROUP DESTINATION_ID:
24.          DEST_ID_LL:    BINARY(15); VALUE IS EQ 13;;
25.          DEST_ID_IDF:   CHAR(3); VALUE IS EQ HEX'C32F01';;
26.          DEST_ID_DATA: CHAR(LENGTH IS DEST_ID_LL-5);;;
27.       END DESTINATION_ID;

28.       GROUP RECIPIENT_LIST:
29.          OCCURS FROM 1 TIMES,
                        WHILE RECIP_ID_IDF = HEX'C30601';
30.          GROUP RECIPIENT_ID:
31.             RECIP_ID_LL:    BINARY(15); VALUE IS EQ 13;;
32.             RECIP_ID_IDF:   CHAR(3); VALUE IS EQ HEX'C30601';;
33.             RECIP_ID_DATA: CHAR(LENGTH IS RECIP_ID_LL-5);;;
34.          END RECIPIENT_ID;

35.       END RECIPIENT_LIST;
36.    END DESTINATION_LIST;

37.    GROUP DOCUMENT_NAME(DOC_NAME_IDF = HEX'C34101'):
38.       DOC_NAME_LL:   BINARY(15); VALUE IS GE 6 AND LE 37;;
39.       DOC_NAME_IDF:  CHAR(3); VALUE IS EQ HEX'C34101';;
40.       DOC_NAME_DATA: CHAR(LENGTH IS DOC_NAME_LL-5);
41.                       LENGTH RANGES FROM 1 TO 32 BYTES;;
42.    END DOCUMENT_NAME;

43.    GROUP USER_DATE_STRING(USER_DS_IDF = HEX'C34801'):
44.       USER_DS_LL:   BINARY(15); VALUE IS GE 6 AND LE 37;;
45.       USER_DS_IDF:  CHAR(3); VALUE IS EQ HEX'C34801';;
46.       USER_DS_DATA: CHAR(LENGTH IS USER_DS_LL-5);
47.                      LENGTH RANGES FROM 1 TO 32 BYTES;;
48.    END USER_DATE_STRING;

49. END REQ_DIST_COMMAND;
```

Figure 7. Detailed DEFINE Example

The concepts of DEFINE will be explained by example. The example is based on the REQUEST_DISTRIBUTION DIU as implemented by the IBM 5520 and described in [9]. A skeleton description of the DIU is shown in Figures 6. The REQUEST_DISTRIBUTION is defined in detail in Figure 7, and is referenced in the following sections to illustrate various features in the language.

3.3 EXPRESSION EVALUATION

Arithmetic and Boolean expressions in DEFINE have the usual syntax found in most programming languages. Operands can be constants, descriptor names (possibly qualified), or built-in function[3] references. Expressions may contain backward and/or forward references to other components. The context of expression evaluation is with respect to the state of the bit-stream cursor, and the descriptor (i.e., the "current descriptor") in which the expression occurs. Backward references refer to components that have already been decoded; these respective descriptors will occur ahead of the current descriptor. In the USER_DS_DATA item descriptor, the length expression contains a backward reference to USER_DS_LL.

Forward references refer to descriptors that follow the current descriptor. The component occurrences corresponding to forward references that have not been decoded (as their descriptors follow the current descriptor). This means the DEFINE interpreter must stack the current bit-stream cursor, and scan ahead in the bit stream (according to the descriptors in the DD) to locate and evaluate the referenced component. This process may recurse, as forward references may occur in the look-ahead scan. In order to preclude ambiguous DEFINE descriptions, the DEFINE interpreter guarantees, from analyzing the DD, that forward references evaluate to a unique component occurrence. This analysis is beyond the scope of this paper. In practice, well designed encoding structures do not require complex look-ahead scans. Examples of forward references are found in the WHILE clauses of the groups DESTINATION_LIST and RECIPIENT_LIST, and in the conditional groups DOCUMENT_NAME and USER_DATE_STRING.

3.4 CONDITIONAL COMPONENTS

A parenthesized Boolean expression after the component name (i.e., item_name, group_name) indicates that the component conditionally occurs in the message. Given a message of m bits, assume that the first n bits have been decoded into components, and that bits n+1 through m remain to be decoded. The DEFINE interpreter must next determine which descriptor to apply in interpreting subsequent bits in the bit stream. Normally, this is done according to the next descriptor in the sequence as defined by the DEFINE description. However, when a conditional descriptor occurs, this may not be the case; namely, if the "be" evaluates _false_, the descriptor is ignored, and the state of the bit-stream cursor remains unchanged. The DEFINE interpreter proceeds with the next descriptor in sequence. The group descriptors named DOCUMENT_NAME, and USER_DATE_STRING (in the above example) are conditional groups. Conditional groups may also result from specifying the "WHILE" clause for a repeating group (see "Repeating Groups").

3.5 REPEATING GROUPS

The _OCCURS clause_ is used for specifying that a group is repeating. An occurrence of a repeating group consists of a sequence of _member occurrences_, where each member occurrence is defined according to the component descriptors in the group. For example, in Figure 7, an occurrence of RECIPIENT_LIST (lines 28-35) consists of one or more occurrences of the RECIPIENT_ID. That is, a single occurrence of RECIPIENT_ID is a member occurrence of the repeating group RECIPIENT_LIST. Similarly, an occurrence of the repeating group DESTINATION_LIST consists of one or more member occurrences, where each member occurrence consists of an occurrence of DESTINATION_ID followed by an occurrence of RECIPIENT_LIST. In parsing repeating groups, the DEFINE interpreter must determine when all member occurrence of the groups have been processed.

The OCCURS clause, with its different variations (as shown in Figure 4) provides a powerful facility for specifying repetition bounds (i.e., via the "FROM" clause). and criteria for determining the number of repetitions in a repeating group. Additional features of the OCCURS clause are described in [6,8]. By specifying a lower bound of _zero_ on the FROM construct, the OCCURS clause gives an alternate means for specifying conditional repeating groups.

Determining the number of repetitions can be computed _a priori_ by computing a repetition count (i.e., "OCCUR ae TIMES;" or "OCCURS ... TIMES, DEPENDING ON ae;"). The arithmetic expression for computing repetition counts contains constants and/or backward references. Alternatively, the end of a repeating group can be signaled by repetitive evaluation of a Boolean expression that contains forward references (e.g., "OCCURS ... TIMES, WHILE be;"). A detailed description of the OCCURS clause is given in [8]. Below, we illustrate the use of the WHILE option.

Consider the processing required for the repeating groups DESTINATION_LIST and RECIPIENT_LIST in Figure 7. Assume that an occurrence of DESTINATION_ID and several occurrences of RECIPIENT_ID have been parsed as pictured in Figure 8.

The bit stream cursor is positioned as shown, following the parsing of an occurrence of RECIPIENT_ID. At this point the DEFINE interpreter proceeds to evaluate the WHILE clause (line 29) for RECIPIENT list to determine if all its member occurrences have been processed. Evaluation of the Boolean expression, RECIP_ID_IDF = HEX'C30601', first requires evaluating the forward reference RECIP_ID_IDF. This evaluation may produce a number of different values, depending on the content of the (unparsed) message (shown by the "???...."). Each case is given below, and the subsequent processing actions of the DEFINE interpreter are described.

1. RECIPIENT_ID_IDF = HEX'C30601' (the IDF for RECIPIENT_ID):

    In this case, the Boolean expression (line 29) evaluates _true_ indicating all members of RECIPIENT_LIST have not been parsed. The DEFINE interpreter proceeds to parse another occurrence of RECIPIENT_ID.

2. RECIPIENT_ID_IDF = HEX'C32F01' (the IDF for DESTINATION_ID):

    The DEFINE interpreter determines that all members of RECIPIENT_LIST have been parsed because the Boolean expression in line 29 evaluates _false_. Next, the DEFINE interpreter evaluates the WHILE clause for DESTINATION_LIST (line 22). In this case, the evaluation returns _true_, indicating that another occurrence of DESTINATION_LIST exists. The next component processed is DESTINATION_ID:

Figure 8. Processing Repeating Groups

3. RECIPIENT_ID_IDF = HEX'C34101' (the IDF for DOCUMENT_NAME):

    As in the preceding case the DEFINE interpreter would proceed to evaluate the

631

WHILE clause for DESTINATION_LIST (line 22). In this case, however, the the evaluation returns false, indicating that all members occurrences of DESTINATION_LIST have been parsed. The DEFINE interpreter proceeds by evaluating the component descriptor following DESTINATION_LIST (i.e., DOCUMENT_NAME). The Boolean expression (line 37), DOC_NAME_IDF = HEX'C34101', evaluates true, and the DEFINE interpreter subsequently parses an occurrence of DOCUMENT_NAME.

4. RECIPIENT_ID_IDF = HEX'C34801' (the IDF for USER_DATE_STRING):

As in the preceding case, the DEFINE interpreter determines that RECIPIENT_LIST and DESTINATION_LIST have been parsed, and then proceeds to evaluate the conditional group, DOCUMENT_NAME (lines 37-42); however, in this case the Boolean expression (line 37) evaluates false; i.e., an occurrence of DOCUMENT_NAME is not present in the message. The DEFINE interpreter continues by evaluating USER_DATE_STRING, the next component in sequence. The Boolean expression for USER_DATE_STRING (line 43) evaluates true, and an occurrence of USER_DATE_STRING is parsed accordingly.

5. RECIPIENT_ID_IDF = HEX'C90381' (the IDF for DOCUMENT_UNIT):

This processing is similar to that of (4) above, except that the DEFINE interpreter determines that USER_DATE_STRING does not exist. Thus, there is no occurrence of either DOCUMENT_NAME or USER_DATE_STRING in the massage. At this point, all the components of the REQ_DIST_COMMAND would have been parsed, and the DEFINE interpreter would proceed to evaluate the next component of the group REQUEST_DISTRIBUTION_DIU (Figure 6), named DOCUMENT_UNIT.

It is of interest to note, in the different cases above, that as long as the evaluation of successive Boolean expressions returned false, the state of the bit stream cursor remained unchanged. In this example, the evaluation of different forward references (e.g., RECIP_ID_IDF, DEST_ID_IDF, ...) produced the same value, because the DEFINE interpreter "looked ahead" the same number of bytes (i.e., 2 bytes) in all cases. Since the legal values for all forward references are mutually exclusive, the description is unambiguous.

3.6 ORDER-INDEPENDENT COMPONENT DESCRIPTIONS

The constructs for specifying repeating groups, in conjunction with conditional descriptors, can be combined to specify that a sequence of components may occur in any order. Suppose in Figure 7 that we wish to change the specification to allow the optional descriptors, DOCUMENT_NAME and USER_DATE_STRING, in any order. The possible cases are given below:

*   no occurrence of either DOCUMENT_NAME or USER_DATE_STRING

*   DOCUMENT_NAME occurrence only USER_DATE_STRING occurrence only

*   DOCUMENT_NAME occurrence followed by USER_DATE_STRING occurrence

*   USER_DATE_STRING occurrence followed by DOCUMENT_NAME occurrence

The DEFINE description for the above definition is shown in Figure 9.

```
GROUP RD_OPTIONS:
   OCCURS FROM 0 TO 2 TIMES,
        WHILE DOC_NAME_IDF = HEX'C34101' OR
              USER_DS_IDF = HEX'C34801';

   GROUP DOCUMENT_NAME(DOC_NAME_IDF = HEX'C34101'):
      DOC_NAME_LL:    BINARY(15); VALUE IS GE 6 AND LE 37;;
      DOC_NAME_IDF:   CHAR(3); VALUE IS EQ HEX'C34101';;
      DOC_NAME_DATA:  CHAR(LENGTH IS DOC_NAME_LL-5);
                      LENGTH RANGES FROM 1 TO 32 BYTES;;
   END DOCUMENT_NAME;

   GROUP USER_DATE_STRING(USER_DS_IDF = HEX'C34801'):
      USER_DS_LL:     BINARY(15); VALUE IS GE 6 AND LE 37;;
      USER_DS_IDF:    CHAR(3); VALUE IS EQ HEX'C34801';;
      USER_DS_DATA:   CHAR(LENGTH IS USER_DS_LL-5);
                      LENGTH RANGES FROM 1 TO 32 BYTES;;
   END USER_DATE_STRING;

   END RD_OPTIONS;
```

Figure 9. Describing order-independent encodings

3.7 INTEGRITY CONSTRAINTS

Previously, we focused on describing the syntactic structure of messages. Another crucial requirement in defining encoding structures for a message class is that of specifying integrity constraints. Integrity constraint specifications define the error checking required by encoding/decoding procedures in distributed processes. In DEFINE, constructs are provided for specifying:

*   Bounds on component (group/item) lengths (LENGTH RANGES FROM min TO max BYTES).[4]

*   Bounds on the number of occurrences of repeating groups (i.e., OCCURS FROM min TO max TIMES).

*   Restrictions on the set of values that an item occurrence may assume (VALUE clause for item descriptors).

*   The item data type. Data type checking can be performed on item occurrences to guarantee that they conform to the specified type. DEFINE provides a powerful "picture" checking capability, which we do not describe here. Type checking is not extensively used for defining messages, as the number of data types is small and the checking is expensive.

*   Existence dependencies. The existence criteria for conditional components, as previously described, defines interrelationships of different components, and serves as an integrity constraint.

In the DEFINE process model, the DEFINE interpreter checks each integrity constraint and issues error messages when violations are detected.

4.0 CONCLUSIONS

In this paper, we have discussed the design of complex messages, for possible use in the context of IBM distributed processing architectures. We presented an overview of the syntax and semantics of the DEFINE data description language. DEFINE provides a simple, yet high-level, and rigorous, message-definition facility. This was illustrated by using DEFINE to describe a complex message (DIU) encoding structure used in the IBM 5520 document distribution system. We stress here that the concepts underlying DEFINE are the significant contribution. The development of an equivalent syntax that is more consistent with a specific programming language (e.g., PL/I) is straightforward.

DEFINE offers several benefits to architecture and product development. Because DEFINE is a very high-level language, less effort is required to understand, and therefore design and modify message encoding structures. The rigorous, unambiguous description provided by DEFINE reduces opportunities for different interpretations of an architecture, and thus product incompatibilities.

If a DEFINE interpreter is implemented, several added benefits are gained. For example, different designs can be evaluated. Typical test messages for different message encoding structures can be run through the DEFINE interpreter; processing times and message lengths can be measured, and size and speed tradeoffs can be made according to engineering principles. In addition, product implementations of an architecture can be validated[5] by passing product-generated messages through the DEFINE interpreter. Lastly, if the DEFINE interpreter implementation is efficient enough, it can provide a generalized, common message encoding/decoding subassembly that may be used in a number of implementations.

FOOTNOTES:

1. A _field_ is also called an _item_, and the terms are used interchangeably. The term _field_ is commonly used in message nomenclature, whereas the term _item_ has been used in the DEFINE language.

2. In DIA the "ID" field has been augmented with an "F" byte to further qualify the identification. Thus, DIA structured fields take the form "LLIDF...."

3. Several special built-in functions have been defined for the DEFINE language. LENGTH(x) returns the length of component x; OFFSET(x) returns the offset from component x to the bit-string cursor; COUNT(x) returns the number of occurrences of group x. The detailed semantics are not be described further in this paper.

4. "Min" and "max" denote arithmetic expressions to compute minimum and maximum values, respectively.

5. Only with respect to message formats.

REFERENCES:

1. Schultz, G.D., Rose, D.B., West, C.H., Gray J.P., "Executable Description and Validation of SNA," _IEEE Trans. on Communications_, Vol. Com-28, No.4, April 1980.

2. IBM Corp.,_Systems Network Architecture Format and Protocol Reference Manual: Architecture Logic_, IBM Form No. SC30-3112, November, 1980.

3. DeSousa, M.R., "Electronic Interchange of Information in an Office Environment," _IBM Systems Journal_, Vol. 20, No. 1, 1981.

4. IBM Corp., _Systems Network Architecture - Sessions Between Logical Units_, IBM Form No. GC20-1868, April 1981.

5. Housel, B.C., Smith, D.P., Shu, N.C., Lum, V.Y., "DEFINE - A Nonprocedural Language for Defining Data Easily," _Proc. ACM Pacific 75_, San Francisco, CA, April, 1975, pp. 62-70.

6. Housel, B.C., Smith, D.P., Shu, N.C., Lum, V.Y., "Data Translation, Part II: "DEFINE - A Nonprocedural Language for Defining Data Easily," IBM RJ1526, IBM Research Laboratory, May 1975.

7. Shu, N.C., Housel, B.C., Taylor, R.W., Ghosh, S.P., Lum, V.Y., "EXPRESS: A Data Extraction, Processing, and Restructuring System," _ACM Trans. Database Syst._ 2,2 (June 1977).

8. IBM Corp., _Data Extraction, Processing and Restructuring System: Define and Convert Reference Manual_IBM Form No. SH20-2177, July, 1979.

9. IBM Corp., _IBM 5520 Administrative System System/370 Host Attach Programmer's Guide_, IBM Form No. SC23-0710, December, 1980.

Barron C. Housel attended the University of Oklahoma where he received a B.S. degree in mechanical engineering in 1963, and an M.S. degree in engineering science in 1965. He has been with the IBM Corporation since 1965. He received an M.S. degree in computer science from Stanford University in 1968, and a Ph.d in computer science from Purdue University in 1973. From 1973 to 1979, Dr. Housel was a member of the IBM Research Laboratory, where he did research in database technology. During that period he was a visiting professor in computer science at Purdue University. Since 1979, Dr. Housel has been a Senior engineer in the communications architecture and technology department at IBM's Raleigh Laboratory.

The Architecture of a Byte Stream Network

A G Fraser
Bell Laboratories, USA

To meet the long-term needs, a data communications service must have a simple specification that is easy to understand, flexible enough to meet diverse requirements, and durable enough to survive changes in the underlying technology. Current protocol standards define a complex interface between a network and its users, and it is suggested that a much simpler service definition is required.

A network is desribed in which the basic service is a virtual circuit carrying an unstructured stream of bytes. The bytes are distinguished as to whether they are control or data. Various user protocols, including well known standards, are implemented on an end-to-end basis using control bytes to give the necessary structure to the data stream. The virtual circuits are implemented using packet switching and statistical multiplexing in a manner that is normally transparent to the end user.

Introduction

With the aid of micro-electronics and digital computers we are evolving steadily towards a society where trade in information could have as much significance for the national economy as the trade in more tangible goods. Our prosperity in the years to come will depend upon an efficient means of information transport. We shall need a ubiquitous data communication network, as ubiquitous as the telephone and road systems now are. To the extent that we fail in this endeavor, we weaken the prospects for a continued healthy economy.

It is against this background that we engineers must evaluate our current efforts to build a data network architecture. Are we developing the framework within which old and new transport facilities can grow and prosper? Certainly, the very active interest in standards suggests a general awareness of the need for a ubiquitous service. But we must strive for a clearer architectural perspective than has so far emerged. Somehow we must develop a description of data communication service that is simple enough for anyone to understand, that is flexible enough for anyone to see how to exploit it, and that is durable enough to survive changing technical and economic priorities. In the following paragraphs I shall suggest an approach to solving this problem while referring to research ongoing at Bell Laboratories' Computing Science Research Center. The opinions expressed are my own and arise out of this research.

Learning from Telephony

We can learn by studying the way in which the telephone system responded to a very similar challenge. Suppose that we were to ask any member of the public what the telephone system is. The answer is quite predictable, but will not be anything like the nuts and bolts view that the average engineer would give. They will explain that the telephone is a thing that usually comes in two parts, one part has a microphone and speaker so arranged that one can easily speak into it and listen to what it says. The other part usually has a dial or some buttons by which one can enter a telephone number. If one does that, waits while the thing gives a few clicks or chirps, most likely one will then be able to talk to whoever is at the other telephone. The average member of the public does not know about its 4000 Hz bandwidth, but there is a strong sense of what a telephone can do. One can talk through it but it is not much good for music and it cannot carry parcels.

I submit that telephone users perceive a service even if it is not clearly defined in their minds. It is a service that has remained remarkably constant for nearly a hundred years. If the same question had been asked of someone living 50 years ago the answer would have been much the same.

The constancy of the service definition for telephony has been crucial to the success of our business over so long a period. During this period the internal structure of the network has undergone drastic surgery with the addition of many new technologies. As new technology has come along, we have taken maximum advantage of it to give increasing economies of scale and steadily improving quality of performance. We have been able to make our own planning decisions without asking our customers what we may do. We have installed the new equipment without telling them, and it has allowed us to maintain a healthy rate of return on investment while the charges to our customers have risen less quickly than inflation. The stability of this service definition has also served us well internally. With a constant definition of purpose, thousands of engineers have been able to make simultaneous changes and improvements to the great machine without going to extraordinary measures to synchronize and plan their activities.

We need an equally simple and robust definition of data communication service for exactly the reasons that the service definition for telephony has served us so well in the past.

Transport as a Common Denominator

Something like one third of all computer terminals are IBM 3270 or similar synchronous devices that use the Bisync protocol [1]. Another one third are asynchronous terminals derived from the Teletype Model 33. Terminals similar to these two classic types are, like Fortran, likely to be around for a long time regardless of the aging technology upon which their designs were based. The future network must support these and new protocols for an increasing variety of computers and terminals. There will be many types of traffic, including synchronous and asynchronous data, telemetry and possibly voice. The network must meet this evolving need while it too evolves in response to advances in technology.

Many of these protocols carry data in packets so that they can obtain the benefits of statistical multiplexing. Bursts of data from different terminals are carried in packets with address information sufficient to steer the data to its proper destination. Thus data from several conversations can share a single transmission line with benefits of sharing and potential low delay. By the same means several conversations can be conducted through a single multiplexed port on a computer and thus reduce network interface costs. Packetised data is also the basis for flow control and error control protocols where the burst of data delimited by one packet becomes a unit of information for control purposes. The fixed format of a packet allows control information to be distinguished from data by virtue of the position it occupies in the packet structure. Thus, in many networks, the packet provides a vehicle for applications level as well as network level controls.

Data packaging is central to the difficulty of keeping the applications level system and the transport system separate. Different terminals tend to want to package data in different ways, in different size units and with different applications significance for each unit. A statistically multiplexed network that works with packaged data has its own requirements for package size and structure if it is to operate efficiently with low delay and/or high throughput. Packaging as a means of distinguishing control from data tends to confuse transport level and applications level functions. It is not surprising therefore that a single approach to packaging leads to an elaborate interface between the transport and applications levels.

To separate applications level functions from transport level functions, we define a basic data transport service in terms of an asynchronous stream of bytes. The packaging of bytes for transport purposes is then separate from and unrelated to the packaging (if any) adopted for a particular data communications application. The bytes are of two types, control and data, and are carried in 9-bit envelopes so that the two types can be easily distinguished. A stream of data and control bytes can support higher level protocols such as Bisync and HDLC, as well as terminals with much simpler requirements such as the character asynchronous devices and telephones. When a data communications application requires that several bytes be packaged as a single unit, control bytes are used to mark the package boundaries. When supervisory information shares the same channel as user data the former is distinguished by using control bytes.

A stream of bytes can be transported, multiplexed and switched in a variety of ways depending upon the required performance level and available technology. There appears to be little difficulty in building a single byte stream network with a mixture of technologies at different points in the network. Indeed, when packet size and packetisation strategy can be selected purely on the basis of transmission requirements and are not constrained by applications level considerations, we find that it is much easier to optimise network design for low delay and good throughput.

In short, the byte stream, simple as it is in concept, can support a wide variety of protocol needs and allows efficient implementation. We are encouraged to explore the possibilities of using it as the basis of a data transport service.

Network Architecture Research

In the Computing Science Research Center at Bell Laboratories we have been experimenting with a collection of data network construction modules, collectively called Datakit [2], from which specific network components can be made. The study of modules seems appropriate in view of the great variety and continual change in user requirements. It also disciplines our thinking since a successful set of rearrangeable modules requires a keen sense of architecture and a clearly thought out partitioning of required functions.

The major components of the architecture are Transmission, Processing, Switching, and Control. Figure 1 shows a network made up of these components.

The switching function can be implemented either in a central switching machine or using a distributed asynchronous bus. In our network, a bus may be used as a local distribution system to collect traffic from several terminals but all circuits are routed through the central switching machines. The arrangement simplifies traffic management, can be implemented in an economical manner and facilitates maintenance procedures. The switching function is controlled from

processors that have access to critical network functions but are otherwise attached to the network as all other processors are. We shall not distinguish between these different processors here.

Transmission systems and processors are the resources of the network. Either may be multiplexed to serve several customers at one time. The resource that is provided to a single user by a (multiplexed) transmission system is called a "channel", and that provided to a single user by a processor is a "process". An integral part of each processor is an interface to the switch or bus, and there is a switch or bus interface circuit at each end of each transmission system. The interface circuits process low level protocols and support the information transfer protocol of the switch or bus. The switch and buses serve to transport information between channels and processes in any combination.

Our research on Datakit has focused entirely on services provided by permanent or switched virtual circuits. The term "virtual" is used to indicate that the circuit carries bursts of data (bytes) and is not simply a pipe with reserved bandwidth. A virtual circuit is a concatenation of channels and processes as defined by connections established in the network switches.

Customer equipment gains access to the network through a transmission line having at one end an interface to the customer equipment and at the other an interface to a switch. The protocol on this line can vary from line to line as indeed it can on all transmission lines in the network. Differences in protocol at the lowest level are accommodated in the interface.

Protocol Hierarchy

It is convenient to discuss protocols in terms of a hierarchy. One such hierarchy is the Open Systems Interconnection Basic Reference Model proposed by Subcommittee 97/16 of ISO [3]. A prominent standard operating within the three lowest layers of the ISO model is CCITT recommendation X.25 [4]. Its three layers, or levels are as follows.

Level-1 The physical interface, includes the electrical representation of information and the lowest level of synchronization.

Level-2 The link level interface, includes procedures for error detection, for error correction (by retransmission), and for segmenting data into blocks. It also includes link flow control.

Level-3 The packet level interface, includes procedures for multiplexing, for end-to-end flow control, and for setting up new virtual circuits.

Datakit employs a slightly different function assignment for the three lowest protocol layers.

Level-A This corresponds to the physical level, level-1, of X.25.

Level-B This level includes procedures for error detection and multiplexing.

Level-C This level handles error correction (by retransmission), end-to-end flow control and segmenting data into blocks.

A summary of the principal differences between the X.25 and Datakit protocol levels is shown in Figure 2.

An architectural objective for Datakit was to keep the innermost parts of the network as simple as possible consistent with providing high performance for a wide variety of traffic types. This is achieved by placing switching at a low protocol level and forcing to the edge of the network any functions that do not have to be performed centrally. Since switching must be in terms of the user's virtual circuits, our strategy forces multiplexing down to the same low protocol level, i.e. level-B.

Multiplexing for bursty traffic involves the transmission of packets containing (abbreviated) addresses and data. Since corruption of the address information could lead to data being wrongly delivered, we chose to perform error detection also at level-B and to discard bad packets before switching them. Error detection at this level also assists with network maintenance because transmission problems are immediately identified with the equipment on which they occur.

Error correction was put at a higher protocol level with the general intention that it should be done end-to-end on a virtual circuit. There is a (usually small) price associated with this in that retransmissions occur across the entire length of the circuit instead of just across the link on which the error occurred. However, this is offset by moving the quite complex procedures and storage management requirements of error control away from the highly multiplexed, high speed central elements of the network. It does not significantly increase the complexity of equipment at the network's edge since that equipment must in any case include provision for dealing with errors occurring between the data terminal equipment and the network. If the user does not require error control on a particular circuit, as would be the case for telephony, or if the user's requirements are very special, these can be accommodated by suitable design of the network interface equipment. These different user requirements do not add to the functional complexity of the inner part of a Datakit network.

The level-A and level-B protocols are implemented on a per-link basis according to the performance and error characteristics of the link. The Datakit switch also has a standard physical interface, with error detection and multiplexing protocol. Thus the interface circuit at the end of a transmission line terminates the level-A and level-B protocols used by that line. The same interface circuit handles the level-A and level-B protocols of the switch. Level-C information passing over a virtual circuit is not altered by these interfaces but is carried unchanged from end-to-end over the virtual circuit (Figure 3).

The Unit of Information

Data communication is concerned with the transmission of data and control. An asynchronous terminal transmits a character each time that a key is pressed and transmits control information (by violating the character transmission format) when the Break key is pressed. File transfer between computers obviously involves data transfer, but control information is also transmitted when, for example, the end of a data record is reached. Control information is transmitted during data transfer in order to effect flow and error control.

Early message switching systems used certain data characters for network control purposes. That made it tiresome or impossible to send binary data and had unfortunate side-effects when erroneously generated data included control characters. Now networks carry data transparently and it should be understood that the transport of end-to-end control information must also be transparent.

HDLC [5] demonstrates a popular method for carrying control information so that it is not confused with user data. The information is assembled into packets having a fixed internal format with control and data separated. In HDLC a bit stuffing procedure ensures that the flag character marking the limits of a packet does not appear elsewhere within the packet. The arrangement serves also as the basis for error control, flow control and segmenting user data into blocks. All of these can take advantage of the bundling provided by a packet structure. Unfortunately this multiplicity of function applied to one data structure makes difficult the separation of function that we have sought with Datakit and which we believe is needed in order to effectively meet the wide range

of cost and performance objectives required of data networks.

Datakit uses the simplest practical information unit, one based upon a single 8-bit byte. Our standard unit of information is a 9-bit envelope (Figure 4). One bit of the nine indicates whether the remaining 8 are data or control. In the case of control information, one bit of the 8 indicates whether the information is for end-to-end control or whether it is supervisory information of interest to the network control process. Examples of supervisory control envelopes are ONHOOK and OFFHOOK which are used to record the state changes in certain types of terminal interface. End-to-end control codes include BREAK which indicates break status to or from an asynchronous terminal, and DELAY which allows a host to control the timing of output to a remotely located terminal. Other control codes are used for flow control and to delimit frames in the user's data.

The range of control codes is divided, for administrative convenience, according to the level of protocol at which the control code may be used. Of the end-to-end control codes, level-B is assigned codes in the range 0 through 7, level-C uses 8 through 63 and higher levels use 64 through 127. Of the codes used for communication with the network control process, 128 through 191 are used for supervision and 192 through 255 are used for maintenance.

There may be some concern that the use of a 9-bit envelope leads to unacceptably low transmission efficiency. That is not necessary, and indeed we can use code compression on long-haul transmission lines taking advantage of the usual low density of control envelopes. The 9-bit envelope allows us to define data transport service in simple terms just as 4 KHz defines a telephone circuit. Neither of these definitions precludes the network from using a variety of coding techniques. For example, on certain trunks we have used a byte-stuffing technique with an escape code to mark the presence of control bytes.

Service Description

Protocol levels A and B implement virtual circuits with the following characteristics:

(a) the virtual circuit is a pipe that carries data bytes (in 9-bit envelopes) asynchronously.

(b) It does not duplicate or rearrange transmitted data.

(c) It does not corrupt individual data bytes. (Corruptions are detected within the network, and bad data is discarded by the network. The intended probability of undetected error is about $10^{**}-12$.)

(d) It may lose data bytes (as a result of corruptions within the network or as a result of network congestion.)

We have found that this type of data transport service can be implemented using simple hardware whose size and performance is more reminiscent of time division equipment than conventional packet switches. Yet we can obtain the transmission efficiency of a packet network by using one of several asynchronous multiplexing techniques on long transmission lines. One indication of the implementation flexibility provided by the architecture is that a switch (typically the bottleneck in large packet switched networks) can itself be replaced by a miniature network without violating the architecture. That suggests the possibility of building large switches from arrays of smaller switching devices (as is of course usual in time division networks). This makes possible a switching machine that can grow gracefully in size and permits one to build the very high throughput switches that will in the future be required for toll switching.

The data communication service implemented by protocol levels A and B is the constant basis upon which different network users might build their particular communications arrangements, and is the constant framework within which the network implementor is free to work. Additions to the Datakit implementation, perhaps using new technology, are made within the constraint that the service definition must remain constant. We have found this to be a quite liberal constraint.

Users are free to choose the communication functions and protocols that best suit their application. Telephony, for example, is not burdened with a packet structure that properly belongs to data communication. At one extreme, a user may choose to use the network as an intelligent "copper wire" that can tell the difference between valid data and idle transmission, and so employs statistical multiplexing for transmission efficiency. In this way the network can efficiently support existing private networks with their own existing protocols. However that is a short term approach which does not easily support effective communication between users. The latter can only take place if users employ common protocols (or protocol converters, see below). In due course we expect users to migrate to new standards at their own convenience. Adoption of new standards is not a precondition for using the service.

When elaborate protocols have to be supported or when there is other reason for extensive processing of transmitted data, we route a virtual circuit through one or more network process. Such a circuit is illustrated in Figure 5. The virtual circuit between users A and B passes through process P. The process P acts like a "filter" in the virtual circuit between A and B. This technique can be used to implement complex protocols such as X.25 and X.29 [6].

Flow Control and Congestion Control

Switched virtual circuits are established by a call set-up procedure the details of which depend upon the type of network interface employed by the terminal. For example, in the case of an asynchronous ASCII terminal, the user types the identity of a host computer and sees in response either an initial (login) message from the host or a rejection message from the network control process.

During call set-up the network control process chooses a route for the virtual circuit and checks that the network has sufficient spare capacity to handle the anticipated additional load. The approach is similar to that proposed for Transpac [7]. Network resources are measured in terms of bandwidth (of a channel), buffer space (in an interface) and processing capacity (in a filter). The characteristics of the anticipated demand placed on the network by a new virtual circuit are based upon the type of service requested and the type of network interface employed. For certain types of traffic (e.g. voice) it may be appropriate to dedicate transmission bandwidth while in other cases (e.g. file transfer) dedicated buffer space may be used.

Once the circuit has been established, the user is expected to stay within the speed and buffer limits set for the virtual circuit. The network interface itself limits the maximum speed of data transfer and the user is responsible for ensuring that the requested buffer space is not exceeded. The network undertakes to provide the agreed amount of buffer space when necessary and the user undertakes never to have more than that amount of data in transmission at one time. There is no need for agreement on the details of the protocol, if any, that the user adopts in order to ensure that his side of the agreement is maintained. However, the network does reserve the right to discard data from a virtual circuit that is not properly controlled at the application level. Just as the byte stream provides a simple interface between the data packaging functions of the transport and applications levels, so this approach to congestion control tends to keep network and applications level control mechanisms apart. The approach does have the disadvantage that it requires more buffer memory within the network than some other approaches do, but memory costs are already sufficiently low that we judge the savings resulting from simplicity to dominate.

Support for Various Protocols

Asynchronous terminals that use an RS232 interface connect directly to a network interface module designed for the purpose. Figure 8 shows the information flow within that module. Data from/to the terminal pass directly through the interface pausing only long enough for packet assembly/disassembly. The maximum time that a byte spends waiting for packet assembly is about 20 msec. The start/stop transmission format used by asynchronous terminals is converted to/from the envelope format used within the network. The RS232 control leads are monitored by the interface module and changes are reported to the network control process by means of a simple protocol using supervisory control envelopes. The data transport protocol is implemented by means of end-to-end control envelopes.

The level B protocols detect corruption in transmitted data and discard anything that is bad. Thus, the level C protocols that are required to provide error correction, must detect lost data but need not check for corrupted envelopes. Usually this is achieved by dividing data into packets with control envelopes used as packet delimiters. Packet length and a sequence number are transmitted as means of detecting data loss.

One technique that is used to support an HDLC terminal employs a network interface module that maps one HDLC frame into one packet at level C. The HDLC functions that correspond to our level B are terminated on the interface module. Thus the CRC is checked and bad frames are discarded. The zero insertion bits are removed and the frame content is transmitted as a series of data envelopes. If the address field contains meaningful address information (as it does in SDLC [8]), that is used to select one of several virtual circuits over which the data are transmitted.

An advantage of this HDLC implementation is that the network virtual circuit is, for most practical purposes, used like a copper wire. The interface module will therefore support most variations of HDLC without change. A disadvantage is that it does little to ease communication between terminals that employ different protocols.

If one disregards the different ways in which various protocols format their packets, the different framing methods and the different degrees of multiplexing, one finds much similarity between many of the packet level protocols in use today. Most use some sort of block error check over the packet, use a sequence number to detect missing packets and retransmit packets when there is an error. Flow control employs either a window based upon the sequence number, or ready/not-ready signals, or both. Such similarities have led us to define a packet level protocol which one can (approximately) map various network access protocols into. In so far as the mapping supports the protocol features actually employed by a terminal, it provides a basis for information exchange between terminals that employ different access protocols. So far our studies indicate that the format conversion required to support this approach can be quite simple to implement and can lead to very efficient network interface hardware.

Summary

I have described briefly the protocol structure of a network that has minimal complexity at its lowest level and which can be molded to fit a wide variety of applications. The design includes a definition of data transport service that should be simple to comprehend and exploit: It provides for switched virtual circuits that carry 9-bit envelopes asynchronously. Data corruption is rare but loss is more common.

The maximum transmission rate and the maximum instantaneous storage capacity of a virtual circuit are not specified by the architecture but may be negotiated when a network interface is installed or a virtual circuit is established.

We have sought to make the transport service transparent to data and to end-to-end control functions. By putting switching and multiplexing at the lowest protocol level and by using virtual circuits for all communications, the network topology is transparent to the user. The properties of a virtual circuit are constant regardless of whether the circuit is delivered to the user through a multiplexed or non-multiplexed transmission line. There is a clear distinction between the virtual circuit and the link level functions of error detection, framing and multiplexing. Thus we have been able to implement local area networks within this architecture and have joined them together with trunk lines keeping the procedure for calling another user independent of the distance covered by the call.

I believe this architecture admits efficient implementation today and can survive new implementations as technology advances in the future. The architecture is flexible enough to encompass both basic transport and enhancements that involve data processing. The rather simple service definition should mean that the network can survive technology changes in either the customer equipment or network implementation without serious impact on the other. In short, it would seem to be a suitable basis for a common carrier data network.

References

1. "General Information — Binary Synchronous Communications". IBM GA27-3004-2, 1970.

2. A. G. Fraser, "Datakit — A Modular Network for Synchronous and Asynchronous Traffic", in IEEE Conf. Proc. ICC79, Boston, June 1979, IEEE CH1435 pp 20.1.1-3

3. "Data Processing — Open Systems Interconnection — Basic Reference Model", ISO Draft Proposal 7498 (1980).

4. "Interface between data terminal equipment and data circuit terminating equipment for terminals operating in the packet mode on public data networks". CCITT recommendation X.25 (1980).

5. "Data communication — High-level data link control procedures — Frame structure". ISO 3309 (1979)

   "Data communication — HDLC balanced class of procedures". ISO 6256 (1981)

6. "Procedures for the exchange of control information and user data between a packet assembly/disassembly facility (PAD) and a packet mode DTE or another PAD". CCITT provisional recommendation X.29 (1980)

7. J. M. Simon and A. Danet, "Controle des Ressources et Principles du Routage dans le Reseau Transpac". Proc. Int. Symp. on Flow Control in Computer Networks, Versailles (Feb 1979) pp33-44, ed. J.Grange and M.Gien, North-Holland Press.

8. "IBM Synchronous Data Link Control General Information". IBM GA27-3093-1, 1975.

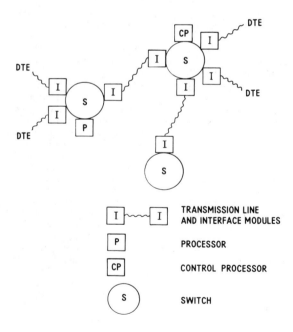

Figure 1: Network Architecture Components

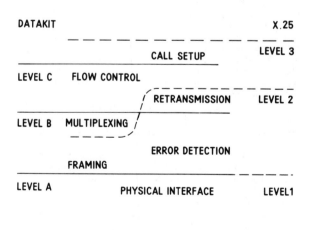

Figure 2: Comparison of X.25 and Datakit Protocol Levels

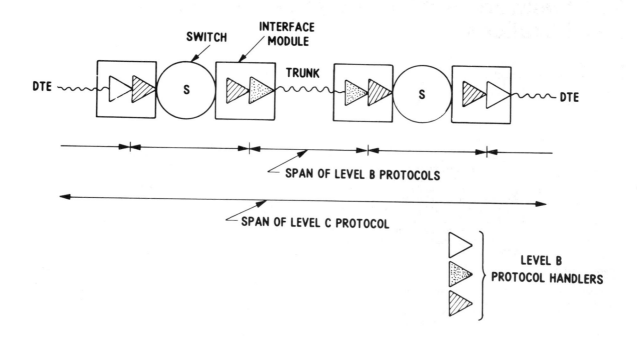

Figure 3: Protocol Handlers for One Virtual Circuit

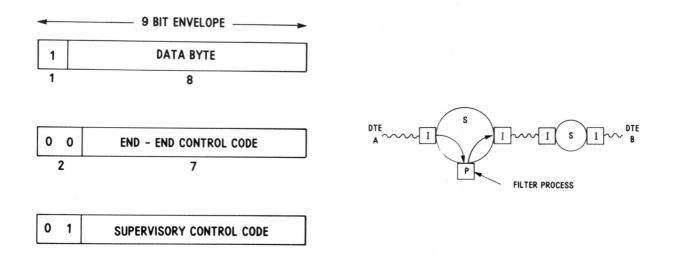

Figure 4: Envelope Structure

Figure 5: Virtual Circuit With Filter Process

SL-10 Network Architecture and Availability Considerations

R Aubin, D E Sproule
Bell-Northern Research, Canada

In order to set and achieve appropriate availability objectives for a data network, one must consider users' needs and derive from them the mission profile of the network as a trade-off between reliability and recoverability. This profile will clearly impact the network architecture. The strategy used in the Northern Telecom SL-10 Packet Switching System for achieving high-availability is presented. On the one hand, high reliability is obtained by applying fault-masking techniques to the areas of the SL-10 System, such as the Backbone Network (DCE to DCE), where faults potentially affect a large number of users. On the other hand, for the Access Network (DCE to/from DTE), where faults affect fewer users, less complex, hence less costly, but efficient error recovery techniques are preferred, yielding a high level of recoverability. Finally, degradation over time is prevented by a complete network management and diagnostic system.

INTRODUCTION

The very high availability standards that have traditionally been applied to voice communication are just as desirable for data communication. They may, however, be more difficult to achieve.

With the architecture of the Northern Telecom SL-10 Packet Switching System, we have developed an approach to availability that adopts a users' viewpoint. In order to provide genuine availability, one must indeed consider the end-to-end performance of a system, in the transmission facilities to and from users' premises as well as the core switching and transmission elements. We also maintain that inherent equipment availability must be matched by a complete and efficient network management system.

After an overview of the SL-10 Packet Switching System, we consider the needs of data network users for availability and derive from them the mission profile of the network as a trade-off between reliability and recoverability together with its architectural impact. We then go on to detail the options taken in the design of the SL-10 Backbone Network, interconnecting Data Circuit-Terminating Equipment (DCE), and the Access Network, connecting Data Terminal Equipment (DTE) to DCE. Finally, we highlight the characteristics of the SL-10 Management System as the key for maintaining availability in the long run.

GENERAL AVAILABILITY CONSIDERATIONS

Overview of the SL-10 System

For the purpose of availability discussions, we break down the SL-10 Network into a Backbone Network and an Access Network. The Backbone Network is made of the SL-10 Switches and the trunk lines between them. The Access Network is made of various types of Line Interfaces (LI) attached to Switches together with the transmission facilities between them and the users.

The SL-10 Switch is a multiprocessor with two classes of switching elements: the Trunk Processors (TP), managing the trunks, and the Line Processors (LP), managing the Line Interfaces and the access lines to the network. Switching elements communicate through a Common Memory element, controlled and administered by redundant load-sharing Control Processors.

Availability Requirements

Before giving a closer look at the SL-10 architecture, we should first ask what are the users' requirements for availability. For this purpose, we can classify the users of a network into two broad categories according to their data traffic: the bulk data users, who perform relatively large, non-real-time operations (e.g., file transfer), and the transactional users, who perform relatively small, real-time operations (e.g., database access). The banking industry is a good example for which both categories of users are found: file transfer may be carried out for daily reporting of customers' accounts while account books are updated on-line at the counter. Both applications require high availability, but their profiles are different.

For bulk data users, the key requirement is a very high probability that their operations be completed without network failure. In other words, they want long network uptime above all. For transactional users, the key requirement is a very high probability that the network be ready to perform their operations. In other words, they want short network downtime above all. As a consequence, the bulk data users' requirement for uptime subsumes the requirement of transactional users; and conversely, for downtime. Implied in both these requirements is that bulk data and transactional users want the network to be scheduled 24 hours a day, 7 days a week.

Availability Objectives

In the design of a packet switching system, what mission profile [1] can be derived from these users' requirements? This profile will emerge as the result of trade-offs and the forecasted system performance will necessarily be probabilistic in nature.

In the appendix, we outline a method whereby perceived users' requirements can be transposed into reliability and recoverability objectives for a network. Reliability is proportional to the network Mean Time To Fail (MTTF), while recoverability is inversely proportional to the Mean Time To Recover (MTTR). The MTTF must be long enough to satisfy the bulk data users and the MTTR, short enough to satisfy the transactional users. An adequate availability objective can then be derived from this judicious mix of reliability and recoverability.

Impact on Architecture

Of course, users' requirements for availability have to be fulfilled at a reasonable cost. And intuitively, the cost functions are not linear. What strategies should one use in order to provide high availability? There is ultimately only one general approach: protective redundancy (of equipment, of operations, of data).

High reliability is achieved by fault-avoidance and fault-masking techniques. Fault-avoidance aims at putting hardware and software in the network that is as nearly fault-free as possible. Fault-masking comes to play in the presence of faults. It allows certain faults to be detected and recovered from without loss of communication for the network users. Loss of performance, however, can be experienced. Fault-masking may be complex because it often involves the real-time replication of operations, either in space, on different pieces of equipment, or in time, by retries. Moreover, it can only be applied if protection against the corruption of users' data can be guaranteed.

Some faults will slip through any reliability scheme and percolate up to the level that some users see their communication lost. In such cases, high recoverability is necessary. It is obtained through automatic error recovery and in the extreme, efficient manual recovery techniques. The purpose of automatic error recovery is to detect the faults visible to users and internally return the network to some possibly degraded but functional state within the shortest time. Finally, should automatic recovery fail, the goal of manual recovery procedures is to provide enough information about the nature and location of faults to make external action efficient.

In the SL-10 System, we have worked toward higher reliability by the extensive use of fault-avoidance and a selective use of fault-masking, and toward higher recoverability by the extensive use of error recovery mechanisms [10].

Indeed, fault-avoidance is applied at all stages of the hardware and software design, manufacturing, and testing process. The production of software, in particular, because of its complexity, makes use of state-of-the-art techniques [7].

Fault-masking is applied to critical elements of the network whose loss would significantly lower the overall reliability. For example, error-correcting memory is used to mask single bit parity errors.

Automatic error recovery in the SL-10 System is built around: complete testing procedures before devices are put to service; reconfiguration after failure; fast software loading; and constant monitoring of devices once in service. For example, if a memory module is found defective, a spare module can be switched in and the programs and data reloaded from disk.

Finally, manual error recovery is facilitated by a complete and efficient network management system. Fault information is available at a central location in the SL-10 Network, the Network Control Centre, as well as at the Switches where the faults are detected.

We believe that this general approach yields a good mix of reliability and recoverability at a reasonable cost. This will be substantiated in the next two sections as we focus on the SL-10 Backbone and Access Networks.

BACKBONE NETWORK AVAILABILITY

The communication service offered by the SL-10 Backbone Network is implemented using two logical layers [9]. At the bottom, the datagram layer provides basic inter-switch communication. At the top, the virtual circuit layer provides end-to-end communication between source and destination Line Processors. Because the Backbone Network supports such a large number of users, extensive fault-masking techniques have been applied to make it very reliable.

The datagram layer is physically implemented by trunks and Trunk Processors, with inter-switch routing administered by Control Processors. In the event of trunk or intermediate Switch failures, the routing system facilitates recovery by redirecting datagrams around the failed component (see Figure 1). The properties of such a system are, however, that no guarantee can be placed on (1) datagrams arriving at the destination in the sequence in which they were transmitted, (2) datagrams arriving at all, and (3) single copies of datagrams arriving at the destination.

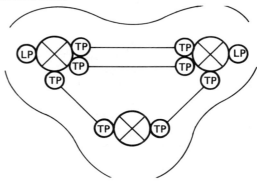

Figure 1. Redundant Backbone Configuration

Such undesirable properties of the datagram layer are masked from users by the virtual circuit layer. The latter is implemented by Line Processors. It provides an error-free, in-sequence, flow-controlled stream of packets across the Backbone Network in the presence of faults.

The virtual circuit layer makes the route between Line Processors extremely reliable (i.e., MTTF of tens of thousands of hours). When this is coupled with the inherent reliability of Line Processors and access facilities (i.e., MTTF of hundreds of hours), we get an end-to-end reliability that is sufficient to satisfy the requirements of bulk data users. Consequently, in the SL-10 System, extensive error recovery techniques have been preferred over complex and costly fault-masking mechanisms in response to faults in Line Processors. Should a Line Processor fail, the virtual circuits anchored on this Processor are terminated. The recovery techniques try to ensure that terminated virtual circuits can be re-established in the shortest period possible, thus answering the requirements of the transactional users. This is the topic of the following section.

ACCESS NETWORK AVAILABILITY

In the foregoing section, we said that the availability of the SL-10 Backbone Network relied on the reliability of the route between Line Processors and the recoverability of the Line Processors themselves. In this section, we expand on how high recoverability is offered by the SL-10 Access Network as a whole.

The Access Network includes such components as the users' access lines, the modems that terminate either end of the lines, the Line Interface devices on the Switch that provide the link level framing protocols, and that portion of the Line Processors that handles the line access protocols. The basic access configuration is shown in Figure 2.

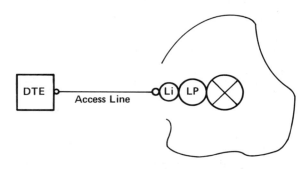

Figure 2. Basic Access Configuration

This basic configuration hides the fact that a single access line often supports many virtual circuits. The availability of this type of access should be increased (by improving on reliability or recoverability), since a single line failure counts for as many failures as the line supports virtual circuits.

Favoring the reliability approach, some packet switching networks have opted for a multiline link protocol for X.25 [4]. Such a protocol enhances virtual circuit reliability across the lines by offering load-sharing at the link level. As a consequence, as long as one of the communication lines is operational, failures in modems or physical facilities will be masked from the users.

It was felt, however, that this approach had shortcomings which made the expected reliability improvement overly optimistic. First, a multiline link protocol necessitates that the frame streams from all access lines be brought together at a single processing point for resequencing. Second, the multiple access lines

must terminate on the same Switch and consequently, tend to use considerable amount of common equipment [8].

Furthermore, one may question if the reliability of access lines is at all an issue. Indeed, studies indicate that data communication over private lines (at least in the United States) has a high MTTF (e.g., 1300 hours) and a poor MTTR (e.g., 2 hours) [8].

As a consequence, the SL-10 approach, as dicussed in what follows, favors the recoverability of the full Access Network.

We maintain that there are two kinds of recoverability requirements for the SL-10 Access Network which give rise to two sets of features. One is intrinsic. It aims at protecting users mainly against whole Switch failure and its exact application depends on the internal policy of the network operating company. The other is extrinsic. It is tailored to individual users' protection needs, especially regarding failures of access lines and even DTE. It is optional and its exact parameters are specified in the users' service data.

Intrinsic Recoverability

Intrinsic recoverability is provided by features such as multiple Control Processors, memory sparing, fast loading devices and algorithms, but above all, where warranted by operating companies, by a redundant Switch. The latter is made of two sections with a Common Memory element and a Control Processor each; every Line Processor on one section can have a spare on the other. This configuration is sketched in Figure 3. By duplicating all switching elements down to the Line Processors, it offers greater overall recoverability than the redundant configurations in other networks [2, 5].

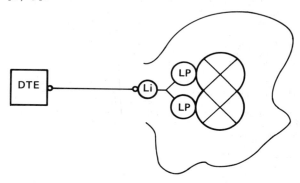

Figure 3. Redundant Switch Configuration

With this capability, high recoverability can be provided transparently and universally to all network users. Both sections of the Switch can share the total load. Should one section of the Switch fail, all virtual circuits originating from and terminating at this section are terminated. A switch-over of users' lines to the redundant section takes place and access lines again become operational. Users may set up communication again through the normal virtual circuit establishment procedure. The virtual circuits that were on the healthy section before the failure do not suffer any interruption.

Gateways (GW) for internetworking form another area of the SL-10 System for which high recoverability has been provided. This is amply justified in view of the number of virtual circuits that these elements can support. Indeed, an international virtual circuit is established from a source Line Processor to the nearest gateway in the network. If multiple gateways are available, they all share the total virtual circuit load. Should a gateway fail, the virtual circuits it supports are terminated and can be re-established transparently on the next nearest gateway [9]. See Figure 4 for an example of such a configuration.

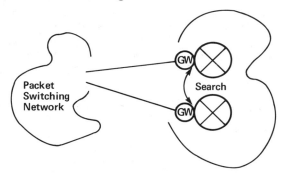

Figure 4. Redundant Gateway Configuration

Extrinsic Recoverability

Individual users may require additional levels of recoverability. In the SL-10 System, three main extrinsic recoverability features are provided: access line hunt groups, access line back-ups, and dial access lines.

With access line hunt groups, several lines on a Switch are connected to the same DTE or to several different DTE. All lines answer to the same network address. When a virtual circuit is established, it may be placed on one or another available line following a search algorithm. Load-sharing on a virtual circuit basis is possible when several lines are operational. Should one access path fail at any point, the virtual circuits on this path are terminated but can be established again on another path in the hunt group. See Figure 5 for possible configurations.

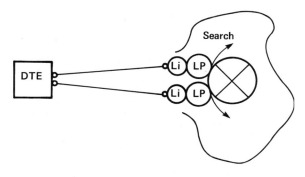

Figure 5. Line Hunt Group Configurations

The hunt group feature provides recoverability from failures on the whole access path from the Line Processors all the way to the DTE themselves. In order to enhance this protection,

e.g., against Switch failure, another option is offered by the SL-10 System at the expense of load-sharing.

The back-up feature makes possible the search for a back-up access line across several Switches. These configurations are drawn in Figure 6. Back-up lines respond to a single address, but offer no load-sharing and a less sophisticated selection mechanism. Since Switches can be geographically distributed, the probability of using common access equipment can be reduced.

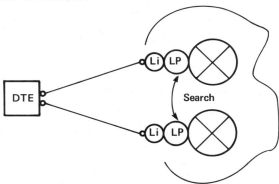

Figure 6. Line Back-up Configurations

Finally, the SL-10 System offers a dial access capability for some services. The precise junction made with the network depends upon the telephone system hunting mechanism. This mechanism searches for a connection across failed lines, modems, Line Interfaces, Line Processors, and even Switches, increasing significantly the availability of access (see Figure 7).

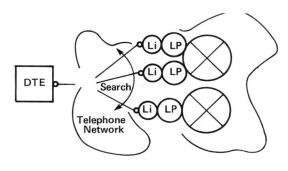

Figure 7. Dial Access Configuration

AVAILABILITY AND NETWORK MANAGEMENT

We have seen that a network must provide users with a judicious mix of reliability and recoverability features. These features are either intrinsic and universal or extrinsic and tailored to individual users. However, no matter how high a level of availability is originally injected into the network, it will slowly suffer from entropy, e.g., spares will be used up. Consequently, a complete and efficient network management is a must to maintain high availability over time.

Network management in the SL-10 System first acts at the network intrinsic level. For the

purpose of short-term action, real-time surveillance processes continually monitor the
various elements of the network. When a fault
or degradation is detected by a Switch, an
alarm is generated containing on-the-spot
information on the nature and location of the
fault. This alarm is sent to a central place in
the network, the Network Control Centre, as
.ell as locally to a console attached to the
Switch. The alarm identifies if immediate or
deferred operator intervention is required.
For longer term planning, the network management system performs the collection of
operational data. From the analysis of such
information, it is possible to keep track of
how well the network behaves and to plan for
further improvements. For example,
non-critical software problems detected by the
software itself are logged for further analysis
and resolution.

The SL-10 network management system also plays
a role at the network extrinsic level. The profile of each user is captured in the service
data. This information is generated by the Data
Control Centre and forwarded through the network to the appropriate Switches where it is
kept securely on tape or disk. Service data
can then be updated selectively for individual
users. Should a user report trouble on his
line, loop back tests can be carried out either
by the Switch Operator or remotely from the
Network Control Centre. These tests are
non-disruptive to other users.

CONCLUSION

We have tried to capture the needs of data network users for availability by categorizing
them into bulk data and transactional users. We
have derived a mission profile for a packet
switching system such that bulk data users
drive the reliability objective and transactional users drive the recoverability
objective, availability being subsidiary to
these two objectives. We have also shown the
trade-offs between reliability and recoverability that have been implemented in the Northern
Telecom SL-10 Packet Switching Network, while
working toward telephony levels of
availability.

More precisely, in the SL-10 System, a good
level of reliability is obtained by the production of high-quality hardware and software
and by the selective introduction of complex
fault-masking features where justified, as in
the virtual circuit layer of the Backbone Network. Various levels of recoverability are
offered by a choice of equipment redundancy,
from memory to a full Switch. Redundant access
facilities can also be specified and used transparently. Finally, an efficient management
system allows the network to be maintained,
especially in the middle and long term.

APPENDIX

The network uptime and downtime probability
laws are often characterized by their means.
The uptime mean is called the Mean Time To Fail
(MTTF) and calculated as follows:

$$MTTF = \frac{\sum_i (\text{uptime seen by user } i)}{\sum_i (\text{no. of failures seen by user } i)}$$

The downtime mean, called the Mean Time To
Recover (MTTR), is calculated similarly:

$$MTTR = \frac{\sum_i (\text{downtime seen by user } i)}{\sum_i (\text{no. of failures seen by user } i)}$$

The MTTF and the MTTR serve as measures of the
network's operational reliability and recoverability respectively. We would like to argue
that this rule is meaningful only if taken in
the context of the complete uptime and downtime
probability laws. This approach is rendered
necessary because of the perceived users'
requirement for guaranteed minimum performance,
whose assessment necessitates some measure of
the spread of the uptime and downtime
densities.

The exponential law is applicable as a law of
time to fail [6] and the normal law approximates a law of time to recover. In the latter
case, we have to recognize that each recovery
mode will possess its own peak. However, we can
often assume, especially with highly recoverable systems, that one peak will largely
predominate, e.g., automatic reconfiguration,
and that its standard deviation will be small
with respect to its mean.

We illustrate how these laws can help setting
objectives to satisfy users' requirements,
thus:

o Suppose that bulk data users would be content if the probability of 1 hour or more
network uptime was at least 0.99. Then, we
want to find r, the failure rate, such that
[6]:
P [t >= 1 hour] = 0.99 = exp(-r).
We deduce that r = 0.01 failure/hour and
consequently, that the network end-to-end
operational reliability objective should
be: MTTF = 1/r = 100 hours.

o Suppose that transactional users would be
content if the probability of 0.02 hour
(1.2 min.) or less network downtime was at
least 0.99. Then, we want to find m, the
mean, and s, the standard deviation, such
that [6]:
P [t =< 0.02 hour] = 0.99 = phi((0.02-m)/s)
where phi is the normal distribution function. We can deduce that, say, m = 0.01
hour and s = 0.003 hour; consequently, the
network end-to-end recoverability objective
(for the main recovery mode) should be an
MTTR of 0.01 hour (given a standard deviation of 0.003 hour).

Availability has not been mentioned so far:
this is because it is subsidiary to reliability
and recoverability [3]. Indeed, in the design
of a network that supports a diversity of
users, the reliability objective is driven by
the requirements of the bulk data users while
the recoverability objective is driven by the
requirements of the transactional users. The
availability objective itself is bound by these
two driving forces, thus:

$$\text{availability} = \frac{MTTF [1]}{MTTF [1] + MTTR [2]}$$

where MTTF [1] is required by bulk data users and MTTR [2] is required by transactional users

To pursue the example above, the MTTF objective of 100 hours and the MTTR objective of 0.01 hour yield an effective availability objective of 99.99%.

REFERENCES

1. R. Bernhard and N. Mokhoff, The Mission Profile, _IEEE Spectrum_, October 1981, 47-49.

2. B. Durteste, Caractéristiques du réseau Transpac, _Proc. Convention informatique_, part I, Paris, 1976, 20-26.

3. H. Kopetz, _Software Reliability_, Springer-Verlag, New-York, 1979.

4. G. Mainguenaud and B. Jamet, A Multiline Data Link Control Procedure, _Proc. Int. Conf. Computer Communication_, Kyoto, 1978, 289-294.

5. C. B. Newport and P. Kaul, Communications Processors for Telenet's Third Generation Packet Switching Network, _Proc. EASCON77_, 8-24 / 12 pp.

6. E. Parzen, _Modern Probability Theory and Its Applications_, John Wiley, New-York, 1970.

7. W. B. Shorrocks, SL-10 Software Production, Testing, and Updating, _Proc. Int. Switching Symp._, Paris, 1979, 1277-1282.

8. J. Spragins, Data Transmission over the Common Carrier Telephone Plant: Factors Affecting its Reliability, _Proc. Int. Conf. Communications_, Toronto, 1978, 3.1.1 - 3.1.5.

9. D. E. Sproule and F. Mellor, Routing, Flow, and Congestion Control in the Datapac Network, _IEEE Trans. Communications_, vol. COM-29, no. 4, April 1981, 386-391.

10. A. Trivedi, C. Bedard, and H. Gibbs, Reliability and Availability Design Consideration in Datapac, _Proc. Int. Conf. Communications_, Toronto, 1978, 3.2.1 - 3.2.5.

Raymond Aubin received the BA degree and the BSc degree (_informatique_) from the _Université de Montréal_ in 1969 and 1972 respectively, and the PhD degree (artificial intelligence) from the University of Edinburgh in 1976. He then joined Concordia University, Montreal, to become Assistant Professor of Computer Science. In 1978, he moved to Bell-Northern Research, Ottawa, to take part in the development of the SL-10 Packet Switching System. He is currently working on a communication architecture for distributed multicomputer systems.

Don Sproule received the BASc degree from the University of Toronto in 1972 and the MIng degree from Carleton University, Ottawa, in 1974. From 1974 to 1982, he worked at Bell-Northern Research Ltd., Ottawa, on the specification and development of the SL-10 Packet Switching System, which was basis for the canadian Datapac Network. Recently, he joined the Mitel Corp., Ottawa, where he is working on data communication applications for PABX's.

A Carefully Structured System Interface

L J Endicott Jr.
IBM, USA

This paper discusses an experimental project at the IBM System Products Division development laboratory in Rochester, Minnesota, USA. The focus of the project, and the subject of the paper, is the empirical development of a system interface which makes available to a non-DP trained user all or most of the business data processing functions required by the owner or manager of a small business. Also discussed are general characteristics of ease of use, some specific problems, and projections into the future.

I   INTRODUCTION

The Nonprocedural System (NPS) project was an experimental project at the IBM System Products Division development laboratory in Rochester, Minnesota. The focus of the project was the empirical development of a system interface to make available to non-DP trained users all or most of the business data processing functions required by the owner or manager of a small business. (Note that this paper describes an experimental activity only and that conclusions are based upon informal observation and anecdotal material, not upon controlled human factors studies. No inferences should be drawn in regard to planned or future IBM products.)

An interface with objectives similar to objectives of the NPS experimental activity should have the following characteristics:

1. It should guide the user and control input to the system in a "friendly" manner; i.e., HELP must always be available and useful, and the user must have the confidence that error recovery is easy.

2. It should introduce the user in a natural manner to DP concepts which the user must understand in order to fully utilize the capabilities of the underlying system.

3. It should provide for hundreds of details and be capable of evolving over time.

The four sections of this paper are: BACKGROUND, which briefly describes the NPS project and the user environment with which it was concerned; EASE OF USE, which offers some general observations about the subject as seen by the NPS project; SOME PROBLEMS, which describes specific problems encountered in the NPS experimental activity; and CONCLUDING REMARKS, which projects into the future of ease-of-use systems.

II   BACKGROUND

The NPS experimental system was operational on an IBM System/34 at the Rochester SPD laboratory long enough to draw some preliminary conclusions even though no formal human factors studies were done. Though the NPS activity had several objectives,[1] one of its central purposes was to investigate the characteristics of a very high level interface that permits non-DP trained users to generate and to quickly and easily modify billing, inventory control, accounts receivable, sales analysis, general ledger, accounts payable, and payroll applications for small businesses.

The NPS project did not address physical characteristics of individuals nor the influence the physical characteristics of an interface have upon its cognitive aspects. It used standard IBM System/34 I/O: an 83-character keyboard, an 80X24 green phosphor display, and a 132-character printer. Within this context, it investigated the interface characteristics and underlying function required to provide very high level ease of use.

The NPS activity was a follow-on to the Nonprogrammer Interface (NPI) project.[2] The NPI experimental system was implemented in APL on the IBM System/370. IBM 5100 and 5110 systems were used as terminals. APL was used on the System/370 because of ease of both implementation and modification, since a largely empirical approach to the problem was planned. The final version of the NPI system was interactive, output oriented, and nonprocedural in nature (other than for pocket calculator type functions). Information could be entered into the system only in response to prompts, and only described data could be entered into the system.

Basically, a set of menus and prompts were provided. The sequencing and tailoring were provided by the system in response to user answers, and user names were substituted where appropriate. The system required fewer than 20 menus and fewer than 75 prompts or questions. Most of these were seen by the user only when an invalid response was provided. Some other significant characteristics of the system were:

° A specific sequence of menus and prompts would not terminate until a legitimate function had been performed or a legitimate algorithm defined. For example, NPI could not generate an application that would not run, although the user could produce a result other than that intended.

○ The user could not "look" inside the system. Information and data were returned to the user only in the format in which they were entered or described to the system.

○ A complete set of system documentation was always available online to the user, and the HELP response was almost always a valid response.

○ Manual office procedure concepts and terminology were employed wherever possible. Traditional DP concepts and terminology were kept to an absolute minimum (some concepts were particularly troublesome--the name of a field versus its content, key fields, control breaks, transaction files, etc., but acceptable approaches were finally found).

○ Processing and file activity were generally derived by implication, but specific manipulation was permitted on request (but only via question and answer, again apart from pocket calculator type functions).

○ Questions were only asked in their "natural" (to the user) sequence (this sequence was determined empirically and is not "natural" to all users). The user was not asked a specific question unless it was one that he would have asked himself at the corresponding point in manual processing.

The NPS system corrected some of the problems discovered within the NPI system. NPS provided considerably improved display capability, utilized a single-level store in place of the NPI APL work space, and added many new functions and interface characteristics. These include: an UNENTER key, a system HELP function to ensure that HELP is always available and easily augmentable by users as well as developers, and an EDUCATION mode of operation.

At the start of the NPI activity, assumptions were made in regard to the class of users who might want to use an NPS-type interface and the general characteristics of the individuals in this class. During the course of the NPI activity, these assumptions changed. It is still not clear how valid the final assumptions were, but they evolved and a fair amount of time and thought went into their evolution.

Potential users of an NPS-type interface are composed of five subclasses:

1. Data entry in both casual and "heads down" mode by all types of users.

2. Application generation and system control and operation by non-DP trained managers and professionals.

3. Modification of prepackaged NPS applications by non-DP trained managers and professionals.

4. Application generation by professional application developers.

5. Casual use of all kinds by DP professionals.

For Subclass 1 above, the individual installation is best able to provide the prompting and HELP text required. This imposes upon the system the requirement to provide facilities to Subclasses 2 and 3, which enables users to enter and change this information in an easy and convenient manner. (For example, the default prompt option is to always prompt using field names within the application plus menu capability to override the prompt. Also, the HELP key is always available when the keyboard is unlocked--in the case of a generated application, the user enters HELP text by: running the application, requesting HELP for each field, and entering the HELP text at that point, thus overriding the default message "HELP text has not been supplied for this field.") In addition, a single display organization should be provided, if possible, equally suitable for both casual and "heads down" use. This was attempted by NPS.

It is assumed that the individuals in Subclasses 2 and 3 have a good knowledge of the job to be automated (i.e., that they can perform the job manually using a typewriter, calculator, and file drawers) but do not necessarily have any knowledge of DP concepts. It is also assumed that they will spend no more than two to three hours with a knowledgeable person or referring to a manual prior to using the machine. It is, therefore, necessary that the system provide three modes of operation: an EDUCATION mode, an inexperienced user mode, and an experienced user mode. This is what the NPS system attempted to do, but again using a single display organization. (The display screen is divided horizontally into three sections: the middle section always reserved for operational data; the lower section for prompt, HELP, and EDUCATION text--mode determines only the relative size, that is, the amount of text in the bottom section of the screen--operational data is always keyed into the middle section; and the top section, used for guidance and always a single line).

It is assumed that the characteristics of individuals in Subclasses 4 and 5 will not impose additional functions upon the system nor affect the characteristics of the interface. Though it was not invalidated, further testing is warranted to validate this assumption.

III EASE OF USE

As previously mentioned, a major purpose of the NPS project was to empirically investigate the cognitive characteristics of an interface to permit non-DP trained individuals to automate record handling in a small business. There are a number of problems involved in this.[3] The NPS project was limited to the application generation and modification aspect. It is assumed that an existing manual procedure is to be automated and that the individual who is generating or modifying the application is able to perform the application manually. The objective of the NPS system was to provide sufficient function, including EDUCATION, MENUS, PROMPTS, and HELP, to permit this.

People who have seen or used the NPS interface have referred to it, probably slightingly, as "interactive RPG," and RPG is considered by many not to be a programming language. The precursor project to NPS was called the "Nonprogrammer Interface" project. Nevertheless, the NPS system is, in B. A. Sheil's terminology, an "open device"[4] and, as such, requires "programming." Sheil, in the same paper in which he discusses open devices, goes on to say:

> If programming is inherently complex, any attempt to simplify it must be based on some property of the programs which some class of people actually want to write which allows a simpler approach. Arbitrary programming would remain complex, but simpler forms would allow nonprogrammers to formulate most of the complex instructions that they need to cope with complex information technology. At the very least, we might expect to be able to construct programming notations which exclude programs whose properties are undecidable. Whether or not this formal restriction improves subjective ease of use, it simplifies many of the technical problems associated with providing programmer support facilities such as program analyzers. This in turn makes it possible for programming environment to provide significantly more advice and assistance to the programmer.[5]

In the following general comments on ease of use in the NPS system, the context is that of minimizing the amount of knowledge and intellectual effort required to generate or modify applications and of enabling (and encouraging) the system user to function with no prior DP experience and without recourse to assistance other than that provided by the system itself.

First, note that ease of use is not absolute—it is relative. Though attempts have been made to quantify ease of use,[6,7] it is probably a subjective measure quantifiable at best by after-the-fact surveys of users. Ordering systems by ease of use will vary both with function and with user class. Assuming this, an obvious corollary is that for the designer/implementer of ease of use, the job is never finished. He is pushing his stone up a hill that becomes ever higher—but at least he can have no complaint in regard to job security. An associated corollary is that unless he plans to deliver an endless number of new

systems, he must design a system that readily permits modification and extension of both the user interface and the underlying support function. In any event, because of individual preferences and what appears to be a wide spectrum of cognitive styles, he must provide for easy modification of the user interface by the user himself—and do so in such a way as to minimize impact upon system maintenance and evolution. (The NPS system only addresses this problem in regard to EDUCATION, MENUS, PROMPTS, and HELP and soft keys, not in regard to alternatives such as APA displays, touch screens, trackballs, and other devices.)

A second general point, and one which many do not recognize or consider simply wrong, is that business data processing is more complex in the amount of both disparate detail and decision processes than is most other forms of computing. Another way of describing this is that it is messy, not elegant. Again, assuming this to be true, the consequence is that users must specify a lot of detailed information (naturally, much can and should be defaulted—but then it is necessary to provide an easy way of 1) overriding the defaults, and 2) respecifying system provided defaults). It appears there is no theoretical way of determining what this detailed information is, when it is complete, how and when it should be presented, what should be defaulted, how should it be overridden, when should it be overridden, and so on. On the NPS project, it was necessary to investigate these problems empirically, and moreover, there was no one best solution. Not only must the NPS experimental system be designed to evolve but most probably any product would have to be designed with a very soft interface (but the "meta interface," so to speak, must be hard—in other words, ease of use cannot be recursive if compatibility is to be retained for application packages, system maintenance, upgrades, etc).

A third point is, though it is necessary to make assumptions of a user's numeracy, literacy, and competence in the job to be automated, no assumptions can be made in regard to the user's knowledge of the physical interface, the cognitive interface, or DP concepts. The hardware interface must be well layed out and labeled, but it also may be necessary to provide keyboard drill programs, perhaps even games. Though these problems must be addressed, the NPS project did not do so.

What was addressed was the cognitive interface and DP concepts. (DP concepts are addressed in the next section.) An education package (a series of system-driven practice problems where the first level HELP text is always displayed) was provided plus the use of the three-partition display including the guidance section (top line) and the prompt/HELP section (bottom portion, under system control varying from four to seventeen lines).

In addition, attention has been focused on the concept of learning by doing. The NPS system tried to provide sufficient test and recovery functions to free the user from the fear of doing something wrong. It is assumed that people will make mistakes, but if they can recover from them, they will feel free to make even more mistakes and learn from them. The UNENTER function is basic to this ability, and an UNDO function was considered.

There are other education-type functions, e.g., a very high level trace, but on the NPS project, since it is impossible to provide "enough" education, only some significant subset could be provided. In the long term, application packages will be available. If these packages are written in a high enough language, such as the NPS system provided, these packages will provide "canned" education. The user may run them as delivered, he may modify them in minor or major ways, or he may simply read them to see how to do what he wants to do and generate a totally new application.

There are other general aspects of ease of use which were investigated or considered by the NPS project. Five should be mentioned here:

1. The NPS interface is largely symmetric, that is, information is presented to the user either identical to, or similar to, the manner in which he entered it. This symmetry seems desirable for ease of use, but it appears difficult either to prove this or even determine when "close" is "close enough."

2. The NPS interface is totally opaque. This appears to be an implicit or explicit assumption about ease-of-use interfaces by most people working in the area. We know of no reason to question this.

3. The NPS interface is highly structured and, therefore, probably restricted. For example, it is not clear whether it is possible in NPS to generate an application which would fully simulate the NPS system interface (for capturing unwary users' passwords, though the planned security option would certainly prevent this). Despite Sheil's contention, the implications of such restrictions, if they exist, are not clear.

4. The NPS interface is largely nonprocedural in nature. It would appear, however, that to date nobody knows how to provide truly easy to use arithmetic and logic other than by expressions.[8] NPS, too, chose expressions. (In the earlier NPI work, an escape to BASIC was provided--it is still not clear what is best.) DO loops were also provided, but control breaks were handled in an RPG-like manner.

5. One final aspect is the relationship of the interface to the underlying system. Although system masking is possible, it appears that building a high level ease-of-use interface on a randomly selected system leads to unanticipated problems. The better approach is to design the underlying system to support the inter-

face, including the use of tagging and program indexing to facilitate run time data checking.

IV   SOME PROBLEMS

It became apparent early in the NPS activity that in order to generate other than extremely simple applications it would be necessary that the user have a fair understanding of a number of DP concepts. Some of these are obvious: the necessity for naming, the difference between the name of something and the thing itself, the concepts of field/record/file, the difference between a primary key and secondary keys, implicit and explicit looping, expression of logic and computation, etc. Some of the less obvious are: collating sequence, data types, transaction files, the necessity for specificity and completeness, etc. Some are moderately surprising, for example, MENUS and their purpose.

Many of these problems and associated studies are discussed by du Boulay and O'Shea[9]. One study made on the NPS project will be described. A college student with no knowledge of DP concepts was employed to generate some applications on the NPS system. She was instructed to keep a diary of her activities and problems. She recorded a great amount of confusion during her first days on the system. She then began to make good progress and her notes were helpful in improving the system's ease of use in regard to some of the areas listed above. It appears that there is some initial global concept required before it is possible to begin to deal with specific DP concepts, though it is possible that the confusion was inherent in this situation (i.e., a young person in a first-time experience) rather than peculiar to the DP aspect.

The major problem that emerges from the employee's diary is that of the necessity for specificity and completeness. She learned quite quickly to generate applications using conditional expressions, but generally did not specify all situations for some particular input. This did not appear to be a problem in conceptualization but a problem in personality and habit--at least we drew no conclusions on the NPS project in regard to what to do about this particular problem.

A second major area of confusion is in naming. Though considerable care had been taken in this area, it was clear from the employee's diary that what had been provided in the NPS project was far from adequate. Originally, unrestricted naming had been permitted--this was a case of too much. The NPS system moved toward a restricted and more highly structured naming support as a system default--unrestricted naming only being supported as a MENU selectable item.

In summary, the findings from this informal study were:

1. In this particular case, familiarization with the system took several weeks with minimal assistance.

2. After familiarity with the system is gained, problems experienced by the novice user are quite similar to those experienced in a classroom environment.

3. For true novices, a highly structured and restricted interface is required, even though this significantly increases the number of options with which the experienced user will have to be familiar.

4. There are some problems which require considerable more work in order to provide a high level ease of use for application generation. These may go beyond the learning and use of concepts.

V CONCLUSIONS

The only thing we can know for certain about the future is that it will be different from what we expect. However, it is probably of some value to speculate about it. Following are some thoughts about ease of use in business data processing arising from our activities on the NPS project.

Because of the wide variation in cognitive styles and in activities to be automated, it is unlikely that we will ever see just one ease-of-use interface—or even a small number. Even for a particular (and truly easy to use) interface, it would appear necessary to develop a "meta interface" to provide a soft interface which can easily be tailored and evolved.

Probably in the future, a large number of individuals, perhaps the majority, coming out of secondary schools will have some DP competence. Nevertheless, it will be necessary, at least during the future that readers of this paper are concerned about, for all ease-of-use interfaces to provide extensive education and help functions. In addition, since only a definite amount is practicable, it will be necessary to assume the existence of application packages which can be easily tailored through the ease-of-use interface or read for their concepts to be acquired.

It is likely that "expert systems" will be developed for the business community; however, this does not appear to be a near-term prospect—and because of the pride we take in our expertise, such systems will not be an unmixed blessing.

Finally, the most exciting development in the next few years may be the availability of optical disks for data storage.[10] Not only will this make more practicable extensive education and help facilities, it may also make possible a return to office procedures which existed in previous centuries, where everything was documented in an orderly and permanent manner.[11] In the words of Huyck and Kremenak: "From someday soon, nothing will be forgotten."[12]

ACKNOWLEDGEMENTS

The author wishes to express his appreciation

to the other members of the NPS project: William L. Batchelor, Roger F. Dimmick, George G. Gorbatenko, E. R. (Jed) Harris, Griff H. Rees, Walter S. Schaffer, and Phil C. Schloss.

REFERENCES

1. Schaffer, W. S., "A High-Level User Interface to a System (NPS Project)," IBM document, IBM Corporation, Rochester, Minnesota.

2. Batchelor, W. L. and L. J. Endicott, Jr., "An Experimental System to Support a Very High Level User Interface," Proceedings of the 1981 NCC Conference, Chicago, IL, May 4-7, 1981, pp 389 to 392.

3. Athey, Thomas H., "Small Business—A Gold Mine for DP Educators," Proceedings of the ACM 1978 Annual Conference, Washington, DC, December 4-6, 1978, pp 99-105.

4. Sheil, B. A., Coping With Complexity, Technical Report, Cognitive and Instructional Sciences Series, CIS-15, April 1981, Cognitive and Instructional Sciences, Xerox Corporation, Palo Alto Research Center, 3333 Coyote Hill Road, Palo Alto, CA 94304.

5. Ibid., p 20.

6. Dunsmore, H. E., "Designing an Interactive Facility for Nonprogrammers," Proceedings of the Annual Conference ACM 80, Nashville, TN, October 27-29, 1980, pp 475-483.

7. Reisner, Phyllis, "Human Factors Studies of Database Query Languages: A Survey and Assessment," ACM Computing Surveys, Vol. 13, No. 1, March 1981, pp 13-31.

8. du Boulay, Benedict, and Tim O'Shea, Teaching Novices Programming, DAI Research Paper No. 132, n.d., Department of Artificial Intelligence, University of Edinburgh, pp 16-30. (Reprinted in Computing Skills and The User Interface, Academic Press, 1981, pp 147-200.)

9. Ibid., pp 15-52.

10. Copeland, George, "What if Mass Storage Were Free?" Papers of the 5th Workshop on Computer Architecture for Nonnumeric Processing, Pacific Grove, CA, March 11-14, 1980, pp 1-7.

11. Crawford, Perry, Jr., "On the Connections Between Data and Things in the Real World," COM 74-10700 Management of Data Elements in Information Processing, First National Symposium, National Bureau of Standards, Gaithersburg, MD, 1974, January 24-25, pp 51-57.

12. Huyck, Peter H. and Nellie W. Kremenak, Design and Memory, McGraw-Hill Book Company, 1980.

<u>Lucian J. Endicott, Jr.</u>
joined IBM in 1960 at
their Endicott, New York,
development laboratory.
He is currently a Senior
programmer in the IBM
System Products Division.

Computer Conferencing and Human Interaction

M Pieper
Institute for Planning and
Decision-Support Systems,
Federal Republic of Germany

With special purpose to clarify the individual and socio-psychological consequences as well as organizational changes which will be caused by computer based communication, GMD's 'Institute for Planning and Decision-Support Systems (IPES)' developed the Computer Conferencing System KOMEX. The first long-termed field-trial of the KOMEX system began in Oct.1980 and was finished in Dec. 1981. It will be shown, that empirical results of the KOMEX field-trial indicate a prevailing lack of originally intended computer assistance for group problem-solving and decision-making processes. Concerning these deficiencies the hypothesis will be advanced, that in systems' design certain principles of 'Interpersonal Relation' or 'Human Interaction' have insufficiently been taken into consideration. These principles, known as the rules of 'role taking', will be explained referring to empirical findings and examples of the KOMEX field-trial as well as to experiences from applications of other Computer Conferencing Systems. Last but not least, the contribution of the Social Sciences in bridging the gap between intention and reality of Computer Conferencing will be exemplified, by showing how empirically evaluated sociological assumptions can possibly be transferred into certain demands for an adequate systems desgin.

1. INTRODUCTION

1.1 Computer Conferencing to overcome the 'Era of Forced Choice' in organizational decision-making

Aggravating economic competition and accellerating technological development forces industrial management as well as public administration to process an expanding complexity of background information, when adequately to preserve economic welfare and social stability of modern societies. In preparing certain decisions, planners in industrial and public administration are forced to select, combine and evaluate informational resources deriving from ever more different enterprise divisions or intervening sectors of public policy. In fact, these activities require an increasing amount of office-hours, and for certain reasons one can assume the evaluation activity to be the most time-consuming.

Evaluating informational resources in planning processes means to elucidate and compare its contentual implications for problem-solving. Therefore, the comparative reference figure needed for any evaluation of problem oriented background information is the problem itself. However, mostly there is no common understanding of difficult problems and hence no commonly accepted criterion to evaluate suggestions for problem-solving. Problem oriented insights are rather preformed by personal convictions and/or professional responsibilities of managers, clerks or officials participating in planning processes. Potentially there will be as many different suggestions and evaluation patterns as there are different professional responsibilities and corresponding problem-solving demands. However, the more different personal intentions, professional responsibilities and problem-solving demands have to be taken into consideration, the more conflictual and there-fore time-consuming it will be, to negotiate commonly accepted decisions.

Beyond that, a certain level of contentual conflicts implied by a certain complexity of problem-oriented background information can be assumed to extend the cognitive capabilities of planners to structure such an informational complexity. For this reason important background information often is simply neglected. So far, wrong or at least less effective decisions can be regarded the result of either an insufficient or an unprocessable amount of background information.

Naturally the idea arised, to exploit the data processing capabilities of computers to moderate these deficiencies of problem-oriented discussions in planning processes. The essential impulse for this intention was set in 1966 by Olaf HELMER, who -at the 'Rand Corporation'- developed a formalized communication procedure of problem oriented expert-ratings, called the DELPHI-method. In 1970, it was Murray TUROFF at the 'New Jersey Institute of Technology', who conducted first experiments to search for possibilities of computer-assistance for such rating and decision-making processes. These origins of Computer Conferencing later on induced GMD's 'Institute for Planning and Decision-Support Systems' to develop the Computer Conferencing System KOMEX.

1.2 The principle of Computer Conferencing

The principle of Computer Conferencing is quite simple: Via a network of computer terminals system participants exchange textual information. These messages (any type of text) are input on computer terminals. The system transmits them to single addresses or certain groups of addresses, to be defined previously, and files the text into an electronic archive. When displaying received messages on display-terminals,addressees are capable of formulating direct responses or of message filing into contentually specified private archives, which can be fallen back upon later on. Partially users are additionally supported by functional features of office-automation, e.g. automated retrieval of documents at a certain date specified previously, and the like.

2. IMPACT-RESEARCH

2.1 Social impact-research to investigate interdependencies of user dispositions and technical facilities

KOMEX originally has been designed as a kind of experimental or prototype system, by which we intended to clarify socio-psychological consequences as well as organizational changes being caused by such systems in advance of their expected widespread employment. Not only because experts as well as the broader public become increasingly aware that technological developments do not only have predictable but also unintended consequences, scientific investigation of technical impacts upon social events becomes increasingly important. Put the case the proviso of restricted calculation concerning technical developments is transferrable to social events to be supported by certain technologies, the importance of impact research becomes immediately evident. Likewise in the sense of unpredicted consequences of certain intentions, problem-oriented communication can succeed or fail from the point of view of certain decision-makers. In applying the computer as a medium of communication, success of communication is no longer a question of only social or psychological dispositions. Social impact research has rather to take the interdependencies of socio-psychological user dispositions and technical facilities into scientific consideration.

2.2 State-of-the-Art of impact-research in the field of Computer Conferencing

Mainly in the United States, extensive investigations have yielded first indications concerning possible impacts of such technical Conferencing facilities upon certain socio-psychological user dispositions. First of all one has to mention the valuable empirical research-work, S.R. HILTZ carried out at the 'New Jersey Institute of Technology' with regard to experimental and practical applications of the EIES -'Electronic Information Exchange System' (HILTZ/ TUROFF 1978). As early as 1974 at the 'Institute for the Future' in Menlo Park (Calif.), the scientific interest of J. VALLEE and his collaborators focussed upon impact research when conducting first field-trials with the predecessor of the PLANET-System, the Computer Conferencing System FORUM (VALLEE et al. 1974, 1975; JOHANSEN et al. 1978). All of these research activities have significantly been stimulated by previous investigations of 'Communication Studies Group' in London, which -sponsored by the British PTT- compared normal face-to-face communication with different modes of technically mediated communication, e.g., telephone, video-conferencing and the like. However, computer assisted communication was out of concern (SHORT et al. 1976).

Up to now, research results concerning social impacts of Computer Conferencing generally focussed upon three dimensions of user dispositions:

- Motivation to participate in Computer Conferencing
- Extent of participation
- Influence of personal argumentation

Motivation to participate in Computer Conferencing decreases underneath and above a certain amount of exchanged information. The 'critical mass' to generate the motivationally required amount of information seems to be reached by at least 8-12 participants. When participants receive permanently more than 7 different messages, 'information overload' minimizes motivation to participate.

Compared with face-to-face communication, opinion leadership is diminished in Computer Conferencing. The extent of personal participation is more equally distributed within the whole group.

On the other hand, diminished opinion-leadership means reduced possibilities of argumentatively carrying into effect certain decisions. There is experimental evidence, that decision-oriented consensus is more often and after a shorter period of time reached within face-to-face discussions than this is the case within a Computer Conference. The influence of personal argumentation upon decision oriented consensus increases, when before informing the rest of the group agreement can be negotiated via private communication channels.

In sum, impact research concerning Computer Conferencing hitherto followed a conceptual framework of considering certain user dispositions being the consequence of certain technical communication facilities. Quite the contrary approach of evaluating and designing technical facilities on the basis of social demands has been fairly neglected. However, for above mentioned reasons of having to take into consideration the interdependencies of socio-psychological user dispositions and technical facilities, social impact research is thrown upon the second approach as well as to the first. In fact, the KOMEX field-trial -as well as practical applications of other Conferencing Systems- indicates essential deficiencies of Computer Conferencing concerning the original intention to support problem-oriented group discussion for purposes of planning and decision-making. Maybe they could have been avoided by focussing upon the second approach nearly as well as to the first.

3. THE KOMEX FIELD-TRIAL

Fifteen months lasting field-trial of the Computer Conferencing System KOMEX was finished in Dec. 1981. The trial involved as pilot-users five subgroups working at different locations on different aspects of a common scientific project on 'Social Network Analysis', founded by the 'German National Science Foundation (DFG)'.

3.1 Analytical interests, design of investigation and general indications

Since Oct. 1980, sociologists of GMD's 'Impact Research Group' analyzed communication among these five subgroups. Gathering appropriate empirical data was guided by analytical interest focussing upon five questions: The first can be outlined by inquiring for what kind of communication a Computer Conferencing System like KOMEX would be used. With regard to the remaining four questions we were interested in how far computer assisted communication among the pilot-users would differ in amount, content, structure and style from conventional modes of communication, e.g. face-to-face, telephone and mailing.

Because of deficient access to indicators of conventional communication by questionaires and by interviewing pilot-users, one should not expect reliable results concerning the comparison of conventional modes of communication and Computer Conferencing. However, there is good reason to expect that efforts of developping a computer assisted method for content-analyzing all texts distributed via KOMEX have resulted in a reliable and detailed description of the entire communication rendered electronically. The total number of different messages was up to 350.

Indications from previous impact-research led us to presume a certain amount of communication to effect 'information overload'. Perhaps for being not far above the motivationally required 'critical mass' factor by involving 14 participants altogether, we could not make out such effects during the whole field-trial.

More equally distributed participation and less opinion leadership could also be assumed concerning structure of communication. We could not confirm this either. Very soon in nearly all of the five subgroups not an opinion-leader but a so called gate-keeper emerged. For the information exchanged between the five subgroups often was redundant for locally centralized participants within each of those subgroups, gate-keepers vicariously received and nearly as often transmitted messages for their respective project groups. Participation in communication process raised in extent within all of the five subgroups. However, by comparing them, amount of participation seemed to be as unequally distributed as -for instance- telephone communication.

Previous indications concerning style of communication could be confirmed. When getting accustomed to the system after a certain period of time, communication more often changed from a rather formal, telegram-oriented style to a style formerly identified by S.R. HILTZ as 'push towards sociability'. By that, she meant presenting oneself by incorporating into the text certain jokes, idioms, modes of expression deriving from verbal speech as well as visual cues, e.g. computer-graphics one could possibly refer to by the term 'computer graffitty'.

3.2 Indications from content-analysis

Impact research hitherto scarely focussed upon empirical indications concerning kind and content of communication, maybe because of the peculiarities implied have been regarded too complex as to be able to classify prevailing communication patterns. Nevertheless, by analyzing all texts distributed via KOMEX, we found out, that at least kind of communication could exhaustively be described by 5 to 7 different categories of personal intentions to communicate. They have been denominated 'to evaluate', 'to document', 'to coordinate', 'to plan', and 'to give administrative support' -for instance, to procure something or settle accounts- for certain activities to be carried out within the project groups. Content of communication was more different to classify in a valid and comparable way, because it was determined by peculiar tasks of the five subgroups. Although being rather peculiar, all subgroup-tasks aimed at the common scientific purpose to evolve conceptual and methodological approaches for Social Network Analysis. From that point of view task-oriented communication contents could be classified by the degree of immediacy in which this general objective was met. We distinguished among five degrees of immediacy:

- 'private communication effected by task-oriented communication' (e.g. getting to know each other),
- 'subordinate tasks' (e.g. announcements of conventionally mailed information),
- 'administrative tasks',
- 'tasks accompanying accomplishment of general scientific purpose' (e.g. official journeys to conferences) and
- 'tasks closely related to scientific results' (e.g. gathering and analyzing empirical data).

Indications concerning kind and content of communication, which were obviously still intercorrelated by our classification, could furthermore be differentiated by a slightly altered analytical approach of BALES' 'Interaction Process Analysis' (BALES 1950). This analytical tool includes 10 categories by which the texts distributed via KOMEX could be coded as 'agreement', 'disagreement' or as giving or asking for 'hints', 'orders', 'personal opinion' or 'scientific argumentation'.

The outlined approach to analyze communication among pilot-users of the KOMEX field-trial confirmed assumptions of a gap between original intentions and practical applications of 'Computer Conferencing'. For the present, the extensive amount above the average of rather short messages concerning administrative orders and coordinative hints for task accomplishment still points to a basic experience whatever special system is applied: Conferencing Systems are mainly used as a kind of comfortable message systems. KOMEX scarcely was used following the original intention of Computer Conferencing to enhance the capacity of information processing for group problem-solving. For instance, processes of relating task-oriented scientific argumentation to reasonable agreements concerning the general purpose of the pilot-users could not be reestablished by content-analyzing group communication via KOMEX. However the extensive amount of content-analyzed messages allowed further differentiation of this general finding.

First of all, administrative and coordinative support for task accomplishment has essentially been executed by straining upon special conferencing facilities to structure information flow. By that, pilot-users could fall back upon comprising subgroup members by defining as addressees certain group names, allowing to send one single message to be distributed electronically to all members of corresponding subgroups. The pilot-users accepted this conferencing facility to adjust coordinative communication referring to its more general or rather special meaning for all or only some of the collaborators in a flexible way to corresponding target-groups. Partly, defined group names referred to only one member of a certain subgroup playing the already described role of a 'gate keeper'. Still in receiving messages labelled by recipient-name or predefined group-name, gate-keepers easily could distinguish whether messages were of private relevance or of general relevance for their respective subgroup. As a side-effect 'information overload' was prevented by relieving the remaining subgroup members from receiving anything but personally relevant information.

In generating commonly authorized scientific reports out of report-parts, which were exchanged for editorial discussion and corresponding modification by the respective authors, so to speak covered argumentative references between the authors could repeatedly be pointed out within KOMEX field-trial. However, argumentative references by explicitly contradicting or consenting to statements of others in the original sense of Conferencing scarcely were provable by content-analysis. For the present, indications from the KOMEX field-trial indicate a prevailing lack of originally intended computer assistance for group problem-solving and decision-making processes.

4. THE GAP BETWEEN INTENTION AND REALITY OF COMPUTER CONFERENCING

4.1 Sociological interpretations

From a socio-psychological point of view, there seems to be one main reason for the deficient application of Computer Conferencing Systems. Industrial as well as political planning generally includes problems of neither a clear and common understanding of measures to be taken nor of the objectives to be met by solving the problem. Therefore the main precondition for successful planning and decision-making is to gain an adaequate understanding of problem-oriented suggestions of others. Maybe it is hence the interactive process of gaining mutual understanding, which has deficiently been taken into consideration when designing Computer Conferencing Systems to enhance the capacity of information processing for group problem-solving. This process can briefly be described by terms of a conceptual framework of the social sciences, to be referred to as 'Symbolic Interactionism' (MEAD 1934, BLUMER 1969).

According to this conception, partners of a conversation face mutually in social roles of 'communicators' and 'recipients'. In communicating to recipients for planning purposes, communicators follow 'personal intentions' for problem-solving deriving from 'personal insights' into the problem. Recipients for their part assign a certain 'meaning' deriving from their 'personal insight' into the problem to the information exchanged. Information becomes meaningful concerning the problem, it becomes a problem-oriented 'message'. Essentially the problem of gaining an adequate understanding of problem-oriented suggestions results from the subjectivity of recipient's insights assigned to received information. Receptive insights into a problem hence normally differ from that of communicators. Problem-solving intentions of others can therefore adequately be understood by recipients only when they are able to reestablish for themselves problem-oriented insights of communicators as complete as possible. Social psychology refers to this so to say empathical ability to 'slip into the shoes of the other' by the term 'role-taking'.

It is the 'role-taking' abilities, which are still restricted by conventional and especially computer based communication systems. No doubt, Computer Conferencing Systems support generation and distribution of information, but there is hardly technological assistance for information processing by recipients. In fact, recipients participating in long termed planning processes are covered by such a flow of different and refining suggestions for problem-solving, which -if at all- they can only rather fussily check by argumentative inconsistencies to find out possible misunderstandings. As a consequence, for recipients very often problem-oriented suggestions become meaningful not before subsequent periods of the planning process have led to a more differentiated understanding of the problem and of respective insights of communicators. By that later moment, however, former misunderstandings are often hardly to revise. Hence, optimized decision-making is restricted.

4.2 General guidelines for an improved systems-design

In how far computer based communication systems can contribute to a better task accomplishment concerning planning and decision-making is among other things caused by the kind of organizational implementation including user-training and the like. Crucial however is technological assistance in unfolding personal 'role-taking' abilities to promote mutual understanding. By that, the necessity to assign meaning to problem-oriented insights leads to at least three standards to be met by systems design.

The first, rather simple standard can be paraphrased as 'proximity of reference'. This means that when building a message, the user must be able to access easily and use any message, to which he refers. Also, the user must be able to easily deal with both a message he is creating, and one to which he refers, for example by means of a split screen feature.

The second standard can be referred to by the term 'reconstruction of context'. That is, in order to understand and give meaning to a received message, the user must be able to collect easily together past messages which can help to reconstruct the context of that message. The system must know that this message is part of a longer conversation and assist the user in access to other messages referring to that conversation.

Advanced standards of 'pattern recognition' or 'pattern matching' are required for long termed planning processes, which normally cause an informational complexity extending the planner's cognitive capabilities to structure such an information overload. These standards should be designed on the basis of two premises:

(1) an argumentation pattern can be established by assigning argumentative references to all problem-oriented statements being expressed

(2) statements as well as references can be qualified by a limited set of contentual indications identically known by all members of the problem-solving group. For instance 'agreement', disagreement' 'refinement' or 'description of facts', 'causal explanation', 'suggestion for action' could be such indications to qualify the content of problem-oriented statements.

Given these two premises, an 'intended reference structure' resulting from respective assignments of communicators can technologically be matched with 'perceived reference structures' resulting from independent but corresponding assignments of recipients. Structural inconsistencies possibly resulting from pattern-matching then can be interpreted as misunderstandings otherwise not to be identified, but now remaining further clarification.

In part, such a concept of an 'Argumentative Planning Information System (APIS)' has technically been realized as an 'Issue Based Information System (IBIS)' and been proved by application (RITTEL 1980). 'Issue Based Information Systems' however similarly to Computer Conferencing Systems only support the generation of information, nevertheless structured by qualified references. By no means the recipient is technologically assisted in processing received information, e.g. by the outlined facilities of 'pattern matching'.

REFERENCES

(1) BALES, R.F. (1950): 'Interaction Process Analysis: A Method for the Study of Small Groups', Reading (Mass.)
(2) BLUMER, H. (1969): 'Symbolic Interactionism: Perspective and Method', New Jersey
(3) BLUMER, H. (1972): 'Symbolic Interactionism: An Approach to Human Communication', in: R.W. BUDD and B.D. RUBEN (eds.): Approaches to Human Communication, New Jersey (pp.401-419)
(4) HELMER, O. (1966): 'Social Technology. Report on Long-Range Forecasting Study', New York
(5) HILTZ, S.R. and M. TUROFF (1978): 'The Network Nation, Human Communication via Computer', Readings (Mass.)
(6) HILTZ, S.R. (1981): 'The Impact of a Computerized Conferencing System on Scientific Research Communities', Final Report to the National Science Foundation, NJIT Research Report, No.15 (pp.739-751)
(7) HILTZ, S.R. (1981a): 'The Evolution of User Behavior in a Computerized Conferencing System', in: Communications (ACM), No.11, Vol.24
(8) JOHANSEN, R. et al. (1978): 'Group Communication through Computers, Vol.5: Effects on Working Patterns', research-report R-41, Institute for the Future, Menlo Park (Calif.)
(9) JOHANSEN, R. et al. (1979): 'Electronic Meetings: Technical Alternatives and Social Choices', Reading (Mass.)
(10)LINSTONE, H. and M. TUROFF (1975): 'The Delphi Method: Techniques and Applications', Reading (Mass.)
(11)MEAD, G.H. (1934): 'Mind, Self and Society', Chicago
(12)RITTEL, H.W.J. (1980): 'A Concept for an Argumentative Planning Information System', working paper no.324 of the Institute for Urban and Regional Development, University of California, Berkely (Calif.)
(13)SHORT et al. (1976): 'The Social Psychology of Telecommunications', London
(14)THAYER, L. (1968): 'Communication and Communication Systems', Homewood (Ill.)
(15)TUROFF, M. (1971): 'Delhi-Conferencing. Technical Memorandum TM-125', Executive Office of the President, Office of Emergency Prepardness, Washington
(16)TUROFF, M. (1972): 'PARTY-LINE and DISCUSSION. Computerized Conference Systems', in: S. WINKLER (ed.): The 1st International Conference on Computer Communication, Washington D.C., (pp.161-171)
(17)UHLIG, R.P. et al. (1979): 'The Office of the Future. Communication and Computers', Amsterdam, New York, Oxford
(18)VALLEE, J. et al. (1974): 'Group Communication through Computers, (Vol.1: Design and use of the FORUM System', research-report R-32, Institute for the Future, Menlo Park (Calif.)
(19)VALLEE, J. et al. (1974a): 'Group Communication throgh Computers, Vol.2: A Study of Social Effects', research-report R-33, Institute for the Future, Menlo Park (Calif.)
(20)VALLEE, J. et al. (1975): 'Group Communication through Computers, Vol.3: Pragmatics and Dynamics', research-report R-35, Institute for the Future, Menlo Park (Calif.)

BIOGRAPHY

Michael Pieper received the degree Dipl.soc. from the Ruhr-University Bochum, in 1978. He is interested in empirically oriented studies of 'Interpersonal Relations'. As a member of the 'Impact-Research-Group' at GMD's 'Institute for Planning and Decision-Support Systems (IPES)', he is engaged in research on organizational applications and social impacts of Computer-Based Communication Systems.

Human Factors in Designing an Electronic Mail System for a Multilanguage Country

D Biran
Israeli Ministry of Communications,
Israel
R Feldman
Jerusalem College of Technology,
Israel

Electronic Mail is rapidly becoming a very useful system in developed countries. A strong effort is applied in making the systems compatible from the point of view of similar services available to users. Multilanguage countries are characterised by special features which have not yet been carefully considered. This paper describes the human factors influencing the proper choice of an Electronic Mail system emphasizing the special needs of multilanguage countries from the users point of view. It should be noted that in addition to the language difference, there is also an alphabet difference, the problem of direction (right to left and left to right), and simultaneous usage of languages in one document.

1. PREFACE

The purpose of this paper is to define outline concepts, and to give guidelines for the development of Electronic Mail Systems which may be used generally, or for multilanguage systems.

Some of the topics discussed {1,2} may be applicable within existing Electronic Mail Systems, or they may be suitable for gradual introduction into new systems, according to the technological possibilities, and future prospective developments.

2. INTRODUCTION

The 1980's is characterized by the convergence of many technologies namely telecommunications, computing, electronics and information systems. As trading distances decrease, and worldwide economics necessitate countries to become more and more dependent upon trade outside national boundaries, no country is able to stand alone, or become isolated, requiring many nationalities and cultures to communicate with each other. Information is transferred by voice, data, video, etc.; and the decision process often has to be made in real time, thus such a demand dictates the requirements of the concepts outlined in this paper.

Countries differ in languages, alphabets, customs and the interpretation of language. Multilanguage needs are presented in terms of understanding and other factors, if acceptable communication is to be carried out, without reverting to a common language throughout the world.

The differences in the languages may be in the spoken language only, or it could be in the differences of alphabet and language, or alphabet, language and direction of writing: e.g. left to right or right to left, plus other criteria.

Further complexities arise when we have to deal with very complex languages such as Japanese and/or Chinese, which cannot be expressed using the agreed concepts of CCITT No. 5 or ASCII codes.

Voice communication introduces its own special complications, and involves a great deal of brain activity when the two communicating parties have to struggle in order to present their meaning, especially when the recipient's language is complex and/or infrequently used.

The application of communicating with text and/or graphics introduces a further complexity and many factors which are quite different to the problems outlined for voice communication alone.

In text and graphics, we are introducing further complex factors in the man-machine-man interface.

Machines are not knowledgeable as yet and their intelligence is limited to the capability built into them by man, as well as to their own inherent limitations in hardware, software and extremely limited programmable decision-processing potential.

Voice communication is simple in comparison to man-machine-machine-man systems, especially when text and graphics are incorporated in the communication process between different languages and cultures, etc.

Figure 1 describes the complexities in voice communication alone, as compared to text and graphic systems.

In voice systems we only need to handle one media, while with the addition of text and graphics the interpretation problems become extensive, although use is made of the same communiction infrastructure as described, in part, in the figure.

3. ELECTRONIC MAIL DEFINITION

Electronic mail (E.M.) {1,3,4} in the broadest sense of the meaning, may be defined as the transfer of any kind of written or graphic information using the telecommunication systems combined or not with teleprocessing from one recipient to the other, through the inter-mediary of one or more computers.

The information may be any typed message using any code (e.g. Baudot, ASCII, EBCIDIC, etc.), any handwritten material or graphics using some facsimile system, or any typed information achieved by translation (e.g. using an optical code reader and a computer) from handwriting. The telecommunication system may be any exist-ing systems or new concepts planned for the future.

The teleprocessing added to the information may include:

1. Editing
2. Any type of office functions
3. Translating to other languages as required
4. Computing
5. Data base access
6. Any type of mailing functions
7. Translation from vocal messages to texts (in future systems)

Figure 2 is shown in the block diagram describ-ing the Electronic Mail System (E.M.S.) and its existing and future potential possibilities. 3,4

4. GENERAL HUMAN REQUIREMENTS FOR AN ELECTRONIC MAIL SYSTEM

The Electronic Mail System has to be designed to encompass many layers of population and different needs. Therefore, one of the most important requirements is flexibility and adaptability.

The E.M.S. has to be very simple from the users' point of view so that the training process is very short and simple.

The system needs to be interactive and all the elements of the E.M.S. should be designed and positioned in the office in a convenient way for solving the office needs and achieving maximum utilization, efficiency and comfort.

The E.M.S. should be reasonably priced so that the widest possible population shall be able to afford it.

The Electronic Mail Flowchart shown in Figure 2 is intended to indicate the various require-ments that the potential user of an E.M. system may need.

These are defined for simplicity as:

1. Electronic Mail Service (general)
2. Data Base access
3. Computer Processing

The flowchart indicates an approach to basic system requirements which are intended only as guidelines for further consideration as the concept develops.

With the eventual development of fifth genera-tion (knowledgeable) processors, it is possible that some of these concepts may be simplified in the future. However, developments in man-machine algorithms could lead to a possible

simplification of some of these complex inter-communication problems, allowing for a simple approach by the human operator to the machine.

5. E.M.S. IN MULTILANGUAGE SOCIETIES

Each nation has its own various specifics in thinking, speaking, mutual understanding and expressing itself. These topics are of utmost importance with regard to E.M.S. for multi-language usage. Some of the main E.M.S. topics in multilanguage systems are:

a. differences in alphabet
b. differences in direction of writing
c. combination of two alphabets while using the same code
d. dealing with various lengths of alphabet; e.g. the Japanese alphabet of some 3000 characters may be dealt with by the CCITT No. 5 code by using a matrix definition of the characters
e. difference in languages
f. differences in understanding of idioms
g. differences in prompting commands
h. comfort in writing simultaneously in two languages in two directions
i. terminal equipment (VDU's, printers, etc.)
j. International prompt signs for office work and mail similar to the traffic signs
k. differences in optical character readers in order to deal with various alphabets
l. translation systems from one language to the other
m. word recognition systems
n. voice recognition systems

The topics described above have, at present, partial solutions to some extent, but with the advances in technology they are likely to be completely solved in the near future.

In the following sections the topics so far introduced will be dealt with in greater detail.

5.1. Concepts of Alphabets

The various alphabets to be employed have to be fully described using the CCITT No. 5 (or ASCII) code as these are the most used codes in current operation.

In order to allow for the use of two to three different alphabets with this code, similar rules to the Baudot teleprinter code must be followed. This means dividing the keyboard into:

a. lower and upper case characters
b. control characters

Such a division may enable us to have at least 100 additional characters. If more than three alphabets are needed, these may be developed in a similar way. In any case, it seems that the maximum number of alphabets used simultaneously will never exceed three.

5.2. Prompting Commands

The prompting commands of an E.M. multilanguage

system have to be very simple and adaptable to the various possibilities of thinking.

Therefore, the utilization of standard type prompts for all languages used is recommended. It may be possible to adopt a very similar approach to that of international road signs which are the same worldwide. Thus the basic commands of the system will be marked on the keyboard and they will have to appear on the screen in the same way. If the terminal does not include graphic possibilities, the prompting will be made using the selected alphabet. In addition to the basic prompting commands, use will be made of specific commands needed by various populations of users.

The prompting commands will include simple possibilities of transfer from the alphabet of one language to that of another in any part of the text.

5.3. Terminal Equipment

The terminal equipment utilized will include, at least, the following items:

- VDU
- facsimile
- printer

The VDU has to be very simple and cheap in either black/white or colour, including options of alphabet and graphics.

The keyboard will be the usual CCITT No. 5 but will have, in addition, the possibilities of overlays for additional language alphabets. One possibility is a very simple keyboard invented in Israel, described in Appendix A. This kind of keyboard does not require the marking of keys as it has only 8 keys and is based on using human memory. The facsimile terminal will be of the conventional type but will include an Analog to Digital converter in order to convert the information to a form recognizable by the E.M.S.

The printer will include a printing head built from some proper matrix, as e.g. a 7 x 9 points matrix, so that all possible characters, graphics and direction of printing could be controlled by software.

5.4. Concepts of Translation Systems

The automatic translation system will be a big data base which will include the possibility of translation from one language to another. The data base has to include proper translation of idioms and the possibility of translating sentences as a whole in order not to change their meanings.

5.5. Recognition Systems

5.5.1. Optical Character Readers

The optical character readers will be software controlled so that they may be changed from one language to another. The character reader has to have the ability to interpret handwriting into typed text.

5.5.2. Word Recognition Systems

The word recognition systems will be constructed so that the user may enter his message using a telephone after the proper prompting for the selected language.

5.5.3. Voice Recognition Systems

The voice recognition system will be an add-on system to the word recognition. This system will be used in order to ascertain that the sender or recipient of the message is the person intended. If the system will not recognize the person he will be automatically logout from the system.

6. PHASED APPROACH TO MULTILANGUAGE SOLUTIONS

There are many prospective solutions available either by hardware and/or software techniques for solving the conversion of one language to another.

The authors have evaluated a number of different concepts based upon the methodology of translation techniques.

A possible approach is shown in Figure 3. The suggested system may be built from a very simple and basic technique to a more complex analysis and derivative of the multilanguage interpretation.

The language data base translator shown in the figure is a separate computer from the E.M.S. Only when translation is needed will the edited message be forwarded to the translation computer. The translation process will be done word by word and sentence by sentence in order to achieve the proper translation. The translated message will be shown on the sender terminal. The sender will have the ability to edit the translation and/or to order the translator to translate back to the original language without referring to the original message. The filing system will always file the original and the translated version unless clearly commanded otherwise.

7. CONCLUSIONS

The multilanguage E.M.S. is a very new field and a great deal of further work still needs to be investigated before real solutions are finalised. The application of Electronic Mail concepts, inter-connectivity and methodology is as yet still ill-defined in terms of standardization.

In the area of multilanguage conversion techniques, the authors have intentionally only indicated general outline parameters and prospective systems concepts that still require a great deal of further in-depth evaluation.

Nevertheless, this is a high technology area which will require eventual solution in order to open up the prospects of international and national E.M. communication in the late 20th and early 21st centuries.

REFERENCES

{1} The Yankee Group, 1979. The Report on
     Electronic Mail.
{2} R. Camrass, Viewdata: A Practical Medium
     for Electronic Mail, Videotex, Viewdata
     & Teletext, Online 1980, 173-183.
{3} GTE Telenet Reference Manual, August 1970.
     Telemail.
{4}

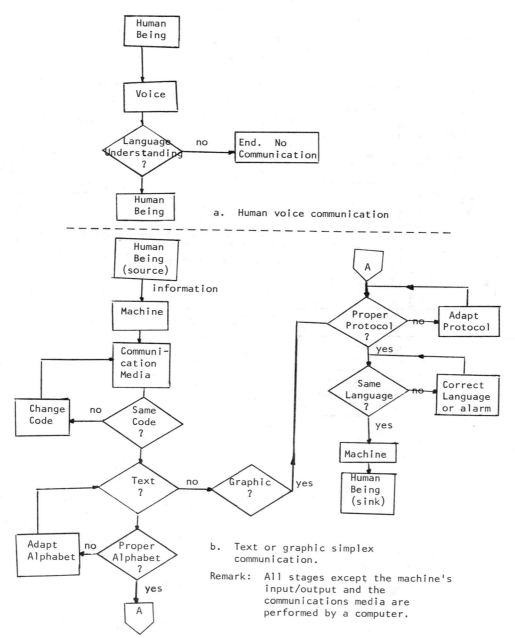

a. Human voice communication

b. Text or graphic simplex
    communication.

Remark: All stages except the machine's
         input/output and the
         communications media are
         performed by a computer.

Fig. 1. Voice communication systems
         compared to text/graphic
         communication system problems.

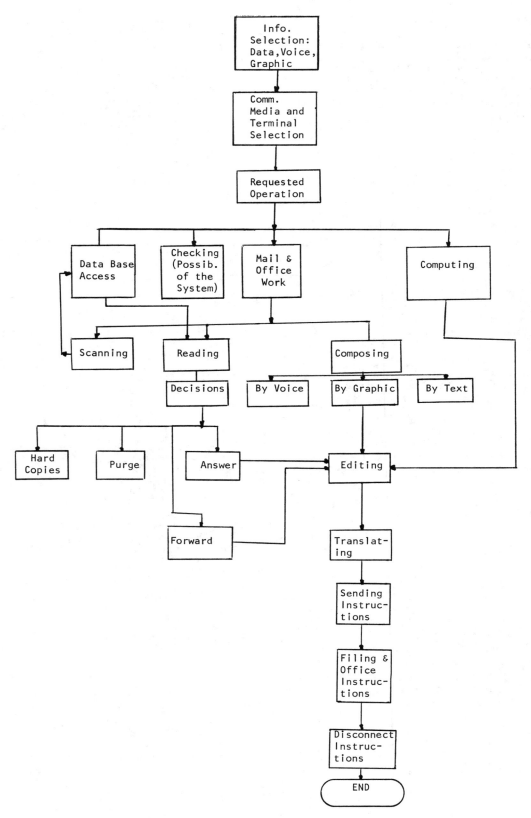

Fig. 2. Electronic Mail System possibilities

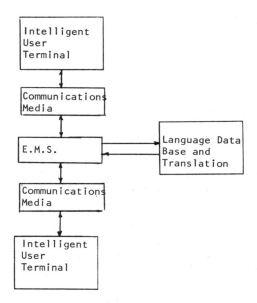

Fig. 3. Multilanguage Translation Scheme.

(The E.M.S. includes all the capabilities of a sophisticated Electronic Mail except the translation process which is done in a separate computer)

APPENDIX A

PRONTO

Product Description

A small, inexpensive, single hand-operated chordic Keyboard having eight keys. Provides a full set of symbols (128 or 64 ASCII). Learning time for the entire symbol set is less than one hour. A high speed data entry rate which exceeds handwriting speeds is realized after further use. Subject of international patent rights and extensive laboratory and field testing.

PRONTO is based on a high-power mnemonic technique which enables an average person to master a 128 character ASCII set within 30-45 minutes. Almost any person, even one of below average intelligence, can master the complete code within one hour.

The number of codes is not limited to 128 and can be expanded via software programming to multiple character sets, specially required control codes, etc.

Due to the strength of the mnemonic technique employed, the amount of restraining after a long interruption is negligable. Laboratory and field tests show that the user returns to his former speed within five minutes after a 6-month interruption.

The PRONTO keyboard is designed for motoric efficiency over the entire code, including

letters, numbers, punctuation and control functions, thereby providing the best results today.

Laboratory and field tests on free text, using managers, secretaries and others as test subjects, have shown that a speed of 150 characters per minute is attained by the average user after less than twelve hours of use. After 25 hours of use, a speed of 200 characters per minute is attained and after 35 hours of use, a speed of 250 characters per minute is attained. Limited testing indicates that a speed of more than 300 characters per minute can be attained by the average user after 50 hours of use. This is twice the speed of ordinary handwriting.

The reaction of the test subjects is extremely favourable and indicates that the majority would accept PRONTO and use it instead of writing by hand.

Human Factors Issues in Network Communication Systems

H T Smith
Nottingham University, UK

This paper discusses some of the human factors issues that need to be addressed before national and international computer-based message systems (CBMS) become widespread in the public domain. An outline is given of the kinds of service requirements that CBMS users need. Several of the requirements raise the issue of standards for user protection. The question of user protection is complicated by the likelihood of mixed communication carriers and differing views about the rights of senders and recipients of messages. The paper explores several issues and suggests an additional class of service to provide more comprehensive user protection.

Introduction

Computer Based Message Systems of the kind provided on research and commercial networks (e.g., ARPA, TELENET, TYMNET, PSS) are the forerunners of larger scale national and international network message systems. Currently, a considerable amount of effort is being devoted to the question of standardisation (e.g., [1,2,3] to allow interworking between different networks and other services such as Telex and Teletex. Much of the standardisation is concerned with the technical specification of protocols and service facilities. As yet, little detailed attention has been devoted to the precise nature of user requirements in CBMS. However, some of these user application considerations have implications for low level system services. For example, service providers have tended to concentrate on facilities for transfer of individual messages; users on the other hand are almost always interested in message transactions - streams of related messages over periods of time. This obviously has implications for basic message structure - even if only to provide uniform schemes for user definable message attribute fields. (Smith [4] gives a more detailed consideration of this topic.)

Similarly, there are many other issues of message system use that still have to be tackled. One particular concern is that of user protection standards. A CBMS enables one user to communicate with many other users quickly and easily. Such facility also brings with it potential penalties through the accidental or deliberate misuse of the communication system. For example, the receipt of volumes of 'junk' mail. It is also possible for the user to incur other penalties (e.g., costs, liability) through the apparently correct use of a system that does not provide adequate user safeguards. With the development of large-scale public and private networks, user protection can be expected to become of pressing importance. Although many of the factors underlying user protection relate to technical constraints, there are also many that relate to matters of social policy. For example, in a world of high communication 'connectivity', the right of an individual to choose whether to be available for communication or not. This paper outlines some of these considerations as they apply to CBMS services.

The following discussion is mainly concerned with basic user-to-user messaging services in a distributed network community. However, much of it will also apply to other communication structures - e.g., Conference and Bulletin Board systems that can be constructed on top of this basic service. A basic messaging service is one that enables users to send and receive messages between private 'mailboxes'. The mailboxes and the connecting networks may either be maintained by a national carrier (i.e., the PT&T), a private carrier/agency, an individual, or a mixture of all three. These kinds of complex carrier arrangement can obviously cause user protection problems, particular those connected with establishing responsibility and liability if there is malfunction or misuse.

Before discussing these issues, it should be observed that CBMS systems offer services that cannot be duplicated by conventional communication systems (e.g., cheap multiple message copying and delivery). These extra services are what makes CBMS use so attractive - and at the same time create such problems as junk mail. It is therefore likely that protection requirements will need to **exceed** those provided by conventional services. At the moment, defining what constitutes acceptable standards for protection is a matter of debate. For example, a message Sender will often wish to operate under a different set of constraints than a Recipient (especially when alternating between these roles).

Messages and Message Related Services

Like most kinds of communication system, CBMS's offer two kinds of access to users:

* User Information Services
* Message Delivery/Receipt Services

<u>User Information</u> services can be divided between Directory type requests and User Status determination. The first kind involves the ability to discover information about a potential recipient or a class of recipients - e.g., all dentists specialising in tooth capping. A CBMS could also allow the recipient to discover information about the sender **before** accepting or reading the message. The second kind provides the facility to discover if someone is available to communicate at a given moment. With conventional mail this can be obtained indirectly by requesting confirmation of mail receipt - or with a phone call, by someone picking up the receiver. An example of a similar CBMS facility would be the 'finger' program on some ARPA hosts[1]. The status information is often used for purposes unrelated to a communication (i.e., checking availability).

Currently there are many difficult issues to be resolved before informa-

___
[1] This program allows an inquirer to ascertain when the `fingered' user last logged in, read mail and (sometimes) whose messages are waiting to be read. Not suprisingly, many sites severely restrict the use of the command.

tion services are realised. For example, so far only basic service primitives have been defined by [5]. These are:

Get Sender/Recipient Address
Get Type of Name
Match Partial Name
Get Sender/Recipient Capabilities
Get Distribution List Members
Modify Entity

Yet to be addressed are such questions as how distributed directories are to be maintained? Who is to be responsible for their updating? What privacy/security problems arise if directories are accessed directly? How do public and private directories interwork. Even the matter of unique naming/addressing identifiers has still to be fully worked out.

<u>Message Delivery/Receipt</u> can involve several separate services. With conventional mail communication it is possible to choose high speed/low speed delivery, guaranteed/non-guaranteed delivery, confirmation and various other options. Depending on the system, CBMS's can offer similar options but also enhanced classes of services - e.g., Schicker [6] discusses a variety of possible confirmation systems. What priority one attaches to these services will depend on the situation and whether the user is a sender or recipient. For example, almost all senders would like to be notified when a recipient **reads** a message as opposed to when it is received. This is a relatively easy matter to arrange in a CBMS system if not in a conventional one - however most recipients (or senders when acting as recipients) are extremely averse to the idea of providing such automatic notification as the default action.

There are other CBMS services that it is not possible to obtain with conventional mail. For example, so-called 'active' messages. These are messages that can invoke processing options **after** delivery/receipt. Such messages might engage in a question/answer dialogue with the recipient and then post themselves back to the sender, or alternatively erase themselves from the recipients workspace after some pre-specified period of time if unread. Again, many recipients have strong reservations about the use of these techniques. They raise the question of who **owns** a message once it has been received into the recipients workspace and what obligations are incurred. Given these problems there is obviously a clear need to keep separate the different domains of the sender, carrier and recipient. This has been recognised in the CCITT message transfer systems model which delineates the message transport system domain from that of the user agent and its workspace by a 'slot'. (The slot may be an abstraction rather than a convenient physical boundary). Thus the message transport system and the users agent engage in an delivery/receipt protocol across (or through) this slot.

User Protection

The service capabilities outlined above clearly establish the need for user protection standards. As a general goal a CBMS should facilitate communication whilst respecting individual rights to privacy and autonomy. This implies that

The system should
(1) preserve message integrity - not introduce errors
(2) be secure - prevent unauthorised disclosure of messages or user status
(3) be predictable - not perform unspecified actions (e.g., must notify sender of undeliverable messages)
The individual should
(4) have access control - the right and means to restrict access to himself/herself
(5) not be unwittingly liable - to costs, legal obligations or unnecessary inconvenience
and above all, there should be
(6) accountability mechanisms - to enable redress when 1-5 don't work.

Most systems do quite a good job on the first three criteria. However, 4,5 and 6 are more difficult. The access control criterion is particularly important and is the focus of the rest of this paper.

Recipient Access

The recipient access problem can be categorised as preventing unwanted or unsolicited communication. Currently, the possession of a conventional mailbox effectively means that the PT&T will attempt to deliver all mail that is correctly addressed. The (increasing) cost associated with conventional mail ensures that not too much junk

mail falls through the user's letter box. However, by default, the user can only stop mail being received if present at the time of delivery. In a CBMS the costs of sending messages are trivial and message generation and multiple copying is easy. It is therefore likely that the number of messages each individual receives will increase enormously[2]. In this situation it is not unreasonable that recipients will want to implement some form of selective access at little cost to themselves.

There seem to be three kinds of approach, Concealment, Cost Barriers, and Selection Filters.

The concealment approach is the most obviously simple strategy and is akin to having an unlisted phone number. Access is not possible to senders who do not know the address. This kind of service should be readily available on CBMS networks. However, it suffers from the disadvantage that addresses are difficult to keep confidential for very long in the age of institutional databases.

The cost barrier approach serves to make it mildly or prohibitively expensive to transmit a message to an individual. Short of making message sending generally expensive, there are two strategies. The first is to make the sender liable to all charges resulting from the transmission and intermediate storage of the message. Thus, until the moment that the recipient reads a message (or deletes it unread) the charges are the senders responsibility. This has obvious advantages for the recipient - e.g., he/she will not have to bear storage costs arising from a quantity of mail arriving whilst away on vacation. It should discourage the prospective sender from speculative mailing. However, a disadvantage of this scheme could be that the charge might convey information to the sender about the recipients communication status. The second, more specific strategy, is to impose a threshold acceptance cost on individual mail boxes [7]. Then, for a message to be transmitted through the recipients slot, the sender (or sender's mail agent) must accept an extra charge.

---

[2] One acquaintance on the ARPA net and a large internal network confesses to getting above 80 messages a day (after removing himself from junk mailing lists)!

This threshold cost would be set by the individual recipient. The problem is that, of course, one would like to be selective about such charging.

The <u>selection filter</u> approach rejects unwanted messages before they pass through the slot. Langsford [8] points out two ways in which the filter could be implemented - by name of sender or by type of content. In the first case one would define a user filter agent that could accept such constraints as

<u>Accept</u> Smith, Jones, Green
or
<u>Refuse</u> Philips, Davies, Anonymous (!)

This might be convenient in fixed circumstances but it does not overcome the problem of unsolicited letters from first time or unlisted correspondents - some of which will be wanted, others will not. A message content solution would be suitable if there were national/international standards for differing types of communication. Thus

<u>Accept</u> Personal, Business
or
<u>Refuse</u> Advertisement, Charity Request

Although this might work well in many situations if it was combined with the selection name facility, it is difficult to believe that it would be easy to enforce such descriptions on the Readers Digests of this world. There have been suggestions that one solution would be the use of independent document certifiers. These would be organisations or individuals who would offer a 'stamp-of-approval' service for documents whose surface description mirrored their contents and/or passed other criteria. Individuals would then arrange for their filter to accept only certified documents for most classes of mail. Even though this is a limited solution, it seems more profitable than other ideas such as fully automatic 'intelligent' document skimmers which would be beset by a host of problems.

These then are just three approaches to recipient access control. However, it is worth noting that once the message has been delivered **through** the slot it is difficult to stop some infringement of privacy/autonomy. The selection filter approach has the definite advantage that unwanted or unsolicited messages are not admitted to the recipients environment. This means that problems of storage charges, active messages of the kind mentioned

earlier, and liability do not arise. Nevertheless, as has been shown, specifying filter constraints is a difficult matter. If they are too restrictive then rejection of potentially wanted communication occurs; in the opposite situation too much is accepted.

One way out of this dilemma is to implement a filter type service that does not pass unspecified messages but generates a a brief 'Request-to-send' message to the recipient. This would only identify the sender, address and affiliation and describe the broad category of mail as above. The Recipient would be notified of the presence of such Request-to-Send messages in addition to delivered messages. (It would be optional whether the recipient chose to look at Request-to-Send messages or ignore them.) If the recipient was interested in a particular communication he/she could generate a 'Permission-to-Send' message that would be transmitted to the sender. This would notify the sender or senders agent that the original message could be retransmitted and (providing it was unchanged) it would be accepted. With sender and recipient agents of similar capability, much of this protocol would be automated in practice. Thus the acceptance of a Request-to-Send could trigger the user agents filter to accept all similar message from that source until further notice. In this scheme all costs up to the transmission of the actual message are borne by the sender (including the recipients 'Permission-to-Send').

Although this scheme sounds clumsy, this would not necessarily be the case. The system overhead need not be high as Request-to-Send/Permission-to-Send could be implemented as datagram type primitives. Whether the carrier or the actual source stores the message for some intermediate period is an implementation issue. In simple situations where only one message transport carrier or agency was involved local storage might be suitable. In other situations the advantage of storing at source is that the sender pays for the inconvenience of storing and maintaining the message. Of course, should the sender delete or alter the message the recipients 'Permission to send' message will not be appropriate and the recipient would be notified. The scheme demands that each message must have a unique identifier that relates to the contents and not just to the posting or delivery time. This is not a difficult requirement, some systems already have such identifiers. Furthermore, other advantages follow from the possession of content identifiers - e.g., the facility to handle embedded message transactions or streams of correspondence (see [4]).

Conclusion

This paper has briefly outlined the need to consider user factors at an early stage in the design and implementation of CBMS services. At the present time there is a natural tendency to increase the provision of communication resources, to bring the facilities that few enjoy to the many. In the not too distant future the emphasis may well switch to the control and limitation of these same resources. Perhaps then communication carriers will earn as much revenue from providing access control services as performing their more traditional function.

References

1. CCITT Study Group VII, _Message Handling Systems_: _Inter-relationships and control procedures_ (_Version 3_), CCITT (1982).

2. D. Deutsch, "Design of Message Format Standard", in _Computer Message Systems_, North-Holland, Ottawa, Canada (1981).

3. C.J. Bennett, _JNT Mail Protocol_, Department of Computer Science, University College, London (1982).

4. H.T. Smith, _Computer-Based Message Systems and Message Structure_, Human Computer Interaction Group Report, Nottingham University (1982).

5. CCITT Study Group VII, _Message Handling Systems_: _Inter-relationships and control procedures_ (_Version 3_), CCITT (1982).

6. P. Shicker, "Service Definitions in a Computer Based Mail Environment", in _Computer Message Systems_, North-Holland, Ottawa, Canada (1981).

7. P.J. Denning, "Electronic Junk", _Commun. ACM_ 25(3), pp.163-165 (March 1982).

8. A. Langsford, "A Consideration of Network Message Services", in _International Workshop on Computer_ _Message Systems_, IFIP WG 6.5 and Gesellschaft fur Mathematik und Datenverarbeitung (GMD), Bonn (1980).

Biography

Hugh Smith is at the University of Nottingham. He is joint editor of the book entitled _Human Interaction With Computers_ and researches in this area. In 1979 he was a visiting professor at the University of Southern California where he lectured on the integration of computer and communication systems. At the present time he is studying the human factor implications of communication systems in the automated office.

Evaluation of the Impact of Different Services on the Access to a Packet Switched Network

L Bella, N Corsi
CSELT - Centro Studi e Laboratori
Telecomunicazioni, Italy

Software tools for the computerized solution of general network optimization problems have been developed at CSELT in the last few years: such tools have been used to solve design problems faced by the network planner when different services and applications with different source traffic characteristics are supported in a packet switched network. This paper presents some results obtained using these tools, to evaluate the cost effectiveness of various alternatives in the access portion (i.e. from user's site to the serving Data Switching Exchange - DSE) of the network. After a review of the access network architectures considered, suitable parameters are introduced in order to define from a traffic viewpoint the services (batch data, interactive data, facsimile, text communication, videotex). Then, the criteria on which the design method is based are outlined. Finally, numerical examples are given showing the impact of various service mixes on the possible network structures which are compared from a technical-economical point of view. Among the relevant conclusions reached under the hypotheses described below, there is the significant advantage of employing in the access network intelligent concentrators rather than pure time division multiplexers; this advantage can be further improved if the concentrators may support a relatively high number of terminations (typically 256) and integrate also local switching capability.

1. INTRODUCTION

The forecasted growth of data applications oriented to large scale usage, such as videotex systems, text communication and electronic mail, is likely to introduce deep changes in traffic profiles and users' distribution as compared to those commonly used by data communication network designers. These changes will be further emphasized by the trend towards the integration of services and applications in a single (multiservice) terminal linked to a single network access; this means that not only the number of services and applications will grow in the next future, but also that various combinations of them will increase the variety of "traffic sources" to be considered in the network design.

On the other hand, it is a common view that the most significant impact of the emerging new services, hereafter referred to as telematic services, will be, at least in the mid-term, on data networks that are a suitable infrastructure offering the necessary flexibility, performance and economics for carrying and managing this new type of traffic. Of course, at the subscriber access level, the data network diffusion will be integrated, when economically justified, by the access capabilities offered by the telephone network, possibly improved by its digital evolution.

In the evaluations that will be made in this paper, reference has been made to a public packet switched data network. It has been considered as divided in two sections: a backbone network, devoted to long-haul traffic handling, and an access network, performing the basic function of conveying data traffic generated at the users' premises to the serving data switching exchange (DSE). Such a configuration includes a high-level meshed network connecting several DSEs, each managing the traffic of a "switching area", and is in line with the architecture of the italian data network described in [1].

Then, a single switching area has been considered as an isolated entity comprising all equipment and links from the user terminal to the DSE (included) and the topological optimization problem has been set in the following terms:

considering given user distributions and traffic source characteristics, the access network architecture, the cost and maximum capacity of available equipment, find the optimal resource amount in each access network section.

The restriction to the access network is only due to the fact that this level appears to represent a more critical aspect from the cost viewpoint and therefore the optimization problem has been considered here with priority.

In the following paragraphs, the results achieved in evaluating some network configurations and structural alternatives are presented.

The paper is structured in three parts which also reflect the three stages of work: the first one outlines the network and system configurations considered; the second one describes the terminal characterization in terms of traffic parameters for the various services and applications as well as the network design method implemented; the final part reports about numerical examples of application of the design method both to various service mixes on a given access network configuration and to various network structures for a given service mix.

In the numerical evaluations for the absolute values relating to subscriber number and distribution, reference has been made to an amount corresponding to 20% of the Eurodata '79 projections for Italy.

2. ACCESS NETWORK CONFIGURATIONS: ARCHI—TECTURE AND EQUIPMENT

In this section the network configurations that have been considered as candidate alternatives in network planning will be discussed in some detail.

Four hypotheses (designated as A, B, C and D) have been taken into account, three of them representing a two level and the fourth a three level tree topology.

The lowest network level, including the subscriber terminal equipment and the access line, is the same in every configuration. Characteristics of the traffic sources and sinks for the various kinds of services will be given in section 3, while the access lines are assumed to be analog telephone subscriber lines, possibly with circuit concentration through the public switched telephone network (PSTN); the speeds vary in discrete steps of 1.2 kbps. As network machine for user interfacing, configuration A uses a traditional time division multiplexer (MUX); then the user traffic is packetized (when needed) in the DSE. The tributary channels (up to 64) are multiplexed on MUX-DSE trunks that are assumed to be digital links whose capacity varies in 4.8 kbps steps.

Configuration B provides at the first network stage an intelligent concentration function (PCE) which also can perform traffic packetization (PAD) thus allowing high utilization of the PCE-DSE links that are of the same type as in case A. The number of access ports is up to 64 and, in order to evaluate the PCE complexity and cost, reference is made to equipment offering CCITT interface support (e.g. X.3, X.25, X.28 and X.29); this type of equipment, in fact, has gained a sufficient degree of maturation to make acceptable economic evaluations possible. The PCE structure is modeled as a multiserver configuration with each server characterized by a traffic handling capacity of 1.2 kbps. As a variant B' of this configuration, the availability of concentrators with higher capacity (up to 256 ports) has been considered as it will be shown in the examples of section 4. In configuration C, the network machine terminating the user line integrates in a single equipment both the concentrator/packetizer function and the local switching capability (this equipment is indicated as LPSE) for a number of user terminations up to 256. The LPSE-DSE network trunks, again similar to those used in configuration A, are in this case off-loaded of local connections, while the equipment complexity and cost is somewhat increased by the additional switching capabilities.

Configuration D provides for the same functionalities in the access network as configuration C, but the concentration and local switching function are physically separated and interconnected by intermediate trunks still with 4.8 kbps (or multiples) capacity. In other words, this configuration introduces a further network level in comparison with the previous ones. The concentrators considered have 64 port capacity.

The final element to be considered in the access network architecture is the DSE. Such unit has been modeled again as a multiserver structure with add-on modules capable of handling 4.8 kbps each. It is worthwhile to underline that a DSE of a given power (i.e. cost) is able to support a different amount of traffic (i.e. users) in different configurations. In particular, the DSE can serve a much higher traffic in configuration B than in A because it has not to deal with packetizing which is a high CPU time consuming and then expensive operation. Again, a DSE in configuration C can handle the traffic of a larger number of users than in configuration B because it is off-loaded both of the locally originated and terminated traffic and of the terminal switch functions (such as user identification, user

facilities manipulation etc.) performed in the LPSE. Similar considerations are applicable for configuration D, where the DSE capacity is the same as in C; this architecture has been considered, in fact, only for the purpose of exploring the potential advantages of reducing the subscriber line length at the cost of introducing a third element in which queueing and processing are performed. The quantitative values assumed for these different capacities will be detailed in sect. 4.

Fig. 1 summarizes the configurations mentioned above.

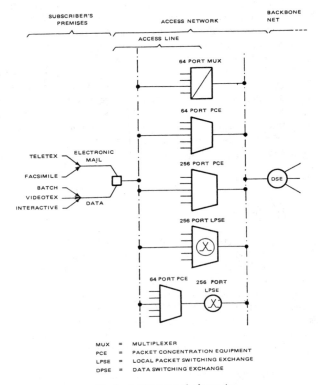

MUX	=	MULTIPLEXER
PCE	=	PACKET CONCENTRATION EQUIPMENT
LPSE	=	LOCAL PACKET SWITCHING EXCHANGE
DPSE	=	DATA SWITCHING EXCHANGE

Fig. 1 - Access network alternatives

3. SUBSCRIBER CHARACTERIZATION AND NETWORK DESIGN METHOD

As already mentioned before, the growth of data networks involves not only an increase of the subscribers number but also a differentiation of the users characteristics depending on the various services requested. In the near future, electronic mail (here intended as text communication and facsimile) and regulated interactive services (such as Videotex) with be developed in addition to public data services. These considerations lead to the need of defining a set of few parameters sufficient to describe quantitatively the characteristics of multi-service subscribers, so that mathematical methods may be applied to the network design. The traffic originated by each subscriber is considered as a sequence of calls interleaved by idle periods,

Service Parameter	DEFINITION	Home Videotex	Text Comm.	Facsimile	Batch mode data comm.	Interactive mode data comm.
r_i	Average transmission rate of source i (bit/s)	0,2 to 0,8	3 to 7	50 to 100	100 to 300	0,5 to 3
b'_i	Message bursty factor for source i	0,01 to 0,2	0,5 to 1	0,5 to 1	0.5 to 1	0,01 to 0,2
b''_i	Call bursty factor for source i	0,002 to 0,005	0,2 to 0,8	0,02 to 0,08	0,02 to 0,08	0,02 to 0,08
ϕ_i	Inverse of the utilization factor for source i	10 to 30	5 to 30	2 to 7	2 to 7	2 to 7
L_i	Average message length (bit)	10 to 10^4	10^4 to 10^5	10^5 to 10^6	10^4 to 10^6	50 to 500

Table 1

each call consisting of a discontinuous sequence of messages, so that the parameters indicated in Table 1 can summarize the user traffic characteristics (in Table 1 also a range of values for each parameter is indicated). In particular, the set of parameters consists of the average subscriber traffic (in bps), message length (in bit), channel utilization factor and, above all, parameters suitable to define the "burstiness" of the subscriber data flow. In fact, the design of the access level to a packet switched network is greatly influenced by the distribution of calls and messages and by the average delay (indicated by D in the following) allowed in the network for the transfer of messages from transmitting to receiving subscribers. A measure of the source "burstiness" may be introduced through the "bursty factor" which is the ratio between the time D previously defined and the message interarrival time (during a call). Therefore, this parameter indicates what average fraction of the time between two subsequent messages may be used to accomplish the transfer from transmitter to receiver. In the same way, a "call bursty factor" can be introduced and also a "total bursty factor" (depending on the preceding bursty factors) can be defined in order to treat already packetized traffic at network levels where messages and calls are not distinguished and only bursts of packets are handled.

The second important aspect that deserves a short comment is the cost optimization criterion adopted. Its basic principle is the research of an optimal subdivision of the total average delay (fixed as quality of service objective) among network units (channels, machines) located at various network levels. In other words, the network resource that is optimally allocated is the "allowed delay"; this resource, in fact, directly defines, if coupled with input traffic, the transmission and switching equipment capacity and, hence, cost.

The main characteristics of the optimization method can be summarized as follows:

- a "channel" of unknown capacity must be designed (it is a portion of the whole network and can represent a link or a node);
- the average delay allowed in the "channel" is less than a fraction K of the whole end-to-end average delay D taken into account in the definition of the bursty factor B that can be one of the previously defined bursty factors depending on the network level.
- the endpoints of the considered "channel" may be equivalent sources replacing a portion of the network;

- the Markovian characteristics are kept through the network, so that each design step may be performed considering the network element at the corresponding network level.

In general it can be shown that the "channel" capacity must be:

$$C \geq \frac{r}{KB} \cdot U\,(C,\,KB,\,r) \qquad (1)$$

where r is the average bit rate of the channel source, K and B are the previously defined factors and U is the factor taking into account the stochastic fluctuation of the source parameters. This expression shows the roles played by these parameters: the capacity of the "channel" must be higher than the average bit rate because of the burstiness of the sources (1/KB) and associated stochastic fluctuations (U).

Assuming an exponential distribution of service time and interarrival time, it can be showed that U = 1 + KB and therefore (1) becomes:

$$C \geq r\,(1 + \frac{1}{KB})\,. \qquad (2)$$

The amount of resources needed at different network levels has been obtained by straightforward application of (1), taking into account the discrete nature of nodes and links. The preliminary optimization of the resource allocation has been performed on the hypoteses of uniform sources and has been carried out, as mentioned above, determining the best subdivision of the total average delay among the various network levels, considering both transmitting and receiving sections. In particular, the partial delay caused by the access network, defined as a given fraction Q of the overall delay, has been considered as a design constraint. In the optimization program, the problem of optimal resource allocation is initially solved supposing continuous capacities for nodes and links, then some extensions are introduced in order to take into account the discrete capacities and the mixage of transmitting and receiving sections. Taking the proper partial derivatives of the total cost function, it can be shown that in the continuous case the determination of the optimal subdivision of the delay between transmission and switching equipment can be carried out separately for concentrators and switching exchanges, and hence a global optimum can be calculated. The consideration of the discrete nature of links and nodes makes the optimization problem rather complex, because no analytical expression in closed form can be found and no independence can be assumed among the parameters. The approach adopted implies that, after the continuous capacity optimization, the maximum possible deviations from the calculated values for the cost parameters are determined taking into account the effects of discrete capacity. In this way, it is possible to define a range of values which is explored, in order to find optimal values, using dynamic programming techniques. Usually, the global solution is reached in a few steps.

In the following section, some results are presented obtained applying this method to the evaluation of the alternative network configurations of section 2 for various service mixes. Each "multiservice" terminal is assumed to be defined by the traffic parameters of Table 1.

4. RESULTS

Different hypoteses about access techniques access schemes and equipment sizes are evaluated with reference to the alternative configurations illustrated in section 2. Some results are shown in Fig. 2 to 5 as examples, assuming Q = 0,70 (it means that the 30% of the total delay is attributed to the backbone network).

A general presentation method is introduced in order to take into account as many significant configurations as possible of new services in a few graphs.

For this purpose, the following parameters are used:

Z represents the ratio between electronic mail (text + fax) and data (batch + interactive) traffic. In the examples, the values Z = 0.25, 1 and 4 are used in each comparison.

X is the percentage of electronic mail traffic in facsimile form (100-X is then text communication traffic percentage).

α is the percentage of data traffic of batch type (100-α is then interactive data traffic).

The last element of the source traffic mix comes from Videotex applications. In this work, only home Videotex has been considered as specific traffic source because business Videotex is likely to present traffic profiles falling into the electronic mail and/or interactive data categories. The evaluations reported in Fig. 2 to 5 have been made considering a fixed percentage of home Videotex traffic equal to 20% of the total traffic. Anyway, this percentage could be again adjusted as a further parameter in order to verify if and how things change depending on different home Videotex diffusion.

Finally, the y variable gives the cost/subscriber of the considered access network configuration normalised to the cost/subscriber obtained in the configuration using packet concentrators with up to 64 terminal ports.

In the first example a comparison between this solution and an access through a TDM multiplexer (see sect. 2) is

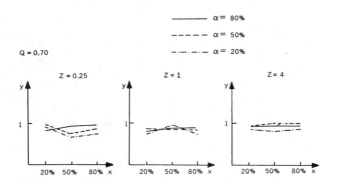

Fig. 2 - *Comparison between different access techniques: y = Ratio between the cost/subscriber for access through a MUX and through a 64 port PCE*

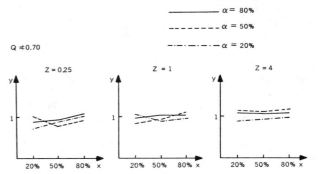

Fig. 4 - *Comparison between switching and non-switching equipment: y = Ratio between the cost/subscriber for access through 256 port LPSE and 64 port PCE*

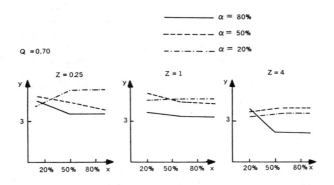

Fig. 3 - *Comparison between different concentrator sizes: y = Ratio between the cost/subscriber for access through 256 and 64 port PCE*

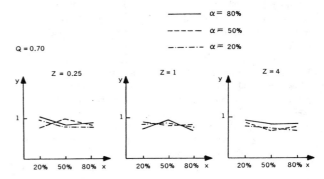

Fig. 5 - *Comparison between different network configurations: y = Ratio between the cost/subscriber for access through 3-level network (64 port PCE plus LPSE) and through 2-level network with 64 port PCE*

carried out. Besides the previous assumptions, further hypotheses are:

- the cost of the MUX is 1/10 of the cost of the PCE
- each server of the DSE can handle a packetized traffic which is three times the one it can handle in case of non-packetized traffic (this is due to the much higher I/O processing required for character mode traffic handling).

Following the described rules, the curves of Fig. 2 show the ratio of the local network costs using the two different access techniques. The significant advantage of the access through packet concentrators is mainly due to the better utilization of the switching apparatus, while the link cost reductions are less determinant because of the relatively short distances in a local area.

The second example concerns the evaluation, within a configuration of B type, of different sizes for the PCE. In particular, potential benefits from the availability of a PCE with up to 256 terminal port capability have been investigated.

In this case, the following data have been inputted to the optimisation program:

- an average increase of the line length (with relative costs) between subscribers and concentrators equal to 30%.
- a cost of the PCE of 2,5 times the cost of the 64 port concentrator.

The curves of Fig. 3 show that the availability of concentrators of larger size lowers the cost per user of the access network for every combination of new services considered, which may only influence the measure of the economical benefit. The average decrease of the cost per user is about 20%.

The third example examines the possible advantages of a type C configuration compared with type B using 64 ports. In this arrangement, further data relating to the addition of a local switching function to the 256 port PCE are:

- a cost of the LPSE equal to 3 times the cost of the small size PCE
- a percentage of 20% of internal traffic, which can be routed directly via the switching concentrator without loading the DSE.

The curves of Fig. 4 show that in this case a 25% average cost reduction may be obtained with a slight improvement in comparison with pure concentration in the access network.

Finally, the evaluation is made of possible advantages of adopting a three level hierarchical structure (configuration D), again compared to a type B with small PCE's configuration.

The following new hypotheses are made (the other parameters remain unchanged):

- the average length (and consequently the cost) of lines between subscribers and concentrators is decreased by 30%.
- the average length (and consequently the cost) of lines between concentrators and the LPSE is three times the length of the lines between subscribers and concentrators
- the capacity (bps) of the new switching equipment is four times the capacity of a concentrator and the cost is about 3 times the cost of a concentrator.

The curves of Fig. 5 show that the insertion of the third network level may decrease the cost of the access network

of some percent (about 5% - 8%) but in a few cases it may also increase it, depending on the burstiness of the service considered. The reason is that a further queueing level introduces a delay which results in a resource increase (to keep the delay within the assigned constraint) not compensated, in some cases, by transmission savings. In general, slight benefits may be achieved in the network adopting three levels instead of two.

These are only few examples of application of the network design method outlined in sect. 3. They have been chosen because of their implications with network planning and equipment design in the national context.

The general conclusions, that can be drawn within the limits of validity of the assumed parameters, can be summarized as follows:

- the access to packet-switched networks through intelligent concentrators is much more economical than through TDM multiplexers
- the use of concentrators of larger size, where applicable, may achieve an average 20% saving, with a slight further improvement if they implement a local switching function
- the introduction of a third network level (beside the existing two) can produce only little advantages.

5. CONCLUSIONS

The characteristics of a network design method to evaluate the impact of emerging new services on the access level of a public packet switched data network has been described and examples of application have been given. Obviously, in the numerical evaluation a series of assumptions has been made about traffic characteristics, possible service mixes, quality of service etc. Anyway, the optimization software handles all these data, from the delay fraction allowed in the access network to the traffic profiles for the various services, from the equipment modularity to the costs etc., as parameters which can be specified as needed by the application context.

It must be also remarked that some simplifications in the system modeling have been made; however, the results obtained can be considered as reliable first approximation quantitative indications for network planners if compared to heuristic or trivial approaches.

The future schedule of work will include refinements of the optimization software for the access level and extensions for covering also the high level portion of the packet network.

The goal is to provide a flexible tool as complete and accurate as possible in order to continuously verify and manage the parallel growth of the packet data network and new telecommunication services by effective monitoring of the cost/benefit parameters.

REFERENCES

[1] .A.Micciarelli, L.Musumeci, R.Parodi: "The public packet switched service in Italy" - proposed paper for ICCC '82, London

[2] A.Micciarelli, C.Mossotto: "Technical aspects in the implementation of a public switched network for data" ISS '79, Paris

[3] S.Lam: "Satellite packet communication multiple access protocols and performance" - IEEE Transaction on communication - Vol. COM-27, n.10, Part I, October 1979

[4] L.Kleinrock: "Queueing Systems" Vol. I-II, John Wiley & Sons, 1975

[5] R.R.Boorstyn, H.Frank: "Large scale network topological optimization" IEEE Transactions on Communication, Vol. COM-25, n.1, January 1977

[6] D.T.Tang, L.S.Woo, L.R.Bahl: "Optimization of teleprocessing networks with concentrators and multiconnected terminals" - IEEE Transactions on computers - Vol. C-27, n.7, July 1978

Luigi BELLA, received his Electronic Engineering degree from the Politecnico of Torino in 1978 with a work on the experimental implementation of an high-speed voiceband modem. In 1978 he joined CSELT, Digital Switching Division, where he worked on the design of digital microprocessor based units for advanced telephone exchange architectures. Since 1980, he started a new activity in the field of technical-economical evaluation of network structures and systems with particular reference to the impact of new telecommunication and telematic services. In 1982, he joined Olteco, Olivetti Telecomunicazioni S.p.A. where he works on terminal protocol support in private packet switching systems.

Norberto CORSI, received his Electronic Engineering degree from the University of Bologna in 1971 with a study on phase jitter accumulation in digital repeater systems. In 1972 he joined CSELT, Data Transmission Department, where he carried out research activities on data network systems in both analog and digital circuit switching environment. Since 1977, he supervised a new research and development work in the field of packet switching systems for large public data networks and in 1980 he actively participated in the working groups who laid down the specifications of the italian public data network and services now under development. Currently, he is responsible of the Protocols Department in the Network and Systems Division at CSELT.

Pricing Interactive Computer Services: a Rationale and some Proposals for UNIX Implementation

W A Gale, R W Koenker
Bell Laboratories, USA

ABSTRACT

This paper suggests a theoretical rationale for pricing interactive computer service and provides some empirical evidence on congestion in UNIX systems which leads to specific proposals for UNIX pricing. Our proposals for UNIX implementation are based on an intensive study of a VAX 11/780 UNIX environment offered by the Murray Hill Bell Laboratories Computer Center. Congestion is an intrinsic problem of shared resources like interactive computer systems: every user contributes to some degree to the general deterioration of service quality (response time) as system loads increase. Prices can be used to encourage the efficient use of shared resources by equating the prices of computer services with value of the *marginal* congestion delay imposed on others. We have constructed statistical models of response time as a function of background load, and models of the cyclical pattern of existing loads which lead to explicit pricing recomendations.

1. INTRODUCTION

An intrinsic problem of shared resources like interactive computer systems is congestion. Every user contributes to some degree to the general deterioration of service quality (response time) as system loads increase. Indeed, it is reasonable to argue that the delay costs created by congestion are the predominant *marginal* cost imposed by users contemplating adding increments to system load. Typically, the capital and operating costs of the system are fixed irrespective of the machine load and therefore an increment in load imposes no direct costs on the administrators of the system. Of course a permanent increase in load may induce additional investment in equipment, but attempts to allocate these capital costs to specific components of the load, however well meaning, are inevitably arbitrary. Nevertheless, a substantial proportion of the literature on pricing computer services takes this approach. See {3}.

Prices can be valuable tools for "encouraging" the efficient use of resources. A well established economic principle, grounded in both equity and efficiency considerations, is that prices should serve to equate private and social marginal costs — individuals should pay for goods and services an amount commensurate with the costs imposed on others by the provision of those goods and services. Thus, users of interactive computer services should pay prices which reflect the value of the incremental congestion delay they impose on others. The equity justification of this principle is self-evident. For efficiency, if prices are lower than marginal congestion costs then users have an incentive to submit tasks whose value is less than the value of the congestion delay they create, while if prices are higher than marginal congestion costs there will be an incentive to withhold tasks whose value exceeds their social cost. Either situation results in inefficient utilization of the system. Unfortunately, both

situations are all too common outcomes of prevailing "cost-recovery" or "fully-distributed cost" pricing schemes. When demand is low these schemes tend to impose high prices, further depressing demand, and resulting in an underutilization of capacity. When demand is high costs may be "recovered" with a modest price, but this frequently results in highly congested service and overutilization of capacity. While the theory of marginal congestion cost pricing is well known, successful applications are quite rare. This is largely due, we believe, to difficulties in measuring congestion costs. Rather than attempting to develop realistic theoretical queueing models for interactive computer systems, we have chosen instead to estimate congestion costs directly by measuring average delay of certain test jobs as a function of actual daily background loads and artificially generated loads. The background loads explain a large fraction of the observed variance in response delay and thus the systematic variation in the level of system loads may be used to calculate plausible marginal congestion cost pricing policies.

2. THE ECONOMICS OF CONGESTION PRICING FOR COMPUTERS

2.1 A Scalar Model of Interactive Computing

To illustrate the foregoing discussion, imagine a simple computing environment with scalar measures of system load, q, and system capacity k. The private cost as seen by an individual user generating an increment dq of system load is composed of two parts: a pecuniary part and a temporal part which we express as,

$$(2.1) \qquad p(dq) = rdq + vw(q,k)dq$$

where r denotes the money price of the service q, $w(q,k)$ is the wait incurred at system load q and system capacity k for a unit of system load, and v is the value of waiting time to users. The *social* cost of doing dq is simply the value of its initiator's wait plus the value of other users' incremental congestion delay, which may be expressed as,

$$(2.2) \qquad s(dq) = vw(q,k)dq + vq \, w_q \, dq,$$

where $w_q = \partial w / \partial q$.

If $p(dq) < s(dq)$ then individual users are apt to initiate tasks like dq which may be justifiable in terms of their private costs, but whose benefits do not exceed their social costs. As a consequence too much congestion will occur. On the other hand, if private costs exceed social costs, some tasks whose benefits exceed their social costs will not be initiated and the service will be underutilized.

The discrepancy between private and social costs is obviously resolved if the following pricing policy is adopted: set

$$(2.3) \qquad r = vq \, w_q.$$

Under this policy, private incentives coincide with social incentives, and efficient utilization of the shared resource occurs. Our pricing rule is a thinly disguised variant of the price — marginal cost rule which pervades economic reasoning. However, marginal costs are borne in this case by other consumers rather than directly by the producer of the service as is usually the case. Pigou {6} developed the essential ideas of marginal congestion pricing in the context of highway tolls, see also {8}. The theory of congestion pricing in queuing models with and without priority classes has been studied in {4} and {5}.

To this point we have said nothing about the direct costs of owning and operating the physical resources which provide the computing services under study. It may seem unseemly, even fiscally irresponsible, to promulgate pricing policies without explicitly considering these costs. Do we know that a system operated with our proposed pricing rule can break even? From the system administrator's point of view this is the first requirement of a pricing policy. To answer this question we must extend our simple model slightly to explicitly incorporate capacity choice.

Under plausible conditions an affirmative answer is possible provided that system capacity has been optimally chosen. A socially efficient investment policy would adjust capacity to equate the value of an incremental reduction in user waiting to the price of an additional unit of capacity, ρ, i.e. it would choose k so that,

$$(2.4) \qquad -q \cdot v \cdot w_k = \rho.$$

Suppose the waiting time function were homogeneous of degree zero in load and capacity, i.e.

$$(2.5) \qquad w(z,k) = w(\lambda q, \lambda k) \quad \lambda > 0.$$

This seems plausible if capacity is expanded by adding essentially independent machines. Further, assume that capacity costs are linear,

$$(2.6) \qquad c(k) = \rho k.$$

If the preceding two quite plausible conditions are met, then not only can the operation of the system break even, but the break-even condition becomes a critical investment signal. The rate of profitability of the system is simply

$$(2.7) \qquad \pi = rq - \rho k$$

which under our proposed pricing rule becomes

$$(2.8) \qquad \pi = q^2 \cdot v \cdot w_q - \rho k,$$

but (2.5) implies

$$(2.9) \qquad q \, w_q + k \, w_k = 0$$

so we have

$$(2.10) \qquad \pi = -q \cdot k \cdot v \cdot w_k - \rho k.$$

Hence $\pi = 0$ is equivalent to the equilibrium capacity condition (2.4). If $\pi > 0$, then

$$(2.11) \qquad -q \cdot v \cdot w_k > \rho,$$

which implies that an increment in k costs less than the value of its resulting reduction in user waiting time. Thus, positive profit is a signal to expand capacity. Conversely, negative profit is a signal to contract capacity. Not only does the marginal cost pricing rule (2.3) induce individual users of the service to behave efficiently, but via the profitability of the system operation it provides an informative signal of socially productive investment opportunities. When conditions (2.5) and (2.6) are violated then the profit signal becomes somewhat ambiguous. For example if (2.5) holds but $c(k)$ is concave (Suppose, for example, that it is linear in k but has a positive fixed cost) then $\pi > 0$ is sufficient but not necessary for capacity expansion.

2.2 Vector-valued Loads and Capacities

Extending the simple scalar model to the much more realistic context of vector-valued load and capacity variables is straightforward. Let $\mathbf{q}$ denote an n-vector of load variables which might be distinguished by generic tasks, time of submission or any number of other considerations. Let $\mathbf{k}$ denote an m-vector of capacity variables. The function w maps load and capacity configurations into a vector of waiting times whose elements correspond to each of the load variables. Now the pricing rule becomes,

$$(2.12) \qquad \mathbf{r} = v \mathbf{w_q}(\mathbf{q},\mathbf{k})\mathbf{q},$$

where $\mathbf{w_q}$ denotes the Jacobian matrix of $\mathbf{w}$ with respect to $\mathbf{q}$. Again, profitability is a signal of productive investment opportunities, but now an entire vector of capacities needs be chosen and we would have to turn to the vector of optimal capacity conditions

$$(2.13) \qquad -v \mathbf{w_k}\mathbf{q} = \rho$$

to decide exactly what mix of capacities should be expanded.

3. EMPIRICAL ANALYSIS OF COMPUTER CONGESTION

Implementation of the pricing policies suggested in the previous section obviously requires detailed empirical study of the causes of congestion in particular computing environments. We need to know how expected response time depends on various measures of system load and capacity, and how load fluctuates over time. In this section we present a detailed analysis based on data from a VAX 11/780 UNIX system operated as part of a general purpose computing facility at Bell Laboratories.

3.1 Experimental Techniques

While we are interested in the delay to various components of the load caused by increments to the load, we can most easily measure the delay to test jobs as functions of the concurrent background. We will then be able to estimate the delay to our test job caused by an increment in the background load.

To facilitate extending the measured results to a typical load, we selected test jobs that exercised primarily one resource. After considerable preliminary study we built test jobs that emphasized cpu use, disk use, and memory use. Two different cpu intensive jobs count for one and two seconds, respectively, on an unloaded machine. Similarly, the disk intensive jobs copy files for one and two seconds. The memory jobs grab several hundred kilobytes of memory then sleep, waking every second for two to ten seconds.

We used these test jobs with two different kinds of backgrounds. The first background was the daily load. Under system control the test jobs were run every fifteen minutes, measurements taken, and the results appended to a file. The second background type was of synthetic loads, each composed of multiple copies of one of the test jobs. These loads were generated between 3 a.m. and 6 a.m. when the activity on the system is normally extremely low. With either kind of background, the information gathered for each test job was the elapsed time it took to run, and the total use of a variety of system resources while the test job was running. These included cpu use by other users and by the system, normal disk access, disk access for swapping, characters transferred on data lines, and references to system tables. These measurements are made by *timex*, a UNIX system utility. Since memory use is not measured by timex, it was measured immediately before each test job ran, using a program that examined system memory tables.

3.2 Functional Form

The literature on queueing provides a reasonable point of departure for specifying the functional form of the congestion function **w**. The expected waiting time in the classical $M/M/1$ queue is given by

$$(3.1) \qquad w = \frac{1/\mu}{1 - \lambda/\mu}$$

where λ is the rate of arrivals, and $1/\mu$ is the expected service time. A much broader class of queues that will give a similar result are the networks of queues

described by Jackson in {1}. Thus for a job testing resource i we have considerable reason to expect a dependence such as

$$(3.2) \qquad w_i = \frac{\tau_0}{1 - \beta_i q_i} .$$

where τ_0 denotes the waiting time for the test job on an unloaded machine, q_i denotes the load of the ith type and $1/\beta_i$ is a measure of system capacity for the ith resource. The Jackson model cited predicts no dependence of waiting time for a job testing resource m on utilization of resources other than m. However, in a real system, it seems prudent to consider this hypothesis empirically. Thus we generalize (3.2) slightly to

$$(3.3) \qquad w_i = \frac{\tau_0}{1 - \sum \beta_{ij} q_j} .$$

Rather than estimate (3.3) directly by nonlinear methods we estimate its reciprocal which is conveniently linear in the parameters β_{ij}. The dependent variable is thus $1/w_i$ which has the interpretation of system throughput of type i.

3.3 Analysis of Daily Background Results

We have specified marginal throughput to depend on three distinct measures of system load. The load on the central processing unit (cpu) is measured in cpu seconds per second. (In practice it is noted by the operating system every 1/60 second whether the cpu is busy or waiting. The cpu load rate is the fraction of "busy" observations of all observations.) The load on disk access is measured in input/output counts per second. One count represents the transfer of one 512 byte block of data from or to the disk. The memory load is conceptually a number of byte seconds/second. In practice we measure the bytes in use at one point of time immediately before a test job runs. While we included many other variables in original exploratory work, these variables explained the bulk of the variance in our observations of response time.

Fig. 3.1-3 illustrate the dependence of cpu throughput on each of the load variables through partial residual plots. A partial residual plot gives a view of dependence of the dependent variable on one among several independent variables by controlling for the influence of all other independent variables. The method of control is to regress the dependent variable as well as the chosen independent variable on the set of other independent variables, taking the residuals in each regression to represent the part of the variable not explained by the other variables. The partial residual plot then is one set of residuals plotted against the other. The coefficient from a simple regression fitted to such a plot is algebraically the same as that for the chosen independent variable in the multiple regression including it and all the variables controlled.

In fig. 3.1, showing the dependence of the cpu intensive probes on cpu load, a linear dependence is clear. The slope of the line is negative, giving a positive β_i, as expected. Fig. 3.2 shows some relationship. The impression of greater dispersion is

677

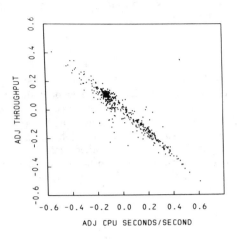

Fig. 3.1. Partial Residual Plot: CPU wait vs. CPU load

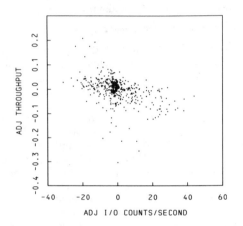

Fig. 3.2. Partial Residual Plot: CPU wait vs. I/O load

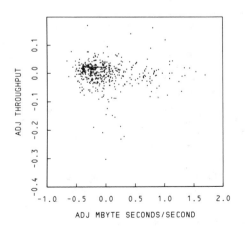

Fig. 3.3. Partial Residual Plot: CPU wait vs. memory load

primarily an artifact of the smaller range of the adjusted marginal throughput in this plot, but there is still a clear negative slope. An important value of a partial residual plot is in examining a lesser effect after controlling for a greater effect, as in fig. 3.3, examining dependence on memory. Here we can see not just a fuzziness induced by the other stronger variables, but a zero slope to an elongated cluster of points, with some outliers near the mean. These figures illustrate our contention that the waiting time function can be measured empirically, even if realistic theoretical models are difficult to construct.

4. LOAD VARIATION MEASUREMENT

A UNIX system utility, the *system accounting report* (sar), gathers information on cpu and disk activity rates. It reports total usage during each hour, and is a rich source of information on cyclical patterns of load variations in cpu and disk activity.

Fig. 4.1 shows plots of hourly loads during the work week. The top panel shows cpu loads, the middle panel i/o loads, and the bottom panel memory loads. The data for cpu loads and i/o loads are from a standard system report detailing all usage. This is preferable to our own data which sample usage, but which had to be used to estimate memory usage. Within each plot the solid dots represent a central estimate from the data — medians for the top two panels which had four or less observations at each hour and 10% trimmed means for the bottom panel which had up to sixty observations at each hour. The vertical bars represent an indication of scale — ranges for the top two panels and 10% trimmed standard deviations in the bottom. The solid line represents a (24 hour period) Fourier fit to the solid dots in each panel. The coefficients were first fitted on a daily basis, but the coefficients were not significantly different by day. For instance, on F test of the hypothesis that the coefficients of the Fourier fit to the i/o load were the same day-by-day yielded 1.18 on 32 and 240 degrees of freedom. Therefore the figures show the results of fitting over the period of a week.

CPU Load

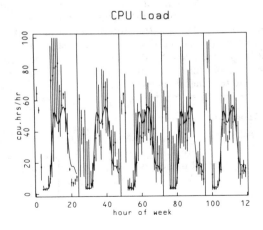

Fig. 4.1. Weekly Load Cycle

I/O Load

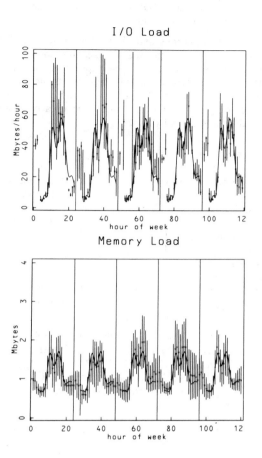

Memory Load

Fig. 4.1. Weekly Load Cycle (Continued)

The figure illustrates several points. First, there is a systematic variation in load by hour of the day. This can be seen from the central points, and is highlighted by the amplitudes of the Fourier fits. Second, there is considerable variation from the central estimate at most hours — especially during the day time. Third, we do not see any need for distinguishing the weekdays. Each day seems fairly well fit by the 24 hour period Fourier fit. A final point is that the usage patterns are quite similar for each resource. The day usage is considerably higher than the night, with the afternoon usage higher than the morning, and with a noon-hour drop. The evening usage exceeds the late night usage.

The variation shown by this figure, and apparently typical of computer loads elsewhere, has led some to suggest dynamic pricing mechanisms that will charge low prices when the actual load is low or high prices where the actual load is high. See {2} and {7} for examples of such suggestions. In discussing this possibility with the system administrators, we were convinced that such a pricing system would have prohibitive administrative costs.

5. IMPLICATIONS FOR PRICING POLICY

In Section 3.3 we illustrated the fitting of a waiting-time (or throughput) function based on VAX-UNIX performance at Bell Labs, and in Section 4 we illustrated the fitting of a smoothed form of the daily load cycle. Using the estimates obtained, we have computed marginal cost pricing policies based on the current load, assuming a value for waiting time. This is doubtless a controversial choice, but for purposes of illustration we have chosen $v = \$50$/hour. Other choices may be accommodated by linearly rescaling the vertical axis in our subsequent figures.

In fig. 5.1 we illustrate the "marginal cost prices" which are implied by the marginal cost pricing rule (2.14) with current loads, our estimated throughput function, and this hypothetical value of time. The solid line in each panel represents the time-varying price of a particular resource: cpu in $ per cpu hour, i/o in $ per megabyte transfer, and memory in $ per megabyte hour. Each price can be decomposed, see eq (2.14), into three components attributed to cpu, i/o, and memory loads. These components are illustrated in fig. 5.1 by dotted, dashed, and dot-dash lines, respectively.

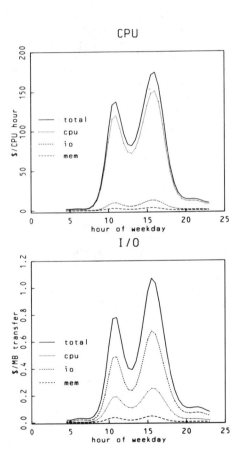

Fig. 5.1. Decomposition of Marginal Cost Rates

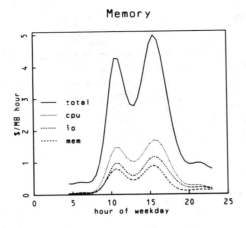

Fig. 5.1. (Continued)

Note that cpu load is the largest effect for both cpu and memory jobs, for cpu it is the predominant effect. I/o activity is the most important determinant of the i/o price. The shape of the price cycle imitates the load cycle illustrated in the previous section, but the peaks are accentuated due to the convexity of the congestion function.

We must emphasize that these prices are designed for current load patterns. Their implementation would doubtless have a serious effect on those patterns whereupon these prices would need to be modified. Nevertheless, these prices do provide valid *directions* for pricing policy changes. A movement in the direction of these marginal cost prices is essentially a gradient step in an iterative pricing scheme.

In contrast to our proposed rates, actual system rates during our study period relied heavily on memory charges. The system rate was non-linear in memory use, but for processes of modest size (more than 100 Kbytes) the rate exceeded *$250* per cpu hour. There was no charge for i/o activity per se. Our finding that current memory loads exert a negligible impact on response time implies that memory prices should be low as illustrated in the last panel of fig. 5.1. We are pleased to report that system memory charges have been recently eliminated. There is still no charge for i/o activity despite the fact that it appears to be a major source of congestion delay. At current system peak loads with our proposed rates the revenue raised by source is roughly 60% cpu, 35% i/o, and 5% memory.

The second important policy recommendation to be drawn from fig. 5.1 is that there should be a much greater daily variation in rates. Current system rates offer a discount of 65% for processes run out of normal working hours. However, current load fluctuations would justify a much more substantial discount. There is an implied discount of about 98% between the recommended peak cpu price of *$175* per hour and the recommended early morning rate of *$3* per hour. The recommended evening discount is about 90%, and the noon discount is nearly 50%. These changes would have the desirable effect of providing users with a more

accurate indication of the real costs which they impose by adding to the system load.

It is thus apparent that actual system rates deviated substantially from marginal congestion costs. While only an exhaustive survey could prove it, we believe that most installations would be found to be similarly deficient. We conclude that a rough intention to charge marginal cost prices would be greatly superior to traditional rules of thumb.

ACKNOWLEDGEMENTS

We are grateful to Debasis Mitra and John Panzer for helpful discussions, and we wish to thank H. Fischer, S. Goldsmith and A. Gross for their cooperation in making the measurements reported here while the system was in daily use.

REFERENCES

{1} Jackson, J. R., Networks of Waiting Lines, *Operations Research*,1957,vol. 5, 518-521.

{2} Kameda, H. and C. C. Gotlieb, A Feedback-coupled Resource Allocation Policy for Multiprogrammed Computer Systems, *Acta Informatica*,1977, vol. 8, 341-357.

{3} McKell, L. J., J. V. Hansen, and L. E. Heitger, Charging for Computing Resources, *Computing Surveys*,1979, vol. 11, 105-120.

{4} Marchand, M., Priority pricing with application to time-shared computers, AFIPS Conference Proceedings, 1968, vol. 33, 511-519.

{5} Naor, P., The regulation of queue size by levying tolls, *Econometrica*,1969, vol. 37, 15-24.

{6} Pigou, A. C., *The Economics of Welfare*, 1920, MacMillan, London.

{7} Shaftel, T. L. and R. W. Zmud, Allocation of computer resources through flexible pricing, *The Computer Journal*,1974, vol. 17, 306-312.

{8} Walters, A. A., The theory and measurement of private and social cost of highway congestion, *Econometrica*,1974, vol. 29, 676-699.

William A. GALE is a member of the technical staff of Bell Laboratories in Murray Hill New Jersey. He received his PhD in 1968 from Rice University and is a member of the American Economic Association and the American Statistical Association.

Roger W. KOENKER is a member of the technical staff of Bell Laboratories in Murray Hill New Jersey. He received his PhD from the University of Michigan in 1974. Prior to joining Bell Laboratories he taught for three years at the University of Illinois at Urbana- Champaign.

Cost-Based Tariffs, Integrated Network Use and Network Competition in the Telecommunication Sector

J Müller
German Institute of Economic
Research, Federal Rupublic of
Germany

The author argues for a move to a cost based tariff policy, instead of the second best pricing policy currently advocated in the literature or the value of service pricing principle currently employed by many PTT administrations. This proposal is not made in isolation, but in conjunction with advocating greater user freedom and the possibility of network competition (either on the basis of service or facility competition) in the face of the emerging technology potential of integrated network services.

I. INTRODUCTION

With the advent of competition in the tele-communications sector, the traditional tariff structure is bound to change. This is apparent from the introduction of network competition in the U.S. and the proposals for network competition in Canada and in the UK. While the American policy makers did not assume that a large network operator will continue to be dominant in the foreseeable future this is a proposition which we in Europe must almost take for granted. With this condition in mind, what strategies are possible, if competition in the network is to take place?

So far, this question has not really been addressed in the literature. Telephone tariffs both theory and in practice have been designed with a simple telephone service in mind and have usually been oriented towards voice services, the major use of the telephone network: In practice, we observe "value of service" pricing with some price differentiation between customers and subsequent cross-subsidization in order to increase network penetration or to achieve other redistributive goals.

In the theoretical literature on telephone ta-riffs one has started with the presumption that economies of scale are present. Marginal cost pricing has therefore been augmented by a second-best tariff policy in the Ramsey and Boiteux tradition, in order to obtain financial self-sufficiency. This seems fine in theory and in the case of a simple voice service. But with the introduction of micro electronics, satel-lites, microware and optical fibre transmission, many new applications and services are becoming economically feasible. The singular technology of the past is being surplanted by a host of new technologies, with different degrees of economies of scale and flexibility. As a con-sequence, the potential for competition in the telecommunication sector has increased signifi-cantly. The second-best pricing policy may,

therefore as mentioned above no longer be sus-tainable under competition and require the con-tinuation of entry restriction.We will,therefore propose a "third best" tariff policy, which is compatible with network competition. This tariff offers four important advantages: First, it results in a telephone tariff that is solely based on attributable costs plus a proportional mark-up. This reduces the allocation and measur-ement problem associated with second-best pric-ing on the demand side.Our approach only uses information on the cost side of the operation. It thus offers ease of implementation.

Second, the resultant tariff is sustainable under network competition. This is an important departure from traditional tariff policy, which was based on the need to protect cross-sub-sidization from competition. Instead, we allow competition to be protected from cross-sub-sidization.

Third, while a second-best pricing policy is welfare or surplus superior in a static world, our simpler cost-oriented tariff may have important effects in a dynamic world,which more than offsets the static welfare losses.

Our proposition rests on two arguments: (1) The static welfare losses due to a change over from a second-best pricing policy to a cost-based tariff tend to be small when economies of scale in the system are small 1). (2) Both second-best pricing and value of service pricing require the introduction of user restrictions to remain sustainable. In a static sense, this reduces the substitution possibilities between services for the user and at the same time raises administrative costs for policing these restrictions. In a dynamic sense, it unduly restricts the users' and producers' participa-tion in an efficient discovery process for a fuller exploitation of the available technology potential. An important aspect of our tariff proposal is therefore to allow competition to function as an efficient discovery process. Tariff policies, which prevent competition from fulfilling this function may, therefore, be dynamically inferior, even if they have static surplus superior properties.

It is precisely these effects on the demand side, and their subsequent effects, that we want to focus on. Because of the emphasis on the regulatory process and the associated measurement and allocation questions, in the traditional discussion on telephone tariffs, we seem to have ignored these dynamic effects on the demand side. Telecommunications application, however, is offering so many new and diverse applications, that only a tariff policy, which allow a decentralized discovery process can hope to exploit the available technology potential more fully.

In addition, competitive in network services may act as a signal for new technology applications for the PTT. Because of their requirement to serve all at uniform tariffs, PTT's usually tend to be slow to innovate, unless the product has proven itself beyond doubt and a nation-wide demand can be taken for granted. Competitive entrants do not have this obligation to serve; they, therefore, face a smaller risk in penetrating only some segments of the market and, therefore, act as an important signal provider of the available technology and demand potential for the larger PTT's.

Fourth, such a tariff policy will also allow competition to function as a regulatory tool. I say this particularly from a European point of view, because we will be faced with a continuing dominance of the PTT's in that sector. As a norm, PTT's either operate under a legal monopoly statute or as privately regulated firms, or more commonly as publicly owned corporations. Empirical evidence suggests, however, that both privately owned and regulated corporations and state-owned enterprises have difficulties in fulfilling their regulatory goals. 2) They, therefore, need to be supervised continuously. A tariff structure which allows competition to function as a regulatory tool is, as can be seen from the behavioural changes experienced in the U.S., an effective regulatory policy. 3) It will help to avoid biased investment decisions for regulated enterprises, such as the Averech-Johnson-Effect 4) and to change the often quite conservative investment and operating policy of state-owned enterprises.
For example, many of them tend to value the reliability of service and avoidance of interruptable services (poor quality would give them a poor public image) often higher than their own customers would. A tariff policy consistent with network competition would allow such customers to choose their own price level of quality, therefore combination acting both as a demand signal to the service providers and as an efficiency signal to the regulators. With that additional information, they can now better assess the efficiency, with which a PTT is providing its services.

II. The Effect of Network Competition on Telephone Tariffs

1. Deaveraging of Tariffs as a Result of Network Competition

Telephone tariffs usually apply uniformly across a service area. They are "averaged". There may be some differentiation in charges according to the size of the exchange, its level of technology (manual or automatic exchange) or the type of network to which the subscriber is connected (i.e. telex versus data), but not all of these differences in tariffs are related to costs. This implies a certain amount of cross subsidization either between services or between customers or different parts of the network with in a certain service. As a matter of fact, telephone companies have often explicitly persued a policy of tariff differentiation (for example between price-elastic privat households and price-inelastic business customers) and used the resulting cross-subsidy from the business subscribers to increase telephone penetration in the household sector.

With a move towards network competition, this cross-subsidization will no longer be sustainable. Entry will take place first in the "lucrative" business market and the most densly used intercity routes, thereby competing away the subsidy to the privat household sector and requiring a readjustment of tariffs ("deaveraging" of tariffs). This "cream-skimming" by new entrants will eventually lead to a and therefore a more cost-oriented tariff structure. It will end the differentiation between customers independent of cost or demand elasticity.

This "idealized effect" of network competition will be limited by the ability of tariffs to correctly reflect costs, by certain accounting conventions, by the behavior of the competitors and the PTT's and by economies of scale and scope. The latter imply some barriers to entry and thereby a lessening of the potential degree of competition.

2. Service restrictions to maintain a cross-subsidy

Against this theoretical ideal we have now to look at the reality of tariff making. An important principle employed by PTT authorities is value of servicing pricing or second best pricing. This is also a type of cost-based tariff, in the sense that it does not ignore the marginal cost of production. The value of service to consumers only plays a role in the allocation of those costs, that exceed the marginal cost of producing that service. However, because of the existence of economies of scale, and due to the need to cover some of the non-attributable costs within a given service, those customers which value their service higher (i.e. have a lower demand elasticity) will be required to pay a higher mark-up to marginal cost. The maintenance of these tariff differenziation rests on the ability to prohibit substitute between services or between customers (through resale) . Therefore, both value of service pricing and second-best pricing, require some restrictions on their users. Thus, even though network competition with the larger variety of new technologies may now be technically possible, substitution by the individual will because of given tariff restrictions not be allowed.

III. A Proposal for a Cost-Oriented Tariff

1. A Proportional Mark-UP

The major argument for a cost created tariff is the old basic principle that prices ought to be related to marginal cost. Where economies of scale are not important and services can be unbundled this policy can be applied directly, so no mark-up is necessary.

Where economies of scale (or the difference between average cost and marginal cost) are large, a mark-up above attributable marginal cost is needed for each service to cover the associated deficit. This is, in a way, an arbitrary allocation process in allocating non-attributable costs. The alternative would have been to allocate these non-attributable costs on the basis of ability to pay,either in the form of a value of service pricing, or a second-best rule. (Which is in some cases equivalent.) This "constant mark-up" approach is in the spirit of Rholfs [5] who argues that price elasticities do not matter because some prices are so clearly above marginal cost, while others lie below, that any other arbitrary decision rule of allocating non-attributable costs will be clearly welfare. Superior if our constant mark-up approach also has the pro-competitive features which we have argued for, then the long term dynamic benefits will more than outweigh the static welfare losses.

Our proposal only makes sense, if most costs can be attributed directly and the accounting system can be tuned to that extend. In that case, the proportion of attributal marginal cost with respect to out put will be the inverse of the scale effect for that particular service. [6] The available evidence suggest that the estimates of economies of scale in the telephone service as a whole are not very large. They may be large in particular services (for example long distance calls and local optical fibre networks) and the required mark-up could then be quite large. Problems do of course arise when a large part of costs is not attributable, for example with a significant component of joint cost in the presence of economies of scope. In that case, network competition and the associated user and producer freedom may not be sustainable, but require further entry regulation.

2. A Tax for Potential Cream Skimmers

Network competition may also not be sustainable, if (above and beyond the need to break even) some services are cross subsidizing others and/or if cross-subsidization within a service takes place. In this case, the proportional mark-up would entail the associated subsidy as well as the non-attributable costs. If entrants, who attempt to cream skimming

through a resale policy, where charged a tax equivalent to that part of the mark-up, then that price vector would be sustainable. No entry restrictions would be necessary and the decentralized discovery process could continue.

We would therefore propose such a tax in all these cases, where "deaveraging" between and within services is not politically feasible. This would, to insist again, help to avoid heavy and unnecessary restrictions on user and entrance - a precondition for what we have termed the decentralized discovery process. The final users contribution for non-attributable network services are then equivalent to those which he would have paid as a direct customer of the PTT. Such a tax on telephone agancies is analogous to the system of value added taxes. Their aim is also to tax the final user in the same way, independent of the way which the purchased product has taken through the production and distribution channels.

This tax would also eliminate the negative effects of cream-skimming, which we have described above. Only those telephone agencies which are just as efficient as the PTT (or better) will be able to survive with positive profits. Only they will therefore have an incentive to enter the market. The other telephone agencies which would survive under this condition are the value added networks, which in essence, produce something different from the PTT.

3. Nationally Uniform Tariffs and Cost Based Tariffs

While a cost oriented tariff normally leads to the abandonment of uniform national tariffs, and an elimination of the resulting cross subsidization - within services, such a policy may also be politically infeasible. This does not necessarily mean that the concept of a cost-based tariff or unrestricted user freedom is no longer possible. But some adjustments are obviously necessary, to combine the benefits of increased user freedom with the political necessity to stop "deaveraging" within services from taking place. Two policies shall be considered here.
In first and most extreme case, we assume that the demand for uniform national tariffs is paramount; even in the face of widely diverging regional costs. In this case, one has to weight the regional and local marginal costs for each service by their relative demand. The resulting, "average marginal cost" of that particular service will then be treated just as before, including the mentioned resale tax. This resale tax would then, entail a subsidy to structurally disadvantaged regions. While this is a further departure from the principle of a cost based tariff, it would at least lead to an equalization of marginal costs between services. In addition, it is an exception by political necessity, which should not hinder the PTT from pursuing a policy in which the price signals reflect costs as close as possible.

In the second case there exist a necessity for the PTT to internally subsidize other services (for example

the mail side of business) as we observe in
a number of countries. This requires the
correct calculation of the cross-subsidization
involved for each particular service, again
not an easy task. But this may well pay for
itself in long term efficiency gains, rather
then a continuous restriction of user freedom
to its current level.

There are of course further combinations
possible, of politically necessary cross-subsidization on one hand and increased user
freedom on the other. But different requirements require different solutions, some of
them administratively more cumbersome then
others. The efficiency costs of maintaining
cross-subsidization and restricting user
freedom should therefore be kept in mind, so
that eventually a direct subsidity program
may overcome such cumbersome arrangement.

FOOTNOTES:

* This paper is based on a larger study on the
issue of competition in the telecommunication
sector. The financial support of the German
Marshall Fund is gratefully acknowledged. The
initial work on this topic was carried out
under a grant from the West German Monopolies
Commission, in collaboration with C.C. von
Weizsäcker and G. Knieps, (Die Möglichkeiten
des Wettbewerbs im Fernmeldewesen, Nomos,
Baden-Baden, 1981). The thoughts of and the
critical discussions with the two co-authors
of that report, and comments of Bernhard
Wieland and Eirik Svindland, have influence
the author in the preparation of this note.

(1) For a summary of empirical studies on
    Economies of Scale, see Charles River Inc;
    The Economics of Competition in the
    Telecommunications Industry, Boston, 1979.

(2) See Littlechild, S.C., the Effects of
    Postal Responsibility and Privat Ownership
    on the Structure of Telephone Tariffs - An
    International Comparison, Working Paper,
    1980.

(3) See also Müller, J., The Potential for
    Competition and the Role of the PTT's,
    Telecommunications Policy, March 1981.

(4) Averch, H. Johnson, L.L., Behaviour of the
    Firm under Regulatory Constraint, American
    Economic Review, Vol. 52, No. 3, 1962. p.
    1052-1069.

(5) Rholfs, J., Economically efficient
    Bell-System pricing, Economics Discussion
    Paper 138, Bell Laboratories, January
    1979.

(6) See Knieps, Müller, von Weizsäcker, ibid,
    for details.

Nonlinear Pricing and Network Externalities in Telecommunications

S S Oren
Stanford University, USA

S A Smith
Xerox Palo Alto Research Center, USA

This paper provides a mathematical framework for modeling demand and determining optimal price schedules in markets which have positive demand externalities and can sustain volume discounts. The theory addressing these aspects applies in particular to electronic communications networks where the benefit derived by a subscriber increases as more subscribers join the network. The paper extends the theory of nonlinear pricing to such markets. A special case of the results has been applied in a case study of a telecommunication network for the hearing impaired. In this context it is demonstrated that a nonlinear pricing strategy will motivate a monopolist supplier to lower the subscription fee. This makes the network affordable to more users and reduces the critical mass of subscribers needed for startup.

1. INTRODUCTION

Non-uniform pricing, i.e., when the unit price of a good depends on the quantity purchased, prevails in the markets for many goods and services and has been the subject of considerable economic research. Recent contributions in this area are due to Spence {10}, Goldman, Leland and Sibley {3}, Mirman and Sibley {5}, Oren, Smith and Wilson {6}, and Willig {12}. Fundamental market characteristics that are necessary to sustain non-uniform pricing are the absence of a resale market and the ability of the supplier to monitor the purchase sizes of his customers. The telecommunication market is an important example in which both of these conditions prevail and non-uniform pricing is common.

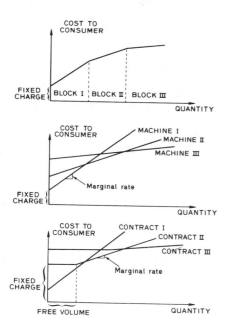

Fig. 1. Alternative Implementations of Nonuniform Pricing.

Operationally, non-uniform pricing can be offered in various ways. Fig. 1 illustrates three alternative types of schedules that are found in telecommunication markets. The first is block pricing in which the consumer pays different rates for subsequent blocks of consumption. In the second case, the consumer can choose among several two part tariffs, each consisting of a fixed charge and a corresponding marginal rate. The third case includes a "free volume" that comes automatically with payment of the fixed charge. In the second case the consumer has the option of choosing a higher fixed charge to obtain a lower marginal rate for service. For example, this may correspond to choosing a more expensive type of equipment that provides better efficiency and reduced marginal charges. The third case arises when the consumer can choose among alternative contracts consisting of a minimum purchase commitment at a fixed rate and a corresponding marginal cost above that commitment. For convenience of analysis, the nonuniform pricing literature typically deals with tariffs that change continuously with quantity. This is equivalent to assuming a continuum of blocks or two part tariffs.

An important characteristic of the telecommunication market which has not been addressed in the nonlinear pricing literature is the externality effect resulting from demand interdependencies. For one and two part tariffs, this has been studied by Artle and Averous {2}, Littlechild {4}, Rohlfs {9}, Squire {11}, and Oren and Smith {8}. This paper provides a framework for determining nonlinear price schedules and analyzing their implications in the presence of demand externalities. The models are developed for heterogeneous markets in which customers differ in their preferences and consumption levels which they select so as to maximize benefit minus cost. For the monopolist supplier case, the model allows the determination of the optimal profit maximizing nonlinear price schedules, the corresponding network size and the "critical mass" of subscribers needed to sustain the network at that price schedule.

* This work was supported by NSF Grant IST-8108350 and by the Xerox Corporation.

685

The results are specialized to a particular specification of the demand function which is used in a case study {1} of a telecommunication network for the hearing impaired (DEAFNET), developed by SRI International. Profitability and consumer welfare implications are discussed in this setting and compared for alternative price structures.

2. FORMULATION

Nonlinear pricing allows the supplier to increase his profits through price discrimination among customers having different demand functions. A fundamental assertion in constructing such pricing schedules is that the supplier knows the distribution of demand functions in the population by customer type. However, he is unable to discriminate directly among customers according to their type, either because he is prohibited from doing so (by regulation) or he cannot identify individual customers' types. Consequently, he will attempt to discriminate according to amount purchased and will rely on the customers' self-selection of purchase quantities. Throughout the paper we shall neglect income effects, and assume that the prices of all alternative modes of satisfying the consumers' demand for communication services (other than the one under consideration) are fixed.

Following {3} an individual consumer's demand may be characterized in terms of a function $W(q,t)$, representing his willingness to pay for the first q units of consumption, $(W(0,t) = 0)$, or equivalently in terms of $w(q,t) = \partial W(q,t)/\partial q$, which is the marginal willingness to pay for the qth unit. It is assumed that $w(q,t)$, is differentiable and satisfies $\partial w/\partial q < 0$, $\partial w/\partial t < 0$. The parameter t is an index that identifies customers' types. Without loss of generality (see {6}), we may further assume that t is uniformly distributed on the interval $[0,1]$.

The supplier chooses the tariff function $R(q)$, defined as the total charge to a customer consuming q, so as to maximize his net revenue. The supplier, who knows $w(q,t)$, assumes that each consumer will select a consumption level that maximizes his consumer surplus, i.e., his benefit minus cost. The conditions this implies are referred to as the self-selection constraints. In general, the tariff function $R(q)$ may have a jump at the origin, reflecting a fixed subscription charge. This may cause consumer surplus to be negative at the "optimal" consumption levels of some consumers, in which case they will choose not to subscribe to the service.

Demand externalities are incorporated in this model by allowing the willingness to pay function of each subscriber to depend on the identity of other subscribers. Thus, for any fixed set $Y \subseteq [0,1]$, representing the set of t indices of all other customers who have subscribed, $W(q,t,Y)$ and $w(q,t,Y)$ will denote the corresponding willingness to pay functions. These functions are assumed to satisfy

$$W(q,t,Y_1) > W(q,t,Y_2) \text{ and } w(q,t,Y_1) > w(q,t,Y_2)$$
$$\text{for } Y_1 \supset Y_2 .$$

i.e., increasing the number of subscribers increases the marginal and total willingness to pay for each purchase quantity. This monotonicity property implies that the demand externalities are always nonnegative, which assumes that congestion effects are negligible.

3. CUSTOMER'S SELF-SELECTION CONDITIONS

In this section we briefly summarize results which are formally proved in {6}.

For any given set $Y \subseteq [0,1]$ and tariff function $R(q)$, let $q*(t,Y)$ denote the optimal consumption quantity for customer t. That is,

$$q*(t,Y) = \arg \max_{q \geq 0} \{W(q,t,Y) - R(q)\} \quad (1)$$

Assuming that $q*(t,Y)$ is well defined, a consumer t will subscribe if and only if his maximum consumer surplus (benefit minus cost) is non-negative, i.e., $t \, \varepsilon \, Y*$ where

$$Y*(Y) = \{t \, | \, CS(t,Y) > 0\} , \quad (2)$$

while

$$CS(t,Y) = W(q*,t,Y) - R(q*) , \quad (3)$$

with $q*$ given by (1).

The "equilibrium" subscriber set Y is then characterized as a fixed point of the set to set mapping defined by (2), or in other words a set Y satisfying the relation $Y = Y*(Y)$. To guarantee that such a set exists, we assume for each t, Y that demand satiates at some finite level $q = Q(t,Y)$, so that it will not exceed $Q(t,Y)$ even at zero marginal charge. This guarantees that $q*(t,Y)$ is finite and $Y*(\cdot)$ is well defined. The existence of a fixed point of $Y*(\cdot)$ then follows from its monotonicity. From a practical point of view, the above satiation assumption is quite reasonable, given some user cost (e.g., time) associated with consumption and the absence of a resale market. For example, people do not spend all their time making local telephone calls although they are free.

In practice, it is also unlikely for a tariff to have fixed charges at quantity levels other than zero. Therefore, we will further assume that $R(q)$ is continuous for all $q > 0$. With that assumption one can show that an equilibrium subscriber set must be an interval $[0,y]$. Accordingly, we simplify the notation, replacing Y with the marginal subscriber's index, y. The subscription conditions (2) and (3) can now be reduced to an explicit condition on the marginal subscriber y.

$$CS(y) = W(q*(y,y),y,y) - R(q*(y,y)) \geq 0 \quad (4)$$

We can also replace (1) by the first order necessary conditions

$$w(q*,t,y) = R'(q*) \quad \text{if } q* > 0$$
$$\leq R'(q*) \quad \text{if } q* = 0 , \quad (5)$$

and the monotonicity condition

$$\partial q*(t,y)/\partial t \leq 0 , \quad (6)$$

which is equivalent to the second-order necessary condition for (1).

The monotonicity of q*(t,y) with respect to t implies that the customer index tε[0,1] is precisely the customer's fractile ranking with regard to his consumption level and, therefore, can be inferred from empirical observations of communication volumes.

4. CRITICAL MASS AND EQUILIBRIUM USER SETS

While our assumptions so far guarantee a unique quantity selection q*(t,y) satisfying condition (5), further assumptions are needed to characterize the values of y that will satisfy condition (4). Specifically, these additional assumptions concern the network externality effect which manifests itself through the dependence of W(q,t,y) on y. For simplicity, we will assume that for any quantity q, W(q,t,0) = W(q,1,y) = 0 for all t,yε[0,1]. That is, the service has no value with zero subscribers, and the lowest volume customer (t = 1) derives zero benefit.

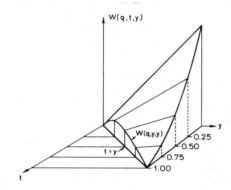

Fig. 2. The utility for consumption level q, as a function of customer index and network size.

Fig. 2 illustrates a typical utility function W(q,t,y) and the corresponding W(q,y,y), which is the cross section of W(q,t,y) along the diagonal t = y. In this illustration W(q,y,y), which is the willingness to pay of the last subscriber, is unimodal. However, as shown in Oren and Smith {8}, one can construct examples where W(q,y,y) has multiple local maxima. For a large class of functions W(q,t,y) it is shown in {6} that the roots of the equation CS(y) = 0 will occur in pairs of adjacent roots between which the function CS(y) is nonnegative. Fig. 3 illustrates a typical form of CS(y) in relation to the marginal subscriber's willingness to pay W(q*(y,y),y,y). In view of condition (4), only values of y in the intervals [y₁,y₂] and [y₃,y₄] define viable subscription levels, since only in these intervals has the marginal subscriber the incentive to subscribe.

The points y_1 and y_3 define "Critical Mass" subscription levels. If, for example, the subscription level is below level y_1, the marginal subscriber has a negative consumer surplus and will therefore leave the network. The same is true for his predecessor, so a chain reaction of subscription cancellations will follow until the network reaches a stable equilibrium (at y = 0). On the other hand, if the network reaches the subscription level y_1, then subsequent customers can obtain a positive

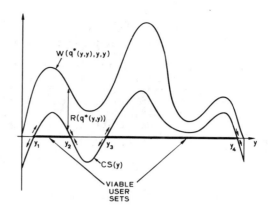

Fig. 3. Typical form of the last subscriber's consumer surplus CS(y).

consumer surplus by subscribing and the network will expand spontaneously to its next "equilibrium user set" [0,y₂]. Beyond y₂ again any additional customer will have no incentive to subscribe unless the network reaches, by some means, level y₃, from which it will again expand spontaneously to y₄. Similar phenomena and concepts have been described previously by Artle and Averous {2}, Rohlfs {9} and by Oren and Smith {8}, in the context of other tariff structures.

5. THE MONOPOLY PROFIT MAXIMIZING TARIFF

As shown in the previous section, the consumption level of each subscriber is influenced by the marginal tariff and the network size, while the equilibrium network size is determined by the last subscriber's fee. Both the usage levels and network size affect the revenues of a monopoly supplier, who controls these quantities by choosing the marginal price schedule R'(q) and the fixed charge R(0⁺). In this section, we derive conditions for the optimal price schedule that maximize the equilibrium net revenues of a monopoly supplier, whose per customer supply cost is given by a function C(q). We assume that C(q) is increasing and continuously differentiable for q > 0, but may have an upward jump k = C(0⁺) at the origin.

We will pursue our analysis by first deriving conditions for the optimal marginal tariff R'(q), q > 0, conditional on a given equilibrium user set y. Then we will obtain conditions for the optimal network size y. To simplify the analysis we will assume from here on that the function W(q,y,y) is unimodal in y. This implies that there may be at most one nonempty equilibrium user set and one corresponding critical mass level.

For any given equilibrium network size y, a monopoly supplier will choose an price schedule which maximizes his net revenue π(y), where

$$\pi(y) = \int_0^y \{R(q^*(t,y)) - C(q^*(t,y))\}dt , \qquad (7)$$

The function q*(t,y) satisfies the consumer self-selection conditions (5), (6) and R(q) must satisfy the boundary condition

687

$$R(q^*(y,y)) = W(q^*(y,y),y,y) , \qquad (8)$$

stating that the smallest purchaser breaks even.

Finding a tariff $R(q)$ that maximize $\pi(y)$, subject to the constraints (5), (6) and (8), is a calculus of variations problem . It can be solved indirectly by determining the function $t^*(q,y)$, which is the optimally induced assignment of subscribers to purchase quantities. Using (5) we then obtain

$$R(q) = K(y) + \int_{o}^{q} w(\theta,t^*(\theta,y),y)d\theta, \qquad (9)$$

where $K(y)$ is a constant of integration determined by (8).

When the monotonicity constraint (6) is inactive, $t^*(q,y)$ is defined implicitly by the first order necessary condition

$$t\partial w(q,t,y)/\partial t + w(q,t,y) - c(q) = 0, \qquad (10)$$

where $c(q) \equiv C'(q)$. Regions of t over which (6) is binding correpond to linear segments in $R(q)$ that can be determined following the approach described in {3}.

An intuitive representation of (10) can be obtained by defining the aggregate demand function $N(p,q,y)$, which is the fraction of customers that will buy at least q units at marginal price p given market penetration y. Let $p(q) = R'(q) = w(q,t^*(q,y),y)$, then (10) can be expressed as

$$1 - 1/e_{Np}(q,y) = c(q)/p(q) , \qquad (11)$$

where $e_{Np}(q,y)$ is the price elasticity of $N(p,q,y)$ defined as

$$e_{Np}(q,y) = - \{p \ \partial N(p,q,y)/\partial p\}/N(p,q,y). \qquad (12)$$

Condition (11) is exactly the classical profit maximizing monopoly condition, parametric on q and y. In other words, for any market penetration level y, the monopoly profit maximizing price schedule $p(q)$ can be determined by treating each qth purchase unit as a separate market having a demand function $N(p,q,y)$.

6. OPTIMAL NETWORK SIZE AND FIXED CHARGE

The optimal equilibrium network size y can now be determined from the first order necessary condition $d\pi(y)/dy = 0$ where $t = t^*(q,y)$. This condition can be reduced to the form

$$R(q^*(y,y))\{1-e_{Wy}\} - C(q^*(y,y)) \qquad (13)$$

$$+ \int_0^{q^*(0,y)} t \ \frac{\partial w(q,t,y)}{\partial y} \bigg|_{t=min\{y,t^*(q,y)\}} dq=0,$$

where e_{Wy} is the partial elasticity of the willingness to pay function with respect to customer index for the marginal subscriber, i.e.,

$$e_{Wy} = -t\{\partial W(q,t,y)/\partial t\}/W(q,y,y)\bigg|_{\substack{q=q^*(y,y), \\ t = y}} \qquad (14)$$

We note that the externality effect, which is reflected by the sensitivity of $w(q,t,y)$ with respect to y, is captured by the integral term in (13). Since $\partial w/\partial y \geq 0$ this term will be nonnegative and will have a similar effect as reducing the supplier's provision cost $C(q^*(y,y))$ for the marginal subscriber. This induces a profit maximizing monopoly to reduce his fixed charge in order to achieve a larger network size (see {6} for a comparative static analysis). If there was no externality effect at all, i.e., $\partial w/\partial y = 0$, then the integral term in (13) would vanish and (13) would reduce to the classical monopoly profit maximization condition for the marginal subscriber's charge $R(q^*(y,y))$.

Another important observation that follows from (13) concerns the issue of cross subsidy. In the absence of network externality, since $e_{Wy} > 0$, it is evident from (13) that $R(q^*(y,y)) \geq C(q^*(y,y))$. In other words, the charge paid by the last subscriber is no less than the cost of supply for his optimal consumption quantity. This is not necessarily true in the presence of network externalities and it is possible to have a whole range of t for which $R(q^*(t,y^*)) < C(q^*(t,y^*))$. Customers in this range will obtain the service below cost. The occurrence of this phenomenon depends on the strength of the externality effect. If this effect is sufficiently strong, the potential increase in demand and willingness to pay of the large users, resulting from increased network size, induces the supplier to subsidize the low-volume users, offering them basic subscription below installation cost. The incentive for doing this is that the additional communications traffic from the larger users to these low-volume users will generate revenues that will more than cover the subsidy. The senders of this extra traffic also increase their surplus as a result.

7. A SPECIAL CASE AND APPLICATION

For a more concrete illustration of the results, we use the following specifications of marginal utility, satiation volume and cost functions

$$\begin{aligned} w(q,t,y) &= 2w_o\{1 - q/Q(t,y)\} \quad q \leq Q(t,y) \quad (15) \\ &= 0 \qquad\qquad\qquad\quad q > Q(t,y) \end{aligned}$$

where $Q(t,y) = 2T y(2 - y)(1 - t), \qquad (16)$

and $C(q) = k + cq. \qquad (17)$

The parameter w_o is the average willingness to pay per unit for all customer types and network sizes, while T may be interpreted as the average volume per subscriber that would be sent in a free maximal network $(y=1)$.

From condition (10) we obtain in this case

$$q^*(t,y) = 2T\gamma(2 - y)y(1 - t)^2 \qquad (18)$$

where $\gamma = (1 - c/2 w_o) . \qquad (19)$

After some laborious algebra, this leads to

$$\begin{aligned} R(q) = (w_o/3)\{6q &- 4[(1-y)\gamma/Q(y,y)]^{1/2}q^{3/2} \\ &+ \gamma^2(1 - y)^2Q(y,y)\}. \qquad (20) \end{aligned}$$

The optimal network size y^* is determined from (13) which can be reduced in this case to the polynomial equation.

$$(1 - y)y(12 - 15y + 5y^2)/6 = k/4\gamma^2 T w_0. \qquad (21)$$

Finally, the critical mass level y_c corresponding to y^* is obtained from the breakeven condition

$$R^*(q^*(y_c,y_c)) = W(q^*(y_c,y_c),y_c,y_c) , \qquad (22)$$

where $R^*(q)$ is given by (20) with $y = y^*$. In this particular example one can show (see {8}) that (22) is satisfied if and only if

$$Q(y_c,y_c) = Q(y^*,y^*) , \qquad (23)$$

from which y_c can be easily determined.

A comparison of these results with those obtained in {8} for the flat rate and two part tariffs (using the same specifications) reveals several distinct advantages for nonlinear pricing.

We demonstrate these observations below in the context of an actual case study {1} sponsored by the National Telecommunication and Information Administration (NTIA) to examine the commercial feasibility of a nationwide communication system for the hearing impaired at a cost comparable to telephone rates. The system under consideration conceived at SRI International is based on regional nodes interconnected nationwide through a Value Added Network (VAN), such as GTE Telenet, for example. Each of these nodes contains computer facilities that multiplex the subscribers' terminals, providing them timeshared access to the VAN. A small scale network (DEAFNET) based on this principle was already built, establishing its technological feasibility. The goal of the economic analysis was to obtain rough estimates of profitability, social benefit, critical mass and typical charges under various tariff structures. The analysis was based on the following inputs assumptions.

• The potential market (maximal network size) is two million subscribers consisting of the deaf population, their relatives, friends, and concerned institutions.

• Willingness to pay for the services, (w_0), averaged over all potential subscribers, is assumed to be 20 cents per call, in addition to any charges for the terminal and for the basic telephone connection.

• Average potential usage in a maximal network, (T), is 200 calls per month per subscriber, assuming free usage. This is close to the current calling rate (local plus long distance) of the average telephone subscriber in the U.S. today.

• Provision cost per subscriber (k) is assumed to be $8.00 per month. This is an optimistic estimate based on projected low cost of computer technology. The cost was assumed to be insensitive to usage which is quite realistic once the network is set up (similar calculations for $k = 20.00 are given in {1}).

The table below summarizes the analysis results corresponding to the above inputs. These numbers should be viewed as a preliminary analysis of economic feasibility rather than a financial analysis in a business sense. A more complete analysis of profit and loss potential would include tax considerations, startup financing cost and many other factors.

Economic Analysis of a Telecommunication
Network for the Hearing Impaired

| | Tariff Structure | | |
	Flat Rate	Two Part	Non-linear
Equil. Network Size	1.14M	1.46M	1.76M
Critical Mass	0.58M	0.32M	0.13M
Mo. Subscription Fee	$28.16	$ 8.00	$ 0.08
Avg. Mo. Usage Payment	-0-	$21.92	$29.19
Avg. Mo. Calls/Sub.	232	148	150
Total Call Volume/Yr.	3.17B	2.59B	3.17B
Total System Costs/Yr.	$ 109M	$ 140M	$ 169M
Total Revenues/Yr.	$ 385M	$ 524M	$ 618M
Total Net Revenue/Yr.	276M	384M	449M
Total Cons. Surplus/Yr.	253M	$ 192M	$ 157M
Total Surplus/Yr.	$ 529M	$ 576M	$ 606M

Notes: M = Million; B = Billion.

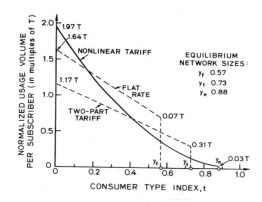

Fig. 4. Usage Distribution by Type of Subscribers.

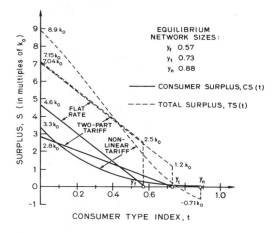

Fig. 5. Total Surplus and Consumer Surplus by Type of Subscriber.

Figs. 4 and 5 illustrate the volume, consumer surplus and net revenue distributions by customer type. An interesting feature of the surplus distribution for the nonlinear tariff is the fact that an entire segment of subscribers at the low end of the market are subsidized by the supplier. This is optimal since the increased revenues from the other subscribers who communicate with those subsidized, more than cover the subsidy and result in increased profit. This does not occur in this example for two part or flat rate tariffs. In general, however, such a subsidy is possible with two part tariffs.

8. CONCLUSIONS

The tabulated figures in the previous section reflect the specific assumptions and specifications used in deriving them. Nevertheless, the comparison of the different tariff structures reveals a fundamental relationship that one expects to find in a more general setting as well. The major difference between the three tariffs considered, lies in the relative allocation of consumer charges among subscription and usage fees. The nonlinear tariff, which consists mostly of usage charges, reduces total consumer surplus but increases supplier's profits and is more efficient in the sense that it increases social welfare. It provides an incentive to the supplier to lower the subcription fee thus making the network more affordable. Thus, it yields a larger network size and than either the flat rate or two part tariffs, and a smaller critical mass, which eases the start up of a new network.

REFERENCES

{1} Allen, D. S., E. J. Craighill, S. S. Oren, C. L. Jackson, S. H. Russell, H. L. Huntley, and J. Wilson, "A Nationwide Communication System for the Hearing Impaired: Strategies Toward Commercial Implementation," SRI International, Final Report, Project 3288 (October 1981).

{2} Artle, R. and C. Averous, "The Telephone System as a Public Good: Static and Dynamic Aspects," The Bell Journal of Economics and Management Science, Vol. 4, No. 1 (Spring 1975), pp. 89-100.

{3} Goldman, M. B., H. E. Leland and D. S. Sibley, "Optimal Nonuniform Pricing," Bell Laboratories Economic Discussion Paper #100, May 1977.

{4} Littlechild, S. C., "Two Part Tariffs and Consumption Externalities," The Bell Journal of Economics and Management Science, Vol. 6, No. 2 (Autumn 1975), pp. 661-670.

{5} Mirman, 1. J. and D. Sibley, "Optimal Nonlinear Prices for Multiproduct Monopolies," Bell Journal of Economics, Vol. 12, No. 1, pp. 659-670, 1981.

{6} Oren, S. S., S. A. Smith and R. B. Wilson, "Nonlinear Tariffs in Markets with Interdependent Demand," PIP Report No. 37 (November 81) Engineering-Economic Systems Department, Stanford University, Stanford, California 94305.

{7} Oren, S. S., S. A. Smith, and R. B. Wilson, "Competitive Nonlinear Tariffs" (to appear in Journal of Economic Theory).

{8} Oren, S. S. and S. A. Smith, "Critical Mass and Tariff Structure in Electronic Communications Markets," The Bell Journal of Economics Vol. 12, No. 2 (Autumn 1981), pp. 467-487.

{9} Rohlfs, J., "A Theory of Interdependent Demand for a Communication Service," The Bell Journal of Economics and Management Science, Vol. 5, No. 1 (Spring 1974), pp. 16-37.

{10} Spence, M., "Nonlinear Prices and Welfare," Journal of Public Economics, 8 (January 1977), pp. 1-18.

{11} Squire, L., "Some Aspects of Optimal Pricing for Telecommunications," The Bell Journal of Economics and Management Science Vol. 4, No. 2 (Autumn 1973), pp. 515-525.

{12} Willig, R. D., "Pareto-Superior Nonlinear Outlay Schedules," Bell Journal of Economics, Vol. 9, No. 1 (Spring 1978), pp. 5-69.

Shmuel S. Oren received his B.S. in Mechanical Engineering in 1965 and an M.Sc. in Materials Engineering in 1969, both from the Technion, Haifa, Israel, and an M.S. and Ph.D. in Engineering-Economic Systems from Stanford University in 1972. From 1972-1980 he was a research scientist at the Xerox Palo Alto Research Center and a consulting faculty at Stanford University. Since 1980 he has been Associate Professor of Engineering-Economic Systems at Stanford. His research interests include optimization, mathematical modeling, technology economics, marketing models and pricing policies. His articles appeared in a variety of journals relating to optimization theory, operations research, systems analysis and economics. He has been a consultant to Xerox Corporation, SRI International and Applied Decision Analysis, Inc. He is a member of TIMS, ORSA, IEEE and the Mathematical Programming Society.

Stephen A. Smith received a B.S. from the University of Cincinnati and an M.S. from Stevens Institute of Technology, both in mathematics, and a Ph.D. in Engineering-Economic Systems from Stanford University. He is currently a Research Scientist at the Xerox Palo Alto Research Center and worked previously at Bell Laboratories as a Member of Technical Staff. His recent research has focused on economic analysis of new communications and information systems technologies, as well as logistics systems modeling. His publications have appeared in a variety of journals in the areas of operations research and economics. He is a member of TIMS, ORSA and the ACM.

The Contribution of Communication and Information Systems to Economic Productivity

C Jonscher, A Balkanski
Communications Studies and
Planning International, USA

Expenditure by the public and private sectors on communications infrastructure and data processing technology is accounting for a large and growing proportion of industrial capital outlays in advanced economies (Jonscher, 1981). Investment in telecommunications and information systems has a wide ranging set of impacts on the national economy. However the effect of greatest significance is the potential improvement investment offers in the productivity or efficiency of economic activity. In this paper we survey some of the evidence available on the benefits which communication and information services can bring to business users.

THE INFORMATION SECTOR OF THE ECONOMY

One of the most striking structural changes observed in industrialised economies over the course of this century has been the shift in the use of human and material resources from the tasks of processing material goods to those of processing information. On the basis of occupational statistics we can identify those individuals whose function is primarily to create, process and handle information rather than physical goods; we will refer to these as information workers. Examples of information workers are administrators, clerks, secretaries, bankers, brokers, lawyers and teachers; the definition corresponds, broadly speaking, to that of 'white collar' occupations. The proportion of the United States labour force accounted for by information workers has risen from less than 18% in the year 1900 to 50.9% in 1979 (Jonscher, 1982a).

Several studies of the size of the information work force have been conducted in the past 20 years.[1] The general conclusion emerging is that about half of all economic activity in the United States can be attributed to the processing of knowledge or facts rather than of physical goods, and that proportion is increasing through time. Studies in several other countries, in particular in the United Kingdom, confirm a consistent pattern of growth in this information-handling sector of the economy.

We refer to this tendency for economic resources to be switched from the traditional productive activities of industrial and agricultural workers to the primarily office-based information-processing activities as the increasing information-intensiveness of societies. It has important implications for the structure and productivity of business organisations, and for the scope for introducing information handling technologies into the economy.

Several hypotheses have been put forward to account for the observed growth in white collar or information-handling occupations at the expense of industrialised jobs. Among the popular explanations are: (i) that the number of scientific and technical experts has increased in line with the increasing technological sophistication of industrial processes, (ii) that the consumption patterns have changed in favour of information-type services such as education, entertainment and the media, and (iii) that the government, largely an information-handling organisation, has grown relative to the economy as a whole. While these factors have contributed to a limited extent to the growth of information occupations, quantitative analysis reveals that they only account for a small part – about one-fifth – of the change in the size of the information sector. The large majority of information or white collar workers are employed in occupations which <u>organise</u>, <u>co-ordinate</u> or <u>manage</u> the functioning of the economy.

It is because the information sector has this organising or co-ordinating role that it is difficult to measure directly its contribution to overall economic productivity. A productivity measure must take account of the effect of information handling activities on the performance of the remaining (non-information) sector of the economy. A rudimentary indication of the relationship between information sector growth is given in figure 1, which covers selected industrial countries over the period 1950-1970. The countries have experienced substantially different patterns of growth of white collar occupations during the past few decades, the rate of change being highest in France and lowest in Canada. The dotted line of the graph shows the relationship between information sector growth (as measured by the proportion of information workers in the economy) and overall productivity growth. The points corresponding to actual values of the two variables under study show a clear (if not high) correlation between the two variables.

The observed relationship is consistent with the hypothesis that technological development brings with it the need for a more extensive information handling capability in the economy.[2]

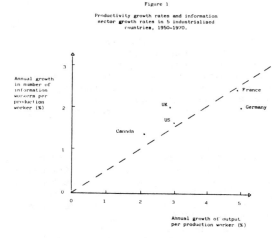

Figure 1

Productivity growth rates and information sector growth rates in 5 industrialised countries, 1950-1970.

Source: Jonscher, 1982b.

THE PRODUCTIVITY BENEFITS OF TELECOMMUNICATIONS SYSTEMS

Whereas broad empirical correlations between information-handling capability and economic output can be identified through micro-economic data such as that presented above, an understanding of the contribution to productivity of specific communication and information systems can only be obtained through detailed micro-electronic research. A programme of studies of this kind is being carried out by a research team (which includes the authors of this paper) at Communications Studies and Planning International Inc (CSP International). The studies are being funded by the International Telecommunications Union and selected other national and international authorities. Their objective is to obtain a more precise and thorough understanding than is available todate of the magnitude of economic efficiency gains which can be obtained through the introduction of more extensive telecommunications facilities.

The models on which these studies are based identify several specific mechanisms through which access to improved telecommunications services can increase the efficiency of private or public sector organisations. While each of the models addresses a different specific example of the application of telecommunications service to business activity, they are all based on the idea that information is a necessary input to economic processes and that communication services enhance the ability of organisations to obtain and transmit information.

Although the models are not exhaustive, they cover many of the situations where a linkage exists between the quality or availability of telecommunications service and the efficiency of economic processes. The types of impacts analysed in our surveys are:

1 Benefits of Business Expansion

Since most industrial processes are characterised by economies of scale in production, the ability to expand output in short run due to improved telecommunication services (and hence improved access to customers, suppliers, or other producers) results in lower unit costs and greater efficiency. Our model of this effect is based on the assumption that most businesses face approximately constant long-run marginal costs.

2 Saving of Managerial Time

There are numerous ways in which access to improved telecommunications services can result in more efficient use of managerial time. Meetings can be held and scheduled more effectively (or indeed replaced by teleconferences), and information relevant to managerial decisions can be obtained more effectively. The benefits obtained through managerial time savings are modelled by taking account of salary and related overhead costs.

3 Saving of Labour Time

The lack of appropriate telecommunications facilities frequently results in wastage of extra labour time such as that of messengers, drivers, and even guards (where security levels are low due to lack of contact with the police). Our model treats the effect in essentially the same way as for managerial time, bearing in mind that the costs involved are lower since a substantial supply of unskilled labour is usually available in the economy.

4 Reduction of Inventory Levels

Higher overall inventory costs are incurred since lack of information forces firms to keep higher stocks (inventories). Our model allows the quantification of this effect by defining a 'safety-stock' level as a function of the level of information available. Improved telecommunications result in a shorter re-ordering delay, hence lower the required level of the 'safety-stock'.

5 Reduction in Production Stoppages

Our model keeps track of the high short-term marginal costs incurred as a result of production stoppages due to machine breakdown, parts shortage, raw material deficiency, or other reasons. Communication problems add to the time elapsed before re-start.

6 Enhanced Transportation Scheduling

Loss of time occurs when destinations are not informed of that timing of vehicle movement. Failure to optimally dispatch vehicles is also measured. The magnitude of these two effects is calculated as they arise in each individual organisation surveyed in the studies.

7 Improved Purchasing Decisions

Telecommunications are crucial to rapid transfer of price information. The problem becomes particularly acute when the purchase need is urgent. Our model attributes a value to added information; we derive a 'price penalty' incurred by lack of information.

8 Increase in Selling Price

The reverse process, seeking out the highest possible selling price, is also assessed. We model this process in the same way as purchasing decisions. The ability to increase selling price is especially important in the case of agricultural exports where access to good price information is essential for the marketing of perishable commodities subject to swings in supply levels.

9 Reductions in Distribution Costs

Telecommunications services are a major part of distribution costs; their quality and availability influences freight handling charges, transport companies' fees, vehicle fleet scheduling and other cost factors. The mechanisms by which these additional costs ariose are varied, and ad hoc methods must be developed to suit each case as it arises.

While the use of these 9 categories to clarify efficiency gains imposes some limitations on the range of impacts measured, it has the effect of introducing a clear and systematic structure to the benefit/cost analysis of communications services. The survey team has found it useful to base its field research on these and closely related categories, adding to the list where necessary to take account of significant impacts which would not otherwise be covered. Initial results of benefit/cost analyses based on this framework are reported in the next section.

RESULTS OF A CASE STUDY: KENYA

The first in the series of studies referenced above has recently been completed (CSP International, 1982); it covered 9 industries in Kenya. As the study was intended to serve only as a pilot test for the methodology, only one business enterprise was selected for detailed analysis within each industry.

The aim of the project was to assess the amount by which each firm would benefit, in terms of net income, if the telephone and telex services were adequate to cope with all demands for exchange lines and calls. These estimated gains are compared with the estimated cost of upgrading the service to each firm to the required level. The cost estimates were based on the average cost, per line and per call, of providing telecommunications services nationwide.

The results of the survey and analysis are summarised in figures 2 and 3. Figure 2 indicates the magnitude of potential benefit which each firm would obtain in each of the 9 categories listed in the previous section. The benefit is expressed as a percentage of gross company revenues. The results show that in each category, except in the case of inventory cost savings, a significant gain (equal to 0.1% or more of revenues) would be obtained by one or more firms. The total benefit to a firm would average about 5% of gross revenues, a proportion comparable to the net profit margin of the enterprise.

Figure 3 compares these gains to the cost of providing the additional telecommunications facilities. The costs are assessed on a national average basis, in accordance with conventional telecommunications authority costing practices. Figure 3 shows that the economic gains identified in the study exceed the costs by factors ranging from 10 to 300; the average potential gain was over 100 times the cost of providing the corresponding increase in telecommunications capacity.

The gains identified by the study are described as potential rather than actual, and thus the improvement of telecommunications facilities is a necessary but not sufficient condition for the realisation of these economic gains. In practice, we would expect benefit-cost ratios to be rather lower than those described in the study. Nevertheless, the margin between potential benefits and costs of telecommunication improvements is so large that even a serious failure to exploit the potential gains would not change the qualitative nature of the study findings.

CONCLUDING COMMENTS

The above results form part of an increasing body of evidence that indicates the extent of private and public benefits which can be obtained through the introduction and information technologies in both industrialised and developing countries. The rise in the proportion of economic activity accounted for by information-related functions, as reported earlier in this paper, further emphasises the need to use these technologies as a means of improving productivity levels.

Yet despite the availability of concrete evidence of this kind, productivity growth in the information sector has remained disappointingly low.

FIGURE 2

EFFICIENCY GAINS FROM IMPROVED TELECOMMUNICATIONS SERVICE:
SUMMARY OF KENYA CASE STUDY

Figures indicate magnitude of benefit as a percentage of
gross enterprise revenues

Industry	Business Expansion	Sales Price Effects	Purchase Price Effects	Inven-tory Costs	Vehicle Use	Production Stoppages	Distri-bution Costs	Labour Time	Managerial Time	TOTAL
Food Processing	5.8	–	0.1	–	0.1	0.2	–	–	0.2	6.3
Industrial distribution	2.5	1.0	–	–	–	–	0.7	0.1	0.5	4.8
Horticultural export	3.6	0.4	–	–	–	–	–	–	–	4.1
Nurseries	3.5	–	–	–	0.2	–	–	–	0.5	4.2
Hotel	2.0	–	–	–	0.1	–	0.4	0.1	0.3	2.9
Freight Transport	0.6	2.5	1.4	–	–	–	0.6	–	0.5	5.6
Travel Agency	–	–	–	–	–	–	–	7.3	–	7.3
Newspaper	6.8	–	–	–	–	–	1.2	0.6	0.5	9.2
Household Products	0.7	–	0.3	–	–	0.1	0.1	–	–	1.3
Simple Average	2.8	0.4	0.2	0	0.1	0	0.3	0.9	0.3	5.1

* Totals may not agree because of rounding

** – means less than 0.05%

FIGURE 3
SUMMARY OF BENEFIT-COST RATIOS IN KENYA CASE STUDY

Figures are expressed in Kenya
Shillings per year

Industry	A* Total Benefits	B Total Costs	A/B Benefit-cost Ratio
Food Processing	4,417,900	14,760	299.3
Industrial Distribu-tion	2,390,000	17,080	139.9
Horticultural Export	2,627,500	31,460	83.5
Nurseries	27,400	2,560	10.7
Hotel	870,000	13,480	64.5
Freight Transport	5,565,000	57,900	96.1
Travel Agency	275,400	2,320	118.7
Newspaper	6,035,600	31,060	194.3
Household Products	11,930,000	125,460	95.1
TOTAL	34,128,800	296,080	115.3

Only those benefits greater than 0.05% of revenue
are included.

Michael Tyler (1980) discusses the various factors which may have brought this about. He suggests that the low growth rate of productivity in the information-handling sector is not inevitable, but rather is a consequence of specific inter-related factors: lack of technological innovation, behavioural factors, and institutional economic factors.

Tyler convincingly explains that the lack of innovation does not result from a lack of invention.

Technical developments have made available service options - for example, electronic mail, teleconferencing, facsimile systems, and advanced methods of document storage and retrieval - which can yield large savings in cost and staff time. Yet, while some of these innovations have been known for at least 10 years, they are not at present widely used. In fact, most office workers have yet to assimilate into their everyday working environment any innovation more advanced than the electric typewriter or perhaps the stand-alone word processing typewriter.

The causes of such a lag in innovation must therefore be found in the remaining 2 factors. The new technologies call for a high degree of change in patterns of behaviour. For example, teleconferencing, in at least some of its applications, gains its economic benefits from persuading managers to substitute tele-communications for part of their travelling. And text processing involves many kinds of changes in the social organisation of typing and document preparation, including interaction between the typist and the author. The complexity and overall poor understanding of these behavioural factors certainly constitutes a barrier to innovation.

Similarly, the economy has a long history of investment in machinery to support production workers, but it has no such tradition in the case of information workers. Corporation and public agencies are not normally accustomed to place a substantial proportion of their total purchases of capital goods in the information area.

These institutional economic factors constitute a further resistance to a greater penetration of information processing tools and equipment.

[1] Fritz Machlup (1962) was the first to attempt to measure the extent of both labour and non-labour resources allocated to the creation and processing of knowledge as opposed to other kinds of products; studies of a similar kind have subsequently been carried out by Peter Drucker (1968). Daniel Bell (1973), Marc Porat (1977), and again by Machlup (1980).

[2] This interpretation of the data is discussed in detail in other papers; see Jonscher, 1982a and 1982b.

REFERENCES

1 Balkanski A. "Modelling benefits of tele-communications." Proceedings of the Tenth Annual Conference on Telecommunications Research Policy (Annapolis, Md 1982).

2 Bell Daniel. The Coming of Post-Industrial Society. New York: Basic Books, 1973.

3 CSP International. "The Impact of Telecommunications on the Performance of a Sample of Business Enterprises in Kenya." A Research Report to the International Telecommunications Union. New York, 1982.

4 Drucker P. The Age of Discontinuity. New York: Harper and Row, 1968.

5 Jonscher C M. "The Economic Role of Telecommunications", in Moss M (ed), Telecommunications and Productivity, Reading, Mass: Addison Wesley, 1981.

6 Jonscher C M. "Productivity Change and the Growth of Information Processing Requirements in the Economy: Theory and Empirical Analysis." Industrial Organisation Seminar Series, Harvard University, Cambridge MA, 1982a.

7 Jonscher C M. "Economic Causes of the Rising Information Intensiveness of Industrial Societies." Seminar to the Massachusetts Institute of Technology, Department of Political Science, 1982b.

8 Machlup F. The Production and Distribution of Knowledge in the United States. Princeton, NJ: Princeton University Press, 1962.

9 Machlup F. Knowledge: Its Location, Distribution and Economic Significance. Princeton, NJ: Princeton University Press, 1980.

10 Porat M. The Information Economy: Definition and Measurement. OT special publication 77-12. Washington DC: US Department of Commerce, 1977.

11 Tyler M. "Telecommunications and Productivity: The Need and the Opportunity." Pp 1-51 in Telecommunications and Productivity. Reading, MA: Addison-Wesley Publishing Company, 1981.

Computer Communications for an International Rescue System

R J Fairhurst
Europ Assistance, UK

The Europ Assistance Group provides medical and technical assistance on a World Wide basis for the Nationals of 12 countries. From its formation in 1963 Europ Assistance built up a vast amount of information relating to all countries of the world. The system handling this is the Geisco Mark III network. The purpose of the paper is to describe the development of the system, the facilities offered and their application to International Medical Rescue with its urgent requirement for accurate and up to date information to allow the safe transport of gravely ill patients on air ambulance flights. It also shows the application of the data in the efficient resolution of less severe medical problems. Further developments of the system including its use for communication between companies of the group and its agents are discussed.

INTRODUCTION

The use of computers and particularly computer communications in medicine is a controversial subject. (1) There are fears that one of our most prized priviliges, the confidential consultation with our patients will be jeopardized. In spite of this there have been many applications of computer techniques to our professional work, particularly in the field of non medical patient records including billing, appointments and recall systems. (2) This paper describes the use of a Computer Communications Network by the Europ Assistance Group in order to provide its Assistance Coordinators and Medical Controllers with the logistic information to enable them to make rational decisions about patient care and transport.

EUROP ASSISTANCE

The Europ Assistance Group provides medical and technical assistance on a World Wide basis for the Nationals of 12 countries. The Group has 600 full time employees and a network of retained agents in 150 countries. Each year more than 7,000,000 subscribe to the service giving rise to 30,000 medical and 50,000 technical cases. Each National Company maintains a 24 hour operations centre dealing with its own subscribers. The group was formed in France in 1963, before then International Rescue of Civilians had been arranged on an ad hoc basis with little expertise in medical transport over long distances and the idea of medical liaison and control was unknown. Patients were treated in the hospitals to which they were admitted, with the locally available facilities. It was most unusual for a patient to be transferred to a more specialist unit. Central to our philosophy is the belief that when people are ill and injured abroad the whole of the treatment must be monitored by physicians, and particularly decisions regarding transport must be taken by them. (3) Since 1963 the demand for international rescue has steadily grown. This growth has been due to two main factors. One

the vast increase in foreign travel made possible by the development of cheap international mass transportation systems, and secondly an awareness on the part of travellers that it is no longer necessary to accept the treatment offered at the site of the incident but that long distance medical repatriation can be safely undertaken. In regard to each case the need for transport arises from a combination of three problems.

1. A lack of medical technology and expertise appropriate to the patients condition at the site of the incident.

2. Differences in the patients expectation of medical care and the locally delivered care. It should be remembered that there is no international uniform system of medicine and that doctors in different countries can follow very different routes to arrive at the same clinical diagnosis.

3. Communications in a foreign society can cause many problems, most obviously when the doctor and nurses speak a different language to that of the patient but simple separation from ones home base and friends often cause severe difficulties.

The Service is based on a subscription which provides for complete medical care backed by an insurance policy. The subscription must be taken out prior to travelling. Subscribers are encouraged to contact the operations centre of their own national company as soon as possible following illness or injury. They are provided with documentary and personal identification to allow contact by third parties in the event of a subscriber being too ill to act in his own right. On each case a file is opened and a dossier of information built up. The medical data is handled by doctors and decisions on the repatriation are taken by these physicians. They consult with their colleagues abroad and in their home country so as to arrange transport for the patient at the optimum time in the optimum conditions. If they feel a lack of information they will inform our agents abroad who may visit the patient and may also obtain medical reports locally. Often the agents abroad may have to arrange primary medical care and we must be aware of the local facilities and their potentials. In some countries we have trained local doctors the techniques of rescue and provided them with specialised medical equipment to allow them to deliver efficient primary care. We believe to transport a patient is a therapeutic procedure which should be prescribed just as carefully and precisely as any other part of medical treatment. The doctor taking the transport decision must be aware not only of the patients likely medical problems but also the transport enviornment and aerospace medicine. (4) He must know and have confidence in his colleagues who carry out the repatriation and understand the limits of any aircraft and medical equipment they may use. This means that in practice the medical controller is also an active member of the repatriation.

THE NEED

By 1978 the Europ Assistance Group activity had produced vast quantities of data on many countries of the world relating to their facilities, ease of access to local services, and of particular idiosyncrasies regarding to operating International Medical Rescue at various locations. The different companies within the group collected different amounts of data and the quality was very variable. There had been many attempts to logically arrange it in operational manuals, guides and lately in microfilm but its rapid and precise application to any particular case was becoming difficult. A study of the problem suggested that a computer based information system had great potential, both for the storage and classification of the data which had already been gathered and to provide a framework for the gathering and classification of future data. The needs of the group were carefully analysed and requirements defined, inclusive 24 hours access for information and modification, access as widely spread throughout the world as possible, 'user friendliness', and a reasonable financial cost. The 'user friendliness' was particularly important because if the system was going to provide the sort of help which we envisage it must be possible for

all our operational staff and eventually agents to be able to use it with very little training.

THE SYSTEM

The final system chosen was the Geisco Mark III, based on Honeywell level 66 machines. The machines operate out of three 'super centre' in Amsterdam, Rockville Maryland and Cleveland Ohio. The centres are linked by a satellite communications network and there is direct access in 32 countries of the world with access via the international telephone and telex network from virtually any country providing its internal system will allow for the speed of the data transmissions. A particular attraction of the system was the fact that with a simple terminal and modem it was easy and cheap to provide access, indeed with the new portable terminals and acoustic couplers almost any telephone can provide access to the system. The system is controlled through our International Relations Department in Paris. They were responsible initially for the development and classification of the original data base. The first major problem involved the language to be used for the display. As a company Europ Assistance has a French parent but it operates in French, English, German, Italian and Spanish. After much discussion it was decided that the base line information should be in French, but that any information put on from national countries in the group would be put on in their own language. The system has nine programmes broken down into two main groups. (5)

1. Programmes giving precise details of services which can be applied to any particular medical case.

SOS2 is the data base programme for France, it was the pilot programme and still contains the most complete information. There is a list of 9,000 towns in France. It is accessed by knowing the geographical department within France followed by the first three letters of the towns name, (table 1). On each town there is an index of 16 specific suppliers, these are airports, ambulances, clinics, garages, stations, hospitals, car hire, doctors, medical emergency service, rail parcel service,

Table 1
Town Access for Grenoble

```
ENTREZ: UNE VILLE (EX:7SPAR) - UN SERVICE (EX:AM99123) - STOP OU BYE
--->?38GRE


   *  38185  GRENOBLE
   ALT 0214M    E   5 ATLAS
   CHAMBERY              058 KMS
   LYON                 104 KMS

   *  38186  GRESSE EN VERCORS
   ALT 1205M    E   6 ATLAS
   CLELLES              019 KMS
   GRENOBLE             047 KMS
```

taxis, travel agents, lawyers, funeral directors, pharmacists and diverse. If in a small town there is no example of a particular supplier an alternative supplier within 20km. is shown. (table 2). Diverse file will eventually be re-classified but is used to build up new sources of information, and on some cities such as Paris the quantity of information stored under diverse is vast.

INTER provides access to four files of general information on each country in the World. These are KNOW HOW providing general administrative details of the country, Correspondants giving details of our own agents within the country, Access giving the immigration conditions of the country, and Diplomatic showing the local Embassies and Consulates. These last two are interesting in that they are interactive in that the information given is that which is relevant to the country requesting it not to the whole group as in other files. Recently the INTER programme has begun to be expanded towards the level of the SOS2 and it is now possible to obtain files on suppliers of services town by town exactly the same way as France. At the moment the information is being completed for Belgium, the United Kingdom, Algeria, Italy, Spain, Tunisia and Morocco. Gradually it will be extended firstly to cover Europe and North Africa and then to any relevant countries in the world where we have a large traffic. (table 3)

2. Co-ordination Group Programmes

This group contains information which is useful administratively to the Assistance Co-ordinators in relation to cases but is not of geographical nature. Programmes in this group are as follows:

INFO is a daily updating of news of importance within the Europ Assistance group, such as new contacts, changes in agents abroad, management meetings and problems of a general nature which might well effect cases such as industrial disputes, communication breakdowns and war zones etc. (table 4)

PRODUIT list the different types of contracts sold by the Europ Assistance group and having chosen the contract by name particular details of it can be extracted including the member of management responsible for servicing that particular contract.

INSOC lists the large international companies who have service arrangements with Europ Assistance to provide care for their employees. It allows us to identify any places in the world where they have large groups of employees and who in those areas is responsible for administratively dealing with Europ Assistance.

APEL is of particular interest to my own profession in that it gives the availability of doctors and nurses to our operations department on a day to day basis. Inevitably we employ many of our medical staff on part time contracts and this file which is updated on a day by day basis shows exactly who is available for work.

DA1 VOL and INTERO are a series of related programmes in which the individual patient file perameters are registered including the medical diagnosis coded according to the international disease code, related to the programme VOL which shows the details of any medical

Table 2
SOS2 Airports for Grenoble

```
ENTREZ: UNE VILLE (EX:75PAR) - UN SERVICE (EX:AM39123) - STOP OU BYE
--->?AE38185


*   381851    040 KMS

GRENOBLE ST GEOIRS   40 KMS   W      TEL.(16) 76 057133 AEROGARE
DOUANES           HJ  HORAIRES HJ
PISTES    DUR   3050M *    45      HERBE      M *
TYPE MILITAIRE   04   OBS.CIVIL TEL.TOUR DE CONTROL:934049
CIE-AER.     PASSAGERS       FRET        CIE-AER.     PASSAGERS         FRET
IT          934055         934055        LP          934372         934372

*   691231    066 KMS

LYON SATOLAS   26 KMS   ESE    TEL.(16) 78 719505 719221
DOUANES              HORAIRES H24
PISTES 1 DUR   4000M *    45      HERBE      M *
TYPE INTERNATIONAL       OBS.
CIE-AER.     PASSAGERS       FRET        CIE-AER.     PASSAGERS         FRET
AH          719502                       LP          719514
AF          719620         719656        IT          719709         719759
AZ          719503                       JU          719507
KL          719861                       LO          719532
SK          719433                       IJ          719430         719863
TU          719501                       UT          719565
SB                         719850        SR                         719856
```

```
                              Table 3
                         INTER Agent in Zambia

ENTER : SOS2,INTER,INFO,MODLIS,PRODUIT,TOWN,INTMAJ OR BYE?INTER

enter: country-service (BXKH) or country-town (4 letters) (BXMADR)?FWCO


==>FW.CO.0000.00


**
    ZAMBIE - LUS
    ************
    LE 28 JANVIER 1982
    .
    JOINTAIR
    P.O.BOX.CH 300
    LUSAKA - ZAMBIE
    .
    GMT.: +2
    .
    HORAIRES :
    .
    .
    TEL.: (MAN.260) 271066   271347
    TLX.: (090200) 40410 ZA JETAIR
    .
    ASSISTANCES :
    * MRS. I. GAUT * 252137 * RESP. ASSISTANCES *
    .
    OBSERVATIONS
    * 1 SUPER KING AIR 200 ET PA 31 - UNE EQUIPE MEDICALE PEUT ETRE
    . FOURNIE PAR LA MINBANK CLINIC
    .
    * CONTACTS MEDICAUX : MINBANK CLINIC - DR. M.BUSH - CAIRO ROAD - LUSAKA
    . TEL.: (MAN.260) 212612 - 216983
    .
    * LES PILOTES ET LE PERSONNEL DE JOINTAIR ONT ETE INFORMES SUR E.A
    . ET PEUVENT ETRE JOINTS PAR "RADIOPAGING".

                              Table 4
                         INFO News for 30/4/82


DOCUMENTATION INTERNATIONALE
****************************

** MJCO : 30.04 **
   ---> VOUS POUVEZ Y CONSULTER LA LISTE DES DERNIERES MISES A JOUR ...


>>> MR TMIRI (CASABLANCA) A DESORMAIS UN NO DE TEL.PERSONNEL
    CONSULTER INTER (DR9999)

>>> NOUVEAU CORRESPONDANT A LA TRINITE (ANTILLES BRITANNIQUES) :
    LA STE : SIMPAUL'S TRAVEL SERVICE
    CE CORRESPONDANT INTERVIENT A LA TRINITE TOBAGO ET GRENADE.
    CONSULTER INTER (FHCO).

>>> LES 1.2.3 MAI SONT FERIES EN GRECE.

>>> ON NOUS SIGNALE QUE POUR UNE MISE A DISPOSITION DE BILLETS A ABIDJAN
    (COTE D'IVOIRE) IL FAUT PASSER PAR AIR AFRIQUE ET NON PAR UTA LES
    JOURS FERIES.

>>> INDTRAVELS NOUS A COMMUNIQUE LES DATES AUXQUELLES SES AGENCES
    LOCALES SERONT FERMEES EN 1982 EN RAISON DE FETES REGIONALES :
    CONSULTER INTER (DRCO0000)

>>> LE CONTRAT AVEC LE MEXIQUE EST EN COURS DE RENEGOCIATIONS.
    DANS L'IMMEDIAT - EXIMTUR N'ETANT JOIGNABLE QU'AUX HEURES D'OUVERTUR
E
    DU BUREAU - EN CAS DE PB. SUFFISAMMENT SERIEUX ON PEUT CONTACTER
    MME FONTAINE (STE HESNAULT) DONT VOUS TROUVEREZ LES COORDONNEES
    DANS INTER (DWCO).
```

transports which are undertaken the same way as an airport departure board and relate again to the INTERO programme which provides the recall of the dossier and transport data for research purposes. In 1981 the companies of the group requested information from the system on 51,862 occasions.

THE FUTURE

The future development includes a rapid completion of the geographical data base on a town by town programme and to proceed with a refinement of the DA1 VOL and INTERO programmes. This will provide very useful statistical information, not only of a medical nature but also of a financial one enabling a close analysis to be kept of the costs of individual cases, and a compilation of costs across the board which help in negotiating with transport companies. As the agents receive access to the computer they will be able to modify their own entries very easily to make sure the information is up to date. They could easily record temporary alternative telephone numbers, or temporary changes in their own administrative arrangements. The system could also provide direct communication for non urgent messages providing that a suitable discipline is developed the systematic recovery of the messages. Eventually we hope the system will become so comprehensive that every decision made by the Europ Assistance Doctors or Assistance Co-ordinators will only be made after access to the computer and that the results of that decision will be recorded on the computer changing the data base. We are very aware that it is vital to keep the information stored on the system is as up to date as possible, it can only be achieved by having an interactive system in which anyone who requires information can also modify information. At this relatively early stage in its development we are very impressed with the flexibility which the computer offers us in providing us with a background of information to help our patients. This information provides choices regarding transport and treatment which might not have been recognized otherwise and could have a great influence for good on the patients ultimate chance of recovery. We see the computer not as a simple extension of our operation manuals and books but as a very useful and practical instrument for the treatment of our patients medical condition.

REFERENCES

(1) Thomas, M., 'Handbook of Medical Ethics' British Medical Association 1982.
(2) McClarkson, D.G., Gray, R.H., Jones, D.H.A., Smith, P.H.S., Jones, I.W., Microcomputer System in an Accident Unit. British Medical Journal 1982, 284: 722-24
(3) Fairhurst R.J., Hurtaud J.P. 'Immediate Prehospital Care' edited by Peter J.F. Baskett p.259-268 (John Wiley & Sons Ltd 1981)
(4) Ivanoff, S, Hurtaud, J.P., de Courcy A., 'Les transports aeriens médicalisés de de longue durée'. La Nouvelle Presse Médicale 7/4/79 1359-61.
(5) Novikoff, C., Antoni, C., 'Nature et Utilisation des Fichiers'. Europ Assistance International Relations (January 1982).

BIOGRAPHY

Richard J. Fairhurst MB.BS WRCP MRCS D.Obst RCOG

Educated University College Hospital Medical School London, qualified in 1969. After junior medical training became a Principle in Genral Medical Practice. Began to work on International Medical Transports in 1973. Chief Medical Officer, Europ Assistance, London 1979. Hon. Member, Department Accident Emergency Medicine, University College Hospital, London 1981. Since 1980 has been particularly concerned with the development of logical systems for the collection and application of medical data on patients abroad to their safe transport over long distances by air. Author of several papers on International Medical Rescue.

The Role of Computer Communications in Disasterology as we approach the Year 2000

M E Silverstein
George Washington University,
USA

There is a vast aspect of our contemporary civilization which begs for the ingenuity of the information scientist. With our leisure time amply supplied by a plethora of computerized amusements and our commercial activities revolutionized by computers and computer communications, late twentieth century man pursues his quotidian activities naked and vulnerable to an increasing threat of injury and death from natural, technologically generated, and conflict spawned catastrophe.

Disasters are the violent subsets of society's collective crises. Students of disaster closely define it as that category of phenomena characterized by permutations of human death and injury, extensive property damage, and disruption of the political and societal fabric calling for extraordinary and extraregional resources. Thus, qualitatively bound together by these common elements, national and international disasters subsume such disparate events as the incapacitation of a single policy maker, moderate urban destruction by fire, flood, explosion, poisonous industrial material, terrorist and other civil violence, the vast effects of extreme weather, vulcanism and earthquake and the civil effects of conventional and strategic war weaponry.

In 1982 we are well on our way toward the death and injury of thousands of ordinary citizens engaged in the process of vacationing or business travel. The toll of the American aggregate highway disaster and the crash of Air Florida 90, the hurrican season in the Caribbean, urban fires, mine tragedies and other catastrophic events will guarantee the destructiveness of this year. The conflicts in the Middle East, the Falklanos, Northern Ireland, and Afghanistan will add to the toll of destruction, as will sporadic, less predictable terrorist episodes.

Last year 250 people died when one Brazilian river boat sank and 300 died when a steamer capsized, 110 were lost in a Taiwan air crash, 225 were lost at sea in a shipwreck in Indonesia, 2500 were killed in two earthquakes in Iran, untold civil casualties were suffered as the result of human conflict, 1553 were lost with the flooding of the Chinese Yangtse, about 200 died or were injured in the geographically distant Kansas City structural accident and a Georgian Soviet train accident. Railroad and bridge accidents in India, a discoteque fire in Eire, and other public building fires around the world killed and crippled hundreds from Keansburg, New Jersey to Ankara, Turkey. 1981 was marked by the death of one policy maker, Anwar Sadat, and the near deaths of Ronald Reagan and Pope John Paul with their actual and potential crisis consequences.

1980 was marred by at least eight international crashes of scheduled airliners, earthquakes in Ecuador, Algeria, Italy and Iran, Hurricane Allen in the Caribbean and the Gulf of Mexico, floods in Africa, collapsing oil platforms at sea, and structural building failures in Columbia, among other unhappy events. The southern Italian earthquake eventually killed 3000, made 200,000 homeless, caused untold property damage and contributed to the political fall of the then current government.

The economic, societal, and political consequences of each year's disasters is being calculated and it is enormous.

The population explosion, the increase in areas of population density, the monumental growth of travel, the increase in stationary and transportable technological hazards, political restlessness, and the increasing ratio of destructive power to size and weight of weaponry have increased the potentiality for and the actual number of disasters occurring worldwide.

Against a global background disastrous events can no longer be regarded as infrequent and remote "Acts of God". Under this definition they are a frequent phenomena of irregular period with the possibility of reasonable predictability.

The actual increase in numbers and significance of disasters has been accompaied by a quite separate trend in the public perception of its rights to security at home and in transit. The last half decade has been marked by an accelerated demand that employer, providers of services, and, particularly, governments singly and collectively provide a safe environment and a sophisticated rescue and postaccident repair capability. What sociologists have termed the "me" generation, which tends to focus on component individuals as opposed to organizational loyalities, has contributed to changing concepts of security as well as responsibility for the provision of security. Coincident with the increase in disaster risk has been the shift in public attitude. Accidents are no longer regarded as "Acts of God" to be dealt with by local, neighborly aid. Society, employer, and government are regarded as culpable when security is breached and citizen or property is damaged. The very spectrum of security is now perceived as extending beyond protection against enemy aggression, criminal acts, and urban fire. The post World War II generations focus their fears on technologically produced hazards and regard the occupational and governmental security umbrella as all encompassing protection accompanied by sophisticated, comfortable, and infallible rescue capability.

This increase in "market demand" for disaster security has actually developed in parallel with technological advances which, if made universally available, would, indeed, provide a significant increase in disaster security which includes prevention, preparedness, rescue, human survival, and reconstruction or reimbursement. The governments of well developed nations acting for themselves or assisted by voluntary agencies have accepted the principle of disaster insurance and at least partial reconstruction responsibility. The UN through UNRRO represents the principle, if not the capability, of international responsibility for lesser and underdeveloped nations. Regional alliances such as NATO, while primarily military, contain this principle within their treaties and at least a minimal appartus for rescue and relief. Advances in computer communication and transportation technology for aerospace and defense suggest that the technological basis for disaster security in a large part already exists. Certainly, the revolution in in-hospital resuscitation and surgical trauma care and the success of small casualty rescue and resuscitation by the

limited emergency medical systems now in place suggest that a major increment in salvage and survival could be accomplished in catestrophic events.

Emergency medical systems do, indeed, provide a limited early response to disasters. Those systems were not designed or intended for such a purpose and should not be expected, in their present configurations, to accomplish that function. The traditional disaster management and response organizations such as the Red Cross, the Red Crescent, CARE, and the international religious relief organizations continue in their traditional function of providing nutrition, shelter, and sanitation in the postevent phase. They are grossly underfinanced and the very nature of volunteer disaster relief agencies implies a lack of coordination and the inability to install high technology rescue systems. Valiant efforts by the Pan American Health Organization, various UN organizations, and the US Office of Foreign Disaster Assistance are blunted by an intrinsic lack of coordination, a lack of access to modern technology and the delicate diplomacy demanded by the sensitivities of the bureaucrats of sovereign states. National governments are limited, less by financial constraints than by pressing, competing political crises, lack of coherent disaster response policies and legislation, inadequate disaster crisis management capability, antiquated and immobile civil response appartus, and, perhaps, most of all, by the lack of a prestigious and well structured research and development system. Public emotion, ignorance, and misinformation based on misconception derived from fiction, rumor and inexpert "experts" tend to limit governmental programs and produce ill advised, ad hoc responses to disaster preparation and actual crises.

When compared with the research structure, the monumental organization, and the funding for other aspects of both national defense and international peace keeping, programs for disaster security are barely existent.

The greatest single need is for a communication system.

The global progress and the geographical enormity of wide spread disasters such as earthquakes and destructive weather phenomena, the need for extraregional resources, the destruction of local communication systems, and the necessity of real time communications within the stricken area point up the need for global intelligence, access to computer information files and a complex communication system.

The frequency of disasters and the extensive preparedness mandated necessitates a permanent command, control and communication system.

Overall supervision must lie with a oversight group from which will be drawn in the event of a disaster an international crisis management team to provide command and control. Nodes in the computer communication system must include files of available resources ranging from medical equipment to special expert manpower to heavy earthmoving gear. Since one key to the management of disasters is advance intelligence, updated hazard assessment files maintained by a constant inflow of information from weather prediction agencies, "earthquake watchers", law enforcement agencies, defense groups, air traffic controllers, and hazardous material shippers, among others must be established.

An overall system requires access to background information concerning hazardous materials, patterns of injury, modes of rescue, and methods of medical treatment.

In the presence of an adequate global system local units can be organized in a reserve fashion with a skeleton permanent force and an adequate command and control center permitting optimum utilization of the existing fire departments, police departments, airport crash response groups, shelter groups, hospitals, and utility companies' field teams.

The communication nodes and linkages required for a disaster system are perhaps best identified in terms of the chronology of disaster.

The predisaster intervals require extensive local HAZARD ASSESSMENT. The local and extraregional resources needed to cope with scenarios constructed around such hazards are then developed.

The specific plans for early response, training, and frequent gaming constitute necessary PREPAREDNESS. Routes, methods, and preparation of reception sites represent the necessary evacuation and relocation segment of preparedness planning.

In conjunction with the larger organization and the inflow of disaster intelligence the probability of a particular event in a particular interval is essential information. In the jargon of "disasterologists" this is termed VULNERABILITY ANALYSIS.

The WARNING SYSTEM has several components:

> The global, national, and regional subsystems of the response network require regular assessments of the status of permanent (i.e. earthquakes) and temporary (i.e. rail or highway transported flammables) hazards.

Frequent updating of relevant information from the global resource files, response technologies and methodologies is a necessity.

Early warnings throughout the system beginning with evidence of an approaching, but not necessarily inevitable, catastrophe are required for regional mobilization.

A warning subsystem which reaches the public is required as threat becomes reality and shelter/relocation action is necessary. An inevitable approaching disaster requires a final public warning. The same broad based subsystem is required for public instruction during an event and for the all clear.

MOBILIZATION and EARLY RESCUE by local first responders requires an elaborate field communications subsystem.

Coincident with action response is the need for assessment of the geographical extent of the disaster, property damage, rescue requirements, level of casualty care, and the eventual need for shelter, nutrition, and sanitation. Local ground evaluation, satellite photos, and appropriate flyovers could provide this information.

Recourse to EXTRAREGIONAL RESOURCES may involve the whole system.

The late phases of disaster care: the provision of food and shelter, reimbursement and reconstruction demand no new communications subsystems.

A disaster communications network faces some special difficulties. Local ground lines and necessary files may be destroyed in the stricken area. Nuclear catastrophes produce an electromagnetic burst and have a potential for radio interference. Present, existing subsystems are plagued by the use of inconsistent radio frequencies and jurisdictional problems.

CONCLUSION

Disaster communications represent an increasing problem for government and society. Present rescue efforts are hampered by the absence of an overall coordinating system and the sparse use of modern computer communications technology. The toll in lives and property on a global level is now large enough to warrant the attention of sophisticated information scientists.

Dr. Martin Elliot Silver-
stein is a university
surgeon long known as a
pioneer in computer com-
munications research.
Over the last two decades
he has worked in the pro-
cessing and transmission
of pysiological data. A
specialist in the surgery
of trauma, he and his re-
search team have developed
portable biotelemetry equipment for the study
and care of the injured patient.

Dr. Silverstein is presently conducting studies
on the optimum management of mass casualties
and the technology of hazard assessment and
disaster response. He has also contributed to
research in the application of communication
and network theory to rural and other distribu-
tive health care systems.

Dr. Silverstein is Associate Professor with the
Department of Surgery and Adjunct Associate
Professor of Optical Sciences at the University
of Arizona. He is currently on sabbatical as a
visiting Scholar at the Georgetown University
Center for Strategic and International Studies
and as an Adjunct Professor of Health Care
Sciences at the George Washington University.

Design of a Two Wire Full Duplex Transmission System on Subscriber Loop

G Panarotto, A Tofanelli, L Varetto
CSELT - Centro Studi e Laboratori
Telecomunicazioni, Italy

This paper deals with high speed digital transmission on subscriber loops. In order to limit the signal bandwidth, baseband two wire full duplex transmission using hybrid circuit is proposed. Spurious signals, due to the loss of the hybrid circuit and to the reflections along the line, can be eliminated by a digital processor which estimates the overall disturbing signal. To update the digital processor, a gradient algorithm is employed using the overall received signal, sampled twice in the signalling period. In order to guarantee the algorithm convergence, a suitable binary code is adopted, which assures a complete absence of correlation between the data flowing in the two directions. The incoming sampled signal, after the cancellation of the disturbances, is filtered by an analog interpolator; the resulting analog signal allows the timing extraction from its zero crossings. Only one fixed equalizer is used for almost all possible link lengths of the subscriber network. Beside the design guidelines, modem performance is reported, checked by simulation and expressed in terms of eye opening at the receiving end and of algorithm convergence rate for various typical link lengths.

1. INTRODUCTION

The possibility of extending high speed digital services to the customer premises depends on the capability of the present loop plant to support the digital transmission. As the transmission in the local area is normally performed on two wire lines, it would be highly desirable that they could be utilized for full duplex digital transmission as well. Several techniques can fulfill this basic requirement, such as time division multiplexing [1], frequency division multiplexing [2] and hybrid balance system. These techniques differ primarily in the way in which the two directions of transmission are separated. In this paper a system (*) working according to the third technique is presented, in which the separation is obtained by means of a hybrid circuit and an echo canceller. The primary problem in implementing this system is the circuit complexity. In this paper two possible solutions are discussed, optimized from the point of view of the operating performance, minimum internal clock frequency and circuit complexity. The above mentioned parameters are of extreme interest in the system integration feasibility and, as a consequence, in the ISDN subscriber loop penetration, as only a very cheap and low power consuming modem can be cost effective compared with the present analog systems in the local area.

2. SYSTEM DESIGN

2.1 General Considerations

Two wire full duplex baseband digital data transmission requires the adoption of a hybrid circuit (HC), for separating the two data streams and preventing the modem from receiving the data transmitted by itself. This goal is achieved only if the balancing network (BN) matches exactly the line transfer function in the frequency band of the signal. The presence of bridged taps and of discontinuities of wire diameter along the link makes impossible the adoption of an unique balancing network. On the other hand, it is desirable to avoid a cumbersome procedure to adapt the BN to each installation condition. The BN can be built up by a rather simple network; with this choice the signal, generated by the BN

_____
(*) Patent pending

mismatch and coming from the transmitting part of the modem (echo signal), must be estimated by a digital processor and subtracted from the overall received signal in order to restore the useful data from the far end terminal. Two methods can be used to cancel the echo. With the first one, the disturbing signal is subtracted once in the signalling period, precisely at the instant where the useful signal eye opening is maximum, in order to allow a correct decision process. In the second method the echo is subtracted more than once in the signalling period. With the first method some problems arise for the timing extraction. In fact it is not possible to use the signal transitions; hence the data aided procedures, requiring a precise shape in the pulse response, can only be used with cumbersome equalizing systems, owing to the wide spread in the link characteristics. This drawback is avoided by adopting the second method, at the expence of a rather larger complexity in the echo estimator implementation. In fact the incoming sampled signal, after the cancellation point, is reconstructed by a low pass analog filter and is fed in a conventional receiver. The timing extraction is then directly performed by using the signal zero crossings and only a fixed delay is needed in order to sample at the optimum eye opening instant. The latter solution is adopted for the modem reported in this paper, whose block diagram is shown in fig. 1.

2.2 Estimation Algorithms

The algorithm used to estimate the echo impulse response is to be adaptive in order to work properly with any mismatch between the BN and the line characteristics, and to compensate for the possible variations in the line impulse response; moreover it should be robust enough to operate also in the presence of the far end information signal, which acts like noise as regards the echo estimation process. The convolution of the estimated echo impulse response with the sequence of the transmitted symbols, which is available within the terminal, gives the echo contents of the incoming signal. Since an estimator operating N times in the signalling period T is equivalent to a set of N interleaved estimators, each operating on a sample every T seconds, and with a $\tau = T/N$ delay with respect to the preceding one, the adopt-

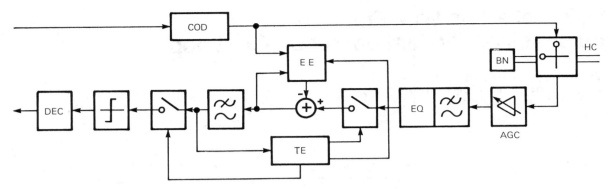

Fig. 1 - Block diagram of the modem. EE = Echo estimator; AGC = Automatic gain control; TE = Timing extraction; COD = 11B-14B coder; DEC = Decoder; EQ = Equalizer (if present)

ed algorithm, referring to a single estimator, will be examined, without loss of generality. Let $\underline{g}$ be the vector of the echo path samples, and $\underline{a}_k$ the vector of the symbols transmitted by the near terminal, associated in $t = kT$ with the vector $\underline{g}$; let $\underline{h}$ be the vector of the channel impulse response and $\underline{b}_k$ the vector of the corresponding transmitted symbols in $t = kT$. The received signal is given by:

$$y_k = \underline{a}_k^T \, \underline{g} + \underline{b}_k^T \, \underline{h}$$

In this system a recursive algorithm, based on the gradient principle, has been chosen, which lends itself to an easy implementation. At time p the estimate $\underline{g}^p$ of $\underline{g}$ is obtained according to the following relationship [3]:

$$\underline{g}^P = \underline{g}^{p-1} + \Delta < e_k \, \underline{a}_k > \qquad (1)$$

where Δ is a coefficient which determines the amount of correction of the previous estimate and e_k is the error between the received signal and its prediction based on $\underline{g}^{p-1}$. To work properly, the algorithm requires that the line code assures the following conditions:

$$\overline{a}_i = \overline{b}_i = 0; \quad \overline{a_i b_i} = \overline{a}_i \cdot \overline{b}_i = 0 \quad \text{with } i,j = 0, 1, 2 \dots \quad (2)$$

and the convergence is guaranteed if:

$$0 < \Delta < \frac{2}{\mu_0}$$

where $\mu_0 = \max_i |\mu_i|$, being μ_i the eigenvalues of the line code autocorrelation matrix.

The direct implementation of the algorithm expressed by eqn. (1) can lead to some difficulties. The evaluation of the time average can slow too much the algorithm convergence. To avoid this drawback, the time average is replaced by the instantaneous value $e_k \underline{a}_k$, at the expence of fluctuations of the echo estimate around its true value, which are equivalent to noise added to the echo estimate.

A problem can arise in the implementation of the multiplications implied by eqn. (1). Employing a binary balanced code, this problem is avoided in the calculations involving the transmitted symbols. To prevent also the multiplication $\Delta (e_k \underline{a}_k)$, there are two methods, both tested in the modem. A first method requires that Δ assumes a power of two value, thus reducing the multiplication to a shift of the operand $e_k \underline{a}_k$ expressed in binary format. The block diagram of the echo processor, implementing the algorithm:

$$\underline{g}^P = \underline{g}^{p-1} + \Delta \, e_k \underline{a}_k$$

is reported in fig. 2.

With the second method $\underline{g}$ is updated only on the basis of the sign of $e_k \underline{a}_k$ and not of its entire value:

$$\underline{g}^P = \underline{g}^{p-1} + \Delta < \text{sgn} \, (e_k \underline{a}_k) > = \underline{g}^{p-1} + \Delta < \text{sgn} \, (e_k) \cdot \underline{a}_k > \quad (3)$$

This avoids the strong limitation on the values which can be assign to Δ. When $\underline{g}^p$ approached $\underline{g}$, sgn (e_k) bears no more information to the updating process and therefore it is necessary to add a dithering noise to the incoming signal [3, 4], uncorrelated with it and having controlled amplitude, to assure the proper convergence of the algorithm. Using this method, strong fluctuations of the estimate g_p can exist, if the time average is performed on not sufficiently long time intervals. This results in a rather low convergence rate, but this disadvantage is well balanced by the possibility of avoiding the A/D converter, acting on the error signal, by

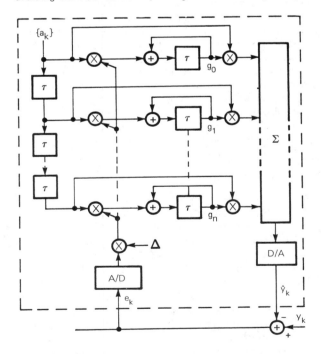

Fig. 2 - Block diagram of the echo estimator operating on the entire value of e_k according to eqn. (1): $\tau = T/N$, $\hat{y}_k$ estimate of y_k based on $\underline{g}^{p-1}$

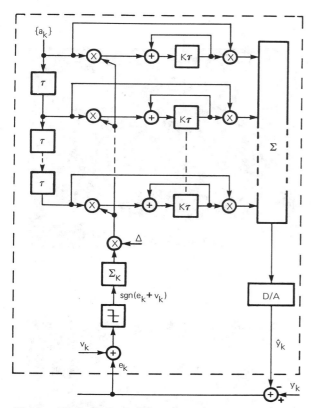

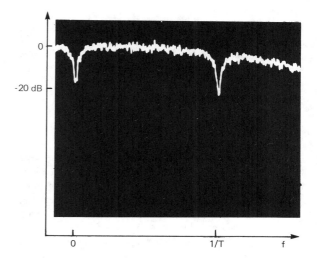

Fig. 4 - *Experimental spectrum of the line code 11B-14B*

Fig. 3 - *Block diagram of the echo estimator, operating on the sign of e_k according to eqn. (3): $\tau = T/N$; Σ_k average over K samples of $e_k + f_k$; f_k dithering noise; $\hat{y}_k$ estimate of y_k based on $\underline{g}^{p-1}$*

using a much simpler threshold device. Fig. 3 reports the block diagram of the echo canceller based on eqn. (3).

2.3 Line Code

The choice of the line code must take into account the relationships (2), which guarantee the algorithm convergence. An 11B-14B balanced line code has been employed, which in particular assures the absence of correlation between the data flowing in the two directions. Its main advantages are: no d.c. component, a relative insensitivity to an imperfect line equalization, it requires no precise automatic gain control (AGC) adjustement and allows an easy timing extraction from the signal zero crossings. Another advantage can be obtained from the format of the transmitted data, being the signalling rate 88 kbit/s, resulting from a 64 kbit/s signal, the PCM encoded voice channel or high speed data, a 16 kbit/s low speed data signal and a 8 kbit/s signal for housekeeping. With the choice of this line code, it is possible to turn the frame alignment into the code word alignment, which is needed in any case. In fig. 4 the experimental spectrum of the selected 11B-14B line code is reported.

2.4 Hybrid Circuit and Filters

The design of a hybrid transformer in the range of frequencies involved, is not an easy task and is economically not convenient. Moreover with direct coupling the transmitted signal is directly fed into the receiver.

A possible scheme for coupling the transmitted signal to the line with inexpensive circuit implementation is represented by the hybrid structure shown in fig. 5.

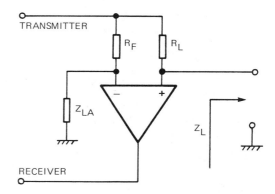

Fig. 5 - *Electrical scheme of the hybrid circuit*

This solution does not require a sophisticated transformer, and, as the frequencies involved are below 1 MHz, it can be easily integrated using bipolar or CMOS technology. For the structure shown in fig. 5 the impulse response of the echo path is given by:

$$\underline{g} = \underline{w} - \underline{q}$$

where $\underline{w}$ is the impulse response of the cable, and $\underline{q}$ is the impulse response of the balancing network. If Z_{LA} is real, the insertion of the BN merely decreases $\underline{g}$. Moreover, even if Z_{LA} is complex and adjusted according to the input line impedance, it cannot reduce the level of reflections caused by discontinuities along the cable.

Moreover low frequency matching is almost impossible due to the large impedance spread shown by the symmetrical pair cables. A good compromise is to reduce the unbalance effects to a level comparable with reflections; in these conditions it is sufficient a simple BN composed by two RC cells.

In order to further simplify the modem complexity, a single fixed equalizing network for a 0.4 mm diameter 3 km long cable is adopted, followed by a raised cosine filter with 80% roll-off. This equalizer is to be inserted for link length above 1 km, as it will be shown later.

709

2.5 Canceller Design

Regardless of which of the two aforementioned algorithms are adopted, the main canceller parameters are: number of taps of the delay line, rate of oversampling, number of bits for internal data representation, correction coefficient Δ, number of bits of the DAC and ADC, if present.

The number N of taps is given by:

$$N = m \frac{\Delta t}{T}$$

where m is the rate of oversampling and Δt is the overall length of the echo impulse response. As the signal spectrum is bandlimited to about 100 kHz, i.e. 1.8 times the Nyquist frequency, m = 2 is adequate. Computer simulations and field testings yielded for Δt a value of about 70 μs, which means N = 14. The values of Δ, of the number of bits for internal representation and of the number of bits for the A/D converter should be jointly optimized, from the point of view of convergence rate, estimate precision and circuit complexity. A good compromise has been found setting Δ to a negative power of two, i.e. 2^{-10}, thus avoiding multiplications, using 6 bits for the A/D converter and 16 bits for the internal representation. Simple estimates of the quantization noise alone indicate that the signal to quantization noise ratio, using M bits for the D/A converter, is [5]:

$$\frac{S}{N} = 10 \log (3 \cdot 2^{2M}/N)$$

With M = 12, N = 14, S/N = 66 dB results, which is adequate for the present application. In order to fully exploit the dynamic of the converters and of the internal numerical representation, an AGC circuit is also provided, as it was said before, with a gain control range of about 40 dB.

3. PERFORMANCE

The performance was estimated by computer simulation. The results are given in terms of eye opening, echo reducing factor and convergence rate of the echo processor considering full-duplex operating mode. Fig. 6 shows eye opening/ /echo peak ratio vs. link length without equalizer and with a fixed 3 km, 0.4 mm diameter cable equalization network. It can be noticed that 1 km is the link length above which the use of the equalizer becomes profitable. Eye diagrams at various link lengths are shown in fig. 7, 8 after cancellation, showing an eye impairement due to imperfect echo cancellation less than 10%. The residual echo during the convergence of the algorithm is reported in fig. 9 in the worst

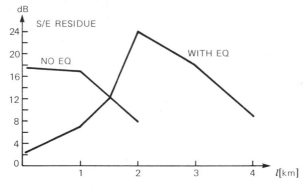

Fig. 6 - *Ratio of eye opening to the peak echo residue vs. link length*

Fig. 7 - *Eye diagram of a 1 km link on a 0.4 mm diameter cable without equalization*

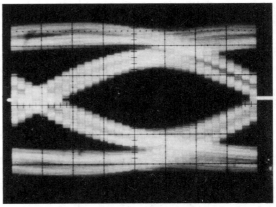

Fig. 8 - *Eye diagram of a 4 km link on a 0.4 mm diameter cable with 3 km fixed equalization*

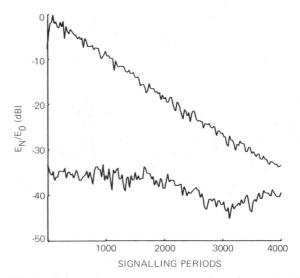

Fig. 9 - *Echo estimate error versus number of transmitted symbols for a 4 km link with equalization, employing the algorithm of eqn. (1); E_n echo estimate at N-th symbol, E_0 actual echo value*

case (i.e. 4 km link length with a 0.4 mm cable); the maximum convergence time is always less than 40 ms. Computer simulations show that, for shorter links, the echo residue is greater and the convergence rate is slightly slower, because the far end signal, acting like noise on the estimation process, is greater for shorter lengths. Nevertheless, being the useful signal higher, the ratios between the eye opening and the echo residue are still good, as can be seen in fig. 6.

Also the algorithm, based on the error estimation sign (eqn. (3)), has been tested. In order to yield performance not too far from those obtained previously, it is necessary to inject a dithering noise with a mean absolute value about twice the eye opening value, to impose to Δ a value of the order of 2^{-12} and to average the error sign over 8 samples. With these parameters, the eye opening, after the convergence, is slightly worse than that obtained previously. The echo residue during the convergence process is reported in fig. 9, from which it can be shown that the convergence rate is about 6 times slower than with the former algorithm.

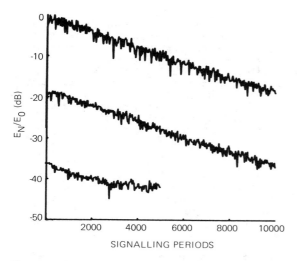

Fig. 10 - Echo estimate error versus number of transmitted symbols, for a 4 km link with equalization, employing the algorithm of eqn. (3)

4. CONCLUSIONS

A system has been described which, by using a hybrid circuit and an echo canceller, provides a full duplex 88 kbit/s digital transmission on two wire lines. Maximum link length attainable is 4 km with 0.4 mm diameter cables. This distance corresponds to about 98% of the Italian subscriber loops [1]. Performance are given in terms of eye opening, convergence rate and echo cancellation capability. In the design particular care has been devoted to the circuit simplicity in view of a possible integration of the entire modem.

REFERENCES

[1] A. Brosio, U. de Julio, V. Lazzari, R. Ravaglia, A. Tofanelli: "A comparison of digital subscriber line transmission systems employing different line codes", IEEE Trans. on Comm., COM-29, N. 11, pp. 1581-1588, Nov. 1981.

[2] P. di Tria, R. Montagna: "Design and simulation of a digital DPSK modem for 80 kbit/s full-duplex data transmission on subscriber loop", ICC '81, Denver 14-18 June, pp. 25.6.1.

[3] G. Panarotto, A. Tofanelli, L. Varetto: "Two-wires full-duplex baseband digital transmission system employing an echo canceller: design guidelines and performance evaluation", CSELT internal report (in italian).

[4] N. Holte, S. Stueflotten: "A new digital echo canceller for two wire subscriber lines", IEEE Trans. on Comm., COM-29, N. 11, pp. 1573-1581, Nov. 1981.

[5] G. Bostelmann: "Simulation of digital full duplex transmission on two wire links", Frequenz, vol. 34 (1980), N. 2, pp. 40-45.

Luigi VARETTO was born in San Mauro (Turin), Italy, on May 1957. He received the P.I. degree in industrial electronics in 1976 from ITIS "G. Peano" of Turin, Italy. In 1977 he joined CSELT where he devoted his activity to scientific computer programming. Nowadays he is working on microprocessor systems applied to digital transmission.

Gianfranco PANAROTTO was born in Turin, Italy, on Febrary 1948. He received the Dr. Ing. degree in Electronic Engineering in 1972 from the Politecnico di Torino, Turin, Italy. Then he joined the CNR (National Research Council) where he was engaged in research concerning image bandwidth reduction.

Since 1974 he has been employed at CSELT, Turin, where he devoted his activity to digital signal processing and computer simulation with application to transmission system design. His present research interests involve microprocessor applications to digital transmission systems and error generation modelling.

Adler TOFANELLI was born in Venaria (Turin), Italy, on October 1949. He received the Dr. Ing. degree in electronic engineering in 1974 from the Politecnico di Torino, Italy.

Since 1975 he has been employed at CSELT, Turin, where he devoted his activity to digital signal processing applied to transmission systems.

At present he is involved in the design of digital transmission systems on subscriber's lines.

The Emerging Digital Transmission Network

W J Murray
British Telecom, UK

Studies of the application of digital techniques to the transmission and switching elements of the British Telecom (BT) telecommunications network showed the considerable advantages and economics over equivalent analogue methods. Digital transmission allows integrated transmission of voice, data and visual services over a common bearer network. Modernisation of the BT transmission network by conversion to digital operation has already commenced using a range of digital transmission systems based on the 2, 8, 34 and 140 Mbit/s internationally agreed hierarchical rates for operation on copper cables, optical fibre cables and microwave radio. It is intended to accelerate the conversion rate so that a telephone service of high quality offering enhanced facilities can be achieved as well as the creation of an integrated services digital network (ISDN) to meet the more complex non-voice customer requirements of the future.

1 INTRODUCTION

Data transmission in the United Kingdom (UK) has been in a dramatic expanding and evolving situation since the introduction of Datel Services by British Telecommunications (BT) in 1965. Both voice band private circuits and the public switched telephone network (PSTN) have been extensively used for data transmission. Customer demand for new and improved services operating at higher bit rates have been met by more complex designs of modems which can cope with the transmission impairments of the analogue transmission network.

However the rapid advances in technology are making available a comprehensive range of sophisticated new customer-located products to augment the basic telephone for business and social purposes. The increasing size and complexity of computing systems associated with data line networks call for higher throughput of information and the provision of intelligent terminal equipments.

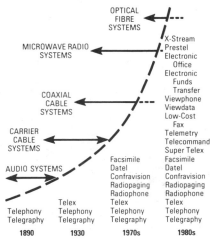

FIG 1. GROWTH IN SERVICES

Figure 1 shows the growth in services offered by BT to date and those likely to be available during the 1980s. Customer information type services are leading towards a convergence of voice, data, text and facsimile services where boundaries between different user requirements are merging and becoming less distinct. The restrictions of the present analogue transmission network and its inability to cope economically with the changing data requirements were taken into account in the studies of applications for digital techniques to both the transmission and switching elements of the BT network. To meet the long term requirements for improved customer facilities and quality of service, as well as giving operational and economic advantages, it was concluded that a digital transmission network offered the essential characteristics because:

- A common transmission path can be used for all services, voice, non-voice and wideband with a high transmission performance virtually independent of distance.

- Integrated digital switching and transmission can be provided for speech and data at rates up to 64 kbit/s.

- New services and terminal devices will generally exploit digital techniques so that the adoption of a digital network will avoid expensive high performance modems and digital/analogue conversion processes.

- Supplementary facilities can be readily provided to augment the basic telephone service and cope with a wide and expanding range of new information services.

Consequently, the BT network is being modernised by replacing existing analogue plant with digital switching and transmission systems, thus forming an all purpose integrated digital network (IDN) between local exchanges which will provide the overall flexibility to meet the ever changing needs to be expected in the future.

This paper outlines the various digital transmission systems in the course of development and production, from the low capacity pulse code modulation (pcm) systems on symmetrical pair type cables to the high capacity, high bit rate systems on coaxial cable, optical fibre cable and microwave radio. Some of the future developments will be mentioned that may further improve the network capability and extend digital transmission into the local network to provide completely digital customer-to-customer links.

2   GENERAL CONFIGURATION OF EXISTING BT TELECOMMUNICATIONS NETWORK

As the telephone and telex networks existed before the demand for data transmission, it was natural for data traffic to be routed over existing telephone transmission line plant and the present telephone and telex services fully exploited to provide economic data communication channels.

The use of a shared network rather than a purpose designed network incurs penalties in that the transmission characteristics of the telephone channel must be taken as the starting point for the development of the data modem – the interfacing device used to convert the customer's binary coded signals into analogue signals that can be handled by the telephone circuit. Where the modems are intended for operation over PSTN connexions, correction must be introduced to compensate for the network impairments that cause errors in data transmission but do not affect speech communication. Restrictions arise in the use of particular frequencies in the available bandwidth but for data transmission rates of up to 1200 bit/s, simple modulation techniques using frequency shift keying (FSK) have proved to be adequate.

For higher transmission rates, more sophisticated modulation techniques using phase shift keying (PSK) or combinations of amplitude and phase modulation must be used to compress the information within the bandwidth available on private speech band circuits and the PSTN. To increase the bit rate without exceeding the permissible bandwidth limitations of the transmission path requires the use of more complex modem devices, which incurs a higher cost. Datel service modems incorporating adaptive type equalisers and medium and large scale integration are currently available for operation at a range of speeds up to 9600 bit/s over voice-band circuits and at 40.8, 48, 50, 64 and 72 kbit/s over group-band circuits. At present there are about 93,000 BT modems in operational use, 60% of which are connected to the PSTN.

There are considerable network constraints in achieving further improvements in bit rates over the present analogue plant and digital alternatives offer the more effective solution in terms of bandwidth utilisation, flexibility and economics in meeting the digital private circuit network requirements of the future.

The BT main network comprises cable and radio transmission systems which provide the traffic circuit routes inter-connecting about 370 Group Switching Centres. Over the years increased traffic has demanded higher circuit capacities of new generation systems. Technology has evolved to meet these needs and at present the basic 12 circuit carrier group is assembled by frequency division multiplex (FDM) for transmission over 24 circuit carrier cables. The formation of larger multichannel assemblies to form the FDM hierarchical structure of supergroups to hypergroups is used for transmission over coaxial cable or microwave radio.

In moving to an all-digital network, a major objective is to have systems offering comparable circuit capacities maximising the use of existing assets in terms of cables, underground equipment housings, power feeding systems, surface intermediate stations and radio towers. These aspects have been given full consideration in the design and development of digital systems, to meet the requirements for speech and data transmission.

3   BT NETWORK MODERNISATION STRATEGY

The main aims of the strategy for modernisation of the BT network are to replace completely the principal analogue network elements with digital equivalents by the early 1990s, comprising large local exchanges trunk and tandem switching and trunk transmission. Replacement of the other elements, such as small Strowger exchanges, crossbar exchanges and the remaining parts of the junction network will be completed some 10 years later.

Implementation of this strategy requires the provision of a digital transmission network to interconnect all primary switching centres within about 10 years and a complete national replacement digital transmission network to interconnect all local exchanges within about 20 years. The methods to be adopted to achieve these objectives take into account the BT intention to exploit the availability of digital plant on routes provided for telephony, and, by the introduction of a limited quantity of specially developed data transmission equipment, to enable digital private data circuits to be offered between major city centres as early as possible. These new X-Stream services – Kilo Stream for services below 1 Mbit/s – Mega Stream for services at 1Mbit/s and above are to provide an overlay digital network until the introduction of Switch Stream – the fully integrated services digital network (ISDN).

Mega Stream is available now and Kilo Stream will be introduced in 1983 offering digital services at speeds of 2.4, 4.8, 9.6, 48 and 64 kbit/s.

4   RANGE OF DIGITAL TRANSMISSION SYSTEMS

It has been planned to make use of a range of digital transmission systems and higher order multiplexing equipment to meet the commitment to modernise the network. The different systems, circuit capacity and the dates for their introduction into service into the network are shown in table 1.

TABLE 1
RANGE OF DIGITAL TRANSMISSION SYSTEMS

EQUIPMENT OR SYSTEM TITLE	CIRCUIT CAPACITY	SERVICE DATES
2 Mbit/s Digital Line System	30	1979
120 Mbit/s Digital Line System	1,680	1980
8 Mbit/s Digital Line System	120	3/83
140 Mbit/s Digital Line System	1,920	8/82
140 Mbit/s OFS – Proprietary	1,920	6/82
140 Mbit/s OFS – Standard	1,920	7/84
11 GHz Digital Radio Relay System (5+1 bothway channels of 140 Mbit/s)	9,600	6/82
4 & L6 GHz Digital Radio Relay System (7+1 bothway channels of 140 Mbit/s)	13,440 per band	7/85
19 GHz Digital Radio Relay System (6 bothway channels at 2 or 8 Mbit/s) (6 bothway channels at 140 Mbit/s)	720 11,520	1981 1986
Multiplex Equipment (2 to 8 Mbit/s & 8 to 120 Mbit/s)	—	1980
(8 to 34 Mbit/s & 34 to 140 Mbit/s)	—	4/83
Codec Equipment Supergroup Hypergroup	60 900	7/84 5/84

The 2.048 Mbit/s DLS, which conforms with the CCITT requirements, is intended primarily for use in the BT junction network but can be extended to customers premises to provide point-to-point private circuits for operation at this bit rate. The latest general purpose 30 channel PCM multiplex (MUX) provides for input signals in both analogue and digital form to be multiplexed together in time division to provide a 2.048 Mbit/s composite digital output signal in HDB3 code. The equipment provides for a combination of services to suit local circumstances as shown in figure 2 by the use of a range of input tributary cards. Where larger groups of 64 kbit/s are required for digital private circuit network applications special dedicated primary MUX will be available with the Kilo Stream Service.

INPUT OPTIONS	
SPEECH	DATA
30 CHANNELS	—
24 CHANNELS	6 CHANNELS AT 64 kbit/s e.g. FOR X-STREAM SERVICES
24 CHANNELS	1 MONO DIGITAL SOUND PROGRAMME CHANNEL
18 CHANNELS	2 MONO DIGITAL SOUND PROGRAMME CHANNELS (2 × 384 kbit/s)
18 CHANNELS	1 STEREO DIGITAL SOUND PROGRAMME CHANNEL (768 kbit/s)
18 CHANNELS	1 MONO DIGITAL 6 CHANNELS AT 64 kbit/s

FIG 2. GENERAL PURPOSE MULTIPLEX

The first high capacity digital system for the main network was designed for operation at a rate of 120 Mbit/s on existing 1.2/4.4 mm

coaxial cable. Each system provides a capacity of 1680 telephone circuits assembled via 2 to 8 Mbit/s and 8 to 120 Mbit/s multiplex equipment. Only a limited number of these systems will be installed in the network as BT subsequently adopted the CCITT recommended hierarchical structure of 34 and 140 Mbit/s rates. Consequently all subsequent systems have been developed for operation at these rates for the different transmission media. As 140 Mbit/s is the rate considered most suitable for the modernisation of the main network systems have been designed for operation at this rate on coaxial cable and microwave digital radio relay systems (DRRS) firstly in the 11GHz band and later in the 4 and lower 6GHz bands. Development work is also in hand for DRRS operating in the 19GHz band at 140 Mbit/s for the main network and at 2 and 8 Mbit/s for junction and local network applications.

Multiplexing equipment has also been developed to provide 8 to 34 Mbit/s and 34/68 to 140 Mbit/s digital multiplex, as shown in figure 3.

The 68 Mbit/s entry port provides for the hypergroup codec and digital television interfacing in the future.

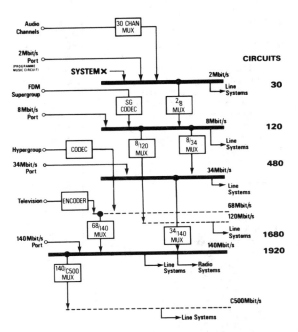

FIG 3. TDM HIERARCHY

These systems are primarily designed to fit existing networks and to establish a digital hierarchical structure. However serious consideration has been given to the use of optical fibres as an alternative transmission media to copper conductor cables. In the main network optical fibres have to compete with coaxial pairs carrying 140 Mbit/s systems and optical fibre systems for operation at 140 Mbit/s have been developed for this application. Following several successful field evaluation exercises by BT and Industry, BT has now gained sufficient experience and confidence to order a substantial quantity of essentially proprietary optical fibre systems for installation and bringing into operational use in the BT trunk and junction network by 1985. The initial order was for a total of 34 systems on 15 different routes using a variety of fibre cables operating in the wavelength region of 850 nm. Six 140 Mbit/s on three routes, four 34 Mbits on two routes and two 8 Mbit/s on one route are for main network use, the remaining twenty-two 8 Mbit/s systems are for short haul application in the junction network. The initial experience with these systems, due for completion in 1982, has encouraged BT to place a further order for a much larger quantity of similar systems involving 224 systems on 65 routes in various parts of the country. Some of these systems will operate at the longer wavelength of 1300 nm on graded index fibre, where one route is longer than 200km. Another route, more than 27km in length, will be equipped with monomode fibre operating at 140 Mbit/s without any intermediate regenerators. This is significant because a system repeater spacing of 30km would mean that for the majority of routes repeaters could be housed in surface stations and power feeding would not be necessary, thus reducing capital costs and improving reliability.

The economic benefits predicted for optical fibre systems compared with coaxial cable and radio system equivalents are indicated in figure 4. Furthermore because of their longer repeater spacing optical fibre systems promise to be easier to install and maintain than digital systems on metallic pairs. Consequently it is a planning objective to derive the maximum potential economic benefits by introducing optical fibre systems as early as possible in the network modernisation programme.

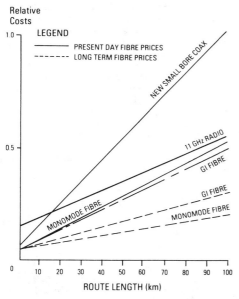

FIG 4. COST COMPARISONS

In the longer term, optical fibre systems have enormous potential to provide very high capacity digital links in an economic manner. Such systems operating at 565 Mbit/s and 1 Gbit/s or using wavelength division multi-

plexing to derive several systems on one monomode fibre will require very few repeaters and will be ideally suited for the large communications capacity required by future information and visual services.

As the proprietary systems are being purchased as cable and equipment packages, this approach results in a number of different designs of system which impose limitations on the exploitation of spare fibre at a later date and cause operational problems such as sterilisation of the routes.

Thus, BT's efforts are currently directed towards the introduction of some standardisation of the optical fibre cable characteristics so that standard systems can be purchased as separately specified cable and equipment.

To derive the maximum benefits indicated previously from using optical fibre systems in the BT trunk network, such systems must be available for use as an alternative to coaxial cable systems as early as possible in the modernisation programme. Thus, current plans aim to order the first batch of standard 140 Mbit/s optical fibre systems for the trunk network in 1983 for installation and bringing into operational use in 1984/85. Larger quantities will be ordered to meet the requirements of the modernisation programme and growth in the network.

5   DIGITALISATION OF THE MAIN NETWORK

Introducing digital transmission systems into the network in an economic manner poses considerable problems, primarily because the established large FDM network, comprising about 1600 hypergroups, must be interfaced with a growing number of digital TDM systems. Initially the digital systems can only be

FIG 5.   MAIN NETWORK DIGITAL SYSTEMS

exploited economically for circuits between
the terminal nodes of the DLS and cannot be
integrated to give the same degree of flexibility as could additional FDM systems.

Strategy studies for network modernisation
established that the most attractive and
economic solution is to minimise the amount of
interworking between analogue and digital plant
by undertaking a rapid modernisation programme
of the PSTN. This calls for a completely
digital main transmission network by the early
1990s and dramatically alters the earlier
planning programme which was based on using
digital transmission systems to meet the growth
only which would have led to a gradual increase
in digital penetration reaching little more
than 50% of the network by the year 2000. The
rapid programme, which BT is now implementing
requires a very large number of 140 Mbit/s
systems to be ordered and brought into operational use to replace all analogue systems in
less than 10 years.

Figure 5 indicates the routes to be equipped
with digital transmission in the early years
of the programme. The planning and provision
dates for these digital transmission systems
also take account of the requirements for the
X-Stream Services.

The percentage penetration of 140 Mbit/s
digital systems on the different types of
transmission media to meet the main network
programme is illustrated in figure 6. To
achieve these aims it will be necessary to
take full advantage of technological advances.
It is expected that about half of the main
network 140 Mbit/s systems will be routed over
optical fibre systems by about 1990. This is
based on the decision not to purchase new
coaxial cable after 1984.

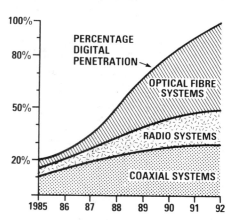

**FIG 6. DIGITAL PENETRATION OF MAIN
NETWORK (140 Mbit/s SYSTEMS)**

6   DIGITALISATION OF THE JUNCTION
TRANSMISSION NETWORK

The introduction of digital transmission into
the BT junction network began over 10 years
ago with the installation of 24-channel pcm
systems which operated at 1.536 Mbit/s on
existing deloaded audio cables. More than
7000 systems have been installed, principally

in the junction network, to increase the
circuit capacity of existing cables. However
as the system makes use of a 7 bit quantisation
law and the line signal structure is not
compatible with System X exchanges or 2 Mbit/s
systems it will not be used in the modernisation programme.

The 2.048 Mbit/s DLS will be fully exploited on
existing types of audio cables as far as
practicable.

Where new cables are the preferred solution to
intercepting existing large cables, a range of
transverse screen cables have been introduced
which offer a higher degree of immunity to
crosstalk and provide increased regenerator
spacing. These systems will be used for
traffic circuits between local exchanges as
well as for customer circuits.

In addition 8 and 34 Mbit/s systems on optical
fibre cable are being used on a relatively
small scale at present. As these systems offer
the advantage of not requiring intermediate
regenerators on most of the junction network
routes a very much larger scale of application
for these systems can be foreseen as the cost
decreases in the future.

7   EXTENDING DIGITAL TRANSMISSION INTO THE
LOCAL NETWORK

The BT digital transmission network potentially
offers customers 64 kbit/s circuits for low and
medium speed data applications and 2 or 8 Mbit/s
and above for higher speed uses. As the number
of System X switching units linked by digital
transmission rapidly increases it will become
progressively possible to provide bothway 64
kbit/s switched transmission paths throughout
the network between local digital exchanges.
By providing digital access from the customers
to System X local exchanges and adding certain
non-voice service facilities the integrated
services digital network (ISDN) will evolve.

Figure 7 shows how the initial implementation
of ISDN is envisaged based on the 80kbit/s
local access which will be used in the 1983
pilot scheme in London. In addition to the
64 kbit/s and 8 kbit/s digital traffic circuits
an 8 kbit/s message based data channel for
signalling and housekeeping ($\triangle$) between the
customer and the local System X exchange is also
provided.

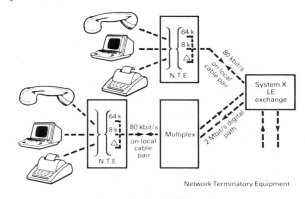

FIG 7. ISDN CONCEPT

In order to reduce the number of 80 kbit/s circuits in the local networks and to serve customers on the fringe of the local distribution cables it is proposed to install primary multiplexers at intermediate sites, possibly housed in cross connexion cabinets and extend the circuits over 2 Mbit/s paths. However it is likely to be many years before national coverage of ISDN facilities can be achieved. The interim period will be covered by the X-Stream services. In the case of Kilo Stream, access from the customer to the network node will be via a 4 wire circuit on standard unloaded local cable pairs using digital baseband WAL2 signals.

Techniques for adding bothway digital paths on the 2-wire telephone pair without causing disturbance to the existing telephone service are being investigated and include burst-mode operation, echo cancellation and frequency division methods. Such systems, which provide additional capacity of at least one bothway 64 kbit/s channel, have the economic advantage of maximising the utilisation of existing local cables but have restricted reach and capacity.

Digital radio systems operating in the 19GHz band can provide a number of bothway channels and could be used for high-capacity customer connections for point-to-point and multipoint distribution application. BT's assessment of the 19GHz digital radio system has indicated that it could provide satisfactory service quickly and economically because the small size of aerials and equipment permits relatively easy mounting on buildings or poles and most applications would not need intermediate repeaters. Such systems are therefore considered ideal for high-capacity customer connections that need to be provided quickly particularly where the connection is required for only a limited duration.

Optical fibre systems are likely to provide the best solution for more permanent long-term requirements for high capacity customer connections. These systems can be designed at any hierarchical digital rate from 2 to 140 Mbit/s, in almost all local network cases without the need for intermediate repeaters. Using the cheapest suitable fibre and simplifying terminal equipment design enables system costs to be minimised. BT is currently evaluating cost-reduced 2 Mbit/s systems.

Optical fibre systems also have great potential for distribution of visual services in the local network. In this application, however, digital transmission may not be optimum and methods of avoiding expensive codec equipment are being studied; the most favoured method at the moment is pulse frequency modulation. Optical fibre systems are featured in both the Visual Services Trial and the CATV system at Milton Keynes.

8   CONCLUSIONS

The decision to modernise the BT telecommunication network quickly has created the impetus to change from analogue to digital transmission at an unprecedented rate posing some problem in planning for both growth and replacement of the analogue capacity.

A new main network is being built to meet both the present telephony and future digital data/information services. This network will make full use of the presently developed digital transmission systems, as well as higher capacity systems as they become available with the exploitation of optical fibre transmission.

The junction network is also being converted to digital operation making use of existing and new types of pair cables pending the availability of fully competitive optical fibre systems for general junction application. Methods of providing digital transmission in the local network are now available for customers to exploit the X Stream Services prior to the full availability of the ISDN to provide network coverage for enhanced data and visual services. Here there is plenty of room for innovation to maximise the use of existing types of local distribution cables, optical fibre-cables and microwave radio in meeting the customers futuristic requirements.

Acknowledgement is made to the Director or Transmission Department of British Telecom for permission to publish this paper.

W J Murray, Head of Section, Trunk Transmission Planning Division of the Network Executive Transmission Department, has been responsible since 1977 for new systems and long term studies of digital transmission in the BT network. Previously he was involved in the introduction of Datel and Dataplex services and was concerned with the technical aspects of data transmission over the BT analogue network.

Adaptive Links – A Methodology for Dynamic Bandwidth Allocation

L F Ludwig
Bell Telephone Laboratories, USA

ABSTRACT

The "digital pipe" concept has been used in the planning of Integrated Services Digital Networks to mean a transmission link which adaptively allocates bandwidth to time varying traffic mixes. Traffic mixes would consist of packet and circuit switched traffic with differing traffic characteristics, directional balances, bit rates, and user perceived service performance grades. The first part of this paper puts forth a formal definition for a general type of digital pipe which is termed an "adaptive link". This is followed by a brief examination of some technical implications via some simple models and elementary performance measures that assume few complicating control considerations. Remarks are made concerning feasibility, design, and implementation. Some control structure considerations are then discussed.

1. SCOPE

There has been considerable interest in a "generalized" digital communications link -- a so-called "digital pipe"[1] -- in Integrated Services Digital Networks. This link would support variable mixes of circuit and packet switched traffic with differing traffic characteristics, directional asymmetries, and bit rates. The purpose of this paper is to pose some analytical problems associated with such a link and offer preliminary examination of a few performance measures. Control structure and penalties required to obtain such flexibility are also examined.

2. THE GENERAL PROBLEM

Traditionally nonhomogeneous traffic between a pair of nodes is segregated onto separate transmission facilities carrying more homogeneous traffic loads. There are, however, considerations making the digital pipe concept of interest as an alternative:

1. Cost:
   - Better utilization of existing low bandwidth plant is preferred to installation of new facilities;
   - Bandwidth is very expensive for all conceivable transport methods, making efficient utilization important;
2. Convenience:
   - ISDN integrated access for PBXs and sophisticated users may require support for time varying mixes of different traffic types;
   - Reconfiguration capabilities within the network may be simplified by transmission links offering a variable channel structure.

Figure 1 illustrates the concept of a digital pipe. The transmission facilities pictured are synchronous and may be unidirectional or bidirectional. A formal definition for a very general view of the "digital pipe" concept is put forth below. To avoid confusion with other uses of the expression "digital pipe", this general view of the concept will be termed an "adaptive link".

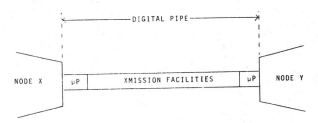

Figure 1. Digital pipe setting, domain, and components.

<u>Definition</u>: An <u>adaptive link</u> is a system comprised of one or more synchronous digital transmission facilities spanning two communications nodes that permits controlled or adaptive aggregation and disaggregation of nonhomogeneous traffic types. One or more of the following nonhomogeneities may exist:

1. Directional balance;
2. Bit rate;
3. Utilization burst characteristics:
   - Number of hierarchical layers into which the resource allocation procedure is partitioned;
   - Traffic characteristics at each layer:
     - Arrival rate;
     - Holding time/packet length;
4. User perceived service performance:
   - Reliability;
   - Error performance;
   - Blocking/delay statistics;

Items 1, 2, and 3 will be discussed in more detail in the next section, taking few control considerations into account. The rationale here is that in some cases significant feasibility statements can be made before complicating control considerations are examined. A subsequent section qualitatively examines control structure considerations. Item 4 is not considered in this paper. We turn now to preliminary study of mixed directional balances, bit rates, and burst characteristics utilizing a finite resource allocation view for transmission facility bandwidth.

3. INDIVIDUAL STUDIES OF DIRECTIONAL, BIT RATE, AND BURST CHARACTERISTIC ADAPTIVITY

3.1 Directional Adaptivity

Many data communications sessions involve asymmetries in the transport bandwidth required by antipodal sources of an end to end connection. During a session of this nature the ratio of bandwidths required may vary or remain fixed, but unless all sessions supported by a link require the same fixed ratio the link will see its overall ratio vary with time. This suggests an application for a directionally adaptive link. In this paper we examine realization considerations and efficiency measures for directionally adaptive links.

The key element of a directionally adaptive link is a transmission facility whose direction can be reversed as shown in the state diagram of Figure 2, such as in the Time Compression Multiplexing technique used for two-wire subscriber loops.[2] If the facility used operates at the same bit rate in either direction, then the average ratio of bandwidths is precisely the average ratio of times spent in states 1 and 3 (see Figure 2). Actual realizations may change states on command in response to traffic or periodically cycle through states 1 through 4 (varying times spent in states 1 and 3 while keeping the sum of these times constant).

Such adaptive facilities should be able to offer a wide range of adaptivity for little or no more cost than for a more narrow range. In cases where a large amount of link bandwidth but little range in adaptivity is needed, it may be desirable to used a combination of directionally adaptive and directionally dedicated facilities. This is true because, for a given amount of bandwidth, adaptive facilities are more expensive than dedicated facilities. Since a link connecting two nodes may consist of a number of facilities, it is therefore of interest to precisely consider how combinations of adaptive and dedicated facilities behave as a directionally adaptive system.

Consider a link comprised of $(k+m+n)$ facilities, of which k are directionally adaptive facilities, m are dedicated for transmission from node X to node Y, and n are dedicated for transmission from node Y to node X. For $i = 1,2,...,k$ let r_i denote the ratio of facility bandwidth available for transmission from X to Y to facility bandwidth for transmission from Y to X, i.e.:

$$r_i = \frac{\text{Bandwidth for X} \rightarrow \text{Y Transmission}}{\text{Bandwidth for Y} \rightarrow \text{X Transmission}},$$

let $E(d_i)$ denote the expected value of the fraction of time spent in states 2 and 4, and let b_i denote the facility bit rate for the ith adaptive facility. If b_i^X, $i = 1,2,...,m$ and b_i^Y, $i = 1,2,...,n$ denote bit rates of dedicated facilities from X to Y and from Y to X, respectively, then the corresponding directional bandwidth ratio for the entire collection is:

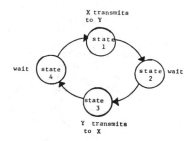

Figure 2. State diagram for a directionally adaptive transmission facility.

$$r_* = \frac{\sum_{i=1}^{k} \frac{r_i}{1+r_i} b_i(1-E(d_i)) + \sum_{i=1}^{m} b_i^X}{\sum_{i=1}^{k} \frac{1}{1+r_i} b_i(1-E(d_i)) + \sum_{i=1}^{n} b_i^Y}.$$

If the state transition cycle is periodically transversed, each $E(d_i)$ is independent of traffic statistics.

If each r_i is substituted with its minimum and maximum value, the maximum or minimum value, respectively, of r_* is obtained. The resulting range of r_* indicates the degree of directional adaptivity of the bandwidth for the entire collection of facilities. The total bandwidth is given by:

$$b_* = \sum_{i=1}^{k} b_i(1-E(d_i)) + \sum_{i=1}^{m} b_i^X + \sum_{i=1}^{n} b_i^Y.$$

For the case where all adaptive facilities are identical (i.e., for all $i = 1,2,...,k$:

$$b_i = b_{adp}, E(d_i) = d,$$

$$\max(r_i) = r_{max}, \min(r_i) = r_{min})$$

and all dedicated facilities are identical (i.e., for $i=1,...,m$ and $j=1,...,n$:

$$b_i^X = b_j^Y = b_{ded})$$

the expressions reduce to:

$$\min(r_*) = \frac{kr_{min}b_{adp}(1-d) + m(1+r_{min})b_{ded}}{kb_{adp}(1-d) + n(1+r_{min})b_{ded}},$$

$$\max(r_*) = \frac{kr_{max}b_{adp}(1-d) + m(1+r_{max})b_{ded}}{kb_{adp}(1-d) + n(1+r_{max})b_{ded}},$$

$$b_* = kb_{adp}(1-d) + (m+n)b_{ded}.$$

These may be used together with the efficiency expressions discussed below in determining optimal configurations as a function of anticipated traffic variational characteristics.

For a directionally adaptive capability to be worthwhile, short-term traffic directional ratios must deviate to some degree. It is therefore of interest to obtain efficiency measures as a function of anticipated traffic variation for comparisons of directionally adaptive and directionally dedicated systems. Referring to Figure 1, let B_X and B_Y denote dedicated bandwidths for transmission from X to

Y and from Y to X, respectively. Then the directional ratio for this directionally dedicated system is $r_{fix} = B_X/B_Y$. Consider the worst case condition where node Y has a block of data to transmit and node X has nothing to transmit. If p_X and p_Y denote the fractions of some random time interval T that nodes X and Y, respectively, have data to transmit, then the fraction of the random time interval T for which this case occurs is $p_Y(1-p_X)$. The wasted bandwidth is then $p_Y(1-p_X)B_X$, or $p_Y(1-p_X)r_{fix}B_Y$. If this bandwidth could be used (via an ideal adaptive capability) for transmission from node Y, the expected value of the resulting <u>throughput gain</u> for this direction (TG_Y) is:

$$E(TG_Y) = \frac{B_Y + p_Y(1-p_X)r_{fix}B_Y}{B_Y} = 1 + p_Y(1-p_X)r_{fix}.$$

Note TG_Y reflects the sensitivity of the possible throughput gain to variational characteristics of the traffic distribution. Note that the effect of varying r_{fix} is to scale the degree of this sensitivity. It is of interest to calculate the expected value of the overall <u>efficiency gain</u> (EG) in a blocking system (i.e., a system where if both X and Y have data to transmit, the one not allocated bandwidth by the directionally adaptive facility is blocked by the system). Note the wasted bandwidth in the antipodal direction is $p_X(1-p_Y)B_Y$. Then:

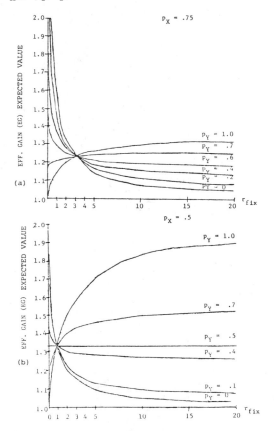

(a)

(b)

Figure 3. Expected value of Efficiency Gain (EG) normalized by $(1-d^*)$ for (a) $p_X = 0.75$, and (b) $p_Y = 0.50$.

$$E(EG) = \frac{(B_X+B_Y)(1-d^*)}{(B_X+B_Y)-p_Y(1-p_X)B_X-p_X(1-p_Y)B_Y}$$

$$= \frac{(1-d^*)}{1 + p_Xp_Y - \frac{p_X + r_{fix}p_Y}{1+r_{fix}}},$$

where d^* denotes the fraction of bandwidth lost due to direction reversal procedures. This relationship is plotted without the $(1-d^*)$ scaling term in Figure 3. Note that, as might be expected, E(EG) is independent of r_{fix} if and only if $p_X = p_Y$. For the blocking system, the directional ratio of the traffic is neatly determined by p_X, p_Y, and r_{fix} and may be shown to be:

$$r_{traffic} = \frac{(1-p_Y+r_{fix})p_X}{(1+r_{fix}(1-p_X))p_Y}$$

using the fact that the fraction of time that contentions are won by Y is $1/(1+r_{fix})$.

3.2 Multiple Bit Rate Adaptivity

The problem of allocating bandwidth to traffics with differing bit rates has generated considerable interest (see[3] for an extensive bibliography). In this section we will examine some specific blocking phenomena relevant to the digital pipe concept via some simple examples based on a well studied queuing model. A number of performance metrics are then introduced and discussed. In the examples, all traffic bit rates are assumed to be integer multiples of a fixed-length TDM frame rate. For a non-delay system a fixed-length TDM frame represents an a priori division of all available link bandwidth into fundamental bit rate units. Thus, extensions to a variable-length frame scheme (such as[4]) are only relevant if some of the traffic is handled by a delay queuing system. These assumptions permit modeling as a blocking, finite server queuing system serving a number of traffic types distinguished by the number of servers each requires from a common server pool, where each server represents a fundamental unit of bit rate, or slot in the fixed-length TDM frame. This has been studied by a number of authors[3]. Although the ideas and methods are easily extended to more traffic types, the examples here, for simplicity, attempt to illustrate phenomenon of interest with only two traffic types.

The examples compare a system where a fixed bandwidth allocation is made to the two traffic types with another system where the same amount of overall bandwidth is adaptively allocated as needed. A fixed blocking probability of 0.05 for each traffic type, equal dedicated bandwidths for each of the two traffic types, and a parametrically specified total bandwidth (total number of servers) is assumed for the Fixed Allocation (FA) case. This determines a traffic intensity for each traffic type in the FA system. These traffic intensities and the overall total bandwidth are then used to calculate blocking figures for the Adaptive Allocation (AA) system via the method of Arthurs and Kaufman[3]. Figure 4 illustrates blocking for both AA traffics as a function of bit rate ratio and the total number of servers (which determines the traffic intensities). It may be seen that as a function of these two parameters the AA blocking is always less than the FA blocking (set at 0.05) for the lower bit rate traffic but may be better, equal, or worse for the higher bit rate traffic. This occurs because for a fixed number of servers and an increasing bit rate ratio the higher bit rate load decreases, giving the lower bit rate traffic a competitive edge for servers in the AA system. Note, however, that improvement for the lower bit traffic independent of these two parameters cannot be guaranteed if all FA blocking probabilities are not equal. In addition, Figure 5 illustrates that higher bit rate traffic intensity cannot be adjusted so as to obtain an equal blocking AA system. This shows that additional schemes must be used in AA systems to insure that lower bit rate traffic does not receive an unfair blocking advantage. One class of methods involves an a

priori limiting of allocations made to lower bit rate traffics. A variety of schemes are possible[5], all of which limit the overall flexibility of the link, however, as a result.

Another performance consideration is utilization of transport bandwidth. For a system S (either AA or some FA scheme) the overall utilization, measuring the effective bandwidth (average number of servers) utilized, may be defined as:

$$U_S = \frac{\sum_i a_i b_i (1-P_i^S)}{N},$$

where parameters are defined as follows:

i: Traffic Type Index (an integer)
S: System Type Index (AA or FA)
a_i: Traffic Type i intensity
b_i: Traffic Type i Bit Rate (Normalized)
N: Total Number of Servers Representing Fundamental Units of Link Bandwidth
P_i^S: Blocking Probability Offered to Traffic Type i by System S

Although an AA system and its associated blocking probabilities $\{P_i^S\}$ are uniquely determined by N and the collections $\{a_i\}$ and $\{b_i\}$, there are many possible FA systems distinguished by how fixed allocations are made to the various traffic types. If FA_θ denotes a particular FA system, it is natural to define a utilization gain comparing utilizations of the two systems:

$$G^\theta = U_{AA}/U_{FA_\theta}$$

Figure 6 shows for the above examples the utilization gain is always greater than unity. It is important to note that the significance of the gain depends on the FA_θ utilization, also indicated in Figure 6. Recall that N denotes the total number of servers. For large N, the FA utilization is very high (90%) so that a 2-3% gain is a significant increase with respect to the highest possible increase, although a small increase overall. For small N, FA utilization is much lower (60%) so that

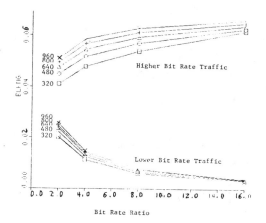

Figure 4. Blocking for two bit rate traffic mixes for bit rate ratios of 2, 4, 8, and 16. Lines connecting points are for clarity. Numbers to the left of curves denote total number of servers.

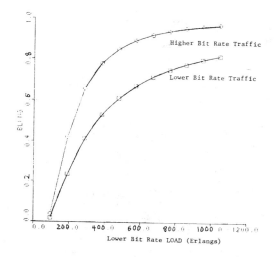

Figure 5. Adaptive system blocking with bit rate ratio 2 and higher bit rate load of 44.5 Erlangs. Note that the lower bit rate load cannot be increased so as to obtain an equal blocking system. Divergence is more pronounced for larger bit rate ratios.

a 4-5% gain is much less significant by either view. This suggests that, independent of control considerations, the mixing of bit rates cannot be expected to contribute to sizable utilization gains.

Since bandwidth may be directly associated with cost, a perhaps more significant metric is the overall bandwidth savings obtained from use of AA rather than a FA_θ scheme. Given a needed bandwidth B, a system S with utilization U_S requires a link bandwidth B/U_S. Thus the fraction of bandwidth saved by the AA system when compared to FA_θ is:

$$\left(\frac{1}{U_{AA}} - \frac{1}{U_{FA_\theta}} \right).$$

The notion of fairness can be coupled to the utilization measure. As in the partial pressure formulation, the utilization may be decomposed into the partial utilizations associated with individual traffic types:

$$u_i^S = \frac{a_i b_i (1 - P_i^S)}{N}$$

It is then straightforward to define a <u>partial utilization gain</u>:

$$g_i^\theta = \frac{u_i^{AA}}{u_i^{FA_\theta}} = \frac{1 - P_i^{AA}}{1 - P_i^{FA_\theta}}$$

which is seen to depend only on blocking comparisons. A measure of pairwise fairness for traffic types i and j with respect to how the overall utilization gain is distributed is then:

$$f_{i,j}^\theta = \frac{g_i^\theta}{g_j^\theta} = \frac{(1 - P_i^{AA})(1 - P_j^{FA_\theta})}{(1 - P_i^{FA_\theta})(1 - P_j^{AA})},$$

optimally near unity. The overall fairness could then be measured as:

$$F^\theta = \min_{i,j} f_{i,j}^\theta$$

optimally near unity.

3.3 Multiple Burst Characteristic Adaptivity

Approaches taken to handling traffic with mixed burst characteristics have traditionally focused on combined circuit and packet switched traffic applied to variable frame length or fixed frame length, movable boundary systems (see bibliography of [4]). Although it is noted that variable frame length schemes have superior performance [4], the intent of this section is not to summarize or add to this line of study but rather to pose a more general view of the basic problem.

Consider the six classical communication strategies: Private Line (PL), Circuit Switched (CS), TASI, Dynamic Virtual Circuit (DVC), Permanent Virtual Circuit (PVC), and Datagram (DG). Each of these may be characterized by a 3-tuple, entries of which denote the use of resource allocation procedures with various time constants and costs. One procedure, referred to as "nailup", involves resource allocation and release procedures with time constants associated with the processing of a service order. Another procedure, referred to as "call setup", has time constants on the order of circuit switched or virtual call setup and release. The third procedure, referred to as "burst", has time constants associated with the transmission and processing of packet headers and trailers or the detections of dead-times in speech. Table 1 illustrates how each of the six schemes are characterized via these procedures. Note that three services

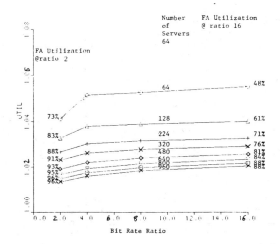

Figure 6. Utilization Gain for bit rate ratios of 2, 4, 8, and 16.

SERVICE	3-TUPLE	NO. OF LAYERS
Private Line	(e,0,0)	1
Circuit Switched	(0,b,0)	1
TASI	(0,b,b)	2
Dynamic Virtual Circuit	(0,e,d)	2
Permanent Virtual Circuit	(e,0,d)	2
Datagram	(0,0,d)	1

TABLE 1. Service characterization by allocation procedure layers and time constants. Entries in 3-tuples denote whether blocking (b), delay (d), either (e), or no (0) use is made of nailup, call setup, and burst procedures, respectively.

involve more than one procedure, and that in this case these procedures are hierarchically related. This suggests a general notion that a resource allocation procedure may be composed of layers of subprocedures, hierarchically invoked according to their respective time constants. Further, each layer may have other characteristics in addition to allocation time constant. For example, TASI and DVC have identical 3-tuples, but differ according to whether blocking or delay is invoked at each layer. Also, each layer's blocking or delay is further characterized by statistics (mean delay or blocking probability, variances, etc.).

In each procedure, delay and processing complexity represent overhead penalities required in the allocation. With respect to adaptive links, the delay between the time a data source has data to transmit and the time the bandwidth is actually allocated may be viewed as a bandwidth loss in many settings. The notion of a layered procedure suggest that a source's transmission statistics are such that this overhead should be distributed over subprocedures of several time constants. Further attributes, such as blocking or delay statistics, may distinguish several procedures with the same time constant. Given a set of procedures, it may be asked how a given user transmission statistic may be optimally matched by combinations of these procedures. The following formalism illustrates how a procedure with a particular time constant may or may not be optimal in reallocating bandwidth during periods of inactivity. The structure of the approach appears extendible to other procedure parameters.

Let $\{P_i\}$ denote a collection of resource allocation procedures distinguished by time constants. Let P_i have time constant t_i with:

$$t_i = (P_i \text{ allocation time}) + (P_i \text{ release time}),$$

and let the P_i be ordered such that $t_i > t_j$ for $i > j$. If c_i denotes the overhead and complexity cost of P_i, then in practice we have $c_i < c_j$ for $i > j$. Let I denote the duration of a given inactivity period for some data source. Then P_i permits resource sharing with some other data source if and only if $t_i < (0.5)I$. If this condition is met and $t_{i-1} \gg I$, then P_{i-1} is a more costly means of resource allocation than P_i. (A simple example is the fact that the handling of a source matching the transmission statistics of a Datagram is more costly when handled over a Circuit Switched or a Private Line connection.) These relationships hold for ranges of values of I, and, together with the probabilities of occurrence of these ranges of I, suggest a formal structure for optimal matching of individual allocation procedures to traffic statistics. Thus variational ranges in the traffic transmission statistics can be directly related to required degrees of burst characteristic adaptivity for the adaptive link. Further development is required.

4. CONTROL STRUCTURE CONSIDERATIONS

4.1 Control Complexity and Bandwidth Requirements

The control structure is ultimately responsible for the management of the individual processes that comprise the adaptive link. It is comprised of local processing occurring within each of the two nodes connected by the link and control messages exchanged between these two nodes. Two considerations important to the feasibility of an adaptive link, then, are the complexity of the local control structures and the bandwidth required for control message exchanges. The complexity issue is a topic commonly addressed in the literature discussing specific implementational approaches (see, for example, the bibliography of [4]). We briefly list four techniques to minimize control bandwidth:

- Precedency: This technique holds a parameter or assignment fixed until a change is deterministically required, reducing extraneous control messages or reassignments generating them;

- Hysteresis: Here a parameter or assignment is held past the point where a change may be otherwise desirable until the cost of further deference of a change exceeds a hysteresis threshold. This technique has application when control messages compete with data or a rush of other control message for transport bandwidth;

- Parallel Procedures: Here, tracking state machines are coordinated by a minimum of control message exchanges. Complex control sequences can then be created locally rather than relying on intimate control message exchanges;

- Huffman Coding: This general message coding technique associates symbols with messages in such a way that shorter length symbols are associated with more frequently occurring messages. This can reduce the mean length of control messages if a statistically adaptive message encoder monitoring the distribution of transmitted control messages is used. The decoder at the opposite node must be in slave relationship with the adaptive encoder.

Each of these techniques relies on reducing redundancy in control message sequences. As a result, information theory arguments show that the control messages are more subject to error. Selective use of these techniques, with or without the use of error correcting codes, should be pursued to obtain minimum mean control bandwidth while insuring required levels of reliability.

One method for comparing performances of a fixed and an adaptive allocation system is to view the data and control as competing for the same bandwidth (there may well be rationales for actually implementing such configurations). The costs of hardware, bandwidth, reliability, and other criterion may then be compared on an absolute basis. It is noted that, in a well designed adaptive link system, the amount of control bandwidth necessary should be monotonically related to the degree of variation seen in the traffic mix.

4.2 Control Structure Characteristics

Formally, the adaptive link is an example of a class of systems referred to as "self-organizing systems" for which an evolving theory exists[6]. Due to the presence of layered user protocols, layered allocation procedures, statistical observers, processers, and multiplexing procedures, it is natural to expect the control structure to be hierarchical in form.

For directional adaptivity, at least one directionally adaptive facility and its associated control system are required. If no dedicated bandwidth exists in each direction for control message transactions, then this control structure must cycle through the state diagram of Figure 2 periodically so as to provide a minimum bandwidth bidirectional channel for control. Otherwise, the control system can be such that the direction is reversed as needed, offering the possibility for reducing the amount of bandwidth wasted in states 2 and 4. From the development in Section 3.2 it is observed that control procedures are required to insure uniform performance and fairness in the handling of mixed bit rate traffic. Also, readings in the literature suggest that a variable frame structure is the key to mixing blocking and delay traffic with varying burst characteristics [4].

4.3 Local Architectures Within Nodes

The architecture within each node will depend on the specific realization. For example, many adaptive link applications may only serve a selective subset of the possible traffic nonhomogeneities. A short list of commonly used architectural features might include:

- Input and output ports for data and control;
- Buffers for delay traffic at these ports;
- Various multiplexers and demultiplexers;
- Control message coordination and processing;
- Statistical observers of traffic characteristics for adaptive subsystems;
- Statistically adaptive encoders and slave decoders for control messages.

5. SUMMARY

A preliminary examination of a number of technical considerations relevant to the "digital pipe" concept has been presented in this paper. Much work remains to be done, not only within the individual topics outlined in this paper, but also in their unification. For example, fixed frame length and variable frame length schemes are optimal for mixed bit rates and mixed burst characteristics, respectively, suggesting complex relationships when both nonhomogeneities are present. Referring to Section 2, a perhaps premature speculation would be that the digital pipe concept may not be as cost effective as might be desired for "cost" oriented applications while also not being as costly as might be feared for "convenience" oriented applications.

6. ACKNOWLEDGEMENTS

The author acknowledges invaluable discussions with W. S. Gifford (posing the problem), L. Y. Ong, D. Y. Burman, and R. G. Holstein, mathematical review and graphics assistance of J. L. Bazley and M. M. Boenke, crucial quantitative results from L Y. Ong, and editorial suggestions of R. L. Pokress and D. M. Tuttleman.

References

1. Dorros, I., "ISDN -- A Challenge and Opportunity for the Eighties", IEEE Communications Magazine, Vol. 19, No. 2 (March 1981).
2. Bosik, B. S., "The Case in Favor of Burst-Mode Transmission for Digital Subscriber Loops", ISSLS Conference Record (1980).
3. Arthurs, E., Kaufman, J. S., "Sizing a Message Store Subject. to Blocking Criteria", in Arato, et al (eds.), Performance of Computer Systems, (North-Holland, Amsterdam, 1979).
4. Maglaris, B., Schwartz, M., "Performance Evaluation of a Variable Frame Multiplexer for Integrated Switching Networks", IEEE Trans. Comm., Vol. COM-29, No. 6 (June 1981).
5. Katzschnor, L., Scheller, "Probability of Loss of Data Traffics with Different Bit Rates Hunting One Common PCM Channel", Proc. 8th Int. Teletraffic Congress, Melborn, Australia (November 1979).
6. Saridis, G. N., "Self-Organizing Control of Stochastic Systems" (Dekker, New York, 1977).

Lester Ludwig was born April 15, 1956, in San Antonio, Texas. He received the BSEE and MSEE in 1978 and 1980 from Cornell University, Ithaca, New York, studying signal processing and bilinear systems theory. He is currently a member of the Digital Network Architecture Department of Bell Telephone Laboratories working on Integrated Services Digital Network architecture and interfaces. He plans pursuit of the PhD degree in computer communications later this year. He is also active in electronic music with many publications in that area. Other interests include pure mathematics and active circuit design.

Some Issues of Transmission of Packetized Voice Through Store-and-forwards Data Communication Networks

D Conrads
Kernforschungsanlage Juelich,
Federal Republic of Germany

P Kermani
IBM, USA

This paper focuses on some issues related to transmission of packetized voice over store-and-forward data communication networks. We first discuss the problem of error checking for voice packets. In contrast to general belief, we show that it is infeasible not to do error checking for voice packets in an environment where voice and data coexist. Furthermore, through mathematical modeling, we demonstrate that there is no significant advantage in providing special, less restrictive, error checking procedure for packetized voice. We then study the capacity and delay requirements in such networks. Through analytic modeling, we draw some basic guidelines on how to design a data network to be able to use it for voice transmission as well. It is shown that even with low data rate vocoder type digitizers, high bandwidth channels (i.e. significantly higher than 50 kbps) are required to meet the delay requirement of voice communication. However, because of the present day high prices of the required hardware, providing packetized voice transmission is yet an uneconomical venture.

1. INTRODUCTION

The ongoing process of more and more digitizing traditionally analog signals - for which voice is no exemption - opens the possibility to use store-and-forward network technology to transmit (digitized) voice [5], [8]. Here, we restrict ourselves to the question of how additional voice traffic would impact existing store-and-forward networks, like for example IBM's SNA.

It turns out that voice traffic has special non-trivial requirements concerning delay and bandwidth and due to its very real time nature needs some kind of guaranteed services [1] [4] [6]. So, the central problems are how to choose network parameters and how to change network procedures such that the appropriate service can be guaranteed without explicitly reserving resources.

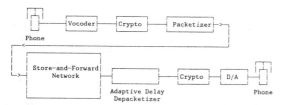

Figure 1. General structure of the environment.

The environment we are facing is shown in Figure 1. At the source speech is digitized, it may be encrypted after digitization and is packetized before it is submitted to the store-and-forward network which is also intended to carry non-voice data traffic. At the destination the incoming packets are depacketized and may be delayed in the "adaptive delay depacketizer" to enforce a more steady flow of information. If applicable, the digital signal is decrypted and then transformed to analog signals and made audible to the listener.

The main topic of this paper is delay studies in store-and-forward networks. First we focus on error handling procedures for voice packets. It is a general belief that for voice packets less rigorous error handling procedures are applicable thereby relieving the delay problem in case of errors. We

show that in an environment which is intended to carry both, data and voice traffic, procedures that avoid retransmission of voice packets impose additional overhead and major changes to existing link protocols such that the overall gain is very marginal even for unrealistic high error rates.

We then study the delay behavior of store-and-forward networks during normal operation. Under deterministic worst case assumptions an expression for the maximum end to end delay can be derived. This expression relates all of the relevant network parameters and therefore enables us to study the interdependencies of these parameters. Furthermore, a probabilistic model for the maximum queue length at a node is also utilized. This model gives more reasonable quantitative results concerning queueing delay, thereby overcoming the main deficiency of the deterministic model. Based on these models, our results indicate that with present-day technology, transportation of a reasonably large volume of packetized voice through existing store-and-forward data networks is physically infeasible and commercially impractical.

2. ERROR HANDLING

It is a general belief that losing a limited number of voice packets does not seriously hurt intelligibility and therefore erroneous voice packets can be discarded in order to avoid the retransmission delay. However, in an environment where both voice and data traffic coexist, the receiver, when sensing a negative CRC-check, has no information whether the related packet is a data packet (in which case requesting retransmission is mandatory) or a voice packet (in which case it simply could be discarded).

There are two, plausible approaches to overcome this problem:

1. Retransmission-decision is made by the sender.

2. Retransmission-decision is made by the receiver.

In the first approach, the receiver of the erroneous packet signals back the error to the sender. The sender which has a valid copy of the packet then makes the decision whether to retransmit it or not. Besides possible problems concerning sequence numbers at the link level protocol, this solution

* This research was done while Dieter Conrads was on leave at IBM Watson Research Center

does not buy too much in terms of delay, especially not in networks which provide node by node sequencing.

In the latter approach, a second CRC is provided for the packet header. Because the packet header is usually significantly smaller than the data part, there is some probability that the header is proved to be valid whereas the data part is in error. In this case the receiver can find out whether the received packet is a voice or data packet. If the packet header is in error there is still a gain in delay because the receiver can request retransmission right after reading the header rather than after reading the entire packet. However, the possible gain in delay and efficiency is not for free:

- The introduction of a second CRC is a major change to most of the existing link protocols[1] and therefore per se an expensive measure in existing networks.

- The header information length is increased by (usually) two bytes for every packet.

The performance of this latter model was analytically evaluated [2]. Our results show that only for unrealistic high error rates and/or very large packets there is a gain in efficiency for the 2__CRC scheme (see Figure 2); with more realistic numbers the 2__CRC scheme is always less efficient. If we change other parameters (such as packet length, header length, etc.), the same behavior prevails [2]. This is an important point because, as we will show in the next section, in order to reduce delay, voice packets should be as small as possible such that the header length is already a critical parameter without these additional CRC-bits and the possible benefit in the error case is also reduced.

When considering procedures which potentially drop packets as the ones described above, the assumption that discarding single packets once in a while will not hurt intelligibility is crucial. We claim that this assumption is no longer valid when employing low voice data rate producing digitizers (vocoders) and/or other data rate reduction techniques where packets may contain information which is pertinent to other packets as well (e.g. silence detection, transmitting delta information, only transmitting parameters which have changed beyond a certain threshold). As a result, such error

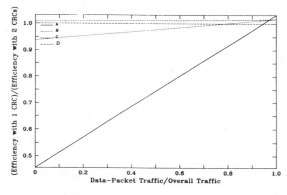

Figure 2. Relative efficiency of two error handling schemes for varying error rates : Packet length=100 bytes, header length=26 bytes, A: error rate= 10^{-3}, B: error rate= 10^{-4}, C: error rate= 10^{-5}, D: line of equal efficiencies.

handling procedures are not applicable in the environment we are investigating.

[1] An exception is, for example, DEC's DDCMP which already for other reasons provides a separate CRC for the packet header.

3. IMPACT OF DELAY REQUIREMENTS

The bandwidth requirements of digitized voice are determined by the voice data rate (VDR) the digitizer generates. The range is from around 1200 bps to 64000 bps. The lower end (less than 5000 bps) being realized by vocoders which in terms of price and performance have not yet reached the point of a broad commercial applicability [3], [7]. Nonetheless, when realizing that most existing networks only support links up to around 50 kbps (per single link, which gives 200 kbps for two full duplex links) it is obvious that only low VDR-vocoders can be employed in such networks.

Concerning delay, there is a consensus that for a voice conversation it should not exceed .5 seconds [4], [6]. This value is therefore made the basis of our delay considerations. Important for speech quality is also the variance of delay. We do not focus on that, but because we only deal with maximum end-to-end delays and have introduced the 'adaptive delay depacketizer' (see Figure 1) we have solved that problem in principle.

In our maximum delay studies we include four types of delay.

1. Packetization delay

   This delay measures the time to fill a packet of length l_v ; it depends on the VDR (voice data rate, V) and the voice packet length (l_v).

2. Transmission delay

   This delay measures the duration of the packet transmission from source to destination (minimum travel time); it depends on the channel capacity (C), the voice packet length (l_v), the packet header length (l_h) and the path length (number of hops, n_h).

3. Queueing delay due to voice traffic

   This delay measures the waiting time a packet encounters at an outgoing link due to interferences with other voice packets; it depends on C, l_v, l_h, n_h and the number of voice sessions, n_v.

4. Interference delay

   This delay measures the time a voice packet may be deferred by interfering data traffic over which voice is assumed to have non-preemptive priority; this delay depends on C, l_h, n_h and the data packet length, l_d.

We have not included propagation delay in our investigations because there is no interaction between this type of delay and other network design parameters. However we should point out, that propagation delay becomes critical and introduces major constraints for satellite links. The maximum delay can be derived under the assumption that the load on all nodes of the path (of length n_h) is the same and that the capacities of the links between adjacent nodes are identical. The maximum delay at a node is encountered when all voice traffic sources are active and continuously generating traffic. In the worst case the delay of a voice packet is the sum of the transmission time of a data packet (the priority is non-preemptive) and of one voice packet per every other source.

Under this assumption the maximum end-to-end delay (D) a voice packet may suffer is given by:

$$D = \frac{l_v}{V} + [\frac{l_d + l_h}{C} + n_v \frac{l_v + l_h}{C}]n_h \qquad (1)$$

with the following constraint

$$n_v V \frac{l_v + l_h}{l_v} \le \beta C \qquad (2)$$

where β specifies the portion of the link capacity which is devoted to voice. By means of the above formula the interdependencies of the different parameters can be studied. For this purpose we set $D = D_{max} = .5$ seconds and look at the maximum number of voice sessions (n_v) over the voice data rate (V) for different parameter settings.

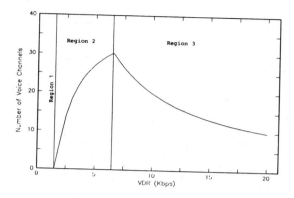

Figure 3. General shape of number of voice sessions vs. VDR curve : parameters are $\beta=1$, $n_h = 3$, $l_v = l_d = 800$ bits, $l_h = 26$ bytes, $D_{max} = .5$ seconds, $C=250$ kbps.

These curves have the general shape shown in Figure 3, which consist of three adjacent regions:

Region 1. Starting with very low VDR no voice traffic is possible because the packetization delay is such that packets cannot be transported from end to end within the D_{max} delay constraint.

Region 2. In this region the end-to-end delay is the limiting factor on the number of voice sessions. This section is the most interesting one because it is determined by interaction of all of the network parameters.

Region 3. In this region the voice data rate is high enough such that $D \leq D_{max}$ is always fulfilled and the number of voice sessions is limited by the bandwidth available.

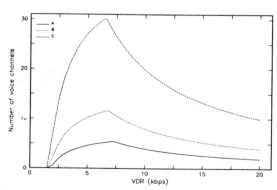

Figure 4. No. of voice sessions vs. VDR for given capacities : $\beta=1$, $l_v = l_d = 800$ bits, $l_h = 26$ bytes, $n_h = 3$, $D_{max} = .5$ seconds, A: $C=50$ kbps, B: $C=100$ kbps, C: $C=250$ kbps.

In the following parameter studies we always assume $l_v = l_d$. The influence of the channel capacity on the number of voice sessions is high (see Figure 4). In Region 3, which is characterized by Eq. (2) this dependency is linear; whereas in Region 2 it is more than linear (increasing C by a factor of α increases n_v by more than α). Region 1 remains unchanged as the packetization delay is not influenced by C. The effect of voice packet length is shown in Figure 5. This figure clearly shows the significance of voice packet length in the system design. Understandably, when delay is the limiting factor (regions 1 and 2) smaller l_v results in larger n_v. However, this trend is reversed when capacity is the bottleneck. The reason for this phenomenon is that for larger voice packet length, l_v, the transmission efficiency is higher (see Eq. (2)).

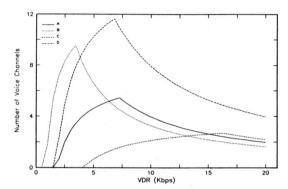

Figure 5. No. of voice sessions vs. VDR for different packet lengths : $\beta=1$, $l_h = 26$ bytes, $n_h = 3$, $D_{max} = .5$ seconds, A: $l_v = l_d = 800$ bits, $C=50$ kbps, B: $l_v = l_d = 400$ bits, $C=50$ kbps, C: $l_v = l_d = 1600$ bits, $C=50$ kbps, D: $l_v = l_d = 800$ bits, $C=100$ kbps.

The path length (number of hops) influences delay types (2) through (4) because they occur at every node (Figure 6).

If we vary β we see that in terms of delay (region 2) it is much more advantageous to achieve a certain bandwidth for voice by devoting a fraction of a high bandwidth link instead of using 100 percent of a lower bandwidth link (Figure 7). This gives an argument for integration of voice and data traffic.

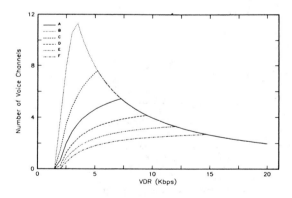

Figure 6. No. of voice sessions vs. VDR for different number of hops : $\beta=1$, $l_v = l_d = 800$ bits, $l_h = 26$ bytes, $D_{max} = .5$ seconds, $C=50$ kbps, A: $n_h = 3$, B: $n_h = 1$, C: $n_h = 2$, D: $n_h = 4$, E: $n_h = 5$, F: $n_h = 6$.

4. CONCLUSIONS

If we assume that 50 kbps per link cannot significantly be exceeded in current networks, we see that they cannot support, by any means, a reasonable number of voice sessions. For high VDR digitizers, bandwidth is the limiting factor. However, low VDR devices do not improve the situation as well. The reason being that with too many low VDR voice sessions, the queueing delay (of type 3) becomes too high.

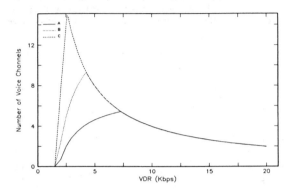

Figure 7. No. of voice sessions vs. VDR for different β : $l_v = l_d$ = 800 bits, l_h = 26 bytes, D_{max} =.5 seconds, n_h = 3, A: β=1, C=50 kbps, B: β=.5, C=100 kbps, C: β=.2, C=250 kbps.

Low VDR, nevertheless improves the situation for data traffic, because there is bandwidth left which is not useable by voice traffic (region 2). So, the only means to increase the number of voice sessions would be a reduction of voice packet length. It turns out that in order to maintain reasonable efficiency the voice packet length should not be significantly less than 800 Bits, as the existing general purpose data networks have fairly large packet headers (e.g. SNA 26 bytes). Beyond that, the processing capabilities of existing nodes would very soon become the limiting factor when reducing packet length.

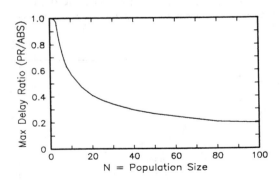

Figure 8. Relative queueing delay : β=1, ε=99%, maximum load applied in both cases.

Admittedly, the model we used to obtain our results is very conservative in the sense that it is based on purely deterministic worst case assumptions. Having these considerations in mind, we developed a probabilistic model for the maximum queueing delay at a node [2]. As expected, the queueing delays derived from that model are much less than in the deterministic case. The ratio between the probabilistic (99 percentile) and the deterministic maximum queueing delay over the population size is shown in Figure 8. Applying these results to our previous problem (Figure 9) we achieve

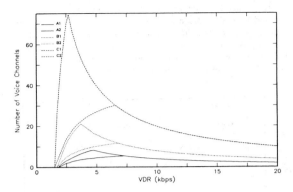

Figure 9. No. of voice sessions vs. VDR for different channel capacities : $l_v = l_d$ = 800 bits, l_h = 26 bytes, D_{max} =.5 seconds, n_h = 3, β=1, ε=99%, A: C=50 kbps, B: C=100 kbps, C: C=250 kbps,

All in all, our results indicate that in order to transmit packetized voice through store-and-forward data networks, very large bandwidth is needed to be able to support a reasonable number of voice sessions. As a result, high nodal processing power is needed to support the high bandwidth; however, such processing power is still not available. Therefore, with present day technology transportation of a reasonably large volume of packetize voice through store-and-forward networks is physically infeasible and commercially impractical.

REFERENCES

[1] Bially, T., B. Gold and S. Seneff, "A Technique for Adaptive Voice Flow Control in Integrated Packet Networks," *IEEE Trans. on Comm.*, Vol. COM-28, No. 3, Match 1980, pp. 325-333.

[2] Conrads, D. and P. Kermani, "A Feasibility Study of Using Store-and-Forward Data Communication Networks to Transmit Digitized Speech", IBM Report RC 9157, Nov. 1981.

[3] Cotton, I.W., "Making Machines Talk: Simulated Speech, Part One," *Data Communications*, Jan. 1981, pp. 75-80.

[4] Coveillo, G.J., O.L. Lake and G.R. Redinbo, "System Design Implications of Packetized Voice," *Proc. of ICC 77*, Chicago, Ill. 1977, pp. 38.3-49 to 38.3-53.

[5] Forgie, J.W., "Speech Transmission In Packet-Switched Store-and-Forward Networks," *Proceedings of National Computer Conference*, June 1975, pp.137-142.

[6] Gitman, I. and H. Frank, "Economic Analysis of Integrated Voice and Data Networks: A Case Study," *Proceedings of The IEEE*, Vol. 66, No. 11, November 1978, pp. 1549-1570.

[7] Gold, B., "Digital Speech Networks," *Proceedings of the IEEE*, Vol. 65, No. 12, Dec. 1977, pp. 1636-1658.

[8] Occhiogrosso, B., "Digitized Voice Comes Out Of Age, Part 2- Techniques," *Data Communications*, April 1978, pp. 63-81.

Dieter Conrads received the diploma in mathematics from the Technical University, Achen, W. Germany in 1968 and the Ph.D. degree in computer science from the University of Dortmund, W. Germany in 1980. Since 1969 he has been a member of the scientific staff of the Institute of Applied Mathematics of the Nuclear Research Center, Juelich, W. Germany. In this position he participated in the design and implementation of a local network of experimental computers and was involved in several joint data processing projects together with other sciences. In a more theoretical area he has worked on paging algorithms, especially prepaging algorithms. During 1981 Dr. Conrads was a visiting scientist at IBM T.J. Watson Research Center, Yorktown Heights, New York, U.S.A.

Parviz Kermani received the B.S. degree from the University of Tehran, Iran in 1969, the M.Math. degree in computer science from the University of Waterloo, Canada in 1973 and the Ph.D. degree in computer science from the University of California, Los Angeles (UCLA) in 1977. From 1974 to 1977 he participated in the ARPA network project and did research in the design and evaluation of computer communication networks. In 1978 he received a postdoctoral fellowship from IBM and was a member of the research staff in the Computer Science Department of UCLA. Since December 1978 he has been with the IBM T.J. Watson Research Center, Yorktown Heights, New York, and has been involved in design of routing and flow control mechanisms for computer networks. His current interests are in the area of design, control, and evaluation of data communication networks and distributed systems.

Maintenance Schemes for DDX Packet Switched Network

K Kuroda, K Fujita, M Nagasawa
NTT, Japan

ABSTRACT

This paper describes maintenance scheme features implemented for the DDX Packet Switched Network expansion.
Packet Multiplexer (PMX) line concentrating and multiplexing functions are required for economical accommodation of low traffic terminals. Maintenance schemes for PMX, such as function sharing principle between Packet Switching unit and PMX, reliability enhancement, and flexible maintenance method for PMX are discussed.
Network expansion procedures, installing a new office and changing over some existing PMX and subscriber accommodations from an existing office to a new office without inconveniencing the customer, are discussed. Subscriber data division, re-routing and permanent virtual circuit reinitialization functions for the adopted procedure are described.

1. INTRODUCTION

Public packet switched networks have been developed in several countries throughout the world these past few years. They are now approaching their enhancement stage, where their capacity will be expanded regionally and quantitatively. In Japan, DDX packet switching service was started in 7 major cities in 1980[1][2], and it has been available in 30 cities since March, 1982.
This paper describes the maintenance schemes which have supported the DDX Packet Switched Network expansion plan. Network expansion has two technical meanings. First is the sole area expansion, and second is the network capacity expansion, according to a traffic increase in the expanded areas.
At the introduction stage for the new network, a leading role in network economization concerns methods to shorten access lines. In the DDX Packet Switched Network, PMX was developed to adopt to geographical concentration.[3] Therefore, it is necessary to establish new maintenance schemes for a remote PMX without maintenance personnel.
Network capacity must be increased, when it is found insufficient due to service area expansion or traffic increase for existing users.
A network equipment growth procedure has been prepared for the small traffic increase. Further, an office division procedure was prepared to handle increasing traffic, which is too high to be handled by existing packet switching (PS) unit.

2. PACKET MULTIPLEXER MAINTENANCE SCHEME

The DDX Packet Switching System configuration is shown in Fig. 1. Packet assemble and disassemble function, line concentrating and multiplexing function are implemented in the PMX, which accommodates low speed and medium speed packet mode terminals and non packet mode terminals. PMX may be located near user terminals and remotely from the PS unit. High speed packet mode terminals and PMXs are directly connected to the PS unit.
In order to realize highly reliable and stable communications, the following maintenance functions, such as subscriber data updating, traffic data observation and collection, fault detection and recovery, fault isolation and testing, command and message handling, and congestion control, are required.
In maintenance functions design, economization, reliability and maintenability must be considered. This section describes the problems involved, how to share functions between PMX and PS unit, how to realize high reliability and how to maintain unmanned PMXs.

2.1 Function sharing between packet switching unit and packet multiplexer

Several PMXs can be accommodated in one PS unit. Virtual circuit control function is decentralized in PMX, as well as in the PS unit. However, maintenance functions are centralized in the PS unit as much as possible and are commonly used for plural PMXs controlled under the PS unit, to realize economical traffic handling.
Maintenance function sharing between the PS unit and PMX is as follows.
1) Hardware; the PS unit is equipped with a Magnetic Bubble memory for file backup storage, Magnetic Tape files for storing bulk data, and Typewriter units for maintenance personnel to use in controlling the system. On the other hand, PMX is only equipped with Typewriter units, as necessary.
2) Software; the maintenance program function in PMX is limited to hardware control in its own equipments, maintenance message handling, and the operation of a process directed by the PS unit. The principal part of the maintenance functions are performed by the program in the PS unit.

2.2 Reliability enhancement

2.2.1 Fault detection and recovery

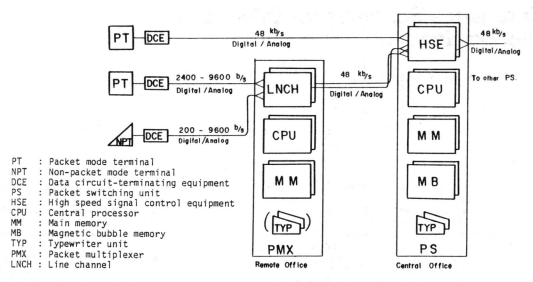

PT   : Packet mode terminal
NPT   : Non-packet mode terminal
DCE   : Data circuit-terminating equipment
PS   : Packet switching unit
HSE   : High speed signal control equipment
CPU   : Central processor
MM   : Main memory
MB   : Magnetic bubble memory
TYP   : Typewriter unit
PMX   : Packet multiplexer
LNCH : Line channel

Fig. 1   DDX Packet Switching System Configuration

(1)   Fault detection by PS unit

In order to reduce the communication service outage resulting from serious hardware failure, PMX is constructed in duplex, one system operating IN Service (INS) and the other for backup Stand-BY (SBY). When PS detects a failure in an INS system, it changes the traffic load onto the SBY system. The faulty PMX is considered under repair, in OUt of Service (OUS) state. A state diagram for PMX maintenance scheme is shown in Fig. 2. The PS unit detects PMX failures by High Level Data Link Control (HDLC) procedure and Health Check procedure. The PS unit regards the PMX as having failed, if the response for an Information frame for the HDLC procedure or a Health Check packet is not received within a fixed time, and initiates restart control to the faulty PMX. A failure can be detected during heavy traffic with HDLC effectively. A failure can be found even with no traffic, using the Health Check procedure. The same Health Check procedure is applied to both INS and SBY PMX system check. Especially, the procedure for INS PMX system is also applied to supervision of the total packet switching system in cooperation with External Supervisory Equipment.

(2)   Self detection

Detecting serious failure which affects PMX normal operation, such as main memory parity error, illegal function code etc., the fault detection program in the PMX collects the failure information and stops PMX operation to make the PS unit detect the failure with the procedures described in above (1).
A failure, which does not affect PMX normal operation at that time but will affect it seriously later, such as power supply unit, fan and fuse failure, is indicated in the maintenance scanner. The periodical program observes it and reports the failure information to call maintenance personnel's attention to the failure.

2.2.2 Restart control

PMX is stored-program-controlled system. A copy of its program and subscribers' data is stored in duplicate in the magnetic bubble memory in the PS unit. The PS unit takes the initiative regarding restart control for PMX. On recovery from fault, the PS unit initiates the restart control to PMX as a result of remote program loading. Restart Control is divided into two procedures, one is Initial Program Load (IPL) procedure and the other is Activating procedure.

(1) Initial program load procedure

From the maintenance point of view, PMX has three states, as described before. ON transition from OUS state to SBY state, PS initiates this procedure. First, PS sends a PMX Stop packet to change the PMX into the status wherein PMX is ready to receive Boot and IPL packet. Then, the PS unit initializes the hardware blocks, except line control block, by Boot packet. When the IPL packet is received, its content is loaded into the main memory in the PMX.

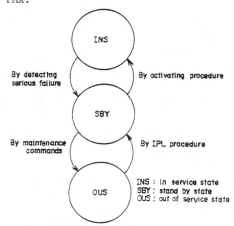

INS : In service state
SBY : stand by state
OUS : out of service state

Fig. 2   State diagram for PMX maintenance scheme

732

After program loading has finished, PMX is brought into the SBY state and sends HDLC procedure SABM command to the PS unit. Thereafter, PMX communicates with the PS unit by HDLC procedure. In order to perform IPL function for PMX, a simple procedure, a reciprocal procedure, is required, because Boot program has extremely fewer functions than the program during normal operation. Certain values of HDLC Address and Command parts, which are not used in usual data link control, are pointed out for this procedure.

(2) Activating procedure

Functions required for the Activating procedure are to load Initialization Program and subscriber data, to take over simplex line control block into its own equipment and to initialize it by executing Initialization Program. The Load packet is used for loading Initialization Program and subscriber data into the main memory, according to the address in itself. Activation packet initiates the Initialization Program execution. It initiates the line control block, on a half and half basis, to smooth the immediate traffic increase after recovery. Completing the initialization, PMX sends back an Acknowledge Activating Procedure packet to the PS unit.

2.2.3 Remote diagnosis

Remote diagnosis is introduced into the fault recovery process to prevent ineffective maintenance personnel distribution and to detect faulty packages simply. Diagnostic command is typed in by maintenance personnel. This command is sent to the PS unit, and delivered to the Diagnostic Control Program if accepted. PMX remote diagnosis is a similar process, on a step by step basis, to that for IPL.

2.3 Remote maintenance

According to packet switching service area expansion, PMXs are newly installed and PMX maintenance areas are subdivided gradually. Then, if maintenance personnel are distributed to every PMX, maintenance cost is increased extremely.
In order to reduce maintenance cost, it is necessary to centralize PMX maintenance work by newly introducing an unmanned PMX, which is controlled by a remote PS unit or other manned PMXs with maintenance command operations.
To implement the above remote maintenance control, the following functions are needed.
1) Maintenance personnel in a manned PMX or PS unit can remotely control plural unmanned PMXs by maintenance command operations.
2) Fault information, which is edited in an unmanned PMX, can be transferred to a manned PMX's typewriter unit. If the manned PMX's typewriter unit is faulty, the fault information can be transferred to another manned PMX typewriter unit or PS typewriter unit in turn.
3) When a new PMX is installed, the above remote maintenance formation can be reconstructed easily by maintenance command operations.
4) It is convenient to be able to use the maintenance functions directly from the unmanned PMX, in case of repairing and testing

its own equipments. Therefore, a portable typewriter unit can be installed and used in the unmanned PMX at any time necessary.

3. NETWORK EXPANSION

3.1 Network growth techniques

A principle of the network equipment growth system in the DDX packet switched network is based on the electronic telephone switching system in NTT, which is composed of offline support programs (Office Configuration Regenerating Program (CGN), Office Data Generating Program (DGN)) for generating new office data and online command programs for changing to the new office data.
However, the DDX packet switched network has a characteristic wherein a copy of PMX office data, which is called PMX back-up office data, is held in the magnetic bubble memory in the PS unit. Therefore, the following growth methods must be newly implemented.
1) A method is incorporated to combine PS unit office data (32 bit/word) and PMX office data (16 bit/word) in response to growth in a new PMX. To realize the method, an offline support program was newly implemented.
2) A method was inaugurated to change the existing PMX office data in the PMX main memory and the existing PMX back-up office data.
To realize the method, office data transfer functions without service interruption were newly implemented as one of the maintenance command functions. In the functions, new office data are transferred from the PS unit to PMX remotely by packets for office data change. PMX back-up office data are changed by sending back the verified PMX office data to PS.

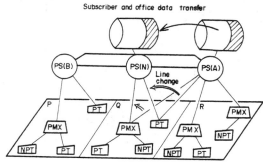

Subscriber and office data transfer

Office service area change from PS(A) to PS(N)

PT   : Packet mode terminal
NPT   : Non-packet mode terminal
P,Q,R : Service area number
PS   : Packet switching office
PS(A) : Existing PS for office division
PS(N) : New PS for office division
PS(B) : Existing PS not relevant to subscriber transfer

Fig. 3   Office division concept

733

3.2 Office division

The office division concept is shown in Fig. 3. When a new PS unit is installed, some existing PMX and subscriber accomodations may be changed over from an existing PS unit to a new PS unit. Some information associated with the PMXs and the subscribers and stored in the existing PS(A) must be transferred from PS(A) to PS(N), as shown in Fig.3 .

However, the structure of and the data-entry system for the subscriber data in the packet switched network are different from that in the electronic telephone switched network. In the DDX packet switched network, a subscriber data has some linked information which indicates another subscriber accommodated to some other PS unit, because of making such services available as the permanent virtual circuit (PVC) service.

3.2.1 Office division alternatives

Considering functions required for the office division, office division schemes are classified into the following three alternatives. Table 1 shows outlines and features for these alternatives.

(1) Individual transfer scheme

In this scheme, to-be-transferred subscribers, subscribers to be transferred from PS(A) unit to PS(N) unit, may be individually transferred from the PS(A) to the PS(N), one by one. This scheme aims at easy work scheduling and smooth work load handling for the office division.

As three kind of subscribers, not-to-be-transferred subscribers, already-transferred subscribers and not-yet-transferred subscribers, are simultaneously accommodated in both PS(A) unit and PS(N) unit during a transient time until the office division completion, the following specific functions must be introduced newly.

On receiving an incoming call packet, either PS(A) unit or PS(N) unit must discriminate whether or not the to-be-called subscriber has already been transferred to the PS(N) unit. If transferred, the packet is to be forwarded from PS(A) unit to PS(N) unit. Otherwise, the packet must be sent out to the called subscriber who is yet accommodated in PS(A) unit.

The above function is called "packet re-routing function" using transfer-state number stored in the subscriber data.

This scheme has not been adopted, due to the following impertinent problems.

1) Program design for the packet re-routing function is difficult, when executing office division in two points of the network simultaneously.

2) Office division procedure is complicated and takes a long time, since the transfer state number must be eliminated after the subscriber transfer, prior to the next office division.

(2) Simultaneous transfer scheme

All to-be-transferred data are simultaneously transferred from PS(A) unit to PS(N) unit by file renewal with office division files in

Table 1   Office division scheme outlines and features

Alternatives / Comparing Items	Simultaneous Transfer	Individual Transfer	Subscriber Management Center (SMC)
System Configuration			
Merit	1 Simple procedures 2 Short construction period	1 Smooth construction work load 2 Easy construction scheduling	1 Simple procedures
Demerit	1 Concentration of construction work load in a short period 2 Difficult construction scheduling	1 Complicated construction procedures 2 Long construction period 3 Difficult program design of a new routing system	1 Increase in call set-up process 2 Change required for packet switching system and network configuration

PS   : Packet switching office
PS(A) : Existing PS for office division
PS(N) : New PS for office division
PS(B) : Existing PS not relevant to subscriber transfer

T : Data terminal equipment

734

which to-be-transferred subscriber data in PS(A) unit file are divided and are added to PS(N) unit file by offline support programs. Therefore, packet switching at the office division execution can be performed as usual, paying no attention to the office division. The office division procedures are simply carried out in a short period. However, changing all to-be-transferred subscriber lines at one time makes the office division work load concentrated. To avoid this problem, it is necessary to reduce the number of to-be-transferred subscriber line changes.
In the DDX packet switched network, this problem can be solved by changing the to-be-transferred PMX's line, connected between the PMX and PS, which enables transferring all subscribers accommodated in the PMX without to-be-transferred subscriber line changes.
As a result, this scheme has been adopted for the following reasons.
1) Office division procedure is simple in a short period.
2) No specific online program functions need be added.

(3)   Subscriber Management Center (SMC) scheme(4),(5)

All subscriber data are centrally administrated by SMC and stored in the SMC memory. On receiving a call request packet, each PS unit always asks SMC about the calling and called subscriber data, which involves a destination office code and so on.
In this scheme, to-be-transferred subscriber data can be changed by maintenance command operations at SMC, as soon as to-be-transferred lines are changed over from PS(A) unit to PS(N) unit. Therefore, the office division work load can be made less and service interruption time can be shortened.
However, this scheme was not adopted, due to the following impertinent problems.
1) Call setup process is increased.
2) Specific interface functions between SMC and each PS unit must be added.
3) Modifications on the existing DDX packet switching systems and network configuration must be required.

3.2.2 Office division functions

An office division scheme, which has the following functions, has been developed.

(1) Office data and subscriber data transfer

Operating office file consists of system programs, office data and subscriber data. The system programs are used in common with all other offices. Office data and subscriber data are generated according to each office configuration and each subscriber service class. In the office division, office data and subscriber data must be transferred from PS(A) unit to PS(N) unit.
In the DDX packet switched network, office data transfer can be realized by the existing programs for network growth, as described in Sect. 3.1. The DDX packet switched network has also implemented the subscriber data division program as one of the offline support programs. Office division files generated by

the offline support programs are respectively loaded into both PS(A) unit and PS(N) unit by the existing file renewal function.

(2) Routing control data change

Routing control functions in the DDX packet switched network are performed by means of the B-link number (BLN) scheme(6). The BLN, which consists of normalized office code assigned to each office and so on, is generated by call setup functions and is added to all packets in the call as a control header for routing control functions.
If the routing control data are not changed, a packet addressed to a subscriber who is going to be transferred cannot be sent to PS(N) unit.
AS the routing control data change must be performed in all PS(B) units, its work load is apt to be concentrated at the office division execution.
To solve the above problem, the DDX packet switched network has implemented a new routing function, called "packet re-routing using translator table", as shown in Fig.4.

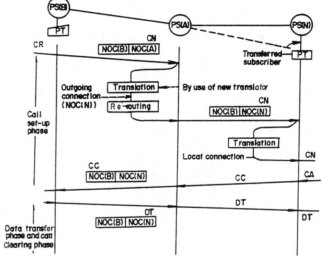

PS   : Packet switching office
PS(A) : Existing PS for office division
PS(N) : New PS for office division
PS(B) : Existing PS not relevant to subscriber transfer
CR   : Call request packet
CN   : Incoming call packet
CA   : Call accepted packet
CC   : Call connected packet
DT   : Data packet

Fig. 4   Packet re-routing using translator table

In this re-routing system, a call request packet addressed to a subscriber who has already been transferred is sent from the existing PS(B) unit to the existing PS(A) unit by using the normalized office code of PS(A) unit. Then it is re-transferred from the PS(A) unit to the new PS(N) unit by translating the to-be-transferred subscriber's number with new translator table in the PS(A) unit and by changing its destination office code to the normalized office code of PS(N) unit. The translater table in every PS(B) unit may be changed at any time conveniently after completing the office division between PS(A) unit and PS(N) unit.

(3) PVC control data reinitialization

The DDX packet switched network provides a permanent virtual circuit (PVC) facility for some users who make use of the DDX network as a private telecommunication circuit.

PVC control data consists of a B-link number, which involves the opposite subscriber's accommodation data. Therefore, if PVC subscribers are transferred to the new PS(N), it is necessary to reinitialize PVC control data of opposite subscriber.

The DDX packet switched network has newly implemented PVC control data reinitialization functions, which can notify the reinitialization by sending a PVC reinitialization request packet from the new PS(N) unit to the other existing PS units at the office division execution.

4. CONCLUSION

This paper describes maintenance scheme features implemented for the DDX Packet Switched Network expansion, such as Packet Multiplexer remote maintenance functions, network growth techniques and office division techniques.

These technologies were successfully employed for commercial network expansion in March, 1982, to meet a packet traffic increase, and have since been operating properly.

ACKNOWLEDGEMENT

The authors wish to thank Mr. M. Matsumoto, ex-chief of the Packet Switching System Section, Dr. Y. Yoshida, chief of the Packet Switching System Section, and Mr. Y. Okuda, who furnished valuable guidances as the group leader. They also wish to thank Mr. K. Ishiguro, Mr. T. Hayashi and other members who contributed to the design and development of the DDX maintenance system.

REFERENCES

(1) J.Iimura, et al. : The DDX Packet Switched Network, Review of the E.C.L., NTT, Jpn., 26, 3-4, p.315, 1978.
(2) M.Matsumoto, et al. : DDX Packet Switched Network and its Technology,ICCC'78,p.583,1978.
(3) R.Nakamura, F.Ishino, et al. : Some Design Aspect of a Public Packet Switched Network, ICCC'76, p.317, 1976.
(4) N.Sone, et al. : Extended DDX Packet Switched Network, Japan Telecomm. Review, 23, 2, p.167,1981.
(5) D.L.Jeanes, A.K.Trivedi, et al. : DATAPAC Subscriber Service Updata System Architecture and Operation, ICCC'78, p.577, 1978.
(6) Y.Miki, M.Nakamura, et al. : DDX Virtual Circuit Control System, Review of the E.C.L., NTT, Jpn., p.925, 1981.

Kenichi Kuroda, Deputy Director, Data Switching Systems Section, Musashino Electrical Communication Laboratory, NTT, has been engaged in developmental research on Packet Switching Systems, and particularly the design and implementation of its maintenance software, since 1978. He received his BE and ME in 1971 and 1973 from Tokyo Institute of Technology. Since joining ECL in 1973, he has been engaged in DDX circuit switching system development and in research on interconnection between public telephone network and DDX Packet Switched Network.

Katsuyuki Fujita, Engineer, Packet Switching System Section, NTT's Musashino Electrical Communication Laboratory, has been engaged in developmental research on DDX Packet Switching System. He received his BE and ME in 1974 and 1976 from Hokkaido University. Since joining ECL in 1976, he has been engaged in DDX Packet Switching System development, particularly the design of PAD protocol and X.25 and X.75 protocols, and the implementation of PMX software and Gateway Switch software which is applied to connection to VENUS of KDD. He is a member of the Institute of Electronics and Communication Engineers of Japan.

Michio Nagasawa was born in 1953. He received his BE in Computer Science from the Electro-Communication University in 1975. Since joining NTT's Musashino Electrical Communication Laboratory in 1975, he has been engaged in developmental research on DDX Packet Switching System, particularly the X.25 protocol design and call (packet) processing program implementation. He is presently working in the field of network expansion system and maintenance system for DDX commercial packet switched network project. He is a member of the Institute of Electronics and Communication Engineers of Japan.

The Bell X.25 Protocol and its Role in the Operations Systems Network

P F Wainwright, G W Arnold
Bell Laboratories, USA

The Bell X.25 protocol, BX.25, is based in its first three layers on the international packet switching standard CCITT Recommendation X.25. Whereas X.25 defines a set of services and procedures provided by a packet-switching network, BX.25 defines how computers communicate with one another through such a network. BX.25 also includes layers of protocol above those defined by X.25. In order to provide a context for the description of BX.25, this paper briefly describes the structure and protocol needs of the internal Bell System Operations Systems Network for which BX.25 was defined. The paper then describes BX.25, with emphasis on the differences between BX.25 and X.25, and discusses the current status of BX.25 implementation in the Bell System. The Bell System's experience with BX.25 demonstrates that a host interface based on X.25, incorporating minor enhancements that do not compromise X.25 network compatibility, affords a data communications interface that is far more versatile than is commonly realized.

I. INTRODUCTION

This paper describes a unified family of protocols based on X.25, called Bell X.25 (BX.25), that is designed to utilize X.25 efficiently and to specify interface procedures for Data Terminal Equipment (DTE) [INT, BEL]. BX.25 has been adopted as the standard protocol for the internal Bell System data communications network, called the Operations Systems Network (OSN). BX.25 differs from X.25 in its ability to support direct DTE-to-DTE communications (both private line and dial-up) as well as access to a packet-switched data network, as shown in Figure 1. This ability enables OSN developers to employ point-to-point links for data communications today, and to evolve gracefully to packet-switched network connections as such networks become ubiquitous.[1]

Besides specifying interface procedures from the DTE perspective, BX.25 also specifies higher level protocols for which there are no equivalent international standards. Examples of these higher levels include session establishment and control, distributed transaction processing, and terminal interface capabilities.

The Bell System's experience with BX.25 demonstrates that a host interface based in its lower layers on X.25, incorporating minor enhancements that do not compromise X.25 network compatibility, affords a data communications interface that is far more versatile than is commonly realized. Such an interface permits a unified protocol for virtual circuit service in a mixed-media private network,[2] thereby affording economy in software development and maintenance by eliminating the need to implement different virtual circuit protocols for different media. These savings are a very significant benefit in a large, heterogeneous private network like the OSN. Furthermore, BX.25 demonstrates that the rich services inherent in X.25, such as multiplexing, flow control, and error handling, permit design of simple higher-level protocols, which, in turn, facilitate implementation in a broad range of systems.

An approach often used in other network architectures, such as Systems Network Architecture (SNA), is to incorporate

---

1. Although at present X.25 specifies only the actions of the DCE, ISO is currently specifying an X.25 DTE protocol [ISOa, ISOb, ISOc], as described in Section IV below.

2. This network could include dedicated host-to-host links, dial-up circuits, shared packet switches, and, potentially, local networks.

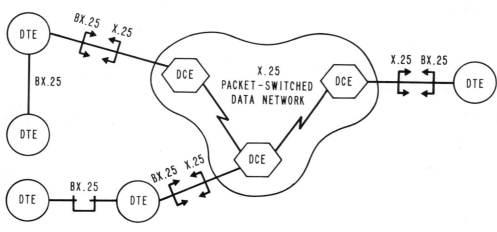

BX.25 Applications
Figure 1

X.25 as a *replacement* for existing lower levels of protocol, typically for the physical and link layers [FPC]. This approach leads to redundancy of functions between existing higher-level protocols, such as contained in SNA, and the rich set of functions afforded by X.25. BX.25 demonstrates that a much more compact, yet robust protocol can be achieved by designing higher-level protocols which effectively utilize the services inherent in X.25.

This paper first reviews the structure and purpose of the OSN in order to provide perspective for BX.25. Next, this paper defines the protocol needs of the OSN in order to provide a rationale for the features of BX.25. Then, the various levels of BX.25 are described, and the differences between X.25 and BX.25 are highlighted. Finally, the status of BX.25 implementation in the Bell System is discussed.

II. OVERVIEW OF THE OPERATIONS SYSTEMS NETWORK

To assist internal operations, the Bell Operating Companies are today using over 90 different types of computer-based systems, termed operations systems, in such diverse areas as marketing, planning, engineering, installation, administration, maintenance, billing, and performance measurement [MMB], and this number is growing rapidly. Many operations systems have dedicated hardware - ranging from large computer systems to minicomputers; others share central computer facilities. The nation-wide collection of operations systems, the terminals supported by the systems, and the data communications elements interconnecting them is termed the Operations Systems Network (OSN). A detailed description of the OSN was presented at the 1980 ICCC [JJA]. Here we review the characteristics of the OSN in order to put the BX.25 protocol into perspective.

In a typical Bell Operating Company, comprising roughly 5% of the Bell System's business and serving about 3 million customers, one would find more than 130 separate operations systems and 7000 computer terminals, together with more than 2000 interfaces to telecommunications equipment. Of the 130 operations systems, about 110 are minicomputer-based, with the remainder running on mainframe computers. In addition to these, a number of systems are run centrally for the entire Bell System and hence are located outside of the company, usually a large distance away.

Operations systems are implemented on a heterogeneous collection of computer hardware and operating system software. Some of the major computer manufacturers represented include IBM, UNIVAC, DEC, Hewlett Packard, and Data General, among others. Numerous operating systems are also used. About 40% of the operations systems utilize some version of the UNIX™ operating system [THC].

Computer-to-computer communication is playing an increasingly important role in the OSN. It is expected that the 150 generic computer-to-computer interfaces now available to the Bell Operating Companies will double by 1985. Telecommunications equipment also interacts with operations systems on a host-to-host basis. Electronic Switching Systems (ESS) incorporate large processors primarily to control telephone switching equipment. Other equipment, such as the newer generation of toll transmission equipment [JRC], incorporates small processors for maintenance and administrative functions. To facilitate the implementation of interfaces to this variety of processors, adoption of standard protocols is essential.

The wide range of equipment and applications on the OSN leads to a diverse set of requirements for OSN protocols. The following section reviews these requirements.

III. PROTOCOL NEEDS OF THE OSN

The basic protocol needs of the OSN have evolved over a period of time. Initially, data communications within the Bell System consisted of isolated pairs of applications that communicated with each other over dedicated links. Such communications required simple, Link Layer protocols to insure data integrity from one point to another. As data communications applications grew in number, situations arose in which several applications in a host needed to communicate with several applications in a distant host. Since implementing multiple parallel data links is not economical, there developed a need for multiplexing permanent virtual circuits on a single (dedicated) logical link. With the advent of packet-switched networks, there arose a need to manage virtual calls through the network. These basic needs suggest a layered approach to the protocol architecture.

In addition to these basic needs, OSN protocols require certain additional features. For example, since some OSN links use the circuit-switched telephone network, and since it is important to minimize the possibility of compromising the integrity of a system, OSN protocols must support security procedures that insure the correspondent host is indeed the intended system.

Because of the diversity of applications, processors, and terminal types in the OSN, there also exists the need for standard higher-level protocols above those defined by X.25. First, a standard layer of protocol is needed to establish, manage, and terminate sessions between hosts, terminals, and telecommunications systems. Above this, end-to-end protocols are needed to facilitate certain types of data communication. For example, host-to-host communication with transaction-oriented applications like IMS or CICS requires an appropriate higher-level protocol to control transaction routing, format control, recovery from system failures, etc. Host-to-terminal communications using a Packet Assembler/Disassembler (PAD) at the terminal end of packet-switched network connections requires a higher-level protocol between the host and PAD. Also, file transfer between hosts can be facilitated by a higher-level file transfer protocol. Moreover, standard protocols for the OSN must be compact and able to be implemented on different vendors' equipment and on a wide range of processor sizes.

OSN protocols must support a transition from the data communications technology of today to the packet-switched network technology of the future. Today, most computer-to-computer interactions are being handled on dedicated facilities or magnetic tape, with some use of a message switching network called the Bell Administrative Network Communications System (BANCS) [SKL, DFL]. BANCS is an important component in the Bell Operating Company data communications environment of today. As the number of these interfaces increases, however, most of the non-bulk data communications will migrate onto a common packet-switched modernized BANCS network. Furthermore, most terminals today are on dedicated lines or dial-up connections, with some use of BANCS data switching. In the future, these too will migrate toward use of a packet-switched network. This state of transition requires that the OSN protocols be applicable to a number of different network technologies.

IV. THE BX.25 FAMILY OF PROTOCOLS

Figure 2 shows the structure of BX.25 in terms of the seven-layer International Organization for Standards (ISO) Reference Model [DAT]. Although BX.25 follows the Open Systems Interconnection philosophy of layering, the exact partitioning of functions differs in some cases. Also, since not all functions contained in the ISO Reference Model are needed in the OSN, BX.25 specifies a subset of the ISO Reference Model functions. The reason for these differences is to reduce complexity so that BX.25 can be implemented in a wide range of processors, including mainframes, minicomputers, and microprocessor-controlled equipment.

This section gives an overview of and rationale for each layer of BX.25, and clarifies the differences between BX.25 and X.25. A detailed description of BX.25 is contained in the BX.25 Protocol Specification [BEL].

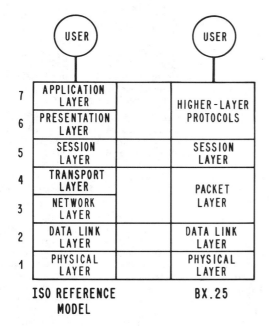

Protocol Layers of BX.25
Figure 2

Overall Architecture

BX.25 is a layered family of protocols that provides a unified set of data communications procedures for use in the OSN. The Packet Layer, which spans the ISO Network and Transport Layers, provides multiplexed virtual circuit services for both DTE-to-DTE and DTE-to-DCE connections. A separate Transport Layer for BX.25 was not deemed necessary because additional multiplexing is not needed, and because end-to-end confirmation can be provided by the Packet Layer functions [ARY]. Furthermore, because the OSN employs either point-to-point (both dedicated and dial-up) links or packet-switches whose reliability approaches that of ESS offices, there is little need for the additional reliability afforded by the Transport Layer. Also, minimizing the number of separate layers facilitates implementation of BX.25 in microprocessor-based systems.

BX.25 provides additional capabilities that have not yet been standardized in the international community. The BX.25 Session Layer provides a standard means to manage sessions between communicating applications. Above the Session Layer, higher-level BX.25 functions facilitate various types of communication such as file transfer and host-terminal interfaces.

Because BX.25 is layered, and because the BX.25 Link and Packet Layers define protocols for both DTE-to-DTE and DTE-to-DCE connections, BX.25 can be used on a variety of network technologies including circuit-switched and packet-switched network access, point-to-point private lines, and, potentially, local networks. It will be possible to use the BX.25 Packet Layer and above on top of a connection-oriented local network protocol such as the emerging IEEE Project 802 Local Network Standard [IEE].

Physical Interfaces

The Physical Layer of BX.25 provides a standard electrical and physical interface between a DTE and any intermediate data communications equipment (such as modems) necessary to establish a data circuit with another DTE or with a DCE. Both the Electronic Industries Association (EIA) RS-232C interface and the higher-speed CCITT Recommendation V.35 interface serve as BX.25 level 1 interfaces. These standards are in complete accord with X.25. In the future, BX.25 will include the EIA RS-449 physical interface standard as well.

Link Layer

The purpose of the Link Layer is to assure that frames are transported reliably across a data link. This is done by providing frame numbering and a cyclic redundancy check, together with Link Layer procedures, such as flow control, error detection, and retransmission, that ensure data integrity. In addition to these basic services, within the OSN there exists the need to permit DTE-to-DTE as well as DTE-to-DCE interfaces, and to provide a security check before a link is established over a dial-up circuit, as discussed in the previous section.

The Link Layer of X.25 provides a good basis for meeting the OSN needs. BX.25 uses, as a link control procedure, Link Access Procedure B (LAPB) of X.25, which is compatible with the Asynchronous Balanced Mode subset of both ISO's High Level Data Link Control (HDLC) procedure and ANSI's Advanced Data Communication Control Procedure (ADCCP).[3] In addition to these X.25 Link Layer capabilities, BX.25 enhances the Link Layer protocol in several ways, for example:

- BX.25 Link Layer procedures specify the actions of the DTE rather than the DCE, and enable direct DTE-to-DTE links without requiring an intermediate DCE. One example of this enhancement is the complete specification of the DTE's response to frame reject and other frames.

- BX.25 utilizes a state table to specify the Link Layer procedures, thereby facilitating the implementation of these procedures.

- BX.25 Link Layer procedures include optional use of the XID (Exchange Identification) frame, a feature of HDLC not contained in X.25, to verify the identity of a host or terminal attempting to establish a circuit-switched connection prior to initialization of the Link Layer interface. This capability is important to the OSN in order to minimize opportunities to compromise the integrity of a system.

- BX.25 provides an optional link assurance service for use during periods of no traffic by periodically initiating a status frame exchange. This enables link failures to be detected even in the absence of data transmission.

Packet Layer

The basic purpose of the Packet Layer is to provide the ISO Transport Services to the Session Layer, independent of the underlying communications media used. For example, the BX.25 Packet Layer provides the individual ISO Transport Connection flow control service by mapping Transport Connections on a one-to-one basis onto DTE-to-DTE virtual calls or permanent virtual circuits, which may or may not involve use of X.25 communications systems. A single Packet Layer protocol is utilized, independently of whether or not an X.25 communications system is employed between the two communicating systems.

The X.25 Packet Layer protocol provides a good foundation for meeting OSN Packet Layer needs. However, the OSN has additional Packet Layer requirements that are not met by X.25. These requirements have resulted in features that are not present in X.25. For example:

- The BX.25 Packet Layer protocol is able to communicate equally well with X.25 DCEs and BX.25 DTEs;

- End system-to-end system parameters needed to establish and manage an end-to-end Packet Layer Connection are able to be negotiated independently of the underlying communications media; and

---

3. Using the Reject Command/Response option and restricting Information (I) frames to being commands only.

- The BX.25 Packet Layer precludes any possibility of there being "deadlock" conditions, regardless of the underlying communications media.

Although X.25 currently defines the actions of the DCE, work is currently in progress within ISO Technical Committee 97/Subcommittee 6 to define a DTE-oriented version of X.25 [ISOa]. The BX.25 specification has been used by ISO as a working document. ISO/TC97/SC6 has identified 31 specific Packet Layer issues to be resolved in order to formulate an X.25 DTE Packet Layer standard [ISOb, ISOc].[4] The BX.25 approach in providing a DTE-oriented protocol satisfactorily resolves most of these issues. [ISOb, ISOc]

Session Layer

The purpose of the Session Layer is to establish, manage, and terminate sessions for use by higher-level protocols or, in some cases, by user applications directly. Within the OSN there exists the need for Session Layer services such as connection and disconnection management of virtual calls, higher-level protocol identification (origin type), and (optionally) transport service disruption recovery. On the other hand, several typical Session Layer functions, such as turn management and quarantine service, are left to individual applications to control directly.

Because of the lack of existing standards, the BX.25 Session Layer is not based on any other protocol but rather is a completely new design. The design principles for the BX.25 Session Layer placed heavy emphasis on not duplicating lower-level functions, thus simplifying the Session Layer and facilitating its implementation on both microprocessor-based equipment and mainframe systems. For example, Session Connection Request messages may be carried as "user data" in Packet Layer Connection Request messages, which may be mapped directly onto virtual circuit connection packets using the X.25 fast select features. These capabilities permit minimization of communication processing, transit delays, and transmission overhead.

The following basic services are provided by the BX.25 Session Layer:

- *Connections*: The Session Layer, upon receiving a request from a higher-level protocol (or an application) to initiate a session with another like higher-level protocol on a distant host (or another application), secures a virtual circuit to the appropriate destination host from the Packet Layer. Alternatively, the Session Layer could be requested to wait for an incoming Session Request message that another host is expected to initiate.

- *Orderly disconnect*: At the end of a session, the Session Layer releases the lower-layer connection after ensuring that all data has been received.

- *Abortive disconnect*: To recover from abnormal conditions, the Session Layer can immediately release a lower layer connection with the possible loss of data.

- *Identification of origin type*: Identifies the type of higher-level entity that is originating the session (e.g., terminal type, or higher-layer protocol type).

As an option, the BX.25 Session Layer also provides resynchronization and recovery functions that provide continuous transparent session services despite lower layer failures.

The BX.25 Session Layer, in its simplest form, requires a minimal amount of processor overhead. If no options are required (i.e., if the session Layer provides only connection, data transfer, and disconnection services), the BX.25 Session Layer allows user messages to be transported without headers using the Q-bit facility.

Higher-Level Protocols

In addition to the protocols described above, the BX.25 family of protocols includes higher-levels that facilitate certain types of application-to-application communications. This section describes some of the higher-level protocols that are being built on top of the other layers of BX.25.

- An OSN PAD protocol uses the Session Layer and lower layers for host-to-terminal communications via a Packet Assembler/Disassembler (PAD). This approach allows terminals to look like remote BX.25 applications. By providing standards for session-oriented PAD functions, BX.25 eliminates the need for different PAD protocols for different terminal types, as is the case for other protocols such as X.29 or Datapac 3303.

- A transaction-oriented Application Layer protocol facilitates host-to-host communications when both applications run on a transaction-based system like IBM's IMS or CICS, or UNIVAC's SPL. Transaction-oriented communication in the OSN typically involves small messages or requests that describe a single unit of work, and may result in a reply being sent back to the originating system (or a different system) at some later time. These services are very important to the OSN since most systems will interface with a transaction-oriented system in order to gain access to company databases. For example, in response to a customer's request for service, a service order is generated on one transaction-oriented system and is forwarded to a second transaction-oriented system for assignment of central office equipment. This service order is then returned to the first system or, alternatively, is forwarded to a third system for further processing.

- File transfer protocols facilitate the transfer of files from one host to another. Specific file transfer protocols that have been formulated for use within the OSN permit the down-loading of generic program files to an ESS office, and the transmission of accumulated billing data files from ESS offices to a Revenue Accounting Office.

- *Other higher-level alternatives*. For special applications where the standard higher-level protocols described above are not sufficient, it is possible for users to implement their own higher-level protocols within their applications and to interface directly with the Session Layer. Although such an implementation is possible, it is discouraged in order to avoid the proliferation of non-standard protocols.

V. STATUS OF BX.25 IN THE BELL SYSTEM

At present, BX.25 is used in thirty-four different applications and/or operating systems used internally by the Bell System. Several hundred instances of these applications are currently deployed in the Bell Operating Companies. Of these systems, seven are based on microprocessor technology, six are based on Western Electric telecommunication processors such as the 3B20 [TFA], twenty are based on general trade minicomputers, and the remaining application is based on a large mainframe computer. These systems utilize a total of ten different operating systems. As a result of this implementation experience we believe that BX.25 is highly flexible, can be implemented on a very broad spectrum of processors and operating systems, and is especially useful in facilitating communication among heterogeneous computer systems.

Because of the large number of different applications that will use the OSN, a BX.25 certification facility is essential to insure that each implementation conforms to the BX.25 standard. Therefore, a certification facility [JAM] has been developed to insure that the various BX.25 implementations conform to the protocol specification.

---

4. The Link Layer part of this X.25 DTE protocol standard is currently out for ballot.

Several specific examples of BX.25 applications provide some insight into the various implementation approaches that have been used successfully. The UNIX™ [THC] operating system for Digital Equipment Corporation (DEC) PDP 11 and VAX computers includes BX.25 above level 2 as a driver within the operating system. Processing associated with the lower levels is off-loaded from the main processor into an outboard DEC KMC 11 microprocessor. A similar approach is used in the Western Electric 3B20 processor.

An alternative approach used in several applications off loads levels 1, 2 *and* 3 to a front-end processor. While this approach is most commonly associated with large mainframe computers, it has also proved useful to the Bell System in selected minicomputer-based applications. An example of the former is the FEP component of the Bell Administrative Network Communications System (BANCS) [DFL], a data switching network used internally by the Bell System. The BANCS FEP is based on a COMTEN 3650 processor and provides BX.25 capability to IBM IMS/BTAM applications.

An example of a minicomputer-based application that utilizes a front end processor to implement the first three levels of BX.25 is the Switching Control Center System (SCCS) [WDB]. This system is used to monitor and control maintenance channels associated with Electronic Switching Systems. Several such channels, providing critical alarm data and more routine exception reports, originate from each switching office and are multiplexed over a single physical link to a central SCCS using BX.25. A microprocessor based front end known as the PDT-2A [JAG] implements the levels 1, 2, and 3 BX.25 protocols for SCCS. The front-end processor routes data on logical channels associated with critical alarms to a critical indicator display, and routes data on other logical channels to a minicomputer system for logging and display to central office maintenance personnel. In this application, the front-end processor approach to BX.25 provides high availability and also permits local switching of data without burdening the main CPU.

A typical application of BX.25 in the Bell System is illustrated by computerized operations support for INWATS (800 Service) and calling card services [GCE, JJL]. These services are provided by the Common Channel Interoffice Signaling (CCIS) network and are controlled by 3B20 data base processors, known as Network Control Points (NCP), currently located in nine U.S. cities. The operation of these processors are supported by a large network of operations systems linked together using the BX.25 protocol. Two centralized PDP 11/70 UNIX™ operating system-based applications, linked by BX.25 to the NCPs, provide real-time remote monitoring and control and software administration support. A third system, which happens to be IMS-based, uses the BX.25 capability of the BANCS FEP to transmit data base updates. Finally, twenty one PDP 11/70 UNIX/RT-based applications located throughout the U.S. interface with selected NCPs using BX.25 to provide data base updates for the calling card service. This network began supporting live service in September 1981.

VI. CONCLUSIONS

The Bell Operations Systems Network will represent one of the world's largest private commercial computer communications networks. Because of the heterogeneous nature of the network, the Bell System has elected to base the network on an internal, vendor-independent protocol standard known as BX.25. The experience with this protocol has demonstrated its versatility. The rich set of functions inherent in X.25, upon which BX.25 is based, permits the design of simple higher-level protocols, leading to a protocol architecture that can be implemented on a wide spectrum of processors.

ACKNOWLEDGMENTS

The design of BX.25 is the result of the efforts of numerous individuals. Key contributors include D. L. Eitelbach, H. L.

Lemberg, J. Lee, D. E. Wallace, K. D. Walter, F. M. Burg, H. H. Moore, G. G. Riddle, T. R. Ryan, H. R. Hronicek, and J. A. Edelman. We would also like to acknowledge the efforts of many other individuals, too numerous to mention here, who are responsible for the many different Bell System implementations of BX.25.

REFERENCES

[ARY] A. Rybczynski, "X.25 Interface and End-to-End Virtual Circuit Service Characteristics," *IEEE Transactions on Communications* Vol. COM-28, No. 4, April, 1980.

[BEL] Bell System Technical Reference, Pub. 54001: "Operations Systems Network Communications Protocol Specification: BX.25, Issue 2," June, 1980.

[DAT] "Data Processing - Open Systems Interconnection - Basic Reference Model," International Organization for Standardization, Second Draft Proposal, ISO/DP7498, August, 1981.

[DFL] D. F. Lee and A. J. Pasqua, "BANCS: A New Outlook on Internal Data Communications," *Bell Laboratories Record*, Vol. 58, No. 1, January 1980, pp. 20-27.

[FPC] F. P. Corr and D. H. Neal, "SNA and Emerging International Standards," *IBM Systems Journal*, Vol. 18, No. 2, 1979.

[GCE] G. C. Ebner and L. A. Tomko, "CCIS: A Signaling System for the Stored Program Controlled Network," *Bell Laboratories Record*, Vol. 57, No. 2, February 1979, pp. 53-59.

[HL] H. Lycklama and D. L. Bayer, "The MERT Operating System," *Bell System Technical Journal*, Vol. 57, No. 6, Part 2, July-August 1978, pp. 2049-2086.

[IEE] IEEE 802 Local Network Standard, Draft B, October 15, 1981.

[INT] "Interface between Data Terminal Equipment (DTE) and Data Circuit-Terminating Equipment (DCE) for Terminals Operating in the Packet Mode on Public Data Networks," CCITT Recommendation X.25, 1980.

[ISOa] "Direct Connection of X.25 DTEs," ISO Document ISO/TC97/SC6 N2106, September, 1980.

[ISOb] "General X.25 DTE Operations Packet Level Considerations," ISO Document ISO/TC97/SC6 N2259, June, 1981.

[ISOc] "X.25 DTE-to-DTE Operations Packet Level Considerations," ISO Document ISO/TC97/SC6 N2258, June, 1981.

[JAG] J. A. Grandle, Jr. and R. R. Plum, "A Versatile Data-Gathering Tool," *Bell Laboratories Record*, Vol. 57, No. 8, September 1979, pp. 227-231.

[JAM] J. A. Melici, "The BX.25 Certification Facility," Proceedings of the Sixth Berkeley Workshop on Distributed Data Management and Computer Networks, Pacific Grove, CA, February, 1982, pp. 283-310.

[JJA] J. J. Amoss, "Planning for the Bell Operations Systems Network," Proceedings of the Fifth International Conference on Computer Communications, October, 1980, pp. 559-563.

[JJL] J. J. Lawser and D. Sheinbein, "Realizing the Potential of the Stored Program Controlled

741

Network," *Bell Laboratories Record*, Vol. 57, No. 3, March 1979, pp. 85-89.

[JRC]   See, for example, J. R. Colton, "Cross-Connections-DACS Makes Them Digital," *Bell Laboratories Record*, September 1980, pp. 248-255.

[MMB]   M. M. Buchner, Jr., "Planning for the Evolving Family of Operations Systems," *Bell Laboratories Record*, May, 1979; pp 118-124.

[SKL]   S. K. Leung, "The Concept and Implementation of BANCS," Computer, January, 1980.

[THC]   T. H. Crowley et al., "UNIX Time-Sharing System," *Bell System Technical Journal*, Vol. 57, No. 6, Part 2, July-August 1978 (entire issue).

[TFA]   T. F. Arnold and W. N. Toy, "Inside the 3B-20 Processor," *Bell Laboratories Record*, Vol. 59, No. 3, March 1981, pp. 66-71.

[WDB]   W. D. Britt and V. L. Thurston, "Improving Electronic Switching Office Maintenance," *Bell Laboratories Record*, Vol. 57, No. 4, April 1979, pp. 110-113.

Paul F. Wainwright received the B.S. degree in physics from Bucknell University in 1972, and the M.Phil. and Ph.D. degrees in physics from Yale University in 1974 and 1977, respectively. Paul joined Bell Laboratories in 1977, and is a member of the Computer Systems Planning Department. He is responsible for developing protocols for local networks, and for initiating a Protocol Testbed Laboratory for doing applied research on network protocols. He is a member of the IEEE Project 802 Local Network Standards Committee. Dr. Wainwright is also a member of Phi Beta Kappa and the Cum Laude Society.

George W. Arnold received the B.A. degree in 1972 and the B.S., M.S., and Eng.Sc.D. degrees in Electrical Engineering and Computer Science in 1973, 1974, and 1978, respectively, from Columbia University. Since 1973 he has been associated with Bell Laboratories. From 1973 to 1978, as Member of Technical Staff, he was involved in planning for Bell System operations systems. In 1978, he became a Supervisor with responsibility for planning internal Bell System data communications standards. Dr. Arnold is a member of ACM, Eta Kappa Nu, Tau Beta Pi, and Sigma Xi.

Network Management: A Common Carrier's Perspective

F M Gilkinson, J A Kennedy, J W
Snow
TransCanada Telephone System, Canada

This paper examines network management from the perspective of the Computer Communications Group (CCG) of the TransCanada Telephone System (TCTS) and presents the Network Management System as an example of CCG's commitment to the network management concept. The Network Management System (NMS) receives status and alarm information from the Dataroute[TM] and Datapac[TM] networks and provides current and historical network status information for presentation on wall sized display boards, colour graphic and standard terminals.

1.0 INTRODUCTION

In less than a decade, data communications networks have evolved from a few remote terminals and a dedicated host into multinational, multipurpose systems with numerous applications on multiple hosts and hundreds of diverse terminals. As a result, data communications users need to be able to ensure the stability of their data networks through continuing growth and change. This need is compounded by the increasing dependency that many users are placing on data communications to do their business. The result is a growing requirement for network management, i.e., the activities necessary to plan, organize, control, maintain and evolve a data network at optimum cost and performance. This paper examines the concept of network management from the viewpoint of a common carrier, the Computer Communications Group (CCG) of the TransCanada Telephone System. CCG's Network Management System (NMS) is discussed as an example of CCG's commitment to the network management concept.

2.0 NETWORK MANAGEMENT

2.1 Technical Requirements

From the preceding definition of network management, it follows that network management encompasses many technical and administrative tools. These tools are necessary to provide network managers with the information and control which allows them to make accurate and timely decisions in such diverse areas of operation as network implementation, resolution of network faults and network design.

From a primarily technical point of view, there are four basic functions which must be provided to ensure effective network management: network surveillance, fault isolation and repair, network control, and collection of network performance data.

Automatic, constant surveillance of different locations within a data network is an essential feature of any network management system. The intent is to identify and quickly resolve service performance problems, hopefully before they become serious.

A network management system must also automatically display and log trouble conditions, i.e., alarms, to provide rapid isolation once a fault has occurred. As most networks are of a hierarchial nature, sympathetic and low order alarms must be masked so that the prime cause of the trouble is immediately evident.

In addition, a network management system must provide sufficient network control capabilities so that the network manager can act to restore service once a fault has been identified and isolated.

The fourth function which is necessary for effective network management is collection of network performance data. In keeping with the previous discussion of the increasing size and complexity of data networks, network performance information is required to evaluate the network's past performance, to identify current network loads, and to plan for future growth. This performance data base must contain a breakdown of traffic flow within the network including transmission delays, as well as service parameters such as availability and reliability.

Finally, the network management system itself must be manageable. The system's architecture must provide for central control and testing as well as system growth. Hence, there must be centralized control points from which all surveillance, trouble isolation, and performance monitoring are controlled. This approach is necessary to provide overall network coordination and to best utilize network management resources. The system must also be modular to allow for expansion in an orderly fashion in order to accommodate planned system growth and new technologies.

2.2 CCG Perspective

CCG is a world leader in the development and management of data networks. To meet the growing demand for data communications, CCG's analogue data network was adjoined in 1973 by the Dataroute network: a national, public digital data network which provides point-to-point and multipoint service at asynchronous speeds of 110 to 1200 bps and synchronous speeds of 1.2 to 56 kbps (Ref. 1). In 1977, CCG added the Datapac network: a public, packet-switched data network based on mini-computer switching nodes interconnected with Dataroute transmission facilities (Ref. 2). Because of the magnitude of these networks, and because of CCG's role as a data communications consultant, CCG has become both a source and a user of network management solutions

CCG's network management solutions combine both organizational and technical elements. For example, the Computer Communications Service Center (CCSC) combines these elements in a centralized customer reporting and maintenance organization (Ref. 3). The CCSC's responsibilities include receiving customer reports, circuit testing, fault sectionalization and repair dispatching. To support this organization, CCG has developed and is developing a number of computerized testing, administrative and management systems. One of these tools, the Network Management System (NMS), is presented as an example of CCG's capability and commitment to the network management concept.

3.0 NETWORK MANAGEMENT SYSTEM

3.1 Background

In 1975, the Dataroute Alarm Reporting and Control System (DARCS) was established to collect, store, and analyze Dataroute alarms and transmission quality information (Ref. 4). DARCS has proven to be an indispensable tool in managing and maintaining the Dataroute network. However, DARCS is being replaced with the Remote Monitoring System (RMS) (Ref. 5), and the Network Management System (NMS), because of the rapid growth of the Dataroute network and the increased need for enhanced network management capabilities.

3.2 NMS System Description

The heart of the NMS is a Tandem NonStop II computer system with two central processing units, each with one megabyte of main memory. The system's peripherals include a magnetic tape unit, a line printer, two 64 megabyte fixed- and moving-head discs and four 300 megabyte moving head discs.

The Tandem system runs under the Guardian Operating System with all control processes implemented as process pairs for high system reliability. The integrity of the system files is ensured by the mirrored data file feature.

The NMS maintains data bases which contain the Dataroute and Datapac network configurations, the RMS network configuration and alarm data for the previous three months. The NMS receives alarm and status information from the Dataroute network via the Remote Monitoring System (RMS) and from the Datapac network via the National Control Centre (NCC). This information is stored in the NMS data

base and processed to provide network management and maintenance information to network management and maintenance personnel throughout the TransCanada Telephone System via visual display boards, colour graphic terminals, standard CRT's and printers (Fig. 1).

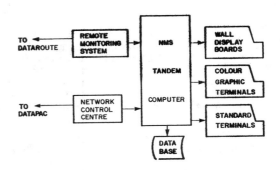

FIGURE I NETWORK MANAGEMENT SYSTEM

The display boards are wall-size mosaic boards which geographically portray the Dataroute and Datapac networks. Network nodes are represented by lamps which change colour under control of the NMS to indicate the network status. Because the display board is updated every five seconds, the user can see the current status of the entire network. Remote display boards are controlled via the Dataroute and Datapac networks.

The colour graphic terminals provide more detailed network status and configuration information about the Dataroute and Datapac networks. Four levels of detail of the network configuration can be selected by the user. Each display is updated by the NMS every five seconds. The graphic terminals can also receive all the NMS management reports that are available to the standard terminals.

For locations which do not justify the more expensive colour graphic terminals, the user can access network status descriptions and all other NMS management reports through a standard terminal or a CRT. Both graphics and standard terminals are supported via the Datapac network.

A two phased development plan has been adopted for the NMS because of its size and complexity. The first phase has entailed the acquisition of the Tandem system, the display boards, and the graphic and standard terminals. At present, the Tandem system can receive Dataroute and Datapac alarms, analyze these alarms and use the information to display Dataroute and Datapac system status on the display boards. Later stages of this first phase will include the display of system status on graphic terminals, and the development of all the reports and user information management features. The second phase will include implementation of alarm correlation and enhanced performance calculations.

3.3 System Functions

The NMS permits the user to manage the alarm information by defining boundaries on the information displayed. Through the use of commands entered from the terminal, the user can limit the information which is displayed by type or duration of alarm, by type of equipment, by system, by location or by customer.

Through the NMS, the user also has the ability to control the Remote Monitoring System to directly obtain unprocessed, detailed alarm information.

The Dataroute network has a three-tier multiplexing hierarchy. Failures in a higher level system produce sympathetic alarms in lower level systems. The NMS will utilize a correlation algorithm based on network topology and alarm times to inhibit display of sympathetic alarms. However, all alarms will be stored in the NMS data base. The NMS will also correlate Datapac trunk alarms with Dataroute system failures.

The NMS will execute a variety of performance calculations to provide an indication of the transmission quality of the network. These calculations will include: percentage error-free seconds, percentage availability, percentage of error-free transmission time, mean time between failures, mean time between errors, and mean time between events.

Because a customer circuit may be derived from several levels of multiplexers and several different multiplexing systems, it has not previously been possible to accurately determine the error performance of that circuit without placing test equipment on both ends of the circuit. The NMS will calculate an estimate of the end-to-end circuit performance as the percentage of error-free seconds that have been experienced by the circuit based on its bit rate of the customer circuits, the alarm history of the multiplexers, the error detection techniques used in the Dataroute equipment and the toplogy of the circuit. This estimate will exclude the local loop performance.

In addition, the NMS will provide the following reports to its users upon request:

(i) geographical location of major alarms (display board and graphic terminals)

(ii) help report

(iii) list report

(iv) alarm history report

(v) alarm status log

(vi) number of circuits per Dataroute system

(vii) network and system performance report

(viii) daily alarm summary report

(ix) RMS continuous monitoring report

(x) alarm cleared report

3.4 System Users

The four major users of the NMS are: the Computer Communication Service Centres (CCSC), the Dataroute System Control Offices (SCO), the Dataroute and Datapac National Data Control Centre (NDCC), and CCG's Account Managers.

The CCSC is the centralized organization responsible for receiving customer reports, testing, analyzing and sectionalizing faults and dispatching for repair activities. In the CCSC, the NMS will provide real-time and historical information helpful in sectionalization of Dataroute and Datapac alarms within the network.

The Display Board and Colour Graphic Terminals will provide CCSC users with the current status of the Dataroute and Datapac network. The Colour Graphic Terminals can also display a specific customers network with network troubles highlighted. With this real-time network information, the CCSC user will be able to perform fault analysis and sectionalization while the customer is on the telephone with the original trouble report.

By requesting the current status of the circuit, the CCSC user receives a list of alarms, if any, on all Dataroute network equipment used by that circuit. In the comment field of the alarms, Dataroute maintenance personnel can enter the cause and the expected repair time of the trouble. An Alarm Cleared Report can be requested on the alarmed system.

If there are no current alarms, an Alarm History Report can be requested. This report will list all the alarms which have occurred on any of the Dataroute equipment used by that circuit. The duration of the history can be controlled by the NMS user, but the default command will search over the last two hours. With this information and the customer description of the trouble, it may be possible to determine if a network problem, which has already been resolved, was the source of the report.

The Alarm Cleared Report provides the NMS user with a message and an audible alarm when a specified system becomes free of alarms. The NMS user can then contact the customer to indicate that the trouble has been resolved so that the trouble report can be closed.

The Display Board or the Colour Graphic Terminal enables the CCSC manager to be aware of major failures as they happen, and thus, he may more effectively coordinate staff efforts.

The Dataroute SCO's are responsible for fault sectionalization at the network level as well as the maintenance of Dataroute and Datapac network equipment. In the SCO's, the NMS provides improvement in the selection of available information.

The SCO user can obtain an alarm log which will identify failures as they occur. To make the alarm log more useful, the SCO user is able to define limits on the alarm information received. These customized alarm limits ensure that only alarm messages meaningful to a particular SCO are directed to it by the NMS.

The List Report and the Alarm History Report will enable the SCO user to more easily solve intermittent problems. The List Report will provide information on the network configuration while the Alarm History Report will provide access to the past ninety days of alarm history on any specified system.

The SCO manager may also use the Statistical Reports or the System Performance Reports to generate a list of systems which have delivered poor performance so maintenance action can be scheduled.

The Number of Circuits Assigned Report provides additional information on the relative severity of simultaneous failures so that restoration activities can be prioritized.

For unusual or difficult to diagnose problems, the SCO user can use the Continuous Monitoring Report and the associated RMS control capability to monitor in detail the alarms being generated by a particular piece of Dataroute equipment.

Finally, because the information contained in a report is an NMS user definable function, an NMS user can receive alarm information for another SCO. This allows a larger manned office to receive alarms normally received in smaller offices which are not continuously manned.

The NDCC has the overall responsibility for Dataroute and Datapac network performance. It continuously monitors the network, records major trouble events and coordinates fault clearing activity. The NMS provides the NDCC user with a number of features useful in monitoring network status and performance. The Display Boards, the Colour Graphic Terminals and the Current Status Report all provide information on the current network status. The List Report provides information on the network topology. The Alarm History Report allows the NDCC personnel to examine events which have occurred during the previous ninety days.

The Statistical Report, the Current Performance Alarm Display and the System Performance Reports also provides the NDCC user with the capability to analyze the performance and the availability of the network and its components.

CCG Account Managers are responsible for interfacing directly with customers. The account Managers will be able to use the Display Board and the Colour Graphic Terminals to illustrate to the customers, in an easily understood format, the scope of CCG's network and the magnitude of the monitoring and maintenance activities.

3.5 System Evolution

The present project plan allows for the evolution of the NMS in a number of ways. Three possible enhancements follow which indicate the system's potential and possible future direction.

Interface with Regional Systems: Dataroute and Datapac are nationwide networks supported by all TCTS member companies. Each member company is developing and implementing network monitoring and management systems for baseband and radio transmission systems, many of which carry Dataroute and Datapac traffic. Interfaces between the NMS and these regional systems will have two significant advantages:

(i) Facility alarms could be correlated with Dataroute and Datapac trunk alarms; and

(ii) It would allow member companies to apply total network management to the systems and services for which they are responsible.

New Network Services: TCTS is currently implementing new value-added and switched data services which will require many of the network management features available in NMS. Because the NMS design allows for expansion and evolution, it is expected that these new services will be added to the NMS to further enhance CCG's total network management capability.

Customer Access to NMS: Many large customers are becoming directly involved in the management of their networks. To be successful, they require access to current and historical information on the performance of their network. The NMS can provide this information on a customer network basis. Future evolution of the NMS may include customer access to this information under controlled and secured conditions.

4.0 CONCLUSIONS

CCG's success in a highly competitive data communications environment has been the result of satisfying customers' rapidly evolving requirements. CCG's attention to all aspects of network management has made a major contribution to this success. The Network Management System is one of the tools used by CCG network management and maintenance personnel to achieve this high level of success.

REFERENCES

(1) D.J. Horton, P.G. Bowie, "An Overview of Dataroute: System and Performance", International Conference on Communications, Minneapolis, Minnesota, June 17-19, 1974.

(2) C.I. McGibbon, et al., "DATAPAC - Initial Experience with a Commercial "Packet Network", ICCC '78, Kyoto, Japan, September 1978.

(3) R.L. Jamieson, "Streamlining Maintenance for a Complex Network", _Telephony_, May 7, 1979.

(4) S. Frankel, G. Pearce and W. Chan "A Minicomputer Based Performance Monitoring System for the Dataroute", _National Telecommunications Conference_, New Orleans, December 2-4, 1975.

(5) F.M. Gilkinson, S.S. Corkovic, J.A. Kennedy, "Monitoring and Management Systems for Dataroute", _National Telecommunications Conference_, New Orleans, December 1981.

Merlin Gilkinson is responsible for design and development of Dataroute surveillance and network management systems. Previous experience includes hardware engineering support and software development on a number of operational and maintenance systems. A graduate with Honours of both University of Toronto (Mathematics Major) and AT&T's Advanced Communication System Training, he has over thirty years of Telecommunications experience with Bell Canada and CN Telecommunications.

James (Jim) Kennedy is the project manager for the Network Management System. He has been with the Computer Communications Group of Bell Canada since graduating with an Honours degree in Computer Science from the University of Windsor, Ontario, Canada in 1974. During this time he has been involved in project management of a computerized test system for data sets and terminals, the evaluation of digital data circuit switching systems and the development of value-added services.

James Snow has been working in the area of network management since he joined Bell Canada's Computer Communications Group in 1980. He received an Honours BSc in Engineering-Physics from Dalhousie University, Halifax, Nova Scotia in 1977 and an MSc (Engineering) from Queen's University, Kingston, Ontario, in 1979. Besides data communications, his areas of experience include meteorology, oceanography, magnetics, and applied superconductivity.

Network Management for Performance and Reliability in the Integrated Text and Data Network of the Deutsche Bundespost

F N Lohwasser
Deutsche Bundespost, Federal
Republic of Germany

The users of data telecommunication expect an extremely high level of availability and reliability on their data connections. The paper to be presented will stress how the Deutsche Bundespost meets these demands by network management on the basis of organization, network operation and maintenance and staff. The central management of data telecommunications is the task of the Telecommunication Engineering Centre in Darmstadt. Maintenance and operation of the data switching and data transmission equipment is done by the staff of the telecommunication offices.

Staff is located on the switch sites. Mobile staff is provided for maintenance and trouble shooting of DCE's. Switches are implemented in large towns. Data transmission centres are installed where there is a heavy concentration of data customers. Central control and testing equipment signalize alarms of transmission systems and single channels. Fault location is provided by transmitting loop commands on the basis of recommendation X.150. Failures are cleared by automatic back-up of transmission lines. Line staff is composed of engineers and technicians. They maintain and operate circuit switched and packet switched equipment. Complex data measurement on trunk and subscriber lines is done by engineers. Staff is trained on courses within the Deutsche Bundespost. When implementing new techniques, basic courses take place in Darmstadt and 'hands-on' courses in Elmshorn. Subsequent courses are performed by the training centres of the regional directorates.

1 Network operation

The operation of data communication equipment at the transmission and switching sites of the Deutsche Bundespost and the maintenance of the telex and data communication equipment on customer premises is performed at the telecommunication office level. The execution of the tasks is supervised by the 18 regional directorates. Overall control is in the hands of the Fernmeldetechnisches Zentralamt in Darmstadt, which is responsible for the provision of the equipment and the establishment of operating guidelines. With the change-over from electro-mechanical to electronic equipment in the telex and data networks, local management at the telecommunication office level has been simplified considerably. The three offices which used to be responsible for switching, transmission and terminal equipment have now been reduced to two, the local staff service and the field engineering service.

2 Transmission and switching sites

The data switching and data transmission equipment are located on sites constituting the nodes of the Integrated Text and Data Network (IDN) and are operated by the staff of the "maintenance and operation of telecommunication equipment". The IDN is terminated by the terminal equipment of the users of the text and data services. The text and data connections are maintained by the field engineering staff "maintenance of text and data equipment".

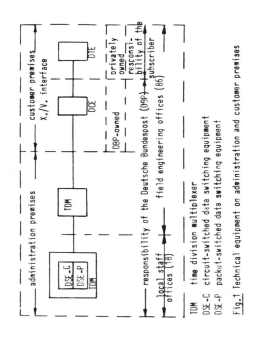

Fig.1 Technical equipment on administration and customer premises

TDM time division multiplexer
DSE-C circuit-switched data switching equipment
DSE-P packet-switched data switching equipment

The data switching equipment for the circuit-switched and packet-switched modes of operation is located at the data switching exchanges. The data transmission systems comprise single-channel equipment and multiplexers. The same type of equipment is also installed at the data transmission centres which do not have staff on site but are maintained by the field engineering service. Terminal stations which are also taken care of by the field engineering service comprise both Deutsche Bundespost-owned data circuit-terminating equipment (DCE) and privately owned data terminal equipment (DTE). The interfaces between the Deutsche Bundespost-owned DCE and privately owned DTE conform to the CCITT Recommendations of the V. and X. series and constitute the boundary between the responsibility of the Deutsche Bundespost and that of the customer.

3 Maintenance organization

The IDN is split up into 18 "control areas", each of which has its own data switching exchange.

3.1

Operation and control of these areas is performed by the 18 operating centres belonging to the 18 data switching exchanges. The staff required for the operation of the technical equipment is located at these centres. Their main functions are:

- acceptance of fault reports
- processing of fault reports concerning national and international traffic
- testing and measuring of subscriber and trunk lines
- network management
- activation of back-up equipment for time division multiplex systems
- keeping the record up to date.

The clearance of faults in data switching and data transmission equipment takes place on the site where the equipment is located. The 18 operating centres are staffed around the clock so that a 24-hour fault clearing service is available to IDN subscribers.

3.2

The allocation of the field staff to particular tasks is controlled and coordinated by staff supervisors at the telecommunication offices. In telecommunication offices without data switching equipment and consequently without an operating centre, the staff supervisors are responsible for the following tasks:

- supervision of the work and allocation of staff
- acceptance and processing of fault reports

- updating of records.

In the field engineering service, the data transmission officers perform the work related to the operation of the network. They are responsible for dealing with data transmission problems and assist customers with the planning and putting into operation of user data networks. They also coordinate the activities of other offices at the telecommunication office and other levels when difficulties arise with the implementation of user data networks (Fig. 2).

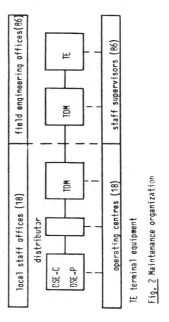

Fig. 2 Maintenance organization

4 Test and measuring equipment

The following central test and measuring equipment for data and facsimile transmission in the public switched telephone network is installed at the telegraph office Frankfurt:

- data test centre
- facsimile test centre

Central protocol test equipment (X.25) which is available to all customers is located at the network control centre of the packet-switched data network DATEX-P at the telecommunication office in Düsseldorf (protocol test centre).
With a view to the future monitoring of the IDN's performance, facilities for a central service test centre are being installed and tested at the Fernmeldetechnisches Zentralamt in Darmstadt.
Regional test and measuring equipment will be implemented at the 18 operating centres. As automatic data test generators, they will be at the disposal of the acceptance staff of the Deutsche Bundespost as well as the IDN subscribers for the purpose of

self-diagnosis. The development of a programme-controlled data measuring equipment project for data terminal equipment conforming to X.21 and X.25 for the Datex, teletex and interactive videotex service is under way. Data network control and test equipment for the 18 operating centres is being designed and implemented. Utilization of the equipment mentioned so far is illustrated in Table 1:

		utilization	
		user	Deutsche Bundespost
Central test and measuring equipment	DTC	-	x
	FTC	-	x
	PTC	x	x
	STC	-	x
Regional test and measuring equipment	ADTG	x	x
	DME	-	x
	CTE	-	x

DTC   data test centre
FTC   facsimile test centre
PTC   protocol test centre
STC   service test centre
ADTG automatic data test generator
DME   programme-controlled data measuring equipment
CTE   control and test equipment

Table 1 Utilization of test and measuring equipment

5 Diagnosis by the customer

For the purpose of data teleprocessing data terminal equipment (DTE) is connected to data processing systems by means of data links (Fig. 3). A data link consists of the transmission path and the data circuit-terminating equipment (DCE) at both ends.

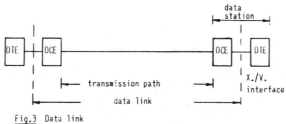

Fig.3 Data link

The data link can consist of a point-to-point or switched connection. A user data network employs a variety of public telecommunication networks (Fig. 4).
For the user of data teleprocessing, the computing centre is the main component of "his" user data network. The computing centre's counterparts for transmission problems are the operating centres of the Deutsche Bundespost. The Deutsche Bundespost strives

to achieve a data link availability of more than 99 %.

$$availability = \frac{observation\ period - fault\ duration}{observation\ period} \times 100\ \%$$

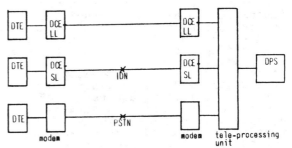

DCE-LL DCE for leased lines
DCE-SL DCE for switched lines (DATEX-L/-P)
DPS   data processing system
Fig.4 User data network

This means that in the case of 99 % link availability, the overall fault duration in a 3-months period amounts to approximately 21 hours. For many data teleprocessing applications, an availability of 99 % does not suffice. Instead, 24-hour availability, i.e. 100 % availability, is required. The Deutsche Bundespost can only fulfill this requirement if, in addition to the 24-hour fault clearing service, it permits the user himself to diagnose and localize any faults which may occur (self-diagnosis). With a view to the diagnosis and localization of faults by trained staff at the computing centre, private test and measuring sets, approved by the Fernmeldetechnisches Zentralamt, are inserted in the digital interfaces between the DTE's and DCE's. Remotely controlled test equipment is located between the DTE and DCE of the customer's remote station. Loop commands conforming to CCITT Recommendation V.54 are transmitted by the measuring and test sets at the computing centre to diagnose and localize faults (Fig. 5).

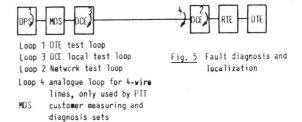

Loop 1 DTE test loop
Loop 3 DCE local test loop
Loop 2 Network test loop
Loop 4 analogue loop for 4-wire lines, only used by PTT
MDS customer measuring and diagnosis sets
RTE remote test equipment

Fig. 5 Fault diagnosis and localization

The values recommended by a working group composed of users, manufacturers and officials of the Deutsche Bundespost envisage the following features:

- optical indication of the interface signals

- acoustic indication of carrier loss
- loop establishment in accordance with CCITT Rec. V.54 (1,3.2)
- monitoring of transmitted and received data
- selective polling of remote stations
- measuring of bit and block error rates.

The remotely controlled test equipment installed at customers' remote stations performs the following functions:

- switching of all interchange circuits during data transmission
- termination of both ends of the interfaces as described in V.28
- establishment of network test loop 2 by buffering the test patterns for the half-duplex mode.

If the diagnosis by the customer reveals that the fault is likely to be found in the IDN, including the DCE's, the data teleprocessing service can be restored either by qualified staff at the computing centres by exchanging the faulty device or by means of the interface switches at the remote stations. In the case of analogue leased lines, the DATEX-L network acts as a stand-by (Fig. 6).

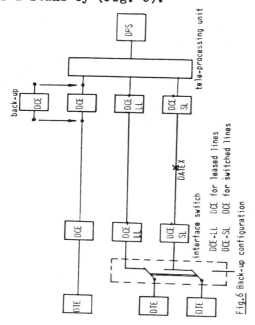

Fig.6 Back-up configuration

6 Network management

The rapid expansion of the synchronous IDN with envelope-structured data channels is dependent on the progress made with the digitalization of the general telecommunication network of the Deutsche Bundespost.
The IDN has already been divided into 18 control areas characterized by the data transmission centre located at the data switching exchange and affiliated operating centre.
In these areas, the data links are routed to the data switching exchange

either direct or via time division multiplexers. To supervise the 18 control areas and to manage the IDN, network control and test equipment is being provided at the 18 data transmission stations connected to the exchanges. As shown in Fig. 7, the following components will be monitored:

1 subscriber lines
2 technical equipment at the data transmission centres
3 multiplexers.

The alarm transmission devices (4) are external units of the control and test equipment at the data transmission centres under the responsibility of the field engineering service. They collect alarms, encode them and transmit them to the control and test equipment.

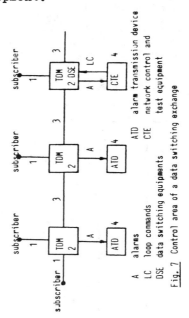

A   alarms
LC   loop commands
DSE   data switching equipments
ATD   alarm transmission device
CTE   network control and test equipment

Fig. 7 Control area of a data switching exchange

Whereas 18 operating centres equipped with control and test equipment are required for monitoring the circuit-switched part of the IDN (Table 2), network management of the packet-switched part of the IDN takes place in a network control centre (NCC). The NCC is located in Düsseldorf and performs the following set of functions:

- coordination of supra-regional fault localization
- evaluation of the alarm protocols of the 17 packet-switched data switching exchanges
- protocal test centre
- central network observation.

751

	total number	
	data switching exchanges	operating centres/NCC
circuit switching equipment	18 + 5	18
packet switching equipment	17	1

Table 2 Data switching exchanges and operating centres

7 Integrated test and measuring procedures

For measurements in the IDN, programme-controlled data measuring equipment is being installed at the 18 operating centres. The CPU of the programme-controlled data measuring equipment controls the protocol testers and monitors via a central bus. As is already the case at the NCC in Düsseldorf, the programme-controlled data measuring equipment is to compile alarm and operating statistics automatically.

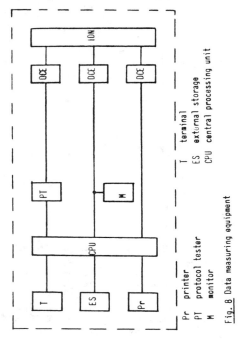

T   terminal
ES   external storage
CPU central processing unit

Pr printer
PT protocol tester
M   monitor

Fig. 8 Data measuring equipment

The protocol testers and monitors collect and analyze both the data streams and bit and byte-oriented data communication protocols. The Deutsche Bundespost supports inter-active videotex service, Bildschirm-text, within levels 1 to 3, and teletex within levels 1 to 7 of CCITT Recommendation X.25.

Biography

Franz N. Lohwasser studied tele-communication engineering at the Technical University in Darmstadt. He graduated as a Diplom-Ingenieur and joined the telecommunication industry 1962. In 1972 he changed to the Deutsche Bundespost, Telecommunication Engineering Centre. Since 1979 he has been heading the section "operation and maintenance of data telecommunication equipments". This task includes operation and maintenance of exchanges on the base of circuit and packet switched techniques. He is responsible for availability and reliability of the Integrated Data Network (IDN) and the data transmission over the public telephone network of the Deutsche Bundespost.

The Influence of Network Bandwidth on the Design of Distributed Database Systems

D A Winscom Clarke
International Computers (Australia),
Australia

The need for interactions with humans imposes practical limits on the acceptable response times for computing systems. Where an application program is separated from one or more database managers by communication links, the delays these impose may make certain design techniques impractical. By roughly estimating these overheads, we can conclude under what circumstances current software technology will be satisfactory and where fresh methods are needed.

1. INTRODUCTION

The pure logic of computing systems is often spoilt by their need for human interaction. Human response times have very definite upper and lower limits for acceptability. Although algebraic equations may be sufficient for relative computation, it is only when absolute values are derived that the practicality of proposed systems can be tested.

This paper is concerned with the effect on the design of distributed databases caused by the speed of communications links. There is no attempt here to consider the relative merits of different protocols nor to allow for the effects of queuing. The figures used are intended only to relate the calculated performance to the scale of human values. Any criticism that they are inaccurate by some percentage figure is entirely merited. It is, however, contended that they are correct in their order of magnitude and it is on that basis that the argument rests.

2. DBMS ARCHITECTURE

Although there are some exceptions, most data base management systems, which allow multiple concurrent users, have the same architecture. A single database manager program acts as server to a number of application programs. These agents and the server communicate by some form of link.

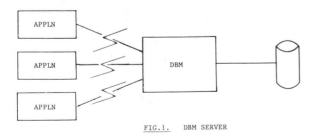

FIG.1. DBM SERVER

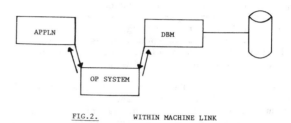

FIG.2. WITHIN MACHINE LINK

In the case of most database systems in service today, both the agents and the server reside in the same computer. The precise nature of the link depends on the operating system in use, though all the mechanisms share certain characteristics. The agent makes a call on the operating system, passing it a number of parameters. The operating system plants these parameters in the address space of the server and notifies it of their availability. The server returns the results of its service in the same way. The cost of the message pair which requests and receives service can be calculated from the number of instructions executed and the processor speed. For large mainframe computers, this will be of the order of 0.5 milliseconds.

3. NETWORK SPEEDS

Up till now, most computer manufacturers have viewed their machines as a closely integrated set of component units. However, the design trend is to view the order code processor as merely one of a number of functional processing units connected by a high-speed area network. In that sense, the future view will be that all databases are distributed.

Accessing a database via a local area network requires the exchange of a message pair. In order to provide some absolute level for the calculations which follow, I am assuming arbitrarily, that such a message pair will require the transmission of five hundred characters. This gives the following table of message rates and transmission times against line speed;

Line Speed (Mbits/sec)	Msg. Pairs (/sec)	Transn. Time (msecs)
50	10,000	0.1
10	2,000	0.5
1	200	5.0

Table 1.

The highest line speed represents the expected performance of the links between the parts of the future multi-processor mainframe computers. Ten Megabits per second is the speed of Ethernet, Cambridge Ring and similar systems. The lowest speed corresponds with the performance of various mini- and micro-computer co-axial cable links.

The table shows clearly that, unless large numbers of agents request service simultaneously and form queues, the separation of a database server from its agents by a local area network does not incur an unacceptably large overhead.

It is instructive to extend the table to encompass wide area networks serviced by communications lines.

Line Speed (Kbits/sec)	Msg. Pairs (/sec)	Transn. Time (msecs)
96	19	52
9.6	1.9	520
2.4	0.5	2080

Table 2.

Here the picture is dramatically different. The small number of message pairs which can be handled makes queuing more probable and even the basic transmission time is one or two orders of magnitude worse than the within - machine case.

4. RECORD ACCESS

In the case of a CODASYL-style database the following sequence of data manipulation language commands is required to read and update a single record;

                    READY
                    OBTAIN recordname
                    MODIFY recordname
                    FINISH

Each command requires a message pair to be exchanged between the application and the database manager. Assuming that the database is being secured by journalising, one disc read and three write operations will be caused. Under normal service conditions, these disc operations will take about fifty milliseconds each.

Using a wide area network at 96K bits per second to connect the application with the database manager, the total elapsed time for the transaction comprises:-

    4 X disc accesses @ 50 msecs   200 msecs
    4 X message pairs @ 52 msecs   208 msecs
                                    408 msecs

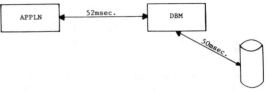

FIG.3.   WIDE AREA LINK

This represents a crude estimate of response time within the computer. In a genuine system, the response time at the terminal would have to allow for queuing for the discs and for the transmission lines between the computer and the terminal.

Taking these things into account, it is clear that the use of a lower speed line between the application and the database manager would degrade response times to an unacceptable extent.

Most of the transaction processing systems in commercial service today have performance characteristics similar to the transaction just considered. There is, however, an increasing demand from users for the ability to use more complex selection criteria. None of the present generation of database management systems supports this facility directly. The selection must be done by accessing successive records and applying the selection criteria e.g. -

    OBTAIN FIRST recordname. PERFORM SELECT-
                                        RECORD.
    PERFORM GETNEXTRECORD
      WHILE RECORDNOTSELECTED.
    - - - - - - -
    - - - - - - -
    GETNEXTRECORD.
      OBTAIN NEXT recordname.
      PERFORM SELECTRECORD.
    GRNEXIT.
      EXIT.
    SELECTRECORD.
      apply selection criteria
    MOVE zero or one TO RECORDSELECTOR. (with
      suitable 88 level)
    SREXIT
      EXIT.

Such selection processes will involve the accessing of between ten and one hundred records. With suitable buffering techniques, the overheads of disc transfers can be greatly reduced, but the use of a wide area network for passing the data manipulation commands between the application and the database manager imposes too great a burden. Single record access to the database is satisfactory over a local area network. Where a wide area network is in use, the database manager must include sufficient intelligence to interpret multi-record predicates.

5. DISTRIBUTED UPDATING

Most database management systems support the concept of a success unit. Within a success unit, a user has sole access to those records which he proposes to update. In the most general case of a distributed database, we can envisage a situation where records of different types are supported by different database managers.

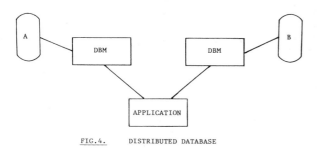

FIG.4.   DISTRIBUTED DATABASE

An application wishing to perform co-ordinated updates of both record types would raise success units with both database managers and use classical hand-shaking techniques to ensure synchronisation.

Using the example of CODASYL-style database systems, the required data manipulation language commands would be:-

```
READY    databaseA
READY    databaseB
OBTAIN   recordnameA
OBTAIN   recordnameB
MODIFY   recordnameA
MODIFY   recordnameB
FINISH   databaseA
FINISH   databaseB
```

Where the links are supported by a high-speed local area network, the delays imposed by the synchronisation messages would, in the above example add less than 40 msec to the elapsed time of the transaction. This is negligible when compared with the 400 msecs involved in accessing the discs.

In the case of a wide-area network at, say, 96Kbit/sec, the synchronisation would cost over 400 msecs. When the disc accessing times, queuing and terminal message transmission are all taken into account, the response time would probably be close to two seconds. This shows that where lower line speeds are used, or where transactions of any complexity are involved, synchronous updating becomes impractical.

Instead a much more sophisticated scheme, which involves secured asynchronous updates, must be used. The essential element of such a scheme is the acknowledgement that the updating of a remote database will take so long that the request for such service must be secured to guard against partial system failure. The required logic is:-

1. Determine the updates to be performed.
2. Secure the update requests locally.
3. Issue remote update requests.
4. Perform remote updates including register-ing the update request.
5. Return a success or failure response.
6. Update the local database and erase the remote service request from the local database.

Once again, this sort of involved processing cannot be invoked on a single-record basis. Acceptable performance requires the use of powerful multi-record predicates.

6. PALLIATIVES AND SOLUTIONS

Although it is intellectually unsatisfying, a practical palliative is to constrain the system design. Many implementations do not require remote update capability. Remote retrieval is adequate. Often the bulk of the database accesses can be satisfied locally, with only a small percentage of transactions incurring the transmission delays on the network. In these cases, the lengthy response times can be made acceptable by informing the terminal user that remote access is about to be invoked and giving him the option to abort the request. These and similar techniques make it possible to build useful systems within the limitations of the current technology.

Since the greatest difficulties are caused by the message traffic between agent and server improvements must be sought by reducing that traffic. One method of achieving that aim is to increase the intelligence of the database server so that the messages are more powerful. Instead of moving the data to meet the porgram logic, the logic is moved to meet the data and executed in the database server. A number of hardware developments are in train which match this objective. Unfortunately, there is little or no sign that the corresponding effort is being made in the fields of software and standards.

7. CONCLUSIONS

The database management systems in service
today are based on the concept of single-
record access. This paper shows that such
software technology can be used to implement
a distributed database with a number of
servers provided that they are connected by a
high-speed local area network. Where a slower
speed wide area network is used, the currently
available technology cannot support the secure
synchronised updating of a distributed database with multiple servers. Such a facility
will be available only when the database
manager servers are able to support more
powerful multi-record access predicates.
Even then, secure asynchronous updating will
be needed to achieve acceptable performance
and this has a number of theoretical
difficulties which will require solutions.

D.A. Winscom Clarke read
Physics at Balliol College,
Oxford. Apart from two years
with an independent software
house, he has worked for ICL
or its predecessor companies
since 1967. He was involved
in the implementation of the
GEORGE 2 operating system and
subsequently worked on the
design of the 2900 series
and its VME software. For
the last eight years he has been a data management
consultant for ICL. He was appointed National
Data Management Consultant to ICL (Australia) in
1980 and has since been responsible for a number
of successful database implementations.

A Communication Oriented Operating System Kernel for a Fully Distributed Architecture

F E Schmidtke
Siemens, Federal Republic of Germany

Starting with a description of the considered network architecture of the loosely coupled multimicrocomputer system SIELOCnet, the basic design principles of our approach are outlined. The currently implemented network operating system called DINOS is based on autonomous system software for all computer nodes which cooperate with other components by well defined protocols. It is based on a state-of-the-art realtime-multitasking kernel managing the local activities of a single node. The DINOS communication mechanism across computer boundaries as well as the overall load balancing and allocation management are embedded within a layered structure of each local operating system. For a programmer there is a unique addressing scheme for local objects within a single computer and remote ones residing elsewhere.

1. INTRODUCTION

Local microcomputer networks seem to fit best the current requirements in computer architecture. Personal computing capabilities are offered by low cost, but fairly powerful microcomputer stations which perform a good deal of activities autonomously. Expensive resources like hard disks, printers and mainframe computers, on the other hand, are provided by dedicated network stations commonly accessible by all users via an uniform interface. Furthermore do such networks contain the ability to implement additional features like runtime parallelism within single programs, distributed databases, user communication (electronic mail) and fault tolerance.

This paper is concerned with the system software of such networks. An approach to implement a network operating system with the mentioned features for a homogeneous microcomputer network is presented. Special emphasis is laid on the communication mechanism among processes scattered around the network. It is based on a layered architecture offering a configuration independent interface to application programmers.

2. SYSTEM ARCHITECTURE

Before going into detail of the network operating system, the architecture of the target system will be introduced. It consists of multiple identical microcomputers loosely coupled by a serial communication system. An example of a possible configuration of SIELOCnet is given by figure 1.

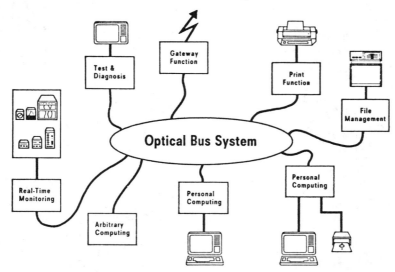

Figure 1 Example configuration of SIELOCnet

The communication medium is a packet switched multiaccess channel based on an optical bus system /SAUE 80/. The first network prototype operates at 16 Mbits per second, and up to 16 computers can be connected to the bus within a maximum distance of 600 meters.

Low level communication up to level three of the ISO Reference model of open system interconnections (OSI) /7/ is performed by dedicated front-end processors, called network controllers, which are attached to every single computer node /8/.

The hardware of the back-end processors, performing the system functions, is build of Multibus connected standard modules like 8086 based single board computers, memory boards and I/O interfaces to peripheral devices.

Although we are considering a homogeneous network, there are three different types of computer nodes in the network. These are distinguished only by their system software defining the functional capabilities. The lower part of figure 1 shows workstations which are dedicated to single users. They run user programms autonomously, to a far extend, and survey the user-system dialogs via the connected terminals. It is possible to connect private peripherals like floppy disks, card readers, printers, ect., to these stations. Workstations represent personal computers of single users and do not offer any network services.

All network node do have access to shared dedicated functional computers, shown in figure 1. Those computers offer network services by accessing and managing shared resources like printers or secondary storage devices (hard disks). They also perform specific network functions like system-test, diagnosis, real-time monitoring and control of industrial environment and communication to external systems (eg. gateway to mainframe computers or networks). It is possible to install arbitrary functional computers at this level, even if they perform specific actions for single users. Their functions include dedicated software tasks like compiling if there is a need for static installation of such services (e.g. in an engeneering environment).

The third type of network computers are denoted as arbitrary processing stations which offer bare computing power to the network. In general they do not have any peripherals connected to them. Instead, they contain certain system software enabling them to load and execute arbitrary user programs, or part of those. Therefore they are most important for system wide load balan-

cing. They also allow running distinct pieces of single user programs concurrently. The network operating system contains mechanisms and strategies for allocation and survey of such parallelisms.

The hardware architecture of the network can be reconfigured arbitrarily within certain limits. Although the result is a static configuration, it is possible to alter this configuration dynamically at system runtime. This provides a fault tolerant behavior in case of single node failures.

3. NETWORK OPERATING SYSTEM

The distributed network operating system (DINOS) of the introduced architecture implements a general purpose OS for different configurations and applications /1,10,13/. DINOS is characterized by its decentralized organization based on the principle of local or cooperative autonomy /3/ offering mechanisms for system wide interprocess communication and load balancing. It is implemented of autonomous operating systems for all nodes controlling their local activities and communicating with other system components by well defined protocols. The structure of DINOS node operating systems is given by figure 2.

Every local OS is divided into two major parts. The upper part contains the so called system-functions, while the lower part implements the DINOS-kernel.

System-functions represent software components offering commonly accessible services like control and management of attached peripherals. They also perform specific tasks like system-test and diagnosis or communication to external systems. At system initialization these functions define their interfaces for reception of requests and data from remote computers. This interface connects "consumers" and "producers" of services via exchange of certain messages defined by protocols.

If a network node is provided with an allocation function, it is capable of allocating (by certain strategies), loading, initiating, and managing one or more code segments, called distribution units, dynamically at runtime. These consist of a (time varying) collection of sequential processes to run independently in a single computer.

An execution unit defines the environment and the scope of an application program as well as the resources required for its execution. This management unit is a frame for an arbitrary

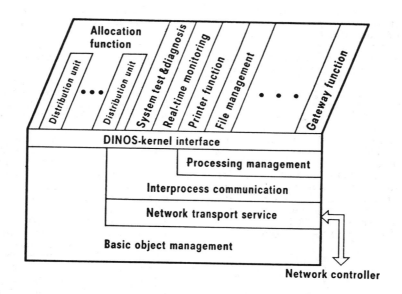

Figure 2   Structure of DINOS node operating systems

number of distribution units each of which is possibly allocated to a different network computer. By that we gain real concurrency at the execution of single programs.

The detailed description of theory and programming technique to structure user programs into execution- and distribution units is out of the scope of this paper and may be found elsewhere /9,14/.

The set of system-functions of a single local operating system defines the capabilities and network services it offers. The assignment of these features is performed by a system generation process. Bound together with the complete DINOS-kernel the set of selected system-functions represents the actual operating system of a node.

The DINOS-kernel is identical for all computer nodes and offers a standard interface to the upper layer, independently of actual configurations.

A kernel is built of four layers.

A basic object management (BOM) layer supervises local building-blocks that are manipulated by a fixed set of operations. It performs the dispatching and context switching of concurrent processes being the basic objects of the software concept. Those represent logical constructs characterized by states that evolve in time according to some rule (e.g. by interpreting instruction sequences) /6/. System-functions as well as the DINOS-kernel consist of processes. The process scheduling operates preemptive, event driven, and priority based, reflecting the realtime requirements of the system.

The BOM layer services interrupts in reaction to external events. It allocates memory objects for code and data and deallocates them if they are no longer needed. Protection mechanisms prevent mutual interferences of independent processes resident within the same node. It handles runtime errors by system routines, which may pass control to user provided error routines if desired.

The BOM layer is reponsible for the local activities within a single node. It is based on a standard real time operating system kernel of a monocomputer system. The remaining parts of the DINOS-kernel are built on top of this layer, managing cooperation and coordination of several network computers. These modules represent a layered architecture and correspond to layers four and partly five of the ISO reference model of open systems interconnection (OSI) /6,7,15/. The different layers are independent from each other and separated by defined interfaces. This allows easy verifying, debugging and modifying of their functions.

The interprocess communication (IPC) layer provides secure, reliable connections between communicating processes independent of their actual allocation to computer nodes /2,4,5/. It implements a datagram service for message exchange, based on an end-to-end protocol achieving error – and flow control characteristics.

The routing of messages to single processes is controlled by symbolic addresses denoted as PORTs /1,13/. Its address scheme is implemented by hierarchical names allowing multicast addressing at a process level /5/. Before messages can be exchanged, a PORT must be created. Its scope, defined by the creation procedure, restricts send - and receive rights to distribution units, user programs (i.e. all distribution units of a single program), users (i.e. all programs of a single user) and system (i.e. no restriction). Since the communication mechanism operates purely unidirectional, for bidirectional message exchange every communication partner must create his own PORT. This relation is illustrated by figure 3.

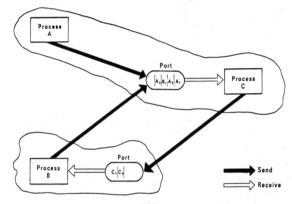

Figure 3 Interprocess communication based on a PORT concept

The lines surrounding processes A and C and process B, respectively, indicate the scope of distribution units. The example of figure 3 shows two distribution units which might reside in different network nodes. This would require internode communication for the message exchange between processes B and C via their respective PORTs. Figure 3 also illustrates the queueing of messages at a PORT by the IPC mechanism.

If a process has send-access to a PORT, it may drop messages there for a receiver. The IPC queues all messages until they are requested. Receiving access to a PORT is restricted to that process which created it.

The IPC mechanism operates fully asynchronous, i.e. senders and receivers are not synchronized for exchange of messages (no-wait-send). The sending process continues operation after a SEND-call. A receiver is suspended only if there is no message available at the specified PORT. Any time a message is accepted at this PORT, the suppended process is marked ready again and may proceed in operation depending on its priority. To avoid possible deadlock situations, a time-out may be specified in a RECEIVE-call.

In order to support the assynchronous behavior of sending and receiving processes, message exchange always results in message duplication. For communication across computer boundaries, messages are buffered in the private memory of the target node. The end-to-end service of the IPC guarantees the delivery of a message to the addressed PORT, not the delivery to a receiver. If this is required, it must be implemented by higher level protocols of system functions or application programs /7,15/.

IPC management tables contain information allowing to check the access rights to PORTs. Access rights are of interest for send - as well as receive operations. For example, it must be prevented that messages of different programs using the same symbolic addresses get mixed.

A sublayer of the IPC mechanism is called network transport service (NTS) which represents an interface to the attached network controllers of a node. These offer a facility for exchange of arbitrary messages on a best effort basis, including send and receive operations as well as certain commands like definition of logical addresses, test functions, etc..

The NTS is responsible for buffer allocation of received messages in order to provide them to local processes. In case a message cannot be accepted because of temporary buffer shortage, it is rejected and an "awake" may be singnalled to the former sender when buffer space is available. The corresponding NTS in the sender, for some time, stores the message in case of a "buffer shortage rejection" and retransmits after reception of the "awake-signal". Retransmission strategies may be influenced by higher levels.

At the DINOS-kernel interface the NTS is not directly accessible by user programmers. Only certain system functions may use this layer for special purposes (e.g. system-test, diagnosis, statistics, downline-loading, ect.). Such functions are clearly separated from normal network access.

The processing management (PM) layer initializes and supervises execution units, distribution units and processes (see above). It also does load balancing within the overall system by allocating those management units to remote network nodes. There is a set of allocation mechanisms resident within the kernel which may be selected and parameterized by programmers and/or compilers /12/ to implement application specific allocation strategies.

Finally the PM handles the naming mechanism. It generates unique identifications for execution units defining the domain for internal communications. This identification is added to all network messages as a logical address enabling the communication system to deliver a message only to a relevant subset of all network nodes (where distribution units of a execution unit are allocated). This equals a dynamic binding of names to network addresses since addressees of a message may reside on arbitrary nodes and each node can represent several logical addresses. This feature is efficently supported by the hardware and the firmware if the attached network controllers.

4. CONCLUSION

This paper described the basic concept of a distributed microcomputer network which is currently being implemented as a prototype system. Taking into account the recent progress in network technology and computer interconnection, the system software is getting of more and more importance. Its primary task is to make the benefits of computer networks available to its users without bothering them with configuration and allocation problems. The network should appear to a user more or less like a single powerful machine.

Our network-operating-system approach tries to tackle some basic problems like decentralized network organization, functional decomposition, interprocess communication and allocation mechanisms. With that concept, we borrowed from ideas recently advanced by other researchers. We are aware of many open questions related to distributed systems. Major ones are management of distributed data-bases, programming techniques and user interfaces. In our future work we shall consider some of those problems.

Remark

This work has been supported under the technological program of the Federal Department of Research and Technology of the F.R.G. (project number IT 1020 5). The author alone is responsible for the contents.

REFERENCES

/1/ Baskett, F; Howard, J.H.; Montague, J.T.: Task Communication in DEMOS, Sixth ACM Symposium on Operating Systems Principles, Nov. 1977, pp. 23-31

/2/ Bellm, H.H.; Schmidtke, F.E.; Schmitter, E.J.: A Distributed Multi-User Microcomputer System with Special Features in Parallel Processing and Fault Tolerance, Proc. of the Third Annual Louisiana Computer Exposition, Febr. 26-27, 1981, pp. 86-92

/3/ Enslow, P.H.: What is a 'Distributed' Data Processing System? Computer, Jan. 78, pp. 13-21

/4/ Eser, F; Schmidtke, F.: Process Communication Within a Distributed Multimicrocomputer System, Microprocessors and Microsystems 1981, Vol. 5, 4, pp. 149-152

/5/ Eser, F.: Interprocess Communication of DINOS, a Distributed Network Operating System, (to appear) 8th Symposium in Microprocessing and Microprogramming, Euromicro'82, Sept. 5-9, 1982

/6/ Fletcher, J.G.; Watson, R.W.: Service Support in a Network Operating System, 20th Internat. IEEE Computer Society Conf., Feb. 25-28, 1980, pp. 415-424

/7/ Kryshow, J.M.; Miller, C.K.: Local Area Networks Overview Part 2: Standard Activities, Computer Design, March 1981, pp. 12-20

/8/ Metcalfe, R.M.; Boggs, D.R.: Ethernet: Distributed Packet Switching for Local Computer Networks, Communications of the ACM, July 1976, Vol. 19, No. 7, pp. 395-404

/9/ Palmer, D.F.: Distributed Computing System Design at the Subsystem/Network Level, Proceedings of 1st internat. Conf. on Distributed Computing Systems, Oct. 1-5, 1979, pp. 22-30

/10/ Rashid, R.F.; Robertson, G.G.: Accent: A Communication Oriented Network Operating System Kernel, 8th Symposium on Operating Systems, Dec. 1981

/11/ Sauer, A; Schwaertzel, H.: A Local Distributed Microprocessor Net with Decentralized Access to an Optical Bus, Proc. of the COMPCON Fall, Sept. 23-25, 1980

/12/ Schmidtke, F.: Programming of Parallel Processes within a Multi-Microcomputer Architecture, Proc. of IMMM Data Comm.80, June 17-19, 1980, pp. 67-75

/13/ Solomon, M.H.; Finkel, R.A.: Roscoe: A Multi-Microcomputer Operating System, 2 nd Rocky Mountain Symposium on Microcomputers, Aug. 1978, pp. 241-310

/14/ Tobiasch,R.; Raffler, H.: Configurating Software- A method for Bridging Over the Gap between Concurrent Processing and Distributed Processing, Proc. of IEEE Infocom 82, March 1982

/15/ Wecker, S.: Computer Network Architectures, Computer,Sept.1979, pp.58-72

BIOGRAPHY

Frank E. Schmidtke was born in Demmin (GDR). He received his diploma in electrical engineering / data processing at the Technical University of Karlsruhe (FRG). Since 1978 he has been with Siemens AG, Munich. His current research interests include loosely coupled microcomputer systems, distributed system software and programming methology.

The Integration of Distributed Hetrogeneous Database Systems based on Entity-relationship Model

S Obana, Y Urano, K Suzuki
Kokusai Denshin Denwa Co., Japan

This paper proposes the virtualization technique, based on the entity-relationship model, for integrating heterogeneous databases distributed world-wide. We first introduce the concept of virtualization of DBMSs (Data Base Management Systems) and users, and propose the symmetric five layered schema structure as an actual technique for this virtualization. Furthermore, we adopt the entity-relationship model for the representation of the conceptual schema in the five layered schema structure and propose the common database access protocol, based on the entity-relationship model, for query processing among these virtualized databases and users. Finally, we show the applicability of this technique to existing database system.

I. INTRODUCTION

In today's world information retrieval systems or database systems are very important components in the computer communication network environment. But these database systems, physically located at different sites, employ different hardware and software and provide different access languages and different data models for users. So network users must be aware of such database system heterogeneity and data distribution in advance.

In previous works, for the purpose of solving these problem, they directly applied the three layered schema structure of ANSI/X3/SPARC to construct distributed database systems based on the bottom-up approach and did not take the distributed processing environments into considerations deeply. In some cases, they introduced, as a common conceptual model, the relational model[9], etc., which do not satisfy the required conditions. In addition, very few papers have discussed the implementation of access protocols for a distributed database system.

In this paper, for the purpose of solving the heterogeneity problem and data distribution problem, we discuss the network architecture of the distributed database system, from the viewpoints of database technique and communication technique. We first introduce the concept of virtualization of DBMSs and users, and propose the symmetric five layered schema as an actual technique for this virtualization. This schema structure is the extension of the three layered schema structure of ANSI/X3/SPARC and exhibits its great power in the case of actual implementation. Furthermore, we adopt the entity-relationship model for the representation of the conceptual schema in the five layered schema structure and propose the common database access protocol for the query processing among these virtualized databases and users.

And then, in order to test our idea of virtualization, we have developed an experimental distributed database system. In this system, users can have access to, using relational query language, the CODASYL[6]-oriented database; Circuit Information System etc., operating in KDD.

II. VIRTUALIZATION OF HETEROGENEOUS DATABASES

2.1 Concept of virtualization for distributed database system

A key to successful structuring of the distributed database system by the bottom-up approach is the solution to the problems of "heterogeneity" and "data distribution". The concept of virtualization is introduced as an optimum means for solving these problems. The techniques of the "virtualization" are widely used in the field of computer communications. There are some activities initiated by the CCITT, ISO, etc. to virtualize terminals and other resources of communication networks.

In this paper, the concept of the virtualization is applied to the distributed database from the viewpoint that data stored in distributed databases itself is considered as a resource of the network.

Under the concept of virtualization, a distributed database system consists of virtual users and servers (referred to as the virtual resources) as shown in Fig.2-1.

This virtualization implies the following two viewpoints:

(1) Virtualization for heterogeneity of resources

A virtual resource has access to another virtual resource without awareness of the heterogeneity of it or as if it had access to a homogeneous network resource. That is, when a virtual user communicates with a virtual server, the user does not need to be aware of the data model and the access language used by the real server, and also, when a virtual server communicates with a virtual user, the server does not need to be aware of the interface used by the real

user such as a high-level query language.
(2) Virtualization for data distribution
    A virtual user can view the
distributed database system without
awareness of the data distribution or as
if it had access to a single server.

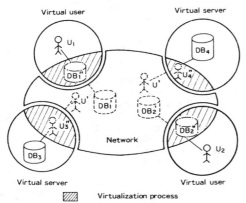

Fig.2-1 Virtualized distributed database

2.2 Symmetric five layered schema structure and entity-relationship model

The ANSI/X3/SPARC study group on databases
has proposed a general architecture for a
database management system.[3] It
constitutes layered architecture of schema
(external schema, conceptual schema and
internal schema). This is used for mapping
the external schemata which describe the data
as seen by the programmers, onto the internal
schema which defines the data as seen by the
system. And this study group uses a three
level organization which introduces three
levels of administration functions, three
levels of schema processors and three levels
of data manipulation modules.
    Actually, the three layered architecture
of ANSI/X3/SPARC is very useful in considering
a single database system. But it can not be
applied to the distributed database system
directly, because the locality of the
processing at each network resource is not
taken into consideration. So in order to meet
the circumstance that network components are
dispersed at different sites, we modify and
expand the model of ANSI/X3/SPARC and propose
a five layered architecture.

2.2.1 Symmetric five layered schema structure

As shown in Fig.2-2, the symmetric five
layered schema structure comprises five schema
levels of LIS (Local Internal Schema), LCS
(Local Conceptual Schema), GCS (Global
Conceptual Schema), GES (Global External
Schema) and LES (Local External Schema).
Around GCS as the centre, LCS and GES, as well
as LIS and LES, are positioned symmetrically.
LES and GES correspond to the virtual user,

and LIS and LCS to the virtual server.
    Generally, difference between the real
users or difference between real servers lies
mainly in the view of data and its
description. To solve the problem of
heterogeneity, it is necessary to use a common
conceptual model to describe the data in the
network.

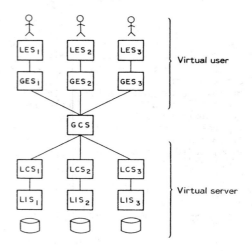

Fig.2-2 Symmetric five layered schema structure

This common conceptual model must satisfy
the following conditions:
Condition 1. The model should provide
              complete and formal description
              of data.
Condition 2. The conceptual model should
              remain unchanged in case of
              modifications in DBMSs.
Condition 3. The change in the conceptual
              world should have little effect
              on other schemata.
Condition 4. The model should be
              understandable.

    In the symmetric five layered schema
structure,
- LIS, which corresponds to the schema or
   subschema of an existing DBMS, is the
   description of data provided by a real
   DBMS. Using the terminology of the
   ANSI/X3/SPARC it also corresponds to the
   external schema or conceptual schema in a
   DBMS:
- LCS, which corresponds 1:1 to LIS, is
   another description of the data structure
   of LIS in a local database using a common
   conceptual model.
- GCS, which is the union of LCSs, is the
   common conceptual model description of all
   the data in the network.
- GES is the common conceptual model
   description which is the subset/fullset of
   GCS and defines the range of the data used
   in user's applications. Therefore, GES is
   the subschema of GCS and corresponds 1:1
   to the LES.
- Finally, LES, which corresponds to a
   subschema of DBMS, is the data structure
   capable of handling user's applications
   directly.

Thus, in the five layered schema structure, the problem of heterogeneity can be treated between LES and GES as well as between LIS and LCS. Also, the problem of data distribution can be treated between LCS and GCS. In other words, a user is able to have access to different databases, via his own view of data or via LES whose data structure is defined with the data model suitable for his application without the awareness of the heterogeneity and the data distribution.

2.2.2 Entity - relationship model

We discussed the necessity of a common conceptual model of the network to solve the problem of heterogeneity and the required conditions for such a common conceptual model. We consider that the entity-relationship[4] model (hereinafter referred to as E-R model) satisfies these conditions fairly well and, therefore, propose its use as the common conceptual model.

The E-R model is similar to the relational model; it is capable of expressing the semantics of data, while the relational model does not have such a capability. In the E-R model, the real world can be expressed by entities and their relationships. For example, a specific "person", "company" and "phenomenon" are entities, and "father and son" is a relationship between two entities called "person".

2.3 Schema integration

"Schema Integration" is the process of defining a GCS from the existing LISs. The general architecture of this design process is discussed here.

There is one LIS for each local database. Each LIS may be expressed by a tree structure type model such as the model used in IMS[10], a network structure type model such as one in CODASYL or a relational model. The first step of the schema integration is to translate LIS into LCS by the E-R model. Mapping information or heterogeneity information is created in this translation. Also this type of information is created in mapping from GES to LES. The second step is to merge LCSs into GCS. To do this an integration database is often created. It contains integration information: location information of data, information about mapping between different data expressions for the same data and other information for reconciling inconsistency between copies of the same data stored at different databases. These heterogeneity information and integration information are used for query processing and other data manipulations.

III. ARCHITECTURE FOR A DISTRIBUTED DATABASE SYSTEM

Now we can define a general architecture for a distributed database system in the same way as that for a database management system in ANSI/X3/SPARC. This architecture is shown in Fig.3-1.

Furthermore, we consider the mapping of this logical architecture into a physical network environment. See Fig.3-2. A

distributed database network consists of virtual users and virtual servers which provide virtual user facility and virtual server facility respectively and a network which provides communication network facilities.

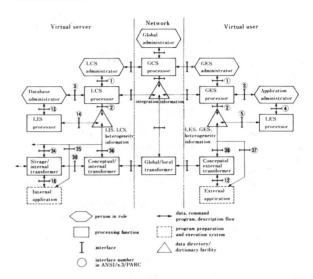

Fig.3-1 General architecture for a distributed database

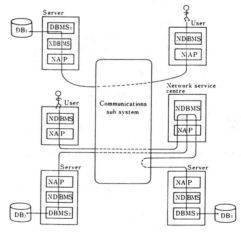

DBMS : Data Base Management System

NDBMS : Network Data Base Management System

NAP : Network Access Processor

Fig.3-2 Physical architecture for a distributed database

3.1 Physical assignment of the distributed database

Although the physical assignment of the virtual resources is not permanent, simply, a virtual user is allocated to a user node, a virtual server to a server node, and a network to a communication subsystem. A node may have both the facilities of the virtual user and the virtual server. When a network has network service centres just as in Fig.3-2, they have the both facilities, and the integrated view of data is provided for users without their awareness of the location of

765

data. So at first a query is transmitted from a user node which acts as a virtual user, to a network service centre as a virtual server, and then the query is transmitted from the network service centre as a virtual user, to a server node as a virtual server.

The facility of the virtual user is to translate a data manipulation, such as a query in the user oriented language, into a conceptual data manipulation using heterogeneity information as well as LES and GES, and to translate conceptual object occurences which are the responses of the conceptual query, into the output data structure visible to users.

The facility of the virtual server is to translate the conceptual data manipulation into local DBMS oriented access procedures using the heterogeneity information as well as LCS and LIS, to have access to the database and to translate its response into conceptual object occurrences.

Furthermore, the virtual user/server facilities at the network service centre are somewhat different from those of the virtual user and the virtual server described above. A conceptual data manipulation from the virtual user is decomposed using integration information. At this time several conceptual data manipulation may be generated for the several virtual server containing the required data, and their responses from the nodes are rearranged and merged.

The communication subsystem carries out the transfer of data between endpoints or provides transport service which corresponds to Level 1, 2, 3 and 4 in OSI reference model[7]. A NAP (Network Access Processor) handles communication subsystem and a NDBMS (Network Database Management System) carries out virual resource facilities, and performs and controls the communication of data manipulations and its result. The NDBMS may include two layers, that is, session and presentation layer in the OSI reference model as shown in Fig.3-3:

Therefore, facilities of the NDBMS are as follows:
- Communication of conceptual data manipulations.
- Communication of status information of virtual resource.
- Communication of conceptual object occurrences.
- Error control and occasional abortion in conceptual data manipulation.
- Flow control of the number of objects generated by each conceptual data manipulation.
- Initiation and termination of sessions.
- Start and stop of processes.

The conceptual data manipulation messages must be exchanged among virtual resources so that they can interact with each other. This includes conceptual requests and its results with associated control. For this purpose, it is proposed to develop a standardized data manipulation protocol.

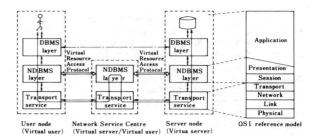

Fig.3-3 Communication network architecture
For a distributed database

3.2 Virtual Resource Access Protocol

Virtual Resource Access Protocol is defined among virtual resources, and facilitates data manipulation (retrieval, update, deletion, insertion, etc.) and database network management. The NDBMS need refer to the LIS (LES), LCS (GES) and heterogeneity information to bind the external objects to conceptual objects and also need refer to integration information to bind the global conceptual objects to local conceptual objects. A virtual resource site does not always have such a meta-database; they may be at another site and may be distributed. In such a case, this protocol can be used in order to have access to them.

Virtual Resource Access Protocol is handled at both the presentation and session layers in NDBMSs. Mainly, commands and responses related to the data manipulation facility are defined as the presentation layer protocols, and those related with the database network management or the process control facilities are defined as the session layer protocols.

In this section, the protocol concerned with data retrieval facitily is described in detail. Commands for request of data retrieval represent queries for conceptual schema (objects). In order to describe these queries, we introduce the query-graph which is superior for representing queries on the entity-relationship model schema.

3.2.1 Query-Graph

To define the query-graph, assume that queries consist of two types of basic operations: one is "data-restriction", which is an operation to find entities satisfied with certain restriction or condition and the other is "data-selection", which is an operation to extract certain functional values about entities selected with "data-restriction". Furthermore, data-restriction allowed in the query-graph is classified as follows:

(1) Simple restriction
  a) type 1 - simple restriction, which is the restriction between an attribute and a constant value, such as SALARY $\geq$ 1,000 $.
  b) type 2 - simple retriction, which is the restriction between attributes in an entity/relationship set, such as SALARY $\geq$ AGE * 100 $.

(2) Relation-restriction, which is the retriction representing relation between

an entity set and a relationship set.

Query graphs are induced with the following procedures;

Step 1

Extract entity sets, relationship sets and arcs connecting them, which appear in a query, in terms of subsets of the conceptual schema represented in the entity-relationship diagram[4].

Step 2

Add simple-restriction operators and data-selection operators to the subset of the conceptual schema produced by step 1 proceduce, relating with the query.

—‖ simple-restriction operator
—○ data-selection operator

Note that relation-restriction is implicitly expressed by arcs connecting entity sets and relationship sets in the diagram.

For example, the query-graph for the following query is illustrated in Fig.3-4.

Query: What are the part numbers of parts used in the project to which the employees working at the department A belong?

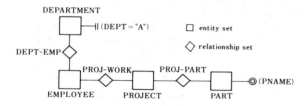

Fig.3-4 Query-graph

3.2.2 Format of the virtual resource access protocol

According to the query-graph, commands of the virtual resource access protocol for data retrieval are created; these contain the information about the operation (simple-restriction and/or data-selection) and semantic path which represents entity sets, relationship sets and arcs connecting these sets. A skeletal format of commands and responses of the virtual recource access protocol for data retrieval is shown in Fig.3-5.

IV. IMPLEMENTATION OF THE INTEGRATED DISTRIBUTED HETEROGENEOUS DATABASES

To make sure of the validity of the concept of the virtualization and virtual resource access protocol, we have been developing an experimental system for distributed database through the packet switched network. The system configuration is shown in Fig.4-1. In this system, a user at the IBM Series/1 mini-computer can have access to the CODASYL databases at the MELCOM COSMO 700III computer and M70 mini-computer, using the relational language SQL(SEQUEL-2)[8]. Each computer is connected with the packet switching equipment, using CCITT X.25 protocol at the speed of 9.6 kbps. The database in

Protocol id.	Operation id.	Field control	Data selection section	Data restriction section	Semantic path section	Constant data section

General format of the protocol for query

Protocol id.

1) Operation command   2) Operation response

Operation id.

1) Retrieve 2) Delete 3) Insert   4) Update

Field control

Assignment of section in the protocol

a) Data selection section

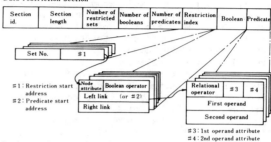

b) Data restriction section

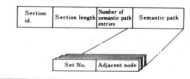

c) Semantic path section

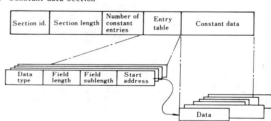

d) Constant data section

Fig.3-5 Virtual resource access protocol

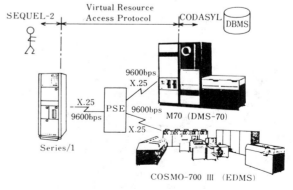

Fig.4-1 Configuration of experimental distributed database system

COSMO 700III is the Circuit Information System, which manages the information on international circuits, equipments and customers, etc. The database in M70 is Equipment Planning System, which manages the information on estimates for equipment, etc. In this system, we have one virtual user node which provides users with the relational view of data and two virtual server nodes for the CODASYL DBMSs, but no network service centre.

V. CONCLUSION

This paper proposed the virtualization technique based on the entity-relationship model for integrating world-wide distributed heterogeneous databases and showed its applicability to existing database systems operating in KDD.

In this paper, for the purpose of solving the heterogeneity problem and the data distribution problem, we discussed the network architecture of the distributed database system, from the viewpoints of database technique and communication technique. We first introduced the concept of the virtualization of DBMSs and users, and proposed the symmetric five layered schema structure as an actual technique of the virtualization. Furthermore, we adopted the entity-relationship model for the representation of the conceptual schema in the five layered schema structure, and developed the common database access protocol.

So far, we have implemented an experimental system which handles heterogeneity problem. In order to evaluate our method further, we are now approaching the data distribution problem and constructing the system which provides the advanced service.

ACKNOWLEDGEMENT

The authors wish to express their sincere thanks to Dr. Y.Nakagome, Managing Director of KDD, and Dr. H.Kaji, Dr. H.Teramura and Mr. Y.Takahashi of KDD R & D Labs for their continuous guidance and kind suggestions. The authors especially express their thanks to Mr. K.Ono, the manager of Information Processing Lab in KDD R & D Labs, for his continuous encouragement and plenty of suggestions during their works.

REFERENCES

(1) Adiba, M., and Delobel, C., "The Problem of the Cooperation between DBMS", Proc. IFIP TC-2 Working Conf. on Architecture and Models in DBMS, Nice France, (Jan. 1977) 165-186.

(2) Adiba, M., Delobel, C., and Leonard, M., "A Unified Approach for Modelling Data in Logical Data Base Design", Proc. IFIP TC-2 Working Conf, on Modelling in DBMS, Freudenstadt, Germany, (Jan. 1976) 311-338.

(3) "Interim Report of the Study Group on Data Management Systems", ANSI/X3/SPARC DBMS Study Group, Report 75-02-08 (Feb. 1975).

(4) Chen, P.P.S., "The Entity-Relationship Model - Toward a Unified View of Data", ACM TODS, Vol.1, No.1, (March 1976) 9-36.

(5) Adiba, M., Chupin, J.C., Demolombe, R., Gardarin, G., and Le Bihan, J., "Issues in Distributed Data Base Management Systems: A Technical Overview", Proc. of the 4th International Conf. on VLDB. Berlin, (Sept. 1978) 89-110.

(6) CODASYL Data Base Task Group Report, Apr. 1971, ACM New York.

(7) International Organization for standardization (ISO/TC97/SC16), "Reference Model for Open Systems Interconnection".

(8) Chemberlin, D.D., "SEQUEL 2: A Unfied Approach to Data Definition, Manipulation, and Control", IBM J. RES. DEVELOP., (Nov. 1976).

(9) Codd, E.F., "A Relational Model of Data for Large Shared Data Bank", Communications of the ACM. Vol.13, No.6, (June 1970) 337-387.

(10) McGee, W.C., "The IMS/VS system", IBM Systems Journal 16, No.2, (1977) 84-168.

Sadao Obana is the member of Information Processing Laboratory, Research and Development Laboratories, KDD. Since he joined the KDD in 1978, he engaged in Computer Communications and advanced Software Engineering. He is interested in Distributed Database systems in computer communication networks. In his university days, he studied computer architectures and database systems. He received the B.S. and M.E. degrees in electrical engineering from Keio University Tokyo, Japan, in 1976 and 1978, respectively.

Yoshiyori Urano is Senior Research Engineer of Information Processing Laboratory, Research and Development Laboratories, KDD. His current research interests include computer communication and advanced software technology. He received the B.S., M.E. and Dr.Eng. degrees in communication engineering from Waseda University, Tokyo, Japan, in 1965, 1967 and 1970, respectively. He received the Yonezawa Prize from I.E.C.E.J in 1973.

Kenji Suzuki is Research Engineer of Information Laboratory, Research and Development Laboratories, KDD, engaging in the field of computer communications. From 1969 to 1970, he was with Philips International Institute of Technological Studies, Eindhoven, The Netherlands, as an invited student. In 1976, he became the winner of IEEE Region 10 Graduate Student Paper Contest. In his university days, he had engaged in the field of magnetic recording. He received the B.E. degree in electrical communication and the M.E. degree in electrical engineering, and the Dr. Eng. degree in electrical engineering from Waseda University, Tokyo, Japan, in 1969, 1972, and 1976, respectively.

Clocked Event Transfer Protocol in Distributed Processing Systems – a Performance Analysis

P Tran-Gia, H Jans
University of Siegen, Federal
Republic of Germany

In modern real-time processing systems the intelligence is distributed among a number of individual processors operating in modes of functional or load sharing. Communication between distributed processors is often organised in the form of message interchanging according to an event transfer protocol. In this paper, a performance analysis is given for the commonly used clocked event transfer scheme, where a two-level queueing system is investigated. For the analysis a dimension-reduction of the two-dimensional description of the imbedded Markov chain is developed. Numerical results for dimensioning purposes are discussed, especially for event delay characteristics under different traffic conditions, clock intervals, and buffer sizes. Finally, the distribution function of the prequeueing delay is presented for the two event transfer disciplines first-in first-out and random.

1. INTRODUCTION

In distributed processing systems, especially in communication applications, the rates of real-time events, which have to be handled by several processors, are very high. These events are generated by peripheral devices or users, or are caused by inter-processor communications.

Fig. 1 illustrates a basic control structure of a multi-processor system where events are preprocessed by peripheral controllers (process level A) and stored in event buffers as valid events in a logical sense. They have to be transferred to another processor (process level B) according to an *event transfer protocol* for further processing. An optimal transfer protocol for this high event rate allows to increase the throughput and to optimize delay characteristics. The most commonly used event transfer protocol is the clocked scheme, whereby events are transmitted between different processors in a batch-wise manner at a scheduled time, initialised by a real-time clock. The event transfer protocol includes the initialisation of transfer, transmission control, acknowledgment etc..

There are a number of studies [1,2,5,6,7] which investigate the performance of event sampling and transfer schemes by means of *one-level* basic queueing models with scheduled batch arrivals. Some of them [1,4] deal with models having infinite waiting capacity. [5] considers dimensioning aspects for models with batch input and finite queue capacity, whereby the blocking probability is calculated for events and batches, which are partly or fully rejected according to the number of free waiting places. Several event transfer schemes with batch arrivals and overhead are discussed in [6], in which a number of events in a batch is considered to be lost when the actual batch is larger in size than the actual number of free waiting places.

In order to analyse the system depicted in Fig.1, a *two-level* queueing system is investi-

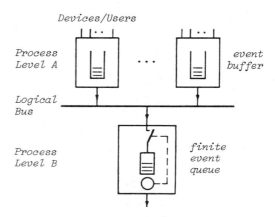

Fig.1   Basic Control Structure for a
Distributed Processing System

gated in this paper, where a clocked event transfer protocol is considered.

In principle an approximation of this model is possible using two separate one-level queues. This method implies an independence assumption for the two queues, the *primary* queue and the *secondary* queue for events to be transferred (c.f. Fig. 2). Because of this assumption the accuracy of the one-dimensional approximation depends very strongly on system parameters. Therefore, an exact analysis requires a *two-dimensional* model which will be presented in the next section. Fortunately, computational efforts can be reduced by the analytical method described in section 3.

2. MODELLING OF CLOCKED EVENT TRANSFER BETWEEN TWO PROCESSORS

The queueing model considered in this paper has the structure shown in Fig. 2. Event arrivals constitute a Poisson process with rate λ. This assumption is based on the observation that the incoming event stream is the superposition of offered traffic from a large number of different devices and users connected to the processor. Taking into account the different types of events and the tasks and programs they may activate, the service time T_{SER} for events is assumed to be negative exponentially distributed with mean $1/\mu$.

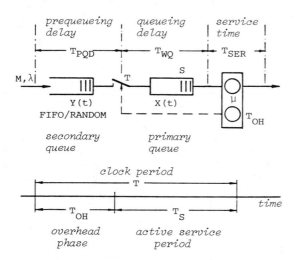

Fig.2 The two-level queueing system

Every event transfer activity which is controlled by the processor is usually performed by the same I/O task and has approximately the same run-time during which the processor is not available for event processing. Therefore, the whole clock period T consists of two parts: the overhead time T_{OH} and the active service period T_S (c.f. Fig. 2). It should be noted here that during the active service period the server is available for event processing but not necessarily busy. In this paper the clock period is chosen to be constant. This is often the case in real systems where the I/O phases are activated by a real-time clock. Another reason for this choice of T can be found in [6]. It is shown there that a well dimensioned clocked scheme is relatively robust with respect to event traffic intensity. The primary queue is considered to have the *finite capacity* S. At a clock instant when the actual batch (i.e. events existing in the secondary queue prior to the clock instant) is larger in size than the number of free waiting places in the primary queue, all free positions will be filled and the remaining events must wait for retrial until the next clock instant.

Each batch consists of two parts, the fresh part and the reattempt part. All arrivals during the clock period form the fresh part; the reattempt part contains events which have been rejected at the previous clock instant.

The total sojourn time of an event in the whole system is composed of three components:

- The prequeueing delay T_{PQD}, i.e. the waiting time in the secondary queue for events to be sent.

- The queueing delay T_{WQ}, i.e. the waiting time in the primary queue, including overhead periods.

- The service time T_{SER}

T_{PQD}, T_{WQ} and T_D will be considered as random variables in the next section.

3. ANALYSIS OF THE TWO-LEVEL QUEUEING SYSTEM

In this section performance measures of the above described two-level queueuing system are presented. Subsection 3.1 discusses queue stability conditions and subsection 3.2 deals with the system state probabilities. Subsequently, system characteristics will be derived in 3.3.

3.1 Queue Stability

Since we consider the overhead time T_{OH} and a finite primary queue capacity S, the system is only stable under certain conditions derived below. For given values of T_{OH}, S, and *offered traffic intensity* ρ ($\rho = \lambda/\mu$) we can calculate a lower and an upper limit for the clock period T, for which the system is stable. The lower limit T_{MIN} is found using the fact that the active service time T_S in which the server is available must be long enough to serve all arriving events on average:

$$T_{MIN} = T_{OH}/(1 - \rho) \qquad (3.1)$$

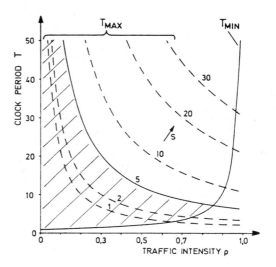

Fig.3 Queue Stability Conditions ($T_{OH}=1/\mu$)

On the other hand, if T becomes too long, the batch sizes are also very large on average and the finite queue is likely to be filled completely at each clock instant and tends to be empty before the next clock. The upper limit T_{MAX} is given by:

$$T_{MAX} = N/\lambda \qquad (3.2)$$

where N = S + 1 is the *primary system size*.

The queueing system is stable for

$$T_{MIN} < T < T_{MAX} \qquad (3.3)$$

The queue stability condition (3.3) is illustrated in Fig. 3. For S = 5 the system is stable in the hatched field. The dashed lines show the upper limit for other values of S.

3.2 The Imbedded Markov Chain and System State Probabilities

In Fig. 4 we consider the two-dimensional random process $\{X(t), Y(t), t\epsilon(0,T)\}$ more closely

$$\Pi(x,y,t) = \Pr\{X(t)=x, Y(t)=y, t\epsilon(0,T)\} \qquad (3.4)$$

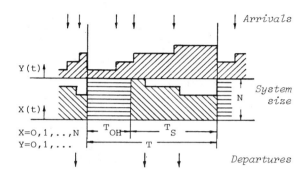

Fig.4 The Two-dimensional Random Process

The system can be analysed using the well-known technique of the imbedded Markov chain. It is here convenient to choose the time-epochs just after the event transfer instants as regeneration points (t=0$^+$), at which the two queues can be considered as connected. This argument allows us to reduce the two-dimensional description of the process into an one-dimensional description at regeneration points. The relationship between the two- and the one-dimensional description of state probabilities is given by

$$P^+(x+y)=\Pi(x,y,0^+) \qquad (3.5)$$

where $\quad \Pi(x,y,0^+)=0$ for $x\neq S+1$ and $y\neq 0$.

Observing two consecutive event transfer periods n and n+1 with state probabilities $\Pi_n(x,y,t)$ and $\Pi_{n+1}(x,y,t)$, $t\epsilon(0,T)$, the main steps of the analysis can shortly be resumed as follows:

1. $\Pi_n(x,y,T^-)=f\{\Pi_n(x,y,0^+)\}$

$x \neq 0$: $\Pi_n(x,y,T^-)=\sum\limits_{i=x}^{N}\sum\limits_{j=0}^{y}\Pi_n(i,j,0^+)\,d_{i-x}\,g_{y-j}$

$x = 0$: $\Pi_n(0,y,T^-)=\sum\limits_{i=0}^{N}\sum\limits_{j=0}^{y}\Pi_n(i,j,0^+)\sum\limits_{\ell=i}^{\infty}d_\ell g_{y-j}$

with $\qquad \qquad \qquad \qquad \qquad$ ...(3.6)

$$d_\ell = \frac{(\mu T_S)^\ell}{\ell!}\,e^{-\mu T_S} \; ; \; g_m = \frac{(\lambda T)^m}{m!}\,e^{-\lambda T},$$

$$\ell,m=0,1,\ldots$$

2. $\Pi_{n+1}(x,y,0^+) = f\{\Pi_n(x,y,T^-)\}$

$x=0,\ldots,N-1; y=0$: $\Pi_{n+1}(x,0,0^+)=\sum\limits_{i=0}^{x}\Pi_n(i,x-i,T^-)$

$x=N; y=0,1,\ldots$: $\Pi_{n+1}(N,y,0^+)=\sum\limits_{i=0}^{N}\Pi_n(i,N+y-i,T^-)$

$$\ldots(3.7)$$

Eqns. (3.6) and (3.7) give us a relationship between state probabilities for two consecutive regeneration points. Using this consideration, the state probabilities at an arbitrary time can easily be derived. Therefore, in general, from a given starting probability vector, transient behaviour of the system can be investigated by means of the power method.

Under stationary conditions

$$\Pi_{n+1}(x,y,0^+) = \Pi_n(x,y,0^+) = P^+(x+y)$$

and after simple algebraic manipulations using (3.6) and (3.7) the system of difference equations for state probabilities can be obtained

$$P^+(k)=\sum\limits_{i=0}^{N-1}P^+(i)\left[g_k\sum\limits_{\ell=i}^{\infty}d_\ell + \sum\limits_{x=1}^{\min(i,k)}d_{i-x}\,g_{k-x}\right]$$

$$+ \sum\limits_{i=N}^{N+k}P^+(i)\left[g_{k+N-1}\sum\limits_{\ell=N}^{\infty}d_\ell\right.$$

$$\left. + \sum\limits_{x=1}^{\min(N+k-i,N)}d_{N-x}\,g_{k+N-i-x}\right]$$

with $\quad \sum\limits_{x=a}^{b}(.) = 0$ for $b < a$. $\qquad$ ...(3.8)

Using eqn. (3.8), the state probabilities of the imbedded Markov chain can be obtained by means of an iteration method with over-relaxation, whereby a proper adaptive truncation of the state space must be provided.

3.3 Time-dependent State Probabilities and System Characteristics

In order to calculate the mean waiting time in the primary queue $E[T_{WQ}]$ and the mean prequeueing delay $E[T_{PQD}]$, it is convenient to use Little's law[8], for which it is necessary to know the mean queue lengths at an arbitrary point in time. Under stationary conditions, we only have to observe the system during *one* clock period ($t\epsilon(0,T)$).

Using the terminology

$$P_k^x(t) = \Pr\{X(t)=k\}$$
$$P_k^y(t) = \Pr\{Y(t)=k\} \qquad \ldots(3.9)$$

we obtain

$$\begin{cases} P_k^x(0) = P^+(k) & k=0,1,\ldots,N-1 \\ P_N^x(0) = \sum\limits_{i=N}^{\infty}P^+(i) & k=N \end{cases} \qquad (3.10a)$$

and

$$\begin{cases} P_0^y(O) = \sum_{i=O}^{N} P^+(i) & k=O \\ P_k^y(O) = P^+(k+N) & k=1,2,\ldots,\infty. \end{cases}$$

(3.10b)

Between two transfer instants, $X(t)$ follows a pure death process $(T_{OH} \leq t < T)$ and $Y(t)$ follows a pure birth process $(O \leq t < T)$.

The mean numbers of events in the primary system $E[X]$ and in the secondary queue $E[Y]$ are given by

$$E[X] = \frac{1}{T} \int_O^T \sum_{k=1}^{N} k\, P_k^x(t)\, dt$$

$$= \frac{T_{OH}}{T} \sum_{i=1}^{N} i P_i^x(O)$$

$$+ \frac{1}{\mu T} \sum_{i=1}^{N} P_i^x(O) \sum_{k=1}^{i} k \sum_{j=i-k+1}^{\infty} d_j \quad (3.11)$$

$$E[Y] = \frac{1}{T} \int_O^T \sum_{k=1}^{\infty} k\, P_k^y(t)\, dt$$

$$= \sum_{k=1}^{\infty} k\, P_k^y(O) + \frac{\lambda T}{2} = E[Y(O)] + \frac{\lambda T}{2}. \quad (3.12)$$

Using Little's law, the mean waiting time in the primary queue $E[T_{WQ}]$ and the mean prequeueing delay $E[T_{PQD}]$ can be given as follows

$$E[T_{WQ}] = \frac{E[X]}{\lambda} - \frac{1}{\mu} \quad (3.13)$$

and

$$E[T_{PQD}] = \frac{E[Y]}{\lambda}. \quad (3.14)$$

The mean total delay of events in the system is

$$E[T_D] = E[T_{WQ}] + E[T_{PQD}]. \quad (3.15)$$

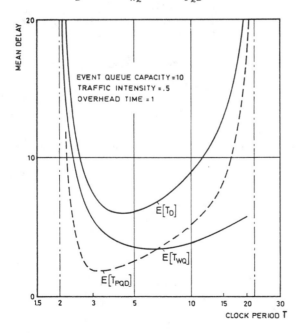

Fig.5 Delays vs Clock Period

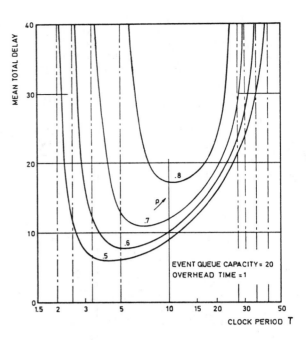

Fig.6 Total Delay vs Clock Period

4. RESULTS AND DISCUSSION

In this section numerical results are presented concerning the mean delays for events in the whole system using a clocked event protocol. All values are normalised by $E[T_{SER}] = 1/\mu = 1$. Fig. 5 depicts the different mean value of delays as a function of the clock period T. By the chosen parameters ($\rho = .5$, $S = 10$, $T_{OH} = 1$) the system is stable for $2 < T < 22$ (c.f.eqn. 3.3). It is clearly shown that a minimum of the total delay for events exists as expected.

In Fig. 6 the total delay is plotted as a function of clock period T and an optimum choice for T can be defined for a given level of offered traffic intensity. The sensitivity of these optimum values has to be taken into account for dimensioning purposes. The best choice $T = 5$ for $\rho = 0.6$ will make the system unstable for $\rho \geq 0.8$, which occurs in overload situations.

The delay characteristics discussed here can be used for dimensioning purposes where the clock period T and the capacity S of the event queue have to be chosen for a given traffic range.

5. PREQUEUEING DELAY DISTRIBUTION FUNCTION

5.1 General Relations

For the following derivation, we consider the two different disciplines FIFO and RANDOM for event transfer from secondary into primary queue. These two strategies can be considered as marginal cases for real systems, whereby FIFO strategy is a more optimistic and RANDOM strategy a more pessimistic case. In order to investigate the distribution function of the prequeueing delay $F_{PQD}(t) = Pr\{T_{PQD} \leq t\}$ in both cases the fate of a *test customer (t.c.)* in a fresh batch is considered (Fig. 7).

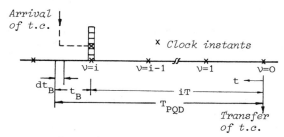

Fig.7 The Prequeueing Delay

As shown in Fig. 7 the prequeueing delay T_{PQD} consists of two components : the delay from arrival until the next clock instant (t_B) and a number i of clock periods (i.T), i=0,1,2,.. The probability that the prequeueing delay varies between $iT+t_B-dt_B$ and $iT+t_B$ is

$$Pr\{iT+t_B-dt_B < T_{PQD} \le iT+t_B\} = w(i,t_B) \cdot \frac{dt_B}{T}$$

with $\qquad 0 \le t_B \le T, \; i \ge 0 \qquad$ (5.1)

dt_B/T :probability that the *t.c.* arrives in dt_B

$w(i,t_B)$:weighted sum over all possible positions in system the *t.c.* can take, who
- arrives t_B before the clock instant
- will be delayed i clock periods.

By integration we obtain from eqn. (5.1)

$$Pr\{iT<T_{PQD} \le iT+t_B\}= \frac{1}{T} \int_{O}^{t_B} w(i,\tau) \cdot d\tau \qquad (5.2)$$

and for the delay distribution

$$F_{PQD}(t)=Pr\{T_{PQD} \le iT+t_B\}$$

$$=Pr\{iT<T_{PQD} \le iT+t_B\}+Pr\{T_{PQD} \le iT\}. \qquad (5.3)$$

Eqn. (5.3) can be solved recursively and after some algebraic manipulations we have finally

$$F_{PQD}(t)=Pr\{T_{PQD} \le iT+t_B\}$$

$$= \frac{1}{T}\left[\sum_{\nu=O}^{i-1} \int_{O}^{T} w(\nu,\tau) \cdot d\tau + \int_{O}^{t_B} w(i,\tau) \cdot d\tau\right] \qquad (5.4)$$

where $i=[t/T]^{-}$, is the largest integer less than t/T.

$i=0,1,2..., \; 0 \le t_B \le T, \; \sum_{i}^{j}(\cdot)=O$ for j<i.

5.2 RANDOM Event Transfer Discipline

In RANDOM case the events are chosen randomly for transfer at clock instants. Based on the stationary state distribution of the imbedded Markov chain we can calculate the probability B_O that the *t.c.* is in the rejected batch part at the first clock instant after his arrival. In this case he has to compete with all customers in the secondary queue at transfer instants (including arrivals during his waiting time). The probability that he will be delayed at those clock instants is denoted by B_1.

From B_O and B_1, which are determined using combinatorial arguments, we obtain the probabilities $w(i,t_B)$ as follows

$$w(O,t_B)=1-B_O \; ; \; w(i,t_B)=B_O(1-B_1)B_1^{i-1} \qquad (5.5)$$

The delay distribution function is found by eqn. (5.4) to

$$F_{PQD}=Pr\{T_{PQD} \le iT+t_B\}= \sum_{\nu=O}^{i-1} w(\nu,t_B)+w(i,t_B) \cdot (\frac{t}{T} -i) \qquad (5.6)$$

The mean pre-queueing delay $E[T_{PQD}]$ and its coefficient of variation c_{PQD} can be found from eqn. (5.6) and can be written in terms of B_O and B_1

$$E[T_{PQD}]= T(\frac{1}{2} + \frac{B_O}{1-B_1}) \qquad (5.7)$$

$$c_{PQD} = \sqrt{\left(\frac{T}{E[T_{PQD}]}\right)^2 \cdot \left(\frac{1}{3} + \frac{2B_O}{(1-B_1)^2}\right) - 1}$$

5.3 FIFO Event Transfer Discipline

In FIFO case the events are transferred between the two queues in order of arrival. Based on the stationary state distribution of the imbedded Markov chain, the prequeueing delay depends *only* on the service process of those customers in front of the *t.c.*. Due to the clocked scheme and the finiteness of the primary queue, idle periods of the server can exist although there are customers still waiting for transfer.

The prequeueing delay distribution function for the FIFO case has been developed analogously to the RANDOM case. However, the extensive derivation of the formula should not be discussed here in more detail.

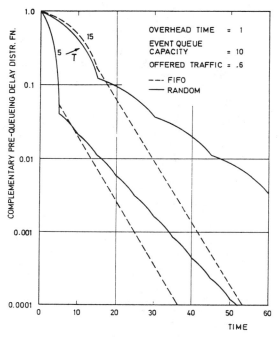

Fig.8 Comparison of $\overline{F}_{PQD}$ for FIFO and RANDOM Event Transfer Disciplines

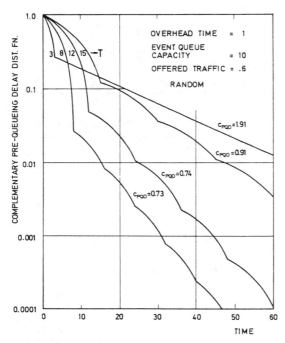

Fig.9 Complementary Prequeueing Delay Distribution Function for RANDOM case

5.4 Results and Comparison

In the following the complementary prequeueing delay distribution function $\bar{F}_{PQD}(t)$ will be discussed for the two considered event transfer disciplines FIFO and RANDOM. As expected the variance of T_{PQD} is higher for RANDOM case as shown by the gradient of the curves in Fig. 8, where $\bar{F}_{PQD}(t)$ is depicted for both disciplines and different values of T. Fig. 9 shows $\bar{F}_{PQD}(t)$ more closely in case of RANDOM for different values of the clock period T. Between T_{MIN} and T_{MAX}, a value of T can be found to optimize the coefficient of variation c_{PQD} for T_{PQD}. This argument can be taken into account together with the optimum choice of the mean total delay for different dimensioning conditions.

6. CONCLUSION

In this paper, a two-level queueing system has been developed and investigated, which models a clocked event transfer protocol between distributed real-time processing systems. In order to analyse the system, an exact one-dimensional description for the two-dimensional process is presented. From the steady state distribution system characteristics as event delays and mean values are derived and discussed. Finally, the prequeueing delay distribution function for events with FIFO and RANDOM transfer disciplines is investigated. The model is applicable for a wide range of distributed computing systems where high rate of real-time events have to be interchanged between processors and the response time is a critical factor. It is shown here that for dimensioning purposes, the queue stability and delay characteristics in overload situations must be taken into account to guarantee proper system performance.

ACKNOWLEDGEMENT

The authors would like to express their thanks to Prof. P.J. Kuehn for fruitful discussions during the course of this work.

REFERENCES

[1] Burke P.J.,"Delays in Single Server Queues with Batch Input".B.S.T.J.,23,830-833(1975).

[2] Chu W.W.,"Buffer Behaviour for Batch Poisson Arrivals and Single Constant Output" IEEE Trans.Comm.,18,613-618 (1970).

[3] Gross D. and Harris C.M.,"Fundamentals of Queueing Theory". Wiley, 1974.

[4] Langenbach-Belz M.,"Two-Stage Queueing System with Sampled Parallel Input Queues". Proc.7th ITC, Stockholm, 1973.

[5] Manfield D.R. and Tran-Gia P.,"Analysis of a Storage System with Batch Input Arising out of Message Packetisation". IEEE Trans. Comm., 30, 456-463(1982).

[6] Manfield D.R. and Tran-Gia P.,"Queueing Analysis of Scheduled Communications Phases in Distributed Processing Systems". Proc. 8th Symp.on Comp.Perf.Modelling,Meas. and Eval.,Amsterdam, 233-250(1981).

[7] Schwaertzel H.G.,"Serving Strategies of Batch Arrivals in Common Control Switching Systems". Proc.7th ITC, Stockholm, 1973.

[8] Little J.D.C.,"A Proof of the Queueing Formula L= λW". Operations Research, 9, 383-387(1961).

[9] Tran-Gia P. and Jans H.,"Delay Analysis of Clocked Event Transfer in Distributed Processing Systems". ORSA/TIMS Meeting, Detroit, April 1982.

P. Tran-Gia was born in Viet Nam and received the M.S. degree (Dipl.-Ing.) in EE from Stuttgart University, West-Germany, in 1977. In 1977 he joint SEL(ITT) in Stuttgart, where he was working in software development of digital switching systems. Since 1979 he has been Assistant Professor at the University of Siegen, Dept. of Communications. His current research activities are in the field of queueing theory and its application in performance analysis for telecommunication systems.

H. Jans was born in Niederkruechten, Germany. He received the Dipl.-Ing. degree in EE from Technical Univ. of Berlin, Germany, in 1975. Since then he has been Assistant Professor at the University of Siegen, Faculty of EE. His current research activities are in the field of queueing theory and its application in computer and communication systems.

Open Systems Interconnection – Basic Concepts and Current Status

B M Wood
Computer Analysts and Programmers
Ltd., UK

This paper provides an introduction to the standards under development for open systems interconnection through a review of the Reference Model for Open Systems Interconnection and of the concepts and principles which it introduces; it provides estimates of the timescales within which standards may be expected to appear; and it discusses the problems to be faced in meeting those timescales.

1.   INTRODUCTION

Open Systems Interconnection (OSI) is a term which is now widely used to characterise communications between computer systems through the use of a set of standards, OSI standards, which allow interworking independently of the nature the systems involved.

The term Open Systems Interconnection originated within the International Organisation for Standardisation (ISO) and formal responsibility for the development of OSI standards rests with the ISO.   The ISO membership comprises the national standards bodies of 88 countries (BSI in the UK, ANSI in the US, AFNOR in France etc.) and the organisation was set up in 1947 as a specialised international agency under the United Nations with responsibility for all standardisation fields except standards for electrical and electronic engineering.

Although ISO has formal responsibility for OSI standards, its work in this particular area is heavily shadowed by the activity of the CCITT (the Comite Consultatif International Telegraphique et Telephonique) which is part of the International Telecommunications Union, also an agency of the UN.   The CCITT is responisble for developing recommendations for the design and operation of telecommunication equipment and services, and its members, nominated by national governments, are agencies responsible for offering public telecommunications services (like British Telecom) and representatives of equipment manufacturers.   Once the recommendations are agreed by the members, they have the force of standards within the telecommunications industry.   The increasing involvement of telecommunication agencies in the provision of data communication networks and data communications based services like Teletex, Videotex and facsimile is facing CCITT with standardisation needs which are very similar to those addressed by work on OSI.
Clearly, it is important that ISO and CCITT should move in step.   Fortunately, this has been recognised on both sides and very great efforts are being made to achieve and maintain compatibility.   The main problem is that, until recently, there have not been the same pressures behind computing standardisation in ISO as there have been behind the work of CCITT and, therefore, there has not been the same level of resources to support it.

Activity on OSI standards started in ISO in 1977 with the setting up, under Technical Committee TC97 (responsible for standards in the area of computers and information processing) of Subcommittee SC16.   SC16 was initially charged with looking at the need for, and possibility of, standards for communications between systems above the level of data transmission standards, which were already the remit of SC6.   This initial activity established the outline of the Reference Model for Open Systems Interconnection, providing the framework for standardisation work, and the definition of work items for standards.   These work items are given in fig. 1 together with their assignment to SC6 and SC16.

The purpose of this paper is to review the nature of OSI standards through a discussion of the Reference Model itself and the concepts and principles which it introduces, to provide estimates of when the first standards can be expected to appear, and to discuss the problems to be faced in developing OSI standards and introducing them into use.

2.   THE REFERENCE MODEL FOR OPEN SYSTEMS INTERCONNECTION

The starting point for looking at OSI standards is the Reference Model for Open Systems Interconnection [1].   The Reference Model has been developed to define a structure for communications between computer systems and to identify a set of communication services and protocols which will support that structure.
The Reference Model is a model of what is termed the OSI environment - a set of open systems interconnected by some medium for the transmission of data.   A system in this context is defined to be a set of one or more computers and the software, peripherals, terminals, human operators, physical processes and means of data transfer that go with them, and make up a single information processing unit. Such a system is open if it can interwork with other open systems using OSI standards.

The Reference Model is concerned with the relationships between four basic elements of the OSI environment:

-     the systems themselves;

-     the medium for transmission of data;

- application-processes carrying out the information processing for particular applications;

- connections joining application-processes and enabling them to exchange information.

Typically an application-process might be:

- a manual application-process: someone operating an automated banking terminal;

- a computerised application-process: a Fortran program executing in a computer centre and accessing a remote data base;

- a physical application-process: industrial process control equipment controlled by a computer linked into a plant control system.

The Reference Model represents the OSI environment and the relationship between the basic elements of it in the way shown in fig. 2. The elements are now abstractions from the real world and in particular:

- a system represents only those aspects of a real open system which are relevant to OSI;

- an application-entity represents those aspects of real application-processes which are relevant to OSI.

2.1 Basic concepts (fig. 3)

The Reference Model goes on to define a structure for communications within the abstract representation of the real world shown in figure 2. In doing so, it defines an internal structure for the abstract systems, as well as a structure for the communications between them. However, it is important to be clear that this internal structure is only defined to help to clarify the external behaviour of systems. The external behaviour of real systems is the subject of OSI standardisation, not their internal structure.

Layering The first concept introduced by the Model is that of layering, building on well established practise which separates communications-oriented functions and the related protocols from processing-oriented functions and higher level protocols.

Each system in the Model is composed, logically, of subsystems which form an hierarchical sequence such that the services provided by one subsystem are offered directly only to the next higher subsystem in the sequence and use directly only the services of the next lower subsystem. A subsystem is made up of a group of entities which perform the functions provided by it. Subsystems of the same rank form a layer.

The entities of a given layer cooperate to provide services to the next higher layer. In order to do so they communicate using the services of the next lower layer, except in the case of the lowest layer where the entities communicate directly using the physical media.

Service-access-points Entities in adjacent subsystems within a system interact through a service-access-point located on the boundary between the subsystems. An entity in one layer offers services to the next higher layer through a service-access-point and requests the services of the next lower layer through a service-access-point.

A service-access-point is identified and located by its address and it is the addresses of service-access-points which tie together the Model and the environment which it is modelling. They correspond to the addresses of systems on a physical network, to the logical communication ports within a system, to service programs etc.

An entity in a given layer is attached at a given time to a specific service-access-point on the boundary with the next lower layer, and it can be reached for communication purposes through this service-access-point. However, the relationship between entity and service-access-point is not fixed. The entity may be detached from one service-access-point and reattached to another by means of management functions within the layer and the relationship between entity and service-access-point is maintained by a directory function in the layer.

Connections Entities exchange data and control information over connections. A connection is an association between two or more entities within one layer which is established and maintained by the next lower layer. The association is set up by agreement between the entities involved and between each entity and the next lower layer. An entity requests, or agrees to, the setting up of a connection through a service-access-point, referencing in a request the service-access-point-address of the entity with which it wishes to be connected. When the connection is established, a connection - endpoint is created within the service-access point and is given a connection-endpoint-identifier by which it can be referenced by the entity and the layer service.

Protocols Communication and cooperation between entities in a layer to provide services are governed by protocols for the layer. A protocol operates through the exchange of protocol-data-units between the entities, using a connection established through the next lower layer.

2.5 Communication Structure

Using the basic concepts that have just been described, the Reference Model defines the communication structure illustrated in fig. 4.

In order for two application-entities to communicate they must request the next lower layer to establish a connection between them through the service-access-points by which they are identified. The entities in the next lower layer, accessed through the service-access-points, establish and operate this connection through the exchange of protocol-data-units, governed by a relevant protocol, over a connection which they, in turn, request from the next lower layer.

Thus, the request for connection by the application-entities results in the establishment of connections down through the hierarchy of layers until the lowest layer is reached, in which the entities can communicate directly using the physical media. The significance of the hierarchy of connections is, of course, that each layer should 'add value' to the connection service which it is offered by the layer below.

2.6 Connection Operation

A connection is established and released by a protocol exchange between the entities supporting it. While the connection is in existence, the entities associated by it can transfer data as service-data-units. The connection service maintains the delimitation of service-data-units and the order of data within each service-data-unit.

The connection service transfers service-data-units as user data in protocol-data-units. The size of the service-data-unit is not constrained by the size of the protocol-data-units exchanged between the entities supporting the service. Service-data-units may map one-to-one on to protocol-data-units, several service-data-units may be blocked into a single protocol-data-unit for transfer, or a service-data-unit may be segmented and carried in a sequence of protocol-data-units.

In addition to providing basic data transfer on a connection, a connection service needs to provide a number of other functions, depending upon the nature of the service it is offering and the nature of the service offered to it by the layer below. Some of these functions are specific to particular layers but some are potentially relevant to a number of layers, these are:

- error detection, acknowledgement and error correction, dealing with the loss or corruption of protocol-data-units;

- sequencing, dealing with the misordering of protocol-data-units;

- flow control across service-access-points and within the layer;

- reset, allowing the data flow over a connection to be set to a known state;
- multiplexing, allowing a number of connections to be supported by a single connection provided by the next lower layer;

- splitting, allowing a single connection to be supported by a number of connections provided by the next lower layer.

2.7 Relaying and routing

It is not always possible to establish a direct connection between two entities in a layer through the next lower layer. This is true, for example, if there is no physical medium connecting the systems in which they are located. When a direct connection is not possible, then communication takes place through intermediate entities in the layer, which provide routing and relaying of the data (e.g. through the nodes of a packet switching network).

2.8 Management

Finally, there is a need for management of the OSI environment and for corresponding management protocols. These protocols provide for the initiation, termination, monitoring and coordination of the activities both of subsystems and of application-processes, and for the handling of abnormal conditions.

3. THE 7-LAYER MODEL

The result of applying the general concepts and principles outlined in the previous section to the modelling of the functions involved in communications between application-processes in the real world is the seven layer structure shown in fig. 5. In this structure, the highest layer, the Application Layer, comprises the application-entities which represent the application-processes of the real world and the layers below provide a step-by-step enhancement of the transmission facilities provided by the physical media.

3.1 The layers of the model

The Physical Layer provides a model for the interface to the physical media, controlling bit transmission between systems, and providing for the activation, deactivation and, where necessary, the linking of data circuits to provide physical-connections.

The Data Link Layer supports data-link-connections. It provides control of data transfer over physical-connections, detection and, if necessary, correction of errors in the data transferred, and allows for the transfer of requests to link data circuits from the Network Layer to the Physical Layer.

The Network Layer supports network-connections and ensures that the characteristics of these connections are independent of the underlying data-link and physical-services except in the quality of service provided. In particular, the layer provides relaying and routing, so that end-to-end connections can be established between transport-entities in systems which cannot be directly linked by data-link-connections. Where relaying and routing are involved the end systems can be represented as communicating through a transit system comprising only sub-systems in the first three layers of the Reference Model (fig. 6), and the transit system may itself represent a network of transit systems which models, say, a PTT data service.

Thus the first three layers of the Reference Model provide system-to-system transmission services and the complexities of different data transmission systems and the means by which they provide end-to-end connections are handled below the Network Layer boundary. The layers above the Network Layer are only concerned with end-to-end operation. An important corollary of this location of functions is that, within the OSI architecture, gateway functions linking different transmission networks are located in the Network Layer.

The bridge between these services and the application oriented services of the upper three layers is provided by the Transport Layer. The Transport Layer supports transport-connections. It expands the end-system to end-system addressing of the Network Layer to provide transport-addresses within the end-systems; it manages the use of network-connections, (for example, providing for the multiplexing of transport-connections on to network-connections where this is cost-effective); and it provides defined qualities of service over network services of variable quality.

Above the Transport Layer the services of the layers are oriented to application needs. The Session Layer supports session-connections allowing the establishment, control and termination of dialogues between application-processes. In particular, it maintains continuity of session-connections over transport-connection failure, provides for the exchange of turn to communicate, and provides synchronisation facilities and support for check-pointing.

The Presentation Layer resolves differences in the representations of information used by application-entities, allowing each entity on a connection to communicate without knowledge of the representation of information used by the other entity.

3.2 Service and Protocol Standards

The importance of the Reference Model is that it allows the development of service and protocol standards for one layer of the model to be decoupled from developments for other layers. The boundary between two layers in the Reference Model identifies a point at which an OSI service standard is to be defined. Agreement on this service standard defines the service that can be used by the protocol of the higher layer and the service to be supported by the protocol of the lower layer, and the functions provided by a layer protocol are constrained by the differences between the service provided at the lower boundary and the service offered at the upper boundary. Fig. 1 shows the work items for service and protocol standards that have been established within ISO. These follow the layer structure up to the Session Layer but currently there are no work items concerned

with services and protocols specific to the Presentation and Application Layers. The reason for this is that, at the time the work items were identified, it was possible to say, in broad terms, that these layers existed, but it was not possible to identify clearly a boundary between them or common mechanisms for their operation which would match the needs of three specific examples of special services which were already clearly identified, namely job transfer, file operations, and virtual terminal operations. Thus it was decided to pursue the development of service and protocol standards for these three specific services in the expectation that this work would lead to a clarification of the structure of the layers.

4. FURTHER DEVELOPMENT OF THE REFERENCE MODEL

Although the Reference Model is now a Draft International Standard (DIS) it is recognised that there is likely to be a continuing need to define extensions to it, or to provide fuller descriptions of some of the concepts defined by it.

One such extension is being prepared as an Addendum to DIS 7498[2] which will cover what is termed connectionless-data-transmission. Currently the Reference Model only talks about communication over connections, implying dynamic agreement between the application-entities involved before communication can take place. Connectionless-data-transmission defines a mode of operation where communication can take place without a dynamically established prior agreement and is seen as relevant to certain kinds of message service and to the modes of operation of many local area networks.

Further addenda are being considered to cover, for example, naming and addressing and security, and the process of refinement of the Reference Model is likely to continue for some time yet.

5. PROGRESS, TIMESCALES AND PROBLEMS

Considering the scale and newness of what is being attempted, progress on OSI standards has been encouragingly rapid, as has the acceptance necessary if standardisation is to be successful. Nevertheless there are significant problems to be overcome and, after giving an estimate of current timescales for OSI standards to appear, this section discusses these problems briefly.

5.1 Timescales

From the point of view of a prospective user of OSI standards it is appropriate to consider two timescales:

- the timescale for effective agreement, corresponding to the acceptance of a working draft for a standard as a Draft Proposal for an International Standard (DP);

- the timescale for full agreement,
corresponding to agreement in ISO on a
Draft International Standard (DIS).

Because of the uncertain timescale involved
in progressing to final agreement on a DIS,
and on the assumption that SC6 and SC16 are
doing their job so that changes through the
voting stages are not changes of substance,
it is reasonable to take the timescale for
effective agreement as providing a timescale
for planning to begin the implementation of
standards.

Estimates of the timescales for effective
agreement are given in fig. 7. These
timescales show ranges of times reflecting
some uncertainty about the time for the
first standard but also indicating that a
family of standards are likely to follow the
first one.

5.2 Problems

In the first place, OSI standards are
'prospective' standards, in that they are
being developed in advance of any widespread
experience of the modes of computer use with
which they are concerned. The aim of the
standards is to allow modes of interworking
between computer systems which are currently
difficult or impossible to achieve except,
in some cases, between computers from a
single supplier. In consequence, there is
only limited and unrepresentative experience
upon which to draw in preparing the
standards, and the work involved is as much
about learning and the development of
understanding as it is about standardisation.

As a result, it has been necessary for the
process of standardisation to start by
establishing a basic conceptual structure
and a language in which to express this
structure. This is reflected in the
Reference Model, which describes
architectural principles and defines common
terms, as well as defining a structure of
services and protocols. It is also reflected
in work on service and protocol standards
where there has been a need to concentrate
effort first on the development of suitable
models in terms of which the specific
services can be described. Crucially, it is
reflected in the problems of providing
precise specifications of services and
protocols, of confirming the completeness of
these specifications, and of measuring the
conformance of implementations.

Second, the scale and complexity of the work
is much greater than normal. The activity
of SC16 covers seven work items directed at
the development of at least 13 interrelated,
independent, and individually complex
standards. Moreover, this work must take
account of related work items on data
transmission standards (the lower three
layers) which are the responsibility of SC6.
The effort available to sustain this work
must be provided by the national
organisations: ISO has no independent source
of funding or of technical experience.
Effective work to support the programme in
the UK alone requires 6-12 man years of

effort each year. Clearly, the coordination
of international effort on this scale
presents formidable problems.

Thirdly, because OSI standardisation is
'prospective' and because experience of
standards development in computing is
limited, OSI work is caught up in a
'reconciliation of cultures'. There are
national/social differences in the way in
which computing has developed in different
countries, in the long term plans for
computer use and computer services, and in
the degree of central control and
direction. There are technical differences
in the way in which ideas about computing
and communications have evolved in each
country. There are professional differences
between standards specialists and computing
specialists on the nature, structure and
content of the standards to be produced.

Finally, there is the fact that work on
standards cannot be successful unless it is
supported in each country by systematic
efforts to develop the understanding and
experience on which the work can build, and
unless conditions are created which
encourage the widespread adoption by the
computing industry and by computer users of
the standards produced. What is involved is
a range of activities which is much wider
than the work of standards organisations
themselves. Examples are:

- research and development projects;

- pilot projects to build up
  implementation experience;

- standards verification and
  certification services;

- education and training programs;

- a strategy for the step-by-step
  introduction of OSI standards into
  general use.

These are problems which do not have simple
'solutions', they are rooted in the fact
that, despite its size and significance, the
computing industry has seen only limited
effective standardisation. The key to
overcoming the problems lies in the
realisation and acceptance by the computing
and communications industries (both
suppliers and users) that they exist and
must be overcome if OSI standards are to
become a reality. In addition there is a
need for the industry to understand the
process of standardisation, to avoid
unrealistic expectations about the timescale
within which a comprehensive and mature set
of OSI standards can be developed, and to
accept the necessity of a step-by-step
evolution of OSI standards as experience in
their use and understanding of the nature of
the requirements evolves. However, in the
end, success or failure will depend on the
will of the industry both to develop the
standards and to bring them into use, and on
the support provided by national governments
for their efforts.

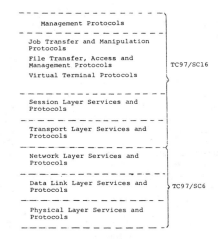

Figure 1   ISO Work Items on Standards for OSI

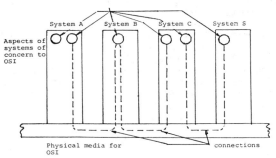

aspects of application processes of concern to OSI....application-entities

Figure 2   Basic elements of the OSI Environment

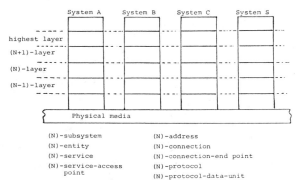

(N)-subsystem   (N)-address
(N)-entity   (N)-connection
(N)-service   (N)-connection-end point
(N)-service-access   (N)-protocol
     point   (N)-protocol-data-unit

Figure 3   BASIC CONCEPTS OF THE REFERENCE MODEL

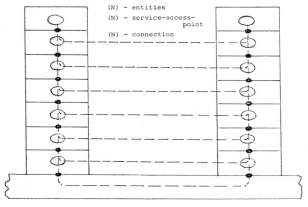

(N) - entities
(N) - service-access-point
(N) - connection

Figure 4   OSI COMMUNICATION STRUCTURE

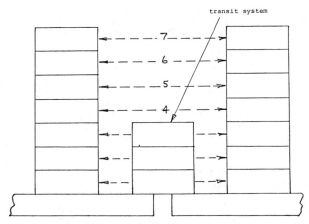

Figure 6   COMMUNICATION INVOLVING A TRANSIT SYSTEM

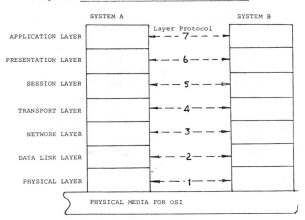

Figure 5   THE REFERENCE MODEL FOR OPEN SYSTEMS INTERCONNECTION

Management	Service & Protocols	1983-84++
Job Transfer & Manipulation	Service & Protocol	1984-5
Files	Service & Transfer Protocols	1983
	Access & Management	1984-86
Virtual Terminals	Service & Protocols	1984-85++
Presentation Layer	Service	1983-84
	Protocols	1983-84++
Session Layer	Service	1983-84
	Protocols	1983-84
Transport Layer	Service	1982
	Protocols	1982-83
Network Layer	Service	1983
	Protocols	1983-84++
Data Link Layer	Service	1983-84
	Protocols	1983-85

** indicates work on additional drafts beyond the dates given

Figure 7   TIMESCALES FOR STANDARDS FOR OSI

6.   REFERENCES

1.   "Data Processing - Open Systems Interconnection - Basic Reference Model". ISO/DIS 7498, April 1982.

2.   Working draft for an Addendum to ISO 7498 covering Connectionless-data-transmission. ISO/TC97/SC16/N911, January 1982.

The Lower Layers of the OSI Reference Model

J Tucker
Logica, UK

The paper introduces the Physical, Data Link and Network Layers of the OSI Reference Model and shows how they may be applied in order to achieve the objective of the lowest three layers, namely providing communications between End-Systems in a standard form that is independent of the types of communications media involved. This objective is expressed in OSI terms as the provision of the Network Service. It provides general solutions to the problems of gateway design.

1. OBJECTIVES

The objective of OSI as a whole is to permit the construction of Open Systems which can interact with each other meaningfully and usefully over a wide range of communications media. A fundamental principle of layered architectures, going back well beyond the beginning of OSI, is that the procedures needed to support different applications, e.g. file access and virtual terminal operation, have nothing to do with the procedures needed to transfer data across networks; and hence these two types of procedure should be carefully decoupled. Thus in OSI, the operation of the upper layers, which are concerned with distributed processing rather than communications, must not depend upon how the communication between the end-systems is maintained or what media are employed.

Each service boundary between OSI layers performs a decoupling function; indeed, it is the precise definition of OSI services that makes explicit and guarantees the independence of layers. The decoupling of distributed processing from communications is achieved in two stages, by the definition of the Network Service (at the Network/Transport Layer boundary) and the Transport Service (at the Transport/Session Layer boundary). The Transport Service, provided by Layers 1-4, is required to be an end-to-end communications service

i. independent of the characteristics of the underlying communications media in the facilities it makes available,

ii. giving the quality of service requested by the higher layers,

iii. in a cost-efficient manner within the quality of service constraints.

Of these three functions, (i) is the responsibility of the Network and lower layers. The Transport Layer, which resides solely in end-systems, then has the task of achieving (ii) and (iii) where possible by such means as multiplexing, error detection/correction schemes and so on.

Thus the OSI Network Service, provided by the lowest three layers, is a standard end-to-end communications service across all kinds of media, singly or in concatenation, such that the operational differences of those media are hidden from the higher layers, which reside solely in end-systems. All gateway operation and use of existing networks, such as X.25 networks, X21 networks and Local Area Networks, are the province of the lowest three layers. A good analogy is provided by the international telephone networks, which offer a standard end-to-end service between any two telephones in the world. Similarly, the objective of the lowest three layers of OSI is to make it possible for any two data terminals to communicate in a standard basic fashion across whichever communications networks, public or private, wide area or local area, are needed to connect them.

2. STRUCTURE

There are a number of possible structures which can provide the Network Service, depending upon the communications media used. The OSI architecture is prescriptive rather than descriptive, and prescribes a three-layer structure into Network Layer, Data Link Layer and Physical Layer. This 'canonical' OSI structure is described first. Since, however, it is not necessarily possible (or sensible) to apply OSI retrospectively to systems designed without the benefit of its framework, it has to be recognised that some systems, in fact communications networks, which will participate in OSI in the future do not themselves fit into its mould. How these are treated is described later.

2.1 The OSI Layers

The purpose of the three layers as a whole has been described in Section 1.

The part played by the Physical Layer is to convey bits over data circuits between systems. The transmission may be parallel or serial, full-duplex or half-duplex.

It has been recognised for a long time that many data circuits do not offer the low error rates required by a number of applications, and so over the years a substantial body of technique has been developed to enable data transfer to take place with an acceptably low residual error rate. Most of these techniques have also introduced framing, or a block structure of some kind. These requirements are represented in OSI by the Data Link layer, the purpose of which may be stated as "to detect and possibly correct errors which may occur in the Physical Layer", together with the provision of block transfer in the form of Data Link Data Units.

The most familiar examples of existing Data Link mechanisms are given by HDLC: but the very large set of HDLC commands and responses was developed with more than the OSI Data Link Layer in mind, and hence the full complexity of HDLC will almost certainly not be required for OSI purposes. Conversely, the development of fibre-optic technology and Local Area Networks imposes OSI Data Link requirements of a kind not exactly matched by HDLC. Thus HDLC should be viewed in OSI terms as a collection of mechanisms a subset of which may be used to provide the Data Link Service in some circumstances, whilst similar but non-identical mechanisms will also be required in others. We shall come back to the subject of Local Area Networks in OSI later.

Finally, given that the Data Link Layer provides reliable blocked data transmission between systems, it is the task of the Network Layer to provide end-to-end communications, pulling together Data Link services as necessary by means of interworking and end-to-end addressing and routing functions to enable the end-systems to exchange data.

2.2 Using Real Communications Networks

That simple analysis of the Physical, Data Link and Network Layers is not by itself adequate to deal with the use of a number of existing and planned communications networks within an OSI environment. First, some networks do not quite seem to fit the model: X.21 networks, for example, may be regarded as offering some Network Layer functions - addressing, call progress signals - during the call establishment phase but only Physical Layer functions during the data transfer phase; nor is there provision in the Reference Model as currently defined for the common channel signalling system proposed for ISDN. Second, other networks such as X.25 networks are more closely aligned to the Reference Model, but cannot be regarded as providing the complete OSI Network Service (with provision for quality of service negotiation, interworking, global addressing, for example).

Whether or not the Reference Model should take explicit account of this diversity of technology is not terribly important. What is important is that it must be possible to offer the OSI Network Service over all these different types of networks, separately or in concatenation; and that implies that methods must be developed for connecting them

together, and offering a standard, technology-independent service over all configurations.

To avoid confusion it is convenient in this context to use the term "subnetwork" when referring to real communications 'networks' such as PSS, Transpac, Ethernet, etc., and to keep the word "network" for use in referring to the third layer of OSI. It is then possible to make explicit the very important distinction between the OSI Network Service, which is to be standardised, and the service provided by particular types of subnetwork, which depends very much on what the subnetwork is. Thus the "subnetwork service" of PSS, say, is very different from that of the Nordic Public Data Network; that again is different from the service provided by a Local Area Network; and the OSI Data Link Service may in this context also be regarded as a subnetwork service, the service provided by an OSI Data Link.

2.3 General Structure

Whilst theoretically possible, it is of little practical value to attempt to redefine the methods of operation of the various types of communications subnetworks now in existence. Each subnetwork has to be seen as providing some subnetwork service ("below" that of the OSI Network Service), which is given and unalterable. The OSI Network Layer then has to contain mechanisms that will

- enhance or level the services of particular subnetworks so that the OSI Network Service can be offered across them

- enable subnetworks to be interconnected in concatenation, in such a way that the OSI Network Service can be offered across them.

These requirements are illustrated schematically in Figs 1 and 2, which also show the very important fact that part of the OSI Network Service Provider lies in the end-systems (despite the name, which could mislead the casual reader into supposing that the Network Service is something provided by an object called "The Network").

The remainder of this paper deals with the development of the Network Layer to meet those requirements, and shows how Local Area Networks fit into the general scheme.

Figure 3 Current Network Service Primitives

Primitive	Parameters
N-CONNECT Request	- Called address, calling address, quality of service, NS-User Data
N-CONNECT Indication	- (as N-CONNECT Request)
N-CONNECT Response	- Responding address*, quality of service, NS-User Data
N-CONNECT Confirm	- (as N-CONNECT Response)
N-DATA Request	- NS-User Data, Confirmation Request+
N-DATA Indication	- NS-User Data, Confirmation Request+
N-DATA ACK Request+	
N-DATA ACK Indication+	
N-EXPEDITED DATA Request*	- NS-User Data
N-EXPEDITED DATA Indication*	- NS-User Data
N-RESET Request	- Originator, Reason
N-RESET Indication	- Originator, Reason
N-RESET Response	
N-RESET Confirm	
N-NOTICE Indication*	- Reason
N-DISCONNECT Request	- Originator, Reason, NS-User Data*
N-DISCONNECT Indication	- Originator, Reason, NS-User Data*

* indicates that further study is needed to see whether or where these items are required

+ indicates a provider option

4. INTERWORKING

As explained above, interworking, by which we mean operation across concatenated subnetworks via gateways which link them, is a job for the Network Layer in OSI. In the past, where there has been no concept of a universal Network Service, designers of gateways have been faced with the problem that the two subnetworks they wish to interconnect offer different services to their users, with the consequence that no one-to-one mapping of the facilities of one to the facilities of the other is possible. The only solution has been to 'level' the two different services to a common 'levelled' service, possibly a common subset of the two original services, and then a gateway can be constructed. But the difficulty arises that the new 'levelled' service used for interworking is different from at least one of the original services, and so end-systems on at least one subnetwork have to have two different modes of operation: one for communication across just the subnetwork to which they are attached, the other for

interworking across tandem subnetworks.

In a nutshell, the interworking problem is that it is not possible to link together two end-systems which have different expectations about what the communications medium provides, without in some way having to change those expectations, and thus also change end-system behaviour.

The OSI solution to the interworking problem recognises that difficulty, but also recognises that the definition of an OSI Network Service is precisely a common formalisation of the expectations of the Transport Entities (or Network Service Users) within end-systems. It may not be possible to interwork across two subnetworks viewed in isolation: but given participation by end-systems in methods of offering an OSI Network Service across different types of subnetwork separately, as illustrated in Figure 1, those 'enhanced' subnetworks can be regarded as providing the same service, and gateways can then be constructed between them. To put it another way, implementation of the Network Service over dissimilar subnetworks makes them look the same, in terms of the facilities they offer. Then the 'levelling' problem does not exist, since the services are already 'levelled', and gateways can be built to map the facilities of each 'enhanced' subnetwork onto those of the other. This approach is illustrated in Figure 4. It applies equally to connection-oriented and connectionless services.

It should be noted that in some cases the implementation of gateways may be simplified by taking advantage of common features of the 'enhanced' subnetworks either side. Such simplifications would be matters of local optimisation, however; the external behaviour of the gateway would still be as prescribed above.

3. THE NETWORK SERVICE

3.1 Definition Criteria

In developing a Network Service, a number of interests need to be taken into account. Clearly the Network Service needs to offer the communications facilities required by the upper layers. It must also offer all the facilities which it is appropriate to perform at the Network layer or below. Thus, if a particular operation should in all cases be performed only in end-systems, then it should not be located in the Network Layer or below; but if in some cases particular operations of inter-mediate equipment (e.g. gateways) are to be invoked, then representative facilities are required in the Network Service - for it is only via Network Service primitives that Network (or lower) Layer operations can be invoked.

Naturally the experience gained in networking technology over the last decade will be relevant to the location of functions, and so the Network Service will to some extent reflect what existing subnetworks provide. Further-more, efficient use of existing subnetworks within an OSI environment is an important requirement, for obvious reasons. On the other hand, OSI standardisation is standardisation for the future; it should prescribe how systems ought to be built, not rigidly constrain future developments through any requirement to encompass any particular existing procedure.

The task of definition of the Network Service is further complicated by the fact that there may be more than one type of service (a) required by higher layers and (b) provided by lower layers. In the past we have seen different approaches taken, for example: (a) to transaction-oriented and connection-oriented communications, (b) to datagram and virtual-circuit operation in networks. And in the future we see new types of requirements for office automation, and new types of network facilities provided by Local Area Networks.

These differences have found expression in OSI as a polarisation between 'connection-oriented' and 'connectionless' operation. A connection-oriented service has three operational phases:

i.   an establishment phase in which one service-user establishes a 'connection' to another, and in the process may negotiate various characteristics of the connection

ii. a data-transfer phase during which data can be transferred, with sequence maintained over the connection, with the possibility (depending upon the particular service) of resynchronisation, flow-control, expedited flow, etc. ....

iii. a release phase during which the connection is released.

It is not so obvious what connectionless operation is, except that it does not have an establishment or a release phase. But even in the remaining data transfer phase, there are at least two kinds of operation that might be required or provided:

i.   where data units are completely independent of one another,

ii. where relationships between data units are maintained - e.g. sequence - such that flow control could be imposed, resynchronisation invoked, etc. ....

For example, one might say that datagram networks provide a service akin to type (i), whereas Local Area Networks provide something more like type (ii). It is the personal view of the author that, given the great difference between those two types, it is inappropriate to subsume them both under the general heading of connectionless operation. In particular, to pursue the example, protocols appropriate for use over datagram networks may not be appropriate for use over LANs.

Nearly all the work done so far has been on connection-oriented operation. Connectionless operation is still the subject of lively debate from the point of view of (a) what it is exactly and (b) which combinations of connection-oriented operation at some layers and connect-ionless at others are useful, and where they might apply.

3.2 The Connection-Oriented Network Service

In Figure 3 we present the set of primitives of the draft Network Service as currently defined by ISO and CCITT. For more detail the reader should refer to ISO/TC97/SC6/N2241, Draft Network Service Definition.

A further advantage to be gained from this approach, where the Network Service is the same whether or not multiple communications subnetworks are used, is that the Network Protocols used by end-systems will depend solely on the type of subnetwork to which they are attached, not upon the types of subnetwork (if any) elsewhere in the chain. Thus, apart from the addresses used and such quality of service aspects as transit delay, end-system operation will be completely independent of the existence or use of gateways to other subnetworks. Gateways will be invisible.

5. LOCAL AREA NETWORKS

The last topic of this paper is the location of Local Area Networks (LANs) within OSI. The first point to make here is that OSI prescribes hierarchies of functions, not interfaces to physical equipment. Local Area Networks may be operated in a variety of different ways, simultaneously; the same LAN may carry voice, data using one protocol, data using another protocol, etc., all at the same time. The question should therefore be: what LAN services should fit into OSI, and where?

There are two basic ways in which a LAN may be part of an OSI environment. The first sees the LAN used in the construction of a distributed processor which, as a whole, plays a defined OSI role: e.g. a gateway or an end-system. For example, a number of processing functions could be distributed around a LAN using some internal communications protocol, and an 'external communications' station of some kind used to present the appearance of an OSI end-system to the outside world. Here the LAN has a role similar to that of the bus-structure of other participating computer systems, and its method of operation is not a matter for OSI.

The second type of operation uses the LAN as a communications subnetwork in the sense used earlier in the paper, i.e. as a communications medium for the interconnection of OSI end-systems. In this case the devices on the LAN would be OSI end-systems in their own right, and would be very similar to OSI end-systems attached to wide-area networks. Here the service provided by the LAN is of concern to OSI, and is the subject of the remainder of the paper. Furthermore, the interworking approach developed above can be applied to the construction of gateways between LANs and one another, or between LANs and other kinds of subnetworks.

It is important to distinguish three different service levels in the discussion. At the bottom comes the service provided by the Local Area Network communications equipment as supplied by the manufacturer; this service depends on the technology and manufacturer chosen, and is the basis on which higher services must be built. At the top comes the OSI Network Service, as discussed earlier in the paper. So far the picture looks much the same as that for wide-area networks: there is a variety of subnetwork services, and each has to be 'levelled' or 'enhanced' so as to provide the OSI Network Service, by means of Network Protocols; and that will permit interworking just as described in Section 4 above.

That is all true. But there is also interest in defining an intermediate level of service, common to all LANs but not WANs, so as to provide a stable base for the development of higher-layer procedures and to make it easier to supply equipment that will be capable of operation over a variety of LANs, especially since it could lead to the development of a standard interface to a variety of different LANs. Indeed this interest exists

independently of OSI, and is the subject of great activity within IEEE. This service level is important to OSI too, since its use would enable OSI work to proceed without the need to recognise the great technological variety of LANs, and conversely it would enable LAN developers to proceed knowing that, if their systems offer the intermediate service, they can readily be incorporated in an OSI environment.

For this purpose, the IEEE have chosen a LAN Service somewhere below the OSI Data Link Service, and have in addition proposed protocols (Local Network Logical Link Control, or LNLLC) which will provide the OSI Data Link Service above the lower basic LAN Service. Furthermore, two versions of LNLLC are proposed: one aimed at providing a connectionless Data Link Service, the other a connection-oriented one. Some more technical work will be required before the OSI Data Link Service(s) and thus the precise location of LAN services within OSI can be regarded as firm, but the major decisions of principle have been taken.

What is needed to complete the incorporation of LANs in OSI is the construction of inter-working procedures by which they can be linked to other communications subnetworks. The principles which must be followed have been discussed above, but some significant questions remain. Connection-oriented and connectionless modes of operation are being defined for both Data Link and Network Services, and, as noted in Section 3 above, it may be appropriate to construct variants of either or both of them to take account of LAN operation. Thus a number of possible combinations (at least four) of modes of operation at the two different service levels are possible, and it is necessary to determine in which circumstances and to meet which requirements the various combinations are appropriate. One hopes that only a small number of combinations will be judged useful; it will then be possible to develop a restricted set of protocols capable of supporting all types of LAN subnetwork use within OSI.

Jeremy Tucker read Mathematics and subsequently Mathematical Statistics at Christ's College, Cambridge. After three years working in the area of Computer Simulation he joined Logica in 1969, where he is now a Principal Consultant. He has worked in data communications and computer networking for over ten years, has been active in the development of HDLC and CCITT X.series Recommendations, and is the convener of the ISO working group (TC97/SC6/WG2) responsible for the Network Layer of the OSI architecture. He is also a member of the FOCUS Information Technology Suppliers' Committee on Standards.

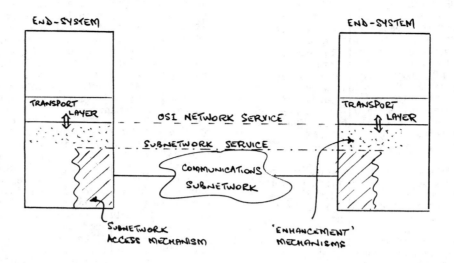

FIGURE 1   PROVISION OF THE OSI NETWORK SERVICE

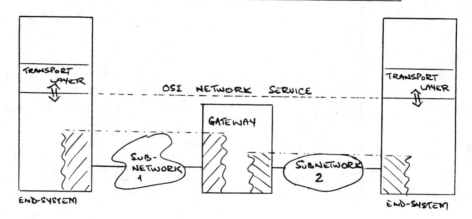

FIGURE 2   REQUIREMENTS FOR INTERWORKING

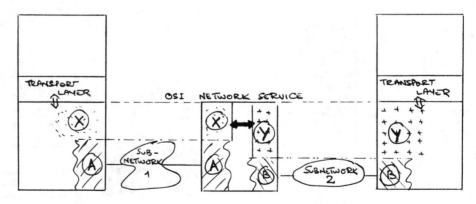

(A), (B) : Subnetwork Access Mechanisms

(X), (Y) : 'Enhancement' Mechanisms

⟷   : Service Mapping Function

FIGURE 4   THE OSI APPROACH TO INTERWORKING

The Transport Layer

K G Knightson
British Telecom, UK

The Transport Layer is of great importance in the OSI model and is being considered by
several standards organisations. The architectural aspects of the Transport and related
layers and the objectives of the Transport Layer will be outlined, together with the
relationship between functions and protocols, leading to the concepts of protocol
classes. The common functionality and the individual functionality of the various
classes will be briefly described, together with the encoding principle.

1   INTRODUCTION

One of the essential requirements within an
Open System Interconnection environment is
the ability for one open system to
communicate with another geographically
remote open system.

The Transport Layer of the OSI Reference
Model [1] is the one layer and the only
layer, in the architecture with the overall
responsibility for controlling the
transportation of data between a source
end-system and a destination end-system. The
Transport Layer has thus been the subject of
intense activity over the last few years.

2   INTERNATIONAL ACTIVITIES

The 3 following organisations are active in
producing standards for the Transport Layer:-

European Computer Manufacturers
Association - ECMA

Comite Consultative Internationale de
Telegraphie et Telephonie - CCITT

International Organisation for
Standardisation - ISO

ECMA was the first international standards
body to produce and ratify a Transport
Protocol which has been published as Standard
ECMA-72[2].

The interest from CCITT arises from the
requirements to internationally standardise
text/graphic and other communications
services that could be offered by CCITT
member bodies, eg Facsimile, Teletex,
Videotex, Message Handling, Electronic Mail
etc. These kinds of services are
applications and thus, necessarily, require
elements of all the layers of the OSI model.
The distinction between pure data
communications and pure data processing has
become less clear. The concepts involved in
advanced office automation and the electronic
office require both raw communications and
processing to be part of the complete
'service' package.

CCITT COM VIII has published
Recommendation S.70, a "Network-Independent
Basic Transport Service for Teletex". S.70
is compatible with a defined subset of the
ECMA - 72 standard (Class 0).

Both ISO and CCITT COM VII are studying the
transport layer in the context of wider
range of usage than S.70, and see S.70 as
a defined subset of the total capabilities.
The amount of official liaison is greater
than ever before and the personal
representation in both CCITT and ISO
committees has increased. There is every
indication that a single standard will be
produced, even though it would appear as
separate publications from ISO and CCITT.

The value of the work of ECMA has been
acknowledged and there is also a strong
desire that as much as possible of the ECMA
standard should be included in the CCITT/ISO
standard.

3   ARCHITECTURAL ASPECTS

Important architectural relationships have
been defined between the Transport Layer and
the Network Layer, and Transport Layer and
Session Layer.

The Transport Layer is the highest layer with
any responsibility for the transportation of
data. Thus the Transport Layer relieves the
Session Layer entities from any concern with
the means of transportation of data between
them.

The Transport Layer is OSI End-System
oriented. Thus Transport Protocols operate
only between OSI End-Systems. Any relay
functions or service enhancement protocols
used to support the Network Service between
the OSI End-Systems are operating below the
End-Systems' Transport Layer.

The service of a layer, in the OSI context,
is the set of capabilities which it offers to
the user in the next higher layer. The
service provided to the next higher layer is
built upon the service provided from the
lower layer, by the addition of appropriate

functions. The functional entities
themselves communicate by means of the
peer-to-peer protocol.

4   OBJECTIVES OF TRANSPORT LAYER

The primary objective of the Transport Layer
is to provide to the Session Layer, data
transportation at a required quality of
service in an optimum manner. The Transport
Layer thus 'bridges' the quality of service
'gap' between that required by the Session
Layer and that offered by the Network Layer.

The quality of service requirements are
expressed in terms of parameters requested by
the Session Layer, eg throughput, transit
delay, residual error rate, establishment
delay, resilience, cost, security, priority
etc.

The Transport Layer must provide all the
functions to meet the quality of service
requirements, and the necessary supporting
protocols.

For example, if the throughput requested were
in excess of the network access rate it might
be necessary to establish more than one
Network Connection, and a protocol for line-
sharing would be necessary. Conversely one
Network Connection might be able to support
more than one Transport Connection, in which
case a protocol for multiplexing would be
necessary.

Extra capabilities for Error Detection and
Correction might be necessary.

It should also be clear by now that the
Transport Layer has to know the quality of
service of the Network Connection before it
can decide which function will have to be
invoked over that Network Connection.

5   TRANSPORT SERVICE [3]

The interaction between the user of the n
layer and the provider of the n layer is
described by a set of named service
primitives. A named service primitive has
one or more related parameters and related
service primitive events. This method of
service definition is accepted by both CCITT
and ISO. Groups of related primitives have
similar names and are qualified to indicate
their procedural role, eg user generated
Requests and Responses, provider generated
Indications and Confirmations.

5.1 Service Primitives

The following service primitives have
been defined:-

Primitive	Parameters
T-CONNECT request	(to transport address, from transport address, options, quality of service, TS-user data)
T-CONNECT indication	(to transport address, from transport address, options, quality of service, TS-user data)
T-CONNECT response	(responding address, options, quality of service, TS-user data)
T-CONNECT confirm	(responding address, options, quality of service, TS-user data)
T-DISCONNECT request	(TS-user data)
T-DISCONNECT indication	(Disconnect reason, TS-user data)
T-DATA request	(TS-user data)
T-DATA indication	(TS-user data)
T-EXPEDITED DATA request	(TS-user data)
T-EXPEDITED DATA indication	(TS-user data)

6   TRANSPORT LAYER FUNCTIONS

The Transport Layer has to invoke functions
in accordance with a set of parameters
tailored to suit the application, over a wide
range of Network Service qualities.

The protocol is the externally visible
representation of the functionality of the
Transport Layer. Since there may be many
separate functions within the layer, every
function has to be represented by a protocol
element. However, the combinations of
parameters and protocols that could result,
could give rise to selection and negotiation
problems. Conversely, a protocol which
accommodates all functions irrespective of
whether they are actually required, would
result in inflexibility and inefficiency.

These considerations led to the concept of
classes of protocol in ECMA-72. There has
been considerable difficulty in agreeing the
grouping of the functions and agreeing the
nature of a group structure. The original
ECMA proposals were based on a strict
hierarchical set of protocol classes, where
protocol Class N was always subset of class
N+1. The consequence of this is that if a
particular function only exists, in say,
Class 3, all the functions of Classes 0, 1,
2 are included irrespective of whether they
are required.

Both the current studies in ISO and CCITT are based on a variation of the ECMA proposals. There has been a relaxation in the requirement for a strict hierarchy of protocol classes and acceptance of the use of options within classes to overcome the disadvantages described above.

7 TRANSPORT LAYER PROTOCOLS [4]

7.1 Protocol Classes

Both CCITT and ISO have agreed on the following 5 protocol classes:-

- Class 0 : Simple Class

- Class 1 : Basic Class Error Recovery Class

- Class 2 : Multiplexing Class

- Class 3 : Error Recovery and Multiplexing Class

- Class 4 : Error detection and recovery Class

With the exception of Classes 0 and 1 transport connections of different class may be multiplexed together onto the same network connection.

Classes and options within classes are negotiated during the connection establishment phase.

Options define additional functions which may be associated within a class.

The choice of class will be made by the transport entities according to:-

- the users requirement expressed via T-CONNECT Request T-CONNECT Response service primitives;

- the quality of the available Network Service;

- the user required service versus cost ratio acceptable for the transport user.

The classes are intended to cater for, among other things, the following types of Network Connection:-

Type A Network connections with acceptable residual error rate (for example not signalled by "clear" or "reset") and acceptable rate of signalling failures.

Type B Network connections with acceptable residual error rate (for example not signalled by "clear" or "reset") but unacceptable rate of signalling failures.

Type C Network connections with residual error rate not acceptable to the TS user.

It should be noted that Types A, B, C have no absolute figures, and that what may by Type A for a given application may be Type B to another.

7.2 Common Elements

The Basic protocol unit is the Transport Protocol Data Unit (TPDU).

TPDUs, in general, classified either as Data TPDUs or Control TPDUs. Unless there is a means of indicating the length of data in data TPDUs, concatenation of Control and Data TPDU can only be achieved by placing Control TPDUs in front of a Data TPDU in a concatenated set of TPDUs.

All classes use the T-Connect Request/ Indication and T-Connect Response/ Confirm. This protocol exchange provides for:-

- Identification of calling and called session entities by use of reference numbers.

- Negotiation of classes and options.

- Negotiate of size of Data TPDU.

- Connection Identification.

- Exchange of parameters.

- Exchange of user data.

Since the Transport Service Data Units are not constrained in size they have to be segmented into manageable protocol sizes. The integrity is maintained by an end of TSDU indicator carried in every TPDU. This permits TPDUs to be chained together to represent a complete TSDU.

7.3 Class 0 - Simple Class

This class has the minimum functionality of all the classes, and is fully compatible with CCITT Recommendation S.70 Teletex Terminals. This class is for use over Type A Network Connections.

Only functions for establishment, data transfer with segmenting, and error reporting are available.

There are no functions for multiplexing, disconnection, flow control, error recovery or expedited data transfer.

Furthermore no exchange of user data is permitted during connection establishment, and only address and TPDU size parameters are allowed.

Since there is no explicit disconnection procedure the life time of the Transport Connection is dependent upon, and the same as, the life time of the Network Connection.

For Class 0 the standard maximum Data TPDU length is 128 octets including the TPDU header.

7.4   Class 1 - Basic Error Recovery Class

The objective of this class is to provide recovery from network signalled errors (network disconnect or reset).

This class is intended for use over Type B Network Connections.

Class 1 provides Transport Connections with error recovery, expedited data transfer, disconnection, and flow control based on the underlying Network Service provided flow control.

Data may be exchanged during connection establishment.

No functions are provided for multiplexing.

It should be noted that the procedures for Class 1 have only recently been finalised. This Class 1 differs significantly from that defined by ECMA-72 and reflects a compromise agreement within ISO and CCITT.

7.5   Class 2 Multiplexing Class

This class provides capability of multiplexing several Transport Connections within a single Network Connection. This class has been designed for operation over Type A Network Connections.

The use of flow control within the protocol is an option of this class:-

Flow Control Option

This option can be used to reduce congestion, optimise response times and resource utilisation. This is required when the traffic is heavy and continuous and/or when there is a high degree of multiplexing taking place.

No Flow Control Option

This will allow multiplexing but with the absence of explicit flow control within the protocol. This can be useful for Transport Connections with non-critical response time requirements, or with infrequent short bursts of traffic with a predictable low total level of utilisation of the underlying Network Connection.

No functions are provided for error detection or error recovery. If the network resets or disconnects, the Transport Connection is terminated without an explicit end-to-end exchange and the TS-users are informed.

Class 2 provides the following functions in addition to those available in Class 0.

- Multiplexing

- Flow Control

- Exchange of user data during connection establishment

- Credit Mechanism (with flow control option)

- Expedited Data Transfer

- Explicit Disconnection

7.6   Class 3 - Error Recovery Class

The objective of this class is to provide Class 2 with the additional functions to permit recovery from network signalled errors (network disconnect or reset). This class is intended for use of Type B Network Connections.

7.7   Class 4 Error Detection and Recovery Class

The objective of Class 4 is to detect lost TPDUs, mis-sequenced TPDUs and duplicated TPDUs and/or parts of TPDUs (control or data type).

Class 4 is designed for use over network connections considered to have an unacceptable residual error rate relative to high level requirements, ie a Type C connection.

The main differences from Class 3 are the addition of time-out mechanisms and resultant extra procedures, and a checksum mechanism.

7.8 General Structure of TPDUs

TPDUs are divided into 4 parts as shown below. All TPDUs contain an integral number of octets.

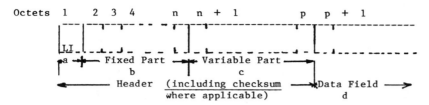

Octets 1 2 3 4   n n + 1   p p + 1

a = Length Indicator Field (LI)

b = Fixed Part

c = Variable Part

d = Data Field

8   CONCLUSIONS

A detailed description [5] has not been possible within the constraints of this paper.

Nevertheless, this account of the work should convince most readers that a great deal of progress has been made and that the availability of an international standard is not far off.

REFERENCES

[1]   Draft Proposal ISO/DP 7498,
      4 February 1982, "Information
      Processing Systems - Open Systems
      Interconnection Basic Reference Model".

[2]   Standard ECMA-72, January 1981,
      "Transport Protocol".

[3]   ISO/TC 97/SC 16 N 860, Newport Beach
      December 1981, "Draft Connection
      Oriented Transport Service Definition".

[4]   ISO/TC 97/SC 16 N 861, Newport Beach
      December 1981, "Draft Connection
      Oriented Transport Protocol
      Specification".

[5]   Knightson K G, "Transport Layer", State
      of the Art Report on 'Network
      Architectures' published by Pergamon
      Infotech, February 1982.

Keith G Knightson is Head of Standards and Protocols Group in the Digital Data Networks Division of British Telecom. He has been an active participant in CCITT in the development of the packet switched Recommendations. He also is involved with Open System Interconnection Standards both in CCITT and ISO, and is currently the CCITT SG VII Special Rapporteur for the Transport Service, Transport Layer, and Network Service. He was actively involved with specification and implementation of BT's Packet Switched Service (PSS) and value-added services.

Keith holds both a BSc and a MSc in Computer Science, is a Chartered Engineer, and a Member of the Institute of Electronic and Radio Engineers.

An Introduction to the ECMA Session Protocol for Open Systems Interconnection

G De Luca, G Rietti
Olivetti Telecomunicazioni, Italy

The ECMA approach to the OSI session layer involves a description of the services provided by the session layer to its users, and a precise definition of the protocol by which these are achieved. This paper provides a description of the ECMA services and an introduction to the protocol. One section of the paper discusses the topic of "subsetting", the technique employed to differentiate the session functions according to the particular user requirements. The concept of subsetting is seen to offer interesting advantages for ensuring flexibility and implementation economy. It is also suitable for various kinds of extensions. The ECMA session standard can thus give a contribution to the success of the OSI architectural concepts.

While the authors trust that the description of the ECMA standard given here is accurate, any additional considerations should not be taken as necessarily representing the official ECMA position.

1. INTRODUCTION.

In the area of Open Systems Interconnection standardization the European Computer Manufacturers Association (ECMA) is one of the most active contributors(#).

\# The following is an extract from the ECMA By-Laws:

The purpose of the Association is:
To study and develop, in cooperation with the appropriate national and international organizations, as a scientific endeavour and in the general interest, methods and procedures in order to facilitate and standardize the use of data processing systems.
To promulgate various standards applicable to the functional design and use of data processing equipment.
The Association shall be a non-profit making organization and shall devote itself to no commercial activity whatsoever.

The following ordinary members are associated in ECMA: AEG-Telefunken, Borroughs International SA, Cii Honeywell Bull, Datasaab AB, Digital Equipment Corporation International (Europe), Ferranti Computer Systems Ltd., IBM Europe, I.C.L. International Computers Ltd, Ing. C. Olivetti & C. S.P.A., NCR Co. Ltd, Nixdorf Computer AG, Philips

At the end of 1980 ECMA issued standard ECMA-72: "Transport protocol" [1]; this has extensively been used by ISO to draft its corresponding document [2]. At the end of 1981 ECMA approved standard ECMA-75: "Session protocol" [3]. This is the first general-purpose OSI session layer standard, and is under study by ISO, together with other proposals, to form the basis of the ISO session standard.

One of the major objectives of a session protocol is to achieve application-oriented functions in a unified way. This is partly different from the objectives of the lower layer protocols whose functions deal with data transportation problems. Roughly speaking, transport and lower layer protocols are designed "looking downwards" (i.e. to the transmission problems), while session and higher layer protocols are designed "looking upwards" (i.e. to the commonality of the actions performed by different communicating applications). In fact, session functions have in the past been embedded into application protocols. By collecting them in the session layer, it is possible to reduce the variety of ad-hoc solutions which have made

---

Data Systems, SEMS: Societe Europeenne de Mini-Informatique et de Systemes, Siemens AG, Sperry Univac.

application-level interworking such a complex and costly effort.

If a more complete description of the OSI layers and their functions is required, the reader is referred to introductory papers such as [5] and [6], and to the current version of the reference model [4].

2. MULTIPLICITY OF OSI PROTOCOLS.

In practice, the protocols to be defined within the OSI framework will need to adapt to a variety of situations.

For the communication-oriented layers 1 to 4, this is due to the difference in the available telecommunication facilities; these may pre-date OSI, but have to be included in an OSI environment. Existing networking facilities roughly cover the functions of the OSI layers up to layers 2 or 3. The service level they provide may have to be integrated by functions in layers 3 or 4 to reach the quality of service needed by the session layer.

As an example, the ECMA transport protocol [1] includes five "classes" of operation, with an approximately increasing range of functions. The various classes cover differences in the underlying network and telecommunication facilities (which may range from data networks, to local area networks, to telephone networks etc.).

The interwork support layers (5 to 7) are also subject to protocol variety, but for different reasons. The layer 5 (application) functions envisaged in the interconnection environment include: file transfer, remote data base access/update, terminal (or generic device) support, telematic services, remote job entry, application and interconnection management. Some of the above functions have already been considered for standardization, and independent protocols are being developed in each case.

It is still unclear whether this multiplicity of application protocols will lead to separate layer 6 (presentation) protocols, or to a single, adaptable presentation protocol. Whatever the choice, even the session layer must adapt to the various modes of user interaction, and has to offer suitable facilities for user cooperation. This problem has been extensively considered in the development of the ECMA standard. The approach taken, which can be summarized in a single session protocol supporting several subsets of services, will be justified, described and discussed in sect. 4.

As a preliminary, an overview of the main session layer concepts and of the ECMA approach is presented in sect. 3.

3. THE SESSION LAYER.

Being the first layer concerned with final users interworking in the OSI environment, the session layer has the main purpose of collecting functions for the management of the user dialogue. These functions are not concerned with communication aspects, nor with the syntax or semantics of the exchanged data (the latter are the concern of layers 6 and 7). Most functions of the session layer complement the connection-oriented transparent data transfer service, and are visible as services to the session users. Before the ECMA approach to the session layer is introduced (sect. 3.2 and 3.3), sect. 3.1 discusses the general objectives of the session services and protocol.

3.1 General Principles.

As already mentioned, the two main objectives justifying the existence of the session layer are:

a) organization of the session user data exchange, and

b) session users synchronization.

Some aspects of the session functions related to objective a) above are:

a1: transparently transferring user data as flows in opposite directions;

a2: increasing the confidence of a user on its data reaching the remote user;

a3: sectioning the data exchange into units of user significance;

a4: identifying these dialogue units to the users;

a5: allowing references to former dialogue points through unit identifiers;

a6: reporting exceptional (error) situations.

Aspects of the session functions related to b) are:

b1: increasing the confidence of a user on the current state of its partner;

b2: regaining user synchronization after an error or loss of cooperation;

b3: managing, where required, the turn to transmit (two-way alternate, TWA-dialogue);

b4: avoiding contention in the request of certain services or resources;

b5: providing expedited data exchange, when this helps users to synchronize directly;

b6: ensuring that the session synchronization also accounts for expedited data;

b7: ensuring mutual agreement for some connection control actions (e.g. establishment, release, changes of synchronization etc.).

3.2 ECMA Session Services.

The ECMA view of the session services can be summarised as follows. Reference is made to the general principles identified in the previous section.

Establishment. The Connect service establishes a session connection with the mutual agreement of both users on the connection parameters and options. It consists in a two-way negotiation during which both users state their requirements; the responder can explicitly accept or refuse the connection (b7).

Termination. The Release service clears a connection in a normal way, with a two-way negotiation involving both users (a2, b7). The Disconnect and Abort services cause the abnormal connection termination: the former is initiated by one user acting unilaterally; the latter is initiated by the session layer (a6).

Data transfer. The Data service transparently passes data units of arbitrary size (a1, a3, b3). Facilities are provided in the protocol to allow:

- submission and delivery of data in segments smaller than the significant units;

- blocking of "small" units into longer messages for optimization purposes.

The Expedited service transparently passes small data units which take precedence over normal data.

Quarantining. Normal data units can be collected into a "quarantine unit"; each quarantine unit is not to be considered valid until closed by an explicit command of the sender. A quarantine unit is stored within the session layer until completed. The Deliver service declares a quarantine unit to be completed. The Cancel service declares the current quarantine unit to be incomplete, and requests its data to be discarded (a3).

Token management. A token is an attribute which can be assigned exclusively to either session user, and moved from one user to the other (see also [7]). Several tokens may exist, and their "ownership" gives a user the "right" to initiate certain services. Hence one of the token functions is to ensure mutual exclusion in service requests (b3, b4, b7).

The Data token, for example, regulates the "turn" to transmit, and may or may not be defined for a connection. If it is defined, only its owner can send data and request other synchronization services as well (TWA). If it is not defined, the dialogue is two-way simultaneous (TWS), although synchronization is still alternate.

The Give tokens service enables the owner of one or more tokens to pass them to the other user. The Please tokens service communicates to the owner of one or more tokens that the other user needs them, but has no other effect.

Synchronization. The services directly concerned with user synchronization offer the following possibilities:

- marking points in the dialogue which users can then reference (a3, a4, a5);

- requesting the remote user to confirm marked points in the dialogue thus making a synchronization (a2);

- committing the session layer to enforce the expected confirmation in various way: no commitment, block of the normal data flow, block of the normal and expedited data flows (b1, b6);

- resetting the dialogue to an agreed point (possibly a previous synchronization point), and repositioning the tokens as required. This resynchronization is typical after error detection, and takes precedence over any other exchange (b2, b4, b6, b7).

The Sync service is used to mark points of the dialogue and to effect a synchronization of the "non committed" or "committed on normal data" type. The End-dialogue-unit service effects a synchronization of the "committed on both flows" type, which completely separates dialogue phases. The Resync service is used to agree on a resynchronization with connection state reset. All of these involve at least a two-way exchange.

The rules for negotiation and contention resolution during a resynchronization cannot be reported here because of lack of space, but give rise to an interesting subprotocol within the overall session protocol.

3.3 ECMA Session Protocol.

Any account of the session protocol which is possible to give here is by necessity incomplete, and references to the ECMA standard are assumed.

The protocol is divided into two sections:

- the SPDU protocol which specifies what messages are carried by Session Protocol Data Units (SPDUs), their encoding and the actions to be taken by the session entities at the ends of the connection;

- the Transport Mapping protocol which specifies how the transport layer must be used by the session entities.

The SPDU protocol describes the behaviour of a session entity when it is triggered:

- by a service request, or response, of the local session user;

- by the arrival of a message.

The actions the session entity undertakes may be:

- sending a message;

- indicating, or confirming the service to the local session user.

The session entity also maintains and updates an internal state, and has some internal storage for quarantine units and for messages which must be temporarily stored while other services are being carried out.

The session entity behaviour is precisely defined in the formalism of finite state machines, with a few ad-hoc features. This formal definition should make it easier to produce correct and conforming implementations.

The encoding of the messages into SPDUs is done with criteria aimed at minimizing the size of the protocol control information normally being transmitted with respect to user data. For messages where data and protocol control information must be transmitted, the most frequent protocol information is encoded in a fixed size header; other less common information can be encoded in the variable field.

The Transport Mapping protocol defines the usage, by the cooperating session entities, of the transport connection. Basically, it states the rules for establishing and releasing the transport connection where SPDUs are transferred. It also states which messages are carried by the normal, and which by the expedited transport flows. In ECMA-75 reference is made to the transport functions as provided by the ECMA transport protocol [1].

ECMA-75 also contains a conformance statement, specifying the minimum characteristics of any system in order for it to conform to the standard. A point of interest of the conformance statement is that it is linked to subsetting: the standard informally defines some subsets of services, and formally identifies the corresponding protocol parts. Subsets are the minimal units for conformance: any equipment needs only implement one of the standard subsets. The next section gives further details on this concept, and on the consequences of its inclusion.

4. PROTOCOL SUBSETTING.

The discussion in sect. 2.3 has pointed out that, even within a single layer of the OSI model, there is a need to differentiate functionalities. For the session layer, this is due to variations in the expected user requirements. This section deals with aspects of subsetting within the ECMA session standard.

4.1 Session Subsetting.

In sect. 3, the introduction to the ECMA session layer approach has mentioned the existence of a single session protocol supporting several services. The standard also describes four subsets of services. The session users agree, at connection establishment time, which subset is to be used; this exactly determines the services available during the connection. Certain selections are possible, at connection establishment, but are limited to some parameters and modes of the subset services.

From each of the defined service subsets follows the identification of a part of the protocol which is necessary and sufficient to support the subset. Any system implementing the session layer is only required to conform to the part of the protocol corresponding to some service subset; hence there is no need for a system to implement the full protocol.

Although the full protocol is consistent in itself, none of the defined subsets requires all its features. (Their union does). There is no notion of a "common core" of all the subsets either, nor there is any hierarchy among the defined subsets. Hence any "reasonable" part of the protocol could be selected to make a "consistent" set of services(#).

4.2 Characteristics of the Approach.

The approach outlined in sect. 4.1 is based on: the concept of service subsets; the uniqueness of the supporting protocol; the statement of conformance on subsets. This approach leads to particular characteristics of the session layer, summarised in the following items.

1. The subset concept caters for the variability of session user requirements: each subset is tailored to a kind of applications "known" at the time of its definition.

2. For economy, implementations may conform to one subset only. When several subsets are required, the uniqueness of the protocol makes implementations simpler and less redundant.

3. The lack of definition of a "common core" for all subsets is due to the "application-orientation" of each subset. This means that a class of applications will be built on top of a given subset and will need the services of that subset and only them. An alternate approach could be to define a "common core" subset and some optional extensions. However this would make it very likely for an application protocol designer to use only that subset, in order to increase the probability of interworking. This would defeat the purpose of the session layer, since most of the more significant session services could not be exploited.

4. Without altering the protocol, it is easy to define non-standard ("ad-hoc") subsets for specific applications. Equipments implementing both standard and ad-hoc subsets still conform to the standard.

5. Still without altering the protocol, it is possible to define new standard subsets. This will be done when applications with a broadly recognised scope define their requirements on the session layer.

6. When there is a need to extend the protocol, if the characteristics of the approach are maintained all the current subsets remain valid even in the extended versions.

An arbitrary part of the protocol is guaranteed to be consistent, but the services it supports may not be complete or useful.

4.3 The Four Defined Subsets.

The four subsets so far defined by ECMA are outlined in what follows. The services they include are indicated in table 1.

A - Basic subset. It gives no enhancement over the services of the transport layer except session connection identification and a kind of "graceful" termination which increases the users' confidence on data integrity.(##) It is provided mainly to support users of communication facilities pre-dating OSI.

B - Basic interactive subset. It provides an organized dialogue structure with:
- selection of interaction type (TWS - TWA);
- possibility to request quarantining;
- negotiated termination;
- token management.
It should be useful to Virtual terminal application protocols.

C - Basic synchronized subset. It provides an organised dialogue structure with all synchronization features:
- selection of interaction type (TWS - TWA);
- possibility to block data units into messages;
- synchronization, dialogue units, resynchronization;
- negotiated termination;
- token management.
The expedited data flow is not provided, since the available synchronization features should support any user requirements for this service. This subset is useful to File Transfer application protocols.

D - Basic TWA subset. It provides a simplified dialogue structure with alternate interactions; it includes management of the data token for the turn to transmit, non-disruptive termination, but no expedited data. This subset should serve normal users without sophisticated requirements.

Finally, it must be mentioned that subsets B and D provide the same services as the partitions of another session protocol presently being defined by the National Bureau of Standards [8].

It must be recalled, however, that in implementations the view of the transport layer may be significantly different from that of the session layer. Besides addressing at session user level, several "value added" functions of local significance may be included to simplify user access.

5. CONCLUSIONS.

This paper has presented a concise introduction to the OSI session layer and to the ECMA approach for a session protocol. The principles underlying the session layer functions, and their specialization in the ECMA approach have been explained.

The ECMA approach involves a description of the services provided by the session layer to its users, and a precise definition of the protocol by which these are achieved. This paper includes a list of the ECMA services, and introduces the protocol; for a more detailed description of the protocol the relevant ECMA documents are referenced.

One section of the paper is devoted to the topic of "subsetting", the technique employed to differentiate the session functions according to the particular user requirements. The principles of the ECMA approach are stated, and the consequences of the adopted solutions discussed. The approach is seen to offer interesting advantages for ensuring flexibility and implementation economy. It is also suitable for extensions, both ad-hoc and standardized. The services of other standardized protocols can also be reproduced by means of an appropriate subset: this is seen as an additional facility for enhancing compatibility between different environments.

Implementations of the ECMA session protocol in actual networking environments, currently under way, will give a final opportunity to evaluate the practical validity of the approach; it will permit the discovery of any shortcomings, and the identification of the required enhancements.

6. ACKNOWLEDGEMENTS.

ECMA-75 is the result of the joint effort of several companies involved in the activities of ECMA Technical Committee 23.

The authors are proud of having been part of the session protocol design group, where they found invaluable expertise and cooperative attitude.

REFERENCES

[1] Standard ECMA-72, "Transport protocol", Jan. 1981.

[2] ISO/TC 97/SC 16/ N 698, "Draft Connection-oriented Transport protocol specification", June 1981.

[3] Standard ECMA-75, "Session protocol", Dec. 1981.

[4] ISO/DP 7498, "Data processing- Open Systems Interconnection- Basic reference Model", Feb. 1982.

[5] K.C.E. Gee, "Introduction to Open Systems Interconnection", National Computing Centre publications, Oxford Rd., Manchester, U.K., 1980.

[6] H. Zimmermann, "OSI reference model: the ISO model of architecture for Open Systems Interconnection", IEEE Trans. on Comm., vol. 28, no. 4, Apr. 1980.

[7] ECMA/TC 23/81/152, "Tokens concept", Contribution to ISO/TC 97/SC 16/WG 6, Dec. 1981.

[8] NBS/ICST/HLNP-81-2, "Specification of the session protocol", draft report, NBS, March 1981.

Table 1 - Summary of subset characteristics.

Subset	Services									Tokens			
	Connect	Release	Disconnect, Abort	Data transfer	Expedited	Deliver, Cancel	Give, Please	Sync, End-DU	Resync	Data	Synchronize	End-DU	Terminate
A: basic	X	X (1)	X	X	X					no	no	no	no
B: basic interactive	X	X	X	X	X	X	X			opt.	no	no	yes
C: basic synchronized	X	X	X	X (2)			X	X	X	opt.	yes	yes	yes
D: basic TWA	X	X (1)	X	X			X			yes	no	no	no

(1): non-negotiable only, i.e. termination cannot be refused

(2): data units can be blocked into messages

Implementation and Applications of the SCIPION Packet Switching Node

**A Bache, D Cheminel, P Louazel,
P Put**
CCETT, France
P A Genel, R Rauche
TIT, France

Until mid 1980, the SCIPION project consisted in proving the feasability of high-throughput packet switching, through the building of a laboratory prototype. Since then, subsequent industrial development, first with TIT inc, then jointly wich THOMSON, is taking place with major emphasis being put on flexibility, in terms of performance, support of different procédures and applications, while retairing very high performance capabilities : up to 20,000 data packets/s per switching unit.

The major features of the system are : high throughput intelligent couplers, multi-level bus architecture, direct access of the packet switching unit to a time division bus for 64 Kbits/s circuit switching.

In smaller configurations, optimized switching software has been designed, which yields a throughput of 800 X25 data packets/s per 16 bit-CPU.
The system has already been chosen by several institutions to provide transit nodes in packet switching networks and front-end processors for high-performance data base or message switching centers. Its application to multi-service networks is being studied.

1. INTRODUCTION

The CCETT (Common Center for Studies in Telediffusion and Telecommunications) located in RENNES, FRANCE, has been involved in the development of packet switching networks since 1972. The SCIPION project, which started in 1978, consisted at first in proving the feasability of high-throughput packet switching nodes. To this end, a laboratory prototype was built and tested. Then it appeared that industrial development was needed, in order to satisfy from 1984 onwards a board range of applications of packet switching : transit nodes, frontend for high performance service providing computers, gateways for private networks.

Therefore, in August 1980, TIT was selected by the French PTT to develop an industrial prototype of the SCIPION Node. This project is now well under way and has led to considerable evolutions with respect to the laboratory prototype.

In the first part of this text, we will describe the hardware architecture of the system; in the second part, the principles of implementation of its operational sotfware, then the last part will describe several applications in development or under study.

2. HARDWARE ARCHITECTURE

2.1 Modularity and flexibility

In order to satisfy very high performance needs (throughput up to 100 Mbits/s full duplex) a modular architecture was chosen. Automous Packet Switching Modules (PSMs) can be interconnected by a very high speed bus. Each PSM can work on a stand alone basis. The maximum throughput of a PSM is 8 Mbits/s full duplex.

However most present needs are convered with a single PSM, some with simpler and cheaper versions of it. Therefore a flexible architecture was chosen for the industrial prototype. A minimal version can be implemented with 4 types of cards and 2 levels of buses.

Increase in performance is achieved in 3 ways to reach the maximum throughput of the PSM :

- using additional cards of the same types,
- using additional levels of buses,
- using new types of cards with dedicated hardware.

In all versions, the parts of the PSM are located in a single direct address space of 16 Mbytes.

2.2 Functions and main units of a module

The operational functions of the system are related to the relevant layers of protocol handled :

- level 1   : connecting analog links (V35 and V11 interfaces) and PCM links (HDB3/6DB)

- sub level 2.1 : HDLC envelope handling

- sub level 2.2 : link level procedure handling

- level 3   : network procedure handling

- level 4 to 7   : storing network service data units
  . before emission (switching node)
  . before transmission to the host (front end system).

In addition, supervision functions have to be performed, for instance

- dialogue with the network management centers,
- testing and measuring the performance of operational functions,
- initialisation, reconfiguration in case of failures.

The main units necessary to build the module are :

- analog and PCM couplers, handling level 1 and sublevel 2-1, storing and extracting data units in a data memory,

- procedure handling and supervision system handling levels 2-2 and 3 operational functions and the supervision functions,

- internal couplers for multi module switching nodes,

- host couplers for front end system.

2.3 Multi level bus based architecture

2.3.1 Time division bus

In several applications, packet mode channels are supported by 64 Kbits/s or nx 64 Kbits/s circuits using one or several time slots in a frame on a 2,048 Mbits/s PCM line (frame formats are defined in recs G732 and G734 of the CCITT). The other time slots in the frame can be used to support voice or data channels, in circuit mode. Therefore a 64 Kbits/s circuit switching capability is included in the system.

Circuit switching is achieved by means of an 8 MHz synchronous bus with a capacity of 64 Mbits/s. It can switch n x 64 Kbits/s channels

- between 2 PCM lines (for synchronous voice or data trafic)

- between a PCM line and a PCM HDLC couplers of the packet switching module.

Command of the bus, i.e. establishment and clearing of circuit connections, is done by a control unit situated in the packet switching module.

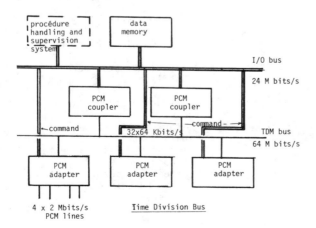

4 x 2 Mbits/s
PCM lines   Time Division Bus

2.3.2 Multi-master buses

A single standard of bus, the XBUS, is used in PSM to interconnect the boards. It is a 16 bits data, 24 bits address bus with asynchronous data exchange and multi-master capability. However, each bus as a specialized function according to the level on which it is used.

- 1 st level : internal to the analog coupler
- 2 nd level : I/O Bus, interconnecting couplers data memory and the Procedure Handling and Supervision System (PHSS)
- 3 rd level and above : System Bus, internal to the PHSS, interconnecting procedure handling operators and memory.

In minimal versions, I/O Bus and system bus can be the same "Common Bus".

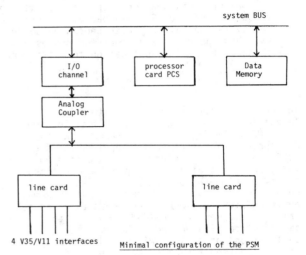

4 V35/V11 interfaces   Minimal configuration of the PSM

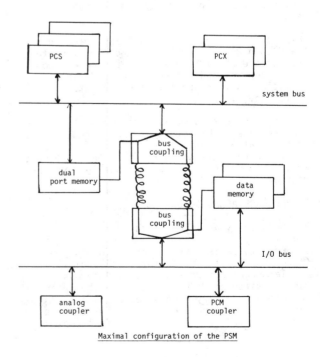

Maximal configuration of the PSM

Coupling between different levels of buses is achieved by 2 methods :

- using dual port memory, direct access through two or several levels of busses. In case of conflicting access request is aborted, resulting in additional wait cycles for the master.

Both functions are implemented by Bus Coupling cards working in pairs, connected by supple connectors.

2.4 Couplers

2.4.1 Analog Coupler

The elements of this coupler are :

- up to 16 lines Cards with 4 LSI multiprotocol chips, supporting 4 V 35 or V10/V11 interfaces

- an input-output channel system on two boards, one with local memory storing frames being received and sent on each line, one with a single high-speed DMA channel controlled by a 16 bit AMD 29116 microprocessor.

2.4.2 PCM Coupler

It is composed of two boards connected to the bus, that can support 32 X 64 K bit/s time slots. It is possible to allocate one or several time slots to HDLC channels under supervision control. Frames received and sent on these channels are stored in local memory.

2 M bits/s HDLC treatment is performed on the second board. The DMA channel and microprocessor are identical to those in the analog coupler.

2.5 Procedure Handling and Supervision System (PHSS)

The minimal version of the PHSS is implemented with a single type of processing card (PCS), with a 16 bit microporcessor, private REPROM/RAM memory and a hardware FIFO used to regulate activation requests received from the system bus.

- memory boards with 256 Kwords capacity, protected by a Hamming code, are used. They support two simultaneous ports of access and can thus be used either as programm extension or "letter-box" memories.

One of the ways to increase performance is to use another type of processing card (PCX) with an AMD 29116 bipolar microprocessor and the same hardware and system interface as the PCS cards, but support a limited volume of software corresponding to frequently invoked functions.

For even higher performance, combinatory operators could be integrated in the system with the same interface.

3. OPERATIONAL SOFTWARE ARCHITECTURE

The software is divided into 2 parts :

- operational software

- management software.

3.1 Definition of operational software

The main operational functions of the Procedure Handling and Supervision System (PHSS) are :

- handling the 2 levels of procedures (link control and network control)
- routing the data packets.

The different tasks activated for switching data packets and treating acknowledgment frames and packets are shown below :

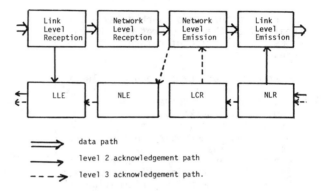

→→ data path

→ level 2 acknowledgement path

- - -> level 3 acknowledgement path.

The first approach is to design the architecture according to these functions.

It means :

- one task to handle the level 2 reception,
- one task to handle the level 3 reception,
- one task to handle the level 3 emission,
- one task to handle the level 2 emission.

These tasks are executed in this order by the same processor or by different processors.

Scheduling consist in :

- task activation,
- exchange between processors of informations necessary to execute the tasks (i.e. context).

3.2 Different ways of increasing software performance

The purpose of the software architecture is :

a) to minimize scheduling overhead,
b) to minimize procedure handling time.

How to minimize scheduling overhead ?

- decrease the number of calls to the scheduler
- decrease the execution delay of each call
  if the scheduling functions are executed by
  a single dedicated scheduler.

How to optimize procedure handling ?

- minimize the number of messages exchanged
  between processors per data packet switched,
  through hardware FIFOS or queues in shared
  memory,
- decrease the execution time.

We are going to study how to acheive this
purpose in a multi-processor environnement.

3.3 Reduction of the number of calls to the scheduler

Almost all treatments are initiated by external
events such as the complete input of a frame.

After the occurence of such an event, the
treatment of the procedures must be carried
on as possible without returning to the
scheduler.

The treatment of the procedure includes

- cheking of the received header,
- routing data packets,
- eventualy transmission on output link,
- generation of necessary service packets and
  service frames,
- eventual transmission of packets or frames
  in reverse direction when the received
  packet or frame brings information unblocking
  a link or a virtual circuit.

The return to the scheduler occurs when there
is no more task related to the initial event
that can be runned on the same processor
because of lack of resource.

The breakpoints are limited to the following
cases :

- a packet or a frame must be queues because
  of flow control,
- the next task must berunned on an other
  processor,
- the switching is completed.

So each processor has to handle all levels of
procedure.

3.4 Reduction of interprocessor traffic

The Procedure handling and Supervision System
is a multi-processor device. The charge has
to be distributed between the processors.

To avoid excess of messages between processors
one solution consists in choosing a processor
at the occurence of an event and in running
all the related treatment on this processor.

Every processor can have access to any of the
contexts which are kept in a shared memory.

So it is necessary to prevent conflictual
access to the contexts and preserve the
sequential order of packets on each link and
virtual circuit.

Unhappily the mechanisms providing these
controls introduce some overhead and furthermore processors may be maintained in a waiting state. Another drawback of this approach
is to limit the throughput of very high rate
trunk line to the throughput of a single
processor.

So another solutions consists in sharing the
links between the processors.

In this case the switching of a packet can
involve 2 processors.

We have 2 cases :

a) local communication : the 2 links L1 and
L2 which support the 2 connected logical
channels C1 and C2 belong to the same processor.

The different tasks are executed by the same
processor.

There is neither return to the scheduler nor
interprocessor exchange.

b) "distant" communication : L1 and L2 do not
belong to the same processor. Messages will
be exchanged between the 2 processors.

Meanwhile the number of messages may be
minimized by a careful choice of the point of
the processing where control is transfered
from the input to the output processor.

In both cases each processor may have access
in its private memory to all the software
necessary for handling all the levels of
procedures, both for reception and emission,
or at least for the normal cases. This standard
software is duplicated in all the private
memories.

This provides :

- better performance,
- flexibility to adapt computing power to
  link traffic,
- reliability by redundancy of type n+1. A
  processor may be isolated and dynamic
  reconfiguration is allowed.

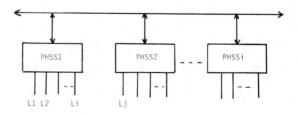

Sharing the links between the processors

3.5 Reduction of procedure handling time inside a processor

Programming is done according to a probability analysis of the procedures.

a) every task is waiting for the most probable events according to the procedure. The other events are put off and can be treated in background or handled by a different processor. Example : the sequence number of every information packet received is assumed to be correct. Any error at this level is a fatal one for the virtual circuit and may be handled in backround after stoping the treatment at foreground level.

In this case, the virtual circuit is inhibited for more packets until the error has been treated.

So we can divide operational software into 2 parts :

- critical software,
- exception software.

3.6 Conclusion

An X25 software has been implemented according to these principles on a 16 bits MOS microprocessor. Its performance is 800 packets switched per second for a single processor.

We are now extending the implemented to a multi processor environment and translating the critical programs for execution on AMD29116 we expect a swtiching power 2 or 3 times better.

4. APPLICATIONS

4.1 Transit Node for packet network

In the near future packet switching networks will evolve towards a two level architecture.

Level 1 : local nodes connecting subscribers with limited throughput but sophisticated operating software offering a wide range of services.

Level 2 : transit node whose main characteristics are :

- no subscribers supported,
- extremely high availability,
- simplified managment software,
- transmission procedures are a standard subset of those supported by first level nodes,
- high throughput is needed as studies have proved : up to 10000 data packets switched per second.

Transit nodes are interconnected to build a strongly meshed transit network which has its proper features. Adapted protocol can be implemented in order to increase throughput. Link speed between the nodes ranges from 256 Kbits/s to 2 Mbits/s.

4.2 Other applications

SCIPION may be used for various applications in the field of electronic-office development.

Software may be implemented to provide front-end processor for high performance "servers".

So SCIPION may be inserted at the heart of a conventional star network in order to increase the throughput of local links operated in base band mode. It will become possible to increase the load of these links by multiplexing high throughput new services with the previously existing remote access to computer facilities. Acting as a central switching node, SCIPION will sort easely the different flows and direct them to dedicated servers.

There is possibility to multiplex data and digitized speech in a PCM environment for which SCIPION will act as a multiservice PABX.

Alain BACHE was born in 1936. He his a graduate engineer of Ecole Nationale Supérieure de TOULOUSE (1961). In 1964, he joined the Centre National d'Etudes des Télécommunications (CNET) in PARIS. He joined the CCETT in RENNES, in 1973. Since then, he has been involved mainly in packet switching software. He has been in charge of the Packet Data Transmission department (TDP) since 1980.

Daniel CHEMINEL is graduate of the Institut National des Sciences Appliquées (1975). He joined the CCETT in 1976 where he was responsible for the study of a tool for the test of a packet switching node. Since 1978 he has been involved in the SCIPION project.

Pierre LOUAZEL received the degree of engineer from the Institut National des Sciences Appliquées in 1972. He joined the CCETT in 1974. Since then, he has been involved first in software for host-computer and front-end computer. Since 1980 he has been engaged in software development on an high throughput packet switching node.

Patrick PUT was born in 1954. A graduate of Ecole Polytechnique (73) and of Ecole Supérieure des Télécommunications, he joined the Centre Commun d'Etudes de Télédiffusion et Télé-communication (CCETT) in 1978. Since then, he has been involved in high-speed packet switching and, to a small extent, in the normalisation of ISDN data services and interfaces. He is now in charge of the SCIPION project.

A Multimicroprocessor Controlled Data Exchange – A Gateway to Public Data Networks

K Rahko, R Juvonen, T Hiltunen
Helsinki University of Technology,
Finland

Until now long haul data transmission has been based on the existing telecommunication networks. Because of the impropriety of these networks for data transmission, new data networks have been constructed. These are circuit or packet switched. Local networks differ quite a lot from public networks and each other being situated at a closed area. This causes difficulties to interface the local networks to other networks. The implementation of interfacing needs a gateway. The functions of the gateway may after all be realized in a local network data exchange. This is possible because even the switching of data in a data exchange can be performed by microprocessors providing thus the necessary intelligence for data transmission. Using new programming methods, like S3A, the implementation of signaling between the levels of layered protocols is easy.

1. INTRODUCTION

The distribution of processing capacity from a centralized data center to the network has recently been a common tendency. The primary reason is economy: the prices of mini- and microcomputers have fallen down. The distribution has also spread eg. data bases around the network. The access of the data bases should after all be possible for those who need them.

On the other hand, the development of public networks has made possible flexible communication over large areas. The public data networks are country wide or even the world wide. For example in the Nordic Countries the Nordic Public Data Network (NPDN) began to offer its connections for commercial use in 1981. The network is also connected eg to Euronet.

The access of public networks from local-area-networks (LANs) demands some kind of a gateway. The use of the gateway gives also savings in the line costs, because it can function as a concentrator or a multiplexer to the public network. If a data exchange is used as a gateway, the integration of all the network processor functions to the same equipment produces usually great economic savings.

2. CHARACTERISTICS OF PUBLIC AND LOCAL NETWORKS

2.1 Public networks

In the most European contries the national PTT's offer some kind of public data transmission services. Until now the services have been based on the existing telecommunication networks, as public telephone network, to which data devices are interfaced with modems, or telex network. /1/

But because of the rapid development of data processsing the PTT's have been forced to develop their data transmission services further. To reach the wished grade or service the improving of the existing network services hasn't been enough, so wholly new data networks have been constructed. In principle there are two types of networks: circuit switched (eg Nordic Public Data Network) and packet switched (eg Euronet).

The circuit switching was basically realized already in the telephone network, but the long connection building times and restrictions in the transmission speeds have lead to new constructions. The principle of packet switching provides more intelligence in the network, so it has been natural to realize it separated.

How ever, it seems that the phase of separate data networks will be only temporary, because digitalization of telephone network is leading to the integrated services digital network (ISDN). /2, 3/

It has always been characteristic for public networks - especially compared with private local networks - that they are tightly standardized at least on the lowest levels of data transmission systems. This is mostly done by CCITT with its recommendations in V- series defining the data transmission over the telephone network and the recommendations in X- series defining the transmission in public data networks. These recommendations are mainly compatible with the corresponding standards of ISO. /4/

To organize the data transmission protocols systematically and to make them modular and flexible it has been introduced so called layered models, of which the most known is the seven layered architecture of ISO.

The four lowest levels define the transport service, which provides the means of moving messages from point to point within the network. The highest three levels (known as user layers) allow the user to interface the network. The defining of all these layers is necessary for two systems to communicate with each others.

2.2 Local networks

Local networks differ quite a lot from public networks and from each other, because they have been designed to operate at a closed area independent from each other. So the network designers have had "free hands" to customize the network according to the special needs of the customer or according to the equipment being available. This causes special difficulties in trying to interface local networks to each other or to public networks.

On the other hand the independence from other networks and even from standars has given the possibility to realize in local networks some facilities which do not exist in public networks. These are eg multiaddress calls, versatile error handling, speed and code conversion, data manipulation, local editing and higher speeds (up to 50 Mbits/s) etc.

There are three basic network structures in local networks: star, ring and bus. The star configuration is the traditional one, which has been commonly used to connect low speed terminals through a data exchange or a PABX to ports of one or more computers. The time sharing networks of Finnish universities are eg of this type /5/. Ring and bus structures are more suitable for distributed systems where large amounts of data is to be transfered. Because of the simplicity the bus structure is also very suitable for office systems where the terminals (eg word processing systems) have enough intelligency to manage the communication protocols.

The variation in the local network protocols is large and mostly dependent on the equipment vendors. Compared with the ISO 7- layer model (OSI, open systems interconnection) some networks provide only two lowest levels, but there are some networks with all the 7 levels, too. Of cource the compability is not yet granted if there are some number of levels. Even in the public networks only two lowest levels are wholly and the third layer only partially implemented (the CCITT recommendations X.21 and X.25).

The public protocols are often too heavy for local networks, so some simplifications are quite common. This causes, how ever, that the direct interconnection of local and public networks is impossible and some kind of a gateway is needed.

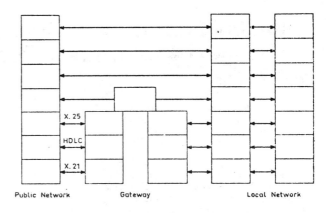

Fig. 1. Interfacing local and public networks

3. INTERFACING DATA NETWORKS USING LAYERED PROTOCOLS

When both local and public networks are using layered protocols and the protocols differ in the lowest levels, the networks can be interfaced using a gateway.

For example, the local network can be a common bus system with CSMA/CD- protocol and the public network is operating according the CCITT recommendations (X.21 and X.25).

The interfacing includes (figure 1) then
-receiving an out going packet through the MAU (media access unit) from the local network
-opening the framing
-converting addresses
-assembling a new packet
-framing according to CCITT X.25
-sending the packet to the public network (X.21)
and vice versa.

In practical implementations there are still a few difficulties: The most important is how to manage the control fields of different meanings and sizes. In HDLC frame, for example, there is no field for the address of the sending unit. When the packet sizes or transmission speeds are not equal, quite a large buffering capacity might be needed.

Additional problems may be caused by special facilities of local networks eg broadcasting.

4. DATA EXCHANGE AS A GATEWAY

The interfaces in local networks can be categorized in two main groups: first, interfaces between users and the local network, and second, interfaces between the local network and other, especially public networks. The problem is how to realize interworking of these interfaces so that a user can reach e.g. public services through a local network, using a traditional interactive terminal. A modular data exchange - or a modular node might be a better name - could be a solution.

As the equipment in the local networks have become more intelligent (intelligent terminals, personal computers, word processing systems, uP- dependent systems and general purpose mini- and microcomputers), the data exchanges have had to grow with them, too. Natural new facilities have been the full availability, which means that any two subscriber equipments can be connected together, and code, speed and even the protocol conversions.

Being in this phase it is only a little step to develop a data exchange into a local network node, which can connect the conventional low speed equipment to a modern high speed local network. This development is especially encouraged by the news that local network standards are getting in some kind of solutions in IEEE 802 Project, which means that the interfacing is becoming easier and cheaper. The high speed network can then interconnect several data exchanges (fig. 2), distributing the exchanges near to users and near to distributed resources.

On the other hand the same basic solutions can be used in interfacing a data exchange to public networks. Because the public networks are already quite well standardised and there are not so many different alternatives as in local networks will probably be, the realisation is even more strait forward.

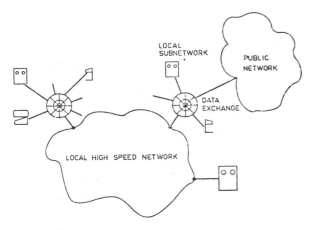

Fig. 2. Data exchange as a gateway to the public network NPDN

5. THE IMPLEMENTED DATA EXCHANGE

The block diagram of the implemented data exchange is in figure 3. The control and io-modules are communicating through an asynchronous bus /8/. The structure and the facilities of the data exchange are described in /6/. The data exchange can be used as a gateway between LAN and public networks, because:

-The data switching is handled by microprocessors. The necessary intelligence in data transmission is thus available.
-The structure is highly modular and flexible.
-The physical interfaces are the units of their own. The interfaces to the dedicated networks are thus easy to implement according to the needs.

To be able to functions as a gateway the data exchange must be able to respond to all the 3 lowest levels of the OSA. The physical level contains the necessary hardware in the subscriber interface unit to send and receive the line signal to and from the transmission media what ever it is. Some low level software is of course needed to control the hardware.

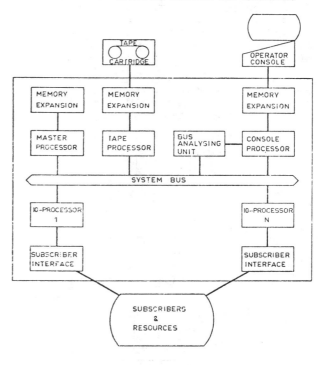

Fig. 3. The block diagram of the data exchange

The level 2 of OSA controls the transmission link. The common protocols used are HDLC and ISO 1745. The handling of the protocols is performed by a process in a slave- processor.

The third level of OSA eg assembles the data packets for transport level and finds a suitable route for data through the network. The former is clearly a task of a slave processor, the latter is rather a task of the master.

The data transmission levels according to the ISO OSA have to communicate a lot with each others. The minimum amount of information transferred between the layers is the transmitted data. In addition some kind of control informations is needed.

The lack of a high level, asynchronous signalling facility in the existing programming methods was one of the most important reasons why a new kind of a programming method, S3A, Structured Software Signalling Architecture, was invented. S3A contains two support languages, a programming language S3L and a graphic description language S3G. S3A and some common programming tools like SDL, CHILL and ADA are compared in /7/.

The way of implementation of OSA levels using S3L is described in figure 4. The signals and messages between processes (= tasks) flow through the signal channels. Each signal is characterized by its identity, format and priority. The identity of the signal is the name of the signal channel. The signal format describes the amount and layout of the information. The signal priority defines the importance of the signal and is used to resolve the order of actions if more than one signal arrives at a process in the same time.

The signalling between tasks in S3A can be expressed in a natural, ie high level and asynchronous, way. The signalling causes thus no noise to the software.

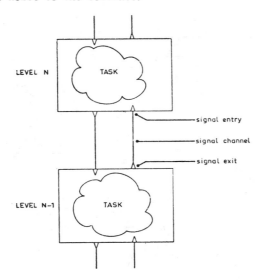

Fig. 4. OSA implemented with S3L

6. CONCLUSIONS

It is economic and efficient to use a data exchange also as a gateway from LAN to public networks. The data exchange can thus function as some kind of a network processor giving to the LAN all the services concerning switching and concentration.

The integration of even the gateway function to the data exchange is made possible by the development in the microelectronics. The speeds of microprocessors are now so high

that even the switching of data can be handled economically by them. A multiprocessor implementation is after all needed.

As data switching is performed by microprocessors, a great deal of intelligence is available in data transmission. The implementation is also flexible, as new fuctions can be implemented mostly just by software.

New enhanced programming methods have been developed to permit the programming of real time functions without noise. The software without noise is easy to develop and maintain.

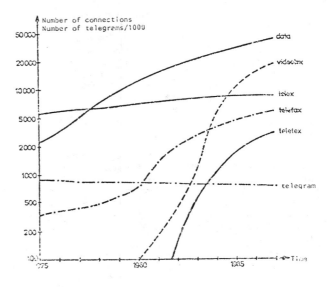

Fig. 5. Forecast of the development of new teleservices in Finland

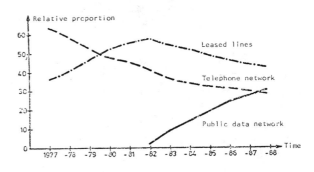

Fig. 6. Portions of different networks in data transmission

7. THE FUTURE

The new teleservices, e.g. videotex and teletex, are growing rapidly with the traditional data communications. Fig. 5 shows a forecast of the growth of different services in Finland. In the public data transmission the NPDN is replacing the telephone network, fig. 6. /9/

In the field of local networks it seems that there can't be any unique solution for network architecture or network standard, because different solutions will be most suitable for different applications. The CSMA/CD bus and token ring have both wide support, but the token ring principle has certain advantages over the CSMA/CD mostly because of its deterministic properties. /10/

In the future the ISDN will integrate especially public services but it will have interfaces to local networks, too, having an important effect to their development. One such effect is the integration of digital voice transmission in packet mode into local networks (IDVD, integrated digital voice data systems). Thus, local networks, other high speed networks (e.g. 5 MHz video) and the ISDN will develop side by side.

The ideas presented in this paper will be applied in the local data network project of Finnish universities. First one of the implemented data exchanges, described in chapter 5, has been installed in the local network of Turku university campus. The interconnection between data exchanges will be implemented with statistically multiplexed lines. In the second phase, more enhanced interconnection methods will be studied in the experimental network of Helsinki University of Technology. The token ring seems to be one of the most considerable alternatives, today.

REFERENCES:

0. Rahko K.: Comparison of different connecting networks – the grid connecting network and its control by microprocessor. ICC'75 conference, San Francisco, 1975.

1. Cardarelli C.: General Considerations on the Development of European Public Data Networks, Telecom '79

2. The Public data network. A brochure produced by the Nordic telecommunications administrations, 1976

3. Kelly P.: The EURONET Telecommunications and Informations Network. The Radio and Electronic Engineer, vol 49, no 11, November 1979

4. CCITT, CEPT, IEEE, ISO and PTT standards.

5. Juvonen R., Rahko K.: Local Computer Networks in Finnish Universities. Proceedings of HICCS, Hawaii, January 1981

6. Rahko K., Hiltunen T.: A Data Exchange for Turku Campus Area, Proceedings of IDATE, Montpellier, October 1981

7. Rahko K., Hemdal G.: Discussion on Development of Integrated Documentation Languages for International SPC-
systems. Report 4/81, Helsinki University of Technology, Telecommunication Switching laboratory, Finland 1981.

8. Leppänen R., Rahko K., Terada H., Tossavainen M.: Software of distributed microprocessor control scheme in an experimental switching system, Report 3/78, Helsinki University of Technology, Telecommunication Switching Laboratory, Finland 1978.

9. Report of the committee for legislation of telecommunications. Ministry of Communications. Helsinki, Finland 1982.

10. Proceedings of the IFIP TC 6 International In-Depth Symposium on Local Computer Networks. Florence, Italy 1982.

ANNEX: THE NORDIC PUBLIC DATA NETWORK

The Nordic Public Data Network, NPDN, began to offer its services for commercial use in November 1981. The network lies in Denmark, Finland, Norway and Sweden. The network is also called DATEX- network and its services DATEX- services.

At first the NPDN offers only circuit switched transmission services. These are implemented using DCE's (Data Circuit-terminating equipments), DMX's (Data Multiplexors), RMX's (Remote Data Multiplexors), CMX's (Customer Multiplexors), DCC's (Data Circuit Concentrators), DSE's (Data Switching Exchanges) and SSC's (Special Service Centers) (figure). The transmission speeds of subscribers are up to 9600 bit/s, in the network the transmission rate is 64 kbit/s.

The basic services of the network are:

- Subscribers are connected to X.21 or X.21 bis (V.24) interfaces.

- Data transmission in the network is symmetric and full duplex.

- Network is fully transparent.

- The network gives the timing signals for synchronous subscribers

- Transmission speeds for synchronous subscribers are 600, 2400, 4800 and 9600 bit/s.

- Transmission speeds for asynchronous subscribers are 50- 2400 bit/s. The asynchronous data is transmitted synchronously in the network.

- Every subscriber has a six digit long subscriber number of its own.

- The connection establishing time is less than 100 ms in 90 per cent of cases.

- The disconnection time is less than 50 ms in

90 per cent of cases.

The auxiliary services offered by the network are:

- direct call
- selective direct call
- abbreviated address calling
- closed user group
- outgoing calls barred
- outgoing international calls barred
- incoming calls barred
- incoming international calls barred
- multiple lines at the same address
- connect when free
- redirection of calls
- calling line identification
- called line identification
- charge transfer
- charge advice
- leased circuit

The telecommunication administrations of the Nordic Countries will follow the development within the telecommunication area, and new services of NPDN will be implemented if needed. One possible new service could be the packet switching based on CCITT X.25 recommendation. This would use the existing X.21- protocol as a physical interface.

BIOGRAPHIES

Kauko J. Rahko is professor in telecommunication switching at Helsinki University of Technology. He holds Dr Tech degree since 1967. Earlier his position was Head of the Research Institute of Helsinki Telephone Company. Now he is also Head of Electrical Engineering Department of Helsinki University of Technology. He has about 200 publications in various fields of telecommunication engineering.

Reijo O. Juvonen received M.Sc degree in 1979 from Helsinki University of Technology and he is currently a project engineer in a university data network project. His special interest areas include local data networks and their switching systems.

Tarmo T. Hiltunen is a project researcher in a university data network project. He is specialised on the software of multiprocessor controlled data switching systems.

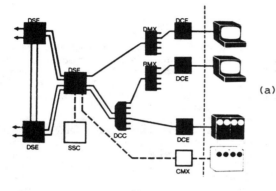

(a)

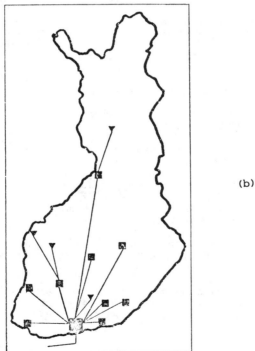

(b)

Figure. The Nordic Public Data Network:
(a) Block diagram and (b) geographical location of network components in Finland.

A Multi-Microprocessor Design for use in a Packet Switched Network

F M Restorick
Plessey Office Systems, UK
B H Pardoe
University of Salford, UK

This paper describes a multi-processor architecture which is particularly suited to act as a node processor in a packet switching environment. The basic concept is that each high speed link entering the node has its own dedicated module, containing its own packet memory, CPU, and operating software. There are two global busses which act as an interconnect between the separate modules. These are the System Bus, and an Inter CPU Bus. Due to the 'loose' coupling between each processor module, the possibility of failure of the whole node is reduced. The basic kernal of the distributed operating system needed to run this multi-processor as a packet switching node is discussed. The recovery mechanisms with regard to a link module failure is also dealt with.

1. INTRODUCTION

Since the advent of packet switching technology it has become apparent that difficulty is experienced in providing enough processing power when more than, say, three high speed links are attached to one node. During the experimental stages of packet switching, off-the-shelf mini-computers were used as the node processors, but as the technology grew, specially designed multi-processor architectures evolved, such as the Pluribus[1]. Plessey have introduced their TP4000 range of multiprocessors which were specifically designed to operate as node processor, and Packet Assembler-Disassemblers (PAD's)[2].

With the view that the future demands of a node processor will be higher link speeds and more links, this paper describes a node multi-processor architecture which will hopefully solve some of the problems.

2. BOTTLENECKS

The main bottleneck in any processor is usually the bus interface, either processor-memory or memory-I/O channel transfers have to compete to access this bus. Some solutions to reduce this contention problem would be to:

1) Use more than one bus.

2) To have a high speed bus, with input and output buffers.

3) To reduce the traffic level going across the bus.

In 3), the action of reducing traffic across the bus may seem impossible, but if a careful study is made of the bus traffic requirements of a node processor, some important criteria can be made.

Each packet entering a node on one link either leaves by another link, or is absorbed by the node. So at first it is seen that each byte of a packet must traverse across the central bus twice. However, if each packet is stored in memory attached to the link, then it need only transfer across the central bus once,

to be transmitted by the outgoing link element.

If each link has its own processor and local executable program, isolated from the packet memory, then the processor could retrieve instructions and process local variables in its own private RAM without interruption from the packet traffic. It would, of course, be necessary to access the header field of packets in memory, but this would not cause a contention problem, as the ratio of packet access instructions to ordinary local RAM access would be very small.

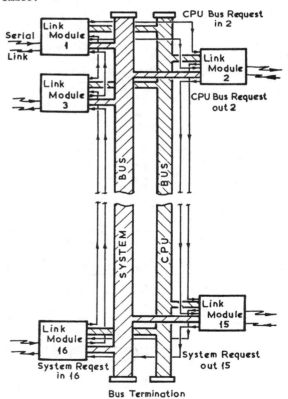

Fig. 1 The NODE Processor.

3. THE NODE PROCESSOR ARCHITECTURE

With the above in mind, a node processor architecture has been developed that would permit
up to 16 high speed links (64kbaud) to be fed
into, and to come out of it.

First we discuss the hardware details of this
architecture and secondly, the basic skeleton
software needed to drive it.

4. THE HARDWARE

With reference to Fig. 1 it is seen that each
high speed link has its own module and these
modules are joined together via two busses.
Namely a System Bus and a CPU Bus. These busses have a totally different operating mode,
owing to the difference in their function as
busses.

5. THE SYSTEM BUS

This bus operates in a time shared round-robin
mode where each module would request use of its
time slot if it was in the process of sending
a packet.

The system bus cycle time is much faster than
the time taken for a DMA memory fetch in a
module, this is in order that the maximum
throughput across the bus can be achieved, and
yet the packet memory in each module need not
have fast access times.

Reference to Fig.2 shows the protocol of the
bus control lines in a typical transfer situation. At (A) we have module 1 using its timeslot to transfer its packet byte across the
bus to link module 2. When this is complete,
then we enter the next time period, and as link
module 2 is not currently sending any packets
at the present time, then link module 3 gets
the slot to send a byte across to link 1 (B).

This continues around until link module 16 is
reached whereupon link module 1 gets another
time slot. If module 1 was the only module
actively sending a packet then it would have the
soul use of the system bus, and provided the
round-robin mechanism was fast enough to go all
the way round the loop in one clock cycle, then
it would use consecutive time slots, assuming
the module's DMA channel can provide the bytes
fast enough!

There is a problem that arises when a particular
module is attempting to send a packet to a module that is already receiving a packet from
another module. The ACK control line would then
inform the sending module that is currently
receiving a packet from another module and to
try again at the next allocated time-slot with
the same information byte (C). Once the other
packet has been received the receiving module
would acknowledge the first module that attempted to send it information in the round-robin
loop.

Of course, the next question to be asked is
'How does the receiving module detect that a
transfer is complete?'. Well, this signal is
transferred by keeping the WRITE control line
active for a further clock cycle, this then
informs the receiving end that this particular
transfer is complete and enables it to acknowledge the next request (D).

It may seem at first sight that a contention
problem exists when a great many links are all
trying to transfer packets to one particular
link module. If this is the case then, it is
more likely that the link would not be able to
send them out of the serial line fast enough
and produce a flow control message which it
would send globally to all other link modules
via the CPU bus.

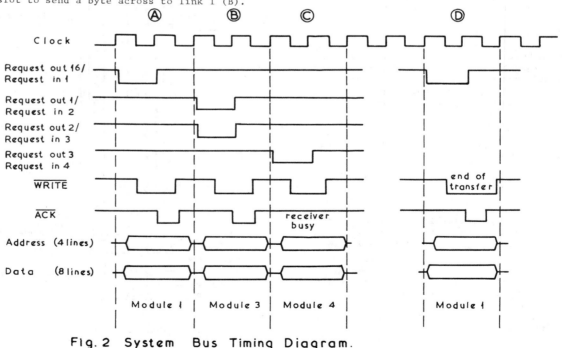

Fig. 2 System Bus Timing Diagram.

6. THE CPU BUS

This 8 bit bus again operates on a round-robin basis, but this time, once a request is granted, then the link module has full use of it until it has completed the transfer. Naturally, the use of the CPU bus by any particular module is low and the length of the messages sent across in one transfer would have to be limited to a set maximum.

Fig. 3 shows the protocol used on this bus. Once a request has been granted then the message is transmitted onto the bus a byte at a time. The first byte acts as a destination address and either addresses a particular link module or addresses all the link modules at once, with a global address. This special address informs all the modules that they should receive the message that follows.

The next byte is the address of the sending module which is then followed by the message itself.

Enough about the busses, lets now look more closely at a link module.

7. THE LINK MODULE

Fig. 4 gives a diagram of the basic architecture of a typical link module. As can be seen, the CPU has its own private ROM and RAM and a Bus Interface to the CPU bus. The CPU would, for most of the time, access the ROM and local RAM during program execution, where it does not compete with any other device for its resources. However, it is also possible for it to access either the packet memory or the DMA devices via the isolation buffer. This is to enable the CPU to act on DMA completion interrupts or to initialize the DMA devices. It also enables access to the packet headers and queue structures within the packet RAM.

The HDLC intelligent controller is already in existence in LSI form under the code name WD2511 by Western Digital[3]. This device carries out all the functions of the level 2 protocol as defined in CCITT recommendation X25[4].

The System Bus DMA interface is rather specialised however, since it contains a FIFO buffer for both outgoing data and incoming data, this enables the system bus to be utilised to its full bandwidth.

8. SOFTWARE ASPECTS

Before we go deeply into the ins and outs of operating systems, let us first view the processes involved in a node processor. The basic process involves reading an input packet from the link, reading the header information for the destination address of that particular packet, from which the required output link is determined. The process then needs to place this packet onto the output link queue. On top of the basic process are the functions of allocation and relinquishing packet memory buffers, virtual channel set up processing and flow control.

This paper does not try to suggest the best type of operating system to fit into this environment, as the purpose of the original research programme was to assess the throughput/delay characteristics of packets travelling through this node. However, to make an assessment of the software involved in the running of this node processor, let us first look at the path of a packet through this node.

Fig. 5 shows the internal queue network of a packet which enters the node on one link and exits the node from another link. As can be seen, there are 2 main processes involved when a packet is received from the link and transferred to the system bus, there operation is described as follows:-

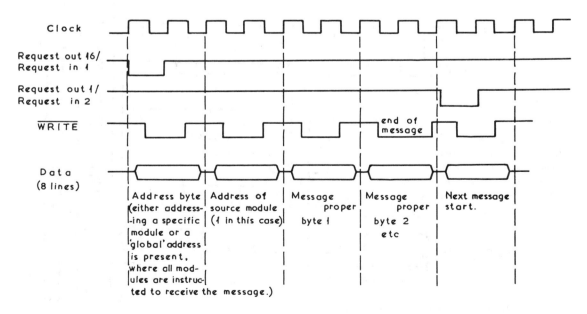

Fig. 3 CPU Bus Timing Diagram.

PACKET INPUT PROCESS - this process would sleep on the receiver interrupt until a packet is received from the link. The process then looks at the header (level 3 X25) information to determine the type of packet, most packets are merely traversed through the node, so if this were a data packet and the virtual channel was already set up, then this process would pass the packet to the system bus output queue, which would hand over the responsibility of sending the packet across the system bus to the intelligent DMA controllers. The Packet Input Process would then request another buffer from the buffer pool and place it into the receiver buffer space and wait for the next frame.

SYSTEM PACKET ACKNOWLEDGE PROCESS - this process would normally be permanently asleep, until triggered by the System Bus Driver, when it would start a timed wait on the CPU Bus input queue. If the receiving module is alive and well, then the packet sent to it would be acknowledged via the CPU Bus before the time-out period of this process. However, if a timeout did occur, then a System Bus timeout recovery mechanism would come into operation. This might involve attempting to (re)send the packet at the head of the acknowledge queue, or if the maximum number of timeouts have occured, then it can be assumed that the receiving module is inoperable, and that a message would be 'broadcast' by the sending module to all other modules that it suspects the receiving module in question. Normally though, an acknowledgement is received within the allotted time, and this process would then relinquish the packet buffer to the buffer pool.

At the output module, we have two main processes also, these are:-

SYSTEM BUS RECEIVER PROCESS - this process would wait forever, until a packet is sent to it via the system bus. When this occurs, then the first task is to build an acknowledgement message, addressed specifically to the sending module, and pass this message to the CPU Bus output driver. The packet header information would then be read and, if necessary, the virtual channel variables within that module would be updated. In most cases however, the packet would contain just information and so the process would send the packet to the link output driver which would arrange for it to be sent out onto the link, and also trigger the link acknowledge timer. The process then obtains another buffer from the pool and places it into the system bus input queue.

LINK ACKNOWLEDGE PROCESS - this process is normally waiting until a packet is sent out to the link, when it is triggered into life and does a timed wait for the acknowledgement of the packet being sent, when the acknowledgement is received within the time limit, then the packet buffer is returned to the buffer pool.

It can be seen then, that each process module requires a multi-tasking operating system, or nucleus, in order that all the processes can be made to run asynchronously. All the software would be contained in ROM, although, there is the possibility of down line loading. Since the software for each link module is almost identical, then the receiving link module would 'broadcast' the whole system onto the CPU bus once it had received and verified its own copy.

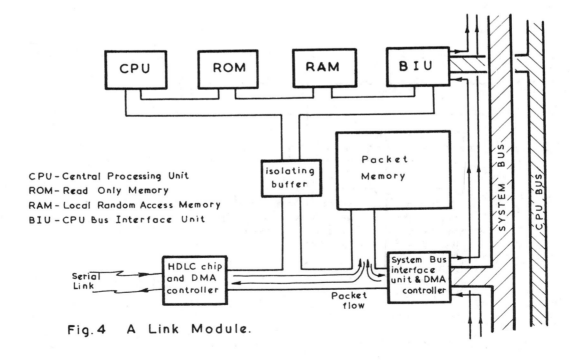

Fig. 4   A Link Module.

CPU - Central Processing Unit
ROM - Read Only Memory
RAM - Local Random Access Memory
BIU - CPU Bus Interface Unit

9. RELIABILITY ASPECTS

Due to the nature of the coupling of each individual module and the fact that we are not reliant on a central, or master operating system, then it is obvious that the system has a high reliability factor. The most vulnerable parts of the node are the busses, since if either of these fail, then the whole node fails. So these need to be designed and built with high reliability in mind.

However, if a link module should fail, then the other module would detect this fact, either by a broadcast message from a module that has timed-out while trying to send a packet to the failed module, as mentioned earlier in this paper, or by a watchdog mechanism described as follows:-

Each link module, at short intervals would 'broadcast' to the CPU Bus that it was still functioning correctly. The other modules would detect this, and keep a table of the modules that are known to be 'active'. However, should a module fail, then all the other modules would detect this by the fact that the failed module did not broadcast its 'OK' message within the allotted time interval. The action by the other modules would be to first prompt the failed module to see if it gives a response. If a response is received, then we assume that the failed module has recovered, so no further action is taken. But if there is no response, and a redundant link module is available and in situ, then a message is addressed to it, indicating that it should take over the role of the failed module and switch it out of the system.

Due to the nature of the architecture, the mean-time-between-failure (MTBF) of the system would be heavily dependent on the MTBF figure

for the busses and interface components. This assumes that any failures occurring within a link module can be detected and rectified by switching in a stand-by link module to replace the failed one.

10. NODE MAINTENANCE

Since a node processor has to be continually 'online' then it is worth mentioning the problem of maintaining this particular multi-processor.

As the architecture is of a modular structure, we can diagnose and test one particular group of links within the system while the other link modules are carrying traffic. It is possible for a link module to be instructed to broadcast via the inter CPU bus that it is going offline, which results in the other modules losing all knowledge of that particular module. This could be done with several modules if desired.

When a link module is ready to go into service again, it would be instructed to broadcast this fact via the CPU bus. The table of active modules within each module would then be updated and the newly activated module would be brought into service at the earliest opportunity.

11. PERFORMANCE MEASUREMENT

Figure 6 shows the throughput characteristic of a 10 link node processor system, using the multiprocessor architecture as defined in this paper, and, for comparison, using a conventional single processor approach. The characteristic was achieved by simulation.

The veritcal axis shows the reciprocal of the delay in order that a straight line approximation

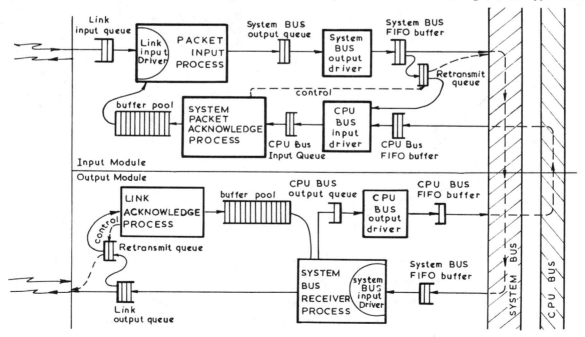

Fig. 5 Diagram showing path of an information packet through node.

of the simulated data can be plotted. It also allows us to find the point at which overload occurs more easily (infinite delay).

The per packet delay for an equivalent single processor system is seen to be half that of the multiprocessor system (namely 0.3 ms (1/3300) against 0.6 ms (1/1500) for low traffic. However, as the traffic level rises, the per packet delay in the single processor rises rapidly, reaching an overload condition at 205 packets per second per link.

With the multiprocessor approach this delay remains relatively constant until traffic levels about 300 packets per second per link are reached.

12. CONCLUSIONS

The mean packet delay of a packet traversing this node would be higher than an equivalent mini-computer configuration at low traffic levels, since the packets have to undergo a store-transfer-store cycle before they are ready to be output onto the outgoing link. However, as the traffic level rises it is easy to see that this particular architecture would result in a lower mean packet delay, since the single processor mini-computer would rapidly run out of available processing power as all the link processes compete for the one processor.

In addition, to increase the throughput of this multi-processor design further, it would be quite feasible to have more than one System Bus, as this is the major contributor to the delay experienced by a packet traversing the node.

13. ACKNOWLEDGEMENTS

This research was funded by the Science Research Council.

REFERENCES

(1) F.E. Heart et al, A new mini-computer/ multiprocessor for the ARPA network. AFIPS Conference Proceedings Vol. 42 1973 p.529-37.

(2) TP4000/2200 Hardware Description - Plessey Controls Ltd, Poole, Dorset.

(3) WD2511 short form data sheet - Western Digital Corporation.

(4) CCITT Recommendation X25 - Yellow Book, Vol. VIII.2.

B H Pardoe received his BSc from Hull University in 1964. This was followed by 6 years in industry equally split between the UK, USA and Australia. He returned to Essex University to receive an MSc (1972) and PhD (1975). He is currently a Lecturer in the Department of Electronic and Electrical Engineering at Salford University and the author of several papers on data transmission and data communication.

M Restorick obtained his BSc in Electrical Engineering from North Staffordshire Polytechnic in 1977. After a one year period in industry, he moved to Manchester in October 1978 to commence postgraduate studies at Salford University. He is currently writing his PhD dissertation on his work carried out at Salford, this consists of a three year simulation study of a multi-microprocessor node computer. Since October 1981 he has held the post of Senior Software Engineer at Plessey Office Systems at Nottingham. This involves the development of systems software for a multi-processor office system under development.

Fig.6 Comparison of throughput characteristic of multiprocessor architecture with conventional single processor approach for a 10 link node.

High Capacity Packet Switching System by means of Multi-microprocessors

T Saito, H Inose, M Wada,
H Shibagaki
University of Tokyo, Japan

Versatility of packet switching principle gave rise to a new possibility to realize a integrated communication service for various information including data, voice and image. However, since the complexity of packet switching made it difficult to realize a high capacity switch, the throughput of the switch ever realized is as small as 0.5 Mbit/sec, in contrast to usual PCM switch having the throughput of 100 Mbit/sec. To use as the switch for more general information, the capacity of a packet switching system should be expanded. This paper proposes a principle of a packet switching system based on multi-micro processor. A number of processors are interconnected through a common memory. Each of processors has its own local memory and to facilitate interprocessor communication, address space of the common memory is designed to be continueing from each local memory. An experimental packet switch with skeltonized scale has been constructed and the results of evaluation for the experimental system indicate the realizability of high capacity packet switch based on the principle.

1. INTRODUCTION

Variety of ideas has been presented to realize combined voice and data communication servece in future. Proposal of integrated service digital network is based on circuit switched system. Combined voice and data communication systems based on packet switching principle has also been proposed.

Comparing the combined voice and data service based on these two principles, the packet switched system generally provides more versatile services.

In conventional data packet switching system for data, however, the highest data speed is 48 kb/sec and total amount of data traffic is much lower than that of telephone traffic. Therefore, traffic handling capacity of a conventional data packet system is too low to handle combined voice and data traffic. To realize a combined voice and data packet switching system therefore a new switching concept is needed to enhance the traffic handling capacity of packet switching systems.

Although packet switching systems are characterized by the use of store and forward concept, the same concept has been basically employed by PCM switching systems in their time slot interchanges. The major differences of the latter to the former are such that the store and forward interval is restricted within the Niquist interval and that the amount of information to be stored is much less. Another major difference to be pointed out exists in the control mechanism of the switching system. In the PCM switching system, the control information to determine the destination of buffered information is stored in the switching system prior to the connection set up. This may be called "preset up control". On the other hand in the packet switching system, the destination of the packet is determined by the information carried in the header of the packet itself. This control mechanism may be called "header driven control".

In preset up control system, processing for switching is performed by a central control which is used only at set up and clear down phase a communication. In the remainder of the communication period, information can be handled by the speech path which is operated independent from the central control. This is the reason why high capacity can be achieved by preset up controlled system.

In packet switching systems also, if control subsystems and information path are able to be separated by providing a number of speech path control circuits, a high-capacity packet switching system may be realized.

The packet switching system described in this paper is essentially X.25 compatible. Types of packets are classified into two categories one is to be handled by the main processor and the other is handled by input and output processors. The packets of the former type includes the packets involved in the setup and release of virtual circuits. Other packets like data packet receive ready packet etc. are handled by input and output processors without intervention of the main processors.

2. PRINCIPLE FOR CAPACITY ENHANCEMENT

Figure 1 shows the outline of the high-capacity packet switching system. An input output (IO) processor module are provided for each of lines which are assumed to be PCM repeatered lines having the transmission rate of 1.544 MHz. The total number of IO processors depends on the percentage of packet to be handled by the main processor module. In typical case, the expected number of possible IO processors is about 50. The main processor module is used as the central control of the system.

An IO processor module is composed of a microprocessor, a local memory and a communication control LSI which is used for HDLC processing.

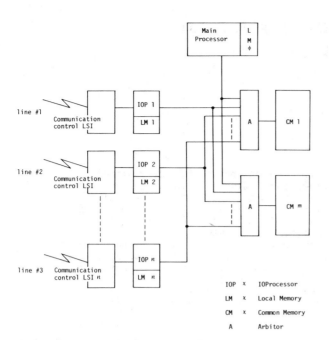

Fig. 1   Overall configuration of high-capacity
packet switching system

Table - 1   Assignment of function to each of module

Information path		Control path
IO processor module		Main processor module
Communication control LSI	Processor	
HDLC procedure	HDLC procedure	Virtual circuit handling procedure
* Flag detection	* Generate address and command	* Analysis of call request
* Insertion and deletion of "0"	* Check command part	* Analysis of call termination
* Check and compute FCS	* Transmission of ACK and NAK	* Establish and release of virtual circuit
* Detection of underrun	* Monitoring of timers	* Establish routing table
* Compute number of byte	Data packet handling procedure	
	* Determine packet types	
	* Flow control	
	* Check packet sequence	

The main processor module is composed of a
micro-processor and a local memory. The processors share common memory modules each of
which has a number of ports. The access to
the common memory is controlled by an arbiter
which schedules the access on first-come-first-
served basis. A local memory is used to store
programs, parameter tables as well as temporary
data for each of the processor. The common
memory is used for packet buffering and inter-
processor communication.

Any processor can access to all the address
space of the common memory to read the information. A processor, however, is permitted to
write only in the assigned address space for
the processor. For this purpose the address
space of the common memory is divided into
portions each of which is assigned to an IO
processors for writing. By this mechanism,
the control processor for the common memory and
the overhead by the control processor is eliminated. Since the address space of the common
memory is divided, the efficiency of the common
memory usage is degraded, however, in view of
the drastic cost reduction of the LSI memory,
the problem is not essential. The assignment
of switching functions to the IO processors and
the main processors is summerized in Table 1.
Since the IO processors are provided for each
of lines, functions of data path are assigned
to IO processors. The functions which needs
the status information of the whole switching
system or other lines are assigned to the main
processor. The computation of the frame check
sequence and the framing pattern processing for
the HDLC procedure is to be performed by the
communication control LSI.

The processing procedure for a packet is as
follows. The packet received by a communication control LSI is transferred to an input
buffer located in a common memory. During the

reception, the frame check sequence is verified
by the communication control LSI. If an error
is found, the IO processor discards the information received at the common memory and start
the usual recovery procedure. If the HDLC
frame is found to be correct, the address and
the command of the HDLC frame are checked.
After this procedure, the packet type is identified. If the packet is a data packet, the
outgoing route is determined by the link table
established at the call establishment phase
and the output request is fed to the IO processor which handled the line of the outgoing
route. When the IO processor of the outgoing
route finds the request, the processor
generates the HDLC frame which includes the
packet stored in the common memory and transmits
the frame through the communication control LSI.
At the transmission phase, the content of the
packet is directly read out from the address
space at which the IO processor of the input
side has written the packet.

On the other hand, if the packet is related to
setup or release of a virtual circuit, the IO
processor informs the arrival of the packet to
the main processor to establish the link table.

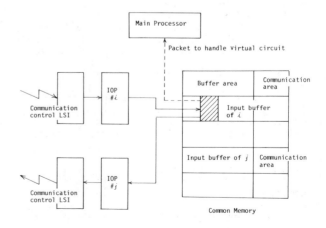

Fig. 2   Flow of packet from IOP #i to IOP #j

The outline of the flow of packet handling is summerized in Fig. 2.

3. ESTIMATION OF TRAFFIC HANDLING CAPABILITY

The traffic handling capacity of the system is expected to be limitted by the following factors.
1. processing capability of an IO prossor.
2. processing capability of the main processor.
3. access contention of the common memories.

The average processing step for a packet is reported to be about 700 steps in typical packet switching system. Viewing from the results, in the present system using micro-processors, required processing step needed for a packet is less than 1000 steps in average. To handle 1.5 Mbit/sec PCM line, if average packet size is 1000 bits, an IO processor module having the processing capability of 1.5 M step/sec is needed.

The traffic applied to the main processor depends on mixture ratio of packet which require attention by the main processor. If the majority of traffic is to carry voice or facsimile, the mixture ratio of packet to be handled by the main processor is small enough. However, if the traffic of interactive data or traffic for X.25-type fast select packets is dominant, the total throughput of the system will be limited by the throughput of the main processor.

As has been described previously, the common memories are accessed on first-come-first-served basis. The access mechanism can be evaluated by
1. average waiting time before served by the memory.
2. probability of reception overrun and transmission underrun.

The reception overrun occurrs in case that, before completion of writing of a data byte, next data byte arrives to be stored. If this case happened, since the access mechanism is still involved in the processing of prior byte, the next byte may be lost. The transmission overrun occurs in case that readout of byte from the memory is delayed to cause inter-ruption of transmission because of the con-gestion of the memory. If the average waiting time is too long, processing capability of the processors are degraded.

The memory access mechanism can be evaluated using the simplified model as is shown in Fig. 3. In this model, processors are repre-sented by IO processors. Each of n IO pro-cessors requests access to the common memory independently. Each of processors waits until the request is permitted.

Assuming the Poisson arrival of request and the negative exponential distribution of the memory service time, the model of the waiting system can be expressed by M/M/1/n.

The average service time corresponds to the memory access time. Since the memory access time is constant, the evaluation by M/M/1/n model will give safety side results. In this evaluation, the memory access time is assumed to be 100 nsec which is not too difficult to attain in near future.

Access to the common memory is requested for packet reception and transmission as well as

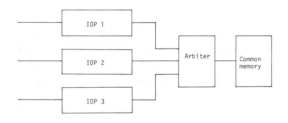

Fig. 3   Model for the analysis of memory congestion

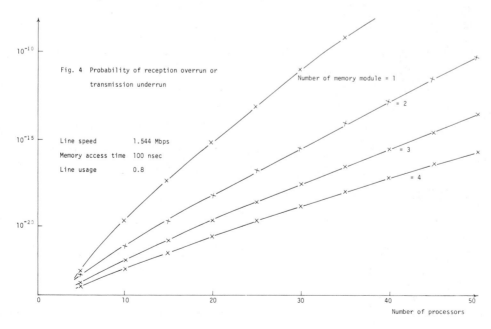

Fig. 4   Probability of reception overrun or
         transmission underrun

Line speed   1.544 Mbps
Memory access time 100 nsec
Line usage   0.8

Number of memory module = 1
= 2
= 3
= 4

Number of processors

inter-processor communication. Access for inter-processor communication is assumed to be 10 times for a packet.

If a plurality of common memory units are provided, access rate to a memory unit will be reduced. Denoting the number of memory unit by m, access rate to one memory will be simply λ/m.

Figure 4 shows the reception overrun and transmission underrun probabilities respectively when the number of common memory modules is 1 through 4. The transmission speed is assumed to be 1.544 MHz and reception overrun probabilitiy is defined as the probability that waiting time is longer than one byte duration, i.e., 5.18 μsec.

If the number of memory module is 3, the average waiting time is as small as 100 nsec and the reception overrun probability is less than 10^{-15}. This means that the structure of the packet switching system using the common memory for inter-processor communication is feasible from the view point of memory access control.

4. HARDWARE OF THE HIGH-CAPACITY PACKET SWITCHING SYSTEM

For the feasibility demonstration of the high-capacity packet switching system, and experimental system has been designed and constructed based on the principle described in 3.

Figure 5 shows the experimental system. This system includes a skeletonized high-capacity packet switching system and some development aids including floppy disk drives, a character display and a serial printer.

The high-capacity packet switching system is composed of two IO processor modules, one main processor and two common memories. in this configuration, three processors may request access to the common memories, so that the feasibility study of the access control to the common memory was made possible which is considered to be the most critical problem in the system design. Z80s are used as the micro-processors as an experiment.

The transmission and the reception is controlled by the Z80SIO and Z80DMA as follows. When a data pattern which is not identical to the HDLC flag pattern (01111110) is received at the receive line of the SIO, the reception start interrupt is generated, which enables the reception operation by the DMA. The received data is transferred from the buffer register in the SIO to the input buffering area in the common memory through the DMA control on byte-by-byte basis. After the completion of data reception, which is identified by the detection of a flag pattern, the SIO will check the frame check sequence which is found just before the framing pattern and SIO will interrupt the IO processor. The interrupted processor disables the DMA and confirms that the result of FCS check is correct and other errors was not found.

When a packet is to be transmitted from the common memory, the IO processor establishes the starting address and the byte count to be transmitted in the DMA. Then the processor enables the DMA. The data is transmitted to the line through the DMA and the SIO byte-by-byte. When the specified number of bytes has been transmitted, the frame check sequence is automatically generated by the SIO and transmitted to the outgoing line. The termination of transmission is noticed to the IO processor by means of an interruption. Then the IO processor disables the DMA.

The common memory module include the arbiter to control the access to the common memory, the request generators which generate the request to the arbiter and to the switches. The request generator and the switch are provided for each of processors which have access to the common memory.

The RAM used for the common memory of the experimental system is static RAM having the access time of 200 nsec. The clock of the common memory module is 4 MHz, which is independent from the processors.

Figure 6 shows the principle of the arbiter used for the common memory. If two requests are applied to the input of the S-R flip-flop, the output of the S-R flip-flop indicates which of the input is given earlier. The output of the S-R flip-flop is inverted and applied to J-K flip-flops.

If n inputs are applied, the required number of flip-flops is $_nC_2$. In the experimental

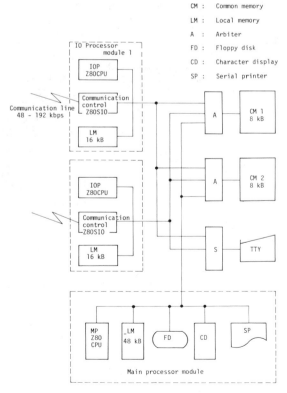

```
CM :  Common memory
LM :  Local memory
A  :  Arbiter
FD :  Floppy disk
CD :  Character display
SP :  Serial printer
```

Fig. 5   Hardware configuration of experimental system

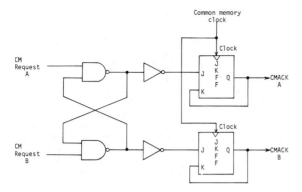

Fig. 6　Principle of the arbiter

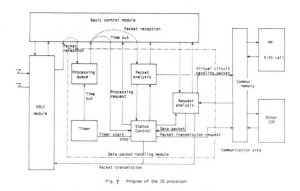

Fig. 7　Program of the IO processor

system, since two IO processors and a main processor is provided, 3 S-R flip-flops are used for the arbiter.

Extending the principle to such cases as the number of IO processors is as many as 50, the arbiter circuit may become too complicated. In such a situation, tree type arbiter can be designed to reduce the number of required components.

When one output from the S-R flip-flop becomes logical "1", the corresponding J-K flip-flop is enabled. The output of the J-K flip-flop is applied to the processor which generated the request for the memory access permission. The signal is called CMACK. The CMACK resets the memeory request signal from the processor and the J-K flip-flop is also resets at the next clock. Thus the selection of the processor is performed in every 250 nsec cycle time of the common memory.

The main-processor module is composed of a CROMEMCO micro-computer system. The system is is also Z80 based system having 48 kbyte local memory and two floppy disk drives.

Total scale of hardware is 700 integrated circuit chips including LSI, which are mounted on 26 circuit boards.

5. SOFTWARE OF THE HIGH-CAPACITY PACKET SWITCHING SYSTEM

The software of the high-capacity packet switching system is composed of the HDLC procedure handling module, the data packet handling module, the virtual circuit handling module and the basic control module. The HDLC procedure handling module and the data packet handling module are assigned to the IO processors. The virtual circuit handling module is assigned to the main processor. All the program has been written by Z80 assembler.

The data packet handling module of the IO processor has the structure as is shown in Fig. 7. The request for data packet processing is applied from the HDLC procedure of the IO processor for packet reception of from other processors for packet transmission. The former request is queued at the processing queue to which request from timer is also applied. The packet is first analyzed by the packet analyzing program. If the packet is to be

processed by the main processor, it is noticed to the main processor. The request from other processor is analyzed by the request analysis program. If it is the request for transmission, the request is passed to the HDLC module. If a packet routed through a different IO processor is acknowledged, the IO processor receives a buffer release request from the IO processor used for packet transmission. The buffer release request is passed to the buffer management program in the HDLC module to release the buffer.

Figure 8 shows the software structure of the main processor used for X.25 virtual circuit handling. When the IO processor #J finds a packet which is related to X.25 virtual circuit handling, the IO processor will give the request to main processor by writing into the communication area. The main-processor maintains the monitoring of the communication area in the common memory. If the request is found, the request analysis module of the main processor program will analyze the content of the request, the logical channel number and the originating IO processor identity. The result of the analysis is reported to the basic control module. The virtual circuit handling module is started by this request and the task to be excuted is determined using the IO processor number, logical channel number, content of the request and the present status of the virtual circuit.

For the control of a virtual circuit, status of all the logical channels of all the IO processors are needed. This table is called the link table which is stored in the common memory and shared by data packet handling module of IO processors.

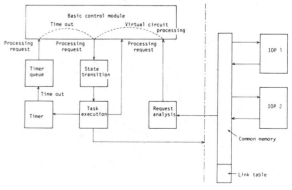

Fig. 8　Program of the main processor module

If some packets are to be transmitted to handle a virtual circuit, the order to transmit the packet is requested from the main processor to the IO processor.

6. EXPERIMENT FOR PERFORMANCE EVALUATION

To obtain the design parameters for an operational high-capacity packet switching system, performance of the experimental system has been evaluated.

6.1 Dynamic Steps for Packet Handling

The throughput of the packet switching system depends upon the kinds of packets transmitted through the network. If the number of data packets transmitted for each of virtual call is large, the loading to the main-processor which handles virtual circuits are reduced. If the acknowledgment is piggybacked on the data packet, the number of recive ready packet used for acknowledgment is reduced.

The experiment was performed in the case that data packets are continuously transmitted after the establishment of virtual circuit and all the HDLC frames are acknowledged by piggyback operation. The average number of dynamic steps for a packet reception was about 430 steps, and that of packet transmission was about 400 steps. In total, dynamic steps to process a packet was about 830 steps.

The average instruction exec ution time of Z80 is about 4.2μ sec when the clock cycle is 400 nsec. Since the CPU is not operational during DMA transfer, assuming that DMA transfer is performed once in every instruction, average execution time is about 4.5μ sec. Therefore the processing capability of one IO processor is about 270 packet/sec. If the average packet length is 1000 bits, the IO processor can handle a line of 270 kbit/sec. The required number of dynamic steps may increase by further development. Using faster microprocessors available in the market in near future, however, it is expected that one IO processor can easily handle a PCM line of 1.544 Mbit/sec.

6.2 Requirement for Memory Capacity

The memory capacity for each IO processor used in the experimental system was 10 kbytes for program memory and 4 kbytes for input and output buffer. If the number of IO processors is 50, the total memory capacity is 700 kbytes. The amount can be attained economically.

6.3 Requirement for Main Processor

Dynamic steps to set up and release a virtual circuit was 150 steps in the experimental system. To handle 50 IO processors by main processor, if identical processors are used for both purposes, capacity ballances when the number of data packets is 10 times larger than the number of virtual circuit controlling packets. If the data packets transmitted by a virtual call is smaller in number, more powerfull processors may be needed for the main processor.

7 CONCLUSION

This paper described the experimental model and the results of the first phase of experiment on the high-capacity packet switching system. The objective of the experiment is to obtain the detailed design parameter to design a prototype model which can handle 50 ∿ 100 T-1 class PCM lines. If the capacity can be realized, the packet switching system can be applicable to commercial quality voice signal as well as bandwidth compressed voice and data. The experimental result indicates that, with reasonable effort to enhance the capacity, above described scale of packet switching system is realizable.

Tadao SAITO is an associate professor of electrical engineering of the University of Tokyo. He received his B.S., M.S. and Ph.D. degrees in electronic engineering from the University of Tokyo in 1963, 1965 and 1968 respectively. Since 1969 he is an associate professor of the University of Tokyo. He was a research associate of Caltech in 1974-1975. His study subject includes digital communication systems, computer networks and protocol standardization.

Hiroshi INOSE has been Professor of Electronic Engineering since 1961, and the Director of Computer Center since 1977, at the University of Tokyo. His work has been concerned with electronic switching, digital modulation, data communication and road traffic control systems. He has received a number of awards for his work including the Second Marconi International Fellowship and Japan Academy Prize. He served as the Program Committee Chairman of the Fourth ICCC. Dr. Inose is a foreign associate of the National Academy of Sciences (U.S.A.), a foreign member of the American Philosophical Society and a Fellow of IEEE.

Masahiro WADA is an engineer of Kokusai Denshin Denwa (KDD) of Japan. He received his B.S. and M.S. degrees from the University of Tokyo in 1979 and 1981 respectively. His study for his M.S. thesis is included in this paper.

Hitoshi SHIBAGAKI is an engineer of NTT Yokosuka Electrical Communication Laboratory. He received his B.S. and M.S. degrees from the University of Tokyo in 1978 and 1981 respectively. His current interest is software engineering to produce application software of on-line systems.

Human Factors in Open System Interconnection

D L A Barber
Logica, UK

This paper is intended to promote a discussion of the relationship of human factors studies to open systems interconnection. It raises questions rather than offering answers for this subject has scarcely been considered so far. Yet it is an important area, ripe for debate, where it seems some fundamental research activities could be undertaken with potentially great benefit to users and systems designers alike.

1. INTRODUCTION

At first sight, there seems little connection between the study of human factors in the design and use of Computer Systems and the current work on the interconnection of Open Systems. Certainly the literature on Open Systems seems largely to have ignored human factors. Indeed it is not clear whether the Human user is seen as part of the top level of the OSI model, or is at some higher level that has not yet been considered.

This confused state of affairs is understandable because the complexity of communications automata and protocols that are necessary to provide services for users is much greater than was imagined in the early days of computer communications systems. Furthermore, the task of describing such protocols in a way that allows them to be easily implemented from specifications seems to be beyond our present capabilities.

The success of the research "Open" systems that have been implemented eg ARPA net, EIN, Euronet etc. have depended upon the efforts of many talented systems designers cooperating in working parties to hammer out the precise meaning of protocol specifications proposed by earlier 'higher-level' Committees. In the light of this experience, the goal of an unambiguous initial specification, supported by formal proving methods for verifying the correctness of a particular scheme, still seems some way off. Yet without this, the ideal of a collection of open systems to which anyone may connect another system, by independently implementing a standard set of protocols, is unattainable.

Small wonder therefore that the intellectual challenge of agreeing upon, and then defining precisely, an architecture for a universal open system is currently attracting so much of our scarce system designing resources.

Perhaps inevitably the development of thinking about protocols has followed a bottom-up path. The basic element that supports the overlaying structure of protocols is the physical communications connection. This provides the essential cement between the distributed components of an open system. The levels of protocol immediately above this connection are designed to disguise the vagaries of the different kinds of communications facilities and these provide well defined criteria with which to measure specific proposals at these levels.

But at the higher levels, criteria for judgement became a catalogue of desirable properties rather than a set of definite requirements and the room for debate expands alarmingly. This lessens the probability of agreement on one or even a few, specific standards. In such circumstances, there appears to be great merit in taking a top-down look at what the users actually require or, perhaps more realistically, what they are prepared to pay for in the way of open system services.

However, as will emerge, this is such a vast subject that we can only touch upon a number of controversial issues with the intention of stimulating debate. This is the purpose of this paper.

2. WHY OPEN SYSTEMS?

Some people are skeptical about the purpose and value of OSI activities, perhaps because the term "Open System" is not well defined and so can be taken to mean a wide variety of things.

To promote better understanding and credibility we must try to consider more closely the terms and objectives of OSI. We might, for example, define an open system to be simply one that comprises a mix of terminals and computers made by different manufacturers; if so, there are already many such in existence. Another definition might be that an open system is one that presents a universally accepted interface to the outside world so that certain kinds of transaction may be conducted with "foreign" systems.

In complete contrast, and more ambitiously, we might postulate some kind of world-wide public open system. By analogy with the public road and telephone networks this would be available for use by any person with the right interfacing equipment, and all parts, somehow, would be interconnected so that access to any one part would be possible from all others.

Put another way, the ultimate goal might be to provide everyone with a pocket "communicator" that enables them to interact using speech, text and pictures both with other pocket communicators and with computer systems and databases, wherever these may physically be located. As portrayed in 'Startrek', the television Science Fiction series.

Somewhere between our present capabilities and the Startrek scenario lies an evolving future "reality" achievable at some rate determined mainly by non-technical issues such as, politics and, indeed, human factors.

The desireability of achieving the Startrek scenario may be questioned by many, but it seems a technologically plausible view of the future that this author, at least, regards as a stimulating and attractive prospect and one, moreover, that justifies the current work on Open Systems Interconnection.

However, a more commercially realistic and, indeed, essential scenario is one where at least a cross section of existing and planned informatics systems may interwork with each other via the present public telephone, packet switched and digital circuit switched networks. Without the development of this capability, the growth the world's economy will be severely constrained over the next few years by having to be developed piecemeal rather than across a broad front. This, then, is really why OSI is such a vitally important matter today.

3. TYPES OF OPEN CONNNECTION

Two kinds of equipment can be involved in an open system. One is a terminal (of whatever kind) that is under the direct control of an active human user; the other is an unattended system such as a database server that operates as an automaton. The behaviour of such an automaton may be highly complex but is deterministic in that it depends on the type and sequence of input messages it receives from its environment, and on the pre programming given to it by people. Insofar as this programming has anticipated all possible eventualities that can occur, the automation will respond reliably and correctly, whatever inputs are received - including, for example, a sudden loss of power.

An important philosophical point here is that for both kinds of equipment it is people who decide what is supposed to happen and so pass judgement on whether or not a system is working correctly. A practical point is that the terminal user is actively and intimately involved in what is happening and can readily direct the course of events; this makes the design of protocols, involving people potentially easier than those for automata.

In fact, because humans are better at recovering from system failures than computer programs acting as automata, a communications system solely for people can omit some of the complex features necessary in a fully automated system to ensure that it always behaves reliably and correctly.

On the other hand, humans differ widely in skill and experience so it is more difficult to design an interactive interface that really suits the unknown user, than it is to match the characteristics of a pre defined automaton.

But the real challenge lies in meeting the requirements of all three kinds of interaction possible in an open system, namely:-

- a dialogue between terminals controlled by people,

- an interaction between a user at a terminal and a server system

- a transaction between two servers.

Perhaps rather oddly, the main thrust of OSI discussions has been directed towards the third and possibly most difficult objective of defining various levels of interacting automata that can establish connections, transfer data, manage a session and present information to applications programs in dissimilar computing systems, all without human involvement.

One of the factors that complicates this problem is that the Hosts or Servers in an open system may be very different in their design concepts. The crunch question is whether they should be adapted to match the communications system, or whether it should be tailored to suit each Host. The purpose of the layered protocol architecture is to

824

provide a basis for automata programs that will perform the matching functions. But where these automata programs are to reside physically is a question that is seldom addressed.

However, in this paper on human factors we are primarily concerned with the first two kinds of connection i.e. user to user and user to server. To consider these we must next examine the nature of the users, the interface presented by the systems they use, and the tasks they are trying to accomplish.

4. WHO IS THE OPEN SYSTEMS USER?

A point of confusion that frequently arises is the use of the term "user" to describe components of an open system as well as the person using it. For example, the session layer protocol is often referred to as the user of the transport layer, and so on. But here, when we are considering human factors, our user is obviously a person. But what kind of a person? This is the key question, because a discussion of human factors that took humanity in general as its subject would be too diffuse to be profitable.

What we must try to do is to define our user, or rather classes of user and then, ideally, develop a formal model that can serve to test and compare different systems so they may be ranked in order of, say, friendliness to the user. The concept of the "friendly" system is an important one as is reflected by the current buzz word "user friendly". But this too needs careful definition because something that is friendly to one user may appear distinctly hostile to another. Indeed, friendliness is seldom synonymous with efficiency so we should qualify the contemporary plea for user-friendly systems by asking that they should also be user-efficient; whatever that may turn out to mean on closer analysis.

But perhaps the greatest difficulty encountered in modelling a user's characteristics, is the variability of the average person's parameters and psychology. To someone in a cantankerous mood, all systems are hostile, while nothing bothers the bouyant soul who welcomes problems as a challenge. "Life's like that", one might say, but should our computer systems be so, too?. We must hope not.

Fortunately the appearance of cheap logic and storage now makes it possible to tame the existing systems by using 'intelligent' black boxes, and also provides the means for new systems to be designed, ab initio, to be easier to use. Indeed, the micro-processor-based personal computers and small business systems are markedly superior to the big

main-frames in this respect, and is one reason why they have been so dramatically successful in the market place.

5. THE USER INTERFACE

The interface presented to its users is arguably the most important aspect of the design of any system, or product. When taken in its widest sense the user interface covers the aesthetic appeal of equipment as well as the ergonomics of its use. Such questions as to why a computer terminal in a wooden cabinet sells better, or worse than a similar one in a plastic case, are aspects of the user interface as important for the initial sales of new systems as the layout of a keyboard or the dialogue used to perform some task. This is because the merits and demerits of these more subtle features do not usually become fully apparent until users have bought the equipment.

The layout of controls and indicators, buttons and displays, is obviously important, as are the procedural interfaces ie the sequences of inputs and outputs and their meanings, that are needed to use the equipment. Most systems today appear to the casual, or untrained user, as difficult to use, because they often seem to have quirks of behaviour that do not accord with 'common sense' experience of everyday life. These quirks are very difficult to identify and resolve, because people soon adapt to them and cease to be aware of them, as they become regular experienced users. However, they remain a potential source of mistakes for the experts, and a continuing irritation to the occasional user.

Unfortunately, there seems to be very little 'science' attached to interface design, and examples of ill-conceived interfaces are legion in computer systems. But there are now some interesting and significant papers on the subject in the literature and some generally accepted criteria are beginning to emerge. These have largely been the result of observations of different systems, and how they are used, rather than the development of any basic theory.

It might be argued that if a better understanding of what constitutes a good user interface can be gained, it may become possible to define a generalised version for use throughout an open system. This seems unlikely in view of the wide spectrum of users and services that will, almost by definition, be the hallmark of open systems. Indeed there is a vital philosophical point that must be appreciated regarding the feasibility of designing a uniform universal interface. It is that the attractiveness of one particular service compared with others must ultimately lie in its unique appeal when measured against the user's requirements.

For example, some databases may be popular for the special information they provide or for the way they present it, or indeed for the ease with which they allow data to be manipulated. The interface to such databases must of necessity, be different from that of others. For example, a legal database will not sensibly be manipulable by medically oriented commands, and vice versa.

Nevertheless, there is no reason why the lower levels of the users procedural interface should not be the same for many services. The Euronet Diane Command Language is an excellent example of what is possible in this respect, and suggests that a dual interface - one a network standard, for more generalised interactions, the other optimised for the local or more advanced users - might be worth consideration. Success with this would allow people to use their own home systems for basic tasks, when away at foreign sites, and also might permit some kinds of interaction with relatively unknown foreign systems.

But there are many problems to be considered in attempting to define a general purpose user interface, not least of these is the level of knowledge, skill and even intelligence of the users for which it is intended. It is often argued that a system cannot suit both casual and frequent users, being either too difficult for one, or too boring for the other. However this view overlooks the potential capability of future systems, and the concepts pioneered by the research projects aimed at developing the "User Agent" approach to interface design.

Essentially, the User Agent is a set of local software processes that can be tailored to an individual user so that he can conduct a transaction using his own language, commands and responses, because these are mapped to and from whatever interactions are required by the particular remote system he has called up. The user agent processes are usually assumed to reside in a local "black box" into which appropriate software may be down-loaded by each called system, using telesoftware techniques.

In the absence of a User Agent, systems could be made more friendly to novice and expert users alike, by arranging for login names to cause the selection of adaptive 'user profiles' that are independently evolved to suit each user's behaviour. This would help people in an active and positive way. The very large number of 'states' in the

state transition diagram describing such an interface, will require a vast amount of logic and storage to implement these "intelligent" systems; but they are bound to appear eventually.

Intuitively it seems plausible that the best human interface is one which matches the input/output mechanisms of people. If so, we may anticipate dramatic improvements from the introduction of speech synthesis and recognition, together with the use of high resolution dynamic picture displays, with windowing facilities, more ergonomic keyboards and specialised display manipulation methods.

But, as not all users will have such exotic facilities in their User Agents, they cannot all expect the same benefits, and so a standard procedural interface able to be used effectively with a very wide range of terminal types is probably an unattainable objective.

6. OPEN SYSTEMS USER FACILITIES

To identify the facilities that should be available to users of an open system it is necessary to identify the tasks they may wish to perform. The main types of activity are person-to-person, person-to-server and server- to-server. The last does not involve people in a direct way, and is not therefore considered here.

For the person-to-person case, a user may wish to:-

a) conduct a real-time interactive dialogue with another user (whether by voice, text or pictures).

b) Conduct a store and forward interaction by exchanging information with another user over a protracted time scale.

c) Broadcast a message to several users

d) Take part in a teleconference of users

In cases a) and d) the interactions will be in the form of short communications (messages) of a length convenient for human dialogues. In the other two cases, the messages may be of any length. ie a user may wish to transmit a file and ask for comments from one other user, or from many.

It may well be that the interactions between users takes place through the medium of a computer system. This almost certainly will be so for a teleconference. However, the users should be aware of this, only when there is no possibility for it to be hidden from them.

For interactions between a user and a server, the options are as follows:-

1) The user engages in a real-time interactive dialogue with the server eg using an interactive database query language.

2) The user exchanges messages with the server, vaguely analagous to a batch processing scheme eg requests a copy of a report from a database.

3) The user broadcasts messages to several servers eg to enquire which is able to assist him.

4) The user is involved in an interaction with several servers eg during a comparison of data from more than one database.

The fundamental difference between a communication that takes place between users, and that which occurs between a user and a server is that people may interact with each other using whatever natural language questions and answers are needed to resolve difficulties or misunderstandings, whereas a server has to be preprogrammed with all necessary (help) messages. The ease with which people may use servers therefore depends on the quality of the training they may receive, on the comprehensiveness of user's handbooks and on the degree of assistance that is available on-line to them during an interaction. It is the manifest weakness of many systems in these areas that has led to the cry for more user friendliness in user interface designs.

In any distributed system we may distinguish two basic aspects of a transaction; firstly, the interaction with the communications medium to establish paths or liaisons between the communicating entities (users or servers), and secondly the subsequent interaction that occurs between these entities.

The path establishment interaction should, as far as possible, be similar, irrespective of from where it is initiated. However, the interaction between the entities themselves can not generally be entirely uniform because it has to be specific in some degree to each particular task being performed. Nevertheless, lower levels of inter entity interaction may well be made the same in similar classes of transaction, with much benefit to users.

In a future ideal distributed system, the user should not be aware of all the various 'standardised' lower levels of protocol. Indeed, if they are truly standard, they can be readily and reliably implemented by automata. If this is so, the user has to come into the picture only at the level when the protocol specific to the task in hand, comes into play. But with today's systems we must to accept that users cannot avoid being involved in an initial setting-up activity, followed by an interaction with a peer entity (either user or server), and concluded by a clear-down action.

The setting up and clearing functions should be implemented in the same way everywhere so that wherever a user may be he or she may go to any terminal and use the same commands and see the same responses. This means the user will be easily able to call-up the familiar facilities at his or her home site. If, in addition, certain basic processing tasks are also implemented identically everywhere, the itinerant user can perform these locally at any site, without the need for retraining. It will then be only the interfaces to specialised facilities, peculiar to particular sites, that will need to be learnt specially by those users wishing to use them.

The key problem facing the international standards bodies is to first select the basic user-level facilities to be provided by all networks and services, and then agree a set of standardised user interfaces to access and operate them. This is likely to prove a very difficult task indeed.

7. SOME BASIC ISSUES

7.1 Naming and Addressing

Before one user may communicate or correspond in any way with another user or a server he must:-

1) be aware that the others exist

2) know what the other is called ie the name

3) know how to reach the other through the communications media ie the address

The existence of a particular correspondent may be known prior to an interaction, or may be established as the first stage by consulting a directory such as the yellow pages (to give an analogy from the telephone service). The name of the correspondent may be known, or, again, may be obtained from a 'yellow pages' database.

The method of addressing the chosen correspondent may be known or may be obtained from a directory, but in this case it is the equivalent of the telephone directory's white pages that is required.

There are two components to an address; the correspondents name and the correspondents location. These are exemplified respectively by the postal service where the correspondents name is part of the address placed on an envelope, and by the telephone service where the number of a telephone extension is the correspondents expected location. The importance of distinguishing these forms of address is that, in principle, automatic redirection is possible when the name of the correspondent is supplied to the communications network or agency.

The suggestion that redirection should be possible highlights a very important aspect of human factors when considered in the light of what users would like to have. It is easy and often very useful to take as a model the services provided by some familiar existing system that is operated by people. But there is a danger that some apparently trivial task that they perform almost incidentally turns out to be crucial to the success of the whole system, yet difficult, if not impossible, to perform automatically. An example is the manual telephone exchange where the operator can provide helpful information that might not have been thought worth including in any automatic directory. Likewise, when someone is not at their telephone extension, another person will often answer and provide valuable and possibly unpredictable information for the caller.

Addressing is usually made hierarchical. With the postal system mail is sorted by people and so the structure of an address does not matter, provided all the information is present. Different countries use different orders for name, room, building, street, town, country, etc. but this presents no problem for manual sorting. However, it means that an automatic sorting (switching) system has to be given knowledge of all possible variations (or must be adaptive in some way) otherwise it cannot cope.

To be really helpful to its users, a future open system should be able to automate functions such as the location of a chosen correspondent given possibly imperfect but redundant information. It will obviously be difficult to agree and standardise on how this should be done and it will be helpful if users can elect to use either names or the network addresses covered by CCITT Recommendation X121. On the particular issue of contacting a user by name, rather than the place where he or she is usually located, it will be contingent on the users to inform the Open System where they are, so that redirection may be possible.

7.2 Security and Privacy

By definition, an open system is one that can communicate with other open systems connected to a public network. The whole purpose of working towards open systems is to ensure that they can communicate freely with each other. It therefore seems strange to be concerned about security and privacy issues. In fact, these two topics are often confused, but here we will use security to mean the freedom of users' information from corruption while it is being stored, transmitted or manipulated by the open system. Privacy will be the term used to cover the protection that the system gives to one user's information from access or corruption by other users.

From the privacy viewpoint, while the systems may be designed so that their users may communicate freely with each other, there will still be a need for each user able to mark his files as being open for access by other people, or accessible only by himself. Indeed, there might be a need for a number of levels of privacy ie access by other workers in the user's own group, access by other people within the establishment, in outside establishments, and so on.

Security aspects must be part of the overall system design and cannot easily be grafted on as a later addition. For example, it is necessary to have proper procedures for making back-up copies of files, programs etc. In the stand alone big systems of today, these functions are usually performed by operators and it is an open question on how this should be done in a distributed system where copies of a users file might conceivably be stored anywhere. It is by no means clear who should be responsible for providing the necessary back-up facilities.

7.3 Accounting and Billing

The problem of charging a user for the resources he uses is often difficult with a Computer Bureau, because the communications charges are due to the network operator while the cost of computing and storage of information are due to the bureau. Sometimes, arrangements are made for users to pay a single bill for all services but this is by no means common. The use of a public network with many open systems that all users may access if they wish, could lead to each user receiving a large number of bills from different places. It would clearly be much more convenient for the user to have one itemised bill and one place to pay whatever is due, and there is need to consider how this might be done.

Apart from the question of how the user is charged, there is the matter of what he is charged for and how he is informed of the rate at which he is being charged. With bureau services it is usual at the end of an interaction, for a message to be printed giving the number of units of various resources that have been used. It would also be useful for users to have a cumulative account given to them whenever they attempt to use a network service, and also to have an indication of how much a particular transaction will cost them, before they decide to make it. These facilities are not common in existing systems and might be difficult to implement in a uniform way in an open system. However, such information would be very useful to users who could select services on the basis of a prior knowledge of what a particular transaction would cost if carried out at different sites.

7.4 Specialised Management and Information Centres

In view of the various requirements indicated above, there may be some advantage in creating special centres which would provide directory information, details of charges for various resources, and other suchlike services. Certain of these centres could also provide some kind of security for critical information that users want to be sure will not be lost, whatever happens in the open system. Yet other centres could assist in the control of privacy, using one of the various encryption methods that have been discussed in the literature. Some of these need a secret key which might well be distributed by a privacy management centre.

8. BIBLIOGRAPHY

The following list of references covers a variety of aspects of Human Factors in Computer System Design and most of the papers contain extensive bibliographies that will be useful to anyone wishing to go more deeply into these topics.

1. Thomas J.C. and Carol J.M.
   Human Factors in Communication
   I.B.M. Systems Journal Vol. 20 No.2
   Page 237

2. Davies D.W. and Yates D.M.
   Human Factors in Display Terminal
   Procedures
   Proc. ICCC Kyoto Sept. 78 p.777

3. Miller L.H.
   A Resource for Investigating Human
   Interaction with Computers
   Proc. IFIP TeleInformatics 79 p.195

4. Anderson R.H. and Gillogly J.J.
   Rand Intelligent Terminal Agent
   (Rita); Design Philosophy
   Rand Corporation R/1809/ARPA Feb 76

5. Morton J. et al
   Interacting with the Computer; a
   framework Proc. IFIP TeleInfomatics
   79 p.201

6. Chevance R.J.
   Principals of a Dialogue Processor
   Proc. IFIP TeleInformatics 79 p.209

7. Guida G.
   Ideas about the Design of Natural
   Language Interfaces to Query
   Systems.
   Proc. Workshop on Natural Language
   for Interaction with Databases,
   IIASA Jan 1977 p.265

8. Gini G. and Gini M.
   Cognitive Information Retrieval by
   Goal - Oriented Languages
   Proc. Conf. on Artifical
   Intelligence; Question Answering
   Systems, IIASA Jun 75 p.216

9. Schicker P.
   Naming and Addressing in a Computer
   Based Mail Environment.
   IFIP WG 6.5 N.21

10. MacNeil D.R.
    Check List of Basic Features for
    C.B.M.S.
    IFIP WG 6.5 N.35

11. Message handling facilities (model
    and services)
    Basis for work on CCITT Q5/V11 5 /
    VII IFIP WG 6.5 N.40

9. CONCLUSIONS

This paper has covered a number of issues and problems that are relevant for consideration of human factors in open systems interconnection. It appears that present OSI work on layered protocols is mainly concerned with communication between computer systems programmed to behave as interacting automata. Further layers might be proposed above the present ones, to provide some kind of user-friendly interface. But this will be difficult because of the problem of defining precisely what is user friendly.

It is therefore likely that the human interface of a User Agent will have to be outside the OSI protocols structure. But the top OSI layer should perhaps offer different sets of commands / responses for the User Agent to map onto for various user types. When person-to-person communication, is considered (for example, a facsimile handwriting exchange system, or a voice store-and-forward system) there may be

no need for some of the layers of the
present ISO model. So, again the
application of the ISO model to support
communication between people seems to
require further study.

It seems unlikely that a general purpose
user interface can be standardised, but
there is some hope that the procedural
interface between a User Agent and say,
a database server might be defined at
some lower level. This might possibly
be at the presentation level the ISO OSI
model. This would then offer a set of
primitives that could be built upon in
developing a User Agent that could be
tailored by users to suit themselves.

In conclusion, this paper has ended on a
note of questioning some aspects of the
ISO model. This is not to criticise the
intensive and invaluable work being done
in this area by the many workers in ISO,
CCITT and elsewhere. It is rather to
suggest that, when the field application
is widened to look at the needs of the
users of an open system, there are many
issues still to be resolved.

Derek Barber is well known
for his work in Computing
and Communications, and is
co author of two books
"Communications Networks
for Computers" and "Com-
puter Networks and their
Protocols".

As head of Information
Systems at the National
Physical Laboratory he was
involved in the pioneering development of packet
switching techniques. He was Director of the
European Informatics Network from 1973-80. From
1976-79 he was chairman of the International
Federation for Information Processing WG 6.1.
In 1980 he joined the Department of Industry
on the Microprocessor Awareness Project and in
1981 he went to Logica Ltd, where he has been
Principal Consultant on a variety of high technology projects. He is now very interested in
personel computing and its effect on future
society.

Progress towards Distributed Database Systems

A P G Brown
International Computers, UK

Database systems are complex and their introduction and widespread acceptance has been slow. Distributed database systems will be even more complex and will not take off overnight. Nevertheless the architects and researchers have made real progress. This paper discusses the options available to designers, the work currently under way and some of the technical and management problems yet to be solved.

ICL's distributed database system is based upon a Codasyl database system, IDMS. It either allows a database to be distributed over several nodes of a network or it supports a virtual database view mapping onto several autonomous databases. The remote data access protocol is closely related to the COBOL DML. The paper covers the architecture of the system and the practical limitations facing designers.

INTRODUCTION

Database systems are among the more complicated software systems and their introduction and widespread acceptance has taken several years. Distributed database systems have another level of complexity and will be similarly slow to gain acceptance. Nevertheless the architects and researchers have made significant gains and progress in related fields is bringing distributed database systems within planning horizons.

This paper reviews the progress of centralised database systems and other related fields. It discusses the options available to software and application designers and some of the technical and management problems to be faced. ICL's distributed database system is based upon a Codasyl database system, IDMS. It will both allow a database to be distributed over several nodes of a network and support a virtual database view mapping onto several autonomous databases. The remote data access protocol is closely related to the COBOL DML. The paper will cover the architecture of the system and the practical limitations facing designers.

The paper discusses the merits of centralisation and decentralisation and the need for data analysis and data dictionaries. In general, the problems, of control of operations over networks and of decentrailised design have not been faced. Possibly a distributed data dictionary will be one of the first requirements for a real distributed database.

EXPERIENCE WITH CENTRALISED DATABASE SYSTEMS

A database is a collection of related data which is designed to serve the needs of a number of application systems or users. In general the database is set up and controlled separately from the applications it serves so that a degree of independence can be achieved between the database design process and the application design.

The need for database systems arose from the growing realisation in the 1960's that many computer applications within the same enterprise needed to share the same data. Early application systems were designed independently of each other and required their own separately organised data maintenance procedures with consequent duplication of data entry, processing and storage.

The increasing availability and decreasing cost of computing power and data storage has made it possible for complex systems to be implemented at reasonable cost. Early pioneers often invented their own database management techniques and there were some spectacular and costly failures. However there are now many good database management systems available and they are among the most successful of computer software products.

Most of the growth in database systems has occured in the last few years. Indeed it is only ten years since the Codasyl DBTG specifications were published (1) and since Dr. E.F. Codd published his pioneering papers on the Relational Database model (2).

The Codasyl and the Relational model can be seen to underlie most modern database management systems. The Codasyl model is characterised by its network data structure in which records are linked to associated records by Codasyl set structures and the program accesses data one record at a time by following or navagating the access paths. By contrast relational databases are comprised of relations or tables and associations between tables are represented by like values of corresponding data elements. Codd (2) used predicate calculus to define the basic operation for selecting and combining relations.

Many early database implementations failed because the designers did not appreciate the difficulties in integrating application systems that had grown up separately over the years.

To meet the needs of many applications simultaneously the database has to be designed as a model of the Real World System it represents. The idea that the data should be analysed separately from the applications led to the concept of the Conceptual Schema (3,4) as a description of the data in pure terms - i.e. separated from both the requirements of particular applications and from the constraints of physical storage.

There have been many arguments on the best form of conceptual schema or data modelling technique. The ISO.TC97.WG3 report contains a detailed account of several approaches(5). ICL users will be familiar with the Entity Attribute Relationship model taught on the Data Administration and Database Design course, which is backed up by the Data Dictionary System (6). We believe that the form of the model is less important than its substance. It is essential that the database designer and users of the data fully understand its semantics and any analysis technique that helps the user to understand the enterprise being modelled is useful. We recommend the techniques for any system design, even if a database is not being considered.

Experience with database systems has inevitably curbed the wilder claims of the early enthusiasts. There is less talk these days of the Corporate Database. Most organisations understand the practical limitations on database size and complexity that result from the hardware in use and the problems of administration and control. Consequently users tend to have a number of databases, each serving a group of loosely related application systems.

The growth of database systems has gone hand in hand with that of Transaction Processing and computing terminals. Many databases are interacting with hundreds or thousands of terminals and processing many enquiries each second. These systems bring the computer right to the worker's desk and make its correct functioning an essential requirement for his job. Consequently a large part of the design effort and the program code for a DBMS (database management system) is concerned with ensuring that system failures do not compromise the integrity of the data, that failures in part of the system effect the minimum number of users, that recovery is swift and that users are always sure what data has or has not been accepted.

In summary the centralised database technology is now mature and an increasing number of users are using it to give them better control over data and to enable them to exploit data more fully. System performance can be predicted reasonably accurately and system availability is high. Systems design and programming costs compare favourably with file based solutions and it is usually simpler to implement changes and enhancement to applications if this should become necessary.

The effects of databases on the organisation have been favourable. Use of common data serves to increase individuals' confidence in each other's systems and motivates all users

to ensure its accuracy.

DISTRIBUTED SYSTEMS AND DATABASES

The centralised database system discussed in the previous section consists of a database and a database management system in a single machine. It may, however be handling messages routed to it from any number of terminals. This amounts conceptually to a star-network as shown in fig.1

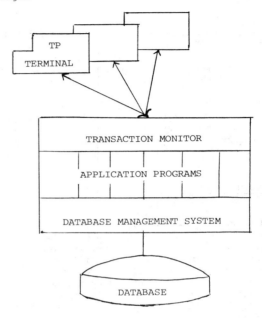

Fig.1: A Shared Central Database System

The communications and transaction monitor are not the concern of this paper. We only note that each interaction with the user at his terminal involves an exchange of messages with an application program near the database.

This system may involve a lot of communications traffic and be subject to loss of service if there are failures or bottlenecks on the communications lines.

On way of improving the efficiency of the system would appear to be to locate some of the data near to terminals that make most use of it. However this must be done in such a way that the integrity of the resulting distributed database is not compromised. The rest of this paper is concerned with various ways of achieving this.

The state of the art for distributed databases lags several years behind that for centralised databases. We are now at the experimental stage equivalent to 1970 database systems. It is an active area of research at various levels but few users have assimilated database techniques sufficiently to be actively planning distributed databases.

The Objectives of Distributed Database Systems

A distibuted database system is one in which a single co-ordinated body of data, the database, is distributed over more than one site and is available to users at more than one site. This definition is valid whether the data is completely replicated at each site or if there is no data duplication. However, if data is duplicated all copies of the data must be kept in step so that the results of processing do not depend on which copy of data is used.

We may expect distributed database designers to be aiming at some or all of the following

*   making less use and better use of communications facilities

*   giving users at terminals or remote sites more control over their processing

*   enabling users to carry on working when other sites are down or cut off by communications failures

*   enabling data to be duplicated or replicated so that the system can survive catastrophies in isolated nodes (e.g. terrorist attack)

*   enabling users to work without having to know the location of data (network transparency).

Before looking at solutions that attempt to provide all the above we will examine two parallel developments.

Distributed Transaction Processing

This facility is currently being released as part of ICL's Information Processing Architecture. It is an extension to the facilities of the TP Monitor to allow transactions to be routed directly from one machine to another without any specific action by the terminal users. It also allows an application program at one site to initiate a transaction for processing at another site and await the response.

DTP therefore allows two databases at different sites to be processed from a single terminal without the terminal user being aware of the site processing his work. However this is not a distributed database system because there are two separate DBMS's which are totally unaware of each other's existence. The "logic" for data distribution is all contained in the TP Monitor and application programs. Nevertheless the system is available now and will satisfy the requirements of many systems.

Distributed Resource Systems

At the small end of the computer market are personal computers and workstations or intelligent terminals. These may be connected to mainframes or may communicate amongst themselves via a local area networks (LAN). A system in which the processing is distributed over several communication nodes is a distributed resource systems. Often nodes have specialised functions such as high speed or high quality printing.

The existence of the extra processing power

near the user raises the question of how best to use it. The system designer now has a choice between sending data from the database to the terminal for processing or sending messages to the database for processing. Some systems are being designed with the terminals definitely in charge and with the data held in a special file server (or database back-end) which services the needs of a number of intelligent terminals.

The file server is not a distributed database (unless there are at least two on the LAN and they co-ordinate their activities) but the fact that the data is remote from the process means that some of their implementation problems are common to distributed databases systems.

User Requirements for Distributed Databases

There are two ways in which distributed databases may be established. Firstly, most of the databases currently existing or planned are monolithic. It is possible that users will be able to produce economies or satisfy new requirements by splitting them up and distributing (or duplicating) substantial parts of them closer to the users.

The second approach is to integrate one or more distinct databases to enable certain applications to process data as if it resided in a single database. In this approach the distributed database is superimposed on existing data. We call this a Distributed Virtual database.

The next section discusses the run-time and compile-time architecture and shows that the software implementation for the systems is very similar.

DATABASE AND DISTRIBUTED DATABASE ARCHITECTURE

The run-time structure of a DBMS, as viewed from the application program is illustrated, using Codasyl terminology, in fig.2. Here the boxes represent layers of software with interfaces between them. Each interface represents a conceptual database machine, making data objects visible to the component above and allowing the objects to be manipulated by the invocation of data manipulation functions at that level.

The subschema is a description of the data available to the application program. The schema is a description of all the data in the database. However it does not describe aspects of the storage which could be changed without impacting subschemas and applications programs. These are typically record placement and indexing strategies which affect the relative performance and costs of various functions. The diagram assumes these are described in a separate storage schema.

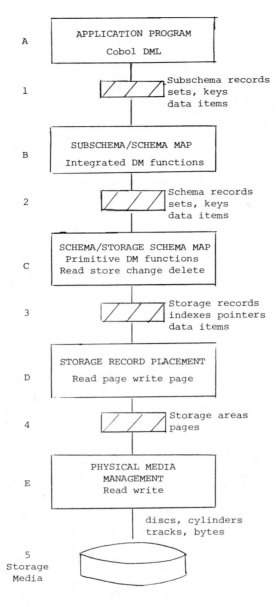

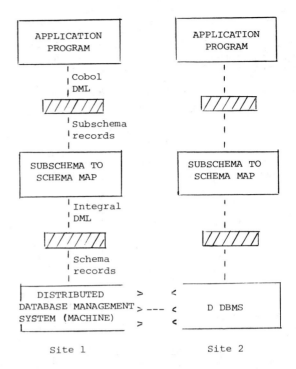

Fig.2: In-line Database Architecture

Fig.3: COBOL view of a Real Distributed
        Database System

In a Real Distributed Database RDDB of fig.3
the schema describes the data available in the
whole database.

This data is physically stored at a number of
sites and the Distributed Database Management
System allows programs (at any site) to access
the data without being aware of its location.

All data manipulation functions are available
to application programs and there is no local
control of the data descriptions operating at
individual sites.

In the Distributed Virtual Databases there are
a number of autonomous databases with their
own schemas. These databases are co-ordinated
so that they appear to co-operate by providing
data to a Distributed Database System whose
data is described by a separate schema.

It would be possible for a single database to
provide data to support several DVDB's.
Extensions of the structure allow DVDB's to be
defined over other DVDB's or Real DDB's since
these all support the same interfaces. Fig.4
illustrates the structure of a DVDB.

In a DVDB each site makes available only a
subset of the data and possibly only a subset
of possible DM functions. For example the
DVDB need not offer STORE or MODIFY functions
since data can be stored and updated using
the site schemas.

In the diagram the Distribution Control
Program carries out the mapping of the data
in individual sites into the form required by
the distributed database schema. The
Distribution Control Program on each site
communicates with similar programs on all the
other sites to gain access to remote data.

Level of Distribution

It is clear that in the DVDB the data objects passing between sites are records since these are supplied at the distribution subschema interface. However for the Real DDB it is theoretically possible to choose the Schema record, storage record or page level as the distribution level.

If an existing DBMS is to be modified to support data distribution then the following points are worth noting.

1. Locking, change-logging and recovery must be handled below the distribution interface to avoid other sites being involved in single site recovery situations.

2. Logical interdependencies between data at different sites and below the distribution interface must be resolved in the distribution control program.

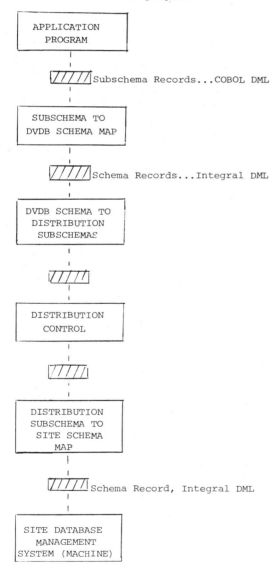

Fig.4: Structure of a Distributed Virtual Database

The requirements for concurrency control and for recovery which pose problems for centralised database systems apply even more to distributed systems but the solution may be different because lock tables are decentralised. In a centralised system there are well known algorithms for detecting deadlock within lock tables. In a distributed system these algorithms would not work unless one site acted as a clearing house for all locks. Usually this would involve so much extra processing that a simple time-out solution is more cost-effective.

Relationships between objects may be spatial, represented in the database, or temporal - to do with the context or currency of DM functions. As an example of a temporal relationship consider a DM function which demands the "Next object". The meaning of this depends on the "sense" of next and what the current object is. But it is possible that "next" involves a switch from an object at one site to one at another site. Even if it involves no switch Distribution Control would need to remember the site supplying the "current" object to supplement the parameters of the DM function.

ICL'S DISTRIBUTED DATABASE SYSTEM

ICL is currently building a DDBMS based upon IDMS (7,8). The architecture is that of the DVDB shown in fig.4. The aim of the initial system is primarily to give the developers experience of the problems of communications and recovery of these systems and to enable performance measurements to be made. It is not envisaged that the system will become a product in its present form.

The DVDB architecture was chosen because it offers a great deal of flexibility. The Distribution Control Program and the Remote Data Access protocol could also support a Real, as opposed to Virtual Distributed Database System.

Most of the software components are identical to the standard IDMS. The only change to the users program is that database keys have to include a site reference because the 4-byte keys are not unique across all sites. Even this change is transparent to most source code as the keys are generally only present in COBOL Data Division entries planted by the IDMS pre-processor.

The DVDB Schema allows IDMS Areas and records to be re-named to avoid clashes that may arise from the site schemas. It may also be necessary to give records that have different names in site schemas the same name in the Distributed Database, assuming of course that they have the same record formats.

In IDMS records are stored in units of storage called Areas, and records may be assigned to areas according to their record type or by the program at the time they are first stored. In practice most databases have all records of the same type in the same area but this is less likely to be the case with distributed databases. Where there is a choice selection may be made either by the application program or by a database procedure supplied by the data administrator and invoked by the Distribution Control program.

One advantage of the approach is that programs that do not need to access data at other sites use the conventional IDMS and by-pass the Distribution Control program. Hence there is no degradation to local working on site when the database is not supporting remote access.

DISTRIBUTED DATABASE DESIGN PROBLEMS

This section discusses some problems of distributed database systems which do not occur with centralised systems. These affect the application systems design and the design of the supporting distributed database management system.

Choice of Site

The choice of site for data is generally made in order to minimise the amount of communication traffic. So there will, hopefully, often be many jobs that require no access to remote data. It is sensible to try to arrange that these jobs are distinguishable from other jobs so that the work done by Distribution Control can be avoided.

However it is likely to be a constraint of DDB's that relationships between sites should be avoided. For example the ICL implementation does not support sets that span sites and there are no record pointers from one site to another. One consequence of this is that it may be difficult sometimes to split up data sets because the wealth of relationships ensures that one way or another nearly all records are inter-related.

One solution to this is to duplicate some of the data. For example we could duplicate part records between a Bill-of-Material application database in the Engineering Office and a Work-in-Progress database near the factory. Duplication of data is easier to handle than cross-site pointers but it creates an extra problem because it is necessary to ensure that all copies are updated together. This prevents local updating of duplicated records independently of other sites.

System and Database Recovery

The mechanism for recovery of a centralised database system involves locking of data on behalf of active processes, logging changes to the database and synchronising processes with the database after failures have occured. These mechanisms have been described at length elsewhere e.g. (9) and there is no need to repeat the discussion here.

Distribution of processing creates two new problems. In a distributed database system each site will handle its own recovery using the techniques of a single database system, but it is necessary to synchronise processing across all sites.

This is achieved by first splitting the processing task into independent success units or commitment units with the property that the system undertakes to process all or none of such a unit. Hence if a success unit fails for any reason the process is set back to the start of the unit and any changes made to the database are rolled back.

In a distributed database the end of a success unit must be signalled to all sites affected by it. This involves a first stage in which each site is informed of the end and asked to secure the process so that both completion and successful rollback can be guaranteed. Only when all sites have acknowledged the "secure" state can the completion of the success unit be assured and at this point each site is told to commit the changes and release the locked data to concurrent running processes. Bachman and Colliat (10) describe the basic mechanism and the exchanges necessary to re-establish synchrony after failure during the commitment process.

A second problem that can occur in distributed databases with replication of data is network fragmentation. If a network gets split into two parts each half may imagine that the other part is dead and continue updating its own copy of the data. When the two halves are reconnected the two copies will need to be reconciled.

I do not believe there is a safe general solution to this problem that would allow each half of the network to continue processing. If it were decided that a "master" copy must be available then one part only would continue. The "master" could be designated by a token so that it is not necessarily bound to a particular site.

The problem can also be alleviated by systems design. Certain types of transaction are time-dependent in that their effect on the database depends on database content and therefore on the sequence in which transactions are applied (e.g. close account and set balance to zero). Others are time-independent and may be applied in arbitrary sequence (add 10 to balance). Clearly if there are network communications problems time-independent changes can be saved and applied to copies by a reconciliation program. Time-dependent transactions should be applied when all copies are in synchrony. The LOCUS system (11) supports fragmented networks working with reconciliation at least for the Operating System's own data.

Performance

In conventional database systems the application program and the database management system can share data in memory. This is equivalent to having a remote database machine with infinite bandwidth. It is not surprising that the interface for the programs to communicate with the DBMS is not the optimum one for distributed systems.

For an optimum distributed system it is necessary to minimise the data traffic between sites. This problem is common to that of file servers and so called database back-end machines. There are two ways of achieving this, and these are not mutually exclusive.

The first is to enable the database machine to select the data needed by the application program as precisely as possible.

The second method is to enable the application program to execute logical tasks near the data. This can be done by linking together separate data manipulation commands and sending a chain of them to be executed before a response is required.

Administration and Control

We can speculate that distributed database application systems will combine the problems of network administration and database administration and so we must look for more help from the system itself. It is certainly the case that early TP and Database Systems required a great deal of skill and care to keep them running, and that over the years they have been deskilled to the point where many can function with no operators at all.

For distributed systems the operator controls must be high level and advisory. Functions like data recovery, system synchronisation after failure and system restart must be completely foofproof.

One of the benefits of distributed computing should be to give individual users more control over their local computing. To achieve this we must identify which aspects of the systems demand system-wide definition, regulation and control and which can be varied to suit local requirements. The most important aspect to control is the definition and meaning of data. We have shown how it is technically easy to define a distributed virtual database that spans local site databases but this approach assumes that the data elements in the site databases are directly comparable or compatible. Achievement of this objective demands a system-wide data analysis, preferably supported by a Data Dictionary System to make the results available throughout the network.

CONCLUSIONS

Distributed Databases are still at an early stage of development. From a purely technological standpoint nearly all the techniques necessary to construct a viable system have been researched and implemented in other contexts. Current developments in Distributed Resource Systems, with file servers and intelligent terminals, and office systems with Local Area Networks will add to users' expectations and confidence.

Users are likely to develop distributed TP systems and loosely coupled Distributed Virtual Databases first since these are available now or can be easily envisaged using available technology.

In the longer term efficient use of distributed data requires higher level data manipulation languages, which will impact conventional

applications design and programming languages. This should simplify the task and bring productivity improvements to applications programming in both centralised and distributed computing environments.

The economics of distributed databases are improving rapidly. Communications speeds and costs have been prohibitive but wider bandwidth connections and more advanced database protocols will be available within three to five years.

REFERENCES

(1) Codasyl DBTG April 1971 Report.
(2) E.F. Codd, A relational model of data for Large Shared Data Bank. In comm. ACM Vol.13, No.6, 1970.
(3) ANSI/X3/SPARC Study Group on Data Base Management Systems: Interim Report 75-02-08 In: ACM SIGMOD Newsletter FDT Vol.7 No.2, 1975.
(4) TSICHRITSIS and KLUG (eds), The ANSI/X3/ SPARC DBMS Framework. Report of Study Group on Data Base Management Systems AFIPS Press, Montvale N.J., 1977.
(5) ISO TC.97-SC5-WG3. Preliminary Report - Concepts and Terminology for the Conceptual Schema.
(6) ICL Technical Publication 6426 - Data Dictionary System.
(7) ICL Technical Publication 6445 - IDMS Data Administration Languages.
(8) ICL Technical Publication 6888-IDMS COBOL DML.
(9) BCS/Codasyl DDLC DBAWG June 1975 Report, published by BCS.
(10) Bachman C.W. and Colliat G.-Commitment in a Distributed Database. Proc 4th VLDB Conference, Berlin 1978.
(11) G. Popek, B.Walker, J.Chow, D.Edwards, C.Kline, G.Rudskin, G.Thiel. LOCUS A Network Transparent, High Reliability Distributed System. Proc. 8th Symposium on Operating System Principles, December 1981.

Graham Brown joined ICT from Cambridge University, where he graduated in Mathmatics. He worked for several years in Sales, specialising in Management Science computer applications. Later he joined Application Systems Division to develop 1900 PERT and production control systems. He has led the design of data management products for a number of years covering both ICL 1900 series and 2900 series machines. As Manager of the Systems Superstructure Technology Centre in the Distributed Systems Development Division he now has design control over data management, transaction processing and compiler products. He has represented ICL on the Codasyl Data Description Languages Committee since 1975 and the Data Base Administration Working Group, which are two groups that have heavily influenced database developments.

Content Addressable Filestore as a Network Resource

L Harding
International Computers, UK

The paper establishes the structure of corporate data processing in terms of a local area network supporting distributed processing and office automation with voice/data terminals connected through a digital PABX which is linked to an area level processing facility. The PABX is also part of a Wide Area Network linked to a Coporate Data Centre. CAFS is seen as a pervasive data handling facility within the communications network. The CAFS hardware is described with an indication of its benefits over a conventional approach to data processing problems. Three specific problems are identified which relate to networked data processing, namely:—data control, data security, and information retrieval. CAFS is shown to offer unique yet simple solutions in each area.

INTRODUCTION

The transition from the computer age to the information age will force fundamental changes in both the role and operational methods of data processing professionals. Office automation and cheap personal computers have provided the means for anyone in an enterprise to create, maintain and process their own data; Local Area Networks provide these users with access to extra processing, storage and output capability; interconnection of LANs and combined voice/data terminals through a digital PABX offer direct access to corporate data and via 'gateways' to national and International networks. A schematic representation of this scenario is shown in fig 1.

The implications of what technology now makes possible in information capture and transfer stretch beyond the data processing considerations into organisation and control of the enterprise. Uncontrolled distributed processing, i.e., dispersed processing, destroys data integrity of corporate files and thus debases central management information. The response of the Central Data Processing service must be to both encourage and control the move to local computing so that local efficiency gains are not off-set by corporate chaos.

Difficulties in implementing or adapting central applications quickly enough to satisfy user needs in a changing business environment are well known; to attempt to apply direct central control to the distributed situation is certainly beyond the resources of a unit established for centralised operation.

The use of a High Speed Search Engine such as an ICL CAFS device provides the enterprise with the capability of managing problems posed by distributed data processing.

Through its supporting software CAFS gives users powerful enquiry facilities on existing files so technical resources can be released to implement distributed systems.

Within the new environment CAFS offers the capability of managing input and security of data and of providing an economic way of creating a global directory of all company information.

CAFS

The ICL CAFS product with its associated software provides a high speed data search facility with the capability of intelligent retrieval of relevant information. A CAFS search is undertaken at disc transfer speeds and is concerned with the content of the file data not its position in or relationship to a record structure. These properties enable a modestly powered processor fitted with a CAFS device to complete a complex search at a rate of several hundred times its equivalent mainframe power.

The principal elements comprising the CAFS hardware are shown diagramatically in fig 2. Details of CAFS design (1) and operational information (2) are described elsewhere so only functional aspects are included below.

The CAFS hardware is designed as an extension to a standard disc control module and operates on conventional exchangeable and fixed disc drives. Each module will handle 16 drives and up to eight modules can be attached to one host computer. An effective transfer rate of over 1 megabyte per second is achieved through each module. At present system limits are in the order of 80 gigabytes maximum storage and an analysis rate approaching 130 megabyte comparisons per second, faster disc units will allow the analysis rate to near 400 megabyte comparisons per second. CAFS can handle existing data file formats so no changes are required to production systems, although text has to be put into a "self identifying" format to facilitate CAFS search. Details of existing files are recorded on a Data Dictionary System; tables derived from this are used by the CAFS Logical Format Unit to interpret data and control the retrieval unit.

In order to use CAFS, a terminal enquiry is formulated directly or via a Query language. The resulting selection criteria are preloaded into key channels a set of which are assigned to a search task. The Logical Format Unit controls the operation of the 16 key channels which compare the incoming data stream with the users target value. The result of the comparison $> = <$ is passed to the Search Evaluation Unit which has 16 serial processors each controlled by a micro-program compiled from the user's selection expression.

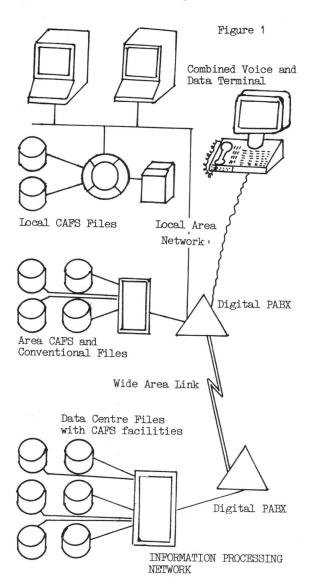

Figure 1

Combined Voice and Data Terminal

Local CAFS Files

Local Area Network

Area CAFS and Conventional Files

Digital PABX

Wide Area Link

Data Centre Files with CAFS facilities

Digital PABX

INFORMATION PROCESSING NETWORK

The Search Evaluation Unit instructs the Retrieval Unit whether or not a record is a hit; if it is, the Retrieval Unit retrieves hit records or specified fields under the control of the Logical Format Unit. Finally when the search task is complete the Retrieval Processor transfers the hit data to the host.

During the selection process the various units can provide functions in addition to simple comparisons. Within the key channels the matching process can be done with bits or

characters not relevant to the comparison masked out. The Search Evaluation Unit has a Quorum Function based on weighting results from the Key channels, it is also able to count the number of hits found in executing a task. The Retrieval Processor can total or find the maximum or minimum values in specified fields, it will discard data not required after totalling and for text searches determine whether hit words are in the correct sequence.

Experience to date

An example of the use of CAFS to improve an existing Data Processing Service has been described in a case study (3) covering the implementation of a Personnel enquiry facility. Some of the measured benefits include a reduction in support staff from 4 to 1 as the need to service batch runs and write ad hoc enquiry programs disappeared; an increase of user ad-hoc enquiries from about 60 per year to some 200 per week; a reduction in batch processing charges to the personnel activity of about 25% or £80k.

Further experience of implementing CAFS systems show a reduction of Design and Development effort of 10 to 40%, a major reduction in ad hoc and tactical batch work resulting in operation savings; improved user service with response times to non standard enquiries reduced from days to seconds and less dependence on specialist staff as the amount of application specific code is reduced.

The distributed environment

The benefits listed above indicate how implementation of CAFS can improve user service, stem the requirement for system changes and so release resources to undertake new work.

Such new work could be establishing the strategy for implementation and control of the distributed processing environment discussed in the introduction. Distributed processing must be justified on business advantage or cost effectiveness grounds. Usually the business advantage argument cannot be quantified so reduced cost or increased efficiency must support the move to local processing. In central computing facilities file control and data security account for perhaps half the operational activity. In order to realise savings when these files are distributed to local offices and plants these and other housekeeping activities must either be automated or abandoned. In practice a central facility is generally retained in one form or another in order to provide technical support and file consolidation capability. The complexity of data communication between sites and to the central facility increases because files as well as messages are now being transferred. As a result, the locating of information will be of critical importance in terms of system efficiency and user service.

As with central processing CAFS offers an

839

effective solution to the distributed processing problem areas mentioned above, data control, data security and data location.

Data Control

In the distributed processing environment common application and system design can be used to impose some standardisation on file structure, however organisation and control of data files will remain a problem.

This will be compounded by LAN technology allowing connection of a multiplicity of terminals with different tasks onto common file servers.

CAFS offers a means of resolving file administration problems by providing an efficient method of creating selected data files from randomly entered and stored data. Input screens simply label data, (for instance: - enquiry, order, despatch, invoice, payment, complaint) and a CAFS search will extract business files as required. Problems associated with overflow and re-organisation are eliminated so the need to maintain local expertise in file or database management is removed. Additionally by searching across the data the system will, for example, create a file of events affecting an individual customer or produce a product introduction analysis by selecting order, dispatch, installation and complaint data associated with that product. The recurrent problem of needing an analysis, not planned into data base design, is eliminated. The saving on ad hoc programming and processing time pays many times over for the cost of storage of redundant or archive data on the the live file if purging runs are not carried out on a regular basis. Again CAFS simplifies the process of purging the file by allowing flexibility in the purging rules. All reference to a customer for instance could be archived at expiry date of product guarantee or on closure of account with simultaneous checks for outstanding debts, complaints or maintenance contracts.

The ability to maintain conventional data files is not affected by the above approach and the appropriate update information can be generated from the CAFS files. For consolidated reports to corporate level either the local files would be created and transmitted to a central site for processing or local processing would reduce the transmitted data to only that information required for corporate purposes.

CAFS therefore provides local users with a practical service to handle day to day business problems, it reduces dependence on local data processing expertise without removing from the data processing function the ability to control corporate information processing.

Data Security

Use of passwords and other checks can be built in to systems to stop unauthorised access to data, while not fool proof such systems are generally effective. The security of data in terms of its protection from deliberate or accidental loss is a problem of greater dimensions.

It follows from the introduction that the inter-connection of word processors work stations and personal terminals through a local area network (LAN) will provide the untrained user with access to extensive data processing and file storage capacity. Further, with the opportunity for distributed processing presented by low cost hardware many current mainframe applications will be split down so that the relevant part of the file resides on the user machine where data is captured or validated. While the importance of securing key files at corporate level is self-evident and justifies investment of significant resources to copy and securely store the data; this is not the case in the distributed situation. In some cases the continued retention of corporate files will be necessary for management information and other central applications. As already stated

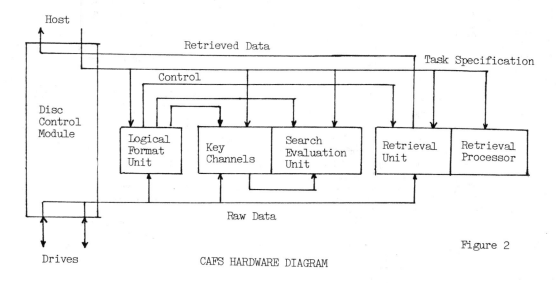

Figure 2

CAFS HARDWARE DIAGRAM

however, the justification for investment in distributed applications and hardware includes assumptions about the reduction in cost of the central facility. Thus the responsiblity for securing data will fall on numbers of local users without the support to ensure continuous implementation of necessary procedures.

The need for a corporate function to provide back up in terms of securing data is obvious, any solution however must be consistent with the cost to the business of losing the data.

In most cases the Corporate Data Centre would organise data security. It would receive information from distributed sites either across the network or through a daily batch update.

In general the cost of retaining masses of data is small, video discs offer the prospect of storing gigabytes of data without attention, for periods consistent with the useful life of most information. The cost of being able retrieve the information is however significant because it assumes the ability to locate relevant data. The cost of managing data files for the sole purpose of security back up is only likely to be justified in respect of key business information. For the rest of the data from distributed systems the secure store on a conventional data processing site will index at the crudest level, by date of batch or even week number. CAFS can provide an effective solution to the problem of secure storage outlined above. It will handle text as well as data. Incoming information can be pre-indexed if sent from a CAFS site or indexed by CAFS before storage. The level of detail in the index will depend on the nature of the information and volumes concerned. A text document could for instance be indexed by author, title, date and its own keyword list or analysed by stop word techniques to provide a more extensive index. Data elements could be indexed for instance by customer, product or service, type of transaction, date etc. Such a store and index system now not only secures data but acts as an archive and provides an audit trail for all corporate information.

Distributed computer sites can follow normal retention procedures and call on the secure store for archived or lost information. Because the data at the site is stored at random there is no problem of integrating retrieved data into files.

Data Location

The move towards distributed processing and associated office automation are based on the premise that business efficiency will improve. In the introduction it is suggested that the use of new techniques will change the way people work and communicate.

First the widespread availability of electronic mail services and Teletex will encourage asynchronous communication; messages will be sent and answers returned when convenient to the communicators separately.

The other effect, that of a reduction in personal secretarial support to office users, will mean more senior technical and management employees setting up their own telephone calls. The loss of productivity that could result from time wasted by senior staff establishing who they need to call, finding the correct number, dialling and awaiting a reply, or leaving a call-back message, could eliminate or seriously reduce gains made by automation in other areas.

The Stored Program Control PABX offers facilities for short form dialing, camp on, ring back when free, call redirect etc., and these will improve the effectiveness of the telephone service. The 'who to call' and 'on what number' problem remains and will grow as the 'information society' opens access to databases and computer facilities world-wide. The possibilities of cutting research, design, development or even production costs by getting to the appropriate data or person will increase demand for an aid to navigating through the information explosion.

As with any requirement to search for and identify information CAFS can assist in resolving the directory problem. Fig 1 depicts three levels of corporate facilities each resourced to meet the specific demands of its users. While local and area directories will handle most enquiry traffic the central CAFS facility is uniquely placed to provide an integrated company service. It can act as a normal telephone directory searching by name, address, company location, job title etc., or parts of any of these. By accessing the company personnel file job descriptions and organisational information can be combined to allow searches by function, technology expertise or authority. If it acts as a secure data store CAFS will have indexed and on file all corporate data and text and so facilitate a search for any specified corporate information. By adding details of other data bases and relevant abstracts a massive store of extra organisational knowledge can be built up. Properly indexed and with large on-line storage capacity CAFS will meet the requirements of a true Corporate Global Directory.

Conclusion

CAFS is a here and now product with massive potential to simplify and improve the service a user gets from information processing systems. The range of tasks it can perform are limited mainly by the DP professional's commitment to traditional solutions.

CAFS is a user engine and as such will have most impact in distributed processing environments where tactical business needs cross boundaries set by file structures and standard enquiry formats. The paper illustrates however that the ability to undertake complex enquiries at very high effective search rates fits it for a long term future at all levels in the information network.

References

(1)   Maller V.A.J. ; 'The content
        addressable file store - CAFS' ICL
        Technical Journal 1979

(2)   ICL Manual CAFS General Enquiry
        Package RP 3024 1980

(3)   Carmichael J.W.S. 'Personnel on
        CAFS: a case study' ICL Technical
        Journal 1981

Mr Harding qualified in
Applied Physics and has a
Post Graduate Diploma in
Management Studies. After
working on development of
electronic instrumentation
with UKAEA, he entered the
computer industry in 1961
with Ferranti. Since then
he has managed engineering
and operations on large
multi computer complexes,
run Management Services and Facilities
Management Divisions and Managed ICL's
Corporate Data Centres. He is presently
Manager of Corporate Networks for ICL,
responsible for voice and data communications
worldwide.

X.21 – The Universal Interface to Distributed Systems Implementations?

S Schindler, T Luckenbach
Technische Universität Berlin,
Federal Republic of Germany

M Steinacker
Siemens, Federal Republic
of Germany

The X.21 is one of the most prominent candidates for a future standard for a universal interface for/to distributed system implementations. This paper provides an appropriate basis for discussing the suitability of the X.21 as a universal interface by explaining the context of the X.21, the philosophy behind it, the architectural issues related to it, and giving a formal specification of it.

1. INTRODUCTION

The development of communications engineering in the immediate future will be marked by two trends: The complete digitalization of all networks and far reaching integration of most networks. Professional discussions relating to these technological developments are pursued under the aegis of several catchphrases, such as Open Systems Interconnections (at the ISO) and Public Data Network Applications (at the CCITT) for the architectural aspects, and Integrated Services Digital Networks (at the CCITT) for the integration of telephone, audio, service and data networks.

For users of these future integrated digital networks the principal question arising from these very broad-based technological discussions concerns the interface which can provide them with access to all these services. There is currently a plethora of different connectors, electrical standards and user procedures for the various networks and services – and this leads to technical and economic problems which are almost insurmountable. It is therefore generally hoped and expected that these interfaces will be simplified in the foreseeable future, and that a "universal service access interface" will be developed /1,2/.

Important though these discussions about the future "universal (ISDN) interface" are, they cannot be understood without some insight into the structure of the associated technical problems and the corresponding efforts to set up international standards. This structure will be outlined and discussed in this paper with reference to the description of the X.21 interface. The X.21 is currently the most-widely discussed candidate for this future universal interface (although it would still require certain obvious extensions for this purpose).

In order to prevent misunderstandings at the outset, it should be mentioned that in this paper the present X.21 is discussed, explained conceptually and technically, and then shown to be describable in simple and precise terms. Thus our present discussion leaves out the extensions which would need to be made to the X.21 so that it may be used as a universal service access interface, but provides the basis for a discussion of these extensions. The pros and cons of a decision in favor of the X.21 – the various potentialities and weak points of the X.21 as well as various structural alternatives to it /3/ – will be treated in detail in a subsequent contribution /4/.

At present, our aim merely is to provide a simple introduction to these topical technological discussions for a wider public.

We will do this by

a) explaining the basic outlines of the standards and recommendations which play a part in these discussions, as far as is necessary for understanding the actual problems involved in specifying a universal service access point and,

b) providing in full the formal specification of one prominent candidate for such a service access convention, rec

X.21, and thus demonstrating the new tenor of these interface discussions.

Point a) will be treated in chapter 2 and point b) in chapter 3.

In reading further it will become immediately clear that our "simplest possible" introduction is very far from being a trivial one. It requires that the reader become familiar with a whole range of technical factors (in chapter 2), and that, in studying the formal specification of the X.21 (in chapter 3) he proceeds with the care usual in mathematics.

In view of the significance of a future universal service access interface, the effort required to become familiar with it appears highly worthwhile – especially as it is just beginning to be extremely topical. For today and in the immediate future the fundamental problem of a universal service access will have to be discussed in every professional meeting dealing with communications technology.

2. THE CONTEXT OF THE X.21

In this chapter we aim to discuss all the standards/recommendations which must be known to obtain a comprehensive understanding of the X.21, so that the following points become clear to the reader:
- firstly, the considerations on the basis of which CCITT divides up the overall task of interface specification (in the X-series), and
- secondly, that although these considerations must be clearly recognised as constituting the "context of the X.21", they have no further significance for a precise understanding of the X.21 itself.

We begin our discussion of the context of the X.21 in section 2.1 with the definitions of the concepts "interface" and "interchange point" and brief explanations of them. In the following section 2.2. the recommendations/standards upon which the X.21 is based (i.e. recommendations X.1, X.24, X.26, X.27, *) and IS 4903) are discussed, inclusive of the reasons for them and how they all interact. We originally intended in a third part of this section to cover another contextual aspect of the X.21, namely recommendation X.21bis, which is designed to regulate the interworking of rec. X.21 with the mostly older recommendations of the V series. Due to space limitations we will deal with this aspect in a separate paper /5/.

It was already pointed out in the introduction that a simple extension of the X.21 (together with its associated specifications discussed here), is suitable as a standardized interface to/for the implementation of a large number of application services of distributed systems. We intend to discuss this aspect in rather more detail in chapter 4 and will thus make no further mention of it at this point.

---

*) This paper was produced in part within the scope of BMFT support project TK 050207 : "Standardized system management in open systems".

---

*) The X-series recommendations discussed in this paper are published in the "yellow book" /R1/.

2.1. Definition of Interface/Interchange point

As we intend to avoid any terminological discussion in this paper, only the two central concepts of "interface" and "interchange point" will be introduced in line with /S1/. Both definitions are translations of the corresponding definitions in the german document, which become more explicit about these issues then the original version.

Interface:
The interface is the totality of specifications regarding
a) the physical characteristics of the interchange circuits
b) the signals interchanged along the interchange circuits
c) the significance of the interchanged signals.

Interchange point:
The interchange point is the location at which the signals on the interchange circuits are delivered in a specified way and at which the interchange circuits are interconnected (e.g. by means of plug-in connectors).

These definitions are clarified in Fig. 2.1. It should be noted that the interchange point describes that part of the interface whose mechanical (or more precisely, geometrical) characteristics require specification, namely the "connector". As against this, the mechanical/geometrical characteristics of the "cables" (insofar as they belong to the interface) do not require to be further specified here. The situation is different with respect to specification of the electrical characteristics of the interface: It is clearly evident that in this case consideration cannot be restricted to the connector alone, but that the electrical characteristics of the entire "wiring", (i.e. of the technical implementation of the interface) must be included.

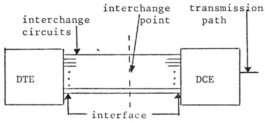

Figure 2.1: Schematic representation of an interface

2.2. The Fundamentals of Rec. X.21

Recommendation X.21 contains the specification of an interface for general use between data terminal equipments (DTE) and data circuit-terminating equipments (DCE) for synchronous operation on public data networks. In this specification, reference is made to various other international CCITT recommendations and ISO standards. Specifically, these are:
- X.1 for identification of user areas for the X.21;
- X.24 for the definition of the interchange circuits of the X.21;
- X.26 and X.27 for the specification of the electrical characteristics of the interchange circuits of the X.21; *)
- International Standard (IS) 4903 /S2/ for the

---

*) By the term "physical characteristics" the text of rec. X.21 occasionally refers to both, electrical and mechanical characteristics. With a view towards new transmission technologies and to stress the conceptual character of this discussion, it would be appropriate also to include optical characteristics of the interchange circuits into the meaning of this general item. But as the X-series recommendations do not refer to optical characteristics at all, we try to avoid the term "physical characteristics" completely, in this paper.

---

specification of the mechanical characteristics of the connector for the X.21.*)
The substance of these documents will be discussed in this chapter. The specifications of the X.21 itself will be described in chapter 3.

2.2.1. Rec. X.1

Recommendation X.1 specifies classes of service for users in public data networks, finally defining a total of 11 classes. These differ with respect to operating mode, transmission speed and permissible character code.

Two operating modes are distinguished: asynchronous and synchronous mode. Over 7 speed levels are distinguished in three speed ranges: 50 to 300 bit/sec, 600 bit/sec to 48 kbit/sec and 24 kbit/sec to 48 kbit/sec. Definitions in respect of the permissible character code exist for both operating modes, but for the synchronous mode only for the administration signals (in the more detailed official terminology in the X.21 these are called: selection sequence, call progress, calling/called line identification and charging information signals).

In the X.21 document is now specified that it should be applied for synchronous transmission as specified in recommendation X.1. Thus classes of service 3-11 are identified in X.1, i.e. X.21 determines transmission speeds 600 bit/sec to 48 kbit/sec and the use of the IA5 character set /R5/ for the administration signals.

2.2.2. Rec. X.24

In recommendation X.24 a total of 10 interchange circuits are designated (see Fig. 2.2.2). These are "conceptual" or "logical" interchange circuits - they can be mapped 1:1 onto actual circuits, but this is by no means compulsory!

These interchange circuits serve to transmit clock signals (not described in rec. X.24), control characters, administration signals and user data. The intended use of the individual circuits for information exchange is directly evident from their names and from Fig. 2.2.2 (synchronous operation is the rule, but isochronous operation is also - temporarily - permissible).

Name	Interchange circuit	Direction from DCE	to DCE
Ground or common return	G		
DTE common return	Ga		+
DCE common return	Gb	+	
Transmit data	T		+
Receive data	R	+	
Control	C		+
Indication	I	+	
Signal element timing	S	+	
Byte timing	B	+	
Frame timing	F	+	

Fig. 2.2.2 Names, abbreviations and directions of the X.24 interchange circuits.

It should be noted, however, that this intended use implies nothing as yet concerning actual implementation. This means that an information exchange is impossible merely on the basis of this specification of the interpretational framework of (still to be defined) signals on these circuits. To allow an information exchange by way of the X.24 circuits, additional and so far detailed specifications of the "signaling ritual" are required, that the transmitted signals and codes can be unambiguously recognized and interpreted.

Rec. X.21 is an example of a part of this more detailed specification (including the specification of the abstract signals, such as "syn" and "plus", and their binary coding by saying that they are from IA5) by means of which one can perform an information exchange via the X.24 interchange circuits; rec X.20 would be another example of the same kind. Another part of a different kind of this more detailed specification would have to describe the physical realisation of the interchange circuits and the physical signaling on these physical interchange circuits. (While the physical realisation of the interchange circuits will be discussed in the two subsequent sections, at present any hope of finding an explicit specification of the physical signaling in the X.21 literature would be vain!)

Let it finally be noted that the part of the detailed specification given by the X.21 (or the X.20) is conceptually independent of the physical characteristics of the circuits, of physical signaling on these circuits, and of the performance of the DCE and DTE between which information is exchanged. The conceptual nature of the X.24 interchange circuits has nothing to do with these physical characteristics.

In the last sentence, a blemish of the X.24 was touched upon, and this can be clarified in a few words. Due to the conceptual nature of the X.24 interchange circuits, they naturally require no ground returns. I.e.: G, Ga and Gb are useful and even necessary circuits in many electrical implementations – but the X.24 has nothing to do with such implementations! They should therefore not be included in this recommendation at all!

Formulating the matter in negative terms we can say: Rec. X.24 defines neither a class of users nor more detailed agreements (such as are required for an information exchange), nor electrical or mechanical characteristics of the interface, nor the number of cables required for its actual physical implementation. In particular it is absolutely legitimate to neglect some of the X.24 circuits in a recommendation which makes use of it. Thus, not all the X.24 interchange circuits occur for example in recs. X.20 or X.21, both of which are based on rec. X.24.

The X.24 is the more recent equivalent of the old V.24 /R4/. Whereas however the V.24 is overloaded with a large number of features which have in the meantime become totally irrelevant, and is additionally made more complex by partial procedural definitions (this recommendation was issued by CCITT as early as 1964), the X.24 is largely free of such technical and structural deficiencies and is correspondingly also very simple. The part which the old V.24 continues to play will be dealt with in /5/.

2.2.3. Rec. X.26

Recommendation X.26 defines the requirements for the electrical characteristics of the DTE, DCE and of the physical interchange circuits which connect them, in case of operation with asymmetrical interchange circuits and lower operating speeds (namely a maximum of 100 kbit/s).

Let us take a look at the confusing change of reference systems which occurs here:
- Whereas in the X.24 the interchange circuits are still conceptual in nature, the unsymmetrical/symmetrical interchange circuits in the X.26/X.27 are very real conductors, in X.26 one cable for each signaling interchange circuit and in X.27 two cables for every one of them.
- Whereas in X.1 the user classes are defined only up to 48 kbit/s, X.26 designates a transmission speed of 100 kbit/s as slow; X.27 even deals with transmission speeds of up to 10 Mbit/s. These inconsistencies have a simple cause: Recommendations X.26/X.27 have been taken over in unchanged form from the V-series recommendations, i.e. from V.10/V.11 /R2,R3/. Since this simple explanation is not known to all outsiders, the confusion is likely to continue.

X.26 is intended for electrical interchange circuits. The signaling performance of such interchange circuits can be described by specifying their electrical characteristics – and this is how X.26 proceeds. If our basis were an optical transmission technology then we could speak in an analogous way of the optical characteristics of the interchange circuits.

Conceptually, however, the concern here is not with the electrical (or in more general terms: with the physical) characteristics of the interchange circuits, but with their signaling performance. The electrical characteristics play a part at all only because our communications system is based on electrical transmission technology.

It is easy to see (see X.26 for further details) that the impairment of the signaling performance will increase as the length of the interchange circuits increases. Fig. 2.2.3 provides experimentally derived guidelines in the form of representative technical parameters relating transmission performance (of acceptable quality) and length of the interchange circuits. Applications with higher (quantitative or qualitative) requirements for the transmission performance must be based on X.27.

Finally it should be pointed out that the signaling characteristics of the interchange circuits, as defined in X.26/X.27, can be used only by terminal equipment of sufficiently high performance. This requirement can always be met by using IC technology. Consequently, X.26/X.27 are (together with the other recommendations/standards described here) ocassionally designated as "IC recommendations".

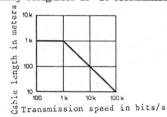

Figure 2.2.3: Transmission performance (acceptable quality) as a function of cable length for asymmetrical conductors.

2.2.4. Rec. X.27

X.27 is the analog to the X.26, but designed for applications with transmission performances up to 10 Mbit/sec or for applications with a qualitative requirement for the transmission performance which cannot be attained by means of the electrical characteristics described in X.26. The relationship between the length of the interchange circuits and the possible transmission speed is illustrated by an example in Fig. 2.2.4.

X.21 lays down that the DCE should in every case be able to operate in line with recommendation X.27. The X.21 interface with the electrical characteristics as described in X.27 is available in the DATEX network of the Deutsche Bundespost.

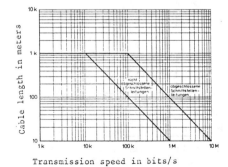

Figure 2.2.4: Transmission performance (acceptable quality) as a function of cable length for symmetrical conductors.

2.2.5. International Standard (IS) 4903

IS 4903 describes the geometrical characteristics of a connector (and an associated jack). This connector has already been available on the market for some time – in the most varied sectors of electronics. It contains 15 pins arranged in two rows and otherwise has the structure which has become usual in this sector.

Apart from specifying the geometrical configuration and its dimensions, IS 4903 also deals with the assignment of the X.24 interchange circuits to the pins. Since IS 4903 through-numbers the pins, this assignation is merely specified in the form of tables (see figs. 2.2.5a and 2.2.5b).

It should be noted that it would be illegitimate to conclude from the X.24 that only a 9-pin connector for it would be required, for example the IS 4902 conector /S3/. Because of the conceptual nature of the X.24 interchange circuits, no physical connector is required for it at all! But a physical connector is required for the physical interchange circuits used for implementing the X.24 conceptual interchange circuits, and these are determined by the X.26/X.27, resp. Consequently, X.21 specifies the IS 4903 with 15 pins and thus also allows implementation of the X.21 interface via this connector for operation according to X.27. In this case each of the 6 signaling interchange circuits is implemented by means of its own pair of twisted cables. For lower transmission circuit requirements (e.g. when operating in line with X.26) only one cable is provided for every interchange circuit and correspondingly only a single pin is used.

Since the DCE always operates in line with X.27 as per X.21, a DTE which operates only according to X.26 has the choice of using any one of the respective pairs of receive signal pins (i.e. 4 or 11, 5 or 12, 6 or 13, 7 or 14).

X.21 itself refers only to the conceptual interchange circuits – it is independent of both of these currently standardized electrical transmission techniques. Consequently X.21 is occasionally designated as "(transmission-)technology-independent". We will have more to say about the meaning of this term in the next chapter.

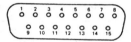 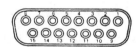

Figure 2.2.5a: Through-numbering of the contacts for the IS 4903 connector (left DTE side, right DCE side).

Pin Number	Interchange Circuit Assignment
1	See Note 1
2	T(A)
3	C(A)
4	R(A)
5	I(A)
6	S(A)
7	B(A)
8	G
9	T(B)
10	C(B)
11	R(B)
12	I(B)
13	S(B)
14	B(B)
15	See Note 2

Note 1: Pin 1 is used for connecting tandem sections of shielded interface cable. The shield can be connected to protective ground or to signal ground at either the DTE, DCE, or both in accordance with national regulations.

Note 2: Pin 15 is reserved for future international use.

Figure 2.2.5b: Pin assigment for the IS 4903 connector to the X.24 interchange circuits used in the X.21.

3. THE DESCRIPTION OF THE X.21 INTERFACE

If we consider the definition of the concept "interface" in 2.1 and the statements in 2.2, then it becomes clear that we have hitherto described only the physical characteristics

of the interchange circuits in the X.21 interface and the characters interchangeable on them (inclusive of those required to set up administration signals). In this chapter we intend to complete the definition of the X.21 interface and it thus remains to define the meaning of the signals which are actually used.

This part of the specification of an interface now shows itself to be especially complicated/subject to misunderstandings/errors, as all experience tends to confirm. In order to make this part more reliable, we have developed a formal specification language for the communications sector, in which definitions of this kind can be expressed very much more easily than in natural language or in any other specification technique known to us. This is due to the "pragmatic profile" of this language. It is called RSPL (Reliable Software Production Language), and its concepts are described in /6,7/. The language description itself and a tutorial can be found in /8,9/ and the formal semantic foundation in /10/. The formal specification of the X.21 given in Figure 3 is stated in RSPL and only briefly described due to space limitations. For its complete explanation we refer to /11,12/.

3.1. A technology-independent formal specification of the X.21

As it is usual for CCITT recommendations of this type, X.21 specifies the behaviour only of the DCE, whereas it prescribes nothing compulsory for the behaviour of the DTE: In fact, X.21 says nothing more about the DTE than how it should behave. Apart from its call collision response during call establishment, the DTE can, following these suggestions, be defined as a mirror image of the DCE. In the formal specification of a DTE given in Figure 3, we followed this procedure. This means in particular that we specified the same time-limit regulations for the DTE as were specified in the X.21 for the DCE.

The X.21 operates with those interchange circuits which are permitted by the X.24, but does without Gb and F. B is optional, is not used in most European countries and will thus also be omitted in this paper. Thus the X.21 in the Federal Republic of Germany manages with seven interchange circuits, of which only four –T, C, R and I– are directly used for information interchange. *)

Only two signals are distinguished on both C and I: ON (i.e. here "continuous 0") and OFF (i.e. here "continuous 1"). The signals on T and R are either "continuous 0", "continuous 1" and "continuous 01" (in the quiescent and the call establishment/clearing phase), or are made up of IA5 characters (in the call establishment phase), or else are binary coded transparent signals (in the data transfer phase). The term "continuous" implies a certain minimum time. It is important to note that the specification given in Figure 3 avoids all references to signal representation issues: The "signals" (or "names" or "events") of an RSPL specification are made known in it by listing them in its FUNCTIONS section. For the specification of the coding of these signals we also refer to /11,12/.

Let us explain this high level of abstraction of our X.21 specification once more and in other words. This formal specification of the X.21 in Figure 3 is based on the fact

*) S is only indirectly concerned with information interchange, since it determines the time raster required for electrical signaling during synchronous operation; for the same reason B is also only indirectly relevant for the description of the functionality of the X.21. Although G and Ga are mentioned in the X.21, they are totally unnecessary for a description of its functionality. As was already explained in section 2.2, both these circuits relate to a totally different semantic aspect, namely to the technical transmission of electrical signals – and this aspect is nowhere referred to in recommendation X.21.

that the DTE can transmit thirteen different signals (these are the functions, the names of which start with "s") and can receive twelve different signals (these are functions, the names of which start with "r"). All the signals are declared in the FUNCTIONS section, but nowhere in Figure 3 it is specified how the signals are actually coded or electrically transmitted. I.e., every unambiguous coding and every transmission technique (e.g. electric, optical or mechanical type) for this hypothetical code can be utilized for the technical implementation of the X.21 interface specified in this way. In conceptual terms, the description of such a technical implementation is nothing other than an "enrichment" or "refinement" of this conceptual X.21 specification (as given in Figure 3).

In this form the X.21 specification is thus actually technology-independent. The X.21 document goes further, however, and prescribes the X.24 interchange circuits for the implementation of the X.21 (with electrical characteristics in line with X.26/X.27 and connector as per IS 4903). By so doing it lays down a specific technological implementation to a great extent. This was by no means a necessary step: a different technological implementation could be selected just as well by interchanging the above 25 signals of the X.21 on only two interchange circuits – one in each direction. The usefulness of the X.21 in this respect will be further discussed in /4,11,12/.

```
MODULE X.21

FUNCTIONS s_C_on, s_C_off, s_C_on_T_0, s_C_off_T_0, s_C_off_T_1, s_T_1, s_T_0,
          s_T_01, s_T_syn, s_T_sel, s_T_plus,
          r_I_on, r_I_off, r_I_off_R_0, r_R_1, r_R_0, r_R_syn, r_R_syn_plus,
          r_R_syn_bel, r_R_pi, r_R_cps_pi;

PARAMETERS t1, t2, t3, t4, t5, t6,
           t11, t12, t13, t14, t15, t16 : TIME : MODULE;

PHASES QST; CSU; DAT; CLR; RES;

DEFINITIONS to_12_13 := IF NX(s_T_sel) = 0 THEN r_R_syn_plus + t12 ELSE s_T_sel + t13 FI;
            to_2_3   := IF NX(r_R_cps_pi) =  0 THEN MAX (s_T_1,s_T_plus) + t2 ELSE r_R_cps_pi + t3 FI;
            to_4     := IF NX(r_R_pi) = 0 THEN s_C_on + t4 ELSE r_R_pi + t4 FI;
            #x#      := DP := x > ! $$;

PSE := { QST → CSU → DAT → CLR }*;

QST := { r_I_off || s_C_off || r_R_1 || s_T_1 }
       → { s_T_01?, DP := r_R_ALL = r_R_1 $$ → s_T_0? → s_T_1}* || { r_R_0 → r_R_1 }*;

CSU := ( s_C_on_T_0 → { r_R_syn_bel? → r_R_syn_plus }#s_C_on_T_0 + t1#
       → ({s_T_syn → s_T_sel+ #to_12_13# → s_T_plus}#r_R_syn_plus + t11#)
         ( s_T_1 #r_R_syn_plus + t12#)
       → { r_R_cps_pi* → r_R_1 || r_I_on }#to_2_3#)
       ( r_R_syn_bel → s_C_on #r_R_syn_bel + t14#
       → {r_R_pi* → r_R_1 || r_I_on }#to_4#),          EXIT(RES,CLR);

DAT := { (s_T_1) (s_T_0) }* || { (r_R_1) (r_R_0) }*;

CLR := r_ALL≠r_I_off_R_0*
       → { ( s_C_off_T_0 || {(r_R_1) (r_R_0)}* → { r_I_off_R_0 → r_R_1 }#s_C_off_T_0 + t5#)
         ( r_I_off_R_0 → s_C_off_T_0 #r_I_off_R_0 + t15# → r_R_1 #s_C_off_T_0 + t6#)
       → s_T_1 }#r_R_1 + t16#,          EXIT(QST);

RES := ( s_C_off_T_1, DP := s_C_on_T_0 + t1 ≤ ! AND s_ALL > 0
                       AND s_ALL = s_C_on_T_0 AND r_R_syn_plus ≤ s_C_on_T_0 $$)
       ( r_R_1, DP := r_R_syn_bel + t14 ≤ ! AND r_R_ALL > 0
                  AND r_R_ALL = r_R_syn_bel AND s_C_on ≤ r_R_syn_bel
                  AND ( s_ALL > 0 => s_C_on_T_0 ≠ s_ALL ) $$),
                                        CONT(QST,CSU);

END_MODULE X.21
```

Figure 3: Formal description of the X.21 in RSPL.

4. ARCHITECTURAL ASPECTS OF THE X.21

Recommendation X.21 is not new – its first version was published as early as 1972. With the rapid development of digital transmission technology it has automatically become more interesting. The breakthrough came in 1976 with the passing of recommendation X.25 – it is included there as the level 1 interface. The X.21 then became both well-known and controversial: this latter was due not to the fact that it contains procedure elements at both level 1 and level 3 of the OSI reference model /S4/ (which would be acceptable), but because it operates with these on level 3 (namely during dialling) even before the level 2 service is available. This pecularity as well as its accompanying recommendations (X.1/X.24/X.26/X.27/IS4903) make it difficult to fit the X.21 into the communications architecture of the OSI reference model, which for its part is generally regarded as defining the perspectives for standards in communications technology.

Happily, the question of the suitability of the X.21 as a universal service access interface has nothing to do with these discussions and problems which beset the use of the X.21 on the lower layers of the OSI architecture.

This can be clarified in a few words. When an application connection is established, this universal interface is located first at the upper edge of the Network layer (of the OSI reference model), i.e. it is initially an interface to a Network service access point. In the initial dialling procedure a user would identify his addressed partner and thus the communications service which he wishes to use as well as the service elements and service primitives which are known at his own interface for the duration of the connection established. The universal interface can, during this period, make accessible a higher layer service (such as the OSI Presentation layer service) or an Application service (such as Teletex, Videotex or Telephony) - it then is an interface to a higher layer service access point or to an Application service accesss point.

In the meantime a large degree of clarity has been achieved regarding the structure of the OSI services. Agreement has meanwhile been reached between the responsible committees of the ISO and the CCITT, particularly with regard to the specifications of the OSI Network/Transport/Session layer services and draft proposals for international standards for them are expected in the coming months. As a result, the question arises regarding a generally acceptable hardware-interface convention for the utilization of these and higher services. Since the X.21 has already on one occasion proved to have the support of the majority in the responsible committees - at least within the CCITT - it appears reasonable to save a great deal of time for elaborate discussions about a new interface project (analogous to the X.21) by agreeing on the X.21 for a second time. The extension of the X.21 then required would not need to give rise to any discussions about fundamentals. (Similar considerations and accelerated procedures are not uncommon. An example of this from the recent past occured in the preparation of the LAN standard: In IEEE project 802 /13/, the LAP-B was taken over as the procedure for layer 2 with minor extensions. This was in fact done because of the resulting procedural simplifications).

It is thus easy to understand the proponents of the slogan "X.21 as the universal service access interface", but it should be clear that interesting alternatives to it also exist. We intend to discuss this question in full in /4/.

REFERENCES

RECOMMENDATIONS

/R1/ CCITT - Yellow Book, Volume VIII - Fascicle VIII.2, Data Communication Networks - Services and Facilities, Terminal Equipment and Interfaces, recommendations X.1-X.29, Geneva 1980.

/R2/ CCITT-Recommendation V.10, identical with X.26.

/R3/ CCITT-Recommendation V.11, identical with X.27.

/R4/ CCITT-Recommendation V.24, List of definitions for interchange circuits between data terminal equipment (DTE) and data circuit-terminating equipment (DCE), Geneva 1976.

/R5/ CCITT-Recommendation V.3, International alphabet Nr.5, Geneva 1972.

International Standards

/S1/ DIN 44302, Datenübertragung, Datenübermittlung, Begriffe, Berlin 1979.

/S2/ ISO IS 4903, Data communication - 15-pin DTE/DCE interface connector and pin assignments, 1980.

/S3/ ISO IS 4902, Data communication - 37-pin and 9-pin DTE/DCE interface connectors and pin assignments, 1980.

/S4/ ISO DIS 7498, Information Processing Systems - Open Systems Interconnection - Basic Reference Model, January 1982.

Individual Contributions

/1/ S. Schindler: Keywords in Communications Technology, Computer Communications, Juni 1982.

/2/ S. Schindler: Open Systems, Today and Tomorrow - A Personal Perspective, Computer Networks 5 (1981).

/3/ H. Burkhardt: Persönliche Kommunikation über das "universal interface".

/4/ S. Schindler, M. Steinacker, T. Luckenbach: Die einheitliche Dienstzugangs-Schnittstelle - Alternativen und Perspektiven, in preparation.

/5/ T. Luckenbach, O. Laumann, S. Schindler, M. Steinacker: Erläuterung und formale Spezifikation der X.21bis, in preparation.

/6/ S. Schindler: The OSA Project: Basic Concepts of Formal Specification Techniques and of RSPL, TU Berlin, FB 20, TR 80-13.

/7/ S. Schindler: RSPL - An Expert Language of Communications Technology, submitted for publication.

/8/ H. Marxen: RSPL-Z Language Reference Manual, TU Berlin, 1981 (available through the authors)

/9/ U. Flasche: Formales Spezifizieren in RSPL-Z - Tutorium und Beispiele, TU Berlin, 1981 (available through the authors).

/10/ S. Schindler, H. Marxen: The OSA Project: Translating RSPL Specifications, TU Berlin, FB 20, TR 79-19

/11/ M. Steinacker, S. Schindler, T. Luckenbach: Description of and Comments on the X.21 Interface, Technical Report, TU Berlin.

/12/ S. Schindler: Handbook of Structured Distributed Systems/Applications and their International Standards, to be published by Springer-Verlag, autumn '82.

/13/ IEEE project 802: Local Network Standard, San Diego, December 1981.

Sigram Schindler studied mathematics and physics, received his diploma degree in mathematical physics and his doctorial degree in numerical mathematics. Since 1974 he is full professor in the Informatics Department of the Technical University of Berlin, heading the research group for operating systems. He actively participates in various national and international committees concerned with communication standards.

Thomas Luckenbach was born 1956 in Berlin. From 1976 to 1981 he studied Computer Science at the Technical University of Berlin where he received his diploma degree in 1981. Currently he is assistant at the TU Berlin, primarily working in the Open Systems area.

Michael Steinacker received the diploma in mathematics from the Free University and the doctorial degree in computer science from the Technical University of Berlin. Since 1980 he has been a member of the Siemens AG, Munich, working in the areas of design and specification methods for communication protocols and services and for distributed systems.

The Upper Layers of the ISO Reference Model

P F Linington
Cambridge University Computer
Laboratory, UK

The paper describes the upper layers of the ISO Reference Model for Open Systems Interconnection, and the way this model can be applied in user applications of distributed data processing. It describes the way communication standards are used in performing the business of an enterprise, the way abstract models aid the definition of such standards, and the division of protocol specifications into application, presentation and session components. The relation of these supporting services to the ISO work on File Transfer, Access and Management, Virtual Terminal Services and Job Transfer and Manipulation is discussed.

1. INTRODUCTION

The work within the International Standards Organization on Open Systems Interconnection (OSI) has been in progress for a number of years now. Most people involved in computer communication have heard of the general concept of OSI and of the existence of the ISO Basic Reference Model which provides a layered framework for protocol standardization [1]. The ideas behind the lower layers of the model are familiar from previous work on communication. However, the upper layers are more complex. The layers concerned are the Application Layer, the Presentation Layer and the Session Layer. They have a close and often subtle relationship with computing, rather than communication, practice. This paper aims to explain the relevance of the OSI standards to the computer user, and outline the internal divisions of the OSI architecture which ease the design of distributed data processing systems.

2. THE OSI VIEWPOINT

When the designer of some distributed application chooses the distinct processing components that are to make up the application, he also decides how much of the internal working of each component is to be made public to the others. Typically, in the interests of modularity, he will share between components only those aspects of their operation necessary for the joint performance of the task in hand. Thus each component has a severely simplified view of its correspondents, seeing them only in their role as respondents to its communication.

Some of the shared behaviour of the communicating components can be expressed in terms of standard protocols. The advantages of standardization are well known. Standards allow the designer to specify certain common behaviour patterns by reference to the standard rather than setting them out in detail; he can do

this in the expectation that implementations of such standard functions will be readily available.

The specification of any interconnection of two elements can be seen as dividing the whole of the distributed application into two parts, corresponding to all the factors influencing the two communicating parties. The other subdivisions of the system are of no concern from this particular viewpoint. If necessary, each link between pairs of components could be specified in a different way.

To take a simple example, consider a large computer with terminals attached via one front-end processor and access to a public data network provided via another (figure 1). This configuration contains a number of connections between components; no two of the links involved need use the same protocols. However, this variablitiy is of no concern in specifying the behaviour of the system as seen by some other user of the public data network. Indeed, as far as electrical characteristics and data link control procedures are concerned, none of these links is visible to the remote user, who is concerned only with the way in which he is himself connected to the public network.

Moreover, if we turn from the matters of simple data transmission to progressively more abstract and application oriented considerations, each action and reaction this remote user sees will be generated by some component in the system which acts as agent for, and shields the corresponding detailed operation of, the other components with which it communicates. Thus program in the front-end processor may be responsible for handling a standard transport protocol, masking the equivalent functions on the interface between the front-end processor and the main processor; operating system functions within the main processor will handle the standard protocols for dialogue and format control masking the details of the actual terminal interfaces; at a very high level

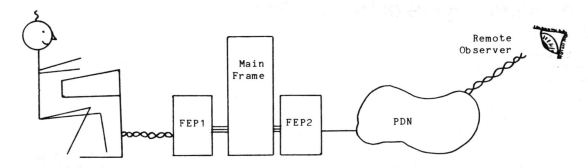

Figure 1 - A Typical System

of abstraction, the whole computing system is but a channel which allows the human users to carry out the exchanges necessary for their enterprise.

Thus, seen from the point of view of the remote user, different aspects of the system are visible as parts of a simplified, communication oriented external view of the system. It is to this external view that the different aspects of the OSI Reference Model correspond (see figure 2).

3. THE TIME COMPONENT

The exclusion of irrelevant local detail from OSI standards can lead to misunderstandings of the constraints placed on the user application. The basic reference model defines connections between systems; this has lead to the criticism by some readers that it requires the components of a distributed application to be in operation at the same time in order to communicate. The missapprehension arises from a failure to realize that some component of the computing system may act as agent for the eventual user, but that any associated queuing or scheduling mechanisms are not externally visible.

To clarify this by analogy, consider the transmission of Telex messages. In the specification of the operational requirements for a Telex terminal, it is implied that the terminal will at least occasionally have a human operator, and that for messages to pass between the two terminals concerned they must be simultaneously available. It is not apparent from the specification of the Telex Service that many large organizations employ a telex operator so that the originator of the message has no contact with the machine. There is no implication that the operation of the receiving machine implies delivery of the message to its addressee. This internal organizational freedom is never questioned, even though it is not expressed in the protocol.

Similarly in distributed applications, use of a connection oriented file transfer protocol to transfer stock control information does not imply that two stock control programs must be executed at the same time; it only implies that the system components concerned with transferring responsibility for the information and flagging a need for further processing must operate concurrently, and that the receiving component should make the information available when the stock control application next runs.

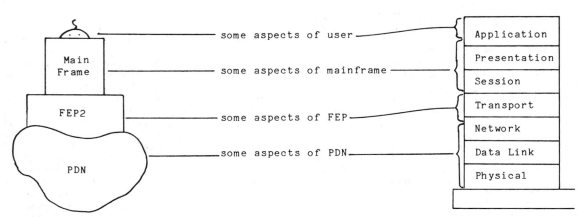

Figure 2 - External View of the System

In this way, connection oriented protocols may be exploited to support asynchronous user activity. If an intermediate system is used to provide a mailbox, no parts of the communicating systems need be active at the same time. The communication between the source or destination and the intermediate component is still described in terms of a connection, however, because this expresses the transfer of responsibility for the data between adjacent components.

4.   THE PROCESS OF IMPLEMENTATION

When reviewing a standard to see if it fulfils his needs, the system designer is offered a suggestion for part of the external view of his system. He must determine whether the view given by the standard is consistent with the activity he wishes the system to perform, and whether he can establish correspondences between the elements of this external view and the internal components of the systems he is designing.

The set of OSI standards and the Reference Model which supports them together form a complex but self-consistent logical structure, defining a large number of concepts each in terms of the others. For example, the Reference Model defines a Session Service User in terms of its relation to the Session Service Provider, and the entity in the Presentation Layer in terms of its relation to entities in adjacent layers.

The system designer does two things. First, he completes the logical structure by defining the relation of his enterprise specific concepts to the terms in the OSI standards. For example, he might define a terminal session to be the means of accessing employment records, or the relation between two application entities as being that between wholesaler and retailer. Second, he must pick correspondences between each term in the logical structure resulting and some piece of software or hardware in his systems that is to be responsible for providing the external behaviour it describes.

This paper is primarily concerned with the first of these two activities, and the way the OSI standards are organized to aid the designer in performing his task. The second, although of vital importance, is the province of the suppliers and users of equipment, not of the definers of OSI standards (although it may be of importance when considering programming language standardization, for example).

5.   DIVISION INTO LAYERS

The Reference Model fulfils its role of providing a framework to support the establishment of a coordinated set of standards by dividing the standardization activity into seven distinct layers. Independent development within each layer is assisted by defining the services offered at the boundary separating each pair of adjacent layers. A service is an abstract statement of the properties of each boundary. It gives the design aims that the protocol below must meet to support its two users; at the same time it indicates the facilities available to the designer of a protocol in the layer above.

Each layer identified by the Reference Model represents some common element needed to support communication. The lower four layers together provide various aspects of decoupling of the application from the supporting communication technology. This process culminates in the definition of a Transport Service [2] which can be provided as a single communication support for any application over a wide variety of networks.

The layers above the Transport Service are concerned with the support of the application oriented aspects of interconnection. The first layer, the Session Layer [3], exists to provide common mechanisms to structure the application dialogue. The service the Session Layer provides includes facilities for managing, where necessary, the right to perform various actions such as the transmission of data, the alteration of shared data or the termination of a dialogue. This is done by providing a generalized token handling mechanism. The Session Service also provides support for the identification and synchronization of actions in a distributed environment, and for application oriented error control. For instance, it provides quarantine facilities which can be used to indicate that the collection of data making up a transaction should either be processed as a whole or discarded, ensuring a consistent state if communication or system errors occur. Alternatively, it also provides resynchronization mechanisms for use in recovery procedures after errors have occurred.

The final layer devoted to the provision of common services is the Presentation Layer. It is the layer most intimately related to the user information exchanged, and will now be described in detail.

6.   THE PRESENTATION LAYER

The Presentation Layer [4] is concerned with managing the problems of encoding and data representation which arise when transferring information between dissimilar systems. To provide such mechanisms in a way which may be used by may different applications is not easy. It requires a means of determining whether the differences between the systems can be overcome, or whether they would affect the correct performance of the work intended.

To achieve this, the concept of abstract data types is used. This concept is, of course, well known in many areas of computing, such as language design, but has not previously been systematically applied in the communication field. In this approach, the Application Layer activity which the Presentation Service has to support can be thought of as the transmission of a series of data items chosen from an agreed set of data types. Once the data types needed are known, the protocols in the Presentation Layer allow selection of a suitable syntactic representation.

For example, if it is known that integers in a certain range and characters from a certain character set are to be transmitted, a suitable numeric encoding and character code can be chosen. Depending on the range of data types or data structures in use, either familiar or user defined, the syntax selection process may be simple or it may be as complex as need be.

A data type definition consists of two parts. First, there is a statement of a structure built up from simpler data types. Second, there is a statement of the operations which may be performed on the data type, and of the effect these operations have on the values and relationships between its component parts.

The presentation service provides facilities for conveying operations on data types, for defining new data types, and for negotiating which well known standard data types are to be available in the dialogue. It also gives access, in a formal sense, to the dialogue control features provided by the Session Service.

7. THE APPLICATION LAYER

The architectural structure up to the presentation service is concerned with the categorization of common functions, and so a linear sequence of layers can be chosen without undue difficulty. However, in the Application Layer we need to support many different types of use, and a more flexible approach is needed. As explained above, the Application Layer completes the logical description of the communication view of the activity. It therefore contains both standard and user defined elements.

In particular, there will be some element in the application layer which mirrors the spark of initiative, probably occurring far from the current activity, which set the communication activity off. This element will generally be an extremely abstract, and hence rather trival sounding statement of the original purpose. Thus a far as the OSI descriptions is concerned,

"Do we have any left hand rear brake couplings?" becomes simply "I want convey a piece of text and expect to receive another piece of text in reply.". Never the less, there is always some element in the logical description of the application layer which corresponds in the designers mind to the complex enterprise originating the activity.

The support for this intent to communicate may involve drawing arbitrary collections of items from the set of tools provided by international or enterprise specific standards. To allow this, the concept of service elements within the application layer has been introduced. In specifying the image a system is to have, the designer can establish any suitable structure of these elements, linking them together by defining their relative roles as user or provider of the particular element. The set of relationships assumed by the two ends of a particular communication must, of course, be the same, so that elements of the same type correspond. The structure chosen by the designer may vary with time, including additional elements in some phases of operation if necessary.

The ISO will define service elements for common activities such as authentication of users or coordination of commitment to change distributed data. It is also defining some service elements which define complete protocols for a particular phase or type of activity. At present this aspect of the work covers File Transfer, Access and Management, Virtual Terminal Protocols and Job Transfer and Manipulation.

In setting out to describe any one of these, the first step is to establish a data model that defines the concepts which are peculiar to the activity. Thus, for instance, an interactive terminal communication may need a model of a text formatting device, while for the specification of a file transfer, a model giving the properties of a filestore would be used. These models are abstract, not relating to any one particular terminal or filestore, and so are called a virtual terminal and virtual filestore respectively. Once such a model has been established, the rest of the specification of an activity consists in stating what protocol messages are possible, and for each protocol message, what manipulations of the model concepts are performed and what supporting services are brought into play.

All the activities described so far have been in terms of exchanges between two parties. Many such pairs may need to interact to perform a distributed task, but their coordination is the job of the system designer since it is outside the scope of the standard protocols. There is one area of work under way within ISO, however, in which the coordination of multiple activities is important, and this is the definition of management protocols. A management protocol is one concerned with the control and coordination of resources, and can involve statements about more than two active parties. For instance, a system would use such a protocol to announce its availability to a group of potential correspondents, or to synchronize data flow to several other systems. The standards for coordinating multiple activities are complex, and therefore likely to be developed internationally on a longer timescale than the simpler two party specifications.

8. CONCLUSIONS

By dividing commonly required functions into three layers in the upper part of the OSI Reference Model, ISO are providing a powerful supporting structure. The provision of the Session and Presentation Services as application independent tools encourages the use of a single solution to support many different kinds of user applications. Where specialization is necessary, the provision of a more flexible approach allowing the combination of various elements within the application layer enables the designers of distributed applications to devise effective and efficient solutions to their problems.

The OSI standards provide the communication component upon which distributed systems, both large and small, can be built. It provides a balance between the advantages of standard elements and the need for flexibility in configuration while retaining a robust modular structure.

REFERENCES

Most of the documents referenced are ISO internal documents, and are therefore subject to revision. The latest versions at the time of going to press are as follows.

[1] DIS 7498 OSI — The Basic Reference Model

[2] SC16 N860 — Draft Connection-oriented Transport Service

[3] SC16 N855 — Draft Connection-oriented Session Service

[4] SC16 N919 — Draft Connection-oriented Presentation Service

[5] SC16 N918 — Issues Pertinent to Application and Presentation Layers

[6] SC16 N880 — OSI Management Framework

Biography: Dr Peter F. Linington has been involved with computer as a users since 1962, and then as a Systems Programmer at Cambridge University since 1971. His involvement with communication protocols started with the participation of the University in EPSS, and increased until it became full time on his secondment to the Department of Industry's Data Communication Protocols Unit at the beginning of 1979.

Dr Linington's standardization work has involved participation in a number of technical committees within BSI, ISO, ECMA and CCITT. He is chairman of the BSI/OIS16 working group on File Transfer, Access and Management and of the PSS User Forum SG3 working group on the Transport Service.

Implications for Canada of Open Systems Interconnection Standards

G P Dallaire
Department of Communications, Canada

The need for a standard computer communication architecture known as Open Systems Interconnection (OSI) has become widely recognized and standard protocols are being developed in the international standards writing bodies of the CCITT and ISO. The Canadian Department of Communications is conducting policy, research and development work aimed at fostering the accelerated establishment of such standards. This paper describes OSI-based programs presently underway in Canada, as well as proposed, future directions, and areas of concentration of effort. It explores the national implications to both information users and providers, and proposes general policy guidelines for its orderly evolution. The importance of current work underway nationally and internationally on Open Systems Interconnection standards (OSI) is emphasized.

1. INTRODUCTION

Much has been said in the past decade regarding the coming of the information society, and the recent introduction in Canada and in other industrialized countries, of a wide array of information systems, services and networks leaves little doubt that the information revolution is indeed well underway and is accelerating at an ever increasing rate. This has been a direct result of developments and innovations in computer and telecommunications technology as sophisticated new networks emerge, linking a variety of data terminals and powerful computers in a wide range of applications.

Significant advances in data transmission techniques have resulted in reductions in the cost of communications and an increase in the type and quality of transmission services. Canadian data communications requirements are being met by the digital packet and circuit switched networks offered by the two domestic carriers, CNCP Telecommunications (CNCPT) and the TransCanada Telephone System (TCTS), as well as Canada's international carrier, Teleglobe Canada. Progress to date in experimentation and implementation of new technology involving digital switching, satellites, and optical fibres promises further reductions in transmission costs in the near future.

In addition, there has been a dramatic fall in the cost and size of computers, while their flexibility and capabilities have increased significantly. Computing power may be purchased today at a small fraction of what it cost a decade ago, and it is predicted that this trend will continue into the foreseeable future.

The merging of computer and telecommunications technologies has economic applications in industry, the business office, and the home. Within such an information economy, the quick and efficient exchange of information will be vital to Canada's economic competitiveness and the Canadian communications industry will play an increasingly important role.[1]

NEED FOR OPEN SYSTEMS INTERCONNECTION

As the number and complexity of new information systems and services increase, however, so do the problems associated with information interchange between systems of different manufacture.

The lack of a standard framework for development of information systems and the resultant incompatibilities between systems has caused computer information users to duplicate investment in equipment or redesign their systems using costly non-standard means in order to facilitate interworking with other computerized devices. In addition, incompatibility of system hardware and software of different type and manufacture has the effect of locking information users to one manufacturer, effectively denying the users the opportunity to employ innovative offerings by other software and equipment suppliers. Furthermore, system incompatibility has placed artifical limits on the extent to which these new tools can be used to perform new tasks and provide new information.[2]

With the dramatic increase in the number of computers and information systems, Canada will not be able to afford a proliferation of incompatible systems if it hopes to maintain its position as one of the world leaders in communication technology and its effective application, in a world where information has become an economic commodity.

Therefore, computer communications standards are required which will provide Canadian industry the necessary framework for the development and application of compatible information system components. The goal of such standards is known as Open Systems

Interconnection (OSI), where systems can work together to accomplish effective information transfer and processing by virtue of their mutual adherence to a set of standards.

The development of OSI standards at the national and international levels is key to maintaining a competitive industrial environment in Canada where distributed processing and telecommunications are playing an increasingly important role in national economic development. Otherwise, a multitude of incompatible proprietary standards could result, and many potential applications of computers and terminals never realized because of basic interconnection problems.[7] The wide-spread entrenchment of such incompatibility in an information-intensive society could have significant negative effects on national productivity and economic growth.

The establishment and implementation in Canada of such standards is fundamental to the full realization, through interconnection via Canadian public telecommunications networks, of new Canadian information services such as the National Library Bibliographic Network, Telidon/Videotex Systems, Office Communications Systems, Electronic Payments, Messaging and Trade Information Systems. In Canada, as in the United States, the requirement for interworking is of particular concern since many of the new and proposed information services will be provided on separate and competitive networks but with the potential requirements for interconnection to meet the needs of various users.

OSI INITIATIVES IN CANADA

Major efforts are being made in Canada to incorporate the Open Systems Interconnection architecture in the development of some of the new systems just mentioned.

A significant project presently in progress at the National Library of Canada involves the implementation of a decentralized nation-wide bibliographic network to ensure the fullest sharing of information and library resources. The development of this library network involves the standardization of procedures and protocols that will enable both existing and emerging library systems, utilizing different computer equipment and different computer programs, to interchange bibliographic data.[3]

This work is being done within the framework of the Reference Model for Open Systems Interconnection presently under study in both the International Telegraph and Telephone Consultative Committee (CCITT) and the International Organization for Standardization (ISO). It is anticipated that draft OSI standards being developed for the transport layer, the virtual terminal, and the common command language for information retrieval will be of direct utility to the library network.[4] A 12-month pilot project commencing mid-1982

will enable the National Library and five other institutions to gain variable experience with electronic messaging, videotex, and access to remote library systems. The benefits of developing a nationwide bibliographic network on the basis of the OSI model include:[4]

- the ability to interconnect a number of currently incompatible systems;

- the ability to utilize a single terminal to access different data bases;

- the de-emphasis of a "central" system and "master" database;

- the opportunity for existing systems of closed networks to retain fairly autonomous development programs as long as their internal system design is compatible with open system standards.

Currently in Canada, several major field trials based on Canadian Telidon/Videotex technology are in progress. The Canadian Department of Communications, where the Telidon technology was developed, plays an important co-ordinating role in these activities, working with educators, provincial agencies, telecommunications carriers, cable television companies, television networks, information providers and software firms. The common goal in these trials is to develop the most flexible and desirable combination of services to meet the current and future needs of Canadians. Above all, integrated system standards are being sought to allow the development of nationwide information services that are as easy to access and use as the telephone.[2]

OSI will significantly impact the development in Canada of the future electronic office where multi-functional electronic devices will be utilized for the processing and transmission of voice, data, text and images - all integrated into a system that will interconnect individual offices by telecommunications.[6]

Two Federal Government departments, namely Communications, and Industry, Trade and Commerce, have initiated, in co-operation with industry, an Office Communications Systems (OCS) program, a major objective of which is to provide leadership for the development of a Canadian-based office automation business infrastructure. Field trials organized under the OCS program, involving prototype office systems, are soon to commence.[6]

In 1980, the passing of revised Canadian banking legislation resulted in the enactment of the Canadian Payments Association which is working towards creation of a National Payments System and the operation of a national clearing and settlement system. This will lead to the growth of an integrated, universally accessible Electronic Payments System which will enable all financial institutions as well as small

855

businesses and individuals to share the benefits of data communications services now enjoyed by the major banks and larger corporations. The development of Open Systems Interconnection protocol standards will be an important and essential building block in the evolution of national and international electronic funds transfer systems.

The growing use of computerized information systems, the steady improvements in telecommunications technology, and the global demand for information of all kinds have contributed to a rapid increase in the amount of data traffic between nations.[2] The application of OSI principles to computerized transborder traffic can contribute significantly to the efficiencies of doing business internationally, with the potential result of opening a wide range of industrial opportunities for Canada with many other countries.

RESEARCH AND DEVELOPMENT IN OSI

The Canadian Department of Communications is conducting a program of research and development in the area of Open Systems Interconnection. The results of this work are being fed into Federal Government, national and international bodies responsible for development of OSI standards. The OSI program is rationalized on the basis of the Department's role in fostering the orderly evolution of telecommunications and contributing to the development of national industrial strength in the area of telecommunications and information system products in Canada. This work provides an important research base for other departmental programs such as the Telidon and Office Communication Systems program. These programs are aimed at technology transfer to private industry and stimulation of national industrial development. A fundamental goal is the establishment of a comprehensive Canadian-based product and system portfolio, developed within the framework of OSI, to ensure compatibility of operation. Acceptance of OSI architecture and standards nationally and internationally will ensure the largest possible market base for these products.

In view of the limited resources available in the Federal Government research and development program, it has been necessary to concentrate on a few high priority areas. These are currently the Transport and Presentation layers of the OSI Reference Model, and formal description techniques for protocol and service specifications. This latter area is regarded as an essential building block in the ultimate development of open systems, since precise and unambiguous specifications are vital to the achievement of compatible implementations. In this particular area, a number of techniques have been investigated and their capabilities for precise representation of complex protocols illustrated. The results of current work indicate that linear program-like techniques,

as well as certain graphical forms, can provide an adequately precise formal description.

At the Transport layer for OSI the Department has actively supported the work in CCITT and ISO, where a significant degree of alignment of draft standards for protocol and service has already been achieved.

At the Presentation layer Departmental experts are working on two fronts. One relates to the establishment of a layer service standard and virtual terminal framework, and the other relates to the establishment of a Presentation layer protocol standard embracing the advanced concepts imbedded in the Telidon/Videotex developments. The importance of maintaining alignment of standards in some of these areas which are closely related, but may be assigned to different national and international study groups, is recognized. In this regard studies are underway to examine relationships and interactions between Teletex, Telex, Videotex and Message Handling services on public data networks, where future user requirements may include the ability to exchange messages among the subscribers to these systems.

An additional dimension of the Department's OSI research program is that of protocol and interface assessment and verification. The complexity of protocol designs, particularly at the higher layers of the OSI architecture, is such that testing and assessment of implementations is itself complex. In many cases, even with a formally specified protocol, implementations will differ. The cost of exhaustive testing of protocols can be excessive for small businesses engaged in OSI protocol implementation.

This fact has led a number of countries to offer a national protocol certification service. In carrying out its own research program the Department is cognizant of the possible need in Canada of such a service. In the event that such a need is clearly identified, the laboratory test bed system and implementation and testing experience would be a very useful asset in establishing a nation-wide service.

NATIONAL POLICY CONSIDERATIONS FOR OSI

For more than a century, Canadians have worked together to build a strong and secure economy. During this period many adaptations have had to be made to accommodate and embrace technological advancement. Never before has there been such a widespread, profound and rapid change in the infrastructure of business and society, as is being wrought presently by the computer. It is essential that such a pervasive change be guided in some fashion so that advantage may be taken of its full potential for enhancing both the social and economic environment in Canada.[8]

The quick and efficient exchange of information between computerized systems is increasingly vital to Canada's industrial competitiveness and economic growth. While the policy and regulatory framework for telecommunications in Canada can perhaps be described as unique, it is also such as to emphasize the need for Open Systems Interconnection.

Data Communications is provided in Canada on a competitive basis by two independent national telecommunications carrier consortia.[9] Of the eleven member companies of these two consortia, four come under Federal Government regulation, while the remaining seven operate under the regulatory authority of the provincial governments. In addition, all cable television companies and national broadcasting undertakings are regulated by an agency of the Federal Government.

A new situation has now developed as a result of a decision last year by the federal regulator to allow certain terminal attachments to the public switched telephone networks of Bell Canada and British Columbia Telephone. This will result in the enhancement of the environment in which companies and individuals choose telecommunications services and supplies from different sources.

This result, as well as the fact that some provincial regulators do not permit terminal attachment, could increase existing problems of effective interworking between systems and equipment. Appropriate mechanisms must be implemented to facilitate such interworkings. As previously discussed, this need for open interworking is increasingly being recognized as of fundamental importance to Canada's industrial competitiveness and economic growth.

The early development and adoption in Canada of Open Systems Interconnection standards are essential to ensure that all required interchange of information between computerized systems of different types and operating characteristics can be achieved in an orderly and cost effective manner. It is essential, therefore, that such Open Systems Interconnection standards provide a conceptual and functional framework for the inter-operability of all computerized systems required to interwork both within and between like and unlike computer information systems. The possible interconnection of future national information systems such as the National Library Bibliographic Network, Telidon/Videotex Systems, Office Communications Systems, Electronic Payments, Messaging and Trade Information Systems, are of special interest because of their potential impact on Canada's social and economic structure.

Such OSI standards must meet the needs of Canada's industry in order to contribute to its competitiveness in offering information systems, products and services both in Canada and abroad. This would include the cable and telecommunications carriers, terminal and mini-computer manufacturers as well as software and information providers. Furthermore, the development of a Canadian Open Systems Interconnection architecture must provide for inter-networking requirements between the various data networks in Canada for the linking of computerized systems served by these different networks.

Finally, it is essential that Open Systems Interconnection allows, where economically and functionally possible, for the equitability of access to and from all information users and providers, including access by the public to government information systems and services.

CONCLUSION

In summary, in Canada, as in numerous other countries, there is now an ever increasing awareness of the significant impact of information technology on future industrial and economic sovereignty.

The rapid development and implementation of new computer communication systems and services is indeed a world-wide occurrence which has been, to a large degree, the result of the input to and output of the intense study activities in the two international standards-writing bodies, the CCITT and ISO.

As is known to those who participate in the work of the CCITT and ISO, both these organizations have recognized for some time now that Open Systems Interconnection is indeed a key element in the successful utilization of information technology.

Since the beginning of work on OSI in the CCITT and ISO some three to four years ago, Canada has maintained a high level of contribution and participation. Only in the past year or so, however, have there been substantive domestic initiatives to develop national OSI standards to meet Canadian objectives and needs. This was emphasized earlier this year by Canada's Minister of Communications, Mr. Francis Fox, when he stated that "OSI impacts on Telidon, Office Communications Systems, transborder data flows, transborder satellite services and almost every other communications activity".[6]

The present pace of work within CCITT and ISO will surely result in International Standards for OSI within the next several years. The present OSI initiatives in Canada must be continued and even accelerated if Canada is to derive the maximum possible benefits from the evolving information society.

Acknowledgements and Disclaimer

The author wishes to thank both Messrs. R.M. Bennett and W.A. McCrum for their editorial assistance, with special thanks to Mr. McCrum for his overall support and specific contribution relating to the area of research and development.

It should be noted that while this paper makes reference to statements of several senior Canadian Government officials, the views expressed are those of the author and do not necessarily reflect the views of the Department of Communications.

REFERENCES

[1]   S. Serafini and M. Andrieu "The Information Revolution and Its Implications for Canada", May 1980, Department of Communications.

[2]   J.T. Fournier, "Transborder Issues and Network Architecture", April 1981, Department of Communications.

[3]   E. Buchinski, Edwin J., and Islam, Mazhural, "The Context of Interconnection for a Nationwide Bibliographic Network", 1980, National Library of Canada.

[4]   E. Buchinski, "National Library of Canada and Open Systems Interconnection", 1981, National Library of Canada.

[5]   COSTPRO Dialogue Report, "A Canadian Trade Information System – A Marriage of Tradition and Automated Systems and the New Technologies", September 1979, Canadian Organization for the Simplification of Trade Procedures.

[6]   The Honourable Francis Fox, Minister of Communications, "Bright Prospects for Informatics Industry in Canada", Canadian Data Systems, pp.64 February 1982.

[7]   R.E. Blackshaw, I.M. Cunningham, "Evolution of Open Systems Interconnection", IEEE '80, October 1980, pp.417-422.

[8]   Report of Ad-hoc Committee of Canadian Ministers, "Economic Development for Canada in the 1980's" Government of Canada Printing Office, November 1981.

[9]   R.M. Bennett, "Canadian Policy Considerations Relating to Teleinformatic Services", Proceedings of the Second CCITT Interdisciplinary Colloquium on Teleinformatics, June 1980.

Gaston P. Dallaire is a graduate engineer from Carleton University and has been Manager, Data Policy Planning in the Policy Sector of the Department of Communications of Canada for the past five years. In this present capacity, he is advisor in initiating policy recommendations involving national and international data communications facilities and services. In addition, he is Chairman of a National Study Group responsible for Canadian contribution to the study activities of CCITT SG VII, Data Communications Networks. Prior to his present position, he was employed with Bell Canada for eleven years.

ECMA Virtual File Protocol – an Overview

P Bucciarelli
Olivetti Telecomunicazioni, Italy
A Poublan
Cii Honeywell Bull, France
J Schumacher
Nixdorf Computer, Federal Republic of Germany
W Thiele
IBM Germany, Federal Republic of Germany

This paper is an overview of the ECMA[1] activity in the area of Virtual File service. Currently ECMA is defining a standard[2] Virtual File Protocol (1) for the Application layer of the OSI[3] architecture.

The role of such a protocol is to allow a standardized handling of files in the context of OSI. This is made possible by the definition of a generalized file model called Virtual File and all services provided by the virtual file protocol are applied to virtual files. At present (April 82) the standard defines only what is needed for a basic File Transfer service but it provides the consistent technical basis for further Virtual File Protocol standards with extended scope.

The aim of this paper is not only to give a description of the standard proposal but primarily to focus on the approach followed in standardization of Virtual File Protocol, to clarify the main concepts and to point out some interesting and largely discussed technical aspects concerning the Virtual File Service.

1   INTRODUCTION

File transfer is one of the most commonly required network services. Since many different implementations of host systems may coexist in a single network, there arises a strong need for standardization of a File Transfer Protocol.

Up till now, specific solutions – normally internal standards – have been adopted inside of closed user groups or for implementations of specific vendors. Extension of those file handling services to new hosts is always possible with costs depending on the flexibility of the existing solution. Implementation cost can, however, grow unacceptably in case of extending those specific solutions to heteregeneous networks between several organizations.

This problem can only be resolved by the definition of a standard File Protocol providing the possibility of file handling in a heteregeneous network at minumum implementation cost.

Adopting a universal standard provides the user with the following benefits:

-   Interconnection of systems from different organizations within a network, and
-   the advantage of a well defined protocol.

The increasing availability of public data networks, encouraging interconnection of computers and exchange of large quantities of data, requires most urgently the definition of a standard solution for file handling and particularly for file transfer. The later such a standard is produced, the more difficult it will be to reach agreement on it, because of growing proliferation of incompatible solutions invented by large users, governments and manufacturers.

Recognizing this urgent need, ECMA started a project aiming at a gradual development of such a standard, covering with its first publication the best understood needs in the

---

[1] ECMA is the abbreviation for 'European Computer Manufacturers Association'. The aims of the Association will be clear from the following extract from the By-Laws:

To study and develop, in co-operation with the appropriate national and international organizations, as a scientific endeavour and in the general interest, methods and procedures in order to facilitate and standardize the use of data processing systems.

To promulgate various standards applicable to the functional design and use of data processing equipment.

The Association shall be a non-profit making organization and shall devote itself to no commercial activity whatsoever.

The following ordinary members are associated in ECMA: AEG-Telefunken, Burroughs International SA, Cii Honeywell Bull, Digital Equipment Corporation Systems Ltd., IBM Europe, I.C.L. International Computers Ltd., Ing. C. Olivetti & C.S.p.A., NCR Co Ltd., Nixdorf Computer AG, Philips Data Systems, SEMS: Societe Europeenne de Mini-Informatique et de Systemes, Siemens AG, Sperry Univac.

[2] DISCLAIMER: The draft standard is at this moment not necessarily endorsed by the companies for which the authors work.

[3] OSI – Open Systems Interconnection.

shortest achievable timeframe.

It defines currently only those services needed for basic file transfer, but by the modularity of its design it can be easily extended to accomodate future requirements.

Brief history of the Standard

When the ECMA effort started, all existing protocols in the field were pre-OSI, a fact that does not decrease their value. Though several of them were examined, one was particularly retained as a source of inspi - ration the NIFTP (3) (4), originally developed in 1977 for the EPSS network in the U.K. The reasons for this preference were, apart from its inherent qualities, the fact that it had been successfully implemented on many diverse installations and therefore constituted a practical experience.

It was of course very important to closely consider any parallel effort in the parti- cular context of Open Systems Intercon- nection. At the beginning the leading contri- bution was the BSI work on the Virtual Filestore, a concept derived from the NIFTP (5) which laid the foundations for all future developments of OSI file protocols.

As time passed, close coordination was maintained with two other standard bodies active in file protocols standardization: the National Bureau of Standards (NBS) and the ISO. The NBS was aiming at producing a file transfer standard for the federal admin- istration within about the same time frame as the ECMA development. The similarity of objectives lead to a close coordination, where each party was informed of the other's progress and this resulted in mutual influence. However, due to the lack of precise unification objectives, the two protocols are similar but not fully compat- ible at the moment.
Concerning ISO, ECMA has been from the beginning a steady contributer to the work of TC97/SC16/WG-5 which is the group within ISO, where standards for file handling in the context of OSI are developed. For the current document see ref. (8). ECMA has taken into account in its design all the major decisions made by the WG-5. But even if ISO and ECMA have the same final goal, their approaches to it are different: while ECMA aims at a gradual development with a first standard publication in the shortest time frame, ISO advances at a much slower pace, trying to encompass as much functionality as possible in its first step. At a certain point therefore ECMA has anticipated ISO in the development of a file transfer protocol.

2 BASIC CONCEPTS

2.1 Standardization approach

In order to provide file transfer inside OSI, syntax and semantics of the messages being interchanged between the two peer entities involved in file transfer have to be stand- ardized. In order to provide a good under- standing of the protocol capabilities, the semantics of the standard are supplied by means of an abstract definition of services. These services are conceptual only and do neither constitute an interface nor define an implementation architecture. The only con- formance requirements are the creation and acceptance of correct protocol elements.

2.2 Relationship between Protocol and Application

File transfer is an application involving two files - source and target - located at different nodes of the network. One of those is local to the system requesting the file transfer, whereas the other one is remote to this system. Access to the local file is outside of OSI standardization, whereas the only means for handling a remote file are those provided by the protocol defined by this standard. The file transfer application is therefore considered as a user of the Virtual File Protocol (VFP). The function- ality added by the application to the services supplied by the VFP and the inter- faces offered to the human as the final user are completely out of the scope of this standard.

It is recognized that file transfer may be initiated by a system not containing any of the involved files (three-party transfer). This case can be reduced to the normal case by sending the request to a system containing one of the involved files. The protocol for three-party transfer has, however, not yet been defined; it is still not clear to which area of OSI it belongs.

2.3 Layering

The file transfer protocol is an application layer protocol of the ISO reference model (2) and is relying on services offered by the presentation layer (7). Some of those services are directly derived from those offered by the session layer (6) i.e., the presentation layer is relaying those services to the appliction layer without adding or hiding any functionality.

2.4 The Virtual File Concept

The major problem faced when trying to design file protocols for a heteregeneous environment are the dissimilarities between the existing file systems. This problem was overcome by the definition of a canonical model of a file: the virtual file.

The virtual file is built on the premise that a standardized representation can be set up for files, including both file structures and the allowed operations on these structures. It removes the differences in style and specifications by using mapping functions to relate the standard descriptions to local resources and vice-versa. Any particular system can then communicate with other different systems in terms which can be mutually understood. Although the objective is to deal with real files, the model and protocol is dealing only with virtual files. The mapping between real and virtual files is considered a local concern, not subject to standardization.

It is ECMA's belief that standardization of virtual files cannot be successful if it imposes major changes to the current file systems, except perhaps in the long term. Therefore the virtual file model does not propose innovations: it is rather aiming at reflecting the major existing file organi — zation.

Another design guideline is to avoid propagation of existing file constructs which are not widely used. It is recognized that such specific file structures may require support in homogeneous networks , but it is believed that this support, where needed, is better provided by specific extensions than by increasing the complexity of the virtual file model. (This is one of the reasons why the ECMA protocol includes a mechanism to facilitate specific extensions without com — promising the open working capability.)

2.5 A Standard developed Step by Step

A gradual approach has been selected for the definition of the virtual file model as well as for the development of the protocol.

The Virtual File Protocol has been designed to provide capabilities for file access and file management, i.e., for handling contents and attributes of files. Currently - December 81 - it defines all those capabilities necessary to support file transfer, covering the most urgent need for standardization in this application area. Design of the protocol has been focused on simplictly , flexibility

and extensibility, such that presently defined simple operations can be easily extended to more complex functions as soon as a need arises.

2.6 Subsetting

Although rather specific requirements have been exempted from standardization, the amount of functionality needed by various implementations is varying to a large degree. While the standard must encompass enough functionality to satisfy the most embracing requirements, it is not desirable to impose more support than required on a particular implementation, resulting in unnecessary development cost and overhead for implemen - tations with simple requirements.

On the other hand, it is not reasonable to allow uncontrolled partial implementations, since it must be insured that workable partial implementations are possible by defining consistent subsets, and communication between different implementations must be possible in case of partial implementations. This is achieved by defining a kernel subset, providing meaningful functionality, but sufficiently small to be acceptable for all implementations. Over and above this kernel, sets of optional extensions are defined. Their use on a particular connection is negotiable.

Both the virtual file model and the services are subsetted this way. There is no dependency between the defined subsets of the virtual file model and of the service: an extended service can be provided for a simple file model and vice-versa.

3   ECMA VIRTUAL FILE PROTOCOL STANDARD – OVERVIEW

This chapter contains a summary of the standard proposal. The virtual file model, the protocol structures and some data presentation aspects are outlined.

3.1 Virtual File Model

The descriptor of the virtual file is made by means of a set of distinct properties called attributes. The values of the attributes define, identify and describe the virtual file completely, allowing correct mapping between real and virtual files. The attributes of a virtual file can be classified into three categories:

- file addressing and protection
- file structure definition
- file history

File addressing must identify a virtual file in a unique way within the OSI environment. A two level addressing scheme is provided:

a) each virtual file is part of a virtual filestore, i.e., a collection of virtual files residing at a particular system and accessible in the OSI through a single Virtual File Service (VFS) entity. The first level of file addressing is therefore the virtual filestore name, a global title necessary to establish an application connection with the appropriate VFS entity.

b) Within the designed virtual filestore, each file is unambiguously designated by its file name. At this moment, no effort has been made to standardize virtual file names: the naming conventions used in the various file systems are too different to allow a general convention easily mappable to and from any local one. Since no rule is established each OSI environment can establish its own naming conventions, if desired.

File protection is the means by which operations on virtual files may be restricted to authorized users. Since there is currently no standard for file protection, two widely used protection schemes have been retained: the file passwords and the access control list, i.e., and explicit list of authorized users. Both are optional.

The file structure definition describes the organization of the file contents. Two models of file structure are supported: unstructured and flat.

An unstructured file has no user defined internal structure: it is seen as a sequence of characters or transparent octets.
A flat file is divided into records, which are the visible units of access defined by the user. There is no relationship beween the records other than sequencing. This category includes most types of conventional files and the relational databases. Further attributes of a flat file specify the record access capabilities (usually called file organization) and describe the record key (if any) and contents. The record contents description may be global: N characters or N transparent octets; this will cover many requirements. It may also include a list of record fields, with their data types and lengths, whenever the virtual filestore can store such descriptions.

File history consists of statistical information about the virtual file usage, like date and time of last modification. Such information may be useful in verifying that the correct version of a file is processed.

The kernel subset of the virtual file model includes only sequentially organized flat files, without record field descriptions.

The prime candidate extension for the next version is the support of hierarchical file structures, i.e., files with multiple record types and hierarchical relationships between these record types. Sufficient gross design has been performed to insure that this introduction will cause no discontnuity in the standard. The support of CODASYL network databases is not intended as long as the service is only file transfer oriented; the reason is that these types of structures are difficult to "flatten" for sequential transfer.

3.2 Protocol Overview

3.2.1 Connection oriented service

In developing a virtual file service (VFS) there are two possible approaches

- A connection-oriented service where each peer entity has two responsible users. Each user is aware of the progress of each operation. Control, incl. interruption is possible during any stage of the process. Service primitives for error recovery and abortion are available to the user.

- A transaction-oriented service providing few but very powerful primitives to one user. These primitives combine multiple function and the whole file transfer is seen as an indivisible operation.

ECMA has chosen the connection-oriented approach, which allows the user to combine protocol functions according to his needs.

3.2.2 Roles of the users at both VFS entities

In the VFS connection between two VFS users, the dialogue is always asymmetrical, i.e., the two users play different and complementary roles. The initiator of the VFS connection (called the Primary) is the one who defines the work to be performed on the Virtual Filestore through the connection in a more or less direct relation with the end user on behalf of whom it acts. The other VFS user (called the Secondary) is executing the work proposed by the Primary and reporting to it; it resides on the same system as the Virtual Filestore and has no relation with the end user.

The VFS users can also assume the roles of Sender (of data) and Receiver (of data). During the life of a connection, these roles can be exchanged while the ones of Primary and Secondary are fixed.

3.2.3 Dynamic structuring of a VFS connection

The VFS allows operations on only one file at a time on a given VFS connection. Multiple files can be handled concurrently through several parallel VFS connections. Furthermore within one VFS connection, operations on the current file are executed one after the other in the order of submission. This is necessary to keep control on the sequence of events.

The work performed on a VFS connection can be dynamically structured as set of nested enclosures which must be opened in the hierarchical order and closed in the reverse order. If the VFS connection breaks or is abnormally terminated by one user, all the currently opened enclosures are considered as being implicity closed.

The enclosures are the following, in the hierarchical order, starting from the outmost one:

(1) Connection enclosure: the VFS connection exists (from establishment to temination of the VFS connection).

(2) File enclosure: a current file exists (from successful file selection to file release). A connection enclosure contains any number of file enclosures (including none).

(3) Open enclosure: the current file is ready for data access (from successful file opening to file closing). A file enclosure contains any number of open enclosures (including none).

(4) Transfer enclosure: file data is being transferred (from transfer start to normal or abnormal transfer end). For file transfer, there is normally only one transfer enclosure within an open enclosure. Once a transfer is open, the roles switch to Sender and Receiver until the transfer enclosure is closed.

3.2.4 Protocol-Descriptive model

The asymmetry of the VFS is reflected in the protocol: the two VFS entities play different and complementary roles, corresponding to the roles played by their respective users:

Primary and Secondary outside of a transfer enclosure. Sender and Receiver within a transfer enclosure.

The Virtual File Protocol is modelled as an abstract machine, with protocol structures between the two VFS entities. A protocol structure is an elementary dialogue for the purpose of an indivisible operation. As such, it is totally successful or totally unsuccessful, never partly successful. It is composed of a request issued by one VFS entity, and for most (but not all) types of structure, of a response issued by the other VFS entity. Each single reponse or request results in a protocol message.

A protocol message contains protocol control information (i.e., one or more parameters) and may contain file data.

Dynamic execution of the VF protocol results in an ordered sequence of protocol structures.

There are two types of protocol structures:

Type 1 structure: request without response

Type 2 structure: request with response

3.2.5 Protocol Structures

This standard defines the following protocol structures:

1. CONNECT (type 2)
   Establishes a VFS connection. Particular parameters are selected or negotiated. They remain effective for the lifetime of the connection.

2. RELEASE (type 2)
   Obtains a clean, non-disruptive release of a VFS connection.

3. DISCONNECT (type 1)
   Obtains, in emergency situations, an unclean, disruptive release of a VFS connection.

4. END-GROUP (type 2)
   Delimits a group of protocol messages. Its purpose is minimization of time delay due to a message exchange (see 4.1). Grouping is selected in the CONNECT request.

5. SELECT-FILE (type 2)
   Establishes a file, which exists within the connected Virtual Filestore as the current file of the connection. All further messages will implicitly refer to this file until RELEASE-FILE, DELETE-FILE or abnormal termination of the connection.

6. RELEASE-FILE (type 2)
   Releases the current file.

7. CREATE-FILE (type 2)
   Creates a new file within the connected
   Virtual Filestore and establishes it as
   the current file. Besides those parameters, which are obvious to this
   service , like file name, passwords or
   file attributes, there are two parameters
   deserving special attention in this
   paper.

   - The clash option specifies the
     action to be applied in case that
     the supplied file name does corre -
     spond to an already existing file in
     the secondary entity. The values
     'reject' 'keep' and 'replace' spec-
     ify the action to be taken by the
     secondary entity.

   - The 'reversible mapping' option
     specifies that mapping between the
     virtual and the real file must be
     reversible. (The role of this para-
     meter will be discussed in chapter
     4.2).

8. DELETE-FILE (type 2)
   Deletes and releases the current file.
   The file is released even if file
   deletion fails.

9. READ-ATTRIBUTES (type 2)
   Returns specified attributes of the
   current file. This does not include
   file-name and file-passwords.

10. OPEN-FILE (type 2)
    Initiates processing of the content of
    the current file. Only sequential
    processing of data is provided for
    reading the contents of the file,
    loading a newly created file, over-
    writing the contents of an existing file
    or extending a file after its current
    end. A failure option specifies the
    action to be taken on the file contents
    in case the data transfer must be
    abandoned. The file might be left with
    undefined contents or a roll-back to its
    previous status might be requested.

11. CLOSE-FILE (type 2)
    Terminates processing of the current
    file data.

12. BEGIN-DATA (type 2)
    Starts transfer of data.

13. DATA (type 1)
    Transfers file data.

14. END-DATA (type 2)
    Signals normal completion of file data
    transfer. No restart is possible after
    acceptance of this structure by the
    receiving node.

15. ABORT-TRANSFER (type 2)
    Specifies the abnormal termination of
    file data transfer. A diagnostic para-
    meter defines, whether the transfer is
    definitely abandoned or if recovery
    might be tried at a later time.

16. RESTART-TRANSFER (type 2)
    Resynchronizes current file data trans-
    fer at a previous point. This point is
    specified in terms of the rank of the
    first record (in case of flat files) or
    octet (in case of unstructured files) to
    be retransmitted.

17. CHECKPOINT (type 2)
    Marks points during data transfer at
    which acknowledgement of processing is
    desired. Other services may be initiated
    by the sender between a checkpoint
    request and the corresponding response.

REFERENCES

(1) European Computer Manufacturers Associ-
     ation, 'Virtual File Protocol', Final
     Draft. ECMA/TC23/159

(2) Data Processing – Open Systems Intercon-
     nection – Basic Reference Model.
     ISO/DP7498

(3) A Network Independent File Transfer
     Protocol. HLP/CP (78)1.

(4) A Network Independent File Transfer
     Protocol – Revised Version. February
     1981.

(5) Open Systems Interconnection – The File-
     store Image – Definition. London
     79-17/BSI/DPS20/WG-6/38.

(6) European Computer Manufacturers
     Association. Standard ECMA – 75.
     'Session Protocol'.

(7) European Computer Manufacturers
     Association. 'Data Presentation
     Protocol' – Final Draft, ECMA/TC23/82/41

(8) ISO: Virtual File Service
     ISO/TC97/SC16/N682

Open Systems Interconnection – Towards a Presentation Service Standard

S Schindler, C Bormann, H Wilke
Technische Universität Berlin,
Federal Republic of Germany

The paper gives a Presentation service specification suitable for the Presentation layer of the Open Systems Interconnection architecture. The Presentation service specified is based on the abstract data type concept. It is expected that a "Draft Proposal for an International Standard" for a Presentation service will become available by the end of this year and that this future International Standard will be very similar to the Presentation service specified in this paper.

OVERVIEW OF THE PAPER

During 1981, far reaching agreements concerning the Presentation service of the Open Systems Interconnection (OSI) communications architecture /1/ have been achieved. It was recognized that the provision of the abstract data type concept by the Presentation service conveniently allows to resolve many information presentation/representation problems in the Application layer.

Introducing this abstract data type concept into the OSI architecture was a major step forward in supporting the design and the use of structured distributed systems. It generalizes the most important concept in classical systems design such as to make it applicable to this area. Thus, the concept of abstract data types is the fundamental support provided by the Presentation service to its users.

A draft proposal for an International Standard for the Presentation service, based on the concept of abstract data types (as currently being discussed in the WGs of ISO/TC97/SC16 and as explained in this paper) may be expected by the end of this year.

The rest of this paper (starting at the next headline) gives a Presentation service specification derived from the current ISO working document on the Presentation service, /2/, by elaborating on its unresolved issues. (The layout of any service specification document for the OSI architecture is subject of a layer independent guideline document - hence the structure of /2/ and of this paper.) Its purpose is to provide a more concise specification of the Presentation service than could be achieved during the short time of the SC16/WG5 Architecture Group meeting which lead to /2/. These elaborations were carried out keeping in mind the requirements of system design and of the future system users, which eventually must be met by the OSI Application services. An explanation of the use of abstract data types for information presentation and representation purposes may be found in /3, 4, 5/.

0. Introduction

This document is part of a set of international standards, produced to facilitate the interconnection of information processing systems. It is positioned with respect to other related standards by the Open Systems Interconnection Basic Reference Model, which defines the subdivision of the whole area of standardization for interconnection into a series of layers of specification.

The aim of Open Systems Interconnection is to allow, with the minimum of technical agreement outside the interconnection standards, the interconnection of information processing systems:

- from different manufacturers
- under different managements
- of different levels of complexity
- of different technologies.

This standard defines the service available to entities within the Application layer of the Basic Reference Model.

The standard recognizes that Application entities may wish to intercommunicate for a wide variety of reasons. Whilst not all systems will share a common method of presenting and representing the information they wish to intercommunicate, they will be agreed about the subject matter of their communication and the meanings to be assigned to that information. The Presentation service supports effecting the intercommunication through transformations of the information presentation and/or representation which leave the meaning unchanged. The difference between presentation and representation of information is, that the former has a meaning for the Application entities, while the latter is of no concern to them.

*) This paper was supported by the BMFT (FRG), under contract No. TK 05020 7: "Standardisiertes System-Management in Offenen Kommunikationssystemen".

This standard describes the service provided to the Application entities using a particular linguistic method known as the abstract data type concept. This method provides a concise unambiguous technique for agreeing on and subsequently communicating units of information and their abstract syntax, while allowing for different local concrete syntaxes of the information which determine the different presentations/representations of this information.

1. SCOPE AND FIELD OF APPLICATION

1.1. Scope

This standard specifies the service of the Presentation layer of Open Systems Interconnection. It specifies the characteristics which are visible to the users of the service.

Matters relating to implementation, testing, and to the local boundary between the users and the provider of the service are outside the scope of the standard.

1.2. Field of Application

The standard is provided for reference by

  - standards for Presentation layer protocols, and
  - standards for Application protocols.

It provides a frame of reference for standards for a wide range of Application services, such as:

  - The Virtual Terminal Service
  - The File Service
  - The Job Transfer and Manipulation Services
  - The Text Preparation and Interchange Service (including: Teletex, Telefax, Videotex, Graphics, Typesetting)
  - The Computer Based Message Service.

2. REFERENCES

(To be included: ISO numbers and titles of the standard documents referred to in this document.)

3. DEFINITIONS, 4. ABBREVIATIONS

(The need for material in these sections is for further study)

5. CONVENTIONS

This standard has been written using the conventions specified in DP xxxx (currently a working draft of ISO/TC97/SC16/WG1).

6. OVERVIEW OF THE PRESENTATION LAYER

In order that the Presentation service users, namely Application entities, can communicate and cooperate, they need to agree upon and deal with the items relevant to their communication. For this purpose the Application entities must be able to interpret each other's references to these items; in other words, Application entities engaged in a dialogue must share a common frame of reference (termed the "common abstract syntax") to these items. The Presentation service provides the means for each Application entity to establish, in a communication, its own "concrete syntax" within this common abstract syntactical frame. (The concrete syntax used by an Application entity in a communication defines its term of reference to the items relevant in this communication.) In addition, the Presentation service supports the reconciliation of the concrete syntaxes established in a communication.

There are three concrete syntaxes (of the common abstract syntax) known by the Presentation layer in any communication: the two concrete syntaxes used by the two communicating Application entities and the concrete syntax used to propagate the references to items between Presentation entities (termed the "transfer syntax" or "common concrete syntax"). Any two or all three of these concrete syntaxes may be identical. The Presentation layer contains functions necessary to transform between the common concrete syntax and each of the other two concrete syntaxes.

As the Presentation service is based on the abstract data type concept, the items relevant to a communication are either object types or objects of these types. A context is a set of names of defined object types and declared objects of these types. A context may be extended/restricted by introducing/withdrawing such names. During the lifetime of a Presentation connection several contexts may be used. By providing a context switch mechanism the Presentation service supports organizing (i.e. grouping/presenting/representing) the items relevant in a communication according to the representation/presentation requirements as stated by the Application entities. The names used to refer to these items are unique in a Presentation connection, i.e. all names are different from each other throughout all its contexts.

7. FACILITIES OF THE PRESENTATION SERVICE

The set of service elements of the Presentation service is partitioned into a number of facilities. Each Presentation facility is explained below. Figure 1 gives the service elements belonging to each facility.

7.1. Establishment Facility

The establishment facility enables an Application entity to establish a Presentation connection with another Application entity. During the establishment of the Presentation connection, the Application entities can exchange values of Presentation connection parameters.

7.2. Termination Facility

Presentation connection termination can be orderly, possibly negotiated between the two Application entities, or forced (and possibly disruptive) by the unilateral action of one Application entity. The Presentation connection can also be terminated due to the action of the Presentation service provider.

7.3. Context Switch Facility

The context switch facility enables the Application entities to exchange the current context, i.e. to make unavailable the names known in the current context and make available those names known in another context. Except those periods of time, when context switching is performed, the same context is provided to the two Application entities using an established Presentation connection.

A context may be left either in a way such that it can be reentered by a future use of the context switch facility or such that it is closed forever.

Note: The question of whether or not a context can be retained for use on a future Presention connection is a management issue and is not considered here.

The context entered by use of the context switch facility can be a new context or an old context left in a reenterable way.

When a context is reentered it will be continued at the point at which it was left.

7.4. Negotiation Facility

The negotiation facility allows the Application entities, in any context, to enter the negotiation phase, to request
the right to negotiate, to perform negotiations and to exit from the negotiation phase. Once in the negotiation phase, the Application entities are able to modify the current context (i.e. to declare names of new objects of types known in the current context, remove names of objects, define new object types and name them and withdraw existing object types).

7.5. Information Handling Facility

The information handling facility allows the Application entities the common execution of an operation on typed objects. The types of the objects involved and the meaning of the operation invoked must have been introduced in prior type definitions known in the current context. The operation is given by name, the objects are given either by name or by value. If the operation has parameters, their actualizations are given by objects.

The difference between giving objects by name and by value is:

- Object names (as well as operation names) are passed to the other Application entity without complex transformations to be performed by the Presentation service.

- Objects given by value may require complex presentation/representation transformations to be performed by the Presentation service, based on information provided in the prior type definitions from which the types of these objects are derived.

7.6. Dialog Control Facility

The dialog control facility consists of all Session service elements except those of the S-establishment and S-termination facility and the S-data service elements.

8. CLASSES OF SERVICE

(To be provided.)

9. THE MODEL

In order to model the Application entities' view of the Presentation service, the "abstract data type" concept is used. The abstract data type concept is concerned with two kinds of items which may be defined/declared, named, renamed, referenced in operation executions, and deleted; they are termed "abstract data types" and "abstract data objects", or "types" and "objects" for short. Both kinds of items are conceptual in nature, i.e. they do not imply and do not restrict any particular implementation. Both kinds of items are identified by means of names which are given to them when they are defined/declared/renamed.

Items of kind "type" and "type name" are made known by defining them, items of kind "object name" are make known by declaring them as being of a known type.

It is left to the Application entities communicating via a Presentation connection, to establish/rescind associations between declared names of abstract objects and existing abstract objects. The latter are known on the Application layer, only, and their implementations are outside the scope of OSI, except when being passed between Application entities in operation executions.

10. PERFORMANCE

(The need for material in this section is for further study.)

Prefix of Name of Service Primitives	Name of Service Element	Type of Service Element
Presentation-Connection Establishment Facility		
P-Connect	Connection establish	confirmed
Presentation-Connection Termination Facility		
P-Release	Connection release	confirmed
P-U-Abort	User initiated abort	non-confirmed
P-P-Abort	Provider initiated abort	provider-initiated
Context Switch Facility		
P-Context	Context selection	confirmed
Negotiation Facility		
P-Neg-Start	Negotiation start	confirmed
P-Neg-T-Give	Neg. token transfer	non-confirmed
P-Neg-T-Please	Neg. token demand	non-confirmed
P-Neg-End	Negotiation end	confirmed
P-Type-Define	Type definition	confirmed
P-Type-Withdraw	Type withdraw	confirmed
P-Obj-Name-Decl	Object name decl.	confirmed
P-Obj-Name-Rem	Object name removal	confirmed
Information Handling Facility		
P-Operation-NC	Object operation	non-confirmed
P-Operation-C	Object operation	confirmed
P-With	Default definition	confirmed
P-Except-Report	Exception reporting	provider-initiated

Figure 1: Summary of Presentation facilities and their service elements (except the dialog control facility)

11. SERVICE ELEMENTS OF THE PRESENTATION SERVICE

11.1. The P-Connect Service Element

The successful execution of this confirmed service element establishes a Presentation connection between two Application entities identified by their names in the request primitive. Initially, this Presentation connection has the context identified by its name in the request primitive.

Simultaneous attempts by both Application entities to establish a Presentation connection between them may result in two Presentation connections.

P-Connect: Implied parameters and

Parameter ! Comment	! Req ! Resp !
!	! Ind ! Conf !
I-Address ! Initiator address	! X ! !
!	! ! !
A-Address ! Acceptor address	! X ! !
!	! ! !
Cont-Set ! Set of names of contexts	! X ! X !
! initially available on this	! ! !
! P-connection	! ! !
!	! ! !
E-C-Name ! Name of initial context	! X ! !

11.2. The P-Release Service Element

The successful execution of this confirmed service element performs the orderly release (i.e. without loss of information) of the Presentation connection.

P-Release: Only implied parameters

Parameter ! Comment	! Req ! Resp !
!	! Ind ! Conf !
(none) !	! ! !

11.3. The P-U-Abort Service Element

This service element provides the means by which either Application entity can unilaterally terminate a Presentation connection. The execution of this service element disrupts any other concurrently active service; in particular, information may be lost.

P-U-Abort:

Parameter ! Comment	! Req !
!	! Ind !
User-Data ! transparent	! X !

11.4. The P-P-Abort Service Element

This service element is the means by which the service provider may indicate the termination of the Presentation connection by reasons internal to the service provider. The execution of the service disrupts any other concurrently active service; in particular, information may be lost.

P-P-Abort:

Parameter ! Comment	! !
!	! Ind !
Reason ! To be defined	! X !

11.5. The P-Context Service Element

The successful execution of this confirmed service element performs a context switch. The selected context must be one of the set of contexts identified within the P-connect service element or it has been subsequently defined, or it is a new context.

This service element identifies also the disposition of the context being left. This permits the context to be left in the reenterable or a non-reenterable manner. A context which has been left in a reenterable manner may be subsequently reentered by a further execution of the P-context element with appropriate parameters. A Presentation context thus reentered is continued in the Presentation state in which it was left.

The Application entities identify the names of type definitions and of objects which are to be passed from the context left to the context entered.

P-Context: Implied parameters and

Parameter ! Comment	! Req ! Resp !
!	! Ind ! Conf !
L-C-Disp ! Disposition of the context left	! X ! !
! (abort, release, save) 1)	! ! !
!	! ! !
E-C-Name ! Name of the context to be	! X ! !
! entered	! ! !
!	! ! !
C-List ! List of names of types and	! X ! !
! objects to be available in	! ! !
! the context to be entered	! ! !

1) The L-C-Disp parameter defines the disposition of the context to be left. If its value is 'abort', the context left is aborted, possibly causing loss of information. If its value is 'release', the context left is closed in an orderly manner, i.e. without loss of information. In both cases the context is left in a non-reenterable manner. If the value is 'save' the context is left in an orderly manner and can be reentered later.

11.6. The P-Neg-Start Service Element

By a successful execution of this confirmed service element the Presentation connection is brought into the negotiation phase in an orderly manner (i.e. without loss of information).

P-Neg-Start: Implied parameters and

Parameter ! Comment	! Req ! Resp !
!	! Ind ! Conf !
Neg-Token ! (req, acc, yc) 1)	! X ! X !

1) The Neg-Token parameter assigns the initial negotiation token in the negotiation phase. If its value is "req"/"acc" the negotiation token is initially held by the requestor/acceptor, respectively. If its value is "yc", the acceptor must set the value to "req" or "acc" in the response primitive.

11.7. The P-Neg-T-Give Service Element

This service element allows the Application entity currently holding the Presentation negotiation token to pass it to the other Application entity. The initial holder of the negotiation token is established through the execution of the P-Start-Neg service element.

P-Neg-T-Give:

Parameter ! Comment	! Req !
!	! Ind !
User-Data ! transparent	! X !

11.8. The P-Neg-T-Please Service Element

This service element allows the Application entity not currently holding the Presentation negotiation token to ask for it. The Application entity holding the negotiation token can then pass it by invoking the P-NT-Give service element, but it is not obliged to do so.

P-Neg-T-Please:

Parameter ! Comment	! Req !
!	! Ind !
User-Data ! transparent	! X !

11.9. The P-Neg-End Service Element

By the successful execution of this confirmed service element the negotiation phase is terminated in an orderly manner (i.e. without loss of information).

P-Neg-End: Only implied parameters

Parameter ! Comment	! Req ! Resp !
!	! Ind ! Conf !
(none) !	! ! !

11.10. The P-Type-Define Service Element

By successful execution of this confirmed service element a new object type is defined and a name within the current context is associated with it.

P-Type-Define: Implied parameters and

Parameter ! Comment	! Req ! Resp !
!	! Ind ! Conf !
Type-Name ! A unique name for the new type	! X ! !
!	! ! !
Neg-Lang ! The name of the negotiation	! X ! !
! language used 1)	! ! !
!	! ! !
Lang-Code ! The coding of the negotiation	! X ! X !
! language 2)	! ! !
!	! ! !
Type-Def ! A type definition 3)	! X ! !
!	! ! !
Obj-P/R ! The presentation and	! X ! (X) !
! representation of the objects of	! ! !
! the type 4)	! ! !

1) The Neg-Lang parameter names the language to be used in this execution of the P-Type-Define service element. It is left to the Application entities to determine this language, e.g. COBOL, PASCAL, ADA, etc. For items related to this type definition this language establishes the common abstract syntax of references to them.

   Note: It would be desirable to have an ISO standard for this OSI negotiation language required, ADA would be a suitable candidate.

2) The Lang-Code parameter informs the service provider about the code repertoire and the character coding used for the Neg-Lang by an Application entity, such as ASCII, EBCDIC, etc. Thus, this parameter would appear only in the request and response service primitives and may have different actual values on both sides. For names of items related to this type definition, these values establish the local concrete syntaxes.

3) The Type-Def parameter contains the new type definition, described in the local concrete syntaxes (as determined by the Neg-Lang and Lang-Code parameters).

4) The Obj-P/R parameter describes the presentation and representation of objects of this type. I.e., for objects given by value (and having this type) by means of this parameter the local concrete syntaxes are established.

   In the former case this parameter would appear in the indication service primitive but not in the response primitive, while in the latter case it would be missing in the indication primitive but not in the response. If this parameter has different values in the request and indication/response primitives, the Presentation service should reconcile these presentation and representation differences in both cases.

   Note: If the negotiation language determined by Neg-Lang allows to describe its objects' presentations and representations, then it contains the constructs for giving the actual value of the Obj-P/R parameter in an execution of this P-Type-Define service element. In order to cover the general case, these constructs would be necessarily pretty complex. But, if only the representation aspect is considered, the problem can easily be solved as can be seen in ADA. In order to remain independant of the negotiation language chosen, we propose to slightly generalize the relevant three constructs from ADA (for giving the size, layout, coding description of objects) such as to make them suitable for our purposes. This would allow the Presentation entities to completely solve the representation problems of the common abstract syntax agreed on by the Application entities, and even the "linear" presentation problem. The solution of the more complex presentation problems in case of n-dimensional presentation spaces then would be left to the Application layer.

11.11. The P-Type-Withdraw Service Element

By successful execution of this confirmed service element a previously defined object type is no longer known in the current context.

P-Type-Withdraw: Implied parameters and

Parameter ! Comment	! Req ! Resp !
!	! Ind ! Conf !
Type-Name ! The name of the type to be	! X ! !
! withdrawn from the current	! ! !
! context	! ! !

11.12. The P-Obj-Name-Declare Service Element

By successful execution of this confirmed service element, a new object name is declared in the current context.

P-Obj-Name-Declare: Implied parameters and

Parameter ! Comment	! Req ! Resp !
!	! Ind ! Conf !
Obj-Name ! A new object name to be declared ! in the current context	! X ! !
Type-Name ! The name of the type of the ! object to which Obj-Name shall ! refer	! X ! !
Cons-List ! A (possibly empty) list of ! objects as required for ! completing the type ! definition given by Type-Name	! X ! !

11.13. The P-Obj-Name-Remove Service Element

By successful execution of this confirmed service element, an object name known in the current context is removed from it.

P-Obj-Name-Remove: Implied parameters and

Parameter ! Comment	! Req ! Resp !
!	! Ind ! Conf !
Obj-Name ! The object name to be removed ! from the current context	! X ! !

11.14. The P-Operation-NC Service Element

By means of this non-confirmed service element an Application entity can indicate to its peer Application entity, that it wants an operation to be performed on one or several objects, where the actual paramters of this operation may be different for different objects.

P-Operation-NC:

Parameter ! Comment	! Req !
!	! Ind !
Oper-Name ! Name of the operation to be ! performed	! X !
Obj-List ! A list of objects (given by name ! or by value) on which the ! operation given by Oper-Name is ! to be performed	! X !
Para-List ! A list of additional objects ! (given by name or by value) ! acting as actual parameters for ! these executions of the ! operation on the objects given ! in Obj-List	! X !

11.15. The P-Operation-C Service Element

By successful execution of this confirmed service element both Application entities indicate to each other that they agree in performing an operation on one or several objects, where the actual parameters of this operation may be different for different objects.

P-Operation-C: Implied parameters and

Parameter ! Comment	! Req ! Resp !
!	! Ind ! Conf !
Oper-Name !	! X ! !
Obj-List !	! X ! X !
In-Params !	! X ! !
Out-Parms !	! ! X !

(see 11.14.)

11.16. The P-With Service Element

By successful execution of this confirmed service element both Application entities may agree on a temporarily constant parameter setting for executions of service elements containing these parameters. A parameter setting remains in effect until another execution of the P-With service element refering to this parameter: if the actual value of a parameter in this execution is "nil" its setting is cancelled, otherwise it is assigned the new value provided.

P-With: Implied parameters and

Parameter ! Comment	! Req ! Resp !
!	! Ind ! Conf !
Oper-Name !	! (X) ! !
Obj-List !	! (X) ! !
Para-List !	! (X) ! !

(see 11.14.)

11.17. The P-Exception Service Element

The Presentation layer will perform some exception detection on its own and will cause exceptions in addition to those of the Session exception reporting service.

P-Exception:

Parameter ! Comment	! Req !
!	! Ind !
Reason ! Not yet defined	! X !

Acknowledgements

This paper reflects many stimulating discussions within the Working Groups 5, 1, and 4 of ISO/TC97/SC16 and within UA16.2 of DIN/NI/AA16.

The authors also would like to express their gratitude to their tutorial and research co-workers: without their voluntary and excellent engagement it would not have been possible to write this paper in due time.

References

/1/ ISO/DIS7498: Information Processing Systems – Open Systems Interconnection – Basic Reference Model, January 1982

/2/ ISO/TC97/SC16/N919: Draft Connection Oriented Presentation Service Definition, March 1982

/3/ S. Schindler, C. Bormann, U. Flasche, H. Wilke: Open Systems Interconnections – The Presentation Service, Computer Communications, April 1982

/4/ S. Schindler, U. Flasche, C. Bormann: Open Systems Interconnections – The Presentation Service Model, Computer Communications, October 1981

/5/ S. Schindler: Handbook of Structured Distributed Systems/ Applications and their International Standards, to be published by Springer-Verlag, autumn '82

A Study of HDLC-NRM Terminal Accommodation Methods to Packet Switched Networks

H Okada, M Nomura, Y Tanaka
NTT, Japan

Three different HDLC-NRM terminal accommodation methods to packet switched networks are considered: X.25 method, Link-by-Link method and End-to-End method. These three methods for packet switched networks and a method for a leased line are compared in terms of PAD processing load, user data throughput, turnaround time and communication cost. It is confirmed that the X.25 method is more economical and superior to the other two accommodation methods to packet switched networks, and to the method for the leased line, in terms of PAD processing load and user data throughput. With regard to X.25 method implementation, conversion methods for HDLC-NRM procedures to X.25 procedures through the PAD function, are discussed.

1. INTRODUCTION

There have been many HDLC-Normal Response Mode (NRM) terminals in data communication systems.(1) With the evolution of data communication needs, there are growing demands for them to be accommodated to the X.25 based packet switched data networks. HDLC-NRM procedures can be applied to multipoint configuration networks. They are economical, because of sharing an expensive leased line, when their applications have low traffic density. These systems, such as transaction processing systems or interactive systems, can be more suitable for packet switched data networks (PSDNs) in service grade and communication cost. HDLC-NRM terminals have been accommodated to several networks. However, details on accommodation techniques and results of comparison with leased line systems are not always clear. It is necessary to confirm an economical accommodation method for HDLC-NRM terminals to PSDNs.

In this paper, three methods of accommodating HDLC-NRM terminals to PSDNs are considered and compared in terms of PAD (Packet assembly and disassembly) processing load, user data throughput and turnaround time. The conversion methods for HDLC-NRM procedures to X.25 procedures are shown.

2. TERMINAL ACCOMMODATION METHODS AND THEIR EVALUATION

2.1 Accommodation Methods

Terminals implementing HDLC-NRM procedures are classified into two categories. One, called primary station or terminal, has the data link control initiative and the other, called secondary station or terminal, is controlled by the primary terminal. A primary terminal, which is usually a host computer, inquires whether or not a secondary terminal is prepared to send and receive data by polling and selecting, respectively.
HDLC-NRM terminal system configuration with leased line is shown in Fig. 1(1). PSDN accommodation methods are as follow:

(a) X.25 method : A secondary HDLC-NRM terminal is accommodated to a PAD and communicates with X.25 packet mode terminals. The PAD polls the secondary terminals and transforms HDLC-NRM procedures into X.25 procedures. As a host computer is connected to a PSDN as a packet mode terminal, it can communicate with HDLC-NRM terminals at the same time through the PAD accommodating secondary terminals.(Fig. 1 (2))

(b) Link by Link (LxL) method : Both host computer and HDLC-NRM terminal are accommodated to PADs. The host computer is accommodated as the NRM procedure primary station. The host polls the PAD which emulates ramified secondary terminals. The HDLC-NRM terminal is accommodated as the NRM procedure secondary station to a PAD, which polls the secondary HDLC-NRM terminals, independently of host computer polling. Data which are sent out from the HDLC-NRM terminal are stored in PSDN until the PAD accommodating the host computer is polled. (Fig.1 (3))

(c) End-to-End (E-E) method : A host computer is accommodated to a PSDN as a primary station and HDLC-NRM terminals are accommodated as secondary stations. In this method, the PADs do not poll HDLC-NRM terminals. The polling frames from the host computer are transmitted to the HDLC-NRM terminal through the PSDN. The response frames from the HDLC-NRM terminal are also transmitted to the host computer through the PSDN. The PADs assemble and disassemble all polling and response frames to and from packets. (Fig. 1 (4))

In the next section, these three methods and the method for leased line are compared under the traffic condition that frame arrival at each terminal follows the Poisson process, the frame length is fixed at 128 byte-length, and the polling interval is fixed at the same interval time in both PAD and host computer. Four terminals are assumed to be ramified on the leased line in the following calculations.

871

2.2 PAD Load

It is expected that the PAD load will be large for the polling process in comparison with the PAD which accommodates HDLC-ABM terminals. Figure 2 shows the load ratio between HDLC-ABM and HDLC-NRM terminal accommodation methods. In the E-E method, it is necessary for a PAD accommodating primary stations to transform an RR frame for polling into a data packet and for a PAD accommodating secondary stations to transform the packet into an RR frame, besides sending and receiving RR frames. Consequently, the PAD load in the E-E method is the largest. As the PAD for accomodating a host computer emulates four ramified secondary terminals on the subscriber line in the LxL method, the host computer cannot poll the other terminals when it receives data from a terminal. Therefore, polling interval for the same terminal by host computer becomes longer. Consequently, the number of wasted polling queries is smaller in the PAD accommodating a host computer than in the PAD accommodating terminals. Therefore, in the LxL method, the load of PAD accommodating primary stations is smaller than the load of PAD accommodating secondary stations.

2.3 Throughput

In this paper, throughput is defined as the maximum data quantity which can be sent from a terminal to a host computer. Figure 3 shows the throughput comparison result for each method. The throughput in the E-E method is lower than in the X.25 method, because the cycle time from one polling to the next polling in the E-E method increases due to delay time inside the PSDN. In the LxL method and the leased line system, the throughput is low because the subscriber line is ramified for four terminals.

2.4 Turnaround Time

Turnaround time is defined as the interval time from when the HDLC-NRM terminal requests to send a frame until it receives its response frame. It contains network transmission delay and poll waiting time. Figure 4 shows the turnaround time comparison result. In the LxL

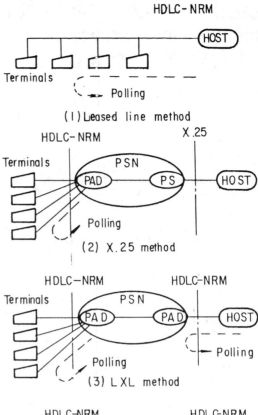

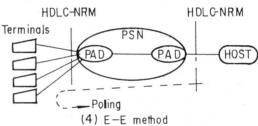

Fig.1 Polling terminal system configurations

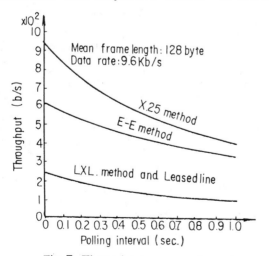

Fig.3 Throughput comparison

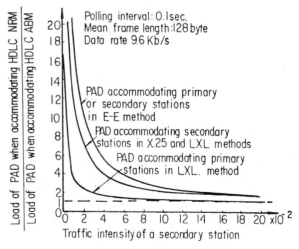

Fig.2 PAD load increase

method, turnaround time is the longest due to the waiting time at the PAD accommodating primary stations. There is an area where turnaround time in the X.25 method is shorter than that in the leased line system, because send waiting time at four ramified HDLC–NRM terminals in the leased line system becomes longer at high traffic intensity.

2.5 Economic Comparison

Figure 5 shows communication cost comparison result for four system configurations in Fig.1, on the basis of the current charges for the leased line and for the DDX packet switched network.(2) There also exists an area where the X.25 method and the LxL method are more economical than the leased line systems.

In the following section, the conversion methods for X.25 method implementation are described.

3. HDLC–NRM TERMINAL ACCOMMODATION

3.1 Packet Switched Network Protocol Structure

Recommendations X.3, X.28 and X.29 were agreed upon in CCITT to accommodate start–stop mode terminals in packet switched networks. (3) Recommendation X.3 defines packet assembly and disassembly facility (PAD), which prescribes mainly non-packet mode terminal attributes. Recommendation X.28 prescribes the protocol between a non-packet mode terminal and a PAD. Recommendation X.29 prescribes the protocol between a PAD and a packet mode terminal (PAD–PT protocol) on top of X.25, and enables a packet mode terminal (PT) to control a PAD.

It is envisaged that the Recommendations will be enhanced for various kinds of non–packet mode terminals to communicate with a packet mode terminal. Bisynchronous terminals, asynchronous basic mode terminals and data telephone terminals, which are intelligent telephone terminals with data transfer capability, will be accommodated to the DDX packet switched network by enhancing the Recommendations. Therefore, if PAD–PT protocol is required for HDLC–NRM terminals, it is necessary that the protocol be compatible with the protocols for the other terminals, in order to maintain communication control program consistency in packet mode terminals. The protocol structure defined for HDLC–NRM terminal accommodation to a packet switched network should, therefore, be aligned with Recommendations X.3, X.28 and X.29. The protocol structure is depicted in Fig.6.

3.2 PAD Parameters for HDLC–NRM Terminals

It is necessary to determine the parameter values and use of optional functions in the HDLC–NRM transmission control procedure at the subscription time, in order to define transmission control procedure definitely. Subscribers will have to register the parameters and optional functions, refered to as PAD parameters, listed in Table 1.

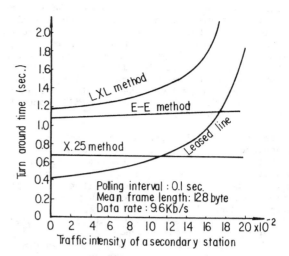

Fig.4 Turn around time

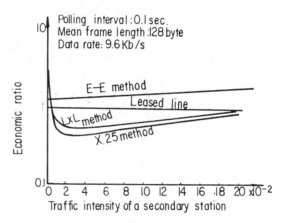

Fig.5 Economic comparison of HDLC–NRM terminal accommodation

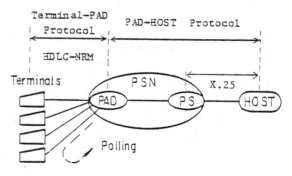

Fig.6 Protocol structure for HDLC–NRM terminal accommodation

3.3 Protocol between a HDLC–NRM Terminal and a PAD

The protocol between a HDLC–NRM terminal and a PAD is divided into a call control phase and a data transfer phase. Since a protocol in the data transfer phase must conform to ISO HDLC standard, a protocol in the call control phase will be the main issue.

873

Packet switched networks provide permanent virtual circuit services and virtual call services. In the permanent virtual circuit services, a pair of terminals communicating with each other is registered in the network at the subscription time, and the virtual circuit is maintained in between them as long as the service is subscribed. The terminals cannot change the destination, but no call control procedure is needed.

In the virtual call services, X.25 call control procedure will be one of the candidate for call control procedures for HDLC-NRM terminals. However, HDLC-NRM terminals will require simpler call control procedure than that for X.25, since the HDLC-NRM control procedure is simpler than the X.25 procedure. X.21, the call control procedure for circuit switched networks, will be the second candidate. It may be the simplest way to accommodate HDLC-NRM terminals, because it is only required to attach a network control unit (NCU), which supports the X.21 call control procedure on behalf of the terminal.

The third candidate will be the use of the UI frame to convey call control signals. Although this method requires the terminal to support the UI frame in the HDLC-NRM procedure, it neither requires X.21 NCU nor sophisticated call control procedure, such as X.25. The call control methods are shown in Table 2.

3.4 Protocol Conversion Methods

Two types of protocol conversion, X.29 based and X.25 based protocol conversion, are considered. Their differences are that X.25 based protocol conversion method converts HDLC-NRM procedure to X.25, while X.29 based protocol conversion method converts a part of the HDLC-NRM procedure to the protocol on top of X.25. In either protocol conversion, information frames, defined for conveying user information in HDLC procedure, are converted into data packets. Their distinction will appear with regard to how to convert unnumbered frames (U frames), which are defined for conveying HDLC procedure commands and responses.

(1) X.29 based protocol conversion

A U frame is converted into a PAD message, a data packet with qualifier bit set to one. The PAD messages will be defined for the U frames used for the HDLC-NRM procedure. In the data link establishment phase, the SNRM PAD message will be issued by a packet mode terminal after the call is established, and it is converted to an SNRM frame by a PAD. The UA frame, which is the response to the SNRM frame, is also converted to a UA PAD message. In the data link disconnection phase, DISC and UA frames are also converted into DISC and UA PAD messages, respectively.

(2) X.25 based protocol conversion

Every U frame is converted into an adequate X.25 control packet, or it is responded to by the PAD. In the data link establishment phase, a PAD will automatically issue SNRM frame to a

Table 1   PAD Function examples

Function	Content
Terminal attribute	Terminal binary speed Full or half duplex mode HDLC system parameters (Timer, Maximum number of outstanding I frames, etc)
Addressing	Address part value assigned to a terminal
Optional frame	Use or non-use of SREJ, REJ, XID frames, etc.
Polling period	Interval of pollings ini- tiated by PAD
Procedure for call establishment	Procedure for call request from, and incoming call to, a terminal
Protocol transformation	Transformation between HDLC frames and X.25 packets, and vice versa

HDLC-NRM terminal after the call is established. The data link is disconnected when the packet mode terminal requests to clear the call.

The signal sequences for the two types of protocol conversion are depicted in Fig. 7. The X.25 based protocol conversion enables a packet mode terminal to communicate with HDLC-NRM terminals by means of X.25. This will be very beneficial to exsisting packet mode terminals, because it is usually hard to change their program. The X.29 based protocol conversion provides the terminals with the capability to exchange end-to-end control information by means of the unnumbered frames and PAD messages. Therefore, the host computer can control the starting time of polling at the PAD to HDLC-NRM terminals. Since both types of protocol conversion have their own benefits, it will be desirable for packet switched networks to provide both protocol conversion.

3.5 Protocol between PAD and Host

(1) PAD-PT protocol selection

PAD-PT protocols will differ, depending on the conversion methods described in 3.4. Therefore, it is necessary for a packet mode terminal to determine, in a call establishment phase, which PAD-PT protocol is to be used. Recommendation X.25 already has a specified protocol identification field in call request and incoming call packets for this purpose. When a packet mode terminal originates a call, it will indicate the requested PAD-PT protocol in the protocol identification field. When a call is originated by HDLC-NRM terminals, it will also be necessary for a packet mode terminal to designate the PAD-PT protocol in a call accepted packet. This requires enhancing X.25 to provide protocol identification fields

Table 2   Three call control methods

	Virtual Call (X.21)	Virtual Call (X.21bis + UI*call control procedure)	Permanent Virtual Circuit (X.21.bis)
Signal Sequence	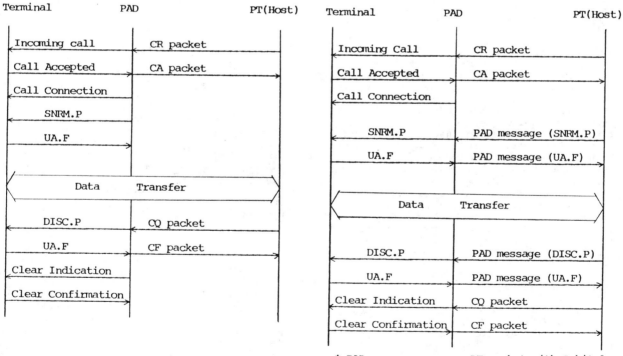 Terminal … PAD Call Request Proceed to Select X.21 Selection Signal CR Call Connection CA SNRM.P UA.F Data Transfer	Terminal … PAD X.21 bis Call Request Call Accepted UI(selection signal) CR UI(call connection) CA SNRM.P UA.F Data Transfer	Terminal … PAD X.21 bis Call Request RQ Call Accepted RF SNRM.P UA.F Data Transfer
Comparison	Network control unit for X.21 is needed. No extension** of NRM procedure is needed.	Network control unit for X.21 is not needed, however, UI call control program is needed. Extension of NRM procedure is needed.	Neither network control unit for X.21 nor UI call control program is needed. No extension of NRM procedure is needed.

*   "UI" means a HDLC UI frame and it conveys call control
     information in its information field.
** "Extension" means that a UI frame can be sent before
     data link is established.

(1) X.25 based protocol conversion
     (PAD initiates the data link
     establishment)

(2) X.29 based protocol conversion
     (Host initiates the data link
     establishment)

* PAD message means a DT packet with Q-bit=1

Fig. 7   Signal sequence comparison for two PAD–PT protocols

X.25 Packet Header (Call Request/ Accept packet)	Protocol Identifier (PID)	User	Data

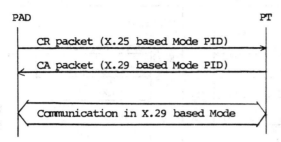

Fig. 8   Negotiation for PAD-PT Protocol

REFERENCES

(1) ISO : Draft International Standard ISO/DIS 6159, 1978.
(2) T. Takatsuki and N. Sone : Inauguration of new public data network in Japan and it's impact, ICCC'80, 1980
(3) CCITT : Recommendation X.3, X.28, X.29, 1980

in call accepted and call connected packets as well as in call request and incoming call packets. An outline of the protocol selection method is depicted in Fig. 8.

(2) User data delimitation

A HDLC-NRM terminal may use a maximum frame length longer than the maximum packet length. A PAD will segment a long signal frame into more than one packet and will set the more data indication to one in the intermediate data packets. Packets having more data indication set to one are considered as a part of the consecutive user data.

4. CONCLUSION

The X.25 method is the best choice among the three HDLC-NRM terminal accommodation methods to PSDN in respect of communication cost, throughput and turnaround time. The X.25 method can realize more economical and higher throughput communication than in a method for leased line system.
With regard to the X.25 method implementation, the polling start time is determined automatically by the PAD in the X.25 based protocol conversion, while it is not necessary for the existing packet mode terminals program to be changed. The X.29 based protocol conversion enables a host computer to control the polling start time at the PAD. Both types of protocol conversion will be needed in PSDN.

ACKNOWLEDGEMENT

The authors would like to express their thanks to Dr. M. Kato, Dr. K. Tsukada and Mr. M. Itoh in Musashino Electrical Communication Laboratory for their continued interest and support.

Hiroshi Okada is a staff engineer in the Data Switching Systems Section, Musashino Electrical Communication Laboratory, NTT. He received his B.S. degree in 1967 from Osaka University. He was engaged in developmental research on on-line banking system and formular manipulation system. He is engaged in research on data communication protocols.

Masayuki Nomura is a staff engineer, Integrated Communication Systems Section, Yokosuka Electrical Communication Laboratory, NTT. He received his B.E. degree in 1971 from Keio University and his M.S. degree in 1973 from Nagoya University. He has been working on the development of packet switching systems. He is researching data network protocols.

Yoshikazu Tanaka is an engineer in the Data Switching Systems Section, Musashino Electrical Communication Laboratory, NTT. He received his M.E. degree in Information Science in 1976 from Kyoto University. He has been engaged in protocol design and verification for packet switching networks. He is currently interested in protocol for message communication systems.

SNA and X.25

G A Deaton Jr., D J Franse
IBM, USA

Recommendation X.25 of the International Telegraph and Telephone Consultative Committee (CCITT) defines interface guidelines for attaching customer data terminal equipment (DTE) to public packet-switched data networks. IBM's Systems Network Architecture (SNA) defines formats and protocols governing interactions among IBM products that are components of an SNA network. X.25 functions used to communicate from one SNA DTE to another SNA DTE and to non-SNA DTEs through packet-switched data networks are described. Functions used at the three X.25 levels - physical, link and packet - are delineated. Rationale for selection of some functions but not others is given. Examples of the use of X.25 in specific SNA products are given.

INTRODUCTION

The idea of packet switching, allowing shared use of network resources among users, originated in the mid-1960s. Experimental packet-switched data networks (packet networks, for short) were developed in the late-1960s; public packet networks were introduced in the 1970s. The International Telegraph and Telephone Consultative Committee (CCITT) developed Recommendation X.25 {1} to facilitate attachment of data terminal equipment (DTE) such as computers, cluster controllers, and terminals to packet networks. The CCITT continues to evolve X.25 as the recommended interface between DTEs and Data Circuit-terminating Equipment (DCE) on public packet networks since first adopting the recommendation at Geneva in 1976 {2}.

Early adoption of Recommendation X.25 was intended to limit the proliferation of unique, incompatible interfaces between using equipment and packet networks that were being developed in various countries. The objective was only partially realized because the original recommendation was subject to individual interpretation by the various carriers implementing packet networks. Consequently, DTEs designed for one packet network might not operate on others {5, 6, 7}, even though their interfaces conformed to Recommendation X.25. The CCITT published a refined X.25 interface as a provisional recommendation in 1978 {3}. After further refinements {4}, the current recommendation (published in the 'yellow book') was approved by the CCITT at Geneva in November, 1980 {1}. Many public packet networks then committed to implement a common subset {7, 8, 9} of the X.25 interface by 1982. When this is completed DTEs conforming to Recommendation X.25 should be able to operate on packet networks in many parts of the world without alteration.

In 1977, Canada's Datapac was the first public packet network to offer an X.25 interface. Transpac in France offered an X.25 interface in 1978. Since that time, several more countries have begun development of packet networks. The European Economic Community (EEC) has sponsored an international packet network called Euronet. Thus, international connections may be established by X.25 DTEs through Euronet, or through two or more national public packet networks that are interconnected.

IBM's Systems Network Architecture (SNA) {10, 13, 14, 15, 16, 17, 18} defines formats and protocols governing interactions among IBM products that are components of an SNA network. IBM first announced X.25 interface capability to packet networks for certain SNA products in January, 1977. In 1979, IBM announced additional SNA products that could communicate with each other, as well as with non-SNA equipment, using X.25-based packet network services. IBM made another announcement in 1980, providing X.25 communication between SNA hosts and non-SNA, non-X.25 equipment attached to packet networks. This announcement also allowed SNA users to provide their own application programs to process X.25 packets.

In 1981, IBM announced X.25 products in the United States. X.25 software that supports SNA host computers was made available as a licensed program product for the IBM 3705 Network Control Program. The program product provides all the previously announced functions plus host-to-host X.25 communication, and physical level interface capability conforming to CCITT Recommendation X.21 {1, 19, 20, 21}. This X.25 capability added flexibility to SNA products that already used a wide range of terrestrial and satellite telecommunications facilities and services based on other national and international standards.

X.25 OVERVIEW

The X.25 interface comprises three levels: physical, link and packet (Figure 1).

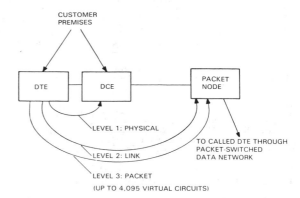

Figure 1: The Three Levels of X.25

The physical level defines the mechanical, electrical, functional and procedural characteristics to activate, maintain and deactivate the physical link between the DTE and the DCE. While the preferred physical level element conforms to CCITT Recommendation X.21 {1, 20}, Recommendation X.21 bis {1} (which includes CCITT Recommendation V.24 {12} and RS-232-C of the Electronic Industries Association {29}) may be used for an unspecified interim period.

The link level defines link access procedures for reliable data interchange across the physical link between the DTE and the packet network. The Balanced Link Access Procedure (LAPB) is the preferred link level element toward which most public packet networks are moving. It is based on the High Level Data Link Control (HDLC) Asynchronous Balanced Mode

(ABM) {28} of operation specified by the
International Organization for Standardization
(ISO).

The packet level element describes the packet
formats and control procedures used to exchange
control and data packets between the DTE and
the packet network. The packet level includes
formats and procedures for permanent virtual
circuit services, virtual call services, and
datagram services, as well as for various
optional user facilities. Only the permanent
virtual circuit and virtual call procedures are
used by SNA X.25 DTEs, since few packet
networks, if any, offer datagram services.

It is important to understand that
Recommendation X.25 defines an <u>interface</u>
between a user's equipment and the packet
network. It does not define the essential
networking architecture for users or for packet
networks. Higher level protocols such as those
provided by SNA are required to allow
meaningful communication between two users'
nodes connected through one or more packet
networks (Figure 2).

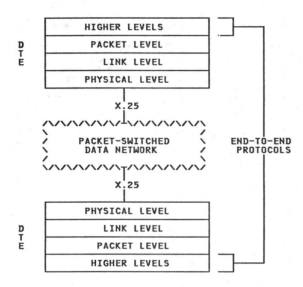

Figure 2: Higher Level DTE-to-DTE Protocols

Recommendation X.25 describes the three levels
and the range of services that may be provided
by public packet networks from the perspective
of the DCE. This paper describes IBM's X.25
architectural and design choices {11} from the
perspective of SNA X.25 DTEs.

ARCHITECTURAL CONSIDERATIONS

Public packet network services provide an
efficient and economical method for
transporting information in some instances.
However, application requirements, geographical
considerations and applicable tariffs often
dictate the use of other services and
facilities for transporting information.
Therefore, virtual circuits (permanent virtual
circuit and virtual call services) are
integrated into SNA in a manner that allows
concurrent use of other services and facilities
offered by Communications Common Carriers,
Telecommunications Administrations and
Recognized Private Operating Agencies around
the world. Relationships between SNA and X.25
are defined for two types of connections:

- SNA-to-SNA Connections that allow SNA X.25
  DTEs to be connected to each other by
  permanent virtual circuit services or
  virtual call services, or both.

- SNA-to-non-SNA Connections that allow SNA
  X.25 DTEs to be connected to non-SNA X.25
  DTEs by permanent virtual circuit services
  or virtual call services, or both.

SNA-to-SNA Connections

One objective of SNA is to afford users the
broadest possible range of choices in selecting
telecommunications services and facilities to
meet their requirements. Figure 3 depicts some
of the data transmission services and
facilities available to SNA customers in
various parts of the world.

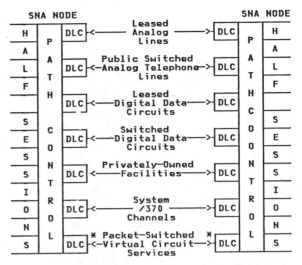

* Includes Logical Link Control (LLC) and
Virtual Circuit Protocol (VCP) components

Figure 3: Coexistence of Services and
Facilities within SNA

Computer network architectures, in general,
provide for the interconnection of physically
distributed functions via various types of data
transmission facilities. Such directly
connected nodes are termed 'adjacent' within
SNA. The Data Link Control (DLC) elements
provide the protocols used to transfer
information between adjacent SNA nodes.

SNA nodes interconnected by packet network
virtual circuit services remain logically
adjacent. The X.25 virtual circuit protocol
(VCP) provides the mechanism to transfer
information between these adjacent SNA network
nodes. Therefore, virtual circuits serve
similar functions in the system as other data
transmission services and facilities and
naturally appear at the same architectural
level within SNA.

This natural fit between X.25 and SNA {23}
permits coexistence of the various data
transmission services and facilities, as well
as a desirable multiplexing capability. For
example, all traffic flowing between adjacent
SNA network nodes is readily multiplexed onto a
single transmission facility.

To permit concurrent use of data link control
and virtual circuit protocol services, all of
the properties of the former must be available
in the latter. SNA X.25 DTEs employ a Logical
Link Control (LLC) protocol to provide certain
adjacent node services in environments where
SNA nodes are connected through one or more
packet networks. This protocol, known as QLLC,
uses 'Qualified' data packets to transfer data
link control information between the two SNA
nodes. Once data link connectivity has been
established, SNA Path Information Units (PIUs)
{10, 13} are transferred in normal,
unqualified, data packets. PIUs that exceed
the maximum user data area of the data packet
are transferred as packet sequences
concatenated by the More Data Mark (M bit).

Note: Some initial SNA X.25 DTE
    implementations do not support the QLLC and
    M-bit procedures. They perform adjacent
    node services and packet

segmentation/concatenation using a Physical
Services Header (PSH) {24}.

SNA-to-non-SNA Connections

The X.25 interface is also used to connect SNA
nodes to non-SNA nodes through packet networks.
SNA-to-non-SNA connections provide a transport
mechanism for data between an application
program in an SNA node and a remote non-SNA
terminal, such as a non-SNA X.25 DTE or a
start/stop terminal attached to a packet
assembly/disassembly (PAD) facility. Three
types of operation are defined for
SNA-to-non-SNA connections - mapped,
transparent and hybrid. No standard protocol
is provided above the packet level of
Recommendation X.25 for SNA-to-non-SNA
connections. These higher level protocols
remain a matter to be agreed upon between the
individual non-SNA terminal and the supporting
customer-written application program within the
SNA node. Figure 4 depicts virtual circuit
connection of non-SNA equipment to an SNA node.

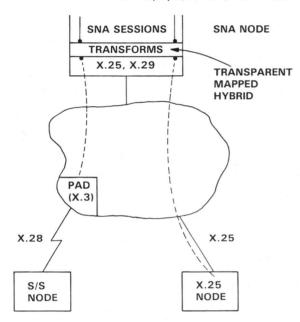

Figure 4: X.25 Connection of Non-SNA Equipment
to SNA Nodes

Mapped operation allows X.25 protocols to be
mapped to and from similar SNA protocol subsets
directly at the SNA X.25 DTE/DCE interface;
thus, virtual circuits are associated with SNA
sessions on a one-for-one basis. An
application in the host can communicate with
the non-SNA node without any X.25 sensitivity.
However, the application and the remote node
must each understand the data streams being
exchanged and process them accordingly.

In transparent operation, the packet level of
X.25 can be implemented in a host application
program. In this case, the packet-level
protocols are transported, transparently,
within the structure of SNA between the host
application and the X.25 interface.

In hybrid operation, X.25 packet-level
functions are neither fully mapped nor fully
transparent. A host application performs some
X.25 packet level functions as in transparent
operation; the remaining packet level functions
are performed at the X.25 interface.

Multiple DTE/DCE Interfaces

Some SNA X.25 DTEs can support multiple X.25
DTE/DCE interfaces. To do so is a
product-specific choice based on traffic
requirements or the need to directly access two
or more networks concurrently, or both. Some

products also permit SNA-to-SNA and
SNA-to-non-SNA connections to coreside at the
same X.25 DTE/DCE interface.

X.25 ELEMENTS IN SNA NODES

The elements of Recommendation X.25 selected
for use at the physical level, link level and
packet level interfaces are described in this
section. SNA-to-SNA and SNA-to-non-SNA
connections differ only at the packet level.
Therefore, descriptions of the physical level
and the link level elements are common to both
types of connection. The reader is referred to
reference 11 for more detail.

Physical Level

The physical level element employs a duplex
(two-way simultaneous) transmission facility.
During an interim period, described in
reference 1, some SNA X.25 DTEs support X.21
bis instead of, or in addition to, the
preferred X.21 at the physical level.

IBM X.21 bis implementations for non-switched
access conform to:

- CCITT Recommendation V.24 {12} with V.28
  {12} electrical characteristics at speeds
  of 19.2 kilobits per second (kbit/s) and
  below.
- CCITT Recommendation V.35 {12} at signaling
  speeds in excess of 19.2 kbit/s.

Other non-X.21 interfaces are supported by some
products.

Switched-circuit access to packet network
virtual circuit services is not supported by
SNA X.25 DTEs because essential DTE and DCE
identification and characterization functions
are still being defined by the CCITT.

Transmission speed is product specific;
however, all SNA X.25 DTEs support at least one
of the X.25 speeds (2.4, 4.8, 9.6 or 48.0
kbit/s) and some may support one or more
additional speeds (e.g., 1.2, 19.2, 56.0 and
64.0 kbit/s).

Link Level

Recommendation X.25 defines a symmetrical link
access procedure (LAP) and a balanced link
access procedure (LAPB) for use as the link
level element. Except for certain early
implementations, SNA X.25 DTEs use only the
(LAPB) procedure since the CCITT has adopted
this as the preferred link level procedure to
be supported by all public packet networks.

SNA X.25 DTEs transmit and receive only frames
containing a single packet consisting of an
integral number of octets and are sequenced
using modulo 8 sequence numbering. They employ
recovery mechanisms that conform fully with
LAPB. Packets transferred across the DTE/DCE
interface are contained within the link level
information field.

Packet Level

Packet types transmitted and received and their
uses with the various services are shown in
Table 1. These packets are used as described
in reference 1. Except for certain early
implementations, the qualifier bit is set
(Q = 1) in data packets to transfer Logical
Link Control (LLC) information. Packet
sequences are generated using the more-data
bit. The delivery confirmation bit (D = 1) in
data packets is allowed only on SNA-to-non-SNA
connections because SNA has its own end-to-end
mechanisms at levels above X.25.

Other X.25 data packet characteristics include
1) packet sequence numbering modulo 8 or,
optionally, 128; 2) maximum user data fields of
128 or, optionally, additional sizes of 16, 32,
64, 512 or 1024 octets; and 3) window sizes, W,
$1 \leq W < 8$ for modulo 8 packet sequence numbering
or $1 \leq W < 128$ for modulo 128 packet sequence
numbering.

TABLE 1 - Packet Types and Their Uses with Various Services				
PACKET TYPE		**SERVICE**		
From DCE to DTE	From DTE to DCE	VC	PVC	I/F
CALL SET-UP AND CLEARING				
INCOMING CALL	CALL REQUEST	X		
CALL CONNECTED	CALL ACCEPTED	X		
CLEAR INDICATION	CLEAR REQUEST	X		
DCE CLEAR CONFIRMATION	DTE CLEAR CONFIRMATION	X		
DATA [AND INTERRUPT]				
DCE DATA	DTE DATA	X	X	
[DCE INTERRUPT]	[DTE INTERRUPT]	[X]	[X]	
[DCE INTERRUPT CONFIRMATION]	[DTE INTERRUPT CONFIRMATION]	[X]	[X]	
FLOW CONTROL AND RESET				
DCE RR	DTE RR	X	X	
DCE RNR	DTE RNR	X	X	
RESET INDICATION		X	X	
	RESET REQUEST	X		
DCE RESET CONFIRMATION	DTE RESET CONFIRMATION	X		
RESTART				
RESTART IND.	RESTART REQ.			X
DCE RESTART CONFIRMATION	DTE RESTART CONFIRMATION			X
DIAGNOSTIC*				X

```
VC = Virtual Call
PVC = Permanent Virtual Circuit
I/F = Entire DTE/DCE Interface
[] = For SNA-to-non SNA Connections only.
* Not necessarily available on all networks.
```

Note: DTE REJECT and DATAGRAM packets are not used by IBM SNA X.25 DTEs.

Table 2. X.25 Optional User Faciltities Provided	IBM SNA X.25 DTEs
Nonstandard Default Window Size	ALL
Default Throughput Class Assignment	User Choice
Incoming Calls Barred	User Choice
Outgoing Calls Barred	User Choice
Single Closed User Group (CUG)	User Choice
Single CUG with Outgoing Access	User Choice
Single CUG with Incoming Access	User Choice
Incoming Calls Barred Within CUG	User Choice
Outgoing Calls Barred Within CUG	User Choice
One-Way Logical Channel Outgoing	Some
One-Way Logical Channel Incoming	Some
Reverse Charging	Some
Reverse Charging Acceptance	Some
Nonstandard Default Packet Size	Some
Flow Control Parameter Negotiation	Some
Throughput Class Negotiation	Some
Multiple Closed User Groups	Some
Multiple CUG with Out Access	Some
Multiple CUG with In Access	Some
Extended Packet Sequence Numbering	Some
RPOA Selection	Some
Fast Select	None
Fast Select Acceptance	None
Packet Retransmission	None
Bilateral Closed User Group	None
Bilateral CUG with Out Access	None

```
All = facilities always provided.
Some = facilities that may be provided.
None = facilities not normally provided.
User Choice = network provided facilities.
```

In addition to the specific significance specified in Recommendation X.25 for bits 8 and 7 of the first octet of the user data field in CALL REQUEST and INCOMING CALL packets, the remaining bits of this octet are used to distinguish between SNA-to-SNA and SNA-to-non-SNA connections that may coexist at the same X.25 DTE/DCE interface.

When subscribed optional user facilities are indicated in INCOMING CALL packets, SNA X.25 DTEs either:

• accept the call with no further comment in the CALL ACCEPTED packet.
• attempt parameter negotiation using the facilities field in the CALL ACCEPTED packet.
• reject the call using the CLEAR REQUEST packet with an appropriate diagnostic indication.

Table 2 shows optional user facilities for SNA DTE's. Some X.25 optional user facilities require that explicit support functions be provided by the DTE; others, designated 'User Choice', do not.

During the data transfer phase, SNA X.25 DTEs process error notification information contained in clear, reset, restart and diagnostic packets. On SNA-to-SNA connections, all DTEs use a consistent set of diagnostic codes that flow end-to-end as the result of clearing, resetting or restarting. Whether an error is detected by the DTE or by the DCE, the DTE notifies the SNA higher levels of the error condition so that recovery procedures can be initiated.

IMPLEMENTATION EXAMPLES

Among the X.25 products offered by IBM are the IBM 5973 Network Interface Adapter (NIA) {26} and a program product for the Network Control Program (NCP) {22} that operates in the 3705 Communications Controller. Both products were developed in IBM's LaGaude, France laboratory. The program product allows SNA host systems to perform X.25 communication with other SNA X.25 nodes and with non-SNA nodes. Selected SNA peripheral nodes (cluster controllers and terminals) and processors with integrated communication adapters (ICA's) use the NIA to communicate using X.25. The NIA converts Synchronous Data Link Control (SDLC) to and from X.25 protocols.

Figure 5 shows the way in which SNA host processors, SNA peripheral nodes, and non-SNA terminals can be interconnected using the NCP program product and the NIA. Six types of communication are shown (dotted lines labelled with numbers in circles in the figure):

1. Remote NIA to NCP
2. Remote NIA to Front-end NIA
3. NCP to NCP
4. NCP to non-SNA X.25 node
5. NCP to start/stop packet assembler/disassembler (PAD) device
6. NCP to non-standardized (N-S) PAD device

The first three connection types adhere to architectural principles for SNA-to-SNA communication using X.25. Connection one allows a peripheral node to communicate with an application program in an SNA host using a permanent virtual circuit or a virtual call between the NCP program product and a remote NIA. Using connection type two, applications in an SNA host can communicate with SNA peripheral nodes. The front-end NIA converts between SDLC multi-drop link protocols and up to four X.25 permanent virtual circuits or one virtual call. Each SDLC multi-drop address maps to a virtual circuit; that is, the maximum of four permanent virtual circuits requires four multi-drop addresses. Each virtual circuit connects the front-end NIA to a remote NIA. It is important to note that none of the connection types require SDLC polling through the packet network. Polling is local between an NIA and the attached SDLC station. The third connection type allows application-to-application and application-to-peripheral node communication using a permanent virtual circuit between NCP's.

The last three connection types adhere to architectural principles for SNA-to-non-SNA X.25 communication. Connection type four provides communication between an application in the SNA host and a non-SNA, native X.25 node (reference 25, for example) using permanent virtual circuits or virtual calls, or both. An SNA session connects the host application program to the NCP program product. Mapped transforms in the

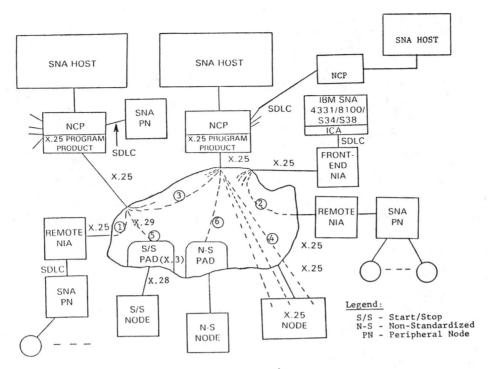

Figure 5: Examples of IBM SNA X.25 Support

program product allow the host application to be free of X.25 packet level processing, whereas hybrid transforms allow host applications to process call control, resetting, restarting, qualified data, interrupt and certain other packets. Start/stop terminals can communicate with an SNA host application using the program product. An X.25 permanent virtual circuit or virtual call connects the NCP to the PAD that resides in the network. The program product uses a built-in, selected set of qualified data packet functions defined in CCITT Recommendation X.29 {1} to control the PAD. The packet network uses Recommendation X.3 {1} to define operation of the start/stop node. There is no X.25 or X.29 functional sensitivity in the host application (mapped transforms are used in the program product).

Should the user want to use X.29 functions that are not built into the program product or should he want to communicate with a PAD-attached node {27} for which there are no attachment standards such as X.3, X.28, and X.29, he can use connection type 6. This enables a host application program to control the non-standardized PAD by processing qualified data and other packets required for PAD control (the program product uses hybrid transforms).

CONCLUDING REMARKS

The three-level X.25 interface provides another alternative for SNA-to-SNA and SNA-to-non-SNA communications. Packet-switched virtual circuit services can coreside in SNA nodes with a large array of other communications services and facilities, giving the user greater flexibility to configure networks considering cost and performance objectives. X.25 functions used in SNA have been selected based on current user requirements. Many of these selected functions have been implemented in SNA products, two of which have been described.

ACKNOWLEDGEMENTS

The authors wish to acknowledge Messrs. Jean-Pierre Davan, Charles Rheinart, Marc Levilion, Lou Butler, Dick Hippert, Andy Kleitsch, Larry Sista, Doug Fraser, and Alan Jones for their efforts in helping to define the X.25 interface used by SNA products.

REFERENCES

{1} CCITT, YELLOW BOOK, Volume VIII - Fascicle VIII.2, Data Communication Networks Services and Facilities, Terminal Equipment and Interfaces, Recommendations X.1-X.29, VIIth Plenary Assembly, Geneva 10-21 November 1980.

{2} CCITT, Orange Book, Volume VIII.2, Public Data Networks, Sixth Plenary Assembly, Geneva (September 27 - October 8, 1976).

{3} CCITT, Gray Book, Provisional Recommendations X.3, X.25, X.28, and X.29 on packet-switched data transmission services, Approved October 1977, Published 1978.

{4} Final report on the work of STUDY GROUP VII during the period 1977-1980, Part III.2: RECOMMENDATION X.25, Document AP VII-No. 7-E, June 1980.

{5} Hess, M. L., Brethes, M. and Saito, A., "A Comparison of Four X.25 Public Network Interfaces", Proceedings of ICC, Boston, 1979, pp. 38.6.1 - 38.6.8.

{6} Rybczynski, A. M. and Palframan, D., "A Common Interface to Public Data Networks", Computer Networks, July 1980.

{7} Karp, R. M. and Lavandera, L., "CCITT Converges on a Universal Public Packet Network Interface", ONLINE Conference Proceedings, June, 1980.

{8} Knightson, K. G., "A Universal X.25 Interface", Proceedings of Networks 80 Conference, Online Publications Limited, London, June, 1980, pp. 405 - 417.

{9} Drukarch, C. Z., et al., "X.25: The Universal Packet Network Interface", Proceedings of the Fifth International Conference on Computer Communications, Atlanta, October 1980.

{10} IBM Corporation, Systems Network Architecture Concepts and Products, Form Number GC30-3072.

{11} IBM Corporation, The X.25 Interface for Attaching IBM SNA Nodes to Packet-Switched Data Networks - General Information Manual, Form Number GA27-3345-0.

{12} CCITT, <u>Orange Book, Volume VIII.1,</u> Data Transmission Over The Telephone Network, Sixth Plenary Assembly, Geneva, 1977.

{13} IBM Corporation, <u>Systems Network Architecture Format and Protocol Reference Manual:</u> Architecture Logic, Form Number SC30-3112

{14} Cypser, R., <u>Communications Architecture for Distributed Systems,</u> Addison - Wesley Publishing Company, 1978.

{15} Hull, D. C., Piatkowski, T. F. and Sundstrom, R. J., "Inside IBM's Systems Network Architecture", <u>Data Communications,</u> February 1977, pp. 34-38.

{16} Sussenguth, E. H., "Systems Network Architecture: A Perspective", <u>ICCC 1978 Conference Proceedings,</u> Kyoto, Japan.

{17} Blair, C. R. and Gray, J. P., "IBM's Systems Network Architecture", <u>Datamation,</u> April 1975, pp. 51-56

{18} Ahuja, V., "Routing and Flow Control in Systems Network Architecture", <u>IBM Systems Journal,</u> Volume 18, Number 2, 1979, pp. 298 - 314.

{19} CCITT "Final Revision of Draft Recommendation X.21", Study Group VII, Geneva, February, 1980.

{20} IBM Corporation, <u>IBM Implementation of the X.21 Interface</u> - General Information Manual, Form Number GA27-3287-0, August 1980.

{21} Ahuja, V. and Barclay, A. S., "Compatibility of Systems Network Architecture and the CCITT X.21 Interface", <u>Proceedings of National Telecommunications Conference,</u> November, 1979.

{22} IBM Corporation, <u>X.25 NCP Packet-Switching Interface</u> - General Information Manual, Form Number SC30-3080.

{23} Corr, F. P. and Neal, D. H., "SNA and Emerging International Standards", <u>IBM Systems Journal,</u> Volume Eighteen, Number Two, 1979, pp. 244-262.

{24} IBM Corporation, <u>X.25 Packet Switching Attachment Working Within ACF/NCP/VS</u> - Program Logic Manual - Program Number 5799-BAK, Form Number LY19-6131.

{25} IBM Corporation, <u>IBM Series/1 Realtime Programming System Packet Network Support</u> - PRPQ Number P10008 - Program Description and Operations Manual, Form Number SC09-1001-1.

{26} IBM Corporation, <u>IBM 5973-L02 Network Interface Adapter Product Description Manual,</u> Form Number GA11-8632-0, 1979.

{27} "A Packet Assembly/Disassembly Protocol Specification for Binary Synchronous Communications", GTE Telenet, April 1980.

{28} International Organization for Standardization <u>Data Communication - HDLC Balanced Class of Procedures,</u> Draft Document ISO/DIS-6256, April 1978.

{29} Electronic Industries Association, <u>EIA Standard RS-232-C - Interface Between Data Terminal Equipment and Data Communication Equipment Employing Serial Binary Data Interchange,</u> EIA Engineering Department, Washington, D. C. (August, 1979).

BIOGRAPHIES

George A. Deaton is Manager of the Network Systems Studies Department in the IBM Communication Products Division at Research Triangle Park, North Carolina. He first began working for IBM in 1962, contributing to manned and unmanned satellite projects under IBM contracts to NASA. In 1970, he became involved in the development of IBM commercial communications products and has since worked with the architecture and design of digital time division systems, in high-speed loop communications systems and more recently in the development of computer communications architecture. He has a B.S. degree in physics in 1961 from Virginia Polytechnic Institute and has done graduate studies in Physics and Astrodynamics.

David J. Franse is an Advisory Engineer/Scientist also with the IBM Communication Products Division at Research Triangle Park, North Carolina. His early telecommunications experience dates to 1947 with Airways and Air Communications Service of the USAF. He joined IBM upon graduation from DeVry Technical Institute in 1956. He made contributions to field engineering for the USAF Semi-Automatic Ground Environment Program. In 1961, he became involved in the development and implementation of various airline reservations systems. Since 1971 Mr. Franse has been involved in the development and analysis of SNA. His current areas of interest include simulation and analysis of data flows in large complex communication networks.

Encryption Implementation in a Layered Network Architecture

W L Price

National Physical Laboratory, UK

The need for assuring the integrity of data carried by computer networks is becoming urgent, defence being required against passive and active intrusion. Data encryption techniques are available, which, if properly applied, can achieve this aim. Standardisation of encryption algorithms and safe modes of operation is proceeding apace, whilst standards for incorporation of encryption as enhancements of the protocols of the lower layers of the Open Systems Interconnection architecture are in preparation. Little has as yet been done at the higher layers. Additional functions required for the creation of a secure network environment include encryption key management procedures, which will call for the setting up of a new network service with the function of encryption key distribution.

1. INTRODUCTION

In this paper we assume that users of communication networks are concerned that the integrity of their traffic be preserved, in other words that its privacy and authenticity be assured. It is by now well understood (1) that data encipherment techniques can be applied to achieving these objectives. It is our purpose here to examine the requirements for encipherment in a data communications context and to discover to what extent current developments are progressing towards fulfilment of these requirements. In particular we shall be concerned to see how encipherment may be fitted into a hierarchical communication protocol structure such as the ISO Open Systems Interconnection (OSI) architectural model.

For widespread acceptance of encipherment techniques it is obviously necessary to create appropriate standards for the encryption function. This work is now quite well advanced. We have had the Data Encryption Standard (DES) published as an American Federal Information Processing Standard (2) since 1977. This same algorithm has recently achieved the status of an American National Standard (3) and it is under consideration by a working group of ISO TC97 for international standardisation. As a result of these developments many manufacturers have produced devices which incorporate the DES; these range from single chips to armoured tamper-proof modules.

It was realised early that to protect a plaintext by simple application of the DES algorithm to successive blocks of data provided inadequate protection against an intruder who might observe repeated ciphertext blocks and so make deductions about the plaintext structure; even worse, no protection was given against an active attack in which the sequence of blocks might be altered by addition, deletion or rearrangement. For these reasons more elaborate modes of use of the DES cipher were conceived; these modes involve feedback paths which establish a dependence of the ciphertext on the position of the corresponding element of plaintext in the data stream,

thereby frustrating attempts to distort a message by interfering with the order of blocks. The recommended modes of use with these properties are known as Cipher Feedback (CFB) and Cipher Block Chaining (CBC); a further recommended mode of use suitable for certain special applications, but lacking some of the strengths of CFB and CBC, is Output Feedback (OFB). Standardisation of the recommended modes of use of the DES cipher is progressing; 1981 has seen the publication of a further Federal Information Processing Standard (4) which gives definitions of the modes of use and work is well advanced within ANSI and elsewhere on similar standards with a wider applicability.

We have seen how a standard encipherment algorithm and methods for its safe use have been developed; these are not by themselves sufficient to allow encipherment devices to be slotted directly into a data communication system, particularly if the latter employs elaborate protocols; further standardisation is inevitable, relating to data formats, methods of key management, integrity checks, etc. Some work in this direction has been carried out in the United States. For some years drafts of a Federal Telecommunications Standard (FTS 1026) have been in preparation; early drafts of this standard laid down the secure modes of operation and also addressed the problem of application of the DES on a simple point-to-point communications link. Data formats were defined, both for enciphered data and for service messages carrying control parameters. Different formats were devised for meeting passive and active threats; in the latter case plaintext chain numbering and manipulation detection codes were incorporated. Recent rationalisation of FTS 1026 has replaced that part of the text defining the recommended modes of operation with a reference to FIPS 81, and has also split the draft standard into two separate drafts, FTS 1025 (5) and FTS 1026 (6). FTS 1025 is concerned with encipherment at network and transport levels of OSI, whilst the new version of FTS 1026 addresses questions of encipherment at the physical and link layers.

The American National Standards Institute (ANSI), the British Standards Institution (BSI), other national standards organisations and the International Standards Organisation (ISO) have also been active in preparing standard definitions of encipherment in a communications context. Drafts for standards at OSI levels 1 and 2 are in an advanced state of development. On the international scene, Working Group 1 of TC97 has already held two full meetings and proposals for standardisation will be sent to TC97.

Further standardisation is also required in the field of device security, in the sense of preventing undetected attacks upon data encipherment equipment. A Federal Telecommunications Standard (FTS 1027 (7), responsibility of the US National Security Agency) has been published recently. This is concerned with those rules for the secure use of cryptographic devices that do not impinge upon interoperability; methods of construction of secure modules and of handling cryptographic parameters are included. Little, if any, standardisation work has been done in this domain outside US Federal Government agencies, though it will certainly be necessary in respect of handling of parameters.

2. ENCIPHERMENT IN DATA NETWORKS

When considering the locations at which encipherment devices should be installed within a data communications network, it is necessary to assess what degree of protection is being sought and, as far as possible, the kind of attack that may be expected. Possibly the simplest measure is to protect each individual data link joining network exchanges or nodes by installing encipherment modules next to the link modems. Key management can be handled easily on a local basis at each link and the impact on the design of the communication protocols is minimised. On the other hand, although the eavesdropper can learn very little by tapping the link, he need only transfer his attention to the exchange or node, where the data is available in clear form. For this reason link encipherment is not generally considered adequate protection for network traffic.

To reduce the vulnerability of data temporarily resident within network nodes, it is possible to set aside secure areas within the storage. Data passing into the secure area is deciphered, but re-enciphered before it is allowed to emerge. Therefore data is always enciphered in non-secure parts of the storage area. Encipherment is carried out according to keys allocated to each attached communication link, the data being re-enciphered with a new key for every new link traversed. Key management is relatively simple for this arrangement, but the security of the whole system depends on the integrity of the secure area of storage in each node.

Maximum security is achieved only if encipherment is implemented on a source to destination basis with no intermediate plaintext state. Data is then enciphered as it leaves the source and does not return to plaintext until

it reaches its ultimate destination. Security is not now dependent on the strength of protection within intermediate nodes. Key management can be in the hands of the source and destination users, but this may present some organisational problems. In a large network there may be many users wishing to communicate on an occasional basis. It is unlikely that each user will wish to maintain a distinct key for each other user; this could require quite a long list of keys, with attendant logistic problems whenever a key is changed. Therefore some key management facilities must be built in to the network design, possibly involving the provision of a key management centre (KMC) attached to the network and providing a service to users.

We should note that end-to-end encipherment does not provide protection against a traffic analysis attack in which the observer makes deductions about the traffic passing on a line based on the volume of traffic and its source and destination. This is possible because end-to-end encipherment must only transform the data field of messages, leaving message headers in clear; the latter information is needed at each node in order to allow routing of traffic. Protection against traffic analysis of this kind can be provided if both end-to-end encipherment and link encipherment are installed. This protects against traffic analysis by observation of a line, but leaves headers readable in nodes. Therefore, from the point of view of preventing traffic analysis, node security may yet be important in an overall scheme.

We can state as a generalisation that the lower the encipherment function is placed in a network hierarchy, the less the header information is exposed. On the other hand, this means that the encipherment function becomes remote from the user, out of the user's control, and the traffic of many users may be enciphered under a common key, which may be unacceptable. This argument again leads us to conclude that encipherment should be installed at more than one level in a network hierarchy. The end-to-end requirement demands encipherment located as close to the users as possible (therefore high in the hierarchy), whilst the need to protect against traffic analysis requires a much lower location.

Faced with a multi-level network hierarchy, as in Open Systems Interconnection, there is a temptation to install the encipherment function at every level, regarding this as necessary for full security. Not only is this unnecessary, but it is very costly, both in terms of the expense of provision of encipherment systems and in terms of the possible operational overheads that are incurred (for example, limited bandwidth of some encipherment systems).

3. ENCIPHERMENT WITHIN OSI

Though it is understood that the OSI definition document has been substantially agreed at the CCITT plenary meeting in 1980, the final definitive text has not yet appeared. Any changes are expected to be of a textual nature and are not expected to change the definition materially. Therefore we can work with the draft document of December 1980 as we consider the application of encipherment.

The draft definition itself makes only one reference to the possibility of including encipherment. This reference occurs in the description of level 6, the Presentation layer. An important function of this layer is to provide services to the layer 7, the Application layer, which achieve independence of character representational data definition, command format, etc., allowing rather diverse applications with different representational conventions to communicate. It seems to be because layer 6 is involved in data transformation that encipherment, regarded as a special purpose transformation of data, is suggested for location here.

It is perhaps surprising to find no other reference to encipherment in the draft definition. Earlier drafts included references for further study of encipherment at layers 3 and 4, respectively Network and Transport. These references have been deleted in the preparation of the present text. We have already seen that encipherment at more than one layer may be necessary in order to provide a specified level of security. The fact that encipherment is mentioned only once in the OSI draft should not be taken to exclude its inclusion at layers other than 6.

Reference has already been made to work within the standards organisations on the preparation of standards for encipherment at layers 1, 2, 3 and 4 of the OSI hierarchy; work is also contemplated at layer 6. Since the lower levels of the OSI model have taken shape before the higher levels, it is natural that proposals for encipherment have followed the same sequence. Though it is possible to outline the definition of encipherment at the higher levels, indeed to design the logical structure of a high level encipherment system, it is not practicable to set out the detailed definition of such a system until the standard definitions of communication protocols at the higher layers are available. The OSI definition provides only a framework on which to structure the work on detailed protocol specification.

If encipherment is installed at the lowest level in OSI, the physical level, this can protect only against a passive attack on the data; it can not protect against attempts to alter the enciphered data. This is because the physical level is required to provide a transparent service; hence it is not possible to introduce the redundancy necessary for the detection of an active attack. The physical layer protocol can not contain a cryptographic negotiation phase and its parameters must be installed by means outside the protocol, for example, the loading of keys by human intervention. For these reasons some users may wish to restrict their proposals for encipherment to the higher layers, where greater flexibility is possible.

An encipherment function at any hierarchical level except the lowest requires not only that the encipherment capability be provided but also that the layer protocol shall be extended to allow for negotiation and secure exchange of cryptographic parameters. It is necessary to achieve agreement between communicating users, firstly on the basic decision to use encipherment, then on the method of encipherment to be used (algorithm and mode of use), on the encipherment key to be applied (known as a "session key") and possibly, on other initialisation parameters. The session key may already be available locally as the result of a visit by a security officer who visits locations and issues keys, it may be exchanged between users enciphered under a shared master key (originally installed at the two users by a visiting security officer) or it may be issued to both communicating users on demand from a key management centre attached to the network and serving either all users or a group of users.

We have already observed that a KMC may be desirable when occasional communication is needed between any pair of a large population of users. As an alternative, it is possible to specify a public key cryptosystem (PKC), by which a user may send enciphered text to a destination under the protection of the public key of the destination user. It is not then necessary to set up a session key between the two users; all that is necessary is to make certain that the public keys of all users are available from some reliable source on the network. Until public key algorithms become available in economically viable implementations this solution must be held in abeyance.

It seems important from many points of view that the various activities in preparing standards should maintain compatibility. Up to the present most of the work on preparing standards within the OSI structure has taken place within the USA. It is therefore disappointing to discover that the work of the Federal authorities and of ANSI on OSI layers 1 and 2 is not keeping step. In part this is due to the pressure on ANSI to accommodate as many existing manufacturers' devices within the standards as possible; in the ANSI drafts it is stated that any pre-existing practice shall be acceptable. Since one of the aims of standardisation is to ensure as much compatibility as possible between equipment from different manufacturers, acceptance of pre-existing practice seems to be an unhappy position from which to start. If incompatible standards become approved in the USA, then manufacturers will find themselves supplying equipment to one set of standards to the Federal authorities and equipment to the other set to non-Federal users. Incompatible standards on the international scene should not be contemplated.

We can mention particular points of detail in which the present draft standards differ. At the physical layer, level 1, though the Federal and ANSI drafts agree on the important issue of recommending the use of 1-bit CFB mode of use, they differ on many other points of detail, including the significant point of the length of initialisation vector to be used for various data formats. At the link layer, level 2, there is also disagreement on the length of initialisation vectors, together with other very important differences. The two drafts agree on the general mode of encipherment to be used, again CFB, but have so far differed on the very important point of the feedback dimension, being 1-bit for the Federal proposal whilst the ANSI draft prefers 8-bit. Initially there was disagreement on the fields to be enciphered; ANSI recommended that the whole of the information field plus the associated address fields should be enciphered, whilst the Federal draft FTS 1026 recommends that only the information field should be enciphered. This is equivalent to saying that ANSI required encryption near the bottom of the link layer, whilst FTS put it near the top of the link layer. The latter approach has the virtue of generality, being applicable within the structure of any of the upper layers of the OSI architecture; the advantage of the ANSI proposal is likely to be easier implementation within layer 2. At the time of writing there are signs that ANSI is coming round to the Federal view on the location of the encipherment function within the link layer.

There is some disquiet at the proposal in the ANSI draft for the inclusion of a by-pass facility in data encryption equipment (DEE) complying with the standard. This is needed by some users in order to test communication equipment; the DEE is required to identify test mode and local or remote loopback signals, then to switch off encipherment. It is feared that it may be possible for the DEE to transmit cleartext when loopback is not actually achieved; herein lies a risk of reducing the level of data protection. It seems undesirable to demand that the bypass mode shall be a feature of all standard DEEs; a better solution is to provide the bypass facility as an option with which not all DEEs need comply.

Above the link layer little has as yet been done, though we have the draft FTS 1025 which addresses layers 3 and 4; this document will require further development. Outside the US Federal domain work above the link layer is proceeding rather slowly.

A more completely developed set of communication protocols is available in the CCITT recommendations for Teletex, the document handling system which has characteristics of a "super-Telex". This has a layered architecture very similar in many respects to the OSI structure, but has only six levels; the sixth level is the document level, the lower levels bearing the same names and roughly the same functions as the OSI layers. Proposals have been advanced for the introduction of encipherment into Teletex. Some of these are described in a paper presented to this conference (8).

4. MESSAGE AUTHENTICATION AND SIGNATURE

Encipherment can also be employed to generate functions which allow the authentication of messages to be demonstrated. This enables communicating parties, sharing the same DES encipherment key, to obtain assurance that messages passing between them have not been altered in transit. Such messages need not necessarily be enciphered in transmission. Federal Information Processing Standard 81, on modes of operation, defines a method in which the DES can be used to generate an authentication field. This function of the DES could prove popular with users, in which case standardisation of authentication methods must be developed within a wider constituency.

Since the secret information on which message authentication depends is possessed both by sender and receiver, message authentication does not provide proof of sending. Authentication cannot therefore be used to resolve disputes between communicating parties. Techniques which allow proof of sending to be generated are potentially very valuable and are possible if public key cryptosystems become practicable; though proposals have been made to use the DES cipher for this purpose, they either involve enormous expansion of data and a mass of expendable key material (9) or they require special secure hardware to be set up at each network node (10).

In public key cryptosystems the key material divides into two categories, that which is public and that which is secret. To encipher a message for secret transmission, the sender obtains the public key of the intended recipient and transforms the message using this key as a parameter in the transformation. The receiver carries out a complementary transformation with his secret key as parameter, thereby retrieving the plaintext message. In at least one PKC (11) the transformations can be carried out in the reverse order, thereby permitting the creation of a digital signature. The sender uses his secret key to carry out a transformation on the message; to establish the validity of the signature, the receiver uses the public key of the alleged sender to carry out the complementary transformation. If the resultant message shows some agreed pattern or redundancy, then it is possible to prove that the sender really did send the message. Positive proof depends on the reliability of the source from which the receiver obtains the public key of the alleged sender. This source should take the form of a public key register, possibly provided by the network authority; this source must provide not only all current public keys, but must also allow for messages signed by public keys which are no longer current. One way of achieving this is to submit signed messages of long-term significance to be re-signed with a public key of the central key registry. Only the public keys of the central registry need then be preserved indefinitely.

Disputes between communicating users are unlikely to arise, because the evidence provided by public keys and associated signatures is positive, not a matter of opinion. However, if this should prove necessary, it is possible to provide a kind of arbitration service which takes the evidence and formally adjudicates the dispute. If this service is provided by the network authority it may seem that it is rather a novel role for such a body. However, provision of evidence of delivery has long been a PTT function in the context of the mail services; proof of origin could be regarded as a natural extension of this function.

It is more than likely that signatures on transmitted documents will be required in the future by users of communication services. Therefore it will be necessary for attention to be given to the standards which will define the precise methods to be adopted for this purpose. Little has as yet been done in this direction. Developments may be expected to await the special purpose hardware which will facilitate efficient implementation of the public key algorithms; when this becomes available it should not be difficult to lay down the necessary standards. An indication of the nature of these standards may be found in Davies and Price (12).

REFERENCES

(1) W. Diffie & M.E. Hellman, Privacy and authentication: an introduction to cryptography, Proc. IEEE, vol. 67, no. 3, March 1979, 397–427.

(2) National Bureau of Standards, Data Encryption Standard, Federal Information Processing Standard, Publication 46, January 1977.

(3) American National Standards Institute, Data Encryption Algorithm, Publication X3 92–1981, July 1981.

(4) National Bureau of Standards, DES Modes of Operation, Federal Information Processing Standard, Publication 81, December 1980.

(5) National Communications System, Telecommunications: interoperability and security requirements for use of the Data Encryption Standard in the network and transport layers of data communication, Proposed Federal Telecommunications Standard 1025, draft of June 1981.

(6) National Communications System, Telecommunications: interoperability and security requirements for use of the Data Encryption Standard in the physical and link layers of data communication, Proposed Federal Telecommunications Standard 1026, draft of June 1981.

(7) National Security Agency, Telecommunications: General security requirements for equipment using the Data Encryption Standard, Federal Telecommunications Standard 1027, May 1981.

(8) D.W. Davies & I.K. Hirst, Encipherment and signature in Teletex, This conference.

(9) S.M. Lipton & S.M. Matyas, Making the digital signature legal – and safeguarded, Data Communications, February 1978, 41–52.

(10) M.E. Smid, A key notarization system for computer networks, National Bureau of Standards, Special Publication 500–54, October 1979.

(11) R.L. Rivest, A. Shamir & L. Adleman, A method of obtaining digital signatures and public-key cryptosystems, Comm. ACM, vol. 21, February 1978, 120–126.

(12) D.W. Davies & W.L. Price. The application of digital signatures based on public key cryptosystems, Proc. 4th ICCC, Atlanta, October 1980, 525–530.

Wyn L. Price received his B.Eng. degree in electrical engineering in 1951 and his Ph.D. in 1955, both from the University of Liverpool. He has been at the National Physical Laboratory since 1954, working on various aspects of computing. From 1970 to 1978 he was leader of the NPL project for the simulation of data communications networks. His present project is a study of data security in networks. He is a Member of the IEE, a Fellow of the British Computer Society and a Senior Member of the IEEE. He is co-author of the recent book "Computer networks and their protocols" (Wiley).

File Transfer Protocols – a Comparison and Critique

R W S Hale
National Physical Laboratory, UK

Many applications of computer communications (document transfer, mail, etc.) have a common requirement, namely to transport data in bulk from one system to another. To do this efficiently requires a specialised protocol, which can support any of these applications. Although many such file transfer protocols (FTPs) already exist, none has yet been used extensively outside the research community. But this is starting to change, and there is a need for a review of the "state of the art". This paper attempts to satisfy that need, surveying as broad a range of FTPs as possible (both technically and chronologically).

1. INTRODUCTION

The problems addressed in heterogeneous file transfer fall into three categories:

A. Translation of information between the conventions of different filestores (e.g. different data codes or record delimiters).
B. Those due to the geographical distribution of the filing systems and the means of communication between them.
C. Provision of a service to systems whose requirements differ widely (from a remote printer to a mainframe with disc filestore).

Each of these is independent of the other two. The first is present irrespective of the communication medium or the sophistication of the systems, and can in part be solved by the presentation service, and in part by the virtual filestore (see section 4).

There are two quite separate aspects to problem B. Firstly, there is the need to communicate at a high level over a physical network. Means to do this have been standardised in the Reference Model for OSI {7}. Secondly, it is sometimes necessary to control one such high level dialogue by means of another (section 3).

Of the three issues, C has by far the greatest impact on the user (the term "user" here refers to any entity that makes use of the file transfer service). In a local environment it may be feasible have a "tailor-made" protocol for each pair of communicating systems, but in an open environment it is not, and (as always) generality is only available at a price.

Our purpose here is to discuss these issues in greater detail, and to examine how far certain real FTPs go towards resolving them. The following protocols have been investigated:

- The ARPANET FTP, published 1973.
- Network Independent FTP (NIFTP), 1977, revised 1981.
- AUTODIN II FTP, 1979, revised 1980.
- Hahn-Meitner Institute's Virtual File Protocol (HMI VFP), 1980.
- UNINETT File Management System (UFMS), 1980.
- Teletex document level protocol, draft recommendation 1980.
- European Computer Manufacturers' Association Virtual File Protocol (ECMA VFP), 1981.
- National Bureau of Standards FTP (NBS FTP), draft report 1981.
- International Standards Organisation FTP (ISO FTP), working draft 1982.

The most recent specifications of each of these protocols are given in {1-6,8,9 & 11}.

The Teletex protocol, although not strictly an FTP, is included here because document transfer (for which Teletex is designed) is potentially a major application of file transfer.

2. THE USER'S VIEW OF FILE HANDLING

Operations on files are of three kinds:

A. Transfer operations, which transfer a single part of the contents of a file. (These form a subset of the access operations, below.)
B. Management operations, which can determine or change the properties, rather than the contents, of a file.
C. Access operations, which are used to examine or alter parts of the contents of a file.

2.1 File Transfer

Any file transfer can be reduced to the following operation:

```
COPY <source file description>
     <sink file description>
     <mode>
     <quality of service>
     <other options>
```

The "mode" parameter indicates the effect that COPY will have on each file. Possible effects on the sink file include:

Cr. Create only (fail if it already exists).
Ow. Overwrite only (fail if it does not already exist).
Ap. Append only (fail if it does not already exist).
CO. Create or overwrite.
CA. Create or append.

The source may sometimes be:

De. deleted on successful completion of the transfer.

Of the many factors that influence the "quality of service", recovery options probably have the greatest importance for the user and for the protocol design. These include:

Ck. "Checkpoint-rollback" mechanisms, which return the transfer to a point of known synchronisation to recover from errors that do not destroy the application (source-sink) connection (e.g. device errors).
Re. Resumption of a transfer which has been interrupted by loss of the application connection, possibly at the user's request.
Su. Suspension of the transfer at the user's request.
Ab. Unilateral abortion of the transfer.

One other important facility is:

P. Partial transfer, i.e. the ability to transfer sections of a source file to update corresponding parts of the sink.

To properly claim to support a particular operation, a protocol must be able to guarantee its atomicity, and so prevent partial completion. Table 1 shows the extent of each protocol's support for the features listed in the text.

2.2 File Management

Cr. Create file (as an atomic action).
De. Delete file (as an atomic action).
Li. List directory (returns a list of all filenames in the directory).
Ex. Examine file (returns properties of the file, e.g. size or history).
Rn. Rename file.
Ch. Change file attributes (e.g. access rights).

The most common management operations are listed above. Examine and change attributes refer to the virtual representation of the file (see section 4).

2.3 File Access

File access provides a more interactive style of working than file transfer, enabling named structural units of the file to be transferred individually. This requires the connection between source and sink files to be maintained while several data transfer operations are performed, and therefore the service elements which make and break this association, "open" and "close", to be separate from those which transfer data. The following service elements might be supported.

Re. Read data unit.
Wr. Write data unit.
Up. Update data unit.

3. SYSTEM INTERCONNECTION

3.1 Connections

File transfer requires the co-operation of three parties: the user, the sender (source filestore) and the receiver (sink filestore), and in general, all three may be at different geographical locations. Clearly, two protocols are needed: a transfer protocol between the sender and receiver, and a management protocol to enable the user to define and control the file transfer. Often, of course, the user will be coresident with one of the other systems, and transfer control will be a local issue.

A file transfer can be controlled in one of two ways. The user may either establish sessions with both sender and receiver, and so have direct control over both, or may choose either the sender or receiver to act as its agent in all communication with the other (see figure 1). The latter requires only one control connection, thereby avoiding the expense of maintaining and synchronising a pair of control connections, with negligible loss of control.

Table 1: Protocol support for service features (described in the text). X indicates mandatory, O optional, and - no support.

	File Transfer Cr Ow Ap CO CA De	P	Recovery Ck Re Su Ab	Management Cr De Li Ex Rn Ch	Access Re Wr Up
ARPANET	- - - X O -	-	O O - O	- O O O O -	- - -
NIFTP	X O O X O O	-	O O O X	- - - - - -	- - -
AUTODIN	- X O X O -	O	O - O X	- O O - - -	- - -
HMI	- - - X X -	X	X - - X	- X - X X X	X X -
UFMS	- - - X X X	-	X - X X	- - - - - -	- - -
TELETEX	Text transfer only	-	O X O X	- - - - - -	- - -
ECMA	O X X O O O	-	O O O X	O O - O - -	- - -
NBS	- - X X X -	-	X X X X	- X X - X -	- - -
ISO	O X X O O O	X	O O O X	O O - O O O	- - -

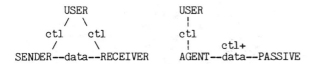

```
       USER                USER
      /   \                 |
   ctl     ctl            ctl
    /       \              |       ctl+
SENDER--data--RECEIVER   AGENT--data--PASSIVE
```

Figure 1: Alternative Control Hierarchies.

Only the ARPANET, AUTODIN, UFMS and NBS FTPs explicitly define remote control mechanisms, and of these all but ARPANET FTP employ the user-agent control relationship. The AUTODIN and NBS protocols provide transfer control as an integral part of file transfer. The others all see it as a secondary issue to be provided perhaps by a separate management protocol.

3.2 Communication Architecture

As the reference architecture for OSI has only recently been defined {7}, it is not surprising that there are significant architectural differences between the protocols. Only three - ECMA, NBS and ISO - conform to the standard architecture, separating file transfer and presentation functions above the session service; the others adopt the more or less ad hoc solutions illustrated in figure 2.

ARPANET FTP is designed for interactive use, and so employs two underlying connections. Commands are transferred as character mnemonics by the TELNET protocol {10}, whereas data is transmitted over a transport connection for better economy.

The NI and AUTODIN FTPs both predate the Reference Model, and are based on the transport service. The AUTODIN "Data Transfer Protocol" performs some presentation functions.

The HMI architecture contains "Status Exchange" and "Synchronisation" layers to effect reliable command and data transfer, respectively. Together these perform a session-like function.

The UFMS transfer protocol is contained in a so-called "Service Layer", extending from the session into the application layer. Above this is the "User Layer" containing applications to use FTP, including the user interface.

Although the Teletex protocol is subdivided into Session and Document layers, these do not resemble ISO layers so much as phases of a single protocol. The session protocol performs connection establishment and manages the interaction of user data (not of the document protocol, as one might expect). The document protocol provides for error-free data transfer.

3.3 Network Independence

For an FTP to be independent of the underlying network, it should make few demands of the lower layer services, and in particular, of the transport and session services. Addressing and resynchronisation issues should be considered.

In order to refer to a particular transfer after a break in the underlying connection, a unique identifier must be allocated to it. The simplest strategy is for the user's system to assign a transfer identifier, and to prefix this with the user's transport (or session) address when referring to it on other systems. However, this address cannot guarantee uniqueness of the transfer identifier unless addresses are globally unique. The AUTODIN, HMI, UFMS, ECMA, NBS and ISO protocols all assume an allocation scheme of this sort; NIFTP does not, but offers no wholly satisfactory alternative for use in resumption. Teletex is designed for a restricted addressing domain, in which unique addresses are assured.

As dialogue synchronisation is implicit in FTP, it is unnecessary for FTP to use session service dialogue control facilities (as is done in ECMA VFP). The only requirement is for a simple "purge" form of resynchronisation. HMI VFP relies on the Status Exchange and Synchronisation protocols to provide dialogue synchronisation.

4. THE VIRTUAL FILESTORE

Underpinning all FTPs is the assumption that dissimilar real files can be described in a common representation, often known as a virtual filestore. This representation is based on a standard set of attributes, which should be sufficiently comprehensive to preserve the form and meaning of most real files. The mapping between real and virtual filestores is done locally. Using this scheme a potentially complex heterogeneous file transfer is reduced to an exchange of attributes and data between homogeneous virtual filestores.

The most important classes of file attributes, and the extent to which the protocols support them, are listed in table 2. The following notes refer to the table.

4.1 Filename

Most FTPs are resigned to the fact that file naming conventions differ widely, and use native conventions in the virtual filestore. However, it is a simple matter, and potentially very useful when examining a file catalogue, to standardise the syntax for components in multi-component filenames. Only ISO FTP does this.

Figure 2:   Communication Architectures

```
 _____    _____    _____   _____   _____   _____   _____
| FTP  Ctrl|  |           |  |    FTP     | |FTP        | |  "User"   | |          | |    FTP    |
|Data ---|--| |           |  | |----------| |Ctrl  Data| |-----------| |          | |-----------|
| |  |   | | |    FTP     |  | |   Data   | | |   .----|-| | "Service" | | Document | |Presentation|
| | |TELNET| | |           |  | | Transfer | |-|--+-.Sync| |-----------| |----------| |-----------|
| | |    | | |           |  | | Protocol | |S|Exch| | | |  Session  | | Session  | |  Session  |
|-V--+---V--| |-----------| |-----------| |-V----+--V-| |-----------| |----------| |-----------|
| Transport |  | Transport |  | Transport | | Transport | | Transport | | Transport| | Transport |
|_____|  |_____|  |_____| |_____| |_____| |_____| |_____|
   ARPANET         NIFTP         AUTODIN        HMINET         UFMS         TELETEX    NBS, ECMA & ISO
```

4.2 File Structure

Except for Teletex which is oriented towards printed output of documents, all the FTPs are suitable for transferring unstructured or flat (record structured) files. The page structure of Teletex documents is more or less equivalent to a variable length record structure.

The hierarchical model adopted by HMI VFP and ISO FTP can describe more complex file structures. In this model a file is represented by an oriented tree in which nodes correspond to structural units in the real file The entire file is represented by the root; and every other node subdivides the structure of its parent into smaller units, as, for instance, a record may be divided into several fields. The advantage of such a model is simplicity coupled with descriptive power; a disadvantage can be the overhead in defining each structural unit. The description of a record structured file using the HMI encoding consumes at least 10 octets per record, whereas AUTODIN FTP, for example, takes only 3. Moreover, the model presumes that the real file structure has a well-defined hierarchy, and so its applicability is limited. It is doubtful that this model will prove significantly more useful than the three level structure (file-record-field) adopted by ECMA.

4.3 Means of Access

Individual structural units of a file may be accessed in many ways. Common means of access include: sequential, by position and by key. Several FTPs support the transfer of indexed files; only ECMA VFP distinguishes positional access from sequential.

Both the ISO and HMI protocols superimpose an "access structure" on the hierarchical file structure by associating names with all data units down to certain level in the structure. Each such data unit can be accessed directly by quoting its name prefixed by the name of its parent node, and so on up the hierarchy.

4.4 Data Types

In the absence of a presentation service, all code conversion must be performed in the FTP process. For this reason most of the older protocols define relatively few data types. The intent of the Teletex protocol is made clear by the absence of non-text data types.

4.5 Unit Sizes

Two views of the size of a file are important in file transfer: the amount of data transferred (current size), and the amount of storage allocated to the file on the receiving system (maximum size). The latter may anticipate future growth of the file.

Record size attributes enable the receiver to anticipate the buffer resources it will need for the transfer, and the distinction between fixed and variable length records may aid the receiver to optimise its use of storage. The transmission buffer size is a separately negotiable transfer parameter in HMI VFP.

For a file containing a mixture of data types, it is not clear how unit sizes should be measured, as these will depend on the encoding. In ISO FTP all sizes are "estimates" in octets, and will be meaningless if tab stops (for instance) are used extensively. In NBS FTP there is a separate size parameter for each data type in the file or record, indicating the number of items of that type. This is cumbersome. Moreover it is not clear how to interpret record size attributes. Does a fixed record size imply that each record is composed of the same number of items of each type? In the ECMA protocol, sizes are measured in octets for binary and text files, and are calculated from the field sizes in heterogeneous files. The fact that field sizes are fixed means that only fixed length records can be subdivided in this way.

4.6 File Security

Various methods of protection are possible: filename passwords, access control lists (ACL), encryption, and non-specific "security level" attributes can all be used to augment the default protection afforded by a filestore.

Access control mechanisms are established by means of file management operations, such as creation or change of attributes; other operations only require these access controls to be satisfied. Thus, an ACL can only be altered during file management. There is no need for an ACL attribute in "pure" transfer.

Only in ISO FTP can full ACL protection be requested. An ACL attribute may be used to specify permissions for individual accessors, depending on their location and the correct specification of a password. Both the HMI and ECMA protocols support ACL's, but limit the choice of access permissions. HMI VFP offers a choice between sole access by the file creator, and access by all users; ECMA VFP only offers the former possibility.

4.7 History

History attributes (identity of last accessor, etc.) are usually maintained locally, and it is a relatively simple matter to make them available in the open system, provided that they refer only to the local copy of the file.

4.8 Text Formatting

Text data is usually formatted in one of three ways. Format characters may be embedded in the text, a carriage control character may be prefixed to each record, or formatting action may be implied by the end of a record.

Translation between different formatting syntaxes should be a presentation function, so that only one syntax is visible to FTP. This is true of the ECMA, NBS and ISO protocols, but in AUTODIN FTP the function is split between presentation and application layers.

4.9 Binary Mapping

When the word size used in a binary file differs from the transfer byte size, conventions must be established for mapping between the two. Words may be packed into bytes or aligned on byte boundaries, or transmitted most or least significant byte first. This cannot be specified in either ARPANET FTP or UFMS.

Again, this should be part of the presentation service, but again it is visible to the user of AUTODIN FTP.

5. THE PROTOCOLS

5.1 Protocol Structure

It has already been noted (in section 2) that the potential capability of a protocol depends to some extent on its structure. If only file transfer is required, it is possible, and more efficient, to identify and open the remote file in a single protocol exchange; but if file management operations are to be supported, then it is necessary to be able to maintain an association with the same file during a succession of management and transfer activities in order to ensure the integrity of the entire sequence of operations. Similarly, it should not be necessary to close and reopen a file between a succession of file accesses. To use several "single shot" partial transfers to simulate file access is not just less efficient, but also splits a single association with a remote file into many separate associations, with no safeguard against being "locked out" before all are completed.

Table 2: Support for certain classes of file attribute.

	Filename	Structure	Means of access	Data types	Sizes of structural units	Security	History	Text formatting	Binary mapping
ARPANET	local syntax	unstruc- tured or flat	sequential	binary or text	max file size only	none	none	embedded or FORTRAN control characters	word size only
NIFTP	local syntax	unstruc- tured or flat	sequential	binary or text, may be mixed	max/current file size, max record size.	password	none	embedded, EOR-implied or FORTRAN control	word size and mapping
AUTODIN	local syntax	unstruc- tured or flat	sequential or by key	private, binary, text or numeric	max filesize fixed or max record size, key size.	password	none	embedded, EOR-implied or FORTRAN control	word size and mapping
HMINET	local syntax	hierarch- ical, any number of levels	hierar- chical	Boolean, text or numeric. Mixed.	max file size, current size of each data unit.	password & simple ACL	none	none	n/a
UFMS	local syntax	unstruc- tured or flat	sequential	binary or text	max file size, fixed/ max record size.	none	none	none	word size only
TELETEX	none	flat (page st- ructured document)	sequential	text and graphic	max file size only	none	none	embedded chars, page boundaries in protocol	n/a
ECMA	local syntax	up to 3 level hierar- chical	sequential by key or by position	binary, text, numeric or mixed	max/current file size, fixed/max record size	password & simple ACL	yes	presentation service functions	
NBS	local syntax	unstruc- tured or flat	sequential or indexed	binary, text, numeric or mixed	max/current file size, fixed/max record size	security level, password	none	presentation service functions	
ISO	standard syntax	hierarch- ical, any number of levels	hierar- chical	basic set (bin/text/ num)+ user defined	max/current file size, max size on each level	password & ACL	yes	presentation service functions	

Thus, each protocol can be structured into phases which are entered and left as corresponding associations are made and broken. In the most general structure the connected phase corresponds to the association of two applications, the file-selected phase to an association between files, the file-open phase to an association between their contents, and the data access phase to the exchange of data. Of the protocols surveyed, only the ECMA, NBS and ISO FTPs are structured in this way. All the others combine the file-selected and file-open phases. Teletex is exceptional insofar as, being a data transfer protocol, it does not support the intermediate file associations at all.

Uniquely, HMI VFP permits several file-open phases to overlap in time. However, the same effect is more simply achieved by multiplexing in the transport or session layer; and for this reason application layer multiplexing is rejected in the OSI Reference Model.

Usually, each phase change involves a handshake (request-respose pair) in the protocol; and this makes the ECMA and ISO protocols rather inefficient for simple file transfer unless pipelining techniques are used. In both of these protocols messages may be grouped, so that "select" and "open" requests, for example, may be sent as a single group, effecting two phase changes in a single group handshake. Response time can be improved in this way. Moreover, if such grouping is mandatory for a kernel subset of the FTP, the number of messages to be recognised by a basic implementation is reduced. This approach has not yet been adopted by any FTP; and consequently the kernel subsets of ECMA VFP and ISO FP, in particular, are larger than they might be.

5.2 Implementation Overheads

A full implementation of any of these protocols is more than many applications require, and it is useful if protocol elements other than those essential to file transfer are not required for for conformance. ARPANET FTP, NIFTP, AUTODIN FTP, ECMA VFP and ISO FTP all distinguish the kernel from the optional parts of the protocols, and all provide means to establish the optional features that both parties are willing to use. HMI VFP, UFMS and NBS FTP all assume full implementation.

Protocol	msgs for file trans.	no. of hdr. bytes/rec.	compression breakeven
ARPANET	3	2 or 3	3
NIFTP	6	>=1	3
AUTODIN	5	3	7
HMI	6	>=10	9
UFMS	5	1	n/a
TELETEX	3	2	n/a
ECMA	12 (6*)	presentation function	
NBS	11	presentation function	
ISO	11 (7*)	presentation function	

Table 3: Protocol Overheads (* = with grouping; counting each group as one message).

For the simplest initiator to responder file transfer, table 3 shows the number of messages exchanged between initiator and responder to initiate and terminate the transfer (i.e. from file selection to the first data message, and from the last data message to release of the file), the number of header octets required for each record transferred, and the minimum number of repetitions of a single data octet for which it is no less economical to use data compression mechanisms (where the protocol defines them). The former figure is more relevant when transferring small amounts of data, the latter two when transferring large files. The table gives a rough indication of the overheads introduced by each FTP, but it should be born in mind that each lower layer of protocol introduces an extra overhead.

Recovery mechanisms may be used to safeguard the data transfer against errors. Most commonly, commitment units are defined by checkpoints inserted in the data stream. If an error (such as a device malfunction) occurs, each party must be prepared to restart the transfer from anywhere within its own domain of responsibility (before/after the last checkpoint acknowledged for receiver/sender). Restart may be immediate, if the data transfer phase has not been lost, or deferred until a later time, if it has. In the latter case, both parties must keep sufficient information about the transfer (addresses, parameter values etc.) to re-establish the previous context before resumption. The same is true when the transfer is voluntarily suspended at the user's request. The extent of support for these facilities is shown in table 1.

There are two further points worth making about recovery. Firstly, HMI VFP does not use application level checkpoints, but instead relies on a lower level "Synchronisation protocol" to maintain synchronism. This is unsuitable for application level resumption. Secondly, UFMS uses checkpoints to provide user level suspension as well as error recovery. The resultant mechanism is not satisfactory, as the Primary must always define checkpoints, and no acknowledgement window can be used.

6. SUMMARY

No absolute judgements can be made, but two considerations are most important to the potential user. Both are obvious. Firstly, a standard protocol should have a long lifetime and good support; and secondly, it should be suitable for the applications that the user really needs.

NIFTP and ARPANET FTP are both backed by a wealth of implementation experience, and NIFTP in particular by detailed documentation. However, it is clear that standardisation will leave them behind. Teletex, and ECMA, NBS and ISO FTPs all promise long term stability and extensive commercial support, but of these only Teletex can yet be implemented.

The greatest advantage of Teletex is its
simplicity. Its ability to interwork with
Telex may well outweigh all drawbacks, but it
is nevertheless only a data transfer protocol.
ARPANET FTP and UFMS are also very simple, but
the former is designed for the human, rather
than machine user, and the latter suffers from
technical problems. NIFTP is economical and
powerful if only file transfer is required
though AUTODIN FTP has greater generality, and
defines a mechanism to perform partial
transfers. NBS FTP offers a very similar
service to AUTODIN FTP. Both these protocols
will be expensive to implement, due to the
inclusion of transfer control in the kernel
subsets.

The ECMA and ISO protocols are also similar in
outlook, ECMA FTP being the more pragmatic of
the two. Both are powerful and well
structured, but may be too expensive for
simpler systems to implement (though the kernel
subset of ISO FTP, in particular, is very
small). The ISO protocol promises file access
capability, but HMI VFP is the only access
protocol defined. However, subsets of this
protocol cannot be negotiated, making it
uneconomic unless file access is a strict
requirement.

Roger Hale was educated at
Trinity College, Cambridge.
He received a BA in mathe-
matics in 1979, and a
Diploma in Computer Science
the following year. Since
leaving university, he has
been working with the
Protocol Standards Group at
NPL.

7. REFERENCES

{1} CCITT Recommendation S.62. Control Proced-
    ures for the Teletex Service. Geneva,
    1980.
{2} Clopper S. and Swanson J. Specification
    of the File Transfer Protocol. National
    Bureau of Standards, December 1981.
{3} European Computer Manufacturers' Assoc-
    iation. Virtual File Protocol. Final
    Draft. ECMA/TC23/81/159, December 1981.
{4} Forsdick H. AUTODIN II File Transfer
    Protocol. Bolt, Beranek and Newman Inc.
    Report no. 4246, February 1980.
{5} Guy M. (ed.). A Network Independent File
    Transfer Protocol, as revised by the File
    Transfer Protocol Implementors' Group of
    the UK Department of Industry Data
    Communications Protocols Unit. FTP-B(80)
    February 1981.
{6} Hahn-Meitner-Institut fur Kernforschung,
    Berlin, GmbH. The Virtual File System.
    Final Draft. HMI-B 333, October 1980.
{7} International Standards Organisation. Data
    Processing - Open System Interconnection -
    Basic Reference Model. ISO/DP7498.
{8} International Standards Organisation.
    Working Draft on File Transfer, Access and
    Management, ISO/TC97/SC16 N1002, March
    1982.
{9} Neigus N.J. File Transfer Protocol for the
    ARPA Network. ARPANET Protocol Handbook.
    Eds. Feinler E. and Postel J. Defense
    Communications Agency, January 1978.
{10}Telnet Protocol Specification. ARPA Doc.
    NIC 18639, August 1973.
{11}UNINETT. The UNINETT File Management
    System. UNINETT Report no.10, July 1980.

Description of a Planned Federal Information Processing Standard for Data Presentation Protocol

J R Moulton
National Bureau of Standards, USA

ABSTRACT

The National Bureau of Standards has developed service and design specifications for internet, transport, session, data presentation, and file transfer protocols for use in computer systems and network procurements. These protocols reside in layers three, four, five, six and seven of the International Organization for Standardization's (ISO) Reference Model of Open Systems Interconnection. This paper describes the services and internal behavior of the data presentation protocol. The specification of the data presentation protocol, as well as specifications for the other protocols, was derived from the most recent developments within ISO. Specific features were selected based on the needs of the agencies of the Federal Government of the United States. These needs are consistent with those of any large organization engaged in the procurements or development of networks of heterogeneous computer systems.

DATA PRESENTATION AND THE NBS NETWORKING PROGRAM

Recent advances in technology have made distributed computer networking and network interconnection rapidly growing fields in computer science. Not only businesses, but also government agencies are planning increased usage of computer networks to share resources and to provide distributed processing. In planning for future networks and in upgrading existing networks, it has been recognized that many networks must be able to support the interconnection of heterogeneous computer systems and components. The optimal way in which this can be accomplished is by providing standard computer network protocols that can be used on a broad spectrum of computer systems. The Systems and Network Architecture Division of the National Bureau of Standards has ongoing projects to develop computer network protocol Federal Information Processing Standards (FIPS), as well as programs to develop computer-based office system and local area network FIPS [1]. The goal of these programs is to provide standards that will support distributed processing within the Federal Government so that computer network components can be procured competitively without the constraint imposed by incompatibilities between vendors' equipment.

One primary aim of the program is the specification of standards that are accepted by industry and available as off-the-shelf implementations. The only way this can be achieved is to develop standards based heavily on standards developed by international standards organizations. Then manufacturers will have one standard that can be used and marketed world-wide. A further aim of the program is to issue standards in a timely fashion so that retrofit costs will be kept to a minimum.

Current protocols under development by NBS include internetwork [2], [3], transport [4], [5], session [6], data presentation [7] [8], file transfer [9] [10], and virtual terminal [11]. The planned protocols for transport [12], session [13], and file transfer [14] are described in papers by Heafner, Blanc, Nielsen, and Moulton. The data presentation protocol is the subject of this paper. Although the services and functions of the protocol are described in some detail, the formal specification cited above should be consulted for a more complete description.

The data presentation protocol was designed and is being implemented by Bolt Beranek and Newman, Inc. (BBN) under contract to NBS. The technical work performed by BBN was done in conjunction with NBS, with the American National Standard Institute (ANSI), and with the International Organization for Standardization (ISO). Additionally, through a liaison agreement, NBS and the European Computer Manufacturers' Association (ECMA) coordinated in developing this protocol. This liaison promoted the exchange of technical solutions to problems encountered by either organization. However, the NBS specification includes design details not found in the ANSI, ISO, and ECMA documents, so that users may reference the NBS protocol specification in procurements and manufacturers may implement directly from the specification.

INTRODUCTION TO THE DATA PRESENTATION

PROTOCOL
Architectural Model

In order to provide a framework for developing computer network standards, an abstract model, the ISO Basic Reference Model of Open Systems Interconnection [15] is used. This architectural model divides computer network functions into seven layers. Each host on a network supports the seven layers so that entities at each layer can communicate with its peer in a different host. The lowest layer models the physical interconnection function such as RS 232 [16]. The highest layer, the user processes, are supported by a set of services. The layers are hierarchically ordered so that each higher layer depends on the services of the next lower layer and provides enhanced services to the next higher layer. The data presentation protocol resides in the sixth layer of the model, the Presentation Layer, and offers services to the file transfer protocol in the Application Layer.

Purpose of the Data Presentation Protocol

As specified by the Reference Model, the Data Presentation Protocol (DPP) exists for the purpose of resolving syntax differences of the data being passed between the DPP-users. The DPP accomplishes this by providing a means for negotiating a transfer syntax mutually understandable by two DPP entities. This syntax also preserves the semantics of the data. For the initial version of DPP, the scope of its applicabiltiy is limited to support file transfer operations. Typical file transfer operations can be divided into an Application Layer protocol and a Presentation Layer protocol using criteria established by the Reference Model [17]. DPP provides the mechanisms needed to negotiate the transfer syntax and the transformations to map the local data syntax to the transfer syntax. The selected transfer syntax and the associated set of transformations comprize the presentation image.

RELATIONSHIP WITH ISO DATA PRESENTATION PROTOCOL

All of the NBS work in the area of network protocols is intended to be compatible with the work in ISO. In fact, due to the extensive work between ISO and NBS, compatibility of protocols has been maintained. In the specific case of the Data Presentation Protocol NBS has been and will continue to be a major contributor to the ISO work on the Presentation Layer Protocol. The current version of the Data Presentation Protocol within ISO includes all of the features of the NBS data presentation protocol. Indeed the protocol services as defined in TC97/SC16/N887 of the current ISO work can be mapped into the services of the NBS Data Presentation Protocol.

There is one minor difference between the work in ISO and that of NBS. ISO has defined a complex session protocol whereas NBS has chosen one of the less complex subsets. This means that the session services available to the application layer in the NBS case do not include the entire set of session services as in the ISO protocol. As services are added to the NBS session protocol they can be made available to the application layer as data presentation services.

DATA PRESENTATION PROTOCOL SERVICE

DESCRIPTION

The DPP provides its users with a connection-oriented data transfer service. The presentation-connection provided by DPP is a logical association between two DPP-entities. In addition to the services associated with the connection- oriented data transfer, there is a set of services to manage the presentation-connection and to describe the syntax of the data.

The following sections present the services provided by DPP to the file transfer protocol by describing the DPP service primitives. Along with each primitive is a brief description of the associated parameters.

Connection Establishment
The connection establishment service is provided by a set of four primitives: P-Connect-Request, P-Connect-Indication, P-Connect-Response, and P-Connect-Confirm. The P-Connect-Request is issued by the DPP-user wishing to establish the

presentation connection. The P-Connect-Indication is issued to the DPP-user with which the initiating DPP-user wishes to communicate. The responding DPP-user issues the connection response primitive, P-Connect-Response, to specify whether the connection is accepted or rejected. The P-Connect-Confirm service primitive announces to the initiator of the DPP connection the result of the connection attempt.

The parameters associated with connection-establishment service primitives include: the names of the two DPP-users, the priority of the connection, and the security associated with the connection. The names of the two DPP-users are symbolic names whose syntaxes are implementation dependent. Each name must, however, uniquely identify a DPP-user in the network or internetwork environment.

Connection Termination

DPP includes two different termination services. The first or normal termination service is a non-destructive close that requires the agreement of both DPP-users. This service is provided by two primitives: P-Close-Request and P-Close-Indication. The P-Close-Request primitive is issued by either DPP-user when he is ready to terminate his half of the connection. The other DPP-user receives a P-Close-Indication notifying him that the connection is being terminated. To complete the termination the other DPP-user must issue a P-Close-Request. When both DPP-users have issued the P-Close-Request primitive, the connection is terminated.

The second connection termination service is a possibly destructive abort service. Again, this service is provided by two service primitives: P-Abort-Request and P-Abort-Indication. As soon as a DPP-user issues a P-Abort-Request, the connection is terminated and the other user receives a P-Abort-Indication.

The only parameter specified in either type of termination is a reason that indicates the cause of the termination.

Status Reporting

The DPP-user may receive unsolicited reports on the DPP connection specified by the P-Status-Indication service primitive. The user also may issue a P-Status-Request service primitive to request DPP to inform him of the current status.

Presentation Image Negotiation

As mentioned earlier, the presentation image defines the transfer syntax and the set of transformations needed to map into and out of the local syntax. Before any data transfers can begin, DPP-users must negotiate the presentation image. DPP provides service primitives that allow each DPP-user to describe the syntax of the data, any constraints imposed on syntax transformations, and the structure of the file being transferred.

DPP-users must describe the syntax for characters, floating point numbers (single- and double-precision), integers (single- and double-precision), and peer-to-peer character syntax. In support of file transfer, DPP recognizes sequential, unstructured, and indexed-sequential files with either fixed or variable length records.

Since some syntax transformations can impact the data semantics, the DPP-user can place constraints on the types of transformations that may be applied. These constraints are: minimum significance for integers, minimum significance for floating point numbers, required destination character code, required file structure, and the use of compression.

Upon completion of the presentation image negotiation, the DPP-user is notified of the results including the structure of the destination file. If the presentation image negotiation fails, the presentation image remains as it was before negotiation.

Data Transfer

The data transfer service consists of two service primitives: P-Data-Request and P-Data-Indication. Associated with the data transfer service primitives is the transformations (including compression algorithms) necessary to deliver data over the previously established connection. The service transfers a unit of data called a presentation-service-data-unit (PSDU). A PSDU has a distinct beginning and end and its length is unlimited. Its integrity is maintained by DPP. PSDUs are delivered in sequence to the corresponding DPP-user.

In order for DPP to apply the proper transformations, the DPP-user must describe the syntax of the data being passed to the DPP. This description includes the type of each data element in the PSDU. The allowable types are: binary string, binary octet, character, integer (single- or double-precision), and floating point number (single- or double-precision).

DATA PRESENTATION PROTOCOL MECHANISMS

The following paragraphs briefly describe the protocol mechanisms that are used to provide the DPP services. For a more complete description, the formal protocol specification [8] should be consulted. The mechanisms are described by the peer-to-peer message exchanges. These exchanges are in terms of protocol data units (PDUs) that are understood by the DPP-entities.

Connection Establishment

Connection establishment uses a two-way message exchange: transmission of ESTABLISH and ACCEPT PDUs. The ESTABLISH PDU initiates the connection establishment attempt and includes protocol class and version information as well as both DPP-user names. The ACCEPT PDU completes the successful establishment of the connection and contains the same information as the ESTABLISH PDU. Figure 1 shows the relationship between the service primitives and the protocol exchanges.

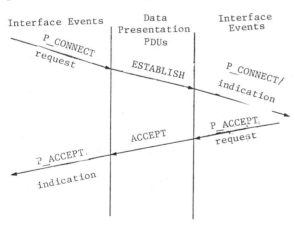

Figure 1. DPP establishment phase

Presentation Image Negotiation

The negotiation of the presentation image requires a three-way exchange. First, the presentation image is sent in a PIM PDU. This PDU contains the proposed transfer syntax description, the DPP-user specified destination file data element constraints, the file key, and the data compression constraints.

Next, the responding DPP-entity returns a PMR PDU containing the same information as the PIM PDU; however, the values contained in the PMR PDU may be modified due to limits on the transformations which the responding DPP-entity can perform and its local user syntax.

The originating DPP-entity validates the values returned in the PMR PDU for the transfer syntax with respect to the constraints of its user. The negotiation of the transfer syntax is considered successful if all received data can be transformed into a syntax acceptable to the DPP-user, none of the DPP-user constraints are violated, and a compatible transfer syntax is selected.

Since the constraints on integers and floating point numbers concern only the number of bits of precision that must be preserved, the transfer syntax is based on the syntax of the local systems. (It is obvious that if a system only supports ten bits of significance then thirty-two bits for the transfer syntax is inappropriate.) DPP verifies that the selected syntax is compatible with its user's constraints. This creates one of three results: the selected syntax exceeds the minimum precision constraints imposed by the user, the syntax exactly equals the constraints imposed by the user or the syntax violates one or more of the constraints.

The third and final exchange is either a PIM-SET PDU or a PIM-NOSET PDU. If the negotiation succeeds then the PIM-SET PDU is sent. If the negotiation fails due to incompatible constraints or formats, the PIM-NOSET is sent. Figures 2 and 3 show the exchanges required for successful and unsuccessful presentation image negotiation.

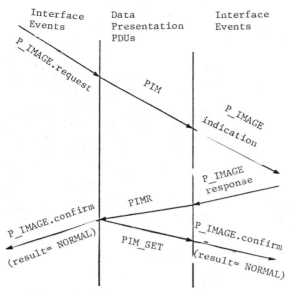

Figure 2. Successful presentation image negotiation

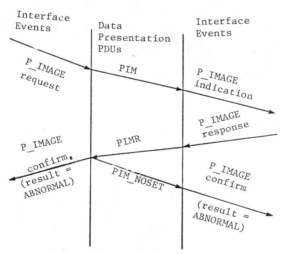

Figure 3.   Unsuccessful presentation image negotiation

Data Transfer

The only PDU sent in the data transfer phase is the DATA PDU. Each DATA PDU contains a complete presentation-service-data-unit (PSDU) and only one PSDU is sent in a single PDU. Since the session protocol is assumed to be reliable there is no peer-to-peer acknowledgement.

CONCLUSION

The data presentation protocol has been defined based on the work of several international organizations while maintaining consistency with the needs of the United States Government. The current NBS specification is a refinement of other existing protocols by including a complete design specification suitable for citing in procurements.

NBS is developing an implementation of the data presentation protocol in the C programming language. Currently, implementations exist for the transport, session, and file transfer protocols. In addition to these protocols, in the near future, NBS will develop draft standards for internetwork and virtual terminal protocols. These standards will provide a basic structure to support more advanced distributed systems.

NBS is committed to producing standards that are compatible with standards produced by ISO. In the case of the Data Presentation Protocol NBS has proceeded ahead of ISO. With a heavy committment to participate in the ISO development process, NBS will continue to negotiate with ISO to achieve a DPP standard acceptable to both ISO and NBS.

REFERENCES

[1]   Blanc, Robert and John Heafner. "The NBS Program in Computer Network Protocol Standards," _Proceedings of the Fifth International Conference on Computer Communication_, Atlanta, 27-30 October 1980.

[2]   Callon, Ross. "Features of Internetwork Protocol." Institute for Computer Sciences and Technology, National Bureau of Standards, May 1981.

[3]   Callon, Ross. "Specification of the Internetwork Protocol." Institute for Computer Sciences and Technology, National Bureau of Standards, May 1981.

[4]   Burruss, John. "Features of the Transport and Session Protocols." Institute for Computer Sciences and Technology, National Bureau of Standards. March 1981.

[5] Burruss, John et. al. "Specification of the Transport Protocol." Institute for Computer Sciences and Technology, National Bureau of Standards, February 1981.

[6] Burruss, John et. al. "Specification of the Session Protocol." Institute for Computer Sciences and Technology, National Bureau of Standards. March 1981.

[7] Clopper, Samuel and John Swanson, "Services and Protocol Mechanisms of a Data Presentation Protocol," Proceedings of Infocom 82. Las Vegas 1982.

[8] Swanson, John and Samuel Clopper. "Specification of the Data Presentation Protocol." Institute for Computer Sciences and Technology, National Bureau of Standards, June 1980.

[9] Clopper, Samuel. "Features of the File Transfer Protocol (FTP) and the Data Presentation Protocol (DPP)." Institute for Computer Sciences and Technology, National Bureau of Standards. October 1980.

[10] Swanson, John and Samuel Clopper. "Specification of File Transfer Protocol." Institute for Computer Sciences and Technology, National Bureau of Standards. June 1981.

[11] Shelton, Carolyn and James Moulton. "Virtual Terminal Protocol Feature Analysis." Institute for Computer Sciences and Technology, National Bureau of Standards. June 1981.

[12] Heafner, John and Robert Blanc. "Description of a Planned Federal Information Processing Standard for Transportation Protocol." Seventh Data Communications Symposium 1981 Mexico City 27-29 October 1981.

[13] Nielsen, Frances, and John Heafner. "Description of a Planned Federal Information Processing Standard for Session Protocol." Proceedings of COMPCON - 1982. San Francisco, 22-25 February 1982.

[14] Nielsen, Frances and John Heafner. "Description of a Planned Federal Informatin Processing Standard for File Transfer Protocol." Proceedings of INFOCOM. Las Vegas, March 30 - April 2, 1982.

[15] Data Processing - Open Systems Interconnection - Basic Reference model. International Organization for Standardization, Draft Proposal ISO/DP 7498. (ISO TC97/SC16/N719) August 1981.

[16] Electronic Industries Association (EIA). RS232: Interface Between Data Terminal Equipment and Data Communications Equipment Employing Serial Binary Data Interchange. Revised 1981.

[17] Moulton, James. "High Level Protocol Layer Boundaries in the ISO Model." Trends and Applications: 1980 Computer Network Protocols, Gaithersburg, Maryland, May 1980.

James R. Moulton is a Computer Scientist with the Institute for Computer Sciences and Technology of the United States National Bureau of Standards. He graduated from the University of Maryland with a Master of Science degree in computer science in 1980. His main research interests are computer network architectures, network protocols, and network security.

The "Red-Book" JTM Protocol and its Application to Distributed Processing

J Larmouth
University of Salford, UK

This paper discusses the support provided by emerging JTM protocol standards for distributed applications. It concludes that, given imagination and flexibility in implementing the protocols on real systems, the standards can provide good support for such applications.

1 INTRODUCTION

This paper is primarily concerned with the needs of an application which involves intermittent activity on a number of computers, proceeding for an indefinite period of time, with no human involvement. The application must be able to continue to operate despite scheduled and unscheduled breaks in service of one or more of the systems involved, and despite short and long-term network failure.

Many such applications do indeed operate at the present time, but they frequently require human involvement after crashes, dedicated machines, continuously running tasks, and considerable coding effort for handling (ad hoc) network protocols and recovery mechanisms.

The paper discusses the support provided for such applications by the emerging Job Transfer and Manipulation (JTM) protocols (JTMPs).

A protocol standard has been developed in the United Kingdom by the Data Communication Protocols Unit of the Department of Industry (Ref 1). This protocol is colloquially known as "Red-Book JTMP" and is part of the "Rainbow series" of protocols currently being implemented on a wide range of equipment. (These protocols have been accepted as "interim standards" by the UK academic community.) The Red-Book JTMP has had a strong influence on the work of the JTM ad hoc group within ISO/TC97/SC16/WG5 - the body producing an ISO standard for JTM activity on open systems. This paper applies directly to the UK Red-book protocol, but in the interests of generality, the terminology of the ISO JTM discussion is used.

Standards for JTM were initially discussed purely as a means of replacing the use of manufacturer's protocols such as IBM Hasp, CDC U200, and ICL 7020. There was, however, an early recognition in the work that what was emerging was a general framework for distributed processing; traditional job activity is fully covered, but is only one part of the field of application of the protocol.

The extent to which actual implementations of the protocol will support the more general features needed for distributed applications is not yet clear. Early implementations, not surprisingly, are concentrating on traditional job activity.

In order to understand the applicability of this protocol, its main features must be understood; the next section provides this necessary background.

2 THE JTM MODEL

The most important step towards understanding any protocol is to identify the underlying model of the real world on which it is based, and the restrictions implicit in that model.

2.1 Communications model

The JTM model recognises open systems, each containing a single JTM application entity. These entities communicate using underlying communication facilities with defined properties. The underlying facilities are assumed to provide

    a)   detection and correction of errors during transfer;

    b)   occasional loss of a connection, with loss of material in transit (reported to both ends);

    c)   defined representations for any necessary data items (such as characters, addresses, end of record, and so on);

    d)   identification of the calling process during connection establishment;

    e)   suitable diagnostics when attempting a connection to distinguish between a site or network which is not functioning at present ("retry later" situation), and addressing errors ("no retry" situation);

The points made in b) and e) above show that "crashes" of open systems and networks are fully visible to JTM; it establishes mechanisms which provide continued service over such crashes. This is one of the main advantages in establishing a distributed processing application using JTM, rather than directly on top of a lower layer service.

2.2 Open systems model

The JTM model of an open system contains (in addition to the JTM application entity and a communications capability) the features of the following sub-sections.

2.2.1 Sources of documents

A document is the unit of data which JTM handles. In many applications it would be large - a complete file, a program, the contents of an A4 sheet of paper, an invoice, or a resource (funds) transfer request or confirmation. JTM does not care what the document contains, nor does it care what the source is. For traditional job activity, a source would be a file-store, or the output queue of a job processor. For more general applications, a source would be any user process running on the system, or the activity of some other protocol handlers (such as those implementing a file transfer protocol - FTP) accessing a remote source. It is this mapping of the very general JTM concept of "a source" onto parts of real systems which determine the breadth of uses to which the protocol implementation can be put. All that is required is that there should be (internal) mechanisms for the local JTM application entity to obtain documents from the source.

2.2.2 Sinks for documents

A sink is the model term for any part of an open system which receives documents. Obvious examples of sinks one would expect to be able to access via the JTM protocol are line-printers and file-stores. Less obvious examples are user processes, remote files (using FTP activity), operators consoles, mail-boxes, letter quality printers, certain VDUs or micro-processor systems, plotters, micro-film devices, and so on. Again, all (!!) that is required is local mechanisms for the JTM application-entity to be able to pass material to these sinks.

2.2.3 Processing elements

A processing element is the most complex part of the JTM model. Put simply, it is a component which acts as a sink for one or more related documents, and some time later acts as a source of one or more new documents. It is clear how this model covers the normal operation of a traditional job processing system, which receives the document(s) defining the job, and later (perhaps a week later) produces

the output of the job. JTM does, however, allow for several different processing elements on an open system. Other examples of the use of such elements would be enquiries addressed to operator terminals with a reply some time later, requests for mounting magnetic tapes with return (later) of the document on the tape, a user process handling orders and generating acknowledgements, and so on. The delay may be very large, or very short.

2.3 Work specifications

The operation of JTM is defined in terms of the above model, that is, in terms of the movement of documents between sources, sinks, and processing elements on different open systems. It does this through the JTM application entities on the open systems involved; these communicate by transferring work specifications (which may, but need not, contain documents). An activity is started by the generation of one or more work specifications on some open system, and the passing of these to the local JTM application entity (which may add documents from locally accessible sources). They are then automatically and reliably sent to the JTMs which must do the work (of moving documents about). Each of these specifications can contain information - so-called proformas - which the target JTM entity will turn into new work specifications, possibly including documents which it has obtained; these are then sent to yet other JTM application entities. Converting proformas into work specifications is called spawning.

Thus we see how one or two initial work specifications can generate a complete cascade of activity. The protocol contains certain recursive features, allowing a spawned work specification to include the proforma used to spawn it. This allows an indefinite chain of activity to be generated.

2.4 Queues

It should be clear from the above that JTM fully recognises the possibility of delays in processing element activity, or due to congestion or temporary unavailability of open systems, networks, or sinks. Thus queues of material waiting for processing or for transfer can build up.

The protocol provides integral facilities (via a work specification) for controlling these queues. Particular activities can be held and released. Moreover, an activity can be held for an arbitrary number of "reasons", each hold being released by some specific work specification generated from a proforma on a remote open system. This will be readily recognised as the basis of a network-wide "semaphore" system. The inclusion of this feature in the JTM protocol initially arose from the need for operator control of printer queues, and for chain jobs. This is one of many possible examples where a careful study of the features needed for jobs showed that general mechanisms were appropriate.

2.5 Other JTM features

There are some features of the JTM operation which are not being covered in detail in this paper, but should be mentioned briefly.

Each work specification can provide information enabling a JTM to generate a new work specification carrying a report to some remote sink. The reports can cover the progress of the activity, or charges which have been levied.

It is worth noting at this point that the protocol recognises that any processing element may generate reports (contents undefined by JTM) at any point in its operation, and may also, more generally, demand the spawning of a specified proforma prior to the end of the task. These two features provide powerful tools for distributed processing.

The final remark to make is that the JTM protocol provides a range of mechanisms for authorisation of activity; these mechanisms do not rely on holding passwords in work specifications and proformas (although this is not excluded). An activity can be established which is secure against attempted interference from other users, but which is itself authorised (at the point of entry to the network) for activity on all the systems it uses. In a closed network these features are often regarded as fairly unimportant, but for open working they are vital.

3 SERVICES PROVIDED BY JTM

It is now possible to expose more clearly the way in which a distributed application can be established, using the services of a JTM implementation on each machine.

There are two main areas to discuss. The first is the advantage of using JTM facilities rather than interfacing directly to some lower level communications feature (such as presentation, sesssion, or transport service). The second is whether the actual features provided by JTM are sufficiently rich to cover the requirements of distributed processing.

3.1 Advantages of JTM

The main advantage of JTM is concerned with reliability. To take a simple example, it is extremely difficult to use a low-level connection to move some material from place A to place B with neither loss nor duplication. Consider the case of printing some mail. Site ALPHA opens up a connection and sends the material. BRAVO prints it, and sends back an

acknowledgement as part of a disconnecting procedure. ALPHA deletes the material if it gets the normal disconnection with acknowledgement, but repeats the transfer if the connection breaks prior to the acknowledgement arriving. This simple protocol causes duplication if the break occurs after BRAVO has sent the acknowledgement and before ALPHA receives it. Adding further hand-shakes does not help. For some applications (like printing a file) the occasional duplication is unimportant. For other applications, however, (such as ordering or funds transfer) it is highly undesirable! In general, a continuous distributed activity requires to know that messages will not be corrupted, lost, or duplicated. The entire operation must provide for controlled movement from one consistent state to another. This requires what are called "commitment mechanisms" to make certain activities atomic over the entire network. JTM uses commitment handshakes in its transfers, and also provides full protection against loss or duplication.

The second main advantage of JTM is that it copes with crashes of the various systems involved, with network unavailability, and with starting up parts of the activity which are intermittent in operation. A task can be started by sending a document - which could just be the task name - to a suitable sink. Once that task has passed a results document or a report to the local JTM entity (by means which the local system can make reliable), it can be sure that the corresponding work specification (with the activity it will cause) will indeed be transferred to the remote system and acted on.

The third and final point is that the mechanisms being used to achieve these effects are all entirely local or use a standard protocol. There is no need for the various parts of the distributed activity to define and code up any protocol in relation to these aspects of communication.

3.2 Support for distributed activity

JTM work specifications are spawned from proformas. Thus a task (initiated by JTM), can demand the spawning of any work specification. Work specifications also contain proformas which are automatically spawned at end of task. Thus part of a distributed application may spawn from a proforma (supplying a document). That document could be carried to a remote filestore, filed, and a proforma automatically spawned which caused a hold to be released on some other work specification. If all holds were now released, that work specification would be activated, and could immediately produce a new (held) copy of itself, then proceed to process the files involved. It might then produce a new document to be carried by a spawned proforma to a remote machine. This time, the sink could be a continuously running part of the operation, and the JTM reporting mechanisms could be used to return an acknowledgement. Alternatively, and probably more usually, the reporting mechanisms could be used simply to generate messages to some central human being who (intermittently or continuously) monitors the operation of the activity.

We see here use of some of the main features of JTM to support a distributed activity:

a) The demand spawning of proformas by a task;

b) The issuing of reports from a task;

c) The automatic spawning of proformas after writing to a sink;

d) Spawning proformas to cause release of (one or more) other tasks on other machines;

e) Automatic start-up of a task by a remote task (by causing activity by a particular processing element).

4   EXAMPLE OF THE USE OF JTM

There are many examples of distributed activity where use of JTM facilities can avoid the need to define protocols and build implementations for handling transfers.

The first example I would give is the handling of electronic mail. All of the reliability and queuing features of JTM are required for this activity, as is the transfer of information (including authorisation) to enable an acknowledgement of receipt to be generated and returned. By using JTM, the work needed to develop a mail protocol and implementations is restricted to details of the format of the actual mail.

The second example I would give is the processing of commercial transactions. The "datagram" nature of JTM work specifications, and the availability of a proforma for returning the response or acknowledgement, makes JTM particularly suitable for these applications.

5   IMPLEMENTATION AND POLITICAL ISSUES

This paper has described an existing protocol definition. Implementations in the UK are in an advanced state, and some will be operating by the time of the ICCC conference.

The protocol definition provides a field for specifying the (local) name of the sink or processing element to which a document is to be passed. The choice of which of the possible sinks (and sources) on a system to make "visible" to JTM in this way is an implementation matter. The protocol standard cannot constrain this. Thus some open systems may have no filestore; others no printer; some may have no background job capability; yet others may not run any "user" processes. This makes it very difficult to specify in a standard the name of sinks to be "connected" to the JTM

system. In particular, it is difficult to ensure that there will be sufficient sinks to be useful for distributed processing.

Present implementations in the UK are (perhaps inevitably) putting the main emphasis on the sinks and sources which are needed for providing simple job submission and output disposal; consideration of demand spawning and allowing user processes to be sinks and sources is coming second. Nonetheless, there is a recognition of the power of the protocol, and it is likely that these features will appear in implementations in due course.

There is also a problem in the standardisation committees. Some experts are very concerned that paying any attention to the more general aspects of distributed processing could slow down the development of standards which are simple "RJE replacements"; other experts are concerned that doing too much with JTM will slow down or prevent the development of standards aimed specifically at distributed processing. This tends to mean that the wider potential of the JTM protocol is hinted at in standards documents, rather than being spelled out – most examples are of traditional job activity. This, together with the name of the protocol "job transfer and manipulation", tends to encourage implementors to cover simple background job activity only. Meanwhile, independent standardisation work proceeds on, for example, mail protocols.

Standardisation activity moves slowly, and understanding and recognition of the issues in this paper is increasing. Many experts who previously concentrated on lower layer protocols are now focussing their attention on higher layer activity, bringing a welcome breath of fresh air. There is little will to develop more protocols than are strictly necessary, and a need now for implementations. I am confident that once basic JTM implementations come into full use on a number of machines, pressure will build up for fully exploiting the protocol, and its advantages will be widely realised.

REFERENCES

{1}   A Network Independent Job Transfer and Manipulation Protocol, DCPU/JTMP(81). The JTMP Working Party of the Data Communications Protocols Unit (Sept 1981). Obtainable from:

Data Communication Protocols Unit
c/o Information Technology Division (IT1c)
Department of Industry
Dean Bradley House
52 Horseferry Road
London SW1P 2AG

J Larmouth began his
career in computing on
the Edsac II at Cambridge
University, and worked in
the Computer Laboratory at
Cambridge on both the
Titan system and the IBM
370/165 (MVT plus Hasp).
He is well-known both for
his work on scheduling
systems and for his
analyses of portability
problems in the old and
new FORTRAN.   In 1976 he
left Cambridge to take up the post of Director
of the Computing Laboratory at the University
of Salford, where he became interested in the
problems of network protocols, particularly
those aspects affecting the services provided
to users.   He was active in the final stages
of the development of the North-West's 'Gannet'
Network, and played a leading role in the
definition of the JTM protocol under the
auspices of the DCPU (a Unit established by
the Department of Industry to coordinate UK
protocol developments).   He is a member of
several BSI Working Groups concerned with
protocol standardisation, and is working very
actively within ISO/TC97/SC16/WG5 to develop an
International Standard for a JTM protocol.
Salford University Computing Laboratory is,
under his direction, developing a portable
package which implements the DCPU JTM protocol;
J Larmouth is also active throughout the
academic networking community in areas ranging
from Local Area Networks to electronic mail
systems.

The Interconnection of Public Electronic Mail Systems

I Kerr
Bell Northern Research, Canada
D J Rhynas
TransCanada Telephone System, Canada

The TransCanada Telephone System provides a public text messaging service with the Envoy 100™ system. To offer Envoy users a larger base of people with whom they can communicate, plans for the interconnection of Envoy with other electronic mail systems in North America and overseas are well underway. This paper discusses the architectural model and protocol structure on which these interconnections will be based. Particular attention has been given to the use of International Standards for electronic mail and for general inter-system communication protocols.

INTRODUCTION

The concept of 'electronic mail' is beginning to catch the imagination of the world. A number of countries have either developed or are currently developing public text messaging services. These are often 'value added' capabilities which are offered in conjunction with a public packet switched data network.

It is worth briefly reviewing the computer based messaging concept. Mail of any form can be defined as the third party delivery of posted envelopes; and in many respects, electronic mail is analogous to letter mail. An originator writes a message and wishes to send it to some recipient. He posts the message and the mail system examines the envelope to determine where it should be routed. (The content of the message is strictly user information and may not even be decipherable by the mail system.) The message is delivered to the recipient's 'mailbox' where it is held and can be read at the recipient's leisure. At this point the message may be annotated, copied, forwarded, filed or discarded. Electronic mail has additional advantages in that it is much faster, easier to file and retrieve, and is rapidly dropping in cost.

This paper provides an overview of the Envoy 100™ text messaging service in Canada. It then discusses the architectural model and protocol structure that will be used to interconnect Envoy with other electronic mail systems, in North America and abroad. We envision an eventual network of public message systems which would encompass the world.

ENVOY OVERVIEW

Envoy 100 is the first in a series of value added services offered by the Computer Communications Group of the TransCanada Telephone System (TCTS). It uses Datapac™, the TCTS packet switched network, as the primary means of access which also interworks with the public telephone and TWX networks.

Envoy 100 is a public text messaging service which has been commercially available in Canada since July of 1981. It allows any user with access to an asynchronous terminal to exchange messages with other users, on a store and forward basis. Since the user is not tied to a specific terminal, he may access his mailbox from anywhere in the world via a packet network accessible to Datapac (over 20 countries).

There are a number of features which facilitate the preparation and organization of messages. A user may interactively prepare, edit and save his text for later action or alternatively 'batch' it to Envoy. He may send the text, as a message, to any number of mnemonic user names, distribution lists or network addresses using a variety of send options (for example, registered or timed delivery). As a recipient, the user may dynamically choose to have his messages auto-delivered (printed at a designated terminal) or call up the system to access his mailbox. Within a mailbox, messages may be read as convenient and answered, forwarded or filed for subsequent on-line retrieval. Envoy 100 has quite a powerful command repertoire which is described in detail in reference (1). Users may interact with the service in either English or French.

The Envoy 100 service is currently supported on a centralized computer system which is connected to Datapac by multiple X.25 access lines. All components are duplexed and user data is dual copied on 'mirrored' disks for high reliability/availability and message integrity.

INTERCONNECTION SERVICE REQUIREMENTS

Why interconnect message systems? Clearly, any communication vehicle becomes more attractive with the largest possible base of potential users. As with letter mail and the telephone network, it would appear socially positive that all public message systems be interconnected. The position within TCTS is to adopt a generally open interconnection policy; this of course benefits the carrier by increasing both Envoy and core network usage and by making the service more attractive to market.

The basic service requirement is the ability for an originator on one system to send a message to a recipient on another. It is important that the user interface be easy to use, a natural extension to the 'home' system. The total complement of messaging capabilities should appear logical and consistent. Yet it is reasonable that the user be aware of some of the limitations of multi-system sending. For example, the sender is expected to know the 'mailing' address of his foreign recipient. In the longer term there will likely be various directory assistance capabilities, but this should not be assumed from the outset.

The addressing scheme for foreign recipients should be similar to the local structure. Where possible, the addresses should be mnemonic and meaningful to humans.

Not all systems will support all features yet they should still be able to interwork. In terms of functionality, this implies that a universally implemented subset will determine the minimum capability between any two systems. Features above this subset should be provided in a standard way. Thus if they are available at both ends of a particular interconnection, they may be used.

CURRENT STANDARDS ACTIVITIES

Many organizations have recognized the need for standards to facilitate the interconnection of electronic mail systems. As a result, groups have been formed to work on the topic within several international bodies. The International Federation of Information Processing (IFIP), though not itself a standards body, has contributed significantly through Working Group 6.5, 'International Computer Based Message Systems'. A subgroup of IFIP, Working Group 6.5 first defined the model of distributed electronic mail systems currently being used as the basis of standards work in the International Telegraph and Telephone Consultative Committee (CCITT).

The CCITT is actively developing standards for electronic mail under question 5 of Study Group VII on 'Message Handling Facilities' (2). The work will take the form of a set of recommendations which will be published at the end of the study period, in 1984. The current status, on which this paper is based, is contained in reference (3).

Also taking place in CCITT is the relevant work of Study Group VIII on Teletex and Facsimile. The Teletex service (4) provides for the transfer of documents between intelligent terminals. It lacks the store and forward and mailbox elements usually associated with electronic mail. However the protocols defined for Teletex have a utility beyond the initial definition of the service, as is discussed below.

In the International Standards Organization (ISO), Sub Committee 18 of Technical Committee 97 (Text Preparation and Interchange) has a work item on the procedures necessary for the exchange of messages.

As a distributed application, electronic mail will make use of the general purpose protocols being developed for Open Systems Interconnection (5), both in ISO and CCITT.

ARCHITECTURAL MODEL

Ultimately, what is required for system interconnection is a set of protocols which define the formats and procedures for the exchange of information. However, before these can be developed, two initial steps must be taken. Firstly, an architectural model of the total interconnected system must be developed, using an initial view of the functions which are to be performed. The architectural model serves to identify components of the system which perform certain functions, and between which, standard protocols are required. Secondly, the services to be provided by the system must be defined in detail, and related to the identified components of the model. There is potential confusion if this step is not taken with care.

The architectural model on which TCTS interconnection plans are based is that which was originally developed by IFIP Working Group 6.5 and is currently the basis of CCITT SG VII work. The model is illustrated in Figure 1 and the components are defined below:

User Agent A set of processes which assists the user in the preparation and inspection of messages and communicates with the Message Transfer Service on behalf of the user. A User Agent may implement mailboxes for incoming and outgoing messages.

Slot The transfer point of responsibility for a message. When the message resides in a User Agent, it is the user and the User Agent who are responsible for it. The User Agent (by direction of the User) submits the message to the Message Transfer Service (MTS) which then assumes responsibility. Similarly, the MTS delivers the message to the receiving User Agent. After completion of delivery, the responsibility for the message lies with the receiving user and User Agent.

Message Transfer Service (MTS) The set of services which provide store and forward delivery of messages. The MTS accepts a message from the originator's User Agent (via the slot), stores, routes and forwards it, and ultimately delivers the message to the recipient's User Agent.

Message Transfer Agent (MTA) The functional entity that is the building block of the Message Transfer Service. The MTS is provided by the union of all Message Transfer Agents.

Management Domain That part of the architectural model which is under the control of one service supplier or Administration.

This model can be mapped onto physical implementations in a number of ways. A stand-alone User Agent may be implemented in an intelligent terminal or workstation. Alternatively the Message Transfer Agent and many User Agents may reside in one computer system. In Envoy 100 the latter approach is taken, although the future support of 'external' User Agents is envisaged.

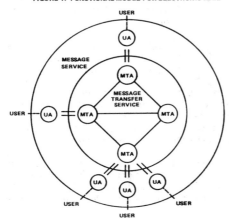

FIGURE 1: FUNCTIONAL MODEL FOR ELECTRONIC MAIL

UA: USER AGENT
MTA: MESSAGE TRANSFER AGENT

SERVICE DEFINITIONS

The model described above leads to the division of electronic mail services into those which are provided by the Message Transfer Service, and those which are provided by the User Agents. The services provided by the User Agent can be divided into those which are entirely local (for example: the editing commands used in the preparation of a message) and those which require co-operation between the User Agents of the originator and the recipient of a message (for example: retrieval of a received message by its subject requires the subject field to have been created in a recognizable form by the originator). The services offered to the user are the sum of these three types.

Many service features can be provided as part of an electronic mail offering. However, our view is that the MTS should offer only a small set of services which are naturally associated with its main function of store and forward delivery. The intention is to allow protocols to be defined to meet urgent interconnection needs. By keeping the Message Transfer Service simple and general purpose, full interconnectability can be offered at this level. A simple, universal standard for User Agent to User Agent interaction will then be able to serve basic communications needs for many users. Those users who have requirements for more advanced features in their User Agents will also be able to communicate using the same Message Transfer Service. This approach is much preferred to having wholly separate systems supporting for example, business forms, graphics or digitized voice communication.

The set of services which we currently envisage being provided by the Message Transfer

System are as follows:

Recipient designation: a simple, user friendly way of uniquely identifying the recipient of a message. This issue is further discussed below.

Originator designation: the provision of a validated identification of the originator of a message, suitable for use as the recipient designation on a reply.

Multi-destination delivery: the ability to post one message with a list of recipient designations and have a copy of the message delivered to each recipient. It should be possible to include recipients from different systems in the 'To' field of a message or in a distribution list.

Envelope identification: unique identification of messages by the Message Transfer Service. This service will support the User Agent in tracking responses to messages and may be used for billing and status reporting functions.

Submission time stamp: the Message Transfer Service will provide the authenticated date and time at which the message was submitted.

Delivery notification: notification to the originator that successful delivery of the message to the recipient's User Agent has occurred. This will not indicate that the receiving user has taken any action or is even aware of the message. This service will be available as a per-message option to the originator.

Non-delivery notification: notification to the originator that successful delivery of the message to the recipient could not be achieved. There will be a defined time limit within which delivery will be attempted. This service will also be available as a per-message option to the originator, but should probably be set up in such a way that the default action is to request non-delivery notification for all messages.

Probe: a means of testing the validity of a particular address on a foreign message system. This could be extended to test for optional capabilities.

Hold for delivery: as a service to stand alone user agents which do not have autoanswer capabilities, the MTS will hold messages until the UA calls in to receive them.

Priority: an indication that a message is to be delivered with either a higher or lower priority than normal.

Conversion: the conversion of the message contents from that provided by the originator to that which can be handled by the recipient; for example, from ASCII to Baudot (Telex).

The co-operating User Agent services can range from the simple transfer of information coded in some standard such as ASCII or Teletex, to the support of complex forms or multi-media documents. Initially, a set of services suitable for handling business memos should be standardized. These services will likely include:

- From, To and CC indications

- Subject indication

- Privacy indication (invokes procedures to prevent unauthorized reading of a message)

- Message Forwarding capability

- Return Receipt capability

PROTOCOL STRUCTURE

A layered representation of the protocols required to support the model and services outlined above is described in (4) and shown in Figure 2. Figure 2 also illustrates the relation between the protocols required for electronic mail and the general purpose layers of the Reference Model for Open System Interconnection.

FIGURE 2: LAYERED MODEL OF ELECTRONIC MAIL PROTOCOLS

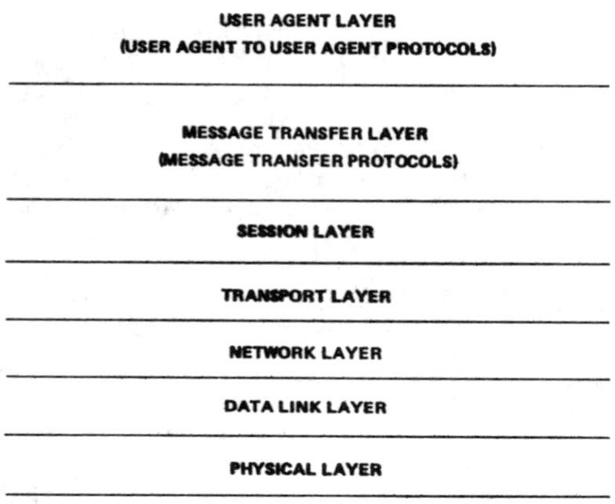

USER AGENT LAYER
(USER AGENT TO USER AGENT PROTOCOLS)

MESSAGE TRANSFER LAYER
(MESSAGE TRANSFER PROTOCOLS)

SESSION LAYER

TRANSPORT LAYER

NETWORK LAYER

DATA LINK LAYER

PHYSICAL LAYER

For layers 1 to 4 of the model, standard protocol specifications already exist (e.g. CCITT Recommendation X.25 for the physical, data link and network layers, CCITT/ISO Transport Protocol class 0 or 1 (6) or CCITT Recommendation S.70 for the transport layer).

The Session Layer protocol will most likely be based on CCITT Recommendation S.62 (7). The combination of the S.62 'Session' and 'Document' procedures is compatible with the Session Layer Service definition (8) and will support the 'Basic Asymmetric Synchronized' subset of the Session Service.

The functionality of the Message Transfer Layer can be divided into two parts:

- Reliable Transfer Server

- Message Dispatcher

The Reliable Transfer Server is responsible for ensuring the reliable transfer of messages

from one MTA to the next, given the MTA address. It achieves this largely by making use of the services of the Session Layer. One or more Sessions may be established between MTAs (to handle different priorities or classes of message). Each Session is used for one-way transfer of messages at any time, and the Session Services of Synchronization and Resynchronization are used to support recovery from failures, either in the communications systems or in the MTA's themselves.

The Message Dispatcher operates the Message Transfer Protocol. It is responsible for end-to-end routing of messages and provision of all the Message Transfer Services. In particular it must discover the address of the next MTA or the recipient UA from the recipient designation provided. The significant characteristics of the Message Transfer Protocol are as follows:

- The information required to provide the Message Transfer Services is contained in an envelope which is essentially the protocol header of the Message Transfer Layer.

- Multi-recipient messages are transferred with designations of all the recipients in the envelope. For transmission efficiency, copies are made only when a divergence of routes is necessary.

- Service messages, such as Delivery Notifications and Non-Delivery Notifications are themselves handled as messages (with a higher priority). They have envelopes and can refer to delivery or non-delivery for more than one recipient.

- If a message is successfully transferred to an MTA, that MTA is responsible for either delivering it or generating the Non-Delivery Notification. No other MTA will monitor the progress of the message. Of course 'off line' tracking, by means of stored records of messages handled, is possible.

- As messages pass through the Message Transfer System, an 'audit trail' is generated. This indicates which Management Domains have handled the message, and what (if any) content conversions have been performed.

The routing of messages by the Message Transfer Layer uses a form of address which is composed of 'attributes'. In one form, which will support Teletex and Facsimile terminals, the only attribute required is an X.121 address (9). For most mailbox systems, the attributes are divided into the 'base attribute set' which identifies the Management Domain of the recipient, and the 'user attributes', which identify the recipient within a Domain. Initially, the base attribute set will consist of a country name and a Management Domain name (e.g. 'Canada', 'Envoy 100') and only one user attribute will be required. This will be an unrestricted field of information which contains whatever is needed to locate the recipient within the Management Domain.

910

Thus, existing systems may be interconnected without the need to change their addressing method, and without the need for internationally accessible electronic directories.

In the User Agent Layer, co-operating User Agent Services must be supported. This requires the message content to be structured in a way that can be handled and processed by each User Agent. For the user information fields, existing conventions can be used such as International Alphabet No.5, or CCITT Recommendation S.61. To support the User Agent Services, the message content may be structured using a digital encoding method such as described in (10).

AREAS REQUIRING FURTHER STUDY

There are several areas which require further consideration. Some initial ideas for the direction of this work are outlined.

User Designation. At present, each Envoy 100 subscriber is identified by a unique character string. In order to be mnemonic and easy to use, this designation is composed of a set of hierarchically ordered fields which identify the user's name, his organization and the division, section etc., in which he works. An example is J.DOE/SPEC.PRODUCTS/SALES/ MARKETING/CENTRAL/XYZ.COMPANY. If there is only one J.DOE on the system then the lowest level is a sufficient identifier; additional levels need only be specified to resolve ambiguity in the case of multiple J.DOE's.

At present, the designations of all recipients are validated immediately prior to submitting a message. In the case of interconnected systems this will not always be feasible. The message will be sent off with the designations of users in other Management Domains unvalidated. The delivery confirmation or non-delivery notification service will indicate the fate of the message.

In order to provide these features with interconnected systems, the definition of the attributes needs extension to allow individual fields to be defined and represented in a standard form. Thus, for example, the sequence 'name/department/organization' would have the same appearance, length restriction and character set in different systems.

Directories. However user friendly the designation system, there is still a requirement for Directories, to assist users. A set of standards is required for the query language and lower level protocols to allow a user to access the directory of any system. Other significant issues are:

- Should directory access be free to users from other Message Domains, perhaps in different countries?

- Can the query language be designed so as to support automatic validation of designations and expansion of distribution lists?

Billing. There are several options with respect to billing for an international service. Settlement could follow the post office precedent, where incoming international mail is reciprocally delivered for 'free', within agreed upon limits. More plausibly, domestic rating could be applied in each country with some premium for the gateway function; in this instance, the originator would likely pay for creating and sending a message while the recipient would pay for reading. Any billing scheme should be volume sensitive and based on characters, messages, holding time or some combination of the three.

User Agent Services. As mentioned above, Envoy 100 currently supports a fairly sophisticated set of User Agent Services. Current work (11) indicates that a useful extension would be a set of facilities to assist in the management of received messages. Some examples are:

- methods for automatically relating messages to particular dialogues or transaction sequences.

- automatic methods for referring to previous messages.

- methods to allow a message to be circulated round a set of recipients with specified actions to be carried out by each recipient.

Thus messages should be seen not as unique and transitory items of information but as part of a growing database of information on various topics. The more methods there are available for searching, filing and retrieving in this database, the more useful it will be.

A second area of User Agent evolution is the transmission of business forms. Invoices, timesheets, bills of lading and other forms make up a large part of business communication requirements. At present Envoy 100 supports a method whereby particular items of information can be requested, validated and entered into a message according to user defined specifications. A standard for the representation of such information would assist the interworking with data processing systems or forms printers.

ENVOY INTERCONNECTION

From the Envoy 100 perspective, interconnection can be viewed at three different levels: domestic, North American and International. While there are peculiarities to each, the same architectural model applies throughout.

Within Canada, one can see a potential demand for connecting private message systems to the public system. There would be a published interconnection standard and any system supporting this standard would be free to participate. This potential would likely not materialize until such a standard were approved within CCITT.

Other TCTS value added services which require messaging capability will conform to the

911

UA/MTA model and connect to Envoy 100 as a public Message Transfer Agent. For example, iNet™, an 'intelligent gateway' service, provides a single user-friendly point of access to a number of computer based information services (12). Envoy 100 and iNet subscribers will be able to freely exchange messages with one another.

Within North America, prior to any standard, Envoy will implement interconnections with message systems in the United States where there is a business case to do so.

Internationally, Envoy 100 will interconnect either directly or indirectly with recognized public message systems overseas. TCTS will continue to support the CCITT standards work and the development of an international network of public MTA's.

CONCLUSION

The TransCanada Telephone System has introduced the Envoy 100 text messaging service and is currently developing other 'value added' offerings. These services can be made more attractive by extending the base of addressable users, which is achieved through interconnection with other message systems in North America and overseas.

There has been considerable progress in the standards arena with regard to Message Handling Facilities. TCTS is actively participating in this work and integrating the architecture and protocols to extend Envoy. The result is a general purpose structure which is suitable for a broad spectrum of message services.

ACKNOWLEDGEMENT

We wish to acknowledge the contributions of our colleagues at both Bell Northern Research and the Computer Communications Group who are involved in the specification and design of message systems.

REFERENCES

(1) Envoy 100 Reference Manual, Computer Communications Group of TransCanada Telephone System, 1981.

(2) CCITT Study Group VII, Contribution No.1, Questions entrusted to Study Group VII, 'Data Communications Networks for the period 1981-1984', Question 5/VII, 'Message Handling Facilities'.

(3) CCITT COM VII No. , 'Message Handling Systems: Interrelationships and Control Procedures', Version 3, March 1982.

(4) CCITT Recommendation F200 'Teletex Service', Yellow Book, Geneva 1981.

(5) ISO Draft Proposal 7498, 'Data Processing - Open Systems Interconnection - Basic Reference Model'.

(6) CCITT COM VII No. , 'Proposed Draft Transport Protocol Specification', Version 2,2, March 1982.

(7) CCITT Recommendation S.62, 'Control Procedures for the Teletex Service', Yellow Book, Geneva, 1981.

(8) CCITT COM VII No. 109E, 'Use of the Teletex Control Procedures to provide the Services of the Session Layer', Bell Northern Research, 1981.

(9) CCITT Recommendation X.121, 'Numbering Plan for Public Data Networks', Yellow Book, Geneva, 1981.

(10) Draft Message Format Standard, U.S. National Bureau of Standards, 1981.

(11) Minutes of IFIP WG6.5, User Environment Subgroup Meeting, Bonn, July 1981.

(12) I.M. Cunningham, H. Williamson, R.T. Begbie, 'The Intelligent Network, iNet', ICCC 1982.

Ian Kerr received a BSc in Chemical Physics and a PhD for work on Molecular Beam Scattering, both from the University of Edinburgh, Scotland. From 1974 to 1979 he was employed by Logica Ltd. in the U.K. and the Netherlands, where he worked on a number of data communication projects. Since 1979 he has been with the Systems Division of Bell-Northern Research in Ottawa, where his responsibilities include international standards for data protocols and messaging, and the specification of communications protocols for new products and services, including iNet.

David Rhynas received his BASc in Systems Design Engineering from the University of Waterloo and has a Masters degree in Electrical Engineering from the University of Ottawa. In 1975, he joined the Computer Communications Group of Bell Canada where he has participated in various system design aspects of Datapac, a public packet switching network. Presently, Mr. Rhynas is Section Manager - Value Added Service Design and is responsible for the technology planning of enhancements to Envoy 100, a public electronic mail service.

Experiences with use of the UK Network Independent File Transfer Protocol on Several Networks

P L Higginson, R Moulton
University College London, UK

At UCL the UK Network Independent File Transfer Protocol has been used to transfer files to and from computers of different makes over three different types of network: X.25, datagram (Arpanet) and local high speed ring. The paper describes the philosophy of the multi-network implementation and highlights the problems encountered, the performance achieved and the impact of network characteristics on file transfer activities.

1. INTRODUCTION

At University College we have a number of PDP-11 computers which are locally interconnected via a Cambridge Ring. Small LSI-11 computers are used as "Gateways" between this local network and three wide-area networks, the British Telecom PSS, the Universities SERCNET and the US SATNET which gives access to the Arpanet. This system has been described in a companion paper [1].

We have developed an implementation of the UK Network Independent File Transfer Protocol (NIFTP)[2] which runs on the PDP-11 Unix Systems which are connected to the Cambridge Ring (two PDP-11/44s and one PDP-11/34 all with large disk stores). Files can be transferred between the Unixes and between a Unix and a computer on any of the three wide-area networks. The connections are shown in Figure 1. The main object of this paper is to discuss our experiences while making the system operational and in using it, but some background information on the implementation is useful and is given in Section 2.

Our experiences fall into several categories, and, in common with others in this field, we have had many more problems with the interfaces to the network and the differences between networks, than with the file transfer protocol itself. Since we can transfer files over four different networks we are in a position to compare them and this is discussed in Section 3. A "Network Access System" hides the peculiarities of the networks from the file transfer programs but also tries to be as general purpose as possible. This has caused particular problems with buffering, flow control and overall throughput and these are discussed in Section 4.

A file transfer protocol is sufficiently complex for it to be likely that two implementations at different sites will contain mutual incompatibilities. This was our experience with both the current and earlier Arpanet and the EPSS experiments[3]. This issue and our general feelings for the file transfer protocol are discussed in Section 5.

An area of major work is the interface between the FTP programs and the host operating system and filestore. This paper is not the place to discuss the local system, but the interface to the user is worthy of discussion. We have adopted a queued interface and on the whole this has been beneficial. Section 6 deals with the interface to the human user while Section 7 deals with our experiences in shipping message files for our computer mail system. We have found some facilities, such as the ability to be told if a transfer succeeds or fails and the ability to have ones mail routed to another machine (which causes a file transfer), which have to be provided with great care.

2. OUTLINE OF THE SYSTEM

The file transfer system is implemented via queues so that users do not have to wait while files are transferred [4]. This facilitates the transfer of files to systems with low connectivity (either because the networks are not always up or the destination computers are not always running the FTP). The FTP program distinguishes between network problems and genuine failures such as incorrect permissions, and retries only in the former case. The queue system could easily be used to do some transfers at certain times or during off-peak charging periods. In order to reduce interference with other network users and to minimise duration charges (on charged networks) only one transfer from each queue is attempted at once. The queues are updated by a number of utility programs and are also linked to the mail system. This is shown in Figure 2.

An entry on a queue gives all the information for the transfer of one file, which may be either a send or a receive operation. Status information on the success or failure of the transfer is added by the file transfer programs. Up to now, the queues have been purged manually so that failures can be examined and either the user given an explanation of why the transfer failed or corrective action taken and the transfer put back into an active state.

Outstanding transfers are attempted hourly until contact with the remote host (source or destination) is achieved. We plan to introduce a limit on the number of attempts and some automatic queue purging shortly. Recently a period of interference with the satellite channel meant that we had no interactive contact with US sites for several days; however

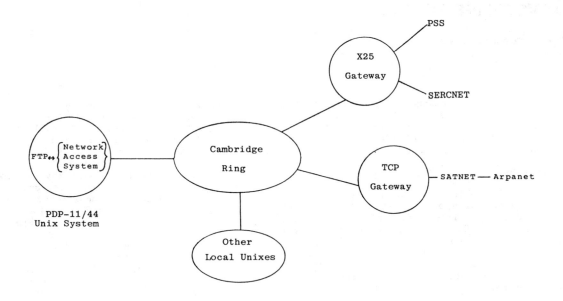

Figure 1   FTP Network Access From Unix

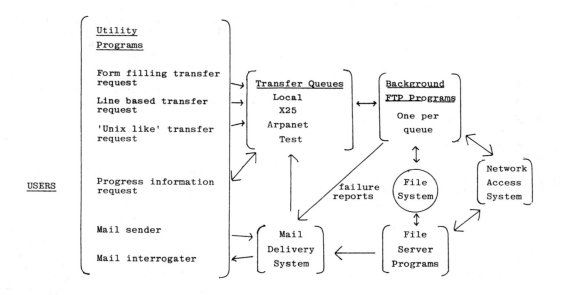

Figure 2   Software Structure on Unix

914

file transfers were still being done (usually around midnight).

The file transfer programs gain access to the networks via a "Network Access System"[5]. This has a uniform "transport service like" interface to the FTP, makes the selection of the route to each network and also manages flow control and buffer size constraints. Other components of the Network Access System manage the network gateways and the server interfaces for incoming transfer requests.

The Network Access System (NAS) permits processes in Unix to make and receive calls to or from the three external networks and between Unixes. It uses transparent data paths provided by the ring interface software to transport control and data blocks between the network gateway machines and the network user machines. Users may be programs running on LSI-11s or (and) programs on Unix. For various reasons the NAS components are "handed" so that an "N" component interfaces to a User and a "U" component manages a Gateway. The LSI-11s have an operating system designed for real time use and hence have message passing primitives available.

The Unix operating system does not have good interprocess facilities (other than via disk) and we did not want to put the NAS components in the operating system itself. Hence each Unix process is treated as if it were a separate machine and each process has its own NAS component. For local Unix to Unix transfers, the server end has a modified NAS component which is a combination of "N" and "U" types and allows the FTP to have the same interface in all modes of use.

3. COMPARISON OF NETWORKS USED

We are dealing with four networks which are very different in hardware terms. The ring is a high speed carrier but the usable bandwidth is severely limited by the use of a Z80 as a front-end to Unix, by interrupt per character mode on the LSI-11s, and because a block mode low level protocol is not used. The connection to Arpanet uses datagrams with and an end-to-end retransmission scheme (the TCP Protocol) whilst both PSS and SERCNET use X.25.

In theory, and mostly in practice, each of these systems provides a highly reliable connection oriented data transmission service. They are highly reliable in the sense that data which is delivered is usually correct; all three types of network may give notification of failure. (Strictly the TCP interface requires the User program to decide when to give up but in practice it turns out the same.) With all the networks we have suffered from the fact that the network interface software has been in an experimental state and as the first heavy users we have been finding some of the bugs.

The ring and its software has been a source of many problems but is now giving reliable, if slow, service. Considering that we use only the hardware level of error detection (as against the block level to which we will shortly convert) we have a remarkably low error rate. The NAS has been enhanced to check for, and report, ring errors. The ring however has no natural buffering and there is almost none in the interface software at either end. We have a severe problem to handle certain messages (such as advance mark acknowledgements and error reports) which the cooperating process is not waiting for. This is partly a function of the Unix interface, which can only read or write at any one time; it causes no problem with wide area networks, because they will happily buffer the small amounts of data involved.

With X.25 networks we have accessed a greater diversity of foreign hosts but had few problems with the actual networks. Because our X.25 software permits further data submissions as soon at the network takes a packet, we need only have limited local buffering; thus single buffering is used between the X.25 Gateway and Unix. The Network Access System has been enhanced to incorporate a minimal Transport Service, although to date our main experience has been with SERCNET where this is generally not needed.

With Arpanet we have done FTPs to one type of host only, and thus have been in control of both the local and remote FTP software. The contrast to the other two cases is marked. The implementation of the TCP protocol requires the user to supply sufficient buffers for the round trip of the acknowledgement or window advancement, and hence the Network Access System provides quad-buffering in the TCP case, and single buffering in the other cases. When it works properly it is good, and we can actually send a file to California faster than to the next room, even though both go across the ring. However, while the ring and X.25 tend to fail in lockup mode (which can usually be analysed and hence fixed), the Arpanet connection is prone to fail into continuous retransmission mode, usually accompanied by a throughput of a few bits a second.

We feel that a consequence of the greater complexity of data protocol involved in the TCP (where retransmission and acknowledgement are done outside the network) is a greater error rate and failure rate in the long term. It is true that these problems can be classed as bugs. However, since every host type has its own implementation of this software, and this software is complex, such bugs will persist; from a user view these bugs may well be permanent features. By comparison, in X.25 the implementation of retransmission and flow control is more modular, is implemented by the network and there is almost no way in which one host's implementation can interfere with another.

4. THE NETWORK ACCESS SYSTEM

The NAS was designed to allow processes to assume that they had a local interface to the network they wished to use, whereas in fact the network was interfaced via a Gateway managed by a Network Access System component. In this way one LSI-11 computer acts as a gateway to both PSS and SERCNET, and four other computers may run processes which access either or both networks. Because network level access is provided, the accessing processes use both the X.29 protocol, the ITP protocol, the Teletex protocol (where the NAS separates experimentation from the service Gateway) and the NIFTP (Network Independent File Transfer Protocol).

The NAS is therefore basically transparent to protocol and to addressing. Between LSI-11s it is also transparent to buffering requests (within limits) and multiplexes multiple user calls to the same Gateway over one data stream on the ring. Each NAS component maintains sufficient information about user calls in progress to notify the user if the Gateway goes down or to clear the network call if the user machine goes down or both if the ring call breaks.

The NAS has proved to be resilient in service, and we allow experimental calls in parallel with service use of the Gateways. Less network problems are caused because calls are cleared when a user machine fails; if the user process was in the same machine as the network process, it would be likely that both would be lost (certainly on the unprotected LSI-11).

LSI-11 based user processes tend to be for specific protocols (e.g. X.29, Teletex) whereas the Unix user processes are mainly the FTPs. Hence we have tried in the Unix NAS components to conceal the nature of the network used from the FTP. This has meant adding more flow control and minimal X.25 Transport Service support to the Unix NAS. The NAS interface has also given us the flexibility to use different transport service interfaces when converting the FTP to run on other systems.

Users nominate remote sites by name. When a transfer is attempted the FTP looks up this name in a file and obtains a real path. The NAS "knows" which machines act as Gateways to which network ids given in the path. We would make the NAS more flexible but the hardware is much more static than the software so this has never seemed worthwhile (i.e. new algorithms are put in more often than new destinations).

5. THE FILE TRANSFER PROTOCOL

The NIFTP was the result of work by a group of UK network users and was written in 1977[2] and revised in 1980[6]. It is designed to encompass both simple and complex systems. Indeed the experience of both ourselves and other implementors has shown that the local filestore interface and the network interface are the major work items rather than the actual FTP protocol implementation.

An FTP designed for heterogeneous systems will of necessity be fairly complex and hence it is likely that two different implementations will contain mutual incompatibilities. We have certainly found this in all our early use; our normal expectation in talking to a new site is to find one new bug at each end.

The recurrent and largely insoluble problems concern format conversion. We have not yet been able to transfer binary files, but we know of an increasing number of users wishing to move load files for micros and facsimile files; we will implement 8 bit binary shortly. Our major conversion problems to date therefore concern text files.

How can the file be transferred so that it prints out correctly on another machine? In any standard FTP, two conversions are done, one from the filestore format of the sender to the standard format, and then from that to the filestore format of the receiver. The main cause of the difficulty is lack of uniformity in the local formats; for example on Unix LF is normally used as newline but it can have a CR added and some programs produce files which do. When sending a file we convert LF into the standard representation of newline, and delete any redundant CRs. Hence we would not expect to get back the exact file we send, nor do we properly support users who do not follow the normal Unix conventions.

All control functions seem to have this problem and underlining has been one serious cause of incorrect transfers. The FTP is specified so that the standard format is unambiguous, however we have discovered that systems use different local formats for different purposes, and the FTP programs cannot easily tell which local convention is used in a particular file. An extreme example of conversion happened when we sent a text file from the US, to a particular system in the UK, and then asked for it back. The target system did not remember whether files were text or binary; when asked for a file (and to specify the mode of the file), it decided it was simpler to send it as binary. Since the source system stored text as five characters to a 36 bit word, and binary as seven bytes in two words, there was no similarity between the file we sent and the file we got back.

We have said little about the FTP protocol in this section because we have found it perfectly adequate for what we have been doing. The negotiation is straightforward, and the options sufficiently rich, to be able to do everything we have wished. The small sub-record size (which results in rather frequent length byte insertions) has been an efficiency worry to some investigators. Certainly in our systems, the O.S. overhead has always exceeded the combined overhead of the FTP and the NAS systems for the same transfer (for example during the transfer of a 20k byte file the NIFTP/NAS used 1 cpu sec while the operating system used 5.7 cpu secs). Hence we have never felt that efficiency of the FTP was a problem. However the need to carry out various error checking and blocking functions on a per byte basis at a low level does result in high processor load.

6. THE USER INTERFACE

The system is operational and files and mail are regularly transferred for users. However, our part of the system, and the whole underlying network infrastructure, are still being improved and made more reliable. A side-effect of the queuing of requests is the low profile kept by the majority of the FTP system. This conceals from users the slow speed at which many files are transferred, and the number of attempts which fail for network or other reasons. Where bugs result in aborted transfers rather than incorrect files, these have often been fixed without the user even knowing that there was a problem with his file. We are, however, in the fortunate situation where there is no other easy way of transferring these files and the users expect network problems anyway. The queuing of requests means that the delay involves no active overheads on the users part.

We have three interfaces for submission of FTP requests, one for local users which is a "form filler" based on our page mode VDUs, one which is a line-at-a-time question and answer system and one which is for use by programs. The use of queues makes having several user interfaces easier and we plan a forth to simplify inter-unix transfers. If a transfer fails the user is sent a message through the electronic mail system giving the reason for the failure. The user may request positive acknowledgement if required.

For the occasional user, receiving messages to report the success or failure of transfers is the most convenient way. For the regular user, a way of listing the status of all his transfers is needed. We currently have ways of listing the status of all transfers but with the increased use, particularly by dial-in users on slower terminals, we urgently need to provide more selective status information. The status program allows queued requests to be cancelled, and allows privileged users to change the status of a transfer (from REJected to PENDing for example).

We are in a position to compare our queued interface with the one used most frequently in the US where the transfer is done on a "while-you-wait" basis. This works well when high speed lines (normally 50 Kbps) connect sites and sites are in a service mode with continuous availability. However, we find that this mode of use is frustrating when used with slower lines or machines which are not continuously available. (At UCL we can often go and find another terminal to use, this is not so easy for a dial-in user.)

As a matter of normal practice FTP requests require several items of control information (two file names, accounts, passwords, modes etc). By contrast electronic mail requires only the name of the addressee which is usually kept short (e.g. name@host) with all common host-names supported. We notice a trend towards users sending files by electronic mail because of the fewer formalities involved and the greater possibilities for onward forwarding. The mail connectivity is greater than the FTP connectivity, because many hosts (including ours) are prepared to accept mail and re-queue it for onward transmission (either to sites not directly available or in different protocols). From an operational point of view it makes no difference to our systems; however at present mail side-steps the protection and accounting which is involved in a true file transfer, and this could have long term implications.

7. USE OF THE FTP BY THE MAIL SYSTEM

The mail system uses the FTP to send mail in an identical way to that in which a normal user would send files [7]. On receipt the FTP has to recognise mail and do a number of special functions. A special file is setup into which the mail can be put and no account information is required for this transfer. At the end of the transfer the mail system is prompted to deliver the received file.

This system has worked well. The queued approach differs from the normal US Arpanet system where one attempt at least is normally made while the user waits. Since most of our mail is staged at least once, it would be of little use for the user to know that the mail had reached the first staging post. (In any case, there is never a guarantee that a user will read his mail).

The queuing has meant that we rarely lose mail and has allowed us to carry some user traffic while making the system operational. We have only had one occurrence of a circulating message other than ones we deliberately constructed for test purposes. The case of the automatic alarm calling the answering machine has unfortunately its electronic mail counterpart, where an automatic reply message "I am on holiday, please send urgent requests to ... " will sooner or later be sent to someone who has just gone on holiday (and setup an automatic reply system). We are very wary of too much automation.

8. CONCLUSIONS

We have succeeded in making the FTP independent of the network it is using, but have had to compromise with the level of software just below it which we had also hoped to make network independent. Buffering and flow control strategies make the difference between the system working as an experiment with short files and working as a service with reasonable transfer rates. We have had to put much effort into this and certainly prefer the more decoupled network strategies implicit in X.25 to the more user dependent algorithms of TCP (in Arpanet).

At the FTP level our only compromises have been in order to interwork with incomplete implementations, and we do not regard this as significant. The decision to adopt a queued strategy has been well vindicated by our experiences. None of our users ever initiate transfers using the interactive interface provided in the US if they can avoid it. The mail system, which is the basis of the JNT Mail Protocol, is in regular use with no serious problems.

9. ACKNOWLEDGEMENTS

We would like to acknowledge the work done by other members of the INDRA group at UCL, particularly D. Frost who did much of the initial work and also the support given under various grants by the Science and Engineering Research Council and the Ministry of Defence, without which this work could not have been done.

REFERENCES

1. Braden, R.T. and Cole, R.H., Some Problems in the Interconnection of Computer Networks (in this volume)

2. High Level Protocol Group, A Network Independent File Transfer Protocol (HLP/CP(78)1), Data Communications Protocol Unit, National Physical Laboratory, Teddington, Middx (December 1977)

3. Higginson, P.L. and Fisher, Z.Z, Experiences with the initial EPSS service, in Eurocomp78 Proceedings of the European Computing Congress 1978 (Online Conferences Ltd., 1978)

4. Frost,D. and Moulton,R., Implementation of a Network Independent File Transfer Protocol, IN 1109 (August 1981)

5. Higginson, P.L., The Design of the Current IPCS System and Possible Improvements, IN 1164 (1981)

6. High Level Protocol Group, A Network Independent File Transfer Protocol FTP-B(80), Data Communications Protocol Unit, National Physical Laboratory, Teddington, Middx (1981)

7. Bennett, C. J., JNT Mail Protocol,TR 74,Dept. Computer Science, University College London (January 1982)

Note: TR and IN indicate internal reports or notes of the Department of Computer Science, University College London.

BIOGRAPHIES

Peter Higginson graduated in 1969 and after taking an M.Sc. in Computer Science went on to work on the software for the hosts at the London node of the ARPA Network. He is now a lecturer in the Department of Computer Science, University College London and is involved in the Department's research projects on various aspects of computer networking.

Ruth Moulton is a science graduate of Westfield College, University of London. She has been working at UCL for 8 years, with the Dept of Physics on a CAL project and now in the Dept. of Computer Science. She is a systems programmer whose responsibilities include the file transfer software.

Automated Protocol Validation: some Practical Examples

H Rudin
IBM, Switzerland

Over the last few years, there has been a growing research effort in the area of computer-communication protocols. Protocols govern the coordination and exchange of information between cooperating systems. An exciting, significant, and successful part of this effort deals with the automated "validation" (or verification) of these protocols. Given a formal definition of a computer-communication protocol, "validation" is an automated process which examines this definition for the presence of various errors which could lead to improper system operation. Results from validating X.25, level 3, and several other examples are presented to demonstrate the power of this approach. The basic technique, recent extensions, and possible future developments are discussed. Overall, the purpose of the paper is to demonstrate that there is a straightforward, practical technique available, today, for improving the reliability of computer communication protocols.

1. INTRODUCTION

The demand for more function in our computer communication systems combined with plummeting digital processing costs result in systems with increasing complexity. The more complex a system is, the harder it is to understand, to design, to document, to debug, and to maintain. A number of ideas helps to ameliorate these difficulties; hierarchical design and structured programming are two key concepts. Both result in a partitioning of function into modules or processes. To do the overall job, these modules or processes must communicate and coordinate with one another. "Protocols" are the rules specifying how this interprocess communication and coordination takes place.

Protocols must function correctly or the system will not have the reliability demanded of it — and, as systems assume increasing numbers of tasks, the demand for reliability increases. Consequently, there is a growing need for techniques to ensure that protocols are in some sense correct. Matching this need, is a growing number of research efforts in the area. Some of the achievements of one of these efforts are described below.

2. AN INTRODUCTORY EXAMPLE: X.25, LEVEL 3

Fig. 1 shows a packet-switched data network with the C.C.I.T.T. recommended interface X.25. The user on the left — at a terminal — gains access to the network through this interface; at the other end of the network, the host computer being accessed is also connected via the X.25 interface. Here we are concerned with the level-3 portion of the X.25 interface recommendation, that part involved with the setup of a logical call over an already existing physical connection {1}.

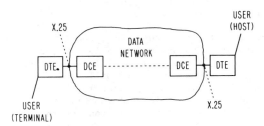

Fig. 1 Use of the X.25 interface recommendation.

Before discussing the validation of this interface recommendation, a brief explanation of how the interface functions is required. Part of the formal specification of the X.25 interface is shown in fig. 2 (ignoring the dashed loop which represents a correction). The DTE (user side) of the interface is shown on the left, the DCE (network side) on the right. Connecting the various states are arcs, labeled with either a (−) sign to indicate generation of the particular type of message involved, or a (+) sign to indicate reception. Starting with the READY state, the DTE can either send a call request to the DCE or receive an incoming call signal from it. Normally the DTE would acknowledge an incoming call by returning a call-accepted signal, alternatively, the DTE would expect to receive a call-connected signal from the DCE after initiating its own call request. The (−) sign implies that the particular message can be sent at any time the DTE or DCE is in the state from which the respective (−) arc departs. Thus, it is possible for a collision (crossing of messages in the connecting medium) to effectively occur between a call request and an incoming call. This collision was anticipated and is resolved in the CALL COLLISION state, favoring the outgoing call. After any one of these possible sequences, both DTE and DCE are in the DATA TRANSFER state and the call has been established.

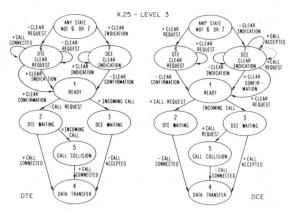

Fig. 2 The formal X.25 interface specification (level 3, corrected 1976 version).

Call clearing is indicated at the top of fig. 1.
Here, from any state (but not state 6 or 7)
either the DTE or DCE may clear a call by sending a clear request or clear indication, respectively, followed by the partner responding
with a clear confirmation.

Validation tries to answer the question, "Is the
specification as shown logically correct?" The
answer in this case was "No". The automated
validation process — which will be described
below — revealed that an unanticipated collision could occur. This collision is shown in
fig. 3. The DTE sends a call request to the
DCE at the same time the DCE sends a clear
indication to the DTE, which enters the DCE
CLEAR INDICATION state. What the DCE should do
upon receiving the call request in state DCE
CLEAR INDICATION is not specified in fig. 2.
A separate table of error conditions in the
1976 specification recommendation, however,
indicates that such a condition should be
flagged as a "local procedure error". This is
inconsistent with fig. 2 which clearly admits
this collision. One recommendation to remedy
this anomaly is the inclusion of the dotted

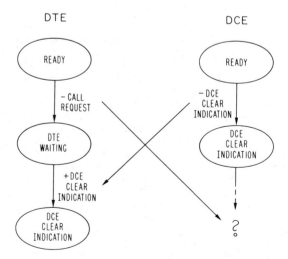

Fig. 3 Unanticipated collision in X.25, level 3.

loop shown in fig. 2 {2}. The DCE would then
simply ignore the call request message when in
state DCE CLEAR INDICATION.

This correction has since been adopted for the
revised recommendation {3}.

It is this kind of inconsistency or anomaly
which protocol validation tries to detect. We
have been concerned with computer-automated
techniques to obtain this objective. Others
have made such an analysis manually; in the
case of X.25, see {4} and {5}.

3. THE VALIDATION TECHNIQUE

Our initial efforts were devoted exclusively to
the syntax of protocols {6}, {7} and {8}. This
means that the investigation was similar to
that performed by a precompiler for a high-
level language. It was not until recently that
we examined protocols for semantic or functional properties.

3.1 Syntactic properties

In the X.25 example above, the design was incomplete in that an "unspecified reception"
could occur, i.e., it was possible for one of
the processes to send a message to another process which could be in a state without provision
for the reception of this message type.

The two other syntactical error types which
could originally be detected, {6} and {7}, are
"unexercised receptions", that is to say,
receptions which could never occur as the protocol is specified, and "static deadlocks",
wherein all processes are waiting for messages
which can never be received. "Unexercised receptions" correspond to "dead code" in a program — part of the program that will never be
executed because of the inherent logical flow.

How are these three kinds of syntactic errors
detected? The approach we find most successful
is the so-called "perturbation" technique {7}.
This is basically an exhaustive search yielding
a tree of global states, the development of
which is shown in fig. 4.

At the top are a number of processes, each
modeled as a finite-state machine and described
in terms of a state-transition diagram, just
like the DTE and DCE processes in the case of
X.25. For N processes, an N × N matrix is
used to record the global states. A global
state is specified as the state of all the
component processes (conveniently along the
main diagonal) and the content of the implicit
channels or communication media between the
various processes. Each process is understood
to send messages to its partner process(es) via
one of these channels. A channel can store one
or more messages for an unknown length of time.
The receiving process then removes the incoming
message from the channel which thus behaves as
a first-in, first-out queue. The contents of the
interprocess channels or queues are recorded
off the main diagonal.

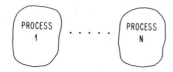

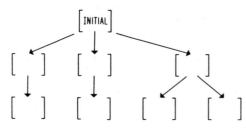

REACHABILITY TREE

Fig. 4 The perturbation technique {7}.

Starting from some specified initial state, successor states are generated and stored in the computer, linked in tree form as shown in fig. 4. The process stops when no new state, i.e., one not previously stored, can be generated. (Termination is guaranteed by setting a limit on the maximum number of messages stored in the channels.) The resulting reachability tree, rooted in the initial global state, is called the global-state graph. Each of the global states can be examined to see whether it is free from the error types listed above.

3.2 Other results of validation for syntax

Historically, the first protocol which we examined — and the one which played the major role in our early thinking — was the CCITT X.21 recommendation for circuit-switched data networks. The results of the validation are described in {9}. Here again, the 1976 version of the protocol was validated and a number of inconsistencies (since repaired) was uncovered.

IBM's System Network Architecture is described in formal, machine-readable fashion {10}. The perturbation approach was modified and has been successfully applied to the validation of SNA. The first application was to the Data Flow Control Layer {11}. To facilitate detection of some additional error types, capability was added to be able to detect "ambiguities", ambiguous global states. These are state combinations or N-tuples where the communication channels are empty and a state in one process

can persist for an arbitrarily long period of time with more than one state in other process(es). A list of such N-tuples can provide much insight to the designer who knows the function he expects his protocol to provide. The list is one of suspect cases only; the designer must decide whether real errors have occurred.

Summarizing, our initial work was devoted to purely syntactic properties of protocols. This led to validation algorithms which are:

1) widely applicable, and

2) easily automatable.

The resulting program packages have been successfully applied to a number of protocols within IBM. These techniques have become the core of our work in validation. What follows are optional additions to this core.

3.3 Weak semantic properties

The validation technique described up to this point can be widely applied, without the user having to make protocol-specific changes to the programs. Given a suitable machine-readable formal definition of the protocol, the validation package can simply be run. This is different from the goals of other researchers in protocol validation whose objectives result in the need to first tune the validator to meet the needs of a specific protocol. However, the techniques discussed above can be extended to answer protocol-specific kinds of issues.

For example, both the "direct store-and-forward" deadlock and the "reassembly" deadlock have been successfully detected {12} in a model of an early ARPANET protocol {13}. This was done automatically but first required that those arcs representing progress or success in some sense be identified {14}. The identification process is a manual one so that the use of the validator is not as automatic as in the case of validation for purely syntactic properties.

3.4 Strong semantic properties

Recently, we have been validating the protocol for a local-area network based on the "token-ring" principle {15} and {16}. The transmission system topology is that of a ring. A token is passed from station to station; the station with the free token may seize the ring to send information to another user {17}.

In this work we were particularly concerned with the behavior of the system in the presence of transmission errors. Special efforts have been made in the system architecture to ensure that there is never more than a single free token on the ring, that the token does not disappear, and that a continuously circulating busy token would in time be removed. For this system, we wanted the validation system to prove that these properties are in fact provided. This is, of course, a question of the system function or semantics.

As in the previous cases, validation starts out by generating the global-system graph. Given some particular starting condition — say the introduction of a particular transmission error — the goal is to demonstrate that some desirable response (expressed as a condition on the global-system state) is reached — say, successful system recovery. First, all those global-system states are found which satisfy the starting condition. For each of the states in this set, the successor state(s) are generated. These successor states are then checked to see whether the conditions corresponding to the desirable response are reached. If yes, then the particular path or trace of states is terminated. If not, the following successor states are generated until either the desirable response is attained or until a maximum number of iterations is reached. In the latter case the system sends the user a warning. The approach just described has proven to be very useful in demonstrating that the token-ring protocol has the various strong semantic properties required of it. The major concern has been recovery from transmission errors which effect the flow of control on the ring but other functional requirements could be examined easily. Because of their semantic aspects, each one of these functional requirements must be explicitly stated by the user.

3.5 Summary of protocol error conditions

The table below summarizes the various kinds of conditions with which we have been concerned. The lower down the table, the more semantic the flavor and the narrower and less automated the application of the validator.

Table 1
Protocol properties

SYNTACTIC

- Unspecified Reception
- Unexercised Reception
- Static Deadlock
- Ambiguities

WEAK SEMANTIC

- Dynamic Deadlock determined by
  - Starvation and
  - Unproductive Cycles

STRONG SEMANTIC

- Functional Properties such as
  - Recovery from Transmission Errors

3.6 Some references

There are other approaches to defining and analyzing protocols, and it is important to mention a number of these here. A tutorial introduction with many references is {8}. Papers emphasizing formal protocol descriptions are {10}, {11}, {18} – {23}. Approaches to the validation of protocols are discussed in {12},

{18}, {20}, {22} and {24}. Several comprehensive collections of papers devoted to protocols have been published in the last few years {25} – {27}.

4. COMPUTER-SUPPORTED PROTOCOL SYNTHESIS

We have been discussing automated tools for the analysis of protocols. The question arises, would it not be possible to provide a protocol designer with an interactive, computer-based support program which would keep him from making some of the kinds of errors discussed above.

The reply is in the affirmative, and we have devoted some effort to this task. One technique consists of the automated application of a number of production rules {28}. Usage of these rules during the design of a protocol ensures that the protocol has neither unspecified nor unexercised receptions.

This much can be done automatically {28} and {29} for two processes. An extension has been made to the more-than-two-process case {30}. For the two-process case, the automated synthesizer has been augmented by an interactive graphics display {31}. Other protocol properties can be checked for by calling special programs at occasional intervals.

In using these techniques, the designer defines a first arc, i.e., the transmission of a particular message type, and the computer follows by applying the production rules to determine the consequences, usually asking the designer where to terminate various reception arcs. After a number of iterations, the procedure terminates and the designer is free to specify another transmission arc.

Sidhu {32} has taken a different approach to synthesis. In his work, a kind of incremental "perturbation" analysis {7} is performed as the design proceeds.

The two techniques — analysis and synthesis — have now been applied to a number of protocols. Our experience has shown that the analysis — perturbation — approach has a much larger area of application than the synthesis approach. The synthesis approach is limited — at least as we have implemented it — to a pure finite-state-machine description. This is not the case for the analytic approach where — as in the case of SNA — finite-state machines may both contain and be imbedded in procedures. But the notion of computer-supported protocol synthesis remains an intriguing one and further research will surely be carried out leading in this direction.

5. LIKELY FUTURE DEVELOPMENTS

The analysis of protocols has made much progress in the last half-dozen years. Not only have automated validation and computer-supported synthesis of protocols been demonstrated on significant examples, but portions of the software implementation of a protocol have been automatically derived (or compiled) from the formal, machine-readable protocol definition {10}. Again based on the formal protocol definition one can imagine that it would be possible to estimate protocol performance; this has in fact been achieved by Bauerfeld using simulation {33}.

Given a validated protocol and a number of different manufacturers implementing this protocol, the question of compatibility arises. It would be exciting — and soon very likely necessary — to be able to certify that a particular implementation does in fact correspond to the protocol as specified in its formal definition. Work has been proceeding along these lines, much of it at the National Physical Laboratory in the U.K. These efforts are described in a number of papers in {26}, particularly in the second volume devoted to protocol testing and certification.

Wrapping all these ideas together — both present achievements and future goals — Piatkowski goes so far as to anticipate a complete engineering discipline for protocols {34}. At the present time there is some distance to travel before this level is reached.

6. CONCLUSION

A number of examples — all taken from the "real" world — has been used here to demonstrate the power of protocol validation. The technique used has an elegant simplicity which makes its use straightforward. Experience has shown that validation reveals significant difficulties in protocols developed even by experienced and careful designers. Very few of the protocols validated have been error free: numerically, say, some five percent! We hope that others will make increasing use of this and related techniques to improve the reliability of computer communication protocols.

Much progress has been made in the formal specification and analysis of protocols but much work remains to be done. The payoff is large, yielding new means of substantially improving the reliability of computer communication systems, even in the face of increasing complexity. Further, the promise is that this will all be achieved at lower overall development cost.

ACKNOWLEDGMENT

The work reported here was done in the main by members of the Data Networks Group at the IBM Zurich Research Laboratory: Colin H. West and Pitro Zafiropulo as long-term members, Dan Brand, Don Cowan, and Rainer Hauser as year-long guests. While initiated within the group, the X.25 validation was done by Matt Hess, at the time from the IBM La Gaude Development Laboratory.

REFERENCES

{1} C.C.I.T.T., Recommendation X.25, Orange Books, Sixth Plenary Assembly, vol. VIII.2, Geneva, 1976, 70-108.

{2} IBM Europe, Technical improvements to CCITT recommendation X.25, submission to Study Group VII, Oct. 1978.

{3} C.C.I.T.T., Recommendation X.25, Yellow Books, Seventh Plenary Assembly, vol. VIII.2, Geneva, 1981, 100-190.

{4} D. Belsnes and E. Lynning, Some problems with the X.25 packet level protocol, Computer Communication Review, vol. 7, no. 4, Oct. 1977, 41-51.

{5} A. A. McKenzie, ed. Computer Communication Review, ACM Special Interest Group on Data Communications, Oct. 1977.

{6} P. Zafiropulo, Protocol validation by duologue-matrix analysis, IEEE Trans. Commun., vol. COM-26, no. 8, Aug. 1978, 1187-1194.

{7} C.H. West, General technique for communications protocol validation, IBM J. Res. Develop., vol. 22, July 1978, 393-404.

{8} H. Rudin, C. H. West and P. Zafiropulo, Automated protocol validation: One chain of development, Proceedings of the Computer Network Protocols Conference, Liège, Belgium, Feb. 1978, paper F4.

{9} C. H. West and P. Zafiropulo, Automated validation of a communications protocol: the CCITT X.21 recommendation, IBM J. Res. Develop., vol. 22, Jan. 1978, 60-71.

{10} D. P. Pozefsky and F. D. Smith, The SNA meta-implementation: language and applications, Proceedings of the International Conference on Communications, Denver, June 14-18, 1981, 9.2.1-9.2.5.

{11} G. D. Schultz, D. B. Rose, C. H. West and J. P. Gray, Executable description and validation of SNA, IEEE Trans. Commun., vol. COM-28, no. 4, Apr. 1980, 661-677.

{12} M. Sherman and H. Rudin, Using automated validation techniques to improve distributed software reliability, Proceedings of the IEEE Symposium on Reliability in Distributed Software and Database Systems, Pittsburgh, July 21-22, 1981, 107-112.

{13} R. E. Kahn and W. R. Crowther, Flow control in a resource-sharing computer network, IEEE Trans. Commun., vol. COM-20, June 1972, 539-546.

{14} J. Hajek, Automatically verified data transfer protocols, Proceedings of the 4th International Conference on Computer Communications, Kyoto, Japan, Sept. 1978, 749-756.

{15} H. Rudin, Validation of a token-ring protocol, Proceedings of the International Symposium on Local Computer Networks, Florence, Italy, April 19-21, 1982, 373-387.

{16} H. Rudin and C. H. West, A validation technique for tightly-coupled protocols, to appear in the IEEE Trans. on Computers, July 1982.

{17} W. Bux, F. Closs, P. A. Janson, K. Kümmerle and H. R. Müller, A reliable token-ring system for local-area communication, Proceedings of the National Telecommunications Conference, New Orleans, 29 Nov. - 3 Dec. 1981.

{18} G. V. Bochmann and C. Sunshine, Formal methods in communication protocol design, IEEE Trans. Commun., vol. COM-28, Apr. 1980, 624-631.

{19} G. V. Bochmann, Finite state description of communications protocols, Proceedings of the Computer Network Protocols Symposium, Liège, Belgium, Feb. 13-15, 1978, F3-1 - F3-11.

{20} G. V. Bochmann, Protocol specification and verification with a general transition model, IEEE Trans. Commun., vol. COM-28, Apr. 1980, 643-650.

{21} A. Danthine, Protocol representation with finite-state models, IEEE Trans. Commun., vol. COM-28, Apr. 1980, 632-643.

{22} P. Merlin, Specification and validation of protocols, IEEE Trans. Commun., vol. COM-27, Nov. 1979, 1671-1680.

{23} T. Piatkowski, Finite-state architecture, IBM Technical Report TR-29.0133, Systems Development Division (now Systems Communications Division), Research Triangle Park, North Carolina, August 1975.

{24} J. Rubin and C. H. West, An improved protocol validation technique, accepted for publication in Computer Networks, possibly April 1982.

{25} A. Danthine, ed. Proceedings of the Computer Network Protocols Symposium, Liège, Belgium, Feb. 13-15, 1978. See also special issue on Computer Network Protocols, Computer Networks, vol. 2, no. 4/5, Sept./Oct. 1978.

{26} D. Rayner and R. W. S. Hale, eds. Protocol Testing - Towards Proof? (an INWG/NPL Workshop), Vol. 1: Specification and Validation, and Vol. 2: Testing and Certification, National Physical Laboratory, Teddington, U.K., May 27 - 29, 1981.

{27} C. A. Sunshine, ed. Communication Protocol Modeling, Artech House, Dedham, Mass., 1981.

{28} P. Zafiropulo, H. Rudin and D. Cowan, Towards synthesizing asynchronous two-process interactions, Proceedings of the Computer Networking Symposium, Gaithersburg, May 29, 1979, 169-175.

{29} P. Zafiropulo, C. H. West, H. Rudin, D. D. Cowan and D. Brand, Towards analyzing and synthesizing protocols, IEEE Trans. Commun., vol. COM-28, no. 4, Apr. 1980, 651-660.

{30} D. Brand and P. Zafiropulo, Synthesis of protocols for an unlimited number of processes, Proceedings NBS - IEEE Computer Network Protocols Conference, Gaithersburg, May 29, 1980, 89-101.

{31} H. Rudin, H. Walther, P. Zafiropulo, D. D. Cowan and N. K. Link, Automated protocol synthesis via graphics, Proceedings of the Fifth International Conference on Computer Communication, Atlanta, Oct. 1980, 391-396.

{32} D. P. Sidhu, Towards constructing verifiable communication protocols, Protocol Testing - Towards Proof? (an INWG/NPL Workshop) National Physical Laboratory, Teddington, U.K., May 27-29, 1981, 75-141.

{33} W. L. Bauerfeld, Description, verification, and performance of computer network protocols, Protocol Testing - Towards Proof? (an INWG/NPL Workshop) National Physical Laboratory, Teddington, U.K., May 27-29, 1981, 253-269.

{34} T. Piatkowski, An engineering discipline for distributed protocol systems, Protocol Testing - Towards Proof? (an INWG/NPL Workshop) National Physical Laboratory, Teddington, U.K., May 27-29, 1981, 177-215.

* * *

HARRY RUDIN received the B.E., M.E., and D. Eng. degrees from Yale University in 1958, 1960, and 1964.

From 1961 to 1964 he served as Instructor in Electrical Engineering at Yale. In 1964 he joined Bell Telephone Laboratories where he worked in the area of data communications, mainly on automatic equalization techniques. He has been with the IBM Zurich Research Laboratory, Switzerland since 1968, where he has worked on computer-communications systems. Here his research first dealt with the problems of dynamic multiplexing, network dimensioning, routing and flow control. Recently his main activities have been on the formal specification of protocols, on their computer-supported design and on their automatic validation.

Harry Rudin is European Editor of the IEEE Transactions on Communications and Correspondent for the IEEE Communications Magazine. He is on the Executive Committee of the Swiss Section of the IEEE and has recently become an editor for the Journal of Telecommunication Networks.

He is a representative to IFIPS TC 6 (Technical Committee on Data Communications) and gives a graduate course on computer and data networks at the Swiss Federal Institute of Technology in Zurich.

Automated Proofing of Communication Protocols against Communication Services

H Eckert, R Prinoth
Gesellschaft für Mathematik und
Datenverarbeitung, Federal Republic
of Germany

One of the merits of the ISO-work on Open Systems Interconnection is the development of a model for the architecture of cooperating systems. The concept of layering results in the definition of services and protocols related to a layer. Services of a layer are defined by a certain set of interactions and the allowed sequences between users and provider of these services. A protocol-specification can be seen as a refinement of a service-specification. Therefore the question should be answered whether such a refinement is "correct". A protocol is correct if the set of interactions and the realized sequences between users and provider are exactly those specifying the service.

O. INTRODUCTION

The purpose of a protocol is to perform the service required. Protocol verification therefore is proving that the protocol guarantees the properties of the service. The service specification cannot be verified, but forms the standard against which the protocol is verified [4].

In this paper we presume that the communication architecutre of a distributed system is structured as a hierarchy of different protocol layers. In verifying that a protocol meets its service specification, it will be necessary to assume the properties of the lower layer's service. We presume that all local components (i.e. the local protocol-machine and the user above) will work without fault. For the underlying transport-medium an error-model is introduced in chapter 3, which has properties similar to the X.25-service in the dataphase [10]. This error-model may be interpreted as (part of the) definition of the lower layer's service. The service required is implemented by local protocol-functions and their execution in prescribed sequences. To prove the correctness of the protocol we <u>first</u> find out all <u>global</u> sequences generated by the protocol-machines and the transport-medium (1st step). This is done by describing the system by a Petri net and analyzing this net with respect to a suitable initialmarking. The reachability-machine of the net consists of all global states and all state transitions. Therefore all sequences possible are found. <u>Afterwards</u> we prove that the properties specifying the service hold true for all system states, provided that firing transitions means executing functions (2nd step). In this paper all local components are state machines [8]. Furthermore all

conditions are tested locally to decide whether a local function is executed or not. So the system designed is near to implementation.

In chapter 1 a service specification in terms of natural language is given, which is part of the problems belonging to session-layer protocol [4]. In this paper we will act with this specification.

In chapter 2 a formal description of the service specification of chapter 1 is given in terms of Petri-nets and local functions. In chapter 3 an error-model for the transport-medium is derived. This error-model may be interpreted as a formal specification of the underlying service. In chapter 4 a simple handshake protocol is introduced. It is verified in chapter 5, that this protocol is a correct refinement of the service specification of chapter 2 if the error-model of the transport-medium is chosen as defined in chapter 3.

1. SPECIFICATION OF A SERVICE IN TERMS OF NATURAL LANGUAGE

Let us consider two user-processes $\bar{L}$ and $\bar{R}$ respectively and a counter Z_L, belonging to $\bar{L}$ and a counter Z_R, belonging to $\bar{R}$. With $J(Z_L)$ and $J(Z_R)$ we denote the value of Z_L and Z_R respectively, which is assumed to consist of non negative integers. Process $\bar{L}$ acts with Z_L and process $\bar{R}$ acts with Z_R such that condition

$$(\ast) \qquad |J(Z_L) - J(Z_R)| \leq 1$$

holds true. Therefore it is necessary to synchronize $\bar{L}$ and $\bar{R}$. Z_L and Z_R are local instances of a <u>dis</u>-<u>tributed counter</u> Z. The process $\bar{L}$ and $\bar{R}$ act on Z due to the following conditions:

- there is no common storage for $\bar{L}$ and $\bar{R}$.
- $\bar{L}$ and R have equal rights (no master/

slave-relation).
- the distributed counter is incremented only if both processes want to do so.
- The operations of $\bar{L}$ and $\bar{R}$ on the distributed counter Z are non-decreasing. This means:

(**) If $(J (Z_L), J (Z_R))$ is reachable from $(J (Z_L^O), J (Z_R^O))$ then $J (Z_L) \geq \min(J(Z_L^O), J(Z_R^O))$ and $J (Z_R) \geq \min(J(Z_L^O), J(Z_R^O))$.

- Condition (*) holds true.

Remark: Altering the contents of a local counter may be considered as an abstraction of a program state change of the local user.

2. SERVICE DESCRIPTION IN TERMS OF PETRI-NETS AND LOCAL FUNCTIONS

In the following, some notions of Petri-net theory are used. The reader who is not aquainted with nets is referred to the literature given at the end of this paper ([1], [7]).

2.1 Definition in the case of normal behaviour

A formal description of the service is given by net A1 and the local functions φ_L, ψ_L, φ_R, ψ_R.

Net A1

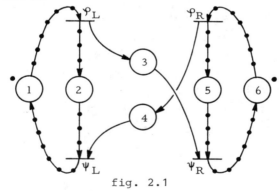

fig. 2.1

In net A1 only local functions are defined: φ_L, ψ_L are local functions of the user $\bar{L}$ ($\bar{L}$ defined by the places 1 and 2) and φ_R, ψ_R are local functions of the user $\bar{R}$ ($\bar{R}$ defined by the places 5 and 6). The initial marking M1 is given as shown in the picture above.

φ_L: If $\bar{L}$ is in state 1 (token in place 1) then function φ_L is enabled. Firing the transitions means executing φ_L: The user $\bar{L}$ which is on top of the local protocol-entity L (see fig. 4.1) gives an increment request to L. A SYNC-signal is sent

from L to the peer-entity and the local state of $\bar{L}$ after execution of φ_L is state 2 (token in place 2). The value of Z_L is not altered.

In quite the same way function φ_R is defined.

ψ_L: If $\bar{L}$ is in state 2 (token in place 2) and if a SYNC-signal is received by the protocol-entity L then function ψ_L is enabled (see fig. 4.1). Firing the transition means executing ψ_L: The incoming signal is consumed and the state of $\bar{L}$ after execution of ψ_L is state 1 (token in place 1). The value of Z_L is incremented by one.

In quite the same way function ψ_R is defined (end of definition).

If we 'execute' net A1 due to the firing rules of a Petri-net, we get the marking M1 to M8 as given in the state-machine E_{A1} (fig. 2.2). Now firing a transition is interpreted as executing local functions. Then we get a global assertion for each marking. In each assertion a relation between the values of the local counters is given (fig. 2.2). For short we write Z_K instead of $J (Z_K)$:

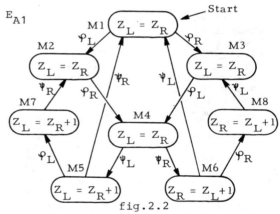

fig.2.2

As can be seen in E_{A1} conditions (*) and (**) hold true.

2.2 Service Description in a more general case

Compared with the service definition given in chapter 1 the formal definition of chapter 2 is a special case of operations on Z_L and Z_R. Taking into account the necessity to recover from loss of data the service definition must be extended. We define:

In each case the local sequences of φ and ψ are defined as in chapter 2.1 (see dotted lines in net A1). If no errors occur then the global sequences of φ and ψ are defined by machine E_{A1} (see fig. 2.2). If errors occur new structure has to be added to E_{A1} and the functions have to be extended (chapter 4). Let E_{B1} be the name of the new machine. Then E_{A1} is part of E_{B1} and in E_{B1} conditions (*) and (**) hold true.

3. ERROR-MODEL FOR THE TRANSPORT-MEDIUM

In this chapter we describe the error-model for the transport-medium which has properties similar to the X.25-service in the data-phase [10]. The error-model may be interpreted as (part of the) definition of the lower layer's service.

3.1 Definition of the underlying service in natural language (properties of the error-model)

1) Messages will be delivered in the same order in which they were submitted.

2) At any time the transport-medium may execute a reset-operation. This is notified to <u>both</u> processes (reset-indication).

3) There may be none or any integral number of messages travelling within the transport-medium when a reset occurs. Messages within the transport-medium are destroyed completely by a reset-operation.

4) Any messages received after a reset-indication at the receiver side has been sent after the corresponding reset-indication at the sender side.

5) If more than one reset-indication occurs during a period of time in which the local process has not reacted to reset-indications, then only one execution of a reset-recovery-procedure occurs.

As messages are transferred as a whole, a message in this model is represented by a token.

3.2 Formal Definition of the error-model

We introduce three places to the net-model namely R_{GL} and R_L and R_R and one transition of special type (R-transition) representing the reset-operation. Fig. 4.1 shows an example.

A token in R_L models the fact that the left protocol-process is notified that a reset-operation has occured (reset-indication) The meaning of a token in R_R is the same with respect to the right protocol-entity.

Transition R is always activated. This is modelled by a loop containing place R_{GL} (which has always a token (see fig. 4.1)).

Firing transition R initiates V1 and V2 as an indivisible set of actions:

V1: All tokens are removed from a pre-defined set of places (modelling the channel).

V2: The number of tokens in R_L and R_R respectively is set to one.

When V1 and V2 are finished, a new system-state is generated. There are no other operations, which may increment the number of tokens of the places R_L and R_R respectively.

(End of definition).

If Mi is the global state (marking) before R fires and Mj is the global state after R has fired, we denote this graphically in the reachability-machine by

Remark: In fig. 4.1 places 3 and 4 define the 'predefined set' with respect to action V1.

Net B1

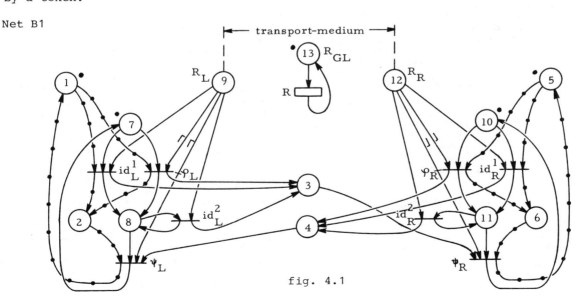

fig. 4.1

4. DESCRIPTION OF A SIMPLE HANDSHAKE-MODEL

In this chapter a refinement of the service specification of chapter 2 is given. In contrast to the service description the transport-medium is not assumend to be reliable. The error-model of chapter 3 is chosen. We have to design a protocol which uses the service of the underlying layer and provides the service required.

4.1 Description of a simple handshake-model

If the transmission medium is not reliable, we have to introduce a strategy to ensure that

- local components react to reset-indications with priority.
- normal behaviour is reached by the system after this reaction (i.e. after error-recovery).
- The relations between the values of the local counters hold true (see fig. 2.2).

The strategy applied is defined as follows:
If there is a local reset-indication a special local function (id-function) is activated which signals the actual state of the local counter to the partner-process. The ψ-function is extended to the effect that the new value of the local counter-instance is evaluated by the minimum of the own counter-value and the received one. We accept a mod 3-folding of the contents of the local counter-instances.
Definition of the protocol in terms of a Petri-net and local functions:

Variables:

For each protocol-entity the local counter-instance, a 'last sent'-variable, an output-queue(FIFO), and an input-queue (FIFO) are defined. We use W to denote the set {SYNC, O, 1, 2, undefined}. The local functions the protocol-processes L and R will activate are defined on vectors of the type (local counter-instance, 'last sent'-variable, output-queue of length 2, input-queue of length 2).
In model B1 the input-queue of the one protocol entity is the output-queue of the peer-entity and vice versa.

Functions:

In case of normal behaviour(that is in absence of local reset-indication) the local functions φ and ψ are defined as follows:

$\varphi : N_o x W^5 \rightarrow N_o x W^5 : \varphi$ puts a SYNC into its output-queue and into its 'last sent'-variable. The value of the local counter-instance is not altered.

$\psi : N_o x W^5 \rightarrow N_o x W^5 : \psi (X,H,...,Y) =$

$$= \begin{pmatrix} x-1 \\ x \\ x+1 \end{pmatrix} ,undef., ...)$$

The partial function ψ is defined by the table below. We assume that X is the value of the local counter-instance. Then the effect of applying ψ is given as follows:

ψ H 'last sent'	Y SYNC	'signal received' (input-queue) O	1	2
SYNC	x+1	-	-	-
O	-	x	x	x-1
1	-	x-1	x	x
2	-	x	x-1	x

If a (local) reset is indicated, the local function id is defined as follows:

id: $N_o x W^5 \rightarrow N_o x W^5$: Let X be the actual value of the local counter-instance. id puts the value X mod 3 into its output-queue and into its 'last sent'-variable. The value of the local counter-instance is not altered.

Remark: The reset-indication is cleared (see fig. 4.1).
Remark: There are two cases of the id-function in net B1 (id[1] and id[2]).

In net B1 sequences are defined with respect to activation of the functions φ, id, and ψ (end of definition).

In net B1 the set of places {7, 8} defines a local protocol-machine process L is running. The set {1O, 11} defines a local protocol machine process R is running [8]. Places 3 and 4 are modelling global conditions. The value of such a condition is an integer (namely the number of token). A condition is true, if the value is an integer > O otherwise it is false [9]. The functions φ, id, ψ, and R are setting a testing (ψ-function) these conditions. This results in the generation of all global sequences (see fig. 5.1).

Remark: We use Petri-nets as a formal tool for modelling concurrency and we use functions to increase the arithmetic power of our tool.
Remark: In this paper we model the logical aspect of the transport-medium rather than the physical aspect. Nevertheless the reader may identify the token in places 3 and 4 with messages of the type SYNC, O, 1, or 2, if the (physical)

transport-medium is able to store at least two messages.

The structure of the service-machine (net A1) is part of the structure of the refined system B1 (see dotted lines).

Remark: Arcs, labelled with '¬' are called <u>inhibitor-arcs</u> [7].

5. ANALYSIS OF THE SIMPLE HANDSHAKE-MODEL (NET B1)

Now we have two fromal descriptions:

- a description of the service required (chapter 2.2)
- a description of a protocol which uses the underlying service (net B1).

We have to show that B1 is a correct refinement of the service specification. This is done in two steps:

First step:

The reachability-machine E of net B1 with initial marking M1 (M1 defined in fig. 4.1) is derived by program. We get E by applying the firing rules for Petri-nets [7] and rules V1, V2 given in chapter 3.2. E has 16 states and generates all sequences possible. Hereby the effect of the functions on variables is not considered.

lines) and every state of E_{A1} is reachable from every state of $\tilde{E}$. There are no deadlocks.

Second step:

The reachability-machine E of the first step together with the definition of the local functions are input for step two. State transitions of the first machine are recomputed with the special functional meaning now given to the transitions (by program).

We get a machine F, which has 128 states. Each state of F is a global vector $V_i \in N_o \times W^6 \times N_o \times Mj$ of the type:

$V_i = (Z_L$, last sent L, channel LR_1, channel LR_2, channel RL_1, channel RL_2, last sent R, Z_R, Mj). Mj is a marking of net B1, i.e. a state in E. So for each vector V_i we can check whether property (::) of chapter 1 holds true. If
$M_\alpha \xrightarrow{f} M_\beta$ is a state-transition in E, then we proceed in the following manner:

For all $V_j = (\ldots, M_x)$ with $x = \alpha$ we execute f (if possible) thus producing a resulting vector $V_k = (\ldots, M_\beta)$:
$V_j \xrightarrow{f} V_k$. The execution of f is an atomic action.

$\tilde{E}$

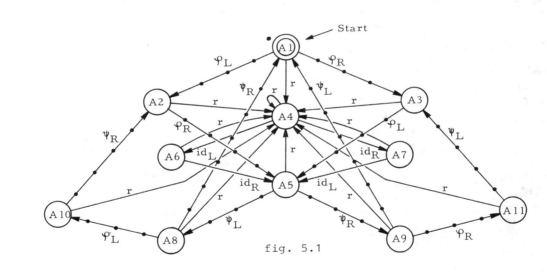

fig. 5.1

In fig. 5.1 a reachability-machine $\tilde{E}$ is shown, which is equivalent to E with respect to the generated language, but has less states than E (minimum state finite automaton [5]). Hereby we presuppose that id^1 and id^2 are labelled with the same symbol id.

Remark: In state A10 (A11) of $\tilde{E}$ place 3 (4) has two token.

The structure of E_{A1} (fig. 2.2) is part of the structure of $\tilde{E}$ (see dotted

Remark: In our example the values of Z_L and Z_R are not bounded. Nevertheless we have a finite set of global vectors $\{V_1, \ldots, V_{128}\}$. This is achieved by introducing a global folding vector. The theory with respect to this folding vector shows that (under certain conditions) properties hold true for infinite sets which are derived for finite sets [2].

Properties of the machine F (tested by program):

- Properties (∗) and (∗∗)of chapter 1 are true for all states of F
- There are no deadlocks
- The structure of E_{A1} is part of the structure of F
- The initial state of F(which is the initial state of E_{A1} too) is reachable from each state of F.

Remark: We use machine E instead of $\tilde{E}$ for the second step because in E we can distinguish whether an execution of id is an interface-operation (id^1) or not (id^2). This information is used by one of the test-programs which derives the 'interface-language' (machine E_{B1}) from the 'protocol-language' ([3], [6]). For further information with respect to the algorithms and programs used the reader is referred to the literature ([2], [9]).

Remark: In our example only two channel-variables are used in vector V_i for each direction because the number of tokens of places 3 and 4 in net B1 is less than three (result of analysis of step 1).

Hans Eckert was born in Dienheim, West-Germany, in 1947. He received the Diplom-Mathematiker from the University of Bonn in 1975. From 1975 to 1977 he worked as a system-analyst at an insurance company. Since 1977 he has been a member of the Institute for Teleprocessing of the Gesellschaft für Mathematik und Datenverarbeitung. He was first engaged in protocol implementation and specification of transport- and session-protocols.Since then he has worked at protocol verification.

Rainer Prinoth was born in Danzig, Germany, in 1941. He received the 'Staatsexamen für Mathematik und Physik' from the University of Frankfurt in 1967.From 1967 to 1969 he worked as a teacher. From 1969 to 1972 he was engaged in operation research projects in the statistic group of the Deutsches Rechenzentrum in Dst., West-Germany, which was merged with the Gesellschaft für Mathematik und Datenverarbeitung in 1972. Since then he has been a member of the Institute for Teleprocessing of the GMD. He has worked at theoretical aspects of distributed systems. Within this work he received his PhD in Computer Science in 1977 from the Technische Hochschule in Darmstadt.

References

[1] Brauer, W. (ed.)
Net Theory and Applications
Proceedings of the Advanced Course on General Net Theory of Processes and Systems
Lecture Notes in Computer Science, Springer, 1979.

[2] Eckert, H.
Ein rechnergestütztes Verfahren zur Verifikation von Aussagen über nicht endliche Erreichbarkeitsmengen
GMD-interner Bericht, 1980.

[3] Eckert, H.; Prinoth, R.
A Method for analyzing Communication Protocols. in:
Papers presented at the Second European Workshop On Application And Theory Of Petri Nets
Bad Honnef, Germany, Sept.28-30,81.

[4] Formal methods for communication protocol specification and verification.
National Bureau of Standards.
Draft Report, June 1980.

[5] Hopcroft, J.; Ullmann, J.
Formal languages and their relation to automata
Addison-Wesley Publishing Company, 1969.

[6] Paule,C.
Epsilon, Ein Programm zur Berechnung der Sprache, welche aus einer vorgegebenen regulären Sprache dadurch entsteht, daß eine beliebige Teilmenge des Eingabealphabets durch das leere Wort ersetzt wird.
GMD-intern 1981.

[7] Peterson, J.L.
Petri-nets
Computing Surveys 9/3, 1977.

[8] Prinoth, R.
Eigenschaften färbbarer Petri-Netze
in: Theoretical Computer Science, 3rd GI-Conference
Lecture Notes in Computer Science, Springer 1977.

[9] Prinoth, R.
An Algorithm to construct Distributed Systems from State-Machines
Second International Workshop on Protocol Specification, Testing and Verification;
North-Holland, 1982.

[10] CCITT Recommendation X.25, "Interface between data terminal equipment (DTE) and data circiut terminating equipment (DCE) for terminals operating in the packet mode on public data networks",
Sept. 1976.

Protocol Implementation Assessment

D Rayner
National Physical Laboratory, UK

Considerable effort is being put into developing international standards for protocols and services in support of Open Systems Interconnection. All this activity will, however, be in vain unless products are produced in conformance with these standards. In order to give users confidence in the products they buy, implementations need to be tested by a trusted independent assessment centre. NPL is currently developing suitable testing techniques for use by such centres. This paper describes the theoretical basis which has been established for this work. This is the subject of international collaborative study, which, it is hoped, will lead to the establishment of international assessment centres using internationally accepted testing procedures.

1. INTRODUCTION

Many people are putting a lot of effort into the development of standards for Open Systems Interconnection (OSI). These standards will include an OSI reference model (1), the services offered by each layer of that model, and the protocols that are needed to provide those services. The objective is to enable any computer or terminal to communicate meaningfully with any other, if mutually agreeable, across whatever series of communications links happens to intervene. This goal will not, however, be achieved unless products are produced in conformance with the standards.

There is therefore a growing interest in establishing centres that can test protocol implementations for conformance to the appropriate standards. For high-level protocols, such testing can be carried out remotely, communication with the client's system being achieved via whatever means is available (e.g. a public data network). These testing centres need to be seen to be impartial and trustworthy. Their credibility will be crucial to their success.

Conformance testing on its own, however, is not enough. Implementations also need to be tested to see that they will meet the user's requirements. In particular, the range of options supported, the performance (throughput and response times), and the robustness (the degree by which an implementation is able to recover from error situations) all need to be measured. The combination of these tests and measurements is termed 'assessment'.

Purchasers of systems containing communications packages can look to Assessment Centres to provide a slimmed down suite of conformance tests for acceptance testing purposes. Some implementors will also require Assessment Centres to provide development aids to assist them in debugging their systems. Current indications are that these two activities will be important revenue earners for the centres.

The need to maintain credibility will lead to Assessment Centres providing an arbitration service. Since testing, however thorough, can only detect the presence of errors not their absence, situations could arise in which two implementations that have received favourable assessment reports fail to interwork properly. An arbitration service could investigate the situation and determine the cause of the problem.

A fuller discussion of this philosophy of assessment, including the nature of assessment reports is given in earlier papers (2,3).

1.1 The UK Position

In the UK, the National Physical Laboratory (NPL) is developing the appropriate testing techniques for protocol implementation assessment. The aim is to establish techniques applicable to the eventual international standards. In the meantime, protocols already in use in the UK provide the basis for developing the techniques. In particular, the initial work is based on the Network Service and Protocol over X.25 (4) which is being used on British Telecom's Packet Switched Service (PSS) and other networks in the UK.

The various aspects of assessment are being tackled in the following order:-

(a) conformance and functional range;
(b) performance and robustness;
(c) development aids and arbitration.

The current plan is that the UK National Computing Centre (NCC) at Manchester will run a pilot service based on the system developed at NPL, probably starting in late 1982, subject to continued funding from the UK Department of Industry.

1.2 International Collaboration

Similar work is going on in other establishments around the world. The Commission of the European Communities (CEC) is part funding collaboration between the groups at NPL, in

Project RHIN of Agence de l'Informatique (ADI) in Paris, and in Gesellschaft fur Mathematik und Datenverarbeitung (GMD) in Darmstadt in W. Germany. ADI has adopted the same basic approach as NPL (see (5,6)), whereas GMD is giving higher priority to development aids and arbitration. The main difference, however, between the three groups is in their initial choice of protocol. The planned collaboration will give full coverage of the Network, Transport and Session layers of the OSI model, with direct application to CCITT Teletex protocols and the ISO Network and Transport services and protocols, once they have become sufficiently stable.

Related work is also going on at the Joint Research Centre (JRC) at Ispra in Italy (7), at the USA's National Bureau of Standards (NBS) (8,9), and at Montreal University in Canada (10). The JRC has developed various tools that can be used by its clients in testing implementations of Euronet protocols, but it does not provide a full assessment capability. NBS is working towards a Certification Center for implementation of the US Federal Protocol Standards that they are in the process of specifying. It is possible that they will also adopt an approach similar to NPL's. On the other hand, Bochmann's work at Montreal has the aim of automatic production of tests from a formal specification of the protocol concerned.

The collaborative project between NPL, ADI and GMD involves JRC Ispra in a technical advisory capacity. There are also moves to extend the collaboration on an informal basis to involve NBS and Montreal. It is hoped that this will lead to internationally accepted testing procedures for international standards, at least within Europe and North America.

2. GENERAL ARCHITECTURE FOR ASSESSMENT

2.1 Layering within the Logical Architecture

The logical architecture for testing can be described in terms of protocol layering, similar to that defined in the OSI reference model (1). The identification of the layers for testing purposes may, however, be different. It may be necessary to subdivide a single OSI layer or to combine two or more of them. Two protocols will be considered to be in separate layers if they are to be tested separately, or in the same layer if they are to be tested in combination and thus considered as a single protocol for this purpose.

For example, the OSI Network Layer can contain both CCITT X.25 level 3, providing a Packet Service, and a Network Protocol above X.25, providing what is sometimes called a "global" Network Service, which is independent of the underlying subnetwork(s). Until recently such a service would have been encompassed by the Transport Service, but it is now clear that the OSI reference model requires the Network Service to have this characteristic; the role of the Transport Layer is now to enhance the quality of service from that provided by the Network Service to that required by the user. A division of the OSI Network Layer into three sublayers has been proposed by ECMA (11), and

this has now been broadly accepted by ISO/TC97/SC6. At present it is convenient to test the upper two of these sublayers together. Thus, the OSI Network Layer can be divided into two assessment layers.

Once the assessment layers have been determined, they can be numbered sequentially. Figure 1 shows an example of how such numbering relates to the OSI reference model numbering for the Transport Layer and below.

OSI layer number	Protocol	Assessment layer number
4	Transport Protocol	4
3	Network Protocol over X.25	3
	X.25 Packet Protocol	2
2	HDLC	1
1	Physical Protocol	

Fig. 1. Example of assessment layer numbering

Once the layers have been so numbered, it is possible to refer to layer N, where N is some positive integer. The protocol in layer N is called the (N)-protocol, the service provided to the layer above is called the (N)-service and the service provided by the layer below is the (N-1)-service. The (N)-protocol is realised by encoding it onto the (N-1)-service. This is shown in Figure 2.

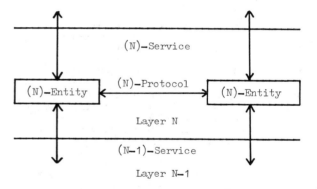

Fig. 2. Layer N protocol and related services

2.2 The Need for a Test Responder

The assessment layers will be chosen so that each implementation under test (IUT) can be treated in isolation from protocol implementations above and below it. Thus, if the IUT is in an assessment layer (N) which is not the highest, it must have some internal interface between it and its higher layer 'users'. Across this internal interface the IUT should provide a realisation of the (N)-service. The (N)-service standard will define the semantics of the service boundary. This may be realised in any way that the implementor choses, provided that the semantics are equivalent. Since the (N)-service boundary must be present for the IUT, there needs to be an (N+1)-entity to operate it. The behaviour of such an entity needs to be predictable, so that, as far as possible, the results of tests are dependent only upon the behaviour of the IUT. To this end, the Assessment Centre will define a Test Responder (TR) for the client to incorporate into his system for assessment purposes.

The TR should ideally be flexible enough to enable any desired test to be run. Since, however, it must be incorporated into every client's system, it should ideally be readily portable onto any system, even one with minimal capabilities. These ideals of flexibility and simplicity conflict and a compromise must be reached.

The TR must be able to inter-relate consecutive connections within the same test. Each distinct sequence of inter-related connections needed during testing is called a 'Test Session'. There is also the need to handle parallel Test Sessions. For simplicity of definition, however, the TR is defined to handle only a single Test Session. For definition purposes, parallel Test Sessions are regarded as being handled by separate parallel Test Responders. These can be incorporated into the client's system as separate instances of a single-threaded process, or as separate threads through a multi-threaded process, or by whatever equivalent means is appropriate in the given system.

The implementation of a TR will use the local realisation of the service boundary provided by the IUT. Since the details of this interface are implementation-dependent, the TR is defined purely in terms of the (N)-service, which provides an abstraction of this interface. It will be left to the implementor to map the TR onto the local realisation of the service boundary. This avoids the need for an Assessment Centre to learn the details of every local interface, and assumes that assessment testing is kept free from local interface considerations.

TR algorithms (12) are defined by means of flow diagrams. These are preferred to any particular programming language because they are less committed to any one way of achieving the required effects. They are therefore easier to translate into the client's preferred programming language. Nevertheless, to assist clients further, reference implementations will be published in those programming languages for which there is known to be a sufficient demand. The first reference implementation of the current TR will be published in Coral 66.

2.3 General Logical Architecture

The combination of hardware and software used by the Assessment Centre to communicate with the client's system during testing is called the 'Active Tester'. Corresponding to each TR, the Active Tester will contain a 'Test Session Handler' (TSH). Each TSH is logically divided into layers corresponding to the assessment layers concerned. In each layer a TSH entity communicates with its peer in the client's system via the appropriate protocol. The

highest layer entity visible in the client's system is the TR, which communicates with a Test Driver via a Test Driver-Responder Protocol. This is a non-standard protocol, defined specifically for assessment purposes. Since it is not used for OSI, it cannot be expected to fit into a layer of the OSI model.

This architecture is shown in Figure 3 below.

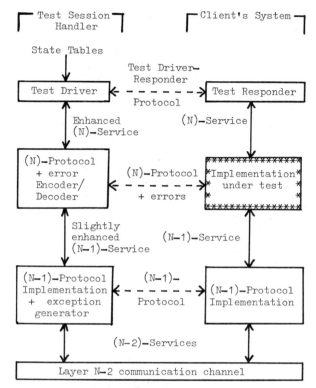

Fig. 3. General Test Session architecture

For the purposes of assessment, the implementation under test will be considered to be a 'Black-box'. It will not be possible for the Active Tester to tell whether the implementation is a single process or a combination of hardware and software such as would be found in an implementation split between a front-end processor and a mainframe. The implementation under test is simply seen as having two service boundaries, one which should provide the (N)-Service and one which should use the (N-1)-Service. The activity across the (N)-Service boundary can be recorded by the Test Responder, but the activity across the (N-1)-Service can only be observed indirectly from the other end of the communication channel.

Thorough assessment of an implementation requires that it be subjected to error situations as well as normal protocol. For this reason, the TSH entity at layer N is not a reference implementation but rather an encoder and decoder of both valid and invalid protocol messages. The service it provides is enhanced because, in addition to the normal (N)-Service, it provides:-

(a) requests for the generation of (N)-Protocol

errors (e.g. syntax violations);

(b) indications of detected (N)-Protocol
errors without any automatic action being
taken;

(c) explicit control over the use of the
slightly enhanced '(N-1)-Service' when
necessary.

Similarly, the TSH entity at layer N-1 is not a
reference implementation, because it too has to
provide an additional service, namely:-

(d) requests for the generation of exceptions
from within layer N-1 that can be
signalled without violating (N-1)-
Protocol (e.g. resets); these may involve the use of messages or parameter
values which should not normally originate
from the service user.

2.4 Simple Physical Architecture

This logical architecture can be mapped onto
the simple physical architecture shown in
Figure 4 below, provided that the (N-1)-Service
is end-to-end. In this architecture the whole
of the Active Tester is implemented in a
computer system at the Assessment Centre's site
and the client's system is tested remotely via
some communications medium, such as a public
data network or the public switched telephone
network.

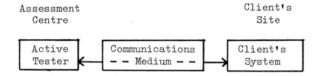

Fig. 4. Simple physical architecture

The initial Active Tester being developed at
NPL will use PSS as the primary communications
medium.

2.5 Advanced Physical Architecture

When the (N-1)-service is not end-to-end, as in
the case of X.25 level 3, a more advanced
physical architecture is necessary in order to
realise the full logical architecture. This
involves the introduction of a transportable
box, called the Environment manipulation and
Monitoring Unit (EMU), between the
communications medium and the client's system,
as shown in Figure 5.

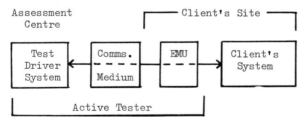

Fig. 5 Advanced physical architecture

3. ACTIVE TESTER DEVELOPMENT

The Active Tester for use in the assessment of
implementation of the Network Service over
X.25 is being developed in two phases. Phase 1
will adopt the simple physical architecture and
will therefore be restricted in the types of
error that the IUT can be subjected to. Phase
2 will incorporate EMU, and could well coincide
with the move to the corresponding ISO Service
and Protocol.

3.1 Phase 1

Phase 1 will be subdivided into four main
stages, as follows:-

(a) A manually driven system has been produced,
enhanced by files containing message
sequences (similar to the NBS scenarios
(9)), primarily for use in debugging the
Network Protocol Encoder/Decoder and
evaluating the Test Responder. It will
only run a single Test Session at a time.

(b) This will be converted into a state-table
driven system for a single Test Session at
a time. Each test will be defined by a
combination of a state table and a
parameter table. The state table will be
automatically constructed from a
programming language-like specification
(similar to the linear form of CCITT SDL
(13,14)). It will operate on a
standardized set of events and actions.

(c) This will then be extended to handle
parallel Test Sessions co-ordinated by a
Test Co-ordinator process, ultimately
under the control of a human operator.

(d) Finally, a more advanced phase 1 system may
be produced, with the Test Coordinator
selecting dynamically the tests to be run
next. The tests would be chosen from a
standard set of simple tests, each defined
in a new language designed specifically for
test definition.

These stages are more fully described in
another paper (15).

3.2 Phase 2

In phase 2, EMU will be a multi-microprocessor
system providing the following range of
functions:-

(a) monitoring of traffic across the client's
X.25 interface;

(b) simulation and generation of errors at X.25
level 3 and in the Network Protocol above
X.25;

(c) generation and absorption of bulk traffic
to reduce the cost and delay that would
otherwise result from sending such traffic
across a public network;

(d) performance measurement, such as timing
and throughput characteristics of the IUT;

(e) X.25 facility matching, where the X.25

facilities subscribed to by the client do
not match those for which the IUT is to
be tested (e.g. use of 'fast select'
where this has not been subscribed to);

Other uses for such a box could include:-

(f) a development aid for implementors;

(g) a general purpose tool for traffic
analysis which could be used as a 'spy'
in an operational network.

A similar box, called Cerbere, is being
developed within Project RHIN (6).

4. CATEGORIES OF TESTS

An informal description of an initial set of
tests for the Network Service has been
published for public comment (16). This
identifies seven categories of tests that will
be needed for full assessment of an
implementation:-

(1) Primitive support;
(2) Individual state transitions;
(3) Parameter variations;
(4) Primitives in combination;
(5) Multiple connections;
(6) Performance;
(7) Robustness.

Primitive support tests are designed to
establish which service primitives are
supported by the implementation. In the case
of the Network Service this involves about 20
individual tests. At the end of this series,
a secondary result will be that it will have
been established whether or not the Test
Driver-Responder Protocol is working
satisfactorily.

Individual state transition tests are the main
tests of conformance. They each involve
driving the IUT into a given state and then
observing its reaction to a specific event.
In the case of the Network Service, this
involves over 100 individual tests.

Parameter variation tests are designed to
investigate the range of parameter values that
the IUT will handle. This includes testing
its reaction to null parameters, ones with
particularly large values, ones with invalid
values, and other special cases, as well as a
selection of 'normal values'.

Tests of primitives in combination are
designed to investigate various sequences of
events to discover whether the IUT's reaction
to a specific event in a specific state is
dependent upon the events leading up to that
state. In particular, they will determine
whether reactions are repeatable, as is
necessary for the reliable handling of bulk
data. These tests can be subdivided into sub-
categories, the most important of which are:-

(a) combinations of data and/or expedited
traffic in both directions;

(b) reset messages combined with data and/or
expedited traffic;

(c) disconnect messages combined with data
and/or expedited traffic;

(d) repeated call set up and break down in
various forms.

Multiple connection tests will investigate any
effects that activity on one connection might
have on parallel connections. In particular,
there will be tests to determine the maximum
number of parallel connections that can be
handled.

Performance tests will measure the maximum
throughput and timing characteristics of the
IUT. Timing characteristics include the
minimum time for call set up and the values of
any timeouts used when waiting for events that
do not occur.

Robustness tests will record the behaviour of
the IUT under a variety of error situations,
and try to determine what circumstances cause
the IUT to generate reset or disconnect
messages.

5. CONCLUSIONS

The philosophy and architecture for assessment
of protocol implementations, as presented in
this paper, is applicable to most if not all of
the layers of the OSI reference model. The
definitions of both the Test Responder and most
of the tests are specific to the service
concerned but not the protocol. Even those
tests that involve the generation of protocol
errors can be defined in terms of a suitably
enhanced service, where the enhancement only
concerns general categories of error. The only
part of the development which has to be
protocol specific is the (N)-protocol
encoder/decoder. Since the interim Network
Service being used is similar in many respects
to the current ISO Network and Transport
Service proposals, most of the work now being
done at NPL will be easy to adapt to the
eventual ISO Network and Transport Protocol
standards.

ACKNOWLEDGEMENTS

The ideas presented in this paper are the
product of the NPL Protocol Standards Group, of
which the author is the leader. Past members
of the group who have contributed to these
ideas are K.A. Bartlett, R.F. Henley,
K. Wilkinson and M. Woodger. Current members
of the group who have contributed to them are
C.M. Coles, G.W. Cowin, D.C. Eason,
R.W.S. Hale, V. Hathway and J.R. Pavel. The
author also acknowledges the contribution made
by I.C. Davidson of the National Computing
Centre.

This work was funded by the UK Department of
Industry's Computers, Systems and Electronics
Requirements Board, which has now been
superseded by the Electronics and Avionics
Requirements Board.

REFERENCES

(1)   Data processing – open systems inter-
      connection – basic reference model,
      ISO/DIS 7498 (November 1981).

(2)   Bartlett, K.A. and Rayner, D., The
      certification of data communication
      protocols, proceedings IEEE Symposium on
      Computer Network Protocols, held in
      Washington D.C., 29 May 1980, Trends and
      Applications 1980 (New York, IEEE, May
      1980) 12–17.

(3)   Rayner, D. (ed.), Protocol implementation
      assessment: philosophy and architecture,
      prepared by the NPL Protocol Standards
      Group, NPL Report DNACS 44/81 (April
      1981).

(4)   Linington, P.F. (ed), A network
      independent transport service, Annex 1 in
      particular, prepared by the Study Group 3
      of British Telecom's PSS User Forum, SG3
      CP(80)2 (NPL, February 1980).

(5)   Ansart, J.P., Test and certification of
      standardised protocols, in: Rayner, D.
      and Hale, R.W.S. (eds.), Protocol
      Testing – Towards Proof?, Volume 2:
      Testing and Certification (NPL, 1981)
      119–126.

(6)   Ansart, J.P., Tools for the certification
      of standardised protocols: Cerbere and
      Genepi, in: Rayner, D. and Hale, R.W.S.
      (eds.), Protocol Testing – Towards Proof?
      Volume 2: Testing and Certification
      (NPL, 1981) 127–130.

(7)   Weaving, K., The verification of high
      level protocol implementations, in:
      Rayner, D. and Hale, R.W.S. (eds.),
      Protocol Testing – Towards Proof?,
      Volume 2: Testing and Certification
      (NPL, 1981) 131–146.

(8)   McCoy, W.H., Colella, R.P. and Wallace,
      M.A., Assessing the performance of high
      level computer network protocols, in:
      Rayner, D. and Hale, R.W.S. (eds.),
      Protocol Testing – Towards Proof?,
      Volume 2: Testing and Certification
      (NPL, 1981) 25–54.

(9)   Nightingale, J.S., A benchmark for the
      implementations of the NBS transport
      protocol, NBS Draft Report ICST/H.NP –
      81–20 (September 1981).

(10) Bochmann, G.V., On the theoretical power
      of some testing methods, in: Rayner, D
      and Hale, R.W.S. (eds.), Protocol Testing
      – Towards Proof?, Volume 2: Testing and
      Certification (NPL, 1981) 15–24.

(11) Network layer principles, prepared by
      ECMA TC24 TGNS, ECMA/TC24/81/123, also
      known as ECMA/TC23/81/169 and
      ISO/TC97/SC6/N2312, (November 1981).

(12) Henley, R.F.L. (ed.), Implementation
      assessment of transport and network
      services: the test responder
      specification, prepared by the NPL
      Protocol Standards Group, NPL Report
      DNACS 46/81 (July 1981).

(13) Recommendations Z101–Z104, Volume VI.7,
      CCITT Yellow Book, output of the VIIth
      Plenary Assembly of CCITT, held in Geneva
      (1980).

(14) Rockstrom, A. and Saracco, R., SDL:
      CCITT specification and description
      language, proceedings National
      Telecommunications Conference, held in
      New Orleans, 29 Nov. – 3 Dec. 1981, NTC
      Record – 1981, Volume 4 (IEEE, 1981)
      G6.3.

(15) Rayner, D., A system for testing protocol
      implementations, to be published in
      proceedings 2nd International Workshop on
      Protocol Specification, Testing and
      Verification, held in Idyllwild,
      California, 17–20 May 1982 (North Holland,
      1982).

(16) Henley, R.F.L., and Rayner, D.,
      Implementation assessment of transport
      and network services: an informal
      description of tests, NPL DNACS TM 5/81
      (July 1981).

Dr D. Rayner was educated at Bristol University from 1969 to 1975, obtaining a BSc in Mathematics with Computer Science and a PhD for his work on formal definition techniques applied to high-level job control languages. Since leaving Bristol he has worked at NPL on user interfaces and high-level protocols, implementing transport service and file transfer protocols for use over the UK Experimental Packet Switched Service. He helped design and revise the UK Network Independent FTP and is chairman of the FTP Implementors' Group. He is leader of the NPL Protocol Standards Group, which is currently engaged in developing techniques for the assessment of high-level protocol implementations.

The Use of ADA Packages for Standard Telecommunications Interfaces

A Langsford
AERE Harwell, UK

M J Norton
British Telecom, UK

The paper describes the concept of a "package" in the ADA programming language. It suggests how the package concept could be used to implement standard data communications protocols. Candidate protocols are indicated, for example, Teletex, X25 Level 3, Transport Service and File Transfer. The paper explores the potential advantages to all sections of the data communications community. For Telecomms Authorities, there is the reduction and simplification of the "Permission to Attach" testing; for the user, a mechanism for hiding the complication and detail of the communications interface; and for the equipment supplier, a standard basis from which to customise individual products.

1. INTRODUCTION

The idea of using Ada packages to provide standardisable software packages for intelligent devices connected to data networks arose in discussion within the Telecommunications Sub-Group of Ada Language UK Ltd. In this paper, we review the way in which the Ada package concept may be used to provide a standard software unit which can be authenticated and approved for installation in telecommunications equipments. We also consider the rationale for selecting suitable candidates to standardise in this way, recognising that there must be a clear advantage for a well identified market to render the exercise economically attractive.

Since the procedures for connection to public communications lines demand a level of acceptance and approval by a licensing body one of the most important points to consider is how such packages may be rendered "tamper proof".

Finally we describe the steps being taken by the Ada Telecommunications Sub-group to develop standard implementations of particular communication protocols. The aim is to reduce the wasteful duplication of effort involved if one had many user/supplier implementations of these protocols.

2. THE LICENSING REQUIREMENT

2.1 The Position Before British Telecom De-regulation

British Telecom, (BT) policy on the licensing of intelligent data communications devices for attachment to the Public Data Services has concentrated on four main areas.

(i)   The attachment of private modems to the public switched telephone network (PSTN), and/or data circuits.

(ii) The use of intelligent "auto-dialling" equipment for central computers to access outstations over the telephone network.

(iii) Attachment to the Public Packet Switched Service (PSS).

(iv) Attachment to the Telex Service.

In all areas, the objective of the licensing policy has been to take all reasonable precautions to prevent attached devices from compromising the integrity of the public networks, both in terms of safety and function.

Topics (i) and (ii) are of little concern for Ada packages, though the potential for creating havoc of a "rogue" auto-dialler has been demonstrated on more than one occasion, despite stringent BT licensing tests on the integrity of the software involved.

Licensing of packet devices for attachment to PSS has proceeded on an almost individual basis. The supplier of a particular implementation of the X.25 packet protocol registers the implementation with British Telecom. This is achieved by completing the standard questionnaire supplied with the PSS Technical Guide, [1]. BT then evaluate the implementation using a protocol tester which emulates the network packet interface and introduces certain fault conditions to check the specific implementation's response. The questionnaire and the assessment visit also confirm compliance with the standard requirements for electrical safety [2].

If all the test results are satisfactory, the implementation is licensed. The implementation or product, when sold to customers will be given approval to connect to PSS on completion of a further, (simpler) questionnaire by the user. This approval is only given if the product is the totally standard unit originally tested, any significant modification may result in BT requiring a complete repeat of the tests. Similarly upgrades to the product may require a further test.

The licensing procedure is thus labour intensive and the cost in manpower and capital resources to BT is high. The tests are however essential to prevent rogue X.25 terminals causing service disruption to other users of PSS.

Licensing for attachment to the Teletex Service [3], is still being formulated for the service launch in Spring 1982. It is anticipated that it will be similar to that already outlined for PSS, though it is hoped that there will be a smaller number of different implementations.

It is very much in British Telecom's interest to reduce the diversity of implementations to be tested and attached to the growing range of data services. (We have not discussed the Prestel or the proposed range of circuit switched data services). Ada UK Ltd believe that Ada packages are a useful tool in achieving this objective.

2.2 The Position Following British Telecom De-regulation

In the short term (by end 1982), it is likely that the British Electro-technical Approvals Board (BEAB) will take on the role of testing for electrical safety and for compliance with the signalling requirements of the PSTN. The responsibility to check compliance with particular services, eg. PSS or Teletex, is likely to remain with BT for at least a further three years. Wherever responsibility lies, the requirement that network integrity be protected will remain. This will still require detailed tests of individual pieces of software.

3. THE MARKET

3.1 Candidate Telecommunication Protocols

As communications networks become controlled more and more by stored program devices and transmission technology becomes digital rather than analogue, there is a growing tendency to place intelligent devices within the communication network. These may be entirely within the network providing switching and accounting services. They may be provided by the network vendor as added value services, e.g. Prestel; and they may be provided as external attachments by users and suppliers for user specific applications. The range of these applications is already diverse and is a fast growing market area.

In order to regulate the potential for product diversity offered by the network supplier, PTTs and other regulatory bodies have recognised that there must be not only national standards to give coherence and unified equipment within a country. There must also be international conventions to enable communications services to operate between countries. The latter are produced as Recommendations of CCITT (International Consultative Committee on Telephony and Telegraphy). They define standard services and interfaces which shall be provided for international telecommunica-

tions. As well as regulating voice traffic, CCITT Recommendations are also available for communication protocols covering packet switching and terminal access. They also define services such as Telex and, more recently Teletex.

In addition, the initiatives within the International Organisation for Standardisation, ISO, to develop standards for Open Systems Interconnections has generated a further range of protocols for data exchange. There is consequently a long list of protocols which are used in conjunction with intelligent data processing instruments. These are summarised in Table 1 where they are grouped according to their application to (i) the communication network, (ii) PTT supplied services, (iii) user operated facilities. Clearly the first two groups are applicable within a different market from the third group.

TABLE I

Protocol for Data Exchange

i) Communication network
 	
    Binary Synchronous
    HDLC
    Ethernet
    ......

ii) PTT supplied services
 	
    X25
    X3, X28, X29
    Teletex
    Videotext
    ......

iii) User operated facilities
 	
    Transport Protocol
    File Transfer Protocol
    Job Transfer (Remote
                Job Entry)
    Banking data (SWIFT)
    Airline date (SITA)
    ......

3.2 Who benefits?

We identify three groups who might benefit from the use of standardised packages with standardised methods for testing and approving them. These are:

(i) the network suppliers (the PTTs)

(ii) systems and software suppliers

(iii) the end users.

When approval in the UK was the province of the Post Office, it was clearly in their interest to encourage the use of standards and standard packages for two principle reasons. Firstly if a standard package can be identified which may be replicated across many systems, the testing and approval procedure has only to be defined and applied the once. Secondly, having a well defined standard with which to conform with ensures that it is, in principle, an easy matter to test for conformance and hence be particularly objective about the criteria for licensing. These arguments should apply in equal measure to the new licensing authority, set up under the 1981 Act. They too will have their work load reduced if approval needs to be given to a single implementation which may then be replicated. The fact that a standard provides grounds for assessing conformance will be even more important for an independent body than for a network supplier. They have to have a firm basis for granting or refusing approval. Granting approval to a product which does not satisfy, for example, the requirements to preserve network integrity could prove too costly to the network supplier. Failing to grant approval to an adequate product stiffles innovation and healthy competition.

The benefit enjoyed by the system and software supplier is less clear cut. Of course there is benefit to the supplier who provides the package in the first instance since he can presumably obtain revenue for licencees who use his product. But what of the organisations which buy a package for incorporation into their own software and hardware products? They have to purchase the same licensed package that others are also installing in competing products. In practice a supplier will buy in components if they meet the requirement and can be obtained at a cost lower than that of internal development. Such an argument is easy to apply when purchasing hardware but less appropriate for a software purchase. Software replication cost is very low. Therefore a supplier may prefer to carry out his own development and pay licensing costs rather than pay a royalty to some other supplier. Yet against this he can set the certain cost of a standard, approved package which minimises the risk taken in embarking on software development. This benefits a system supplier whose product has a small software content (other than the standard package) and whose software expertise is limited. It is particularly likely to benefit the smaller company.

The user benefits provided that the cost of the product is lower than it otherwise would have been and that its quality has not been impared. He also benefits if it gives him a wider choice of products from which to select. Finally he benefits (like the licensing body) from being presented with a product which complies with an externally maintained standard. This ensures that his equipment can be assured of a stable environment in which to operate.

Yet the very stability conferred by adopting standard packages has its negative side. There is the danger that innovation is stiffled. A standard package which carries non-standard extras may have to be licensed as a new package. This increases cost.

Clearly these are all important considerations in any move made to develop and licence standard software for communication protocols.

4. IMPLEMENTATION CONSIDERATIONS

4.1 Why Ada?

Since the initial consideration of standard software package arose in an Ada sub-group, the question could be rhetorical. But there are important issues to be raised. CCITT have under review a PTT sponsored programming language called CHILL which has many (if not all) of the features offered by Ada and is being developed with telecommunications systems in mind. Telecommunications was not a primary requirement when developing the Ada language which was designed for programming embedded (military) systems. There is considerable evidence that large stored program telecommunication systems are not embedded in the sense defined for Ada.

However, those equipments which make use of telecommunications facilities or add value to a telecommunications network closely match the Ada view of an embedded system. Also their primary function is not telecommunications but some other aspect of information processing. It is likely that the coding of these other aspects can be very effectively carried out using the Ada language. It is in this context that the standard communication protocol handling package can be conveniently expressed as an Ada "package".

Ada packages are one of the three forms of Ada program units. Packages allow the specification of logically related entities. Through their visible parts they offer a precise interface to other components which comprise the Ada programme. The private part of the package protects the inner working of the package from external influence.

In many ways the concept is that of a "software library", made machine independent, and thus more widely useful, by use of the Ada language. It will be evident that not all aspects of a communications protocol implementation can be made machine independent, there will always be a driver module concerned with machine dependent hardware interfaces. This machine dependent module is small compared to the total implementation of a communications protocol, for example, in X25 it; might represent one quarter of the layer two software and none of the layer three, probably less than ten percent in total. In Teletex the machine dependent part is less than five percent. The prime objective is to de-mystify communications protocols, essentially reducing them to software library calls.

4.2 Who will produce standard packages?

Software packages usually arise as a commercial venture where a market is identified and is ready to be won over by a product. If there is a clear market advantage then one could expect software houses to be keen to develop packages, at least for certain protocols and services.

Although the market for intelligent, communicating information processing systems is readily identified, that for standard telecommunication packages is more defuse. The benefits are more strongly identified as being those associated with the licensing body and the user. It was in recognition of this problem that the Ada Telecommunication Sub-group saw that some preliminary and even pump-priming activity is called for. The work could therefore be commissioned from a software producer by a consortium of the likely beneficiaries. They would share the speculative risk and enter into agreements with manufacturers seeking a licence to use the package. Being a group of interested parties they could oversee package production and help ensure that the objectives of package Certification, Licensing and Maintenance were adequately handled. Such a consortium would constitute a Commercial Authority in respect of any product. They could also provide, or would assure the provision of a corresponding Technical authority.

4.3 Protection

If the integrity of a public communication network is to be protected by this procedure of licensing standard software packages, some mechanism is needed to render them tamperproof. This is a problem for hardware devices but, in the event of a dispute with a licensing or common carrier authority the modification of hardware to contravene the licence can usually be readily seen.

It is rather more difficult to "police" software but doubtless certain audit techniques could be used. In suspicious circumstances, the machine object code for the package in use could be compared with a suitably compiled reference version of the package. The "Ada" source version of the package would normally be invisible to the user, however there are conflicting requirements on control of this source code. The prospective purchasers and users of the package must have the source version available to them, such that they may be convinced that it is well written, documented and in so far as is possible, error free. The package must however be tamperproof. This conflict of interest could be resolved by building a security package within the communications package. This security package would take no part in the operation of the communications protocol package except to verify its integrity, thus the source version of this embedded security unit would not be publicised. In cases of dispute over "tampering" the security package would be used by an authorised inspector to verify the main package integrity. Software is intangible, it is almost impossible to stop an illicit modification, the objective must be to render it easily detectable.

4.4 Certification, Licensing and Maintenance

Once a standard package exists, it has to be launched. This requires that it is tested to see that it conforms to:

(a) the Ada standard (so that the product is portable between different software or hardware systems);

(b) the communication protocol standard (to ensure that the product meets its telecommunication requirements).

There is at present very little experience in either of these two aspects of conformance testing. Nor is there experience of the legal aspects of certifying a software product of this nature to see that it conforms with the requisite standards. Yet such conformance testing and certification will be required by the licensing authority if they are to approve the package. There is clearly a need for a pilot project to explore how these matters can best be attended to. The Ada Telecommunications sub-group have considered candidate protocols to see which would be the most appropriate for such a pilot project.

Such a project could also yield valuable insight into the important issue of package maintenance. It seems likely that the Technical Authority responsible for the package would handle maintenance issues that must inevitably arise during the product lifetime.

5. CONCLUSIONS

It is not possible to be definitive, at this stage, as to which protocol or protocols should be selected for a pilot implementation as a standard Ada package. But it is possible to set guide lines. To avoid device dependent code, the protocol should be at a reasonably 1high level in the communications hierarchy. It should have general applicability with a ready market from a number of equipment suppliers. These considerations favour the choice of X25 level 3, Transport and Teletex as suitable protocols.

It should not be thought that licensing a standard Ada Package removes the need for all licensing. The hardware still needs to be assessed, though this is a better understood task. Buying a standard Ada Package for inserting in a system is then analogous to buying say a licensed protection circuit for a V24 interface.

But above all, serious study is required to establish that the standard Ada Package offers not only a technical solution but that it is commercially viable. Everyone is prepared to support standards as a "good thing" but it is hard to persuade people to pay for them when the benefits are intangible. The main recommendation of this paper is therefore to encourage the Telecommunications Subgroup of Ada Language UK Ltd to press ahead with their proposed study. They must pay particular attention to the market forces which will influence the acceptability of such packages, will establish guidelines for technical and product certification authorities and will identify the ways in which such products can be marketed. They must assess the economic benefit, the costs and the likely returns.

ACKNOWLEDGEMENTS

The authors acknowledge thier colleagues within the Ada Telecommunication Sub-group for their comments, advice and encouragement.

AL acknowledges the UK Department of Industry for their support of his work on Open Systems Interconnection Standards.

REFERENCES

[1] British Telecom Technical Guide 17 (PSS).

[2] British Telecom Technical Guide 26 (Electrical Safety).

[3] British Telecom Teletex Service Technical Guide.

The Effect of Line Errors on the Maximum Throughput of Packet Type Computer Communication and a Solution to the Problem

M C Davies, I W Barley, P E Smith
British Telecom, UK

One of the problems of inter-computer communication at high bit rates over long distances is the effect of line errors on the overall data throughput even at modest bit error rates (eg 1 error in a million bits).

To compensate for these line errors some form of error-correction is applied either by protocol at the data link level or by forward error correction at the line transmission level.

This paper looks at forward error correction and some recent data link level protocols in terms of throughput efficiency, finally presenting a new selective repeat protocol which has the advantages of both types of error correction.

INTRODUCTION

Distributed processing and inter-computer communication are on the increase, not just in the field of local area networks, but also in terms of communication with distant computers. Any remote communication will involve a transmission link which will be prone to bit errors, to remove the effect of these errors some kind of error-correction must be applied. In a packet switching system this correction is normally carried out by some form of protocol at data link level, although there are other techniques for removing these errors.

Any error-correction procedure will have an effect on throughput efficiency and it is this relationship between throughput efficiency and error-correction that this paper explores. Finally, a new error-correcting protocol is introduced which combines the properties of data link level selective repeat protocol and forward error correction.

ERROR-CORRECTION BY PROTOCOL AT DATA LINK LEVEL

While communication distances remained small and data rates low (hence a low probability of a bit being in error) then the conventional Go-Back-N type protocol was quite sufficient for good data throughput. However once the distance and speed increase Go-Back-N protocols are not good enough as it would be unreasonable to expect a bit error rate better than 10^{-6} for most long transmission links, especially if satellite hops are involved. Therefore, to be useful, any protocol at data link level must be able to give a reasonable performance at this bit error rate and preferably at an order or two higher (ie 10^{-4}). The throughput performance of a modified Go-Back-N protocol is shown in figure 1; the reduction in throughput as distance and/or bit rate increase is quite apparent. (The protocol shown is the Towsley Stutter Go-Back-N protocol where transmitter idle time is used to retransmit unacknowledged packets in an attempt to preempt requests for retransmission.)

The ideal solution is a selective repeat protocol that only retransmits packets that have been corrupted, but this is an impractical solution (due to the large buffer space required at intermediate switching nodes when the error rate is high) if the packets are to arrive at the destination in sequence. The trade-off then is between protocol complexity and buffer requirement if a practical protocol is to be found.

There has been a lot of work carried out in this area [1,2,3] and figures 2 and 3 show some examples of recent protocols. Both the example protocols use selective repeat retransmission for normal working, if however the repeated packet fails to be correctly received then (after a predetermined number of tries) the protocol reverts to another mode.

Figure 2 shows the throughput performance of the Selective Repeat + Go-Back-N (SR + GBN) protocol, where the second mode is a reversion to the conventional Go-Back-N type of protocol after one try at Selective Repeat type retransmission.

Figure 3 shows the throughput performance of the Selective Repeat + Stutter (SR+ST) protocol devised by Miller and Lin[3], where the second mode of operation is a continuous retransmission of the erroneous packet until it is received correctly. Both figures show the improvement of these new (and more complex) protocols over the modified Go-Back-N shown in figure 1.

Thus it can be seen that error-correction by protocol at data link level is possible, providing a non-simple protocol is used, however there is an alternative solution at the line transmission level.

FORWARD ERROR CORRECTION

One way of reducing the number of re-transmissions required is to use forward error correction (FEC) techniques to improve the effective error probability of the transmission link used by the packets. When applied correctly, the extra redundancy introduced by

the forward error correction can be swamped by
the increased throughput of the packet system
gained from the improved error performance.
In order to illustrate this a block code of
length n bits each block carrying k packet
bits is assumed. Then, according to the
Hammond bound [4] the maximum number of errors,
T, that can be corrected is given by:-

$$1 + \binom{n}{1} + \binom{n}{2} + \binom{n}{3} + \ldots + \binom{n}{T} \leqslant 2^{n-k}$$

$$(1)$$

where $\binom{n}{r} = \dfrac{n!}{r! \ (n-r)!}$ \qquad (2)

and it is assumed that the errors occur at
random.

Thus, the probability that a block after
decoding contains an error is equal to the
probability of there being more than T errors
in a block of n bits. Thus, if E_b is the
probability of a decoded block being in error

$$E_b = \sum_{r=T+1}^{\infty} \binom{n}{r} P^r (1-P)^{n-r} \qquad (3)$$

where P is the basic line error probability.

Then, if there are B bits in a packet, the
probability P_p of a packet being in error is
given approximately by:-

$$P_p = 1 - (1-E_b)^{(B/k)} \qquad (4)$$

Without forward error correction this would
be:-

$$P_p = 1 - (1-P)^B \qquad (5)$$

As an example, Fig. 4 shows the block error
probability E_b plotted against the line error
probability P for k = 32 and various values of
n. In each case the minimum value of n
required to obtain the value of T shown was
used. Results of this type may be used in
conjunction with those given in the previous
figures and with equations 4 and 5 to determine
the throughput factors of the various packet
re-transmission protocols in the presence of
forward error correction. An example is shown
in Fig. 5 where the effect of applying forward
error correction to the Stutter Go-Back-N
protocol is shown. As expected, the throughput of the system with forward error correction
is better than the system without forward error
correction when the line error probability is
high. However, once the forward error
corrector has been designed, the throughput
factor due to the forward error corrector is
independent of error probability. Hence, as
the line error probability decreases, the
system without forward error correction has a
throughput approaching unity, while the system
with forward error correction has a throughput
that approaches a value of less than unity.
Thus, when thinking of applying forward error
correction to a line for carrying packets it
is important to decide on the correct balance
between reasonable efficiency during the
periods of poor line-error performance and the

loss in efficiency during the periods of good
line-error performance.

PROPOSED SELECTIVE FORWARD ERROR CORRECTION
AND SELECTIVE REPEAT PROTOCOL

An obvious requirement of a selective repeat
protocol is that it creates the best opportunity possible for the correct reception of
the previously erroneously received packets,
obviously if correct reception on the first
re-transmission could be guaranteed so much the
better.

The protocol proposed in this paper comes near
this criteria, it is the Selective Forward
Error Correction and Selective Repeat Protocol
(SFEC & SR), it operates like this:-

On the reception of an erroneous packet the
receiver sends a Negative Acknowledgment of
Content (ie packet received in error) - NACKC -
to the transmitter while holding the corrupt
packet and continuing to receive subsequent
packets. The transmitter then sends not the
packet, but the forward error correction bits
for that erroneous packet. On reception at the
receiver these FEC bits (which themselves can
be corrupted) plus the held erroneous packet,
can be used to re-construct the original packet.
In the unlikely event of the packet still being
in error, the transmitter on receiving a second
NACKC for the same packet will re-transmit the
packet in question and immediately follow it
by a packet containing the FEC bits - thus
giving the receiver two more chances at getting
the packet. The transmitter would then on
receipt of a further NACKC discard the packet
entirely.

If the packet is not received at all on the
first transmission, this is indicated by the
receiver sending a Negative Acknowledgment of
reception (because it will have the subsequent
and previous sequence numbers) - NACKR - or the
transmitter timing out the original transmission, in either case the transmitter will
repeat the packet and immediately follow it by
the packet containing the forward error correcting bits. The transmitter would then allow
one NACK (of any sort) and subsequent retransmission of both packets to take place before
discarding the packet. In any event, whatever
combination of timeouts and NACKs is used, the
transmitter will always have transmitted two
packets containing the forward error correction
bits and three original packets before the data
packet is deemed irretrievably lost.

Figure 6 gives a logical decision tree for the
protocol.

CALCULATIONS ON SOME ASPECTS OF THE (SFEC & SR)
PROTOCOL

It is assumed that the bits in the packet are
re-ordered so that the distribution of errors
can be taken as uniformly random. Then, if
each packet is divided into sections containing k bits and the second (FEC) packet
containing the extra bits required in order to
apply forward error-correction is similarly
divided, the value of n as defined previously
is 2k. Thus the probability of a section still

being in error after applying the forward error-correction information contained in the second packet is E_b as given by Equ(3). The probability P_k of the packet being corrupt after application of the forward error-correction is given by:-

$$P_k = 1 - (1-E_b)^{(B/k)} \qquad (6)$$

Values of P_k for various values of k are shown in Table (1) for B = 1024 and P = 10^{-3}.

It can be seen from table (1) that, if k is made large enough, the probability of any uncorrected errors is extremely small.

However the above calculations are based on the assumption that the packets are recognised in spite of any errors. If the data link level is being considered, then all the detecting systems must do to recognise a packet is to detect the flags.

The probability E_f of an 8-bit flag containing an error is given by:-

$$E_f = 1 - (1-P)^8 \qquad (7)$$

The probability E_c of an 8-bit byte becoming a fictitious flag was determined by setting E_c equal to the average probability of each of the possible byte combinations becoming a flag. This was given for each byte by $P^H (1-P)^{8-H}$ where H is the Hamming distance of the byte from the flag. At P = 10^{-3} then:-

$$E_f = 8*10^{-3} \qquad (8)$$

and

$$E_c = 3.13*10^{-5} \qquad (9)$$

Then, if byte synchronisation is achieved by some other method, a nonsynchronous packet system will fail to recognise a packet properly if either the leading flag contains an error or if the packet contains a ficticious flag ie the probability of the packet not being properly recognised is (for the example discussed):-

$$1 - (1-E_f) ((1-E_c)^{B/8}) = 1.2*10^{-2} \qquad (10)$$

For the example used in the calculations the probability of the packet being in error is 0.641, thus there is a high probability that the first retransmission will be caused by having an erroneous packet. Subsequent to that it is more likely that the packet will go unrecognised due to flag errors rather than be uncorrected. This shows the effectiveness of the SFEC retransmission policy as problems due to erroneous packets are soon swamped by normal packet recognition problems.

The efficiency of the protocol may be increased further by having constant packet lengths and, if gaps in transmission occur, making sure the gaps are an Integer number of packets long. Then the receiver may be packet synchronised and several errors would be necessary before the system would lose synchronisation or fail to recognise a packet.

The throughput factor of the protocol is given

by:-

$$(1-A_L)/(1+S_1) \qquad (11)$$

where

$$S_1 = Q_L'P_0 + 2Q_L + 2[(Q_L')^2 P_0 P_K + Q_L'P_0 Q_L +$$
$$Q_L(Q_L')^2 P_0 P_K + Q_L^2 Q_L'P_0 + Q_L^2] \qquad (12)$$

$P_0 = 1-(1-P)^B$, the probability of a packet containing an error. P_k, given by Equ(6), is the probability that the packet is still in error after application of the FEC packet.

$Q_L = 1-(1-P_L)^2(1-E_b)$ is the probability that any given packet will be treated by the transmitter as being lost (ie either the transmitted packet has been lost, or the acknowledgement [which is assumed to be forward error corrected] from the receiver is not recognised by the transmitter).

P_L, given by Equ(10), is the probability that a packet will not be recognised as a packet. (P_L was set equal to zero for the packet synchronised case).

$$Q_L' = 1 - Q_L$$

The proportion A_L of the packets abandoned by the protocol is given by:-

$$A_L = [(Q_L')^2 P_0 P_K + Q_L'P_0 Q_L + (Q_L')^2 Q_L P_0 P_K +$$
$$Q_L'Q_L^2 P_0 + Q_L^2][Q_L + Q_L'P_0 Q_L + Q_L'P_0 P_K] \qquad (13)$$

Figure 7 shows the throughput factor of the SFEC & SR protocol plotted against P for the cases of byte and packet synchronisation. It is seen that provided the appropriate data conversion to allow the protocol to be used is performed, the protocol is, at least according to these preliminary results, superior to the other protocols at high data rates and at low error probabilities.

Although this protocol requires an increase in processing power, it appears to have potential where maximum throughput is more important than savings in processor power, since the number of retransmissions is minimised while forward error correction is applied only when necessary. The protocol also has the useful property of the throughput being independent of both line length and bit-rate.

CONCLUSIONS

For efficient inter-computer communication the effect of line errors must be minimised without invoking the need for over complex protocols or limiting throughput because of the redundancy inherent in forward error-correction. This paper has looked at a number of solutions to this problem, and presented a new type of selective repeat protocol where there is a very high probability that the packet will be correctly received (or reconstructed) on the first repeat. This leads to a need for less buffer space at the intermediate nodes and a potential of maximum possible throughput when the line error rate is low.

REFERENCES

[1] Yu, P.S. and Lin, S., An Effective
    Selective Repeat ARQ Scheme for Satellite
    Channels, IEEE Transactions on
    Communications, March 1981, Vol. Com 29,
    353-363.

[2] Towsley, D., The Stutter Go-Back N
    Protocol, IEEE Transactions on
    Communications, June 1979, Vol. Com 27,
    869-875.

[3] Miller, M.J. and Lin, S., The Analysis of
    Some Selective - Repeat ARQ Schemes with
    Finite Receive Buffer, IEEE Transactions
    on Communications, Sept 1981, Vol. Com 29,
    1307-1315.

[4] Hamming, R.W., Error Detecting and Error
    Correction Codes, BSTJ, April 1950,
    Vol. XXVI No. 2, p 147.

TABLE 1

THE PROBABILITY P_k OF A PACKET STILL BEING IN
ERROR AFTER RECEPTION OF THE PACKET CONTAINING
THE FORWARD ERROR CORRECTING BITS FOR VARIOUS
VALUES OF k

For $P = 10^{-3}$ and $B = 1024$

k	E_b	P_k
8	$5.55*10^{-7}$	$7.10*10^{-5}$
16	$1.97*10^{-10}$	$1.26*10^{-8}$
32	$4.21*10^{-15}$	$1.35*10^{-12}$

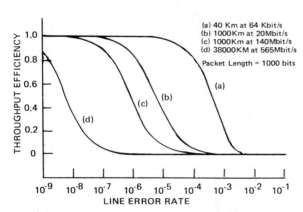

FIGURE 1 THROUGHPUT EFFICIENCY v LINE ERROR RATE
FOR A STUTTER GO—BACK—N TYPE PROTOCOL

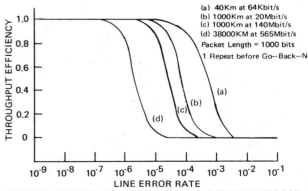

FIGURE 2 THROUGHPUT EFFICIENCY v LINE ERROR RATE FOR
THE SELECTIVE REPEAT + GO—BACK—N PROTOCOL

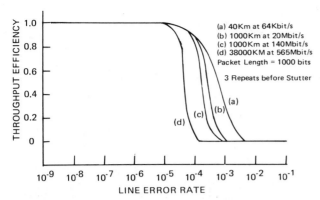

FIGURE 3 THROUGHPUT EFFICIENCY v LINE ERROR RATE FOR
THE SELECTIVE REPEAT + STUTTER PROTOCOL

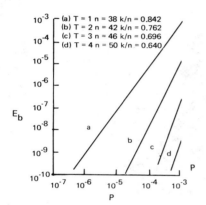

FIGURE 4   The Block Error Probability E_b
Plotted Against the Line Error
Probability P for k = 32 and n
= Minimum Value for the Value
of T Shown.

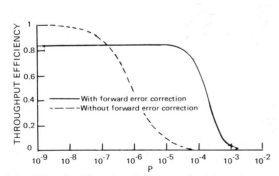

FIGURE 5— The Effect of Adding Forward Error Correction to the
Towsley Stutter Go-Back-N Packet Re-transmission
Protocol. The throughput efficiency is plotted against
the line error probability P.
B = 1000 Line Length = 1000 kM Bit-rate=140 Mbit/s
k = 32 n = 38 T = 1 k/n = 0.842

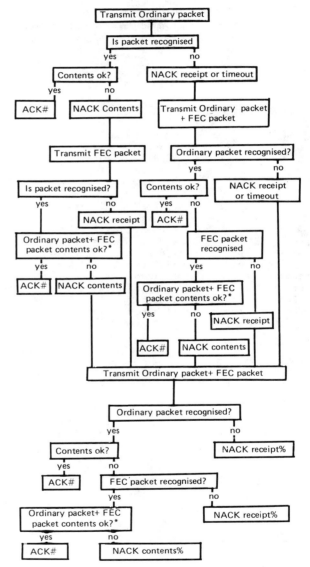

* After using the FEC packet contents to correct those of the Ordinary
packet

Packet successfully transmitted

% Packet abandoned

FIGURE 6 —
LOGICAL DECISION TREE FOR THE (SPEC & SR) PROTOCOL

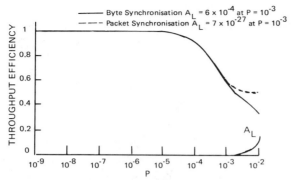

FIGURE 7— The Throughput efficiency and the Probability A_L that
the Protocol will Abandon a Packet are plotted Against
the Line Error Probability P for the SFEC & SL Protocol.
B = 1024 K = 32.

Dr M C Davies

Dr Mark C. Davies (Ph.D.,
M.Inst.P., M.I.E.E.)
joined GEC Hirst Research
Centre in 1957. While
there he worked on the
development of microwave
couplers and filters for
trunk radio-relay systems
and on microwave valves
his Ph.D. thesis was on
parametric processes in electron beams. In
1968 he joined The British Post Office Research
Centre. He lead a Group investigating the
theoretical aspects of digital trunk radio-
relay systems. Since 1980 he has been leading
a Section studying the theoretical aspects of
a system with variable bit-rate switching.

I Barley

Ivan Barley joined the
British Telecom Research
Department in 1964 and until
1975 worked on various
aspects of microwave radio
transmission. From 1975 to
1980 he was engaged on
theoretical studies relating
to submarine cable trans-
mission. He is now with the
Systems Evolution and Standards Department of
British Telecom and leads a group studying
theoretical aspects of variable bit-rate
systems. He is a member both the Institution
of Electronic and Radio Engineers and the
British Institute of Management.

P Smith

Paul Edward Smith, born
20th February 1956.
Bsc (Physics) at Hull
University, 1977. Taught
Physics for two years before
joining British Telecom in
1981. Has since been
involved in the study of
Variable-Bit-Rate systems.

Acknowledgement is made to The Director of
Systems Evolution and Standards Department,
British Telecom, for permission to publish
this paper.

948

Routing to Multiple Destinations in Computer Networks

K Bharath-Kumar, J M Jaffe
IBM, USA

Algorithms for effectively routing messages from a source to multiple destination nodes in a store-and-forward computer network are studied. The focus is on minimizing the Network Cost (NC) which is the sum of weights of the links in the routing path. This measure is compared to the Destination Cost (DC) which is the sum of the shortest path distances to all destinations. The two measures are shown to be quite different in that the path with optimum DC may have a NC which is O(m) times worse than the NC of the optimum NC path and vice versa, where m is the number of destinations. A scheme of algorithms is given which trade off between NC and DC. Several heuristic algorithms are examined for finding the NC minimum path (which is an NP-complete problem). While the minimum spanning tree algorithm has the best worst case performance among all algorithms, a detailed, empirical study of the "average" performance of the algorithms on typical, randomly chosen networks reveals that simpler heuristics are almost as effective. The empirical study also leads to an extensive set of additional conclusions.

1. DEFINITION OF THE PROBLEM

This paper considers the problem routing a message from a single source node to a subset of the other nodes in a store and forward computer communication network. We refer to this problem as the Multi Destination Routing (MDR) problem. There are several practical applications for MDR in data networks. An important application is in the office system environment where a file needs to be distributed to a subset of users connected to the network. Another is the scenario where multiple copies of a data base exist at various nodes within the network and these need to be updated from a central node.

As usual, a computer communications network is modeled as an undirected graph with node set N and link set L. In order to evaluate the quality of routes between the network nodes, a positive cost $c(l)$ is associated with every link $l \in L$. In this paper it is assumed that costs are equal on both directions of a link.

An instance of a *multiple destination routing* (MDR) *problem* consists of a graph (N, L), a *source* node $s \in N$ and a set of *destination* nodes $D \subset N$, with $s \in D$. If $|D| = 1$ then the problem is a *single destination routing problem* and if $|D| = |N|-1$ then the problem is a *broadcast problem*.

A *routing tree* for an MDR problem is a rooted subtree of the graph (N, L) whose root is s, that contains all of the nodes of D, and an arbitrary subset of (N - D), and whose leaf set consists only of a subset of nodes of D. The intuitive interpretation of a routing tree or "routing" is that node s sends a copy of the message (to be sent to D) to each son of s in the tree. These sons in turn transmit the message to their sons until all nodes in the tree (and thus all nodes in D) have received the message.

The *network cost* (NC) of a routing R is defined by:

$$NC(R) = \sum_{l \in R} c(l) \qquad (1)$$

Thus, NC(R) is the weighted sum of the links of R, weighted by the cost of each link. An (NC) *optimal routing algorithm* is one that given N, L, s, D and cost function c produces the R that minimizes NC.

The *destination cost* (DC) of R is defined by:

$$DC(R) = \frac{1}{|D|} \left[\sum_{d \in D} \sum_{l \in p(d)} c(l) \right] \qquad (2)$$

where p(d) is the path in R from s to d. If $c(l)$ were the delay of l, then DC(R) would represent the average delay experienced by the destinations. A third measure that is sometimes of interest is:

$$DC_{MAX}(R) = \max_{d \in D} \sum_{l \in p(d)} c(l) \qquad (3)$$

DC is minimized if the message to every $d \in D$ is sent on the shortest path betwen s and D, and thus DC may be minimized by any standard shortest path algorithm [1]. On the other hand, minimizing NC is equivalent to finding a minimal Steiner tree and thus is NP complete [2].

The MDR problem has been discussed briefly by Dalal [3] MCQuillan [4] and in detail by Wall [5]. Wall considers heuristic algorithms for minimizing NC as well as DC. In minimizing NC, he focuses on constructing a routing tree in a distributed environment.

Due to the application environment of file distribution that we envision, in this paper, we emphasize NC optimization rather than DC optimization. First of all, the transfer of large file consumes a great deal of network resources placing a premium on any algorithm that reduces this utilization. Secondly, in such a "batch" transfer, the actual delay in transferring a file to the destinations is relatively unimportant.

In an attempt to understand the differences between the two measures, Section 2 of this paper investigates using DC optimum path as an approximation for NC optimization. If there are m destinations then the optimal DC path may be m times worse in NC than that of the optimal NC path.

In Sections 3 and 4, several heuristic algorithms for optimizing NC are proposed and their worst case behavior is examined. Section 3 focuses on algorithms that require essentially "global" information at the source; specifically, the shortest distances between the source and destination nodes as well as between all destination nodes. The main heuristic is based on minimum spanning tree (MST) construction. The MST has the best worst case behavior among all the heuristics - it is at most twice worse in cost than the optimal NC. Section 4 presents heuristics that do not have as good worst case behavior as MST but use only "local" information (i.e., shortest paths from source to destinations) and are thus more appropriate to a distributed environment. The heuristics are modifications of optimal DC routing algorithms.

Section 5 returns to the question of trading off NC versus DC by examining a class of algorithms that permit one to approximate optimum NC performance and DC performance simultaneously. For any value of k, an algorithm is given whose DC performance is at most k times worse than optimal and whose NC performance is at most $O(m/k)$ times worse than optimal.

In terms of the practical usefulness of the heuristic algorithms, their "average" performance on some "typical" networks rather than the worst case behavior is of interest. With this in mind, Section 6 compares the average performance of the algorithms on a large set of networks. The main conclusion is that the DC minimization algorithms perform surprisingly well in terms of NC - typically only 20 percent worse than MST. Hence, given the advantages of a local information base and low computational requirements, these algorithms are very attractive in practice.

2. AN ANALYSIS OF THE COST MEASURES

In this section we compare the seemingly complementary goals of good NC and good DC performance. Intuitively, both are minimized when short trees of low cost links are used. Here, it is shown that minimizing NC and DC yield quite different results in the most extreme cases.

In the following discussion, p* denotes the NC optimal routing and p' the DC optimal routing. The analysis studies the worst case DC performance of p* and the worst case NC performance of p'.

Theorem 1. For any network N, cost function c, source s, and destination set D with $|D| = m$, and for all m,

$$\frac{NC(p')}{NC(p^*)} \leq m. \tag{4}$$

Proof. $NC(p') \leq mDC(p')$ since $NC(p')$ counts $c(l)$ for every $l \epsilon p'$ once and $mDC(p')$ counts each $c(l)$ at least once. $mDC(p') \leq mDC_{MAX}(p')$ since DC_{MAX} is the maximum cost to a destination while DC is the average cost. Finally, $mDC_{MAX}(p') \leq mNC(p^*)$ since $DC_{MAX}(p')$ is the smallest cost way of getting to the most costly destination. Since p* gets to that destination (among other things) NC (p*) must be at least $DC_{MAX}(p')$.

We will now show that the bound of Theorem 1 is tight in the sense that it is achievable in a specific instance. This implies that in the worst case, any algorithm that optimizes DC can perform very poorly (m times worse) with respect to optimizing NC. Even with this we do not rule out the possibility of using a DC optimization algorithm as an approximation for NC since, as we shall see later, on the average the difference may not be as bad as the worst case predicts.

Theorem 2. The bound of Theorem 1 is achievable. That is for any ϵ there exists a N, c, s, and D with $|D| = m$ such that

$$\frac{NC(p')}{NC(p^*)} \geq m - \epsilon.$$

Proof. Consider the m+2 node network pictured in Figure 2.1. The label on link l is $c(l)$, its cost. Routing p* consists of sending the message first to node I who then forwards it directly to each destination with $NC(p^*) = x + m$. On the other hand, in p', s sends the message directly to each destination with $NC(p') = mx$. Thus

$$\frac{NC(p')}{NC(p^*)} = \frac{mx}{x + m}.$$

As $x \to \infty$, $NC(p')/NC(p^*) \to m$.

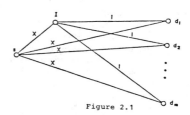

Figure 2.1

We now briefly consider the reverse problem of approximating the optimum DC routing tree with an optimum NC routing tree. While using p* as an approximation for the optimal DC routing would not be appropriate in practice, it is nevertheless interesting to understand this from the theoretical viewpoint of analyzing the intrinsic difference between the two measures. The following results can be proved [6].

Theorem 3. For any N, c, s and D with $|D| = m$, and for all m

$$\frac{DC(p^*)}{DC(p')} \leq m \tag{5}$$

Theorem 4. There exists a N, c, s, D with $|D| = m$ such that

$$\frac{DC(p^*)}{DC(p')} = \frac{(m + 1)}{2} \tag{6}$$

3. GLOBAL INFORMATION ALGORITHMS

In this section we discuss heuristics for the MDR problem which attempt to minimize NC. A common feature of these heuristics is that in order for a source node to determine the routing it requires "nearly" global network information. Specifically, the source needs to know the shortest distance between all pairs of destination nodes. This is in addition to the shortest distance from the source to all destinations, usually the basis for single destination routing. One way of having this information involves each node of the network maintaining an updated topology data base consisting of the weights of all the links of the network.

The Minimum Spanning Tree (MST) Heuristic

Here, we recall the well-known MST heuristic for the Steiner tree problem [7] and discuss its applicability in the networking environment.

Given G, s, and D, with $|D| = m$, we define the induced graph of G, I(G), to be the complete graph on $m+1$ vertices (one vertex for s and one for each $d \epsilon D$) with cost sd(i,j) associated with edge (i, j) where sd(i,j) is the shortest distance from i to j in G. The algorithm executed by s is:

    1. Gather shortest distance information to construct I(G).

    2. Determine the minimal spanning tree, T, for I(G).

    3. Route according to T as follows:

        a. For each neighbor of s in T, s sends a copy of the message. Node s includes in each message the portion of T rooted at that neighbor.

        b. Each node receiving such a message sends out copies if it is not a leaf of the tree, using the same distribution algorithm as the source.

Let NC(MST)/NC(p*) denote the worst case performance of the MST algorithm as compared to the optimal NC routing. An important result (basically from [7]) is:

Theorem 5.

$$\frac{NC(MST)}{NC(p^*)} \leq \frac{2m}{m+1} \qquad (7)$$

From the point of view of "worst case performance," MST cannot be improved for a certain class of algorithms [8]. There are, however, practical enhancements to MST that might be considered in implementing the algorithm which may result in the lowering of NC. They take advantage of the fact that MST uses only the induced graph information; additional information about the original graph G can result in savings.

One such improvement, which we refer to as *basic optimization,* recognizes that if a source node s bifurcates its routing to more than one destination (e.g. d_1 and d_2), and routes to them along the edges connecting s to them in I(G) that these edges may consist of several common links in G. For example, in Figure 3.2 both l_1 and l_2 in I(G) traverse l in G. In cases such as these, the basic optimization involves sending one copy of the message to I and then bifurcating. Thus the cost of link l need not be counted twice, saving on NC. This complicates step 4 of the MST protocol slightly, but is certainly worth it.

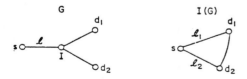

Figure 3.2

There is yet another improvement of the MST algorithm reported recently in [9]. This algorithm requires complete global information - the network topology and link weights. For additional information on the algorithm refer to [9]. Finally, we note that the heuristics for the traveling salesman problem (TSP) can be adopted to approximate optimum NC routing. An example is the "insertion" heuristic for TSP wich requires global information. For details of some of these algorithms and their worst case behavior see [6].

4. LOCAL INFORMATION ALGORITHMS

In this section we introduce a few additional algorithms for NC routing. These use *local information,* which we define to be the shortest path information from the source to all destinations (which would be usually needed for single destination routing). While the performance of these algorithms is not as good as MST, the fact that they do not require significant amounts of information makes them attractive from an implementation point of view.

The first algorithm, called the MINDC algorithm, is to choose the routing that minimizes DC, i.e., the message is sent from the source to each destination node on its shortest path routes. Clearly, this algorithm uses local information. As in Section 4.1, the *basic optimization* is employed here, too. In Section 3, it has already been shown that MINDC has performance which is m times worse than optimal.

The second algorithm that uses local information is called the nearest neighbor algorithm (NN). This is based on a traveling salesman heuristic [10]. Each node, I, that has responsibility to route to certain destinations sends the message on the shortest path to the destination nearest to I. Also, responsibility for *all* other destinations is transferred to that destination. In [10]. NN is analyzed as a TSP heuristic and is proved to have performance of at most

$$\frac{\log_2 n}{2} + 1/2$$

for n nodes. Based on this it can be shown that the performance for the optimal NC routing is bound by $\log_2 m + 1$ for m destinations [6].

5. TRADE-OFF ALGORITHMS

Due to the importance of minimizing NC and the relative simplicity of minimizing DC, the last few sections have concentrated on NC. In some environments, however, there may be a need to minimize NC and DC simultaneously. For example, assume that each link suffers roughly the same delay. Then a cost of 1 may be assigned to each link. Simultaneously keeping NC and DC small then keeps network utilization as well as average delay small. Also, in some applications the objective may be to minimize NC without exceeding a certain DC (if possible).

The obvious way to obtain better DC performance given a particularly good NC routing is to find the destination whose DC performance is degraded most by the good NC routing, and change its route. The more destinations that we do this for, the better DC will become and the worse NC will become. This statement is formalized as follows:

The following represents m different trade-off algorithm, parameterized by the variable i (i = 1, ..., m).

    1. Let p = MST routing, p' = MINDC routing.

    2. Do i times:

        a. Find $d \epsilon D$ with largest difference between the cost of getting to d in p, and the cost of getting to d in p'.

        b. Update p by replacing the path to d (or at least that portion not used by any other destinations) with the minimum DC path to d.

    3. Perform the basic optimization of Section 4.1

951

Let p(i) be the resulting routing. Clearly p(0) is the MST routing and p(m) is the MINDC routing. We now give a number of facts about p(i) which are used to demonstrate that the above is a "trade-off algorithm". Proofs of these results are detailed in [6].

Lemma 1. Let p' be the optimal DC routing, p^* the optimum NC routing. Then:

$$\frac{NC(p(i))}{NC(p^*)} \frac{DC(p(i))}{DC(p')} \le O(m). \tag{8}$$

Lemma 1 does not yet describe how to tradeoff between NC and DC. In principle, it is possible that for every i, either NC (p(i)) is bad or DC (p(i)) is bad. The following results address this issue.

Theorem 7. For any $k \ge 2$, and any G, s, D, there is an i, such that:

$$\frac{NC(p(i))}{NC(p^*)} \le k \text{ and } \frac{DC(p(i))}{DC(p')} \le \frac{4m+2}{k-1} \tag{9}$$

Corollary. For any G, s, D there is an i such that

$$\frac{NC(p(i))}{NC(p^*)} \le \sqrt{m} \text{ and } \frac{DC(p(i))}{DC(p^*)} \le O(\sqrt{m}).$$

The corollary guarantees performance within $O(\sqrt{m})$ of optimal for both measures of interest!

6. AVERAGE PERFORMANCE OF THE ALGORITHMS

From a practical viewpoint of using the optimum NC algorithms in "real" networks a more valid measure than the worst case performance is the one that captures the "average" performance of the algorithms. This section presents a comparison of the global as well as local information algorithms in terms their average behavior.

We obtain the average performances by averaging over a set of randomly generated MDR instances with a fixed number of nodes, fixed average degree (degree being the number of links attached to a node), and a fixed number of destinations. With such parameters fixed, each MDR instance is generated by randomly choosing the source and destination nodes, and using either a fixed or randomly generated network topology. Our method for randomly generating topologies starts with a ring network of a fixed number of nodes (with degree 2). We then randomly add links between node pairs (with equal probability) so that the resulting network has the desired degree. The link costs that we assign are unit costs for some experiments, and are randomly drawn from set {1,2,3,4} for others.

The performance measure we adopt indicates how each algorithm compares to th MST hueristic as follows. Running an algorithm on an instance of MDR yields a value for NC. To evaluate an algorithm, we compare its NC to the NC of the MST algorithm by computing:
NCr=(NC (MST) - NC of algorithm)/NC (MST).

The (experimental) average network cost ratio, ANCr, is the average value of NCr, averaged over a number of instances of MDR.

Another performance measure we use is the computational requirement; in our experiments, actual average computation time, ACT, for each algorithm is kept track of.

The networks considered in our experiments consist of a fixed 19 node network topology based on a early version of the ARPANET topology (Figure 2-10 in [11].) as well as three random topology networks of 19, 38 and 100 nodes. Due to space limitations we present only a subset of the results; for additional details see [6]. Specifically, Figures 6.1 and 6.2 show ANCr performance for the fixed topology 19 node network with unity link weights and unequal link weights respectively as a function of the number of destinations m. The unequal link weights are generated randomly as indicated earlier. Each point on the curve is an average of 100 instances of MDR; this is true for all the experiments reported below. Figure 6.3 shows the ACTs of the algorithms (in ms) again as a function of the number of destinations (for the unity link weight case). (ACTs for unequal link weights are essentially the same.) Figures 6.4 depicts the ANCr performance of 19 node, 2.5 degree random networks with equal link weights. Figures 6.5 depicts the ANCr performance of 38 node, 3.5 degree random networks with unequal link weights.Finally, Figure 6.6 depicts the same for 100 node, 6.5 degree random networks.

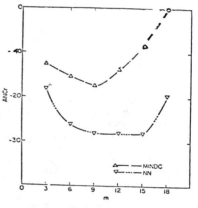

Figure 6.1

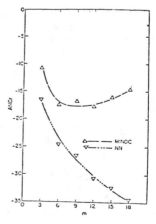

Figure 6.2

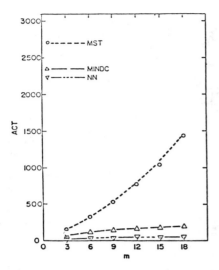

Figure 6.3

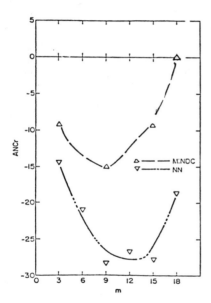

Figure 6.4

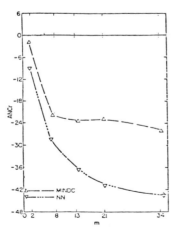

Figure 6.5

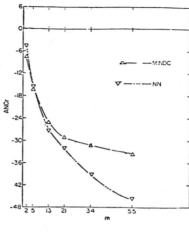

Figure 6.6

The following conclusions can be deduced from our experiments.

A: NC performance of algorithms:

MINDC's performance as compared to MST is surprisingly good particularly when we take into account the differences in the information base and computation times required for the two algorithms. To elaborate, MINDC's performance is at most 15, 20 and 30 percent worse than MST's in the 19 node, 38 node and 100 node cases, respectively. MST is favored in this comparison since we have not taken into account the cost of gathering the additional information required for MST. In terms of ACT, MST requires almost an order of magnitude additional computation (for example, see Figure 6.3).

The traveling salesman heuristic considered here performs very poorly even though their worst case performance is better than that of MINDC. Intuitively, the reason for this is as follows. The NN algorithm is based on constructing a circuit containing the source and destinations. This results in no bifurcation of the routing. Furthermore, there can be a significant amount of retracing of path particularly for a large number of destinations. Since NN and MINDC use the same information and since performance of MINDC is superior, we believe that NN is unattractive in spite of its small ACT.

B. Effect of various parameters:

By comparing Figures 6.1 and 6.2 we see that the results are approximately the same irrespective of whether the weights are all unity or chosen randomly. The exception to this is that as m approaches the total number of network nodes, *most* algorithms perform close to optimum for unity weight networks whereas this is not true for unequal weight networks.

As the size of the network grows the the ANCr of the local information algorithms becomes larger (Figures 6.2, 6.5 and 6.6). This is due to the increasing gap between local and global information.

C. Other observations:

Even though the ANCr measure does not compare the performance of the algorithms to the optimum NC, we can conclude that the average behavior of the algorithm is far better than the worst case behavior derived in the earlier sections even compared to the optimal routing. Consider, for example, the results for 19 node, 2.5 degree, equal weight random set of networks (Figure 6.4). For m=12, the optimum NC is at least 12 since the networks have unity weights. The observed average NC cost for MST turns out to be 13.7 which is at most 14 percent worse than optimal The theoretical worst case is NC=24 or 100 percent more than optimal for the MST. Further, from Figure 6.4, we observe that MINDC is only about 12 percent worse than MST. With MST being at most 14 percent worse than optimum NC, we can conclude that MINDC is at most 28 percent worse than optimum which is much better than the 1100 percent predicted by the absolute worst case.

In networks with equal link weights, most algorithms perform optimally for m=n-1 (see Figure 6.1, for example). This is because these algorithms almost always produce a routing that is a spanning tree and any spanning tree of the network is a minimum spanning tree (which is optimum for m=n-1).

REFERENCES

[1] A. V. Aho, J. E. Hopcroft, and S. D. Ullman, "The Design and Analysis of Computer Algorithms", Addison-Wesley, Reading, MA, 1974.

[2] M. R. Garey and D. S. Johnson, "Computers and Intractability: A Guide to the Theory of NP-Completeness", W. H. Freeman and Co., 1979.

[3] Y. K. Dalal, "Broadcast Protocols in Packet Switched Computer Networks", PhD thesis, Stanford, CSL Techn. Report 128, 1977.

[4] J. M. McQuillan, "Enhanced Message Addressing Capabilities for Computer Networks", IEEE Proceedings, Vol. 66, No. 11, 1978.

[5] D. W. Wall, "Mechanisms for Broadcast and Selective Broadcast", PhD thesis, Stanford, CSL techn. Report 190, 1980.

[6] K. Bharath-Kumar and J. M. Jaffe, "Routing to Multiple Destinations in Computer Networks", IBM Research Report, RC 9098, 1981.

[7] E. N. Gilbert and H. O. Pollak, "Steiner Minimal Tree", SIAM J. Appl. Math., Vol. 16, 1968.

[8] J. M. Jaffe, "Distributed Multi-destination Routing: The Constraints of Local Information", IBM Research Report, RC 9243, 1982.

[9] L. Kou, G. Markowsky, and L. Berman, "A Fast Algorithm on Steiner Trees", Acta Informatica, Vol. 15, 1981.

[10] D. J. Rosenkrantz, R. E. Stearns and P. M. Lewis II, "An Analysis of Several Heuristics for the Travelling Salesman Problem", SIAM J of Compt., Vol. 3, No. 6, 1977.

[11] M. Schwartz, "Computer Communication Network Design and Analysis", Prentice Hall, Englewood Cliffs, NJ, 1977.

K. Bharath-Kumar received his Bachelor's degree in Elecrical Engineering (1972) and Master's degree in Automation (1974) -- both at the Indian Institute of Science, India. He then joined the Electrical Engineering Department at the University of Hawaii, Honolulu, where he obtained a PhD degree in 1979. Since February '79 he has been with the IBM T.J. Watson Research Center at Yorktown Heights, New York, as a Research Staff Member. His main current interest is in the area of Computer Communication Systems.

Jeffrey Jaffe received a BS degree in Mathematics and an MS and PhD degree in Computer Science from Massachusetts Institute of Technology in 1976, 1977 and 1979 respectively. He was a National Science Foundation fellow while a graduate student. He is currently employed by IBM at the T.J. Watson Research Center where he is the Manager of the Network Architectures and Protocols Group. He is actively involved in research on network algorithms, combinatorial optimization and queueing theory applied to networks. He is a member of IEEE, ACM and Phi Beta Kappa.

954

Approximate Analysis of Priority Scheduling Disciplines in Queueing Network Models of Computer Systems

J S Kaufman
Bell Laboratories, USA

Queueing network models which can be exactly analyzed unfortunately excludes CPU priority scheduling disciplines, conspicuously present in most computer systems. A popular approximation technique which we denote the reduced occupancy approximation, is often used to analyze such priority service disciplines because of its simplicity and intuitive appeal. However, despite its widespread use, questions about its accuracy and applicability have received very little attention. In this paper we show where and more importantly why the roa fails. This understanding naturally lays the foundation for a significantly improved approximation technique. Although our primary focus is on a two class preemptive priority closed network structure, the basic idea is quite general and extensions to multiclass and nonpreemptive priority structures are indicated.

1. INTRODUCTION AND SUMMARY

Queueing network models of computer systems are widely used to evaluate a variety of relevant performance measures, such as mean response time, resource utilization and thruput. Because the present state of the art limits exact analysis primarily to the class of product form or BCMP network models [1], a large body of approximate analysis methods has accumulated to cope with currently intractable models.

Central processing unit (CPU) priority scheduling disciplines are perhaps illustrative of this trend. Commonly encountered in practice, these priority disciplines cannot be modelled within the BCMP class of networks, and hence a number of approximate techniques have been suggested and used [2-7]. The most popular and intuitively appealing of these techniques, which we denote the reduced occupancy approximation (roa), attempts to analyze preemptive resume priority disciplines. Despite its popularity and apparently wide usage [2-5], the roa has not been critically examined to determine, for example, regions of applicability. Further compounding this situation, is the existence of proprietary software packages which purport to "analyze" such preemptive resume scheduling disciplines, but which in fact exhibit behavior remarkably similar to the roa.

Motivated in part by the work of Morris [8] and Sevcik [3], we began this study to determine where the roa fails - that is can perform very poorly was appreciated by Morris, Sevcik [9] and undoubtedly other workers in the field. Our major finding is that the roa uses a structurally flawed mean service time for the fictitious "equivalent" low priority server which the roa creates to accomodate the BCMP network structure. Surprisingly, the correct mean service time for this "equivalent" low priority server has a simple characterization which holds for virtually any preemptive model - regardless of stochastic assumptions and network structure. Moreover, we conjectured that if this correct mean was folded into a modified roa (m-roa), much of the error associated with

the roa would typically be eliminated.

To "test" this conjecture we had to narrow our focus and create a test-bed priority network model in which exact results (primarily mean response times) could be obtained efficiently. Although of necessity somewhat simplistic, the test-bed priority network model adequately illustrates the significant potential for improvement conjectured.

2. The Reduced Occupancy Approximation

Consider the central server type network shown in figure 1a. The CPU has a preemptive resume priority service discipline, class 1 (high priority) and class 2 (low priority) customers have exponentially distributed service times at the CPU with mean service rates ν_1 and ν_2 respectively. N_i and ρ_i $i = 1,2$ denote the population size and CPU occupancy respectively of class i customers. The I/O subnet is as yet unspecified.

The roa technique replaces figure 1a by figure 1b, in which both high and low priority customers at the CPU now see dedicated (exponentially distributed) servers with mean service rates ν_1 and $\nu_2(1-\hat{\rho}_1)$ respectively. $\hat{\rho}_1$ is an estimate of the a-priori unknown high priority CPU occupancy. The roa network in figure 1b can be efficiently analyzed (for mean performance measures) assuming that the I/O subnet is itself a product form network. To estimate ρ_1, Sevcik [3] suggested using the fixed point of $\rho_1^a(\cdot)$ where $\rho_1^a(\alpha)$ is the high priority CPU occupancy of the roa network given that the low priority mean service rate is $\nu_2(1-\alpha)$. That is, Sevcik suggests using $\hat{\rho}_1 = \alpha_1$ where $\alpha_1 = \rho_1^a(\alpha_1)$. It is easy to plausibly argue the existence of such a fixed point, and in all examples we considered, the sequence $X_n = \rho_1^a(X_{n-1})$ $n = 1,...$ rapidly converged to α_1. Such a procedure is of course unnecessary in an open and/or mixed network where λ_1 is a given exogenous rate and ρ_1 is consequently known a-priori.

We will generally concern ourselves with the class i mean response time (mean time per job in

955

the network), denoted by $\overline{T}_1$ and $\overline{T}_1^a$ for the exact network and the roa respectively.

Clearly,

$$\overline{T}_1^a = \frac{N_1}{\alpha_1} \nu_1^{-1} \quad \text{and} \quad \overline{T}_2^a = \frac{N_2}{(1-\alpha_1)\rho_2^a(\alpha_1)} \nu_2^{-1}$$

where $\alpha_1 = \rho_1^a(\alpha_1)$ and $\rho_2^a(\alpha_1)$ is the utilization of the "equivalent" low priority server in the roa. Obviously, the mean delay and sojourn time per node by class are also easily obtained from the roa.

The roa, of course, has considerable intuitive appeal. Thus, $\nu_2(1-\rho_1)$ not only is an obvious candidate for the effective low priority service rate, but its reciprocal is perhaps a reasonable guess for the low priority mean completion time [10]. The completion time, discussed in section 3 below, arises naturally and plays a role analogous to service time in the analysis of priority queues.

We conclude this section with two examples which illustrate the use of the roa.

Example 1: Consider a "head of the line" preemptive resume single server queueing system with two priority classes as shown in figure 2a. The arrival processes are independent and Poisson and the service time distributions are exponential. The exact mean low priority sojourn time $\overline{T}_2$ is well known [10] and may be written:

$$\overline{T}_2 = \frac{\nu_2^{-1}(1-\rho) + \rho_1\nu_1^{-1} + \rho_2\nu_2^{-1}}{(1-\rho)(1-\rho_1)} \qquad (1)$$

where

ρ_i = server utilization due to class $i = \lambda_i/\nu_i$

$\rho = \rho_1 + \rho_2$

Now consider the roa approximation shown in figure 2b. In this case, the mean low priority sojourn time given by the roa is just the M/M/1 mean sojourn time:

$$\overline{T}_2^a = \frac{[\nu_2(1-\rho_1)]^{-1}}{1 - \lambda_2[\nu_2(1-\rho_1)]^{-1}} = \frac{\nu_2^{-1}}{(1-\rho)} \qquad (2)$$

If $\nu_2^{-1} = 0$, $\overline{T}_2$ is non-zero for all $\rho_1 > 0$ whereas the roa (eqn. 2) is identically zero for all ρ_1. This reflects the failure of the roa to account for the high priority busy period that often precedes a low priority completion time. Eqn. (1) can also be rewritten as

$$\overline{T}_2 = \frac{(1-\rho_1)+(\rho_1/s)}{(1-\rho_1)} \cdot \frac{\nu_2^{-1}}{(1-\rho)} \qquad (3)$$

where $s = \nu_1/\nu_2$. Note that for large s, the roa is quite accurate, but for small s (the case mentioned above) it "falls apart".

Example 2: Consider the subnetwork in figure 1a to consist of a single processor sharing node with distinct service rates ν_{01} and ν_{02}

corresponding to high and low priority customers respectively. If we let

n_i = number of class i customers at CPU (in queue and in service)

then the corresponding product form roa network shown in figure 1b has a state distribution $p(n_1,n_2)$ which can be shown to depend on the four parameters N_1,N_2,r_1,r_2, where $r_i = \nu_{0i}/\nu_i$ $i = 1,2$ [12].

Note that r_i has the interpretation: ratio of CPU utilization to I/O utilization for class i customers in the original network (figure 1a). Now

$$\rho_1^a = 1 - \sum_{n_2=0}^{N_2} p(0,n_2) \qquad (4)$$

So it is clear that the fixed point $\hat{\rho}_1 = \rho_1^a(\hat{\rho}_1)$ and all performance measures which are obtainable from $p(n_1,n_2)$ depend only on the four parameters N_1,N_2,r_1,r_2. Just as in example 1, the parameter $s = \nu_1/\nu_2$ does not appear in the roa. As we will see in section 4, the priority network whose roa we are considering in this example depends on five parameters: N_1,N_2,r_1,r_2 and s.

The failure of the roa to capture the parameter s, in both of these examples, is symptomatic of a basic underlying problem. This basic problem is the failure of the roa to capture the effective mean low priority service time and is the subject of section 3.

3. Completion and Service Position Times

The completion time (c_2), sketched in figure 3a for a preemptive resume discipline, is the period which begins the instant a low priority customer begins service, and ends the instant the server becomes free to serve the next low priority customer (if any are present) [9]. Thus, as shown in figure 3a, the completion time for a preemptive resume discipline consists of the intervals $x_{21},...,x_{2n+1}$ during which a single low priority customer receives service interlaced with high priority busy periods $b_{11},...,b_{1n}$ which interrupt the low priority customers service.

As is well known [10] the mean of c_2 for the M/G/1 HOL preemptive resume model is $[\nu_2(1-\rho)]^{-1}$, which is precisely what the roa uses as the mean service time at the dedicated low priority server. In [3], Sevcik comments that the roa's assumed exponential low priority service time distribution fails to capture the often significant variability of c_2. Although true, this is overshadowed by the failure of c_2 to capture the correct mean of the roa's dedicated low priority server.

To obtain the correct mean, we view arriving low priority customers to the preemptive priority server as if they had a dedicated server - which is, after all, the basic approximation idea. Thus, if low priority customers are ignorant of the fact that their service is being interrupted by higher priority customers, what do they _perceive_ their service time to be? For ease of exposition, we think of a fictitious service position (s.p.) which low priority customers enter and remain in (figure 3b) during their perceived service time.

As in section 2, denote the number of class 1 (2) customers at the preemptive resume node (in queue + in service) by $n_1(n_2)$ and partition all low priority arrivals into three types as follows:

type i : customer finds $n_2 > 0$ upon arrival to preemptive node

type ii : customer finds $n_2 = 0$ and $n_1 = 0$ upon arrival to preemptive node

type iii: customer finds $n_2 = 0$ and $n_1 > 0$ upon arrival to preemptive node

Type i low priority customers enter the service position (s.p.) and perceive their service to begin at the instant a low priority customer completes (actual) service and they are simultaneously selected for service. Thus type i low priority customers perceive their service time to be an ordinary completion time. Type ii customers enter the s.p. upon arrival and their perceived service time also corresponds to an ordinary completion time. Note that both type i) and ii) customers perceive their service time to begin when it actually does. In contrast, type iii) low priority customers arrive to find $n_2 = 0$ and immediately enter the s.p., perceiving their service time to begin when in fact the server is busy servicing high priority customers ($n_1 > 0$). Thus type iii customers enter and remain in the s.p. for the _forward recurrence time of the high priority busy period they encounter_ - denoted by b_f - in addition to (but before beginning) their completion time.

Thus, whereas c_2 is the correct effective low priority service time for type i and ii customers, $c_2 + b_f$ is the appropriate effective low priority service time for type iii customers.

It is obvious that the service position time $s_2 > c_2$ since

$$s_2 = \begin{cases} c_2 & \text{if low priority arrival is type i or ii} \\ c_2 + b_f & \text{if low priority arrival is type iii} \end{cases}$$

For our purposes, we are interested in the mean service position time $(\bar{s}_2)$ which fortunately has a characterization which is both simple and completely general.

Theorem 1: consider a general two class preemptive priority single server queue (shown in figure 3b) in equilibrium with arbitrary stochastic assumptions (it may be part of some general network or it may be isolated). Then

$$\bar{s}_2 = \frac{\nu_2^{-1}}{1 - p(n_1 > 0/n_2 > 0)} \qquad (5)$$

Proof: See [12] for a detailed proof. The essential idea is as follows: $\bar{s}_2 = U_2/\lambda_2$ where

U_2 = mean utilization of the "equivalent" server.

The preemptive discipline implies that $\lambda_2 = P(n_1 = 0, n_2 > 0)\nu_2$ and the low priority customers view that they have a dedicated server implies that $U_2 = P(n_2 > 0)$. Therefore we find that $\bar{s}_2 = P(n_2 > 0)\nu_2^{-1}/P(n_1 = 0, n_2 > 0)$ which together with the identity

$$P(n_2 > 0) = P(n_1 > 0, n_2 > 0) + P(n_1 = 0, n_2 > 0)$$

yields (5).

Intuitively, we expect that the events $\{n_1 > 0\}$, $\{n_2 > 0\}$ are strongly dependent when $\nu_1/\nu_2 \to 0$ and essentially independent when $\nu_1/\nu_2 \to \infty$. This implies that $\bar{s}_2$ has an indeterminate form (0/0) as $\nu_1/\nu_2 \to 0$ (it generally has a finite non-zero limit) and tends to $\nu_2^{-1}/(1-\rho_1)$ as $\nu_1/\nu_2 \to \infty$.

4. A Network Test-Bed Model

Choosing a test-bed network model from the class of models shown in figure 1a, subject to the requirement of being able to exactly and efficiently analyze it, seemed to exclude all but single I/O node networks. Further, the only service disciplines (for the I/O node) which offered much hope of success were a) preemptive priority, b) random selection, and c) processor sharing.

Choice a) has been analyzed by Morris [8], and although interesting, has the disadvantage that the high priority performance measures are independent of perturbations to the low priority service mechanism. Choice b) while a good deal more realistic as a model of I/O than c) restricts the choice of service rates. That is, if

ν_{0i} = mean service rate of class i customers at the I/O node then the corresponding roa network is product form if and only if $\nu_{01} = \nu_{02}$. The processor sharing choice (c) does not impose such a restriction and in addition, lends itself nicely to an efficient recursive solution.

Thus, our test-bed model is shown in figure 4a, with all service time distributions exponential, and with state transition diagram as shown in figure 4b. The roa for this model was briefly studied in example 2 of section 2 and as there, we define

N_i = population of class i customers

$r_i = \nu_{0i}/\nu_i$ = ratio of class i CPU utilization to I/O utilization

In addition, and unlike the roa, we must also introduce the critical parameter $s = \nu_1/\nu_2$. The Markovian global balance equations defining the state distribution $p(n_1, n_2)$ for this test-bed model are easily written and involve the five parameters: (N_i, r_i) i = 1,2 and s.

Solving the resulting linear system of equations which define $p(n_1, n_2)$ for large N_1 and/or N_2

was rejected for obvious (cardinality) reasons, and standard interation methods were also ruled out. A method for reducing the dimensionality to N_1(or N_2) due to Herzog, Woo and Chandy [11], and in spirit identical to the analytical method used by Morris [8] was briefly considered, before we developed a purely recursive (and hence very efficient) scheme described in [12].

We note as an aside that our recursive scheme applies directly to two other previously studied priority network models which have identical state transition diagrams to the test-bed model (although some transition rates are different). The first is a priority queueing network model discussed by Chow and Yu [6] whose analysis boils down to analyzing a preemptive priority node with state dependent arrival rates and exponential service times. The second is a model considered by Sevcik [9] and discussed in [12], in which both customer classes are generated by distinct finite sources.

In the following section, we use the recursion developed in [12], to compare and contrast the roa and the modified roa with the exact (mean response times) for several test-bed examples. We will be primarily interested in the mean time spent in system for a class i customer, and for convenience we normalize by the mean work incurred by a class i job $\left(\nu_i^{-1} + \nu_{oi}^{-1} \right)$ while in system.

5. Network Examples and General Observations

Using a variety of test-bed network examples, we contrast the roa with the exact results obtained as described in section 4. Each example also illustrates the potential for improvement by showing the modified roa (m-roa) in which the exact value of $\bar{s}_2/\nu_2^{-1}$ is used.

As discussed earlier, we focus on mean response time (time in system) normalized by the mean work required. Each figure referred to in the examples, includes a table contrasting $\bar{c}_2(roa)/\nu_2^{-1}$ with $\bar{s}_2/\nu_2^{-1}$ which is useful in explaining the trends observed.

Example 1: (figure 5) High and low priority customers have equal mean CPU service times (s=1) and are both perfectly balanced between CPU and I/O ($r_1=r_2=1$). The exact and m-roa high priority response times are indistinguishable, and the high priority roa response time is also an excellent approximation. The low priority roa response time poorly approximates the exact result, with the m-roa offering significant improvement.

Example 2: (figure 6) The CPU/I/O balance of both high and low priority customers in example 1 has been disrupted: both low priority and high priority customers bottleneck at the I/O for $N_2 > 2$. High priority response time comparisons are similar to example 1. The low priority roa varies from very poor (N_2=1) to very good (N_2=6). The improved low priority roa behavior for large N_2 is primarily due to the fact that most of the low priority delay occurs at the I/O. The low priority m-roa is uniformly better than the roa, and dramatically so when the low priority multiprogramming

degree is small.

Example 3: (figure 7) All parameters except for s are as in example 2. The high priority mean service time at the CPU is now ten times larger than the low priority (s=0.1). The low priority roa is extremely poor, especially at lower (low priority) multiprogramming degrees. The m-roa is uniformly and significantly better than the roa, reducing the low priority relative error to the range 10 - 20 percent. Note that the high priority roa also exhibits significant error which the m-roa reduces.

Example 4: (figure 8) High and low priority customers are balanced between CPU and I/O (as in example 1) and have equal mean service times at the CPU (s=1.0). Low priority multiprogramming varies from 2 to 12. The low priority roa is extremely poor - it approximates the exact high priority result far better than the low priority result! In contrast, the m-roa low priority result does a fine job, with a relative error of 3 - 4 percent. In contrast to the low priority approximation, the high priority roa (and m-roa) is indistinguishable from the exact result.

Example 5: (figure 9) This example is identical to example 4, except for low priority mean service times which are now ten times larger than high priority (s=10.0). Conclusions drawn are the same as in example 4. Note that the roa, being independent of the parameter s, yields results identical to example 4. The low priority m-roa essentially eliminates the significant roa error.

General Observations

a) The low priority roa is typically very poor consistently and significantly underestimating mean response time. This failure of the roa is primarily due to the use of $\bar{c}_2$(roa) as the mean low priority service time. Thus, as the tables associated with each example show, the correct effective low priority mean service time $\bar{s}_2$ is often hundreds of percent larger than $\bar{c}_2$(roa).

b) The high priority roa is typically quite good.
This is not surprising since incorrect "interference" at I/O - due to the low priority customers there - is the only source of high priority roa error. Thus when N_2 is small, this error must be small. When N_2 is large, the population of low priority customers at I/O (and therefore the potential for interference) is larger - but $\bar{c}_2$(roa) is more nearly the correct low priority mean service time, and hence the resulting I/O interference is more nearly correct.

c) The potential for improvement demonstrated by the m-roa is very significant.
Thus by using the correct effective low priority mean service time, the low priority mean response time approximation improves - often dramatically - and simultaneously also improves the high priority approximation.

d) The residual error in the low priority m-roa can largely be explained by two effects

i) variability error - the random variable s_2 is generally nonexponential, and in fact often has a coefficient of variation much greater than 1. Failure to model this variability in the m-roa accounts for part of the residual error observed. It is important to note however that when $N_2 = 1$ (examples 4 and 5 for example), this type of error is not present, since queueing at the "equivalent" low priority server cannot occur. The second type of error (which is responsible for all the m-roa error in examples 4 and 5) is due to a synchronization effect.

ii) synchronization error - a low priority customer departing the CPU preemptive priority server in any network depicted in figure 1a) will find all high priority customers in the I/O subnetwork. Both the roa and m-roa fail to capture this synchronization phenomenon and this helps to explain why the m-roa low priority mean response time underestimates the exact result in the test-bed network examples just presented. Clearly, this effect is most noticeable when the I/O subnet consists of a single node (common to both high and low priority customers) - as in our test-bed network.

Additional Comments

a) The two node priority network analyzed by Morris [8] and referred to earlier has also been used to evaluate the m-roa [12]. Conclusions reached are entirely consistent with those presented here.

b) Commercial software packages exist which approximately analyze the mean response time for networks such as that in figure 1. One of the more popular of these is "Best 1", marketed by BGS Systems (Boston) as a tool for the Performance Prediction of Computer Systems. The "Best 1" approximation is shown in figures 5-9 and often cannot be distinguished from the roa. It also shares the roa liability of being independent of the parameter $s = \nu_1/\nu_2$ (illustrated in figures 8 and 9). Thus by appropriate choice of s, Best 1 can do very well (contrived in figure 9) or very poorly (in figure 8). Note that the m-roa tracks the changing exact mean low priority response time closely.

6. Generalizations and Concluding Remarks

It can be shown that our results generalize to multiple classes and non-preemptive priority disciplines [12]. Thus consider the CPU in the model shown in figure 1a) to consist of $K \geq 2$ priority classes with class i having preemptive priority over classes $i + 1,...,K$. Let $\overline{s}_i$ and $\overline{\nu}_i$ denote the mean service position time and the mean service rate respectively for a class i customer. The following results generalize theorem 1 of section 3.

Theorem 2: The mean service position time for class i customers $i = 2,...,K$ at a K class preemptive priority single server facility in equilibrium, is given by

$$\overline{s}_i = \frac{\nu_i^{-1}}{1 - P(m_i > 0/n_i > 0)} \qquad (6)$$

where $m_i = n_1 + ... + n_{i-1}$ $i = 2,...,K$ and as before $n_j = $ # of class j customers at the facility (in queue + in service) at a random point in time.

Theorem 3: The mean service position time for a class i customer $i = 1,...,k$ at a K class nonpreemptive priority single server facility in equilibrium, is given by

$$\overline{s}_i = \frac{\nu_i^{-1}}{1 - p\left(n_i^c > 0, x \neq i/n_i > 0\right)} \qquad (7)$$

where x = class of customer currently in service and

$$n_i^c = \sum_{j \neq i} n_j$$

By suitably approximating the effective mean service position times ($\overline{s}_i$), the roa can be modified to produce an approximation which realizes much of the potential demonstrated in this paper. The resulting effective service approximation is uniformly better than the reduced occupancy approximation and is described in detail in [12].

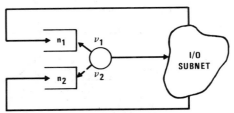

FIGURE 1a) A CENTRAL SERVER NETWORK WITH PREEMPTIVE PRIORITY CPU SCHEDULING

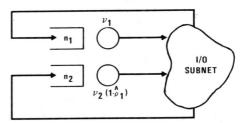

FIGURE 1b) THE REDUCED OCCUPANCY APPROXIMATION

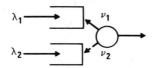

FIGURE 2a) A HOL PREEMPTIVE PRIORITY NODE

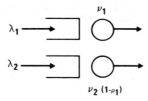

FIGURE 2b) THE REDUCED OCCUPANCY APPROXIMATION

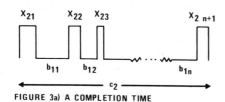

FIGURE 3a) A COMPLETION TIME

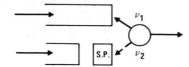

FIGURE 3b) AN ARBITRARY PREEMPTIVE PRIORITY
FACILITY WITH A FICTITIOUS
"SERVICE POSITION"

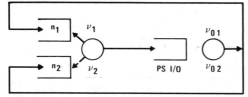

FIGURE 4a) THE TEST-BED MODEL

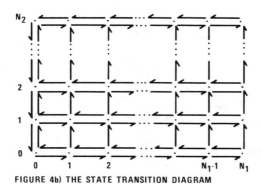

FIGURE 4b) THE STATE TRANSITION DIAGRAM
FOR THE TEST-BED MODEL

MEAN RESPONSE TIME/MEAN WORKLOAD s=1.0, r_1=1.0, r_2=1.0, N_1=3

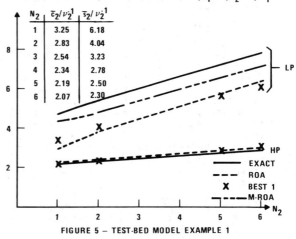

N_2	$\bar{c}_2/\nu_2^{-1}$	$\bar{s}_2/\nu_2^{-1}$
1	3.25	6.18
2	2.83	4.04
3	2.54	3.23
4	2.34	2.78
5	2.19	2.50
6	2.07	2.30

EXACT
ROA
BEST 1
M-ROA

FIGURE 5 — TEST-BED MODEL EXAMPLE 1

MEAN RESPONSE TIME/MEAN WORKLOAD s=1.0, r_1=1.5, r_2=0.2, N_1=3

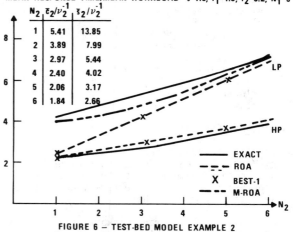

N_2	$\bar{c}_2/\nu_2^{-1}$	$\bar{s}_2/\nu_2^{-1}$
1	5.41	13.85
2	3.89	7.99
3	2.97	5.44
4	2.40	4.02
5	2.06	3.17
6	1.84	2.66

EXACT
ROA
BEST-1
M-ROA

FIGURE 6 — TEST-BED MODEL EXAMPLE 2

MEAN RESPONSE TIME/MEAN WORKLOAD s=0.1, r_1=1.5, r_2=0.2, N_1=3

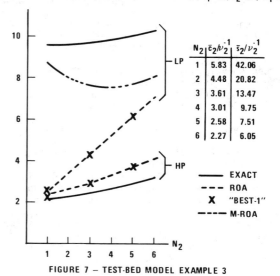

N_2	$\bar{c}_2/\nu_2^{-1}$	$\bar{s}_2/\nu_2^{-1}$
1	5.83	42.06
2	4.48	20.82
3	3.61	13.47
4	3.01	9.75
5	2.58	7.51
6	2.27	6.05

EXACT
ROA
"BEST-1"
M-ROA

FIGURE 7 — TEST-BED MODEL EXAMPLE 3

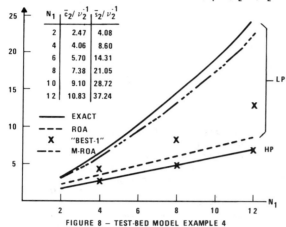

MEAN RESPONSE TIME/MEAN WORKLOAD   s=1.0, r₁=1.0, r₂=1.0, N₂=1

N_1	$\bar{c}_2/\nu_2^{-1}$	$\bar{s}_2/\nu_2^{-1}$
2	2.47	4.08
4	4.06	8.60
6	5.70	14.31
8	7.38	21.05
10	9.10	28.72
12	10.83	37.24

——— EXACT
----- ROA
X "BEST-1"
– – – M-ROA

FIGURE 8 — TEST-BED MODEL EXAMPLE 4

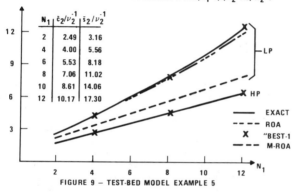

MEAN RESPONSE TIME/MEAN WORKLOAD s=10.0, r₁=1,0, r₂=1.0, N₂=1

N_1	$\bar{c}_2/\nu_2^{-1}$	$\bar{s}_2/\nu_2^{-1}$
2	2.49	3.16
4	4.00	5.56
6	5.53	8.18
8	7.06	11.02
10	8.61	14.06
12	10.17	17.30

——— EXACT
----- ROA
X "BEST-1"
– – – M-ROA

FIGURE 9 — TEST-BED MODEL EXAMPLE 5

REFERENCES

[1] Baskett, F., Chandy, K. M., Muntz, R. R. and Palacjos, F. G., "Open, Closed, and Mixed Networks of Queues with Different Classes of Customers," Journal of ACM, Vol, 22, April 1975, 248-260.

[2] Reiser, M., "Interactive Modeling of Computer Systems," IBM Systems Journal, No. 4, 1976, 309-327.

[3] Sevcik, K. C., "Priority Scheduling Disciplines in Queueing Network Models of Computer Systems," Information Processing 77, Gilchrist, B., ed., IFIP, North Holland Publishing Co., 1977.

[4] Reiser, M., "A Queueing Network Analysis of Computer Communication Networks with Window Flow Control," IEEE Trans. on Comm., Vol. COM-27, No. 8, August 1979, 1199-1209.

[5] Seaman, H., "Modeling Considerations for Predicting Performance of CICS/WS Systems," IBM Systems Journal, No. 1, 1980, 68-80.

[6] Chow, W., Yu, P. S., "An Approximation Technique for Central Server Queueing Models with a Priority Dispatching Rule," IBM Watson Research Center Research Report, RC 8163, March 17, 1980.

[7] Dowling, C. B., Uspenski, A., "Approximation Method for Closed Loop Model with Priority Discipline at CPU," 13th Asilumer Conference on Circuits, Systems and Computers, 1980.

[8] Morris, R. J. T., "Priority Queueing Networks," Bell System Technical Journal, Vol. 60, No. 8, Oct. 1981.

[9] Sevcik, K. C., Personal Communication.

[10] Jaiswal, N. K., "Priority Queues," Academic Press, New York, 1968.

[11] Herzog, O., Woo, L., Chandy, K. M., "Solution of Queueing Problems by a Recursive Technique," IBM J. Res. Develop., May, 1975.

[12] Kaufman, J. S., "Approximation Methods for Networks of Queues with Priorities," Submitted for publication to Performance Evaluation.

JOSEPH S. KAUFMAN, B.E.E., 1965, Pratt Institute; M.S.E.E., 1966 and Ph.D., 1970 (computer, information, and control engineering), University of Michigan; Assistant Professor of Electrical Engineering and Computer Science, Columbia University 1971-1973; Bell Laboratories, 1973-1979, 1980- ; Visiting Scientist with the Computer Science Department, Technion-Israel Institute of Technology during the '79-'80 academic year. Since joining Bell Laboratories, he has been involved with the modelling and analysis of teletraffic and computer systems.

The Use of Distributed Topology Databases for Network Routing

C L Doss II, T D Smetanka
IBM, USA

A unique centralized node (as in TYMNET), a group of locally centralized nodes, or every node (as in ARPANET) in the network can contain the topology databases required for route generation. In large networks, it may become undesirable to maintain network topology information in either a centralized database within one node or distributed among all nodes. The introduction of locally centralized network topology database nodes (henceforth known as LOCTOD nodes) is useful in minimizing the network topology database size in any one node. When an origin node wishes to establish a session with a destination node which is not in the origin's topology database, the origin will query all adjacent LOCTOD nodes. These LOCTOD nodes will in turn query other LOCTOD nodes to obtain topology information pertaining to the destination node.

INTRODUCTION

Many current data communication networks are founded upon statically defined routing tables. Static routing tables are simpler to implement and in many cases require less storage as compared to dynamic tables. On the other hand, dynamic routing tables are preferable in networks which change over time. The dynamic tables are responsive to the network changes by allowing the addition and deletion of network nodes and links to be reflected in the route determination algorithm. Pertinent link or node characteristic changes may also instigate updates to routing tables.

Both ARPANET and TYMNET make use of dynamic routing. One supervisory node contains the entire network topology and performs the shortest path routing algorithm in TYMNET[1][2]. In very large networks (Tymes[1] considers at least 5000 nodes as a requirement for a large TYMNET II network), a single centralized supervisor may not be practical. On the other hand, in ARPANET the network topology and shortest path algorithm are distributed among every node[3]. MERIT (a network intended to connect many of the state of Michigan's (USA) universities) also maintains the topology and shortest path algorithm at each node in the network[4]. This paper considers distributing the topology supervisory function among several network nodes. Each node within the network will determine the optimal route and instigate session (i.e., virtual circuit) establishment.

Many algorithms regarding optimal network path derivation have been discussed in the literature and will not be further discussed here[5][6].

ROUTING TABLE DEFINITION

Figure 1 depicts a typical transcontinental data communications network. Nodes are represented numerically while logical links (including those containing more than one physical link) are depicted alphabetically. For example, assume the current path from Philadelphia to Brussels traverses nodes 3, 2, 7, 8, and 9. A path has the property of being bi-directional. If a new logical link (l-link) is added between nodes 4 (Washington, D.C.) and 10 (Paris), routing tables in nodes 3 (Philadelphia), 4, 10, and 9 (Brussels) would be impacted if such a path is now to be used. See Figure 2. Other nodes desiring the new l-link may also be affected.

The contents of the routing table in each network node is independent of the type of routing (i.e., static or dynamic). The information in the table includes the next l-link to transmit the data over and the status of the route (e.g., inactive, pending-active, or active). The routing table is indexed by origin node, destination node, and route identification.

$$f(origin, destination, Rt\ ID) \rightarrow (next\ l\text{-}link, route\ status)$$

The route identification allows for more than one path between the origin and destination nodes. For example, interactive transactions may desire a separate path as compared to batch transactions between the same nodes. IBM's Systems Network Architecture (SNA) ACF Release 3 requires similar routing tables in various nodes. The SNA ACF Release 3 implementation is slightly different in that destination routing (source independence) is used rather than source-destination routing[7].

The routing tables in the network defined previously in Figure 1 are shown in Figure 3. A message to be transmitted from Philadelphia to Brussels (on Route ID 4 traversing nodes 3, 2, 7, 8, and 9) indexes the following table entries:

1. In the origin node (node 3), f(3, 9, 4) -> (c, active)

2. In node 2, f(3, 9, 4) -> (h, active)

3. In node 7, f(3, 9, 4) -> (i, active)

4. In node 8, f(3, 9, 4) -> (j, active)

5. In node 9, f(3, 9, 4) -> (*)

The destination node is represented by *. Figure 4 highlights the changes in the routing tables for the addition of 1-link o between nodes 4 and 10. Since the new 1-link (Route ID 6) is a more desirable route between Philadelphia and Brussels, a data packet transmitted between these two nodes indexes the following table entries:

1. In the origin node (node 3), f(3, 9, 6) -> (d, active)

2. In node 4, f(3, 9, 6) -> (o, active)

3. In node 10, f(3, 9, 6) -> (m, active)

4. In node 9, f(3, 9, 6) -> (*)

In adding one 1-link, the routing tables in four of the eleven nodes are altered to reflect the route between Philadelphia and Brussels with Route ID 6 as shown in Figure 4.

DYNAMIC ROUTING

In one dynamic routing approach, each node requires knowledge of network topology, not just the information pertaining to routes passing through the node. Two techniques for obtaining the network topology follow. The first involves the initial definition and generation of the network topology at each node. Once the nodes are initialized, changes to the network topology will be conveyed via a Link Alter data packet being propagated through the network. The second alternative is to use the Link Alter packet exclusively to build the network topology database. This technique does not require an initial network definition at each node within the network. As stated earlier, LINK ALTER may also be used to update topology databases when 1-link characteristics (e.g., performance, security, etc.) change. In TYMNET, a packet similar to LINK ALTER is transmitted to the supervisory node any time the network capabilities change[1]. Similarly, in ARPANET[3] a "routing update" is periodically sent to all other nodes while in MERIT NETCHANGE messages[4] are transmitted as nodes or links are brought on-line or taken off-line.

Figure 5 illustrates how topology information can be distributed for nodes between Philadelphia and Brussels. Similar packets are sent involving the other nodes depicted in Figure 1, but are not shown in Figure 5. At 1-link bring up time, each adjacent node to the nodes bringing up the 1-link is notified of the new 1-link via the Link Alter packet. This Link Alter packet will then be propagated to other connecting nodes. In the example, when the 1-link between Philadelphia and New York is brought up, no Link Alter packets can be propagated as there are no currently connected adjacent nodes to either Philadelphia or New York. A Link Alter packet is not needed between Philadelphia and New York since all required information is passed during 1-link bring up. On the other hand, when the 1-link between Amsterdam and Brussels is brought up, a Link Alter packet is sent from Amsterdam to London since these two nodes are already connected via 1-link i. The Link Alter data packet contains the 1-link identification of the 1-link that is activated, the two nodes which are connected via this 1-link, along with the properties of the 1-link. These properties can include bandwidth (e.g., 4800 BPS, 9600 BPS, etc.), delay (e.g., propagation + modem transit), reliability and security characteristics. An instance of propagation is shown when the 1-link between New York and London is brought up. Here the Link Alter packet is sent to Amsterdam and propagated to Brussels. Similarly, a Link Alter packet corresponding to the 1-link from Philadelphia to New York is transmitted to London with further propagation to Amsterdam and Brussels. To prevent looping of the LINK ALTER packet, if a LINK ALTER packet is received by a node which has previously transmitted or propagated this packet, then this packet is discarded. Notice that each node's network topology database contains information regarding all other network nodes (see Figure 6). The entries in the topology database are represented as (node, 1-link to adjacent node, adjacent node). A second dynamic routing approach is that of the Locally Centralized Network Topology Database technique.

LOCALLY CENTRALIZED NETWORK TOPOLOGY DATABASE TECHNIQUE

The Locally Centralized Network Topology Database (henceforth known as LOCTOD) technique decreases the routing table storage requirements. Every node is not required to maintain the total network topology information as previously depicted in Figure 6 (see Figure 8). For example, if New York and Amsterdam are LOCTOD nodes, then Philadelphia only records topological information pertaining to Washington, D.C., Atlanta, Miami, and New York. In a similar fashion to Figure 5, Figure 7 shows topological information distribution for the Locally Centralized Topology Database approach. The difference between the flows in Figure 5 and Figure 7 is that when a Link Alter is received at a LOCTOD node, it is not propagated. Philadelphia's network topology database contains no information pertaining to Cleveland or the European nodes. The Link

Bring Up and Link Access packets contain information regarding LOCTOD nodes. Thus, after the Link Bring Up packet is transmitted between Philadelphia and New York, Philadelphia recognizes New York as a LOCTOD node.

In order for Philadelphia to be able to transmit data to Brussels, a route must be established between these two nodes. Since Philadelphia's topology database does not contain information regarding the Brussels node, Philadelphia queries the adjacent LOCTOD nodes (i.e., New York) to obtain data regarding routes to Brussels. This query is shown in Figure 9 as the Request Topology Information packet. Similarly, the Request Topology Information packet is then sent to all other LOCTOD nodes in the network (i.e., Amsterdam) in order to obtain topology data of routes among Philadelphia and Brussels. A Request Topology Information packet is not propagated to an adjacent LOCTOD node if the adjacent LOCTOD node was previously queried via this Request Topology Information packet. It should be noted that if the origin node's topology database contains information regarding the destination node, then querying adjacent LOCTOD nodes is not required. In this case, performance is improved by eliminating the Request Topology Information packet flows at the expense of not being capable of using routes which pass through more than one LOCTOD node to the destination node.

The Topology Information Reply contains information in regards to the topology of the destination node obtained from the LOCTOD nodes' topology databases. A given LOCTOD node waits for replies to all outstanding Request Topology Information packets sent as a result of this nodes receiving a Request Topology Information packet before returning its reply to the received Request Topology Information packet. Numerous techniques for determining "loss of Request Topology Information packet" are possible (e.g., timeout, node or 1-link inoperative packet, etc.). If such a loss occurs, it is treated as if the destination LOCTOD node does not exist and only topology information from other adjacent LOCTOD nodes is propagated to the originating node. Therefore, a less than optimal route may be chosen by the origin. Information in the Topology Information Reply includes the route's nodes, 1-links traversed, and the properties associated with the 1-links (Figures 9 and 10 do not depict properties). Note that this information may be included in the end node's topology database, but this is not a requirement. In Figure 9, the Amsterdam LOCTOD node returns information regarding the topology of Brussels in respect to Amsterdam. The New York LOCTOD node appends data describing the topology of Amsterdam in respect to New York and transmits this information to Philadelphia. Upon receipt of Topology Information Reply, Philadelphia constructs the Route Setup packet containing data from the reply. Route Setup is required in order to establish the desired route chosen via the route generator algorithm using the topology data received in the Topology Information Reply packets. Route Setup is propagated along the path to Brussels. This is analogous to the "needle" in TYMNET II[1]

and ER_SETUP as proposed by K. Bharath-Kumar, et. al.[8] Each node records the origin node (Philadelphia), destination node (Brussels), route identification, and the corresponding mapping to next 1-link and route status in the routing table (see Figure 3).

The dynamic routing approach allows the addition of 1-links into the network. A 1-link is added to Figure 1 between Washington, D.C. and Paris as seen in Figure 2. In order to reduce the local topology database size, New York, Washington, D.C., Amsterdam, and Paris are defined as LOCTOD nodes. Link bring up for 1-link o between Washington, D.C. and Paris will not cause any Link Alter packets to be propagated into the rest of the network since both Washington, D.C. and Paris are LOCTOD nodes.

Route set up will include the new 1-link, o, in determining which is the optimal route from Philadelphia to Brussels. When Philadelphia wants to establish a route to Brussels, Philadelphia will send a Request Topology Information data packet to its adjacent LOCTOD nodes (i.e., New York and Washington, D.C.). The Request Topology Information sent to New York will function as previously shown in flows 1-4 of Figure 9 except that the topology of 8,k,10; 8,l,11; 9,m,10; and 10,n,11 is obtained as a result of the Amsterdam LOCTOD node querying the Paris LOCTOD node. The topology representation is a list of entries of (node, 1-link to adjacent node, adjacent node). Flows 1-8 of Figure 10 illustrate how the Request Topology Information packet sent to Washington, D.C. is processed by the network. Philadelphia will wait on the Topology Information Reply packets from both New York and Washington, D.C. before determining the optimal route to Brussels. When both replies have been received, Philadelphia determines the optimal route to be that traversing nodes 3, 4, 10, and 9. A Route Setup packet is sent along the optimal route which includes 1-link o as one of the 1-links in the route.

CONCLUSION

The first dynamic routing approach presented required each node to maintain knowledge of the entire network topology. In networks consisting of many nodes, such knowledge may require large databases. Thus, the Locally Centralized Network Topology Database (LOCTOD) dynamic routing technique is proposed. In LOCTOD, each node only maintains the topology of a neighborhood of the node. The neighborhood includes only a subset of the entire network topology. This clustering of nodes into a neighborhood reduces the topology information packet flow (i.e., Link Alter) as seen in Figure 5 and Figure 7. The Locally Centralized Network Topology Database dynamic routing technique maintains distributed topology databases while decreasing storage requirements for these databases. This is as a result of each node only maintaining topology information in regards to a neighborhood which is a subset of the entire network.

ACKNOWLEDGMENT

The authors are grateful to F. Brice, N. Cowder, F. George, R. Hayward, J. Jaffe, R. May, F. Moss, D. Pozefsky, J. Rusnak, B. Smith, and R. Weingarten for their various contributions.

REFERENCES

1. La Roy W. Tymes, "Routing and Flow Control in TYMNET," IEEE Trans. Commun., Vol. COM-29, No. 4, 392-398, April 1981.

2. A. Rajaraman, "Routing in TYMNET," presented at the European Computing Conference, London, England, May 1978.

3. J. M. McQuillan, "New Routing Algorithm for the ARPANET," IEEE Trans. Commun., Vol. COM-28, No. 5, 711-719, May 1980.

4. W. D. Tajibnapis, "A Correctness Proof of a Topology Information Maintenance Protocol for a Distributed Computer Network," Commun. of the ACM, Vol. 20, No. 7, 477-485, July 1977.

5. D. Bertsekas, "Dynamic Models of Shortest Path Routing Algorithms for Communication Networks with Multiple Destinations," Proceedings of the 1979 IEEE Conference on Decision and Control, Fort Lauderdale, Florida, December 1979.

6. E. W. Dijkstra, "A Note on Two Problems in Connexion with Graphs," Numerische Mathematik 1, 269-271, 1959.

7. V. Ahuja, "Routing and Flow Control in Systems Network Architecture," IBM Syst. J., Vol. 18, No. 2, 298-314, 1979.

8. K. Bharath-Kumar, J. M. Jaffe, and F. H. Moss, "Method for Dynamic Distributed Generation of Explicit Routes," IBM Technical Disclosure Bulletin, Vol. 24, No. 10, 4974-4978, March 1982.

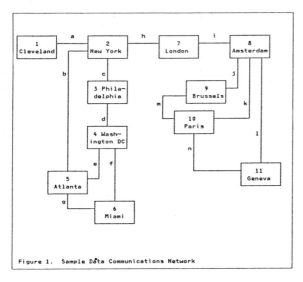

Figure 1. Sample Data Communications Network

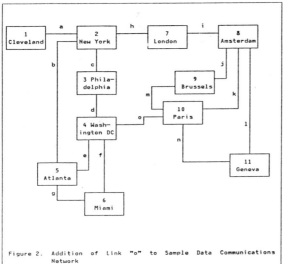

Figure 2. Addition of Link "o" to Sample Data Communications Network

Figure 3. Routing Tables of Sample Network

```
Node 1 (Cleveland)
    f( 1, 10,  3) --> (a, active)      f(10,  1,  3) --> (x, active)
Node 2 (New York)
    f( 1, 10,  3) --> (h, active)      f(10,  1,  3) --> (a, active)
    f( 2,  4,  1) --> (c, active)      f( 4,  2,  1) --> (x, active)
    f( 2, 11,  2) --> (h, active)      f(11,  2,  1) --> (x, active)
    f( 3,  9,  4) --> (h, active)      f( 9,  3,  4) --> (c, active)
    f( 6,  9,  1) --> (h, active)      f( 9,  6,  1) --> (b, active)
Node 3 (Philadelphia)
    f( 2,  4,  1) --> (d, active)      f( 4,  2,  1) --> (c, active)
    f( 3,  9,  4) --> (c, active)      f( 9,  3,  4) --> (x, active)
    f( 3,  9,  6) --> (d, active)      f( 9,  3,  6) --> (x, active)
Node 4 (Washington, D.C.)
    f( 2,  4,  1) --> (x, active)      f( 4,  2,  1) --> (d, active)
    f( 3,  9   6) --> (o, active)      f( 9,  3,  6) --> (d, active)
Node 5 (Atlanta)
    f( 6,  9,  1) --> (b, active)      f( 9,  6,  1) --> (g, active)
Node 6 (Miami)
    f( 6,  9,  1) --> (g, active)      f( 9,  6,  1) --> (x, active)
Node 7 (London)
    f( 1, 10,  3) --> (i, active)      f(10,  1,  3) --> (h, active)
    f( 2, 11,  2) --> (i, active)      f(11,  2,  2) --> (h, active)
    f( 3,  9,  4) --> (i, active)      f( 9,  3,  4) --> (h, active)
    f( 6,  9,  1) --> (i, active)      f( 9,  6,  1) --> (h, active)
Node 8 (Amsterdam)
    f( 1, 10,  3) --> (k, active)      f(10,  1,  3) --> (i, active)
    f( 2, 11,  2) --> (j, active)      f(11,  2,  2) --> (i, active)
    f( 3,  9,  4) --> (j, active)      f( 9,  3,  4) --> (i, active)
    f( 6,  9,  1) --> (j, active)      f( 9,  6,  1) --> (i, active)
    f( 9, 11,  1) --> (l, active)      f(11,  9,  1) --> (j, active)
Node 9 (Brussels)
    f( 6,  9,  1) --> (x, active)      f( 9,  6,  1) --> (j, active)
    f( 3,  9,  4) --> (x, active)      f( 9,  3,  4) --> (j, active)
    f( 3,  9,  6) --> (x, active)      f( 9,  3,  6) --> (m, active)
    f( 9, 11,  1) --> (j, active)      f(11,  9,  1) --> (x, active)
    f( 9, 11,  2) --> (m, active)      f(11,  9,  2) --> (x, active)
Node 10 (Paris)
    f( 1, 10,  3) --> (x, active)      f(10,  1,  3) --> (k, active)
    f( 3,  9,  6) --> (m, active)      f( 9,  3,  6) --> (o, active)
    f( 9, 11,  2) --> (n, active)      f(11,  9,  2) --> (m, active)
Node 11 (Geneva)
    f( 2, 11,  2) --> (x, active)      f(11,  2,  2) --> (l, active)
    f( 9, 11,  1) --> (x, active)      f(11,  9,  1) --> (l, active)
    f( 9, 11,  2) --> (x, active)      f(11,  9,  2) --> (n, active)
```

Figure 4. Routing Tables of Sample Network with Additional Link "o"

Figure 5. Example of Topology Information Packet Flow

```
   1 a  2      2 h  7
   2 b  5      7 i  8
   2 c  3      8 j  9
   3 d  4      8 k 10
   4 e  5      8 l 11
   4 f  6      9 m 10
   5 g  6     10 n 11
```

Figure 6. Topology Database (for all nodes)

Note: ' distinguishes this node as a LOCTOD node.

Figure 7. Example of Topology Information Packet Flow with LOCTOD Nodes

```
Cleveland
   1 a 2'
Philadelphia, Washington, D.C., Atlanta, Miami
   2' b  5      4 e  5
   2' c  3      4 f  6
   3  d  4      5 g  6
London
   2' h  7      7 i 8'
Brussels, Paris, Geneva
   8' j  9      9 m 10
   8' k 10     10 n 11
   8' l 11
New York
   1  a  2      4 f  6
   2  b  5      5 g  6
   2  c  3      2 h  7
   3  d  4      7 i 8'
   4  e  5
Amsterdam
   2' h  7      8 l 11
   7  i  8      9 m 10
   8  j  9     10 n 11
   8  k 10
```

Note: ' distinguishes this node as a LOCTOD node.

Figure 8. Topology Database for Nodes in LOCTOD Environment

Figure 9. Route Setup with LOCTOD Nodes New York and Amsterdam

```
         Philadel-  Washington  Paris  Amsterdam  Brussels  New York
         phia       DC
         3          4           10     8          9         2

           REQ_TOP_INFO (9)
(1)      ─────────────────>
                       REQ_TOP_INFO (9)
(2)                  ─────────────────>
                                   REQ_TOP_INFO (9)
(3)                              ─────────────────>
                                             REQ_TOP_INFO (9)
(4)                                        ──────────────────────────>
                                             TOP_INFO_REPLY (null)
(5)                                        <─────────────────
                                   TOP_INFO_REPLY (8,j,9)
(6)                              <─────────────────
                       TOP_INFO_REPLY (8,j,9; 8,k,10; 8,l,11; 9,m,10;
                                       10,n,11)
(7)                  <─────────────────
           TOP_INFO_REPLY (8,j,9; 8,k,10; 8,l,11; 9,m,10; 10,n,11;
                           4,o,10)
(8)      <─────────────────
           RT_SETUP (RT_ID=6; 3,d,4,o,10,m,9)
(9)      ─────────────────>
           RT_SETUP RESPONSE
         <••••••••••
                       RT_SETUP (RT_ID=6; 3,d,4,o,10,m,9)
(10)                 ─────────────────>
                       RT_SETUP RESPONSE
                     <••••••••••
                                   RT_SETUP (RT_ID=6; 3,d,4,o,10,m,9)
(11)                             ─────────────────>
                                   RT_SETUP RESPONSE
                                 <••••••••••••••••••
                                   RT_REPLY
(12)                             <─────────────────
                       RT_REPLY
(13)                 <─────────────────
           RT_REPLY
(14)     <─────────────────


Figure 10.   Route Setup  with LOCTOD Nodes  NY, Amsterdam,  Wash DC,
             and Paris
```

Mr. Doss received a B. S. degree in computer science and mathematics from the University of North Carolina at Wilmington in 1976 and a M. S. degree in computer studies from North Carolina State University in 1979. He received a research assistantship in May 1977, where his responsibilities were to design application algorithms for the Edit Processor component of the Integrated Photogrammetric Instrument Network (IPIN). This effort led to the analysis of high-level languages which allow concurrent programming. In January 1979 he joined IBM's Communication Products Division at Research Triangle Park, N. C. where he designed and developed the subarea routing function for TCAM (Telecommunications Access Method). His works have appeared in SIGGRAPH (a special interest group of the ACM), NCSU Technical Report, and American Society of Photogrammetry.

Mr. Smetanka received a B.S. degree in mathematics from the University of Toledo (Ohio) in 1974. He then joined IBM's Communication Products Division at Kingston, N.Y. in July of that year where he designed and developed both analytic and simulation performance models of various computer communication's products. He worked in the Distributed Systems Analysis area until 1977 when he joined the TCAM (Telecommunications Access Method) Design and Performance group in Research Triangle Park, N.C. Terry developed the analytic performance model of TCAM as well as designed various components of the product. He obtained his M.B.A. in 1979 from Duke University. His past works have appeared in the IBM Journal of Research and Development, Mini-Micro Systems, Data Communications, as well as various IEEE sponsored conferences.

Some Problems in the Inter-connection of Computer Networks

R T Braden, R H Cole
University College London, UK

In the US and the UK, academic research on wide-area internetting has been largely dominated by either the DARPA Internet or by the PTT/VAN X.25 networks. Researchers in the Department of Computer Science at University College, London (UCL) have been building an interconnection facility for UK and US researchers, linking these two major internet systems. The services to be supported by this facility include interactive terminal traffic, file transfer, and electronic mail.

This paper briefly describes the two internetting worlds and then describes the protocols, services, and hardware used for UCL's interconnection facility. It concludes with a discussion summarising the general interconnection problems we have encountered.

1. INTRODUCTION

This paper is concerned with "internetting", that is, the interconnection of independent packet switching networks to create larger communication domains. In the US and the UK, much academic research on wide-area internetting has been concerned with either the DARPA Internet (hereinafter called the Internet) or with the PTT/VAN X.25 networks. Researchers in the Department of Computer Science at University College, London (UCL) have been active in both areas.

At UCL we have been building an interconnection facility for UK and US researchers, by linking the Internet with two X.25-based networks in the UK. The services to be supported by this facility include interactive terminal traffic, file transfer, and electronic mail. This paper discusses this facility, with particular attention to the significant problems in linking the the two internetting systems. We begin with a brief overview of the two internetting worlds, and then describe the protocols, services, and hardware required for the UCL facility.

1.1 The DARPA Internet

The Defense Advanced Research Projects Agency (DARPA) of the U.S. Government has been sponsoring research into packet-switched computer networks since 1968. This research program has created the "Internet", the interconnection of a number of networks, employing a wide variety of technologies, by gateways. The Internet provides a workbench for research into all aspects of communications using packet switched computer networks. The orientation of the research is towards military systems, hence there is a strong emphasis on survivability.

In practice the Internet is centered on the ARPANET, on which most of the service hosts reside. Attached to the periphery of the ARPANET, by gateways, are a number of local area networks, packet radio networks, distributed computing networks, and SATNET. SATNET [1] is a transit network, having no hosts other than gateways. Also attached to SATNET are UCL and RSRE in the U.K., NDRE in Norway, and DFVLR in West Germany.

The basic Internet architecture consists of a number of networks interconnected by gateway hosts. Each constituent network has its own internal data transmission protocol, used to transport internet datagrams as the smallest unit of transfer. The gateways only process datagrams; there are no virtual circuits at the internet level, and the gateways contain no call state information. The use of datagrams enhances the Internet's ability to survive wide-spread 'outages' and to allocate resources dynamically. Dynamic load-sharing across alternative paths is a nearly-automatic consequence of the use of datagrams.

Internet datagrams are routed individually by the originating hosts and intermediate gateways, based only on the destination network specified in each packet. If the network is not the local network number, a routing table is consulted to choose a gateway. The routing table is built dynamically, based upon routing information in packets exchanged by the gateways.

The datagram protocol [2] IP is used to carry a number of higher level protocols, the most important of which is the Transmission Control Protocol [3] (TCP). TCP is the connection-oriented ("virtual call") protocol which is used between Internet hosts. TCP call state information exists only in the TCP modules of the source and destination hosts.

Although the constituent networks are independent and the network protocols are used to carry the internet protocols, the IP protocol does constrain the address space of a constituent network. The IP protocol uses a 32 bit address field, at least 8 bits of which are used for the network number, so a local network address space must not exceed 24 bits.

1.2 PTT X.25 Internetting

Packet-switching services are being provided by a number of the national PTT (Postal, Telephone, and Telegraph) agencies and in the U.S. by Value Added Networks (VANs). These public data networks have adopted the CCITT recommendation X.25 [4] as the standard service interface.

X.25 encompases three protocol layers; a physical access protocol, a local network access protocol ("Level 2" or "Link Level"), and a user service protocol ("Level 3" or "Network Level"). We will be concerned in this paper with the last, and will refer to it as simply "X.25". The X.25 interface enables a user to create and manage virtual calls, providing reliable, ordered, flow-controlled delivery of packets.

In particular, British Telecom (the PTT agency in the UK), offers X.25 service over their Packet Switched Service (PSS) [5]. The UK academic research community is also being served by a nationwide private network SERCNET, operated by the Science and Engineering Research Council (SERC). SERCNET has been moving as rapidly as possible towards full PSS protocol compatibility, including both X.25 and the user-defined protocols above it [6]. Other private and local networks in the UK are very likely to follow this example and conform to the PSS interfaces and protocols.

To allow internetting of public data networks, the PTTs have defined a global (both logically and physically) 12-digit numeric address space, very much modelled on the international telephone system (X.121) [7]. Using this addressing scheme and the interface recommendation X.75 [8], the PTTs are building gateways to interconnect the national networks. In particular, PSS is connected to the US Value Added Networks via British Telecom's International Packet Switching Service (IPSS).

The resulting world-wide PTT internet system is being based on virtual calls, as opposed to datagrams. A multi-network call will be formed by "concatenation" of virtual calls across individual networks. The resulting service, intended for civilian rather than military use, is not designed to provide either dynamic rerouting in case of wide-spread outages or dynamic load sharing across alternative routes. The PTTs are conscious of the need to sell a service to paying customers and this reflects the design of the PTT internet. To maintain a quality of service the internal operation of the network is divorced from the user by the X.25 interface.

2. PROTOCOLS AND ARCHITECTURE

In order to interconnect the two diverse internet systems described in the preceding section, UCL must deal with the differences in protocols, addressing, and routing mechanisms. These problems will be outlined in this section.

2.1 Protocol Levels

The functions required of UCL's internetting link can be described most conveniently in terms of the familiar multi-layered ISO model [9]. To indicate the relative position of two protocols in the hierarchy, we use the notation "A > B"; here A, a protocol in layer i, is implemented using the facilities offered by protocol B in layer i-1.

We are concerned here with the network and transport layers of the ISO model. The layers above level 4, the transport layer, are used by the higher-level protocols for interactive terminals and file transfer.

More general definitions are possible, but for our purposes:

a. The network layer provides reliable, ordered transmission across virtual circuits spanning a single network or address domain.

b. The transport layer provides reliable, ordered transmission across end-to-end virtual circuits, possibly spanning multiple networks and address domains.

The transport layer must provide complete communication facilities for the application layer. The protocol used in the transport layer, the "transport service", may be regarded as providing an enhancement to the services provided by the underlying network layer. Of course, if the "real service" of the network layer is itself adequate for the higher-level protocols, then the network service can serve as the transport service as well, and the transport layer becomes null.

A UK users group has defined a Network Independent Transport Service [10] (NITS) which enhances the facilities of the PTT X.25 network PSS. NITS provides end-to-end error reporting, and a more powerful addressing mechanism than X.121. In particular, NITS provides arbitrary source-route addressing across multiple naming domains. This is necessary in the UK, since SERCNET uses an addressing scheme which allows both symbolic names ("titles") and numeric addresses, with the numeric addresses being independent of the PTT (X.121) space. The use of NITS thus allows concatenated virtual calls through transport gateways connecting SERCNET and PSS. NITS is also used to extend calls into the many local area networks being attached to SERCNET and PSS.

Figure 1 shows the (approximate) protocol hierarchies with which UCL is concerned.

Within the DARPA Internet, TCP > IP is the transport service. However, TCP > IP, like the PTT X.25 internet, assumes a single global address space. Therefore, TCP > IP fails to provide a general end-to-end addressing between an Internet host and an X.25 host, and for this reason is not an adequate transport service for UCL's interconnection.

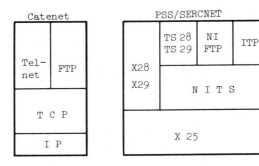

Figure 1 **Protocol hierarchies**

2.2 Interconnection Architecture

The interconnection of networks at UCL is shown in figure 2. Each separate network in the DARPA catenet discussed in this paper is indicated, with the interconnecting gateways.

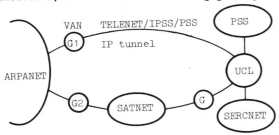

Figure 2 **UCL interconnection architecture**

UCL is a host on the X.25 networks SERCNET and PSS. PSS uses X.121 addressing which allows UCL a 2-digit sub-address field for service selection. SERCNET relies on symbolic sub-addressing in the transport level (NITS). The interconnection facility similarly operates as an Internet host, and the TCP port number is used for service selection. In addition, UCL has a local-area network, based on a Cambridge Ring [11]. This network appears as a component of the Internet, i.e., it has its own network number.

There are two paths from UCL to the ARPANET. One path, SATNET, uses the Atlantic Packet Satellite network as a transit network. The operating costs of the SATNET connection in the U.K. are provided by the Ministry of Defence (MoD); thus, the MoD (and British Telecom) will permit SATNET use only for work which is sponsored by the MoD or by DARPA.

To allow access to ARPANET for non-MoD sponsored users, for example academic users supported by SERC, there must be a second path using a PTT-provided service. In particular, we use the three-network concatenation: PSS-IPSS-Telenet to cross the Atlantic.

This requires the "encapsulation" of IP datagrams within X.25 packets over PTT virtual calls. We call this arrangement an "IP Tunnel". One end of the tunnel is at UCL, the other is in an Internet Gateway in the US called the "VAN Gateway" [12]. There will be a single X.25 call open between the two whenever datagrams are to be passed. This call is initiated at UCL on PSS by giving the X.121

address of the VAN gateway in the US. The gateway then believes it is talking to a network and functions as a normal DARPA Internet gateway. The tunnel is merely a mechanism for transporting datagrams for non-MoD users across the Atlantic in a legal manner.

Note that UK users would be able to connect directly to the VAN gateway over the PTT internet, but the higher-level protocols in the Internet are quite different from those of the X.25 world in the UK. Hence, UCL's interconnection facility must be in the middle.

UCL has the constraint that all non-MoD traffic be routed via the IP tunnel. Ideally we would like a DARPA catenet host to say "this is a MoD user" and decide to use gateway G2 to SATNET (see figure 2); or "this is a non-MoD user" and decide to use G1 the tunnel link to UCL. Unfortunately, Internet hosts and gateways route datagrams purely on the basis of their routing tables, which return a unique destination gateway for each network number. They do not make the more complex routing decisions which we require, particularly on a packet-by-packet basis.

We must therefore force the Internet hosts to use the 'correct' paths to the UK. To do this, we make UCL appear to Internet gateways and hosts as two different networks, called UCLNET and PSSNET, with no link between the two. The interconnection facility is thus "multi-homed", appearing on both apparent networks. MoD users reach the facility via UCLNET, while non-MoD users reach it via PSSNET. An Internet host having traffic for "PSSNET" will choose G1 as the only gateway, for example.

This model works very well until one of our links to the ARPANET fails. Then we would like to be able to use the other path, given restrictions on usage, for the UK-US traffic. However, since we have forced traffic down a single path by insisting it is the only route, the traffic cannot get through if that route breaks.

The most obvious way to overcome a break in one of the paths is to inform the Internet gateways that the network on the broken path is now reachable via the good path. Unfortunately there are no gateways under UCL control that we can use for this. At present we do not plan to implement gateway functions to perform this task as we do not need a gateway for any other purpose. As the terminal gateway at UCL is multi-homed on PSSNET and UCLNET, we can continue to use the good path by only using the host address on the reachable network for all users. However, a TCP module recognises datagrams as belonging to a particular call by comparing the source and destination address of the call with those in the datagram. Thus all calls from the unreachable net have to be abandoned and new calls made.

Finally, there are important access control issues. A US user is assumed to have the sanction of DARPA and will normally use the SATNET path to reach UCL. At UCL we will allow that user to make a call on PSS or SERCNET if there is accounting information that allows us to charge someone for the call. However, if the SATNET path fails, and the US user knows the PSSNET address of the UCL system, he can use the X.25 tunnel, incuring significant charges in merely reaching UCL. There is very little we can do about this until complex access control is placed in the VAN gateway. Since the gateway operates at the IP datagram level, it has no information on which to base such user-level access control decisions.

3. UCL INTERCONNECTION FACILITY

The circle marked UCL in figure 2 shows connections to a number of dissimilar networks. These connections are used for various purposes, research and service. To allow ourselves maximum flexibility with these scarce resources all the networks terminate on computers attached to our Cambridge Ring. Note that not all the networks terminating at UCL are shown in figure 2 neither are all the interconnections. Figure 3 shows the UCL ring and those computers on the ring discussed in this paper.

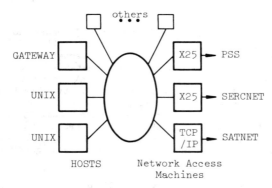

Figure 3 **UCL ring configuration**

Each network terminating at UCL is connected to the ring by what we call a "network access machine". There is one for X.25 networks (both PSS and SERCNET) and one for SATNET [13]. The network access machine contains the network protocols for that network and processes to direct data to and from other ring hosts. To enable the user processes in the hosts to manipulate calls in a network access machine, an inter-process protocol is used.

As shown in Figure 3, the hosts include: a GATEWAY, which implements the terminal and file transfer interconnection facility discussed in this paper, and two UNIX systems. The UNIX systems support NIFTP which can be used to reach PSS, SERCNET, and Internet hosts, and also the Internet terminal protocol TELNET. NIFTP is used for both file and electronic mail transfers [14] between the UK and US.

The obvious advantage of this distributed approach is in the use of 'network independent' protocols, such as NIFTP, where one implementation is used to communicate with hosts on very different networks.

4. SOFTWARE

We will now describe the implementation of terminal and file transfer service in the UCL interconnection facility. Electronic mail introduces a number of additional considerations which cannot be dealt with in the current paper.

4.1 Terminal Service

In the DARPA domain, the terminal protocol is Telnet [15], using TCP as the transport service. Within the UK (X.25) domain, there are three alternatives. The CCITT terminal protocol X.28/X.29 [16] uses X.25 as the transport service. TS28/TS29 [17] is a flavour of X.28/X.29 that uses NITS > X.25. Finally, the SERCNET uses a private terminal protocol ITP >NITS > X.25, in addition to the two flavours of X.28/X.29.

UCL must therefore provide a terminal gateway which performs the conversion of terminal protocols:

```
Telnet <=> X.29
Telnet <=> TS29 > NITS
Telnet <=> ITP
```

In addition to these conversions, the terminal gateway must implement the full protocol hierarchies:

```
Telnet > TCP > IP,
TS29 > NITS > X.25,
X.29 > X.25,
ITP > NITS > X.25.
```

Like any gateway, this terminal protocol converter appears as hosts in each of the three domains: Internet, SERCNET, and PSS. For reasons discussed earlier, it has two different host addresses on the Internet.

Since the terminal protocols differ significantly in the functions they offer, fully-automatic conversion is not generally possible or in fact desirable. For this reason, the terminal gateway at UCL includes commands which allow the user to modify or override various aspects of the conversion.

The terminal gateway forces a user to login, to provide access control. After logging into the gateway, the user may enter an "open" command specifying the address in the target domain of the desired server host. The access control enables the terminal gateway to select the correct path to the ARPANET (if necessary) depending on the class of user. Thus access control at UCL is vital to the 'correct' operation of the interconnection facility.

Note that the adddressing facilities of NITS used on the X.25 side would allow the open command to be issued implicitly by the gateway. That is, the NITS source routing mechanism is capable of handling the Internet addresses as well as any other naming domain. With suitable tables in the originating host and intermediate transport gateways, the end-to-end addressing could be invisible to the user. In any case, the lack of an equivalent facility on the

Internet side will force explicit opens on US users.

4.2 File Transfer

The Internet uses a file transfer protocol known as FTP [18], while the UK users have developed a Network Independent File Transfer Protocol or NIFTP [19]. Direct protocol translation between them is infeasible. Instead, a store-and-forward or "relay" host which implements both protocols must be available.

The current choice for relay host is a machine in the US on the ARPANET on which both FTP and NIFTP are implemented. The relay function on this host must currently be done manually. We plan to implement an automatic means, although there are awkward problems with password integrity.

In order to provide a path from NIFTP > NITS > X.25 to NIFTP > TCP > IP, UCL provides a "Transport Service Gateway" (TSG) which connects two "equivalent" transport protocols (NITS > X.25, and TCP), supporting a common protocol (NIFTP) in the application layer. The TCP connection will effectively be concatenated with the X.25 call.

NIFTP was designed to use NITS and assumes that the transport service will take care of the addressing problems. NITS provides a source-routed address string, which may be used by a UK host (on SERCNET or PSS) to reach the UCL TSG, and then to provide the TSG with the address of the Internet host on which NIFTP executes.

However, the return path is impossible with the current Internet protocols, since TCP does not provide the multiple-domain addressing of NITS. Thus, an NIFTP in the Internet is unable to open a call directly to a UK host through the UCL TSG. NIFTP itself has no primitives for addressing, and TCP cannot express addresses outside its own domain.

There are also serious problems of access control. NIFTP differs in a very important way from terminal interaction in that NIFTP is designed to operate in the background, and all current implementations operate in this fashion. Thus, explicit user login and open commands are not possible. The access control problem will be solved by requiring that the necessary account and password information be imbedded in the appropriate point in the NITS address string [20].

5. DISCUSSION

We have described two major internet systems, the DARPA Internet and the PTT X.25/X.75/X.121 system, and the interconnection between them that UCL is building for UK researchers. Despite the very disparate protocols (NITS > X.25, TCP > IP) of these two systems, UCL's interconnection is able to transfer application-level data across two distinct catenets under the control of three distinct administrations.

However, the implementation of the UCL facility has brought to light a number of general problems.

1. The addressing mechanism provided by the Internet and the PTT protocols are not extensible into other internetting domains. Thus, we say that TCP and X.25 are not complete transport services outside their home domains.

   In the PTT X.25 case, NITS solves this problem where it is used. However, the lack of universal adoption of NITS, especially by British Telecom, leaves the problem only partly solved. For example, PSS PADs use X.29 over 'bare' X.25, without a transport service.

   In the Internet case, Bennett has proposed an implementation of NITS over TCP to supply the missing addressing generality [21].

2. Both internetting systems need better mechanisms for passing accounting and user identification information. In addition, this accounting and identity information can be required at quite low levels of the protocol hierarchy. The identification information is essential to UCL to identify the class of user, and hence the restrictions on the selection of a route.

   There is no mechanism in X.25, and therefore X.75, for passing identification and accounting information. The addition of such information into the NITS protocol has been identified by the U.K. Transport Service Implementors Group as a topic requiring further study, although there is an existing proposal (to embed the accounting information in the address string), as described earlier.

   The Internet end-to-end protocol TCP has no facilities for identifying a user, nor is there any mechanism for passing such information to the IP protocol level. A problem for protocols such as TCP and IP, where there is no state information within the catenet, is to find an efficient mechanism to carry the potentially infinite variety of identification information.

In summary, we would suggest that a transport level protocol, such as NITS is required where calls are made to cross administrative boundaries or where data protection laws are in force. Such a transport protocol would have to be universal in order to allow general interconnection of internet systems.

6. ACKNOWLEDGEMENTS

The work described in this paper is supported by the Ministry of Defence under grant 2047/84, and the Science and Engineering Research Council under grants A/75695 and N2BIR0188. Nearly everyone in the INDRA group of the Department of Computer Science has contributed to this work. We are grateful to our colleagues and to Vint Cerf for valuable comments and criticisms of the paper. We would also like to acknowledge useful discussions with Jack Haverty of BBN concerning UCL's Internet routing problems.

References

1. Jacobs, I., Binder. R., Hoversten, E., "General Purpose Packet Satellite Networks", Proc. IEEE vol 66,11 pp1448-1467, November 1978.

2. Postel, J., "The DoD Standard Internet Protocol", RFC 791, September 1981.

3. Postel, J., "The DoD Standard Transmission Control Protocol", RFC 793, September 1981.

4. CCITT, "Recommendation X.25, Interface between DTE and DCE for Packet Mode Terminals", ITU Geneva, 1980.

5. Medcraft, D., "Development of the UK Packet Switched Services", Proc. Conf. on Data Networks, ONLINE, p173, 1980.

6. Girard, P., "Protocols for the SRC/NERC Network", Issue No.5 Rutherford Laboratory, September 1980.

7. CCITT, "Recommendation X.121, International Numbering Plan for Public Data Networks", Study Group VII, ITU Geneva, 1978.

8. CCITT, "Recommendation X.75: Terminal and transit call control procedures and data transfer system on international circuits between packet-swithced data networks", ITU Geneva, 1978.

9. ISO DP 7498, "Reference model for Open Systems Interconnection", International Standards Organisation, 1980.

10. PSS User Forum SG3, "A Network Independent Transport Service", Study Group 3, February 1980.

11. Wilkes, M., "Communication using a Digital Ring", Proc. PACNET Conf. Sendai, Japan, pp47-55, August 1975.

12. Haverty, J., "VAN Gateway: Some Routing and Performance Issues", IEN 154, May 1981.

13. Cole, R. & Lloyd, P., "The SATNET access machine", IN 1113, June 1981.

14. Bennett, C., "The JNT mail protocol", TR 74, November 1981.

15. Postel, J., "TELNET Protocol Specification", IEN 148, June 1980.

16. CCITT, "Recomendations X.3, X.28, X.29, on Packet-switched Data Transmission Services", ITU Geneva, 1980.

17. PSS User Forum, "Character Terminal Protocols on PSS", Revision 1, February 1981.

18. Postel, J., "File Transfer Protocol", IEN 149, June 1980.

19. PSS High Level Protocol Group, "A Network Independent File Transfer Protocol", Data Communication Protocols Unit, NPL, Teddington, UK, February 1980.

20. Dunn, A., "A User Authorisation Scheme for SRCNET", Rutherford Laboratory, Abingdon, December 1981.

21. Bennett, C., "Realisation of the Yellow Book above TCP", IEN 154 (IN 965), August 1980.

Note:
TR and IN indicates an internal report or note of the Department of Computer Science, University College, London.
IEN indicates a DARPA Internet Experiment Note and RFC indicates a Request For Comments, both of which may be obtained from: Defense Adavnced Research Project Agency, IPTO, Arlington, VA. USA.

Biographies

A Computer Science graduate of Essex University, **Robert Cole** is a qualified teacher. He was a lecturer at the Polytechnic of the South Bank, London for 5 years before joining the networks research group at UCL in 1979. He has also written a text book on computer comunications.

Robert Braden is an Associate Research Fellow in the UCL Computer Science Department, on leave from the Office of Academic Computing of UCLA. He has been concerned with host software for the ARPANET since 1969, and has been working in the computer field for twenty years. He obtained an MS degree in Physics from Stanford University.

Recent Developments in the DARPA Internet Program

J Postel, C Sunshine, D Cohen
USC Information Sciences Institute,
USA

The U.S. Defense Advanced Research Projects Agency (DARPA) has sponsored research and development in computer networking for many years. These developments have often paved the way for public and commercial systems. Today the DARPA-sponsored networking system includes a variety of networks and second-generation protocols. This paper outlines some of the recent developments in the DARPA Internet Program. In particular the specific areas of protocols, interconnection with public networks, gateways, network monitoring, and transition planning are discussed.

1. INTRODUCTION

The U.S. Defense Advanced Research Projects Agency (DARPA) has sponsored research and development in computer networking for many years. These developments have often paved the way for public and commercial systems. Today the DARPA-sponsored networking system includes a variety of networks and second-generation protocols. This paper outlines some of the recent developments in the DARPA Internet Program. Note that the views expressed are those of the authors and should not be assumed to represent the position of DARPA.

After giving some background on the DARPA Internet system, we discuss recent developments in specific areas including protocols, interconnection with public networks, gateways, network monitoring, and transition planning. It must be stressed that this paper is a very brief overview of the recent developments; the reader should turn to the references for information on the technical aspects of the DARPA Internet Program.

1.1. Background

The DARPA Internet Program involves the interconnection of several different types of networks. These networks include a large land-line network (ARPANET) [1], satellite networks (SATNET, WBNET) [2,3], radio networks (PRNET) [4], and local networks (ETHERNET, LCSNET) [5,6]. These networks share the property of being digital packet networks, but are dissimilar in that they operate at vastly different data rates, and with different reliability, packet sizes, and distribution characteristics (point-to-point vs. broadcast). The motivation for the interconnection of these networks is to allow communication the among host computers on these networks.

DARPA has developed an interconnection strategy that uses a datagram protocol, called the Internet Protocol [7], as the basic universal protocol. This protocol provides a uniform address space as well as the mechanisms for routing datagrams through the connected set of networks and for sizing datagrams to fit into the packet size of each network.

.....

This research is supported by the Defense Advanced Research Projects Agency under Contract No. MDA903 81 C 0335. Views and conclusions contained in this report are the authors' and should not be interpreted as representing the official opinion or policy of DARPA, the U.S. Government, or any person or agency connected with them.

This strategy is different in important ways from that of the public data networks which assume compatible virtual circuit protocols (X.25/X.75) in all networks connected. The DARPA approach is partly motivated by the desire to allow interconnection of a variety of existing and future networks with different characteristics and protocols.

Since many applications require a reliable data stream transmission service, the Transmission Control Protocol (TCP) [8] was developed and is widely used in the DARPA Internet. TCP provides end-to-end reliable connections for data stream traffic, using mechanisms such as checksums, positive acknowledgments and timeouts with retransmission, and flow control.

Other applications, however, are well suited to the datagram approach. For these a User Datagram Protocol (UDP) [9] has been developed. Examples of such applications are simple transaction services such as a Time-of-Day server and a Directory-Assistance server.

In general concept, the DARPA approach is quite similar to the Xerox approach in the Experimental Ethernet using the PUP protocols [10] and the approach in the Ethernet using the Network System protocols [11,12].

1.2. A Comparison of DARPA and ISO Architectures

The general models of protocol architecture used by the ISO and by the DARPA groups are not so far apart as might first be assumed because of the differences in terminology and descriptive style. Both assume a layered model with the lowest layers being physical and the highest being user or applications.

```
ISO                    DARPA

Application            Application
Presentation               "
Session                    "
Transport             Transport (TCP, UDP)
-----                 Internetwork (IP)
Network               Network
Link                  Link
Physical              Physical
```

Protocol Layers
Figure 1.

There are two principal differences between the ISO and DARPA models: (1) the ISO Application, Presentation, and Session layers are all combined in one Application layer in the DARPA model, and (2) the DARPA model explicitly stresses the need for an Internetwork layer.

These differences may be said to be differences of principle as well. In the DARPA design, the universal protocol is the datagram based Internet Protocol, while in the ISO design the key protocol is the virtual circuit based transport protocol. In the DARPA design, the applications are quite varied with distinctly different needs for connection management and data format conversions, while in the ISO design the standardized mechanisms are specified for these functions in the ISO session and presentation layers [13].

In practice the differences in the architectures are not as great as they might appear. The DARPA transport layer protocols implement some functions that are similar to the ISO session functions, and some DARPA applications are of a utility nature and provide some of the functions of the ISO presentation layer. Also, recent work on the ISO network layer has begun to define a distinct internetwork sublayer.

Another difference is the focus of the ISO on one protocol at each layer, while DARPA allows a multiplicity of protocols at each layer except the Internet layer. In fact the DARPA model is like a tree with the IP as the main trunk; below this the roots spread out (representing the use of different networks, link protocols, and physical interfaces), and above IP branches spread out (representing the use of different transport and application protocols). The ISO attempts to reduce this difference in protocol philosophy by establishing classes of service within a protocol, but this is still limiting in that a low class of service is a subset of a higher class of service. In the DARPA model there is no necessary relationship between protocols at the same level of the tree.

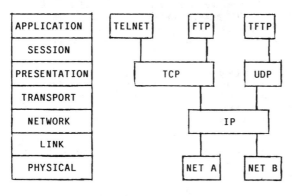

ISO   DARPA

Protocol Structures
Figure 2.

This flexibility of allowing multiple protocols at each layer extends in two ways: recursion and encapsulation. In protocol recursion, a high level protocol is used as a lower level protocol for another application. For example, a mail protocol may be used to provide a sort of network-level transaction service in building an internet mail system (see Section 5.2). In protocol encapsulation, the protocol messages of one system are sent through another system by using or "wrapping" them in the protocols of the second system. For example, DARPA IP packets may be sent through the Xerox Ethernet system encapsulated in PUPs. When two (or more) protocol systems provide for encapsulating each other's protocols, the result is called mutual encapsulation [14].

1.3. The Evolution of IP and TCP

Early DARPA work on the interconnection of networks envisioned one protocol to provide the services now provided by the combination of IP and TCP. This was the first version of TCP [15]. It was clear from the earliest work on the problems of network interconnection that end-to-end mechanisms were needed to ensure reliability, flow control, duplicate detection, and sequencing, and that

network-by-network mechanisms were needed for routing, fragmentation, and congestion control.

Other work in uses of packet-switched networks led to the realization that different applications require different types of services and that the very reliable sequenced data stream service provided by TCP was not the best choice for some other applications, for example, digital packet speech communication.

Problems also developed in the interaction of mechanisms to control errors end-to-end with those to provide the network-by-network functions. For example, the need to have an end-to-end checksum on the data conflicts with the need to allow fragmentation by gateways for transmission through "small packet" networks.

At this point the transport layer TCP was separated into two distinct protocol layers with completely independent mechanisms (although for efficiency TCP uses some information carried in the IP header). This division also allowed the development of completely separate transport protocols to support other types of applications (e.g., transaction and real-time). This separation greatly reduces the complexity of mechanism and description of each of the transport protocols.

The IP provides the network-by-network functions of routing and fragmentation and is used by several higher level protocols in addition to TCP. The TCP provides the end-to-end reliability, flow control, and data-sequencing functions for applications which need this type of service.

2. INTERNET PROTOCOL

As noted above, the basic function of IP is to route individual datagrams to their internet destinations. For this purpose, IP modules must be present in source and destination systems and in the "gateways" or forwarding nodes that interconnect networks. IP will also "fragment" packets if necessary into small enough packets to traverse each individual network encountered on the way to the destination. The fragments need not be reassembled until they reach their destination. A full presentation of IP may be found in [7], and the specification in [16].

IP provides several important additional features, including Type Of Service (TOS), Time To Live (TTL), Security, control messages, and source routing.

The TOS provides a way to specify the desired service characteristics to each network transmitting the datagram. The TOS is specified in terms of virtual service parameters (such as precedence, delay, throughput, and reliability), and this specification is mapped at each network into the actual service parameters available.

The TTL provides an upper bound on the lifetime of a datagram in the internetwork system. Most reliable transport protocols depend for their correct operation on some assumption (often implicit and unstated) that datagrams (or packets, or segments, ...) cannot persist in the communication system longer than some maximum lifetime.

The Security provisions in the IP allows datagrams to be marked with security classes appropriate to military security needs. IP does not make datagrams secure, but it does provide the facility to properly identify the security class of datagrams transmitted in a secure environment. These security markings could be used in a multilevel secure computer system to control access to the information communicated.

To assist in managing datagram traffic a set of control messages have been identified and codified as an Internet Control Message Protocol (ICMP) [117]. These messages are sent as ordinary datagrams but are addressed to the IP module itself. For example, control messages indicate that a destination is currently unreachable, or that a more optimal route would result if datagrams addressed to a certain host (or network) were sent via a different gateway.

The initial version of the IP specified a fixed format 32-bit internet address which allowed only 256 networks. The current version allows many more networks (over 2 million) and also reserves some addresses for future allocation. The addresses used in IP are hierarchical addresses because they explicitly indicate the network and the address within the network.

Another feature of IP is the optional use in a datagram of a source route to specify a number of intermediate gateways through which the datagram is to be routed. This feature allows the source to add routing information to that normally available in the gateways to reach destinations that may be new or for some reason not generally known in the internet.

3. TRANSPORT PROTOCOL

A full presentation of an earlier version of TCP may be found in [8], and the current specification in [18].

3.1. Features of TCP

The TCP mechanisms operate somewhat differently from the transport protocols considered for standardization by ISO and CCITT.

For example, the TCP flow control is octet oriented rather than record oriented. This is important in that significantly different buffering strategies are made available to the implementer.

Also, data is transferred as a stream of octets with no record markers at all, although record markers may be employed at the application level by the users of TCP if desired. The sending user or application may indicate that the data submitted so far is to be pushed through the internet and delivered to the destination user or application.

This is a modification of an earlier, intermediate version of TCP which had introduced an interaction between TCP transmission segments (called letters) and buffer boundaries. This linkage caused complications in the flow-control procedure. The TCP flow-control procedure has been simplified by eliminating any interaction between buffer sizes, push points, and flow control.

The connection opening and closing procedures of TCP are very careful, always using a three message exchange. For opening a connection, this provides greater confidence that the connection is between the correct parties and not due to old duplicate datagrams. For closing, this provides a "graceful" close ensuring that the last data sent is delivered to the user.

TCP provides a service to signal an "urgent" condition to the remote user. This signal may be delivered ahead of previously sent data. The arrival of an urgent signal is reported promptly to the receiving user, although closely spaced urgent signals may be merged, with only the last one indicated to the user. The urgent signal is intended to prompt special treatment of the data stream by the receiving user, but no special data is associated with the urgent signal itself. The TCP urgent mechanism is inherently synchronized with the data stream; in addition, some applications explicitly synchronize the data stream with the use of the urgent signal by transmitting a special data mark in the regular data stream.

Finally, TCP uses TCP-level addresses called "ports" for multiplexing connections between processes. Some standard, well-advertised ports are assigned to provide common services. For example, the File Transfer server can always be contacted on port 21. A connection is distinguished by the concatenation of the addresses (including ports) on both ends, thus one port number may be engaged in many connections to different other ends.

3.2. Implementation Strategies of TCP

The management of TCP connections involves the control of two major parameters: (1) the window, and (2) the acknowledgment. The window is the flow control parameter and indicates how many more octets can be transmitted. The acknowledgment is the error control parameter and indicates which data have been received, thereby stopping further retransmissions of that data.

It is important that these two parameters be managed separately. A TCP must send acknowledgments promptly enough to stop wasteful retransmissions, but must send window updates cautiously to avoid stimulating the transmission of unnecessarily small segments. In many other virtual circuit protocols (e.g., X.25) these two functions are coupled, preventing this important flexibility.

Another connection-management concern is the retransmission timeout. Performance studies have shown that the best results will be obtained by using an exponential-decay, smoothed, dynamically-measured value for the retransmission timeout.

4. APPLICATION PROTOCOLS

The application protocols include the terminal access protocol (Telnet) [19] and the file transfer protocol (FTP) [20]. These are essentially the same as they were in the original ARPANET, simply modified to accept internet addresses and to use TCP connections rather than the connections of the old ARPANET transport protocol. A new generation of these protocols is currently under study by Systems Development Corporation for the U.S. Defense Communications Agency.

The procedures for handling computer mail are being separated from those for file transfer and augmented for improved efficiency. Added features of the mail transfer protocol (SMTP) [21] include multirecipient message transmission and explicit provision for relaying messages.

Some new protocols are available in the Internet including a block-at-a-time "trivial" file transfer protocol (TFTP) [22] and a name server protocol [23]. These two examples of transaction-oriented protocols use a simple user datagram protocol (UDP) [9] at the transport level above the IP layer.

Protocols supporting the combination of voice, facsimile, and graphics data with text in computer mail are under development and in experimental use [24].

Also under investigation are protocols to support real-time voice communication, in both point-to-point and conference modes [25].

5. GATEWAYS AND NETWORK INTERCONNECTION

The original gateways in the DARPA Internet were small model PDP-11 computers. One of the main goals of the DARPA architecture with datagram internet protocol was to use relatively simple gateways with limited buffering since no connection management or retransmission would be required. A simple routing metric counting each network as one unit of cost was implemented and worked satisfactorily as long as internet traffic load was light.

Current plans call for the replacement of original gateways with more powerful processors and implementation of more sophisticated routing procedures that will monitor link status between each pair of gateways. The procedures for congestion control, debugging, monitoring, measurement, and fault detection, isolation, and recovery are also being improved. The expanded gateway capacity will allow a whole set of second order problems to be addressed: multihoming, network partitions, mobile hosts, source routing, and access controls [26].

5.1. Interconnection with Public Networks

One development already accomplished is a "VAN gateway" (to value added public nets). This gateway functions at the Internet Protocol level much like other gateways in the DARPA Internet but employs the X.25 network-access protocol on its interfaces to public nets (currently Telenet). X.25 virtual circuits are initiated and accepted as needed to transfer IP datagrams to their destinations. This experimental capability is being used to determine the performance of the DoD standard protocols on public data networks. Access to the VAN gateway is restricted to a small set of authorized users [27].

To use the VAN gateway, hosts on the public network must implement the DARPA protocols above the X.25 network level just as any other hosts. This approach will also be used in the Computer Science Network (CSNET) of U.S. University Computer Science Departments connecting university research computers [28]. Experiments are also being performed with "protocol translation" machines that attempt to interconnect systems with differing higher level protocols (e.g., for virtual terminals or file transfer) [29].

5.2. Interconnection of Mail Systems

Another recent development has been in the area of computer mail. A strategy for interconnecting specialized services (in this case computer mail) where there is no transport level connectivity or commonality has been devised. This involves use of a "private" host able to invoke the mail services in the two systems, and agreement on some conventions for placing intersystem instructions within the "text" as seen by either mail service. The private host performs as a seemingly "normal" mail destination on one system, and then extracts the forwarding instructions from the text of the message, reformats it, and transmits it to the specified mailbox in the second system. Hence the host acts as an application-level relay. Such a service has been implemented at ISI between the Telemail and ARPANET mail systems [30,31], and between the UK NIMAIL and Arpanet mail [32].

6. MEASUREMENT AND MONITORING

There is a program for monitoring the gateways and measuring the traffic and error levels [33]. The normal condition is for gateways to periodically send a report to a measurement center of the number of datagrams they have received from and sent to each network and the number of errors they have detected. The measurement center makes up a daily report summarizing the traffic through each gateway and the error statistics.

In addition, the gateway implementers may enable other specialized reports from particular gateways to study the behavior in more detail. These include both periodic reports and "trap reports" that are triggered by the gateway detecting an internal error condition or resource-utilization threshold.

7. CURRENT STATUS AND TRANSITION PLANS

7.1. Current Installation Status

As of May 1982, there are approximately 50 host computers using these protocols, including the Digital Equipment Corporation models LSI-11 (MOS), PDP-11 (UNIX), VAX (UNIX,VMS), PDP-10 (TOPS-20, TENEX), the Honeywell H6800 (Multics), the International Business Machines 3033 (MVS), and the Hewlett-Packard HP3000. There are 12 Gateways interconnecting 15 Networks.

In addition to experimental and development work, the system carries routine daily operational traffic from over 50 interactive terminal users in the UK and Norway via the broadcast packet SATNET and from users on a local area packet radio network at Ft. Bragg.

7.2. Transition from the old ARPANET Protocols

The DARPA community has been using the ARPANET and its protocol family quite successfully for some years. This Internet protocol family has been developed in parallel by a subset of that community. Starting in 1980 plans were developed for the conversion of the whole of the DARPA community to use these Internet protocols, and at the end of 1981 a concerted effort was begun to carry out the conversion. The goal is to retire the old ARPANET protocols by the end of 1982. This is a very ambitious plan for quite a large change in an operating communication service.

This conversion will be gradual. Hosts will convert when they are ready, and there is no "flag day" on which everyone must switch over. For a conversion of this type to succeed, a procedure must be available for communication between the two protocol environments (old ARPANET and new Internet) for each of the principal services. The procedure is to provide several "relay hosts" for each service. In essence one concatenates the use of the service from the source host to the relay host (using one set of protocols) with the use of the service from the relay host to the destination host (using the other set of protocols) [34].

8. FORMAL MODELLING OF PROTOCOLS

The original ARPANET protocols were specified rather informally using natural language (English), with little separate attention to the services they provided. Recent work has underscored the need for more rigorous specification and verification of protocols and the services they are intended to provide [35,36]. A variety of specification techniques adapted from more general software engineering have recently been applied for this purpose, but state machine models seem the most widely used.

One particular state machine model has been developed by SDC, and used to rigorously specify TCP and IP services and protocols [37,38]. This parallels the work going on within ISO TC97 SC16 on formal definition techniques and similar work in support of U.S. National Bureau of Standards protocol development efforts [39]. Even when completely formal specifications cannot be obtained, the process of developing more rigorous specifications has always revealed a significant number of errors or ambiguities in previous specifications.

Some more theoretical work is tackling the problem of formal verification of protocol designs. An extremely unlikely bug in the connection-establishment procedures of the TCP was discovered using the Affirm automated verification system developed at ISI [40,41] and a repair suggested. Other work on TCP verification is under way with the Gypsy system at the University of Texas [42].

9. SUMMARY

Over ten years ago, the ARPANET broke new ground and stimulated a revolution in computer communication. Recently, a second generation of networks and protocols has been incorporated into the DARPA Internet system. Major design goals of flexibility and robustness have led to an architecture with a common datagram-based internet protocol, allowing a variety of networks to interconnect. The second generation of protocols up through the transport level is firmly in place and operational. Existing application-level protocols have been revised to use the new internet transport services, while work on new application-level protocols is in more exploratory stages.

ACKNOWLEDGMENT

We would like to acknowledge the active support and guidance Dr. Vinton G. Cerf of the U.S. Defense Advanced Research Projects Agency has provided for this paper and the work described here. It must of course be noted that the work described here was performed by many companies, universities, and research centers either under contract to or otherwise cooperating with DARPA, and important contributions were made by many individuals.

REFERENCES

[1]   Roberts, L., and B. Wessler, "Computer Network Development to Achieve Resource Sharing," Proceedings of the Spring Joint Computer Conference, AFIPS, V. 36, pp. 543-549, May 1970.

[2]   Jacobs, I.M., R. Binder, E.V. Hoversten, "General Purpose Packet Satellite Networks", IEEE Proceedings Special Issue on Packet Network Technology, V. 66, N. 11, pp. 1448-1467, November 1978.

[3]   Kahn, R.E., "The Introduction of Packet Satellite Communications", Conference Record, V. 3, National Telecommunications Conference, Washington, D.C., IEEE Catalog Number 79CH1514-9, November 1979.

[4]   Kahn, R.E., S.A. Gronemyer, J. Burchfiel, and R.C. Kunzelman, "Recent Advances in Packet Radio Technology", IEEE Proceedings Special Issue on Packet Network Technology, V. 66, N. 11, pp. 1468-1496, November 1978.

[5]   Metcalfe, R.M., and D.R. Boggs, "Ethernet: Distributed Packet Switching for Local Computer Networks," Communications ACM, V. 19, N. 7, pp. 395-404, July 1976.

[6]   Clark, D.D., K.T. Pogran, and D.P. Reed, "An Introduction to Local Area Networks", IEEE Proceedings Special Issue on Packet Network Technology, V. 66, N. 11, pp. 1497-1517, November 1978.

[7]   Postel, J., C. Sunshine, and D. Cohen, "The ARPA Internet Protocol", Computer Networks, V. 5, N. 4, pp. 261-271, July 1981.

[8]   Postel, J., "DOD Standard Transmission Control Protocol", USC/Information Sciences Institute, IEN-129, RFC 761, NTIS ADA082609, January 1980. Appears in: Computer Communication Review, Special Interest Group on Data Communication, ACM, V. 10, N. 4, October 1980.

[9]   Postel, J., "User Datagram Protocol", USC/Information Sciences Institute, RFC 768, August 1980.

[10]   Boggs, D.R., and others, "PUP: An Internetwork Architecture," IEEE Transactions on Communications, V. COM-28, N. 4, pp. 612-624, April 1980.

[11]   Dalal, Y.K., "Use of Multiple Networks in Xerox' Network System," Proceedings 24th IEEE Computer Society International Conference (COMPCON), February 1982.

[12]   XEROX, "Internet Transport Protocols", XSIS 028112, Xerox Corporation, Stamford, Connecticut, December 1981.

[13]   Postel, J., "Internetwork Protocol Approaches", IEEE Transactions on Communication, V. COM-28, N. 4, April 1980. Also in "Tutorial: Office Automation Systems", K. Thurber, ed., IEEE Computer Society, September 1980.

[14]   Shoch, J., D. Cohen, and E. Taft, "Mutual Encapsulation of Internetwork Protocols", Proceedings Trends and Applications 1980: Computer Network Protocols, NBS, Gaithersburg, Maryland, May 1980. Also in "Tutorial: Office Automation Systems", K. Thurber, ed., IEEE Computer Society, September 1980. Also in Computer Networks, V. 5, N. 4, pp. 287-301, July 1981.

[15]   Cerf, V., and R. Kahn, "A Protocol for Packet Network Intercommunication," IEEE Transactions on Communications, V. COM-22, N. 5, May 1974.

[16]   Postel, J., ed., "Internet Protocol - DARPA Internet Program Protocol Specification", RFC 791, USC/Information Sciences Institute, September 1981.

[17]   Postel, J., "Internet Control Message Protocol - DARPA Internet Program Protocol Specification", RFC 792, USC/Information Sciences Institute, September 1981.

[18]   Postel, J., ed., "Transmission Control Protocol - DARPA Internet Program Protocol Specification", RFC 793, USC/Information Sciences Institute, September 1981.

[19]   Postel, J., "Telnet Protocol Specification", USC/Information Sciences Institute, IEN 148, RFC 764, June 1980.

[20]   Postel, J., "File Transfer Protocol Specification", USC/Information Sciences Institute, IEN 149, RFC 765, June 1980.

[21]   Postel, J., "Simple Mail Transfer Protocol", USC/Information Sciences Institute, RFC 788, November 1981.

[22]   Sollins, K., "Trivial File Transfer Protocol (Revision 2)", MIT/Laboratory for Computer Science, RFC 783, June 1981.

[23]   Weinstein, C., and M. Heggestad, "Multiplexing of Packet Speech on an Experimental Wideband Satellite Network", Proceedings 9th AIAA Communications Satellite Systems Conference, San Diego, California, March 1982.

[24]   Postel, J., "Internet Name Server", USC/Information Sciences Institute, IEN-116, August 1979.

[25]   Finn, G., and J. Postel, "Data Structures and Presentation Control for Multimedia Computer Mail", Proceedings EASTCON, November 1981.

[26]   Sunshine, C.A., "Addressing Problems in Multi-Network Systems," Proceedings IEEE INFOCOM 82, Las Vegas, March 1982.

[27]   Cerf, V.G., and P.T. Kirstein, "Issues in Packet Network Interconnection," Proceedings of the IEEE, V. 66, N. 11, November 1978.

[28]   Landweber, L.H., and M. Solomon, "Use of Multiple Networks in CSNET," Proceedings 24th IEEE Computer Society International Conference (COMPCON), February 1982.

[29]   Braden, R.T., and P.L. Higginson, "Development of UK/US Network Services at University College, London", Department of Computer Science, University College, London, IEN-185, INDRA Note 1101, May 1980.

[30] Cohen, D., "Internet Mail Forwarding," Proceedings 24th IEEE Computer Society International Conference (COMPCON), February 1982.

[31] Cohen, D., and J. Postel, "Internet Mail Forwarding: Mail Interchange Between Incompatible Systems", IFIP Working Group 6.5 Workshop on International Computer Message Services, Rocquencourt, France, April 1982.

[32] Bennett, C., "A Simple NIFTP-Based Mail System", Department of Computer Science, University College, London, IEN-169, INDRA-1025, January 1981.

[33] Flood Page, D., "Gateway Monitoring Protocol", Bolt Beranek and Newman, IEN-131, February 1980.

[34] Postel, J., "NCP/TCP Transition Plan", USC/Information Sciences Institute, RFC 801, November 1981.

[35] Bochmann, G., and C. Sunshine, "Formal Methods in Communication Protocol Design", IEEE Transactions on Communication, V. COM-28, N. 4, April 1980.

[36] Sunshine, C., "Formal Modeling of Communication Protocols", USC/Information Sciences Institute, RR-81-89, March 1981. To appear in Computer Networks and Simulation II, S. Schoemaker, ed., North-Holland, 1982.

[37] System Development Corporation, "DCEC Protocols Standardization Program, Protocol Specification Report, TM-7038/204/00, July 1981.

[38] System Development Corporation, "DCEC Protocols Standardization Program, Transmission Control Protocol Standard," TM-7038/207/01, December 1981.

[39] National Bureau of Standards (USA), "Specification of the Transport Protocol," Vols. 1-4, Report Nos. ICST/HLNP-81-11 to -14, September 1981.

[40] Schwabe, D., "Formal Specification and Verification of a Connection-Establishment Protocol", USC/Information Sciences Institute, RR-81-91, April 1981. Also in Proceedings 7th Data Communications Symposium, ACM/IEEE, Mexico City, pp. 11-26, October 1981.

[41] Thompson, D., and others, "Specification and Verification of Communication Protocols in AFFIRM Using State Transition Models", USC/Information Sciences Institute, RR-81-88, March 1981. To appear in IEEE Transactions on Software Engineering, 1982.

[42] Good, D., and R. Cohen, "Verifiable Communications Processing in Gypsy", COMPCON, pp. 28-35, 1978. Appears in: "Communication Protocol Modeling", C. Sunshine, ed., Artech House, 1981.

Danny Cohen is a project leader at USC/ISI. His research interests include aircraft cockpit information systems, interactive real-time systems, flight simulation, voice communications, computer architecture, VLSI, computer networking, and graphics.

Danny received the BSc degree in Mathematics from the Technion (Israel Institute of Technology) in 1963 and a Phd degree in Computer Science from Harvard University in 1969.

Danny has been on the Computer Science faculties of Harvard University, the Technion and CALTECH.

Jonathan Postel is a project leader at USC/ISI. His current research interests are the interconnection of computer networks, multimachine interprocess communication, and multimedia computer mail.

Jon received his BS and MS degrees in Engineering and his PhD in Computer Science from the University of California, Los Angeles. Jon has worked for the MITRE Corporation in McLean, Virginia and SRI International In Menlo Park, California.

At UCLA he was involved in the development of the ARPANET Network Measurement Center and the installation of the first host on the ARPANET. Since that time, he has participated in the development of many of the higher level protocols used in the ARPANET.

Carl Sunshine is with USC/ISI where he is engaged in research on computer networks and their protocols. He is particularly interested in protocol design, modeling, and analysis, and network interconnection.

Carl received a PhD in computer science in 1975 from Stanford University where he worked on the first major network interconnection projects within the ARPA and IFIP communities. From 1975 to 1979 he worked at the Rand Corporation on various protocol design and network planning projects.

Carl is active in IFIP, ISO, and ANSI network groups and is Vice Chairman of the ACM Special Interest Group on Data Communication. He serves on the editorial board of Computer Networks journal, and is Associate Editor for Protocols of the IEEE Transactions on Communications. He has lectured and published widely.

X.75 Interconnection of Datapac with other Packet Switched Networks

M S Unsoy
TransCanada Telephone System, Canada

Recently, agreement has been reached within CCITT with respect to standards for the inter-connection of public packet switched networks (PSNs). CCITT Recommendation X.75 describes the standards for the internetwork signalling procedures required to interconnect these networks. The Datapac network, as well as several other PSNs, has already implemented the X.75 procedures. This paper discusses the methodology used and the operating experience gained by the introduction of X.75 interfaces between Datapac and other PSNs, including GTE Telenet, Tymnet, Teleglobe Canada, IPSS, PSS, Datex-P, Transpac KDD and NTT (the last six through Teleglobe Canada).

1. INTRODUCTION

Several public data networks based on packet switching technology are operational around the world. Datapac™ in Canada, GTE Telenet and Tymnet in the U.S., PSS and IPSS in the U.K., Transpac in France, and Datex-P in West Germany are some of them. Many more such networks are being developed in numerous other countries. By interconnecting public PSNs, international data services are offered to network users. Before any standards were reached for internetworking, interim gateways were installed to connect these public networks (Ref. 1), thus achieving early intro-duction of international packet switched data network services.

CCITT (International Telegraph and Telephone Consultative Committee) has agreed upon Recom-mendation X.75, an internetwork signalling procedure for the interconnection of public PSNs (Ref. 2). Datapac and several other PSNs have implemented the CCITT X.75 procedures to interconnect with other networks (Ref. 3, 4). Datapac has established direct X.75 intercon-nections with GTE Telenet and Tymnet in the U.S. Through the IPACS (International Packet-Switched System) transit network services of Teleglobe Canada, Datapac has also intercon-nected, via X.75, with IPSS and PSS of the U.K., Transpac of France, Datex-P of West Germany, KDD and NTT of Japan, Italy, Switzer-land, and Austria for two-way and over 20 other countries for one-way (incoming only) traffic. This paper discusses the operating experience in introducing these X.75 inter-faces between Datapac and other PSNs.

The rest of this section presents a brief description of Datapac. Section 2 outlines Datapac X.75 internetworking characteristics. Section 3 describes procedures that have been agreed upon between Datapac and other PSNs, to complement the CCITT X.75 procedures. The X.75 tests conducted by Datapac and other PSNs and the experience gained from these tests are the subject of Section 4. Finally, Section 5 describes operational aspects of the X.75 interconnections between Datapac and other PSNs. The performance, traffic engineering, troubleshooting and accounting issues are also discussed.

Datapac is a public packet switched data communications network operated by the Computer Communications Group (CCG) of the TransCanada Telephone System (TCTS). The basic service offering provides the capability to set up a virtual circuit between a pair of Data Terminal Equipments (DTEs). The network topology presently comprises 23 packet switch-ing nodes interconnected in a mesh of 56 kbps digital transmission facilities and supplying service to 66 Datapac Serving Areas across Canada. Each node consists of the SL-10 packet switch developed by Bell Northern Research and manufactured by Northern Telecom Ltd. The SL-10 is a multi-microprocessor which can be modularly extended to support the required number of access lines and a mix of software-based access services (Ref. 5).

Datapac started commercial international services with GTE Telenet and Tymnet in the U.S.A. in May, 1978. The interconnections were achieved through interim gateways imple-mented on minicomputers and connected to networks via X.25 interfaces. The Datapac international overseas service was inaugurated in January, 1980 through an interim gateway developed by Teleglobe Canada, and connected to Datapac via an X.25 interface. Teleglobe Canada maintains a transit packet switched network (IPACS), administering calls between Canadian and overseas networks. These interim gateways proved very useful, not only in supporting the ever increasing international traffic between Datapac and other PSNs, but also in providing us with expertise in inter-networking (Ref. 6).

2. DATAPAC X.75 INTERNETWORKING

CCITT Study Group VII defined Recommendation X.75 in 1978 to accomplish the interconnection of public PSNs. The revised version of this recommendation was approved by CCITT in February 1980 (Ref. 2). This section briefly describes the implementation of X.75 proce-dures and international addressing on Datapac. For further details, see Ref. 3.

2.1 X.75 Procedures

The CCITT Recommendation X.75 defines procedures at the interface between two stations called Signalling Terminal Equipments (STEs). Like X.25 (Ref. 7), these procedures are specified at three distinct levels: physical, frame and packet levels. The physical level defines the electrical and functional characteristics of the interface between two STEs. The frame level specifies the use of the data link control procedure LAPB which is compatible with the High-Level Data Link Control (HDLC). The frame level procedures guarantee the correct exchange of information across the international link.

The packet level defines procedures by which switched virtual calls are established, maintained and cleared across the X.75 interface. The procedures and packet formats for X.75 are very similar to those for X.25. The X.75 Call Request and Call Connected packets contain an additional field for utilities used to signal network-oriented information between STEs.

An STE initiates a call by transmitting a Call Request packet across the X.75 interface. The Call Request packet contains the Logical Channel Number chosen by the STE which identifies all packets associated with the call. It also includes the calling and called DTE addresses or international data numbers as defined in CCITT Recommendation X.121 (Ref. 8). The utility, facility and user data fields follow. Utilities are used to signal network oriented information between STEs. The facility field may only be used for national facilities. User data may be a maximum of 16 octets in length.

The calling STE will receive a Call Connected packet if the called STE can accept the call. Similar to the Call Request, the Call Connected packet contains an address field, network utility field and a user facility field. When a switched virtual call cannot be established, the called STE will transmit a Clear Request packet containing the appropriate call progress signal as defined in CCITT Recommendation X.96 (Ref. 9).

The CCITT X.75 Recommendation defines several network utilities in order that network oriented information may be signalled between the STEs in the Call Request and the Call Connected packets. Datapac X.75 implementation includes the following utilities (Ref. 3):

- Call Identifier
- Throughput Class Indication
- Window Size Indication
- Packet Size Indication
- Transit Network Identification
- Reverse Charging Indication
- Utility Marker
- Tariff

2.2 Datapac International Addressing

One of the basic elements of international network connections is the international numbering plan. The CCITT Recommendation X.121 defines the international numbering plan for identifying public network addressing. Each public data network is assigned a Data Network Identification Code (DNIC), a four-digit number with the first three digits identifying the country and the fourth digit identifying a particular public data network in that country. Datapac's DNIC is 3020.

An international address contains a DNIC, followed by a Network Terminal Number (NTN) which specifies the address of the terminal within the public data network. The NTN comprises up to 10 digits and is assigned to a particular terminal by the network administration.

For outgoing international calls from a network, an international prefix digit is allowed in CCITT Recommendation X.121. The composition of this prefix digit is a national matter since the prefix digit does not form part of the international data number. The prefix digit for Datapac is 1. All international addresses supplied by DTEs on Datapac must be preceeded by this digit. Thus, when a Datapac user wishes to establish an international virtual circuit, he specifies the destination DTE address using the following format: 1 DNIC NTN.

3. CHARACTERISTICS OF DATAPAC X.75 INTERFACES

CCITT Recommendations X.75 and X.121 do not cover all areas of public PSN internetworking. There are several issues that have to be discussed and negotiated between the networks involved. The values for various parameters defined in X.75 should also be agreed upon by the networks.

An X.75 gateway consists of 2 STE stations in neighbouring PSNs with an X.75 link between them. Datapac has such direct X.75 gateways with GTE Telenet and Tymnet in the U.S.A., and with IPACS of Teleglobe Canada for interconnecting with overseas PSNs.

Datapac and the neighbouring PSNs agreed to use the Single Link Procedure (SLP) only. The Multi-Link Procedure (MLP) is not supported at Datapac X.75 interfaces. These administrations also agreed to use MOD-8 numbering at both the frame and packet levels. Since no satellite links are expected at this time, the MOD-128 numbering is not supported at Datapac X.75 interfaces.

The SLP in CCITT Recommendation X.75 is based upon the Link Access Procedure (LAPB) described in Section 2 of CCITT Recommendation X.25. When Datapac X.75 interconnections with the neighbouring PSNs were introduced, LAPB procedures were under development in Datapac. To achieve early introduction of the X.75 interconnections, Datapac and other PSNs agreed to base the SLP upon the Link Access Procedures (LAP) described in the same section of Recommendation X.25 (Ref. 7). As soon as LAPB became available and was tested on Datapac, X.75 interfaces between Datapac and other PSNs supported LAPB.

To reduce the occurrence of call collisions,

STEs assign logical channel numbers in a reverse order. It is agreed that the Datapac STEs assign logical channels in descending order, starting with the highest numbered available channel, while the neighbouring PSNs use the logical channels in ascending order, starting with the lowest numbered available channel.

It is agreed to provide multiple X.75 gateways between Datapac and each neighbouring network, thus enhancing the availability of X.75 interconnections. Datapac routing procedures for outgoing international calls select the closest (in terms of hops) and the least loaded (in terms of VCs) gateway at call setup time.

To ensure availability of the X.75 interface, the Datapac STE periodically sends a Clear Request packet as an idle line probe to the neighbouring STE on an idle logical channel. If a Clear Confirmation packet is not received within the specified time (e.g., 3 minutes), a major failure must have occurred at the neighbouring STE. The Datapac STE declares the interface down, generates an appropriate Datapac alarm, and further outgoing calls are routed through other X.75 gateways.

The Datapac and neighbouring network STEs verify the DNICs of all addresses on incoming and outgoing Call Request and Call Connected packets. By specifying the authorized DNICs in the STEs, all networks can enforce any policy bilaterally agreed upon, with regards to incoming, outgoing and transit calls.

It is agreed between Datapac and the U.S. networks (i.e., GTE Telenet and Tymnet) that collect calls over the X.75 gateways will be accepted, thus allowing reverse charging between Canada and the U.S. The reverse charging requests and confirmations are exchanged between the networks using the Reverse Charging Indication utility. However, it is agreed not to support collect calls between Datapac and the overseas networks through IPACS. As a result, the X.75 gateways between Datapac and IPACS will block such calls.

The CCITT X.75 specifications do not allow permanent virtual circuits; thus only switched virtual circuits are supported through Datapac X.75 interconnections.

The network access services permitted to establish international calls via X.75 between Datapac and other PSNs are limited to X.25 and X.28 (Interactive Terminal Interface - ITI) access services on Datapac. Datapac currently supports the first 12 of the international ITI parameters, as specified in CCITT Recommendation X.3. Datapac and other PSNs also offer sets of national ITI parameters. For international calls, the International ITI parameters can be used transparently through the Datapac X.75 interfaces. For national parameters, users have two choices: (i) the ITI terminal user may set the local national parameters, or (ii) the host can specify and set the national ITI parameters of a foreign network if they are delimited from the Inter-

national ITI parameters with a National Parameter Marker (NPM), as indicated in CCITT Recommendation X.29 (Ref. 10).

4. TESTING OF DATAPAC X.75 INTERFACES

The X.75 interface between two public PSNs has to be tested thoroughly before it is introduced to commercial service. This section describes the testing conducted by Datapac and other PSNs for X.75 interconnections.

4.1 Testing Stages

Recommendation X.75 specifies the signalling procedures between two STEs. However, the X.75 interface is only a portion of the international end-to-end (DTE-to-DTE) connection. Thus, testing the X.75 interconnection of two or more networks involves two stages: (i) X.75 interface testing, and (ii) end-to-end testing.

The purpose of X.75 interface testing is to verify that the implementation of X.75 procedures on each network's STE conforms to the procedures specified in CCITT Recommendation X.75 and other additional interface requirements. Datapac has developed a test plan which includes over 500 individual tests to verify the functional correctness of the Datapac STE implementation. These tests cover not only the normal procedures but also abnormal conditions in cases of invalid frames or packets.

Other networks have developed similar test plans to verify the correctness of their STEs. Using these plans and various automatic test tools, Datapac and other networks conducted the X.75 interface testing separately.

The purpose of end-to-end testing is two-fold. Firstly, it verifies that the X.75 implementations and interface parameters of all involved networks are compatible. Secondly, it verifies that the international virtual circuits from DTE to DTE can be established, maintained and cleared as specified. This stage of testing requires the full cooperation of the networks involved. Datapac has conducted end-to-end testing with each of GTE Telenet, Tymnet and several overseas networks jointly. A description of some of these tests and their results is provided in the next section.

4.2 End-to-End Testing

The current X.75 interconnections between Datapac and most other PSNs support virtual circuits between X.25 DTEs and/or X.28 DTEs (ITI terminals). Thus, end-to-end tests can be classified into four basic categories:

(i) Datapac X.25 DTE to foreign PSN X.25 DTE
(ii) Datapac X.25 DTE to foreign PSN X.28 DTE
(iii) Datapac X.28 DTE to foreign PSN X.25 DTE
(iv) Datapac X.28 DTE to foreign PSN X.28 DTE.

In addition to these categories, end-to-end tests were conducted with some networks' non-standard DTEs (e.g., Tymcom and Tymsat DTEs on Tymnet).

Each category included a series of tests for call setup, data transfer, call reset, and call clearing, in both foreign PSN-to-Datapac and Datapac-to-foreign PSN directions. These tests were designed to check every possible end-to-end situation in every phase of a virtual call. For example, the data transfer phase was tested by sending data packets with/ without the M-bit, with/without the O-bit, with different data field lengths, and by sending interrupt packets under various conditions (e.g., busy or non-busy channels).

During this exhaustive testing, incompatibilities between Datapac and other PSNs were encountered and resolved. For example, immediately following initialization of the X.75 link between Datapac and GTE Telenet, it was found that X.75 logical channel ranges did not match. Even though 64 logical channels were agreed upon, GTE Telenet implements 64 logical channels from 0 to 63, while Datapac implements them from 1 to 64. This problem was corrected by increasing Telenet's logical channel range by one (Ref. 11). Similarly, when the X.75 link between Datapac and IPACS' Engine gateway was first initialized, it was found that 32 of the 64 logical channels on Engine were incoming and the other 32 were outgoing only. Tymshare, the Engine manufacturer, corrected the problem by modifying the software.

Another difficulty was the incompatibility in the X.75 Call Connected packet format. The format used by Datapac STE followed the CCITT X.75 version provisionally approved in 1978. However, Telenet's STE was using the format specified in the 1980 version of X.75. The problem was resolved by Datapac modifying the Call Connected packet format in accordance to the 1980 version of CCITT X.75.

One problem at the call setup phase related to a bilaterally agreed utility field called the Tariff utility. This field was missing in the Call Connected packets sent by Telenet's STE but was expected by Datapac's STE. This was resolved by modifying Telenet's STE to include the Tariff utility in the Call Connected packets.

One other problem was the incorrect signalling of clear and reset causes, experienced in Datapac - GTE Telenet and Datapac - IPSS/PSS interconnections. Both GTE Telenet and IPACS undertook software modifications to assure proper signalling of clear and reset causes over the X.75 interface and also end-to-end.

The only problem encountered in the Datapac - Datex-P interconnection via IPACS was a mismatch in the treatment of utility fields by the three networks involved. Since the treatment of utilities at X.75 interfaces is parameterized, the problem was resolved by fine-tuning the parameters at the Datapac - IPACS and IPACS - Datex-P X.75 interfaces.

The last problem that surfaced as a result of end-to-end testing was incompatibility in the use of the Protocol Identifier Field of Call Request packets generated by the ITI PADs. According to CCITT Recommendation X.29 (Ref.

10), the 4-octet field should be specified as X"01000000". Datapac ITI PADs expect the protocol identifier field to contain this value. However, GTE Telenet, IPSS and PSS use the second and third octets of this field to specify the type and speed of the ITI terminal. This non-standard use of the protocol identifier field caused call clearing by the Datapac PAD. Telenet agreed to provide the protocol identifier field as X"01000000" in Datapac-destined ITI calls. Similarly, IPACS agreed to remove the non-standard octets of this field in Call Request packets originating from PSS and IPSS and destined for Datapac.

4.3 Customer Trials

After verifying the functional correctness of the Datapac X.75 interfaces, some network users were asked to participate in customer trials. The purpose of these trials was to test the acceptability of X.75 interconnections, the X.121 addressing node, and of end-to-end performance. It also provided users with an opportunity to test and modify their own software, taking advantage of X.75 interconnections between Datapac and other PSNs.

5. OPERATIONAL ASPECTS OF DATAPAC X.75 GATEWAYS

Traffic engineering, performance and accounting are among the several operational aspects of the PSN interconnections not covered by the CCITT standards.

5.1 Traffic Engineering

The number of gateways, their locations, line speeds and the number of logical channels on each are the main traffic engineering issues in Datapac X.75 interconnections. Datapac X.75 gateways can be located on any node in the network and many such gateways can be supported on a single node. Various synchronous speeds up to 56 kbps can be used, and a wide range of logical channels can be assigned to each gateway.

Datapac traffic engineers are provided with various tools based on traffic statistics collected periodically from the X.75 gateways. These statistics provide the number of frames and packets sent and received, the packet length histogram for each direction, and minimum and maximum numbers of simultaneous virtual circuits over an X.75 gateway during a 15-minute interval. Using these statistics, Datapac traffic engineers determine the need for (i) additional gateways, (ii) upgrading the speed, or (iii) more logical channels on existing gateways. Accounting statistics also provide Community of Interest (COI) tables, which are used to determine the best locations for Datapac X.75 gateways to other PSNs.

Neighbouring PSN administrations also gather information regarding the internetwork traffic. Decisions to add new gateways, or increase the speed or numbers of logical channels on existing gateways, are made jointly by Datapac and neighbouring PSN administrations based on the traffic information available.

5.2 Performance

Datapac X.75 internetworking provides various means of enhancing the performance of international calls. Since Datapac X.75 gateways are implemented within the network and as part of the network, Datapac operational personnel have wide control and monitoring capabilities. This 24-hour, 7-day monitoring of all gateways significantly increases the availability of interconnections. The idle line probe, described in Section 3, also enhances this availability.

There are multiple X.75 gateways between Datapac and each neighbouring network. The Datapac routing scheme for an outgoing international call is such that the gateway that is the closest (in terms of hops) and the least loaded (in terms of VCs) is chosen for the call. If a gateway to a network is down, then one of the other gateways will be chosen. This routing scheme not only improves the availability as perceived by the user, but also selects the best path within Datapac, thus improving the end-to-end delay performance.

As described in Section 2, X.75 internetworking also provides an opportunity for networks to negotiate throughput classes, and window and packet sizes at the X.75 interface on a per call basis. Values for these three network utilities can be selected, bearing in mind the objective of meeting user delay and throughput performance requirements while making efficient use of network resources (Ref. 12). Currently, Datapac X.75 gateways negotiate these values to defaults agreed bilaterally between the networks. However, it will be possible in the near future to negotiate a wide range of throughput classes, window sizes and packet sizes, to enhance virtual circuit performance.

5.3 International Accounting

On international calls, one DTE is billed for the total charges arising from a call, excluding local access charges. If a single flat rate tariff exists, no additional signalling is required. But, for cases of non-flat rate tariffs, (e.g., a duration charge for dial port usage, city density sensitivity), a mechanism is required to allow the remote network to send tariff parameter information to the billing network. The billed DTE may be the calling or called DTE since reverse charging is optionally available between Datapac and the U.S. networks.

Tariff parameters can be exchanged between the end networks during call establishment by using the Tariff utility field. These tariff parameters are stored in Datapac and in the foreign network for the call duration. When the call is cleared, these parameters are sent to the Datapac Data Collection Centre (DCC) in the call accounting records, along with the call's data volume and duration, the calling and called addresses and other service information.

CONCLUSIONS

By interconnecting public packet switched data networks, international data services are offered to network users. The interconnection of Datapac and other PSNs has been provided through interim gateways since May 1978. However, after the CCITT standards for interconnection were firmly established, standard interconnection procedures (i.e., X.75 and X.121) were implemented.

Before X.75 interfaces between the networks were introduced, network administrations conducted discussions and negotiations to agree on bilateral and/or multilateral internetworking issues. These negotiations were followed by detailed testing of both X.75 interfaces and the end-to-end connections. All incompatibilities were identified and resolved. Harmonious operation of the X.75 interfaces was demonstrated. Finally, customer trials were held to verify the acceptability of the X.75 interconnections.

As a result of these tests and trials, X.75 interfaces between Datapac and other networks were introduced to commercial service (Figure 1), thus enhancing the quality and scope of the international virtual circuit services offered to the network users.

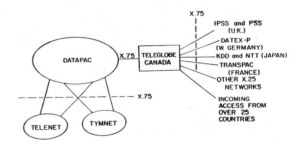

FIGURE I. DATAPAC X.75 INTERCONNECTIONS

ACKNOWLEDGEMENTS

The successful development, implementation and testing of the Datapac X.75 interfaces were the result of team efforts. Essential roles were played by many individuals in the Computer Communications Group of the Trans-Canada Telephone System and in Bell Northern Research. Their considerable efforts are gratefully acknowledged. The author would also like to acknowledge the contributions of many individuals from GTE Telenet, Tymnet, Teleglobe Canada, British Telecom Inc., Deutsche Bundespost, Transpac, KDD and NTT who participated in technical discussions and end-to-end testing with Datapac.

REFERENCES

(1) Rybczynski, A.M., Weir, D.F., and Cunningham, I.M., "Datapac Internetworking for International Services", ICCC '78 (Kyoto, Japan, Sept. 1978).

(2) CCITT Revised Recommendation X.75, "Terminal and Transit Control Procedures and Data Transfer System on International Circuits between Packet Switched Data Networks", COM VII - No 441 as amended and approved by Study Group VII (Feb. 1980).

(3) Rybczynksi, A.M., Palframan, J.D., and Thomas, A., "Design of the Datapac X.75 Internetworking Capability", ICCC '80 (Atlanta, October 1980).

(4) Weir, D.F., Holmblad, J.B., and Rothbert, A.C., "An X.75 Based Network Architecture", ICCC '80 (Atlanta, October 1980).

(5) McGibbon, C.I., et al., "DATAPAC - Initial Experience with a Commercial Packet Network", ICCC '78 (Kyoto, Japan, Sept. 1978).

(6) Unsoy, M.S., Rybczynski, A.M., and Rhynas, D., "Datapac International Packet Switching Services", ELECTRO '81 (New York, April 1981).

(7) CCITT Revised Recommendation X.25, "Interface between Data Terminal Equipment (DTE) and Data Circuit-Terminating Equipment (DCE) for Terminals Operating in the Packet Mode on Public Data Networks", as amended and approved by Study Group VII (Feb. 1980).

(8) CCITT Revised Recommendation X.121, "International Numbering Plan for Public Data Networks", CCITT Grey Book, as amended and approved by Study Group VII (Feb. 1980).

(9) CCITT Revised Recommendation X.96, "Call Progress Signals in Public Data Networks", approved by Study Group VII (Feb. 1980).

(10) CCITT Provisional Recommendation X.29, "Procedures for the Exchange of Control Information and User Data between a Packet Mode DTE and a PAD Facility" (1978).

(11) Unsoy, M.S., and Shanahan, T., "X.75 Internetworking of Datapac and Telenet", Seventh Data Communications Symposium (Mexico City, Mexico, October 1981).

(12) Rybczynski, A.M., and Unsoy, M.S., "X.75 Internetworking Flow Control Considerations", ICC 81 (Denver, Colorado, June 1981).

AUTHOR

Mehmet Unsoy received his BSEE from Middle East Technical University, Turkey, in 1973, and M. Math and PhD in Computer Science from the University of Waterloo, Canada in 1974 and 1980, respectively. Since 1978, he has been working as a manager with The Computer Communications Group of the TransCanada Telephone System. He has been responsible for the X.75 internetworking between Datapac and other public data networks. At present, he is responsible from Datapac services planning, including CCITT activities. He has published several papers on Datapac.

Interconnection of Public and Private Packet Networks

D L Jeanes
Bell-Northern Research, Canada

This paper outlines the emerging requirements for connection to public packet switching networks in those countries where private data networks exist. It reviews the progress of international standards discussions regarding such connections. Connection methods using standard X.25 interfaces are described, together with ways for private networks to resolve addressing and routing problems. These methods appear to be a viable alternative to private systems using dedicated lines. When an administration will provide the necessary interfaces and address assignments, the private network must still have additional capabilities for the interconnection to be effective. These are feasible with Northern Telecom's SL-10 * packet switching system, which is now in widespread use as the basis of both public and private data networks.

SUMMARY

Requirements of the private data network market for interconnection are identified. The networking capabilities of modern private telephone exchanges are seen as an example that may well be followed for data networks. Standardization issues and progress of discussions in the international standards bodies are reviewed. There are various numbering plan possibilities and configurations for interconnecting private systems via public facilities. The capabilities of Northern Telecom's SL-10 Packet Switching System and an X.25 "gateway" service for use in private networks are described. Although there is potential for further study and improvements, it is concluded that, where public networks will provide the necessary interfaces and address assignments, X.25 now permits effective interconnection.

MARKET REQUIREMENTS FOR INTERCONNECTION

In countries where private data networks are permitted, there are increasing requirements for their interconnection with public packet switching networks. Two developments provide the impetus. First the number and size of private data networks is advancing beyond traditional systems based on a single host computer. Second the maturing system of national data networks, with standard X.25 packet mode interfaces, (reference 8), and international X.75 connections, offers new opportunities for national and worldwide interconnection. X.25 concentrators have proved attractive in reducing the customer cost of terminal access to public networks. In some countries there is now the opportunity for switching as well as concentration within such systems, (reference 3).

Where private networks are permitted, public network access can provide increased geographic coverage, extra capacity on demand, or low-cost backup. In some cases the public network can replace all dedicated lines between private network locations.

There are two general requirements of private to public network interconnection methods. The first is universal accessibility for private network Data Terminal Equipment, (DTE), which must be able to originate and accept calls to and from any DTE reachable via public networks. The second is adequate cost control mechanisms for administration of the private networks.

Accessibility is the ability for terminals on public and private packet networks worldwide to communicate conveniently and efficiently. Addressing schemes should allow world-unique addresses for private network terminals. Co-ordinated numbering plans within private networks should be possible. If the addressing scheme only permits some of the terminals on a private network to be addressable from a public network, then administrative problems and user confusion will result. Numbering plans which allow full addressing avoid problems as private networks grow. Numbering methods should make efficient use of the address space, but private networks must be able to have sufficiently large address spaces, both for DTE addressing and for internal routing purposes.

The addressing information should be handled in such a way that it can transit public networks even if they do not recognize private networks. Intercommunication should not require a DTE to implement extensions to X.25, (or X.29 for interactive terminal support). Access from

----

* SL is a registered trademark of Northern Telecom Limited.

public terminals to a private DTE should preferably use the same address, regardless of the location of the calling terminal. In countries where private networks may connect to more than one public packet network, access codes for users to reach these networks must be convenient and unambiguous.

Cost control is important to an organization which must allocate internal data communication costs to users. Access to public facilities, which may be expensive, must almost always be subject to accounting and control. Accounting can be handled from public network billing information if the calling private network terminal is identified. Private network accounting data, if used, must identify the actual far-end address for off-net calls. Some private networks may wish to make use of cost-related information provided directly by the public network, such as a charge information facility in X.25. Control requirements include restricting public network access or calling options to specific terminals or users. These restrictions may be applied to individual private DTEs. They may differ between on-net and off-net calling. Normally controls are implemented at the calling point.

Many potential network customers have indicated to Northern Telecom their requirements for public network interconnection. Both the purpose and the degree of interconnection vary considerably. For example, one customer required interworking with five domestic and international public packet networks for extended geographic coverage. Another specified interconnection with from two to seven public networks for automatic back up of dedicated facilities. A third wished to interconnect via X.25 with three public networks. One required connection to a national public network for support of both X.28 and IBM 2780/3780 terminals.

There are several commercial reasons for the private network owner to want interconnection. For small private networks requiring wide geographic coverage with low data volumes, long haul transmission over public networks may be cheaper than dedicated facilities. Public network connection can also provide on-demand backup for nonredundant dedicated trunks. Regulatory restrictions and high tariffs in some countries make networking over dedicated facilities infeasible. Some administrations are discouraging use of dedicated lines in favour of their public data networks. Dedicated lines on heavily used routes can be supplemented with public network switched connections to permit economical wide geographic coverage.

THE INTERCONNECT EXAMPLE OF THE TELEPHONE PBX

Connection between the public switched telephone network (PSTN) and private switching systems has been allowed in some countries for many years. The Private Branch Exchange, (PBX), is extensively used in the United States. The term "interconnect" is now used in the U.S. to mean the market for privately owned telecommunications equipment connecting to public networks. Some modern private branch exchanges have rich feature sets to support networking using both dedicated lines and switched public network connections. The Electronic Switched Network (ESN), based on the the Northern Telecom SL-1, is an example of a system with these features, (reference 7).

PBX systems effectively function as switching extensions of the public network. Several signalling protocols are supported for public to private telephone network interconnection. Some of them permit direct dialling for both calling directions between the PBX and PSTN. Some provide the calling PBX extension number to the PSTN for accounting purposes. These features require the extension numbers to be part of the public telephone numbering plan. Where extension numbers are not in the public plan, they can only be reached from outside by a two-stage process through a human attendant. PBX systems are often directly connected by dedicated facilities such as "tie" trunks. Features such as automatic route selection permit the building of private networks of multiple PBXs. Routing of calls between PBXs over dedicated or public facilities is performed automatically based on the called number.

Private switching systems can also provide customized cost control features to facilitate interconnection. Call detail recording provides accounting for PBX calls using the PSTN. Individual telephones on the PBX can have various "class-of-service" restrictions which may limit access to potentially expensive public facilities. Access to specific public network area codes or even individual phone numbers may be restricted. Password controlled authorization code mechanisms allow a normally restricted terminal or even a terminal on the public network to access the controlled facilities.

Users will expect private data networks to ultimately have the same capabilities as are currently provided by sophisticated telephone private branch exchange networks. These extensive capabilities for PBX interconnection are a result of similar user requirements to those which are now emerging in the private data network market. They indicate the features and capabilities which should be planned for in the design of such networks.

STANDARDIZATION ISSUES FOR INTERCONNECTION

Active discussion of private network interconnection has begun within the various international standards committees. So far there is no common position among telecommunication administrations. The X.25 packet mode interface appears to be the best protocol that will be generally available to private packet switching networks. However, interconnection also poses problems of addressing, routing, availability, and accounting that are beyond X.25 and that must be resolved by the private networks. The influence of international standards on data network product requirements has grown, largely because of the widespread acceptance and use of X.25 by national public networks and by an increasing number of computer and terminal manufacturers, (reference 4).

Much of the concern about connecting private networks to public data networks has been raised in meetings of the ISO/TC97/SC6 subcommittee and subsequently in CCITT study group VII, (reference 2). Some of the issues to be studied include: conveying a private network DTE address, amount of numbering space required, multiple circuits between networks, connecting to multiple public networks, exchanging accounting information, reverse charging acceptance and closed user groups, problems with X.25 timeouts, passing of call progress signals, (such as clearing cause), unambiguous identification of the calling party and network, and methods for choosing routes where alternative public networks exist.

Interconnection depends on the method used to assign addresses to private network DTEs. If private and public network managers can agree on consistent schemes, many problems and restrictions disappear. The standards bodies have placed a high priority on finding suitable private network addressing methods. Proposals for addressing extension through the X.25 facility field and X.121 numbering plan extensions to permit private network addressing are under study. Currently there are three active proposals, which are discussed in the next section of the paper. Suggestions to allow the call user data field for addressing have been rejected because such use violates the reference model for open systems interconnection (OSI), and because the addressed end system may also need to make use of the user data, for example as a security password.

Private network requirements will initially have to be met without any special interconnection mechanisms beyond standard X.25. It will be the only suitable transparent packet interface offered by most public networks. Other standard protocols, such as X.28, are not suitable for interconnection due to limitations on transparency, multiplexing, efficiency, and error control. Public networks should not have to know the internal structure of private networks or the characteristics of individual

private network terminals. There appears to be a growing concensus that public/private network interconnection must be provided for and that X.25 is the appropriate protocol.

PRIVATE NETWORK NUMBERING PLANS

CCITT recommendation X.121 defines the international numbering plan for public data networks, (reference 9). It provides for international addressing within the 15-digit limit of X.25. Three or four digits are used to identify the country, and possibly a network within the country. Up to eleven or ten digits respectively are available for use as national addresses. The remaining digit is unspecified but would normally be used for an international calling prefix.

Three approaches to private network numbering that are compatible with X.121 have been identified. Each differs in the demands that it makes of DTE, private network, and public network capabilities. They are referred to in this paper as shared address space, private local numbering, and private network national numbering.

Shared address space assigns addresses to private network DTEs within the numbering plan of a single public network. Public networks may permit subscription to blocks of consecutive addresses, and then route calls for all the addresses to one or more X.25 links. This method has several advantages but some problems. Each private DTE has a world unique address which conforms to X.121. Any standard DTE with access to a public packet network can therefore call a DTE on an interconnected private network. Public network accounting can identify usage by individual private DTEs. A user has the same address for both local and public network calling. However, problems arise when a private network connects to more than one public network or when public networks are unable to assign sufficiently large blocks of numbers to private networks.

Private local numbering assigns DTE addresses that are chosen independently from the public network numbering plan. These addresses can normally consist of fewer digits than a normal national address. They are similar to extension numbers in private telephone systems. This approach has several advantages. Administration and local user calling is usually simpler due to the use of shorter addresses. The private network can connect to multiple public networks or have ports with different addresses on a public network. Users still have unique DTE addresses within the private network, but more than one private network access address may be used. Outside callers can combine any such address with the private local number when calling.

Local addresses may be passed through the public network as extra digits following the public address of the private network. These digits are not interpreted by the public network, but the public network must allow them. The overall X.25 limit of 15 digits, (including any prefix), must not be exceeded. Incoming calls from public networks have all preceding digits stripped from destination address fields. Outgoing calls must have these digits re-inserted in source address fields. There is no requirement for these stripped or inserted digits to be the same for all points of interconnection. The advantage of this approach is that it conforms to X.25, does not require extensions to existing DTEs or public networks, and provides for unique DTE identification in call setup and accounting.

An alternative local numbering approach is now under discussion in CCITT. The local address may have a larger number of digits, but it is carried through public networks in a facility field separate from the public address. This scheme eliminates the impact on public network address space or number of address digits. By permitting two addresses, (or more), it also allows the caller to indicate the preferred route to reach the private network. However, it requires changes to the X.25 standard, changes to all DTEs that wish to indicate double addresses, and provision to accept the facility in public networks, (whether or not they support private networks directly).

Private network national numbering has been proposed in ISO and CCITT discussions, (reference 6). This scheme is similar to integrated national numbering from the private network viewpoint; however, the numbers are not assigned from the numbering plan of a public network. Instead one or more separate four-digit Data Network Identification Codes are assigned to cover all the private networks within a given country. Each private network has a nationally agreed Private Network Identification Code, (PNIC), of two or more digits following the DNIC. A coding scheme was proposed for these codes that would permit definition of a large number of networks with compact internal numbering plans, as well as a small number of networks with very many addresses.

This method recognizes the problems of multiple public network interconnection and of excessive address space demands on public networks. The scheme would only be used in countries which needed such a capability. It would still provide world unique private network DTE addresses. However, PNICs may cause severe problems for public networks. They preclude the hierarchical routing which most networks use currently. Potentially large lists are required to map addresses to private network access ports. These lists must be either centrally stored or duplicated in some or all nodes of the public network.

PRIVATE NETWORK CONNECTION CONFIGURATIONS

Several possibilities are available for interconnection of privately owned packet switching systems with the public networks. They include single systems operating as private data exchanges, co-ordinated systems with public interconnections, and private packet networks. These configurations can be viewed as stages in the orderly growth of a private packet switching network. They introduce more complex routing situations as a private system grows, while reducing communication costs through use of switched public facilities, particularly in the initial stages.

The single system provides a local switching capability but has connections to the public network. These permit interworking between private terminals and public DTEs. It is suitable where there is a strong local community of interest with more than one host computer and some remote users. This configuration is equivalent to a telephone PBX or to a local area data network.

In co-ordinated systems users served from different sites can call each other via the public network. Private SL-10 packet switching systems can be co-ordinated so that dedicated trunk connections are also possible. Calls between sites may use these or the public network route. Calls from the public network can only use the gateway leading directly to the destination system. Although this configuration can act as a network internally, the public network sees it as separate DTEs.

The private packet network has its own dedicated internal trunks and does not depend on the public network as a connection path. When connected to a public network it appears as a single entity. The private network is responsible for routing calls between DTEs among its own internal sites. It may be impossible to route a call between two such DTEs over a path part of which includes public network facilities. This is because the public network will not distinguish between the different parts of such a private network and will therefore not be able to determine the appropriate destination gateway.

SL-10 INTERCONNECTION CAPABILITIES

SL-10 has evolved from its origins as one of the world's first commercial packet switching systems. Originally built for the Canadian Datapac network in 1976, (reference 1), the system is now also in service or being installed for public packet switching networks in Germany, Austria, and Switzerland. There are private SL-10 networks in Belgium, (Société

990

Générale de Banque), and the United States, (Federal Reserve System), and others are on order in the United Kingdom and in the U.S. and Canada. SL-10 is a leader among public packet switching networks and is establishing an equally strong place in the market for large private data networks.

SL-10 supports CCITT standard interfaces such as X.25, X.3/28/29, and X.75, as well as IBM-compatible 3270, 2780/3780, HASP Multileaving, and other protocols. Existing SL-10 capabilities and features for public and private networks provide the elements needed for interconnection. They include flexible routing, multiple circuit services, a variety of call restriction options, comprehensive accounting, network user identifiers, and flexible address formats. There are also some X.25 extensions, such as optionally permitting call progress signals from the DTE, (for example the call clearing cause).

SL-10 based public networks have considerable flexibility, (subject to pricing and regulatory considerations), to assign address ranges to private networks. Depending on the national address length, subaddress extension digits may be assigned. Variable length addresses are possible, allowing subaddress assignment of various sized address blocks within the overall national plan. Multiple addresses can also be independently assigned to a single X.25 link.

THE SL-10 X.25 GATEWAY

The approach to be used for private networks based on Northern Telecom's SL-10 Packet Switching System is an X.25 DTE interface. It is referred to as a "gateway" to correspond to the use of this term in X.75 and other internetworking methods, (reference 5). It should be noted that a gateway in this sense is a function that does not require a physically independent device. Interworking between non-X.25 terminals through the gateway is possible because it is a transparent facility.

The X.25 gateway provides methods for the routing and transmission of incoming and outgoing calls from or to a public data network. Both functions differ from previous uses of X.25 as a purely DTE/DCE protocol for public network access. An incoming call from a public network can address a DTE on the SL-10 private network through subaddressing. This means that the public network will not examine the entire destination address but will pass all the signalled digits to the DTE. Further address analysis is then done in the private system. (This is similar to direct extension dialling on private telephone systems). Outgoing calls can use international standard destination addresses to facilitate routing, with subaddressing used to fully identify the source.

These calls are routed by the X.121 Data Network Identification Code.

Subaddressing is not supported by all public networks. However, there are other ways of assigning multiple consecutive addresses to a circuit which may be available, (subject to pricing or regulatory constraints). It is not necessary for a public network to reduce the number of digits in its national addresses in order to allow multiple address assignment. Where there is direct connection to more than one public network, the private network can avoid numbering inconsistencies by using short-form addresses, (e.g. two to four digit extension numbers), instead of the full national address. Some address modifications will be supported as options to accommodate these special situations.

Incoming calls from a public packet network to an SL-10 private network are forwarded by the gateway to the private network terminal identified by the destination subaddress in the call packet. Use of a single X.25 circuit, (or multiple circuits with the same public network address), permits world unique terminal numbers on the private network. This is an example of the use of shared address space. Addresses on the private network conform to X.121 and lie within the range allowed by the public network. The gateway may modify address fields between the public and private networks to permit short form terminal addresses within the private network. Call progress signals are passed back by the gateway to indicate clearing causes, (if the public network allows them). The gateway can include public network charge facility information in the private network accounting data, if required by the private network manager.

Outgoing calls from the private to a public network use the same gateway but are routed to it by DNIC. The gateway supports load sharing and network administration features. The public network, however, sees only an X.25 DTE and need not be aware of the gateway function. The called DNIC may identify either the public network or another network accessible through it. When there are connections to multiple public networks the network manager can choose which DNICs to route via each network. The terminal user cannot presently select transit network routings.

ISSUES FOR FURTHER STUDY

There are a number of additional requirements for the existing and proposed interconnection mechanisms. These are currently under study in ISO and CCITT. The rapid evolution of the private network market and growth in use of X.25 will encourage the finding of solutions.

In some cases public networks will wish to assign non-contiguous blocks of addresses to a private network. This may result from interconnection with multiple public port addresses or from unplanned growth in numbering requirements. It will then become impossible to pass correct source addresses to the public networks. User confusion and ambiguous private network accounting may result. However, the experience from telephony indicates that contiguous blocks of public numbers can be assigned to private systems. Use of multiple circuit connections such as hunt groups may also interfere with the correct passing of addresses. Preferably the public network will offer a multiple circuit arrangement with a single address. The X.25 protocol could be extended to facilitate interconnection. Additional signalling mechanisms could be defined to allow call progress signals from the private to the public network. X.25 multilink procedures are being studied and will eventually appear in some public networks, providing improved gateway performance and reliability.

For nonstandard addresses which are not unique within the X.121 plan, the second address gateway or "port method" may be necessary. It is similar in principle to attendant intervention or "second dial tone" in telephony. On a PBX the caller is connected to the attendant, orally gives a second number, and is then connected to the requested extension via a second call placed by the attendant. Alternatively, a second dial tone may be given to prompt the caller to dial additional digits. Such manual methods are not normally considered for data switching. The method for handling a second address on a private data network is to use the first address to select the port or gateway. The gateway then accepts the second address automatically. A virtual circuit in the called network can then be set up by the caller and concatenated with the original virtual circuit from the caller to the gateway.

CONCLUSION

The rapid growth of public networks supporting X.25 and the widespread acceptance of the standard by suppliers of computer and data communications systems have created a new environment for private networking. Although explicit standards for interconnection between private and public packet switching networks are still under study, X.25 can be used effectively, as presently defined, to provide standard gateways to public networks. The only additional required capability can be implemented in the private network, (such as in SL-10), and is transparent to the public network.

REFERENCES

1. Clipsham, W.W., Glave, F., Narraway, M.; "Datapac Network Overview"; International Conference on Computer Communication, Toronto, August 1976, pp. 131-135.

2. ISO/TC97/SC6; "Private Data Network Interface to X.25 Public Data Networks"; Contribution N2107, January 1981.

3. Tenkhoff, P.A.; "Private and Public Networks: A Role for Each?"; Networks 80 Conference, Online, May 1980, pp. 49-62.

4. Knightson, K.G.; "A Universal X.25 Interface"; Networks 80 Conference, Online, May 1980, pp. 405-417.

5. Unsoy, M.S.; "X.75 Interconnections of Datapac with other Packet Switched Networks"; International Conference on Computer Communication, London, September 1982.

6. CCITT Study Group VII; "Private Network DTE Addressing"; Contribution COM.VII-37, February 1981, 9 pp.

7. Dayem, R., Faletti, R.; "Electronic Switched Network", International Switching Symposium, Montreal, Canada; 21-25 September 1981, 7 pp.

8. CCITT Recommendation X.25; "Interface between Data Terminal Equipment (DTE) and Data Circuit-terminating Equipment (DCE) for Terminals Operating in the Packet Mode on Public Data Networks"; CCITT Yellow Book, Geneva, 1980.

9. CCITT Recommendation X.121; "International Numbering Plan for Public Data Networks"; CCITT Yellow Book, Geneva, 1980.

David Jeanes studied Computer Science at the University of Toronto, receiving his B.A.Sc. in Engineering Science in 1969. He worked as Chief Programmer of the Computer Systems Research Group at the University until 1973, then studied for an M.Eng. in Electrical Engineering in 1974. Joining Bell-Northern Research to work on the development of the Datapac Network, he was responsible for managing a major software architectural redesign of the SL-10 Packet Switching System in 1977. He has also worked on radio paging, local area networks, software engineering methods, and on development and planning for the SL-1 PBX. He is now manager of SL-10 Product Planning. He is a member of ACM and the IEEE Computer Society.

Response Times over Packet Switched Networks – some Performance Issues

J Chammas
TransCanada Telephone System, Canada

For most interactive computer communication applications, response time is a primary parameter of performance. With the rapid development of private and public packet switching data networks (PSNs), evaluation of user-perceived response times over PSNs becomes of particular importance. This paper addresses some of the main issues and implementation alternatives to consider when assessing response times over a PSN. The first part of the paper presents a response time analysis for three typical interactive oriented data terminal equipments (DTEs) accessing a packet switched network: a packet-mode X.25-based DTE, an IBM 3270 compatible DTE and a start-stop mode DTE. The second part of the paper introduces the concept of packet interleaving of multi-packet messages over X.25 access lines and analyzes its impact on response time.

1. INTRODUCTION

In recent years, packet switching technology has gained wide acceptance as a means of implementing public and private data communication networks. The advantages related to packet switching networks (PSNs) such as increased reliability, universality and cost reductions are well known and frequently reported in the literature. Improvement in network delay achieved by message packetization is also frequently mentioned.

For most interactive computer communication applications, response time is a primary parameter of performance. Although response times over private multipoint networks have been extensively analyzed (2), (3), (7), user response time issues over PSNs have only recently gained attention (14). It is thus the purpose of this paper to provide further insight into this subject.

In Section 2, the possible definitions of response times for any data network are presented. In Section 3, the hypothetical reference connections that will serve as a basis for our discussions are established. The response time components and special considerations in estimating the response time for each reference connection are then examined in Section 4. Finally, Section 5 analyzes the effect on response time of packet interleaving of multi-packet messages over X.25 access lines. During the initial implementation of some X.25 users, packet interleaving of multi-packet messages was observed and identified as a potential source of increased delay. The impact of packet interleaving on user response time will thus be analyzed and comparisons made with the non-interleaved case for various message length distributions.

2. RESPONSE TIME - DEFINITIONS

Response time can generally be defined in two different ways. The first and probably most common definition (1) is the elapsed time from the last user keystroke, which terminates a service request, until the first meaningful character is displayed at the user's terminal. For a buffered terminal, the first character displayed is equivalent to the receipt of the last character of the first block of a multi-block message, since block error checking is normally performed prior to display.

Response time can also be defined as the elapsed time from the last user keystroke until the last message character is received at the user's terminal. This definition is probably more accurate than the first as it is related to the interactive turnaround time, which is the amount of time required to perform a specified task (generally an input-output message pair). In fact, from an organizational point of view, turnaround time is the most significant measure of interactive computer service as it is directly related to the organization's cost of performing a given amount of work during a unit of time. For a buffered terminal, the last character displayed is thus equivalent to the receipt of the last character of the last block of a multi-block message.

Response time is usually expressed in terms of its mean and percentile values. A percentile value X implies that the response time will be less than or equal to a given value, say T seconds, X percent of the time. Typical values used for X are 90 and 95. The percentile value is probably considered more important than the mean, because it is closely related to the variability of the response time. Large variances are negatively perceived by the users as long response times, although infrequent, are long remembered and heavily weighted(10). In fact, in some user systems, dummy host delays are intentionally added in order to achieve a reasonable degree of uniformity in response times.

3. HYPOTHETICAL REFERENCE CONNECTIONS

The basic access method to PSNs is Recommendation X.25 of the International Telegraph and Telephone Consultative Committee (CCITT) which defines the procedures for interfacing general purpose synchronous data terminal equipments

(DTEs) to public PSNs. Three levels characterize the X.25 interface (RYBC 80): (i) a physical level that is responsible for establishing, maintaining and disconnecting the physical link between the DTE and the data-circuit terminating equipment (DCE), (ii) a link level, that is responsible for the orderly and error-free exchange of frames, (iii) a packet level that specifies the packet formats and the procedures to be used by DTEs to establish, maintain and clear concurrent virtual circuits (VCs) over a single physical link.

The use of PSNs by pre-packet era DTEs is widespread and growing, and led PSN carriers and communication product manufacturers to introduce specialized interfaces called packet assemblers/disassemblers (PADs). The main function of these PADs is to perform protocols conversion to X.25 and to support the agreed-to higher end-to-end protocol levels. PADs may be integrated with the packet switch as a software component or they may be external devices attached to the PSN by X.25 links. An extensive description of the services offered by Datapac, the TransCanada Telephone System's packet switched network, through the use of PADs can be found in Reference (8).

Currently, the most widely used interactive oriented DTE types accessing PSNs through PADs are the start-stop mode and IBM 3270 compatible terminals. Start-stop mode compatible devices operate at low speeds (300 to 1200 bps) on an asynchronous (character at a time) basis. The IBM 3270 compatible terminals considered operate under Binary Synchronous Communications (BSC) half-duplex line control procedure (5) at speeds ranging from 1200 to 9600 bps. Attachment of these typical terminals to PSNs will also be examined. Integrated PADs will be considered for simplicity of analysis and because this is currently the case for Datapac. The study of external PAD connections is a simple extension of the X.25 TC access method analysis.

Three reference connections will therefore be examined (Figure 1). The first reference connection is between an X.25 terminal controller (TC) and an X.25 host computer. The X.25 terminal controller, to which may be attached low speed teleprinter or display devices, communicates with the host via an X.25 access line and the agreed-to higher level end-to-end protocol. A communication controller or front-end (F/E) is attached through a high speed I/O interface to the host computer, and is responsible for the communication functions such as the support of the X.25 interface and higher end-to-end protocol levels required. The second reference connection considered is between a BSC terminal controller and the X.25 host computer. Finally a virtual communication path between a start-stop mode device and the X.25 host computer will serve as the third reference connection.

In the next section, the components of response time and special considerations in estimating response time for these three reference connections are addressed.

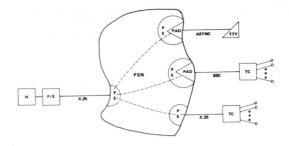

H ≡ Host Computer
F/E ≡ Host Front-End Processor
PS ≡ Packet Switch
PAD ≡ Packet Assembler/Disassembler
PSN ≡ Packet Switched Network
TC ≡ Terminal Controller
TTY ≡ Start-Stop Mode Device

Figure 1: Hypothetical Reference Connections

4. RESPONSE TIME ANALYSIS

For the purposes of this section, it is assumed that the device input message length requires only one packet while the host ouput message requires multiple packets. This message structure assumption is not critical and is typical of multiple conversational applications in use today.

4.1 X.25 TC to X.25 Host Connection

For any device attached to the TC, response time is usually defined as the elapsed time from the last user keystroke until the first character of the first error-free output packet is displayed (assuming that packets can be displayed as they are received). The response time can be subdivided into the following components:

(i)   queuing time for the input packet, in the TC to DCE direction
(ii)   propagation and input packet transmission times over the TC access line
(iii)   PSN transit delay for the input packet
(iv)   queuing time for the input packet, in the DCE to F/E direction
(v)   propagation and input packet transmission times over the F/E access line
(vi)   host and F/E processing times
(vii)   queuing time for the first output packet, in the F/E to DCE direction
(viii) propagation and first output packet transmission times over the F/E access line
(ix)   PSN transit delay for the first output packet
(x)   queuing time for the first output packet, in the DCE to TC direction
(xi)   propagation and first output packet transmission times over the TC access line (as packet error checking is normally performed prior to display).

Queuing time components (i), (iv), (vii) and (x) are a function of the access line speed, unidirectional access line utilization, message length characteristics and of the packet and frame window rotation mechanisms.

The access line utilization is in turn a function of the packet length characteristics, the packet arrival rate, the access line speed, the access line information frame retransmission rate and the frame and packet acknowledgement (Receive Ready) levels, as the amount of frame and packet acknowledgements may significantly increase the line utilization.

The X.25 frame and packet window sizes must be properly chosen so that frame or packet window closures are normally avoided.

The PSN transit delay is defined as the time interval between the correct receipt of the last bit of the packet at the source DCE and delivery of the last bit of this packet to the transmit queue of the destination DTE. The network transit delay depends on the processing and queuing times at the source, intermediate and destination packet switches (PSs) and on the queuing, propagation and transmission times over internodal trunks. With Datapac, customers may select between two priority schemes, resulting in shorter transit delays for priority packets (13).

On the other hand, if the selected response time of interest is as defined to the last character of a multi-packet output message, the additional delay components are obtained as shown in Figure 2. In this figure, it is assumed that (i) the output message from the host to the TC consists of three consecutive full packets, (ii) that no delays are introduced because of frame, packet or higher level flow control and (iii) that the network trunk delays are relatively small compared to the access line packet transmission times. An expression for the total output message delay is presented and shows that overlaps in some delay components lead to a smaller total delay than the sum of all delay components. In general, if N consecutive full packets are sent, and if assumptions (ii) and (iii) are satisfied, the total output message delay can be expressed as $T_{WHS} + NT_{LS} + T_N + T_{WLS} + T_{HS}$ where the delay components are as defined in Figure 2.

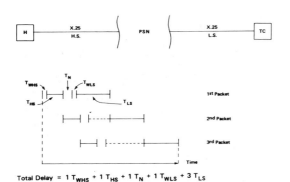

Total Delay = $1 T_{WHS} + 1 T_{HS} + 1 T_N + 1 T_{WLS} + 3 T_{LS}$

T_{WHS} ≡ Queuing time over the high speed access line

T_{HS} ≡ Propagation and Transmission times over the high speed access line

T_N ≡ Network Transit delay

T_{WLS} ≡ Queuing time over the low speed access line

T_{LS} ≡ Propagation and Transmission times over the low speed access line

Figure 2: Total Delay for a
Three-Packet Output Message

Finally, it is assumed that packets are sent consecutively. This may not always be the case as it will be shown in Section 5.0, where packets belonging to a multi-packet message may be interleaved with other message packets.

It can be noted that one way to improve response time is to use shorter packets but at the expense of increased X.25 packet and frame level overheads.

Assuming mutual independence among the component variables, the mean and variance of the response time is derived from the sum of the mean and variance of each delay component respectively. Following Martin (7), the percentile value can be estimated from a Gamma distribution with parameter R equal to the ratio of the square value of the mean over the variance of the response time.

4.2 BSC TC to X.25 Host Connection

In a large number of IBM 3270 compatible implementations, output messages are typically sent in one data block (initiated by STX and concluded with ETX control characters) to the selected devices. An X.25 F/E will thus normally break the output message in packets linked with the More data (M) bit (11). Since, by definition, the M-bit function implies that the user considers these packets as belonging to one message entity, the PAD will normally buffer the entire message, before it is actually sent to the selected device. It is clear that the response time of interest is defined to the last character of the output message block received.

Assuming that (i) the output message is transmitted in consecutive packets, (ii) that no delays are introduced because of frame, packet or higher level flow control and (iii) that the network trunk delays are relatively small compared to the host access line packet transmission times, the components of the response time are:

(i)   queuing time for the input message block
(ii)   propagation and input message block transmission times over the TC access line
(iii) PSN transit delay for the input packet
(iv)   queuing time for the input packet, in the DCE to F/E direction
(v)   propagation and input packet transmission times over the F/E access line
(vi)   host and F/E processing times
(vii) queuing time for the first output packet in the F/E to DCE direction
(viii) propagation and transmission times for all packets, in the F/E to DCE access line
(ix)   PSN transit delay for the last packet
(x)   queuing time for the output message block
(xi)   propagation and output message transmission times over the TC access line.

Queuing time components (i) and (x) are a function of the access line speed, access line utilization and message length characteristics. The remaining delay components are as described in Section 4.1.

The delay components for a three packet output message are depicted in Figure 3. From the total delay expression derived it is clear that a portion of the delay component overlaps, as depicted in Figure 2, will not occur if the PAD buffers the entire message.

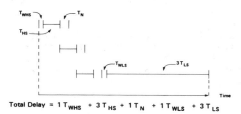

Total Delay = $1 T_{WHS} + 3 T_{HS} + 1 T_N + 1 T_{WLS} + 3 T_{LS}$

$T_{WHS} \equiv$ Queuing time over the X.25 high speed access line

$T_{HS} \equiv$ Propagation and Transmission times over the X.25 high speed access line

$T_N \equiv$ Network Transit delay

$T_{WLS} \equiv$ Queuing time over the BSC low speed access line

$T_{LS} \equiv$ Propagation and Transmission times over the BSC low speed access line

Figure 3: Total Delay for a Three-Packet Output Message-PAD buffers entire output message

Two alternatives can be used to reduce the total delay and allow for overlaps. The first possible approach is a PAD implementation where following receipt of the first N packets linked by the M-bit, the device is selected and transmission of these N packets initiated. If following transmission of these first N packets the remaining packets were not received (because of VC flow control or any other reason), the message will be aborted by the PAD (ENQ sent). N's optimal choice is a tradeoff between delay and the probability of message abortion. The second alternative is a host-F/E implementation whereby the output message is broken into sub-messages. This procedure will permit display of the initial part of the message and will allow for delay overlaps as depicted in Figure 2. Once again a tradeoff must be made since TC line overhead and utilization will increase as additional device selections (5) must be initiated by the PAD.

Finally, the potential existence of packet interleaving of multi-packet messages on the host access line may further increase the response time. This topic is addressed in Section 5.

4.3 Start-Stop Mode Terminal to X.25 Host Connection

For a low-speed start-stop mode device, response time is usually defined as the interval between the last user keystroke and the display of the first meaningful character. The response time components are the same as presented in Section 4.1 except that components (i) and (ii) of Section 4.1 are replaced by

the propagation and last character (input message block, for block-mode devices) transmission times over the terminal access line and components (x) and (xi) are replaced by the propagation and first characters (control characters plus first meaningful character) transmission times over the terminal access line.

5. PACKET INTERLEAVING OF MULTI-PACKET MESSAGES

This section studies the effect of packet interleaving on user response time, as defined to the last received character of an output multi-packet message, and compares it with the noninterleaved case.

Packet interleaving is defined as the interleaving of packets belonging to a multi-packet message with other single or multi-packet messages over the same X.25 physical link. These messages may be associated with separate VCs or they may be associated with the same virtual circuit if it is shared by multiple users. Packet interleaving of multi-packet messages is illustrated in Figure 4, which presents possible ways of sending two multi-packet messages, from an X.25 DTE to the DCE.

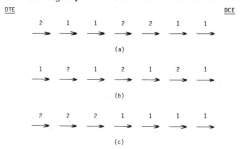

Message #1 = 4 packets
Message #2 = 3 packets

(a) Two packets sent at a time
(b) One packet sent at a time
(c) Non-interleaved case (FCFS)

Figure 4: Packet Interleaving of Multi-Packet Messages

Two possible circumstances may cause packet interleaving. First as already mentioned, some observed host-F/E implementations of packet level and frame level buffer management lead to packet interleaving. As it will be demonstrated in the following subsection, packet interleaving introduces a form of priority scheme that may be attractive for some systems. Second, packet level flow control may result in some form of packet interleaving since, in the event of a flow controlled VC, the F/E will normally release queued packets belonging to other VCs.

5.1 A Mathematical Analysis

To analyze the impact of packet interleaving on response time, a Round-Robin (RR) queuing system is applied as a model of the interleaving process for a host-F/E implementation. It is assumed that no frame, packet or higher level flow control is experienced.

As shown in Figure 5, the RR queuing system comprises a single first-come-first-served (FCFS) queue and a server. A newly arrived message joins the end of the queue and waits until it finally reaches the server. A message will not be served for longer than the pre-assigned maximum time called a quantum q. If the message's service is completed, it departs from the system, and the server immediately serves the next message waiting at the head of the queue. If the message service has not been completed, it is cycled back to the end of the queue. The queue represents the F/E frame queue and the server depicts the F/E access line. The quantum can be viewed as the time required to transmit a given fixed number of consecutive full packets belonging to the same message.

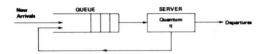

Figure 5: Round-Robin Queuing Model

The RR and processor-shared (or zero quantum RR) systems have been studied extensively in References (4),(6),(9), and (12). In Reference (12) it has been shown, for a Poisson arrival process and general service time distribution, that the mean waiting time is approximately a linear function of the required service. Thus this discipline implicitly favours messages with shorter service times. On the other hand, for the FCFS scheduling algorithm (which is equivalent to the non-interleaved case) the mean waiting time is independent of the service time. These conditions are shown in Figure 6, where the average conditional waiting time (conditioned on the required service time t_s), $w(t_s)$, is sketched as a function of the service time, t_s, for the RR ($q \geq 0$) and FCFS systems (9), (12).

For the Processor-shared (PS) system, the average conditional waiting time, $w(t_s)$, is given by (6): $W(t_s) = \frac{\rho}{1-\rho} t_s$

where ρ is the server (line) utilization.

Thus the system average waiting time, w_{ps}, is equal to:

$$w_{ps} = \int_{o}^{\infty} w(t_s)\, f(t_s)\, dt_s = \frac{\rho}{1-\rho}\, \bar{t}_s$$

where $f(t_s)$ is the service time density function and $\bar{t}_s$ is the expected service time.

Conversely, for the FCFS model, the system average waiting time is given by (6):

$$w_{fcfs} = \frac{\rho}{2(1-\rho)}\, \bar{t}_s\left[1 + \left(\frac{\sigma t_s}{\bar{t}_s}\right)^2\right]$$

where σt_s is the standard deviation of the service time.

It can be seen that

$$w_{fcfs} \geq w_{ps} \text{ if } \bar{t}_s \leq \sigma t_s$$

where the equality occurs at $\bar{t}_s = \sigma t_s$

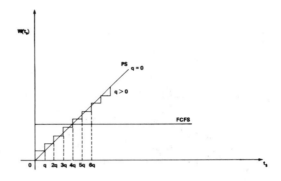

Figure 6: Behaviour of the Average Conditional Waiting Time for the RR ($q \geq 0$) & FCFS Systems- General service time distribution

Since the PS model results can be used to estimate the general RR discipline (12), it is implied that the system average waiting time (and hence system average response time) is better for the FCFS (non-interleaved case) if the service time follows a Gamma distribution that lies somewhere between the constant and exponential distributions. The RR system is however preferable for hyperexponential service time distributions as $\sigma t_s > \bar{t}_s$

In References (4) and (9), the variance of the conditional waiting time for the exponential service time distribution has been solved. The result is presented in Figure 7, where the conditional waiting time variance is represented as a function of the service time, t_s, for the RR ($q \geq 0$) and FCFS systems (9). It can be seen from this figure that the Round-Robin scheduling discipline can result in significantly higher variance in response time over the FCFS discipline (non-interleaved case) particularly for longer service times (4),(9).

Since the FCFS discipline is a limiting case of the RR system ($q \longrightarrow \infty$), the larger is q, the smaller will be the response time variability and vice-versa.

Three important results have been derived in this section: (i) packet interleaving of multi-packet messages introduces a form of priority scheme that improves short message response times at the expense of long messages, (ii) if the message length distribution is hyperexponential, it is demonstrated that the system average response time is lower for the interleaved case. However, if the message length distribution follows a Gamma distribution that lies between the constant and exponential distribution, which is generally the case, then the system average response time is larger for the interleaved case, (iii) packet interleaving leads to a larger response time variability, which is very annoying to the end user.

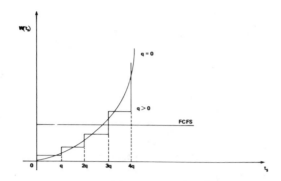

Figure 7: Behavior of the Conditional Waiting Time Variance for the RR(q≥0) and FCFS Systems-Exponential service time distribution

It should be noted that the preceding analysis applies only to the second definition of response time (i.e., defined to the last received character of an output multi-packet message). Moreover, these results have a greater impact when the PAD buffers the entire message prior to transmission to the destination device or, for an X.25-to-X.25 connection, when the source access line speed is lower than or equal to the destination access line speed. If however, the response time of interest is based on our first definition (i.e., defined to the first displayed output character) then packet interleaving is clearly an attractive approach because the first packets of a multi-packet message are more rapidly released to their destination.

CONCLUSION

In this paper, the definitions and components of user perceived response times over packet switched networks have been presented. It was shown that response time estimation is largely dependent on the network access method and the PAD and host-F/E implementations.

Packet interleaving of multi-packet messages was also introduced and analyzed. It was shown that if response time is defined as the interval between the last user keystroke and receipt of the last output message character, and if the message length distribution lies between the constant and exponential distributions, then packet interleaving should be avoided as it increases the system average response time. In addition, packet interleaving increases the variability of the response time which is a very undesirable situation from a user point of view. On the other hand, packet interleaving favours short messages at the expense of larger size multi-packet messages, thus creating an implicit priority mechanism instrument. Packet interleaving is also the preferred approach if the response time of interest is defined to the first displayed output character and if no PAD buffering is allowed for PAD-based accesses.

REFERENCES

(1) ACM, "Guidelines for the Measurement of Interactive Computer Service Response Time and Turnaround Time", Computer Communication Review, January 1979.
(2) J. Chang, "Terminal Response Times in Data Communications Systems", IBM J. Res. Develop., May 1975.
(3) W. Chou, "Terminal Response Time on Polled Teleprocessing Networks", Computer Networking Symposium, 1978.
(4) E. Coffman, R. Muntz, H. Trotter, "Waiting Time Distributions for Processor-Sharing Systems", Journal of the ACM, January 1970.
(5) IBM, "IBM 3270 - Information Display System Component Description" (IBM, 1980).
(6) L. Kleinrock, "Queuing Systems - Vol. 2" (John-Wiley & Sons, 1976).
(7) J. Martin, "Systems Analysis for Data Transmission" (Prentice-Hall Inc., 1972).
(8) M. Matsubara, "Datapac Network Services", Proc. of National Electronics Conference, October 1981.
(9) R. Muntz, "Waiting Time Distribution for Round-Robin Queuing Systems", Proc. of the Symposium on Computer Communications Networks and Teletraffic, 1972.
(10) W. Nugent, "A Fast Incomplete Gamma Function for Improved Measures of Response Time Quality", Proc. of Computer Communications Networks, 1978.
(11) A. Rybczynski, "X.25 Interface and End-to-End Virtual Circuit Service Characteristics", IEEE Trans. on Communications, April 1980.
(12) M. Sakata, S. Noguchi, J. Oizumi, "An Analysis of the M/G/1 Queue Under Round-Robin Scheduling", Operations Research, 1971.
(13) D. Sproule, M. Unsoy, "Transit Delay Objectives for the Datapac Network", Proc. of the 5th International Conference on Computer Communications, 1980.
(14) P. Verma, "Customer Perceived Delays in a Packet Switched Network", National Telecommunications Conference - Vol. 2, 1980.

AUTHOR

Joseph Chammas received his B.A.Sc. and M.A.Sc degrees in electrical engineering from the University of Montreal, Canada, in 1976 and 1979, respectively. Since 1978, he has been with the Computer Communications Group of the Trans-Canada Telephone System where he has been involved in the areas of customer data network design, Datapac access services development and Datapac network planning. He is presently Senior Engineer with the Datapac network planning group in Ottawa. He is currently pursuing the M.B.A. program as a part time student at the University of Ottawa and is a member of the Association of Professional Engineers of Ontario and IEEE.

Testing Packet Switched Networks

B R Spiegelhalter, C G Miller
British Telecom, UK

The paper describes the method used by British Telecom to test packet switched networks. The rationale behind the approach is discussed i.e. to test networks from an independent user's point of view. The high speed multi-protocol tester developed by British Telecom to verify the complex interfaces is described and its versatility is considered.

The control of software faults in networks is discussed and the build-up of a library of repeatable tests is demonstrated to be a rapid, effective method for assessing software releases. The experience gained from testing small, co-located and large, widely-dispersed networks is described and the paper concludes with a discussion of the lessons learnt and some future developments.

INTRODUCTION

British Telecom (BT) have been involved with packet switching since 1973, initially with the "Experimental Packet Switch Service" (EPSS) then with Euronet and BT's International Packet Switch Service (IPSS). In 1981 BT opened a national public network known as the Packet Switch Service (PSS).

UK PSS NETWORK

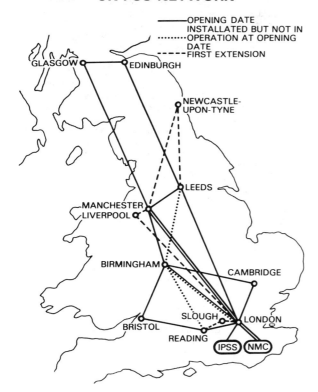

The general principles of packet switching have been described elsewhere but it is worth highlighting the PSS system which opened service as a nine node network covering the whole of the UK: the system has since nearly doubled. Each node contains one or more packet switches based upon a multiple microprocessor architecture with each switch capable of handling up to 128 ports. The system is controlled by a Network Management Centre (NMC) based on duplicated minicomputers each with 600 Mbytes of disc storage. In addition to packet terminals, the system handles character-mode terminals using its built-in Packet Assembler/Disassembler(PAD). This paper is concerned with the testing problems posed by the implementation of packet switched networks, the development of a test tool (AUTOFLOOD) to overcome these problems and the experiences in testing PSS.

TESTING OBJECTIVES

The primary aim of testing a system is to find any errors in its operation in order that these may be corrected: without such correction, testing merely confirms the status of the system.

Hitherto, British Telecom has bought off-the-shelf packet switched systems from commercial suppliers in this country and abroad, suitably modified to meet BT's requirements for compliance with CCITT. Therefore, since BT normally plays no part in the design and development of the system, formal acceptance testing takes place with little prior knowledge of the system. Consequently, it is important that the testing be comprehensive and that all the necessary tests can be carried out in the limited time allowed in order to ensure conformity to the specification and to verify that the system meets the complex CCITT recommendations for packet switched systems.

Table 1

CCITT Protocol Standards for Packet Networks	
X.25	Packet Mode Terminals
X.3	Packet Assembler/Disassembler
X.28	Access for Start/Stop Mode Terminals
X.29	Packet Terminal/PAD interworking
X.75	International Interworking

Since it is impractical to test each of the enormous number of possible combinations of events that can take place, the aims of testing have to be examined and then priorities established. In this way a meaningful set of tests can be produced. However, such is the nature of software systems that even in areas of the system where testing is concentrated, undetected errors will still arise after the tests have been successfully completed.

PRINCIPAL TEST AREAS

The basic concern of a public administration is to offer a satisfactory service to its customers and this, together with the above considerations, leads to the following main test areas:

Protocols - To verify that the network interfaces are in accordance with the CCITT recommendations so that customer terminals from a number of manufacturers may operate on the network and that the network may interwork with other packet networks.

Performance - To verify that the network can handle the throughput specified and that the system reacts reasonably under overload conditions, e.g. congestion control.

Reliability - To verify that the network as a whole and its component parts meet the specified failure rates for both software and hardware.

Routing - To verify that packets reach the destination terminal by the most efficient path without loss, duplication or corruption and that the network is tolerant of link failures.

Security - To verify that the system is immune to illicit or accidental changes to data structures (e.g. billing information) or software.

Billing - To verify the accuracy and security of data acquisition for the formation of customers bills.

Network Control - To verify that the network can be controlled efficiently, including the introduction of new customers, maintenance of the network database, monitoring of the network, diagnostics, etc.

HIERARCHICAL APPROACH

Having established the aims of testing and accepted that complete testing is not feasible, a practical approach to the validation of the packet switch network has been devised. The approach recognises that the time allowed for testing is limited and that the main test areas have many interdependencies.

A bottom-up approach is advocated where each level is verified before going on to test the higher levels. The hardware is first tested, followed by the physical and electrical interfaces. The lower level of the protocol is then tested e.g. X.25 level 2, followed by X.25 level 3. The same bottom-up technique is adopted for X.3, X.28 and X.29.

After the protocols have been tested, the bottom-up approach breaks down slightly as there are several parallel functions. Here, the priority allocated to each area dictates the order of the testing and the amount of

effort to be expended on each test. For example, load testing and routing testing may be performed in any order but the accounting tests should be undertaken after these, even though the latter may have a higher priority.

Errors may be found at any time, in which case testing may have to suspended while the error is corrected. The consequences of a correction in a complex software system are difficult to predict as further errors may be introduced. In addition, the current series of tests may become invalid. Extensive retesting is then necessary which incurs penalties in time and manpower. Even with well structured systems it is wise to return to the lowest level of tests when corrections have been made to the system. This leads to the conclusion that the testing methods should be rapid and simple to execute, without compromising their effectiveness.

TEST TOOL REQUIREMENTS

Manual methods of testing are not sufficient and some form of automated test tool is necessary. The requirements for such a tool are examined below:

1. Independence

    As stated earlier, one of the primary reasons for testing is to ascertain the acceptability of the network to customers. This necessitates the investigation of the network from the user's point of view. The only interfaces that the test tool should have with the network should be the same as those offered to users or other external systems e.g. gateways. The tests are concerned with what the system actually does rather than how it does it.

    Methods of testing using equipment similar to that under test e.g. back-to-back testing, often bypass the external interface by interconnecting using some internal method. This method is suitable for debugging individual subsystems but may not give a correct impression of the way in which the total system performs. In addition, if the same software modules and hardware interfaces are used in both the testing and tested systems, they can mask each other's idiosyncracies.

    Therefore the test tool should not only test the system via the user interface but also should be configured with independent hardware and software.

2. Repetition of tests.

    When a correction is made to a system a certain amount of retesting is necessary. A tool is therefore required where the suite of test programs can be easily rerun and also where individual tests can be repeated in isolation.

3. Speed and Capacity

    In conjunction with the ability to retest easily is the requirement to retest quickly so that new versions of the system can be rapidly assessed. Furthermore, the test tool should have the ability to subject the system to sustained peak load.

4. Versatility

As well as load testing, the test tool should be capable of testing each aspect of the protocols and exception conditions.

5. Ease of use

Although predominantly required for acceptance testing, such a test tool will be used as a maintenance aid during the life of the system and so the skill required to operate the test tool should be kept to a minimum in order to reduce training commitment. In conjunction with this is the requirement to modify and add new tests with relative ease as enhancements are added to the system or particular aspects of the system are singled out for special investigation.

6. Transportability

It should be possible to transport the tester to the manufacturer's premises so that close liaison can be maintained with the system developers.

TEST TOOL IMPLEMENTATION

Having identified these requirements, it was necessary to find a way of implementing them within the tight timescales and with the rather limited resources at our disposal. Fortunately, some similar work had been carried out by the British Post Office (as it then was) concerning testing of EPSS [2]. Indeed, the approach to functional testing was similar in that a pre-defined series of stimulii was applied to the network under test, and the responses compared with those anticipated.

The design for the PSS tester – dubbed AUTOFLOOD – arose from the concepts embodied in the EPSS version and the requirements above. Considerable expertise and some BT software existed for the Ferranti Argus 700 minicomputers, so AUTOFLOOD was based on a newer version of the same machine.

AUTOFLOOD was built into two half-height racks to ease transportation; these could be used as desk pedestals.

A test language was devised by which AUTOFLOOD would be controlled, based on the parlance in CCITT recommendation X.25 Geneva 1978 (the most up to date document at the time).

TEST TOOL FACILITIES AND FEATURES

A form of compiler has been written which operates on a source file containing commands written in the test language, and generates intermediate data structures and files. These are used by another part of the AUTOFLOOD software (the test sequencer) to execute the specified commands, typically sending out packets and character strings and comparing those received from the network under test with those specified in the source (test) file.

If the tester finds the network response differs from that specified, it will immediately stop that stream of the test, print out the observed and expected responses, and indicate at what point in the test the failure occurred. These can then be studied to determine if the network response was incorrect, or if the test had been written so as to expect the wrong response.

AUTOFLOOD HARDWARE

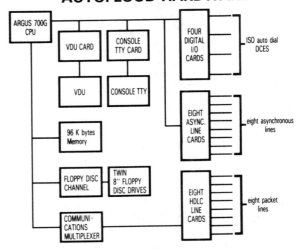

The hardware and software of AUTOFLOOD have been able to meet a very wide range of requirements. AUTOFLOOD has eight HDLC ports and up to eight asynchronous test ports, enabling simultaneous testing of network ports of widely varying characteristics. For example, one tester port might be connected to a network port with incoming calls barred, another to one with outgoing calls barred, another might have reverse charging inhibited, some could be in a closed user group, another might be allowed to make fast select calls, while yet another might not. This enables the tester to check the correct functioning of all these different network options.

The asynchronous capability permits testing of the PAD and it's interaction with the packet side of the network. This has proved to be one of the unique features of AUTOFLOOD, since to the network it can look like a separate host and terminal.

Since the throughput of AUTOFLOOD approaches four hundred frames per second, it has also been very useful in performing stress tests on the network – indeed at present, it appears to be a very effective way of performing a check on the hardware of the existing BT network nodes, and has had considerable use in screening new hardware modules before they are placed in the network.

AUTOFLOOD features some very useful monitoring facilities. Keyboard commands enable the tester to display on a fast Visual Display Unit (VDU) screen a mimic diagram of the tester showing exactly how many packets per second are flowing in and out. This is very useful when carrying out traffic and soak tests, since one can see at a glance if there is a port causing trouble. Details of an individual port can also be presented, giving more information than the throughput display. Similarly one can display details of a particular logical call.

A keyboard command to instruct the tester to timestamp data packets enables measurement of the time taken for packets to cross the network. Although this does include a certain amount of time taken with low level queuing and transmission, the figures obtained are very similar to those a customer on the network will observe, and AUTOFLOOD has been used on several occasions to provide intending users of PSS with information to help them decide on the right balance of packet length and window size for their particular application. Separate fields at the top of the screen are continuously updated with information concerning the processor utilisation of the tester, the current number of free buffers, time, date and the current position in a test, so the user can always see if the test is progressing satisfactorily.

Since the tester has twin floppy discs and a reasonably sophisticated file handling system, it is much the same as any other minicomputer to operate, and it is easy for semi-skilled personnel to use. The test files are entered directly "key-to-disc" on the VDU or console terminal, and can be edited on the tester. The

SOFTWARE SCHEMATIC

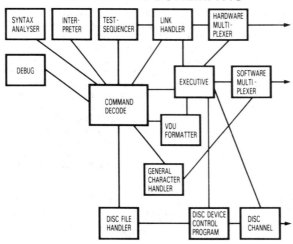

language used to control the tester can be somewhat compact if full use is made of the abbreviations and macro expansion facilities available. For this reason, an "interpreter" has been provided which takes the compiled test and prints out a much more verbose version, rather more like English than the test language: this has been found helpful when studying a particular portion of a test (e.g. that someone else has written). In practice, the interpreter is infrequently used because, although the test language looks a little cryptic at first sight, anybody who is familiar with packet switching very quickly becomes adept at reading tests directly.

ADDITIONAL TEST FACILITIES

The tester can also be used for carrying out tests in a number of areas which do not involve

protocol testing, e.g. billing. When running an AUTOFLOOD test, it is always known exactly what calls have been set up, and how many data packets sent. This precision enables a check to be made on the integrity of the accounting of various different types of call by comparing the billing information generated by the network with that expected from examination of the AUTOFLOOD test.

It is also found useful for testing some of the Network Management Centre (NMC) facilities such as controlling, testing, and monitoring lines. In all of these cases AUTOFLOOD establishes confidence that the NMC has done what is expected.

Congestion control is tested using AUTOFLOOD by writing tests that are deliberately designed to try and run the network out of buffers. This is achieved by forcing the network to hold data for a number of calls for a DTE (in this case AUTOFLOOD) which claims not to be ready to receive data, and then allowing in all the data to ensure none has been lost.

FAULT DETECTION

When testing systems it is inevitable that conditions will be detected where there will be initial doubt whether the system under test is at fault, the problem lies with the test itself, or indeed whether a fault exists at all. Initially (and despite exhaustive checks), there will be bugs in a new suite of test tables. If the fault is in the tests, the tables are easily modified and a reliable suite of test programs soon emerges. If it is found that the network is at fault, a fault report is generated and sent to the contractor's system support organisation. One is then left with a number of alternatives as to how to proceed. Testing could stop until the fault is fixed, or testing could continue on an independent aspect of the system. Alternatively the individual test which failed could be skipped and testing continued on the same aspect. Although it is recognised that further testing may be rendered invalid by a correction to the original fault, the latter alternative is often adopted so that more information surrounding the fault can be found. In addition, further faults may be found which can be fixed at the same time as the original fault. This option tends to reduce the number of software releases needed to establish a fault free system.

With an automated test tool, the correction of a fault takes significantly longer than its detection. The correction of one fault may reveal others which were masked by the first and so corrected versions of the software are subjected to the whole test suite. With AUTOFLOOD the X.25 test suite takes only 30 minutes to run and so the software can be rapidly assessed. The results can then be fed back quickly to the programmer for any further corrections which may be necessary. The tester can easily become an effective debugging tool with the danger that because of its rapid response a 'suck-it-and-see' approach will be taken by the implementers and ill-conceived fixes will be tried.

As faults are fixed, the verifying tests are

incorporated into the standard test suite forming a valuable check that a fault that has been cleared does not reappear in later versions of the software (a problem familiar to many system developers!). In this way a library of tests can be built by which any new software release can be judged.

The testing phase of the fault clearing cycle is reduced and the majority of time in the cycle becomes that taken to make the software change, and to build and release new systems.

EXPERIENCE WITH PSS

The majority of BT's experience of testing packet switch networks using the approach described has been with the UK National Packet Switching Service (PSS). The contract for this network was placed with Plessey Controls Ltd in 1978 but the design and development was performed by GTE-Telenet in the USA.

It was felt the system software acceptance testing should take place at the contractor's premises so as to reduce the fault clearing time. The contractor provided a test configuration consisting of three packet switches and a single network management centre and suitable port profiles for the test network were agreed.

Prior to the arrival of the tester in the USA a number of BT modems had been shipped and commissioned so that the compatibility of the equipment could be assessed. The modems were dispensed with having established that the equipment was compatible.

THE TEST ENVIRONMENT

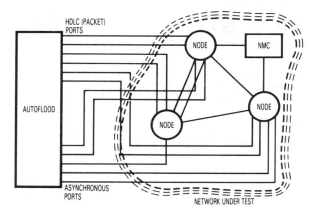

HDLC (PACKET) PORTS
NODE
NMC
NODE
NODE
AUTOFLOOD
ASYNCHRONOUS PORTS
NETWORK UNDER TEST

The test team had to overcome the contractor's reservations about AUTOFLOOD which were understandable as in some cases the tester software was newer than the software under test. To compound this situation there was an initial period when many of the tests produced discrepancies. The problems were partly due to some invalid assumptions having been made by the writers of the test tables (who were fairly new to X.25) but the majority were due to the presence of some ambiguities in the X.25 recommendations available at the time. The problems were dealt with in one of 4 ways:

1. A network fault report was raised

2. A test table fault was identified and the test modified.

3. A specification interpretation problem was identified which would then be discussed at contractual level.

4. A fault was identified in the tester software.

It was sometimes necessary to use a passive line monitor on the test circuit to arbitrate between the tester and the network but fortunately very rarely was the discrepancy found to be due to the AUTOFLOOD software.

After a time the test suite stablised and the tester came to be accepted as a reliable tool by the contractors. Indeed, it was frequently used to aid debugging.

Eventually the software was considered sufficiently satisfactory to transfer testing to the UK so that those parts of the system which could not be tested on the contractor's test environment could be checked on the large widely-dispersed network.

The approach to network tests was firstly to repeat the factory tests on the UK switches and then to perform tests which involved the whole network. A temporary network of data links to switches remote from London was established enabling calls to be generated at any of the packet switches and received at any other packet switch, as all of the special links terminated on the packet tester: in effect the tester became a DTE on every switch. In this way routing, reconnection, loading, billing and failure tests were performed on the whole network although the maintenance of the temporary network and the coordination of the activities at the remote sites did present problems. In addition a considerable number of hardware problems were experienced with the main network which disrupted the system tests.

It was recognised that no testing can be exhaustive and that faults will always be found under normal service operation and so it was envisaged that part of the acceptance testing should involve selected customers using the network. However, due to the earlier delays, customers were already using the trial national network to verify their own DTE implementations. This caused additional problems during the testing phase as breaks in service had to be limited, and occasionally their random traffic had to be stopped so that tests where the exact traffic profile had to be known could be performed e.g. billing and statistics. The customers' traffic did throw up some faults but the number was limited.

The operational network is expanding rapidly and the customers' traffic is increasing. One would expect this combination of circumstances to lead to the discovery of more system errors, but in practice, the occurrence rate has been very small. The role of testing continues as new software, containing enhancements and fixes to old faults, is released. Subjecting new releases to the test suite on a captive test network has been effective in minimising the problems encountered in using new software operationally.

EXPERIENCE WITH OTHER NETWORKS

Similar test techniques have also been used on other networks although not as extensively as with PSS. Before being shipped to the USA the tester was used with the Euronet packet switch network where it was able to isolate some suspected faults. More recently the techniques have been applied by BT's International Packet Switching Service when testing their X.75 connections to other packet networks throughout the world, e.g. Spain, Japan. In addition the PSS-IPSS gateway was tested and also gateways to other services e.g. telex.

In each case the same basic approach has been used but the test tables have normally undergone some modifications.

FUTURE DEVELOPMENTS

Our approach is being served very well by the AUTOFLOOD tester but consideration is being given to separating the software systems for the functions and traffic so that higher speed switches may be tested. At present more than one tester is required for throughput testing of the faster minicomputer-based switches.

As far as the tester is concerned, a microprocessor based system is also being considered for ease of portability, wider capability and cost reduction.

CONCLUSIONS

The techniques used by BT to test packet switch networks do not form a strict methodology but rather an approach which experience has proved to be effective. This would not be possible without a test tool such as AUTOFLOOD.

With the advances in specification and design languages, and structured development techniques, the number of errors remaining at system integration time should be small but some will exist nonetheless and so good system test techniques will be necessary for some time to come.

We feel that the low level of faults that have been found by other parties (customers, operators, etc) since formal testing ceased vindicates the time spent on testing and fully justifies our approach.

ACKNOWLEDGEMENTS

The views expressed here are the authors' personal views and do not represent British Telecom policy statements. Acknowledgement is made to the Senior Director of Technology Executive for permission to make use of the information contained in this paper.

REFERENCES

[1] CCITT Recommendations X.25, X.75, X.3, X.28 and X.29.

[2] M.J.Norton "Experience in Software Test Techniques for Packet Switching Exchanges" Proceedings of the Third International Conference on Software Engineering for Telecommunications Switching Systems.

[3] C.G.Miller and M.J.Norton "Autoflood - A Flexible Test System for Packet Switched Networks". NATO Advanced Study Institute on Advances in Distributed Computing 1980

THE AUTHORS

Brian Spiegelhalter graduated from Southampton University in 1971 with an Honours Degree in Mathematics and joined the Research Department of the British Post Office.

In 1974 he moved to the Computer Systems Engineering Division where he was involved in the development and testing of the MAC telephone network performance monitoring system.

In 1979 he became leader of the packet switching group responsible for software liaison, network testing and packet switch tester development. Since 1982, he has led the local area networks implementation group.

Christopher Miller graduated in 1977 from Durham University gaining an Honours Degree in Applied Physics. He joined the British Post Office and after assisting with software maintenance of EPSS, wrote much of the software for the British Telecom packet tester - Autoflood.

He was heavily involved with testing PSS software, spending some months at the manufacturer's premises in the USA.

His current work includes maintenance of Autoflood software, and the development of a second generation packet tester.

Participants in the Sixth International Conference on Computer Communication

Abramson N - **xiv**
Adams C J - **379**
Adams G C - **379**
Anderson G M - **367**
Andrews M C - **xv**
Arita T - **19**
Armstrong J T - **202**
Arnold G W - **737**
Aubin R - **640**
Austin S S - **485**
Axford J G - **xv**

Bache A - **799**
Bain W P - **373**
Balkanski A - **691**
Baker K - **1**
Barber D L A - **xvii, 823**
Barbera S J - **158**
Barley I W - **943**
Barnard P - **543**
Barnes A C - **237**
Begbie R - **295**
Bella L - **669**
Bharath-Kumar K - **949**
Biran D - **658**
Blanc R - **xvii**
Boose E F - **491**
Bormann C - **865**
Braden R T - **969**
Brenner J B - **109**
Brown A P G - **831**
Brown R S - **97**
Bucciarelli P - **859**
Burren J - **442**

Caneschi F - **601**
Cantwell B D - **206**
Celandroni N - **425**
Chammas J - **993**
Chan G K - **455**
Chang Jin-Fu - **219**
Cheminel D - **799**
Cheng S S - **485**
Chilver H - **xv**
Chow A C - **31**
Clancy G J
Clark R A - **277**
Clarke D A W - **753**
Clarke K E - **206**

Cohen D - **975**
Cole R H - **969**
Compton J P
Conrads D - **725**
Cook J S - **485**
Corsi N - **669**
Coulter A W - **xviii**
Cozza L M - **163**
Cunningham I M - **295**

Dallaire G P - **854**
Dallas I N - **137**
Daniels R - **442**
Danthine A A S - **xi**
daSilva J S - **455**
Davies D W - **401**
Davies M C - **943**
Day J F - **367**
Deaton Jr G A - **877**
De Luca G - **792**
deMercado J B - **455**
De Micheli S - **55**
Dewis I G - **xiii, 259**
Di Pino D - **55**
Dickson H C - **479**
Divakaruni R S - **362**
Donohue III B P - **179**
Doss II C L - **962**
Drake P - **307**

Eckert H - **925**
Edmonds I A - **xiv**
Eikeset P - **73**
Endicott Jr L J - **647**
Erskine S B - **xvi**
Etherington R - **467**

Fairbairn D R - **xv**
Fairhurst R J - **697**
Farber D J - **xii**
Faust R U - **167**
Feeney W R - **549**
Feldman R - **658**
Fergus E - **407**
Ferro E - **425**
Forster J F S - **103**
Franse D J - **877**
Frantzen V - **25**
Fraser A G - **634**

Fratta L - **xiv**
Fujita K - **731**
Fussgaenger K - **518**

Gagliardi D - **197**
Gale W A - **675**
Gambling W A - **xiv**
Gassmann H P - **555**
Genel P A - **799**
Gilkinson F M - **743**
Giorcelli S - **37**
Girling C G - **395**
Goldstein B - **225**
Graves J - **237**
Green W H F - **103**
Gregory D N - **xiii**
Griffiths J W R - **442**
Gustawson C E - **327**

Hale R W S - **889**
Hammond N - **543**
Handler G J - **121**
Harding L - **838**
Hardy J H M - **43**
Harris J R - **xii**
Harris K B - **507**
Hasegawa K - **115**
Hashida Y - **345**
Hawk R C - **357**
Heard K S
Hegenbarth M - **212**
Hensel P - **513**
Higginson P L - **913**
Hilsz J P - **319**
Hiltunen T - **805**
Hiltz S R - **577**
Hirst I K - **401**
Hooper R - **xii**
Hoppitt C E - **43**
Horton D J - **xi**
Housel B C - **627**
Hubley J S - **155**
Huckle B A - **589**
Huet M - **241**
Hughes C J - **13**
Hughes P A B - **564**
Huitema C - **431**
Hull A - **571**
Hunkin D J - **513**

Reviewers for the Sixth International Conference on Computer Communication

Abramson N
Ackzell L
Ahuja V
Akesson B
Andrews M C
Axford J G

Barber D L A
Benedetti M
Bennett J F
Biran D
Blanc R
Boggs D
Bothner-By H
Bouillie M
Burkhardt H
Butler L

Chang J H
Chilver Sir Henry
Clark D D
Collyer E A
Coulter A
Cowie J B

Danthine A S
Davies D W
Despres R
Dewis I G
Drozhinov V I
Duncanson L A
Dzida W

Edmonds I A
Erskine S B
Evans B O

Fairbairn D R
Fairclough J W
Farber D J
Fraser J W
Fratta L

Gambling W A
Gregory D N

Harris J R
Hay W
Heard K
Hills M T
Hodson K

Hooper R
Horsley A

Horton D J
Howarth C I
Hughes C J
Hunt D G

Ishino F

Kalin T
Kato M
Katzeff K
Kirstein P T
Kohiyama K
Komari K
Kuemmerle K

Larmouth J
Lazarev V G
Le Moli G
Linington P

Maruyama K
Meisel R
Merriman J H H
Midwinter J E
Myers T J

Naughton M
Niblett B

Ono K

Palonen V
Parodi R
Paul M
Pedersen J
Picard Ph
Port E
Pouzin L
Price W L

Raubold E
Rayner D
Read C N
Ritchie W K
Rohlfs S
Rosner R A
Routhorn G A
Ruzza G

Sarbinowski H
Scantlebury R
Seifert L C
Serrure A
Shackel B
Sibley D S
Silverstein M E
Smith H T
Spaniol O
Staudinger W
Strack-Zimmermann H
Strich W E
Sunshine C

Texier A
Thomas J R
Thomas J S
Thompson G B
Tietz W
Toda I
Tombs D

Verma P K
Vogt F H

Wedlake J O
West A
Wilbur S
Woldaw B
Wood B M

Yoshida Y

Zitzmann F R

Executive Committee of the International Council for Computer Communication

PRESIDENT

Douglas F Parkhill
Dept of Communications
Canada

EXECUTIVE VICE-PRESIDENT

Dr Phillip H Enslow Jr
Georgia Institute of
Technology, USA

SECRETARY GENERAL

Dr Maurice Karnaugh
IBM, USA

DEPUTY SECRETARY GENERAL

Dr M Clayton Andrews
IBM, USA

EXECUTIVE SECRETARY

Dr Pramode K Verma
American Telephone &
Telegraph Company, USA

TREASURER

John D McKendree
Defence Communications
Agency, USA

HOUSE COUNSEL

Fred Israel
USA

VICE-PRESIDENT

Louis Pouzin
CNET, France

VICE-PRESIDENT

Dr Carl Hammer
Research Consulting
Services, USA

VICE-PRESIDENT

Edward J Grenier Jr
Sutherland Asbill
& Brennan, USA

VICE-PRESIDENT

Edward E Boyar
Defence Communications
Engineering Centre, USA

VICE-PRESIDENT

Dr Nathaniel Macon
USA

PAST PRESIDENT

Dr Stanley Winkler
IBM, USA

PAST PRESIDENT

Dr Peter E Jackson
Northern Telecom
Canada

Executive Committee of the Sixth International Conference on Computer Communication

CONFERENCE CHAIRMAN

J S Whyte
British Telecom

CONFERENCE GOVERNOR

Dr S Winkler
IBM

CONFERENCE VICE-CHAIRMAN

P T F Kelly
British Telecom

PROGRAMME CHAIRMAN

Professor A S Douglas
London School
of Economics

MEMBER FOR GENERA⁜ CO-ORDINATION & EDITOR OF PROCEEDI⁜

M B Williams
British Telecom

MEMBER FOR FINANCE

J A Urquhart
British Telecom

MEMBER FOR PUBLICITY & SOCIAL PROGRAMME

P W Hefford
British Telecom

REPRESENTATIVE, DEPARTMENT OF INDUSTRY

P H Poole

International Programme Advisory Committee of the Sixth International Conference on Computer Communication

Programme Committee of the Sixth International Conference on Computer Communication

Chairman
Prof A S Douglas
London School of Economics
& Political Science

Vice-chairman & Programme Co-ordinator
M B Williams
Consultant to British Telecom

Vice-chairman
Dr J H Merriman
Consultant

Dr J B Cowie
British Telecom

D W Davies
National Physical Laboratory

Dr L A Duncanson
ICI

J W Fairclough
IBM UK Laboratories

C J Hughes
British Telecom

P A B Hughes
Logica

P T F Kelly
British Telecom

Prof P T Kirstein
University College London

G Peake
ICL

P H Poole
Department of Industry

C N Read
Inter-Bank Research Organisation

Dr R A Rosner
Computer Board & Research Councils
Joint Network Team

B M Wood
Computer Analysts & Programmers

Date Due
